D0075014

American Theatre Companies, 1931–1986

American Theatre Companies, 1931–1986

EDITED BY

WELDON B. DURHAM

GREENWOOD PRESS
NEW YORK • WESTPORT, CONNECTICUT • LONDON

Library of Congress Cataloging-in-Publication Data

American theatre companies, 1931–1986.

Includes index.
1. Theater—United States—History—20th century—
Dictionaries.   I. Durham, Weldon B.
PN2266.A54   1989   792′.0973   88–32039
ISBN 0–313–25360–9 (lib. bdg. : alk. paper)

British Library Cataloguing in Publication Data is available.

Library of Congress Catalog Card Number: 88–32039
ISBN: 0–313–25360–9

First published in 1989

Greenwood Press, Inc.
88 Post Road West, Westport, Connecticut   06881

Printed in the United States of America

The paper used in this book complies with the
Permanent Paper Standard issued by the National
Information Standards Organization (Z39.48–1984).

10 9 8 7 6 5 4 3 2 1

Contents

Preface

American Theatre Companies, 1931–1986 is the third and final book in a series of three providing essential facts about resident acting companies in the United States.

The breakdown of the world economy in the late 1920s and the Great Depression of the 1930s eliminated all but a few commercial troupes in the United States. A handful of noncommercial groups and workers' theatres also survived the economic collapse. In 1935 the federal government established the Federal Theatre Project (FTP), a work-relief program wherein dozens of acting companies were assembled and put to work in cities all over the country. The FTP died in 1939, the victim of a Congress annoyed by the Left-leaning political posture of the project's managers and artistic decision-makers. The demise of the FTP was tantamount to the death of the resident acting company in America.

The resurrection of this mode of organization began at the end of World War II as a few art theatres and community theatres gathered the financial and organizational strength to support a company of actors working year-round. The revival gathered force in the fifties, under the leadership of a generation of visionary and dauntless founders and managers. In the mid–1960s the Ford Foundation gave crucial, life-giving support to struggling companies. Dozens of new companies sprang up in the seventies, inspired by the success of organizations in Washington, D.C., Minneapolis, Minnesota, Seattle, Washington, San Francisco, California, and Dallas and Houston, Texas. Resident theatre companies radically altered the American theatre by decentralizing it. Moreover, the nonprofit commercial organizations that sustained the resident acting companies became vital elements in the cultural renaissance sweeping the United States. They have taken their place in the cultural life of major and smaller cities alongside new or revitalized ballet and opera companies, symphonies, museums, and galleries.

American Theatre Companies, 1931–1986 contains biographies of seventy-eight organizations, forty-eight of which continued to produce plays after the closing date for entries in this book, June 30, 1986. Some of the thirty that have not survived were elements of the FTP; others were workers' theatres and art theatres of the thirties and early forties; still others were nonprofit commercial groups that failed to set roots deep enough in the cultural life of their communities. Among the groups covered are some of the longest-lived resident theatre companies in the history of American theatre. The Cleveland Play House was founded in 1915 but did not achieve professional status until 1954, hence the appearance of its entry in this rather than the earlier book. The Barter Theatre of Abingdon, Virginia, was organized in 1933, Houston's Alley Theatre in 1947, and the Arena Stage of Washington, D.C., in 1950.

In total, these group biographies establish unequivocally the basic elements of a formula for the survival of a modern resident theatre organization. Imaginative, energetic, and indomitable managers who accept the limitations of the local situation while exploiting to the limit its possibilities are a feature of most successful groups. A responsive and responsible community given some power to determine the theatre's future through a board of directors and through auxiliary, support organizations has been a key to success for many organizations. Ownership of a theatre building insulates the resident acting company from the worst effects of inevitably variable artistic and financial conditions. Subsidies in the form of gifts and grants and low-cost leases bridge nearly ineludible gaps between operating expenses and earned income. Constructive, cooperative relations with theatrical labor unions have smoothed the path to labor contracts adaptable to a variety of situations in the workplace. Clearly, ingenious, occasionally inspired management is the key to the durability of the modern acting company.

The seventy-eight entries in this book are arranged alphabetically, and cross-references provide access to entries on companies known by alternate names. An asterisk (*) after the mention of a company in a narrative indicates that the book includes an entry on the company named. Authors of the entries have distilled vital information from published and unpublished sources relating to the dates, places, personnel, policies, and repertories of the most durable acting companies assembled to produce more than one nonmusical play while residing for at least twenty consecutive weeks in a single location. Each entry includes dates and locations of the company's operations, the manager's name(s), and an analysis of the group's artistic and business practices. An assessment of the company's commercial and artistic significance adds a critical dimension to each entry. All but one of the articles includes a list of names of known performers, designers, technicians, and other support and managerial personnel. This list is omitted from the entry for the long-lived Cleveland Play House, because these names, several hundred of them, are given in a recently published company biography. Dates of the association of key persons (names in italics) are included in parentheses after the person's name. Because the book purports to cover the history of ongoing companies only through the end of the 1985–86 season, and because this aim is announced in the title of the book, the editor elected to close all dates, even those of potentially ongoing personnel in the predominantly transient world of the resident theatre artist, with 1986. All the articles, save that on the Cleveland Play House, include a list of all plays known to the compiler to have been produced by the group. Each entry concludes with a bibliography of published and unpublished sources consulted by the author as well as a guide to archival resources for further study, when such primary material is known to exist. An index of persons and plays referred to in the narrative portion of each group biography provides the user with further means of cross-referencing the entries. Plays and persons named in the appendices to each entry are not indexed.

American
Theatre Companies,
1931–1986

A

A CONTEMPORARY THEATRE, INC., originally called "Act, Inc.," opened in 1965 in Seattle, Washington, with Arthur Kopit's *Oh Dad, Poor Dad*. The summer stock venture was privately sponsored by Jean and Greg Falls. A professional company including two scene designers, two directors, a technical director, part-time administrative personnel, and actors primarily from New York and Los Angeles presented the season, which consisted of five shows, each seen in a two-week run. The only competitor in town was the Seattle Repertory Theatre*, which had just completed its second fall and winter season of classic repertoire.

Act, Inc. (ACT) proposed to produce the important plays of its time, while they had particular meaning and impact. Since its opening, ACT has produced seven world premieres and fifteen American or West Coast premieres. The children's theatre wing of ACT has produced eight American premieres and over thirty world premieres.

The first year proved successful with 8,931 (35 percent of capacity) attending sixty performances. ACT, Inc., then incorporated as a nonprofit organization under the direction of a six-member board. It soon changed its name to A Contemporary Theatre, Inc., and expanded its second season to seven plays. *The Fantasticks*, by Tom Jones and Harvey Schmidt, ACT's first musical, played to 92 percent of capacity through a regular run and two extra performances; 5,475 attended that production alone. Overall attendance for the summer of 1967 was 25,640.

Because of the success of the summer seasons of 1966 and 1967, ACT expanded to a 21-week, 126-performance season of 7 plays and hired Robert Gustavson as general manager. However, the theatre suffered a financial crisis in 1968 when anticipated audiences did not materialize. Attendance for the season was 24,173, and the house played to 45.4 percent of capacity. Even though ACT cut expenses and borrowed money, the season's deficit was $27,200.

ACT planned its 1969 season more cautiously and returned to a two-week run of each production. The success of the production of Peter Weiss' *Marat/Sade* set in motion the process of financial recovery, and under the general management of Terence C. Murphy in 1970, the remainder of the debt was retired. Attendance in 1970 reached 27,605 when the company was playing to 77.7 percent of the theatre's capacity. When in 1971 Clark Gesner's musical *You're a Good Man, Charlie Brown* was extended for two weeks, ACT attained a sixteen-week season of ninety-nine performances. ACT traditionally retains the last slot for a possible season expander, while extra matinees are used to extend the other season productions.

By 1972 ACT held an Equity Class C rating, and its season consisted of a world premiere, three Obie Award winners, and a Pulitzer Prize winner. That year ACT announced plans to operate year-round and to purchase the building it had rented since 1965.

ACT and the University of Washington Continuing Education Department cosponsored a series of postperformance lectures and discussions beginning in 1966. ACT continues to involve audiences in discussions and has sponsored "Dialogues" on Monday nights during the fall as well as the performance-related "Prologue" and "Epilogue," which occur before and after a production. During the 1971 season ACT began publishing *Playfacts*, which provides information on the season's shows, playwrights, and directors. ACT also publishes a quarterly newsletter, *Backstage*, and an annual report.

The company produced in the Old Queen Anne Hall, a three-story brick building erected in 1911 and listed on the National Register of Historic Places. Originally a meeting hall, the building has also served as a popular ballroom and dance studio and as home of the Queen Anne Badminton Club. Architects David Hewitt and James Sanders worked with Ibsen Nelson in remodeling the building. The first season ACT spent over $30,000 on capital improvements. The theatre's first fund-raising campaign netted a grant of public money for improvements of the theatre; ACT expanded seating in its theatre to 423, installed a ventilation system, and built a thrust stage twenty feet deep by thirty feet wide. ACT purchased the building and adjacent parking lot in February 1973 at the cost of $275,000, and with generous public and foundation assistance ACT was able to raise $125,000 for the down payment. ACT board members provided an additional $60,000, while the group secured a mortgage of $95,000. The loans were to be amortized from operating income and rental of three office spaces in the building. ACT had made a good buy, for a 1975 insurance assessment set the value of the building and parking lot at $525,000. In order to protect its investment the board launched a "Masterplan for Building Development," calling for improvements to be made on a funds-available basis over four to six years at an estimated cost in 1975 of $302,500. Under this plan the company expanded the scenery and costume shops and built a cabaret theatre adjoining the mainstage. At the close of the 1980 season ACT began renovation of the stagehouse, auditorium, lobby, and restrooms, adding seats to bring the total to

454, and an elevator to provide handicapped access. Work continued on the office space and exterior of the building.

In 1966 the Eleven O'Clock Theatre, a children's theatre, was formed. The children's company, primarily consisting of actors from the University of Washington, played Wednesday through Saturday matinees during July and August. The second season the children's company began to tour and to call itself "ACT." During its first two seasons the Eleven O'Clock Theatre performed Brian Way's participation scripts. In 1969 ACT moved into its second phase with directors choosing recent plays, some of which the directors themselves had written. At the same time Arne Zaslove reduced the number of productions to two per summer. In 1971 Zaslove wrote *An Original, Absurd Musical Revue for Children;* that fall Zaslove rewrote the play and ACT sent it on tour under the auspices of the Washington State Cultural Enrichment Program. The tour played to 55,000 schoolchildren and expanded the ACT season to six months, running from June to December. From 1972 to 1976 ACT concentrated on improvisation-based revues and on scenic effects. Since 1977 it has concentrated on adapting narrative fiction for the stage.

The most active period in ACT's history began in 1973 with the appointment of Andrew Witt as general manager. Witt worked closely with Greg Falls to lead ACT through some of its most productive years. Greg Falls, founder of the Champlain Shakespeare Festival in Vermont and executive director of the School of Drama at the University of Washington for ten years, is ACT's founder and only artistic director. Each year he directs for the mainstage, and his adaptation of Charles Dickens' *A Christmas Carol* remains ACT's biggest money-maker. Before his appointment as general manager, Andrew Witt was technical director for the Bathhouse Theatre in Seattle and technical assistant for the National Playwright's Conference at the O'Neill Center in Waterford, Connecticut. He also acted, stage-managed, and served as assistant general manager at ACT.

In 1974 ACT began to expand beyond its original conception as a summer theatre featuring a contemporary repertoire. ACT 2, an outgrowth of the earlier off-season productions of the Young ACT company (YAC), emerged in a repertoire of classic plays. Also, by 1974 YAC was touring six western states under the auspices of the Western States Art Foundation. When it was upgraded to professional status it became the only such children's theatre in the Northwest. The ACT season, originally scheduled to run from June to September, was extended until November 10, 1974, because of a seven-week run of the musical *Godspell*, by John Michael Tebelak and Stephen Schwartz. In order to ensure an orderly growth for ACT, in 1975 Witt arranged with the League of Resident Theatres, the management cartel representing nonprofit resident theatres in negotiations with theatrical labor unions, to allow ACT to play a twenty-one-week season, while YAC played a thirty-week season. ACT thus began a three-week run of each of its seven productions in a season that extended from June 19 to October 18.

By 1976 ACT had assets of $385,000 and a long-term debt of only $175,000. The mainstage season ran from May to November, and the YAC toured from October to April. ACT received federal grants in both "Professional Theatre" and "Theatre for Youth" categories.

ACT's burgeoning growth prompted the Ford Foundation and the Kresge Foundation to request information about the future of the company. At a long-range planning retreat in Port Ludlow, Washington, on October 14, 1978, the board decided to continue ACT as a two-company organization, with the resident company producing plays in five-week runs from April to October. They projected a conservative expansion of both the ACT and the YAC season. The board also announced plans to continue to commission and develop new scripts, as well as to organize exchanges with other companies and persons from abroad. Finally the board established a permanent long-range planning committee that would meet quarterly.

In 1979 inflationary costs and unsold bookings on its western states tour forced YAC to abandon the tour and establish a residency at ACT in Seattle. The series sold out, so YAC planned a resident subscription season in 1980. The children's theatre played at other sites while ACT remodeled in 1980–81. The organization later merged with the Seattle Junior Theatre and expanded its Seattle marketing staff. It continued to play a January-through-April season to compliement ACT's May-through-November mainstage season until 1986 when the YAC residency was terminated as a cost-cutting measure.

ACT reorganized in 1980 when Andrew Witt left to become managing director of the Tacoma Actor's Guild. During his term with ACT, subscription sales rose 267 percent while earned and unearned income more than doubled. By 1980 ACT had a year-round season with an annual income of $1.13 million, and performances ran Tuesday through Sunday with matinees on Wednesday and Saturday. Attendance at resident company productions was over 60,000, and the theatre was playing to 94 percent of capacity. Witt started and then expanded the policies of offering discounts to senior citizens and students and of reducing admission prices for premieres. Under Witt's management the Seattle Arts Commission and the King County Arts Commission provided low-income residents with free tickets for one matinee of each production.

Although originally committed to producing contemporary plays, the repertoire of ACT has changed in recent years. In 1977 audiences selected ACT's production of Shakespeare's *As You Like It* as the most popular, and ACT produced more classics for a time. Moreover, ACT's competitors, Intiman Theatre Company*, Empty Space Association*, Seattle Repertory Theatre, and Pioneer Square, although primarily recognized for their revivals of traditional and classic plays, produced modern plays and premieres of new plays. By the mid–1980s ACT had returned to its commitment to contemporary British and American plays.

Despite the shifting emphasis in its repertoire, ACT audiences have been loyal. The renewal rate for subscribers is between 70 percent and 80 percent and a

1976 audience analysis revealed that only about one-sixth of those surveyed regularly attended Seattle's other professional theatres. Attendance at mainstage ACT productions continues to mount through the 1980s, and the company's annual budget has grown to nearly $2 million.

Actors who appeared regularly in early ACT productions included Elsa Raven and Michael Dunne. Ben Tone has appeared repeatedly throughout ACT's history. A list of regional actors of reknown working at ACT would include Ted D'Arms, Denis Arndt, Michael Santo, Eve Roberts, and Marjorie Nelson. ACT holds annual auditions in New York and Los Angeles but casts ever more frequently from Equity and non-Equity auditions in Seattle.

Currently it is difficult to assess the overall effect of ACT's 1980 reorganization. They continue to concentrate on contemporary plays, but the new scripts are less experimental than in the past. The board is determined to keep ACT's income high in relation to its expenses, and remodeling continues only as funds are available. Indications are that ACT will look more to foreign playwrights and use its cabaret theatre primarily for commissioned works and revues written by Jean Falls. ACT is currently raising money for a new facility with two performing spaces to open in 1990.

ACT has received the Award of Excellence of the American Theatre Festival, the Washington Governor's Arts Award, and the Jennie Heiden Award. When ACT's theatricalization of Homer's *The Odyssey* was performed at the Terrace Theatre in the John F. Kennedy Center for the Performing Arts in Washington, D.C., in 1979, national attention focused briefly on the fledgling company. Moreover, YAC was one of four American companies selected to perform at the Louisiana World Exposition in 1984. ACT is recognized by the National Endowment for the Arts, the Ford Foundation, and the Washington State, King County, and Seattle arts commissions as one of Seattle's six major cultural institutions. Regular funding from foundations, government, and quasi-governmental agencies and astute management by its board maintains ACT's position as the second largest theatre in Seattle.

PERSONNEL

Artistic Director, later Producing Director: Greg Falls (1965–86).

General Managers: Gregory Eaton (1966–67), Robert Gustavson (1968–69), Terence C. Murphy (1970–73), William S. Taylor (1965–66), Andrew M. Witt (1974–80).

Administrative Manager: Susan Trapnell Monitz (1980–83).

Producing Manager: Phil Schermer (1983–86).

Company Managers: Anne Denise Ford (1984–86), Jody Harris (1977–79), Karen O'Shea (1982), Karen Rotko (1979–81), Larry K. Walden (1983), Michael Weholt (1977).

Directors: Malcolm Black (1969, 1971), Margaret Booker (1975), Joy Carlin (1982), Fred Chappell (1984), Raymond Clarke (1977), Don Correll (1973), *Clayton Corzatte* (1970, 1972, 1979, 1981–82), John Dillon (1980, 1985), Richard Edwards (1979, 1981–82), Robert Egan (1981), *Greg Falls* (1965–82, 1984–86), Margaret Faulkes (1966–67), Anne-Denise Ford (1984–86), Aaron Frankel (1986), Rita Giomi (1986), Gary Gisselman

(1984), Susan Glass [Burdick] (1985), Moses Goldberg (1971), Thomas Gruenewald (1979), Jim Hancock (1981), Gerald Harte (1968), Judith Haskell (1977–78, 1980), Israel Hicks (1971), James Higgins (1975), Thomas Hill (1966–67), *John Kaufman* (1973–74, 1979, 1981, 1986), Paul Lee (1976), Roberta Levitow (1982), *Robert Loper* (1967, 1971, 1973–76, 1978–81), William Ludel (1977–78), Pirie MacDonald (1968, 1971–72, 1974), *Eileen MacRae Murphy* (1976–77, 1979–82), Sharon Ott (1983–84), Eleanor Owen (1972), Kent Paul (1977), Tawnya Pettiford (1980), Ralph Rosinbum (1970), W. Duncan Ross (1966), Lou Saterni (1983), Ronald Satlof (1966), Mel Shapiro (1965, 1984), *Jeff Steitzer* (1983–86), Jack Sydow (1974–75), *M. Burke Walker* (1973–75, 1977–78, 1980, 1983), Douglas Turner Ward (1983), William West (1967, 1972, 1974, 1979), Allie Woods (1971–73), Tunc Yalman (1972–73), *Arne Zaslove* (1968–71, 1973–74, 1985).

Resident Directors: Greg Falls (1965–86), Anne-Denise Ford (1984–86), Jeff Steitzer (1984–86).

Fight Director: David Boushey (1977–78).

Jugglers: Timothy Daniel Furst (1986), Paul David Magid (1986), Randy Nelson (1986), Howard Jay Patterson (1986), Sam Williams (1986).

Scene Designers: Kent Bishop (1968), Felix E. Cochren (1983), Robert Dahlstrom (1983–84), Alanson B. Davis (1966), Joseph Dodd (1986), Thomas M. Fichter (1982), *Bill Forrester* (1972–73, 1975–77, 1981–86), Gloria Fricke (1965), Karen Gjelsteen (1975, 1977–80, 1982, 1984), Jim Hancock (1981), Richard J. Harris (1986), *Shelley Henze Schermer* (1972–82, 1984–86), Bruce Jackson (1985), Robert Lewis (Robert Lewis Smith) (1966), Jennifer Lupton (1986), *S. Todd Muffatti* (1965–74, 1978), Dwight Richard Odle (1970), Michael Olich (1985–86), *Bill Raoul* (1966–68, 1971–73, 1980–81, 1983, 1985), Richard Salabaugh (1966), Debra Sanderson (1981), Philip Schermer (1967, 1972, 1976, 1981), *Scott Weldin* (1979–83, 1985–86), *Jerry Williams* (1966, 1969, 1974–78), Carey Wong (1980), Gilbert Wong (1984).

Lighting Designers: Peter W. Allen (1986), Christopher Beardsley (1983), John R. Bradford (1968–69), Cathy Breen (1968–70), *Jody Briggs* (1970–73, 1978–82, 1984–86), Paul Bryan (1977–80), Randall G. Chiarelli (1981), Peter Dansky (1986), Lee DeLorme (1984), Richard Devin (1976), Bill Forrester (1985), *Donna Grout* (1980–86), Scott Hawthorn (1971), Allen Lee Hughes (1983), Rich Kennedy–Paulsen (1984), Jennifer Lupton (1985), Richard Montgomery (1968–69), S. Todd Muffatti (1970, 1974), *Al Nelson* (1975–78, 1984–85), Grace Nunes (1969, 1971), Rick Paulsen (1985–86), Lloyd S. Riford III (1986), Jeff Robbins (1983), *Philip Schermer* (1966–69, 1972–86), Frank Simmons (1980), James Verdery (1984, 1986), Judy Harris Wolcott (1975).

Costume Designers: Faith Adams (1970), Abigail Arnt (1968), Linda Bachmann (1973), Alexandra B. Bonds (1984), Nanrose Buchman (1981, 1984–86), Sarah Campbell (1986), Celeste Cleveland (1986), Sheryl Collins (1985), Liz Corey (1985), *Jim Crider* (1965–72), Laura Crow (1980, 1986), Shay Cunliffe (1982–83), Judy Dearing (1983), A. Devora (1986), Donna Eskew (1975), Josie Gardner (1982–84), Sarah Nash Gates (1984), Marian Hill [Cottrell] (1982–83), *Julie James* (1979–82, 1985), Lynn Lewis (1974), Jane McGillivray (1972–73), Susan Min (1978), Catherine Paxton (1982), Rose Pederson (1985–86), Ronn Talbot Pelle (1969), Sally Richardson (1981), *Don Klovstad* (1976–79, 1982), Mike Lowther (1977–80), A. I. Nelson (1984–85), A. W. (Al) Nelson (1976, 1983–84), Howard Neslen (1986), John Savage (1980), Frank Simons (1980), Maynard Smith (1982), Alan Templeton (1982), Skip Templeton (1981–82), Mylor Treener (1981), Richard Weil (1977–79), Al Weldin (1983).

Choreographers: Jan Bonzon (1977–79), Carol Borgmann (1984), Rebecca Brown (1976–77), Kenneth Carr (1971), Lee Champion (1972), Christopher Duncan (1970–71), Valerie Dunne (1981–82, 1986), William Earl (1973), Susan Glass [Burdick] (1982, 1984–85), Judith Haskell (1978), Ben Johnson (1969), Christopher Joy (1971), Marian Ladre (1965), Ursula Meyer (1985), David Nash (1986), Tawnya Pettiford (1980), Susan Richardson-Glass (1979–80), David Vaughan (1970), Arne Zaslove (1968).

Composers/Arrangers/Orchestrations: John Biddle (1972), Robert Billig (1986), Andrew Buchman (1982), Robert Davidson (1968–70), Roger Downey (1967), Rob Duisberg (1979–80), Michael Fause (1984), Chad Henry (1985), *Stan Keen* (1971–73, 1975, 1977–78), David Hunter Koch (1982, 1986), Robert MacDougall (1976–79, 1985–86), Alan Menken (1986), Robby Merkin (1986), Richard C. Peaslee (1969, 1976), Kathryn Sestrap (1979), Joseph Seserko (1980).

Sound/Sound Designers/Coordinators: Abigail Arnt (1965), Kent R. Bishop (1965), Robert Bulkley (1984), Bill Carswell (1984), Greg Eaton (1965), Ernest Hibbard (1981), Michael Holten (1986), Steven M. Klein (1986), David Hunter Koch (1984–86), Sally Lansing (1965), Regge Life (1983), *Mac Perkins* (1973–81, 1986), Martin Pavloff (1978), Carmine Simone (1983), Lindsay Smith (1984–85), James Verdery (1984–85).

Stage Managers/Production Managers/ Production Stage Managers: Kent Bishop (1966, 1968), Jody Briggs (1970–71), Karen Brilliande (1986), Denise Cooperider (1970–71), Don Correll (1972–73), Sandra L. Cruse (1975–78), Susanita Dacula (1971), William Davidson (1965), Edward DeShae (1983), Bruce Alan Elsperger (1985), Bonita M. Ernst (1982–84), Anne-Denise Ford (1981–83), Bruce Halverson (1968), Joan Kennedy (1983–84), E. Allen Kent (1966), Joan Klynn (1967–68), Janice C. Lane (1983), Eileen MacRae [Murphy] (1974–81), James S. Martin (1968–69), Sarah S. Mixson (1986), Richard Montgomery (1968), Jim Royce (1976–77), Debra Sanderson (1981–82), Lisa Schilling (1984), Theresa Updegrove (1985), James Verdery (1985–86), Jorie Wackerman (1984–86), *Michael Weholt* (1972–76, 1981–82), Michael Wise (1985), Andrew Witt (1972–73), Jonathan Wright (1967).

Actors and Actresses: John Abajian (1969–71), Brian Abiram (1971), Loretta Ables (1986), Lori Abrahamson (1976), Arni Adler (1984–85), Sara Ahmedi (1970), Roderick Aird (1985), Wil Albert (1966), Rex E. Allen (1984–85), Linda Alper (1982), Tony Amendola (1980), Mark Anders (1985), Daryl D. Anderson (1972, 1975), Stanley Anderson (1968), Tobias Anderson (1972–73, 1975, 1985), Jill Andre (1970), Adrienne Angel (1978), Gwen Arment (1980), C. W. Armstrong (1968, 1971–73, 1975), John Armstrong, *Denis Arndt* (1978–79), Richard E. Arnold (1975–76), Abby Arnt (1965), Eric Augusztiny (1975), Calliandra Austin (1980), Shaun Austin-Olsen (1978–79), Brian Avery (1975), *Jack Axelrod* (1965, 1968, 1971–72, 1974), *John Aylward* (1967–69, 1971, 1973, 1975–77, 1979–82, 1985), D. Quinton B. (1972), Robert Bailey (Baily) (1971), Henry Kaimu Bal (1973, 1979), *Laurence Ballard* (1985–86), Stewart Ballinger (1967, 1969, 1979–80), Peter Ban (1969), Edward Baran (1977–81), Allison Barcott (1985), Erik Barnes (1976), Don Barnett (1967), *Edwin Barron* (1965), *Patricia Barry* (1974), *Don Bartholomew* (1965), Sarah Baskin (1986), Ariel Basom (1985), Don Bearden (1972–73), Kurt Beattie (1975–77, 1985), Nicholai Beck (1981), Jahnna Beecham (1983), Anne Beecher (1969), Regina Bell (1974), Gayle Bellows (1980, 1984, 1985), Chappelle Benet (1971), Katherine Benfer (1977), Dianne Benjamin [Hill] (1985–86), Robert Benson (1971), Jackie Benster (1970, 1974), Barbara Bercu (1975–77, 1979), Barbara Berge (1977), Jason Bernard (1966), David Berry (1972), Tom Besse (1967), Shana Bestock (1985–86), Laurie Bialik (1980), Leon Bibb (1975), Lyle Bicknell (1978),

James Bigham (1973), Beatrice Bischofberger (1965), Denice Bischofberger (1965), Henry Bischofberger (1965), *Kent Bishop* (1965–68), Jack Bittner (1978), Diane E. Bivens (1980), Robert Blackburn (1975, 1979), Michelle Blackmon (1986), Ralf Blair (1975), Nesbitt Blaisdell (1981), Jean Bonard (1977), *Edwin Bordo* (1974–75), *Frank Borgman* (1984), Barbara Borland (1968), Peter Boynton (1979), J. V. Bradley (1974, 1979), Stam Bradley (1981), Ken Branch (1978), Alan W. Brandon (1971, 1974–75), *John Brandon* (1974), Jane Bray (1975), Keve Bray (1966), Conni Marie Brazelton (1980), Elizabeth Briggs (1970), Jerry M. Brinkman (1974), Elaine Bromka (1981), Sarah Brooke (1985), Dorothy Brooks (1984), William Brower (1967), *Charles Brown* (1983), Joan Brown (1969), Patricia Brown (1967, 1977–78), Tamara Brown (1974), Steve Brush (1986), Mark Buchan (1976), Ray Bumetai (1986), *Jean Burch* (1965–69, 1972), Gene Burk (1979), Jan Burrell (1971), *Catherine Butterfield* (1977), *Glenn Buttkus (Buttkins)* (1971–75), Marky Buxton (1969), Michael Byron (1971, 1974–75), James M. Caddell (1986), *Adolph Caesar* (1983), William Cain (1981), Gisela Caldwell (1968), Nancy Callman (1980), Karen Kee Campbell (1976), J. Kenneth Campbell (1981), Pat Campbell (1970), David Canary (1978), Rose E. Cano (1985), Colleen Carey (1985), Leslie Carlson (1970), Colleen Carpenter (1982, 1985), Elizabeth Carter (1984), Barbara Caruso (1974), Robert Casper (1969), George Catalano (1985), Dorothy Chace (1978), *Kathleen Chalfant* (1984), Michael Chambers (1970, 1973), Lee Champion (1970–71), Randal Chicoine (1969), Michael Christensen (1969–70), Dale Christopher (1978), Gina Citoli (1969), Alan L. Clark (1966), Shane Clark (1985), Marlene Clary (1965), Gordon Coffey (1971), Alice Coffin (1965), *Frederick Coffin* (1975), Cherry Coggins (1969), David Colacci (1978–82), *Elizabeth Cole* (1978), *Megan Cole* (1984), Phil Coles (1968), Alexander Conley III (1965), Steve Conley (1966), Thomas Connolly (1967), Katherine Connors (1967), Sid Conrad (1972), Maury Cooper (1976, 1980), Cecelia Cordova (1972), *Robert Cornthwaite* (1970, 1972, 1976–77), Frank Corrado (1986), Lee Corrigan (1977, 1979), *Clayton Corzatte* (1973–75, 1977, 1979–80, 1984–85), Patricia Cosgrove (1977), Walter Cotton (1971), Jeffrey Covell (1981), Scott Creighton (1984–85), Saylor Creswell (1977), *Michael Cristofer* (1973), Sheila Crofut (1981), Toni Cross (1982), Darryl Croxton (1973), Amy Crumpacker (1984), Sandra Cruse (1977), Daniel Daily (1980–81), *Kathy Danzer* (1983), Cynthia Darlow (1981), *Ted D'Arms* (1973–74, 1978–81), Diana Darzins (1969), Vincent D'Augelli (1982), Jean David (1972), Phillip Davidson (1985), *Richard M. Davidson* (1985), Robert Davidson (1969), William Davidson (1965), *David Davies* (1983), Heidi Helen Davis (1981), Montgomery Davis (1971), Megan Dean (1973–74, 1976–77), *Justin Deas* (1977), Diane DeFunis (1972), Robert Deitrich (1973, 1975), Carole Demas (1967, 1969), Alexis Denisof (1978–79), Teotha Dennard (1977), Theresa DePaolo (1981), Chris DeVore (1981), *John Dewey-Carter* (1983), Thomas Diggs (1986), *Mary Diveny* (1984), Fred Dobler (1971), Charles Doherty (1969), Cameron Dokey (1981, 1986), Bridget Donahoe (1971), *Robert Donley* (1974–75), *Judith Doty* (1966), B. J. Douglas (1984, 1986), Inga Douglas (1972), Ann Driscoll (1968, 1970), Mark Drusch (1982, 1985–86), Stuart Anderson Duckworth (1982), *Patrick G. Duffy* (1969–72), *O. L. Duke* (1983), Christopher Duncan (1971, 1976), *Michael Dunne* (1965–67), Morgan Dunne (1969, 1971), Rosheen Dunne (1979–80), Adrienne Dussault (1978), Douglas Easley (1978), Karen Eastman (1976), Billie Eaton (1965–66), Gregory Eaton (1967), Sue Van Eaton (1968), Thomas Eberle (1983), Mitchell Edmonds (1979, 1982), Ashley Eichrodt (1984–85), Gregory Elliot (1975), Bayne (Wayne) Ellis (1968), Richard Eng (1979), James Engelhardt (1967), Annette Ensley (1972), *Ben E. Epps* (1983), Jonathan Estrin (1974), Patricia Estrin (1974, 1976), Anne Etue (1972),

Mary Ewald (1984), Frank Ewbanks (1975), Donald Ewer (1974–77), Mary Fain (1977), Brian Faker (1983), *R. A. Farrell* (1978–82, 1984–86), Joerle Farwell (1967), Jonathan Farwell (1966–67, 1969), Sara Farwell (1967–68), Jay (Peter J.) Fernandez (1975–77), *Katherine Ferrand* (1976, 1979–82, 1984), Frank Ferrel (1976), William Ferriter (1981), Kevin Field (1982), Joe J. Fields (1975–76), Sparkle Finley (1967), Susan Finque (1985–86), Kelly Fitzpatrick (1978), Neil Fitzpatrick (1981), Bonnie Flagg (1966), Paul Fleming (1977), Michael Flynn (1981–82), Julie Follansbee (1982), Danny Follette (1965), Judy Ford [Taylor] (1986), Loren Foss (1971), Michael Fox (1970), Gabrielle Franchot (1970), Charles Frank (1967), *Bernard Frawley* (1969, 1978, 1980), *Erik Fredericksen* (1978), Susan French (1971), *Ray Fry* (1986), Dan Fuller (1968, 1974), *Janice Fuller* (1974, 1978), *Timothy Daniel Furst* (1986), Cyprienne Gable (1970), Sandra Galeota (1985), Allen Galli (1985), Dean Gardner (1973–77), Kurt Garfield (1975), *Gale Garnett* (1983), June Garre (1969), Sylvia Gassell (1975, 1978), Mark Geiger (1976), Linda George (1967), Anne Gerety (1977), Rod Gibbons (1969), *John Gilbert* (1966–67, 1970, 1973–82, 1984–85), Steven Gilborn (1971, 1974), Stuart Gillard (1968, 1970), Joshua Gillow (1984), Joey Ginza (1972), Paul Gladstone (1984–85), Michael Glenn-Smith (1969), John Glennon (1970), Steven J. Goddard (1974), *Danny Goldring* (1983), Ruby Goldschmidt (1984), Sonny Gorasht (1972), Ki Gottberg (1984–85), Gordon Gould (1969), Kenneth Gray (1966), Melissa Gray (1985), Robert Gray (1969, 1971), *Vernon Gray* (1965), Richard Greene (1965), William (Bill) Greenwood (1965–66), Melody Greer (1965), Michael Griswold (1970), Nathan Haas (1984), Eric Hagerman (1985), *Davis Hall* (1984), Bruce Halvorson (Halversen) (1968), Patricia Hamilton (1970, 1982), Mark Hammer (1970), Susan Hammergren (1966–67), Tom Hammond (1986), Lloyd Hardy (1972), *Brian Hargrove* (1984), Ginger Harmon (1966), *Jerry Harper* (1981, 1984), Helen Harrelson (1967), Harriet Harris (1982), Jackie Harris (1965), Joyce Harris (1985), Gerald Harte (1967–68), Linda Hartzell (1985), Hugh Hastings (1985), Eileen Hawkins (1979), Maureen Hawkins (1974), *Richard Hawkins* (1977–80), *Suzanna Hay* (1983), Doris Hayes (1986), *Gardner Hayes* (1974), Christine Healy (1979, 1982, 1984), Kathleen Heaney (1977), Gail Hebert (1974–75), Deborah Hedwall (1972), Don Henline (1971), Nels Hennym (Hennum) (1966), Chad Henry (1970), Gregg Henry (1974), Andrew Hepburn (1969), Tara Herivel (1986), *Jety Herlick* (1965), Steven W. Herrmann (1975), Randy Herron (1971), Hillary Hicks (1970), Kyra Hider (1986), James Higgins (1968, 1973–75), Robert A. Higgins (1975), James Hilbrandt (1982), Tom (Thomas) Hill (1976, 1981), Malcolm Hillgartner (1983), Margaret Hilton (1971, 1974–76), *Earl Hindman* (1974), Lizabeth Hinton (1985), Jill Hirsh (Hirsch) (1965), *Gerald Hjert* (1965–66), Patricia Hodges (1969, 1972–74), Bern Hoffman (1971), *Henry Hoffman* (1975), Randy Hoffmeyer (1985), Edward Holmes (1971), Nicholas Hormann (1977), John Horn (1975), John Hosking (1976–79), Paul Hostetler (1985), Brenda Hubbard (1978–79, 1981), Wayne Hudgins (1970–74), Will Hughes (1976), Marceline Hugot (1985), Jay Humphrey (1969), Neil Hunt (1973), *Suzy Hunt* (1980–83), Bonnie Hurren (1972), Frances Hyland (1973), Michael B. Ingersoll (1975), William Inglis (1965), Yolly Irigon (1973), Suzanne Irving (1986), Estelle Jackson (1965), Gwen Jackson (1979), Leonard Jackson (1971, 1973), *Samuel L. Jackson* (1983), Cathy Jamerson (1972), Jim Jansen (Janson) (1975–76), William Jay (1973, 1981), *Mark Jenkins* (1980), Glenn Johnson (1968), Greg Thomas Johnson (1986), Mel Johnson, Jr. (1976), Randy Johnstad (1975), David Jones (1971, 1978), Edward L. Jones (1970), *Steven A. Jones* (1983), Kim Joseph (1979), Karen Joshi (1976–77), Christopher (Christopher) Joy (1971), Scott Kaiser (1986), Stephanie Kallos (1986), Janet Kapral (1970), *John Kauffman* (1967–68, 1972–73, 1978–

79), Stan Keen (1975), Peter Kelley (1979–80), *Daren Kelly* (1984), Henry M. Kendrick (1973, 1975), Laura Kenyon (1973), *Nicholas Kepros* (1971), Kathy Kernohan (1969), Peter Killy (1986), Maureen Kilmurry (1981), Kathy Kinder (1970), Cindy King (1968), Karen Kingsley (1976–77), *Jean Marie Kinney* (1969–71, 1973–74), *David S. Klein* (1985–86), Jill Klein (1985–86), Joanna Klein (1980, 1985), Katherine Klekas (1985), Joan Klynn (1966), Sally Kniest (1965, 1974), Richard Knisely (1977–78), Eric Knudson (1967), David Koch (1980–82, 1985), Noel Koran (1974–75), *Richard Kuss* (1967–68), William L. Kux (1975–76), Barbara Kyle (1970), Rene Laigo (1972), Diana LaMar (1985), Michael Landrum (1971), Keith Langsdale (1983), Sally Lansing (1965), Charles Lanyer (1972), Laurie Lapinski (1973, 1978), *Martin LaPlatney* (1972–73, 1976, 1985), Bob Larkin (1973), Jess Larsen (1965–66), Lori Larsen (1969, 1985), Philip Larson (1971), Charles Layne (Layner) (1971–72), *Eugene Lee* (1983), Ki Lee (1969), Paul Lee (1976), Richard Lee (1977–79), Jo Leffingwell (1970–76, 1985–86), *Zoaunne LeRoy* (1973–74, 1978–79, 1981, 1985), Len Lesser (1970), Barbara Lester (1977), Kathy Lichter (1977), Judith Light (1973), *Marion Lines* (1977), Diana Lingwood (1967), Peter Lohnes (1981, 1984–85), Joanne Long (1971), John Long (1965–67), Kevin C. Loomis (1984–85), *Robert Loper* (1968–69, 1973, 1978, 1981, 1984), Malcolm Lowe (1986), Susan Ludlow (1973, 1975, 1977, 1985), Terry Lumley (1965), Allan Lurie (1978), Kathryn Luster (1974), Kevin Lynch (1985), Diane McBaine (1981–82), Ann McCaffray (1969, 1971–73), Helene McCardle (1984), Robert McCormack (1974), Andy McCutcheon (1986), Scott McDade (1969), Art McDonald (1971), Beth McDonald (1976), Lindsay MacDonald (1969), *Tanny McDonald* (1975–76, 1978), Constance Jean Blake McDougall (1971), Robert MacDougall (1976), Rex McDowell (1976–77, 1985–86), Janice McElroy (1970–71), Katherine McGrath (1971), Patricia McGregor (1968), Pernell McGuire (1977), David H. MacIntyre (1984), *John MacKay* (1986), Michael McKee (1978), Karen McLaughlin (1977), Melinda McLean (1973), Lachlan Macleay (1979), David McMahan (1975), Dermot McNamara (1973), Doug McQuain (1966), Terri McRay (1978), Diane Maggio (1978), *Paul David Magid* (1986), Robert Maguire (1984–85), Daniel Mahar (1974, 1981–82), Juanita Mahone (1980), David Mainer (1985), Kris Mainz (1979–80), Jimi Malary (1979–80), Robert Manzari (1980), *Adrienne Marden* (1974), *David Margulies* (1986), Paul Marin (1971), Richard Marion (1976), *Peter Marklin* (1984), *Christopher Marks* (1979–82, 1984–86), Noah Marks (1981–82), Karen Marra (1982), Dylan Marshall (1985), Brian Martin (1984–85), James Martin (1968), Peter Martin (1965), Whitney Mason (1971), Marie Mathay (1977–79), Marcy Mattox (1977–79), Daniel Mayes (1985), Jan Maxwell (1986), *Glenn Mazen* (1977, 1980, 1984), Alfred Mazza (1971), Joseph Edward Meek (1975, 1977), Dean Meland (1977), Elizabeth Melcher (1970), Craig Kenyon Menteer (1986), *Eda Reiss Merin* (1973), Christine Merino (1986), Karen Mesney (1982), Kathryn Mesney [Hetler] (1984, 1986), Ursula Meyer (1982, 1984), Jerry Mickey (1965), Ivars Mikelson (1975), David Milbert (1968), Daniel Milder (1985–86), Constance Miller (1977), Julian Miller (1971, 1973), Monica Miller (1970), Nancy Miller (1978), Patricia Miller (1983), Robert Milton (1966–68), Hau Minn (1969–70, 1979), Jack Mitchell (1972), Paul T. Mitri (1986), Medora Moburg (1974), *Tony Mockus* (1985–86), Margit Moe (1979), William Molloy (1968–69, 1973), Bob Molock (1973), David Mong (1980–81, 1985), *James W. Monitor* (1975–79, 1981, 1984), Cathy Monk (1970), Barbara Montgomery (1973), Richard Montgomery (1965–66, 1968, 1973), Judith Moore (1977), Todd Moore (1986), William Moreing (1978), Rene Moreno (1984), Clark Morgan (1966), Gerald Morgan (1968), Michael Morgan-Dunne (1984), Barbara L. Morin (1979–80, 1982), Sherry Morrison (1969), *Jacqueline Moscou* (1981,

1984), Marnie Mosiman (1976), Brian Muehring (1971), Jayne Muirhead (1979–80, 1982, 1985–86), Barry Mulholland (1978), Bill Mullikin (1974), Mark Murphey (1977), Ric Murphy (1965), Anne Murray (1972), Patricia Murray (1975), Joyce Mycka-Stettler (1985), Bill Myers (1975), *Lynda Myles* (1967, 1969, 1980), Steven Nabors (1978), Maryann M. Nagel (1975–76), Don Nahaku (1986), Elaine Nalee (1978), Pat Namara (1978), Allen Nause (1979, 1981–82, 1986), K. Nelsen (1976), Gail Nelson (1975), *Marjorie Nelson* (1969, 1974–75, 1980, 1985), Novella Nelson (1966), *Randy Nelson* (1986), Darrell Neumeyer (1967, 1970), William Newman (1972), Gun-Marie Nilsson (1967, 1969–70), Nancy Nolan (1974), Tatum Nolan (1986), Clare Nono (1981), Jessie Nores-Haas (1972), Joan Norton (1973–74), Gretchen O'Connel (1986), K. Lype O'Dell (1967–69), Pat Ojendyk (1970), Bill O'Leary (1982–83), *Henry Oliver* (1966), Tanner Oliver (1966), Merritt Olsen (1977–79), Rosella Olson (1965), Liz O'Neal (O'Neil) (1971), Robert E. Oram (1976), James D. O'Reilly (1973), Gretchen Orsland (1985), Anne O'Sullivan (1984), Christopher Owens (1973), Michael Palmer (1969), D. H. Panchot (1971, 1973, 1975), Hershey Parady (1972, 1974, 1981), Constance Parker (1970), Reed Parsley (1969), Tony Pasqualini (1985), Sue Patella (1974), *Howard Jay Patterson* (1986), Liann Pattison (1984), *Jeanne Paulsen* (1983–84, 1986), Larry Paulsen (1984), *Jeanne Paynter* (1965), Pamela Peadon (1970), James W. Pearl (1977), Matt Pelto (1969, 1972), John Pendleton (1977), Christopher Pennock (1968), Mark Pesola (1968), James Pestana (1986), *Tawnya Pettiford-Wates* (1986), Mary Petzold (1986), David Pichette (1982, 1984–86), *James Pickens, Jr.* (1983), *Rod Pilloud* (1975, 1980–82, 1984–85), *Demetra Pittman* (1973–75, 1979–80, 1982, 1985), Anne Postma (1972), Benjamin Prager (1981), Jeffrey L. Prather (1976–79, 1981), Barry Press (1984), John Pribyl (1986), Sally Prichard (1965, 1976, 1981), Molly Pritchard (1977), *John Procaccino* (1979–81, 1984), Dan Putman (1968), Nancy Anne Quense (1966), *Maureen Quinn* (1969, 1971, 1974), Arlene Quiyou (1980), Rex Rabald (1983, 1985–86), Eileen Ramsey (1972), Rich Rand (1984), Jerome Raphel (1967), Andrew Ratshin (1984–85), *Elsa Raven* (1965–66, 1968, 1979), William Earl Ray I (1986), Russel J. Reed (1986), Joyce Reehling (1974), Susan Rees (1967), Roxanne Reese (1980), Michael Regan (1966), Cynthia Reid (1972), Orrin Reiley (1973), Gary Reineke (1968, 1970), John Renforth (1973, 1975), Gwynne Rhynedance (1984), Rikki Ricard (1985), Gerald Richards (1979), Paul Richards (1967), Cecelia Riddett (1979), *Richard Riehle* (1980, 1981, 1983, 1985), Robert Riner (1969), Leslie Rivers (1971), Ruth Kidder Roats (1973–76), *Eve Roberts* (1978, 1980, 1986), Les Roberts (1977), Susan Roberts (1971), Freddy Robinson (1972), Randy Roger (1985), Annette Romano (1986), William Rongstad (1971, 1973–75), Steven Rose (1981), Jeff Rosen (1970), Clive Rosengren (1980), Duncan Ross (1967–69), Kimberly Ross (1976), *Jim Royce* (1966, 1969, 1971–74, 1976–80), Elizabeth Rukavina (1980–81), Judith Rumsby (1973), Jane Ryan (1981–82), Edward Sampson (1982, 1984–85), *Alvin Lee Sanders* (1975, 1984–85), Clark Sandford (1985), Ethan Sandler (1984), *Michael Santo* (1980–81, 1984), *Mark Sather* (1976–78), *Ronald Satlof* (1965–66), *Isao Sato* (1979), Jessie Saunders (1973), Nick Savian (1968), *Ron Lee Savin* (1986), Marco Sawrey (1981), Janine Sawyer (1978), John Scanlan (1967), Alan Scarfe (1969), Michael V. Schauermann (1984–85), Julian Schembri (1973–74), Diane Schenker (1981), Shelley Henze Schermer (1978), Leo Schmidt (1978), *Stefan Schnabel* (1984), Peggy Schoditsch (1983), David Scott (1976–77), Lucian Scott (1974), Mara Scott-Wood (1982), Dan Sedgwich (1969), Jeff Selters (1985–86), John Seward (1971), Judith Shahn (1985), Lee Shallat (1972), Joan Shangold (1980, 1984), Paul Shapiro (1986), Patricia Sheehan (1967), Kura D. Shepard (1978), Michael Shepard

(1966), Mark G. Sheppard (1970), Armin Shimerman (1978), John Shuman (1978), *Ruben Sierra* (1978), *Peter Silbert* (1984–86), Adam Silver (1984), Ben Silver (1984), Phyllis Silver (1971), David Silverman (1984–86), Curt Simmons (1982), Jonathan Simmons (1979, 1982), Alex Sinclair (1975), Daniel Singer (1985), *Marc Singer* (1968–70), Cameron Sisk (1982), Lisa Sisley (1978), Allyn Sitjar (1979), Warren Sklar (1971, 1973), *Leah Sluis (Leah Stuis)* (1976, 1979), Jean Smart (1977–78), Audrey Smith (1972), Brady Smith (1977), Casey Smith (1984), Frank Smith (1985), Lara A. Smith (1984), *Lois Smith* (1986), Parker Smith (1968), Marcus Smythe (1977), Steve Sneed (1981), *Barbara Sohmers* (1984), Tony Soper (1984–86), Adrian Sparks (1971–73), Don F. Spencer (1968), Frederick Sperberg (1976), Thomas Spickard (1978), Thomas Spiller (1973, 1975), Sharon Squires (1973), Kathryn Stalter (1976–77), Bradley Stam (1979–80), Andrea Stein (1984–85), Jeffrey Steitzer (1979), Amy Steltz (1979–82), Brian Sterling (1967), David Stettler (1985), Anita Stewart (1967), Mada Stockley (1975), Margaret Stockton (1971), Randall Stuart (1984), Rebecca Stucki (1985), Gregory P. Suenaga (1986), Eric Sumerall (1985), Faye B. Summers (1982), Elizabeth Swain (1968), William Swan (1972), Jenni Swanson (1970), *Jack Sydow* (1985), *William Szymanski* (1986), *Robert E. Taeschner* (1971, 1973–74, 1976, 1985), Tremaine Tamayose (1986), Tom Tangney (1972), Barbara Tarbuck (1978), Bill (William) Taylor (1965), Holland Taylor (1968), James Taylor (1976), Sue Taylor (1969), Vern Taylor (1975, 1982, 1984), Bill Terkuile (1981–83, 1985–86), Ray Thach (1973), Mary Thieten (1984–85), *Eberle Thomas* (1983), G. Vallmont Thomas (1985), Brian Thompson (1978), *Gary Thomsen (Thompson)* (1970, 1972), *Ian Thomson* (1973), Steve Tomkins (1977, 1979), Jim Tompkins (1968–69), *Ben Tone* (1967, 1972–73, 1975, 1977, 1979–80, 1982, 1984), Ann H. Topping (1975), John Towey (1973), Casey Trupin (1984–86), Marie Truty (1974), Sergei Tschernisch (1967, 1977), Richard Marlin Tutor (1980, 1982–86), Lyn Tyrrell (1982), Donna Uno (1972), Deems Urquhart (1970–71, 1973), Carolyn Val-Schmidt (1977), Henrietta Valor (1973), Mary Van Arsdel (1984), Floyd Van Buskirk (Giannove-Van Buskirk) (1984–85), *David Vaughan* (1966–70), Jo Vetter (1985–86), George Vogel (1966), Anne Walker (1967), Suzanne Walker (1977), Patricia Walter (1970), Kelly Walters (1969, 1971–72, 1976–78), Dori Warren (1972), Richard S. Watson (1968, 1975), Laurel Watt (1981), A. C. Weary (1975–76), Paul Anthony Weber (1985), Casey Webster (1971), Vernon Weddle (1967), Michael Weholt (1971), William Weir (1986), Charles Weldon (1971), Rebecca Wells (1983), Diane Weyrick (1986), Geoffrey Weyrick (1986), David White (1980), *Joan White* (1970–71, 1974), Laurel Anne White (1986), David P. Whitehead (1985), Shay Whitman (1968), Mason Whitney (1971), Dick Wilkens (1978), Mark Wilkinson (1970), Amy Beth Williams (1979–80), David B. Williams (1974), Edward R. Williams (1986), *Sam Williams* (1986), Nina Cole Wishengrad (1979–81, 1983–84), Andrew Witt (1972), William C. Witter (1972, 1974–75), *Catherine Wolf* (1984, 1986), Tim Wolfe (Woolfe) (1970), Paul Wollangk (1970), Christopher Wong (1981), G. Wood (1975), Lynn Wood (1971), Carol Woodbury (1969–70), Russell Woodbury (1972), Allie Woods (1971, 1973), Steve Worthington (1971), Jonathan Wright (1967), R. Hamilton Wright (1980, 1985–86), Roald Berton Wulff (1985), Stanley Yale (1976), *Stephen Yoakam* (1984), Will York (1976), Jerri Lee Young (1986), *Joan Young* (1965), Arne Zaslove (1968, 1970), Robert Zenk (1977–80, 1984), *Stephen Zettler* (1983), Joe Zimmerman (1969).

REPERTORY

1965: *Oh Dad, Poor Dad, Cat on a Hot Tin Roof, Who'll Save the Plowboy, Dark of the Moon, The Private Ear* and *The Public Eye*.

1966: *In White America, The Typist* and *The Tiger, The Mirrorman* and *The Hat, On Trial* and *The Ladder, Tiny Alice, A Thurber Carnival, The Physicists, Arsenic and Old Lace, The Collection* and *The Room.*

1967: *Luv, The Crossroads, The Decision, The Deputy, Out at Sea* and *Strip Tease, After the Fall, The Unwicked Witch, Behind the Scenes, The Great Divide, The Fantasticks, The Caretaker.*

1968: *Slow Dance on the Killing Ground, Jack and the Beanstalk, Eh?, Royal Hunt of the Sun, The Lion in Winter, Black Comedy, Captain Fantastick Meets the Ectomorph, The Dancing Donkey, A Delicate Balance, Waiting for Godot, Androcles and the Lion.*

1969: *Celebration, The Homecoming, The Brave Little Tailor, Rhinoceros, Inadmissable Evidence, Rumpelstiltskin, Marat/Sade, Philadelphia, Here I Come!, Crabdance.*

1970: *The Birthday Party, Professor Filarsky's Miraculous Invention, The Balcony, Rosencrantz and Guildenstern Are Dead, The Adventures of Br'er Rabbit, The Caucasian Chalk Circle, The Prime of Miss Jean Brodie, Endgame, Your Own Thing.*

1971: *Hadrian VII, The Puppet Prince, Jack and the Beanstalk, The Boys in the Band, The Night Thoreau Spent in Jail, An Original, Absurd Musical Revue for Children, Ceremonies in Dark Old Men, Plaza Suite, A Cry of Players, You're a Good Man, Charlie Brown.*

1972: *The Indian Experience, The Me Nobody Knows, The Cow in the Kitchen, What the Butler Saw, The Effect of Gamma Rays on Man-in-the-Moon Marigolds, Courageous Ki and the Serpent, Echoes, Trial of the Catonsville Nine, Moonchildren, Butterflies Are Free, An Original, Absurd Musical Revue for Children, The Christmas Show.*

1973: *Under Milk Wood, No Place to Be Somebody, How the Camel Got Its Hump, Old Times, One Flew over the Cuckoo's Nest, Skits and Other Silly Things, The Contractor, A Conflict of Interest, A Day in the Death of Joe Egg, An Original, Absurd Musical Revue for Children, The Cole Porter Review, The Indian Experience, The Christmas Show.*

1974: *Three Early Farces (The Brute, The Marriage Proposal, The Anniversary), The Locomotion Show, The Heiress, The Hot l Baltimore, And They Lived Happily Ever After, Twigs, A Streetcar Named Desire, Count Dracula, In Celebration, The Chairs* and *The Bald Soprano, Godspell, The Christmas Show.*

1975: *The Hollow Crown, Sleuth, The Resistible Rise of Arturo Ui, When You Comin' Back, Red Ryder?, Quiet Caravans, Of Mice and Men, Oh, Coward!, Oh, Coward!* (Alaska tour), *An Original, Absurd Musical Revue for Children, The Whistlestop Review, We Three, The Christmas Show.*

1976: *The Whistlestop Review, An Original, Absurd Musical Revue for Children, Fire!, See the Players, Sizwe Bansi Is Dead, The Time of Your Life, Scapino!, Desire Under the Elms, Relatively Speaking, Boccaccio, A Christmas Carol.*

1977: *The Whistlestop Review, As You Like It, Travesties, Ladyhouse Blues, Streamers, The Club, Absurd Person Singular, The Odyssey, A Christmas Carol.*

1978: *The Odyssey, Henry IV*, Part I, *Shadowbox, Ballymurphy, Sea Horse, Makassar Reef, Anything Goes, Forgotten Door, A Christmas Carol.*

1979: *Forgotten Door, Seattle Eclectic, The Odyssey* (includes tour to Washington, D.C., and Victoria, British Columbia), *Man and Superman, Fanshen, Otherwise Engaged, Holy Ghosts, Water Engine, The Fantasticks, A Wrinkle in Time, A Christmas Carol.*

1980: *A Wrinkle in Time, Seattle Eclectic, For Colored Girls Who Have Considered Suicide/When the Rainbow Is Enuf, Catholics, Artichoke, Wings, Buried Child, Starting Here, Starting Now, A Christmas Carol.*

1981: *A Pushcart War, Doors, Custer, Getting Out, Billy Bishop Goes to War, Night and Day, Loose Ends, Whose Life Is It Anyway?, A Christmas Carol.*

1982: *Ali Baba and the Forty Thieves, Five-by-Five, Da, Fridays, Waiting for the Parade, The Gin Game, The Greeks, A Christmas Carol.*

1983: *Aladdin and the Magic Lamp, A Soldier's Play, The Dining Room, Crimes of the Heart, Educating Rita, Cloud 9, A Christmas Carol.*

1984: *Not Just Kidstuff, The Persian Princess, Amadeus, Top Girls, Angels Fall, Thirteen, Fool for Love, The Communication Cord, Tendencies, A Christmas Carol, Tendencies, None of the Above, Uncle Bonsai.*

1985: *The Persian Princess, Beauty and the Beast, What's in It for Me?, Step on a Crack, The Odyssey, King Lear, True West, Doctors and Diseases, A Little Bit o' Lehrer, Maydays, Other Places, End of the World, "Super Heroes," "Or Can We Talk?" Quartermaine's Terms, A Christmas Carol, Uncle Bonsai, None of the Above.*

1986: *Juggle and Hyde, Theseus and the Minotaur, A Wrinkle in Time, The Navigator, A Story of Micronesia, Ming Cycle, Uncle Bonsai, 18 Wheels, Bridge to Terabithia, On the Razzle, Painting Churches, Tales from Hollywood, Brighton Beach Memoirs, Jail Diary of Albie Sachs, Little Shop of Horrors, A Christmas Carol.*

BIBLIOGRAPHY

Published Sources:
Seattle Post-Intelligencer, 1965–86.
Seattle Times, 1965–86.
The Weekly, 1985–86.

Archival Resources:
Seattle, Washington. A Contemporary Theatre. Scrapbooks, programs, subscription brochures, *Backstage*.
———. Seattle Public Library. Scrapbooks, 1965–86; press releases, 1967–86.
———. University of Washington Libraries. Manuscripts Section. Reports, annual meeting information, programs, reviews, correspondence, financial records, subscription records, box-office records, building plans.

Liz Fugate

ACT, INC. See A CONTEMPORARY THEATRE, INC.

ACTORS, INC. See ACTORS THEATRE OF LOUISVILLE.

ACTORS' LABORATORY, INC., was established in Hollywood, California, in 1941 by actors, mostly former members of the Group Theatre*, who were disenchanted with opportunities then available in the film capital for developing their craft. More than two dozen actors and actresses met first in December 1940 to discuss their needs. A workshop for professional actors met first at the Music Box Theatre but soon moved to a rented studio over the Ontra Cafeteria on Vine Street and then to a loft over Sharkey's Bar at 5873 Franklin Street. By the end of the first session of the workshop in July 1941 the group numbered more than seventy.

Actors' Laboratory, Inc. ("the Lab"), in part an offspring of the Hollywood Theatre Alliance, a small art theatre group, set out to establish workshops and to conduct classes to perfect the acting skills of Hollywood performers. Public performances of workshop projects and much lauded major theatre productions followed from this initial impulse to reform Hollywood's working environment. Former Group Theatre actors thus hastened the introduction into the American film industry of acting techniques inspired by the teachings of Russian actor-director Konstantin Stanislavsky. More important perhaps the Lab featured the politically committed actor in an assault on the social ills of American society, especially racism and economic exploitation. The group met overwhelming resistance from authorities in the film industry and in government.

The Lab founders first set up an executive board, which remained the group's ruling body throughout its nine-year existence. The board developed a curriculum, organized the laboratory, and engaged teachers. Former Group Theatre performers Roman Bohnen, Mary Virginia Farmer, and J. Edward Bromberg as well as Jules Dassin, formerly of the Jewish Art Theatre, were the first faculty of the Lab. Students, accepted to the workshop after an interview with the board, paid $12.50 to attend classes meeting two nights each week. Teachers were salaried but actually paid only sporadically. Shortly after establishing the workshop, the board organized the Forum, a venue for guest speakers who provided instructional and inspirational lectures for the Lab's members. A statement of policy adopted in May 1941 stressed the close tie between social and political beliefs and actorly craftsmanship.

The first public performance of the Lab occurred December 8, 1941, in the loft over Sharkey's Bar. Roman Bohnen directed members of the Lab in the second act of Clifford Odets' *Paradise Lost*. The performance went on despite hysteria created by the Japanese bombing of Pearl Harbor and an apparent threat to military installations on the West Coast. The Lab then produced *Brother Rat*, a comedy about the misadventures of three cadets at the Virginia Military Institute, by VMI graduates John Monks, Jr., and Fred F. Findlehoffe. It toured area air and naval bases and introduced the Lab to the fulfilling task of producing plays for tours to training camps and hospitals and to American military bases overseas. In the next three years the Lab produced eight shows for the Hollywood Victory Committee and the United Service Organizations (USO).

The spring workshop in 1942, whose faculty included film and stage director Daniel Mann, attracted fifty-four students, some of whom were on scholarships given by the board according to need and talent. In March 1943 the Lab moved to 1455 Laurel Boulevard, just behind Schwab's Drugstore on Sunset Boulevard. The wood-frame house, already converted to a theatre with a small stage and large rehearsal room, and an outbuilding used for classes was the home of the Lab until its demise in 1950. The Lab incorporated in 1943 and hired a permanent head of the workshop in Mary Tarcai. Tarcai, a graduate of Columbia University's drama department, had studied with Maria Ouspenskaya and Richard Boleslavsky, former members of Stanislavsky's Moscow Art Theatre, and she had taught acting for six years at the Neighborhood Playhouse School of Theatre in New York City. By May 1944 the Lab boasted 144 members. The board also established "work groups" in 1944 to provide members opportunities to work on their craft outside the productions, which could not accommodate all the members, and beyond the classroom, a setting that did not appeal to some members. The leadership of Roman Bohnen in most affairs of the Lab was well established by this time. Until his death from a heart attack during a performance of a Lab production in 1949, Bohnen was the source of the group's vision and the mediator of its many internal struggles.

In 1945 the Lab reorganized, introducing a number of committees and councils into its structure. The ploy did little to democratize the group, however, for the executive board exercised ultimate control of policy. The Lab also enlarged its faculty to accommodate veterans studying acting under the G.I. Bill and contract players sent to classes by the film studios that retained them. A faculty of ten, including actor Anthony Quinn, conducted day classes, while a faculty of four, including Hume Cronyn, offered night classes. Studio contract players such as Marilyn Monroe and Audie Murphy and veterans such as Joe Papirofsky (later Broadway director and producer Joe Papp) encountered a variety of approaches to acting, most based on Stanislavskian principles.

The Lab also expanded its schedule to include "major" productions at the Laurel Avenue Theatre and, since the Laurel Avenue Theatre was restricted by zoning laws to weekend use at other locations in Hollywood, most notably at the Las Palmas Theatre. The Lab's workshop and USO productions had garnered it a small reputation, but the major productions of dramatic classics, recent Broadway hits, and new plays by southern California writers during the period from 1945 to 1950 established it as one of the most effective acting companies in the United States. Lee J. Cobb was noted for his work in the title role of Andre Obey's *Noah*, presented in March 1945 at the Laurel Avenue Theatre. Lab member Morris Carnovsky then directed his own adaptation of Ben Jonson's *Volpone*, which became the organization's greatest hit. It was seen first in 1945 at the Laurel Avenue Theatre and then at the Las Palmas Theatre, where it ran for twenty-five performances in 1946 and twenty-five performances in 1947. The cast included Phoebe Brand, Lloyd Bridges, J. Edward Bromberg, Norman Lloyd, and Rhys Williams. The combination of successful productions and heavy enrollment at the workshop in 1945–46 made the Lab financially solvent, a condition it seldom enjoyed before or after this period.

In 1946 the Lab began to cultivate an interest in new plays, trying but failing to duplicate the success of the Group Theatre in this regard. The organization also experienced internal dissension as students in the workshops chafed for more consideration for work in major productions. By 1947 a clique of some board members and their friends dominated casting for major productions, a hold unbroken to the end of the life of the group. However, actors paid for their work in Lab productions typically endorsed their checks and returned them to the Lab as a contribution to its welfare. In 1948, in an effort to streamline decision-making, the executive board, which numbered as many as thirty at times, appointed an executive arm committee to deal with day-to-day business. The committee never functioned effectively, however, because the board never relinquished its authority to permit the committee to act.

As early as November 1945, undocumented accusations of Communist party influence in the affairs of the Lab were printed in the *Hollywood Reporter*. Questions about the loyalty of actors and other artists in the theatre and film industry surfaced during hearings of the Un-American Activities Committee of the U.S. House of Representatives in 1947. The California Senate followed the lead of the U.S. Congress in establishing the Fact-Finding Committee on Un-American Activities. Hearings of the committee into allegations of Communist infiltration into the film industry commenced in Los Angeles in February 1948. Committee chair, State Senator Jack B. Tenney, subpoenaed four members of the Lab's executive board: Roman Bohnen, Will Lee, Rose Hobart, and J. Edward Bromberg. The Tenney Committee accused these board members, on the basis of hearsay evidence alone, of suborning students with un-American teachings. Shortly thereafter the film industry blacklisted these four and other actors associated with the Lab. Some players, such as Jeff Corey, stayed in Los Angeles and struggled to survive without film-acting work. Corey became an influential acting teacher, conducting classes in the privacy of his home, but warned students to disavow any association with him. Others left the film colony for the stages of New York, London, and the capitals of Europe. Lee J. Cobb, for instance, rebounded from the blacklist with his heralded portrayal of Willy Loman in Arthur Miller's *Death of a Salesman*. Others struggled for a livelihood without work in Hollywood. The Tenney Committee accusations also destroyed the tenuous balance of power among the leaders of the Lab. After Bohnen's death in 1949, the organization collapsed on the occasion of an uprising among students in the workshop clambering for more participation in major productions. The Lab mounted its last production in February 1950.

PERSONNEL

Executive Board: Membership changed from year to year; these names appear repeatedly in extant minutes of meetings of the executive board: Alan Baldwin, John Berry, Roman Bohnen, Jack Bragin, Phoebe Brand, Lloyd Bridges, J. Edward Bromberg, Phil Brown, Morris Carnovsky, Howland Chamberlin, Araby Colton, Jeff Corey, Louise Craig, Hume Cronyn, Howard Da Silva, Jules Dassin, Mary Davenport, Katherine De Mille, Howard Dimsdale, Edward Dymtryk, Mavis Eliofson, Rayne Ellis, Mary Virginia Farmer, Richard Fiske, Jody Gilbert, Michael Gordon, Lloyd Gough, Rose Hobart, Ben Irwin, Robert Karnes, Gia Kent, George Kilgen, Henry Koster, Hy Kraft, Will Lee, Sam Levene, Daniel Mann, Winifred Mann, Virginia Mullen, Ruth Nelson, Joe Papirofsky, Larry Parks, Abe Polansky, Gene Reynolds, Waldo Salt, S. Sylvan Simon, Helen Slote, Art Smith, Elliot Sullivan, Mary Tarcai, Jane Taylor, Ray Teal, Irene Tedrow, George Tyne, John Vernon, Herman Waldman, William E. Watts, John Wexley, Frances Williams, Mervin Williams, Marjorie Winfield, Ned Young.

Directors (Major Productions, 1945–50): David Alexander, Roman Bohnen, Lloyd Bridges, J. Edward Bromberg, Phil Brown, Morris Carnovsky, Jacobina Caro, Michael Chekhov, Bert Conway, Hume Cronyn, Jules Dassin, Danny Dare, Whitford Kane, Sam Levene, Robert Lewis, Daniel Mann, James O'Rear, Alfred Ryder, Vincent Sherman, Art Smith, Arthur Spencer, George Tyne.

Designers (Major Productions, 1945–50): Boris Aronson, Robert E. Andjulis, Charles Boswell, Gene Callnon, Sidney Dubin, Duane Finn, Mordecai Gorelik, John Hubley, Boris Karmas, Peter Klain, Les Marzolf, Thomas O'Neill, Nicholas Remisoff.

Actors and Actresses (Major Productions, 1945–50): Joe Agnello (1945), Marlene Aims (1947), Sara Allgood (1947), Pat Alphano (1946), Dick Anderson (1947), James Anderson (1947, 1948), John Arnold (1945), Jan Arvan (1948), Leonard Auerbach (1946), Richard Avonde (1947), Ruth Avonde (1946), Georgia Bachus (1948), Anton Backus (1946), Ken Bader (1946, 1947), Edward Bajian (1948), Allan Baldwin (1945), Paul Barrett (1945), Art Batanides (1948), Steve Bennett (1946), Helen Beverly (1945), Whit Bissell (1947), *Roman Bohnen* (1946–49), Anita Bolster (1947), Charles Boswell (1947, 1948), Frank Bowers (1948), *Phoebe Brand* (1945–48), Janet Brandt (1946, 1948), Lennie Bremman (1945–48), Beau Bridges (1948), Dorothy Bridges (1946), *Lloyd Bridges* (1945–48, 1950), Fred Briggs (1948), *Peter Brocco* (1946–48), *J. Edward Bromberg* (1945–49), Jay Brooks (1948), Barney Brown (1945, 1946), Evans Brown (1948), Phil Brown (1946, 1948), Steven Brown (1946), Cicily Browne (1950), George Buchanan (1948), Frank Cady (1946, 1947), William Cain (1946), *Morris Carnovsky* (1945, 1946, 1950), Camille Cassady (1948), Howland Chamberlin (1946, 1947), Richard Chandlee (1946, 1948), Guy Christian (1946), Angela Clarke (1948), Ruth Clifford (1947), *Lee J. Cobb* (1945), Muriel Coburn (1946), Leon Colker (1945), John Compton (1948), Bert Conway (1947, 1948), Charles Cooper (1948), *Jeff Corey* (1946, 1948), Jon Coslyn (1946), William Cottrell (1946), Walter Coy (1948), Helen Craig (1945), Oliver Crawford (1946, 1948), Howard Da Silva (1950), Mary Davenport (1947, 1948), Don Davis (1946), James Davis (1946), Richard Davis (1947), Robert A. Davis (1948), Olive Deering (1949), Dick Dickerson (1945), Alan Douglas (1948), Constance Dowling (1945), Joe Du Val (1948), Sid Dubin (1946), Marjorie Dunfee (1947, 1948), Al Eben (1946), Barry Eddy (1946, 1947), Rayme Ellis (1947), Nick Elsmore (1945), Leif Ericson (1946, 1947), Doris Fesette (1948), Joel Fluellen (1945, 1948), Helen Ford (1950), Ruth Ford (1945), Paul Frees (1945), David Fresco (1945, 1946, 1948), John Garfield (1946), Sam Gary (1945), *Jody Gilbert* (1946, 1947, 1948), Ned Glass (1948), Lloyd Gough (1948), Hugo Haas (1945, 1946, 1947), John Halladay (1948), Alvin Hammer (1945, 1946, 1947), Sammy Hill (1946), Rose Hobart (1946), Bob Hoffman (1948), Maynard Holmes (1946, 1948), Rod Holton (1945), Ray Hyke (1948), Anthony Joachim (1948), Russell Johnson (1946), Ken Jones (1945, 1946, 1948), Whitford Kane (1947), Robert Karnes (1946), Doris Karnes (1946, 1948), Max Lamb (1948), Frank Lattimore (1945), Mark Laurence (1946, 1947), Leon Lenoir (1945), *Norman Lloyd* (1946–47), Ian McDonald (1948), Sean McGlory (1947), Danna McGraw (1946, 1947), Kitty McHugh (1948), Paul McVey (1948), Joseph Mantell (1946, 1947), Adrienne Marsden (1947), Martin Mason (1946, 1948), Melle Matthews (1948), Ed Max (1948), Hal Melone (1946), Rolf Meyer (1948), Carl Milletaire (1945, 1946), John Mitchell (1948), John Montell (1945), Marilyn Moore (1946), Henry Morgan (1947), Danny Morton (1948), Marjorie Nelson (1946, 1948, 1950), Ruth Nelson (1945, 1949), Arthur O'Connell (1948), James O'Rear (1946), Jerry Oser (1948), Wendy Oser (1948), Joy Page (1945), *Jerry Paris* (1948), Jim Parker (1948), Larry Parks (1945), Bot Patten (1948), Kenneth Patterson (1946, 1948), Nigel H. Pelham

(1945), John Pelletti (1948), Leo Penn (1946, 1949), Marilee Phelps (1948), Bill Philla (1946), Philip Pine (1946, 1948), Vincent Price (1947), Frances Rey (1945), Gene Reynolds (1946, 1948), Armand Roland (1945), Amerlia Romano (1945), Clinton Rosemond (1947), Alfred Ryder (1946, 1947), Leonard Salvo (1948), Beth Sanderson (1948), Carlo Schipa (1945), Virginia Sharpe (1946, 1947), Manny Shipow (1946), Robin Short (1945), Semford Siegel (1945), George Slocum (1948), *Art Smith* (1946–49), Billy Smith (1948), Dean Smith (1947), Emmet Smith (1948), Stewart Stern (1948), *Houseley Stevenson* (1945–48), F. Carrington Strong (1948), Philip Sudano (1945), Jessica Tandy (1947), Alan Tanner (1945), Arno Tanney (1948), Mary Tarcai (1946), Irene Tedrow (1946), Oliver Thorndyke (1945), Joe Thornton (1945), Anthony Trager (1946), *George Tyne* (1945–48), *Peter Virgo* (1945–48), Herman Waldman (1946), Ray Walker (1947), Harlan Warde (1946, 1947), Stanley Waxman (1948), Francis S. White (1945, 1947), Napoleon Whiting (1948), Mack Williams (1946), Mervyn Williams (1946, 1948), *Rhys Williams* (1945–47), Majorie Winfield (1945), Ian Wolfe (1945), Adrian Wood (1946), Buddy Yarus (1946).

REPERTORY

1941: Loft on Franklin Avenue: *Paradise Lost*, Second Act.

1941–44: USO Tours: *Brother Rat, Three Men on a Horse, The Male Animal, The Night of January 16th, Girl Crazy, Mr. and Mrs. North, Kiss and Tell, Arsenic and Old Lace*.

1944: Laurel Avenue Theatre: *The Bear, The Curse of the Coffin Nails, Sweet and Simple, Shall We Improvise?, Hello Out There, Evils of Tobacco, All Aboard, Shy and Lonely, A Pound on Demand*.

1945: Laurel Avenue Theatre: *Noah, Volpone, A Bell for Adano, All Aboard, Craig's Wife* (a scene), *Evils of Tobacco, All A-Bored*. Philharmonic Auditorium: *Same Boat Brother, All Aboard*.

1946: Las Palmas Theatre: *Volpone, Awake and Sing!, Home of the Brave, Inspector General, To the Living, Birthday, Wizard of Oz*. Laurel Avenue Theatre: *Birthday, Mooney's Kid Don't Cry, Pierre Patelin, The Shewing Up of Blanco Posnet, Green Cockatoo, A Sound of Hunting*.

1947: Laurel Avenue Theatre: *The Front Page, Paul Thompson Forever, A Talk in Darkness, Pastoral, $4.40, Peer Gynt, Aria de Capo, Rising of the Moon, Summer Comes to the Diamond O, 27 Wagons Full of Cotton, Portrait of a Madonna, Great Man's Whiskers*. Las Palmas Theatre: *Portrait of a Madonna, The Last of My Solid Gold Watches, Mooney's Kid Don't Cry, End of the Beginning, Juno and the Paycock, All Cultural Levels Eat Here, Volpone*.

1948: Laurel Avenue Theatre: *Dragon, Declaration, A Pound on Demand, Trial by Jury, Red Peppers, The Mask, The Cause of It All, Plant in the Sun, Freight, All You Need Is One Good Break, Androcles and the Lion, Shoemaker's Holiday, Abe Lincoln in Illinois, Exuberanza, Now Is the Winter*. Las Palmas Theatre: *All My Sons*. Strauss Auditorium: *Plant in the Sun, Freight, World by the Tail*. Musart Theatre: *Another Part of the Forest*.

1949: Coronet Theatre: *Now Is the Winter*. Laurel Avenue Theatre: *Distant Isle, Monday's Hero, Proud Accent*.

1950: New Globe Theatre: *The Banker's Daughter*.

BIBLIOGRAPHY

Unpublished Source:

Salvi, Delia N. "The History of the Actors' Laboratory, Inc." Doctoral dissertation, University of California, Los Angeles, 1969.

Delia N. Salvi

ACTORS' REPERTORY COMPANY, New York, New York, produced plays of social and political protest in commercial theatres from 1935 to 1938. The group was formed from the company of the Theatre Union's* production of Albert Bein's *Let Freedom Ring*, and further solidified while producing a bill of radical one-act plays on Sunday nights during the run of *Let Freedom Ring*, beginning January 12, 1936. On March 14, 1936, they offered the premiere of Irwin Shaw's forceful *Bury the Dead*, and in April they brought the Shaw antiwar drama to Broadway for a run of 110 performances.

The group's succeeding efforts never achieved the level of popularity or artistry of *Bury the Dead*. In November 1936 they produced E. P. Conkle's *200 Were Chosen*, which ran for thirty-five performances. *Washington Jitters* by John Boruff and Walter Hart, their final effort, opened, with Theatre Guild backing, at the Guild Theatre in May 1938 and ran for three weeks.

The John Lenthier Troupe, a satellite of the company committed to politics and reform more radical than the generally centrist main body, joined Actors' Repertory Company regular Will Geer in summer tours performing militant Left-wing material for audiences of workers throughout the United States.

In addition to Geer, whose career as a featured player on Broadway, in films, and in television spanned nearly fifty years, Actors' Repertory Company players of note included John O'Shaughnessy, later a director for the Arena Stage*, Washington, D.C., and the Theatre of the Living Arts*, Philadelphia. Robert Porterfield, founder of the Barter Theatre*, Abingdon, Virginia, also performed with the group.

PERSONNEL

Producer: Sidney Harmon.

Directors: Walter Hart, Worthington Miner, J. Donald Shugrue.

Playwrights: Walter Hart, J. Donald Shugrue.

Actors and Actresses Appearing in at Least Two Actors' Repertory Company Productions: Paula Bauersmith, Aldrich Bowker, Dorothy Brackett, Norma Chambers, David Clarke, Edwin Cooper, Charles Dingle, Will Geer, Kathryn Grill, Charles Jordan, Rose Keane, Gordon Nelson, Neill O'Malley, John O'Shaughnessy, Douglass Parkhurst, Robert Porterfield, Anthony Ross, Garland Smith, Lesley Stafford, Fred Stewart, Lucille Strudwick, George Oliver Taylor, Robert Thomsen, Bertram Thorn, Frank Twaddell, Eric Walz, Herta Ware, Robert B. Williams.

REPERTORY

Bury the Dead (1936), *Prelude* (1936), *200 Were Chosen* (1936), *A Town and Country Jig* (1937), *Washington Jitters* (1938).

BIBLIOGRAPHY

Published Sources:

New York Times, 1935–38.

Goldstein, Malcolm. *The Political Stage: American Drama and Theater of the Great Depression*. New York: Oxford University Press, 1974.

Archival Resource:

New York, New York. New York Public Library. Billy Rose Theatre Collection. Actor's Repertory Company scrapbook and John Lenthier Troupe clippings file.

Weldon B. Durham

ACTORS THEATRE OF LOUISVILLE was founded in Louisville, Kentucky, in 1964 by Richard Block and Ewel Cornett. Block, a native of Louisville, educated at Carnegie Institute of Technology and the University of Washington, organized a group called Theatre Louisville in the spring of 1963. While Block tried to raise money for a professional theatre, Cornett formed another group called Actors, Inc. Cornett's troupe produced five plays in the summer of 1964 and then Block and Cornett merged their organizations to form Actors Theatre of Louisville (ATL). ATL opened December 18, 1964, in a tiny converted loft at 617½ South Fourth Street. The first season of six productions ran for twenty-four weeks and played to almost 16,000 admissions. Receipts of $34,000 were supplemented by a grant of $15,000 from the Rockefeller Foundation. The second season of eight productions ran for thirty weeks on a budget of $98,000. Block and Cornett then acquired a lease on the abandoned Illinois Central Railroad Station at Seventh Street and Ohio River for use in 1966–67.

ATL grew rapidly under the Block–Cornett management. In 1967 its subscription sales campaign peaked at 5,700, an increase of more than 300 percent since 1965. The budget stood at $198,000, allowing the compactly organized group to produce eight plays in a season of thirty-six weeks. Critical response was increasingly warm, and the group acquired grants from the National Endowment for the Arts, the Kentucky Arts Commission, the U.S. Department of Health, Education, and Welfare, and the Ford Foundation, allowing it to enlarge and extend its services.

Then in January 1969, with subscription sales declining and public enthusiasm cooling, Block asked his board of directors to seek a new producer-director, one who could better marshal community support. Block's achievements were impressive, but the task of selling ATL had become oppressive.

Block's replacement was Jon Jory, formerly associated with the Cleveland Play House* and cofounder and artistic director of the Long Wharf Theatre* of New Haven, Connecticut. ATL under Jory's management has become a vitalizing force in the cultural and economic life of Louisville and an organization with few, if any, peers among contemporary regional theatres. Jory, educated at the University of Utah and Yale University but an actor since childhood, was the showman and leader the group needed. He set about rebuilding all aspects of ATL. He lengthened the run of each production and decreased the season from eight to seven shows. He deemphasized the production of the demanding European masterworks that Block had favored and produced lighter, contemporary fare. He also reduced the size of the resident company of actors, hired more temporary performers, and used the savings to pay higher salaries to those remaining in the resident company. He warmed and loosened the ambience of the theatre and organized the theatre's operations to make theatre-going a total entertainment experience by offering attractions other than the plays themselves. Moreover, he vigorously solicited community support and inventively promoted theatre and other arts as Louisville's least expensive and most effective stimulant for economic growth. Active leadership in the Louisville Riverfront Development Project, in the Louisville Fund, and in united arts fund-raising inserted ATL into the total cultural life of the city. Cooperation with business and industrial interests helped to focus national interest on Louisville as a place to visit or relocate to. All types of involvement in the life of the community—a speaker's bureau, tours of productions to public schools and colleges, poetry programs in residential settings, drama classes, study materials on difficult plays, auctions, an autumn boutique, volunteer auxiliaries, and theatre rentals—strengthened the bond between ATL and the citizens of Louisville.

In Jory's first season attendance was up 50 percent over 1968–69. Subscription sales increased from 5,017 in 1969–70 to 8,216 in 1970–71, when season tickets accounted for 95 percent of admissions during a sold-out season.

In 1972 ATL moved to its current location in the old Bank of Louisville Building at 316–320 West Main Street in midtown Louisville. Adaptation of the national historical landmark, with its attractive Greek Revival lobby, cost $1.7 million, over 70 percent of which was raised locally. The renovation netted ATL the 641-seat Pamela Brown Auditorium, with a modified thrust stage, and the 160-seat Victory Jory Theatre, with its three-quarter arena stage. A short-lived children's theatre affiliate produced six plays in 1973–74 under the management of ATL regular Vaughn McBride. In 1974 ATL was designated the State Theatre of Kentucky. At its new home ATL continued to grow, serving 175,000 patrons in the 1978–79 season of seventeen productions in the two theatres. By 1985, twenty-one years after its founding, ATL was budgeted at more than $3.5 million per season.

ATL's 1971 production of *Tricks*, a musical adapted by Jory from Molière's *Les Fourberies de Scapin*, with a rock score by Jerry Blatt and lyrics by Lonnie Burstein, enjoyed a highly successful run in Louisville. In the spring of 1972 Jory moved it to Washington's Arena Stage*, where it played to warm critical and audience response, and then in January 1973 it opened at New York's Alvin Theatre to nearly universal critical oppobrium. It closed after five previews and eight performances. *In Fashion*, another Jory–Blatt–Burstein musical, pleased Louisville audiences in February and March 1973 and was selected for production on WNET's "Theatre in America" series and televised nationally on PBS in 1973 and 1974. Audience and critical acceptance of *Tricks, In Fashion, Kentucky!* (1973), and *Chips 'n' Ale* (1974) led to a major commitment to new plays, increasingly evident in 1976 when the group produced Paul Hunter's *Scott and Zelda* as well as the American premiere of Charles Marowitz's version of *Hamlet*. In the season of 1976–77 came D. L. Coburn's *The Gin Game* and John Orlock's *Indulgences in the Louisville Harem*. ATL offered the first of its now world-famous Festival of New American Plays in 1977–78. In the next nine years the group presented more than a hundred short and full-length new or nearly new plays, including such notably successful works as Marsha Norman's *Getting Out*, Beth Henley's *Crimes of the Heart*, James McClure's *Lone Star*, William Mastrosimone's *Extremities*, John Pielmeier's *Agnes of God*, Wendy Kesselman's *My Sister in This House*, Patrick Tovatt's *Bartok as Dog*, and Mary Gallagher's *Chocolate Cake*. In 1986 Jory announced that the new play festival would begin to emphasize the revival and development of plays that have had one professional production but little visibility. Through most of its history ATL has produced few premodern plays, less than one per season on the average, but in 1985–86 Jory launched a project called "Classics in Context" with a production of *The Misanthrope* and a number of events focused on the life and works of Molière. Otherwise, seasons in the early eighties, while dominated by the new play festival, have offered audiences a selection of familiar forms, plays, and authors, as exemplified by a series of Agatha Christie and Frederich Knott murder/mystery melodramas beginning in 1979.

The Festival of New American Plays focused national and international attention on ATL, as did the award of the 1978 Pulitzer Prize for Drama to D. L. Coburn for *The Gin Game*. In 1978 Jory and ATL received the Margo Jones Award for achievement in regional theatre and in 1979 the Shubert Foundation's James N. Vaughn Award for development of new plays.

The company continues to attract awards and recognitions. In 1978 *Getting Out*, by ATL's playwright-in-residence Marsha Norman, was cited as an "outstanding new play" by the American Theatre Critics' Association, and in 1979 Norman, a Louisville native, received a Rockefeller Foundation Award in support of her work. The 1980 Antoinette Perry Awards included a special Tony for ATL, and in 1981 the Pulitzer committee selected Beth Henley's *Crimes of the Heart*, a play discovered and first produced at ATL.

ATL's artistic personnel are typically young performers and designers, graduates of theatre programs in universities and conservatories. In the decade of the seventies they came to ATL after two or three years in other regional theatres; Jory has recruited maturer and more experienced performers in recent years. Resident performers commonly stay with ATL for only two or three years, though there are notable exceptions to this rule. Adale O'Brien joined the company in 1969 after performing leading roles at the Cleveland Play House, the Long Wharf Theatre, and Arena Stage. With only brief departures she has been a mainstay of the acting company, performing as many as eight roles each season. Lee Anne Fahey, a graduate of the Goodman School in Chicago, has performed regularly with ATL since 1970. The best known of ATL's former players is probably Ned

Beatty, who performed in Louisville in 1966. Beatty's fame has come as a supporting actor in such motion pictures as *Deliverance* and *Superman*.

Similar stability is evident in the technical departments of the theatre. Paul Owen has been resident scenic designer since 1971, after ten years at Houston's Alley Theatre. Kurt Wilhelm, like Fahey a graduate of the Goodman School of Drama, was resident costume designer from 1972 to 1985, after stints at Memphis' Front Street Theatre* and at the Pittsburgh Playhouse.

A considerable measure of credit for the extraordinary success of ATL must go to an administrative team made up of Jory, Alexander Speer (administrative director and with ATL since 1965), Trish Pugh (associate director from 1969 to 1981), and her successor, Marilee Herbert Slater. While Jory concentrates on the artistic direction of the company (he also directs several plays each season), Speer oversees the administrative staff, physical plant operations, budgets, relations with the ATL board of directors, and ATL's auxiliary enterprises, such as the Starving Artist Cabaret located in the basement of the theatre, and Pugh (later Slater) manages public relations and audience development activities. The expansion of ATL's programs and their integration into the life of the community are achievements traceable to the efforts of these company leaders.

PERSONNEL

Producing Directors: Richard Block (1964–69), Jon Jory (1969–86).

Administrative Directors/General Managers: Allan Longacre (1967–69), Alexander Speer (1967–86).

Associate Directors: Ewel Cornett (1964–66), Trish Pugh (1969–81), Marilee Herbert Slater (1981–86).

Directors: Steven Albrezi (1981–82), Kathy Bates (1984–85), Conrad Bishop (1985–86), Sam Blackwell (1981–82), *Richard Block* (1964–69), Kent Broadhurst (1983–84), Thomas Bullard (1984–86), *Larry Deckel* (1978–80, 1981–86), Rahda Delamarte, Alan Duke, Richard Dyas, Oskar Eustis, Robert Falls (1982–83), *Ray Fry* (1975–79, 1983–86), Susan Gregg (1982–83), Tom Gruenewald, Michael Hankins (1978–80), Israel Hicks (1974–76, 1980), Norris Houghton (1982–83), Elizabeth Ives (1974–81), *Ken Jenkins* (1969–72, 1980–85), Walton Jones, *Jon Jory* (1969–86), Victor Jory, Barnet Kelman, Charles Kerr (1973–79), Mladen Kiselov (1985–86), Vaughn McBride (1982–85), Perie McDonald, William McNulty, Peter Maloney, Emily Mann (1982–83), *Frazier W. Marsh* (1981–86), Lazlo Marton (1983–86), Christopher Murney (1969–72, 1974–76), Marsha Norman, *Adale O'Brien* (1974–76, 1981–86), Bill Partlan, John Pielmeier, Jackson Phippen, Teri Ralston, Mary Robinson, L. Susan Rowland, Amy Saltz (1979–82), Bekki Jo Schneider (1981–82), Theodore Shank (1981–83), *Robert Spera* (1982–86), Anthony Taccone, Kathleen Tolan (1982–83), Dierk Torsek (1982–83), Patrick Tovatt (1971–73), Russell Treyz (1982–83), Alexa Visarion, Julian Webber, B. J. Whiting.

Musical Director: Peter Ekstrom.

Choreographers: Sherry Barnard, Margaret Castleman [Schwartz] (1978–80), Lynne Gannaway, Michael Sokoloff.

Scenic and Lighting Designers: Jack Collard (1964–66), Geoffrey T. Cunningham (1971–76), Virginia Dancy, David S. S. Davis (1984), Thomas B. Dean, Miklos Feher, David Gano, Karen Gerson (1981–83), Jess Goldstein (1981–83), Karl Haas (1978–83),

David B. Hagen (1978–80), *Jeff Hill* (1979–86), James Joy, Brooke Karzen (1965–69), Geoffrey L. Korf, Hugh Landwehr, Grady Larkins (1972, 1980, 1981–83), Richard Mix (1965–69), *Paul Owen* (1972–86), Joe Pacetti, Myles Smith, Jim Sandefur, Karen Schulz, Sandra Strawn, Hal Tine (1969–72, 1980), Joseph A. Varga, Johnny Walker (1969–72), Elmon Webb, Richard Kent Wilcox (1981–83).

Costume Designers: Karen Anderson-Fields, Katherine Bonner, Marie Chiment, Fran Collard (1964–66), *Marcia Dixcy* (1983–86), Nancy Flanagan, Karen Gerson, Holly Jenkins-Evans, Katherine E. Kraft, James Larsen, Mary Lou Owen, Paul Owen (1978–80), Lucile Paris (1965–68), Ann Wallace, *Kurt Wilhelm* (1972–85).

Composers and Lyricists: Jerry Blatt, Lonnie Burstein.

Playwrights (two or more new plays produced): Lee Blessing, Roy Blount, Jr., Kent Broadhurst, David Campton, Anne Croswell, Peter Ekstrom, Gary Leon Hill, Ken Jenkins, Trish Johnson, Jon Jory, Wendy Kesselman, Vaughn McBride, James McClure, Jane Martin, William Mastrosimone, Marsha Norman, John Pielmeier, Robert Schenkkan, Adele Adeling Shank, Daniel Stein, Jeffrey Sweet, Patrick Tovatt, Jim Wann, Ara Watson.

Actors and Actresses (appearing in two or more productions in a single season; dates given for persons two or more years in the company): Leta Anderson, *Stanley Anderson* (1970–72), Walter Atamaniuk, Irwin Atkins, *Andy Backer* (1980–86), *G. W. Bailey* (1972–74), *Jim Baker* (1975–79), *Lenny Baker* (1966–68), Mary Bartlett, Peter Bartlett, Kathy Bates, *Ned Beatty* (1965–67), Wanda Bimson, Robert Blackburn, Jonathan Bolt, Eric Booth, Patrick Boxill, Rand Bridges, Thomas Martlett Brimm, *Kent Broadhurst* (1978–81), Robert Brock, Cheryl Lynn Bruce, Susan Bruyn, Timothy Burfield, *Leo Burmester* (1975–81, 1982–83), *Bob Burrus* (1974–79, 1983–86), Clyde Burton, *William Cain* (1973–77), James Carruthers, Susan Cash, Kathleen Chalfont, Grace Chapman, Patricia Charbonneau, *Bryan Clark* (1965–67), Kirstan Conn, *Christopher W. Cooper* (1980–82), *Dale Carter Cooper* (1969–73), *Jack Collard* (1964–66), Melody Combs (1984–86), Barbara Cornett, Joseph Costa, *Peggy Cowles* (1969–74, 1976–79, 1982–83), Gloria Cromwell, Jeanne Cullen, *Donna Curtis* (1971–73), Anthony DaFonte, Stephen Daley, Andrew Davis, Marguerite Davis, *Jo Deodato* (1965–67), *Dawn Didawick* (1976–78, 1982–83), Mary Diveny, Beth Dixon (1984–86), Sally Douglass, Alan Duke, Deanna Dunnagan, *George Ede* (1969–71), Jeanne Even, *Lee Anne Fahey* (1969–74, 1975–77, 1979–81, 1982–83, 1984–85), Clarence Felder, *Denise Fergusson* (1964–65, 1969–70), John H. Fields, Lanny Flaherty, *Mitzi Friedlander* (1965–69), *Ray Fry* (1975–86), Gwen Gautsch, George Gerdes, Reedy Gibbs, Janna Gjesdal, Lisa Goodman, Haskell Gordon, Patrick Gorman, Kathryn Grady, Rueben Green, Harry Groener, *Michael Gross* (1973–77), Max Gulack, Murray Guyer, Marilyn Hamlin, John Hancock, Sheila Haney, Jan Leslie Harding, Gerald Harte, Suzanna Hay, Gardner Hays, Anthony Heald, Debra Hedwall, *Laura Hicks* (1980–82), Dorothy Holland, *Vinnie Holman* (1974–75, 1977–78), Lori Holt, *Katherine Houghton* (1970–72), *Max Howard* (1966–68, 1972–73), Holly Hunter, Patrick Husted, Jeffrey Hutchinson, *Jean Inness* (1969–80), Jane Ives, Robert Jackson, Christine Jansen, Daniel Jenkins, *Ken Jenkins* (1969–72, 1980–81, 1982–83, 1984–85), *J. S. Johnson* (1964–69), Leona Johnson, Geffrey Duncan Jones, Jessie K. Jones, *Victor Jory* (1969–80), Cynthia Judge, Christine Kauffmann, Brian Keeler, Gretchen Kehda, Dolores Kenan, Will Kennon, *Michael Kevin* (1975–85), Kerstan Kilgo, *Susan Kingsley* (1969–70, 1974–84), *Charles Kissinger* (1965–68), Lee Kissman, Kevin Kling, Rob Knepper, *Bruce Kuhn* (1982–86), Cliff Lambert, Larry Larson, Ken Latimer, Levy Lee, Andrea Levine, *Judith Long* (1970–72), Bryan Lynner, Saundra MacDonald,

Frederic Major (1982–86), Deborah May, *Vaughn McBride* (1969–86), *Sandy McCallum* (1970–74), Pirie McDonald, Pat McNamara, *William McNulty* (1976–83, 1985–86), Margo Martindale, *Randle Mell* (1981–83), Theresa Merritt, William Mesnik, Nancy Mettle, Barry Michlin, Lynn Milgrim, Dana Mills (1984–86), Debra Monk (1984–86), Fred Morsell, Joe Morton, *Christopher Murney* (1969–72), William Myers, Tania Myren, *Adale O'Brien* (1969–86), K. Lype O'Dell, Gene O'Neill, Sally Parrish, Guy Paul, Patricia Pearcy, David O. Peterson, *John Pielmeier* (1974–79), *Anne Pitoniak* (1977–81), Mary Ed Porter, Scott Porter, Peggity Price, *Teri Ralston* (1973–75), *Steve Rankin* (1982–86), *Sally Fay Reit* (1980–83), Harriet Dean Richards, Marilyn Rockafellow, Brian Rose, Cristine Rose, Marcell Rosenblatt, Nada Rowand, Elizabeth Ruscio, Sheryl Ryunhart, Albert Sanders, *Fred Sanders* (1982–84), Robert Schenkkan, *James Secrest* (1976–78), *John Seitz* (1964–66), *Grant Sheehan* (1965–68), John Shepard, Harold Lee Sherman, John Short, Sylvia Short, Peter Silbert, *Jane Singer* (1966–68), Robertson Smith, Melodie Somers, John Spencer, Fritz Sperberg, June Stein, Sherry Steiner, Patricia Stewart, William Swetland, Jeffrey Tambor, David Tarleton, Hal Tenney, Ellen Tobie, *Dierk Toparzysek* (later *Torsek*) (1979–85), *Patrick Tovatt* (1972–74, 1976–79, 1981–82), Wayne Turney, John Turturro, Stephen Van Benschoten, *John C. Vennema* (1982–84), Bill Verderber, *Paul Villani* (1969–71), Basil Wallace, *Paul Watson* (1965–67), *Sherri Watson* (1965–67), *Jane Welch* (1965–69), Gretchen West, Kathryn Wheeler, Andre Womble, *James Woodall* (1964–68), Nan Wray, *Max Wright* (1970–72), John Wylie, Janet Zarish, David Zirlin, Daniel Ziskie.

REPERTORY

1964 (Actors' Inc.): *The Lady's Not for Burning, The Visit, Desire Under the Elms, The Zoo Story, The American Dream.*

1964–65: *Amphitryon, The Glass Menagerie, Arms and the Man, John Brown's Body, The Caretaker, Rashomon.*

1965–66: *Death of a Salesman, Waiting for Godot, The Importance of Being Earnest, No Exit, The Public Eye, Private Lives, A Doll's House, The School for Wives, The Tavern.*

1966–67: *All My Sons, Charley's Aunt, Miss Julie, The Knack, In White America, Slow Dance on the Killing Ground, Nathan Weinstein's Daughter, A Streetcar Named Desire.*

1967–68: *All the King's Men, The Hostage, Long Day's Journey into Night, Endgame, The Firebugs, A Night of the Dunce, Misalliance, Thieves' Carnival.*

1968–69: *The Member of the Wedding, The Birthday Party, Uncle Vanya, Rhinoceros, After the Fall, Summer and Smoke, The Cresta Run, The Imaginary Invalid.*

1969–70: *Under Milk Wood, The Killing of Sister George, Staircase, Star-Spangled Girl, See How They Run, Hamlet, Cat on a Hot Tin Roof, Beyond the Fringe.*

1970–71: *The Taming of the Shrew, Charley's Aunt, Our Town, The Lion in Winter, Thurber Carnival, The Tenth Man, Feiffer's People, Joe Egg, Major Barbara, Dracula.*

1971–72: *Play It Again, Sam, The Prime of Miss Jean Brodie, The Glass Menagerie, Tricks, Night Must Fall, Angel Street, A Midsummer Night's Dream, Marat/Sade, Hedda Gabler, Dear Liar, My Three Angels, Death of a Salesman.*

1972–73: *A Man for All Seasons, You Can't Take It with You, The Pirates of Penzance, Kentucky!, In Fashion, Macbeth, What the Butler Saw, Just Between Us, Adaptation* and *Next, Old Times.*

1973–74: *Long Day's Journey into Night, The Boor, The Man of Destiny, Play Strind-berg, Rendezvous, The Last of the Red Hot Lovers, Tartuffe, One Flew over the Cuckoo's Nest, The Journey of the Fifth Horse, The Boys in the Band, The Miracle Worker, Chips 'n' Ale, Dames at Sea, The Apple Tree, Thumbelina, A Christmas Carol, Saint George and the Dragon, Gabriel Ghost, Rumpelstiltskin, Cinderella.*

1974–75: *That Championship Season, Frankenstein, Countess Dracula, The Real In-spector Hound, Red Peppers, Swan Song, The Threepenny Opera, A Flea in Her Ear, The Ballad of the Sad Cafe, Relatively Speaking, Female Transport, Jacques Brel Is Alive and Well and Living in Paris, Noon, Welcome to Andromeda, Luv, Sleuth.*

1975–76: *Arms and the Man, The Hot l Baltimore, Ten Little Indians, Oedipus the King, Scapino!, The Last Meeting of the Knights of the White Magnolia, The Sunshine Boys, Dear Liar, The Sea Horse, Scott and Zelda, Measure for Measure* (adapted by Charles Marowitz).

1976–77: *The Best Man, Sexual Perversity in Chicago, Vanities, Reunion, Medal of Honor Rag, Tea with Dick and Jerry, Much Ado About Nothing, A Christmas Carol, The Resistible Rise of Arturo Ui, The Matchmaker, Who's Afraid of Virginia Woolf?, The Diary of Anne Frank, The Gin Game, Indulgences in the Louisville Harem, Table Manners, Round and Round the Garden, The Rainmaker.*

1977–78: *Round and Round the Garden, Living Together, Getting Out, Does Anybody Here Do the Peabody?, Andronicus, The Front Page, Luann Hampton Laverty Ober-lander, The Mousetrap, Peg o' My Heart, Daddies, The Bridgehead, Sizwe Bansi Is Dead, Third and Oak, A Christmas Carol, An Independent Woman, The Louisville Zoo* (various writers), *The Lion in Winter.*

1978–79: *Whose Life Is It Anyway? The Splits, The Runner Stumbles, The Play's the Thing, A Christmas Carol, What Every Woman Knows, Circus Valentine, Matrimonium, Find Me, Crimes of the Heart, Lone Star, Holidays* (various writers), *Room Service, The Gin Game, The Shadow Box, Gold Dust.*

1979–80: *Mornings at Seven, The Slab Boys, Childe Byron, Otherwise Engaged, A Christmas Carol, The Time of Your Life, The Incredible Murder of Cardinal Tosca, Tarantara! Tarantara!, Lone Star, Louisville Zoo Two*; Fourth Annual Festival of New Plays: *Today a Little Extra, Power Plays, Agnes of God, They're Coming to Make It Brighter, Sunset and Sunrise, Remington, Doctors and Diseases, The America Project* (various authors); *In Fashion.*

1980–81: *Sea Marks, Terra Nova, Cyrano de Bergerac, A Christmas Carol*; Shorts Festival: *Chocolate Cake, Semi-Precious Things, Final Placement, Just Horrible, Morn-ing Call, Propinquity, Ching, The Most Trusted Man in America, Let's Us; Sly Fox, On Golden Pond, Black Coffee*; Fifth Annual Festival of New Plays: *Future Tense, Auto-biography of a Pearl Diver, Early Times* (various authors), *Extremities, My Sister in This House, A Full-Length Portrait of America, SWOP, Shorts* (various authors); *Getting Out, Bus Stop.*

1981–82: *Lone Star, Chug, The Three Musketeers*; Shorts Festival: *Clara's Play, A Pale Lion, The Boy Who Ate the Moon, Damn Everything But the Circus, The New Girl, The Eye of the Beholder, The Groves of Academe, Singles, Gun for the Roses, In Between Time, Intermission, Lunch Break, Merry-Go-Round, Private Showing, The Saint of the Day, Wash, Rinse, Spin, Dry*; Humana Festival of New Plays: *The Informer, Clara's Play, The Grapes of Wrath, Oldtimer's Game, Full Hookup, Cemetary Man* and *Rupert's Birthday, Solo, Talking With, A Different Moon; The Gift of the Magi, The Spider's*

Web, The Arabian Nights, Tintypes, Billy Bishop Goes to War, The Oldest Living Graduate.

1982–83: *Julius Caesar;* Shorts Festival: *I Love You, I Love You Not, The Cameo, In the Bag, Bartok as Dog, The Happy Worker, Partners, Good Old Boy, A Tantalizing, The Value of Names, The Habitual Acceptance of the Near Enough, Flight Lines, I Want to Be an Indian, Coup, Clucks, Mine, The Art of Self-Defense, Nice People Dancing to Good Country Music; A Christmas Carol, The Gift of the Magi, Murder at the Vicarage, Misalliance, Mass Appeal;* Humana Festival of New Plays: *Eden Court, A Weekend Near Madison, Neutral Countries, Courage, Food from Trash, In a Northern Landscape, Sand Castles, Thanksgiving, Fathers and Daughters, A Tantalizing, The Value of Names; The Hasty Heart, Key Exchange, Wuthering Heights.*

1983–84: *A Midsummer Night's Dream, Holy Ghosts, A Christmas Carol;* Shorts Festival: *Flickers, The Death of King Philip, Comrade, A Gothic Tale, Businessman's Lunch, Graceland, Husbandry, Trotsky's Bar Mitzvah, Cheek to Cheek, Cuffs, Arts and Leisure, Sweet Sixteen, Five Ives Get Named, American Tropical, Shasta Rue, Coastal Waters, Girl in Green Stockings, What Comes After Ohio?, Approaching Lavendar, The Renovation, Well Learned, Creative Pleas; The Gift of the Magi, Of Mice and Men, The Three Sisters, A Coupla White Chicks Sitting Around Talking;* Humana Festival of New Plays: *Danny and the Deep Blue Sea, Independence, The Octette Bridge Club, Courtship, Execution of Justice, Lemons, The Undoing, 007 Crossfire, Husbandry; Dial "M" for Murder, The Middle Ages.*

1984–85: *True West, The Caine Mutiny Court Martial;* Shorts Festival: *Summer, The American Century, The Black Branch, The Dog Isn't Fifteen, My Early Years, The Person I Once Was, I'm Using My Body for a Roadmap, The Love Suicide at Schofield Barracks, The Roots of Chaos, Private Territory, The Cool of the Day, Advice to the Players; The Dining Room, The Gift of the Magi, A Christmas Carol, The School for Wives, Uncle Vanya, 'night, Mother;* Humana Festival of New Plays: *Available Light, Tent Meeting, The Very Last Lover of the River Cane, War of the Roses, Days and Nights Within, Ride the Dark Horse, Two Masters (The Rain of Terror* and *Errand of Mercy); Wait Until Dark, K2.*

1985–86: *Traveler in the Dark, Cloud 9, And a Nightingale Sang . . . ;* Shorts Festival; *The Gift of the Magi, A Christmas Carol, The Royal Comedians, The Misanthrope, Master Harold . . . and the boys;* Humana Festival of New Plays: *Smitty's News, To Culebra, No Mercy, How to Say Goodbye, Some Things You Need to Know Before the World Ends, A Final Evening with the Illuminati, Astronauts, The Shaper, 21A, How Gertrude Stormed the Philosopher's Club; A Streetcar Named Desire.*

BIBLIOGRAPHY

Published Sources:

Best Plays, 1969–70 through *1984–85.* New York: Dodd, Mead, & Co. 1970–85.

Harris, Albert J., Jr. "Actors Theatre of Louisville." *Dictionary of Literary Biography.* Vol. 7. Detroit: Gale Research Co., 1981, Pt. 2, pp. 405–11.

Kaminsky, Laura J., ed. *Nonprofit Repertory Theatre in North America, 1958–1975: A Bibliography and Indexes to the Playbill Collection of the Theatre Communications Group.* Westport, Conn.: Greenwood Press, 1977.

Novick, Julius. *Beyond Broadway: The Quest for Permanent Theatres.* New York: Hill and Wang, 1968.

Pevitts, Robert R. "At the Crossroads: Actors Theatre of Louisville." *Southern Theatre* 27 (Spring 1986): 27–28.

Theatre Profiles. Vols. 2–7. New York: Theatre Communications Group, 1975–85.

Theatre World. Vols. 26–42. New York: Crown Publishers, 1969–86.

Zeigler, Joseph W. *Regional Theatre: the Revolutionary Stage*. Minneapolis: University of Minnesota Press, 1973.

   Unpublished Sources:

Playbill. Collection of the Theatre Communications Group (microfiche) includes programs 1964–75.

Volk, Thomas W. "Actors Theatre of Louisville, 1963–1971." Master's thesis, Wake Forest University, 1973.

Weldon B. Durham

ACTORS THEATRE OF ST. PAUL (ATSP) was founded in 1977 by Michael Andrew Miner in the Foley Theatre, a 260-seat proscenium facility located at 2115 Summit Avenue, St. Paul, Minnesota. In 1983 the group moved to a 350-seat proscenium theatre at 28 West Seventh Place. Miner was an actor and director in several Minneapolis and St. Paul theatres as well as at the Milwaukee Repertory Theatre* before establishing ATSP. The group is committed to the development of a cohesive acting ensemble capable of meeting the demands imposed by a varied repertoire of modern and contemporary plays.

   Although not a collective, the company assists the artistic director in selecting plays that offer specific performance challenges. In its first season ATSP produced four plays focused in a study of the impact of the family on individual development. The next season the group produced three plays illustrating the uses of history: John Dos Passos' *U.S.A.*, Joseph O'Conor's *The Iron Harp*, and Robert Ingham's *Custer*. The group has committed a portion of recent seasons to the development of new plays through residencies for playwrights, staged readings, and full productions. Amlin Gray's *The Pavilion Room: A Victorian Reverie* was seen in 1980 and the same author's *Outlanders* in 1981. *The Gift of the Magi*, adapted by playwright-in-residence John Olive from the O'Henry story, was seen in 1980 as well. Olive's *Careless Love* premiered in 1985. Plays by other Minneapolis writers have included Lee Blessing's *Nice People Dancing to Good Country Music* (1984) and Paul D'Andrea's *Bully* (1985). The plays of Irish lyricist Brian Friel have been a regular feature of the ATSP repertory of contemporary drama.

   In addition to producing a season of six or seven plays, ATSP conducts regional tours and workshops and sponsors readings for new plays and residencies for young playwrights. The group also maintains an internship program and a children's theatre.

   Under Miner's direction ATSP has grown remarkably. Five actors and actresses formed the first resident company; in 1981 the group supported an acting company of sixteen. Similar development is evident in technical and management areas. The 1984–85 subscription list numbered 2,400; the company boasts as well a long list of patrons whose gifts have significantly supplemented box-office receipts.

PERSONNEL

Artistic Director: Michael Andrew Miner.

Managing Directors: Janet Miner, Martha Sloca Richards.

Directors: Martha Boesing, Michael Brindisi, James Cada, Jon Cranney, Janie Geiser, D. Scott Glasser, David Ira Goldstein, Dawn Renee Jones, David Kwait, Robert Mailand, Michael Andrew Miner, Emily Moon, Kevin Olsen, Sharon Ott, Kristin Overn, David Parrish, Louis Rackoff, Scott M. Rubsam, Louis Schaefer, David Schmalz, Jeff Steitzer, George C. White.

Scenery and Lighting Designers: Tom Butsch, Bob Bye, James Guenther, Mary Ellen Horty, Chris Johnson, Larry Kaushansky, Dick Leerhoff, Michael Andrew Miner, Jean Montgomery, Paul Peloquin, Doug Pipan, Nayna Ramey, Arthur Ridley, Paul Scharfenberger, Michael Vennerstrom, Rick Walsh, James Michael Water, Don Yunker.

Costume Designers: Christopher Beesley, Tessie Burdick, Margaret Churchill, Janie Geiser, Jill Hamilton, Rich Hamsen, Michael L. Hansen, Chris Johnson, Karen Nelson, Nayna Ramey, Arthur Ridley, Anne Rubin, Sandra Schulte, Don Yunker, Nan Zabriskie.

Playwrights: Lee Blessing, James Cada, Barry Casselman, Paul D'Andrea, Steven Dietz, Elaine Garonzik, Janie Geiser, Scott Ira Gertner, Amlin Gray, Ken Jenkins, Mark Keller, Wendy Kesselman, John Klein, Grace McKeany, Jaime Meyer, John Olive, George Sand.

Actors and Actresses: Carol Jean Anderson, Oscar Backlund, Nancy Bagshaw, Leslie Ball, Jim Baron, *Spencer Beckwith* (1979–83), Jeanne Blake, Paul Boesing, *James Cada* (1978–83), Virginia Calhoun, Jon Cavenaugh, John P. Connolly, James Craven, Mike Czeranko, Mary Ann Dempsey, Kevin Dewey, Suzanne Egli, Elizabeth English, Chris Forth, Charlotte Gibson, *D. Scott Glasser* (1982–83), *Louise Goetz* (1980–84), *Daniel J. Goodwin* (1985–87), Barbara Granning, David Gutmann, James Harris, *Terry Heck* (1985–87), Starri Hedges, *Diane Benjamin Hill* (1979–83), Lee Humphries, Craig Johnson, Prudence Johnson, Timothy M. Jopek, Gene Jundt, *Barbara Kingsley* (1980–85), Ben Krielkamp, *David M. Kwiat* (1979–85), John Lilleberg, Nancy Lillis, *David Linthall* (1985–87), Cynthia Dunbar Lohman, M. Merle McDill, Mark McGovern, Ruth Mackenzie, Chuck McQuary, Patrick Martin, Michael Andrew Miner, Margit Moe, Ken Morgan, Dolores Noah, Nancy Olesen, Steven J. O'Toole, Bryan Poffenberger, Mary Preus, Fay Price, Steve Pringle, Gary Rayppy, Mari Rovang, Vada Russell, Deborah Ryter, Mark Scanlon, *Louis Schaefer* (1986–87), Gale Sears, *Tim Seibert* (1985–87), James Stowell, Bernadette Sullivan, Bart Tinapp, Robert Wagner, Lizanne Wilson, *Sally Wingert* (1981–85), *Alan Woodward* (1979–85).

REPERTORY

1978: *Scenes from American Life, The Farm, Down by the Gravois (Under the Anheuser-Busch), Arms and the Man.*

1978–79: *The Waltz of the Toreadors, The Mandrake, Androcles and the Lion, The Iron Harp, Custer, U.S.A., Two for the Seesaw.*

1979–80: *Philadelphia, Here I Come!, The Lady's Not for Burning, The Three Sisters, A Touch of the Poet, The Two-Character Play, The Pavilion Room: A Victorian Reverie.*

1980–81: *Fighting Bob, How the Other Half Loves, The Gift of the Magi, Spokesong, Miss Julie, Outlanders, Ring Round the Moon, Vikings.*

1981–82: *Old Explorers, Hedda Gabler, Absurd Person Singular, How I Got That Story, Waiting for the Parade, The Subject Was Roses, The Increased Difficulty of Concentration, Tartuffe.*

1982–83: *The Sea Gull, Fallen Angels, Sea Marks, Disability: A Comedy, Angel Street, Pantomime, Have You Anything to Declare?.*

1983–84: *The Grand Hunt, Translations, The Hothouse, My Sister in This House, Nice People Dancing to Good Country Music, The Woods, Pygmalion.*

1984–85: *Awake and Sing!, Season's Greetings, The Faith Healer, We Won't Pay! We Won't Pay!, Careless Love, Bully, Scapin.*

1985–86: *Much Ado About Nothing, Joyous Noel!, And a Nightingale Sang, More Fun Than Bowling, Blood Knot, Trakkers Tel, The Barber of Seville.* First Stage series: *Among Dreams, Blue Nights, Painting It Red.*

1986–87: One-Act Play Festival: *Minnesota, Bitter Harvest, An Educated Lady, Chug, 4:45 AM, Bluegrass, The Coming of Mr. Pine, Photograph, Burning Desire, The Blue Mercedes. The Real Thing, I Love You, I Love You Not, Peg o' My Heart, Uncle Vanya, How I Got That Story.* First Stage series: *Ten November, Merry-Go-Round.*

BIBLIOGRAPHY

Published Sources:
Best Plays, 1978–79 through *1984–85*. New York: Dodd, Mead, & Co., 1979–86.
Theatre Profiles. Vols. 4–7. New York: Theatre Communications Group, 1979–85.
Theatre World, 1985–86. New York: Crown Publishers, 1987.
                                                                Weldon B. Durham

[THE] ACTOR'S WORKSHOP (TAW) of San Francisco, California, had its origins in a theatre study group organized in 1952 by San Francisco State College drama professors Jules Irving and Herbert Blau and their wives, Beatrice Manley (Mrs. Blau) and Priscilla Pointer (Mrs. Irving). Its off-Broadway contract of April 15, 1955, with the Actors' Equity Association (the first ever awarded to a group outside New York City) marked the beginning of the most recent wave of decentralization in the professional theatre of the United States. TAW gained international acclaim for its American premieres of plays by Samuel Beckett, Harold Pinter, Bertolt Brecht, and Jean Genet, and it was, for a time, a true repertory theatre, presenting a number of plays in nightly rotation at two theatres. It offered employment and training for an ensemble of performers that numbered more than one hundred at its largest. It knew crushing failure both in its artistic endeavors and in its efforts to win the support of San Francisco theatre patrons, but it also established a reputation for conceptually brilliant and technically adroit productions. According to Keith Fowler, whose history of the organization is exhaustive and definitive, TAW was not only "a good theatre, . . . it was heroic. [It] survived fourteen years while maintaining what was possibly the most rigorously serious and experimental schedule of plays in the country" ("A History of the San Francisco Actor's Workshop," doctoral dissertation, Yale University, 1969, p. 2).

Blau and Irving rented a studio in a loft above a judo academy at 275A Divisadero Street and invited friends in the theatre to join the group. Among those who met on January 15, 1952, were Hal J. Todd, a drama student at Stanford (where Blau and Irving were working on graduate degrees); Richard Glyer, a teacher at San Francisco State; Paul Cox, an actor-playwright; and Dan Whiteside, a student at San Francisco State. Both Blau and Irving had studied at New York University (Blau in chemical engineering) and at Stanford University. Irving had Broadway directing and acting experience; Priscilla Pointer had trained at the Tamara Daykaronova School for the Stage and had served during World War II as a civilian actress-technician for the U.S. Army; the others were talented and intelligent amateurs.

The theatrical workplace in San Francisco offered few opportunities for professional development. Professional road shows came regularly to the Geary, Curran, and Alcazar theatres; the Civic Light Opera produced musicals; and a few amateur groups flourished in the area. Driven by an intense anti-Establishment motive, Irving and Blau wanted a workshop in which each individual could perfect his or her talents and in which untried and esoteric drama could be experimentally produced.

Irving and Blau chose Philip Barry's *Hotel Universe* for the group's inaugural presentation (to an invited audience of about fifty on February 28, 1952) because, as Blau later explained, "it had substantial roles for all the actors, and because it could be done in modern dress around the unused brick fireplace [in the loft on Divisadero]" (*The Impossible Theatre* [New York: Macmillan, 1964], p. 139). Irving directed, the company designed the setting and costumes, and San Francisco State College students designed the lighting. Expenses of the production were minimal, though the company solicited donations from the invited audiences.

A little over a year later, after five successful productions for invited audiences and a glowing review in the *San Francisco Chronicle* of their work on Federico Garcia Lorca's *Blood Wedding*, the company incorporated as The Actor's Workshop of the San Francisco Drama Guild.

In August 1953 TAW abandoned the studio on Divisadero and moved to the second floor of a warehouse at 136 Valencia Street, in San Francisco's "market" district. This flexible theatre, seating 200 to 500 (depending on the configuration of the playing space) on folding metal chairs, was called the "Elgin Street Theatre" because the box office (where $1.50 admissions were sold) was located at the back door on Elgin Street. Irving's warmly received production of Aristophanes' *Lysistrata*, selected because several women in the company needed work, opened the theatre. Later that season (1953–54) Irving's production of Arthur Miller's *Death of a Salesman* was a major critical, artistic, and popular success and a turning point in the company's history. TAW was firmly established in San Francisco, though its financial position remained precarious.

The company's greatest asset was a roster of over seventy volunteers who acted, built scenery and costumes, staffed the box office, and underwrote all the group's functions with their time and energy. All productions were cast from among members of the group wherever possible, but outside talent was occasionally used. Each production received about one month of rehearsals, exclusive of readings and preliminary discussions. Casts rehearsed seven nights a week and on weekend afternoons. Company members were seldom paid for any of their work.

The senior members of the company included Beatrice Manley, a character actress known for her *hauteur* and technical control; Priscilla Pointer and Norma Jean Wanvig, leading women graced with youth, beauty, and intelligence (Pointer was gifted with especially clear diction and a capacity for intense emotionality; Wanvig with a sophisticated comedic air); and Joseph Miksak, a muscular and masculine leading man with a deep, resonant voice and a commanding demeanor. Tom Rosqui had studied theatre at the College of the Pacific in Stockton, California, before embarking on an acting career that took him to New York, where he appeared off-Broadway and in national tours, and to Milwaukee, where he acted at the Fred Miller Theatre. Rosqui played a wide range of principal roles, including the callow George Dillon in *Epitaph for George Dillon*, by John Osborne and Anthony Creighton; the dashing revolutionary Richard Dudgeon in G. B. Shaw's *The Devil's Disciple;* the sensitive, agonized Tom in Tennessee Williams' *The Glass Menagerie;* and the malevolent Aston in Harold Pinter's *The Caretaker*. Robert Symonds, a student of B. Iden Payne at the University of Texas before stints at the Ashland (Oregon) Shakespeare Festival and at San Diego's Old Globe Theatre, was an effective character actor in roles such as Falstaff in Shakespeare's *Henry IV*, Part I, General John Burgoyne in *The Devil's Disciple*, and Goldberg in Harold Pinter's *The Birthday Party*.

The next milestone for TAW was the production of another Arthur Miller drama, *The Crucible*, which opened December 3, 1954, at the Elgin Street Theatre. Previous productions had run for a maximum of twenty-two performances (most about twelve); *The Crucible* attracted more than 22,000 patrons to nearly one hundred performances. Buoyed by the group's success, Blau flew to New York to negotiate a special Actors' Equity contract that contained many concessions, allowing TAW to continue to operate as it had (with few paid performers) but with the status and prestige of recognition by the professional actors' union. Meanwhile Irving arranged the lease of a 630-seat theatre on the second floor of the Marines' Memorial, just a block off Geary Street in the heart of San Francisco's theatre district. The Marines' Memorial Theatre offered an awkwardly shaped auditorium, inadequate offstage space, little room above the stage to hang scenery, and no room for offices or for scenery and costume construction and storage, but its size and location more than made up for its inadequacies.

In August 1955 TAW began to produce plays at the Marines' Memorial and the Elgin Street theatres. However, poor audience support of the productions of the 1955–56 season brought the group to the brink of financial disaster. A revival of *The Crucible* in the spring brought temporary relief, but TAW was shortly evicted from the Elgin Street Theatre, for it was to be razed to make room for a freeway.

A subscription sales campaign in 1956–57, headed by new business manager Alan Mandell and stimulated by a production of August Strindberg's *Miss Julie*, directed by George Tabori and starring Viveca Lindfors, provided resources to launch the season, though only 900 subscriptions were sold. The group inaugurated an annual children's show in 1956, producing *The Princess Who Was Twice as Nice*, by Jules Irving, who also directed. Most of the children's scripts produced subsequently were written or adapted by Irving, and featured him, Priscilla Pointer, the Irving children (David, Katie, and Amy), and Alan Mandell. Better public support permitted TAW to rent a studio theatre, the Bella Union Theatre in Chinatown.

The third milestone for TAW was a U.S. Department of State invitation for the group to represent the American regional theatre movement at the 1958 International Exhibition in Brussels. Irving and Blau offered the workshop's production of Samuel Beckett's *Waiting for Godot*, given its American premiere by TAW in February 1957. TAW had to raise $12,000 to transport the company and its baggage to Brussels; about two-thirds of the amount was raised in San Francisco, while the remainder came from the proceeds of a six-week run of the show off-Broadway. *Godot* was enthusiastically received in Brussels, though some critics complained that TAW hadn't presented an American play, while others took issue with director Herbert Blau for staging choices that departed from European practice. The production also became the center of an international scandal when anonymous policymakers in the U.S. State Department objected, for reasons never made public, to the employment of James Kershaw, the company's stage manager. After long and complicated protestations, TAW was forced to leave Kershaw in the United States.

In May 1958 Irving and Blau established a new corporate structure for TAW by forming the San Francisco Actor's Workshop Guild, Inc., a nonprofit corporation that paralleled for a time the already existing for-profit structure. Sources of income other than box-office receipts were vital to the growth of the company. Since Equity affiliation in April 1955, TAW had produced eighteen major works, including four original plays and one American premiere of a foreign play. As of the beginning of the 1958–59 season, it operated as a weekend theatre and paid some performers only as much as $10 per performance. Its only source of income was box-office receipts (except for the funds raised for the *Godot* tour), which were growing rapidly, but not fast enough to permit the upkeep of the Marines' Memorial Theatre and the maintenance of a full-time ensemble. The need for a studio continued to press on the company, for the use of the Bella Union Theatre had proved unsatisfactory. The group located a better space just around the corner from the Marines' Memorial. The Encore Theatre, as the 140-seat facility was called, opened May 10, 1959, with a production of Samuel Beckett's *Endgame*. Notable design work was being done by James Hart Stearns and Robin Wagner; the acting ensemble was growing in size, strength, and artistic range; and Irving, Blau, and David Sarvis were becoming established as brilliant directors. The greatest artistic and popular success of 1958–59 was Irving's production of John Osborne's *The Entertainer*, featuring Robert Symonds.

More milestones followed in 1959–60: the Ford Foundation granted TAW $47,000 (which the company had to match, dollar for dollar) to guarantee seasonal contracts for ten performers, who should be paid a minimum of $200 per week. The grant was for a total of three years with a cap of $52,000 per year. TAW struggled each year to match the grant with local gifts, but it managed. The grant stipulated that funds should be used to bring in fresh talent, though, ultimately, Irving and Blau were permitted to reward company stalwarts Rosqui, Symonds, Michael O'Sullivan, and Ray Fry with full-time employment. The new "Ford actors," as they were known, contributed less than had been expected, and their presence and work habits, in some cases, undermined the stability of a company already somewhat weakened by factionalism. The grant also permitted the use of guest directors of some repute; visitors this year were Alan Schneider, William Ball, and Glynne Wickham. Wickham's production of Harold Pinter's *The Birthday Party* became the single most popular production of TAW and one of its most heralded artistic successes.

In 1960–61 TAW abandoned its weekend-only performance schedule and then struggled to fill the theatre because several of the season's offerings were weak. Blau's *King Lear*, the group's first Shakespearean production, was an unqualified success; Irving's *Henry IV*, Part I, was the next season's greatest popular and artistic success. These two works established TAW's proficiency in still another genre; subsequent productions of Ben Jonson's *Volpone*, Shakespeare's *Twelfth Night* and *The Taming of the Shrew*, and William Wycherly's Restoration comedy classic, *The Country Wife*, sustained the company's reputation for vibrant, innovative revivals of classics of the English theatre. In 1961–62 subscription sales climbed to 3,100 (low in comparison to sales experienced by other groups at this time), and the season's offerings drew well, permitting TAW to retire its debts from past years. The Ford Foundation, recognizing the group's high ideals and its communal, self-sacrificing spirit, provided an outright grant of $197,000 to continue the professional salary scale it had helped to establish. Other signs of the group's growing reputation included notices in *Nation* and the *New York Times* as well as an invitation to present its productions of *The Birthday Party* and *Waiting for Godot* at the Seattle World's Fair.

The 1962–63 season was the group's most successful, both financially and artistically. It featured ten new productions in a new seasonal format (rotating repertory was abandoned when it proved ineffective in increasing attendance at midweek performances and because nightly changeovers from one setting to another proved exhausting) and two holdovers at the Encore Theatre. Blau's productions of Bertolt Brecht's *Galileo* and Jean Genet's *The Balcony* became further milestones for TAW. Critics called *The Balcony* "sensational" but "repellent"; large audiences, however, turned out to view the spectacle of feverish eroticism. Growth in the size of the ensemble (now including twenty staff personnel and thirteen resident actors, as well as nearly one hundred part-time assistants and volunteers) and increasing specialization seem not to have impeded TAW's ability to mount productions that unified acting styles with vivid scenic spectacles. Eighty-five thousand patrons attended the group's functions. Using apprentices and junior company members, TAW initiated a thriving theatre-in-the-schools program. Tours to area communities by the senior company were also well received and lucrative. On the other hand a vocal and artistically effective splinter group appeared within the company, the R. G. Davis Mime Troupe. Davis, who was later to found the San Francisco Mime Troupe*, regarded TAW as a conservative, excessively institutionalized theatre. To the general public, however, TAW seemed to be becoming ever more avant-garde, experimental, and negativistic.

The last year of the Ford Foundation Resident Theatre Grant, 1963–64, saw the continuation of TAW's financial growth. Its budget peaked at $345,000 and its subscription list grew to 4,500. Despite the absence of any box-office "hits," the group ended the year nearly $33,000 in the black. Only six major productions were planned for the 1964–65 season, as well as an appearance of Emlyn Williams reading from the works of Charles Dickens, but early on Irving and Blau were asked to take over the artistic direction of New York City's Repertory Theatre of Lincoln Center*. Loyalty to the company and to the idea of a decentralized American theatre slowed their response, but ultimately the extraordinary facilities, budgets, and talent in New York City led Irving and Blau to accept the offer to build a repertory company in the nation's theatre capital. Robert Symonds and several other performers followed their leaders, but the majority of the group dispersed after TAW's curtailed season ended on March 1, 1965. Reaction to the decision of Irving and Blau was mixed; some regarded it as self-serving; some congratulated them on the opportunity presented them. Ironically Robert Brustein, drama critic for *New Republic*, had only recently spent a week with the company and had been struck by its intelligence and discipline, calling TAW a "close-knit family group cooperating in a common pursuit" ("Health in an Ailing Profession," *New Republic* 152 [January 30, 1965]:32).

The final season of TAW, conducted under the management of Kenneth Kitch and John Hancock, featured a virtually new company hired, for the most part, through auditions in New York City. The 1965–66 season was adventuresome, but it was a financial flop and only modestly successful artistically. Hancock's direction of Bertolt Brecht's *The History of the Lamentable Reign of Edward II* met with critical approval, but his production of *A Midsummer Night's Dream* was regarded by some as gratuitously bizarre and grotesque, by others as innovative. TAW permanently disbanded at the close of the 1965–66 season, having lost the support of its founders, its local allies of influence, and the Ford Foundation.

PERSONNEL

Producing Directors: Herbert Blau (1952–65), Jules Irving (1952–65).

Managing Director: Kenneth Kitch (1965–66).

Artistic Director: John Hancock (1965–66).

Business Manager: Alan Mandell (1956–65).

Directors: Maurice Argent (1956), William Ball (1960), *Herbert Blau* (1953–65), Lee Breuer (1962–63), John Clark (1956, 1958), Leon Forbes (1957), Robert W. Goldsby (1959, 1961), Tom Gruenewald (1965), John Hancock (1965–66), *Jules Irving* (1952–65), Mitchell Lifton (1959, 1964), Robert Loper (1960), Vincent Porcaro (1959), Robert Ross (1954), *David Sarvis* (1956, 1958, 1960), Alan Schneider (1961), *Robert Symonds* (1959–65), George Tabori (1956), Morgan Upton (1959), Timothy Ward (1962–64), Carl M. Weber (1963), Stan Weese (1954), Glynne Wickham (1959).

Scenic Designers: Alonzo (1962), George Armstrong (1953–55), Ernest Baron (1955–56), John Blankenship (1956), Tom Borden (1956), Leonard Breger (1955), R. Cushing (1963), Judith Davis (1962), Michael Devine (1963), Jim Dine (1966), Bruce Harrow (1964), Ann Elizabeth Horton (1963–64), Wallace Jonason (1955), William Stewart Jones (1964–66), Alan Kimmel (1960), Joan Larkey (1965), *Robert LaVigne* (1959–66), Ralph McCormic (1953–54), Jean Parshall (1956), Bernard Perry (1954), Neil Pinney (1962), Vincent Porcaro (1959–60), Herb Reynaud (1957), David Sarvis (1960), Keith Snider (1964), Eric Stearne (1955), *James Hart Stearns* (1956–65), Knute Stiles (1961), Ian Strasfogel (1966), James Thompson (1960), Lydia Modi Vitale (1952–53), *Robin Wagner* (1957–58, 1959, 1962), Stan Weese (1954), Irle White (1961).

Lighting Designers: Joe Carillo (1954), Donald Childs (1966), Virginia Cox (1952), Daniel Dugan (1963–64), Lyn Fischbein (1962), Judah Holstein (1952), Ann Elizabeth Horton (1962–64), Al Jutzi (1966), Kay Kaggie (1959–60), Joan Larkey (1965), Robert LaVigne (1962), F. Leon Leake (1965), Roland Loomis (1956), Ralph McCormic (1952–55), James McMillan (1959–63), Ima G. Mahin (1959), Don Metcalfe (1961–63), Jean Parshall (1955), Elias Romero (1963), Jim Rynning (1965–66), *Jose Sevilla* (1962–65), Robin Wagner (1962), Stan Weese (1954), Judy Harris Wolcott (1960).

Costume Designers: Alonzo (1962), Ruth Argent (1954), Rivka Berg (1959–60), Bere Boynton (1960), Helen Breger (1953), Judith Davis (1962), Jim Dine (1966), Herman George (1965), Ann Elizabeth Horton (1963–64), William Stewart Jones (1964–66), Robert LaCloutier (1961), Carol LaFleur (1963), Robert LaVigne (1965), Jan Parr (1954–56), Jean Parshall (1956–57, 1960, 1962–63), Priscilla Pointer (1954), Stephen Morgan (1955), Alexander Orloff (1962), Jeanene Schilling (1955), Shan Slattery (1959), Keith Snider (1964), *James Hart Stearns* (1956, 1959, 1961, 1963–64), Rebecca G. Stearns (1956), Lydia Modi Vitale (1952), Stan Weese (1953–54), Dori White (1960).

Actors and Actresses: Ed Abajian (1954–55), Trigger Addis (1954–55), *Maurice Argent* (1953–61), Richard Armbruster (1953–54), Jack Aranson (1961–62), George Baron (1957–58), Donald Buka (1960–61), Wolfe Barzell (1961–62), Frank Bayer (1961–63), Robert Benson (1962–66), Lorraine Bergstrom (1959–60), Patricia Beverly (1953–55, 1959), Nancy Bond (1962–63, 1965–66), Philip Bournef (1960–61), Bere Boynton (1960), *Bert Brauer* (1952–64), Ruth Breuer (1961, 1963), Richard Bright (1965–66), Alan Brody (1958–60), Hal Burdick (1961–62), Roberta Callahan (1962–63), Joe Carillo (1952–54), Kathe Chapman (1959–60, 1962), Najean Cherry (1954, 1957), Virginia Chesse (1954), John Clark (1952–61), Doris Cole (1953–54), C. David Colson (1965–66), Don Cross (1954, 1956), Susan Darby (1957–63), R. G. Davis (1959–63), Roger

DeKoven (1961–62), Alan Dewitt (1962–63), James Donohue (1960–62), Margaret "Peggy" Doyle (1955, 1959–63), Robert Doyle (1959–61), Joel Fabiani (1959–60), Leon Forbes (1952), William Fortinberry (1962–65), Neva Fowler (1958–61), Barbara Franger (1952, 1954), *Ray Fry* (1954–65), Dwight Frye (1959–60), *James Gavin* (1960–61, 1962–63), Rhoda Gemignani (1963–66), Mara Alexander Gilbert (1955–60), Richard Glyer (1952, 1954, 1955, 1959), Sheila Goldes (1962–63), Dean Goodman (1960–62), Dorothy Gordon (1955), Michael Granger (1961–62), Robert Hagopian (1952–55), Barbara Heald (1953–54), Marian Hailey (1962), *Robert Haswell* (1952–64), Charlotte von Herberg (1953–54), Barton Heyman (1965–66), *George Hitchcock* (1957–c.1965), *Elizabeth Huddle* (1962–65), Laurence Hugo (1960–61), *Jules Irving* (1952–59), Irving Israel (1959–64), *Wallace R. Jonason* (1956–64), Robert Karnes (1962–65), Patricia Katz (1952), Elizabeth Keller (1959–62), K. K. Kitch (1960–64, 1965–66), Milt Kogan (1965–66), Norma Leistiko (c.1957–61), Edmond Lewis (1952–53), Abe Liberfeld (1965–66), Vivica Lindfors (1959), Michael Linenthal (1959–60), Frances Lipson (1953–54), William Major (1960–61), Alan Mandell (1959, 1962), *Beatrice Manley* (1952–65), *Winifred Mann* (1954–66), *Monte Markham* (1962–65), *Glenn Mazen* (1962–65), Burgess Meredith (1959), *Joseph Miksak* (1952–62), Edward O'Brien (1959–62), *Michael O'Sullivan* (1957–61), Edwin Owens (1962–63), Albert Paulsen (1960–61), *Robert Phalen* (1959–65), *Priscilla Pointer* (1952–65), Herbert Propper (1963–64), Paul Rebillot (1962–63), Frances Reid (1960–61), *Eugene Roche* (1955–60, 1962), *Tom Rosqui* (1952–65), Katharine Ross (1960–63), *Robert Ross* (1952–54), Hope Sansberry (1960–61), William Sibley (1954–55), Ann Siena (1953–54), Robert Skundberg (1965–66), Colette Slightam (1952–53), *Malcolm Smith* (1953–57, 1959, 1961–64), Rudi Solari (1955), Erica Speyer [Rosqui] (1960–64), David Ogden Stiers (1965–66), Willis Stiver (c.1957–61), Dan Sullivan (1963–64), John Sullivan (1955–56), Bill Sweeney (1954–55), *Robert Symonds* (1954–65), Tom Tarpey (1965–66), Alexis Tellis (1952–53), Malachi Throne (1961–62), Morgan Upton (1959–66), Abe Vigoda (1965–66), David Vilner (1963–64), *Shirley Jac Frazier Wagner* (1957–65), *Norma Jean Wanvig* (1952–61), *Stan Weese* (1952–55, 1960), *Edward Winter* (1961–65), *William Witt* (1954–64), Stan Young (1956–57).

REPERTORY

1952: *Hotel Universe, I Am a Camera.*

1952–53: *Hedda Gabler, Blood Wedding, Playboy of the Western World, Summer and Smoke, The Miser.*

1953–54: *Lysistrata, Venus Observed, Death of a Salesman, Playboy of the Western World, The Cherry Orchard, Tonight at 8:30.*

1954–55: *Oedipus Rex, Master Pierre Patelin, The Crucible, Camino Real, The Girl on the Via Flaminia, Captive at Large.*

1955–56: *The Importance of Being Earnest, Deirdre of the Sorrows, A Pound on Demand, Mother Courage, The Crucible.*

1956–57: *Miss Julie, The Stronger, The Plough and the Stars, The Flowering Peach, Waiting for Godot, The Country Wife, Hotel Universe, The Ticklish Acrobat.*

1957–58: *The Potting Shed, Tiger at the Gates, A Gift of Fury, The Miser, The Iceman Cometh, Prometheus Found* and *The Housewarming.*

1958–59: *Waltz of the Toreadors, Garden District, The Entertainer, Waiting for Godot, The Infernal Machine, Endgame, Three Modern Noh Plays, Cock-a-Doodle Dandy, The Crucible.*

1959–60: *The Busy Martyr, The Plaster Bambino, Epitaph for George Dillon, Jack, or, The Submission, The Chairs, The Devil's Disciple, The Marriage of Mr. Mississippi, The Birthday Party, Saint's Day.*

1960–61: *The Birthday Party, The Rocks Cried Out, The Alchemist, A Touch of the Poet, Twinkling of an Eye, Krapp's Last Tape, The Zoo Story, The Widow* and *The Maids, King Lear, Misalliance, The Maids* and *The Sandbox.*

1961–62: *The Birthday Party, Krapp's Last Tape* and *The Zoo Story,* and *King Lear* continued from previous season; *Serjeant Musgrave's Dance, The Three Sisters, Becket, Friedman & Son, Dance of Death, Henry IV,* Part I, *Waiting for Godot.*

1962–63: *The Birthday Party, Waiting for Godot* continued from previous season; *Happy Days, Twelfth Night, The Glass Menagerie, Galileo, The Dumb Waiter* and *A Slight Ache, Telegraph Hill, Volpone, The Balcony, Major Barbara, The Underpants.*

1963–64: *The House of Bernarda Alba, The Taming of the Shrew, The Caretaker, The Master* and *There! You Died, The Caucasian Chalk Circle, The Defense of Taipei, The Ginger Man, The Firebugs, The Night of the Iguana, The Chalk Garden, The Birds, Volpone.*

1964–65: *The Wall, The Country Wife, Uncle Vanya, The Rooming House* and *The Collection.*

1965–66: *The Milk Train Doesn't Stop Here Anymore, The History of the Lamentable Reign of Edward II, Point Conception* and *The Cage, The Last Analysis, Don Juan, The Father, The Empire Builders, A Midsummer Night's Dream, A Man's a Man.*

Children's Theatre productions: *The Princess Who Was Twice as Nice, The Magic Butterfly, La Cenerentola (Cinderella), The Brave Little Tailor, Gretchen and the Lonely Goblin, Simple Simon.*

BIBLIOGRAPHY

Published Sources:

Blau, Herbert. *The Impossible Theatre.* New York: Macmillan, 1964.

Brustein, Robert. "Health in an Ailing Profession." *New Republic* 152 (January 30, 1965): 32–35.

Dukore, Bernard. "The First Actor's Workshop: A Balance Sheet." *Player's Magazine* 42 (December 1965): 76–77.

———. "West Coast Theatre: The Pleasure of Companies." *Tulane Drama Review* 9 (Spring 1965): 198–207.

Eichelbaum, Stanley. "Theatre USA: San Francisco." *Theatre Arts* 44 (March 1960): 57–61.

Theatre World. Vol. 22. New York: Crown Publishers, 1966.

Zeigler, Joseph Wesley. *Regional Theatre: The Revolutionary Stage.* New York: Da Capo Press, Inc., 1977.

Unpublished Sources:

Bazarini, Ron. "The Organization and Management of the Actor's Workshop of the San Francisco Drama Guild, Inc." Master's thesis, Stanford University, 1957.

Fowler, Keith Franklin. "A History of the San Francisco Actor's Workshop." Doctoral dissertation, Yale University, 1969.

Archival Resource:

New York, New York. New York Public Library. Billy Rose Theatre Collection. "The Story of the Actor's Workshop" by Cliff Levy; clippings, correspondence, financial records, 1952–65; biographies of company, structure of company, c.1964;

programs, 1953–64; clippings re 1961 financial crisis; clippings 1965 re Blau and
Irving move to Lincoln Center; box-office statements, 1961–64; floor plans, light
plots for numerous productions; ledgers, checkbooks, account books.

Weldon B. Durham

[THE] ALASKA REPERTORY THEATRE (ART), the state's first nonprofit,
professional theatre, was founded by Paul V. Brown in June 1976 and opened
March 1, 1977, with a production of *Scapino!* Housed primarily in the munic-
ipally owned Sidney Lawrence Auditorium in Anchorage, performances are also
given in the University of Alaska, Fairbanks auditorium.

The company was part of the second wave of regional theatre development,
the first having taken place during the 1960s. Anchorage had, at the time of the
ART's founding, several nonprofessional community theatre organizations, including the Anchorage Theatre Guild, the Anchorage Community Theatre, and
the Anchorage Opera Guild. Additionally, the University of Alaska Theatre
Department and Arts in Alaska, Inc., a nonprofit organization that toured skits
and short programs, contributed to an active theatrical scene. There was some
concern on the part of these rival groups at the ART's founding that the new
theatre would reduce the public's interest in and contribution to community
theatres; Brown reassured them, however, pointing out that the ART could spur
growth and, through leadership, promote higher standards and quality.

Brown, with Robert J. Farley, founded the company with the aim of providing
theatrical productions and services to all residents of the state, whether in villages
or cities. They also envisioned the company as a resource for other arts organizations. Brown is a member of the executive committee of the Alaska Arts
Alliance and a founding member of the Anchorage Arts Commission. Farley
began his career with the APA–Phoenix Theatre* in New York and has worked
in a variety of regional theatres, including the McCarter Theatre Company* in
Princeton, the Intiman Theatre Company* in Seattle, and the Alliance Theatre
in Atlanta.

The ART began with strong support from the business community as well as
from the state. The budget for the first season was projected as between $350,000
and $400,000, funding of which came from the business community, the state,
and subscriptions. By fiscal year 1980 the company received 75 percent of all
the funds distributed by the State Arts Council ($750,000 that year). In fiscal
year 1985 the company still received that amount of money from the Council,
now 60 percent of that organization's disbursements; however, the ART received
as well that year a $400,000 line item grant from the state legislature. Community
support is evidenced by the construction of a performing arts complex in Anchorage, completed in 1988, which provides permanent housing for the opera,
community theatre, and the ART. The company's original ambitious touring
program had to be somewhat curtailed, since sets, properties, costumes, and
equipment had not only to fit into trucks, but into small planes and boats as
well, which made touring a complicated and expensive proposition; touring to

outlying districts, although limited, still exists, however, and the company continues to offer statewide consultation for theatrical production as well as educational services.

Critical response to the ART has been positive. The appropriateness of casting and play selection and the level of production standards have inspired comments such as, "Not a miscast role," and "Direction . . . didn't allow for any lag in action" (Anchorage *Times*, March 10, 1977, p. B2).

In its first ten seasons the ART has mounted forty-five productions, ranging from Shakespeare (*The Taming of the Shrew, A Midsummer Night's Dream, Twelfth Night*) and Molière (*Tartuffe*) to G. B. Shaw (*Major Barbara*) and Neil Simon (*Brighton Beach Memoirs*). The majority of the company's productions have been comedies; more serious works, however, have been successfully presented, including works by Ibsen (*An Enemy of the People*), Arthur Kopit (*Wings*), and Ted Tally (*Terra Nova*). In addition, the company has presented productions such as the McClain Family Band, the Alec McCowen production of *St. Mark's Gospel*, and the Joffrey II Dancers. Finally, the ART has presented a series of educational programs on playmaking and playreading.

Paul V. Brown has, since the company's inception, acted as the producing director, and Robert J. Farley has, for the same period, served as artistic director for all productions; Farley has been the stage director for the majority of plays, although the company has at times used the services of guest directors. Additionally, the ART has regularly employed production, lighting, costume, and sound designers, stage and production managers, and, when necessary, choreographers and musical directors. The acting company has been composed of a large number of actors and actresses (many of whom have appeared in only one production), and guest stars. Chief among those actors and actresses who have appeared in several productions are William Arnold, Mitchell Edmonds, Harry Frazier, Sharon Harrison, Steve McKean, Joe Meek, James Morrison, Richard Riehle, Donn Ruddy, Luan Schooler, James Hotchkiss, and Philip Pleasants. Many of the company's actors and actresses have gone on from the ART to perform at such theatres as the Guthrie Theatre, the Mark Taper Forum, the Alabama Shakespeare Festival, and the Portland (Maine) Stage Company, as well as moving into television.

The ART's first season was a short season, with only three productions in the spring of 1977; all others have been full seasons. With ten successful seasons completed the ART anticipates an equally successful future.

PERSONNEL

Management: Gary D. Anderson, production manager (1978–80); Paul V. Brown, producing director (1977–86); Robert J. Farley, artistic director (1977–86); Vince Liotta, production manager (1977).

Stage Directors: Gary D. Anderson (1978–80), Margaret Booker (1979–80), Dennis Bright (1977–78), Roy Brocksmith (1985–86), Clayton Corzatte (1977–78, 1980–81, 1984–85), Robert J. Farley (1977–86), John Going (1981–83), Walton Jones (1980–81,

1985–86), Irene Lewis (1981–82), Michael Murry (1984–85), Martin L. Platt (1978–79), Dan Sedgewick (1981–82), Meridee Stein (1982–83), Russell Treyz (1979–80).

Musical Directors: Joseph Church (1982–83), John Clifton (1979–80), Mary Pat Graham (1981–82), Mark Hardwick (1984–86), Richard Stillman (1980–81).

Technical Director: Hugh Hall (1978–80).

Choreographers: Laurie Boyd (1980–82), Lisa Brailoff (1981–82), Susan Mendel (1979–80), Linda Reiff (1982–83).

Stage Managers: Gary D. Anderson (1977), Carol Chiavetta (1981–85), Pamela Guion (1983–84), Emil Holloway (1979–80), Steven W. Login (1977–78), Ann Mathews (1979–82), Dan Sedgewick (1978–79, 1980–81), Gretchen Van Horne (1984–86), Vita Zingarelli (1979–80).

Production Designers: Timothy Ames (1980–81), Karen Armstrong (1980–81), Karl Eigsti (1984–85), Karen Gjelsteen (1980–81, 1983–85), Jamie Greenleaf (1977–80, 1981–82), Hugh Landwehr (1981–82), Connie Lutz (1984–86), Michael Olich (1984–85), David Potts (1983–84), Kevin Rupnik (1981–82, 1983–84), William Schroder (1981–83), Oliver Smith (1982–83), Michael Stauffer (1983–84), Robert Zentis (1979–81).

Lighting Designers: Pat Collins (1981–82), Victor En Yu Tan (1981–83), Hugh Hall (1980–81), Neil Peter Jampolis (1984–85), E. Allen Kent (1977), Laurie MacKenzie Miller (1981–82, 1984–85), Spencer Mosse (1981–83, 1984–85), Robert Peterson (1984–85), Judy Rasmuson (1981–82, 1983–85), James Sale (1978–82), Michael Stauffer (1980–81, 1983–84), Robert W. Zentis (1980–81).

Costume Designers: Christine Andrews (1982–83), Nanrose Buchman (1978–82), Deborah M. Dryden (1984–85), Linda Fisher (1981–82), James Burton Harris (1981–82), William Ivey Long (1980–81), Michael Olich (1980–81, 1983–84), Dunya Ramicova (1981–82, 1983–84), Sally Richardson (1984–85), Jennifer Svenson (1984–85), Mariann Verheyen (1984–85).

Sound Designers: Steve Bennett (1980–84), Bruce Crouch (1984–86), Bill Henderson (1983–84), Michael Schweppe (1979–80), Jerry Summers (1984–85).

Actors and Actresses: John Abajian, John Ahearn, James Aiken, Dennis Allen, Brooks Almy, Matthew Amson, Christine Andreas, *Charles Anatolsky* (1978–82), Marina Arakelian, Betty Arnett, *William Arnold* (1978–82), Frances Asher, Linda Atkinson, *Tom Bade* (1979–82), Marian Baer, Maggie Baird, Brett Baker, Rose Marie Barbee, Nicola-Marie Barthen, Dennis Bateman, Emery Battis, John Bauer, Deborah Bauman, Lissa Bell, Charles Berendt, Jill Bess, Nesbitt Blaisdell, Lada Boder, *Marshall Borden* (1978–85), Eric Borland, Joseph Botz, Ed Bourgeois, Tom Bower, Laurie Boyd, Nancy Boykin, Tom Bradley, Lisa Brailoff, Gunnar Brauson, Roy Brockett, Ivan Brogger, Kermit Brown, Kim Brown, Matthew Brown, Robert Browning, Shirley Bryan, Bill Buell, Elizabeth Burr, James Burton, Kristina Callahan, Ed Campbell, Thomas Carson, Amanda Chase, *Nora Chester* (1981–84), Daniel Church, Mike Chybowski, John Clarkson, Kirtan Coan, Marc Cohen, Megan Cole, Edward Conery, John Conley, Sid Conrad, Maury Cooper, Albert Corgin, *Clayton Corzatte* (1978–85), *Nicholas Cosco* (1978–80), A. D. Cover, Kevin Craig, Adam Crenshaw, Steve Crosby, Joseph Culliton, Kevin Daly, Jeff David, Adam Davidson, Curt Dawson, Marty Decker, Debra DeHass, Carolyn DeLany, Kim Delgado, Davian Delise, Doreen Delise, Mary Anne Dempsey, Liz DeVivo, Susan Diol, Damon DiPietro, Kathy Donlan, Gene Dugan, Gerard Dure, Dan Diggles, Robert Donley, Robert Miller Driscoll, Cara Duff-MacCormick. *Mitchell Edmonds* (1978–86), Warren Elkins, Sasha Ensign, Shannon Eubanks, Ron Evans, Randy Fader, Lou Favreaux, Michael Feigin, Sarah Felcher, Katherine Ferrand, John Finn, Douglas Fisher, Justine

Fitzgerald, Tom Flagg, Lucy Flynn, Freda Foh Shen, Will Folson, Larkin Ford, Susie Foster, Vanya Franch, *Harry Frazier* (1978–82), Ron Frazier, Danny Frichman, David Fuller, Elliot Gagnon, Mary Gallacher, Kim Gambino, Karl Gaskin, Martha Gearheart, Frank Geraci, Anne Marie Gerard, Sue Anne Gershenson, *June Gibbons* (1981–86), Beth Gilles, Kerry Gilman, Gerald Gilmore, Jenny Golden, Ruddy Goldschmidt, Joan Gossett, Ben Gotlieb, Samaria Graham, Helen Green, Valerie Green, Zack Grenier, Mike Hadani, Bebo Haddad, Bruce Haines, Arthur Hammer, Stephen Haraden, Jerry Harper, *Sharon Harrison* (1980–82), *Dana Hart* (1978–82), Therese Hayes, Mike Haynes, John Heginbotham, Sherrie Heginbotham, K. C. Helmeid, Derek Hensel, Dorothy Hill, Geoffrey Hill, Kevin Hills, Margaret Hilton, James Hindman, Karen Hoins, Erika Honda, J. R. Horne, *James Hotchkiss* (1977–82), Nancy Houfek, Max Howard, Jane Hurdle, Michael Hureaux, Annie Stokes Hutchinson, Dana Ivey, Peter Jack, G. D. Jacobson, Tim James, J. J. Jigliotti, Michael Johnson, John Frederick Jones, Peter Josephson, Cynthia Judge, Margaret Kallstrom, Brian Keeler, Daren Kelly, John Kelly, Rena Kliot, Georgianna Lane, Marta Lastufka, Richard C. Lavin, Terry Layman, Michelle League, Arlene Lencioni, Lynn Lentz, John Lenz, Barbara LeVine, Bram Lewis, Miller Lide, Phillip Lindsay, Joel Lockman, Carole Lockwood, Jay Louder, Conan McCarty, Kenneth McClendon, Stacey McClendon, Andy McCutcheon, Pirie MacDonald, *Tanny McDonald* (1978–81), James McDonnell, Ann McDonough, Edwin J. McDonough, Elizabeth McGovern, Mark McGrath, *Maeve McGuire* (1981–85), *Gary McGurk* (1982–84), Gannon McHale, Craig Lee McIntosh, Lizbeth Mackay, *Steve McKean* (1978–80), Karen McLaughlin, Gina McMather, Jonathan McMurty, Jean McNally, Dermot McNamara, Peter MacNicol, Frederic Major, Kathleen Manousos, John Mason, James Maxwell, Glenn Mazen, *Joe Meek* (1978–85), Kathleen Melvin, *Susan Mendel* (1978–80), Scott Merrick, Monica Merryman, Suzanne Miles, Dan Millen, John Milligan, Michael Mitchell, Alan Mixon, Jane Moore, Tim Morrisey, *James Morrison* (1978–80), John W. Morrow, Jr., Lora Morrow, Jody Morse, *Perrin Morse* (1981–85), Kate Mulgrew, *Jack Murdock* (1982–85), Peter Murphy, Gregory Murrell, Caitlin Murry, Jane Murry, Nancy Nichols, Ed Nolde, Patricia Norcia, Elizabeth Norment, *Ernie Norris* (1978–81), Patrick O'Connell, Edie Ogando, Ken Olin, Merritt Olsen, Etain O'Malley, Deirdre Owens, Jim Oyster, Elizabeth Parrish, Leon Parsons, Moultrie Patten, Virginia Patterson, Guy Paul, Michael Paul, Larry Paulson, Guy Payne, Stephen Pelinski, John Perkins, Ryan Pernela, Richard Perrin, Ethan Phillips, Rick Piaskowski, John Pielmeier, Beverly Pina, Philip Piro, *Philip Pleasants* (1977–85), J. Courtney Pollard, Mary Porter, Marina Posvar, Jeffrey L. Prather, William Preston, Marian Primont, Michael Purcell, Lori Putnam, Christine Ranck, Ralph Redpath, Gavin Reed, Susan Reilly, Eleanor Reissa, *Richard Riehle* (1982–86), Marc Riffon, Julian Rivers, Linda Robertson, Charles Shaw Robinson, Wendy Rockman, John Roderick, Philip Rodriguez, Reno Roop, David Roth, *Donn Ruddy* (1977–86), Joan Rue, Michael Rutherford, Richard Ryder, Benjamin Ryken, Dick Sabul, John Salazar, Diane Salinger, *Mary Nell Santacroce* (1978–86), Michael Santo, Candace Sassman, Ellen Schafroth, Stefan Schnabel, Jana Schneider, Annie Schooler, *Luan Schooler* (1978–81), Ben Schwartz, Betsey Scott, Donovan Ward Scott, James Secrest, Susan D. Servos, Tracy Shaffer, Joan Shangold, Harold Shepard, William Shephard, John Shuman, *Bob Sieger* (1981–82), Douglas Simes, Jean Smart, Jeff Smith, Rich Smith, Lynne Sofer, Mary Lou Spartz, Wayne Spector, Marco St. John, Fran Stevens, Richard Stillman, Dorothy Stinnett, Guy Strobel, Pete Sugden, Dennis Sullivan, William Swetland, Paul Szopa, Corliss Taylor-Dunn, Freyda Thomas, Paul Thomas, Judith Tillman, Robert Tornfelt, Duane Tucker, Eric Tull, Eric Uhler, Joan Ulmer, Richard Ussery, Mary Van

Dyke, Diane Van Fossen, Mark Varian, Justin Vaughn, Jennie Ventriss, J. J. Vincent, Tony Vita, Ian Wagreich, Steven Ward, Sussane Ward, David Westgor, Ryal White, David Whitehead, Raymond Wiberg, Cynthia Wilson, Gerald Wilson, Claire Wipperman, Catherine Wolf, John Wylie, Janet Zarish.

REPERTORY

1977: *Scapino!, Private Lives, Clarence Darrow.*

1977–78: *Sherlock Holmes, The Fourposter, The Eccentricities of a Nightingale, Diamond Studs.*

1978–79: *The Fourposter, A Christmas Carol, Terra Nova* (West Coast premier), *The Taming of the Shrew, Slow Dance on the Killing Ground, Deathtrap.*

1979–80: *Diamond Studs, Talley's Folly* (West Coast premier), *A Christmas Carol, Something's Afoot, Sly Fox, Loose Ends.*

1980–81: *Will Rogers' U.S.A., On Golden Pond, The Elephant Man, A Midsummer Night's Dream.*

1981–82: *The Man Who Came to Dinner, A Christmas Carol, An Enemy of the People, The Hot l Baltimore, Fools.*

1982–83: *Nightingale, Major Barbara, Ain't Misbehavin'.*

1983–84: *All My Sons, Wings, The Philadelphia Story, Tartuffe.*

1984–85: *Noises Off, Translations, Brighton Beach Memoirs, Pantagleize, Billy Bishop Goes to War.*

1985–86: *Pump Boys and Dinettes, Twelfth Night, or What You Will, Watch on the Rhine, Greater Tuna, Tintypes, The New American Musical.*

BIBLIOGRAPHY

Published Sources:
Anchorage *Daily News*, 1977–86.
Anchorage *Times*, 1977–86.
Fairbanks *Daily News Miner*, 1977–86.

Krystan V. Douglas

ALLEY THEATRE, established in Houston, Texas, in 1947, is the oldest of the nation's resident theatres. Its founders, lead by Houston high school drama teacher Nina Vance, were protesting the intellectual superficiality of community and professional theatre in Houston at the time. Under Vance's leadership until her death in 1980 and subsequently under the artistic direction of Patricia Ann Brown, the Alley Theatre has become a centerpiece in the cultural life of the fourth largest city in the United States. Its current home overlooks Jones Plaza, a majestic civic center in downtown Houston. Nearby are located the Jesse H. Jones Hall for the Performing Arts, home of the Houston Symphony, as well as the newest opera house in the United States, the Wortham Theatre Center, with two stages housing the Houston Opera and the Houston Ballet.

Vance had been educated in speech arts at Texas Christian University (B.A., 1934), and she had studied theatre at the University of Southern California, Columbia University, and New York's American Academy of Dramatic Art before returning to Texas to teach drama in Houston's high schools and direct plays for the Houston Jewish Community Center. Vance had also acted in Houston community theatre troupes directed by Margo Jones.

In October 1947 Vance, Robert and Vivian Altfeld, and Sidney Holmes cleaned out purses and pockets and used the $2.14 they found to buy 214 postcards, which they sent to friends possibly interested in founding a permanent facility for the serious pursuit of theatre art. Nearly one hundred showed up for the meeting.

The group first set up in a dance studio operated by the Altfelds at 3617 Main Street. The theatre was little more than a large room at the end of a long alley into a collection of artist's studios. Production conditions were very primitive: the theatre had to be set up and taken down every night to permit use of the space as a dance studio in the day; it was tiny and cold, and a large sycamore tree enclosed in the building was part of every set. The first production was *A Sound of Hunting*, which opened a ten-performance run on November 18, 1947. Harry Brown's war drama had been a recent commercial failure in New York, but the Alley troupe (the moniker had been picked by the founders, over Vance's protest, because of the narrow but charming access to the theatre) garnered positive reviews. They presented six plays at the eighty-nine-seat Main Street theatre before the city fire marshal closed it.

Robert Altfeld then located an old fan factory on Berry Avenue, and volunteer laborers, using donated materials, made it over into a 230-seat arena theatre, which opened February 8, 1949, with a production of Lillian Hellman's then controversial *The Children's Hour*. Good press notices attended the opening, not only for the production, but also for the space. Through a combination of serendipidity, good judgment on the part of many artistically talented volunteers, and Nina Vance's rapidly growing command of the principles of arena staging, the fan factory on Berry Avenue had been converted into an attractive and theatrically effective space. However, auxiliary spaces (offices, dressing rooms, scenery and costume shops, and storage) were inadequate, and houses nearby had to be rented and converted into support spaces.

By 1949 the company had only three persons on salary: Vance, a janitor, and an office manager. In 1949–50 Ronald Alexander's *Season with Ginger* (later, as *Time Out for Ginger*, a Broadway success and a long-time community theatre standby) was developed at the Alley and premiered with Alexander in attendance. The production set Alley Theatre attendance records, but it was soon eclipsed by a thirty-six-performance run of Moss Hart's *Light Up the Sky*.

The Alley experienced another banner season in 1950–51. The patron list was growing (though the organization subsisted wholly on box-office receipts and the volunteer efforts of designers and performers), and regular runs were extended to twenty-six performances. In 1950 Iris Siff and Blake Davis founded the Alley Academy, a school to provide training for the adults working at the theatre. In time it became a school for children and adults, offering a curriculum designed to stimulate theatre appreciation. However, in March 1950, the presence of a fully professional troupe at a nearby theatre, The Playhouse, undermined the appeal of the Alley group and ultimately forced the Alley Theatre to professionalize.

Vance promoted professionalization, but the Altfelds saw the trend as a betrayal of the original purposes of the organization and of the selfless amateurs who had built it. The Altfelds resigned from the Alley Theatre Board of Directors in 1952, leaving Vance in complete control of the troupe. The slow drift toward professionalization (use of guest stars such as Albert Dekker and occasional use of other paid performers) culminated in 1954, when the Alley management signed a contract with Actors' Equity Association, the professional actor's union, whereby the Alley should maintain a company of six professional performers and guarantee that half the members of each cast should be Equity performers. The Playhouse suspended operations in 1954.

Full professionalization and the demise of The Playhouse brought nothing like instant success to the Alley Theatre. For the next eight years the group struggled through cycles of box-office success and failure. Brooks Atkinson's favorable notice of the Alley's 1952 production of August Strindberg's *Miss Julie* focused national attention on the group, as did the presentation in 1958 of a segment of an Alley production on NBC-TV's *Wide, Wide World*. Alley Theatre chronicler Ann Holmes suggests that the artistic success of the company far surpassed its popular success. Holmes thought that the Alley troupe of the early fifties was fearless in its commitment to drama that looked at timely issues, undaunted in its celebration of literary excellence, and adept at getting at the truth of human situations. However, lack of sustained attention to promotion and sales by a professional staff undermined the Alley's economic stability.

In 1958 Vance launched a new promotional initiative by putting together a new board of directors consisting of thirty-six civic leaders who were committed to promoting the Alley as a civic asset. Formerly, board members had been current and former volunteers at the theatre. However, incentives offered to groups failed to attract audiences, and the Alley experienced its poorest attendance to date in the season of 1958–59, despite fine productions of Jean Giraudoux' *The Madwoman of Chaillot* and Eugene O'Neill's *The Iceman Cometh*. As the season neared an end, the Ford Foundation offered Vance a job in New York. She prepared to leave for New York while also establishing for the board the conditions under which she could be persuaded to stay in Houston: a permanent general manager and a larger sales and promotion staff, two or three dark months each year (the Alley operated year-round), and a substantial salary increase for herself. The board responded affirmatively and Vance stayed in Houston.

In 1959 F. McNeil Lowry of the Ford Foundation cited the Alley Theatre as "probably the most significant professional theatre in the United States, outside of New York" (quoted in Robert M. Treser, "Houston's Alley Theatre," doctoral dissertation, Tulane University, 1967, p. 104). The Ford Foundation granted the Alley $156,000 (to be matched by local funds) with which to hire actors over the next three seasons. Attendance was up slightly in the first season of the "Ford actors," but it leveled off again in 1960–61, despite the first season ticket drive in the organization's history. The need for a new facility was pressing, as most observers agreed that Houston wouldn't go to a theatre in a converted fan factory. The national press continued to focus favorable attention on the Alley and its productions, but to no local avail.

The company of 1961–62, the first full Equity resident company, the strongest to date in the view of Robert Treser ("Houston's Alley Theatre," p. 119), failed to attract large audiences in its first two shows, but attendance was up sharply thereafter. Ben Jonson's *Volpone* was very well attended in its run of forty-one performances, and William Gibson's *The Miracle Worker* was the biggest hit since *The Iceman Cometh* in 1958. More important, efforts to build a new theatre for the Alley troupe gathered force. The Ford Foundation expressed interest, as did the Houston Endowment, Inc., which donated a tract of land adjacent to the Civic Center as a site for the new theatre. In October 1962 the Ford Foundation granted $2.1 million (requiring a $900,000 local matching fund) for the construction of a new theatre in Houston and for the development of the Alley Theatre company over a ten-year period. Still later the Ford Foundation granted another $1.4 million for the construction of the very special building designed for the Alley by Ulrich Franzen.

Fund-raising was the main activity of the season of 1962–63. The season subscription campaign peaked at only 2,700, more than double the year before but less than half the established goal. Vance scrapped the use of seasonal contracts for performers and let the run of each production be determined by audience demand. The level of artistry dropped, but the fund-raising campaign was a success, owing in great measure to the widespread and enduring support of Houston media.

Vance tentatively announced 1963–64 as a "dark" season to allow time for planning the new building and beginning its construction. Mounting public pressure and last-minute permission from the Ford Foundation to use interest accruing to its grant and matching assets to underwrite the season's projected deficit persuaded Vance to keep the theatre open. Season sales reached 4,200, and Vance's production of Anton Chekhov's *The Three Sisters* became the first in Alley history to play to over 100 percent of the Berry Avenue theatre's capacity.

The design and construction of the new theatre was a protracted affair not concluded until the fall of 1968. Meantime the Alley continued to produce five or six plays per season until 1967–68, when they ended their stand on Berry Avenue with a three-play season. In 1965 the Alley premiered Paul Zindel's *The Effect of Gamma Rays on Man-in-the-Moon Marigolds*. It went on to a Pulitzer Prize–winning Broadway run.

The new Alley Theatre was dedicated October 13, 1968, and it opened officially November 24 with a preview of Bertolt Brecht's *Galileo*, with Tony van Bridge in the title role. Clive Barnes of the *New York Times* called the new Alley Theatre "one of the most attractive and striking theatres in the world." Indeed, Ulrich Franzen's postmodernist design, an unlikely blend of medieval and southwestern United States motifs, received a 1972 Honor Award from the American Institute of Architects. The structure is a warm and textured amalgam of concrete and native stone. Nine towers emphasize the solidity of the building while also housing fire stairs and well-insulated air conditioning machinery. Audience promenades and balconies circle the upper levels. Winding staircases provide a sense of mystery while rich colors, sandblasted concrete, and carved wood blend opulently for an effect at once graceful and intimate. The Large Stage (seating 800) is innovatively designed such that the audience is enveloped by caliper stages. Tunnels at the side facilitate entrances to the open stage. Franzen eliminated a major problem found in most open-stage theatre—large volumes of space surrounding a comparatively small stage—by lowering the auditorium ceiling. The George Izenour–designed lighting system features a gridiron from which lights are suspended only nineteen feet above the stage. The effect is a large theatre with excellent acoustics and an uncanny feeling of intimacy. A 296-seat Arena Stage duplicated many of the most successful features of the Berry Avenue theatre. Workshops, offices, and storage spaces honeycomb the $5.5 million building.

The inaugural season on Texas Avenue was made up of monumental and demanding plays for which the company was not suited. Subsequent seasons have featured more compact and more realistic plays, usually of American origin, though works from the international repertory of established drama are also quite common. The production of new plays has not been an Alley priority.

Throughout the 1970s efforts to develop a resident company fell short as Vance and other directors made heavy use of jobbed-in performers. The Alley management could find no way to lure more than a few high-quality performers to Houston for long residencies. Moreover, as early as 1973, Vance was ill from the cancer that was to claim her life in 1980. The energy to drive the organization to new heights of achievement in its new theatre was not hers to give. The company languished, for no new leader was able or willing to provide the profoundly committed and astutely practical leadership Vance had given for nearly thirty years. Vance's close friend Herschel Wilkenfeld served as executive producer in the late seventies; Vance, though largely inaccessible during the period of her decline, remained executive director. After her death in February 1980, longtime managing director Iris Siff became acting artistic director.

After considerable deliberation and while a team of four directors managed the company in 1980–81, a search committee selected Patricia Ann Brown to succeed Vance as artistic director. Brown, like Vance, was Texas-born; she had been educated in the public schools of Houston and had acted (as Pat Horn) with the Alley Theatre intermittently from 1947 to 1951. She was producing director of the Magnolia Theatre of Long Beach, California, from 1954 to 1968 and then a Los Angeles–based theatre consultant and free-lance director until 1981.

Brown immediately set about revitalizing the Alley. The 1981 Summer Fair, heretofore a film festival, offered theatre to Alley patrons. Brown introduced rotating repertory on both the Large Stage and the Arena Stage in 1981–82 and negotiated an exchange of companies and productions between the Alley and Alan Ayckbourn's Stephen Joseph Theatre in England (Ayckbourn, a prolific writer of contemporary comedy of manners, is Pat Brown's directing specialty). Brown also initiated a Lunchtime Theatre to better develop the downtown corporate audience, and she installed a university-affiliated director training program. The Alley's apprentice and actor-training programs received greater emphasis, as did an effort to establish and maintain a permanent acting ensemble. Brown also increased the number of productions on the Alley calendar, and she has begun to liberalize the politically and aesthetically conservative programming typical of the Alley under Nina Vance.

Aggressive telemarketing by new managing director Tom Spray boosted subscription sales to about 30,000 for 1985–86, while operating expenses for expanded operations neared $5 million. In 1985 and 1986 the Alley inaugurated the season with a benefit gala, raising an average of $300,000 each year. The National Endowment for the Arts has offered the Alley a challenge grant of $500,000 to be matched three-to-one by local contributions over a three-year period. This grant is part of a two-phase, $9.8 million endowment campaign initiated by the Alley board of directors in 1985. The Challenge Endowment was seeded by an anonymous gift of $1 million. Despite an enduring depression in the energy market, on which Houston and all of Texas are so dependent, Houstonians have rallied to Brown's efforts to rejuvenate the Alley Theatre.

PERSONNEL

Founders: Robert Altfeld, Vivian Altfeld, Sidney Holmes, Nina Vance.

Artistic Directors: Patricia Ann Brown (1981–86), Nina Vance (1947–80).

Managing/Executive Directors: Arthur J. Keeney (1966–69), Iris Siff (1964–82), Tom Spray (1981–86).

Directors: Josephine R. Abady (1985–86), Charles Abbott (1982–83, 1985–86), George Anderson (1982–83, 1984–86), Alan Ayckbourn (1981–82), Cliff F. Baker (1983–84), William Ball (1959–60), B. H. Barry (1981–82), *Pat Brown* (1969–70, 1979–86), Roderick Cook (1979–80), *Louis Criss* (1966–69, 1979–81), Kirk Denmark (1969–70), Ted Follows (1976–77), Burry Fredrik (1970–71), James Gardner (1984–85), John Going (1982–84), Robert Graham (1982–83), *William Hardy* (1965–67, 1968–71), Neil Havens (1981–83, 1984–85), John Pynchon Holmes (1981–82), Jerome Kilty (1969–70), Michael LaGue (1982–83), Arthur Laurents (1978–79), *R. Edward Leonard* (1969–76), Romulus Linney (1982–83), Robert David McDonald (1968–69), Sherman Marks (1968–69), James Martin (1985–86), Michael Meacham (1968–69), Philip Minor (1969–70), Malcolm Morrison (1985–86), Jim O'Connor (1984–85), Horenca J. Ormes (1982–83), Vance G. Ormes (1982–83), Joyce Randall (1962–64), Ivan Rider, Jr. (1981–82), Joseph Ruskin (1965–67), *Beth Sanford* (1968–86), Alan Schneider (1959–60), Milton Selzer (1969–70), Lee Shallat (1984–85), *Robert Symonds* (1973–74, 1979–81), Joan Vail Thorne (1983–85), *William Trotman* (1971–72, 1973–76), *Nina Vance* (1947–77), Calina Volchyek (1977–78), *John Vreeke* (1979–85), Jack Westin (1972–73), Clifford Williams (1980–81), Mervyn Willis (1984–85), Angela Wood (1961–62), *John Wylie* (1955–68), Leslie Yeo (1976–79).

Designers: Frances Aronson (1985–86), Ariel Baliff (1980–81), Barbara A. Bell (1985–86), Keith Belli (1983–84), Robert Blackman (1981–83), William Bloodgood (1981–82), *Don Bolen* (1958–63), *John Bos* (1979–83), Dennis Bradford (1981–83), Lewis Brown (1985–86), Ainslie G. Bruneau (1983–85), Lucie Caldwell (1968–70), Joanie Canon (1984–85), Michael J. Cesario (1977–78, 1979–81), Jan Cole (1984–86), George Collins (1958–59), James Cornick (1958–60), Richard D. Cortright (1969–72), Barbara C. Cox (1973–76), John Custer (1962–63), Tom Dean (1981–83), Richard Devin (1981–83), Fontini Dimou (1983–85), Patricia E. Doherty (1985–86), Deborah M. Dryden (1981–82), *Jonathan Duff* (1970–76, 1977–83), Paul Dupree (1975–76), Jean Eckart (1978–79), William Eckart (1978–79), Richard Ellis (1985–86), *James F. Franklin* (1981–85), Ferruccio Garavaglia (1971–72), Carlin Glynn (1959–60), Richard H. Graham, Jr. (1970–71), *Matthew Grant* (1976–83), Pam Gray (1984–85), Jane Greenwood (1979–80), Paul Gregory (1974–75), John Hagen (1969–71), Keith Hein (1981–83), Mo Holden (1984–85), Michael Holt (1984–85), Stephen J. Houtz (1979–80), Robert Howery (1959–60), Rosemary Ingham (1981–82), John Jensen (1981–83), Jim Jeter (1959–61), Richard W. Jeter (1983–86), Tony Johnson (1982–83, 1984–85), Dale F. Jordan (1983–85), Charles S. Kading (1984–86), Jack Kammerman (1969–70), Howard Tsvi Kaplan (1985–86), John Kenny (1974–75), Grady Larkins (1968–69), *Marie LeMaster* (1959–65), Edward Lipscomb (1981–82), Jim Love (1959–60), Francis Lynch (1981–82), Tom McKinley (1980–83), Henry McNally (1959–60), Arthur Meister (1981–83), John Michener (1985–86), Harris Milam (1960–61), Michael Miller (1981–83), Sarajane Milligan (1985–86), Sean Murphy (1981–83), Pat Nielson (1969–70), *Michael Olich* (1976–77, 1979–80, 1981–83), Al Oster (1979–83), Mary Lou Owen (1968–69), *Paul Owen* (1960–69), Elizabeth Poindexter (1981–83), Florine (Sissy) Pulley (1965–66), Tom Rasmussen (1981–83), Penny Remsen (1981–83), Michael Ryan (1985–86), Ellen Ryba (1978–80), James Sale (1981–82, 1985–86), Jeff Seats (1979–80), Debbie Smithee (1981–83), Jack Spain (1958–59), James E. Stephens (1979–80), Judge Stevens (1958–59), Greg Sullivan (1982–86), John Carter Sullivan (1981–86), Byron A. Taylor (1984–85), Paul Tremaine (1960–61), *William Trotman* (1959–60, 1961–62, 1972–74, 1975–76, 1980–81), Linn Vercheski (1981–83), Mariann Verheyen (1981–83), John Vreeke (1979–80), Ann Wallace (1981–83), Dale White (1981–83), George Williams (1959–61), Jerry Williams (1969–73, 1979–80), John Wylie (1968–69), Art Yelton (1985–86).

Actors and Actresses: Paula Abbott (1985–86), Jim Adams (1968–69), John Adams (1975–76), Ruth E. Adams (1983–84, 1985–86), David Adamson (1971–73), Janet Williams Adderly (1985–86), Nathan Adler (1980–81), Dell Aldrich (1959–60), *Jo Alessandro* (later *Jo Marks*) (1947–50, 1951–52, 1954–55, 1961–62, 1982–84), Danny Alford (1981–83), J. Brent Alford (1981–82, 1985–86), Ira Allen (1957–58), Michael Allinson, (1978–79), Richard Allton (1964–65), Robert Altfeld (1947–49, 1950–52), Vivian Altfeld (1947–48, 1950–51), Luisa Amaral-Smith (1984–86), Allen Amason (1970–71), Marty Ambrose (1973–74), Barbara Anderson (1980–81), Clint Anderson (1954–55, 1956–57, 1970–74), George Anderson (1960–61, 1962–63, 1965–66), Jensie Anderson (1985–86), Scotty Anderson (1949–51), Suzanne Anderson (1967–68), Bill Andes (1969–70), Susan Andre (1973–74), Pamela Anson (1978–79), Charles Armsby (1956–58), John Armstrong (1979–80), Sidney Armus (1968–69, 1974–75), *Timothy Arrington* (1981–86), Martin Ashe (1955–56, 1959–60), Maggie Askey (1976–77), John Astin (1959–60), Claudene Atkinson (1955–57), Rene Auberjonois (1961–62), Anthony Auer (1972–73), Basil Augustine (1968–69), Lynn Autmann (1964–65), Caroljean Avera (1951–53), Mary Ayres (1980–81), Beth Babbitt (1965–66), Rob Babbitt (1981–82), Donald Babcock (1959–

60), Neil Badders (1981–82), Leopold Badia (1963–64), Ken Bahn (1985–86), *Jim Bailey* (1948–49, 1951–55), Al Baker (1956–57), Michael Ball (1976–77), Ric Ballad (1948–49, 1953–54), *Jerome Ballew* (1964–66, 1968–70), Margaret Bannerman (1957–59), Ann Barber (1962–63), Margaret Bard (1979–80), Mildred Barnes (1954–55), Barbara Barnett (1972–73), Gertrude Barnstone (1958–60), Roger Baron (1974–75), Joe Barrett (1980–81), Dianna Barrington (1977–78), Holly Barron (1985–86), Robert Barrows (1958–59), Ivar Barry (1980–81), Kenneth Barry (1967–68), Mary Barry (1982–83), David Ray Bartee (1985–86), Jimmy Bass (1951–54, 1956–57), Sue Batchelor (1983–84), Dolores Baum (1985–86), Louis Beachner (1963–64), William Beckhame (1948–51, 1953–54, 1956–57), Claude Bede (1977–78), Cal Bedford (1974–76), *James Belcher* (1981–83, 1984–86), Collins Bell (1957–59), Glynis Bell (1972–74, 1982–83), Jack Bell (1968–71), Jay Bell (1981–82), John Bell (1962–63), Liz Bell (1963–64), Morris Bell (1949–50, 1952–53), Susan Bell (1961–62), Betty Bellune (1963–64), Herb Bennett (1949–51, 1952–54, 1956–57), Jeff Bennett (1984–86), June Bennett (1952–53, 1956–57), Carl Bensen (1951–52, 1953–54, 1959–60), Robert Benson (1979–80), Jem Bentz (1949–52, 1954–55), Eddie Bergson (1979–80), Alexandra Berlin (1966–67, 1968–69), Jim Bernhard (1958–59, 1982–83, 1984–86), Charlene Bigham (1973–74, 1985–86), Thomas Bish (1958–59), Ronald Bishop (1961–62, 1974–75), Chalyce Blair (1981–82), Steven Blair (1985–86), Milton Blankenship (1979–82), Robin Bludworth (1980–81), Mickey Bobkoff (1960–61), Barbara Bollman (1962–63), Terry Bone (1963–64), Victoria Boothby (1985–86), Nancy Boykin (1985–86), Maralyn Boysen (1952–53), Mary Bozeman (1958–59), Robin Bradley (1977–78), Celia Braswell (1981–82), *Charles Braswell* (1957–59), Peter Breck (1952–53, 1955–57), Ted Brenner (1949–50), Cathy Brewer-Moore (1978–79), Jean Brewington (1954–56), Tony van Bridge (1968–69), Bill Bridges (1960–62), Lei Broadstone (1979–80), James Broderick (1969–71), James E. Brodhead (1982–83), Sheri Tyrell Brogden (1982–83), John Broglio (1968–69), Pamela Brook (1976–77, 1980–81), Myrtis Brooks (1951–52), Franklin Brown (1973–74), Linda Brown (1965–66), Pat Brown (1969–70), Richard C. Brown (1985–86), Sarah Brown (1982–83), Linda Brumfield (1970–71), Steve Brush (1983–84), Frank Bryans (1956–57, 1958–59), Geoffrey Bryant (1959–60), Geneva Bugbee (1961–62, 1963–64), Joseph Buloff (1955–56, 1958–59), Hal Burdick (1960–61), Lee Burnett (1972–73), Joseph Burns (1962–63), *Bob Burrus* (1981–83), Norman Burton (1959–60), Michael Butler (1981–82), Patrick L. Byers (1977–78), Peggy Ann Byers (1976–77), John Cagan (1982–84), Thonnis Calhoun (1958–59), Joseph Campbell (1949–50), Les Campbell (1956–57), *Polly Campbell* (1952–56), Joyce Campion (1977–78), Ralph Capezutti (1948–50), Ray Carlson (1949–50, 1952–53), Lauren Ann Carner (1971–72), John Carpenter (1969–70), Mimi Carr (1974–76), Tom Carrins (1952–53), Carol Carter (1961–62), Dan Carter (1974–75), Timothy Casey (1971–72), Charles Cashmere (1958–59), Steve Cassling (1981–83), Brea Cavazas (1958–59), David Cendric (1972–73), David E. Chadderdon (1976–77), Julie Challenger (1981–82), Grace Chapman (1970–71), Jonathan Charles (1985–86), Randy Cheramie (1976–78), Kay Chevalier (1962–63), Gale Childs (1977–80), David Christmas (1978–79), Kendall Clark (1968–71), Frederick Clay (1979–80), *Jeannette Clift* (1949–51, 1952–55, 1956–58, 1961–62, 1965–71, 1972–73, 1980–81), Mabel Cochran (1958–59), Laura Coffee (1960–61), Waldo Coffman (1949–50), Arlene Cohen (1960–62), Melody Kay Coker (1985–86), Christopher Combest (1985–86), Michelle Condre (1957–58), Darlene Conley (1972–73, 1974–75), Marguerite Conner (1957–59), Charles A. Cook (1959–60), Lisa Cook (1980–81), Roderick Cook (1962–63, 1975–76, 1978–79), Connie Cooper (1961–62), Dale Carter Cooper (1969–70), Judy Cooper (1961–

62), Maury Cooper (1962–64), Renate Cooper (1948–49, 1951–52), Robin Cooper (1973–74), Michael Copan, Jr. (1959–60, 1961–62), Carolyn Cope (1984–85), James Cornick (1958–59), Robert Cornthwaite (1973–74, 1984–85), Joseph Costa (1974–75), A. D. Cover (1974–75), Franklin Cover (1963–64), Barbara Cox (1973–74), Mary Agen Cox (1984–85), *Rutherford Cravens* (1971–74, 1975–77, 1979–80, 1982–83), Dan Crego (1961–62), Georgia Creighton (1973–74), Jack Creley (1979–80), Kay Crews (1973–74), Louis Criss (1966–67), J. T. Cromwell (1972–73), Pat Crowder (1956–57), Caroline Crystal (1974–75), Barry Cullison (1969–70), *Bob Cummins* (1949–50, 1951–55), Michael Cunningham (1981–82), Richard Curnock (1977–78), Carl DaGilis (1952–54), Zan Dailey (1973–75), Stephen Daley (1961–62), Laurie Daniels (1982–83), David Dannenbaum (1957–60), Henry Dardenne (1981–82), Ted D'Arms (1968–69), *Philip Davidson* (1974–78), Lane Davies (1973–74), Carl Davis (1975–77), Dan Davis (1950–51, 1955–56), David Davis (1955–56, 1960–61), Pat Davis (1950–51, 1952–53), Rick Davis (1951–52), Sue Carol Davis (1962–64), Vivan Lee Davis (1973–74), Barbara Daytree (1974–75), Blue Deckert (1979–80, 1981–82, 1984–85), *Albert Dekker* (1953–55), Jerry Delony (1951–53), Dante DeLoreto (1983–84), *Margaret Denney* (1948–51, 1952–54, 1958–59, 1961–62), Leslie Denniston (1980–81), William Denny (1947–49, 1950–51, 1959–60), Caroline Diamond (1948–50), Fritz Dickmann (1980–81, 1984–85), Walt Dickson (1964–65), Therese Diekhans (1979–80), *J. Robert Dietz* (1964–67), Kenneth Dight (1976–78), Dick Dobbyn (1961–62), Michael Donaghue (1978–79), *Robert Donley* (1960–61, 1980–82), Ron Dortch (1971–72), Richard Dow (1978–79), Thorne Dreyer (1962–63), Steve Driscoll (1964–65), Alice Drummond (1966–67), Jonathan Duff (1973–74), Todd Duffey (1984–85), Matt Duffin (1981–82), David Dukes (1969–70), Joan Dunham (1980–81), Paul Dupree (1972–74), Jack Dupuy (1971–72), Peter Duryea (1962–63), Marilyn Earl (1952–53), Holmes Easley (1956–58), George Ebeling (1970–71), James Edmonson (1975–76), Daryl Edwards (1984–85), Michael Egan (1953–55), Barbara Elliott (1952–53, 1954–55), Glenn Elliott (1966–67), Jack Ellis (1963–64), *Jim Ellis* (1959–60), Woody Eney (1971–73), Sheldon Epps (1972–73, 1976–77), Richard Erdman (1959–60, 1980–81), John Etheredge (1973–74), *Lillian Evans* (1966–75, 1976–85), Jack Van Evera (1978–79), Robert Fairfax (1960–61), Ed Farmer (1952–54), Frances Farmer (1948–49, 1953–54), June Farquharson (1952–54), Jonathan Farwell (1970–71), Christopher Fazel (1974–75), Alan Feinstein (1980–81), Clarence Felder (1968–70), Iris Fenton (1951–52, 1953–54), Moya Fenwich (1979–80), Gillie Fenwick (1979–80), Lou Ferguson (1984–85), Darcey Ferrer (1980–81), *James Field* (1959–60), Karen Filer (1969–71), *Joe Finkelstein* (1949–50, 1951–52, 1953–55, 1970–72, 1981–83), *Philip Fisher* (1962–65, 1972–74, 1980–83, 1984–85), *Bettye Fitzgerald* (1957–67, 1973–86), Haskell Fitz-Simons (1974–76), Neil Flanagan (1980–81), Pauline Flanagan (1977–78), Walter Flanagan (1950–51, 1952–53), Michael Fletcher (1979–81), Gertrude Flynn (1970–71), Tom Flynn (1982–83), Charles Folwell (1973–74), Forrest Folwell (1973–74), Brenda Forbes (1975–76), Larry Ford (1975–76), Ruth Ford (1982–83), Ann Forgy (1985–86), Fred Forrest (1963–64), Frances Foster (1976–77), Ken Fowler (1983–84), *Robert Foxworth* (1957–58, 1959–61), Roy Frady (1969–70), Richard Francis (1968–69), *Bernard Frawley* (1976–78, 1980–81), Ronnie Freed (1950–51, 1952–53), Cyndy Freedman (1961–63), Marilyn Fried (1959–60), *Karen Friman* (later *Karen Morris*) (1959–64), Kristina Friman (1985–86), Lauren Frost (1971–73), Scott Fults (1984–86), I. G. Futor (1964–65), Harold Gaardner (1952–53), Wayne Gagne (1975–76), Kimberley Gaisford (1979–80), Sandra M. Galeota (1985–86), *Roland Gallian* (1956–57, 1958–60, 1961–63), Pat Galloway (1978–79), Bonnie Gallup (1983–84), Kim Garcia (1973–74), Peter Angel Garcia (1985–

86), Craig R. Gardner (1975–76), Karen Garelick (1981–82), Martin Garner (1964–65), Christopher Gaze (1976–77), Faith Geer (1958–59), Stephen Geer (1959–60), Ted Gehring (1955–57), Doug Gens (1976–77), Johnny Nelson George (1949–52), Ellis Gilbert (1948–50), Brian Gilmar (1967–68), Shawn Glanville (1977–78), Kayce Glasse (1984–86), Charlotte Glenn (1948–50, 1959–60), William Glover (1971–72), *Carlin Glynn* (1956–59), *Russell Gold* (1961–62, 1975–76), Beryl Goldberg (1950–51), John Goldsmith (1970–71), Maurice Good (1977–79), Robyn Goodman (1970–71, 1978–79), John Paul Goodwin (1948–49, 1950–51), Carl Gordon (1976–77), Cynthia Gorman (1985–86), Gil Gorman (1952–53), David Gould (1982–83), Elaine Graham (1982–83), *Robert Graham* (1981–83), Barbara Dennison Grant (1974–75), Calvin Grant (1957–59), Ernest Graves (1957–58), Charles Gray (1952–55), Joan Smith Gray (1961–62), Melissa Ann Gray (1983–84), Spalding Gray (1966–67), John Green (1972–73), Lanny Green (1981–82), Francine Greenfield (1949–50, 1957–58), Helen Greenwood (1948–49), David Gregory (1985–86), Michael Alan Gregory (1984–85), Paul Gregory (1973–74), Christian Grey (1979–80), Gary Griffin (1959–60), James Griffiths (1968–69), John Grimes (1948–49), Gene Gross (1964–65), *Vernon Grote* (1976–79), Ambrosio Guerra (1985–86), Michael Guido (1977–78), Philip Gushee (1968–69), Deborah Gwillim (1973–74), Paul Haggard (1968–69), Daydrie Hague (1982–84), Bruce Hall (1963–64, 1969–70, 1973–74), Michael Hall (1971–73), Helen Halsey (1980–82), Margaret Hamilton (1969–70), Rick Hamilton (1962–63, 1968–69, 1984–85), Timothy Hanlon (1985–86), William Hansen (1963–64, 1972–73), *Jerry Hardin* (1964–67), Sarah Hardy (1976–77), *William Hardy* (1952–54, 1955–60, 1961–73), Wiley Harker (1980–81), Mary Harrigan (1963–64), Lenore Harris (1977–78), Patrick Harrison (1961–62), Mike Hartman (1980–81), James Harvey (1973–74), Roger Hatch (1972–74), Dorothy Ann Haug (1977–78), Betty Havens (1966–67), Sandy Havens (1954–56), Lila Hawthorne (1959–60), J. Rorey Hayden (1981–82), Pauline Hecht (1950–51, 1956–58, 1959–60, 1961–62), Teresa Heck (1981–83), Nelson Heggen (1976–77), Cyndy Heinrich (1960–62), *Dale Helward* (1957–58, 1964–67, 1968–69, 1975–76, 1977–78, 1979–81, 1982–83, 1984–85), Stephen McKinley Henderson (1984–85), Maxwell Hendler (1949–52), Anthony Hendrix (1983–84), Dee Hennigan (1982–83), Sean Hennigan (1982–83), Richard Herbine (1954–55), Tito Hernandez (1985–86), Wes Hickle (1950–51), Diane Hill (1965–66), Richard Hill (1982–84), Sarah Hill (1985–86), Brian Hinson (1981–82), I. M. Hobson (1968–71, 1972–73), Ted Hoerl (1971–72), Dominic Hogan (1969–70), Irene Hogan (1969–70), Burk Holaday (1971–72), Tommy Hollis (1980–81), Bertha Holmes (1948–50), Edward K. Holmes (1962–63), Sidney Holmes (1947–48, 1949–50), George Honea (1977–78), Rosamond Hooper (1974–75), Paul Hope (1984–86), Pat Horn (1948–50, 1956–57), Derek Horton (1985–86), Eric House (1977–79), Gary Hubbard (1972–73), David Hudson (1978–79), I. M. Hudson (1971–72), Rodney Hudson (1981–82), Ron Hudson (1971–72), Jack Hughes (1947–48, 1955–56), Ross Hughes (1951–53), Lynn Humphrey (1981–83), Margaret Humphreys (1978–80), Leslie Hunt (1947–50), Kim Hunter (1980–81), William Hutson (1972–73), Mark Hymen (1985–86), Mary S. Irey (1974–75), Joe Isaacs (1970–71), Mary K. Isaacs (1970–71), Stephen Isbell (1975–76), Charles Jackson (1981–82), George Jackson (1975–76), Lazette Jackson (1961–62), Samuel L. Jackson (1982–83), Spence Jackson (1973–74), Len Jacob (1967–68), Max William Jacobs (1962–64), Michael Jamail (1950–52), Donald W. Janeck (1960–61), *Bella Jarrett* (1961–62, 1964–65, 1966–68, 1975–76, 1977–78, 1979–80), Sharon Jarvis (1980–81), Jane Jeanes (1954–56), Carthal T. Jenkins (1962–63), *Trent Jenkins* (1963–65, 1966–69, 1974–75, 1976–77, 1978–79, 1983–84), Louise Jenkins (1976–77), *Jimmy Jeter* (1947–52, 1953–58,

1960–61), David K. Johnson (1976–77), Fiona Johnson (1957–58), Jack Stubblefield Johnson (1985–86), Kent Johnson (1983–84), Marilyn J. Johnson (1985–86), Rick Johnson (1973–74), William Johnson (1982–83), Don Jones (1966–67), Jerry Jones (1973–74), *Jerome Jordan* (1950–53, 1957–58), Sidney Kaplan (1948–50), Lillian Kaufman (1951–53), Clarence Kavanaugh (1950–52), Sidney Kay (1959–60), Robert R. Kaye (1973–74), Mark Keeler (1974–75), James Kelly (1976–77, 1978–79), Veronica Kemp-Henson (1981–82), *Richard Kennedy* (1955–57), James Kenney (1960–61), John Kenny (1973–74), Joel Kenyon (1978–79), Lynn Kevin (1963–65), Toney Keyes (1974–75), Jonathan Kidd (1972–73), Mike Kiibler (1974–75), Patricia Kilgarriff (1980–81, 1982–83), Charles Killian (1956–57), Jerome Kilty (1969–70), Floyd King, Jr. (1963–64), Murray Klater (1950–51, 1952–53), Jim Kleeman (1964–66), Varney Knapp (1964–65), Billie Knight (1947–50), Don Knuijt (1950–51, 1952–53), Arthur Korman (1979–80), Nikjon Kovalevsky (1976–77), Melissa Kraft (1979–80), Gary Krawford (1979–80), Charles Krohn (1963–64, 1985–86), Fred Kuchlin (1947–51), *Michael LaGue* (1981–83), Jeff Laite (1982–83), *Cynthia Lammel* (1981–85), Carol Lee Lang (1976–77), Raymond Lankford (1950–53), Bob Larkin (1970–71), *Dan LaRocque* (1981–84), Bill Larsen (1954–56), Fred Latham (1949–50, 1953–54), Danny Lawrence (1963–64), Dennis Lebby (1984–85), Willie LeBlanc (1961–62), Denise LeBrun (1972–73), Ray Ledbetter (1960–61), Eva Le Gallienne (1980–81), Johanna Leister (1984–85), *Marie LeMaster* (1956–58, 1960–61, 1963–64, 1965–66, 1968–69), *Nancy Evans Leonard* (1968–72), Robert Edward Leonard (1969–71, 1973–74), Eugenie Leontovitch (1959–60), Lynne Levine (1956–57), Marc Levine (1956–58), Dorothy Levy (1955–57), Simon L. Levy (1974–75), Bobo Lewis (1985–86), Chris Lewis (1976–77), Gilbert Lewis (1976–77), Gwendolyn Lewis (1981–82), Joel Ronston Lewis (1960–61), Pamela Lewis (1984–85), Raan Lewis (1984–85), Rick Lieberman (1971–73), Marilyn Lightstone (1964–65, 1977–78), Vivica Lindfors (1978–79), Priscilla Lindsay (1972–73), William C. Lindstrom (1973–74), Stuart Litchfield (1982–83), Alan Litsey (1981–82), Ann Lloyd (1954–55, 1956–58), Bruce Lloyd (1951–52, 1953–54, 1956–57), *Tom Lloyd* (1958–60), Carol Locatell (1981–82), Timmy Locke (1952–53), Richard Loder (1980–81), Walter Lodge (1948–51), Walter Loewenstern (1951–53), Ralph Longley (1956–57), Carolyn Lovelady (1962–63), *Dede Lowe* (1981–83), Deloris Lowman (1979–80), J. Frank Lucas (1954–55, 1957–58), Lynn Lucas (1956–58), Robert Lynn (1950–51), Susan McClintock (1963–64), J. Shane McClure (1978–81, 1982–83), Cassie McCollum (1981–82), David McCracken (1982–83), Margo McElroy (1973–74, 1975–77), Victor McElwee (1954–56), Malcolm McGee (1970–71), Elizabeth McGrath (1979–80), Joe McHale (1956–58), Marilyn McIntyre (1985–86), Jane MacIver (1976–77), Jay McKee (1973–74), John McMurtry (1967–68), Henry McNally (1959–60, 1961–62), *Jim McQueen* (1981–83, 1985–86), Meg McSweeney (1982–83), Richard McWilliams (1979–80), Bob Magruder (1958–59), Patsy Magruder (1958–60), Joseph Maher (1972–73), Laurie Main (1972–73), Eddie Mallett (1959–60), *Anthony Manionis* (1972–74, 1976–79), John Mansfield (1973–74), Steven Marcus (1984–86), Bob Marich (1985–86), Marietta Marich (1985–86), Marijane Maricle (1955–56), Russ Marin (1971–72), Lealan Markham (1977–78), Stephen Markle (1981–82), Loree Marks (1958–59), Barbara Marshall (1960–61), Nan Martin (1963–64), Nancy Mason (1951–52), Terry Masters (1981–82), Gerry Matthews (1950–53), David Mauro (1971–72), Wayne Maxwell (1960–61), Jerry Mayer (1981–82), Irena Mayeska (1978–79), Amanda Mayo (1971–72), Caroline Mead (1960–61), Lawr Means (1984–85), Joseph G. Medalis (1968–69), Jack Medley (1979–80), Elizabetta Melchiori (1985–86), S. Epatha Merkerson (1982–83), Peter Messaline (1979–80), Robert John

Metcalf (1973–74), Lorraine Meyer (1962–66, 1968–70), *Yvonne Meyer* (1948–50, 1951–52, 1953–55, 1956–58), Dale Mikulenka (1955–58), Lou Ann Miles (1985–86), John Milford (1970–71), Michael Miller (1962–63), Nancy Miller (1981–82), Patrick Miller (1960–61), Georganna Mills (1985–86), Ann Minor (1970–71), Sharon Montgomery (1981–82), Che Moody (later Che Knight) (1959–61, 1963–64, 1977–78), Sarah Jane Moody (1983–84), Daniel Mooney (1969–70), Jonathan Moore (1962–63), Richard Moore (1961–62), James Richard Morgan (1970–71), Monique Morgan (1978–79), Ronald Morgrave (1964–65), Michael Moriarty (1970–71), Aileen Morris (1948–50, 1951–53), Keith Morris (1973–74), Vernon Morris (1981–82), *Fred Morrow* (1947–48, 1950–53, 1970–71, 1973–74), Kathryn Mosbacher (1974–75), *Robin Moseley* (1978–80, 1981–85), Norman Moses (1982–83), Bill Mueller (1951–53), Judy Mueller (1972–73, 1976–78), Ruth Mueller (1951–53), Betty Mulders (1957–59), William Munchow (1963–64), Bob Mundell (1973–74), George Mundine (1953–54, 1958–59), Sara Munson (1952–53, 1955–56), *Warren E. Munson* (1961–64), Mark Murphy (1975–76), Frank Myers (1962–63), John Napierala (1972–73), Patrizia Narcia (1980–81), Floyd T. Nash (1985–86), Myron Natwick (1960–61), Alexandra Neil (1985–86), Ruth Nelson (1980–81, 1982–83), Bennie Nipper (1958–59, 1962–64), Frances Nohl (1950–53), Jim Nolan (1975–76), Celia Nolte (1980–81), Bill E. Noone (1969–70), Kathleen O'Meara Noone (1969–70), Michael Normandy (1984–85), Bruce Norris (1983–85), Kristin Norton (1985–86), Billy Nowell (1981–82), Valerie Noyes (1978–79), Bruce Nozick (1985–86), Patrick Nugent (1983–84), Roy Oakes (1956–57), Donna O'Connor (1969–73, 1977–78), K. Lype O'Dell (1984–86), Stephen O'Dwyer (1985–86), David Okarski (1974–75), Colleen O'Kit (1981–82), George Olsen (1950–51), Margret O'Neill (1963–64), Joel Ontiberoz (1970–71), David Opatoshu (1978–79), Steven Ortego (1978–79), Lee Hickle Osborne (1950–52, 1953–54), Fowler Osburn (1958–60, 1961–62), Michael O'Sullivan (1969–70), *Paul Owen* (1960–64), Reginald Owen (1953–54), David Palmer (1964–65), Tom Palmer (1959–60), *Tony Palmer* (1951–57, 1958–60, 1968–69), Chip Pankey (1975–77, 1978–79), *Amelia Parker* (1947–60, 1963–64, 1965–66, 1974–75), Bruce Parker (1974–75), Roxann Parker (1980–81), Joel Parks (1977–78), Mitchell Patrick (1983–84), Moultrie Patten (1962–63), Kathryn Paul (1978–80), Albert Paulsen (1978–79), Bonnie Pavia (1958–59), *Virginia Payne* (1961–64, 1965–67, 1968–69), Patricia Pearcy (1970–71), Paris Peet (1980–82), Susan Pellegrino (1984–85), Mel Pennington (1958–59, 1962–63), Wheade Peoples (1962–63), Susan Peretz (1969–70), Robert Phalen (1980–81), Garry Phillips (1970–71), Miriam Phillips (1963–64, 1977–78), Renae Pickens (1972–73), Byrne Piven (1968–69), *Richard Poe* (1983–85), Priscilla Pointer (1973–74), Paul Polk (1985–86), Rand Porter (1975–76), Matthew Posey (1981–82), K. K. Preece (1985–86), Dorothy Price (1968–70, 1972–73, 1977–78), Greg Price (1949–50), John Baker Prickett (1948–50), Jean Proctor (1974–75, 1981–83), *Robert Quarry* (1960–61), Gerald J. Quimby (1985–86), Elaine Rabin (1958–59), Rex Rabold (1975–76), Ed Radabaugh (1957–58), David Radford (1982–83), Guy Rall (1949–50, 1955–56), Kevin Ramsey (1985–86), *Joyce Randall* (1958–64), James Ray (1980–81), James Ream (1985–86), Alexander Reed (1969–70), Jennifer Reed (1972–73), Richard Reed (1975–76), Kate Reid (1976–77), Paul Reimann (1962–63), Margie Repass (1950–51, 1952–53), Anne Revere (1964–65), Alice J. Rhoades (1976–77), Judy Rice (1972–73, 1978–79), Jess Richards (1985–86), Carl Richter (1948–50, 1952–53), Caroline Richter (1948–50, 1954–55), Emily Riddle (1980–82), Ron Rifkin (1981–82), Rozanne Ritch (1959–61), Pam Ritter (1985–86), Martin Rizley (1973–74, 1977–78), Betty Roach (1953–54, 1955–56, 1959–60), Oris Robertson (1958–60), Charles Robinson (1970–72), Carol Rodesney

(1951–52), Lou Rodgers (1969–70), Patricia Roe (1984–85), Brent Rogers (1981–82), William Rohrig (1985–86), Richard Rorke (1975–76), *Christine Rose* (1975–78), Joann Rose (1961–62, 1972–73), Marilyn Rosenblum (1950–51, 1951–53), Scott Roser (1981–83), Caroline Ross (1960–61), Beatrice Roth (1963–64), Gregory Ruhe (1984–85), Bob Rumsby (1984–85), Joseph Ruskin (1965–67), Shelley Russell (1973–74), Michel Rutrough (1970–71), Greg Ryan (1975–76), Lee Ryan (1951–52, 1953–54), Charles Sanders (1984–86), Tommy Sands (1950–51, 1953–54), *Beth Sanford* (1962–64, 1965–66, 1967–68, 1970–71, 1983–84), John Sanford (1980–81), Chesley Santoro (1973–74, 1977–78), Marcia Saxman (1959–60), Michael Scanlon (1968–69), Craig Schaeffer (1978–79), William Schlottman (1962–63), Larry Schneider (1982–83), George Schroeder (1950–51), Dwight Schultz (1975–76), David Schuster (1973–74), Philip Schuster (1979–80, 1981–82), Cheryl Scott (1967–69), Nancy Scott (1979–80), Florence Sebesta (1956–57), Bernice Selber (1952–54), Leigh Selting (1985–86), Milton Selzer (1968–69), Sol Serlin (1964–65), Sandi Shackelford (1981–82), Karen Shallo (1971–72), Ntozake Shange (1985–86), John B. Shanks (1949–51, 1954–55), Teresa Shanline (1973–74), Taubey Shedden (1973–74), Jay H. Sheffield (1968–70), Rita Shelton (1961–62), Sharon Shepley (1981–82), Don Shewey (1973–74), Anne Shropshire (1971–72), Ethel Shutta (1949–50, 1954–55, 1957–58), Iris Siff (1948–49, 1951–53), Max Silverman (1979–80), Michael Silverman (1979–80), William Simington (1984–85), Audrey Simons (1965–66), Constance Simons (1957–58), Johnny Simons (1965–66), Barbara Singer (1958–59), E. A. Sirianni (1974–75), *Woody Skaggs* (1970–74), Gram Slaton (1981–82), Curt Sleight (1954–57), Erika Slezak (1969–70), Fred Sliter (1963–64), Patti Slover (1977–79), Betsy Smith (1956–57, 1959–61), *Brandon Smith* (1979–80, 1981–86), Carol Smith (1956–59), Carter Smith (1955–58, 1959–60), Gram Smith (1977–79), Lee Smith (1972–73), Miriam Smith (1949–51), Norma Smith (1957–59), Sally Larsen Smith (1948–51), Al Smither (1965–66), Andrew Smoot (1982–83), David Snell (1980–81), Barry Snider (1965–66), Arlen Snyder (1959–60), Marcus Soloway (1979–80), Mark Soper (1984–85), Jack Spain (1958–59), Leann Sparacina (1981–82), John Spargur (1959–60), Paul Speyser (1964–65), Nancy Spivay (1970–71), Jeff Spivey (1953–55), Alan Stack (1980–81), Talmadge Stands (1965–66), Tom Stansbury (1966–67), Joel Stedman (1970–72, 1977–78), Judye Stephen (1958–60), Judge Stevens (1958–59), Walker Stevens (1981–82), Leonard Stewart (1950–51), Judith Stoskopf (1960–61), Robert Strane (1985–86), John Strano (1982–83), Morris Strassberg (1964–65), John Straub (1961–62), *Ray Stricklyn* (1949–50, 1962–63, 1964–65, 1970–72, 1984–85), Jerry Strickler (1959–61), Sheppard Strudwick (1974–75, 1980–81), Peter Strugess (1979–80), Harold Suggs (1978–79, 1984–86), Bobby L. Swain (1977–78), Sharon Swink (1974–75), *Robert Symonds* (1973–74, 1975–80), Daniel Szelag (1979–80), Lyle Talbot (1975–76), Jill Tanner (1985–86), Patricia Tanner (1958–59), Dixie Taylor (1971–72, 1977–78), Jordan Thaler (1982–83), Stephen Joseph Theatre in the Round Company (1981–82), Daniel Therriault (1975–76), Paul C. Thomas (1973–74, 1984–85), Sharon Thomas-Montgomery (1981–82), Bob Thompson (1976–77), *Emory Thompson* (1952–53, 1954–56, 1957–60), Joyce Thompson (1960–61), Tracy Thorne (1984–85), Linda Thorsen (1978–80), Concetta Tomei (1975–77), Jess Tomlinson (1978–79), Gary Tomson (1959–60), *Tom Toner* (1950–62, 1965–69), Mildred Torres (1949–50), Harry Townes (1973–74), Carmen Townsend (1950–53), Paul Trahan (1959–60), Howard Trapp (1959–60), Brian Tree (1976–77), *Paul Tremaine* (1960–62), *William Trotman* (1959–60, 1961–62, 1964–65, 1967–76), Mark Troy (1961–63), Neil Tucker (1954–55, 1958–59), Anne Twomey (1980–81), Michael Tylo (1977–78), *Robert Van Hooten* (1958–60, 1962–63), Sara Van Horn (1964–65),

Marijane Vandivier (1985–86), Mark Varian (1971–72), Frank Vega (1985–86), Holly Villaire (1980–81, 1982–83, 1985–86), Ernest Villarreal, Jr. (1958–59), Mark Volland (1980–81), John Vreeke (1983–84), Barbara Waddill (1964–65), Irving Wadler (1949–51, 1954–55), Ann Walker (1971–72), Connie Wallace (1959–61), Barbara Walleston (1953–55, 1959–60), Patricia Walter (1964–65), Audrey Ward (1965–66), Monica Ward (1979–80), Kathy Paul Warren (1981–82), Wyn Warren (1980–81), Justine Wasielewski (1971–72), Camille Waters (1964–65), Len Wayland (1962–63), Timothy Wayne-Brown (1973–74), Sallie Weathers (1981–82), Melissa Weaver (1970–71), Robb Webb (1968–70), Penni Weeks (1960–61), Ingeborg Weigel (1953–54), Dorothy Weiss (1950–51), Susan Welby (1985–86), Jennie Welch (1985–86), Dennis Wells (1981–82, 1984–86), Scott Wentworth (1980–81), Duval West (1950–51, 1952–53), Guy West (1960–61), Stephen Weyl (1961–62), Anthony White (1953–54), Jim White (1960–61), Joan White (1979–80), Laurel White (1982–83), Bernedette Whitehead (1955–56), Lee Whiting (1964–65), Donn Whyte (1984–85), Kenneth Wickes (1976–77), Chris Wiggins (1961–62), Buel Will (1973–74), *Ann Williams* (1960–61), *Betty Williams* (1951–52, 1953–54, 1955–56, 1958–61), Brenda Williams (1981–83), Chalethia Williams (1985–86), David Williams (1979–80, 1984–85), George Williams (1958–61), Greg Williams (1985–86), Morris Williams (1950–52), Chris Wilson (1948–49, 1955–57, 1963–65), Eleanor Wilson (1960–61), Milton Wilson (1950–52), Nathan Wilson (1961–63), Dustye Winniford (1980–81), Cary Winscott (1981–82), Kathy Jo Witt (1978–79), Edward Wittner (1974–75), Ben Wolf (1973–74, 1975–76), *Angela Wood* (1960–61, 1980–81), Lynn Wood (1969–70), Norma Jean Wood (1969–70), Linda Woodruff (1976–77), Allie Woods (1965–66), John Woodson (1982–84), *Ginger Wright* (1962–65, 1968–69), *David Wurst* (1973–81), *John Wylie* (1953–69, 1985–86), Nancy Wyman (1968–69), Gary Wynn (1981–82), Sandra Yarber (1960–62), Leslie Yeo (1975–77), Denton Yockey (1985–86), Marifran Yoder (1971–72), *Sally Zelker* (1954–59), Victoria Zussin (1968–69, 1976–77).

REPERTORY

At 3617 Main Street:

1947–48: *A Sound of Hunting, Payment Deferred, Another Part of the Forest, Caroline.*

1948–49: *Clash by Night, John Loves Mary.*

At 709 Berry Avenue:

1948–49: *The Children's Hour, Another Language, The Warrior's Husband, Desire Under the Elms.*

1949–50: *The Gentle People, No Exit, Season with Ginger, Dark Lady of the Sonnets* and *Man of Destiny, Light Up the Sky, Wingless Victory, Summer and Smoke.*

1950–51: *Joshua Beene and God, The Magic Fallacy, On Time and Nightmares, Golden Boy, Angelica, The Hasty Heart, The Enchanted.*

1951–52: *Goodbye, My Fancy, Thunder Rock, The Man, Miss Julie, Life with Mother, Home of the Brave, The Barretts of Wimpole Street.*

1952–53: *The Skin of Our Teeth, Burlesque, Stalag 17, The Rose Tattoo, My Dear Delinquents, Elizabeth the Queen.*

1953–54: *Miranda, I Am a Camera, The Play's the Thing, Death of a Salesman, Mrs. McThing, The Shrike, Affairs of State.*

1954–55: *Open House, Picnic, My Three Angels, All My Sons, Dial "M" for Murder, The Lady's Not for Burning, Light Up the Sky, The Remarkable Mr. Pennypacker.*

1955–56: *The Rainmaker, The Glass Menagerie, The Tender Trap, Hedda Gabler, The Fifth Season, A Roomful of Roses, Detective Story, Career.*

1956–57: *Sabrina Fair, Anastasia, Anniversary Waltz, A View from the Bridge, The Lark, Wedding Breakfast, Time Limit, Time Out for Ginger, Seventeen.*

1957–58: *The Chalk Garden, Will Success Spoil Rock Hunter?, The Matchmaker, The Reluctant Debutante, Three Love Affairs (A Phoenix Too Frequent, Bedtime Story, Still Life), Julius Caesar, Middle of the Night, Champagne Complex, The Remarkable Mr. Pennypacker.*

1958–59: *Gigi, The Madwoman of Chaillot, The Spider's Web, The Tunnel of Love, The Crucible, Say, Darling, Orpheus Descending, Holiday for Lovers, The Iceman Cometh, Once More with Feeling.*

1959–60: *Waiting for Godot, Who Was That Lady I Saw You With?, Rashomon, Waltz of the Toreadors, The Caine Mutiny Court Martial, The Cave Dwellers, Nude with Violin, A Moon for the Misbegotten, Sunrise at Campobello, Make a Million, Mister Roberts.*

1960–61: *Library Raid, Jane, Ondine, The Little Foxes, An Enemy of the People, The Happy Time, Six Characters in Search of an Author, Friends and Lovers* (three one-acts by Chekhov, O'Neill, and O'Casey), *The Winslow Boy, Period of Adjustment, John Brown's Body.*

1961–62: *Misalliance, Come Back, Little Sheba, Volpone, A Majority of One, Hamlet, Garden Spot, U.S.A.,* Jeannette Clift's *One Woman Show, The Miracle Worker, Amphitryon 38, Toys in the Attic, The Ponder Heart.*

1962–63: *Becket, The Hostage, Life with Father, The Taming of the Shrew, An Inspector Calls, Long Day's Journey into Night, Bernardine.*

1963–64: *The Queen and the Rebels, The Imaginary Invalid, Harvey, The Three Sisters, The Best Man, The Aspern Papers, Oh Dad, Poor Dad, Mamma's Hung You in the Closet and I'm Feelin' So Sad.*

1964–65: *The Trojan Women, The Tenth Man, A Sound of Hunting, The Knack, The Effect of Gamma Rays on Man-in-the-Moon Marigolds.*

1965–66: *The Devil's Disciple, Right You Are (If You Think You Are), You Can't Take It with You, Duel of Angels.*

1966–67: *The World of Sholom Aleichem, Diary of a Scoundrel, The Physicists, The Sea Gull, The Great Sebastians, The Caretaker.*

1967–68: *A Delicate Balance, The Miser, Candida.*

At 615 Texas Avenue:

1968–69: *Galileo, Don Juan in Hell, Saint Joan, Billy Liar, War and Peace, Charlie* and *Out at Sea, Light Up the Sky, All the Way Home.*

1969–70: *The Rose Tattoo, Everything in the Garden, Tartuffe, The Andersonville Trial, Dear Liar, Charley's Aunt, The World of Carl Sandburg, Blithe Spirit.*

1970–71: *Mourning Becomes Electra, Ring Round the Bathtub, The Night Thoreau Spent in Jail, Our Town, The Prime of Miss Jean Brodie, Dial "M" for Murder, Tango.*

1971–72: *Camino Real, U.S.A., A Flea in Her Ear, What the Butler Saw, My Sweet Charlie, Spoon River Anthology, Hadrian VII, The Taming of the Shrew, Child's Play.*

1972–73: *Pantagleize, Happy Birthday, Wanda June, Life with Father, The Hostage, All Over, Colette, The School for Wives, Jacques Brel Is Alive and Well and Living in Paris.*

1973–74: *Inherit the Wind, The Purification, Ah, Wilderness!, Encore, an Evening of Songs with Denise Le Brun, A Midsummer Night's Dream, Comedy of Marriage, Count*

Dracula, The Decline and Fall of the Entire World as Seen Through the Eyes of Cole Porter.

1974–75: *Wilson, The Man Who Came to Dinner, A Christmas Carol* (William Trotman adaptation), *Twelfth Night, A Streetcar Named Desire.*

1975–76: *Indians, The Cocktail Party, The Front Page, A Christmas Carol, Scenes from American Life, The Last Meeting of the Knights of the White Magnolia, Tiny Alice, Juno and the Paycock, The Show-Off, Purgatory, The Harmful Effects of Tobacco.*

1976–77: *The Sty of the Blind Pig, The Collection* and *The Dock Brief, You Never Can Tell, The Corn Is Green, Loot, The Runner Stumbles, Endgame, How the Other Half Loves.*

1977–78: *Mary Stuart, The Importance of Being Earnest, Denise Le Brun: Lifesize, The Root of the Mandrake, Echelon, The Shadow Box, Absurd Person Singular.*

1978–79: *Scream, Alice in Wonderland, The Happy Time, Artichoke, Don Juan in Hell, Side by Side by Sondheim.*

1979–80: *Indulgences in the Louisville Harem, Wizard of Oz* (Elizabeth Goodspeed adaptation), *Black Coffee, The Cherry Orchard, The Gospel According to St. Matthew, Sylvia Plath: A Dramatic Portrait* and *Three Women, Oh, Coward!, The Goodbye People.*

1980–81: *To Grandmother's House We Go, The Adventures of Tom Sawyer, The Threepenny Opera, Strider, Fathers and Sons, On Golden Pond, Betrayal, Romeo and Juliet, Da, Ten Little Indians, The Mousetrap.*

1981–82: *Cyrano de Bergerac, You Know Al He's a Funny Guy, The Red Bluegrass Western Flyer Show, The House of Blue Leaves, The Elephant Man, And If That Mockingbird Don't Sing, Paradise, Way Upstream* and *Absent Friends, Heidi* (John Vreeke adaptation), *The Wall, Talley's Folly, The Unexpected Guest.*

1982–83: *Close Ties, The Rivals, The 5th of July, Nuts, Family Business, The Visit, How I Got That Story, The Dining Room, Holy Ghosts, Taking Steps, Wait Until Dark.*

1983–84: *The Dresser, Donkeys' Years, Cloud 9, All My Sons, True West, Crimes of the Heart, Angels Fall, Uncle Vanya, Amateurs, 'night, Mother, Angel Street.*

1984–85: *The Sorrows of Frederick, Season's Greetings, Starry Night, Quartermaine's Terms, Extremities, Sweet Bird of Youth, Fool for Love, Much Ado About Nothing, Sizwe Bansi Is Dead, Open Admissions, And a Nightingale Sang . . . , A . . . My Name Is Alice, Kind Lady.*

1985–86: *Execution of Justice, Kiss Me Kate, Painting Churches, The Miss Firecracker Contest, Balm in Gilead, Pack of Lies, Traveling Lady, Spring's Awakening, Orphans, The Foreigner, What the Butler Saw, How the Other Half Loves.*

1986–87: *Another Part of the Forest, The Death of Bessie Smith* and *Counting the Ways, Trelawny of the "Wells," The Marriage of Bette and Boo, Glengarry Glen Ross, The Normal Heart, The Immigrant, The Perfect Party, A Lie of the Mind, The Common Pursuit.*

BIBLIOGRAPHY

Published Sources:

Barnes, Clive. "Theater: *Galileo*'s Challenge Is Met: Alley Troupe Presents Play in New Building." *New York Times*, December 1, 1968, p. 88.

Best Plays, 1961–62 through *1985–86*. New York: Dodd, Mead, & Co., 1962–87.

Holmes, Ann Hitchcock. *The Alley Theatre: Four Decades in Three Acts: A History of One of the Nation's Resident Theatres*. Houston: Alley Theatre, 1986.

Hulbert, Dan. "From Houston, a Touch of British Fun." *New York Times*, June 30, 1985, sec. 2, p. 4.

Kaminsky, Laura J., ed. *Nonprofit Repertory Theatre in North America, 1958–1975: A Bibliography and Indexes to the Playbill Collection of the Theatre Communications Group*. Westport, Conn.: Greenwood Press, 1977.

"Repertory: The Playhouse Is the Thing." *Time* 92 (December 6, 1968): 71.

Schmidt, Sandra. "Regional Theatre: Some Statistics." *Tulane Drama Review* 10 (Fall 1965): 52.

Taite, W. L. "Alley of Aspirations." *Texas Monthly* 12 (April 1984): 178, 180–81.

————, and Alice Gordon. "Striking the Set (Nina Vance, Founder and Executive Director of the Alley Theatre)." *Texas Monthly* 8 (May 1980): 194, 196.

Theatre Profiles. Vols. 1–7. New York: Theatre Communications Group, 1973–86.

Variety, October 15, 1986, p. 182.

Unpublished Sources:

Playbill Collection of the Theatre Communications Group (microfiche) includes programs from 1947–48, 1958–67, 1968–75.

Treser, Robert Morris. "Houston's Alley Theatre." Doctoral dissertation, Tulane University, 1967.

Archival Resources:

Houston, Texas. Alley Theatre. Financial records, programs of productions, minutes of meetings of the board of directors from 1959, minutes of the meetings of the executive committee from 1959, correspondence, history file.

New York, New York. New York Public Library. Billy Rose Theatre Collection. Clippings to 1968, programs 1948–60, photos, posters, press books.

Weldon B. Durham

[THE] AMERICAN ACTORS COMPANY (AAC), also known as the American Actors Theatre, was formed in New York City by Horton Foote (playwright), Mary Hunter (director), and Helen Thompson (business manager), students of Tamara Daykaronova's School of the Stage (1935–71). Their philosophy was determined in 1937; by 1938 the resident company occupied a studio at 256 West Sixty-ninth Street. Although they would eventually produce plays in their studios, their first production, *The Trojan Women* by Euripides, translated by Edith Hamilton, opened at the Master Institute Theatre, the Roerich Museum, New York City, January 24, 1938. Later the company performed at other locations: 108 West Sixteenth Street, the Montowese Playhouse in Branford, Connecticut, and the Provincetown Playhouse.

Disenchanted with the insecurities and inadequacies of a Broadway that was unable to absorb the talents of the young, trained, but inexperienced New York actor, the AAC aimed to provide a space for the young actor to perform, in true ensemble fashion, and to learn through their performances. The group was also devoted to the development of young American playwrights. The AAC performed short plays and new plays by American authors until 1944. From 1945 to 1946 an associate group of the AAC carried on the objectives of its mother company.

This company did not strive to develop a unified artistic vision, and it had no artistic director. Mary Hunter directed the majority of its productions, and leaders of the AAC concentrated on developing the talents of members; consequently the company provided a stimulating atmosphere in which a young theatre practitioner could experiment without the pressures of commercial theatre. Also, the AAC tried to build an ensemble in which practicality and artistic cooperation were central considerations. The group emphasized developing the actor as both an artist and a technician. Moreover, the play and the actor's role in it, not the actor's personality, received closest attention. The company added classes in acting, speech and diction, and movement and dance techniques to further develop its members.

Generally, its plays were experimental and produced, appropriately, in small spaces. Its first experimental theatre was a garage at West Sixty-ninth Street, a space that held approximately forty persons. Later the group used other spaces. Little is known about the AAC's finances, except that, in general, it solicited support through associate and founding memberships.

During the eight years the AAC produced plays, critics frequently noted its unusual play selection, especially its devotion to works depicting life in America's geographic regions, and its admirable acting and directing. Little attention was paid to technical production. Curtis Pepper of the *New York World-Telegram* called the company "a rare, stimulating group. They breathe American in appearance . . . The actors have scored again in frankly presenting a play of the American scene with force and charm" (American Actors Company clipping file, New York Public Library, Library and Museum of the Performing Arts). Of their production of *American Legend*, George Freedley noted: "There is a spontaneity and gaiety about the revue which is guaranteed to warm even a critic's heart" (AAC clipping file, New York Public Library).

After the company's early performance of Euripides' *The Trojan Women*, it selected the "American Scene" as its theme. Plays utilizing American folk dance and song, such as *American Legend* and *Virginia Overture*, were also a significant feature of its repertoire. In 1941 the company left New York City and produced a series of plays at the Montowese Playhouse. When the associate group reestablished the AAC, it continued the early philosophy of working with young actors, directors, and playwrights on material related to America. AAC helped to develop the talents of playwrights such as Horton Foote, Paul Greene, Thornton Wilder, E. P. Conkle, Irwin Shaw, Stephen Draper, Lynn Riggs, Arnold Sungaard, and Madeline Wallen.

The AAC consisted of approximately eighteen to twenty members. Production staff members, such as scenic artist Joseph Anthony, were often called on to act. When the company mounted a special production, such as its *American Legend*, it used numerous dancers and singers from outside the company. The AAC also engaged professional actors to play roles that could not be cast from within the company.

The AAC disbanded in 1944. Mixed reviews of its Broadway production of Horton Foote's *Only the Heart* (forty-four performances at the Bijou Theatre) may have contributed to its demise. An "associate group" from the AAC performed in 1945–46.

PERSONNEL

Management: Mary Hunter, director (1938–44); Horton Foote, playwright (1938–44); Helen Thompson, business manager.

Scenic Technicians: Joseph Anthony, scene designer (1938–44); Henry Elbaum, Robert Franklin, Ronald Sherman, Joseph Sullivan.

Stage Managers: John Hampshire, Ronald Sherman.

Stage Directors: Joseph Anthony, Mary Hunter.

Actors and Actresses (partial listing): Frances Anderson, *Joseph Anthony*, Baldwin Bergersen, Phyllis Carver, *Patricia Coates, Gertrude Corey, Virginia Donaldson, Mildred Dunnock, Horton Foote*, John Forsht, Elizabeth Goddard, Perla Gomez, *John Hampshire, William Hare, Mary Hunter*, Lucy Ladd, Virginia Palmer, *Betine Prescott, Jane Rose*, Fanya Selinskaya, *Ronald Sherman*, Inez Spears, *Lorraine Sturat, Joseph Sullivan*, Tony Taylor, Russell Thorson, Jeanne Tufts, Madeline Wallen, *Beulah Weil, Perry Wilson*, Sarah Winfree, *Roland Wood*.

REPERTORY

1938: *The Trojan Women*.

1939: *Sump'n Like Wings* by Lynn Riggs; four short plays by E. P. Conkle and Paul Greene.

1940: *Shroud My Body Down* by Paul Greene; nine short plays by E. P. Conkle, Thornton Wilder, and Horton Foote; five television performances for the National Broadcasting Company from a series of short plays on the American scene.

1941: *Texas Town* by Horton Foote; *American Legend* assembled and directed by Mary Hunter in collaboration with Agnes de Mille; Montowese Playhouse season—*Broadway 1941* by Philip Dunning and George Abbott, *Gaslight* by Patrick Hamilton, *Green Grow the Lilacs* by Lynn Riggs, *Far-Off Hills* by Lennox Robinson, *Mr. and Mrs. North* by Owen Davis, *The Male Animal* by James Thurber and Elliot Nugent, *The Swan* by Ferenc Molnar, *Brief Moment* by S. N. Behrman.

1942: *Out of My House* by Horton Foote; *Only the Heart* by Horton Foote (Provincetown Playhouse).

1943: *Playboy of Newark* by Ben Simkhovitch; three short plays by Irwin Shaw and Tennessee Williams—workshop.

1944: *Only the Heart* (Bijou Theatre) by Horton Foote; *Virginia Overture* by Arnold Sungaard, choreography by Valerie Bettis; *Donna Rosita* by Garcia Lorca—workshop.

1945 (associate group): Four short plays by Madeline Wallen, Horton Foote, Paul Green, and Thornton Wilder—workshop.

1946 (associate group): Three short plays by Stephen Draper, Gwen Pharis, and Thornton Wilder—workshop. (Program Note, American Actors Company clipping file. New York, New York. New York Public Library. The Library and Museum of the Performing Arts.)

BIBLIOGRAPHY

Archival Resource:
New York, New York. New York Public Library. The Library and Museum of the
    Performing Arts. American Actors Company clipping file.

Nancy Kindelan

AMERICAN ACTORS THEATRE. See AMERICAN ACTORS COMPANY.

AMERICAN CONSERVATORY THEATRE (ACT), San Francisco, California, originated with a manifesto written by Chicago-born actor-director William Ball. ACT was officially formed on May 27, 1965, when Ball, Jules Fisher,
Edward Hastings, Jr., Kristin Linklater, and Robert Whitehead signed incor-
poration papers for nonprofit foundation status in Delaware. The original board
of trustees was composed of theatre professionals from New York.

Ball had just directed a successful production of Molière's *Tartuffe* for the
Repertory Theatre of Lincoln Center*, but the firing of that company's artistic
directors, Elia Kazan and Robert Whitehead, impressed on Ball the fact that the
motives of business-oriented boards of directors often diverged from those of
artists. Ball recognized the vulnerability of the creative decisions of theatre
professionals to the influence of the financial motives. This experience, along
with his awareness of New York's grip on American theatre, induced Ball to
establish what he hoped would be a national theatre not based in New York;
specifically, he envisioned a true repertory theatre with an ensemble acting
company and a functional conservatory.

With the help of a grant of $115,000 from the Rockefeller Foundation, further
funding from the Andrew Mellon Foundation, and the assistance of the Pittsburgh
Playhouse and the Drama Department at Carnegie Institute of Technology (Ball's
alma mater, now Carnegie-Mellon University), Ball restaged his production of
Tartuffe in Pittsburgh, Pennsylvania, on July 15, 1965, the debut performance
of ACT. A production of Luigi Pirandello's *Six Characters in Search of an
Author* followed on July 28. For its first six-month season ACT produced fourteen
plays in simultaneous double repertory in the playhouse's two theatres—the
Craft, with 540 seats, and the Hamlet, with 340 seats. They met with good
critical reception but little public support. Furthermore, by the end of the first
season ACT was experiencing internal conflict, and as Ball had anticipated, both
the board of the Pittsburgh Playhouse and the academics from the Carnegie
Institute of Technology were trying to gain control of ACT's artistic direction.

The Rockefeller Foundation averted ACT's first threat of extinction with an-
other grant of $160,000, allowing it to move to New York to train for ten weeks.
Although the group was able to schedule a tour of its productions from Westport,
Connecticut, to Stanford University in Palo Alto, California, with stops in Ann
Arbor, Michigan, and Phoenix, Arizona, ACT was a company in search of a
home.

Serendipitously for ACT, in 1965 most of the core members of the Actor's Workshop*, founded in 1952 by Herbert Blau and Jules Irving in San Francisco, followed the founders to New York to become part of a new company at Lincoln Center, leaving the culturally vibrant city slightly embarrassed at having failed to maintain its first regional theatre company.

ACT contacted San Francisco's Chamber of Commerce, which sent a delegation to view the ACT performance at Stanford. Favorably impressed, banker Mortimer Fleishhacker, chair of the newly formed California Theatre Foundation, promised Ball he would raise the $200,000 necessary to support ACT in San Francisco for one year. Thirty-five thousand dollars came directly from three sponsors: department store magnate Cyril Magnin, influential hotel owner Melvin Swig, and Fleishhacker, whose enthusiastic support allowed the fledgling company to take root in its early years.

On January 21, 1967, ACT opened a twenty-two-week season of sixteen productions in two San Francisco theatres, the Geary (seating 1,049) and the Marine's Memorial (seating 640). The forty-seven members of the conservatory also staged twenty-eight performances in thirteen other California cities. However, because its future was still insecure, the company also entered negotiations with the Chicago Action Committee for Theatre for support for a part of the 1967–68 season. In September 1968, after considering the problems of physical logistics, they chose San Francisco as their permanent home. During its second (forty-week) season in the city, ACT offered an ambitious repertory of thirty-one plays. The repertory emphasized classics with a positive message as Ball tried to counteract the negativistic image of theatre fostered by the Actor's Workshop and to reach the widest possible audience. Subscriptions climbed to 17,000, but ACT's decision to accentuate the positive earned the company the unfortunate nickname of "American Confectionary Theatre." ACT produced only five premieres in its first five San Francisco seasons and has never abandoned the classics in favor of new plays.

Until 1968 ACT's ambitious program was possible largely because of funding from the Ford, Mellon, and Rockefeller foundations, the National Endowment for the Arts, and the California Theatre Foundation (CTF). After exhausting these sources, ACT again faced financial crisis and ended the 1968–69 season a half million dollars in debt and playing to only 30 percent of capacity in its two theatres. In the fall of 1969 ACT appeared at a theatre festival in New York, while the Gerome Ragni, James Rado, and Galt McDermott musical *Hair* occupied the Geary Theatre for a very profitable run. The proceeds from *Hair* helped ACT through its twenty-two-week season of eleven plays in 1970. Then, in 1970–71, ACT reduced its membership from 250 to 157 members, abandoned the Marines' Memorial Theatre to produce less complicated seasons (eight to ten plays) at the Geary, and reduced its dependence on the revival of past hits. These management initiatives, accompanied by successful ticket sales and fund-raising campaigns, stabilized the company for five years. After another period of financial stress in 1977, a further streamlined ACT again regained financial security as well as critical and popular success until the early 1980s, when it was again forced by economic pressures to reduce the scope and quality of its activities.

ACT's periods of financial hardship paralleled internal difficulties. The first major clash in San Francisco came in 1969 over Ball's insistence on artistic control of the company in opposition to pressure from his staff and his board of directors. Several key ACT administrators and directors resigned, and Ball maintained his personal control of ACT.

The next major crisis began in 1981 when Cyril Magnin resigned as director of the California Association for the American Conservatory Theatre (formerly the CTF), and Ball disbanded the organization. Ball was subsequently elected president of a reorganized CAACT, and he filled the board with his friends and associates from around the country, thereby further consolidating his control over ACT. He went so far as to decline a $1 million grant to refurbish the Geary that year because it had "strings attached." In 1983 James B. McKenzie, Executive Producer since 1969, left the company, and finally, Ball himself resigned in 1986. By 1985 Ball had begun to lose his absolute control when financial pressure necessitated the addition of community members to the board of directors.

Despite its financial and managerial difficulties, ACT has remained true to Ball's vision of an American theatre conservatory. Sparked by what he thought was inadequate training in universities, Ball sought to raise the standard of American acting by reacting against a strict reliance on the Method and by modeling his program on the concept of ensemble articulated by Michel St. Denis. In the founding year of 1965 ACT worked closely with students from the Carnegie Institute, and by 1967 a conservatory was established in San Francisco under the direction of Mark Zeller. It enrolled six students; forty more were soon added, and Robert Goldsby became director. In 1968, 200 students entered ACT's first Summer Training Congress, and in 1969 the company established the Conservatory Advanced Training Program under the direction of Allen Fletcher. In 1972 the Conservatory became a two-year program, and Fletcher ultimately abandoned the classically oriented St. Denis model and developed a more eclectic acting program. Grounded in a *commedia dell'arte* style, ACT training emphasized comedy and physical development in a highly technical course of study. However, new avenues of exploration opened under the guidance of new artistic director Edward Hastings, Jr.

PERSONNEL

General Director: William Ball (1965–85).

Executive Director: Edward Hastings, Jr. (1965–82).

Artistic Director: Edward Hastings, Jr. (1985–86).

Executive Producer: James B. McKenzie (1969–83).

Managing Directors: William Bushnell (1966–68), Charles Dillingham (1969–77), Omar K. Lerman (1965–66), Benjamin Moore (1983–85), John Sullivan (1985–86).

Conservatory Directors: Allen Fletcher (1970–84), Robert Goldsby (1968–70), Lawrence Hecht (1985–86), Mark Zeller (1967–68).

Directors: *William Ball* (1965–86), *Eugene Barcone* (1967–69, 1972–73, 1976–77, 1980–81, 1982–86), Robert Bonaventura (1972–73), Helen Burns (1982–83), Edward Payson Call (1965–67), Joy Carlin (1985–86), Gower Champion (1968–69), Francis Ford Coppola (1971–72), Louis Criss (1970), Peter Donat (1971–72), James Dunn (1974–75), *James Edmonson* (1981–84), Sabin Epstein (1976–77, 1985–86), Dolores Ferraro (1976–77), *Allen Fletcher* (1965–84), John C. Fletcher (1980–81), Rick Foster (1979–80), William Francisco (1965–66), Gerald Freedman (1965–66), Janice Garcia (1980–81), Joseph J. Garry, Jr. (1979–80), Edward Gilbert (1970), Robert Goldsby (1966–67, 1968–69), James Haire (1976–77, 1980–81), David Hammond (1976–77, 1979–81), Jay Harnick (1965–66), *Edward Hastings* (1968–69, 1970–77, 1978–86), Mark D. Healy (1965–66, 1970), Lawrence Hecht (1983–86), Elizabeth Huddle (1980–82), Janice Hutchins (1983–86), *Nagle Jackson* (1967–69, 1972–73, 1976–77, 1978–82, 1984–86), Jon Jory (1975–76), John Kauffman (1980–81), Jerome Kilty (1966–68), Michael Langham (1982–83), Omar K. Lerman (1965–66), Dakin Matthews (1982–83), *Tom Moore* (1976–83), Gilbert Moses (1970), Richard Nesbitt (1967–69), *Jack O'Brien* (1970, 1972–74, 1976–77, 1980–81), Arthur Pepine (1965–66), Stephen Porter (1977–78), Ellis Rabb (1970, 1970–72), Byron Ringland (1966–68), Larry Russell (1980–81), Andrei Serban (1974–75), Edwin Sherin (1968–69), Robert Six (1967–68), Harold Stone (1965–66), Jerry Turner (1980–81), *Laird Williamson* (1975–77, 1978–83, 1984–86), Michael Winters (1981–82), William Young (1965–66).

Designers: Lani Abbott (1982–83), *Joseph Appelt* (1981–85), Maurice Beesley (1971–72), *Robert Blackman* (1971–82, 1983–85), Paul Blake (1972–73, 1976–77), William Bloodgood (1980–81), Randy Bobo (1981–82), Gregory Bolton (1974–76), Robert Bonaventura (1967–68), Debra Booth (1984–85), Marshall Booth (1965–66), Mark Bosch (1981–82), James Edmund Brady (1972–73), Lewis Brown (1967–68), *Martha Burke* (1978–82, 1983–84), *Michael Casey* (1981–85), Regina Cate (1970, 1985–86), Michael Clivner (1968–69), Steven Cohen (1965–66), Elizabeth Covey (1971–72), Robert A. Dahlstrom (1976–77), *F. Mitchell Dana* (1972–76, 1977–81), Robert Darling (1970–71), Jeannie Davidson (1985–86), Jackson DeGovia (1970, 1970–71), *Richard Devin* (1977–81, 1985–86), Robert Charles Dillingham (1976–77), Arthur Dinsmore (1972–73), Derek Duarte (1985–86), Stan Dufford (1965–66), Milton Duke (1970), Rick Echols (1982–83), *Cathleen Edwards* (1976–80, 1983–84), Mariana Elliott (1966–67), *Dirk Epperson* (1974–75, 1977–83), John Sergio Fisher (1966–67), Jules Fisher (1965–67, 1970), *Robert Fletcher* (1970, 1970–75, 1977–79, 1980–81), Dorothy Fowler (1967–68), *Ralph Funicello* (1972–75, 1976–83, 1984–85), Richard Goodwin (1984–85), Jane Greenwood (1965–66), Mark Harrison (1973–74), Richard Hay (1980–82), J. Allen Highfill (1974–75), Jesse Hollis (1985–86), Kent Homchick (1980–81), Dennis Howes (1979–80), John Jensen (1974–75, 1976–77), Les Kane (1972–73), Fritha Knudsen (1985–86), Fred Kopp (1972–74), Katharine E. Kraft (1984–86), Ralph Lee (1965–66), Alfred Lehman (1970), Dawn Line (1984–85), *John McLain* (1966–70), William Matthews (1965–66), Henry May (1978–79), Michael Miller (1978–79), Ralph Miller (1979–80), Christopher D. Moore (1983–85), *Robert Morgan* (1972–75, 1977–82, 1984–85), Mark Negrin (1965–66), William Nelson (1965–66), *Michael Olich* (1979–82), David Percival (1984–85), Robert Peterson (1982–83, 1984–85), Bartholomeo Rago (1974–76), M. Celestine G. Ranney (1979–80), Charles Richmond (1970–71), Carrie Robbins (1979–81), Ann Roth (1965–67; 1970–72; 1973–74), Carol Rubinstein (1965–66), Ward Russell (1970; 1970–71), James Sale (1980–82), *Duane Schuler* (1979–83, 1984–85), Karen Schultz (1979–80), Jean Seemiller (1966–67), *Richard Segar* (1976–83, 1984–85), D.

Hudson Sheffield (1965–66), Rick Shrout (1984–85), Vicki Smith (1981–82), Julie Staheli (1971–72), Paul Staheli (1968–69, 1970, 1971–72), Thomas P. Struthers (1965–66), Greg Sullivan (1982–83, 1984–85), Alfred Tetzner (1981–82), James Tilton (1970–72), David Toser (1965–66), Warren Travis (1979–80, 1985–86), Patricia Von Brandenstein (1968–69), *Walter Watson* (1967–75, 1977–79, 1981–82), Stuart Wurtzel (1965–69), Parker Young (1968–69).

Actors and Actresses: Frank Abe (1975–76), Linda Aldrich (1983–86), Hugh Alexander (1965–66), Phoebe Alexander (1972–73), Wayne Alexander (1975–78), Hope Alexander-Willis (1974–76), Al Alu (1965–67), Mark Amarotico (1984–85), Brian Ames (1965–66), Lynne Arden (1965–68), Robert Ari (1971–72), Peter Arnoff (1976–77), Carol Aronowitz (1965–66), James Arrington (1973–74), Janie Atkins (1972–74), *Rene Auberjonois* (1965–68, 1974–75), Len Auclair (1973–74), Andy Backer (1972–75), Karen Bailey (1973–74), Jim Baker (1970, 1970–71, 1985–86), Lance Baker (1985–86), *Candace Barrett* (1974–79), Barbara Barrie (1965–66), Paul Bates (1980–81), Barbara Baxley (1965–66), William Bechtel (1970), Phillip Beck (1973–74), Peter Belden (1979–80), Cliff Bemis (1979–80), Annette Bening (1982–85), Martin Berman (1968–69, 1970–72), *Ramon Bieri* (1965–69, 1972–73), *Joseph Bird* (1970–79, 1980–86), *Raye Birk* (1973–83), Scot Bishop (1984–86), Carolyn Blakey (1970–71), Nancy Blossom (1970–71), Roberts Blossom (1965–66), Allen Blumenfeld (1976–77), Earl Boen (1973–77), Jane Bolton (1975–76), Robert Bonaventura (1965–66), Terri Boodman (1965–66), Libby Boone (1976–80), Barbara Bosson (1965–66), Heather Bostian-Vash (1985–86), Ronald Boussom (1973–76), Peter Bradbury (1985–86), Bonita Bradley (1973–75), *Mark Bramhall* (1965–69, 1970–71), Peter Bretz (1983–84), Catherine Brickley (1976–77), Kate Brickley (1984–86), Betty Bridges (1973–74), Bess Brown (1980–81), Jay Brown (1965–66), Julie Brown (1976–77), Light Brown (1970–71), R. Aaron Brown (1972–73), William Brown (1980–81), Sandy Bull (1985–86), Cynthia Burch (1975–76), Traber Burns (1975–76), Dennis Cameron (1965–66), Karie Cannon (1971–72), Christopher Cara (1972–73), *Joy Carlin* (1970, 1970–81, 1985–86), Nancy Carlin (1983–84), John Carpenter (1965–66), Larry Carpenter (1971–72), *Mimi Carr* (1980–84), Gene Carroll (1973–74), Barbara Caruso (1965–66), Michelle Casey (1984–86), Marilyn Kay Caskey (1976–77), Kraig Cassity (1975–76), John Castellanos (1985–86), Michael Cavanaugh (1970, 1970–71), George Ceres (1976–77), Jeff Chandler (1970, 1970–71), Robert Chapline (1970, 1972–75), Dion Chesse (1966–68), Richard Christopher (1976–77), Ludi Claire (1965–66), Charles Coffey (1975–77), Barbara Colby (1966–68, 1972–73), Elizabeth Cole (1973–74), Megan Cole (1974–76), Suzanne Collins (1970, 1970–71), Katherine Conklin (1972–73), Linda Connor (1975–76), Lee Cook (1971–72), Suzanne Corot (1965–66), Jim Corti (1972–73), Nicholas Cortland (1975–76), Richard Council (1971–72), Penelope Court (1977–79, 1980–81), Joe Coyle (1965–66), Kathryn Crosby (1972–74, 1978–79), David Croyden (1965–66), Joan Croyden (1965–66, 1982–83), Martin Curland (1980–81), Joan Darling (1965–66), *Peter Davies* (1976–80), *Daniel Davis* (1974–80), *Heidi Helen Davis* (1976–80), Patra Dawe (1980–81), Jennifer Dawson (1972–73), George Deloy (1982–83, 1984–85), Tom DeMent (1965–66), John DeMita (1983–84), Richard Denison (1978–80), Robert Dicken (1972–73), Mariano DiMarco (1980–81), *Barbara Dirickson* (1972–85), *Peter Donat* (1967–86), Katy Donovan (1970), Raymond E. Dooley (1976–77), Franchelle Stewart Dorn (1975–78), William Douglas (1970), Nike Doukas (1984–86), *Jay Doyle* (1965–72), Brigid Duffy (1965–66), David Dukes (1966–69), Gary Dumas (1965–66), Richard A. Dysart (1965–67), George Ede (1967–69), James Edmondson (1982–84), Elizabeth Eis (1965–66), Dana Elcar (1972–

74, 1980–81), Bobby F. Ellerbee (1972–75), Geoffrey Elliott (1984–86), Julia Elliott (1985–86), Karl Ellis (1973–74), Jessica Epstein (1973–74), *Sabin Epstein* (1973–79, 1985–86), John Erlendson (1985–86), Nancy Erskine (1976–77), Drew Eshelman (1983–86), Donald Ewer (1972–73), Patricia Falkenhain (1967–69), Robert Feero (1967–68), Larry Ferguson (1967–68), Gina Ferrall (1980–83), William Ferriter (1975–77), Jill Fine (1984–86), Kate Fitzmaurice (1977–79), Jerry Fitzpatrick (1972–73), Ed Flanders (1972–73), Allen Fletcher (1983–84), John C. Fletcher (1980–82), Julia Fletcher (1979–82), Robert Fletcher (1970, 1970–71), Melvin Buster Flood (1977–78), Ann Foorman (1976–77), Lois Foraker (1970), Herbert Foster (1970, 1971–72), Clement Fowler (1965–66), Jerry Franken (1968–69), Gina Franz (1975–76), David O. Frazier (1979–80), *Harry Frazier* (1965–70), Amy Freed (1984–85), Scott Freeman (1984–85), Steve Fryer (1973–74), Cynthia Fujikawa (1985–86), Mike Gainey (1976–77), Robin Gammell (1965–66), Janice Garcia (1975–77, 1978–79, 1980–81), Janice Garcia-Hutchins (1981–82), Ellen Geer (1966–68), Sandra Gentile (1965–66), Lynn R. George (1965–66), Bruce Gerhard (1975–76), Robert Gerringer (1967–69), David Gilliam (1970, 1970–71, 1972–73), Jerry Glover (1970–71), Richard Glyer (1966–67), Dean Goodman (1985–86), Patrick Gorman (1970–72), Lou Ann Graham (1973–76), *Ross Graham* (1972–76), Sarina C. Grant (1972–73), Kenneth Gray (1968–69), Wendell Grayson (1984–86), Tim Greer (1985–86), David Grimm (1966–68), Robert Ground (1970), Bennet Guillory (1975–76, 1977–79), Nathan Haas (1975–76), David Haier (1985–86), Jill Hall (1979–80), Charles Hallahan (1972–77), *Rick Hamilton* (1973–76, 1985–86), Harry Hamlin (1975–77), John Hancock (1970, 1970–71, 1972–73, 1976–77), Lydia Hannibal (1981–82), Mark Harelik (1980–81, 1983–84), Tom Harmon (1985–86), Kathleen Harper (1970, 1970–71), Leslie Harrell (1973–74), Thomas Harrison (1980–82), Kate Hawley (1967–68), *Lawrence Hecht* (1973–83, 1984–86), Emily Heebner (1980–81), Jean Heimer (1965–66), Barta Heiner (1975–77), Barbara Herring (1972–73), John Herring (1966–67), John Noah Hertzler (1981–84), Ian Hewitt (1985–86), Leslie Hicks (1978–79), Jill Hill (1980–82), Michael Hill (1976–77), Scott Hitchcock (1984–85), Ed Hobson (1980–81), Henry Hoffman (1972–74), Nancy Houfek (1982–85), Stephen Hough (1984–85), Elizabeth Huddle (1972–73, 1985–86), David Hudson (1977–78), Michael Hume (1972–73, 1974–75), David Hurst (1965–66), Janice Hutchins (1982–86), John Hutton (1980–82), Scott Hylands (1965–68), Charles Hyman (1973–76), Karen Ingenthron (1967–68), Amy Ingersoll (1976–77), Robert Insabella (1972–73), Paul Itken (1965–66), Gregory Itzin (1975–77), Lisa Ivary (1984–85), *Johanna Jackson* (1980–82, 1983–86), Todd Jackson (1984–85), Peter Jacobs (1984–86), Katherine James (1976–77), *Carol Mayo Jenkins* (1966–70), Byron Jennings (1980–81, 1983–84), Stephen Johnson (1980–81), Jane Jones (1980–82, 1984–85), Benjamin Louis Jurand (1976–77), Nicholas Kaledin (1980–82, 1983–84), Maureen Kelley (1973–74), Dennis Kennedy (1970), Enid Kent (1966–68), Daniel Kern (1972–80), Philip Kerr (1968–70), Michael Keys-Hall (1975–77), Margaret Kienck (1976–77), Randall Duk Kim (1974–75), Lauren R. Klein (1980–81), Judith Knaiz (1972–74), Dudley Knight (1970–72), *Ruth Kobart* (1965–68, 1973–75, 1977–78), Noel Koran (1976–77), Kay Kostopoulos (1984–85), Barry Kraft (1967–68), Robert Krimmer (1980–81), Chris Kuhlman (1973–74), Claudette Kukitsis (1965–66), Richard Kuss (1981–82), Poppy Lagos (1965–66), Ray Laine (1967–68), Kimberley LaMarque (1985–86), Carl Lambrecht (1965–66), Gerald Lancaster (1977–79), Robert Lanchester (1968–69), Charles Lanyer (1973–75), Dana Larson (1966–69), Richard Larson (1965–66), *Anne Lawder* (1970–84), Ron Lazar (1973–74), *Michael Learned* (1967–72), Brianna Lewis (1984–85), Gilbert Lewis (1970), Lorna Lewis (1965–66), Steve Liska (1965–66), Theresa Liteo (1979–80), Gary Logan

(1980–81), Mary Loquvam (1980–81), John Loschmann (1985–86), Fanny Lubritsky (1966–67, 1970, 1970–71), Laurence Luckenbill (1965–66), Ken Lutz (1965–66), Lee McCain (1970–72), Jeff McCarthy (1979–80), Carolyn McCormick (1983–85), John McDill (1966–67), Nancy McDoniel (1971–72), Terry Mace (1967–68), Barry Mac-Gregor (1968–69), Matt McKenzie (1980–81), *William McKereghan* (1977–84, 1985–86), Anne McNaughton (1982–84), Jennifer MacNish (1968–69), Dom Magwili (1973–74), David Maier (1984–85), Claire Malis (1973–74), Winifred Mann (1970–72), David Margulies (1965–66), Douglas Martin (1983–85), Larry Martin (1971–72), Michael X. Martin (1978–79), Marsha Mason (1972–73), Richard Mason (1984–85), *Dakin Matthews* (1980–86), *Deborah May* (1972–78, 1982–83, 1984–85), Anita Maynard (1976–77), Glenn Mazen (1967–68), *DeAnn Mears* (1965–68, 1978–79, 1980–84), Judith Mihalye (1965–68), Carol Miller (1976–77), James Milton (1968–69, 1970), *Delores Y. Mitchell* (1975–81, 1982–83), Don Mitchell (1965–66), Ed Mock (1970), Robert Mooney (1972–75), Judith Moreland (1984–85), Clarence Morley (1965–66), *Mark Murphey* (1977–83, 1984–86), Thomas M. Nahrwold (1978–80), Sharon Newman (1981–83), Josephine Nichols (1966–68), Richard Niles (1965–66), Robin Nordli (1985–86), Terrence O'Brien (1980–81), Thomas Patrick O'Brien (1982–84), Michael O'Guinne (1978–79), *Michael O'Sullivan* (1965–69), Michael Oglesby (1978–79), *Thomas R. Oglesby* (1976–82), *Fredi Olster* (1973–76, 1985–86), *Frank Ottiwell* (1970, 1970–75, 1977–79, 180–86), Elizabeth Padilla (1984–86), Victor Pappas (1972–73), *William Paterson* (1967–86), Angela Paton (1967–70), Greg Patterson (1980–82), Christopher Payne (1968–69), Carole Payot (1972–73), William Peck (1975–76), *Susan E. Pellegrino* (1975–80), Victor Pelles (1965–66), Austin Pendleton (1965–67), Jane Percival (1968–69), Dennis Percy (1966–67), Kimo Perry (1967–68), Robert Pescovitz (1980–81), Stefan Petrov (1965–66), H. C. Pettey (1965–66), Patricia Ann Pickens (1973–74), Marty Pistone (1984–85), John Pitts (1965–66), Marcia Pizzo (1984–86), Richard Poe (1970, 1972–73), Charlene Polite 1965–68), Herman Poppe (1967–69), Duane Porter (1965–66), Jim Poyner (1984–85), Stephen Pratt (1984–85), *E. Kerrigan Prescott* (1971–75), Duncan Quinn (1965–66), Ellis Rabb (1965–66, 1970), Wendi Radford (1980–82), James Ragan (1966–68), Beth Raines (1973–74), Eileen Ramsey (1968–69), Jean Rasey (1973–74), Marguerite Ray (1967–68), Mary Ellen Ray (1966–68), Stacy Ray (1980–82), Kate Redway (1980–81), Michael T. Rega (1976–77), *Ray Reinhardt* (1965–70, 1971–79, 1980–85), Shanti Reinhardt (1985–86), Daniel Renner (1980–81), Juanita Rice (1974–75), Phyllis Rice (1968–69), Randall Richard (1980–83), Richard Riehle (1984–85), Eve Roberts (1974–75), Jeremy Roberts (1982–83), Stephen Rockwell (1985–86), Jill Romero (1984–85), Carol Rossen (1965–66), Mary Ellen Roy (1965–66), Joe Rudnick (1968–69), John Rue (1972–73), Gretchen Rumbaugh (1980–81), *Ken Ruta* (1965–73, 1982–83), Stephen St. Paul (1976–77), Diane Salinger (1977–78), Rebecca Sand (1972–73), Jay O. Sanders (1977–78), Tom Savini (1965–66), Frank Savino (1980–83), Mark Schell (1967–68), Stephen Schnetzer (1973–76), John Schuck (1967–68, 1970), Peter Schuck (1975–76), Craig Scott (1973–74), Donovan Scott (1972–73), Charles Seibert (1965–66), Evelyn Seubert (1973–74), Priscilla Shanks (1976–77), Freda Foh Shen (1976–77), *Paul Shenar* (1965–69, 1970, 1971–74), Howard Sherman (1971–73), Warner Shook (1972–73), Sandra Shotwell (1973–76), Stephanie Shroyer (1984–85), Cynthia Sikes (1978–79), Douglas Sills (1984–85), Garland J. Simpson (1980–82), Mark Simpson (1984–85), R. E. Simpson (1970, 1971–72), Marc Singer (1971–74), Shelley Slater (1965–66), Shirley Slater (1972–73), Anna Deavere Smith (1974–76), Caroline Smith (1975–76), Izetta Smith (1966–69), Randall Smith (1974–75, 1977–79), Robertson Smith (1977–79), Rosemarie Smith (1984–85), Sharon Smith

(1965–66), Sally Smythe (1980–83), Josef Sommer (1970–71), Ronald Stanley Sopyla (1976–77), Michael Spera (1965–66), Katherine Stanford (1985–86), Katharine Stapleton (1975–76), James Stephens (1973–74), Lannyl Stephens (1985–86), Melissa Stern (1980–81), Mary Lou Stewart (1975–76), Raymond Stough (1965–66), Robin Strasser (1965–66), John Stuart-Morris (1985–86), Harold Surratt (1982–84), *Deborah Sussel* (1967–72, 1980–83, 1985–86), Francine Tacker (1975–77, 1982–83, 1984–85), John Talt (1966–67), Tom V.V. Tammi (1970), Bonnie Tarwater (1978–79), Anthony "Scooter" Teague (1965–66, 1974–77), Carol Teitel (1965–67, 1968–69, 1982–83), Judy Teran (1973–74), Angie Thieriot (1973–74), Scott Thomas (1965–66, 1970–72), Tynia Thomassie (1983–84), Sada Thompson (1965–67, 1973–74), Sandy Timpson (1972–73), Terrence Todd (1966–67), Patrick Tovatt (1965–68), Alice Travis (1976–77), Todd Tressler (1973–74), Carl Turner (1980–81), Gil Turner (1967–68), James Turner (1965–66), Cicely Tyson (1965–66), Bernard Vash (1984–86), Joan Vigman (1973–74), Edward Walker (1965–66), Jewel Walker (1965–66), Marjorie Walker (1965–66), Patti Walker (1973–74), *Sydney Walker* (1974–85), Lee Wallace (1965–66), Francy Walsh (1972–73), *Marrian Walters* (1974–86), Don Watson (1966–68), James Watson (1968–69), Marshall Watson (1980–81), Henry Watt (1985–86), Kenn Watt (1984–86), *Ann Weldon* (1967–72), Mark Wheeler (1970, 1970–72), Al White (1974–77), Collis White (1973–74), *J. Steven White* (1972–78, 1982–85), Isiah Whitlock, Jr. (1978–79, 1980–82), Mary Wickes (1972–73), Nancy Wickwire (1973–74), *Bruce Williams* (1976–79, 1980–85), Kappy Williams (1965–66), Michael Williams (1979–80), Teresa Williams (1984–85), Laird Williamson (1974–76), Stefan Windroth (1980–81), James R. Winker (1973–78), *Kitty Winn* (1965–70), *Rick Winter* (1971–75), *Michael Winters* (1977–81), Alicia Wollerton (1984–85), Christopher Wong (1976–77), *G. Wood* (1968–73), Kathleen Worley (1972–73), Henry Woronicz (1984–86), Robert Wortham-Krimmer (1981–82), Laura Ann Worthen (1982–83), Shela Xoregos (1979–80), Stephen Yates (1972–73), *D. Paul Yeuell* (1980–84), Janis Young (1965–66), Taylor Young (1984–85), William Young (1965–66), Daniel Zippi (1975–76, 1985–86).

REPERTORY

1965–66: *Tartuffe, Six Characters in Search of an Author, Tiny Alice, The Rose Tattoo, King Lear, Death of a Salesman, The Apollo of Bellac, Antigone, Noah, The Servant of Two Masters, The Devil's Disciple, In White America, Under Milk Wood, Beyond the Fringe.*

1967 (Six-month San Francisco season): *Beyond the Fringe, Endgame, Charley's Aunt, Man and Superman, Arsenic and Old Lace, Our Town, Dear Liar, The Torch-Bearers, Long Day's Journey into Night, The Sea Gull, The Zoo Story, Krapp's Last Tape, Tartuffe, Tiny Alice, Six Characters in Search of an Author, Death of a Salesman, Under Milk Wood.*

1967–68: *Two for the Seesaw, The Crucible, Thieves' Carnival, Twelfth Night, An Evening's Frost, The Misanthrope, A Delicate Balance, A Streetcar Named Desire, Hamlet, Don't Shoot, Mable, It's Your Husband, Deedle, Deedle Dumpling, My Son God, Long Live Life, In White America, Caught in the Act, The Zoo Story, The American Dream, Dear Liar, Under Milk Wood, Tartuffe, Tiny Alice, Our Town, Long Day's Journey into Night, Charley's Aunt, Endgame.*

1968–69: *A Flea in Her Ear, The Devil's Disciple, Little Murders, Staircase, The Three Sisters, The Promise, Rosencrantz and Guildenstern Are Dead, The Architect and the Emperor of Assyria, Room Service, Glory! Hallelujah!, The Hostage, Oh Dad, Poor*

Dad, Mama's Hung You in the Closet and I'm Feelin' So Sad, A Delicate Balance, In White America.

1970 (Short season): *The Importance of Being Earnest, Oedipus Rex, Saint Joan, The Blood Knot, Little Malcolm and His Struggle Against the Eunuchs, Hadrian VII, The Rose Tattoo, The Tempest, The Tavern, Rosencrantz and Guildenstern Are Dead, Six Characters in Search of an Author.*

1970–71 (No double repertory): *The Merchant of Venice, The Relapse, The Latent Heterosexual, The Time of Your Life, An Enemy of the People, The Selling of the President, The Tempest, Hadrian VII.*

1971–72: *Caesar and Cleopatra, Antony and Cleopatra, Dandy Dick, Paradise Lost, Private Lives, The Contractor, Sleuth, Rosencrantz and Guildenstern Are Dead, The Tavern.*

1972–73: *Cyrano de Bergerac, The House of Blue Leaves, The Mystery Cycle, A Doll's House, You Can't Take It with You, That Championship Season, The Merchant of Venice, The Crucible.*

1973–74: *The Taming of the Shrew, The Hot l Baltimore, The Miser, The House of Bernarda Alba, Tonight at 8:30, The Cherry Orchard, Broadway, Cyrano de Bergerac, You Can't Take It with You.*

1974–75: *King Richard III, Pillars of the Community, Horatio, Jumpers, Street Scene, The Ruling Class, The Threepenny Opera, Cyrano de Bergerac, The Taming of the Shrew.*

1975–76: *Tiny Alice, The Matchmaker, Desire Under the Elms, General Gorgeous, The Merry Wives of Windsor, Equus, Peer Gynt, The Taming of the Shrew, This Is (An Entertainment).*

1976–77: *Othello, Man and Superman, Equus, A Christmas Carol, Knock Knock, The Bourgeois Gentleman, Valentin and Valentina, Travesties, Peer Gynt.*

1977–78: *Julius Caesar, The Master Builder, The Circle, A Christmas Carol, All the Way Home, Hotel Paradiso, Absurd Person Singular, The National Health, Travesties.*

1978–79: *The Winter's Tale, A Month in the Country, Ah, Wilderness!, The Circle, A Christmas Carol, Heartbreak House, The 5th of July, The Visit, Hay Fever, Hotel Paradiso.*

1979–80: *Romeo and Juliet, Buried Child, Hay Fever, The Little Foxes, A Christmas Carol, The Crucifer of Blood, The Girl of the Golden West, A History of the American Film, Pantagleize, Ah, Wilderness!.*

1980–81: *Much Ado About Nothing, Ghosts, Hay Fever, The Trojan War Will Not Take Place, A Christmas Carol, Night and Day, Another Part of the Forest, The Rivals, The Three Sisters, The Little Foxes.*

1981–82: *Richard II, I Remember Mama, The Three Sisters, The Admirable Crichton, A Christmas Carol, Happy Landings, Black Comedy, The Browning Version, Mourning Becomes Electra, Cat Among the Pigeons, Another Part of the Forest.*

1982–83: *The Gin Game, Dear Liar, The Chalk Garden, A Christmas Carol, Uncle Vanya, Loot, Mornings at Seven, The Holdup.*

1983–84: *Arms and the Man, Dial "M" for Murder, A Christmas Carol, John Gabriel Borkman, A Midsummer Night's Dream, Angels Fall, The Sleeping Prince, The Dolly.*

1984–85: *Old Times, The School for Wives, A Christmas Carol, Translations, Macbeth, Our Town, Painting Churches, Mass Appeal.*

1985–86: *The Majestic Kid, Opera Comique, A Christmas Carol, 'night, Mother, You Never Can Tell, Private Lives, The Passion Cycle, The Lady's Not for Burning.*

BIBLIOGRAPHY

Published Sources:

Ball, William. *A Sense of Direction: Some Observations on the Art of Directing*. New York: Drama Books, 1984.

Best Plays, 1979–80. New York: Dodd, Mead, & Co., 1981.

"Bill Ball: The ACT Years," *San Francisco Examiner and Chronicle*, October 11, 1981, pp. 34–43.

Kaminsky, Laura J., ed. *Nonprofit Repertory Theatre in North America, 1958–1975: A Bibliography and Indexes to the Playbill Collection of the Theatre Communications Group*. Westport, Conn.: Greenwood Press, 1977.

Kutt, Inge. "The American Conservatory Theatre, San Francisco," *Dictionary of Literary Biography*, Vol. 7. Detroit: Gale Research Press, 1984, pp. 411–17.

Theatre World 1967–68 through *1985–86*. Vols. 24 through 41. New York: Crown Publishers, 1969–87.

Wilk, John R. *The Creation of an Ensemble: The First Years of the American Conservatory Theatre*. Carbondale: Southern Illinois University Press, 1986.

Winn, Steven. "The Enigmatic Man Behind ACT," *San Francisco Sunday Examiner and Chronicle*, October 4, 1981, pp. 16–21.

Unpublished Source:

Playbill. Collection of the Theatre Communications Group (microfiche) includes programs from 1965 through 1975.

Archival Resource:

In *The Creation of an Ensemble* John R. Wilk mentions the existence of the ACT Archive at the Geary Theatre, San Francisco.

Rodney Simard
Personnel list compiled by Weldon B. Durham

[THE] AMERICAN NEGRO THEATRE (ANT) was established June 11, 1940, by Abram Hill and Frederick O'Neal in the Harlem district of New York City. Hill, the company's director until 1948, and other original members (Howard Augusta, Ruby Wallace Dee, Stanley Greene, Betty Haynes, James Jackson, George Lewis, Claire Leyba, Kenneth Mannigault, Helen Martin, and Virgil Richardson) stressed the need to develop an ensemble as closely knit as a family. ANT incorporated as a cooperative, with members sharing expenses and profits. Part-time salaries were paid to some officers under the auspices of a grant from the Rockefeller Foundation, but most members contributed their services. In addition to producing plays in its first home, a converted lecture room at the 135th Street Library, and later at the Henry Lincoln Johnson Lodge of the Elks at 15 West 126th Street, ANT organized workshops, a school of the drama, and a radio show production unit. In its nine-year history, ANT produced nineteen legitimate dramas, of which twelve were world premieres.

Abram Hill, a native of Atlanta, Georgia, was raised in New York City and educated at the City College of New York and at Lincoln University (Pennsylvania). He studied playwriting at the New School for Social Research and perfected his talent while reading and writing plays for the Federal Theatre Project.

The Project collapsed before his Living Newspaper on black life in America, *Liberty Deferred*, could reach the stage. Hill's *On Striver's Row*, a comedy of black life in a wealthy section of Harlem, was produced by the Rose McClendon Players of New York City in 1939. *On Striver's Row* opened September 1, 1940, ran fifty performances in ANT's tiny Library Theatre, and called the group to the attention of the black community of Harlem and the New York City press. Hill's *Walk Hard* (1944), based on Len Zinberg's novel of the same title about the trials of a black boxer, fared less well with audiences and critics but was moved to Broadway for a few weeks. Hill directed five ANT productions and served as company director and chairman of the executive committee.

Frederick O'Neal met Hill while performing in the Rose McClendon Players' production of *On Striver's Row*. O'Neal trained at the New Theatre School in New York City, organized a short-lived community theatre in his home town of St. Louis, and appeared briefly on Broadway in a Civic Repertory Theatre production in 1936. O'Neal played major roles in several ANT productions and served as company manager throughout the life of the group.

ANT's educational programs began in 1941 when Alvin Childress developed a summer workshop for the community and for other ANT members. In 1943 the group incorporated a school of drama under the headship of Osceola Archer. Acting, movement, voice, and stagecraft techniques were taught to nearly 200 students, among whom were Sidney Poitier and Harry Belafonte.

ANT set out to counteract the stereotype of the stage Negro and to create a new, more honest stage image. Its repertory reflected this purpose. ANT produced plays by black writers Abram Hill, Theodore Browne, and Owen Dodson, as well as by white writer Philip Yordan. Browne's *Natural Man*, featuring the legendary John Henry, was first seen in Seattle, Washington, where Browne served as assistant director of the Negro unit of the Federal Theatre Project. Owen Dodson, who later chaired the Howard University Department of Drama, directed his *Garden of Time* for ANT in 1945. In it players blended poetry, music, and dance in a retelling of the Medea legend. Philip Yordan's *Anna Lucasta* was ANT's greatest financial success. Adapted by Abram Hill from a Polish to a black setting, *Anna Lucasta*, under the direction of Harry Wagstaff Gribble, opened June 16, 1944, at the Library Theatre, where it ran for five weeks before being moved to Broadway by producer John Wildburg. There it settled in for a two-year stay to become the longest-running all-black drama in Broadway history. After 1945 ANT turned to the production of well-known plays such as *Rain*, by Clemence Randolph and John Corbin, and J. M. Synge's *Riders to the Sea*, largely abandoning its efforts to produce realistic images of black life.

Several ANT performers went on to productive careers in commercial theatre. Ruby Wallace Dee came to ANT while a freshman at New York's Hunter College. She appeared in seven ANT productions and on Broadway in *Anna Lucasta*. Alice Childress acted in four ANT productions, taught acting workshops, and served on the group's playreading committee. She devoted her later professional life to playwriting. Alvin Childress, Maxwell Glanville, Hilda Simms (the original Anna Lucasta), Claire Leyba, and Earle Hyman capped their ANT experience with significant careers as actors on stage and in film and television and as teachers of acting. Roger Furman, ANT's only black designer, studied design at the New School for Social Research, designed sets for Walter Carroll's *Tin Top Valley* (1946) and *Rain* (1947), as well as costumes for Kenneth White's *Freight* and *Riders to the Sea* in ANT's final season.

Ironically, ANT's greatest commercial success, *Anna Lucasta*, was also the most significant cause of the organization's decline. The production drew the group out of Harlem to Broadway, and many of the members never returned to the company.

PERSONNEL

Manager-Producers: Austin Briggs-Hall, Abram Hill (1940–1948), Hattie King Reavis.

Company Manager: Frederick O'Neal.

Business Manager: J. Deveaux Davis.

Art Director: Oliver Harrington.

Secretary: Vivian Hall.

Studio Director: Osceola Archer.

Playwright: Abram Hill.

Directors: Harry Wagstaff Gribble, Abram Hill, John O'Shaughnessy, Benjamin Zemach.

Technicians/Designers: Roger Furman, George Lewis, Charles Sebree, Perry Watkins.

Actors and Actresses: Lillian Adams, Sally Alexander, Edward Alford, Roy Allen, Jacqueline Andre, Ismay Andrews, Osceola Archer, Howard Augusta, Audrey Beatrize, Harry G. Belafonte, Elsie Benjamin, Charles Benton, Doris Block, John Boule, Edwin Breen, Austin Briggs-Hall, Sadie Browne, Sylvan Buch, Dorothy Carter, *Fred Carter* (1944–48), *Alice Childress* (1940–48), *Alvin Childress* (1940–48), Draynard Clinton, Robert Coren, Billy Cumberbatch, William Daniels, Bootsie Davis, *Ruby Wallace Dee* (1940–48), Vivian Hall Dogan, Hazel Dykes, Bently Edmonds, Alfredo Elkins, Geneva Fitch, Fred Fitzgerald, Ruth Ford, Vernon Ford, Oliver Gandi, *Maxwell Glanville* (1941–49), Charles Glassoff, Glen Gordon, Milton Gordon, William Greaves, Stanley Greene, Evelio Grillo, Vivian Hall, Inge Hardison, Lula Hariston, Carol Harms, Bill Harris, *Betty Haynes* (1940–48), Gordon Heath, Charles Henderson, Owen Tolbert Hewitt, Raymond Hill, Buddy Holmes, William Horace, Sally Howard, Betty Humphries, *Earle Hyman* (1943–45), James Jackson, Willie Lee Johnson, Joseph Kamm, Blanch Kirkland, William Korff, Verneda Laselle, Urylee Leonardos, George Lewis, *Claire Leyba* (1940–46), James Lightfoot, Maurice Lisby, Michael Lloyd, William Loguen, Yvonne Maedchen, Kenneth Malory, *Kenneth Mannigault* (1940–49), Aida Marlowe, Ray Marlowe, Helen Martin, Mary Mason, Mildred Meekins, Jill Miller, Lionel Monagus, Joe Nathan, Dean Newman, Charles Nolte, Courtney Olden, *Frederick O'Neal* (1940–47), Ruby Orange, Cathy Parson, Yolanda Paterno, Lawrence Pepper, Alberta Perkins, Ann Petry, Fernan Phillips, Oliver Pitcher, Sidney Poitier, Bessie Powers, Geraldine Preillerman, John Proctor, Marion Randolphs, Nadya Ramanov, Hattie King Reavis, Roger Reynolds, Virgil Richardson, Vincent Rourke, Maynard Sandridge, Isabel Sanford, Dale Shell, Hilda Simms, Morris Singer, Martin Slade, Claude Sloan, Laurence Smaulding, Elwood Smith, Joan Smith, Muriel Smith, Bette Snyder, Paul Steiner, Samuel Stone, Javotte Sutton, *Clarice*

Taylor (1940–48), George Taylor, Lance Taylor, Franklyn Thomas, Salvador Thomas, Maurice Thompson, *Letitia Toole* (1941–46), Charles Trent, Mel Tyler, William Veasey, Edith Marie Whitman, Bob Wilkes, Frank Wilson, Jane Wyatt, Leonard Yorr, Estelle Young.

REPERTORY

1940–41: *Hits, Bits, and Skits: A Variety Show, On Striver's Row*, Second Variety Show, *Natural Man, On Striver's Row* (musical).

1941–42: *Starlight.*

1942–43: *Three Is a Family.*

1943–44: *Three Is a Family, Anna Lucasta.*

1944–45: *Walk Hard, Garden of Time, Henri Christophe.*

1945–46: *Home Is the Hunter, On Striver's Row, Angel Street, Juno and the Paycock, You Can't Take It with You.*

1946–47: *The Peacemaker, Tin Top Valley, The Fats, Christopher Bean, Rope, The Show-Off.*

1947–48: *Rain, The Washington Years, Sojourner Truth, Almost Faithful.*

1948–49: *The Fisherman, Skeleton, Riders to the Sea, Freight.*

BIBLIOGRAPHY

Published Source:

Walker, Ethel Pitts. "The American Negro Theatre," in *The Theatre of Black Americans*. Vol. 2. Edited by Errol Hill. Englewood Cliffs, N.J.: Prentice-Hall, 1980.

Unpublished Source:

Walker, Ethel Pitts. "The American Negro Theatre, 1940–1949." Doctoral dissertation, University of Missouri-Columbia, 1975.

Weldon B. Durham

AMERICAN REPERTORY THEATRE, INC., was organized in New York City in 1945 by Cheryl Crawford, Eva Le Gallienne, and Margaret Webster. In June 1946 they acquired a year's lease on the International Theatre, located at 5 Columbus Circle. This theatre, variously known as the Majestic, the Park, the Park Music Hall, the Cosmopolitan, and the Columbus Circle, opened in 1903 and was demolished in 1954. After try-outs in Princeton, Philadelphia, and Boston, the company opened on November 6, 1946, with Shakespeare's *Henry VIII*, on the eighth with J. M. Barrie's *What Every Woman Knows*, and on the twelfth with Henrik Ibsen's *John Gabriel Borkman*. G. B. Shaw's *Androcles and the Lion*, preceded by Sean O'Casey's *Pound on Demand*, opened on December 19. These played in repertory until February 22, 1947.

The company then abandoned repertory because of financial difficulties, and opened Sidney Howard's *Yellow Jack* for a single-play run on February 27. In conjunction with Rita Hassan, they produced *Alice in Wonderland*, which opened on April 5, 1947.

In 1946 the American theatre had no permanent company playing in repertory in New York, and had had none since 1933 when Eva Le Gallienne's Civic

Repertory Theatre closed its doors at the Fourteenth Street Theatre. The American Repertory Theatre was an attempt to fill that void.

All three of the founders, Crawford, Le Gallienne, and Webster, were experienced women of the theatre. At this point in their careers their combined credits for plays produced, directed, or acted totaled roughly 235. Crawford, one of the few successful female producers in New York, began her career with the Theatre Guild, was one of the founders of the Group Theatre* (1930), founded the Maplewood Theatre (1940), and, as an independent producer, brought such hits as *Porgy and Bess* (1942) and *One Touch of Venus* (1943) to Broadway.

Eva Le Gallienne, after beginning her career in England, made her New York debut in 1915 and became a star with her portrayal of Julie in *Liliom* (1921). She opened the Civic Repertory Theatre in 1926. Underwritten by private donations, this theatre played thirty-four productions in repertory during its six-season life. Le Gallienne's dream of repertory persisted.

Like Le Gallienne, Webster also had her start in England. By the time she came to New York in 1937, as the director of Maurice Evans' *Richard II*, she had acted in fifty productions, some of them at the Old Vic, and she had directed twelve. She continued directing with, among others, Maurice Evans' *Hamlet* (1938), his *Henry IV*, Part I (1939), four productions of Shakespeare at the New York World's Fair (1939), *Twelfth Night* (1940), Maurice Evans' *Macbeth* (1941), Paul Robeson's *Othello* (1943), and *The Tempest* (1945), produced by Cheryl Crawford.

The American Repertory Theatre was founded for a number of reasons, not least among them to build an acting company for the American theatre that would compare with England's Old Vic and the Moscow Art Theatre. The founders hoped to benefit the public, the actor, and the playwright: the public, by giving them the opportunity to see masterworks not generally available in the Broadway theatre; the actor, by challenging him to polish his craft in a constantly alternating series of roles, and to perfect the ensemble playing that only the security of the permanent company could provide; the playwright, by having a company that could give his work more exposure than the instant hit or flop methods of Broadway were capable of doing.

Financially, the American Repertory Theatre was an anomaly. In response to financial advice from legal counsel, a corporation was formed on October 15, 1945, offering 600 shares of class A common stock for an aggregate of $300,000. One share of preferred with one share of class A common sold for $500. The voting stock, class B common, was offered privately. But it was not until November 2, 1945, when Joseph Verner Reed donated $100,000 to Webster, that the project got off the ground.

A National Advisory Committee of seventeen was formed, which included such luminaries as Leonard Bernstein, Robert Edmond Jones, Jo Mielziner, and Tyrone Power. A list of 141 sponsors, included in the program, gave recognition to those who bought shares.

Eventually the money was raised and then carefully budgeted to cover the formation of the company and the mounting of six productions. The total production costs, through *Yellow Jack*, were $186,750.34. However, the New York running costs were increased by several unexpected union rulings. Because there was no established code for stagehands working in repertory, Local 1 of the IATSE (International Alliance Theatre Stage Employees) made an arbitrary decision late in October 1946 regarding the American Repertory Theatre. The size of the permanent crew was based on the demands of the largest production, *Henry VIII*, which the union judged needed a crew of twenty-eight. The company was then saddled with this crew when play requirements dropped, as they did in each of the other plays. This ruling, combined with those of Local 802, American Federation of Musicians, regarding *Henry* and *Androcles*, that they were "dramas with music," raised expenses across the board by almost 20 percent.

The company played every night except Monday, with a matinee on Saturday and Sunday. Prices ranged from a top of $4.20 to $1.20, with a $7.20 top for opening nights. In January 1947 a new policy was inaugurated that gave the customer a 10 percent reduction on the purchase of tickets to two shows and a 20 percent discount on the purchase of tickets to three.

Crawford's budget had allowed for two seasons playing at a small loss with a break-even point of $16,000 a week. When the weekly "nut" leaped toward $20,000 and the box-office demand lagged, the company ran out of money.

A meeting was held at the theatre on January 21, 1947, to review the situation, which resulted in some impressive gestures of goodwill from other sectors of the theatrical community.

The American Repertory Theatre received unanimous initial encouragement from the press. The idea of a permanent American company in repertory was soundly endorsed, as were the founders. A collaborative "Good Luck" ad appeared in the *New York Times* and in the *Post* on November 6, 1946, signed by Actors' Equity, the Dramatists' Guild, the Theatre Guild, and others, seventeen in all.

This ground swell of enthusiasm was tempered somewhat in the critical comment on *Henry VIII*. *What Every Woman Knows* prompted several reviewers to compare June Duprez' performance with that of Helen Hayes (1926) and even with that of Maude Adams (1908). Duprez ran a poor third. *John Gabriel Borkman* was described as "brilliant" on one hand and as "theatrical claptrap" on the other; as a "bore" by one critic and as "inspired" by another.

While acknowledging the magnificent physical beauty of *Henry VIII* and the handsome mounting of all the other productions, and while citing the talents of members of the troupe, critics of the first three productions consistently questioned the selection of scripts. With *Androcles and the Lion* the company received unqualified support from everyone, including the paying public.

In seventeen weeks of repertory the American Repertory Theatre presented 121 performances of the plays of Barrie, Ibsen, Shakespeare, O'Casey, and Shaw. Then repertory was replaced by plays produced for a single extended run.

Sidney Howard's *Yellow Jack* had first been presented by the Theatre Guild in 1934, when it was a critical but not a popular success. The American Repertory Theatre's production repeated this bit of theatre history. It closed on March 15, 1947.

The final production of the season was *Alice in Wonderland*, adapted by Le Gallienne and Florida Friebus, which opened on April 5, to an enthusiastic press, and continued to run for 110 performances. This was the same *Alice* that had been the final production of Le Gallienne's Civic Repertory Theatre in 1932.

A major consideration in the selection of plays had been the selection of players. It was difficult to decide on productions without knowing who would be in the cast. The plays were therefore chosen for ensemble playing with little attempt to spotlight a featured performer.

The company consisted of a technical and administrative staff of twenty and a troupe of twenty-six actors and actresses, with twelve supernumeraries. All the personnel were signed to two-year contracts, which offered them more job security than did most runs of single plays.

The featured players were Le Gallienne, Victor Jory, Walter Hampden, Ernest Truex, and Margaret Webster, all of them well known in theatre and film circles. They were supported by June Duprez, Philip Bourneuf, and Richard Waring. Of the younger players, several achieved success later: Eli Wallach with *The Rose Tattoo* (1951) and the film *Baby Doll* (1956); Efrem Zimbalist, Jr., with the television series "77 Sunset Strip" (1958–63); Julie Harris, who joined the troupe for *Alice in Wonderland*, followed with Frankie in *Member of the Wedding* (1950), Sally Bowles in *I Am a Camera* (1951), and Jeanne D'Arc in *The Lark* (1955). Anne Jackson, who became Mrs. Eli Wallach, Philip Bourneuf, John Becher, Cavada Humphrey, Richard Waring, and William Windom all continued successful careers in theatre, film, and television.

In June 1947 *Alice* was moved to the Majestic Theatre for a run of six weeks, after which the company disbanded for the summer, intending to tour the show during the 1947–48 season. They opened in Boston in September to excellent notices and a weekly gross of $25,000, but because of heavy running expenses they lost $3,500 the first week. The tour was abandoned. Crawford resigned in June 1947 and in May 1948 the American Repertory Theatre, Inc., was officially dissolved.

PERSONNEL

Management: Cheryl Crawford, managing director; John York, general manager; Newbold Morris, treasurer; Wolfe Kauffman, press director; Paul Morrison, technical director.

Designers: Remo Bufano, masks and animals for *Alice* and *Androcles;* David Ffolkes, sets and costumes for *Henry*, costumes for *What Every;* Paul Morrison, sets and costumes for *John Gabriel*, sets for *What Every;* Robert Rowe Paddock, sets for *Alice;* Wolfgang

Roth, sets and costumes for *Pound on Demand, Androcles, Yellow Jack;* Noel Taylor, costumes for *Alice*.

Musical Directors (responsible for composing and arranging): Richard Addinsell, *Alice;* Marc Blitzstein, *Androcles;* Lehman Engel, *Henry, John Gabriel, Yellow Jack*.

Stage Directors: Eva Le Gallienne, *John Gabriel, Alice;* Victor Jory, *Pound on Demand;* Martin Ritt, *Yellow Jack;* Margaret Webster, *Henry, What Every, Androcles*.

Actors and Actresses: Emery Battis, John Becher, *Philip Bourneuf*, Angus Cairns, *June Duprez*, Marion Evensen, Raymond Greenleaf, *Walter Hampden*, Cavada Humphrey, Ann Jackson, *Victor Jory*, Arthur Keegan, Donald Keyes, *Eva Le Gallienne*, Mary Alice Moore, Robert Rawling, John Straub, Eugene Stuckmann, Theodore Tenley, *Ernest Truex*, Eli Wallach, *Richard Waring, Margaret Webster*, William Windom, Ed Woodhead, Efrem Zimbalist, Jr. Supernumeraries were a stable part of the company, appearing in all of the productions where extra people were needed. They were Don Allen, John Behney, Michel Corhan, Will Davis, Thomas Grace, Bart Henderson, Frederic Hunter, Robert Leser, Gerald McCormack, Ruth Neal, Walter Neal, James Rafferty. Before the opening of *Yellow Jack*, the following players voluntarily requested and received the permission of Actors' Equity to go off the payroll: June Duprez, Walter Hampden, Ernest Truex, and Richard Waring. Alfred Ryder was added to the cast of *Yellow Jack*, and Robert Carlson, Julie Harris, Henry Jones, Rae Len, *Bambi Linn*, Jack Manning, Eloise Roehm, Dan Scott, and Charles Townley were added for *Alice*.

REPERTORY

1946–47: *Henry VIII, What Every Woman Knows, John Gabriel Borkman, Pound on Demand*, and *Androcles and the Lion;* also, *Yellow Jack, Alice in Wonderland*.

BIBLIOGRAPHY

Published Sources:

Crawford, Cheryl. *One Naked Individual*. New York: The Bobbs-Merrill Company, 1977.
Le Gallienne, Eva. *With a Quiet Heart*. New York: Viking Press, 1953.
Webster, Margaret. *Don't Put Your Daughter on the Stage*. New York: Alfred A. Knopf, 1972.

Archival Resource:

New York, New York. New York Public Library. Library and Museum of the Performing Arts. Cheryl Crawford Collection. Scrapbooks of Cheryl Crawford.

Nancy R. McClave

AMERICAN REPERTORY THEATRE (ART) was established at Harvard University, Cambridge, Massachusetts, in 1979 by Robert Brustein, actor, director, critic, educator, and administrator. The group included about thirty-five performers, administrators, artisans, and technicians from the Yale Repertory Theatre*, which Brustein had headed until 1979. The ART negotiated a five-year contract with Harvard University whereby ART used, rent-free, the Loeb Drama Center for forty weeks each year. Harvard agreed to subsidize about 11 percent of ART's operating budget to cover the cost of maintaining the facility. Brustein, formerly a drama professor at Cornell, Columbia, and Yale universities and Vassar College, was appointed professor of English at Harvard, director of undergraduate activities at the Loeb Drama Center, and artistic director of the professional repertory company.

The Loeb Drama Center, designed by Hugh Stubbins and Associates, opened in October 1960. This prototype of the flexible, fully mechanical theatre of the future featured revolutionary electromechanical systems designed by Yale University's noted theatre design engineer George C. Izenour. Lift systems permitted six configurations of the auditorium and of the stage. Remotely controlled, synchronous electric winches were designed to facilitate precise and rapid movement of scenery above the stage. The theatre also provided generously sized and tastefully decorated public spaces, adequate dressing and rehearsal rooms, shops for scenery construction and costume construction, outstanding acoustical properties, and good sound insulation. ART replaced or augmented the theatre's lighting, sound, and synchronized winch systems in its first two seasons in Cambridge.

ART's abbreviated inaugural season began in January 1980 with a revival of a piece from the repertory of the Yale company, the Alvin Epstein–directed *A Midsummer Night's Dream*, with music composed by Henry Purcell (1659–95) for his opera *The Fairy Queen*, based on Shakespeare's classic comedy. The first season included a new American play, *Terry by Terry*, by Mark Leib; Bertolt Brecht's seldom-produced Chicago gangland fable, *Happy End* (1929), with a jazzy score by Kurt Weill; and a new translation/adaptation of Nikolai Gogol's *The Inspector General*, directed by Peter Sellars. Thereafter, the resident acting ensemble of fourteen to eighteen dedicated itself to presenting five to seven productions in rotating repertory in a forty-week season. Staged readings of new plays, a New Stages Series of minimally produced new scripts at Harvard's Hasty Pudding Theatre, cabarets, poetry readings, and guest productions have given ART patrons an ample bill of fare. In recent years summer-fall tours have lengthened their year to fifty-two weeks.

Works in three categories have dominated ART's repertory. Classics, such as *Sganarelle, an Evening of Molière Farces*, and early modern dramas, such as Jean Genet's *The Balcony*, have been set in new locales and infused with contemporary references by directors devoted to finding new ways to express the author's intent. Andrei Serban's direction transformed Anton Chekhov's usually somber *The Three Sisters* into a knockabout farce, in which the Pozorov sisters and their suitors "pout like children on a stage strewn with toys, . . . [and] earnest philosophizing about suffering and social evolution is played as vapid bourgeois chitchat" (William A. Henry III, "Reinventing the Classics," *Time* 121 [February 7, 1983]: 85). Andrei Belgrader's treatment of *Waiting for Godot* relied on images of Charlie Chaplin, Buster Keaton, and other American movie clowns to lend immediacy to the cosmic plight of Samuel Beckett's central European circus clowns. JoAnne Akalaitis' controversial *Endgame* was set in a subway station and included a musical overture composed by Philip Glass. This *Endgame* provoked legal action by Beckett's U.S. agent. ART settled out of court and ran a strongly worded rejoinder from Beckett in the *Endgame* playbill. Michael

Feingold merged two plays by German dramatist and actor Frank Wedekind (*The Earth Spirit*, written in 1895, and *Pandora's Box*, written in 1903) in *Lulu*, set by director Lee Breuer in 1970s Hollywood and other contemporary locales redolent of an all-consuming sexuality. Breuer's treatment of Wedekind's sex tragedies as a film being dubbed by actors in a post-synch studio alienated ART's subscribers but found the group another, younger audience. *Lulu* was well received on ART's 1982 European tour. Finally, one might include in this category Euripides' *Alcestis*, as adapted from the Dudley Fitts–Robert Fitzgerald translation by Robert Wilson (who also directed and co-designed the production). Wilson reconstructed the text to dislocate the narrative line and emphasize a bird motif, adding a prologue by Heiner Mueller, and then, after the intermission, introducing a Japanese Kyogen farce, *The Birdwatcher in Hell*, with an electronic score by performance artist Laurie Anderson. This was Wilson's first complete work produced in the United States since the epochal *Einstein on the Beach* in 1976. It was also his first foray into staging classic drama and using professional actors.

Neglected works of the past, frequently involving music and having a particular appeal to contemporary audiences, constitute a second category. The collaborative works of Bertolt Brecht and Kurt Weill had been a specialty of the Yale Repertory Theatre and continued to be part of the ART repertory the first two seasons. In 1981 Mark Leib blended two plays of Pierre-Augustin Caron de Beaumarchais, *The Barber of Seville* and its sequel, *The Marriage of Figaro*, in *Figaro*. Conductor-composer Stephen Drury added the music of Wolfgang Amadeus Mozart. Peter Sellars' staging of George Frideric Handel's *Orlando* in 1982, in which the hero appears as a space explorer launched from Cape Canaveral on a mission to Mars, was warmly received in some quarters. The Andrei Serban–directed production of Carlo Gozzi's commedia scenario, *The King Stag*, featured additional original music by Elliot Goldenthal and Julie Taymor's visually stunning costumes, puppets, and masks. Serban squeezed Sergei Prokofiev's *The Love of Three Oranges* (from a scenario by Gozzi) into a madcap, twenty-five-minute afterpiece.

New works, including those bound for Broadway, but especially those unique ventures that challenge conventional notions of what constitutes a meaningful theatrical experience, form the pillar thrusting ART above the plane occupied by the finest regional repertory companies into the plane of world-renowned theatres. Jules Feiffer's biting *Grownups*, in which a beleaguered husband struggles to maintain his integrity, went on, with Bob Dishy and other ART performers, to eighty-three performances on Broadway in 1981–82 and to considerable critical acclaim. Robert Auletta's surreal evocation of the mental landscape of a half-psychotic Vietnam veteran, *Rundown*, was well received in Cambridge, and Marsha Norman's *'night, Mother*, a Gorkyesque prelude to a young woman's suicide, garnered the 1982 Pulitzer Prize. ART also premiered *Orchids in the Moonlight*, a dialogue between Mexican screen goddesses Dolores del Rio and Maria Felix, by Carlos Fuentes, one of Mexico's most distinguished and controversial men of letters and a leading spokesman for its political left. *Orchids* was Fuentes' first major work written in English, and his first play produced professionally in America. Christopher Durang's surrealistic satire of modern parenting, *Baby with the Bathwater*, was developed at ART before its eighty-four performances off-Broadway in 1983–84.

The 1983–84 ART season featured four world premieres, including *Traveler in the Dark*, Marsha Norman's despairing exploration of the failures of an eminent physician to be a loving human and an effective healer, and the Roger Miller–William Hauptman musical, *Big River*. A revised version of this adaptation of Mark Twain's *The Adventures of Huckleberry Finn* won the 1985 Tony Award for best musical, as well as Tonys for Hauptman (best book), Miller (best music), Heidi Landesman (best scenery), and Des McAnuff (best direction of a musical). The spate of new plays continued in 1984–85 with Hauptman's *Gillette*, in which two drifters in Gillette, Wyoming, experience tests of the very possibility of love and friendship, and Ken Friedman's *Claptrap*, a farcical spoof of Ira Levin's *Deathtrap*. *The Juniper Tree*, a minimalist opera based on a fairy tale by the brothers Grimm, composed by Philip Glass and Robert Moran, with a libretto by Arthur Yorinks, stirred critical encomia when produced in December 1985.

American premieres have attracted significant critical attention while affording ART audiences unique and challenging experiences. The American premiere of Milan Kundera's homage to French encyclopedist Denis Diderot, *Jacques and His Master*, attracted attention not only because of the fine literary reputation of its author, an exiled Czech novelist, but also because Brustein engaged the well-known social and literary critic Susan Sontag to direct. But perhaps no ART production has drawn and polarized critics and audiences alike as did the segment of Robert Wilson's *Civil Wars* produced in March 1985. Wilson, probably the United States' most heralded scenarist and director in the style of postmodernism, conceived a twelve-hour mixed media extravaganza depicting primal myths of civil strife and reconciliation to be produced in self-sufficient sections in each of several countries and then assembled in its entirety at the Los Angeles Olympic Games in 1984. The project was never fully realized, but portions were produced. The ART production, consisting essentially of parts done first in Cologne, West Germany, baffled some viewers and stirred others, while taxing to the limit the descriptive powers of reviewers and commentators.

ART's devotion to nonnarrative theatre and opera, to revitalized classics, both obscure and famous, to committed political commentary, and to the infusion of aesthetically demanding music into nonmusical works, has thrilled some of its clients and distracted and overwhelmed others. Naturalism has been all but excluded from the Loeb Drama Center stage (*'night, Mother* is a notable exception to the rule), and literary works of the sort commonly anthologized in college textbooks have been avoided for the most part (productions of Richard Brinsley Sheridan's *The School for Scandal* and Luigi Pirandello's *Six Characters in Search of an Author*, and a guest production of Eugene O'Neill's *A Moon for the Misbegotten* excepted). ART has thrived despite an uncompromising commitment to risky work.

ART's achievements while undertaking such a challenging repertory have earned the troupe a position at the very forefront of U.S. theatre in the 1980s, a position it has reached after traversing difficult financial terrain and passing through periods of cool, occasionally hostile responses from its audience. In its first full season of operation, 1980–81, ART subscribers numbered 13,000; total attendance stood at 140,000. Earned income accounted for about half the $2.065 million budget, and the season ended with ART experiencing a significant deficit of about $200,000. Sexually explicit imagery in the costumes worn for Shakespeare's *As You Like It*, Lee Breuer's deconstruction of *Lulu*, and the apparently unfocused direction of *Has "Washington" Legs?*, a satirical jibe at Hollywood, turned subscribers away. Only 7,500 responded to the season sales campaign of 1981–82, and the group experienced another $200,000 deficit. The next season, 1982–83, total attendance surpassed the record of 1980–81, though only 8,166 patrons subscribed to the season. In 1983–84 ART operated at 93 percent of capacity, and the next season it was filled to 99.75 percent of capacity, including 11,000 season subscribers. Since 1982, ART's productions have drawn patrons to 95 percent of capacity and above. Budget growth has been measured and controlled, gaining ART a reputation for careful financial management, an attractive counterpoint to its reputation for presenting an adventurous repertory. Support from the Massachusetts Council on the Arts and Humanities and from the National Endowment for the Arts was substantial in the period from 1980 to 1985; individual and corporate support was slight at first but has steadily grown.

In 1984 Harvard renewed its contract with ART. Then in 1985 ART's achievements began to be substantially recognized on the national front. The National Endowment for the Arts awarded the group a challenge grant in the amount of $750,000 and an "ensemble" grant of $843,000. Shortly afterward the National Arts Stabilization Fund, established in 1983 by the Ford, Mellon, and Rockefeller foundations to reward arts groups for sound fiscal management and for setting and maintaining high artistic goals, granted ART $950,000 with which it might retire its deficit and establish an endowment. In 1986 the Jujamcyn theatrical real estate company gave ART the 1986 Jujamcyn Award of $50,000 and the American Theatre Wing honored ART with the Tony it gives annually to an outstanding resident company outside New York. The honors have solidified ART's position at the forefront of American resident theatres, and the grants have permitted the group to enlarge its ensemble, lengthen its season, increase salaries, hire resident designers and acting and voice coaches, and launch a campaign to create a permanent endowment fund.

ART's relations with Harvard have warmed and expanded. In 1979 conservative elements at Harvard, which had never offered a theatre course in its 350-year history, responded coolly to the idea of a professional theatre company on campus. Students were also concerned that the presence of the professional theatre group would impede student access to the Loeb Drama Center. In a few years the faculty seemed reconciled and students were happy with the opportunity to work with professionals. In 1980 Brustein negotiated an arrangement whereby members of ART would teach acting, directing, design, dramaturgy, and theatre history courses, in essence giving Harvard an undergraduate theatre program for the first time in its history. Courses are offered through the Harvard School of Continuing Education and the Harvard Summer School. In 1982 the Musical Theatre Lab moved from the John F. Kennedy Center for the Performing Arts in Washington, D.C., to Cambridge to become a joint project of the Stuart Ostrow Foundation, the ART, and Radcliffe College. In 1986 Harvard approved the establishment of the ART Institute for Advanced Theatre Training. This two-year certificate program (no formal advanced degree would be given) commenced in 1987 when twenty students were admitted to the first class to study acting, directing, design, and dramaturgy.

PERSONNEL

Artistic Director: Robert Brustein.

Managing Director: Robert J. Orchard.

Production Manager: Jonathan Seth Miller.

Directors: JoAnne Akalaitis (1984–86), Andrei Belgrader (1980–81, 1982–84), Michael Bloom (1985–86), Lee Breuer (1980–81), *Robert Brustein* (1980–86), Philip Cates (1983–84), Gerald Chapman (1983–84), Barbara Damashek (1985–86), Robert Drivas (1983–85), *Alvin Epstein* (1979–81, 1982–83), William Foeller (1982–83), John Grant-Philips (1982–83), Joann Green (1981–82), Adrian Hall (1981–82), Walton Jones (1979–80), Jerome Kilty (1984–85), Michael Kustow (1980–81), David Leveaux (1983–84), Mark Linn-Baker (1982–83), Des McAnuff (1983–84), John Madden (1979–80), Jonathan Miller (1982–83, 1984–85), Tom Moore (1982–84), Travis Preston (1980–81), Peter Sellars (1979–80, 1981–82), *Andrei Serban* (1981–83, 1984–86), Susan Sontag (1984–85), David Wheeler (1981–82, 1983–85), Robert Wilson (1984–86).

Set Designers: Loy Arcenas (1985–86), Kate Edmunds (1980–82), Andrew Jackness (1979–81), Tom Kamm (1984–85), Heidi Landesman (1982–84), Adrianne G. Lobel (1979–81), Tom Lynch (1980–81, 1982–83), Beni Montresor (1982–83), Alexander Okun (1985–86), Patrick Robertson (1982–83), Kevin Rupnik (1981–83), Karen Schulz (1984–85), Don Soule (1982–83), Elaine Spatz-Rabinowitz (1981–82), Douglas Stein (1983–85), *Tony Straiges* (1979–83), George Tsypin (1985–86), Brian Vahey (1983–84), Robert Wilson (1984–85), *Michael H. Yeargan* (1979–82, 1983–86).

Costume Designers: Robert Blackman (1983–84), Zack Brown (1979–81), Nan Cibula (1979–80, 1981–82), Karen Eister (1984–86), Jane Greenwood (1984–85), Lynn Jeffrey (1982–83, 1984–85), Heidi Landesman (1982–83), Adrianne G. Lobel (1980–81), William Ivey Long (1979–80), Patricia McGourty (1983–84), Beni Montresor (1982–83), Alexander Okun (1985–86), Liz Perlman (1982–83), *Dunya Ramicova* (1979–82, 1983–84), Kevin Rupnik (1981–82), Rita Ryack (1980–81, 1982–83), Julie Taymor (1984–85), Nancy Thun (1980–83), Brian Vahey (1983–84), Rosemary Vercoe (1982–83), Constance R. Wexler (1984–85), Kurt Wilhelm (1983–85), Yoshio Yabara (1984–85), Michael H. Yeargan (1983–84, 1985–86), Kristi Zea (1985–86).

Lighting Designers: William Armstrong (1979–81), Paul Gallo (1979–81), *James H. Ingalls* (1980–84), Beni Montresor (1982–84), Spencer Moss (1984–86), Thom Palm

(1982–85), Richard Riddell (1985–86), Donald Edmund Thomas (1983–84), *Jennifer Tipton* (1982–86).

Literary Directors: Michael Kustow, Jonathan Marks.

Composers: Ruben Blades, Barbara Damashek, Stephen Drury, Philip Glass, Elliot Goldenthal, Hans Peter Kuhn, Karl Lundeberg, Richard Peaslee, Elizabeth Swados.

Musical Directors: Stephen Drury, Gary Fagin, Michael S. Roth, Paul Schierhorn, Craig Smith, Daniel Stepner.

Choreographers: Johanna Boyce (1985–86), Carmen de Lavallade (1980–81), Kathryn Posin (1982–83).

Technical Director: Donald R. Soule.

Production Coordinator: Thomas C. Behrens.

Actors and Actresses: S. Mark Aliapoulios (1985–86), Michael Allio (1982–83), Rose Arrick (1984–85), Linda Atkinson (1980–81), Michael Atwell (1980–81), Dennis Bacigalupi (1984–85), Sharon Baker (1981–82), Gerry Bamman (1980–81), Ian Bannen (1983–84), John Bellucci (1981–82, 1983–84), Paul Benedict (1981–82), Nina Bernstein (1983–84), *John Bottoms* (1979–86), Amy Brenneman (1983–84), Janet Brown (1981–82, 1985–86), Sandy Brown (1983–84), Robert Brustein (1979–80), Jane Bryden (1981–82), Rosilind Cash (1981–82), Marilyn Caskey (1979–80), Philip Cates (1979–80), Lynn Chausow (1984–85), Chris Clemenson (1979–81), Glenn J. Cohen (1982–83), William Cotten (1985–86), Hume Cronyn (1983–84), Diane D'Aquila (1984–86), Cynthia Darlow (1980–81), Hugh D'Autremont (1983–84), Robertson Dean (1979–80), *Thomas Derrah* (1980–86), Walter van Dijk (1979–80), Bob Dishy (1980–81), John Drabik (1979–81), Ursula Drabnik (1984–85), Mark Driscoll (1982–84), Robin Driscoll (1981–83), Robert Drivas (1984–85), Albert Duclos (1980–81), Jennifer Dundas (1980–81), *Eric Elice* (1979–81), Alvin Epstein (1981–83), Ben Evett (1983–84), Margaret Fleming (1979–80), Bill Foeller (1982–83), Jeffrey Gall (1981–82), Jennifer Geidt (1979–80), *Jeremy Geidt* (1979–86), Cheryl Giannini (1980–81, 1982–83), Francois de la Giroday (1981–82), *Seth Goldstein* (1982–86), Pamela Gore (1981–82), John Grant-Philips (1983–84), Ellen Greene (1980–81), *Richard Grusin* (1979–85), Martha Hackett (1982–83), Martha Hageman (1982–83), *Ben Halley, Jr.* (1983–86), Jamie Hanes (1982–83), Maja Hillmold (1981–82), Lise Hilboldt (1983–84), Ruby Hinds (1985–86), Ellen Holly (1981–82), Robert Honeysucker (1980–82), Rodney Hudson (1984–86), Alden Jackson (1983–84), Mark Jackson (1980–81), *Cherry Jones* (1980–85), Robert Joy (1983–84), Gayle Keller (1984–86), Mary Sego Kendrick (1981–82), *Jerome Kilty* (1981–85), Sue Ellen Kuzma (1985–86), Susan Larson (1981–83), *Carmen de Lavallade* (1979–81), Linda Lavin (1983–84), Geraldine Librandi (1980–81), Frank Licato (1981–82), Mark Linn-Baker (1979–80), Mary Linn-Baker (1982–83), Jack Luceno (1979–80), John McAndrew (1979–81), Brian McCue (1979–80), *Karen MacDonald* (1980–84, 1985–86), Tim McDonough (1985–86), William McGlinn (1980–81), Joan MacIntosh (1985–86), James Madelena (1981–82), Jonathan Marks (1981–83), George Martin (1980–81), Nancy Mayans (1979–80), Eric Menyuk (1985–86), Maria Moessen (1982–83), Christopher Moore (1984–86), Kathleen Mulligan (1982–83), *Harry S. Murphy* (1980–86), Kate Nelligan (1983–84), Frederick Neumann (1980–81), Elizabeth Norment (1979–81, 1985–86), Barbara Orson (1979–81), *Marianne Owen* (1979–84), Andrew Parker (1979–80), Deborah Phillips (1982–83), Anne Pitoniak (1982–83), David Ripley (1980–81), *Stephen Rowe* (1979–84), Paul Rudd (1985–86), Anthony Rudie (1983–84), Kenneth Ryan (1979–81), Lisa Saffer (1985–86), Robert Schaffer (1979–80), Damon Scheller (1983–84), Frances Schrand (1984–85), Kim Scown (1980–81), Nicole Shalhoub (1983–84), *Tony Shalhoub*

(1980–84), Paul Shierhorn (1982–83), Grace Shohet (1979–80), Catherine Slade (1980–81), Lis Sloan (1979–80), Priscella Smith (1984–85), Phyllis Somerville (1983–84), *Richard Spore* (1980–84), Robert Stattel (1983–84), Jack Stehlin (1984–86), David Stoneman (1985–86), Joan Storey (1982–83), Guy Strauss (1983–84), Sanford Sylvan (1981–82, 1985–86), Peter Tamm (1979–80), Alison Taylor (1982–84), Ann Titolo (1979–80), *Maggi Topkis* (1979–80, 1982–84), Lynn Torgove (1985–86), Valerie Walters (1985–86), Sam Waterston (1983–84), Nicolette Webb (1981–82), Charles Weinstein (1985–86), Gregory Welch (1984–85), Jane West (1985–86), Kathleen Widdoes (1981–82), *Shirley Wilber* (1981–86), Treat Williams (1984–85), Max Wright (1979–80), Nick Wyse (1982–84).

REPERTORY

1979–80: *A Midsummer Night's Dream, Terry by Terry, Happy End, The Inspector General.*

1980–81: *As You Like It, The Berlin Requiem* and *The Seven Deadly Sins, Lulu, Has "Washington" Legs?, Figaro.*

1981–82: *Sganarelle, an Evening of Molière Farces, Orlando, The Journey of the Fifth Horse, Ghosts, Orchids in the Moonlight, True West, Rundown.*

1982–83: *The Three Sisters, 'night, Mother, Waiting for Godot, The Boys from Syracuse, The School for Scandal, Baby with the Bathwater.* Three one-acts: *Hughie, Footfall, Rockaby.*

1983–84: *Measure for Measure, A Moon for the Misbegotten, Traveler in the Dark, Big River, Six Characters in Search of an Author, Angel City, Holy Wars, Strokes, Sganarelle, The School for Scandal.*

1984–85: *The King Stag* and *The Love of Three Oranges, Endgame, Jacques and His Master, The Civil Wars: A Tree Is Best Measured When It Is Down* (Act III, Scene I; Act IV, Scene A and Epilogue); *Love's Labour's Lost, Gillette, Claptrap, Sganarelle, An Evening of Molière Farces, Six Characters in Search of an Author.*

1985–86: *The Changeling, The Juniper Tree, The Balcony, Alcestis, Olympian Games, The Day Room,* and guest productions of *Mistero Buffo* and *Tutta Casa, Letto, e Chiesa.*

BIBLIOGRAPHY

Published Sources:

American Theatre, 1984–86.

Boston Globe, 1983–86.

New York Times, 1979–87.

Theatre Communications, 1980–84.

Berc, Shelley. "Lee Breuer's *Lulu.*" *Theater* 12 (Summer 1981): 69–77.

Best Plays, 1979–80 through *1985–86.* New York: Dodd, Mead, & Co., 1980–86.

deGaetani, Thomas. "The Adaptable Theatre in the American University; and the Loeb Drama Center." In *Adaptable Theatres,* edited by Stephen Joseph. London: Association of British Theatre Technicians, 1962, pp. 17–21.

"Drama Center for Harvard." *Architectural Record* 128 (September 1960): 151–60.

Henry, William A., III. "Reinventing the Classics." *Time* 121 (February 7, 1983): 85.

Land, Dick. "Harvard's Loeb Drama Center: The First Three Years." *Theatre Design and Technology* 1 (May 1965): 12–18.

Moynihan, D. S. "Sarah Pearson: On a Roll at ART." *Theatre Crafts* 20 (March 1986): 40, 49–63.

Smith, Ronn. "Wilson Weaves Classical Magic." *Theatre Crafts* 20 (November 1986): 30–32, 88–92.

Theatre Profiles, Vols. 5–7. New York: Theatre Communications Group, 1981, 1983, 1985.

Theatre World, 1979–80 through *1985–86*. Vols. 36 through 41. New York: Crown Publishers, 1980–86.

Wallach, Susan Levi. "Robert Brustein and Robert Orchard: Art and Management Mesh at the ART." *Theatre Crafts* 16 (October 1982): 12–15, 43.

Weldon B. Durham

AMERICAN THEATRE COMPANY (ATC) was founded in New York City in 1968 by Alice Scudder Emerick and Richard Kuss as a theatre in which fledgling professionals could showcase their talents for agents and producers. It presented its first production, a revival of Charles H. Hoyt's 1890 play *A Texas Steer*, in the parish hall of the Church of the Holy Communion for eight weekend performances beginning October 26, 1968.

Though there were several showcase groups off-off-Broadway, the ATC was founded for the express purpose of exploring America's theatrical heritage, which Kuss and Emerick considered an ongoing development. Emerick and Kuss selected each season's plays so they represented four periods in the nation's drama: the early period until 1870, the development period to 1920, 1920–45, and contemporary and experimental plays. About half the plays each season were revivals, half original, and during the early years half the plays were fully staged, while the rest were done as workshop productions. In the last five years of the company's existence all plays were fully staged for runs of twenty performances.

Alice Scudder Emerick, an actress and producer of off-Broadway plays, was most responsible for forming the ATC. Her husband, Richard Kuss, a graduate of Ithaca College, had acted and directed both in New York and in summer stock. When Ellis Santone came to the first open call, he brought two one-act plays by Henry James that he wanted to direct, and these became the company's second offering. Santone, with a Master's degree from Purdue University and six years' directing experience, primarily in Washington, D.C., became associate artistic director for the company. Kuss directed twenty-one of the plays ATC produced and Santone, seventeen.

For its second season the company moved into a studio on East Fourteenth Street, where it remained until 1977. Its last season, 1977–78, was presented at the Nameless Theater on West Twenty-second Street. The ATC was incorporated as a nonprofit corporation in 1970. Emerick was managing director, Kuss was artistic director, and Santone was associate artistic director. Charles Gillette, who had been with the company from the beginning, was scenic director. Everyone volunteered his or her time, and there was never a paid administrative staff. Each year a company was engaged for the season, but contracts were signed only for individual plays, and an actor could leave if something better turned up. Rehearsals lasted for four weeks, and the season ran from September through

June. In the beginning the Showcase Code of Actors' Equity Association did not allow donations, and Equity rules stipulated that no one could be paid if Equity members were not paid. The next few years saw the beginning of hat-passing, then guaranteed carfare for performers, and eventually a $35 weekly honorarium. For the last seasons ATC charged a $2 admission and accepted Theatre Development Fund vouchers. The New York State Council on the Arts, the National Endowment for the Arts, the Josephine B. Crane Foundation, the Simon Foundation, the CBS Foundation, and other funds and individuals provided additional support. A board of advisors included, among others, Harold Clurman and Jean Dalrymple.

The small stage in the studio on Fourteenth Street limited the staging of plays, but Kuss and Santone usually managed by avoiding gimmickry and allowing the play simply to speak for itself. Plays with large casts presented insurmountable problems. The company was also limited by uneven acting. ATC was not widely reviewed, but two original plays received particular attention: Charles Hallett's *Aaron Burr* and Barbara de la Cuesta's *Why I Am Here*. Though prompted by political tensions of the 1960s, the significance of this company lay in its presentation of American classics such as *A Texas Steer*, William Vaughn Moody's *The Faith Healer*, Rachel Crothers' *He and She*, and Colonel Robert Munford's *The Patriots* (1776), produced by ATC as part of the 1976 American Bicentennial.

In 1978 it was clear to Emerick, Kuss, and Santone that the company could not continue on its showcase contract with Actors' Equity Association. Moreover, the organizers realized that professionalization, with a salaried staff and acting company, would be too much. ATC closed after presenting "The Best of the Revolution," based on scenes and songs from plays written during the Revolutionary War period, a staged reading still occasionally presented. Among those who remained for all nine years were Thomas Connolly, Susan Tabor, Walt Gorney, and John Carpenter. Actors who have gone on to prominence are Christopher Lloyd, Gary Sandy, and Kevin Conway. Kuss has continued to act on stage, in films, and on television, while Santone briefly formed another company before pursuing a teaching career. Alice Emerick died in 1986.

PERSONNEL

Management: Alice Scudder Emerick, managing director (1968–78); Richard Kuss, artistic director (1968–78); Ellis Santone, associate artistic director (1968–78).

Scenic Directors: Charles Gillette (1968–77), Robert Perkins.

Scenic and Lighting Designer: Robert Perkins (1970–74).

Technical Director and Production Manager: Greg Smith (1970–74).

Scenic Technicians: Lee Aguillo, Larry Alboum, David H. Bosboom, Edwin Byrd, Susan Caldor, Mary Calhoun, Paula Davis, Joe Gasparino, Tobias Haller, Joan Haymes, Lynn Kable, Paul Krampe, Ilse Kritzler, Jerry Lee, Kevin Lewis, Kenneth Longert, Bo Metzler, John Orberbe, Ellis Santone, Marie Tripp, Peter Zirnis.

Costumes: Cheryl Bell, Pat Barker, Mauriak Carpenter, Paula Davis, Ann Dunbar, Agnes Gray, Ann Jones, Poppy Lagos, Barbara Lee Maccarone, Marie Miller, Mary Aliva Oute, Lucetta Perohiano, Barbara Ragan, Emmett Streetman, Evelyn Thompson.

Stage Managers: Jay Adler, J. J. Alexander, Martha Barrett, Mary Chase, James Curtan, Ann Dalbrivitz, Aaron Davis, Jennifer Dawson, D. J. Donnelly, Jack Dugger, Susan Dunfee, Georgia Fleenor, Susan Ford, John Handy, Patricia Hannigan, Stephanie Hawthorne, David Hutchinson, David Jason, Donald Keyes, Ross Klahr, Jim Knape, Douglas Kolbo, Joe Lane, Faye Lipsky, Suzanne O'Connell, Ed Oster, Lewis Pshena, Lisa Robbins, Cal Smith, Marie Tripp, Susan Unger, Peter Vistor, Cam Williams (1970–75), Judy Williams, Peter Zirnis, Ellen Zock.

Musical Director: Paul Spong (1974–77).

Stage Directors: Albert Amateau (*The Mulligan Guard Ball*—scenes), Les Barkdull (Robert Frost masques), Sonia Berman (*Shenandoah*), Dorothy Chernuck (*Money-Back Guarantee* and *The Petition, Ticket, The Reverend Griffith Davenport, For Her Enchanting Son, Fashion*), Milt Commons (*The Price of Life*), Thomas Connolly (*All the Old Familiar Places, Found Objects, The Contrast*—scenes, *A Better Place, The Fan Club*), James Curtan (*Poor Aubrey*), Frank Errante (Dietz one-act plays), Lee Falk (*Eris*), Stephan B. Finnan (*Here We Are, Hughie*), Georgia Fleener (*This Piece of Land*), Gordon Gray (*Isy Monk—We Ain't What We Was*), Richard Harden (*Aaron Burr*), John Hogan (*Something That Matters*), Richard Kuss (1968–78), Amy Saltz (*Round Trip*), Ellis Santone (1968–78), Thurmon Scott (*Soldiers of Freedom*).

Actors and Actresses: *Albert Amateau* (1968–71), Marshall Anker, Fran Anthony, Lynn Archer, Allison Argo, Peter Armstrong, Madison Arnold, Lynn Arollea, Ray Ascensio, *Robert Baines* (1969–75), Leslie Barrett, Hermine Bartee, Norman Beim, Wendall Bentley, Marcia Blau, Rosemary L. A. Borello, Nancy Boykin, Lawrence Broglio, Arthur Brook, Doris Brook, Gardner Brooksbank, Robert Browning, Elaine Bullis-Orms, Jon Peter Bumstead, Peter Burnell, Edwin Byrd, James F. Cade, Dennis Cameron, Beth Carlton, Jo Carpenter, *John Carpenter* (1968–78), *Chris Carrick* (1969–75), Betty Chambers, *Eleanor Charris* (1968–75), Jerry Chase, Tyrus Cheney, Yolanda Childress, Jose Cintron, Myotte Coker, Milt Commons, Matt Conley, *Thomas Connolly* (1968–78), Kevin Conway, Tom Craft, Mark Curran, John Daley, Jay Davis, Todd Davis, Jennifer Dawson, Rosemary DeAngelis, Jay Devlin, Howard DeWitt, Beth Dixon, Kathy Doyle, Billy E. Drago, Nat Drayton, Ann Dunbar, Herb DuVal, *Alice Scudder Emerick* (1968–78), Robert Fitzsimmons, Ann Freeman, Richard Friesen, Cyprienne Gabel, Donna Gabel, Julie Garfield, Mimi Garth, Anne Gerety, Jack Godby, Fredric Good, *Walt Gorney* (1968–78), Shanton Granger, Ruth Grant, Gayle Greene, Sharon Hall, Joseph Hamer, John Handy, Susan Handy, Jay Hargrove, Brian Hartigan, Pen Hartzell, Kerann Havilland, Robert Heine, Michael Hennessy, Charles Herrick, John High, Leila Holiday, Susan Hufford, *Annette Hunt* (1968–71), Megan Hunt, *David Hutchison* (1970–75), Claudia Inglis, *Joseph Jamrog* (1968–72), Michael Jeffers, Seth Kaplan (1968–72), *Anita Keal* (1968–75), Tom Keena, Clyde Kelley, *Dennis Kilbane* (1968–72), Jeffrey C. Kramer, *Carolyn Krigbaum* (1969–73), Ron Kuhlman, Richard Kuss, Joe Lane, Gene Law, Christopher Leahy, Jan Leighton, Judith Morley Levitan, Robert LeVoyd-Wright, O. B. Lewis, William Linton, Ruth Livingston, *Christopher Lloyd* (1970–72), Don Lochner, Bill Loggan, Winston Loggins, Poppy Logos, John Long, Robert Lorick, Larry C. Lott, Chuck Lulinski, *Shawn McAllister* (1970–72, 1976), Roger McIntyre, Anna Marie McKay, Charles Maggiore, Ric Mancini, Uriel Mendelson, Robert Milton, Mel Minter, Bill Moher, Kelly Monaghan, Isy Monk, Allyn Monroe, James Moody, Jeannine Moore, Carol Morgan, Christopher Murray, William Newman, *Garrett Nichols* (1969–74), Douglas Nigh, *James O'Connell* (1968–72), William Van O'Connor, Steve Orr, Edwin Owens, Joseph Pantaliano, *Ed Penn* (1970–73), Lucetto

Perchiano, Keith Perry, Susan Peterson, Judith Piatt, Paula Pierce, Edward W. Powell, Jr., James Pritchett, Jim Quinn, Jeramie Rain, Marilyn Randall, Lourette Raymon, Alex Reed, Hal Reese, Cecilia Riddett, Lisa Robbins, Mary Rocco, Frank Rohrbach, Gene Romeo, Norman M. Rosenbaum, Steven Rosenthal, Jan Ross, *Jeanne Rostang* (1970–72), Gene Ruffini, Gail Ryan, Cari Sanborn, Gary Sandy, Ellis Santone, Thurman Scott, Tom Scott, *Richard Scribner* (1969–72), *Edward Seamon* (1970–75), Judith Searle, James Paul Sherman, Gwen Simmons, Kendly Smith, Kitty Alice Snead, Patricia Snead-Hill, Robert Snively, Dennis Soens, Richard Sterne, Jack Swanson, *Susan Tabor* (1968–78), Kay Tornborgh, Alethea Turner, Robert Van Der Berg, Kathryn Venet, Gwendolyn Wahman, Jessica Wahman, Terrance Wallace, Joseph Warren, Milton Wasserman, Geoffrey Webb, Richard Weiss, John Hilburn Wells, Sally Westerman, Allister Whitman, Robert Wilde, Ronald Willoughby, John Wylie.

REPERTORY

1968–69: *A Texas Steer, Pyramus and Thisbe/The Salon* (one-acts), *The Double Axe* (dramatization of Robinson Jeffers' poem), three one-acts: *Solid Walls, The Dog School, Shenandoah.*

1969–70: *The Faith Healer, The Truth, Vietnam U.S.A., Soundings, Ponteach* (Act 1)/*The Candidates* (adaptation). Workshop Productions: *Deus Ex Machinist, I Used to See My Sister,* and *Noah Webster's Original Unabridged Electric Ark* (one-act plays by Dietz); *Reconciliation; Money-Back Guarantee* and *The Petition.*

1970–71: *Cop!; Eris, Ticket,* and *The Puppet Pusher,* a bill of one-act plays; *The Patriots; He and She; Rocket to the Moon; The Reverend Griffith Davenport; Round Trip.* Workshop Productions: *The Man Who Raped Kansas, All the Old Familiar Places, The Truth, The Mulligan Guard Ball* (scenes), *Poor Aubrey, For Her Enchanting Son, The Gladiator, The Widow's House.*

1971–72: *The Candidates, Margaret Fleming, The Battle of Brooklyn, Hotel Universe, The Broken Swing.* Workshop Productions: *Found Objects, The Contrast* (scenes), *The Price of Life, A Better Place.*

1972–73: *The New York Idea, The Fan Club, Fashion, A Masque of Reason* and *A Masque of Mercy, In the Cage.*

1973–74: *Here We Are, Hughie, The Male Animal.*

1974–75: *It Pays to Advertise, Aaron Burr, Gladys and Victor* and *This Piece of Land* (one-act plays), *Ponteach, Something That Matters, The Private Secretary.*

1975–76: *Why I Am Here, The Fall of British Tyranny, The Patriots, The Battle of Brooklyn, Aaron Burr.*

1976–77: *The Mulligan Guard Ball, Soldiers of Freedom, Isy Monk—We Ain't What We Was.*

1977–78: *The Best of the Revolution: The Spirit of '76.*

BIBLIOGRAPHY

Published Sources:
Back Stage, 1968–78.
Show Business, 1968–78.

David M. Price

[THE] APA (ASSOCIATION OF PRODUCING ARTISTS) was organized in January 1960 in New York City by Ellis Rabb as an itinerant repertory company. Together with Rosemary Harris, Rabb's wife at the time, the organization mounted a repertory, rehearsing in borrowed space at the Sullivan Street Playhouse in Greenwich Village. Inspired by the work of Sir Tyrone Guthrie, the artistic policy of the APA was to present plays of enduring popularity. The APA was dedicated to establishing a repertory theatre in its purest sense by mounting a series of plays with casts drawn from members of the company and presenting them on alternate evenings of performance. And the APA wanted to establish repertory in New York City, a feat not accomplished since the days of Eva Le Gallienne's Civic Repertory Theatre in the late twenties.

Rabb, a graduate of the Carnegie Institute of Technology, gained a strong foundation in classical theatre at the Antioch (Ohio) Shakespeare Festival, at the American Shakespeare Festival in Stratford, Connecticut, and while appearing in Broadway and off-Broadway productions. In 1957 he won the Clarence Derwent Award for acting in an off-Broadway production of Molière's *The Misanthrope*, and in the fall of 1957 he appeared in a minor role in the Phoenix Theatre production of Friedrich von Schiller's *Mary Stuart*, directed by Tyrone Guthrie and starring Irene Worth, Eva Le Gallienne, and William Hutt. These personalities helped to shape the future spirit of the APA.

The APA was invited to perform for the summer of 1960 in Hamilton, Bermuda, by the Bermuda Theatre Festival. Its opening repertory was a musical version of Arthur Schnitzler's *The Affairs of Anatol*, G. B. Shaw's *Man and Superman*, Anton Chekhov's *The Sea Gull*, and Shakespeare's *The Taming of the Shrew*. Critical success with a residency at the McCarter Theatre, Princeton, New Jersey, in the fall of 1960 assured a return to Princeton in February 1961, when the group presented a Shakespearean repertory that included *King Lear, As You Like It, Twelfth Night, A Midsummer Night's Dream*, and *Hamlet*. Among the directors of these productions was Stephen Porter, who became one of APA's most successful in this line of work. The group spent the summer and fall of 1961 in Boston and Falmouth, Massachusetts; at the Bucks County Playhouse in Pennsylvania; and in East Hampton, Long Island; Olney, Maryland; and Milwaukee, Wisconsin. The last residence in Milwaukee was a financial disaster, almost demolishing the organization.

APA finally regained its feet and moved closer to its goal by leasing the Folksbiene Playhouse in lower Manhattan, where they played a successful run in early 1962. The beginning of their salvation as a viable company was guaranteed by the University of Michigan's Professional Theatre Program under the direction of Robert Schintzer. The APA accepted Schintzer's invitation to a fall residency, even though APA had to abandon its repertory scheme and present extended runs of single plays. Nevertheless, critical acclaim in Ann Arbor established them as an extraordinary and versatile company. Eva Le Gallienne, a longtime friend of Rabb and an ardent supporter of the repertory idea, directed Henrik Ibsen's *Ghosts* and played Mrs. Alving, the lead in it, in one of five productions that fall. For the next three years the company returned to Ann Arbor each fall for increasingly longer stays. In 1964 they returned to New York to perform at the Phoenix Theatre* on East Seventy-fourth Street.

The association with the Phoenix Theatre was propitious for both organizations. Since 1953, when T. Edward Hambleton and Norris Houghton formed the Phoenix Theatre, the group had struggled to present noncommercial fare at affordable prices. By 1964 the Phoenix Theatre had sound management, an established subscription audience, and an artistic philosophy compatible with that of APA, which by then possessed impressive critical credentials compiled by a highly skilled company performing an extensive repertory. In one month at the Phoenix Theatre, beginning on March 30, 1964, the APA produced Luigi Pirandello's *Right You Are (If You Think You Are)*, George M. Cohan's *The Tavern*, Molière's *Scapin* and *The Impromptu at Versailles*, and Maxim Gorky's *The Lower Depths*. The critical reaction was generally good and augured well for a return to New York.

The next fall (1964) in Ann Arbor APA mounted a new production of *Man and Superman*, with Rabb as Tanner, Rosemary Harris as Violet, and Nancy Marchand as Ann. The show was a critical success when produced at the Phoenix Theatre. The APA had scored a modest triumph, for across town the more prestigious and much heralded Repertory Theatre of Lincoln Center* struggled to overcome negative press notices and continuing administrative and artistic turmoil. Comparisons of the APA with the Lincoln Center group regularly cited the APA as the proper model for a repertory company. The 1964–65 season included a dazzling production of *Judith* by Jean Giraudoux, with Rosemary Harris and Paul Sparer, as well as a new theatrical adaptation of Leo Tolstoy's *War and Peace*, which Hambleton had been anxious to produce.

On the basis of these successes Rabb and Hambleton signed an agreement on March 16, 1965, to create the APA-Phoenix. For the five-year venture, beginning with the 1965–66 season, Rabb was to be the artistic director and Hambleton the managing director. However, the agreement was premature, since it was based on an expected grant from the Ford Foundation that would permit the new company to move into larger quarters in the Lyceum Theatre on Broadway. The grant was not forthcoming and the merger appeared doomed.

The APA, riding the crest of critical acclaim, decided to return to Ann Arbor rather than to wait in New York for other funding. There they mounted another season of repertory that included *You Can't Take It with You* by Moss Hart and George S. Kaufman. The play's rousing success prompted the board of the Phoenix Theatre to advance $45,900 to secure a short-term lease of the Lyceum Theatre and to bring the production to New York. The APA-Phoenix finally settled into the Lyceum and the merger was consummated in late March 1966. *You Can't Take It with You* continued to run to capacity audiences for 255 performances. What the APA had accomplished with this play was to be the hallmark of their work. They had taken a standard American work and breathed fresh life into it under Rabb's direction, thereby stamping it with their own style and confirming its status as a classic.

Facing a sizable deficit, the combined company sought federal aid, and in June 1966 the National Endowment for the Arts approved a matching grant of

$125,000. Other foundations, including the Avalon Foundation and the Rock-efeller Foundation, quickly matched the federal money. In the next year the company enlarged and played residences in Los Angeles and Ann Arbor. APA-Phoenix adopted a system of "repertory within repertory," with shows being double cast and specific casts not announced until the night of performance. Helen Hayes and John Houseman added a further star luster when Hayes joined the acting company and Houseman directed.

The New York season of 1966 began in typical repertory fashion with Richard Brinsley Sheridan's *The School for Scandal* and *Right You Are (If You Think You Are)* opening on successive nights. However, rising costs and increasing misunderstanding between artists and management brought about an irreparable rift. Nevertheless, the company continued at the Lyceum with occasional residencies in California, Michigan, and Canada. In July 1967 the Ford Foundation made a three-year grant of $900,000 to the APA-Phoenix. This, one of the Ford Foundation's largest ever grants, was intended to guarantee the continued artistic development of the company. However, even with such largesse and with the star appearance of Helen Hayes in George Kelly's *The Show-Off* (which opened in the summer of 1967, was later revived and sent on a national tour in 1968 and 1969), the company experienced increasing debt that reached over $1 million in 1969.

The final chapter of the story of the APA-Phoenix was written as the 1968–69 season came to a close. In New York the repertory consisted of four plays: T. S. Eliot's *The Cocktail Party*, Molière's *The Misanthrope*, Sean O'Casey's *Cock-a-Doodle Dandy*, and *Hamlet*. Of these, only *The Misanthrope*, directed by Stephen Porter, with Brian Bedford, Richard Easton, and Christina Pickles, was a critical success. *Hamlet* was an afterthought presented in a black box setting. Rabb both directed and acted in this, the last new production of the company, and it was a critical failure. Rabb, speaking for the APA, agreed to complete the third year (1968–69) of the Ford grant with the Phoenix, but he was unwilling to continue with the Phoenix beyond that. The board of directors of the Phoenix Theatre was unwilling to underwrite another season at the Lyceum, so, on April 26, 1969, the curtain came down on *The Misanthrope* and with it came the end of the merger of the APA and the Phoenix Theatre.

The APA continued independently for one more fall season in Ann Arbor. One of its productions there, Noel Coward's *Private Lives*, starring Brian Bedford and Tammy Grimes, was brought to New York by producer David Merrick. The close of *Private Lives* in 1970 marked the demise of the APA. The Phoenix continued independently, mounting first a production of Mary Chase's *Harvey*, with Jimmy Stewart and Helen Hayes, and then several more classic and new plays.

The APA and the Phoenix had a considerable impact on the American theatre from 1960 to 1969. The APA and the APA-Phoenix had mounted more than forty major productions, each production part of a revolving repertory. More than 300 actors were employed for lengths of time varying from a few weeks to ten years. They established, for almost two years, continuous revolving repertory in New York and in other sites, and they played on Broadway for almost five years, becoming the first repertory company to do such a thing in more than thirty years. They attracted substantial grants, and in so doing they helped to establish the principle that such enterprises had to be subsidized in order to survive. They also revived major classics of the American theatre and lesser known works of important European dramatists.

PERSONNEL

Management: Ellis Rabb, artistic director (1960–69); Robert Gold, APA manager (1960–65); T. Edward Hambleton, managing director (1965–69); Norman Kean, general manager (1965–69); Marilyn Miller, assistant general manager (1965–69).

Scenic Technicians: James Tilton, scene and lighting design (1965–69); Nancy Potts, costumer (1965–69).

Stage Directors: Richard Baldridge (1962–63), Vinette Carrol (1966), John Houseman (1966–67), Eva Le Gallienne (1962, 1968), *Stephen Porter* (1960–69), *Ellis Rabb* (1960–69), Alan Schneider (1965).

Actors and Actresses: Philip Andrus, *Tucker Ashworth* (1960–62), Edward Asner, Claribel Baird, Laurinda Barrett, Louis Beachner, Brian Bedford, *Joseph Bird* (1963–68), Ronald Bishop, Rod Bladel, Barry Bostwick, Alan Brasington, Donald Briscoe, Jacqueline Brooks, Geoffry Brown, Kermit Brown, Edward Cambria, Peter Coffield, Olivia Cole, *Patricia Conolly* (1965, 1967–68), *Clayton Corzatte* (1962–65, 1967–68), Paddy Croft, Chase Crosley, *Keene Curtis* (1960–65, 1967–68), Anita Dangler, Edward D'Arms, Thayer David, Jack Dodson, Peter Donat, Gwyda Donhowe, Ralph Drischell, Olive Dunbar, Michael Durrell, *Richard Easton* (1960–61, 1967–68), Michael Ebert, Robert Einenkel, Morris Erby, Jan Farrand, Jonathon Farwell, Edward Flanders, Michael Forest, Ann Francine, Alan Fudge, Ellen Geer, Kate Geer, *Will Geer* (1961–63, 1967), Robert Gold, Russell Gold, Jim Goldsmith, *Gordon Gould* (1963–65, 1967), James Greene, Esther Gregory, Evelyn Gregory, Tammy Grimes, George Grizzard, Edward Grover, Jane Groves, Uta Hagen, Jennifer Harmon, Adrienne Harris, *Rosemary Harris* (1960–65), Brooke Harrow, Claude Harz, Helen Hayes, Betty Hellman, Katherine Helmond, David Hooks (1960–62), Cavada Humphrey, Tom Jennings, Page Johnson, Richard Jordan, William Kerr, Joel Kramer, William Larsen, Louise Latham, Eva Le Gallienne, Peter Levin, Amy Levitt, Diane Linders, Larry Linville, Laurence Luckenbill, Robert Lumish, Jane McArthur, Michael McCarthy, Jack McQuiggan, Nancy McQuiggan, *John Macunovich* (1963–64), *Nancy Marchand* (1963–64), Enid Markey, *Nicholas Martin* (1960–61, 1965–68), Anne Meacham, Joanna Merlin, Betty Miller, Philip Minor, *Donald Moffat* (1960, 1964–65, 1968), Earl Montgomery, Cathleen Nesbitt, Eulalie Noble, Jack O'Brien, Etain O'Malley, Deborah Packer, John Paoletti, *George Pentecost* (1963–64, 1967–68), *Christina Pickles* (1961, 1964, 1968), Herbert Popper, *Ellis Rabb* (1960–61, 1963–68), John Ragin, Patricia Ripley, Rex Robbins, *Eve Roberts* (1960–61, 1963–64), Joanna Roos, Janet Saltus, Michael Shapiro, Nat Simmons, Drew Snyder, *Paul Sparer* (1960–61, 1964–64), Philip Stamps, Frances Sternhagen, Margot Stevenson, David Stewart, Helen Marie Taylor, James Tripp, *Dee Victor* (1960, 1964–66), Nancy Walker, *Sydney Walker* (1963–65, 1967–68), Paulette Waters, Elizabeth Weil, Mark White, James Whittle, Ralph Williams, *Richard Woods* (1962–65, 1967–68), Pamela Payton Wright, Stephen Wyman, Janet Young.

REPERTORY

1960: City Hall Theatre, Hamilton, Bermuda: *Anatol*, musical version by Arthur Schnitzler and Tom Jones, *Man and Superman, The Sea Gull*. Outdoor Theatre, Hamilton, Bermuda: *The Taming of the Shrew*. Bucks County Playhouse, New Hope, Pennsylvania: *Man and Superman, The Sea Gull, Anatol*. Theatre-by-the Sea, Matunuck, Rhode Island: *Man and Superman, The Sea Gull, Anatol*. John Drew Theatre, East Hampton, L.I.: *Man and Superman, The Sea Gull, Anatol*. McCarter Theatre, Princeton, New Jersey: *Man and Superman, Anatol, The Lady's Not for Burning, Right You Are (If You Think You Are), The Tavern, The Sea Gull, Scapin, Box and Cox, The Cat and the Moon, The Importance of Being Earnest*.

1961: McCarter Theatre, Princeton, New Jersey: *King Lear, A Midsummer Night's Dream, Twelfth Night, As You Like It, Hamlet*. Boston Arts Festival, Boston, Massachusetts: *Twelfth Night, The Tavern*. Highfield Theatre, Falmouth, Massachusetts: *Twelfth Night, The School for Scandal*. Bucks County Playhouse, New Hope, Pennsylvania: *The School for Scandal, The Tavern, Twelfth Night*. John Drew Theatre, East Hampton, L.I.: *The School for Scandal, The Tavern, Twelfth Night, The Sea Gull*. Olney Theatre, Olney, Maryland: *The Tavern, The Sea Gull*. Fred Miller Theatre, Milwaukee, Wisconsin: *A Midsummer Night's Dream, The Sea Gull, The Tavern, The School for Scandal, Fashion*.

1962: Folksbiene Playhouse, New York City: *The School for Scandal, The Sea Gull, The Tavern*. Bucks County Playhouse, New Hope, Pennsylvania: *A Penny for a Song*. John Drew Theatre, East Hampton, L.I.: *A Penny for a Song*. Mendelssohn Theatre, Ann Arbor, Michigan: *The School for Scandal, We Comrades Three, The Tavern, Ghosts, A Penny for a Song*. Michigan Tour: *The School for Scandal, The Tavern*.

1963: Trueblood Theatre, Ann Arbor, Michigan: *A Midsummer Night's Dream, The Merchant of Venice, Richard II*. Michigan Tour: *A Midsummer Night's Dream*. Boston Arts Festival, Boston, Massachusetts: *A Midsummer Night's Dream*. Trueblood Theatre, Ann Arbor, Michigan: *Much Ado About Nothing, A Phoenix Too Frequent, Scapin, Right You Are (If You Think You Are), The Lower Depths*. Michigan Tour: *Much Ado About Nothing*.

1964–65: Phoenix Theatre, New York City: *Right You Are If You Think You Are), The Tavern, Scapin, Impromptu at Versailles, The Lower Depths*. Boston Arts Festival, Boston, Massachusetts: *Scapin, Impromptu at Versailles*. Mendelssohn Theatre, Ann Arbor, Michigan: *War and Peace, The Hostage, Judith, Man and Superman*. Michigan Tour: *Man and Superman*. Phoenix Theatre, New York City: *Man and Superman, War and Peace, Judith*.

1965–66: Mendelssohn Theatre, Ann Arbor, Michigan: *You Can't Take It with You, The Wild Duck, Herakles, Krapp's Last Tape*. Lyceum Theatre, New York City: *You Can't Take It with You*. Huntington Hartford Theatre, Los Angeles, California: *You Can't Take It with You, The School for Scandal, Right You Are (If You Think You Are)*. Greek Theatre, Los Angeles, California: *War and Peace*.

1966–67: Mendelssohn Theatre, Ann Arbor, Michigan: *The School for Scandal, Escurial, Sweet of You to Say So, The Cat and the Moon, Right You Are (If You Think You Are), We Comrades Three, The Flies*. Royal Alexandra Theatre, Toronto, Canada: *We Comrades Three, The Wild Duck, The School for Scandal*. Lyceum Theatre, New York City: *The School for Scandal, Right You Are (If You Think You Are), We Comrades Three, The Wild Duck, You Can't Take It with You, War and Peace*. Huntington Hartford Theatre, Los Angeles, California: *The Wild Duck, Right You Are (If You Think You Are), The Show-Off, Pantagleize, The King Dies* (called *Exit the King* after this engagement).

1967–68: Mendelssohn Theatre, Ann Arbor, Michigan: *Pantagleize, You Can't Take It with You, Right You Are (If You Think You Are), Exit the King, The Show-Off.* Theatre Maison Neuve, Montreal, Canada: *You Can't Take It with You, Right You Are (If You Think You Are).* Royal Alexandra Theatre, Toronto, Canada: *You Can't Take It with You, Right You Are (If You Think You Are), Pantagleize, The Show-Off, Exit the King.* Lyceum Theatre, New York City: *Pantagleize, The Show-Off, Exit the King, The Cherry Orchard.* Stanford University, Stanford, California: *Pantagleize, Exit the King, The Show-Off, The Cocktail Party.* Royal Alexandra Theatre, Toronto, Canada: *The Misanthrope, The Cocktail Party.*

1968–69: Lyceum Theatre, New York City: *Pantagleize, The Show-Off.* Mendelssohn Theatre, Ann Arbor, Michigan: *The Misanthrope, Hamlet, Cock-a-Doodle Dandy.* National Tour: *The Show-Off.* Lyceum Theatre, New York City: *The Cocktail Party, The Misanthrope, Cock-a-Doodle Dandy, Hamlet.*

BIBLIOGRAPHY

Published Sources:
Ann Arbor News, 1960–69.
Boston Daily Record, 1961–63.
Boston Globe, 1961.
Boston Herald, 1961–67.
Christian Science Monitor, 1961–69.
Cue, 1960–69.
[New York] *Daily News*, 1962–69.
Detroit Free Press, 1962–69.
Equity News, 1960–69.
Michigan Daily [Ann Arbor], 1962–69.
Nation, 1960–69.
New Republic, 1960–69.
Newsweek, 1960–69.
New York Herald Tribune, 1962–65.
New York Journal American, 1962–65.
New York Post, 1962–69.
New York Times, 1962–69.
New York World Telegram and Sun, 1962–65.
New Yorker, 1962–69.
Philadelphia Inquirer, 1960–68.
Time, 1960–69.
Variety, 1962–69.
Village Voice, 1965–69.
Wall Street Journal, 1964–69.
Women's Wear Daily, 1962–69.

Archival Resource:
New York, New York. New York Public Library. Library and Museum of the Performing Arts. Letters, scrapbooks, reports, playbills of the APA Company, 1960–65, and the APA-Phoenix Repertory Company, 1965–69.

Robert F. Falk

APA-PHOENIX THEATRE See APA (ASSOCIATION OF PRODUCING ARTISTS).

ARENA STAGE, Washington, D.C., was founded in 1950 by Zelda Fichandler, a recent graduate (M.A., Dramatic Art) of George Washington University and her theatre professor, Edward Mangum. Mangum acquired a lease on the Hippodrome Theatre located on Mount Vernon Square, and he and Fichandler raised $15,000 from people who became stockholders in Arena Stage, Inc. They spent $12,000 remodeling the former movie and burlesque house and opened it August 16 with Oliver Goldsmith's eighteenth-century comedy classic, *She Stoops to Conquer.* The founders, influenced by the work of Margo Jones, promoter of "arena" staging, and driven by the need to hold down production costs and use the building efficiently, arranged the Hippodrome's 247 seats on the four sides of a rectangular playing space. Fichandler ran a successful publicity campaign to open the theatre and attracted excellent promotional support from the Washington press. She also helped in the box office, designed sets, which were built in the alley outside the theatre, and directed seven of the seventeen productions of the first season. For this she was paid $65 per week, as was Mangum; a few performers made as much as $55 per week. The company met encouraging but tough criticism, suffered several financial crises and several failed productions, but survived and began to flourish. In the next five years the group mounted fifty-five productions. Mangum resigned in 1952, after appointing Fichandler managing director.

The group's repertoire was a mixture of classics, modern but well-known dramas and comedies, and revivals of Broadway failures deemed worthy of a second chance, such as Edwin Justus Mayer's *Children of Darkness.* Successes at the Hippodrome included *Three Men on a Horse*, by George Abbott and John Cecil Holm, which ran for seventy performances in 1952, John Patrick's *The Hasty Heart*, seen in 1952, and Robert Anderson's *All Summer Long*, seen the next season. Newly appointed artistic director Alan Schneider directed *The Hasty Heart* and *All Summer Long.* Finchandler invited Schneider, a theatre faculty member at Catholic University of America since 1941, to direct Tennessee Williams' *Glass Menagerie* in 1951, and Schneider directed two or more plays a year each of the seventeen years he was associated with Arena Stage. Schneider became one of the foremost directors in the United States, noted especially for his work on plays by Samuel Beckett, Harold Pinter, and Edward Albee.

Strong acting has been a tradition at the Arena Stage. Early performers of note include George Grizzard, a student of Schneider's who performed six roles at Arena Stage between 1950 and 1952. Grizzard made his Broadway debut in 1955 and appeared as Nick in the Broadway production of Edward Albee's *Who's Afraid of Virginia Woolf?* (1962), Schneider directing. Washington, D.C.–born Frances Sternhagen appeared with Arena Stage in 1953–54, had her Broadway debut in 1955, and then went on to a Tony Award–winning appearance in Neil Simon's *The Good Doctor* in 1972. Lester Rawlins was a company member from 1950 to 1955, his first professional engagement of note before his Broadway debut in 1955 and a long career as a classical actor on Broadway, in regional theatres, and on many Shakespeare festival stages.

On July 17, 1955, Arena Stage suspended operations at the Hippodrome while Fichandler searched for a larger theatre. Arena Stage, Inc., also dissolved, and Fichandler formed a new organization of stockholders, Arena Enterprises, Inc. In the summer of 1956 the group acquired a new facility, the Hospitality Hall of the old Christian Heurich Brewing Company in the "Foggy Bottom" section of the District of Columbia. The "Old Vat," as it was called, seated 500 in four tiers of seats around an eighteen-foot-by-twenty-four-foot playing space. A resident company, featuring eight members of Actors' Equity Association, the professional actor's union, opened in Arthur Miller's *A View from the Bridge* on November 7, 1956. Subscription drives at the Hippodrome had failed, but campaigns at the new location were successful. The season of 1957–58 attracted 2,300 subscribers; the next season appealed to 3,300, and the final season at the Old Vat, 1960–61, won the support of 6,400 season ticket buyers. Continued solvency permitted Fichandler to expand her acting company and her support staff. Her husband, Tom, joined the staff as associate producer in 1957; Fichandler added a business manager (Cay Knockey, formerly an actress with the group and for a time Fichandler's personal assistant) and a full-time costumer (Mariana Elliott, who came to Arena Stage after five years with the Barter Theatre*) about the same time.

The repertory (forty-one productions in five seasons) continued to be a substantial mix of older literary drama and new but previously produced works. Productions of little-known and seldom seen plays dotted the calendar, pieces such as Bridget Boland's *The Prisoner* seen in 1956 (and the group's worst commercial failure in its early years). Revivals of plays that had failed in commercial theatres continued as the group produced Denis Cannan's adaptation of Jean Anouilh's *Mademoiselle Colombe*, Ray Lawler's *Summer of the Seventeenth Doll*, *Epitaph for George Dillon*, by John Osborne and Anthony Creighton, and *The Disenchanted*, by Budd Schulberg and Harvey Brett.

In 1959 a grant from the Ford Foundation freed Fichandler from her day-to-day duties to look for funding for a new theatre. F. Cowles Strickland, formerly a theatre professor at Stanford University and cofounder of the Berkshire Playhouse, replaced her as resident director for the 1959–60 season. The Playwright's Program of the Ford Foundation also supported a premiere of Josh Greenfeld's *Clandestine on the Morning Line*.

Resident performers and well-chosen jobbers continued the Arena Stage tradition of good acting. Performers of note included Carnegie Institute of Technology graduate Sada Thompson, who had made her professional debut in 1947 and had appeared with the Henrietta Hayloft Theatre, a Rochester, New York, stock company, and the Barter Theatre. Thompson went on to a productive career at the American Shakespeare Festival, Stratford, Connecticut, at the American Conservatory Theatre*, and on television. Fellow Carnegie Tech graduate William Ball, an accomplished classical actor and founder of the American Conservatory Theatre, bolstered the group in 1957–58. Philip Bosco appeared in twenty roles between 1957 and 1960, these forming but the first chapter in a

significant career as a classical actor with the American Shakespeare Festival
and the Repertory Theatre of Lincoln Center*, New York. Tom Bosley, a 1959
Tony winner in the title role of the musical *Fiorello!* and a familiar face and
voice to viewers of television's *Charley's Angels*, appeared from 1956 to 1958.
Robert Prosky, an Arena Stage mainstay for twenty-four years, appeared first
in 1958, and then became a company regular in 1960. The stock character actor
played over 135 roles with the company, leaving in 1984 to take over the
continuing role of Sergeant Stan Jablonski in television's *Hill Street Blues*.

Supported by steadily competent, occasionally brilliant work by the acting
company, and sustained by steady patronage at the box office, the organization
experienced remarkable success in a $850,000 building fund campaign launched
in November 1959. Support from the Twentieth Century Fund, the Old Dominion
Foundation, the Rockefeller Foundation, and many local friends of the theatre
rocketed the fund to $647,500 by March 1960. On October 18, 1960, ground
was broken for a new theatre designed by architect Harry Weese at Sixth Street
and Maine Avenue, an urban renewal site on the riverfront in southwest Washington. Weese's notes for the building, the first theatre in America built expressly
for professionals playing in arena style, suggest a "sober, undecorated, almost
neutral environment, . . . a background for the art, . . . definitely subdued, . . . a
permanent building without commercial overtones, yet alive and responsive to
its public" ("Notes on the Arena Stage Building," unpublished manuscript,
n.d., p. 2). Longtime *Washington Post* critic Richard Coe detected in the building
a "faintly cold, intellectually striving atmosphere," and commentator Joseph
Zeigler found it "an abstract and efficient building without embellishment—an
expression of the mind behind Arena Stage—Zelda Fichandler" (Joseph W.
Zeigler, *Regional Theatre* [New York: Da Capo Press, 1977], p. 37). The playing
space is large, a thirty-foot-by-thirty-six-foot-by-twenty-four-foot neutral cube,
best formed by light, a space in which, Zelda Fichandler has noted, "the audience
feels as if they're viewing a medical operation" (quoted in Susan Lieberman,
"The Right Stuff: Three Decades of Talent at Arena Stage," *Theatre Crafts* 18
[March 1984]: 33).

The company left the warm ambience and the romantic charm of an old,
abandoned brewery and opened their new facility on October 30, 1961, with
Bertolt Brecht's *The Caucasian Chalk Circle*. The building had cost $935,000,
but Arena Stage received an $863,000 Ford Foundation grant allowing them to
occupy their building debt-free and to invest income from ticket sales in production and administration. Subscriptions grew from 9,200 in 1961–62 to 15,600
in 1964–65. Charging a top price of $3.95, the group had average weekly receipts
in 1962–63 of $15,000 when the 811-seat theatre was filled to 90 percent of
capacity. With a break-even point at $11,000 per week, the group prospered,
experiencing the most successful season in its financial history. The Fichandlers
(Tom became a full-time executive director in 1961) continued to attract Ford
Foundation support for actors' salaries, for administrative interns, and for play-

wrights in residence (Herbert Boland in 1962–63 and Shelby Foote in 1963–64). An acting workshop and a production intern program sprang up.

In 1965 Arena Stage established the Living Stage Company, a multiracial, improvisational touring ensemble under the direction of Robert Alexander. In 1986 the Living Stage Company, still directed by Alexander, began its twentieth season of workshops and free performances, mainly for people who have little chance to attend a theatre, the disabled and the incarcerated, for instance. Living Stage material is company developed and commonly interweaves music, poetry, dance, acting, and improvisation into an experience dedicated as much to illuminating the artistic process as to entertaining.

Starting in 1964 Fichandler tried to enrich the group's repertory with the addition of more intellectually complex and emotionally demanding plays such as Brecht's *The Threepenny Opera* and *Galileo*, Ben Jonson's *Volpone*, George Bernard Shaw's *Misalliance, Heartbreak House*, and *Saint Joan*, John Whiting's *The Devils* (a U.S. premiere), and John Arden's *Serjeant Musgrave's Dance*. In 1965–66 subscription sales dipped to about 8,000, just half the previous year's total, as audiences indicated disapproval of the repertory. Fichandler retreated from her enrichment scheme and offered a safer, more familiar season of six plays in 1966–67. Significantly, Arena Stage's second production of Brecht's *Galileo*, celebrating the opening of the group's thirtieth season, was the most heavily attended production in its history up to that time. Subscription sales, the backbone of the earned-income portion of a modern regional theatre's budget, turned up, peaking at 19,000 in 1968–69.

Since 1961 Arena Stage has steadily increased its commitment to the production of new American plays and to U.S. premieres of plays from Great Britain and Europe. The 1967 Arena Stage production of Howard Sackler's *The Great White Hope*, a biographical play about the black boxing champion Jack Johnson, imposed a heavy financial burden during its two-month run, but the piece thrust the company into national view and established that regional theatres could assume a function heretofore reserved for Broadway—developing new plays and new playwrights. The play, produced by Herman Levin, opened on Broadway in 1968 with the Arena Stage director Edwin Sherin, the star of the Washington production, James Earl Jones, and many of the company's performers. It won the Pulitzer Prize. Arthur Kopit's *Indians*, with Stacy Keach, was developed at the Arena Stage but produced on Broadway by others to considerable critical acclaim. Michael Weller's *Moonchildren* followed a similar path.

Since 1961 the Arena Stage acting company has been an artistically resplendent mixture of jobbed-in stars and resident performers in long (fifteen-to twenty-year) and short (two- to three-year) terms of employment. Stanley Anderson came to Arena Stage in 1972, just five years out of college at San Jose State University, after short stints with several regional companies, including the Seattle Repertory Theatre* and the Actors' Theatre of Louisville*. In 1985–86 he was one of the group's most honored, versatile, and durable members. Richard Bauer joined the company in 1966 after graduate theatre studies at Washington,

D.C.'s Catholic University of America (a trait he has in common with many another Arena Stage performer). His wife, Halo Wines, became a company regular in 1972. Other performers who have appeared ten or more years with Arena Stage include Leslie Cass, Terrence Currier, Dorothea Jackson Hammond (who has appeared intermittently with the group since 1950), and Mark Hammer. Stability has also been a significant feature of other parts of the organization: In addition to Zelda Fichandler and Alan Schneider, directors Edwin Sherin, Norman Gevanthor, Martin Fried, David Chambers, Douglas C. Wager, and Garland Wright have made sizeable contributions to the artistry of the company. Designers Marjorie Slaiman, Karl Eigsti, Ming Cho Lee, Santo Loquasto, and Tony Straiges have shaped the costumes and scenic environments of many of the most successful Arena Stage productions.

In 1970 Arena Stage built a new theatre adjoining its nine-year-old facility. David Lloyd Kreeger, a Washington insurance magnate, contributed $250,000 toward the total cost of $1.5 million, the Ford Foundation granted $800,000, while the Old Dominion Foundation, the Eugene and Agnes E. Meyer Foundation, and the Twentieth Century Fund made major contributions. The result was a warm, intimate 514-seat theatre "strikingly different from the Arena. The stage has a back wall and wings. The seats are a lively purple, the carpet a burnished gold, the long curved auditorium wall richly paneled in a brown velour" ("The Kreeger Theatre." Unpublished notes by Harry Weese and Associates, September 1, 1970). The Kreeger opened January 15, 1971, with the U.S. premiere of Peter Barnes' *The Ruling Class*.

Since 1971 Arena Stage has opened two additional performance spaces. In 1975 the Kreeger Theatre basement was converted to a 160-seat space for the development of new plays. It opened January 13, 1976, with Steven Stosny's *Singers* and functioned as intended until the end of the 1978–79 season. Not used for public performances in 1979–80, it emerged in 1980–81 as a 199-seat cabaret featuring Steven Wade in Banjo Dancing. Wade has appeared there regularly through 1986. In 1983 the organization converted another Kreeger Theatre space, formerly a rehearsal hall, then a scenery construction shop, to a 150-seat theatre for the development of new plays and for the presentation of works best served by an intimate room. "The Scene Shop" opened with Emily Mann's *Still Life*.

Writing in 1968, Julius Novick observed that Arena Stage was "materially and artistically" one of the most successful theatres in America (*Beyond Broadway* [New York: Hill and Wang, 1968], p. 40). In some respects its history has paralleled that of the regional theatre movement in the United States; in other respects it is the paragon of that movement. It was the first American resident company to represent the United States in the Soviet Union (1973), the first theatre outside New York to receive an Antoinette Perry (Tony) Award for theatrical excellence (1976), and the first American company to perform at the Hong Kong International Arts Festival (1980). Zelda Fichandler has received the Margo Jones Award for "significant contribution to the dramatic art through the production of new plays," the Brandeis University Creative Arts Citation in Theatre, the Acting Company's John Houseman Award for "commitment and dedication to the development of young American actors," and the 1985 Commonwealth Award for distinguished service to the theatre. Perhaps even more important, Fichandler is one of the best grant writers in the regional theatre movement and "an acknowledged genius of theatrical subsidy" (Zeigler, *Regional Theatre*, p. 35). By 1978 an organization originally budgeted at $800 per week had an annual operating budget of $2.871 million, with attendance in three theatres of 250,000 generating $1.829 million in earned income. The budget for 1980–81 exceeded $4 million at a time when the *Washington Post* noted that "some of Arena's most enterprising productions faced an uncommon number of empty seats" (June 28, 1981, p. K1a). Budgetary pressures have increased in recent years despite extraordinary fund-raising successes. When Arena Stage opened its doors in 1950, the only other professional theatre in town, the National, had just closed its doors. The renovation of Ford's Theatre, the erection of the John F. Kennedy Center for the Performing Arts (with three theatres), the establishment of professional resident theatre companies at the Folger Theatre, the founding of small professional and semiprofessional companies in the District of Columbia and in suburban Maryland, and the renovation of the National Theatre have created intense competition for Arena Stage. Although Arena Stage commonly wins the bulk of critical laurels and remains the foremost theatre in the nation's capital, a future of artistic achievement and financial solvency is by no means assured.

Despite extraordinary success in attracting grants and gifts, small deficits are common. In 1983 the National Endowment for the Arts (NEA) granted $750,000 but required Arena Stage to garner a $3 private gift for every federal dollar granted. Concurrently, Arena Stage hired a not-for-profit fund-raiser to conduct a campaign to establish in two years an endowment fund of $6 million. The campaign was a success. Then, in 1984, Arena Stage received the first installment of a five-year matching grant from NEA to provide year-round employment for the acting ensemble and to expand other artistic resources. At the grant award ceremony, Hugh Southern, NEA deputy chair for programs, referred to Arena Stage as "the flagship theatre of the not-for-profit professional theatre movement" (*Washington Post*, September 6, 1984, p. B1d).

PERSONNEL

Managing Directors: Zelda Fichandler (1952–57), Edward Mangum (1950–52), William Stewart (1985–86).

Producing Directors: Zelda Fichandler (1957–86), Alan Schneider (1973–74).

Associate Producing Directors/Producers: David Chambers (1978–80), Edwin Sherin (1964–69), Douglas C. Wager (1984–86).

Executive Director: Tom Fichandler (1957–85).

Associate Producer: George Touliatos (1974–76).

Directors: Jerry Adler (1971–72), Patrick Adriarte (1977–78), *Robert Alexander* (Children's Theatre and Living Stage Company, 1966–86), Howard Ashman (1980–81), Paul

Austin (1972–73), Vernel Bagneris (1980–81), William Ball (1958–59), Jeff Bleckner (1971–72), Lee Breuer (1983–84), Edward Payson Call (1974–77), Lawrence Carra (1953–54), Jacques Cartier (1983–84), *David Chambers* (1975–83), *Liviu Ciulei* (1973–74, 1976–80), Edward J. Cornell (1978–79), J. Robert Dietz (1954–55, 1956–57), John Dillon (1973–76), Donald Driver (1971–72), Susan Einhorn (1977–78), Warren Enters (1957–58, 1961–62, 1963–64), *Zelda Fichandler* (1950–61, 1969–70, 1972–73, 1974–76, 1977–78, 1981–84), Aaron Frankel (1953–54), Gene Frankel (1968–69, 1970–71), *Martin Fried* (1975–78, 1980–82), *Norman Gevanthor* (1969–74, 1975–77), Thomas Gruenewald (1976–77), Charles Haid (1973–74), Iza Itkin (1956–57), Walton Jones (1978–79), Milton Katselas (1966–67), Hy Kalus (1966–67), Lawrence Kornfeld (1972–73), Ron Lagomarsino (1980–81), Basil Langton (1952–53), Sheldon Larry (1978–79), Michael Lessac (1979–80), Gene Lesser (1971–72, 1974–76, 1980–81), Richard Maltby, Jr. (1977–78), *Edward Mangum* (1950–52), Christopher Markle (1984–85), Marshall W. Mason (1977–78), Tom Moore (1975–76), Donald Moreland (1967–69), Gilbert Moses (1969–71, 1982–83), Earl Mowery (1951–52), James Nicola (1982–83, 1985–86), Sharon Ott (1985–86), Edward Parone (1965–66), John Pasquin (1975–76), Gary Pearle (1978–80, 1982–84), Lucian Pintilie (1984–86), Robert Prosky (1978–81), Richard Russell Ramos (1978–79, 1980–81, 1983–84), Elinor Renfield (1984–86), Steven Robman (1977–78), Alfred Ryder (1968–70), Amy Saltz (1984–85), *Alan Schneider* (1950–54, 1956–63, 1971–73, 1974–77, 1978–79), Carl Shain (1953–54), Mel Shapiro (1970–71), *Edwin Sherin* (1963–69), George L. Sherman (1963–64), Elliot Silverstein (1954–55), Harold Stone (1967–68), *F. Cowles Strickland* (1959–62), Elizabeth Swados (1977–78), Horacena J. Taylor (1978–79), Joan Vail (1954–55), Nina Vance (1962–63), *Douglas C. Wager* (1975–86), Carl Weber (1973–75), David William (1966–67, 1970–71), *Garland Wright* (1981–86).

Costumiere: *Marjorie Slaiman* (1966–86).

Costume Designers: Jared Aswegan (1984–85), Miruna Boruzescu (1984–86), Noel Broden (1981–83, 1985–86), Zack Brown (1976–77), Kate Carmel (1977–78), Rebecca Carroll (1977–78), Marie Ann Chiment (1981–83), Liviu Ciulei (1973–74), *Gwynne Clark* (1970–76), Jo Ann Clevenger (1980–81), John Conklin (1968–69, 1971–72), Laura Crow (1977–78, 1983–84), *Mariana Elliott* (1957–65), *Linda Fisher* (1969–77), Sandra Yen Fong (1980–81), Jess Goldstein (1978–79), Bruce Harrow (1973–74), Judith Haugan (1966–67), Desmond Heeley (1979–80), Anne Hould-Ward (1981–84, 1985–86), Ghretta Hynd (1984–85), Georgianna Jordan (1971–72), William Ivey Long (1978–79), Santo Loquasto (1977–78), Carol Luiken (1975–76), Jennifer von Mayrhauser (1976–77), Carol Odetz (1979–80), Martin Pakledinaz (1985–86), Alvin Perry (1978–79), Nancy Potts, (1966–67), *Mary Anne Powell* (1979–85), Dunya Ramicova (1978–79), Leigh Rand (1967–68), Sheila Roman (1977–78).

Scenic Designers: *John Arnone* (1981–86), Laurence E. Bahler (1958–59, 1963–64), David R. Ballou (1970–72), John Lee Beatty (1975–76, 1977–78), Robert Bookatz (1962–63), Radu Boruzescu (1984–86), Zack Brown (1976–77, 1978–79, 1981–83), Lloyd Burlingame (1954–55), Liviu Ciulei (1973–74), Albert Colbath (1951–52), John Conklin (1968–69, 1970–73), Robert Conley (1956–57), Curtiss Cowan (1959–61), Sally Cunningham (1976–78), Bill H. Demos (1960–61), *Karl Eigsti* (1964–66, 1973–84), Jules Fisher (1966–67), John Raymond Freiman (1961–62), Robert Green (1962–63), David Lloyd Gropman (1978–79), Judith Haugan (1966–67), Desmond Heeley (1979–80), Al Hurwitz (1951–52), David Jenkins (1972–75, 1983–85), Marjorie Kellogg (1973–74), Leo Kerz (1969–71), Mesrop Kesdekian (1957–59), Heidi Landesman (1981–83), Grady

Larkins (1975–77), Eugene Lee (1970–71), *Ming Cho Lee* (1966–68, 1970–71, 1972–76, 1977–79, 1981–83, 1984–85), Hugh Lester (1971–72, 1978–79), *Adrianne Lobel* (1980–83, 1984–86), *Santo Loquasto* (1970–73, 1975–78, 1979–80), Kert Lundell (1968–69), Thomas Lynch (1979–84, 1985–86), Russell Metheny (1985–86), Vera Mowry (1950–51), Dick Nelson (1957–58), Franne Newman (1970–71), Christopher Nowack (1977–78), Alexander Okun (1983–84), Rick Paul (1971–72), Lance Pennington (1980–81), Vincent Piacentini, Jr. (1963–64), William Ritman (1971–72, 1978–79), Nicholas Russiyan (1967–68), Douglas W. Schmidt (1967–68), Kenneth Scollon (1950–51; 1954–55), Loren Sherman (1984–85), Jane Stanhope (1951–52), Douglas O. Stein (1985–86), Robert Burns Stevens (1951–52), Walter Stilley (1952–53), *Tony Straiges* (1976–84, 1985–86), Robert U. Taylor (1972–73), Wynn Thomas (1978–79), Robin Wagner (1965–68, 1969–70), James Waring (1950–51), Peter Wingate (1961–62), Patricia Woodbridge (1977–78, 1984–85), Alison Yerxa (1984–85), Robert Yodice (1978–79), Marshall Yokelson (1952–53).

Lighting Designers: Julie Archer (1984–85), Frances Aronson (1983–86), Liviu Ciulei (1973–74), Robert Crawley (1975–77), William Eggleston (1966–70, 1973–74), Beverly Emmons (1984–86), *Arden Fingerhut* (1973–74, 1979–84), *Leo Gallenstein* (1950–68), Paul Gallo (1983–86), Henry R. Gorfein (1971–72), *Allen Lee Hughes* (1975–76, 1979–86), *Hugh Lester* (1970–71, 1972–79, 1980–83), Roger Milliken (1978–79), *William Mintzer* (1972–84), John J. Mulligan (1977–78), Nora Pepper (1973–74), Shirley Prendergast (1978–79), *Nancy Schertler* (1980–86), Duane Schuler (1979–80), Vance Sorrells (1970–73), Cheryl Thacker (1977–78), Lee Watson (1970–71).

Music Composers: Norman L. Berman (1977–78), Nick Bicat (1979–80, 1985–86), Robert Dennis (1974–78, 1979–80), Tim Eyermann (1978–79), John Gray (1979–80), Alan Laing (1974–75), John McKinney (1978–79, 1985–86), Mel Marvin (1976–80), Richard Peaslee (1974–75), David Shire (1977–78), Elizabeth Swados (1977–78), Stanley Walden (1977–78).

Choreographers: B. H. Barry (1977–78), Virginia Freeman (1978–79), Mary Kyte (1978–79, 1980–81), Ethel Martin (1977–78), Theodore Pappas (1982–83), Tommie Walsh (1978–79).

Musical Directors: Robert Fisher (1982–84), David Loud (1985–86), John McKinney (1982–84), Mel Marvin (1973–74, 1982–83), Steven Ross (1974–75), Eric Stern (1980–81).

Technical Directors: David M. Glenn (198?–85), Henry R. Gorfein (1974–86).

Playwrights in Residence: Herbert Boland (1962–63), Conrad Bromberg (1965–66), Shelby Foote (1963–64).

Actors and Actresses: Dan Ahearn (1969–71), *Jane Alexander* (1965–68, 1970–71), Lyn Alstad (1958–59), Maureen Anderman (1971–72), *Stanley Anderson* (1972–86), Joan Van Ark (1963–64), Dimitra Arliss (1968–69), *Rene Auberjonois* (1962–65), William Ball (1957–58), Joyce Ballowy (1958–59), *Richard Bauer* (1966–86), *Gary Bayer* (1971–77), Art Beatty (1970–71), *Ned Beatty* (1963–65, 1967–70), Mary Bell (1962–63), Doris Belock (1964–65), *Harry Bergman* (1958–64), Casey Biggs (1985–86), *Philip Bosco* (1958–60), *Tom Bosley* (1956–58), *James Bostain* (1961–63), Tom Brannum (1963–64), *Damon Brazwell* (1965–67), Conrad Bromberg (1966–67), Roscoe Lee Browne (1962–63), Geneva Bugbee (1962–63), *Yusef Bulos* (1968–70), Joe Bunner (1959–60), Adolph Caesar (1966–67), Laura Campbell (1968–69), Kathleen Carothers (1962–63), Anna Carparelli (1967–68), *Marie Carroll* (1961–63, 1964–65), *Ethel Casey* (1950–52, 1954–55, 1956–60), *Marilyn Caskey* (1982–85), *Leslie Cass* (1970–82), *Anne*

Chodoff (1950–52, 1954–55, 1956–57, 1961–62), Leonardo Cimino (1977–78), *Kendall Clark* (1961–63), *Jeannette Clift* (1958–60), *Alan Coates* (later *Alan Oppenheimer*) (1954–55, 1957–63, 1964–65), Joel Colodner (1977–78), *David Congdon* (1965–68), Albert Corbin (1950–51, 1970–71), Clayton Corzatte (1957–58), Ralph Cosham (1985–86), Veronica Costang (1977–78), *Nicholas Coster* (1957–59), *Ronny Cox* (1963–66, 1967–69), Shirley Cox (1961–62), Darryl Croxton (1968–69), *Terrence Currier* (1972–83, 1984–86), *Henry Danilowicz* (1950–51, 1952–54), Randy Danson (1985–86), Jennifer Darling (1966–67), *David Darlow* (1968–70), *Ted D'Arms* (1964–66), Sefton Darr (1956–57), Donald Davis (1960–61), Humphrey Davis (1969–70), Anne Diamond (1959–60), *J. Robert Dietz* (1954–55, 1956–57, 1960–64), Melinda Dillon (1961–62, 1968), Richard Dix (1966–67), *Gywda Donhowe* (1959–61, 1963–64), *Kevin Donovan* (1982–84), Judith Doty (1960–61), Tony Dowling (1958–59), Jacqueline Dudley (1950–51), Pamela Dunlap (1969–70), John Dutra (1960–61), *George Ebeling* (1963–67, 1972–73), Joyce Ebert (1959–60), *Louis Edmonds* (1957–59), Ronnie Clair Edwards (1960–61), Heather Ehlers (1985–86), Jill Eikenberry (1970–72), Elizabeth Eis (1966–67), Dana Elcar (1957–58, 1965), Tom Ellis (1957–58), Robert Elston (1958–59), *Morris Engle* (1968–72), Christine Estabrook (1977–78), Michael Fairman (1970–71), Mary Farrell (1953–54), *Jonathan Farwell* (1962–64), Zelda Fichandler (1951–52), Pauline Flannigan (1957–58), Jay Fletcher (1968–69), *Robert Foxworth* (1965–68), Richard Frank (1978–79), Carl Mikal Franklin (1971–72), Orville French (1950–51), David Garrison (1976–77), John Gegenhaber (1985–86), Lou Gilbert (1963–64, 1967–68), Joseph Gistirak (1952–53), Russell Gold (1960–61), Sarah Gorham (1967–68), *Grayce Grant* (1966–72), Ernest Graves (1979–81), *George Grizzard* (1950–54), Gene Gross (1956–57, 1972–73), Carol Gustafson (1969–70), Clay Hall (1952–53), Frank Hamilton (1952–53), *Mark Hammer* (1973–86), *Dorothea Jackson Hammond* (1950–53, 1956–58, 1959–60, 1962–63, 1965–66, 1969–76, 1985–86), William Hansen (1969–70), Jerry Harden (1956–57, 1958–59), Margot Hartman (1956–57), James Harwood (1956–57), Hurd Hatfield (1963–64), Martha Henry (1966–67), Edward Herrmann (1971–72), Tom Hewitt (1983–84, 1985–86), Burton Heyman (1967–69), Tana Hicken (1967–68, 1985–86), *Michael Higgins* (1954–55, 1956–57, 1966–67), Thomas Hill (1952–53), Richard G. Holmes (1967–68), David Hurst (1961–62), Craig Jackson (1961–62), *Charles Janasz* (1980–84), Leon Janney (1959–60), Bella Jarrett (1962–64), Zena Jasper (1970–72), Jerry Jedd (1956–57), *Analee Jeffries* (1978–81), James Jenner (1978–80), Timothy Jerome (1979–80), *Allen Joseph* (1953–55, 1956–58), Stephen Joyce (1961–62, 1965–66), Katherine Justice (1964–65), Jim Kelly (1959–60), Laurie Kennedy (1976–77), *James Kenny* (1964–69), Gerry Kiken (1953–55), Jerome Kilty (1954–55), Hilary Knapp (1952–53), Trent Knepper (1954–55, 1960–61), Marion Kraczmar (1950–51), Mara Lane (1964–65, 1966–67), William Larson (1966–67), Louise Latham (1957–59), Elizabeth Lawrence (1963–64), Jean LeBouvier (1961–62), John Leonard (1984–86), Barbara Lester (1958–59), Michael Lewis (1970–71), Judith Long (1972–74), Richard Longman (1957–58), Melissa Loving (1965–67), Michael Lyston (1958–60), Macon McCalman (1971–72), Bill McGuire (1950–51), Christopher McHale (1978–79), Richard McKenzie (1967–68), Ronald McLarty (1971–72), Emily McLaughlin (1954–55), Gloria Maddox (1969–70), Valerie Mamches (1966–67), Mary Mangum (1950–51), Maurine Marlowe (1960–61), John Marriott (1969–70, 1972–75), *Gaylord Mason* (1957–60), *Anne Meacham* (1954–55, 1956–57, 1959–60), John Megna (1962–63), Eda Reiss Merin (1962–63, 1969–70), Joanne Merlin (1963–64), *Michael Mertz* (1973–77), Robert Miller (1960–61), Skedge Miller (1958–59), *Christina Moore* (1978–84), Marion Morris (1958–61), Richard Morse (1952–53), Frank

Muller (1978–79), William Myers (1972–73), Tania Myren (1976–77), Henry Oliver (1950–52), *Joe Palmieri* (1978–81, 1982–84), Joan Pape (1975–76), Robert Pastene (1972–73), Angela Paton (1951–52), Jeanne Paynter (1964–65), Brock Peters (1962–63), Kelly Jean Peters (1962–63), Lauri Peters (1965–66), Miriam Phillips (1961–62), Phyllis Phillips (1952–53), *Stanley Pitts* (1951–54), Ray Poole (1951–52), *Robert Prosky* (1960–84), Robert Quarry (1961–62), Thomas Quinn (1985–86), Douglas Rain (1966–67), *Lester Rawlins* (1951–57), Marion Reardon (1952–54), *Ray Reinhardt* (1961–64), George Reinholt (1965–67), Anne Revere (1962–63), *Pernell Roberts* (1950–52), Mark Robinson (1971–72), John Rodney (1952–53), Ed Rombola (1968–69), Roberta Royce (1960–61), Jack Ryland (1965–66), Jay O. Sanders (1976–77), *Richard Sanders* (1969–73), Janet Sarno (1965–66), Garrett Saunders (1968–69), Roy Scheider (1962–63), Jane Schmidt (1950–51), Walter (or Warner) Schreiner (1950–52), James Secrest (1960–61), Toni Seitz (1964–65), Anna Shaler (1967–68), William Shust (1960–61), Jane Singer (1963–64), Marion Sittler (1950–51), Lisa Sloan (1976–77), Donegan Smith (1970–72), Barbara Sohmers (1978–80), Phyllis Somerville (1968–70, 1971–72), *Cary Anne Spear* (1978–80, 1985–86), Kim Staunton (1985–86), Gordon Sterne (1950–51), Frances Sternhagen (1952–53), *Henry Strozier* (1982–86), Inga Swenson (1962–63), Dick Sykes (1953–54), Glenn Taylor (1972–73), Carol Teitel (1958–59), Dell Tenney (1956–57), Sada Thompson (1956–57), James Tolkan (1976–77), Tom Toner (1962–64), John Madden Towey (1977–78), Kathryn Tracy (1966–67), Michael Tucker (1970–71), *Richard Venture* (1965–69), Jon Voight (1965–66), Howard Weirum (1960–61), *Bruce Weitz* (1970–72, 1974–75), *Dianne Wiest* (1972–77), *Astrid Wilsrud* (1957–60), *Halo Wines* (1972–86), *Howard Witt* (1968–77), Eugene R. Wood (1967–68), George Wright (1966–67), *Max Wright* (1967–68, 1969–70, 1971–76), Wendell Wright, Jr. (1972–74), John Wylie (1978–79), Edward Zang (1963–64), Iona Zelenka (1950–51), *Anthony Zerbe* (1963–65).

REPERTORY

1950–51: *She Stoops to Conquer, Of Mice and Men, The Firebrand, The Delectable Judge, The Taming of the Shrew, Pygmalion, Alice in Wonderland, The Playboy of the Western World, Children of Darkness, The Adding Machine, The School for Wives, The Inspector General, The Glass Menagerie, Mr. Arcularis, Twelfth Night, The Scarecrow, The Importance of Being Earnest.*

1951–52: *Julius Caesar, She Stoops to Conquer, Ladder to the Moon, Burning Bright, Twelfth Night, The School for Scandal, Three Men on a Horse, Dark of the Moon, The Importance of Being Earnest, The Hasty Heart.*

1952–53: *Desire Under the Elms, Tonight at 8:30* (a bill of one-act plays, including *Fumed Oak, Ways and Means*, and *Still Life*), *Lady Precious Stream, All Summer Long, The Country Wife, Our Town, Arms and the Man, The Country Girl, Boy Meets Girl, My Heart's in the Highlands.*

1953–54: *Two Plays* (a bill of short plays, including *A Phoenix Too Frequent* and *The Happy Journey*), *The Bad Angel, Thieves' Carnival, Charley's Aunt, Ah, Wilderness!, Summer and Smoke, Blithe Spirit, The Cretan Woman, All My Sons, Room Service.*

1954–55: *The Crucible, Androcles and the Lion, Golden Boy, The Miser, The World of Sholom Aleichem* (including *A Tale of Chelm, Bontche Schweig*, and *The High School*), *Rain, The Mousetrap.*

1955–56: Dark.

1956–57: *A View from the Bridge, Tartuffe, The Prisoner, The Girl on the Via Flaminia, Dream Girl, Three Plays* (a bill of short plays, including *Bedtime Story, Portrait of a Madonna*, and *Man of Destiny), The Three Sisters, Witness for the Prosecution.*

1957–58: *The Doctor's Dilemma, Answered the Flute, Brother Rat, Juno and the Paycock, Pictures in the Hallway, Two Plays* (a bill of short plays, including *Apollo* and *The Browning Version), Romeo and Juliet, Mademoiselle Colombe, Summer of the Seventeenth Doll.*

1958–59: *The Front Page, Three Plays* (a bill of short plays, including *Once Around the Block, The Purification*, and *A Memory of Two Mondays), The Hollow, The Devil's Disciple, A Month in the Country, The Plough and the Stars, The Lady's Not for Burning, Epitaph for George Dillon.*

1959–60: *Major Barbara, Clandestine on the Morning Line, Three Men on a Horse, The Cherry Orchard, The Caine Mutiny Court Martial, The Iceman Cometh, Ring Round the Moon, The Disenchanted.*

1960–61: *The Gang's All Here, The Egg, The Rivals, Six Characters in Search of an Author, Silent Night, Lonely Night, Tiger at the Gates, Three Plays* (a bill of short plays, including *Krapp's Last Tape, The End of the Beginning*, and *In the Zone), Man and Superman.*

1961–62: *The Caucasian Chalk Circle, Two Plays* (a bill of short plays including *The American Dream* and *What Shall We Tell Caroline), The Madwoman of Chaillot, The Moon in the Yellow River, Misalliance, The Burning of the Lepers, Uncle Vanya, The Time of Your Life.*

1962–63: *Once in a Lifetime, Under Milk Wood, Volpone, Twelve Angry Men, The Hostage, All the Way Home, Othello, The Threepenny Opera.*

1963–64: *The Devils, Battle Dream, Hotel Paradiso, The Wall, The Affair, The Taming of the Shrew, Enrico IV, Dark of the Moon.*

1964–65: *Galileo, The Rehearsal, Billy Budd, Heartbreak House, He Who Gets Slapped, Long Day's Journey into Night, Two Plays* (a bill of short plays, including *The Lonesome Train* and *Hard Travelin'), Spoon River Anthology.*

1965–66: *Saint Joan, The Skin of Our Teeth, Project Immortality, The Three Sisters, Serjeant Musgrave's Dance, Three Plays* (a bill of short plays, including *Mr. Welk and Jersey Jim, The Lesson*, and *The Collection), Oh What a Lovely War.*

1966–67: *Macbeth, The Magistrate, The Crucible, The Inspector General, Look Back in Anger, The Andersonville Trial.*

1967–68: *Major Barbara, Poor Bitos, The Great White Hope, The Blood Knot, The Tenth Man, Room Service, The Iceman Cometh.*

1968–69: *The Threepenny Opera, Six Characters in Search of an Author, King Lear, The Persecution and Assassination of Jean-Paul Marat as Performed by the Inmates of the Asylum of Charenton Under the Direction of the Marquis de Sade, Indians, The Cage, Jacques Brel Is Alive and Well and Living in Paris.*

1969–70: *Edith Stein, You Can't Take It with You, The Cherry Orchard, The Chemmy Circle, Two Plays* (a bill of short plays, including *Enchanted Night* and *The Police), Dance of Death, No Place to Be Somebody.*

1970–71: *The Night Thoreau Spent in Jail, Mother Courage, The Ruling Class, Jack MacGowran in the Works of Samuel Beckett, Pueblo, Wipe-Out Games, Awake and Sing!, What the Butler Saw, The Sign in Sidney Brustein's Window.*

1971–72: *Pantagleize, Moonchildren, Twelfth Night, The House of Blue Leaves, A Conflict of Interest, Uptight, Status Quo Vadis, Tricks.*

1972–73: *I Am a Woman, The Hostage, The Foursome, Our Town, A Public Prosecutor Is Sick of It All, A Look at the Fifties, Enemies, One Flew over the Cuckoo's Nest, Raisin.*

1973–74: *Two by Samuel Beckett: Krapp's Last Tape* and *Not I, Our Town, Inherit the Wind, Tom, Three Men on a Horse, The Resistible Rise of Arturo Ui, Leonce and Lena, The Madness of God, Two Plays in Repertory: In Celebration* and *Relatively Speaking, Horatio.*

1974–75: *Death of a Salesman, Who's Afraid of Virginia Woolf?, Boccaccio, The Front Page, Julius Caesar, The Last Meeting of the Knights of the White Magnolia, The Dybbuk, The Ascent of Mount Fuji, Sizwe Bansi Is Dead* and *The Island.*

1975–76: *Long Day's Journey into Night, An Enemy of the People, Once in a Lifetime, Emlyn Williams as Charles Dickens, The Tot Family, Heartbreak House, What the Babe Said* and *Total Recall, Madmen, Waiting for Godot, Busy Dyin', Dandelion Wine;* an "All-American Repertory," including *Death of a Salesman, The Front Page,* and *Our Town.*

1976–77: *Saint Joan, Emlyn Williams' Dylan Thomas Growing Up, Saturday, Sunday, Monday,* a bill of short plays by Samuel Beckett: *Play, That Time,* and *Footfalls, Streamers, Singers, Three Plays* (a bill of short plays, including *Porch, Scooping,* and *Exhibition), The Autumn Garden, Living at Home, Catsplay, The Lower Depths, A History of American Film.*

1977–78: *Nightclub Cantata, The National Health, Starting Here, Starting Now, The Caucasian Chalk Circle, Comedians, A Streetcar Named Desire, Hamlet, Gemini, Separations, Duck Hunting, The Desert Dwellers, Trappers.*

1978–79: *Tales from the Vienna Woods, The 1940's Radio Hour, The Past, Disability, Casualties, Ah, Wilderness!, Curse of the Starving Class, Tintypes, Loose Ends, Don Juan, Nevis Mountain Dew, Idiot's Delight.*

1979–80: *The Winter's Tale, Tiebele and Her Demon, Design for Living, You Can't Take It with You, After the Fall, Billy Bishop Goes to War, Plenty, Emigres, An American Tragedy.*

1980–81: *The Flying Karamazov Brothers, Gertrude Stein Gertrude Stein Gertrude Stein, Galileo, One Mo' Time, The Man Who Came to Dinner, The Suicide, The Carousel of New Plays* (presented in rotating repertory: *Disability: A Comedy, The Child,* and *Cold Storage), Kean, God Bless You, Mr. Rosewater, American Buffalo, Pantomime.*

1981–82: *Major Barbara, A Lesson from Aloes, A Midsummer Night's Dream, Tomfoolery, A Delicate Balance, Undiscovered Country, K2, Animal Crackers.*

1982–83: *Home, On the Razzle, Cymbeline, The Imaginary Invalid, Screenplay, Geniuses, Buried Child, Candida, Still Life.*

1983–84: *The Importance of Being Earnest, Beyond Therapy, As You Like It, The Three Sisters, Accidental Death of an Anarchist, Quartermaine's Terms, Cloud 9, Happy End.*

1984–85: *The Tempest, The Gospel at Colonus, Passion Play, Man and Superman, Tartuffe, Isn't It Romantic, Execution of Justice, Real Estate.*

1985–86: *The Good Person of Setzuan, 'night, Mother, Women and Water, Restoration, The Wild Duck, The Philadelphia Story, The Taming of the Shrew.*

BIBLIOGRAPHY

Published Sources:
American Theatre, 1984–86.
Theatre Communications, 1980–84.

Washington Post, 1974–86.

Best Plays, 1973–74 through *1985–86*. New York: Dodd, Mead, & Co, 1974–86.

Lieberman, Susan. "The Right Stuff: Three Decades of Talent at Arena Stage." *Theatre Crafts* 18 (March 1984): 28–33, 52–54.

Novick, Julius. *Beyond Broadway: The Quest for Permanent Theatres*. New York: Hill and Wang, 1968.

Schneider, Alan. *Entrances: An American Director's Journey*. New York: Viking Penguin, 1986.

Theatre Profiles, Vols. 1–7. New York: Theatre Communications Group, 1973–85.

Theatre World, 1973–74 through *1985–86*. New York: Crown Publishers, 1974–86.

Zeigler, Joseph W. *Regional Theatre: The Revolutionary Stage*. New York: Da Capo Press, 1977.

Unpublished Sources:

Coyne, Bernard A. "A History of the Arena Stage, Washington, D.C." Doctoral dissertation, Tulane University, 1964.

Playbill Collection of the Theatre Communications Group (Microfiche) includes programs from 1957 to 1975.

Weese, Harry. "Notes on the Arena Stage Building." Mimeographed, Harry Weese and Associates, Architects and Engineers, Chicago, Illinois, n.d.

————. "The Kreeger Theatre." Mimeographed, Harry Weese and Associates, Architects and Engineers, Chicago, Illinois, September 1, 1970.

Weldon B. Durham

ARIZONA CIVIC THEATRE. See ARIZONA THEATRE COMPANY.

[THE] ARIZONA THEATRE COMPANY, then the Arizona Civic Theatre, began its first season in rented space at the Santa Rita Hotel in Tucson in 1967. With a budget of only about $4,000 and a dream to "establish quality professional theatre for the people of Arizona," the company presented an ambitious season of eleven productions in 1967–68 under the artistic direction of Sandy Rosenthal (d. 1986). Despite serious financial problems in its first years, Arizona Civic Theatre pursued an extensive production schedule, rapidly built a loyal following, and in 1971 moved from rented space to a permanent home in the city-built Tucson Community Center Little Theatre. With Rosenthal's leadership, Arizona Civic Theatre achieved professional status in 1972. In 1973 Rosenthal, who until then had continued to hold onto his interior decorating business, assumed his position as artistic director on a full-time basis. The 1976–77 season saw the first performance of an Arizona Civic Theatre production in Tucson (*Vanities* at the Scottsdale Center for the Arts). The company changed its name in 1978 to Arizona Theatre Company (ATC). In 1979 Rosenthal took a leave of absence from the company and was replaced on an interim basis by Mark Lamos. In 1980 Rosenthal retired from the theatre and was replaced on a permanent basis by the current artistic director, Gary Gisselman. One of Gisselman's priorities was to reduce the large debt ATC had incurred during its first thirteen years of operation. With the help of managing director David Hawkanson, Gisselman was able to secure a major Ford Foundation Stabilization Grant, and in 1982 the company became debt-free.

Although ATC had been touring productions to Phoenix since 1976–77, it was not until 1983–84 that all ATC productions were presented in both Tucson, the company's home base, and Phoenix. Although the problems inherent in such a schedule are enormous, ATC remains committed to the idea and seeks permanent performance space in the planned Herberger Theatre Center in Phoenix. In addition, ATC seeks new space in the Tucson Temple of Music and Art in order to meet ticket demands that the Tucson Community Center Little Theatre cannot handle.

The 1986–87 season marked the twentieth anniversary of ATC, an anniversary suggesting that the dreams and visions of the founders were good, and that the support of Arizonans has never waivered. For the anniversary season the theatre chose a season focusing on the American Dream.

Local and national critics have been supportive and positive in their assessment of ATC's progress as an artistic institution, but not all other producers in the state believe that ATC has contributed enough toward the development of local performers. Gary Bacal, director of marketing and public relations for ATC, admits that the nature of ATC's two-city schedule has not allowed it to develop a full company of actors. Although ATC has some semiregular performers, local talent is employed only in small roles. Most ATC performers, especially those in major roles, are jobbed-in on single-play contracts.

Over the years ATC has increased its commitment to public service in Tucson, Phoenix, and the state. Among those services are outreach ticket programs for the handicapped and disadvantaged, preperformance and postperformance lectures and demonstrations, special ticket programs for senior citizens, students, and military personnel, special residency programs (e.g., Childsplay, a professional children's theatre from Phoenix), and the Student Services Program, which includes the School Tour, bringing live theatre to the classroom, and the Student Matinee program.

In addition to its regular-season productions, ATC has instituted a program of staged readings and fully mounted productions to develop new plays. Related to this program but not actually part of it was the theatre's work in the 1986–87 season to develop a new play based on the work of Studs Terkel. The company-developed piece was the last production of the season.

The current budget for the theatre is approximately $2.5 million, 56 percent of which comes from earned income. In 1985–86 ATC employed more than 150 actors, technicians, and administrators. ATC's 250 performances in 1985–86 were attended by more than 110,000 persons—more than 90 percent of capacity.

PERSONNEL

Artistic Directors: Gary Gisselman (1980–86), Mark Lamos (1979–80), Sandy Rosenthal (1967–79).

General Manger: Nancy Thomas.

Managing Directors: Richard Bryant, David Hawkanson.
Resident Director: Walter Schoen.
Other Personnel: Not available.

REPERTORY

1967–68: *Generation, The Mousetrap, The Best Man, The Fantasticks, The Owl and the Pussycat, Hansel and Gretel, The Sign in Sidney Brustein's Window, No Exit, A Case of Libel, A View from the Bridge, What's New.*

1968–69: *Love in E-Flat, The Threepenny Opera, Time of Your Life, A Thousand Clowns, Chicago* and *Birdbath, The Subject Was Roses, Lysistrata, A Delicate Balance, The Private Ear* and *The Public Eye, The Littlest Tailor, A*B*C*, Pinocchio.*

1969–70: *Carnival, Dear Friends, Don't Drink the Water, A Day in the Death of Joe Egg, Rosencrantz and Guildenstern Are Dead, A Man for All Seasons, Have You Any Dirty Washing, Mother Dear?, Spoon River Anthology, Little Red Riding Hood, The Hobbit, The Dandy Lion.*

1970–71: *You Know I Can't Hear You When the Water's Running, Summertree, The Price, Ceremonies in Dark Old Men, The Odd Couple, The Boys in the Band, Adaptations/Next, Calm Down, Mother/Keep Tightly Closed in a Cool Dark Place, Celebration.*

1971–72: *West Side Story, The Effect of Gamma Rays on Man-in-the-Moon Marigolds, Cyrano.*

1972–73: *Conflict of Interest, Norman, Is That You?, Stop the World—I Want To Get Off!, Child's Play, The Gingerbread Lady.*

1973–74: *Inherit the Wind, A Christmas Carol, Promenade, All!, Jacques Brel Is Alive and Well and Living in Paris, The School for Wives, Of Mice and Men.*

1974–75: *A Streetcar Named Desire, Sherlock Holmes, The Hot l Baltimore, That Championship Season, Berlin to Broadway with Kurt Weill, The Taming of the Shrew, Diamond Studs.*

1975–76: *Dybbuk, The Sunshine Boys, Rashomon, Diamond Studs, The Sea Horse, The Devil's Disciple, Moonshine and Sassafras.*

1976–77: *In Fashion, Sizwe Bansi Is Dead, Ah, Wilderness!, Vanities†, Jacques Brel Is Alive and Well and Living in Paris.*

1977–78: *Pygmalion, Slow Dance on the Killing Ground, Equus†, Black Comedy* and *On the Harmfulness of Tobacco, Shadow Box, Rodgers and Hart, Starting Here, Starting Now.*

1978–79: *Cold Storage, A Christmas Carol, Tartuffe†, The Royal Hunt of the Sun†, Boesman and Lena, The Show-Off.*

1979–80: *A Flea in Her Ear†, Twelfth Night, The Glass Menagerie†, Father's Day, The Sea Gull, The Threepenny Opera.*

1980–81: *The Rivals†, Custer†, Indulgences in the Louisville Harem, The Elephant Man, A Little Night Music, Talley's Folly.*

1981–82: *The Rainmaker, A Christmas Carol, Waiting for Godot, Misalliance, As You Like It†, The Gin Game†, Tintypes†.*

1982–83: *What the Butler Saw†, A Christmas Carol, Journey's End, Mass Appeal†, Uncle Vanya†, The Dining Room†, A Funny Thing Happened on the Way to the Forum.*

1983–84: *A Streetcar Named Desire, Billy Bishop Goes to War, The Taming of the Shrew, Our Town, 'night, Mother, Quilters.*

1984–85: *And a Nightingale Sang, Master Harold . . . and the boys, The Learned Ladies, Death of a Salesman, Goodbye Freddy, The Robber Bridegroom.*

1985–86: *Fool for Love, The Real Thing, Galileo, The Government Inspector, Private Lives, My Fair Lady.*

1986–87: *The House of Blue Leaves, A Delicate Balance, The Matchmaker, The Marriage of Bette and Boo, Glengarry Glen Ross, An Original Play* (created by ATC).

Note: Beginning with the 1983–84 season, all ATC productions were presented in both Tucson and Phoenix. † indicates plays presented in both cities before 1983–84.

BIBLIOGRAPHY

Published Sources:
Arizona Daily Star (Tucson), 1967–86.
Arizona Republic (Phoenix), 1967–86.

Unpublished Sources:
Arizona Theatre Company. "Mission Statement." 1983.
Bacal, Gary. Letter to author. No date.
Schoen, Walter. Personal Interview. No date.

Archival Resource:
Tucson, Arizona. Arizona Theatre Company. Programs, season ticket brochures, and fact sheet.

Timothy D. Connors

[THE] ARTISTS' THEATRE was formed in New York in 1953 and operated for two decades as a modern American "art theatre," seeking to revolutionize prevailing dramatic and theatrical practice, much as had the independent theatres directed by André Antoine, Paul Fort, and Aurélien-Marie Lugné-Poë in turn-of-the century Paris.

The company's founders, contemporary art dealer John Bernard Myers and theatre director Herbert Machiz, were uniquely prepared for such an undertaking, as both were influenced by apprenticeships spent among a vanguard of European artists, authors, and theatre practitioners. John Myers had served as New York condottiere for the European artists in exile during the Nazi occupation of Paris, and his surrealist-inspired ideals for collaborations between poets, painters, and performers led him to begin performance collaborations informally in the late 1940s and early 1950s, combining the talents of later luminaries of the New York School poets and the "second-generation" New York School painters. Herbert Machiz' firsthand experience with the postwar theatres of Louis Jouvet and Jean-Louis Barrault—and their repertoire of sophisticated theatre poetry—spawned in him on his return to America a desire to liberate the American dramatic repertoire from what he felt was its "limited realistic formula," and to develop in its place a repertoire of plays by "poets and original thinkers," plays with a double life of literary and theatrical value ("The Challenge of a Poetic Theatre." *Theatre Arts*, February 1956, p. 74).

Myers and Machiz established a forum for experimentation with nonnaturalistic dramas mounted with abstract settings by modern painters. An examination of the history of the three periods of activity of the Artists' Theatre discloses the struggle of a poet's theatre in the shifting contexts of experimentation in American theatre.

Operating as a nonprofit corporation between 1953 and 1956, the Artists' Theatre produced a series of fourteen abstract, poetic, and philosophical plays, thirteen of which were by young American authors. America's most respected theatre critics and men of letters applauded the group for its courage, for some of these experimental works were too fragile in feeling, too private in reference, and written with too little sense of the requirements of theatrical production. On the other hand, Eric Bentley called *The Screen* "the best new work to appear off-Broadway in the 1952–53 season" (*New Republic*, June 15, 1953, p. 23, and *The Death of Odysseus* "the best new writing of the 1953–54 season" (*New Republic*, December 14, 1953" p. 21. In 1954–55 The Artists' Theatre produced *The Immortal Husband*, which John Gassner applauded as one of the best-realized poetic dramas to be presented on or off-Broadway between 1951 and 1957. In 1955–56 the group's efforts were crowned with both the *Show Business* magazine award and the first *Village Voice* Obie Award given to *Absalom* as the "Best New Play."

The Artists' Theatre encouraged young American poets and authors to write for the theatre at a time when no other outlet for poetic drama existed. Moreover, a large number of the playwrights produced by the Artists' Theatre, including Tennessee Williams, Robert Hivnor, Frank O'Hara, Barbara Guest, Kenneth Koch, James Merrill, John Ashbery, James Schuyler, and Lionel Abel, went on to write plays that were to be produced by such avant-garde companies as the Living Theatre*, the American Theatre for Poets, and the Judson Poet's Theatre. Working as director and dramaturg, respectively, Machiz and Myers shaped the early efforts of these unconventional playwrights and helped them to become aware of the theatre as a means of aesthetic expression.

In 1956 efforts to achieve tax-exempt status failed, in part as a result of the founders' attempts to raise capital to finance their productions, while awaiting Internal Revenue Service determination of their status. Machiz and Myers closed down their stalemated company. Although a financial failure, the company had succeeded in fomenting a brief renaissance of nonrealistic drama off-Broadway and in paving the way for other groups committed to the unconventional.

Machiz and Myers revived the Artists' Theatre intermittently between 1960 and 1965. In their more commercial ventures of the early sixties the founders submitted to the need for more conservative production values, but they maintained their goal of premiering nonrealistic, poetic, and otherwise experimental dramas. The seven plays presented in the four programs of this second period included Lionel Abel's *The Pretender* (1960), which examined the issue of white supremacy and black pride and power at the very advent of the American civil rights movement; two absurdist plays by Holly Beye, winner of poetry awards from the Woodstock foundation and the *Quarterly Review of Literature;* and the American premiere of Fernando Arrabal's first full-length play, the apocalyptic *The Automobile Graveyard.*

Harold Clurman noted the originality and sophistication of Abel's "jeu d'esprit," *The Pretender*, which, Clurman contended, was rendered in a style likely to confuse American audiences conditioned to realism. Richard Gilman found *The Automobile Graveyard* an extraordinarily provocative and farsighted choice, while John Simon admired Machiz and Myers' encouragement of playwrights of such obvious talent and insight as Holly Beye. Finally, Elizabeth Hardwick and Pauline Kael joined these champions of the Artists' Theatre as they and other members of New York's literati took the stage in postperformance discussions to defend Machiz and Myers' production of Lionel Abel's *The Wives*, an existentialist treatment of Sophocles' *Trachiniae*. Subsequently twenty-nine artists, authors, and critics published an open letter in the *New York Times* explaining the play's significance to the increasingly philistine audiences and critics of off-Broadway theatre.

Machiz and Myers abandoned production off-Broadway after a tenacious battle to present their innovative repertoire and after much personal anguish and financial loss. The Artists' Theatre experience in two successive periods illustrates that off-Broadway was rapidly becoming a "commodity" theatre, fully deserving Robert Pasolli's derisive appellation: "Broadway, junior grade" (*Village Voice*, May 27, 1965, p. 18). It also suggests that the economic and cultural forces responsible for a theatre movement *off*-off Broadway were already operating by 1960.

Machiz and Myers revived the Artists' Theatre at the Southampton College campus of Long Island University during the summers of 1968 and 1969. The founders sought to develop an enduring Artists' Theatre festival, modeled after those held annually in Edinburgh, Scotland, and Spoleto, Italy, as well as a permanent acting company dedicated to the presentation of poetic plays. Owing to the scarcity of suitable new scripts and to Machiz and Myers' desire to build audiences through the production of more well-known plays, the two produced works by post–World War II European authors in styles redolent of Parisian theatre of the late 1940s. Accordingly, they mounted revivals of classic works of a highly imaginative character: Jean Cocteau's *The Knights of the Round Table*, Roger Vitrac's *Victor, or the Revolt of the Children*, a late visionary play by Henrik Ibsen, *Little Eyolf*, and Vladimir Nabokov's dream play, *The Waltz Invention*. To these they added two revivals of more recent plays by American poets of the 1950s: Jane Bowles' *In the Summer House* and the Artists' Theatre's own 1955 discovery, *The Immortal Husband*, by New York School poet James Merrill. The only two premieres presented in these festivals were the seriously unresolved *Lady Laura Pritchett, American*, by John White, and Machiz' own musical dramatization of Gertrude Stein's children's stories, *The First Reader*.

Southampton reviewers greeted the Artists' Theatre's efforts to challenge the mind and the imagination with a number of positive critical notices. Unfortunately these reviews stimulated no large and appreciative audience. Hampered by inadequate theatre facilities, by conflicts with the Long Island University administration over funding, and by tight production schedules and inadequate rehearsal time, and troubled by the provinciality of Southampton audiences, Machiz and Myers ended this last period of the Artists' Theatre in 1969. In an ironic coda to their years of work in the United States, critics at the Dublin, Ireland, International Theatre Festival, where the company had been invited to perform in the fall of 1969, lavished praise on the group.

An analysis of the production photographs, original designs, and critics' descriptions of all thirty-one Artists' Theatre productions reveals that the secondary goal of this art theatre—the reinvigoration of American scenic practice through the introduction of decors by contemporary American abstract artists—was achieved. From 1953 to 1956 Machiz and Myers presented the work of second-generation New York School painters such as imaginative realists Larry Rivers and Jane Freilicher, abstract expressionists Alfred Leslie and Grace Hartigan, astigmaticist sculptor Elaine de Kooning, and collage artist Julian Beck in signal experiments in scenic design and stage decoration. The visual and critical evidence further indicates that Machiz and Myers carefully integrated the personal vision of each of these artists into the theatrical whole.

In the second period of the Artists' Theatre its subsidiary goal of revitalizing theatrical decor was hampered by the commercial circumstances under which off-Broadway for-profit productions were mounted. Commercial production necessitated the use of designers sanctioned by United Scenic Artists, the union of scenic, lighting, and costume designers. Although settings for the seven plays produced in this period were tastefully, even elegantly conceived and executed, they show little evidence of the abstract and painterly style of the unconventional and nonprofessional designs of the first period.

The nonprofit, noncommercial nature of the summer festivals at Southampton College permitted a greater measure of artistic freedom. Once again productions of the Artists' Theatre became a magnet attracting the most important progressive artists of the era, including the celebrated pop artist Alex Katz, color-field abstractionist Kendall Shaw, and abstract figurationists Robert Cato and Allan d'Arcangelo.

The Artists' Theatre's experiments in scene design in the early 1950s were among the first consistent postwar expressions of a flight from naturalism in the American theatre. Moreover, painter-designers such as Robert Soule, Robert Fletcher, Larry Rivers, Jane Freilicher, Robert Cato, Alex Katz, and Alfred Leslie, whose early work was first seen in Artists' Theatre productions, continued to render decors for off- and off-off-Broadway productions in the 1960s and 1970s.

The remarkable record of critical success of the complex and eclectic repertoire of the Artists' Theatre is, to an extraordinary degree, directly attributable to Herbert Machiz' keen sense of the expressive potential of actors, the stage, and its settings. Machiz viewed the director as an analytic and interpretive artist whose first responsibility was to render each play in the scale, mood, and tempo most expressive of the intentions of its author. This point of view, conditioned by Machiz' experiences with Jouvet and Barrault, accounted for his special reverence for the dramatic text. Machiz' conception of the director's task led him to insist on employing only professional actors who were dedicated to finding for each nuance of meaning the appropriate vocal and gestural equivalent.

To be sure, Machiz made errors in some of his thirty-one productions for the Artists' Theatre. His all-black-cast treatment of Federico Garcia Lorca's *Don Perlimplin* (1953) and his Feydeau-like rendering of *The Automobile Graveyard* (1961) were overly ambitious. His artistic failures were few, however, and reflected in some measure the constraints of inadequate rehearsal time in which to realize challenging conceptions. None of the Artists' Theatre productions could be termed a complete failure, and most elicited special critical praise for Machiz' directing. In all three periods of the Artists' Theatre's activities, critics celebrated the originality of his staging, the carefully modulated ensemble acting of his casts, and his integration of all elements of the production into a unified whole.

It was an irony of Herbert Machiz' fate to have arrived in New York with a passion for developing a nonrealistic American repertoire, for encouraging imaginative, painterly rather than constructivist settings rendered by contemporary artists, and for exploring the European "test and technique" approach to acting and directing at a time when the American theatre was inhospitable to each of these aims. He found Actors' Studio or "method" acting objectionable for its extreme emphasis on the psychology of the actor and for its complicity in the proliferation of the outworn formulae of realism. He lived to see this approach seriously challenged in the 1960s by what he found to be only slightly less troubling, an aesthetic deemphasizing language and setting, favoring improvisation and communal authorship, and exploring a "transformational" approach to acting. In light of these shifting contexts the record of the Artists' Theatre is an all the more remarkable testament to Machiz' vision and abilities.

The experiments of the Artists' Theatre appealed to a small audience of poets, artists, and intellectuals and to the critics of art and literary quarterlies. Throughout most of its existence the "popular" daily critics and the popular audience for whom these critics were the arbiters of taste, avoided the company's unconventional productions. Although the avant-gardists deeply appreciated the group's work, they were far too few in number and the reviews in the quarterlies appeared too late to be of significant financial benefit to the company. Nevertheless, the Artists' Theatre acquired a reputation that invites attention to the details of its history.

PERSONNEL

Management: Herbert Machiz, John Bernard Myers.

Scene Designers: Julian Beck (1954), Neil Blaine (1953), Robert Cato (1969), Alan D'Arcangelo (1969), Jane Eakin (1969), Robert Fletcher (1956), Jane Freilicher (1953), Paul Georges (1953, 1968), Richard V. Hare (1955), Grace Hartigan (1953), Alex Katz (1968), Elaine de Kooning (1953), Al Kresch (1953), Alfred Leslie (1953–54), Leo B. Meyer (1965), Kyle Morris (1968), Larry Rivers (1953), Kendall Shaw (1968–69), Robert Soule (1954, 1960, 1962), Kim Swados (1961).

Composers: Sarah Cunningham (1954), John Gruen (1954–56), Teiji Ito (1956), John Latouche (1953), Ned Rorem (1968), Mordechai Sheinkman (1961), Billy Strayhorn (1953), Ann Sternberg (1969).

Actors and Actresses: Leroy Adams (1960), Nancy Andrews (1968–69), Tige Andrews (1954), *Alan Ansara* (1956), Michael Anthony (1969), Michael Arquette (1961), Richard Astor (1956), *Conrad Bain* (1962, 1968–69), Jay Barney (1953), Emory Bass (1968), Richard Baublitz (1956), Kurt Bieber (1956), Emilie Boselli (1954), Mark Breaux (1954), Carolyn Brenner (1954), *Jacqueline Brookes* (1968–69), Roscoe Lee Browne (1960), Joseph Brownstone (1954), Larry Bryggman (1962), Donald Buka (1969), Elizabeth Burke (1962), Peggie Cahill (1969), *Mary Grace Canfield* (1954–55), *Jack Cannon* (1953–54), Michael Capanna (1954), Irwin Charone (1954), Virgilia Chew (1968–69), Stanley Cobleigh (1953), Alan Coleridge (1969), John Conwell (1953), Mildred Cook (1954), Peter Coury (1954), Scott Cunningham (1960), Jon Cypher (1965), *Frank Dana* (1954), *Leora Dana* (1968–69), Doris Davis (1953), Gabriel Dell (1961), Jack Delmonte (1954), Lawrence Dukore (1961), Mildred Dunnock (1968), Louis Edmonds (1953), Jean Ellyn (1955), Richard Fourman (1953), Elizabeth Franz (1968–69), Edward G. Fuller (1968–69), Kazimer Garas (1965), Jimmy Gavin (1961), George Gaynes (1956), Avril Gentles (1965), Frank Giordano (1969), Michael Goodwin (1968), Walter Gorney (1954), *Charity Grace* (1953), Dylan Green (1969), Catherine Guilford (1953), John Hallo (1953), *Jack Harpman* (1953), Michael Higgins (1962, 1968), Chris Hoffer (1953), *June Hunt* (1953–54, 1965), Irma Hurley (1956, 1962), Veronica Hyland (1969), Robert Jacquin (1953), Eric James (1968), James Earl Jones (1960), Constantine Katsanos (1968), Will Klump (1956), Bruce Kornbluth (1968–69), Roland Laroche (1953), Jennie Lawrence (1954), Pegeen Lawrence (1965), Sondra Lee (1969), John Leighton (1969), Calvin Lockhart (1960), Leo Lucker (1956, 1965), Pat Lysinger (1969), Carole McCrory (1954), Leila Martin (1961), Walter Mathews (1954), Guy Mayor (1953), *Anne Meacham* (1953–55, 1965, 1968), Scott Merrill (1955), Jan Miner (1965), Robert Morris (1956), Craddock Munro (1953), *Alec Murphy* (1965, 1968–69), Jack Naylor (1956), Edwin Owens (1968), Bruce Parker (1953), Estelle Parsons (1961), Nancy Pollack (1953), Joseph Raymond (1953), Robert Raymond (1954), Patricia Ripley (1954), *Gaby Rodgers* (1953, 1962), Frederick Rolf (1955), Fran Ross (1968), Joseph Ruskin (1954), Eileen Ryan (1953), Jack Ryland (1969), Tessa Sapan (1969), Lee Saunders (1953), Joy Saxe (1968–69), Sol Serlin (1956), *Alan Shayne* (1953–54), William Sheidy (1955), Dan Shilling (1954), Patricia Sinnott (1969), *Garn Stephens* (1968–69), Sydney G. Stevens (1954), Sam Stewart (1953), *Sylvia Stone* (1953, 1962), Rex Thompson (1968), Sandra Thornton (1969), Barbara Torrance (1954), Richard Towers (1953), Art Vasil (1969), *Fiddle Viracola* (1965, 1969), Royce Wallace (1960), Dan Williams (1953), Stephen Wolfson (1956), *Forrest Wood* (1953–54).

REPERTORY

1953: *The Screen, Try! Try!, Little Red Riding Hood, Presenting Jane, Auto Da Fe.*

1953–54: *The Love of Don Perlimplin for Belisa in the Garden, The Death of Odysseus, Fire Exit, The Ticklish Acrobat.*

1955: *The Immortal Husband.*

1956: *Absalom.*

1960: *The Pretender.*

1961–62: *The Automobile Graveyard, Thus, It's All over Now, On Circe's Island, A Summer Ghost.*

1965: *The Wives.*

1968: *The Knights of the Round Table, Little Eyolf, The Immortal Husband, In the Summer House.*

1969: *Victor, or the Revolt of the Children, Lady Laura Pritchett, American, The Waltz Invention*, musical revue, *The First Reader.* At Dublin International Theatre Festival: *The Immortal Husband, In the Summer House.*

BIBLIOGRAPHY

Published Sources:

Commonweal, 1953–69.

New Republic, 1953–69.

New York Herald Tribune, 1953–69.

New York Mirror, 1953–69.

New York Times, 1953–69.

Partisan Review, 1953–69.

Saturday Review, 1953–69.

Theatre Arts, 1953–69.

Village Voice, 1953–69.

Gruen, John. *The Party's over Now.* New York: Viking Press, 1967.

Machiz, Herbert. "Introduction." *The Artists' Theatre: Four Plays.* New York: Grove Press, 1960.

————. "The Challenge of a Poetic Theatre." *Theatre Arts*, February 1956, pp. 72–74, 88–89.

Myers, John Bernard. "A History of the Artists' Theatre." *Southampton College Summer Windmill*, July 3, 1968, pp. 1–2.

————, ed. *Tracking the Marvelous* (exhibition catalogue). New York: New York University (Grey Art Gallery and Study Center), 1981.

————. *Tracking the Marvelous: An Autobiography.* New York: Random House, 1981.

Unpublished Sources:

Myers, John Bernard. Letter to author. July 13, 1979.

————. Personal interview. August 9, 1979.

Archival Resources:

Austin, Texas. University of Texas. Humanities Research Center. Playbills, press releases, photographs, business records.

Cambridge, Massachusetts. Harvard University. Theatre Collection. Papers Related to Herbert Machiz, John Myers, and their Artists' Theatre.

New York, New York. New York Public Library. Library and Museum of the Performing Arts at Lincoln Center. Playbills, press releases, clippings, photographs, business records.

Lawrence Jasper

ASOLO STATE THEATRE had its beginning in 1949 when the state of Florida, owner and operator of the Ringling Museums in Sarasota, Florida, purchased the fittings installed in 1798 by impresario Antonio Locatelli in the audience hall of the fifteenth-century castle of Queen Catherine Cornaro in Asolo, Italy. Some of Europe's most famous actors and actresses, notably Eleanora Duse, who considered the Asolo her home theatre, performed on this stage. The lovely little hall was dismantled in 1930 and a movie theatre was installed in its place. A Venetian antique dealer purchased the curving walls of the front of the two upper tiers of boxes, the valences of the box openings, the ceiling decorations, the proscenium arch, and other ornamental details, and stored them in Venice, where Ringling Museum director A. Everette Austin, Jr., discovered them some nineteen years later. In 1957 the theatrical fittings, including the original lamps and medallion portraits of Queen Catherine, Dante, Petrarch, Tasso, Ariosto, Goldoni, and others, were moved from Gallery 21 of the Ringling Museum of Fine Art to the current Asolo Theatre. The old theatre's horseshoe floor plan was slightly modified to provide two entrances for the audience, and some nonsupporting columns were removed to improve sight lines. The current theatre in Sarasota also boasts air conditioning, modern theatre lighting and sound systems, 319 seats, and a box office.

The Asolo State Theatre began in the summer of 1960 when two professors from Florida State University (FSU), Arthur Dorlag and Richard G. Fallon, staged six eighteenth- and nineteenth-century comedies in Ringling's Asolo Theatre on a budget of $5,000. Utilizing FSU students and faculty, they gave twenty-five performances of works by Molière, Richard Brinsley Sheridan, Carlo Goldoni, John Gay, and George Etherege, using authentic wing-and-back staging. The next summer the company, now named the Asolo Theatre Comedy Festival, hired several actors, including Polly Holliday, Paul Weidner, and Bradford Wallace, on small stipends, a first step toward professionalization. Also in 1961, patrons in Sarasota formed the Asolo Theatre Festival Association (the Asolo Angels) to support the young company.

Arthur H. Dorlag (b. 1922), associate professor of speech and director of theatre at FSU, was general director of the theatre for its first three seasons but left that post to become the Asolo's director of research. He later left the company. Cofounder Richard G. Fallon (b. 1923) remained with the Asolo, most of the time as its executive director, for many years.

Fallon, raised in New York City, interrupted studies at Brown University to serve in the U.S. Army from 1942 to 1945. Afterward he earned a Certificate of Excellence at the Old Vic Theatre School in London. He completed his formal education with B.A. and M.A. degrees (1951) from Columbia University, after private study with several theatrical luminaries. Fallon, the first chairman of FSU's department of theatre (1969), was also the first dean of FSU's School of Theatre, established in 1973. He also founded and directed the Charles MacArthur Center for American Theatre. He has served as the president of the American Theatre Association (1983–84) and is a member of its College of Fellows.

Two faculty members in the inaugural company, Robert Strane and Eberle Thomas, shared the company's artistic leadership. In 1962, 1963, and 1964 they continued the emphasis on classical plays, but in the fourth season (1963) they included Christopher Fry's *The Lady's Not for Burning*, a modern poetic drama.

The next season two more modern classics (*The Importance of Being Earnest*, by Oscar Wilde, and *Tiger at the Gates*, by Jean Giraudoux) appeared on the bill of four plays. The Asolo's first truly contemporary drama was Eugene Ionesco's *The Bald Soprano* in 1966.

The Asolo introduced plays by George Bernard Shaw and Anton Chekhov in 1967, but the next year it abandoned classical programming altogether, producing Archibald MacLeish's *J.B.*, *Look Back in Anger*, by John Osborne, *The Visit*, by Frederich Dürrenmatt, and *The Caretaker*, by Harold Pinter. Since then the Asolo's yearly repertory has carefully blended revivals, current dramas, and musicals. It currently produces mostly contemporary plays.

In 1972 Eberle Thomas resigned as co-artistic director to become a full-time playwright. Robert Strane continued alone as artistic director until 1981. Stuart Vaughan served as "artistic advisor" for only one season, 1982. In 1983 John Ulmer became the Asolo's artistic director and brought experience and a clear sense of mission to the job. He had been artistic director of Stage/West and the Carnegie-Mellon Theatre Company as well as managing director of the La Jolla Playhouse of the Stars. He had directed at Pennsylvania's Bucks County Playhouse, New York's Roundabout Theatre, Virginia's Wayside Theatre, New Jersey's Shakespeare Festival, Syracuse Stage, and the Coconut Grove Playhouse. Ulmer formulated three artistic guidelines for the Asolo: (1) do the best theatre possible for the widest possible audience, (2) make each show of the season carry its own weight, and (3) do only shows with metaphors that remain meaningful beyond the two hours' playing time. The Asolo offers few experimental or avant-garde productions because Ulmer does not believe in asking a local, narrowly focused audience to support experimental theatre. He also says that a theatre automatically commits itself to excellence when it accepts public subsidies.

The Asolo's annual budget steadily increased. Fallon urged the Florida legislature to designate the Asolo as the "state theatre" of Florida in 1965. In another appeal Fallon asked the state of Florida to support an "Enrichment in the Schools" program wherein an Asolo touring company would perform in the public schools, thus encouraging and supplementing the study of drama and theatre arts. The state's grant to the Asolo State Theatre in 1966 increased its budget from $65,000 to $440,000 and made the theatre more than a summer operation.

Fallon made Sarasota, not the FSU campus in Tallahassee, the center of the school touring operation. He established and staffed scenic and costume shops in Sarasota, and the Asolo State Theatre became a year-round operation, even though the Ringling Museums' opera season still controlled the Asolo's stage during December, January, and February. Fallon next set up a performance laboratory for FSU's graduate students of acting. FSU's Master of Fine Arts program in Professional Actor Training, begun in 1968, moved to Sarasota in 1973, where it now flourishes as the FSU–Asolo Conservatory of Professional Actor Training. At least six Asolo staff members, including three of the conservatory's faculty, draw salaries as FSU faculty members. Although the Asolo State Theatre producing company originally belonged to FSU, no person or supporting entity owned more than 18 percent of the Asolo. This diversity, Fallon felt, protected the Asolo from vested interests.

However, in 1968, because its relationship with FSU was unclear, state auditors cut the Asolo adrift from FSU. The termination of federal grant money at about the same time precipitated a crisis, and only the generosity of private resources made the 1970 season possible. Fallon and others incorporated the Asolo as a nonprofit corporation in 1969 and hired a managing director, Howard J. Millman, to conduct its accounting, business, and budgeting affairs. Millman stayed at the Asolo until 1980. The Asolo continued to develop other funding strategies. In 1971 Florida's legislature began to appropriate funds directly to some of the Asolo's statewide programs. Earlier the legislature had designated the theatre a "state agency" under the Division of Cultural Affairs of Florida's secretary of state. In 1972 the Ford Foundation offered the Asolo a challenge grant of $176,955, spurring the belated appointment of a board of directors. The Curtain Raisers, discussed later, were formed at the same time. By 1979 the Asolo's annual budget passed the $1 million mark. In 1983 it reached $1.5 million and in 1985 it exceeded $2 million. In 1980 Florida established the State Theatre Program to distribute legislative allocations not only to the Asolo, but also to two other theatres: the Hippodrome State Theatre* and the Coconut Grove Playhouse. Locally, the Asolo receives funds from the Asolo Theatre Festival Association (Asolo Angels), which was chartered as a nonprofit corporation in 1962, fully six years before the Asolo State Theatre itself was chartered. The Angels' three goals are (1) to raise a major portion of the Asolo's yearly subsidy, (2) to provide trained volunteers, and (3) to act as a liaison between the audiences and the Asolo company. In their first twenty-two years the Angels raised more than $3.5 million for the Asolo. In 1985 the Angels pledged to raise $350,000, roughly 17 percent of the Asolo's budget, through membership solicitation ($25 to $500+), a "co-producer" contribution program, and a conservatory scholarship sponsorship program. Angels also organize galas, opening night parties, rummage sales, and telethons to raise funds. Because many of the Angels are highly skilled retired professionals, the administrative costs are very low, 13 cents for every dollar raised. Another local support group, the Curtain Raisers, was founded in 1972. The group initially enabled the theatre to meet a Ford Foundation challenge grant of $176,955. The program solicits annual memberships from the business community in categories ranging from $50 to $9,999. The Asolo also receives support from the National Endowment for the Arts and the Southern Arts Federation, along with grants from businesses and gifts from private philanthropic sources.

Touring has helped the Asolo broaden its audience. Beginning with a statewide Education Enrichment Tour, the Asolo played to Florida audiences from 1966 to 1975. Federal and state grants supported the touring program from 1966 to 1968. When these resources dried up, private sponsors continued the program.

The Asolo Children's Theatre, in conjunction with FSU, toured two plays annually from 1971 through 1976. Actors-in-the-Schools, a third touring program, brought Equity actors directly into high school classrooms from 1972 to 1974. In 1975 it was succeeded by the Asolo Touring Theatre, which added a second Equity company in 1982 to specialize in audience participation, a theatrical style made popular by the initial touring company. Asolo On Tour (distinct from the Asolo Touring Theatre) was organized in 1981 to resume mainstage trouping throughout Florida and the Southeast. It receives funding from Florida's State Touring Program and the Southern Arts Federation. In nineteen years of touring the Asolo companies performed sixty-two different plays in 2,700 locations both in and out of Florida, traveling 382,000 miles and playing to more than 2 million persons.

Asolo productions have also played in New York City. Its premiere production of Daryl Boylan's *Transcendental Love*, a play about the home life of Ralph Waldo Emerson and Margaret Fuller, transferred to the Provincetown Playhouse on September 25, 1980, where it ran for fourteen performances (plus four previews). In 1985 the Asolo's revival of *Dames at Sea* played at the Lambs' Theatre for a longer period of time.

The Asolo has never featured star performers. However, some of its alumni have achieved stardom, notably Polly Holliday, Pamela Payton-Wright, and Paul Weidner.

The longevity of the Asolo's technical and office staff is truly remarkable. Some of them have been with the theatre for twenty years. Although the Asolo management was unusually stable in its first twenty years, it saw many changes in the 1980s. David S. Levenson succeeded Howard Millman as managing director from 1980 until 1984. Subsequently Fallon hired Stephen Rothman, who has B.A. and M.F.A. degrees from FSU, as associate executive director.

Rothman is well known in American regional theatres. A founding member of the Hartman Theatre Company* in Stamford, Connecticut, he left to become the producing director of the Paramount Arts Center in Aurora, Illinois (1977–78). He was the executive director of the Pasadena Playhouse (1979–84), where he supervised a massive and expensive restoration project, as he had in Aurora. He was also theatre management consultant for the $5 million restoration of the Pantages Center for the Performing Arts in Tacoma, Washington. He is a stage director as well.

Fallon and Rothman planned to expand the Asolo operation, and movie star Burt Reynolds, an FSU alumnus, lent his name and financial support to the project. In October 1984 Ringling Museums trustees donated a building site on nearby museum property. However, in the spring of 1986, Fallon resigned in a dispute with the Asolo's board of directors over a projected deficit of $2 million. Gil Lazier, dean of FSU's School of Theatre, took charge of the theatre. Fallon was reassigned as dean emeritus and director of professional programs at FSU's School of Theatre. Although FSU indicated it would continue its commitment to the $10 million expansion project, Steve Rothman did not renew his contract as associate executive director of the Asolo. Later Lazier appointed Don Creason of the FSU faculty as acting director of the Asolo.

The boards of the Asolo State Theatre and The Theatre, Inc., as the expansion project is called, were merged. The resultant Asolo Performing Arts Center will be built on another Ringling Museums property site. The original Asolo Theatre will remain in the current building, while a new 500-seat theatre will contain the interior of an ornate Victorian theatre, the Dunfermline Opera House from Scotland. Along with the Asolo State Theatre company, the center will contain the Asolo Conservatory and the Asolo Television and Film Studio.

The Asolo State Theatre has been a mighty force in the development of theatre in Florida. The Asolo's various touring programs serve the entire state, and the Asolo's productions draw an audience from all of central Florida. In addition, the conservatory has consistently offered training of the highest caliber. Finally, the Asolo pioneered Florida's State Theatre Program, an admirable example of legislative support for regional theatres.

PERSONNEL

Management: Richard G. Fallon, general director (1960–68), executive director (1968–86); Arthur H. Dorlag, general director (1960–62), director of research (1962–?); Howard J. Millman, managing director (1968–80); David S. Levenson, managing director (1980–84); Stephen Rothman, associate executive director (1984–86); Robert Strane, artistic director (1968–82), Eberle Thomas, artistic director (1968–74); John Ulmer, artistic director (1982–86).

Directors: Gregory Abels (1982), Alan Arkin (1985–86), Paul Barry (1977–78), Cash Baxter (1984–85), Jonathan Bolt (1982), Jamie Brown (1985–86), John Dillon (1974–76), Bernerd Engel (1979–81), Sheldon Epps (1983–85), Mark Epstein (1978–79), *Richard G. Fallon* (1960–79), Robert Falls (1983–84), Peter Frisch (1970), Moses Goldberg (1971–72), Susan Gregg (1985–86), Thomas Gruenewald (1977–78, 1982), John Gulley (1984–86), Sandra C. Hastie (1974–76, 1978–79), Richard Hopkins (1973), *Jim Hoskins* (1973–84), Norris Houghton (1983), Max Howard (1978–79), Amnon Kabatchnik (1973–75, 1976–77), George Keathley (1977–78), *Neal Kenyon* (1975–77, 1979–81, 1984–85), James Kirkland (1983), Robert Lanchester (1971, 1972), Gene Lesser (1979–81), Philip Le Strange (1976–77), Bill Levis (1985–86), Donald Madden (1982), Peter Maloney (1976–77), Lucy Martin (1984–85), M. Jean-Louis Martin-Barbaz (1972, 1984–85), *Richard D. Meyer* (1969, 1970, 1972, 1973–74), Robert Miller (1985–86), *Howard J. Millman* (1970–81), Salli Parker (1974–76), John Reich (1979–81, 1984–85), *Stephen Rothman* (1974–75, 1976–77, 1978–79, 1984–85), Peter J. Saputo (1973–74), Jon Spelman (1971, 1972), *Robert Strane* (1963–81), *Eberle Thomas* (1960–74, 1979–81), *Isa Thomas* (1976–77, 1978–81, 1983), *John Ulmer* (1975–77, 1978–79, 1983–85), Porter Van Zandt (1985–86), Stuart Vaughan (1982), *Bradford Wallace* (1971–79), Paul Weidner (1967–68), Thomas Edward West (1977–79), Paxton Whitehead (1974–76), William Woodman (1975–76, 1979–81), Tunc Yalman (1973–74).

Scene Designers: *Bennet Averyt* (1975–76, 1977–81, 1983–86), Sam Bagarella (1981–83), William Barclay (1981–82), *Robert C. Barnes* (1975–80, 1983–84), Howard Bay (1978–80), Peter Dean Beck (1981–82), Thomas Michael Cariello (1981–82), David Chapman (1975–76), Jim Chesnutt (1975–76), Franco Colavecchia (1980–81), Robert

Darling (1979–81), *Jeffrey Dean* (1976–79, 1983–86), John Doepp (1982–84), *Holmes Easley* (1969–72, 1975–76, 1977–78, 1980–82, 1985–86), David Emmons (1977–80), *John Ezell* (1971–73, 1980–83, 1984–86), Peter Harvey (1975–76, 1984–85), Kenneth Hurt (1984–85), William King (1971–72), Kenneth N. Kurtz (1983–84, 1985–86), Sandro La Ferla (1976–77, 1978–81), Kevin Lock (1985–86), Gordon Micunis (1982–83), Joseph Nieminski (1975–76), Charles T. Parsons (1985–86), Ray Perry (1967–69, 1971–72, 1976–77), Rick Pike (1971–75, 1977–78), Charles I. Reimer (1960–63), John Scheffler (1975–79), Henry Swanson (1971–73, 1983–84), James Tilton (1971–73).

Costume Designers: Diane Berg (1978–80), Mitchell Bloom (1985–86), Joy Breckenridge (1967–68), Barbara J. Costa (1971–72), Peter Harvey (1984–85), Vicki S. Holden (1980–83), *Flozanne John* (1973–81), *Catherine King* (1970–86), *Sally A. Koss* (later *Sally Koss Harrison*) (1978–85), Harlan Shaw (1963, 1968–69), Paige Southard (1974–75, 1981–82), Ellis Tillman (1981–82).

Lighting Designers: Richard C. Evans (1968), John D. Gowans (1968–71), Robert Hardin (1968–69), Richard Kamerer (1967), James Meade (1970–73), Mark Noble (1985–86), *Martin Petlock* (1972–86), Kenton Yeager (1984–85).

Actors and Actresses: Lewis Agrell (1973–76), Denny Albee (1973–75), David Aldrich (1967), Deborah Allen (1980–81), Donna Anderson (1984–86), Porter Anderson (1977–80), August Antilla (1963), Ellen Antilla (1963), Kathleen Archer (1976–79), Adam Arkin (1985–86), Anthony Arkin (1985–86), Donna Aronson (1973–75), Judith Ashe (1983–84), Karen Bair (1985–86), D. H. Baker (1978–80), Irene Ballinger (1972–73), Lisa Barnes (1985–86), Barbara Barringer (1983–84), Maryann Barulich (1976–79), Louis Beachner (1984–85), Normand Beauregard (1976–78), John Behan (1973–75), Janet Bell (1968–69), Jay Bell (1968–69), Charles Bennison (1979–82), Susannah Berryman (1978–81), Robert Beseda (1977–80), Denise Bessette (1981–82), Carolyn Blackinton (1977–80), Bill Blackwood (1978–80), Karen Blair (1984–85), *Raye Blakemore* (1977–81), Susan Borneman (1976–78), Carolyn Bowes (1980–81), Gregory Bowman (1978–79), Howard A. Branch, Jr. (1976–79), George Brengel (1976–77, 1978–79), Kevin Brief (1981–84), Elizabeth Brincklow (1972–73), *Ritch Brinkley* (1975–79), *Robert Britton* (1967–71), Alan Brooks (1981–82), Martha J. Brown (1974–77), Lydia Bruce (1983–85), Howard Brunner (1984–85), Tara Buckley (1978–81), Donald Buka (1985–86), Peter Burnell (1980–81), Linda Burnham (1975–77), Susan Esther Burnim (1979–80), Marnie Carmichael (1978–81), Hal Carter (1977–79), Vicki Casarett (1972–74), Tom Case (1976–78), Laurel Cases (1985–86), Phillip Cass (1982–83), Cathy S. Chappell (1974–77), Dion Chesse (1981–83), Nora Chester (1974–77), Mark Ciokajlo (1983–86), Ralph Clanton (1975–76), Janice Clark (1974–77), Burton Clarke (1973–76), James Clarke (1978–80), Randy Clements (1983–85), C. David Colson (1967–69), Diane C. Compton (1983–85), Linda Cook (1985–86), Ken Costigan (1975–76), A. D. Cover (1983–86), Patrick Crean (1973–75), Jim Crisp, Jr. (1974–77), Sheridan Crist (1985–86), Dub Croft (1981–82), Charles Cronk (1979–82), Joan Crowe (1983–85), Mac Crowell (1985–86), Lou Ann Csaszar (1976–79), Joseph Culliton (1982–83), Stuart Culpepper (1970–71), Valery Daemke (1983–84), *Laurence Daggett* (1980–84), *Stephen Daley* (1982–86), Barbara Dana (1985–86), James Daniels (1978–81), Kay Daphne (1983–86), Charles Davis (1972–73), Fred Davis (1975–78), Justin T. Deas (1971–73), *Dottie Dee* (1973–76, 1979–80), Donna A. Delonay (1985–86), Molly DePree (1975–78), Paula Dewey (1978–82), Curzon Dobell (1985–86), Art Dohany (1985–86), Darra Dolan (1983–85), James Donadio (1974–75), James Donlon (1976–77), Phillip Douglas (1981–84), Bairbre Dowling (1979–80), Cynthia Dozier (1982–83), Ann Ducati (1985–86), Deanna

Dunagan (1976–79), Marc Durso (1985–86), George Dvorsky (1984–85), *Patrick Egan* (1968–74, 1979–80), Paul M. Elkin (1981–82), Robert Elliott (1979–81), Paul J. Ellis (1983–85), *Bernerd Engel* (1973–76, 1980–82), Ellia English (1981–82), Brit Erickson (1977–79), Dov Fahrer (1977–80), Richard G. Fallon (1983–84), Robert Ferguson (1979–82), Deborah Fezelle (1980–81), John Fitzgibbon (1982–83), Kelly Fitzpatrick (1975–78), Joleen Fodor (1983–85), Marilyn Foote (1977–80), Michele Franks (1981–82), Ray Frewen (1980–83), Barry Friedman (1979–80), Neil Lee Friedman (1982–83, 1984–85), David Gaines (1980–82), Lawrence Gallegos (1980–81), Leo Garcia (1980–83), Frank Georgianna (1967), Jack Gilhooley (1976–77), George Gitto (1983–84), Jeanann Glassford (1979–82), Marc H. Glick (1979–82), Ron Gold (1967), Mary Francina Golden (1982–83), Lawrence Gordon (1963), John Gray (1974–77), John Green (1976–79), Fred Greene (1979–80), Suzanne Grodner (1981–84, 1985–86), Rita Grossberg (1972–73), Richard Grubbs (1981–84), Pam Guest (1978–80), Max Gulack (1974–76), Daniel Hagen (1980–81), Judith Halek (1984–85), Helen Halsey (1978–81), Jacqueline Hammond (1975–76), *Arthur Hanket* (1976–79, 1982–83), Elizabeth Harrell (1979–82), Terence R. Harris (1978–79), Nancy Hartman (1984–86), Mark Hattan (1985–86), Dan Haughey (1978–79), Yvette Hawkins (1985–86), Kelley Hazen (1981–84), Anthony Heald (1967–79), Judith Heck (1978–79), Jeffrey Herbst (1985–86), Neil Herlands (1980–81), Bill Herman (1975–78), Lisa P. Hermatz (1984–85), Elizabeth Herron (1985–86), James Hillgartner (1975–77), Margaret Hilton (1963), Mark Hirschfield (1978–81), Michael Hodgson (1979–82), *Donald C. Hoepner* (1967–79), P. J. Hoffman (1981–82), *Polly Holliday* (1963, 1967, 1968, 1970–73), *Richard Hopkins* (1970–74), Bob Horen (1975–76), Mary Elizabeth Horowitz (1977–79, 1981–82), Jayne Houdyshell (1983–85), *David S. Howard* (1975–82), Max Howard (1977–80), Bruce Howe (1977–79), Richard Hoyt-Miller (1982–85), Arthur Glen Hughes (1979–82), Tresa Hughes (1985–86), James Hunt (1980–82), James Hurdle (1973–74), Pat Hurley (1973–76), Randy Hyten (1981–84), Joan Inwood (1973–75), Peter Ivanov (1975–77), Richard Jacobs (1972–74), Mark Jacoby (1980–82), William Jay (1975–76), Christine Joelson (1977–80), Stephen Johnson (1973–76), Nancy Johnston (1983–84), *Douglas Jones* (1981–86), Jerry Allan Jones (1983–85), Stephen Joseph (1974–77), Lee Kalcheim (1976–77), Margaret Kaler (1966–69), Diane Kamp (1985–86), Linda Kampley (1966–68), Coleen B. Kane (1982–85), Donna Kane (1984–85), Arthur Kanket (1985–86), Katie Karlovitz (1983–85), Paul Kassel (1981–84), Kenneth Kay (1982–83), Doug Kaye (1972–74), Michael P. Keenan (1963, 1967, 1968–69), *Rory Kelly* (1982–86), Tom Kendall (1981–84), *Neal Kenyon* (1975–79), Jaye Keye (1980–83), *Henson Keys* (1972–76), Ruth Kidder (1980–81), Jody Kielbasa (1983–86), Graves Mark Kiely (1980–83), Sammy Kilman (1963), Grant Kilpatrick (1963), Alan Kimberly (1978–81), *Jeffrey Bryant King* (1977–82), Barry Klassel (1973–76), Kathleen Klein (1971–73, 1981–82), Dane Knell (1985–86), Rob Knepper (1983–84), Denise Koch (1980–81), Jack Koenig (1985–86), Susan Koenig (1984–85), Robert Kratky (1979–82), David Kwiat (1974–77), James La Ferla (1963), Michael Laird (1985–86), Robert Lanchester (1971–73), Beth Lane (1985–86), Keith LaPan (1981–84), Michael Lee Larisey (1984–86), Mare Launder (1984–86), Terry Layman (1983–84, 1985–86), *William Leach* (1971–78), Carol Lee (1973–75), Barbara Lester (1984–85), *Philip LeStrange* (1971–75, 1981–82), David B. Levine (1981–82, 1984–85), Bill Levis (1985–86), Pamela Lewis (1975–77), Beth Lincks (1975–78), Jillian Lindig (1973–75), Robin Llesellyn (1979–82), Angela L. Lloyd (1976–79), Michael L. Locklair (1977–80), Philip Lombardo (1980–83, 1984–85), Tim O'Neal Lorah (1982–85), Gretchen Lord (1982–84), Kirk Lumbard (1984–85), Macon McCalman (1968–71), Carol McCann (1980–83),

Innes-Fergus McDade (1982–83), Jean McDaniel (1976–79), Brian McFadden (1976–78), Barbara Reid McIntyre (1972–75), David Mallon (1969–71), Clardy Malugen (1978–81), Patrick Manley (1982–85), Susan Jones Mannino (1983–86), Marti Maraden (1968–69), Vicki March (1980–83), Lowry Marshall (1979–81), John J. Martin (1983–84), Carol Martini (1983–86), Peter Massey (1979–81), Patricia Masters (1980–82), Terri Mastobueno (1974–75), Morris Mathews (1972–74), Kyndal May (1985–86), Theodore May (1980–81), Richard Maynard (1985–86), Carolyn Ann Meeley (1977–80), C. W. Metcalf (1973–74), Holly Methfessel (1982–85), William Metzo (1979–80), Dennis Michaels (1975–77), Jonathan Michaelsen (1979–82), Carolyn Michel (1984–86), Mark Mikesell (1980–83), Carolyn Ann Milay (1981–82), Paul Milikin (1981–82), Sharron Miller (1979–80), Devora Millman (1970–71), Joyce Millman (1970–71), Charlotte Moore (1968), Kathy Morath (1980–81), Monique Morgan (1978–81), John Moskal, Jr. (1972–73), Stephanie Moss (1968–69), Kim Ivan Motter (1976–79), Mary Ann Mullen (1977–78), *Robert Murch* (1973–76, 1978–83), Paul Murray (1975–77), Janet Nawrocki (1978–80), Cynthia Newman (1982–85), *Clark Niederjohn* (1974–77, 1979–80), Douglas R. Nielsen (1980–81), Maria Niles (1974–75), Bill E. Noone (1970–73), Kathleen O'Meara Noone (1970–73), Virginia North (1967), Ellen Novack (1973–75), *Patricia Oetken* (1974–77, 1978–80), Ellen Olian-Bate (1973–74), *Bette Oliver* (1974–82), Frederic-Winslow Oram (1974–77), Valerie Ososky (1973–75), Viveca Parker (1981–82), Evan S. Parry (1977–80), Chuck Patterson (1978–80), Pamela Payton-Wright (1963), Donna Pele (1974–77), Lynne Perkins (1984–86), William Perley (1968–69), David O. Petersen (1966–69), Michael Piontek (1983–86), Nona M. Pipes (1972–75), *William Pitts* (1968–71, 1977–80), Jerry Plourde (1981–84), Brant Pope (1981–84), Mary Ed Porter (1976–78), Robb Pruitt (1985–86), Gerald Quimby (1975–76), Thomas Quimby (1973–76), Steven J. Rankin (1975–78), Katherine Rao (1975–76), Kenn Rapezynski (1983–86), Karen Rasch (1983–86), Rupert Ravens (1985–86), *Karl Redcoff* (1981–86), *Barbara Redmond* (1968–73, 1979–80, 1981–82), Joseph Reed (1976–79), Barbara Reid (1975–77), Diana Reis (1984–85), Michael Reynolds (1967–69), *Walter Rhodes* (1966–68, 1970–75, 1976–78), Kathryn Riedman (1983–86), Jennifer Riggs (1983–86), Anthony Ristoff (1963), Lance Roberts (1981–82), Chuck Rosenow (1984–85), Mark Rosenwinkel (1979–81), Jane Rosinski (1980–83), B. G. Ross (1971–73), Connie Rotunda (1979–82), Joan Rue (1974–76), Steve Ryan (1975–78), Richard Sabelloco (1984–85), Susan Sandler (1970–72), Anne Sandoe (1973–76), Peter J. Saputo (1968–69), Wendy Scharfman (1981–84), Howie Seago (1984–85), Kerry Shanklin (1972–74), Cynthia Simpson (1983–84), Paulette Sinclair (1967), Paul Singleton (1978–81), Victor Slezak (1982–83), Christine Sloan (1985–86), Albert L. Smelko (1963, 1967–69), Jane Smillie (1981–82), Alan Smith (1973–76), Burman Smith (1973–75), Christine Smith (1974–75), Leslie J. Smith (1981–84), Michael O. Smith (1985–86), Richard Smolendki (1985–86), *Barbara Sohmers* (1978–80, 1984–86), Georgia Southcotte (1984–86), Jon Spelman (1972–73), Sharon Spelman (1969–72), Steve Spencer (1983–86), Frederick Sperberg (1976–78), James St. Clair (1977–79), Ann Stafford (1978–80), *Robert Stallworth* (1974–77, 1979–80), John Starr (1963), Duncan Stephens (1981–82), Allan Stevens (1983–84), Leon B. Stevens (1983–85), Wesley Stevens (1981–82), Edward Stevlingson (1980–81), Deborah Stewart (1974–75), Parry B. Stewart (1983–86), Robert Strane (1968–81), Elizabeth Streiff (1979–82), Marcie Stringer (1983–85), Henry Strozier (1969–71), James L. Sutorius (1971–72), Dolores Sutton (1985–86), Milt Tarver (1976–78), Maggie Task (1983–84), Eric Tavares (1983–86), Pam T. Taylor (1982–85), Alex C. Thayer (1985–86), *Eberle Thomas* (1968–74, 1975–82), *Isa Thomas* (1968–86), Powys Thomas (1973–74),

William L. Thomas (1982–85), Peter Gregor Thompson (1985–86), Lizbeth Trepel (1981–84), William Turner (1973–75), Deborah Unger (1975–78), Carlos Valdes-Dapena (1980–83), Stephen Van Benschoten (1975–79), William Van Hunter (1980–81), Vikkian (1973–75), Mary Colleen Vreeland (1984–85), John Thomas Waite (1985–86), Robert Walker (1976–79), John C. Wall (1975–78), Bradford Wallace (1963, 1968–86), Carn N. Wallnau (1983–84), Colleen Smith Wallnau (1982–84), W. Francis Walters (1982–83), Andrew Watts (1982–83), Steve Weaver (1974–75), Paul Weidner (1963), Jane Welch (1980–81), Cynthia Wells (1980–81), Ronald Wendschuh (1980–81), Chris Wheeler (1980–81), Vince Williams (1984–86), *Carol Williard* (1969–71, 1983–85), Jack Willis (1982–85), Penelope Willis (1971–74), Roy Alan Wilson (1983–84), Jill Ann Womack (1985–86), Jim Wrynn (1972–73), Rebecca Young (1963), Romulus E. Zamora (1974–77), Mark Zimmerman (1983–84).

REPERTORY

1960–62: Not available.

1963: *Cyrano de Bergerac, The Mistress of the Inn, The Rivals, The School for Wives, The Taming of the Shrew*.

1964–66: Not available.

1967: *As You Like It, The Cherry Orchard, Eleanora Duse, The Fan, The Madwoman of Chaillot, Major Barbara, Romeo and Juliet, Scapin*.

1968: *Henry IV*, Part I, *Servant of Two Masters, Tartuffe, J.B., Look Back in Anger*.

1968–69: *A Midsummer Night's Dream, Antigone, The Alchemist, The Visit, Wilde!, The Caretaker, Arms and the Man, The Misanthrope, Oh What a Lovely War, The Lion in Winter, The Homecoming, Two Gents*.

1970: *Blithe Spirit, The Glass Menagerie, Misalliance, The Physicists, Oh Dad, Poor Dad, Mama's Hung You in the Closet and I'm Feelin' So Sad, Doctor Faustus, A Flea in Her Ear, Life with Father, All's Well That Ends Well, The Price, The Tortoise and the Hare*.

1971: *Born Yesterday, Candida, Charley's Aunt, The Comedy of Errors, Indians, A Day in the Death of Joe Egg, Love for Love, Our Town, The Puppet Prince, The Snow Queen, The Subject Was Roses*.

1972: *The Front Page, The Best Man, Hay Fever, Dracula, The House of Blue Leaves, The Matchmaker, The Devil's Disciple, War and Peace, The Time of Your Life, Just So Stories, The Yellow Laugh, The Legend of Sleepy Hollow, The King Stag*.

1973: *Pygmalion, Angel Street, The Philadelphia Story, The Crucible, Hotel Paradiso, The Effect of Gamma Rays on Man-in-the-Moon Marigolds, Little Mary Sunshine, The Rose Tattoo, The Merchant of Venice, Big Klaus and Little Klaus, Aladdin, The Canterville Ghost, The Wind in the Willows*.

1974: *The Brave Little Tailor, Reynard the Fox, Private Lives, Trelawney of the "Wells," The Devil's General, Broadway, A Delicate Balance, Arsenic and Old Lace, Inherit the Wind, Ring 'Round the Moon, Macbeth, Don Quixote of La Mancha, Story Theatre*.

1975: *Guys and Dolls, Heartbreak House, King Lear, Mistress of the Inn, The Sea, Tartuffe, There's One in Every Marriage, Tobacco Road*.

1975–76: *The Patriots, The New York Idea, Hogan's Goat, Boy Meets Girl, A Streetcar Named Desire, Look Homeward, Angel, Trolls and Bridges, Going Ape, The Quibbletown Recruits, The Music Man, Win with Wheeler, 1776 . . . and All That Jazz*.

1976–77: *The Ruling Class, Cat on a Hot Tin Roof, Waltz of the Toreadors, Desire Under the Elms, Knock Knock, The Sea Horse, Oh, Coward!, Two for the Seesaw, Serenading Louie, Mummer's End, My Love to Your Wife, Cyrano de Bergerac, Saturday, Sunday, Monday, Cromwell.*

1977–78: *The Royal Family, Juno and the Paycock, She Stoops to Conquer, The School for Wives, Travesties, Richard III, A Troupe in a Trunk, The Man Who Came to Dinner, The Inspector General, Catsplay, Archy and Friends.*

1978–79: *Design for Living, The Shadow Box, Volpone, Let's Get a Divorce, Long Day's Journey into Night, A History of the American Film, Othello, Stag at Bay, The Cherry Orchard, Merlin.*

1979–80: *Ah, Wilderness!, The Tempest, Da, Tintypes, Man and Superman, Idiot's Delight, The Warrens of Virginia, Transcendental Love, Stand-Off at Beaver and Pine.*

1980–81: *On Golden Pond, The Beggar's Opera, Terra Nova, The Song Is Kern!, The Three Musketeers, Picnic, Once in a Lifetime.*

1981–82: *A Midsummer Night's Dream, Mrs. Warren's Profession, The Show-Off, The All Night Strut!, Charley's Aunt, The Male Animal, The Girl of the Golden West.*

1982–83: *The Dining Room, A View from the Bridge, Misalliance, Man with a Load of Mischief, Sherlock Holmes, The Winslow Boy, Dark of the Moon.*

1983–84: *Arms and the Man, Waiting for Godot, The Gin Game, Promenade, All!, Death of a Salesman, The Drunkard, Rashomon, The Importance of Being Earnest.*

1984–85: *Children of a Lesser God, Amadeus, And a Nightingale Sang . . . , The Little Foxes, Dames at Sea, A Month in the Country, You Can't Take It with You, Twice Around the Park.*

1985–86: *A Christmas Carol, Greater Tuna, A Moon for the Misbegotten, A Life in the Theatre, Sleuth, Orphans, Spoon River Anthology, Tartuffe, How the Other Half Loves, As Is, Forgive Me, Evelyn Bunns, Hamlet.*

BIBLIOGRAPHY

Published Sources:

"The Asolo Theatre." *25th Anniversary Season Program: Waiting for Godot.* Sarasota, Fla.: Asolo State Theatre, 1985.

"Fallon Exits Asolo After Board Powwow." *Variety,* 323 (May 28, 1986): 85.

"The First 25 Years: Asolo on Tour." *Asolo State Theatre, 1984–85 Season Program: Amadeus.* Sarasota, Fla: Asolo State Theatre, 1985.

LaHoud, John. *Theatre Reawakening: A Report on Ford Foundation Assistance to American Drama.* New York: Ford Foundation, Office of Reports, 1977.

Theatre Profiles. Vols. 1–7. New York: Theatre Communications Group, 1973–85.

Theater World, 1960–61 through *1985–86.* New York: Crown Publishers, 1961–87.

Unpublished Sources:

Fallon, Richard G. Personal interview. March 11, 1985.

Lewis, Bettilu. Personal interview. March 13, 1986.

Playbill Collection of the Theatre Communications Group 1957–75 (microfiche).

Ulmer, John. Personal interview. March 11, 1985.

(Personnel and Repertorg compiled by Weldon B. Durham) Donald H. Wolfe

ASOLO THEATRE COMEDY FESTIVAL. See ASOLO STATE THEATRE.

AT THE FOOT OF THE MOUNTAIN was founded in 1974 by Martha Boesing in Minneapolis, Minnesota, and is currently located in the Cedar Riverside People's Community Center on the west bank of the Minnesota River.

Its 1974 season opened with *Pimp*, written and directed by Boesing. This first effort focused on the way women are trained to live their lives within socially dictated limits.

Feminist theatre companies were a natural outgrowth of the women's movement, which had gathered strength in the late sixties and early seventies. Boesing's original goal was for the experimental ensemble "to create plays and music out of the company's own feelings and life experiences." Although two years passed before they officially dedicated themselves to feminist issues, early productions indicate evidence of a strong feminist orientation. At the Foot of the Mountain has become a major force in American feminist theatre, and its unprecedented eight years of continuous operation locates it among the country's most significant professional women's theatres.

The company's Mission Statement describes how they hope to empower audiences both artistically and politically. Central to its political stance is the commitment "to revolt against misogyny, racism, and all related violations of the human spirit whereby one person (or group of persons) has power over another." The core of its artistic goals illustrates its attempt to "create theatre directly out of the lives, values, and visions of women," and identifies the centrality of their feminist concerns.

In 1976 Phyllis Jane Rose, who had directed *Pimp* at Southern Illinois University at Carbondale, moved to Minneapolis to work as a director with the young company. At the Foot of the Mountain had been commissioned to present a piece at San Francisco's Firehouse Theatre for a Demeter Festival. The play was to be written by Boesing about the relationships between mothers and daughters. However, the piece was postponed until the ensemble could discover its "company voice." In order to do this, the members decided to spend a year performing existing texts.

They discovered in their search for a text that no script avoided demeaning women in some respect. As a result, they decided to adapt Bertolt Brecht's *The Exception and the Rule* by interrupting the story with testimonies of rape. The adaptation, *Raped*, was its first production as a committed feminist theatre and remained a popular feature of the repertory for four seasons. In later productions audience members were invited to further interrupt the text with their own rape testimony. This experience became the basis of "Ritual Drama," a form of transformational theatre "structured to stimulate and incorporate spontaneous audience testimony into the production." The company has dedicated itself to developing this form and has featured it in its productions of *Junkie!* and *Ashes, Ashes, We All Fall Down*.

As have many feminist theatre companies, At the Foot of the Mountain has struggled to exist. The group incorporated in 1974 as a nonprofit organization and has operated since then on donations, both corporate and private, and box-office receipts. For the first five years the company's core artists, Martha Boesing, Jan Magrane, and Phyllis Jane Rose, were the sole members of the board of directors. In 1980 they shifted from a collective to a collaborative ensemble and decided to separate the functions of the performance company from those of the management company. They invited ten women from outside the theatre to serve on the board of directors, which has worked closely with the management company to expand audience and community support. The operating budget has increased from $60,000 in 1980 to $250,000 in 1985. The company has grown to include full-time artistic and producing directors with three to eleven performers, musicians, and technicians. The management company, with its managing director, is a full-time ensemble of six.

At the Foot of the Mountain developed the Emergent Artists Series to provide performance opportunities for segments of the women's community seldom included in more traditional theatres. The series features four projects: Broadcloth: A Sampler of New Scripts by Women Writers, Broadcloth: A Series of New Work by Women Performers, The Coming of Age Project, and Differences. The two Broadcloth projects are biennial series in which selected authors and performers are brought to Minneapolis from all over the country to present their work. The Coming of Age Project provides workshops to encourage the expression of two groups of women: those aged thirteen to seventeen ("our daughters") and those aged sixty to eighty ("our grandmothers"). Workshop participants create performances from the stories and experiences in their lives. Differences features a four-week series of public forums focused on issues that divide the women's community in an effort to confront the fears engendered by this diversity.

In order to reach a larger audience, the company has expanded to include touring and media projects. Its production of *Raped* sold out its entire run during the original performance in July 1976 and became the first project to tour. Since then *Head over Heels: Teenage Rites of Passage* and *Las Gringas* have played to warm receptions in more than ten states. As a result of this success, At the Foot of the Mountain was chosen by the Northwest Area Foundation, the Minnesota State Arts Board, and the Affiliated State Arts Agencies of the Upper Midwest to be part of the 1984–85 "Twin Cities Performing Artists on Tour" program. Two of its productions, *Junkie!* and *Ashes, Ashes, We All Fall Down*, have been recorded on film and are available to interested individuals and organizations. In addition to performing and holding workshops, the company offers a variety of classes to the public, the fees for which are based on the participant's income. A multiracial, multicultural orientation emerged in 1983.

After ten years with the company, artistic director Martha Boesing resigned her position to accept an eighteen-month grant from the Bush Foundation that allowed her to write full-time. While her full-time involvement with the theatre has ceased, she intends to return for projects of special interest.

In 1984 Phyllis Jane Rose was appointed executive director, a new position created after Boesing's departure. The duties of the executive director include the coordination and articulation of the theatre's artistic, programmatic, and organizational long-range planning; development (with the board) of financial policies that support the long-range needs of the theatre; and the final staff approval of and overall responsibility for all theatre expenses, activities, and growth. The identification of these duties as vital to the continued life of the company indicates its growth from a small, six-person collective operating only part-time and dedicated to personal vision to a full-time professional theatre.

The critical response to ten seasons of productions by At the Foot of the Mountain has been mixed. While some journalists have criticized Boesing for indulging herself that her personal images are relevant to a wider public, continued strong audience support has fueled the company's rapid growth. At the Foot of the Mountain has weathered the difficulties encountered by many young companies and emerged as a central force in American feminist theatre.

PERSONNEL

Management: Martha Boesing (1974–84), Jan Magrane (1974–86), Phyllis Jane Rose (1974–86).

Production Company: Marion Angelica, Ellen Anthony, Aurora Bingham, Martha Boesing, Paul Boesing, Kay Bolstad, Barrie Jean Borich, Leslie Bowman, Sue Carter, Jaehn Clare, Dorothy Crabb, Susan Delattre, Meredith Flynn, Kathryn Hill, Kim Hines, Endesha Mae Holland, Carla Jester, Judith Katz, Jenifer Keefe, Terri Kruzan, Marilyn Lindstrom, Jan Magrane, Pam Marshall, Arisa Morgan-Lewellyn, Chris Parker, Debra Parks-Satterfield, Quimetta Perle, Phyllis Jane Rose, Martha Roth, Naomi Scheman, Danielle Sosin, Loretto Stanton, M. Sue Wilson, Theresa Ziegler.

Designers and Technicians: Jeff Bartlett, Tony Bingham, Leslie Bowman, Lucinda Frantz, Linda Gellman, Peg Grifin, Deb James, Carla Jester, David Krchlech, Jan Magrane, Joan Mikelson, Ardith Morris, Donna Nelson, Morgan O'Brien, Clancy O'Reardon, Liz Olds, Linda Osborne, Phyllis Jane Rose, Nancy Seaton, Lisa River Stacy, Lisa Stephens, Carol Wisewomoon, Corine Zala.

Stage Directors: Martha Boesing, Paul Boesing, Chris Cinque, Jan Magrane, Phyllis Jane Rose, Erica Tismer, Phyllis Jane Wagner, Barbara Wiener.

Actors: Lucy Bacon, Jan Badger, Carah Balkman, Lorraine Barr, Betsy Benjamin, Barbara Bloom, Martha Boesing, Jennifer Boesing, Joyce Boesinger, Kay Bolstad, Anne Bowman, Karen Carlisle, Margo Carper, Marie Cartier, Chris Cinque, Jaehn Clare, Annie Clark, Judy Cooper, J. A. Crane, Jenise Didier, Shannon Doheny, Randa Downs, Leah J. Erickson, Kathryn Esslinger, Ruth Ever, Danielle Renee Fagre, Rhonda Feiman, Bethleigh Flanagan, Holly Franzen, Trudy Fulton, Annie Gage, Rebecca Gant, Amy Gold, Susan Graves, Kathleen Hardy, Marya Hart, Roubye Hart, Lisa Heffley, Audreia Henderson, Kathryn Hill, Judith Katz, Marianne Keller, Lara Kokernot, Denise Konicek, Dora Lanier, Cecilia Lee, Stephani Lourie, Jan Magrane, Amy Del Main, Anita Makar, Miriam Monasch, Arisa S. Morgan-Lewellyn, Susie Mudge, Marcia K. Mueller, Rachel Nelson, Linda Osborne, Esther Ouray, Deb Parks, Dennis Paul, Pauline Pflander, Mary Preus, Elizabeth Pringle, Susan Pritchard, Elizabeth Reese, Cathy Rieves, Liz Robbins, Phyllis Jane Rose, Carolyn Russell, Robyn Samuels, Phaedre Sanders, Carol H. Santucci, Jeanette Sarmiento, Robyn Sue Schnidt, Barbara Schwalbe, Meredith Sedlachek, Bridget Siobhan, Bebhinn Dubhain Smuda, Madeleine Sosin, Loretto Stanton, Melissa Stoudt, Renee Sugrue, Erica Tismer, Pamela Wagner, Phyllis Jane Wagner, Melanie Williams, Laurie Witzkowski, Jennie C. Yngsdahl, Theresa Ziegler.

REPERTORY

1974: *Pimp, The Gelding.*
1975: *River Journal.*

1976: *Love Song for an Amazon, Raped.*

1977: *Babies in the Big House, The Moon Tree, Raped.*

1978: *The Story of a Mother, The Clue in the Old Birdbath, Raped.*

1979: *The Life, Prehistoric Visions for Revolting Hags, Raped.*

1980: *Dora Dufan's Wild West Extravaganza: Or the Real Lowdown on Calamity Jane, Pizza, Raped.*

1981: *Junkie!.*

1982: *Ashes, Ashes, We All Fall Down.*

1983: *Low Life on a High Planet, Haunted by the Holy Ghost, Antigone Too: Rites of Love and Defiance.*

1984: *Las Gringas, The Girls Room.*

1985–86: *The Clue in the Old Birdbath, Head over Heels, Going to Seed, The Ladies Who Lunch, Neurotic, Erotic, Exotics* (with Spiderwoman Theatre Company).

BIBLIOGRAPHY

Published Source:

At the Foot of the Mountain Anniversary Newsletters. Ten volumes. Minneapolis: At the
    Foot of the Mountain, 1975–85.

Archival Resources:

Minneapolis, Minnesota. At the Foot of the Mountain Theatre Company.

Seattle, Washington. University of Washington. School of Drama. Complete collection
    of programs; articles of incorporation and bylaws.

Juli A. Thompson

B

BALTIMORE THEATRE PROJECT, Baltimore, Maryland, was founded in 1971 by Philip Arnoult, then professor of theatre at the Baltimore campus of Antioch College. Arnoult leased two floors of a historic brick building at 310 Preston Street (near Baltimore's famous Lyric Theatre and across the street from the Meyerhof symphony hall). He and Colin Heath, the theatre's first technical director, then designed and built open-space performance areas on both floors. The theatre opened on September 7, 1971, with a reading of new work by the feminist poet Robertoh Fava. The first theatre performance in the new theatre took place on November 15, 1971—an original, experimental work titled *The Kaakamakakoo* by the Otrabanda Company, a group of American and Asian performers under the direction of Tone Brulin, a Belgian theatre and television director.

From the beginning Arnoult conceived of the Theatre Project as a producing and presenting institution, rather than as an acting company. The theatre has, nevertheless, formed and housed numerous professional acting companies for productions of original plays and performance projects (among them Theatre X, Milwaukee, Wisconsin; Iowa Theatre Lab, Catskill, New York; and Blackbird Theatre Company, Tulsa, Oklahoma). Although its in-house productions and resident theatre companies have been successful and well received, the theatre is primarily known for its year-round presentation of the work of visiting theatre artists and companies from across the United States and from other countries. During the 1970s the Theatre Project became a widely copied model for community-based, nontraditional performing arts centers in the United States and in Europe. The Theatre Project has had no competitors in the Baltimore area. It remains one of the few theatres outside New York City to consistently present experimental work from the world's stages.

Philip Arnoult began his career as an actor, director, and producer in Memphis, Tennessee, at the Front Street Theatre. In 1963 he founded the short-lived Market

Theatre in Memphis. From 1965 to 1968 he served in Germany as an entertainment director for U.S. Army Special Services. In 1969 Arnoult directed the
WeatherVane Playhouse in Akron, Ohio. In 1970 he moved to Baltimore and a
faculty position with Antioch College. By this time Arnoult knew he wanted to
create an alternative to traditional commercial and regional theatres. He was
appalled by the small, demographically narrow, traditional American theatre
audience. He was determined to make the Theatre Project accessible and desirable
to large numbers of ordinary people who seldom, if ever, attended a theatre
performance. The most important influence on Arnoult's plans for the theatre,
including its name, was the Depression-era Federal Theatre Project and the goals
of its director, Hallie Flanagan. Arnoult was most strongly influenced artistically
by the work of Jerzy Grotowski and the Polish Laboratory Theatre. Although
he supported and encouraged works in a wide variety of styles, he was most
closely attuned to artists with an unconventional and nontraditional vision.

Until 1985 the Theatre Project had no box office, and admission was free.
Donations were requested from the audience after each performance. In its early
years the Theatre Project was strongly subsidized by Antioch College. The
balance of its funding came from grants from the National Endowment for the
Arts, the Maryland State Arts Council, and from private contributions. In 1976
funding for Theatre Project activities dramatically increased as the theatre entered
into contracts with federal, state, and local agencies to provide performances
and arts instruction for a variety of programs. The Theatre Project pioneered in
the use of CETA (Comprehensive Employment Training Act) jobs and funds
for arts activities. In the 1980s, faced with the disappearance of many sources
of nonprofit theatre funding, the Theatre Project instituted a subscription plan
and began charging admission to performances. The plan provided a new, albeit
more traditional base of financial support. In 1971 the Theatre Project's total
income was $41,000. In 1980 that figure was nearly $500,000. The theatre
operated with an annual budget of approximately $150,000 in 1986.

The Theatre Project has presented an astonishing number of performances in
its fifteen-year history. More than 400 separate performance groups and solo
artists have presented more than 3,000 performances in the theatre's main performance space alone. The theatre has also presented more than 2,000 performances outside the building in Baltimore communities and neighborhoods, in
the Baltimore-Washington region, and in national tours of Theatre Project productions. These figures represent performances by the Theatre Project's resident
acting companies and by visiting artists from twenty-nine states and twenty
foreign countries. In 1976 and 1977 the Theatre Project also produced, in collaboration with the University of Baltimore, the well-known TNT (The New
Theatre) festivals, the first international experimental theatre festivals to be held
in the United States. From 1976 to 1981 the Theatre Project's in-house productions of original plays and its special projects became integral features of the
theatre's operations along with its presentations of the work of visiting artists.
During those years the theatre produced the Baltimore Neighborhood Arts Circus,

a summer program that provided hundreds of performances by professional artists in parks and playgrounds throughout the city. The theatre gained national recognition with its production of *Baltimore Voices*, a model oral-history theatre production funded in part by the National Endowment for the Humanities.

The Theatre Project formally separated from Antioch College and became an independent organization in 1976. At that time it was incorporated as a nonprofit community arts center with a board of directors and a core staff, which included an artistic director, a managing director, and a technical director. The theatre employed actors, designers, and administrative personnel on a project-to-project basis. In 1980, for example, the Theatre Project maintained its regular season of performances in the theatre, two acting companies presenting performances in the theatre and on tour, a city-sponsored training program, and its program of summer performances, all operating at the same time. During that year the theatre employed approximately 200 persons.

For most of its history the Theatre Project's internal organization was that of a hierarchical collective. Arnoult retained final decision-making authority in every phase of the theatre's operations, but subordinate staff members, project directors, and artistic personnel enjoyed considerable freedom in planning and executing the theatre's programs. The full theatre staff met regularly for planning and review, and every staff member had a voice in shaping Theatre Project operations.

Influential artists and theatre companies who have appeared at the Theatre Project include the following: Le Plan K, Brussels; Teatre Vicinal, Paris; Krishnan Nabmudiri, New Delhi; Shalako Company, New York; Medicine Show Theatre Ensemble, New York; Pilobolus, Boston; Bread and Puppet Theatre, Vermont; Iowa Theatre Lab, Catskill, New York; The Play Group, Knoxville; Omaha Magic Theatre, Omaha; Spiderwoman Theatre, New York; Bob Carroll, San Francisco; The Dance Exchange, Washington, D.C.; Independent Eye, Chicago; Friends Roadshow, Amsterdam; Kipper Kids, London; Les Enfants Du Paradis, Montreal; Studio Scarabee, Amsterdam; Paul Zaloom, New York; Squat Theatre, Yugoslavia; and Florida Studio Theatre, Sarasota.

The Theatre Project operated from September 1971 to March 1982. It closed, except for occasional performances, in 1983 and 1984. The theatre reopened in December 1985. It is currently operating with year-round performances.

PERSONNEL

Management: Philip Arnoult, founder and director (1971–86); Carol Baish, associate director (1971–86); Benjamin F. Carney, associate director (1976–81); John Strausbaugh, associate director (1981–83); John Wilson, house manager (1978–81).

Technical Directors: Timothy Duke, (1979–81), Colin Heath (1971–74), James Houstle (1978), Steve Walker (1976–78).

Actors and Actresses (Theatre Project residents): Tone Brulin (1974), Paul Iorio (1974–75), Jill Kline (1977–81), Barry Meiners, J. W. Rone, Helen Szablya (1979–81), Andy Trompeter (1980–81), Ric Zank.

Throughout its history the Theatre Project employed numerous project-related management, administrative, technical, and artistic personnel. In-house productions, training programs, and other special projects all required full staffing that disbanded when the projects were completed. Data concerning the many shorter-term personnel employed by the Theatre Project can be found in the Ben F. Carney archival collection and the Theatre Project archives.

REPERTORY

1971–72: *Oedipus, The Future King, Double Bill.*

1972–73: *Boxes, But It Is Nothing, Stump Removal, Colin Heath and Friends* (music).

1973–74: *Theatre Project Puppets*, Daniel Mark Epstein (poetry).

1974–75: *The Work I've Done, Theatre Project Orchestra* (music).

1975–76: *Theatre Project Dance Company* (dance), *The Naming, Dancer Without Arms, Moby Dick, Sweetbird, Judas Pax* (Iowa Theatre Lab).

1976–77: *Come True, Tales Tall and True, Dutchman, The Dumbwaiter, The Zoo Story.*

1977–78: *Tale of the Groundhog, Space Director, Metamorphosis, Blackbird Theatre.*

1979–80: *Baltimore Voices, Theatre Project Dance Festival.*

1980–81: *Baltimore Voices, John Strausbaugh.*

1981–82: *New Wave Festival.*

Comprehensive data concerning Theatre Project Productions and performances by visiting artists and companies may be found in the Theatre Project archives.

BIBLIOGRAPHY

Published Sources:

Baltimore Sun, 1971–86.

New American (Baltimore), 1971–86.

New York Times, 1972–86.

Washington Post, 1971–86.

Unpublished Source:

Carney, Benjamin F. "The Baltimore Theatre Project, Inc., 1971–85: Toward a People's Theatre." Doctoral dissertation, University of Missouri, Columbia, 1985.

Archival Resources:

Baltimore, Maryland. The Theatre Project. Baltimore Theatre Project archives, 1971–86.

New York, New York. Personal collection of Benjamin F. Carney relates to period 1971–83.

Benjamin F. Carney

[THE] BAM (BROOKLYN ACADEMY OF MUSIC) THEATRE COMPANY

PANY was actually two separate attempts (1977–78 and 1980–81) at forming a classical repertory company. For each attempt, the idea and original impetus came from Harvey Lichtenstein, president of the Brooklyn Academy of Music, a nonprofit, multitheatre complex located at 30 Lafayette Avenue in a section of downtown Brooklyn undergoing gradual gentrification. The Academy itself was originally built in 1859 and moved to its current location in 1903. It served as both a cultural center and social meeting hall for the residents of Brooklyn until the 1930s, when it fell into disuse as its neighborhood deteriorated. Renovation work on the entire complex was begun in 1974 after Lichtenstein, a former dancer and fund-raiser for the arts, became president in 1971.

The renovated BAM consists of four theatres: the Opera House (2,100 seating capacity) and the Playhouse (1,022 seats), both proscenium-equipped theatres; the Lepercq Space, a former ballroom with flexible bleachers (550 capacity); and the Attic Space (199 seats). The BAM Theatre Company mounted productions in all spaces except the Attic.

In 1976, as part of the bicentennial celebration, the BAM and the Kennedy Center (Washington, D.C.) coproduced revivals of three American classics (*Sweet Bird of Youth, The Royal Family*, and *Long Day's Journey into Night*). Their successful critical and financial reception at the BAM convinced Lichtenstein that the New York City theatre was ready for another attempt at establishing a true, classical repertory company such as had been tried (and had failed) at New York's Repertory Theatre of Lincoln Center* in the 1960s. He wanted to present classic plays (American and otherwise) not being seen in New York, using America's best stage actors while training new ones. He approached many of the American theatre's leading directors, such as Mike Nichols, Ellis Rabb, and Edwin Sherin, to take charge of the company, but he was universally rejected, as it was felt that the repertory concept was not workable, given the structure of the American theatre. Instead, Frank Dunlop, the English director of the Young Vic (which had played at BAM in 1974), was offered and accepted control of the company. Although he wanted, in the long run, to have a core repertory company, Dunlop felt it best to begin by casting each play separately and performing each for its separate run (as was done in other off-Broadway ''repertory'' companies, such as the Circle in the Square and the Public Theatre). He understood that this would enable him to attract the ''star'' names necessary to attract audiences.

Along with Dunlop, Lichtenstein hired Bernice Weiler, a veteran of theatre management, to serve as general manager, and the already existing marketing and technical facilities and resources of BAM were utilized.

Dunlop's first season, in the spring of 1977, consisted of two plays, the questionably classic *The New York Idea*, Langdon Mitchell's rarely (if ever) revived 1906 farce, and the more solidly classic *The Three Sisters*, by Chekhov. Both productions were directed by Dunlop and utilized Broadway designers. The strong casts were headed by such Broadway stars as Blythe Danner, Rosemary Harris, Tovah Feldshuh, Stephen Collins, and Denholm Elliott. The appearance of recent Motion Picture Academy Award winner Ellen Burstyn may, as much as any production values, have accounted for the sold-out houses for *The Three Sisters*. Critical reception, while not overwhelming, was polite.

Dunlop's second season, from February to June 1978, saw four plays mounted: G. B. Shaw's *The Devil's Disciple* (a joint production with the Ahmanson Theatre of Los Angeles), Ferenc Molnár's *The Play's the Thing*, and Shakespeare's *Julius Caesar*, all three directed by Dunlop; and Samuel Beckett's *Waiting for Godot*, directed by Walter Asmus and based on Beckett's own production mounted in the early 1970s in Berlin. Again, professional designers were employed, and an impressive array of Broadway talent, such as Barnard Hughes, George Rose, Austin Pendleton, Rene Auberjonois, and Sam Waterston, appeared (some in more than one production). And again, an entire run was sold out with the help of an Oscar. In this case, Richard Dreyfuss won the Oscar during the run of *Julius Caesar*. Still, by the end of the second season, it was obvious that Dunlop's successes were those of the commercial American theatre and not the classical repertory Lichtenstein had envisioned. Also, his late choices of plays and actors had made marketing (particularly on a seasonal basis) difficult. It was decided to replace him with another English director, David Jones, formerly an associate director of the Royal Shakespeare Company, who, like Dunlop, had gotten to know Lichtenstein when his company had previously performed at BAM.

Unlike Dunlop's seat-of-the-pants approach to production, Jones shared Lichtenstein's desire for a permanent company, but he realized that he would be unable to sign big names to long-term contracts. So his company consisted entirely of lesser-known actors, the best-known being the British actor-director Brian Murray. Possibly the biggest box-office name associated with the company was American stage and film director Arthur Penn, who would share directing duties with Jones.

Thanks to a $400,000 grant from the Ford Foundation, Lichtenstein was able to hire the complete supporting staff of a true repertory company. Charles Dillingham, formerly general manager of the American Conservatory Theatre* in San Francisco, was the managing director, playwright Richard Nelson was the dramaturg, and there were resident staffs of designers, stage managers, composers, and administrators, as well as both vocal and choreographic residents. In addition, Jones attempted to perform in a limited true repertory schedule, rotating two or three productions on a weekly basis. However, the cost of set storage and technical turnaround time for this schedule proved extravagant.

Jones' repertory for the 1980 season was varied and featured two little-known and rarely revived American plays, *Johnny on a Spot*, by Charles MacArthur, and *He and She*, by Rachel Crothers, in addition to Shakespeare's seldom-performed *The Winter's Tale*, the American premiere of Maxim Gorky's *Barbarians*, and a double bill of romantic farces by Georges Feydeau and Bertolt Brecht (!). The combination of unknown plays, poor reviews, and unknown casts resulted in half-full houses. For his second season Jones scheduled better-known plays and playwrights (Shakespeare, George Farquhar, Henrik Ibsen, Bertolt Brecht, and Sophocles), but the reviews were no longer even polite, and New York City theatre audiences, with the vast array of choices open to them, stopped making the trip to Brooklyn almost entirely. His funding gone and the BAM in debt, Lichtenstein was forced to concede that New York City wasn't interested in a true classical repertory and to disband the company. Instead, the

BAM turned to the promotion of avant-garde theatre, music, and dance and has been successful with its annual Next Wave festival begun in 1983.

PERSONNEL

President of BAM: Harvey Lichtenstein.

Dunlop Company, 1977–78:

Artistic Director: Frank Dunlop (1977–78).

General Manager: Bernice Weiler (1977–78).

Directors: Walter D. Asmus (1978), Frank Dunlop (1977–78).

Set Designers: Carole Lee Carroll (1978), Santo Loquasto (1978), William Ritman (1977), Carl Toms (1978).

Costume Designers: Dona Granata (1978), Nancy Potts (1977–78), Carl Toms (1978).

Lighting Designers: F. Mitchell Dana (1977–78), Shirley Prendergast (1978).

Actors and Actresses: Norman Abrams (1978), Terry Alexander (1978), *Rene Auberjonois* (1977–78), Earl Boen (1978), *Ellen Burstyn* (1977), Ralph Clanton (1977), Jerome Collamore (1977), *Stephen Collins* (1977–78), George David Connolly (1977), Robert Cornthwaite (1978), *Blythe Danner* (1977), Stephen Davies (1978), Justin Deas (1978), Paul Diaz (1978), *Richard Dreyfuss* (1978), Michael Egan (1978), *Denholm Elliott* (1977), Sheldon Epps (1978), *Tovah Feldshuh* (1977), Michael Gennaro (1978), *Margaret Hamilton* (1977–78), *Rosemary Harris* (1977), Luise Heath (1978), *Barnard Hughes* (1977–78), *Thomas Hulce* (1978), Justine Johnston (1977), *Kurt Kasznar* (1978), David Patrick Kelly (1977), Diana Kirkwood (1977), Philip Kraus (1978), Ken Letner (1978), Allan Lurie (1978), George McDaniel (1978), Sharon Morrison (1978), R. J. Murray, Jr. (1978), John Orchard (1978), *Milo O'Shea* (1978), Stuart Pankin (1977), Randy Pelish (1978), *Austin Pendleton* (1977–78), Paul Perri (1978), Alek Primrose (1977), Betty Ramey (1978), Peggy Rea (1978), Rex Robbins (1977–78), *George Rose* (1978), Leon Russom (1977), *Chris Sarandon* (1978), *Carole Shelley* (1978), Slone Shelton (1978), Rex Stallings (1978), Fred Stuthman (1978), Holly Villaire (1977–78), *Sam Waterston* (1978), Edward Zang (1978).

Jones Company, 1980–81:

Artistic Director: David Jones (1980–81).

Associate Director: Arthur Penn (1980–81).

Managing Director: Charles Dillingham (1980–81).

Literary Manager: Richard Nelson.

Directors: Edward Cornell (1980), Andre Ernotte (1980), David Jones (1980–81), Emily Mann (1980–81), Arthur Penn (1981), Laird Williamson (1981).

Set Designers: John Lee Beatty (1980–81), Robert Blackman (1981), David Gropman (1980), Andrew Jackness (1980), John Jensen (1980–81), Heidi Landesman (1980), Ming Cho Lee (1981), Santo Loquasto (1981).

Costume Designers: Susan Hilferty (1981), William Ivey Long (1980), Santo Loquasto (1981), Carol Oditz (1981), Dunya Ramicova (1980–81), John David Ridge (1980), Jennifer Von Mayrhauser (1980–81), Julie Weiss (1980).

Lighting Designers: F. Mitchell Dana (1980–81), Arden Fingerhut (1981), William Mintzer (1980).

Actors and Actresses: Sheila Allen (1980–81), C. B. Anderson (1980–81), Gerry Bamman (1980–81), Gary Bayer (1980), Dominic Chianese (1981), Jerome Dempsey (1980–81), Christine Estabrook (1980), Laura Esterman (1981), Boyd Gaines (1980),

Avril Gentles (1980), Sam Gray (1981), Tracy Griswold (1981), Michael Gross (1981), Ben Halley, Jr. (1981), Michael Hammind (1980), James Harper (1981), Olivia Virgil Harper (1981), Helen Harrelson (1980), Roxanne Hart (1980), John Heffernan (1980), Patrick Hines (1980), Richard Jamieson (1980–81), Cherry Jones (1980), Cheryl Yvonne Jones (1981), Laurie Kennedy (1981), Stephen Lang (1980), Anna Kluger Levine (1980), Kevin McClarnon (1980), Beth McDonald (1981), MichaelJohn McGann (1980–81) (Note: First names as are), Frank Maraden (1980–81), Marti Maraden (1980), Randle Mell (1981), Guy Michaels (1980), Bill Moor (1980), Keith Moore (1980–81), Joe Morton (1980–81), Brian Murray (1980–81), Joan Pape (1980–81), Peter Phillips (1980), Jon Polito (1980), Scott Richards (1981), Kristin Rudrüd (1981), Robert Rutland (1981), Don Scardino (1981), John Seitz (1980), Priscilla Shanks (1981), Norman Snow (1980), Ted Sod (1981), Sherry Steiner (1980).

REPERTORY

1977: *The New York Idea, The Three Sisters.*
1978: *The Devil's Disciple, The Play's the Thing, Julius Caesar, Waiting for Godot.*
1980: *The Winter's Tale, Johnny on a Spot, Barbarians, He and She, The Marriage Dance: The Wedding, The Purging.*
1981: *A Midsummer Night's Dream, The Recruiting Officer, The Wild Duck, Jungle of Cities, Oedipus the King.*

BIBLIOGRAPHY

Unpublished Source:
Daykin, Judith, BAM general manager. Personal interview. No date.

Archival Resources:
New York, New York. Brooklyn Academy of Music. Programs, press clippings, reviews.
New York, New York. New York Public Library. Library and Museum of the Performing
        Arts, Lincoln Center. Programs, press clippings, reviews.

Fredric Berg

BARTER THEATRE, also known as Robert Porterfield's Barter Theatre of Abingdon, Virginia, the State Theatre of Virginia, and the World Famous Barter Theatre, was founded by Robert Porterfield as a nonprofit regional repertory theatre. Its initial performance of John Golden's *After Tomorrow* played to a capacity audience at the Town Hall/Opera House in Abingdon, Virginia, on June 10, 1933.

During the winter of 1932–33, Porterfield gathered from friends and acquaintances at the Actor's Dinner Club in New York a company of twenty-five seasoned and versatile actors and actresses. These players agreed to perform in Abingdon and the surrounding mountain towns in exchange for room, board, and a share of one-half the season's profits. The other half went to the Actors' Relief Fund.

From the town of Abingdon, with a population of under 2,000, Porterfield obtained a rent-free lease on condition the company not perform on Sundays. The Depression-closed Martha Washington College campus across the street from the Opera House provided housing for the artists lured from New York for the summer.

The first play was rehearsed in New York. Each person found his or her own transportation to Abingdon. To combat Bible Belt beliefs that actors were evil, all members of the company attended church regularly during the season.

Each play opened in Abingdon and then went on the road. A rented farm truck and school bus provided transportation for the company. Thirty cents in cash was welcome, but almost any item that could be used was accepted in exchange for admission, including bartered food. Playbill advertising was traded for muslin to be used for sets and for necessities that could not be made over or borrowed. Draperies, curtains, and old clothes were transformed into costumes. Salvaged lumber was used in sets, which were designed to telescope to fit a variety of playing areas. Some towns, situated on the regular touring route between New Orleans and New York and Philadelphia, still had town hall theatres. In other locales the company performed in courtrooms, schoolrooms, and hotel dining halls.

As the season ended, the company had collected one sow, temporarily the group's mascot, but really being fed for slaughter, a few country hams, and a tiny margin of cash profit. Three barrels of jam and $4.30 in cash went to the Actors' Relief Fund as its share. *East Lynne*, the only costume play, drew the largest audiences. Two of the seven plays in the first season had never before been performed.

In 1934 Hume Cronyn and his wife, Emily Woodruff, bought an interest in the season. Cronyn, acting as production director, coordinated productions and freed Porterfield to promote and book engagements. Alan Williams staged all nine productions, the first of which was rehearsed in New York before the company arrived in Abingdon. Six of the first season's company returned.

Changes came in 1935. A motion picture distributor obtained a year-round lease to the Abingdon Town Hall theatre and the Martha Washington campus was rented to a hotel chain. Porterfield then leased the campus of the Stonewall Jackson College, also closed by the Depression, on the edge of town but not on the national highway. The new quarters provided a larger theatre in which to perform, rehearsal space, shop space, and living space surrounded by acres of open hillside. Signs were erected to point all traffic to the theatre.

An apprentice training program was added, with each apprentice paying room and board. Directors Edward Forbes and Owen Phillips, actress Grace Mills, and dancer Elise Graham were the faculty. The first play was rehearsed in New York, but the remaining eleven had open try-outs on the campus, with Equity performers or apprentices playing roles as cast by the director. A system of two interchangeable companies allowed two plays to be in rehearsal at all times and assured longer rehearsal periods for each play. Each play opened in Abingdon and remained in the repertory until the end of the season. The last week of the season the six most popular productions were given a final performance on the Barter stage in Abingdon. Performances were normally on the Barter stage on Thursday, Friday, and Saturday with an admission price of 40 cents or the equivalent in barter. Of the initial apprentice class, only one, Jeffrey Lynn, went on to a successful career in films.

Movies attracted the cash customers, while the bartering ones favored the live theatre, so the theatre almost closed. Judge Temple Bodley of Louisville, Kentucky, gathered 300 cash customers for a benefit, a premiere of Lula Vollmer's *The Hill Between*. Bodley's gesture saved the theatre.

During the winters, when not acting, Porterfield toured the lecture circuit promoting the Barter Theatre and lobbying for a national theatre made of state touring companies. He invested the income derived from his lectures in Barter Theatre salaries and equipment.

The seasons continued in the pattern set in 1936, and the company grew to nearly one hundred members. Classic plays and untried scripts were included in each season's bill. From 1936, beginning with Wendell Whitten, a playwright in residence was included in the company. This playwright might also act, direct, design, or promote as well as write. Standard plays as well as plays by members of the acting or technical staff were produced. As many as five new scripts were mounted each season.

In 1936 the audiences grew by half and the percentage of cash income began a steady increase. At the end of the season Porterfield took his company to New York, where they presented *Two Women of Abingdon*, an Elizabethan-style comedy, to a standing-room audience of 540 at the New School for Social Research. The season's profits netted $50 for the Actors' Relief Fund.

In 1937 Margaret Wycherly joined the company, after a successful season in New York. The audiences continued to increase, and the season again ended in New York, at the Heckscher Theatre, where the company presented *Macbeth* with Miss Wycherly as Lady Macbeth. Reviews were favorable.

In 1939 Porterfield established the Barter Award to acknowledge the season's efforts of an American-born actor or actress. At a gala event in New York Eleanor Roosevelt made the first of these presentations to Laurette Taylor. A ham, a platter with the Barter logo, and the deed to an acre of land near Abingdon were presented each year except during World War II and while Porterfield was on leave in 1966. Each Barter Award recipient then selected from a day-long audition an actor and actress to be awarded an Equity contract at Barter. Larry Gates and Edith Sommers were the first to receive the coveted contracts.

Workshops for public school teachers were added to the program for the summer, and Porterfield successfully lobbied the Virginia legislature for funds to take his theatre into the schools during the winter. In 1941 the state of Virginia awarded Barter $15,000 to instigate a schools program, but funding did not materialize because of World War II. Gas and tire rationing caused a much smaller touring radius with a smaller company during the 1942–43 season. The theatre closed for the seasons of 1943–44 and 1944–45.

In the interim a tornado destroyed the building in which the theatre's assets were stored, scattering props, sets, and costumes across the mountains. The town of Abingdon wanted the Barter Theatre, so in 1945 it offered a ten-year, rent-free lease on the Town Hall, and it agreed to build an annex to the Town Hall for dressing rooms and scenery storage. Washington County underwrote the mortgage on the purchase of the Stonewall Jackson College dormitory building, and surplus military furniture furnished the rooms occupied by the company. The company then acquired a warehouse in Abingdon and used it as a scene shop. It also reached an agreement with a New York theatrical supply business whereby touring sets about to be discarded were instead trucked to Abingdon. Heavy fabrics necessary for period costumes were unavailable, so women's clubs across Virginia gathered draperies, velvets, and brocades for the theatre. Furthermore, Abingdon went to the legislature to help Porterfield lobby for funds. The legislature granted $10,000 a year toward equipment, asked Barter to provide residencies at the state colleges, and endorsed the Barter Theatre as "the State Theatre of Virginia."

As the 1945–46 season began, technicians built productions in Abingdon while Owen rehearsed Noel Coward's *Blithe Spirit* in New York. This season featured a system whereby two plays toured while a third occupied the Barter stage. The three-part company of about one hundred included designers, directors, and actors. A two-week festival at the end of the season featured twelve plays.

Ticket prices after World War II were 90 cents and $1.20, and barter gradually diminished. The federal government levied a tax on entertainment tickets sold in the war years and immediately after, and collectors frowned on barter because produce was hard to tax. Moreover, playwrights wanted cash, not ham, for royalties. Although barter was accepted during the summer, the theatre encouraged cash admissions.

In 1948 the Barter Theatre was invited to take a production of *Hamlet* to Denmark to represent the United States at a *Hamlet* festival at Kronberg Castle in Elsinore. The U.S. State Department agreed to sponsor the trip, but funds were not available to finance it. Porterfield turned to the American National Theatre and Academy (ANTA) for sponsorship, and Blevins Davis, then president of ANTA, pledged ANTA's support on the condition that he select the director and the designers. Davis chose Robert Breen, who cast himself in the title role and toured with the company in the winter of 1948–49. As departure time neared, Breen decided New York stage stars should play the leading roles in Denmark, and he threatened to cancel the trip if Porterfield objected or failed to cooperate. Porterfield withdrew the Barter billing from the company when Walter Abel, Ruth Ford, Clarence Derwent, and Aline Macmahon replaced the regular Barter players. Frederic Warriner, Jacqueline Logan, Jerry Jedd, and Leo Chalzel were demoted to minor roles. As a result of this administrative debacle, the Danes were denied a chance to see the ensemble acting for which the Barter Theatre had become famous.

In 1953 the old Empire Theatre, built on Broadway in 1893 and long the flagship theatre of the Frohman brothers, was demolished, and many of its fabled interior decorations were given to the Barter Theatre and used to dress up the Abingdon Town Hall.

Mason Bliss, Barter's booking agent, opened his own agency in Richmond and booked Barter, along with other companies, during the 1950s. However, competition from less expensive companies, stricter union regulations, the expense of travel, and the rapid deterioration of the theatre's touring equipment forced Porterfield to temporarily discontinue the winter touring season in 1959.

During the summer of 1959 Barter staged its first children's production, *Rumpelstiltskin*, with early curtain times for evening performance. A clamor for more children's performances conflicted with adult demands for regular fare. Thus *Rumpelstiltskin* earned a short touring season of its own.

By 1961 Barter opened an alternate theatre in a nearby chapel dating from 1830, used for shops and storage in years past. "The Playhouse on the Green" operated during July and August, offering children's matinees, avant-garde plays, cabarets, try-outs, and showcases for work by company members. Performances in the Playhouse were scheduled concurrently with those on the Barter stage.

In 1961 the Old Dominion Foundation provided Barter with a matching fund grant of $100,000 to reorganize its board of directors into one more directly involved in the operation of the theatre, and to establish the Barter Foundation to assure the theatre's future. In May 1962 author James Hilton's widow, Alice, who was Barter's executive secretary and chief fund-raiser, died, leaving her estate to the Barter Foundation. The Barter Foundation then purchased the Martha Washington campus, and operated it as a resort. The profits funded the Barter Theatre until 1981, when Barter sold the campus to local businessmen.

The Barter season was extended until near Thanksgiving in 1962. The company then opened in December at the Renaissance Theatre in Richmond, a small house attached to a restaurant. Severe winter weather made mountain roads unsafe, so the company's promise to return to Abingdon in February 1963 was unredeemed until April. At this time Porterfield obtained permission from the actors' union to schedule matinees at irregular daytime hours five days a week in the early spring, to which schoolchildren could be bused. He also arranged for Friday and Saturday evening performances to be open to the public. This preseason, initiated in 1963, continues, with the regular season beginning near the end of May.

Peter Culman, who served as Porterfield's production coordinator from 1960, was about this time being prepared to succeed Porterfield. After Porterfield's marriage in 1965, Culman was promoted to assistant executive producer and vice president of the Barter Foundation. At the end of the 1965 season Porterfield and his bride departed on a year's leave of absence, leaving Culman in charge. At the same time many designers, technicians, and performers departed in the largest turnover of personnel in the history of the theatre. During Porterfield's absence twenty-five truckloads of furniture, props, and memorabilia were discarded. Porterfield returned to find the theatre stripped of twenty years' accumulation of what Porterfield regarded as the company's valuable assets. Porterfield fired Culman and began rebuilding his store of material.

When Porterfield died October 26, 1971, the Barter Foundation board of directors [in accordance with Porterfield's wishes,] appointed Rex Partington as artistic director and manager. Partington, a member of the 1950–51 Barter company, had managed other theatres in the meantime. His wife, Cleo Holladay, who had been a Barter actress during the 1940s and 1950s, returned as a member of the acting company. Partington has attempted to retain the Barter image and to adhere to its traditions. Ensemble acting remained a primary aim. For several years Partington retained the repertory festival in August as a three-play program, but he discarded it in 1980, thus completing a revision of company policy begun by Porterfield, who was phasing out the festival at the time of his death.

As early as 1964, Norfolk, Virginia, was offered as a winter home for Barter, but no theatre could be found in which to perform. In 1975 the Chrysler Museum Theatre became available, and Norfolk began raising funds to underwrite a Barter Company winter residency. Barter played the winter of 1975–76 in Norfolk, and has established intermittent winter residencies in Richmond and at George Mason University, Fairfax, Virginia.

In 1980 the Virginia legislature increased Barter's annual stipend to $15,000 a year. Patron donations and season ticket sales have increased sharply in the 1980s, and operating expenses surpassed $1 million in 1982. The company continues to play an eight-show season in Abingdon from April to October. In late winter and early spring the Barter Players tour the Southeast while a second company tours high schools and community centers in Virginia.

PERSONNEL

Management: Robert Porterfield, founder and managing director (1932–71); Peter Culman, managing director while Porterfield was on leave (1966); Rex Partington, artistic director and manager (1972–86); Helen Fritch Porterfield, business manager (1933–42), C. Alden Baker, business manager (1947–50); Alice Hilton, executive secretary (1951–61); Pearl Price Hayter, executive secretary-business manager (1962–86).

Set Designers, Scenic Artists: Gary Aday (1985–86), Bennet Avery (1970–83), Ruth Ball (1952–53), Howard Bane (1949–50), Barbara Benziger (1952–53), Fred Boyce (1951–52), Dennis Bradford (1984–85), Gregory Buch (1977, 1979), Peter Buchnell (1947–48, 1951–52), Warren Cauthen (1950–51), Robert Chace (1940), F. Leonard Darby (1979), Richard David (1972), Stuart Day (1946–49), John DeVries (1939), Don Drapeau (1971), Ben Edwards (1935); D. R. Edwards (1972); Daniel Ettinger (1982–86), Jack Fawcett (1933), Hugh Fettis (1937), Fitz-Hugh (1948–50), John Edward Friend (1946–47, 1953–54, 1956–58), James Frankel (1973), Peter Frye (1948–49), Bill Gammon (1963–64), G. Carr Garnett (1970), Hal George (1964), Margaret Glass (1934), Will Gould (1948–50), Montgomery Hare (1948–49), F. Hazzard (1968), Clarence L. Hundley (1980–82), Virginia Johnston (1950–51), William J. Kelly (1967), Jack Landau (1955–56), John C. Larrance (1982–84, 1985–86), Frank Lemmon (1946–47); Laurie Leonard (1936), Don Liberto (1962–63), Galen M. Logsdon (1980); Marjorie Lutz (1933), Eve Lyon (1965), Thomas McKeehan (1964), Carl B. "Mac" MacLaughlin (1966), Carol Madeira (1969), Richard Martin (1946–47), David Massey (1951–52), Elizabeth Matta (1962–63), Henry May (1942, 1954–55), Virginia Mealy (1938), Katherine Moore (1971), Roger Morgan (1959–63), Frank Moss (1971), David Murphy (1971), Jim Newton

(1964), Randall O'Neill (1949–50), Henry Packer (1965–66), Webster Parker (1949–51), *Lynn Pecktal* (1954–65, 1982–85), Bob Phillips (1981–82), Lester Polakov (1938), David Reed Pursley (1967), Bruce Rayvid (1976), Raymond Recht (1970–74), Marvin Roark (1969), Ruth Saada (1966), Maynard Sampson (1934), Henry E. Scott (1967–68), Dana Seefield (1972), Craig Smith (1940–41), Jim Stauder (1984–85), Michael Stauffer (1968–70), Mack Stratham (1951–56), Frances Strauss (1937), Ralph Swanson (1967), Ray Sylvester (1938), Sheldon Thompson (1939), Henrietta Van Gelder (1941), Jean Vickery (1964), William James Wall (1966), Ernest Walling (1940), T. Park Warne III (1979), Mary R. Wayne (1977), David W. Weiss (1981–82), Parmalee Welles (1976–80), Arthur Whitehead (1976), Bill Wilson (1962), Marilyn Wooten (1968), Elizabeth Young (1963).

Lighting Designers: Bryan E. Ackler (1971), Stephen Arnold (1976), Bennet Averyt (1980–81), *Albin Aukerlund* (1946–66), John Baker (1967–68), Charles Beatty (1982–83), Bruce Lyman Blackmore (1970), Roger Lee Bright (1968), Kenneth Brumbeloe (1951–52), Peter Buchnell (1947–48), Michael Casteel (1969), Gregory Christiansen (1970), Don Coleman (1976), Wallace Dace (1948–49), Daniel H. Ettinger (1982–83), Robert Gallico (1952–53), Margaret Glass (1934), Will Gould (1949–51), Patricia Green (1971), Jack Hagy (1947–48), Robert Hammel (1968), Gary N. Harris (1979), Jean Hodgin (1948–49), Edgar Kaufman (1946–47), Barbara Kreshteal (1972), Jerry LeFaver (1949–50), Cindy Limauro (1978–80), Grant Clifford Logan (1976–77), Edmund Lynch (1960–61), Robert Marshall (1970), Gene Massey, Jr. (1966), David Mazikowski (1973), Henry Millman (1969), Parker Mills (1936–37), Sara Ross Morgan (1978), George Neiman (1936–40), Arthur Oslag (1940), Al Oster (1982–86), Ben Packer (1966), *Anthony C. Partington* (1977–83), Vernon Keith Phillips (1977), John Poulton (1964–66), Robert Prestis (1942), Stuart Richman (1971), Michael J. Rosati (1971), Christopher H. Shaw (1982–83), John T. Sloper (1941), Frank Stevens (1948), Larry Untermeyer (1946–48), Paul Wasserman (1942), Karen Wenderoff (1962, 1980–81), Byron White (1973–74), Marshall Yorkelson (1946–47).

Costume Designers: Eleanor Anton (1941), Stephen Arnold (1978), Nancy Atkinson (1980–82), Karen Bacon (1966), Prudence Bacon (1968), Lucille Baille (1965), Georgia Baker (1979, 1982–85), Betty Bellune (1962–63), Barbara Benziger (1951–52), Carol Blevins (1980–81), Dorothy Brentliner (1949–50), Karen Brewster (1984–86), Fred Boyce (1951–52), Peter Buchnell (1947–78), Becky Bynum (1972), Warren Cauthen (1951–52), Joanne Chalfont (1958–59), Walta Chandler (1959–62, 1963–64), Elizabeth Cove (1978), Marianne Custer (1983–84), Sue Carol David (1961–62), Judith Dolan (1979–80), Patricia Elgas (1934–35), Mariana Elliott (1954–59, 1961–62), Laren Farr (1952–53), Barbara Forbes (1982–86), John Edward Friend (1953–54, 1956–57), G. Carr Garnett (1976–80, 1984–85), Hal George (1964), Peri Grenell (1962), Martha Hally (1984–86), Mary Jo Hamilton (1978), Patricia Havens (1940–41, 1946–47), Jo Horne (1968–70), Clarence L. Hundley (1960, 1980–82), *Sigrid Insull* (1974–81, 1982–86), Virginia Johnston (1950–51), Josephine Jones (1957–58), Martha Kelly (1971–72), Rachel Kurland (1979–81), Carmen Lewis (1936), Tiffany Lobianco (1953–54), Galen M. Logsdon (1980–81), Mary Jane McCarty (1981–82), Elizabeth McFadden (1935), Judianna Makovsky (1981–82), Desiree Mavros (1963), Lisa Michaels (1985–86), Rhonda Minnick (1971), Maida Murray (1964), Barbara van Ornham (1950–51), Mildred Orrick (1933), Anne Duff Parker (1979–80), Nina Partridge (1935), Jo Patterson (1947–48), Maryanne Powell-Parker (1973), David Reed Pursley (1967), Bess Reitzel (1946–51), Eleanor Roberts (1933), Clyde Robinson (1934), Mary Ross Russo (1972), Lyn

Sams (1970), Shelley Heng Scheoner (1980), Pamela Simmons (1975), Robert Stark (1954–55), Frances Strauss (1937), Lucye Thoma (1938), Elizabeth Ann Tullis (1967), Mell Turner (1948–51), Jerry Uchin (1941), Jo Waffle (1946–47), Harriett Wallace (1961–62), Lois Warnshius (1946–47), Eric Warren (1952–53), Anne St. Clair Williams (1967), Constance Winde (1939).

Stage Directors: Prentice Abbott (1933), Larry Alford (1979), Rae Allen (1972, 1974), Clinton Atkinson (1964–65), Albin Aukerlund (1963), Valgene Axelrad (1956–57), Theron Bamberger (1938), David Barlow (1974), Ned Beatty (1961–62, 1967), Walter Beckel (1962–63), Marsha Bennett (1972), Paul Berman (1982–83), George Black (1975), Lyn Bothe (1966), Robert Breen (1948–49), Robert Brink (1967–68), Rocco Buffano (1961–63), Kristina Callahan (1972), Virginia Card (1954–55), Patricia R. Carmichael (1980), Fred Chappell (1981–82), Richard Clark (1937), Milton Commons (1962–63), Frances Conley (1972), Dale Carter Cooper (1959–60), Ken Costigan (1973, 1982–86), Jack Cowles (1965), Hume Cronyn (1934, 1938), Peter Culman (1965–66), Miranda D'Ancona (1967), Severn Darden (1956–57), Alan Delano (1935), Harry Ellerbe (1983–84), Paul Emerson (1967), Sherman Ewing (1941), Fitz-Hugh (1949–50), Tennyson Flowers (1971), Edward Forbes (1934–36), Kenneth Frankel (1973–75), John Edward Friend (1947–48, 1953–54, 1966, 1970), Peter Frye (1948–49), Richard Gaines (1941), Larry Gates (1967), Hal George (1964), John Going (1972, 1975–76, 1981), Will Gould (1949–50), Elise Graham (1935), Gordon Greene (1967), Thomas Gruenewald (1982–83), Pat Hale [Whitten] (1962–63, 1969), Adrian Hall (1963), William Hammond (1960–61), Jerry Hardin (1957–58, 1963), Montgomery Hare (1946–50), Carl Harms (1956–57), Fred Harris (1939), Don Hart (1940–41), Judith Haskell (1985–86), Linde Hayan (1968), Jeffrey Hitch (1984–85), Jordon Hott (1966), Paul Huber (1940), Ronald Lee Huffman (1966), Pamela C. Hunt (1980, 1982–85), Howard Hunter (1950–52, 1954–58), Jeffrey S. Hurst (1984–85), Mitzi Hyman (1953–54), Graham Jarvis (1959–60), Rashad Jamal (1964), Roland C. Keller (1978), Voight Kempson (1979), William van Keyser (1983–86), James R. Kirkland (1980), Lawrence Kornfeld (1981–82), Jack Landau (1955–56,) Jerome Lawrence (1979), Frank Lowe (1956–59, 1960–63), Norman McDonald (1941–42, 1954–55), Leslie McLeod (1939–40), Dorothy Marie (1972–74, 1976–78), Richard Martin (1946–47), Charles Maryann (1975–76), Pierrino Mascerino (1968), Ada Brown Mather (1977–78, 1980–82), Jeff Meredith (1978–81), Grace Mills (1935, 1941), Parker Mills (1938, 1950–51), Greg Mooney (1936), Michael Morrell (1971), Conrad Nagel (1941), Jerry Oddo (1964, 1971), Pierre Olaf (1968), John Olon-Scrymgeour (also John Olon) (1974, 1976–78, 1980–82), *Rex Partington* (1980–81, 1982–83, 1985–86), Kent Paul (1967), Margaret Perry (1948–53), *Owen Phillips* (1935–37, 1946–56, 1963, 1968–80), Evelyn Pierce (1940), *Robert Porterfield* (1933–71), Peggity Price (1976), Trip Plymale (1985–86), George Quick (1947–49), Susan Rae (1966), John Ritchie (1962), Kenneth Robbins (1976–79), Dorothy Marie Robinson (1982–83), Donna Search (1974), Georgia Shott (1966), John Sillings (1959), Alan George Smith (1939), Arthur Stennings (1933), Edward Stern (1979), Fred Stewart (1938–40, 1946–47, 1949–50), Mark Sumner (1981–82), Margaret Swope (1938), Arnold Sundgaard (1941, 1952–53), Gregory Taylor (1963), Samuel Taylor (1939), Bertrand Thorn (1938), George Touliatos (1974, 1981–82), William Tost (1978), Jerry Uchin (1946–47), Ernest Walling (1940–42), Ray Walling (1938), Frederic Warriner (1957–60, 1960–61), Don Weightman (1958–63), Alan Williams (1934, 1937, 1939), Walter Williamson (1968–70), Edwin Wilson (1964), William Woodman (1966), Margaret Wycherly (1942), Paul Yost (1936), Peter Zeisler (1946), Ira Zuckerman (1966).

Music Directors: Roger A. Brown (1963), Elizabeth C. Cummings (1965), Byron Grant (1976–79), Marvin C. Jones (1980), Karl Lucas (1946–47), William Schleuter (1974), Carey Sparks (1940), Frances Stewart (1939–40).

Resident Playwrights: Marsha Bennett (1972), Virginia Card (1954–55), Sydney Carter (1937), Patricia Conley (1972), Paul Dellinger (1970), Sherman Ewing (1938), Edward Forbes (1939), Robert Gallico (1953–54), Pat Hale [Whitten] (1959–64, 1969), Montgomery Hare (1947–50), Jamie Heron (1937), Frank Lowe (1963), Leslie McLeod (1939–40), *Jerry Oddo* (1957–58, 1961–62, 1964, 1967, 1971), Margaret Perry (1952–53), Margaret "Peggity" Price (1975), Kenneth Robbins (1979), Edith Sommer (1942), Fred Stewart (1939), Arnold Sundgaard (1938, 1946–47, 1952–53), Barbara Tarbuck (1973), Peter Taylor (1971), Wendell Whitten (1935–36).

Actors and Actresses: Prentice Abbot, John Charles Abegglen, George Abel, James Abernathy, Brian Acworth, Phyllis Adams, Gary Aday, William Adler, Jeni Agar, Andra Akers, Claude Akins, Carella Alden, Anne Alexander, Doug Alexander, *Fred Alexander* (1939–41), Irena Alexander, *Lee Alexander* (1981–83), Joanne Allaband, Richard Allan, Elizabeth Allen, Harriet Nichold Allen, Jean Allen, Lyman Allen, Mary Ruse Allen, William B. Allen, Ann Curtiss Allison, Amy Allston, Clay D. Alsup, Nancy Altizer, Warren Altman, Marianne Amato, Eric Amen, Laura Amlie, Gregory Amsterdam, Adel Anderson, Charles Anderson, *Eunice T. Anderson* (1980–83), George Anderson, Haskell Anderson, *Hugh Anderson* (1938–40), *Judith Anderson* (1953), McKee Anderson, Ruth Anderson, Timothy Anderson, *Vienna Cobb Anderson* (1957–59, 1960–61), Wallace Anderson, William Dallas Anderson, Williamene Anderson, Edward Andrew, James Andrews, Florence Anglin, Joseph Anthony, Eleanor Anton, Eathleen Arey, Gwen Arment, Frances Armitage, Charlotte Armstrong, Fred Armstrong, Jacob Arnold, Beth Asbury, Claudette Asbury, Lee Asbury, Jerry Atkins, *Clinton Atkinson* (1964–65, 1968), Nancy Atkinson, *M. H. "Rickey" Austin* (1933–34), Carl S. Azzara (1967), Richard Babsock, Walter Backel, Karin Bacon, Marnie Bacon, Prudence Bacon, James Baher, Nick Bakay, James Bailey, Leroy Bailey, Lucille Baillie, Ray Baillie, Beryl Baker, *C. Alden Baker* (1948–50), Christine Baker, Frances Baker, Jerry Baker, Kenneth Baker, Uradell Baker, Valley Baker, Virginia Baker, Jerome "Nick" Bakewell, Jonathan Ball, Ruby Ball, Kathryn Ballard, *Peter Ban* (1969), Pat Banks, Frances A. "Frank" Bara, Aza Bard, Margaret Barker, David Barlow, Alice Barnard, Jo Barnard, Mary Barnard, Martha Barnes, Mary Ellen Barnes, Arthur Barnett, Cynthia Barnett, Harry Barnfeld, Ruth Barnhill, George Baron Barrachlough, *Ellen Barrett* (1962–64), Leslie Barrett, Paul Barry, Arthur Barsamian, Annie Sue Bass, Emory Bass, Georgia Bates, Peter W. Baxhill, Ayers Baxter, Marilyn Baxter, *Daphne Bayne* (1936), Deborah Bays, John Beary, Jack Beasley, Charles Beatty, *Ned Beatty* (1958–64, 1967), Shirley Beaver, Carolyn Porter Beck, Dennis Beck, Antoine Becker, Stuart Becker, Vernon E. Beckman, Warren Beckman, *Don Oscar Becque* (1938), Louise Beddingfield, James Daniel Beebe, Raymond Beech, Adele Beekman, Richard Belcher, George Belk, Emily Bell, Gene Bell, Glynnis Bell, *Jay Bell* (1967–68, 1971–72), Elaine Bellis-Orms, Betty Bellune, Paul Bement, Donald Benedict, Kenton Benedict, John Bennes, Pamela J. Bennet, Fern Bennett, *Georgia Bennett* (1955–57, 1960–63), Gordon Bennett, Marcia Bennett, Andrea Benson, Ann Benson, Mary Benson, Andy Bernard, Clifton C. Bernard, Paul Bernard, Lynn Bernstein, Sheila Bevan, Jack Bezek, Allison Biggers, *Ross Bickell* (1981–86), Michael Birne, David Birney, Jean Birney, John Bishop, George Black, Michelle Black, Ann Blackburn, Dorothy Blackburn, Robert Blackburn, Frederick Blackmer, Jan Blackwell, Perry Blackwell, Samuel S. Blackwell, Peggy Blair, Bonnie Blake, Judy Blake, Sydney Blake, James

Blevins, Ted Blevins, Terry Bliss, Gloria Blondell, Nancy Blonder, *Eric Blore* (1953),
Ronnie Bloxham, Ron Bobko, Nicco Boccio, Oxie Bodine, Robert Boehm, Gian Bog-
giano, Rudy Boisseau, Leta Bongel, Guy Bongiovanni, Constance Bonner, Helen Bons-
telle, Leta Bonynge, Michael Boone, Nancy Boone, Barbara Booth, Edwin Bordo, Harry
Borenfeld, *Ernest Borgnine* (1945–50), Robert Bormarth, Jim Boswell, Lyn Bothe, Dor-
othy Bourne (1940–41), Richard Bowden, Ginger Bowen, Scott Bowen, Thornton Bow-
man, *Ford Bowmar* (1937–38), Jerry Allen Bowter, Arthur Boyd, Barbara Boyd, Rodney
Boyd, Duane Boyer, *Mary Boylan* (1939–42, 1946–47), *Ray Boyle* (1947–49), Francis
Braddock, Don Bradford, Randolph Bradford, Gwendolyn Brady, Jennie Brady, Karen
Braga, Jocelyn Brande, Jim Branson, Kenneth Brauer, Ralph Braun, *Robert Breen* (1948–
49), Sherry Breitburg, Carolyn Brenner, Randy Brenner, Dorothy Brentlinger, Joan
Briggs, Roger Lee Bright, Ann Brillhart, Robert Brink, Rudolph Brinkley, Brigit Bris-
good, Mary Elizabeth Briton, Thomas Brittingham, Peter Brock, Pope Brock, James E.
Brodhead, Kathy Brom, Frank Brook, Al Brotherton, Bud Brown, Chris Brown, Dorothy
Brown, Eleanor Brown, Gwendolyn Brown, Henry Brown, James Dennis Brown, James
E. Brown, Janet Blaine Brown, *Landon C. Brown* (1959–63), Peter Brown, Robert
Brown, Roger Brown, Ted Brown, Robert Browning, Mary Ann Brownlow, Dennis
Brubaker, Elaine Brubaker, Robert Brubaker, Colin Bruce, Kenneth Brumbelow, Marlene
Bryan, Bill Bryant, Yolande Bryant, Betty Bryson, Alice Buchanan, Frank Buchanan,
Doris Ann Bucher, Andre Buckles, *Ann Buckles* (1950–52, 1954–55, 1971–74), Sherri
Buckles, *Rocco Bufano* (1956–57, 1960–61), Elaine Bullis-Orms, Harwood Bullock,
Leigh Burch, Jeffrey Burchfield, Alexander Burke, Gerald Burke, Sarah Burke, *Robert
Burns* (1947–48, 1949–51), Nell Burnside, Lessie Burnum, Fred Burrell, *Caddell Bur-
roughs* (1947–53), James Burrows, Tom Burrows, Joseph Burson, James Buss, Sarah
Buxton, Becky Bynum, James Cahill, A. D. Caldwell, John W. Caldwell, Ted Caldwell,
Edward Payson Call (1954–55, 1962–63), Kristine Callahan, Roger Callis, Virginia
Calvert, Holly Cameron, James Cameron, Sandy Camora, C. W. Campbell, Virginia
Campbell, William Campbell, Doris Campner, Vivian Capps, Virginia Card, Chet Carlin,
Katherine Carlson, Robert Carlson, Richard Carlyle, Robert Carlyle, David Carmack,
Wilson Carmen, Candace Carmicelli, James R. Carnelia, Jr., Mary Carney, Lang Car-
pentier, Tony Carpisi, Vickie M. Carr, Liz Carrington, Kyra Carroll, Rhoda Carroll,
Wally Carroll, Carrotte, Bill Carrouthers, Micael Carson, Gladys Carter, Sydney Carter,
Tinsley Carter, Tiina Cartmell, Carleen Caryl, Patty Cassidy, Ron Castle, Susie Castle,
John L. Caulfield, Warren Cauthen, George Cavey, Richard Cesaiti, Dorothy Chace,
Jane Alic Chaffin, Joanne Chalfont, Helen Chalzel, Leo Chalzel, Sally Chamberlin,
Norma Chambers, Mike Champaigne, John W. Chandler, Robert Chandler, Waltar Chan-
dler, William Chandler, Bonnie Chapman, *Tomes Chapman* (1936), Keith Charles, *Mi-
chael Charles*, Jeffrey Charles-Reese, Ann Chase, Jerry Chase, John Chase, Mary Chase,
Michael Chase (Keith Michael) (1949–52), Sandra Chesley, Allan Chester, Tom Chil-
dress, Carol Chitton, Martha Christian, Donald Christopher, Geraldine Chronowit, *Diane
Cilento* (1949–50), Luci Claire, Howard Clancy, Betsy Clark, Burt Clark, Carolyn Clark,
Christie Clark, Elijah Clark, John Clark, Katherine Clark, Phillip A. Clark, Richard
Clark, Robert Clark, Maryann Clarkson, Marlene Clary, Ray·Clary, Dennis Clay, Jane
Cleaveland, Thomas Clifton, Del Close, Caryl Coan, Alan Coats, Mel Cobb, Herman
Coble, Victor Coe, Fabio Coen, Lillian Coffey, Kip Cohen, Gregory C. Colan, Lennie
Colby, Beatrice Cole, Constance Coleman, Gene R. Coleman, Hank Coleman, Kelly
Coleman, Nancy Coleman, Thomas Coley, Clifford Collier, Gary Collins, Paul Collins,

Peggy Collins, Schery Collins, Sarah Collingwood, *Frederick Combs* (1953–55, 1964), Nell Combs, Milton Commons, Millie Condon, Carolyn Condron, Edward Conery, Eric Conger, Abram Conley, Elizabeth Conley, Cary Connell, Carolyn Cononico, Ed Conquest, Katherine Conrad, Jeffrey Coogle, Cynthia Cook, Richard Cook, Ruth Cooke, *Dale Carter Cooper* (1960–61, 1968, 1970–71, 1973–74), David Cooper, Elaine Cooper, James Cooper, Nancy Cooper, Muriel Copeland, *Catherine Coray* (1982–85), Albert Corbin, Barry Corbin, Elyse Corbin, Betsy Cornell, Don Cornett, Daryle Ann Corr, William Corrie, Chapel Cory, Clayton Corzatte, Joseph Costa, Nicholas Coster, *Ken Costigan* (1982–85), Phoebe Cotes, Lee Cotterell, Arthur Countis, Harriet Courney, Carolyn Cowles, *Jack Cowles* (1965, 1967–68), Shirley Cox, Spencer Cox, Colin Craig, Edwin Craig, Garrett Craig, Harry Cramer, Eddy Craven, Robert Craven, William Crayton, Saylor Creswell, Barbara Crickenberger, John Cromwell, *Jane Cronin* (1964, 1970), *Hume Cronyn* (1934, 1938, 1948), David Cross, Frances Cullen, Jack Cullers, Jane Culley, Joseph Cullingham, Joseph Culliton, Peter Culman, Jason Culp, Elizabeth Cummings, Lance Cunard, *Ruby Cunningham* (1956–58, 1959–60, 1962–63), Caryl Cuskey, *Augustus Dabney* (1938), Linda Dahl, Tessa Dahl, David Dahline, Eleanor Dale, Ray Daley, Clay Dalferes, Jeffrey Dalton, Kenneth Dalton, Virginia Daly, Gary Daniel, Tommy Daniel, Pamela Danser, Mike D'Antuone, Janey D'Arcy, Sophia D'Arcy, *Severn Darden* (1954–58), Bob Dare, William Dare, David Darlow, Phena Darner, Don Dart, William E. Dauphin, Jeff David, Nawane David, Tom David, Gordon Davidson, Jim Davie, Alison Davis, Ed Davis, Jack L. Davis, Jenny Davis, Mark Davis, Olive Davis, *Sue Carol Davis* (1961–63), Tracy Davis, Matthew D. Davison, Suzanne Dawson, Bill Day, Caroline Day, Gerry Day, Stuart Day, J. J. Deadmore, Frank Deal, Dalton Dearborn, Dick DeCicco, Dorothy A. Dee, Marcy Degonge, James DeGraff, Margaret deGroff, Ian Deitch, Marsha C. Delafield, Paul Dellinger, Marsha V. DeLong, Mark Dempsey, Mary Ann Dempsey, Sally Dennison, Elfrida Derwent, Emmy Deturler, *Joan DeWeese* (1946–49, 1960–62), Mary Dewing, Susan Dias, Jane Reilly Dibble, John Dickens, Thomas Leigh Dickman, Walter Dicks, Dean Dietrich, Bob Diggers, Frances Dillard, Jeanne Dillen, William Dinsmore, Murray Dinzes, Walter Dix, Beth Dixon, Billy Dixon, Ellen M. Doak, Walter Dobson, Rebecca M. Dobyns, Judith Dolan, Barbara Dole, Carl Don, Ellen Donkin, Peter Donnelly, Edna Dooley, Nathaniel Doolittle, Lucille Dopp, Phoebe Dorin, Melinda Dotson, Mary Ellen Doubles, *Adrienne Doucette* (1978–79), Agnes Dougherty, John Douglass, Peter Dowling, Virginia Dowling, David Doyle, Kathleen Doyle, George Drake, Ronald Drake, Margaret Draper, Virginia Dreher, Mabel Driscoll, Ralph E. Driscoll, Wards Drummand, *Robert Dryden* (1937–38), Dorothy Dubel, John DuBois, *Dortha Duckworth* (1938, 1968), Ethan Kane Dufault, Lucille Duff, Winifred Duff, Darlene Duling, Jorge Dumas, Howard Duncan, Bartlett Dunlap, Helen Dunlap, Louise Dunn, Joseph Dunnea, Ann Dunnigan, Charles Durand, Barbara Durcky, Sydney Durrant, Herbert Duval, Lyle Dye, Elizabeth Dyer, Michael Dyer, Cheryl Earp, Shelton Earp, Edward Eastland, Helen Eastman, Ed Easty, John Eaton, Frank Eben, Pat Echeverria, Joseph P. "Pete" Edens, Lou Edmister, Eddie Edmonds, D. R. Edwards, Roland Edwards, Susan Edwards, Leigh Eisenhauer, John Ekston, Jean Elgard, Flora Elkins, Cherie Elledge, Frances Eller, *Harry Ellerbe* (1980–85), Richard Ellington, William Ellington, John Elliot, Mariana Elliott, Pat Elliott, Brad Ellis, Tom Ellis, Walter Ellis, Cornelia Ely, Paul Emerson, Donna Marie Emmert, Mary Lou Endean, Stephen Eoff, Alex Ericson, Andrea Erskine, Betty Eskew, Shannon Eubanks, Bill Evans, David Evans, Donna Evans, *Gwyllum Evans* (1973–77, 1984–86), *Josephine Evans* (1938, 1940), Nick Evans, Terry Everett, *Aileen Ewart* (1939–40, 1946, 1953–59), Elinor Ewart,

Sherman Ewing, Christine Fagan, Richard Fagan, John Falk, *Bedelia Falls* (1938–39), Claire Fanning [Perry], Karl Fanning, Toni Fanning, Roy Fant, *Evelyn Fargo* (1940–41), Doris Farmer, James Farmer, Natalie Farmer, Patricia T. Farmer, Dinah Farr, Jean Farragut, Gilbert Fates, Roger Fawcett, Rusty Fawcett, Brendan Fay, John Fedoruk, Michael Fender, Gretchen Fennel, Jock Ferguson, Virgil Ferguson, Jim Fern, Walter Richard Fern, Winifred Fethergill, Mary Fielding, Mary Fields, Mel Fillini, Travis Fine, Joel Fink, Alex Finlayson, Mary Finney, Al Fiorello, Jr., Douglas Fisher, Frances Fisher, John FitzGibbon, Walter Fleenor, Kathy Fleig, Broke Fleming, William Fletcher, Theodore Flicker, Kelly Flint, Rieta Flood, Stanley Flood, Catherine Flye, Joleen Fodor, *Bob Fogle* (1933), Paul Foley, *Robert Foley* (1964–65, 1967–69, 1971–72), George Fontaine, Eugene Foote, *Edward Forbes* (1934–36), Mary Ford, Michael Forgas, John Forker, Charles Forrester, Jane Fortner, Robert Fortune, Anne L. Foster, Elaine Foster, *Helen Foster* (1936), Nellie Jean Foster, Ann Fowler, Maria Fowler, Kimberly Fox, Margaret Fox-Roberts, Eileen Frank, James Franklin, Arthur Frantz, Scott Frazier, Linda F. Friedlob, *Constance Friend* (1938), *John Edward Friend* (1946–47, 1953–54, 1956–57), Ernie Fritz, Peter Frye, Elinor Fuchs, Mattie Fugua, George Fuller, Barbara Fulton, Walter Fulton, Stephen Gabis, John S. Gage, Richard Gaines, Mary Gallagher, *Robert Gallico* (1952–54), Lisa Galloway, Bill Gammon, Marion Garber, Henry A. Gardner, Jane Gardner, Jim Gardner, John Gardner, Laura Gardner, Rita Gardner, Valerie Gardner, Vincent Gardner, G. Carr Garnett, Cindy L. Garrett, Estelle Garrew, Carolyn Gary, Vaughn Gary, Frances Gaskins, Edward Gasper, *Larry Gates* (1939–40, 1946–48, 1949–50, 1955–56), Stuart Gates, Sylvia Gawryla, Ann Gaylord, Paul Genge, Mary Gentry, Hal George, Thomas George, Tom Gerhardt, Anne Gerhart, Edward Gero, Mary Gershank, David Gerstein, Elizabeth Gery, William Gibson, Peggy Gilbert, Barbara Gillespie, Christie Gillespie, James Gillespie, Marvine Gillespie, Betty Gillette, Linda Gillin, Jackson Gillis, John Gilpin, Louis Girard, George Gitto, David Givens, Margaret Glass, James Glazebrook, Regina Gleason, William Gleason, *Rosamond Gleason* (1935), James Glenn, Libby Glenn, Stephanie Glick, John Glover, Georgia Gobble, Ruth Gobble, Katrina Gober, Leta B. Gold, Russell S. Gold, Judith Goldschmidt, Linda Goldsmith, Betty Gooch, Joanne Good, Gerry Goodman, Bev Goodwin, Charles Goodwin, Edith Gordon, Haskell Gordon, Sander P. Gossard, Marguerite Gould, Richard Gould, Will Gould, Sally Gracie, Betty Graham, Byron Grant, Elinor Grant, Mary C. Grant, Joan Grant, Katie Grant, Judith Grantham, Michael Graves, Houston Gray, Nancy Gray, Donald Green, Katherine Green, Nancy Green, Patricia Green, Del Greene, *J. Gordon Greene* (1958–62, 1967), Jerry Greene, Sam Greene, Skip Greenlee, Bobbi Greer, Kate Greer, Claude Greever, Doris Gregory, Frank Gregory, Peri Grenell, Arlene Griffin, Carole Griffith, Margaret Griffith, Walter Griffith, Windy Griffith, George Grimes, Tarje Grimstad, Herman Grisby, Tracy Griswold, Karen Grubb, James Grubb, Ginger Guffee, *Michael Guido* (1978–81), *Max Gulack* (1955–56, 1960–61, 1973–74), Yve Gumbelle, Olen Gumley, Helen Gunderson, Elizabeth Ann Gunn, David Gurstein, *Ruth Gutterman* (1933), Virginia Haberman, Phyllis Haddix, Gilbert Haggart, James Scott Hagger, Jack Hagy, Eric Halbig, Pat Hale, Ronald Hale, Sandra Kay Hale, Adrian Hall, Andy Hall, Prentiss Hallenbeck, George Halloras, John Hallow, Mary Hamil, Jackie Hamilton, James Hamilton, Jane Hamilton, John Hamilton, Leigh Hamilton, Marcia Hamilton, Peter Hamilton, Edward Hammersley, William Hammond, Charlotte Hampden, *Lynn Hampton* (1934–35), Robert Hancock, Jerry Hanken, Essie Hanover, Larry Hansen, Thomas Wayne Hanson, Ted Hardcastle, *Jerry Hardin* (1955–59, 1960–69), Jane Hardwick, May Hare, Meredith Hare, Kevin Hargreaves, James Harlan, Carl Harms, Charles Thomas Harper,

William Harper, Burt Harris, Fred Harris, Gloria Jean Harris, James Harris, Jan Harris, Rosalind Harris, Bennie Harrison, Jr., Naomi Harrison, *Nell Harrison* (1933, 1935–39, 1949), Sandy Harrison, Kitty Harrold, David Harsheid, Don Hart, Peter Hart, David Hartley, Jack Hasler, Sally Hassenfelt, Edith Hatcher, Gloria Hatrick, Darlene Hauge, Frederick Haut, Carla Ann Haven, William Hawley, *Mary Hayden* (1946–48, 1949–50, 1956–57), Gloria Hayen, *Linde Hayen* (1969, 1971), Barton Hayman, Carol Haynes, *Storrs Haynes* (1933), Betty Hayter, John Joseph Hayworth, Pat Hayworth, Jean Hazelwood, P. Hazzard, Georgia Heaslip, Horton Heath, Al Hedison, Elizabeth Ann Hedrick, Walter Heeb, Audrey Heffernan, William Wilder Hegman, Tim Heier, Karl Heist, Dennis Helfend, *Eric Hellborg* (1933), Betty Hellman, Anne Helm, Bernard B. Helton, Alan Hemingway, Raili Hemsing, James Henaghan, Jo Henderson, Mary Jo Henderson, Delbert Henegar, William Henninger, Frederick Henry, Katherine Ann Henry, Harold Herman, Sara Hermstadt, *Jamie Heron* (1937–40, 1949–51), Harry Hess, Iphigeau Hickman, Eddie Hicks, Norma Hicks, Wally Hicks, Drew Hierholtzer, Mary Higgins, James Hilbrandt, *Diane Hill* (1958–63, 1968–69), Kathy Hill, Ray Hill, William Hill, Judy Hiller, Shelton Hillman, Margaret Hilton, Donald Hinchey, *Darthy Hinkley* (1935, 1937), Terry J. Hinz, Nina Hirschfield, Libby Hisey, David Hodge, Syd Hodgin, Richard Hoetzel, Aaron Hoffman, Joanne Hoffman, Rachel Ann Hoffman, Ralph W. Hoffman, Sarah Hoffman, Rebecca Holderness, *Cleo Holladay* (1952–53, 1955–56, 1976–86), Dorothy Holland, Eugene Holland, *John Talbot Holland* (1950–53), William Hollenbeck, Barbara Holleran, Gary Holley, Edward Holmes, Kyle Holmes, Peggy Ann Holmes, Janet C. Holmstrom, Douglas Hopkins, Becki Hood, Bob Horen, Parl Horn, Chaucey Horsley, Katherine Horst, Vickie Horton, *George Clark Hosmer* (1973–77, 1981–83, 1984–85), Jordon Hott, Theodore P. Houck, Jr., Robert Houser, Bert Housle, Theodore Houston, Druck Howard [Fenka], Mary Louise Howard, Sharon Howard [Kantowitz], Betty Howe, Harland Howe, William Howell, Gina C. Howerton, Janet Hubbard, Stephan Hubbart, *Paul Huber* (1938–40), *Marcie Hubert* (1956–61), Francis Hubley, Al Hudson, Bill Hudson, Charles Hudson, Delores Hudson, Helene Hudson, Joyce Hudson, *Robert Hudson* (1933–35), Steven Hudson, Gary Huffman, Susan Hufford, Ronald Lee Hufham, Tom Hughes, *Lawrence Hugo* (1940, 1949–50, 1973), Helene Hulbert, *Kalita Humphreys* (1935–40, 1947–48, 1949–50, 1953–54), George Humphries, Clarence L. Hundley, Annette Hunt, Ernest W. Hunt, Nancy K. Hunt, Pamela C. Hunt, Percy Hunt, *Howard Hunter* (1948–58), Marie Goodman Hunter, Marion Hunter, Jane Huntington, Michael Elizabeth Huston, Theodore Huston, Helen Hutchinson, Mary Dix Hutt, Campe Summerson Hyatt, James Hylan, *Mitzi Hyman* (1947–49, 1952–53), Liz Ingelson, Juliet Ingram, Donald Inman, Patricia Irvin, Diorien Israel, *Agnes Ives* (1933–34), *Anne Ives* (1959–60, 1962–63), *Alexander Ivo* (1942, 1947–48, 1950–51), Dorothy Jackson, George Jackson, Lisa Jacobson, Tina James, Virginia James, Richard Janiver, Rochell Jarrett, *Scott Jarrett* (1939), *Grahame Jarvis* (1957–69), Bobbi Jay, *Jerry Jedd* (1947–49, 1961–62), Judith Jeffrey, Priscilla Jenerette, Agnes W. Jenkins, Virginia Jenkins, Beverly Jensen, Lee Roy Jines, Anthony Johnson, David Johnson, Eve Johnson, Kay Johnson, Elizabeth Johnston, Peter Johnston, Ray Johnston, Scott A. Johnston, Archdale Jones, Charles Jones, Jackie Lee Jones, Jacqueline Jones, James Jones, Jennifer Ann Jones, John Christopher Jones, John Randolph Jones, Marvin C. Jones, Rebecca Sue Jones, *Richard Jones* (1960–62, 1964), Robert Jones, Tom Jones, Carroll Jordon, Rose Marie Jordon, Cynthia Judge, Obie Floyd Julian, Evelyn Justice, Kelli Kahn, Stanley Kahn, Rashad Kamal, Ben Kapen, Joyce Kaplan, Katisha Karel, David Karp, Kay Kasberger, Eugene Kaskey, Susan Kaslow, Emily Katz, Patricia Katz, Ed Kaufman, Stephen Kaye,

Vivian Kaye, Kenneth Keene, Lillian Keene, Kermit Kegley, Drew Keil, *Ian Keith* (1949–50, 1956–57), Virginia Keith, Roland Keller, Kathy Kelly, William J. Kelly, Bernice Kelmanson, William Kemp, Jena Kemper, Kay Kendall, Richard Kendrick, Shawn Kennedy, Mike Kennon, Arthur Kent, Herbert Kenwith, Sam Kester, Richard Kevlin-Bell, William Van Keyser, Guy Kibbee, Robert Kidd, Elaine Kilden, *Bruce Kimes* (1935–37), Gregory Kindle, *Dennis King* (1959), Gilbert King, Jerre C. King, Jerry King, Jolly King, Junior King, Rachel King, Virginia King, Edith Kingdom, Susie Kingsley, Richard Kinter, Linda Kirchman, James Kirkpatrick, Cheryl Lynn Kitz, James Kleeman, Martha Kleeman, Tom F. Kletchka, Franklyn Kline, Judith Kling, Sue Kling, Sue Klug, Dane Knell, Wayne Elliot Knight, Jane Ridley Knobelock, Gretchen Knorr, Michael Kolba, Bradley Kolling, Christine Kolling, Susan Kolling, Philip Kolturski, Alan Kootsher, Ethel Koreman, Doris Kornish, Roger Kozol, Mark Krause, Barbara Kreshtool, *Kitty Kreutz* (1957–59, 1961–62), Richard Kronold, Carol Kross, Carolyn O. Kruse, Craig Kuehl, Maggie L. Kuypers, Boyd Lackey, David Laden, *Jerry LaFavor* (1948–50), Barbara Lail, Peggy Lambert, *Louise Lamont* (1938–39), *Syl Lamont* (1938–40, 1949–50), Jean Lancaster, Joan Lancaster, Oliver Land, Jack Landau, Lucy Landau, Gayle Kelly Landers, Katherine Lane, *Doreen Lang* (1947–49), Jacqueline Lanza, Kim Lapsley, R. Scott Lark, Adrian Larkin, Frances Larson, Patricia Larson, Sally Larson, Andy Lasley, Robert Laturno, Sandra Laufer, Peter Laurie, Frederick Lawrence, David Lea, Damien Leake, Campe Leary, William Lechie, Heyden LeClaire, Howard Ledig, Bryarly Lee, Frank Lee, Gary Lee, Harry Lee, Jonathan Lee, Dempster Leech, Bert Leefmans, Betty Ann Leesburg, Jay LeFarge, *Richard Leigh* (1971–73), Arlene Lencioni, James Lentz, Carole Loeber, Angeline Leonard, John Leonard, Mark Leonard, Philip Leonard, Victor Lessor, David Lethcoe, Lynn Ann Leveridge, *Dorothy LaVerne* (1950–56), Stephen Levi, Robert Levis, Harry Levy, Bernadette Lewis, David A. Lewis [Ossian], Michael Lewis, *Don Liberto* (1961–63), David Licht, Kathy Light, Elizabeth Ligon, *Donald Linahan* (1959–61), Mary Elizabeth Linahan, *Howard Lindsay* (1958), Norma Jean Linkous, Kate Greer Linville, Larry L. Linville, Kathleen Lipp, Jessica Lippman, Richard Litt, Arthur Little, Michael Little, Ruth Littleton, Ruth Livingston, George Lloyd, Henry Lloyd, John Lloyd, Sherman Lloyd, *Francis Lobiance* (1952–54), Tiffy Lobianco, Beatrice Lociento, Philip Locker, Rosemary Lockhart, Lily Lodge, Alma Loftness, Jacqueline Logan, William Logan, David Lohoeter, Virginia Lomas, Grislaine Loree, George Loros, *Frank Lovejoy* (1935), Marjorie Lovett, *Melissa Loving* (1962–64, 1967), Nancy Loving, Ellen Lowe, *Frank Lowe* (1950–52, 1956–59, 1960–63, 1985–86), *Inez Lowe* (1956–57, 1959–63), Nadine Lowe, Margaret Athens Lowell, Kristen Lowman, Jane Lowry, Ken Lowry, Barbara Lucas, James Lucas, Roxie Lucas, *Claire Booth Luce* (1963), Jean Ludwig, Salem Ludwig, Karl Lukas, Susan Lund, Rebecca Lundahl, *Margaret Lunsford* (1974–77), Libby Lyman, Edmund Lynch, Elise Lynch, Pat Lynch [Aurelia Troy], Raymond Lynch, *Jeffrey Lynn* (1935, 1962–63), Eve Lyon, Mildred Lyons, Michael McArthur, Patsy McAuley, Raymond McBride, David McCall, James McCall, Joe McCall, Charles McCauley, June McCauley, Lucy McClanahan, Keith McClelland, *H. H. McCollum* (1933), Carroll McComas, Myron Glenn McCoy, Jack McCracken, Nellie McCracken, Susie McCrae, Mat McCullock, *Miranda McDermott* (1946–47, 1955–56), *Tom McDermott* (1946–50, 1956–57), Beth McDonald, Carol McDonald, *Norman MacDonald* (1941–42), Edwin J. McDonough, Margo McElroy, Gertrude McFarland, Owen MacFarland, Catherine McFarlane, Kathleen McGee, Shawn McGill, Donald McGoldrick, Ray McGoldrick, Betsy McGowen, George McGuire, William McIlwinnen, Lester Mack, Alta McKay, Randolph McKee, *Thomas McKeehan* (1951–

56, 1962–63), Gale McKeeley, Phillip McKenna, Beverly McKenzie, *Richard McKenzie* (1955–59, 1961–62, 1963, 1964), Randall McKey, *Blanche McKinney* (1951–54), Byron McKinney, James McKinney, Mary McKinney, Jo McKinnon, Paul Mackley, Edith Meiser McKnight, John McLain, Carl B. "Mack" McLaughton, Jr., Richard Mc-Laughlin, *Leslie MacLeod* (1939–40), Cole McMartin, Andrew McMillan, Robert McNamara, Anne Sue McNeely, Gale McNeely, Glenn McNeill, John McNulty, Bruce McPherson, Fillmore McPherson IV, Robert Macray [Ward], Phoebe McSheer, Nan Macy, Donald Madden, William Madden, Gloria Maddox, W. Eric Maeder, George Maguire, Walter Mahala, Lydia F. Mahan, *Kate Mahew* (1938–39), William Mahone, Becky Maiden, Bess Malone, Betty Manley, Curtis Mann, Jane F. Mann, Paula Mann, Katherine Manning, Martha Manning, *Michael J. Mantel* (1974–78), Ellen March, Frank Margrum, *Dorothy Marie* [Robinson] (1968–69, 1972–74, 1976–78), Alan Marks, Ben Martin, Catherine Martin, Helen Martin, Lee Martin, Susan Martin, Tom Martin, Emily Martinet, Charles Maryann, Donald Marye, Pierrino Mascarino, Tom Mason, David Massey, Gene Massey, Peter Masterson, Tojan Matchins, Charles Matlock, Anderson Matthews, Billy Matthews, George Matthews, Morris Matthews, Robert Matthews, *Virginia Mattis* (1947–49, 1971, 1976–77), Ellen Maupin, Gary Maupin, Desiree Mavros, Andy Maxey, Henry May, Monie May, Kathleene Maye, Janet Maylie, David Mazikowski, Carlo Mazzone, Paul Meacham, Randall Meade, Murray Mealand, Virginia Mealey, Michael Mears, David R. Mease, Michael Mederos, John Medici, Alfred Medinets, Leslie Lynn Meeker, L. Richard Meeth, Frederick Meister, George Meister, Sarah Melici, Laura Mellencamp, Paul Melton, Jeff Meredith, Paul Merrill, John Meyer, Gigi Meza, Keith Michael [Michael Chase], Kenneth Michael, Robin Michael, Raf Michaels, John Michalski, Madison Mickel, Louise Miles, Paul Miliken, Michelle Milks, Hugh Millard, Betty Miller, Frances Miller, Freda Miller, Mark Miller, Melvin Miller, Monica Miller, Patrick Miller, Tod Miller, Michael Milleville, John Milligan, Betty Rose Milliken, Henry Millman, Doug Mills, *Grace Mills* (1934–35, 1937), Ann Mingea, David Mink, Frederick Minte, Earl Mitchell, Mary Mitchell, James Mitchum, Steve Mittman, Ann Moffat, Gary Mohr, Deborah Moldow, June Moncure, Betty Monday, Blair Mongerson, Roy Monsell, Ted Montague, Rusti Moon, Greg Mooney, Becky Moore, Donley Moore, Dorothy Moore, *Elizabeth Moore* (1941–42, 1946–47), Randall Moore, Thomas Moore, David More, Peter More, Donald Moreland, Michael Morese, Alice Morgan, Bronwyn Morgan, Cassandra Morgan, Elisa Morgan, Elizabeth Ann Morgan, Gabrielle Morgan, Laura Morgan, Lorraine Morgan, *Roger Morgan* (1959–63), *Donald C. "Serafin" Mork* (1963), John Morley, Mach Morris, Robert Morris, Jane Morrisey, Betty Jane Morrison, Nancy Morrison, Sharon Morrison, *John Morrow, Jr.* (1974–75, 1977–78), Patricia Morrow, Janet Morse, Jewell Morse, Otis Morse, Jean Mortimer, George Morton, Tim Morton, William Morwood, Dennis Moser, Edward Moser, Stuart Moses, Hugh Mosher, Peggy Jean Moss, William Mowry, Xandra Moyon, C. Leslie Muchmore, Charles Muckle, George L. Muckle, Janice Faye Mullins, Duncan Munsey, Alec Murphy, Rosemary Murphy, Russ Murphy, Sarah Jane Murphy, Anne Murray, Maida Murray, Margaret Murray, James F. Murtaugh, Georgia Musaser, Alfred Musekari, Mary Musekari, Wayne Musick, Betty Musser, David Myers, Gregory Myers, Michael Myers, Mary Ellen Naff, *Conrad Nagel* (1941), Ruth Nagel, George Nahoon, Bernadette Nance, *Nadine Nash* (1937–38), Amy Nathan, Paul S. Nathan, Taffy Nathanson, Cal Naylor, Emily Neal, Joyce Neal, *Patricia Neal* (1942), Michael J. Necreto, Jr., *Bela Negie* (1946–48), Olivia Negron, Anne Neifert, George Neiman, Adele Nelson, Dawn Nelson, Dewitt Nelson, Douglas Nelson, Dusty Nelson, Erica Nelson, *Herbert Nelson* (1940, 1946–48,

1949–50, 1960–62), James F. Nelson, Janet Nettles, Mary D. Neufield, Mary Neuman, Toni Neumark, Anne Newhall, Bill Newitt, Jean Newton, Jim Newton, Richard Newton, Barry Nichols, Harriet Nichols, Josephine Nichols, Roxie Nichols, *Barbara Niles* (1980–85), James Noble, *Charlotte Nolan* (1949–50, 1951–52, 1954–55, 1960–61), Michel Norell, Donald Norris, Alfred Norton, Kitty A. Norton, Nancy Norton, Steve Novelli, Mary Nunley, Wendy Nute, Shirley Nye, Helen Oakes, Jean Oates, Rita Oakes, Michael O'Brien, Patty O'Brien, Patricia O'Connell, Regan O'Connell, Richard C. O'Connell, Jerry O'Conner, Evelyn Oddo, *Jerry Oddo* (1951–55, 1957–58, 1964–65, 1967, 1970), David Oden, Dillon O'Ferris, George O'Halloran, Jeffrey Ohlrick, Alexander O'Karma, *Pierre Olaf* (1962–63, 1968), Kevin O'Leary, Anthony Oliver, Burns Oliver, Frederick Olmstead, Merritt Olsen, Dale Olson, Frances O'Neill, Claire Ordway, Daniel Oreskes, Cynthia Ann Orr, Martha Orrick, Hubert Osborne, Karen Osborne, Robert Osborne, Shirley Osborne, David Ossian, Shirley Oxford, Ben Packer, *Elizabeth Lyman Packer* (1965–67), Henry Packer, *Peter Pagan* (1949–51, 1955–56, 1961–62), Melinda Page, Victoria Page, Clara Ellen Painter, Anthony Palmer, Lamont E. Palmer, Gracie Paris, Lamar Parish, Barbara Parker, Buck Parker, Carolyn Parker, David Parker, Josephine Parker, Margaret Parmenter, Hunter Parris, Frank Parrish, Don R. Parsons, Jack Parsons, Joel Parsons, Dixie Partington, Rex Partington, *Rex Partington III* (1981–83, 1985–86), *Tony Partington* (1978–83), Nina Partridge, Cynthia Parva, Keiran Pascall, Robert Pascall, *Robert Pastene* (1941, 1946–47, 1948–49, 1958–63), Moultrie Patten, Jo Patterson, Michael Patterson, Robert Patterson, David Patton, David Pauker, Kent Paul, *Morgan Paull* (1961–62, 1963), Mary Payne, Michael Peake, Susan Pellegrino, Bill Pember, *Brock Pemberton* (1947), Ralph Pendleton, Amelia Penland, *Lydia Perera* (1937), Mary Perkinson, Antoinette Perry, Claire Perry, *Margaret Perry* (1949–55), *Mary Perry* (1949–52), Karen Peterson, Wally Peterson, David Pevsner, Margaret Peyton, Sara Peyton, Charlene Phillips, *Margaret Phillips* (1942, 1962–63), *Owen Phillips* (1935–36, 1946–56, 1962–63, 1968–81), Steven Phillips, Ronald Philput, Celia Pickens, Allison Pickrell, Elinor Pickrell, Joclyn Pierrel, Kim Pigman, Charron Pitts, Denise Pitts, Patricia Place, Walter Plinge, Lester Plummer, Trip Plymale, Debra Poland, Sherrard Pollard, Susan Pomerance, Edward Pope, Granville Pope, Arthur Porlar, *Norman Porter* (1940–42), Jay Bird Porterfield, Jean Porterfield, Robert Porterfield, Robert Neal Porterfield, Shelley Post, *John Poulton* (1963–66), Betsy Powers, Charles Powers, Doug Powers, *Eleanor Powers* (1933), Pauline Preller, Sartel Prentice (1938), Cindy Prescott, Algernon Preston, William Preston, David Allen Price, Donna Price, Elizabeth Ann Price, Kenneth Price, *Margaret "Peggity" Price* (1973–77, 1980–81), Phillip Price, Dan Priest, *William Prince* (1937, 1955–56), Jerry Probst, Hamilton Proctor, Jr., Edward Prostak, Edward Proyan, Robert E. Proyer, Rudy Pugliese, J. Shaw Purnell, David Reed Pursley, Robert B. Putnam, Barbara Quacy, Milo Dale Quan, Letha Queen, Barbara Quel, George Quick, *Mildred Quigley* (1933), *Charles Quinlivan* (1952–53, 1955–56), Alicia Quintano, Stephen Radisch, Gerome Ragni, *Katherine Raht* (1937), Sam Rainen, Mark Rainsford, Robert Raleigh, Mary Ramos, Judy Ramsey, Martha Ramsey, Clement Ramsland, Charles D. Randall, Jeanette Randall, Mike Randall, Bobbie Lee Rankin, Caroline Ransom, Michele Raper, Jack Rauchenstein, Susan Rea, Patricia Gilbert Read, Nancy Reardon, Elizabeth Ann Reavey, Ralph Redpath, Daniel Reed, Gavin Reed, James Reese, Carole Ann Reich, Geoffrey Reid, Charles Reilly, Jane Reilly, Michelle Reilly, Susan Reilly, Gretchen Rennell, Pierre Ressingnal, Christine Reusswig, Diane Reynolds, Glenn Reynolds, Harold Reynolds, Joanne Reynolds, Lee Reynolds, Robert Reynolds, Catherine Rhea, Ruth Rhea, Bryan C. Rice, Judy Rice, Doris Rich, Paul Rich, Donald Richard,

Jean-Paul Richard, Jean Richards, Douglas Richardson, Ruth Richardson, John Richie,
David Richmond, *Randy Richmond* (1937–38), Steven Rickert, Rebecca Riddick, George
Riddle, Rosamond Riddle, Jane Ridley, Jon Riffle, Jerry Rifkin, Orvis L. Rigsby, Jr.,
John R. Riordon, *Naomi Riseman* (1954–55, 1957–58, 1961–62), Susan Riskin, George
Ritner, Charles Rittenhouse, Michael Rives, Elizabeth Robbins, Landon Robbins, Art
Roberts, Jane Roberts, Justine Roberts, Margaret Roberts, Edward Robertson, Naomi
Robin, Susanne Robins, Clide Robinson, Delores Robinson, Keith Robinson, Susanne
Robinson, Con Roche, Ken Rockefeller, *Gaby Rodgers* (1950–51, 1952–53), Sandy Roe,
Carol N. Rogers, Linda Rogers, Elizabeth Rogerson, Jane Roggio, Reginald Roland,
Michael Romero, *Woodrow Romoff* (1946–48, 1949–53, 1955–56, 1960–61, 1972), Kim-
berly Ross, Roger Rowitz, Mary Lee Rowland, Thomas Rowland, Paul Ruber, Narii
Ruesch, Mary Lee Ruffin, Gayle Ruhlen, Carol Ann Runion, Ray Rush, Joseph Ruskin,
John Russe, Sally Russe, Michael Russell, Ralph Russell, Joe Russo, Lee Rutherford,
Robert Rutland (1973–77), Chilton Ryan, *Mitchell "Mitch" Ryan* (1954–55, 1957–60,
1963–64), Nora Louise Ryan, Ruth Saada, David Sabin, *Elizabeth St. Clair* (1957–69,
1961–62), Jane St. Clair, George Salerno, Jackie Saloman, Colgate Salsbury, Maynard
Sampson, Lynn Sams, Mark Samuels, Jamie Sanches, Hattie Sue Sandefer, Richard
Sanders, Warren Sanders, Jeanne Sanderson, Phyllis Sanderson, James Sargent, Claude-
Albert Saucier, Frank Savage, Joyce Savage, Allen F. Savitz, Donald Sawyer, *Bigelow
Sayre* (1934), Betty Scanlon, Sue Scarborough, *Maud Scheerer* (1937–38), Evelyn Schie-
felbein, William Schilling, William Schleuter, Joan Schleuter, Jane Schmidt, Steven
Schmidtz, Allen Schoer, Judd Schreidfeder, David Schroeder, Betty Schultz, Carol
Schultz, Mary Schulz, William Schurling, Debra Schut, Madeira Schwartz, Katherine
Scoggins, Frank Scott, Henry Scott, *J. A. Scott* (1962–67), Morgan Scott, Dee Scribner,
Lang Scruggs, Mary Seaman, Bunty Seams, Marian Seams, Donna Searcy, James Secrest,
Dana Seefield, Boyd Seghers, *Gretchen Seidel* (1934–35), Steven Seidel, Virginia Seidel,
John Seitz, Claudeis Selby, *Earl Selfe* (1947–48, 1951–54), Marilee Sennet, Roger
Serbagi, Mary Lee Settle, Kathryn Setzer, Robert Sevra, Roland E. Seward, Victor
Seymour, Cynthia Shallat, Richard Shapik, Larry Alan Sharp, Mac Shaw, Vanessa Shaw,
Lloyd Sheets, Christine Sheffey, John Sheffey, David Lynn Shelby, Mary Shelley, John
Shepard, Julia Sheppard, Blanche Sheridan, Ann Sherry, Sam Sherwell, Mary Sherwood,
Armin Shimerman, Steven Sheuer, Sylvia Short, Gloria Shott, Virginia Shuey, Alan
Shufflebarger, Constance Shulman, Cynthia Shulz, John Shuman, Kenneth Shuman, Luke
L. Sickle, John B. Sillings, Elliott Silverman, Donna Simerly, Alice Simon, Ellen Simons,
Jerry Simpson, Randy Sinclair, Ellen Singleton, Kermit Singleton, Ann Siranco, *Mumsey
Slack* (1933), *S. Slaughter* (1933), Victor Slezak, Earl Slofe, John T. Sloper, Douglas
Smeltzer, Maurice Smeltzer, Alan Smith, Alan George Smith, Anna Chandler Smith,
Carl Smith, Charles Smith, Charles Smith, Jr., Charles W. Smith, Cleo Smith, Cora
Smith, Corine Smith, Dana Smith, Doreen Smith, Helen Smith, Meredith Smith, Piper
Smith, Roy Smith, Terry Smith, *W. Craig Smith* (1940–41), Freda Miller Snapp, James
Snapp, Douglass Sneed, Douglass Snodgrass, Lucille Snodgrass, Anne Snow, Richard
Snow, Amy Snyder, Barry Snyder, Doris Snyder, Nancy Snyder, Judy Soffian, Clarissa
Somers, *Edith Sommers* (1939, 1942), *Gordon Sommers* (1946–50), Rytva Soni, *Leeka
Sopin* (1934), Daniel Sorrell, John Sorsby, Robert D. Soule, Sari Sozan, Kevin Spacey,
Shirley Greig Spalding, Susan Spalding, David Spangler, Carey Sparks, Dusty Spear,
William Spear, Ronald Harrison Spears, Edwin Spencer, Gilliam Spencer, John Spencer,
Mark Spencer, Nancy Spencer, Elizabeth Spies, Maxine Spigel, Barbara Spink, Clifford
Spitzer, Edie Spitzer, Nicholas Stanor, Marjorie Stapp, Hilda Roe Stark, Richard Stark,

Robert Stark, Lee Starkey, Charles Starrett, Donald Stauffer, Larry Steele, Ann Stell, John Steneck, *Arthur Stenning* (1933), Donna Stephen, Fred Stephen, Bill Stephens, Nancy Stephens, *Tyson D. Stephenson* (1971, 1975–76, 1979), Ernest Stepney, Edward Jules Stern, Joseph W. Stern, Charles Sterriett, Frank Stevens, Peter Stevens, Susan Stevens, Warren Stevens, Phillip Stevenson, Edward Stevlingson, Betty Stewart, *Fred Stewart* (1938–41, 1946–47), *Dorothy Stickney* (1958), Bob Stillman, Margaret Stoddard, Thomas Stolz, Diane Stopnel, Lucy Storm, Janet Stout, Susan Strandburg, Renata Strauss, Robert Strauss, Joan Streuber, Sylvia Strickland, Frances Stringfellow (1937–38), Peter Strong, Susan Strong, *Henry Strozier* (1960–63, 1969), Danold Strubbe, *Anna Stuart* (1967–69), Catherine Stuart, Donald Stuart, Ian Stuart, Floyd Sullins, Jean Sullivan, Robert Summers, Richard Summit, Arne Sundergaard, Patricia Swanson, Adolphus Sweet, Kenneth L. Swiger, Kitty Swink, *Margaret Swope* (1938–39), Donald Symington, Kathy Taaffe, Richard Tabor, Edward Tallaferro, Barbara Tarbuck, Marguerite Tarrant, Cindy Tarver, Milton Tarver, Deborah Tate, Richard Tatro, George C. Taylor, Gregory Taylor, Harold Taylor, Helen Marie Taylor, Jack Taylor, Luke Taylor, Rebecca Taylor, Sandra Taylor, Gerald Teaster, Ilsebet Tebesli, Deborah Jean Templin, Barbara Terrell, Terrence F. Tessen, Robert Thames, Donna Thatcher, Barbara Therry, Peter Thoemke, Jean Thomas, Nicholas Thomas, *Rosemary Thomas* (1947–51), Shirley Thomas, Timothy Thomas, William Thomas, Daniel Thompson, David Thompson, James Thompson, Margaret Thompson, Martha Thompson, Sada Thompson, Virgil Thompson, Walter Thompson, William Thompson, *Robert Thomsen* (1933), Frank Thomson, Raymond Thorne, Sally Thurber, Carell Tice, Thornton Tice, Belle T. Tierney, Michael Tierney, Shirley Tirlet, Kenneth Tobey, John Tobias, Donna Todd, Elizabeth Todd, Michael Tolaydo, Colen Tolbert, Verda Tolbert, James Tolkan, Wayne Tolman, Sonia Torgeson, William C. Tost, Dianne Totten, Duane Totten, Gloria Totten, Cynthia Towne, Mildred Trares, *Chester Travelstead* (1933), Katie Sue Trent, *Neal Trent* (1958–61, 1963), Nancy Tribush, Roberta Trigg, Eugene Troobnick, Ben Tudor, Haynes Tuell, Harriett Tumlin, Maidel Turner, *Mell Turner* (1942, 1946–47, 1948–53), Patrick Turner, William Turner, William Turpin, David Tyler, Susan Tyler, Tom Tyrrell, Jerry Uchin (1940–41, 1946–47), David Upson, Roy Urhausen, Tom Vail, John C. Vance, Patricia Vance, Bruce Van Cott, Carole Van Dermier, Jane Van Dusen, Deborah Van Nostrand, Barbara Van Orman, Edna Varney, Jim Varney, Joan Varnum, Mary Vaughn, Richard Vaughn, Ann Verley, Mary Kate Vought, Harold D. Vencil, James Vickers, Jean Vickery, John Vivyan, R. C. Vliet, Charles Vocalis, David Vogel, Richard C. Voigts, John Wade, Marion Wade, Mary Wadsworth, Jo Waffle, Mary Ann Wages, Cheri Wagner, Jane Ann Wagner, Nancy Wagner, Martin Waldron, Pat F. Waldruff, Elizabeth Tipton Walker, Lucye Walker, Mary Ann Walker, Scott Walker, Susan Walker, William Wall, Charles Wallace, Jeff Wallace, Ira Wallach, Gerald Walling, Roy Walling, Stratton Walling, William Walsh, *Erik Walz* (1935, 1938–40), Barbara Ward, Sandra Ward, Benjamin Warfield, Josef Warik, Cynthia Limauro Warne, Marsha Warner, Beverly Warren, Jennifer Warren, Marjorie Warren, Wayne Warren, *Frederic Warriner* (1946–50, 1951–61, 1967), Paul Wasserman, Charles Waterman, Janet Watkins, Peggy Watkins, Ara Watson, Nancy Watts, Lawrence C. Way, Henry Wayne, Eleanor Weal, Daniel Weaver, *Francis "Fritz" Weaver* (1951–53), Gary Weaver, Nancy Webb, Erin Weber, Mary Weed, Peter Week, Susan Weeler, Van B. Weeler, *Don Weightman* (1958–61, 1963), Susan Rae Weinstock, Roslyn Weiss, Beatrice Weller, Betty Cole Wells, Irving Wells, Marcia Wells, Marion Wells, John Welz, Paul Westbrook, Shelly Westebbe, Marvin Wheeler, Carol Whipple, Edwina Whipple, Juin Whipple, Becky White, Glenn White, Jack White, Janet White,

Joyce White, June Daniel White, Arthur Whitehead, Robert Whitehead, Terrese Whitler, Iris Whitney, Wendell Whitten, Terry Whittington, Jeff Wicke, Lynn Wieneke, Edmund Wilde, Ian Wilder, Nancy Wilder, Richard Wilder, Curt Williams, Florence M. Williams, Grant Williams, Hugh Williams, Jeff Williams, Joe Jackson "Joey" Williams, Joseph Williams, Mike Williamson, Ruth Williamson, W. H. Williamson, *Walter Williamson* (1968–70), *Marion "Matt" Willis* (1935–36), Susan Willis, Martha Wilnot, Charlotte Wilson, Douglas Wilson, Ed Wilson, *Elizabeth Wilson* (1942, 1946–47, 1948–49, 1950– 51, 1952–53, 1959–60, 1962–63, 1964), George Wilson, Glen Wilson, J. J. Wilson, Lee Wilson, Lionel Wilson, Marion Wilson, Rebecca Wilson, Kay Wilt, Bill Winslow, Eric C. Winterling, Marsha Wisehousen, Walt Witcover, Raymond Witherspoon, Walter Wood, James Woodall, William Woodman, Emily Woodruff, Glenn Woods, Paul Wood- ville, Richard Woodworth, Marilyn Wooten, Carole Lee Worden, Charles Michael Wright, Christopher James Wright, Elinor Wright, Fred Wright, Marilyn Wright, Michael Charles Wright, *Margaret Wycherly* (1937, 1939, 1942), Phyllis Wynn, Estelle Wynor, *Betty Wysor* (1949–53), Elaine Yarber, Mary Yarbrough, Evelyn Yionoulis, Carroll York, Michael York, *Paul Yost* (1937–38), Dan Young, Libby Young, Mattie Jefferson Young, Paul Young, Alice Yourman, Gloria Zablool, Zeke Zaccaro, Ida Zahl, Margaret A. "Peggy" Zajone, Alan Zampese, Edward Zang, Jr., Peter Zeisler, Helen Zelen, Jean Zell, Donna Zimmerman, Twink Zirkle, Jacqueline Zoty, Ira Zuckermann.

REPERTORY

1933: *After Tomorrow, Monkey Hat* (new play by Tom Powers), *Salt Water, Caught Wet, East Lynne, Three Wise Fools, The Bob-Tailed Nag* (new play by Frances Mellor Gregory).

1934: *Ten Nights in a Barroom, Dangerous Corner, The Late Christopher Bean, Mountain Ivy* (new play by Anne W. Armstrong), *Coquette, Three-Cornered Moon, He Knew Dillinger* (new play by John Crump), *Death Takes a Holiday, The Second Man, Holiday.*

1935: *Smilin' Through, Little Journey, Forever and Forever* (new play by Courtney Savage), *The Pursuit of Happiness, March Hares, Tommy, The Hill Between* (new play by Lula Vollmer), *Double Door, Storm Child* (new play by Griff Morris and John Houston), *Lorella's Holiday* (new play by Edward Forbes), *The Flattering Word, Dungarees, Troublesome Wives* (bill of three one-acts).

1936: *The Minuet* (curtain-raiser for) *Bury the Dead, Post Road, The First Year, Moonshine and Honeysuckle, Solid South, Everyman, Two Women of Abingdon* (bill of two short plays), *The Eternal Ingenue* (new play by Wendell Whitten), *Candida, Personal Appearance, Mrs. Moonlight, The Vinegar Tree, Nor All Your Tears* (new play by Kate Horton), *Shall We Join the Ladies?, If Men Played Cards as Women Do, The Old Lady Shows Her Medals* (bill of three one-acts).

1937: *Hay Fever, The Distaff Side, Macbeth, The Long Night* (new play by Frederick Jackson), *The Petrified Forest, Storm over Betsy, A Living Motion Picture* (curtain-raiser for) *The Cradle Song, Wild Swan* (new play by Sherman Ewing), *Private Lives, Alice* (new play by John Cromwell and William Killcullen), *Fly Away Home, Patrick Henry* (new play by Jamie Heron), *For Charity* (new play by Sydney Carter), *Sun-Up.*

1938: *Penny Wise, Mad Hopes, Spring Dance, Romeo and Juliet* (mountain version anonymously adapted from William Shakespeare), *Friday at Four* (new play by Ralph Holmes), *The Dunce Boy, Jail for Sale* (new play by Samuel J. Park), *Tonight at 8:30, Kind Lady, The Barker, Stage Door, Idiot's Delight, High Tor, Everywhere I Roam* (new play by Arnold Sundgaard), *Prelude, Fine Feathers, Here We Are* (bill of three one-acts).

1939: *Our Town, Springtime for Henry, We'll Take the Highroad* (new play by Leslie McLeod), *What a Life, Lady Baltimore* (new play by Fred Stewart), *Pygmalion, First Lady, Blind Alley, Susquehanna, Dear Octopus, Saturday's Children, Cannons and Crinolines* (dramatic sketches), *Henry IV*.

1940: *Bats in the Woodhouse, or, Button, Button, Ah, Wilderness!, Roller Shades* (new play by Bess Breene), *The Last Straw* (new play by Lydia Perera), *Accent on Youth, Family Portrait, On Earth, As It Is* (new play by Leslie McLeod), *Lee of Virginia, Peg o' My Heart, Excursion, Once upon a Time* (new play by Achmed Abdullah and Robert Osborne), *Edward III, Margin for Error, Davy Crockett*.

1941: *The Philadelphia Story, The Servant of Two Masters, Night Must Fall, The Astonished Heart, The Petrified Forest, The Old Maid, Little Women, The Male Animal, The Bo Tree* (new play by Frank Gabrieldson), *The Farmer Takes a Wife, Jorislund* (new play by Arnold Sundgaard), *Ladies in Retirement*.

1942: *Heart of a City, French Without Tears, Outward Bound, There's Always Juliet, Thunder Rock, No Boys Allowed* (new play by Edith Sommer), *Letters to Lucerne, The Man Who Came to Dinner, Guest in the House, Love Is a Verb* (new play by Karl Widenbach), *He Who Gets Slapped, Family Portrait*.

1943–45: Theatre closed because of World War II.

1946–47: *Blithe Spirit, My Sister Eileen, State of the Union, Wings over Europe, The Women, Much Ado About Nothing, The Happy Journey* (curtain-raiser for) *Virginia Overture* (new play by Arnold Sundgaard), *Three Men on a Horse, Arms and the Man, Stage Door, Oh My Aching Back* (musical revue by Fred Stewart and the Barter Company), *Our Town, Accent on Youth*.

1947–48: *John Loves Mary, East Lynne, Arsenic and Old Lace, State of the Union, Years Ago, Payment Deferred, Arms and the Man, The Barretts of Wimpole Street, The Hasty Heart, The Importance of Being Earnest, Candida, Twelfth Night, The Month Is March* (new play by Montgomery Hare), *Harvey*.

1948–49: *Petticoat Fever, The Glass Menagerie, Papa Is All, Voltaire* (new play by Sherman Ewing), *Voice of the Turtle, Death Takes a Holiday, Pursuit of Happiness, John Loves Mary, Dear Ruth, Cain's Keep* (new play by Montgomery Hare), *Widow's Walk, Hamlet, The Hasty Heart*.

1949–50: *Jenny Kissed Me, Angel Street, The Master Builder, For Love or Money, The Show-Off, You Can't Take It with You, Ladies in Retirement, Keepers of the House* (new play by Julia Brinkman), *Count Your Blessing* (new play by Carl Allensworth), *Accent on Youth, The Torch-Bearers, The Hasty Heart, The Imaginary Invalid, Baa-Baa, Black Sheep* (new play by Montgomery Hare), *Thunder Rock, Dangerous Corner*.

1950–51: *The Heiress, Life with Father, Passing of the Third Floor Back, Claudia* (new play by Rose Franken), *Comedy of Errors, Two Mrs. Carrolls, Tonight at 8:30, The Corn Is Green, The Shining Hour, The Vinegar Tree, The Male Animal, Sun-Up, The Glass Menagerie, The Show-Off*.

1951–52: *Light Up the Sky, The Hasty Heart, The Merchant of Venice, Pursuit of Happiness, The Vinegar Tree, Mrs. Moonlight, Broadway, Two on an Island, Mr. Thing* (new play by Mary Chase, which opened on Broadway as *Mrs. McThing*), *Some Sweet Day* (new play by Anne W. Armstrong), *See How They Run, Sun-Up, Charley's Aunt, The Rivals*.

1952–53: *The Curious Savage, The Twelve Pound Look* (curtain-raiser for) *Trial by Jury, Carolina Charcoal, Good-bye My Fancy, The Kilgo Run* (new play by Arnold Sundgaard), *The Detective Story, The Merchant of Venice, Biography, Sweet Fire* (new play by Lee Marion), *Light Up the Sky, Port in Seven* (new play by Betty Wysor), *The Virginian* (adapted by Margaret Perry from a novel by Owen Wister), *The Late Christopher Bean, George and Margaret.*

1953–54: *A Streetcar Named Desire, George and Margaret, Ten Little Indians, Street Scene, Born Yesterday, Ah, Wilderness!, Scribblers Three* (new play by Bunter Blore Beeton [Eric Blore]), *Family Portrait, The 13 Clocks* (adapted by Robert Gallico and Frank Lowe from a story by James Thurber), *Two Gentlemen of Verona, Mr. Pim Passes By.*

1954–55: *My Three Angels, Mister Roberts, The Barber of Seville* (adapted by Virginia Card from the Rossini opera), *Stalag 17, Heart of a City, Clutterbuck, The 13 Clocks, Macbeth, Death of a Salesman, Lolita* (new play by Mary Chase), *Granny's Millions* (new play by Anne W. Armstrong), *The Moon Is Blue.*

1955–56: *Dial "M" for Murder, The Caine Mutiny Court Martial, The Cocktail Party, I Remember Mama, Julius Caesar, The Little Foxes, The King of Hearts, Affairs of State, The Moon Is Blue, Sabrina Fair, The Time of Your Life, Murder in the Old Red Barn.*

1956–57: *The Tempest, The Lady's Not for Burning, Bus Stop, Dark of the Moon, The Tender Trap, Picnic, Oh, Men! Oh, Women!, The Seven Year Itch, Hall of Mirrors* (new play by Pat Hale), *The Bad Seed, The Rainmaker, The Living Theatre, or Nine by Six, A Cry of Players.*

1957–58: *The Great Sebastians, Anniversary Waltz, The Desperate Hours, Teahouse of the August Moon, Thieves' Carnival, The Reluctant Debutante, Anastasia, Come Back, Little Sheba, The Rainmaker, The Golden Lanterns* (new play by Rebecca Franklin and M. K. Stevens), *The Fourposter.*

1958–59: *Visit to a Small Planet, No Time for Sergeants, Mousetrap, The Crucible, Inherit the Wind, Tea and Sympathy, Six Characters in Search of an Author, Jada* (new play by Paul S. Nathan), *The Play's the Thing, A Lovely Light* (premiere of adaptation of life and work of Edna St. Vincent Millay into one-person performance by Dorothy Stickney), *The Reluctant Debutante.*

1959–60: *Separate Tables, Bell, Book and Candle, Gigi, Solid Gold Cadillac, Cyrano de Bergerac, Voice of the Whirlwind* (new play by Pat Hale), *Cat on a Hot Tin Roof, Auntie Mame, Rumpelstiltskin.*

1960–61: *The Golden Fleecing, The Disenchanted, The Boy Friend, The Regions of the Moon* (new play by R. G. Vliet), *The Dark at the Top of the Stairs, Don Juan in Hell, Two for the Seesaw, Fallen Angels, Rumpelstiltskin, Sleeping Beauty, The Skin of Our Teeth.*

1961–62: *The Pleasure of His Company, Teahouse of the August Moon, Where's Charlie?, Warm Peninsula, The Marriage-Go-Round, Send Me No Flowers, Rain, Idiot's Delight, Land of the Dragon, Under Milk Wood, To God in Italian* (new play by Jerry Oddo).

1962 (summer): *Janus, Five Finger Exercise, This Wooden "O"* (new play by Edith Meisner), *The Waltz of the Toreadors, Write Me a Murder, The 13 Clocks, Where's Charlie?, Under the Yum-Yum Tree, The Bald Soprano, Act Without Words* (bill of two short plays), *Night of the Awk, No Exit, The Zoo Story* (bill of two short plays), *The Fantasticks, 27 Wagons Full of Cotton, Lady of Larkspur Lotion, This Property Is*

Condemned (three one-acts), *The Adventures of Br'er Rabbit* (new play for children by Pat Hale and Paul Spong).

1962–63 (winter): *Misalliance, Uncle Vanya, The Taming of the Shrew, Ring 'Round the Moon, Christmas Special* (from York, Hegge, and Wakefield cycles), *The Fantasticks, The Miracle Worker, Period of Adjustment, Under the Yum-Yum Tree.*

1963 (summer): *Invitation to a March, Sunday, Sunday in New York, Come Blow Your Horn, Bye Bye Birdie, Period of Adjustment, The Guardsman, The Moon Is Blue, Look Homeward, Angel, George Washington Slept Here, Long Day's Journey into Night, The Milktrain Doesn't Stop Here Anymore* (revised version try-out), *Young Abe Lincoln, Beauty and the Beast* (new play for children by Ellen Stuart), *Bremen Town Musicians* (new play for children by Pat Hale), *Frog Prince, Rip Van Winkle* (new play for children by Pat Hale), *The Dumb Waiter, The Lesson* (two short plays), *Serraffin* (one-man show mime), *Three for the Show* (new musical revue by Barter Company).

1964: *A Midsummer Night's Dream, A Shot in the Dark, Oh Dad, Poor Dad, Mamma's Hung You in the Closet and I'm Feelin' So Sad, Critic's Choice, Little Mary Sunshine, The Queen and the Rebels, Take Her, She's Mine, Witness for the Prosecution, The Night of the Iguana, Robin Hood* (new play for children by Pat Hale), *Wizard of Oz, The Adventures of Br'er Rabbit, Androcles and the Lion, Three by Oddo* (new one acts by Jerry Oddo), *Impromptu, The Sandbox, The Stronger* (bill of three one-acts).

1965: *Julius Caesar, The Threepenny Opera, The Happiest Millionaire, Mary, Mary, Waiting for Godot, Pictures in the Hallway, Who's Afraid of Virginia Woolf?, Never Too Late, A Man for All Seasons, Hay Fever, Tartuffe, The Knack, Leader of the Pack* (new play by Sherman Ewing), *The Brave Little Tailor, Pinocchio, The Red Shoes, Man vs. Woman* (adapted from George Bernard Shaw), *The Private Ear, The Public Eye.*

1966: *Twelfth Night, You Can't Take It With You, The Importance of Being Earnest, Absence of a Cello, The Cave Dwellers, The Bat, The Crucible, The Madwoman of Chaillot, The Devil's Advocate, You Never Can Tell, Any Wednesday, Fugitive Masks* (new play by David Madden), *The Fatal French Dentist* (new play by Oscar Mandel on a bill with) *The Joy of Life* (new play by Henry F. Salerno), *A Bird in Hand* (new play by Stephen H. Yafa on a bill with) *Conditioned Reflex* (new play by Curtis Zahn), *Inner Space* (happening by Vernon Lobb), *Marat/Sade, Beyond the Fringe, Golden Sandals, Gabriel Ghost, Winnie the Pooh.*

1967: *Hamlet, Charley's Aunt, Blithe Spirit, Luv, Five in the Afternoon* (new play by Elizabeth Blake), *Barefoot in the Park, Stop the World—I Want to Get Off* (Barksdale Company), *The Odd Couple, Annie and Mike* (new play by Jerry Oddo), *A Certain Young Man* (new play by Thomas deWitt Walsh), *Anniversary, Who's Afraid of Virginia Woolf?, The Adventures of Br'er Rabbit, Beauty and the Beast, Romeo and Juliet, Look Back in Anger.*

1968: *Romeo and Juliet, The 13 Clocks, Pursuit of Happiness, Wait Until Dark, Present Laughter, The Impossible Years, Cactus Flower, Ten Nights in a Barroom, Swan Song* (curtain-raiser for) *Black Comedy, The Caretaker, Fair Harvard* (new play by Sam Brattle), *U.S.A.* (revue), *Catch Me if You Can, Dick Whittington and His Cat* (new play for children by Ellen Stuart), *Cinderella, A Gift for Cathy* (new play by Ronald Alexander).

1969: *The Incomparable Max* (new play by Jerome Lawrence and Robert E. Lee), *U.S.A., Arms and the Man, The Show-Off, See How They Run, Here Today, The Winslow*

Boy, The Hasty Heart, Merton of the Movies, There's a Girl in My Soup, Money, The Little Mermaid, Names and Nicknames, Cinderella, The Dragon's Secret (new play for children by Helen Byrd, Shirley Byrd, and Rebecca Mitchell).

1970: *The Hasty Heart, Plaza Suite, The Lion in Winter, The Petrified Forest, Arsenic and Old Lace, The World of Carl Sandburg, The Stolen Prince, Rumpelstiltskin, Rat Race, Star-Spangled Girl, Macbeth, The Devil's Disciple, Peter of the Round Table* (new play for children by Pat Hale Whitten).

1971: *Arsenic and Old Lace, Much Ado About Nothing, A Stand in the Mountains* (new play by Peter Taylor), *I Do! I Do!, Forty Carats, Don't Drink the Water, Too Young for Spring* (new play by Jaspar "Jerry" Oddo), *The Glass Menagerie, Angel Street, Spoon River Anthology, The Rivalry, Dick Whittington and His Cat, Reynard the Fox.*

1972: *Much Ado About Nothing, Our Town, Dracula, Last of the Red Hot Lovers, The Country Girl, Butterflies are Free, Harvey, Summer and Smoke, Dear Liar, You Know I Can't Hear You When the Water's Running, Apple Pie, An Evening with Tennessee Williams* (in person), *Brecht on Brecht, A Thurber Carnival, Magical Musical Mountain* (new play for children by Marsha Bennett and Pat Conley), *Gammer Gurton's Needle.*

1973: *Spoon River Anthology, The Comedy of Errors, Life with Father, The Hostage, Cocktails with Mimi* (new play by Mary Chase), *The Imaginary Invalid, Night Must Fall, Candlelight, The Subject Was Roses, The Marriage-Go-Round, Voice of the Turtle, The Frog Prince, Who Am I?* (new play for children by Barbara Tarbuck), *Collision Course, By Way of Introduction.*

1974: *Candida, Scapin, The Torch-Bearers, The Odd Couple, Ten Nights in a Barroom, Champagne Complex, Private Lives, Straitjacket* (new play by Howard Koch), *Beyond the Fringe, Silent Night, Lonely Night, Who Am I?, Winnie the Pooh, Bremen Town Musicians, Collision Course, Under Milk Wood, The Nature of Comedy* (dramatic sketches), *William Shakespeare, Poet and Playwright* (reader's theatre).

1975: *The Devil's Disciple, The Diary of Anne Frank, The Beaux' Stratagem, The Male Animal, Broadway, Light Up the Sky, Biography, Sleuth, Two on an Island, The America Experiment* (new play by Margaret Price), *La Ronde, Subreal.*

1976: *The Diary of Anne Frank, You Can't Take It with You, Ten Nights in a Barroom, Biography, The Glass Menagerie, The Threepenny Opera, Democracy, The Matchmaker, Relatively Speaking, Sweet Mistress* (new play by Ira Wallach), *Beyond the Fringe, Jack Tales, Asterian Canticles, The Great Sebastians, Transformations, A Midsummer Night's Dream.*

1977: *The Matchmaker, The Taming of the Shrew, Relatively Speaking, All My Sons, Hay Fever, The Playboy of the Western World, Man with a Load of Mischief* (adapted by John Clifton and Ben Tarver from a play by Ashley Dukes), *Bubba* (new play by Sam Havens), *The Mousetrap, Never too Late, Memory Cake, Balloons, Buffoons and Bubbles, The Context, Pretext, Love, Intrigue and Majesty* (compiled from William Shakespeare), *By Appointment Only, Afterwards.*

1978: *Two Gentlemen of Verona, I Do! I Do!, The Mousetrap, Born Yesterday, The Corn is Green, Tartuffe, The Apple Tree, The Second Man, How the Other Half Loves, The Owl and the Pussycat, Oh, Coward!, Vanities, The Hare and the Tortoise,* Part II, *A*B*C** (America Before Columbus).

1979–80: *Hay Fever, I Do! I Do!, The Wonderful Ones, A Doll's House, Same Time Next Year, Misalliance, Dames at Sea, Absurd Person Singular, Side by Side by Sondheim, Luv, The Fantasticks, The Private Ear* and *The Public Eye.*

1980–81: *Misalliance, The Odyssey, The Importance of Being Earnest, The Royal Family, Ah, Wilderness!, The Desperate Hours, The Heiress, Blithe Spirit, Berlin to Broadway with Kurt Weill, Riverwind, Starting Here, Starting Now, The Fantasticks, Home of the Brave.*

1981–82: *Dulcy, On Golden Pond, Arms and the Man, Deathtrap, Talley's Folly, Oh, Coward!, Gallows Humor, Two by Five, The Corn Is Green, The Heiress, Love's Labour's Lost.*

1982–83: *You Can't Take It with You, Hedda Gabler, The Matchmaker, Tintypes, I Ought to Be in Pictures, The Mousetrap.*

1983–84: *Bus Stop, Fallen Angels, Da, The Dining Room, Side by Side by Sondheim, Relatively Speaking, Tintypes.*

1984–85: *Tintypes, Crimes of the Heart, The Good Doctor, Artichoke, Mass Appeal, Promenade, Bell, Book and Candle, Calling on Lou.*

1985–86: *And a Nightingale Sang, Agnes of God, My Fat Friend, Painting Churches, The Guardsman, Greater Tuna, Twice Around the Park, Billy Bishop Goes to War, Sea Marks, Educating Rita, I Ought to Be in Pictures.*

BIBLIOGRAPHY

Published Sources:

Theatre Profiles, Vols. 1–8. New York: Theatre Communications Group, 1973–88.

Theatre World, 1979–80 through *1985–86*. New York: Crown Publishers, 1981–87.

Williams, Anne St. Clair. "The Barter Theatre: A History." *Southern Theatre* 20 (March 1972): 5–19.

Unpublished Source:

Williams, Anne St. Clair. "Robert Porterfield's Barter Theatre: The State Theatre of Virginia." Doctoral dissertation, University of Illinois, Champaign-Urbana, 1970.

Archival Resource:

Abingdon, Virginia. Barter Theatre. Business and production records, scrapbooks.

Anne St. Clair Williams

BERKELEY REPERTORY THEATRE was founded in 1968 by Michael Liebert and a group of drama students from the University of California at Berkeley. Liebert and his associates converted a storefront into a theatre with a stage surrounded on three sides by seating for eighty-four. The theatre was located at 2980 College Avenue, one mile south of the University of California, in a commercial zone occupied by small restaurants, art galleries, bookstores, and craft shops. The group dedicated itself to the presentation of rarely performed classics in an effort to cultivate the tastes of an audience not served by Berkeley's university and community theatres. Initially the Berkeley Rep scheduled performances on weekends only, but by 1972 it was operating six days a week throughout the year in an enlarged theatre seating 153. The size and configuration of its theatre space and budget constraints meshed with other interests of the group to make it an actor's theatre. Sets and costumes were simplified as directors sought to emphasize the performer's potential for stirring an emotional response in the audience.

In 1975 Berkeley Rep began raising funds to support an enlargement of its theatre, and in 1978 the group began to produce new plays by local playwrights. By the end of its first decade, 4,000 subscribers supported Berkeley Rep, and the company operated on a budget of more than $250,000. In 1979, with the help of an unprecedented Urban Development Action Grant, Berkeley Rep began construction of a 400-seat theater, the centerpiece of a plan to revitalize downtown Berkeley. The new theatre at 2125 Addison Street was inaugurated in 1980. It included not only a mainstage in thrust configuration, but also a 70-seat (later 150-seat) flexible performance space. The subscription list rocketed to more than 11,000, and the fifty-member company played to near capacity for its eight-show season in 1980–81. Sharon Ott succeeded Michael Liebert as artistic director in 1984 and the company has continued to grow.

PERSONNEL

Management: Michael W. Liebert, artistic director (1968–83); Joy Carlin, acting artistic director (1983–84); Sharon Ott, artistic director (1984–86); Mitzi Sales, general manager and managing director (c.1971–86).

Directors: Tony Amendola (1981–82, 1983–84), Larry Berthelot (1981–82), Dennis Bigelow (1979–81), Ann Bowen (1982–83), Gregory Boyd (1981–82), Joy Carlin (1981–84), John Dillon (1983–84), Peter Donat (1977–78), Oskar Eustis (1984–85), John Raymond Freimann (1978–79, 1982–83), Edward Hastings (1983–84), Douglas Johnson (1975–77, 1983–84), Alex Kinney (1981–82), George Kovach (1976–78), Peter Layton (1979–82), Michael W. Leibert (1975–82), James Moll (1981–82), Robert Moss (1984–86), William I. Oliver (1979–81), Maureen O'Reilly (1977–79), Sharon Ott (1984–86), Shazo Sato (1983–84), Steven Schachter (1984–85), Joe Spano (1977–78), Jeff Steitzer (1985–86), Anthony Taccone (1984–85), Albert Takazauckas (1979–85), H. Burke Walker (1985–86), Don West (1979–81), Richard E. T. White (1984–86).

Scenic Designers: Gene Angell (1975–79, 1981–83), George Barcos (1979–81), Robert Blackman (1977–78), William Bloodgood (1979–81, 1984–86), Gene Chesley (1976–77), Lauren Cory (1978–79), Andrew DeShong (1976–78, 1979–81), Mark Donnelly (1981–84), Kent Dorsey (1984–85), William S. Eddelman (1984–85), Kate Edmunds (1985–86), John Raymond Freimann (1977–79), Ralph Funicello (1979–81, 1983–84, 1985–86), Karen Gjelsteen (1981–85), Richard L. Hay (1979–81), Jesse Hollis (1979–85), Christopher M. Idoine (1977–78), George Kovach (1977–78), Laura Maurer (1984–85), Henry May (1981–83), Richard G. Norgard (1981–83), Tom Odegard (1977–78), Michael Olich (1985–86), Ron Pratt (1975–79, 1981–83), Tom Rasmussen (1981–83), Shazo Sato (1983–84), Barbara Sellers (1978–79), Lesley Skannal (1975–77), Vicki Smith (1981–86), Warren Travis (1979–83), Noel Uzemack (1978–81), Bernard Vyzga (1981–84), Scott Weldin (1985–86), Jeff Whitman (1975–78).

Costume Designers: Beaver Bauer (1984–85), Robert Blackman (1981–83), William P. Brewer II (1982–83), Deborah Brothers-Lowry (1982–83), Debra Bruneaux (1984–85), Marie Anne Chiment (1976–78), Eliza Chugg (1984–85), Jeannie Davidson (1982–86), Rondi Davis (1978–79), Deborah Dryden (1979–81, 1982–84), Cathleen Edwards (1979–81), Lorraine Forman (1982–83), John Raymond Freimann (1977–78), Susan Hilferty (1984–86), Michael Krass (1985–86), Toni Lovaglia (1982–83), Sarajane Milligan (1978–81), Robert Morgan (1982–83), Merrily Ann Murray (1978–81, 1983–84),

Colleen Muscha (1984–85), Syrell Myers (1977–78), Michael Olich (1984–86), Tom Rasmussen (1982–83), Sally Richardson (1983–84), Shazo Sato (1983–84), Lesley Skannal (1975–78), Diana Smith (1975–78, 1979–81), John Carver Sullivan (1985–86), Warren Travis (1978–81, 1982–83), Walter Watson (1982–83), Kurt Wilhelm (1983–84).

Lighting Designers: Joan Arhelger (1981–83), S. Leonard Auerback (1979–81), George Barcos (1979–81), Mark Bosch (1981–83), John Chapot (1979–81), Matthew Cohen (1975–78), Kent Dorsey (1984–86), Derek Duarte (1981–86), Barbara DuBois (1981–83), Dirk Epperson (1979–81), Larry French (1981–83), Ken Hein (1977–78), Christopher M. Idoine (1977–78), Lynn Koolish (1977–81), Dan Kotlowitz (1983–86), Joan Liepman (1975–76), Peter Maradudin (1985–86), Robert Peterson (1979–83, 1985–86), Tom Ruzika (1981–84), Shazo Sato (1983–84), Betty Schneider (1979–83), Greg Sullivan (1979–85).

Actors and Actresses (1983–85 only are available): Tony Amendola (1983–85), David Booth (1983–85), Joy Carlin (1983–84), James Carpenter (1984–85), Charles Dean (1983–85), Ken Grantham (1984–85), Alexander-Williams Hope (1983–84), Irving Israel (1983–85), Judith Marx (1983–85), Michelle Morain (1983–85), Barbara Oliver (1984–85), Richard Rossi (1983–84), Brian Thompson (1983–85), Michael Tulin (1984–85).

REPERTORY

1968–71: Unavailable.

1971–72: *The Alchemist, Angel Street, Julius Caesar, Who's Happy Now?, Love's Labour's Lost, For Promised Joy, She Stoops to Conquer.*

1972–73: *Father's Day, Crime on Goat Island, Mostaleria, The Dance of Death, Loot, Subject to Fits, The Sea Gull, The School for Scandal, Arms and the Man, The Comedy of Errors.*

1973–74: *Charley's Aunt, Heartbreak House, The Master Builder, The Petrified Forest, The Misanthrope, Dracula: A Musical Nightmare, The Front Page, London Assurance, Born Yesterday.*

1974–75: *Blithe Spirit, The Little Foxes, A Midsummer Night's Dream, The Devil's Disciple, Continental Divide, Uncle Vanya, The Hostage, Much Ado About Nothing, Hamlet, The Merchant of Venice.*

1975–76: *Seven Keys to Baldpate, The Iceman Cometh, Arsenic and Old Lace, Cat on a Hot Tin Roof, Of Mice and Men, Yankee Doodle, Rope, The Importance of Being Earnest.*

1976–77: *Candida, Bus Stop, The Philanthropist, Mann ist Mann, The Country Wife, Private Lives, Our Town.*

1977–78: *A Flea in Her Ear, Rep!, Major Barbara, Mad Oscar, The Servant of Two Masters, A Moon for the Misbegotten, Wait Until Dark, Arms and the Man, As You Like It, They Knew What They Wanted, Misalliance.*

1978–79: *The Skin of Our Teeth, She Stoops to Conquer, The Tavern, He Who Gets Slapped, The Last of the Marx Brothers' Writers, Room Service.*

1979–80: *A Delicate Balance, Children of Darkness, Waltz of the Toreadors, Hedda Gabler, What the Butler Saw.*

1980–81: *Galileo, Fallen Angels, My Heart's in the Highlands, Pygmalion, Measure for Measure, The Shadow Box, A Life in the Theatre, The Norman Conquests.*

1981–82: *The Cherry Orchard, The Belle of Amherst, As You Like It, Savages, After the Fall, Heartbreak House, The Diary of Anne Frank, Tonight at 8:30.*

1982–83: *Happy End, Chekhov in Yalta, The Glass Menagerie, The Show-Off, Beyond Therapy, A Lesson from Aloes, U.S.A., Geoff Hoyle Meets Keith Terry.*

1983–84: *American Buffalo, The Way of the World, Season's Greetings, Awake and Sing!, Filumena, The Margaret Ghost, Kabuki Medea.*

1984–85: *A Touch of the Poet, Otherwise Engaged, Tartuffe, Kingdom Come, Misalliance, The Tooth of Crime, Execution of Justice.*

1985–86: *The Playboy of the Western World, In the Belly of the Beast, The Art of Dining, The Sea, The Diary of a Scoundrel, The Normal Heart, Twelfth Night.*

BIBLIOGRAPHY

Published Sources:

Theatre Profiles. Vols. 1–8. New York: Theatre Communications Group, 1973–88.
Theatre World, 1983–84 through *1984–85.* New York: Crown Publishers, 1985–86.

Weldon B. Durham

BOARSHEAD: MICHIGAN PUBLIC THEATRE in Lansing, Michigan, also known as the BoarsHead Theatre, was originally organized as a summer theatre in 1966 by John Peakes and Richard Thomsen. For the first five seasons they produced plays in the 350-seat thrust stage–equipped Ledges Playhouse located in Fitzgerald Park, Grand Ledges, Michigan (a small town about ten miles west of Lansing), while on summer vacation from their college teaching positions. The producers left teaching in 1970. They rented a local church and converted it into a theatre, which they operated as a nonprofit company. The theatre opened in September with a production of *Feiffer's People*, an offbeat comedy by Jules Feiffer. In 1975 the company moved into its current home, a 250-seat thrust stage theatre designed especially for it within the Center for the Arts in Lansing at 425 South Grand Avenue.

Initially Peakes and Thomsen planned to settle in the eastern United States, where they hoped to raise their families and continue college teaching careers in drama. They believed that their summer project would be a periodic diversion from teaching that would also provide an opportunity for their personal artistic development. Their intentions changed when the producers gradually became more involved with the cultural life of Lansing. They were concerned about well-meaning but underequipped amateur groups producing seasons of warmed-over Broadway hits, and profit-minded dinner theatre presenting television stars in second-rate acting vehicles. They were also distressed by the passing of many nascent theatre companies that attempted to produce better fare, but lacked the managerial acumen to remain solvent.

Despite these gloomy conditions, the success they were experiencing with their summer group in Fitzgerald Park convinced them there was an audience for higher-quality theatre in Lansing as well as a market demand that could, under the right conditions, sustain a professional company for the long term. Armed with this knowledge plus their own high artistic standards and business experience, the producers modified their earlier resolve and organized a permanent company to produce drama they believed would be important to the lives of the people of Lansing. Their mission was "to make a difference." Specifically, the producers were committed to American plays, and dedicated to the idea that an important theatre must grow from within to become the voice of the community it serves. Half of each season would be devoted to new works, preferably those with regional origins and a distinctly theatrical style.

In 1971 the theatre established a board of directors and became incorporated as a not-for-profit enterprise. Official Michigan tax status for the operation was granted in 1976 and an Actors' Equity Association Letter of Agreement was signed in 1979. The BoarsHead Theatre has shown a steady rise in attendance, increasing its earned income from $135,680 in 1977 to $309,455 in 1986. Major expenses incurred by hiring full-time staff have somewhat dimmed the financial picture recently, but a new policy of fiscal restraint has been introduced to correct the temporary difficulty. Increased attention has been given to corporate sponsorship, and mainstage seasons in the future will include more established contemporary plays instead of experimental scripts.

Overcoming the handicap of a small population (300,000 metro area), the BoarsHead Theatre has established and maintained a reputation for a continuously high-quality theatrical product. Critics admire how the company has faced the inevitable difficulties with optimistic determination. There is high praise for the company's strong commitment to community involvement, and there is also respect for its tough-minded endurance, a quality Midwesterners like to see in themselves.

In sixteen years of continuous full-time operation the company has produced an average of six plays annually, bringing the total to more than one hundred full-length plays and musicals. Variety has characterized play selection over the years, but contemporary American plays have dominated the repertory. Lanford Wilson, Eugene O'Neill, William Saroyan, and Milan Stitt are a few of the most prominent dramatists whose plays have been produced, along with those of scores of newcomers. The company is particularly effective portraying traditional American values and ideals. In 1984 the producers decided to rely more on established contemporary plays in an effort to increase box-office revenues. Most new scripts are currently produced as staged readings in a midwinter second season called "Winterfare Festival of the Arts," which features Michigan artists in music and dance performances as well as theatre.

The resident acting company is made up of twelve members, constituting 75 percent of each production. The company is supplemented with interns and guest artists (often BoarsHead alumni) hired from auditions in New York City, Chicago, or Detroit. The theatre sponsors a continuous program of affiliated activities consisting of a four-play summer season in Muskegon, Michigan, internships, artists-in-schools residencies, acting classes, All Peoples Theatre (for handicapped individuals who want to explore their creative potential), plays for children, touring youth theatre, and the Young Playwrights' Festival.

PERSONNEL

Artistic Directors: Nancy-Elizabeth Kammer (1984–86), John Peakes (1970–84), Richard Thomsen (1970–84).

Directors: Arthur Athanson, Robert Burpee, Charles S. Burr, Jim Burton, Barbara Carlisle, Kyle Euchert, Claude File, Robert Hall, Gus Kaikkonen, Nancy-Elizabeth Kammer, Mark Klein, Peter Link, B. Rodney Marriott, Andrew Mendelson, Marcial Milgrom, Michelle Napier, Penny Owen, John Peakes, Leonard Peters, Nina Simons, Patricia K. Smith, Kristine Thatcher, Maggie Thatcher, Richard Thomsen.

Designers: Peter P. Allburn, Donna Arnink, David Arnold, Glen J. Clements, Sea Daniel, Charlotte Deardorff, John Eckert, Fran Engelgau, Fred Engelgau, Kyle Euckert, Joseph Grigaitis, Ann Gumpper, Jeff Guzik, Kim Hartshorn, Ed Kruis, Margaret Lee, Ruth Long, Johanna Lubkowski, Arthur Meister, Bill Mikulewicz, Richard Oman, Robert Palmateer, John Peakes, Kenneth L. Peck, Gordon Phetteplace, Sidney Poel, A. J. Rocchio, Kerry Shanklin, George Sherlock, Dennis Sherman, Patricia K. Smith, Tim Stapleton, Barbara Thomsen.

Actors and Actresses: Not available.

REPERTORY

1970–77: Not available.

1977–78: *Last of the Red Hot Lovers, Living Together, Who's Afraid of Virginia Woolf?, Private Lives, Equus, Stop the World—I Want to Get Off, The Runner Stumbles, Vanities, The Sunshine Boys, Cabaret, Fiddler on the Roof, The Male Animal.*

1978–79: *The Last Meeting of the Knights of the White Magnolia, The Underpants, Dandelion Wine, A Life in the Theatre, Uncle Vanya, Steambath, Time Steps, The House of Blue Leaves, Harvey, Man of La Mancha, George M!, Same Time Next Year.*

1979–80: *The Passion of Dracula, Brontosaurus Tales* (Gus Kaikkonen), *Sly Fox, A Christmas Carol, The Glass Menagerie, Back in the Race* (Milan Stitt), *The Collected Works of Billy the Kid* (Michael Ondaatje), *Sizwe Bansi Is Dead, Minnesota Moon* (John Olive), *A Blue Note Memory of Harvey and Rickey* (Doug Clark), *California Suite, Hello, Dolly!, Broadway Spirit, Twigs* (George Furth).

1980–81: *Waltz of the Toreadors, Gemini, The Palace of Amateurs* (John Faro PiRoman), *A Christmas Carol, Letters from Bernice* (Jeanne Michaels and Phyllis Murphy), *Ah, Wilderness!, Clara's Play* (John Olive), *Oh, Coward!, Total Abandon* (Larry Atlas), *Uncle King Arthur* (Milburn Smith), *You're a Good Man, Charlie Brown, Godspell, Deathtrap.*

1985–86: *The General's Daughters* (Linda Brumfield), *The Foreigner, Our Town, Home, Jacques Brel, The Sonneteer* (Larry Atlas), *Bitter Harvest* (John Olive), *Neidecker* (Christine Thatcher), *Give the Queen a Dollar* (Steven Metcalfe), *Waterwalker* (Steven Metcalf), *Shards* (David Thomsen), *Potholes* (Gus Kaikkonen), *Power, Sex and Boogie* (John Faro PiRoman), *Stage Struck Blues* (Jeanne Michaels and Phyllis Murphy), *Waiting Rooms* (Andrew and Adriana Johns).

1986–87: *Greater Tuna, In the Sweet Bye and Bye* (Donald Driver), *The Time of Your Life, Bullets to the Gun* (Justin Peacock), *The Only Song I Know* (John C. Cameron), *A Picture of Oscar Wilde* (Peter D. Sieruta), *Two Beers and a Hook Shot* (Kent R. Brown), *Valentines and Killer Chili* (Kent R. Brown), *Joe's Friendly* (Bruce Gadansky), *Photographic Memory* (Kim Carney), *Careless Love* (John Olive), *Man Enough* (Patty Gideon Sloan), *Frankenstein* (Bob Hall and David Richmond), *Bridging the Gap* (Ron Osborn), *Stop Me If You've Heard This One* (Rodney Vaccaro).

BIBLIOGRAPHY

Published Source:

Theatre Profiles. Vols. 4–7. New York: Theatre Communications Group, 1979–86.

Unpublished Source:

Sauers, Timothy. BoarsHead Theatre director of marketing and public relations. January 15, 1987.

Archival Resource:

Lansing, Michigan. Lansing Center for the Arts. BoarsHead Theatre programs, season brochures, annual reports.

James Thomas

C

CENTER STAGE was founded in 1962 when Edward Golden, finding commercial theatre at a low ebb in Baltimore, Maryland, aspired to start a regional theatre in that city. The old Ford's Theatre was about to be torn down; the Mechanic was not yet foreseen, and Painters Mills was open only in the summer. No dinner theatres had yet appeared, and Baltimoreans in search of professional theatre usually went to the Arena Stage* in Washington. Golden assembled a group of people to sell shares in a profit-making theatre corporation. The founders were naive—they hadn't talked to theatre people in other cities, so they believed that money could be made on a regional theatre. Accordingly, they began selling shares and telling friends they were a good investment.

The shares proved to be just that, but not as originally conceived. The new group incorporated in September 1962 and set out to find a site. After several unsuccessful attempts, Golden and his backers found the second floor of a building at 45 West Preston Street, owned by the Greek Orthodox Church. An area seventy feet by thirty-six feet could house arena productions for a maximum of 200 patrons. Backstage facilities were totally inadequate, but the Center Stage opened with Arthur Schnitzler's *La Ronde* on January 15, 1963. The fire department threatened to close them that afternoon, but the theatre's attorney successfully pleaded for a dispensation, and the show opened to mild praise. Later that season the Center Stage scored its first real hit with Edward Albee's *The Zoo Story*, in which Colgate Salsbury played a highly praised Jerry. Center Stage had only 600 season subscriptions by the end of the first season. Total attendance for the eight productions was 17,000 and the box office had taken in $36,885, but the "profit-making investment" had lost $8,473.

The second season opened October 15, 1963, with Moss Hart's *Light Up the Sky*. By midseason losses had mounted to $15,000, despite a subscription audience of 900, so Center Stage decided to convert to nonprofit status. Although the second half of the season showed a profit of $4,000 (owing in part to a $7,500 fund-raising campaign), the season's costs outpaced income by more than $11,000.

In the third season new executive director William H. Bushnell, Jr., began to expand the theatre's activities. With a $15,000 grant from the state of Maryland, the Center Stage began touring to schools, becoming one of the first regional theatres in the nation to do so. Bushnell also put one of the company's actresses, Vivienne Shub, in charge of a children's theatre operation. Artistic changes followed as guest directors were brought in for four of the season's productions. Nevertheless, after one of its more successful seasons, with contributions and grants increasing to $35,000, the Center Stage again had an $11,000 deficit. That summer, however, Golden left Center Stage and Center Stage left Preston Street. The company moved to the old Oriole Cafeteria at 11 East North Avenue, which it converted to a larger stage with greater (315) seating capacity, a move made possible by a loan of $40,000.

On November 28, 1965, the new theatre opened to positive response. A new director, Douglas Seale, began his three-year stint in Baltimore. England-born Seale acted and directed to mixed reviews, but during his tenure subscriptions rose steadily to 7,000. Unfortunately deficits also increased, reaching $60,000 by 1967–68. Oddly, several of Seale's Shakespearean productions, his specialty, failed: *Titus Andronicus, As You Like It*, and *Hamlet*.

Other changes followed. In October 1966 Bushnell left for the American Conservatory Theatre* in San Francisco, taking several members of the company with him. After an uncomfortable interlude the company hired Peter Culman from the Barter Theatre* in Virginia as the new administrative head.

Seale's departure in June 1968 left the Center Stage without an artistic director for 1968–69. Culman reviewed 1967–68 and considered it the Center Stage's worst season so far. He further noted that whereas the Center Stage had begun 1967–68 with 8,000 subscribers, they entered 1968–69 with barely half that number. Changes had to be made. Culman kept only two of the previous season's actors, trimmed the budget by $40,000 (about 10 percent), but increased the performers' salaries in the belief that actors and actresses accounted for at least 70 percent of the success of a theatre company.

The company abandoned the notion of maintaining a resident acting company and began jobbing in actors and directors for most productions. Financially, the 1968–69 season was a disaster. Expenses rose to $170,000; box-office receipts and grants dwindled; and Center Stage ended the season with a deficit of $110,802, bringing their total debt to almost $185,000. Banks were unwilling to loan the theatre any more funds.

This marked the nadir thus far for Center Stage. John Stix became consulting director in 1969 and artistic director in 1970, bringing with him a greatly needed quiet stability. The Center Stage began to solve its problems. From 1969 to 1971 Culman reduced expenses by $35,000 the first year and $15,000 the next. He and the board president, Sewell S. Watts III, managed to increase grants and contributions, and, for the first time, Center Stage operated in the black, paying off as well $16,000 a year in interest on its outstanding debts. Still, the theatre was close to going under. One of the banks, Equitable Trust, donated the company the money it had borrowed but told them not to come back for more.

In the summer of 1971 Watts suggested one more push for grants and contributions, after which the company could decide whether to continue. Center Stage raised $100,000 in the immediate neighborhood, but then the Ford Foundation awarded the theatre a grant of $320,000, part of which was a matching grant to pay off the debts. By 1973 the debt was paid off; the budget was balanced, and, for the first time, Center Stage ended a season with no debt and money in the bank. The 1972–73 season, with Culman as executive director and Stix as artistic director, opened with the first Center Stage sellout, Dale Wasserman's dramatization of Ken Kesey's *One Flew over the Cuckoo's Nest*. As the theatre celebrated its tenth anniversary, it was an established part of the Baltimore community and the national theatre scene, as evidenced by a National Endowment for the Arts grant to sponsor a tour of one of its mainstage productions.

During the summer of 1973 the board promoted Culman to managing director, demoted Stix, who had been accused of spending too much time in New York, to consulting director, and engaged Jacques Cartier as artistic director. Cartier's first move was to cancel four of the six productions Stix had scheduled, replacing them with his own choices. The National Endowment for the Arts had offered the Center Stage $85,000 for a regional tour; Cartier felt the group needed $100,000 to break even, so he cancelled the tour.

Cartier came to Baltimore after five years with the Hartford [Connecticut] Stage Company. His success in Hartford and his hardheaded action immediately on assuming his post in Baltimore boded well for the future, and Baltimoreans looked forward to the next decade of the Center Stage.

Then the theatre burned down.

On January 10, 1974, two disgruntled drunks, having been thrown out of Benny Goodman's Beef and Beer, a restaurant next door to the theatre, set fire to the building. The blaze wrecked the theatre and speeded up the search for a permanent location for the group. Meanwhile, the company transferred its current production to the Baltimore Museum of Art Auditorium, missing not a single performance. After playing for a weekend at the Museum of Art, the company moved to the College of Notre Dame.

Then, after heated discussions, the board decided to cancel the mainstage season, locate a permanent site, and raise funds for a new building. The search for a permanent site settled on the old St. Ignatius complex in the 700 block of North Calvert, built in 1855 to house Loyola College. Byzantine negotiations led finally to acquisition of the building (42,000 square feet), which would take nearly $2 million to renovate. The city of Baltimore bought the building from the Jesuits, paying them $200,000, with the understanding that Center Stage would raise money for the renovation. To further assist Center Stage the city of Baltimore loaned $200,000 to be used in the renovation. The National Endowment for the Arts granted $100,000, and the Ford Foundation made an unprecedented loan of $750,000. Finally, a consortium of Baltimore banks loaned $300,000 on security put up by members of the Center Stage board of directors. Center Stage pledged $150,000, two-thirds of which was to be raised by a capital fund drive. The Ford Foundation loan, by far the largest contribution, was a tribute to the Center Stage's meticulous fiscal procedures. The Foundation examined every aspect of the Center Stage—its financial management, its board structure, its operation management, its artistic worth and management. So impressed was the Foundation with the Center Stage's accounting methods that they recommended them to similar organizations throughout the country.

The new theatre complex was designed by James R. Grievs of Baltimore in association with New York lighting and theatre consultant Roger Morgan. Although some windows had to be blocked up for soundproofing purposes, the building's facade was left essentially as it had been. In 1978 the Center Stage won one of fifteen awards for successful restoration granted by the American Institute of Architects.

On December 9, 1975, twenty-three months after the fire, the Center Stage opened a sellout production of Moliére's *The Miser* in its own 500-seat theatre. The renovation was only the first phase of the intended development; phase two would add a 300-seat proscenium theatre, and phase three called for transforming the huge rear courtyard into an outdoor theatre. By May 1976, however, it became clear the season was neither a financial nor an artistic success. The board accepted the resignation of Jacques Cartier.

Thus the second season in the new quarters opened under the artistic direction of Stanley Wojewodski, Jr., while Peter Culman remained as managing director. Wojewodski had been director of the theatre's young people's company and was named as a temporary artistic director. The next year he was selected as the permanent artistic director. He designed a mainstage season of six plays, including classics and modern scripts, for a small resident company supplemented by New York actors. The Center Stage also toured annually, playing to more than 100,000 students throughout the state. Wojewodski launched an internship program for secondary-school students, performance workshops, and an accredited directing seminar for teachers. Other additions were staged readings, workshop productions, and an internship for local playwrights.

As the Center Stage prepared for 1978–79, they had 11,070 season subscribers, up 3,000 from the previous year. The renewal rate was 82 percent, 12 percent above the national average for regional theatres. In addition, the list of contributors had increased 300 percent in eighteen months. The Center Stage was carrying no deficit and had been meeting its fund-raising goals. Wojewodski's leadership appeared to be a critical part of the Center Stage's newfound formula for economic stability.

As the Center Stage expanded its offerings, striving toward a fifty-two-week use of the building, several kudos came its way. *Bartleby*, adapted from the Herman Melville short story and produced at the Maryland Center for Public

Broadcasting, enhanced Center Stage's national reputation when it was broadcast nationally. It was selected as the best regionally produced public television drama by the Corporation for Public Broadcasting and the best program of the year by the Southern Educational Communications Association.

By the 1979–80 season the Center Stage was playing to 93 percent of capacity. In order to prevent subscribers from filling every available seat, runs were extended from four and a half to five and a half weeks. Guest directors such as William Devane and Robert Allan Ackerman had high praise for the operation, and the *Washington Post* called it the equal of the best regional theatres in the nation.

The year 1980 marked the beginning of the First Stage series, designed to provide workshops for new scripts, a means for testing new conceptual approaches to proven scripts, and the discovery of appropriate performance styles for them.

By 1983 Center Stage operated on a $2 million budget, including $1.4 million earned income. Annual attendance had risen to 180,000 and subscribers numbered 15,083 for a season that ran from September to June.

Today the Center Stage enjoys substantial local respect and loyalty. As an assured part of the Baltimore cultural scene, its greatest achievement has been the scenario for its own survival.

PERSONNEL

Artistic Directors: Jacques Cartier (1973–75), Edward Golden (1962–65), Douglas Seale (1965–68), John Stix (1970–73), Stanley Wojewodski, Jr. (1975–85).

Executive Directors: William H. Bushnell, Jr. (1965–66), Peter W. Culman, Jr. (1966–85).

Directors: Robert A. Ackerman (1977–79), Larry Arrick (1972–73), Edward Berkley (1977–78), Paul Berman (1984–85), Lenore Blank (1981–82), Roy Brocksmith (1984–85), Jacques Cartier (1973–74, 1975–76), Leanardo Cimino (1967–68), Kenneth Costigan (1963–64), *Peter Culman* (1968–72), Walter Dallas (1981–82), John Henry Davis (1976–77), William Devane (1978–79), Charles Eastman (1975–76), Nathan George (1969–70), Bernard Hiatt (1963–64), Ronald L. Hufman (1967–68), Mesrop Kesdekian (1964–65), Woodie King, Jr. (1976–77), Albert Laveau (1975–76), Irene Lewis (1979–81, 1983–85), Robert Lewis (1970–72), John Lithgow (1971–72), Robert H. Livingston (1972–73), John Marley (1964–65), Michael Murray (1973–74) Mitchell Nestor (1972–73), John Olon-Scrymgeour (1964–65, 1967–69), John Pasquin (1983–84), Sheldon Patinkin (1970–71), Kent Paul (1968–69), *Jackson Phippin* (1979–85), Ben Piazza, (1969–70), Travis Preston (1983–84), J. Ranelli (1979–81), Steven Robman (1978–79), Marcia Rodd (1977–78), Dennis Rosa (1968–69, 1969–70), David Rounds (1969–70), Alfred Ryder (1971–72), Lee D. Sankowich (1971–72), Carl Schurr (1973–74), Douglas Seale (1967–68), Geoffrey Sherman (1980–81), *John Stix* (1968–74), Lee Theodore (1969–70), Richard Ward (1970–71), Ruth White (1968–69), *Stan Wojewodski, Jr.* (1975–85), Garland Wright (1980—81), Arne Zaslove (1976–77), Stephen Zuckerman (1983–84).

Scenic Designers: Bennet Averyt (1972–73), John Baker III (1967–68), John Boyt (1972–73), Wally Cobert (1981–82), Charles Cosler (1976–79), Clark Crolius (1977–78), Kate Edmonds (1983–84), Eldon Elder (1970–72, 1976–78), *Richard Goodwin*

(1980–84), Peter Harvey (1975–78), Desmond Heeley (1980–81), Andrew Jackness (1978–79), David Jenkins (1975–76), John Jensen (1975–76), John Kasarda (1978–79, 1980–81), Marjorie Kellogg (1971–72), Leo Kerz (1970–72), Thom Lafferty (1970–71), *Hugh Landwehr* (1977–85), Peter Larkin (1978–79), Whitney J. LeBlanc (1970–71), Eugene Lee (1975–76), Kert Lundell (1968–69, 1975–76), Henry Millman (1979–81), David Mitchell (1970–71), Roger Morgan (1968–69), Joan Olsson (1970–71), Jason Phillips (1969–70), Raymond C. Recht (1972–74), W. Scott Robinson (1969–70), Barry Robison (1979–81), C. Mitch Rogers (1969–70), Jay Scott (1970–71), Douglas Seale (1966–68), Phillip Silver (1966–67), Preston Sisk (1970–71), Ritchie M. Spencer (1969–70), Douglas Stein (1983–85), *Tony Straiges* (1981–82, 1983–85), Charles Vanderpool (1970–71), Robert T. Williams (1968–69), Nancy Winters (1984–85), Ed Wittstein (1981–83), Paul Wonsek (1980–81).

Lighting Designers: Frances Aronson (1979–80), Bennet Averyt (1972–74), *Bonnie Ann Brown* (1978–83), Ian Calderon (1975–78), Pat Collins (1983–85), Charles Cosler (1976–78), Peter Culman (1971–72), Lee Dunholter (1966–68), Eldon Elder (1971–72), *Arden Fingerhut* (1976–83), Paul Gallo (1979–81), John Gleason (1979–81), Gilbert V. Hemsley, Jr. (1975–76), Ann Howell (1980–81), James F. Ingalls, Jr. (1983–85), Neil Jampolis (1978–79), Leo Kerz (1971–72), Craig Miller (1981–84), Roger Morgan (1975–76), Spencer Mosse (1978–79, 1980–81), *Judy Rasmuson* (1977–85), Raymond C. Recht (1972–74), Jane Reisman (1978–79), David Rogers (1964–66), John Sichina (1971–72), Phillip Silver (1966–67), Stephen Strawbridge (1984–85), Donald Edmund Thomas (1981–82), Jennifer Tipton (1983–84), John Tissot (1981–82), Richard Winkler (1983–84), *Ann G. Wrightson* (1979–83).

Costume Designers: Melissa F. Binder (1979–81), John Boyt (1972–73), James Edmund Brady (1966–68), Jim Buff (1984–85), Lawrence Casey (1984–85), Laura Castro (1977–79), Liz Covey (1975–76), Laura Crow (1973–74), Kate Edmunds (1983–84), Eldon Elder (1971–72), *Linda Fisher* (1973–74, 1979–85), Jess Goldstein (1983–85), *Dona Granata* (1977–84), Desmond Heeley (1980–81), John Jensen (1975–76), Leo Kerz (1971–72), Jean Levine (1973–74), Kert Lundell (1975–76), Mimi Maxmen (1983–84), Tiny Ossman (1980–81), Elizabeth P. Palmer (1975–78), Walter Pickette (1981–82), Nancy Potts (1975–76), Raymond C. Recht (1972–73), Del W. Risberg (1981–85), *Carrie F. Robbins* (1979–81), Barry Robison (1979–81), Hilary Rosenfeld (1977–78), Hilary Sherred (1978–79), Lesley Skannal (1980–82), Ritchie M. Spencer (1968–69), Mary Strieff (1971–73), *Fred Voelpel* (1979–81), Jacqueline Watts (1981–82), Juliellen Weiss (1972–73), *Bob Wojewodski* (1977–83).

Acting Company Members (partial): Lach Adair (1973–74), Mathew Anden (1970–71), Eunice Anderson (1973–74), Madison Arnold (1973–74), Peter Bailey-Britton (1970–71, 1973–74), K. T. Baumann (1973–74), Paul Benedict (1973–74), Steven Blanchard (1983–84), Dwight Bowes (1973–74), Pamela Burrell (1973–74), Emmy Lee Butler (1962–63), Burke Byrnes (1965–66), Myra Carter (1973–74), Grace Chapman (1964–65), Rose Chappel (1962–63), Frederick Coffin (1969–70), Maury Cooper (1968–69), John Costopoulos (1971–72), Sally Cotton (1970–71), Julia Curry (1973–74), Carolan Daniels (1970–71), Jack Deisler (1972–73), Constance Dix (1962–63), Richard Dix (1972–73), Richard Dmitri (1973–74), Robert Donley (1978–79), Jamie Donnelly (1973–74), Greg Dubbs (1973–74), Doreen Dunn (1973–74), Carol DuPont (1972–73), James Eames (1973–74), Lori Ehudin (1973–74), Mike English (1962–63), Rhea Feiken (1962–63), Ellen Fields (1964–65), John Fields (1964–65), Stephen Fleagle (1972–73), Barbara Frank (1969–72), Patricia Gage (1975–76), Kay Gates (1973–74), Steven Gilborn (1970–

71), John Gray (1973–74), Michael A. Hartman (1973–74), Shirley Herrmann (1962–63), Tana Hicken (1977–78), Jeffrey Hildner (1965–66), Dale Hodges (1973–74), Paul Holmes (1973–74), Judith Hordan (1971–72), Bert Houle (1970–73), Christopher Johnson (1969–70), Page Johnson (1973–74), Douglas Jones (1970–71), Bruce M. Kornbluth (1967–69), Marcia Jean Kurtz (1973–74), Juanda LaJoyce (1973–74), Mark LaMura (1973–74), Sharon Laughlin (1965–66), Michael Lewis (1973–74), Richard Lieberman (1973–74), Mark Lonow (1973–74), *Will Love* (1970–74), Jane Lowry (1973–74), Tanny MacDonald (1973–74), Dale McIntosh (1972–73), William McKereghan (1965–68), Heather MacRae (1972–73), Woodward Mann (1971–72), Robert Manuel (1973–74), W. T. Martin (1973–74), Michael Medeiros (1973–74), Robert Murch (1964–65), P. H. Murray (1971–72), Peter Murray (1972–73), John Newton (1970–72), John O'Leary (1962–63), Terry O'Quinn (1979–80), Susan Peretz (1973–74), David O. Petersen (1983–84), Ralph Piersanti (1962–63), Louis Plante (1971–72), Don Plumley (1973–74), Ed Preble (1965–67), James Pritchett (1973–74), James L. Pryor (1973–74), Margaret Ramsey (1971–72), Jerome Raphel (1973–74), Robert R. Reilly (1970–71), William R. Riker (1983–84), Rozanne Ritch (1962–63), Jan Rothman (1972–73), John Rothman (1971–72), Colgate Salsbury (1962–63, 1968–69), Janet Sarno (1973–74), Frank Savino (1973–74), John Schuck (1965–67), Dwight Schultz (1973–74), Carl Schurr (1972–73), Jimmy Seibold (1971–72), Susan Sharkey (1973–74), *Vivienne Shub* (1962–65, 1966–67, 1969–70, 1971–73, 1973–74, 1975–76, 1978–80), Charles Siebert (1967–68), Maureen Silliman (1973–74), Jane Singer (1964–65), Jonathan Slade (1970–71), Deborah Smith (1971–72), Robert A. Smith, Jr. (1973–74), Peter Steward (1962–63), Betsy Stoll (1970–71), Gabrielle Strasun (1973–74), *Henry Strozier* (1970–74), Margaret Stuart-Ramsey (1972–73), Margaret Sullivan (1969–70), Shana Sullivan (1970–71, 1972–73), Donald Symington (1965–67), Daniel Szelag (1983–84), Henry Thomas (1975–76), Paul C. Thomas (1976–77), Elizabeth Thurman (1965–66), Michael Tolaydo (1973–74), Ellen Darrel Tovatt (1965–67), Patrick Tovatt (1965–67), Charles Traeger (1973–74), Sylvia Traeger (1973–74), Dan Tyra (1970–71), David Tyrrel (1971–72), Ann Ulvestead (1972–73), Glenn Walken (1973–74), Sophie Wibaux (1970–73).

REPERTORY

1962–63: *Amphitryon 38, Arms and the Man, Beyond the Horizon, La Ronde, The Maids, The Zoo Story, The Mousetrap, You Touched Me!*.

1963–64: *Bedtime Story, The Importance of Being Earnest, Light Up The Sky, The Room, The Shadow of a Gunman, Silent Night, Lonely Night, The Sketches, Summer of the Seventeenth Doll, Twelfth Night, U.S.A.*

1964–65: *The Country Wife, The Doctor's Dilemma, Galileo, The Hostage, The Lady's Not for Burning, The Physicists, Six Characters in Search of an Author, A Touch of the Poet.*

1965–66: *Ardele, As You Like It, The Birthday Party, Caesar and Cleopatra, The Chinese Wall, The Days Between, The Tavern.*

1966–67: *The Balcony, Benito Cereno, The Death of Bessie Smith, Lady Audley's Secret, The Miser, Noah, A Penny for a Song, Titus Andronicus.*

1967–68: *The Devil's Disciple, An Enemy of the People, Hamlet, The Member of the Wedding, The Royal Family, Waiting for Godot, Et Cetera '68.*

1968–69: *Boy Meets Girl, A Doll's House, The Journey of the Fifth Horse, The Merchant of Venice.*

1969–70: *Fire in the Mindhouse, The Knack, Long Day's Journey into Night, Park, Slow Dance on the Killing Ground, The Tempest, Who's Got His Own.*

1970–71: *A Cry of Players, Marat/Sade, Twelfth Night, The Lover* and *The Collection, Ceremonies in Dark Old Men, Fire in the Mindhouse.*

1971–72: *Andorra, The Beaux' Stratagem, Death of a Salesman, The Sea Gull, Staircase, The Trial of the Catonsville Nine.*

1972–73: *Dandy Dick, Gimpel the Fool, Julius Caesar, The Me Nobody Knows, One Flew Over the Cuckoo's Nest, The Petrified Forest, St. Julian the Hospitalier.*

1973–74: *Happy Birthday, Wanda June, Hay Fever, The Hot l Baltimore, Uncle Vanya, A View from the Bridge, Who's Afraid of Virginia Woolf?.*

1974–75: No mainstage series.

1975–76: *Tartuffe, Busy Bee Good Food All Night Delicious, Dream on Monkey Mountain, Old Times, The Cherry Orchard, Under the Gaslight.*

1976–77: *She Stoops to Conquer, When You Comin' Back, Red Ryder?, Misalliance, Toys in the Attic, The First Breeze of Summer, Knock Knock, A Sorrow Beyond Dreams.*

1977–78: *The Goodbye People, The Rivals, The Runner Stumbles, Ashes, The Night of the Iguana, Blithe Spirit.*

1978–79: *The Shadow Box, Born Yesterday, A Christmas Carol: Scrooge and Marley, G. R. Point, You Can't Take It with You, Measure for Measure, Bonjour, là, Bonjour.*

1979–80: *Mother Courage and Her Children, Lone Star* and *Private Wars, A Christmas Carol: Scrooge and Marley, Watch on the Rhine, A Day in the Death of Joe Egg, Crimes of the Heart, Cyrano de Bergerac.*

1980–81: *The Front Page, Agnes of God, The Duenna, A Man for All Seasons, Sally's Gone, She Left Her Name, Inherit the Wind.*

1981–82: *A Lesson from Aloes, Much Ado About Nothing, The Amen Corner, The Workroom, Terra Nova, Savages, Griffin! Griffin!*

1982–83: *Last Looks, The Miser, Division Street, Wings, The Woman, Love's Labour's Lost, Yes, I Can!.*

1983–84: *Crossing the Bar, Our Town, The Sleep of Reason, You Never Can Tell, Another Part of the Forest, Ohio Tip-Off.*

1984–85: *Danton's Death, Henry IV,* Part I, *Execution of Justice, On the Verge; or, The Geography of Yearning, Native Speech, Hedda Gabler, Who They Are and How It Is with Them, A Flea in Her Ear, Painting Churches.*

1985–86: *She Loves Me, Boesman and Lena, Bedroom Farce, The Normal Heart, The School for Wives, Buried Child, In a Pig's Valise, Deadfall, Reunion.*

BIBLIOGRAPHY

Published Sources:

Meersman, Roger. "Center Stage." *Players Magazine* 46 (April-May 1971): 190–92.

Theatre Profiles. Vols. 1–7. New York: Theatre Communications Group, 1973–86.

Theatre World, 1969–70 through *1985–86.* New York: Crown Publishers, 1971–87.

Zeigler, Joseph Wesley. *Regional Theatre: The Revolutionary Stage.* Minneapolis: University of Minnesota Press, 1973.

Unpublished Source:

Playbill Collection of the Theatre Communications Group (microfiche), 1957–75.

Archival Resources:
Baltimore, Maryland. Enoch Pratt Free Library. Clippings, programs.
Baltimore, Maryland. Historical Society of Maryland. Clippings, programs.

Stephen M. Archer

CHEKHOV THEATRE PLAYERS, organized in 1939, was also known as Chekhov Theatre Productions, Inc. Actor-director-teacher Michael Chekhov (1891–1955) and his staff organized this touring company and selected its members from among students in Chekhov's Ridgefield, Connecticut, studio. On October 24, 1939, at the Lyceum Theatre in New York City, the company made its debut with a production of *The Possessed*—a play adapted by George Shdanoff from Fyodor Dostoyevsky's novel, as translated by Elizabeth Reynolds Hapgood.

Both Chekhov studios, Dartington Hall, England (1936–38), and Ridgefield, Connecticut (1939–42), were devoted to revitalizing actors, designers, playwrights, and directors. Chekhov's artistic vision, reflective of his rich Russian heritage and influenced by his association with the Moscow Art Theatre, was formal, eclectic, and experimental. His system of acting, which stressed imagination and inspiration over observation and personalization as the keys to creating truthful characters, was practiced at both studios and applied in the professional touring company's productions.

Like the Group Theatre*, the Chekhov Theatre Players utilized an approach based on Russian actor training, developed an ensemble, and, occasionally produced its plays on Broadway. Although the two groups differed in many respects, both sought to improve the quality of acting in America. After two successful touring seasons, two Broadway productions, and one off-Broadway production, the Chekhov Theatre Players disbanded.

Chekhov, the nephew of Anton Chekhov and a student of Konstantin Stanislavsky, Eugene Vakhtangov, and Vsevolod Meyerhold, was the director of the Second Moscow Art Theatre, acting coach in New York and Hollywood, and author of four books detailing his theatre aesthetics: *The Actor's Path* (1929), *The Problem of the Actor* (1946), *To the Actor* (1951), and the posthumous *To the Director and Dramatist* (1965). Realizing that his was an ideal theatre needing specially trained actors, Chekhov established, with the aid of Mr. and Mrs. Leonard Elmhirst and Beatrice Straight, the Chekhov studios. The touring repertory company was an offspring of the three-year training program. Chekhov believed that the experience of touring would help the student actor bring his talent to full maturity while experiencing the security of full employment. The tours also enhanced Chekhov's efforts to recruit new talent for his school.

Profit was not a central consideration for the company. The Chekhov Theatre Players was privately funded by Beatrice Straight and the William C. Whitney Foundation. During rehearsal periods and while on tour the players' expenses were absorbed by the Chekhov Studio. A small stipend was provided for personal expenses. While on Broadway the casts of both *The Possessed* and *Twelfth Night* were paid the union minimum.

After opening on Broadway in 1939 the Chekhov Theatre Players toured from Maine to Texas for two seasons, primarily performing to college audiences. Their repertoire included *Twelfth Night* and *King Lear* (second touring season), Charles Dickens' *Cricket on the Hearth*, and Michael Chekhov and Arnold Sundgaard's *Troublemaker-Doublemaker*, a fairy tale for children. *Twelfth Night*, the group's second Broadway production, opened December 2, 1941, at the Little Theatre. Although *The Adventures of Samuel Pickwick, Esq.*, by Michael Chekhov and Henry Lyon Young, was rehearsed, it did not join the tour. A 1942 benefit performance for Russian war relief, of the Anton Chekhov sketches *Happy Ending*, *After the Theatre*, *The Story of Miss NN*, *The Witch*, and *I Forgot*, at the Barbizon-Plaza Theatre in New York, was the last time the Chekhov Theatre Players performed.

Although *The Possessed* and *Twelfth Night* earned mixed reviews from New York critics, the company received very favorable notices on the road. Critics spoke of the vividness of their productions, of their fast pace, their skilled, youthful performances, and their strong sense of ensemble.

The Chekhov Theatre Players was devoted to developing a strong ensemble, so no emphasis was placed on stars. Indeed, the company program did not include actors' biographies; instead it noted that of those twenty-two members of the permanent company, seventeen were American-born, three were Canadian, and one was Austrian. Beatrice Straight, Hurd Hatfield, Yul Brynner, and Ford Rainey, all Chekhov students, were successful in professional theatre and in films.

PERSONNEL

Management: Beatrice Straight, president (1939–42); Michael Chekhov, artistic director and vice president (1939–42); Eugene Somoff, general manager (1939–42); Deirdre Hurst, secretary (1939–42); Oliver M. Sayler, press manager (1939–40).

Playwrights: Michael Chekhov, George Shdanoff, Arnold Sundgaard, Henry Lyon Young.

Stage Managers: R. T. Jones (1939–41), Robert Woods (1939–41).

Scenery and Costumes: Michael Chekhov, Mstislav Doubojinsky, Alan Harkness, Oliver Smith.

Music: Andre Singer, Joseph R. Wood.

Technical Advisors: Al Boylen, Robert Gundlach, David Heilweil, Keith Palmer, Robert Woods.

Actors and Actresses: Lester Bacharach, Eleanor Barrie, *Ronald Bennett* (1939–42), Donald Boeche, Alfred Boylen, *Yul Brynner* (1940–42), Erika Chambliss, Woodrow Chambliss, Burke Clarke, *Blair Cutting* (1939–41), Louise Dowdney, *Margaret Draper*, Jeanne Elgart, Dorothy Whitney Elmhirst, Katherine Ann Falder, John Flynn, Arthur Franz, Peter Frye, *Alan Harkness* (1939–41), Nelson Harrell, *Hurd Hatfield* (1939–42), Mary Haynsworth, David Heilweil, Alonzo Hinkley, Thomas Hughes, *Deirdre Hurst* (1939–42), Richard T. Jones, James Legendre, Daphne Moore, Reginald Pole, *Ford Rainey* (1940–42), Penelope Sack, Sam Schatz, *Beatrice Straight* (1939–42), Mary Lou Taylor, Iris Tree, Peter Tunnard, Ellen Van Volkenburg.

Associate Members: Gena Canastrarri, secretary to E. Somoff (1939–42); Norris Houghton, lecturer in theatre history; Elizabeth Reynolds Hapgood, translator of *The Possessed;* Tamara Daykaronova, American representative, Chekhov Studio; Sergius Valiliev and Frances Deitz, assistants; M. Daykaronova, Andrius Jilinsky, and Vera Soloviova, student auditions; Serge Strenkovsky, makeup teacher; Mme. Bailiev, makeup teacher; Mstislav Doubojinsky, designer of sets and costumes for *The Possessed;* Woodman Thompson, designer of *The Adventures of Samuel Pickwick, Esq.;* Oliver Sayler, public relations; Helen Thompson, theatre parties, public relations, and bookings.

BIBLIOGRAPHY

Unpublished Source:
Kindelan, Nancy. "The Theatre of Inspiration: A Critical Analysis of the Acting Theories of Michael Chekhov." Doctoral dissertation, University of Wisconsin, 1977.

Archival Resource:
du Prey, Deirdre Hurst. "The Actor Is the Theatre, Archival Collection: 1935–1942." New York, New York. Library and Museum of the Performing Arts, Lincoln Center. The Michael Chekhov Clipping File.

Nancy Kindelan

CHEKHOV THEATRE PRODUCTIONS, INC. See CHEKHOV THEATRE PLAYERS.

CHILDREN'S THEATRE COMPANY, Minneapolis, Minnesota, was organized as "The Moppet Players" in 1961 by University of Minnesota graduate Beth Linnerson and her friend Martha Pierce. It opened its first season with David Morgan's *Pecos Bill* in Mama Rosa's restaurant, located in Minneapolis' West Bank neighborhood. The Moppet Players operated out of the restaurant for one year before affiliating with the Pillsbury-Waite Settlement House. Under that affiliation it moved into an abandoned firehouse in the West Bank neighborhood, renovating the building (at 1826 South Fourth Street) as a 150-seat theatre.

Under Linnerson, The Moppet Players followed a pattern born with the establishment of the first children's theatres in the United States around 1900. As were most early American children's theatres, The Moppet Players was a social, not an artistic, institution, concerned more with the recreational and cultural needs of the neighborhood than with the artistic integrity of its productions. At its inception the company drew all its resources from the neighborhood. To keep expenses low, child and adult volunteers mounted productions of original skits and adaptations of traditional children's stories. Admission to Saturday afternoon performances was only 25 cents. Linnerson and Pierce attempted to raise no money within the community because of the organization's social focus and because of the community's poor economic condition. But The Moppet Players, Minnesota's first full-time children's theatre, soon outgrew its affiliation with the settlement house, and it broke away from that organization's restrictions on fund-raising to begin a struggle to prosper as an independent artistic institution.

The company's transition from a social orientation to an artistic one really began in 1962, when John Clark Donahue joined Linnerson and Pierce at the new theatre. Donahue had attended the University of Minnesota with Linnerson. A painter, actor, and art teacher, he had been working for several years as a jazz musician. His background as a painter and a musician played a major role in directions the company took. Donahue's orientation toward the visual arts was evident in a renovation of the theatre and in the well-received design of productions for the 1962–63 season. Commentators also noticed improvement in the group's acting skills. In 1963–64 Donahue wrote and directed plays, and he served as technical director and designer. At the beginning of the 1964–65 season he was named artistic director, a position he maintained until his resignation from the Children's Theatre Company in 1984.

By 1964 major conflicts had developed between Linnerson, who still saw the primary focus of the company as the socialization of children, and Donahue, who sought artistic excellence. But Linnerson was no longer a dominant figure in the company. The theatre's patron, the Pillsbury-Waite Settlement House and the Pillsbury Citizens' Service, had set up a board of directors to guide the theatre. Because of the company's rapid growth the board appointed John Davidson as administrator of The Moppet Players in August of 1963. In the fall of 1964 the board of directors dismissed Linnerson as a staff member of the company and offered her a seat on the board. Linnerson refused the seat and at the end of the 1964–65 season left the company, taking with her the name "The Moppet Players," which she had formally registered under her own name.

At the end of the 1964–65 season Donahue and Davidson sought out a new, more artistically oriented organization and a larger theatre. They moved their company, by then named "The Children's Theatre Company," to South Minneapolis, where it joined the Minneapolis Institute of Art as a department of the Minneapolis Society of Fine Arts. There, sponsored by the Institute on a year-to-year basis, the company opened its 1965–66 season in a 646-seat auditorium.

The company continued the success experienced as The Moppet Players, filling its new facility to 96 percent of its capacity. It produced five plays, giving a total of forty performances to 28,500 audience members. Admission to the plays was 95 cents and $1.25, and ticket sales accounted for 77 percent ($25,460) of the $33,091 season budget.

Over the next fifteen seasons, first under the sponsorship of the Institute of Art and the Society of Fine Arts and then in 1976 as an independent nonprofit organization, the Children's Theatre Company greatly increased its operational scope. The number of productions each year ranged from five to sixteen as the company expanded its operations to include tours, workshops, residencies, and the Summer Theatre Institute, as well as film and video productions. In the 1985–86 season the company presented seven mainstage and two studio productions, giving 415 performances to 221,516 paying patrons with ticket prices ranging from $4.75 (day) and $5.75 (evening) for children to a top price of $14.95 for adults. During that season the theatre earned $2,261,000 of its $3,420,000 budget.

Staff and facilities also changed substantially. In the second season of The Moppet Players, Linnerson, Donahue, and Pierce were paid $200 a month. By the 1965–66 season four staff members of the Children's Theatre Company were paid a combined salary of $19,500. The full-time resident staff of the theatre and its school now numbers close to one hundred, and the list of part-time and temporary employees and guest artists is extensive.

In 1972 the Rockefeller Foundation awarded the company a $500,000 matching grant for construction of a new theatre, only the third such grant awarded by the foundation up to that time. In 1973–74 the Minneapolis Society of Fine Arts renovated and expanded its physical facilities, including in it a new theatre for the Children's Theatre Company. For a year the company had no theatre, but the Society of Fine Arts paid to keep the staff intact and in production. The company rented space in which to rehearse, it toured, and it conducted residences at several schools. In September 1974 the Children's Theatre Company moved into its new $4.5 million, 750-seat, proscenium-style theatre. The facility at 2400 Third Avenue South included scenery and costume construction shops, rehearsal studios, classrooms, and offices.

Under Donahue's direction the company developed a unique focus and style. From the beginning Donahue thought theatre for children should play to children's sense of wonder, mystery, and amazement. To that end he frequently used flashbacks, montages, slow motion, and cross fades. He also made extensive use of mime, dance, and music, integrating the various arts to create strong sensual images. He proposed to create mystery rather than meaning and to help his audience learn "through sensory means and through participating in the mysterious 'child-poet' vision." With Donahue's approach and direction the Children's Theatre Company won the 1973 American Theatre Association's Jennie Heiden Award for excellence in children's theatre.

The Children's Theatre Company owes much of its national and international renown to its repertory. From its beginning the company has featured a blend of original adaptations of classic children's works with original plays. Since 1961 The Moppet Players and the Children's Theatre Company has produced 208 plays, six videos, and a film. Thirty-five additional productions have been revivals from the company's repertory. Donahue is himself a playwright and has written or collaborated in the writing of more than twenty original plays and twelve adaptations. He wrote and directed *Good Morning, Mr. Tillie*, which the company toured to Washington, D. C., in 1970 for the convention of the American Educational Theatre Association. In 1972 his *Hang on to Your Head* attracted both controversy and praise when presented for the International Association of Theatre for Children and Youth in Albany, New York. The play received an exceptional production, noted for its technical brilliance and overall professionalism. Playwrights who have worked for the company include Frederick Gaines, whose adaptation of *A Christmas Carol* is periodically remounted by the Children's Theatre Company and presented regularly by the Guthrie Theatre. Gaines' adaptation of Washington Irving's *The Legend of Sleepy Hollow* is also a favorite of Minneapolis audiences. For the 1975–76 season British playwright and guest artist Michael Dennis Brown adapted Hans Christian Anderson's *The Snow Queen* for the company. One of the company's playwrights, Timothy Mason, has written many plays, but he is best known for his adaptation of Theodore Geisel's *The 500 Hats of Bartholomew Cubbins*. The Children's Theatre Company was the first organization Geisel (Dr. Seuss) allowed to adapt and stage one of his books. The 1980 production of *The 500 Hats of Bartholomew Cubbins* drew acclaim for the company once again as being outstanding in American children's theatre.

The company also produced adult plays on its mainstage from 1969 to 1978. The first of these productions was Donahue's *"A Wedding" and Variations*, developed out of improvisational work on Anton Chekhov's *A Wedding*. Other seasons have included Maxim Gorky's *The Lower Depths*, Richard Brinsley Sheridan's *The School for Scandal*, Richard Rodgers and Lorenz Hart's *Babes in Arms*, and Shakespeare's *Twelfth Night*.

But it is, of course, the children's plays that form the heart of the company's repertory. Numerous playwrights, often working in collaboration with actors, musicians, composers, dancers, and all the other theatre artists, have contributed an extensive volume of work to the corpus of America's dramatic literature for children. In 1981 the Children's Theatre Company received the Margo Jones Award for outstanding commitment to the development of new plays and playwrights.

John Clark Donahue resigned as artistic director of the Children's Theatre Company in the summer of 1984, and the theatre's directorship was assumed by Jon Cranney. Cranney had served for many years as stage director, production director, and performer with the Guthrie Theatre Company* in Minneapolis. With the assistance of a core artistic staff of about twenty, most of whom have been with the company from seven to twenty-one years, Cranney continues to lead the Children's Theatre in its development of productions that carry on the tradition of creativity and excellence begun by Donahue and his colleagues a quarter of a century ago.

Integral to the development of the Children's Theatre Company has been the growth of the school, part of the organization since the second season of The Moppet Players. In the winter of 1963 Martha Pierce opened afterschool classes in the old firehouse theatre, offering classes in art, creative dramatics, and dance. In 1969 a theatre school began offering a range of courses in performance studies and technical theatre for which students could earn credit through their home high schools. In 1981 the school became a fully accredited conservatory offering a full schedule of academic and fine arts classes. The students also work closely with the theatre company in its production work. A summer theatre institute provides five weeks of day-long classwork as well as production experience to both regional and international students. The company also provides apprenticeships and internships to students who have completed their high school education. In this way the company continues to draw talent from the community that has played and is playing a vital part in the company's growth.

PERSONNEL

The vast number of artistic and administrative employees and volunteers who have worked with the Minneapolis Children's Theatre prohibits a complete listing of the company's personnel. Also, because of the variety of jobs done by individual artists within the company, categorizing personnel under a single specific heading can be misleading. The following is a list of artistic personnel who have each worked with the company for at least five years and have been instrumental in the creative growth of the Minneapolis Children's Theatre Company.

Jack Barkla, nonresident scenic and costume designer (1968–86); Carl Beck, actor (1966–86); Gary Briggle, nonresident stage director (1973–86); Maggie Belle Calin, designer coordinator, scenic and costume designer (1972–86); Roberta Carlson, nonresident composer (1967–86); Gary Costello, actor (1979–86); Jon Cranney, artistic director (1984–86), stage director (1970–86); John Clark Donahue, artistic director, stage director, scenic and costume designer, playwright (1962–84); Gerald Drake, actor (1966–86); Thomas Dunn, actor (1974–86); Myron Johnson, stage director, choreographer, actor (1965–86); Robert Jorissen, nonresident sound designer (1974–86); Wendy Lehr, stage director, choreographer, actress (1966–86); Jason McLean, actor (1976–86); Timothy Mason, nonresident playwright (1966–86); George Muschamp, actor (1973–86); Thomas Olson, literary editor, playwright (1969–86); Leslye Orr, actress (1974–86); Oliver Osterberg, actor (1976–86); Alan Shorter, musical director, composer (1979–86); Hirum Titus, nonresident composer (1970–86).

REPERTORY

The Moppet Players:

1961–62: *Pecos Bill, Bill Eden's Magic Carnival, The Reluctant Dragon, Why the Chimes Rang, Sleeping Beauty, The Sorcerer's Apprentice, The Nightingale, The Magic Fishbone, The Magic Horse, Hansel and Gretel.*

1962–63: *The Reluctant Dragon, Madeleine, Winnie the Pooh, The Swineherd, Merry Tyll's Pranks, Alice Through the Looking Glass.*

1963–64: *The Emperor's New Clothes, Shoofly Pie for Christmas, Budelinck and the Three Billy Goats Gruff, The Nightingale, Ozma of Oz, Hansel and Gretel.*

1964–65: *Ali Baba and the Forty Thieves, A Christmas Fantasy in Dance, Bremen Town Musicians, The World of Mother Goose, The Princess and the Pea, Mr. Muffie's Magic Mimes: Jack and the Beanstalk.*

The Children's Theatre Company and School:

1965–66: *The Sleeping Beauty*, adapted by John B. Davidson; *A Christmas Carol*, adapted by William Hillard; *Good Morning, Mr. Tillie*, by John Clark Donahue; *Rumpelstiltskin*, adapted by John Clark Donahue; *The Pied Piper of Hamelin*, adapted by John B. Davidson.

1966–67: *King Arthur and the Magic Sword*, adapted by John B. Davidson; *Cinderella*, adapted by John B. Davidson; *The Emperor's Nightingale*, adapted by William Hillard; *Hang on to Your Head*, by John Clark Donahue; *Johnny Appleseed*, by John B. Davidson.

1967–68: *Oliver Twist*, adapted by Jonathan Gilman; *The World of Mother Goose*, adapted by John Clark Donahue; *Beauty and the Beast*, adapted by David Merkle; *Old Kieg of Malfi*, by John Clark Donahue; *The Emperor's New Clothes*, adapted by John B. Davidson; *Variations on a Similar Theme*, by John Clark Donahue.

1968–69: *Ali Baba and the Forty Thieves*, adapted by William Hillard; *A Christmas Carol*, adapted by Frederick Gaines; *The Little Mermaid*, adapted by Barbara Nosanow; *How Could You Tell?*, by John Clark Donahue; *Johnny Tremain*, adapted by Barbara Nosanow; *"A Wedding" and Variations* by John Clark Donahue.

1969–70: *The Legend of Sleepy Hollow*, adapted by Frederick Gaines; *Cinderella; Kidnapped in London*, adapted by Timothy Mason; *Good Morning, Mr. Tillie; Alice in Wonderland*, adapted by Frederick Gaines; *Goldilocks and the Three Bears* and *Little Red Riding Hood*, adapted by John Clark Donahue; *The Lower Depths*.

1970–71: *Rip Van Winkle*, adapted by Frederick Gaines; *The Little Match Girl*, adapted by John Clark Donahue; *Moliére's "Le Bourgeois Gentilhomme,"* translated and adapted by John Lewin; *The Princess and the Pea*, adapted by John Jenkins; *The Three Little Pigs* and *The Three Billy Goats Gruff*, adapted by Wendy Lehr; *Jerusalem*, by Frederick Gaines; *Little Women*, adapted by Bain Boehlke; *The Adventures of Huck Finn*, adapted by Frederick Gaines; *A Wall*, by John Clark Donahue from a scenario for improvisation by Alvin Greenberg; *Children*, by Frederick Gaines; *Goodbye, Goodbye*, by Bain Boehlke.

1971–72: *Robin Hood: A Story of the Forest*, adapted by Timothy Mason; *Peter and the Wolf* and *The Ugly Duckling*, adapted by Wendy Lehr and Guy Drake; *Under Milk Wood; Spoon River Anthology; Sleeping Beauty*, adapted by Richard Shaw; *Hansel and Gretel*, adapted by John Jenkins; *The School for Scandal; The Cookie Jar*, by John Clark Donahue; *The Sitwells at Sea*, adapted by Gar Hildenbrand; *Madeleine and the Gypsies*, adapted by John Clark Donahue; *A Suitcase* and *Variations on a Similar Theme*, by John Clark Donahue; *An Evening of Leonard Cohen*, adapted by Hiram Titus; *Hang on to Your Head; Potpourri*, adapted by John Clark Donahue; *The Boy Friend*, by Sandy Wilson; *Musical Chairs*, by Timothy Mason.

1972–73: *African Tales: Rumpelstiltskin* and *Kalulu and His Money Farm*, adapted by Timothy Mason; *Raggedy Ann and Andy*, adapted by John Clark Donahue and Gar Hildenbrand; *Bellavita* and *Sicilian Limes*, by Luigi Pirandello; *The Steadfast Tin Soldier*, adapted by Richard Shaw; *The Netting of the Troupial* by John Clark Donahue; *Johnny Appleseed*, adapted by Gar Hildenbrand; *The Cookie Jar; African Tales; Rutabaga Follies*, adapted by John Clark Donahue; *Babes in Arms*.

1973–74: *The Legend of Sleepy Hollow, A Christmas Carol, The Nightingale*, adapted by Timothy Mason; *The Boy Friend, The Fourposter; Hansel and Gretel, Memory Petals*, by John Clark Donahue; *Changes*, by John Clark Donahue.

1974–75: *Pinocchio*, adapted by Timothy Mason; *Ukranian Tales: The Fat Cat* and *The Chatterbox*, adapted by Timothy Mason; *On the Harmfulness of Tobacco; The Swan Song: A Celebration*, by Anton Chekhov; *Cinderella, The Nightingale, He Who Gets Slapped; Peter and the Wolf* and *The Ugly Duckling, The Imaginary Invalid*, adapted by John Clark Donahue; *No Strings*, by John Clark Donahue and Timothy Mason; *The Squeeze*, by John Clark Donahue.

1975–76: *The Treasure Island*, adapted by Timothy Mason; *The Sea Gull; The Little Match Girl; Mother Goose*, adapted by Myron Johnson and Steven M. Rydberg; *The Snow Queen*, adapted by Michael Dennis Browne; *Twelfth Night; A Room in Paradise*, musical adaptation by Timothy Mason and Hiram Titus of Georges Feydeau's *Hotel*

Paradiso, translated by Anne Rosen; *The Nightingale; Paul Bunyan Meets His Match*, adapted by Mark Frost; *The Empty Place*, by John Clark Donahue.

1976–77: *The Adventures of Tom Sawyer*, adapted by Timothy Mason; *Goldilocks and the Three Bears* and *Little Red Riding Hood; The Importance of Being Earnest; Cinderella; The Dream Fisher*, by John Clark Donahue; *Romeo and Juliet; Oliver!' A Suitcase* and *Variations on a Similar Theme, Of Mice and Men; The Oracle*, by Michael Braun; *Three Can't Fit in a Rickshaw*, by John Clark Donahue.

1977–78: *Aladdin and the Wonderful Lamp*, adapted by Timothy Mason; *Thieves' Carnival*, translation by George Muschamp; *The Little Match Girl; Beauty and the Beast*, adapted by Timothy Mason; *A Circle Is the Sun*, by John Clark Donahue and Frederick Gaines; *The Pied Piper of Hamelin*, adapted by Thomas W. Olson; *The Rivals; Punch and Judy* and *The Three Sillies*, adapted by Timothy Mason; *Butley; A Taste of Berries*, by Frederick Gaines.

1978–79: *The Legend of Sleepy Hollow; Hansel and Gretel*, adapted by Thomas W. Olson; *A Christmas Carol, The Little Mermaid*, adapted by Timothy Mason; *Good Morning, Mr. Tillie, Pinocchio, The Green Beetle Dance*, by John Clark Donahue; *The Sitwells at Sea; Bullseye*, by John Clark Donahue; *Summer Matters*, by Kirk Ristau.

1979–80: *Treasure Island, The Emperor's New Clothes*, adapted by Timothy Mason; *Sleeping Beauty*, adapted by John Clark Donahue and Thomas W. Olson; *The Hound of the Baskervilles*, adapted by Frederick Gaines; *Falling Moons*, by Kirk Ristau; *The 500 Hats of Bartholomew Cubbins*, adapted by Timothy Mason; *Moon over Rio*, by Gene Davis Buck; *The Festival of Our Lord of the Ships*, by Luigi Pirandello; *Equinox*, by Frederick Gaines; *Stargazer*, by Marisha Chamberlain.

1980–81: *The Adventures of Huckleberry Finn*, adapted by Timothy Mason; *The Story of Babar, the Little Elephant*, adapted by Thomas W. Olson; *Cinderella, The Three Musketeers*, adapted by Frederick Gaines; *The Clown of God*, adapted by Thomas W. Olson; *The Virgin Unmasked*, by Sharon Holland; *Desert in Flower*, by Marisha Chamberlain; *The Great American Family*, by John B. Davidson; *Merely Players*, by Sharon Holland.

1981–82: *Kidnapped in London, Puss in Boots*, adapted by Sharon Holland; *The Little Match Girl, The Cookie Jar, Phantom of the Opera*, adapted by George Muschamp and Thomas W. Olson; *Alice in Wonderland*, adapted by Sharon Holland; *Alice in Wonderland* (video): *Puss in Boots* (video); *Brothers and Sisters*, by Steven Dietz; *The Night of January 16*, by Ayn Rand; *The Maids; Lids*, by John Clark Donahue; *The Woods*, by David Mamet; *d'Art*, by Frank Pike; *Album*, by David Rimmer; *Ned and Jack*, by Sheldon Rosen; *Across Town*, by Frank Pike; *The Contenders*, by Sharon Holland; *Ten-and-a-Half*, by John B. Davidson.

1982–83: *The 500 Hats of Bartholomew Cubbins, Pippi Longstocking*, adapted by Astrid Lindgren and Thomas W. Olson; *Mr. Pickwick's Christmas*, adapted by Thomas W. Olson with George Muschamp; *The Clown of God, The Red Shoes*, adapted by John B. Davidson and John Clark Donahue; *The Adventures of Tom Sawyer, The Wind in the Willows*, adapted by Sharon Holland; *Brothers and Sisters; Hand in Hand*, adapted by Leslye Orr; *Irma's Dream*, by Warren Green; *The Indian Wants the Bronx; Trial by Jury; The Unseen Hand*, by Sam Shepard; *A Midsummer Night's Dream; Aviation*, by Marisha Chamberlain; *Catch Me a Z*, by Steven Dietz; *The Convention Grill*, Part I, by John B. Davidson and James Martin; *One That Goes Out*, by Barry Goldman and Roberta Carlson.

1983–84: *The Secret Garden*, adapted by Thomas W. Olson; *The Adventures of Babar*, by Thomas W. Olson and Laurent de Brunhoff; *Cinderella, Frankenstein*, adapted by

Thomas W. Olson; *The Nightingale*, adapted by Marisha Chamberlain; *Pinocchio, Hand in Hand, Lids; Raisin' Cain*, by Jan Quackenbush: *Raymond in Space*, by Peter Tolan; *The Troubles*, by Thomas W. Olson.

1984–85: *The Legend of Sleepy Hollow, Madeleine and the Gypsies, The Little Match Girl, The Mystery of the Tattered Trunk*, by Wendy Lehr, Thomas W. Olson, and Richard Russell Ramos; *The Princess and the Pea*, adapted by Barbara Field; *Penrod*, adapted by Thomas W. Olson; *By Invitation Only* by Phil Eaton; *Hand in Hand; The Byrdz*, by Aristophanes, adapted by Jon Cranney and Laurie Bohne; *The Do-It-Yourself Manual on the American Dream*, by Michael Kinghorn.

1985–86: *King Arthur and the Magic Sword*, adapted by Frederick Gaines; *The Adventures of a Bear Called Paddington*, by Michael Bond and Alfred Bradley; *Goldilocks and the Three Bears* and *Little Red Riding Hood*, adapted by Wendy Lehr; *Cinderella, The Adventures of Mottel*, adapted by Thomas W. Olson and Judith Luck Sher; *Harold and the Purple Crayon*, adapted by Myron Johnson; *Little Women*, adapted by Marisha Chamberlain; *The Emperor's New Clothes; Peter Pan; Fortune and Men's Eyes; Woyzeck.*

BIBLIOGRAPHY

Published Sources:

Minneapolis Star, 1961–86.

Minneapolis Tribune, 1961–86.

Donahue, John Clark. *The Cookie Jar and Other Plays*, edited by Linda Walsh Jenkins. Minneapolis: University of Minnesota Press, 1975.

Donahue, John Clark, and Linda Walsh Jenkins, eds. *Five Plays from the Children's Theatre Company of Minneapolis*. Minneapolis: University of Minnesota Press, 1975.

Unpublished Source:

Hicks, John V. "The History of the Children's Theatre Company and School of Minneapolis 1961–1981." Doctoral dissertation, University of Wisconsin, 1982.

Archival Resource:

Minneapolis, Minnesota. The Minneapolis Children's Theatre. Letters, flyers, press releases, and programs.

Tim Budke

CHILDREN'S WORLD THEATRE, New York City, was founded in 1947 by Monte Meacham, Jo Ann Sayers Bliss, Bette Butterworth (Meacham), Sarah Newmeyer, Julie Thompson, and Sheldon Thompson. Using the Barbizon-Plaza, a theatre with a tiny stage and no fly or wing space, the group presented its first production, Charlotte Chorpenning's *Jack and the Beanstalk*, on November 1, 1947. Twenty thousand children attended matinee performances on weekends and during school holidays at the Barbizon-Plaza from November 1947 to December 1948. The group's success led to the addition of tours, with Chorpenning's *Little Red Riding Hood* being the first show taken on the road. Additional actors were hired to accommodate touring engagements that, during the eight years the company existed, took them from Canada to Florida and included bookings in Cincinnati, Indianapolis, St. Louis, Rochester, and Syracuse. The company also played in Bennington, Vermont, Jackson, Mississippi, Lexington and Louisville, Kentucky, and at the 1950 Chicago World's Fair. In addition to its regular season at the Barbizon-Plaza and its tour, United Parents Association hired Children's World Theatre to give three weekend performances a month for five months in school auditoriums in three boroughs of New York City. The company maintained productions in New York and on tour until the summer of 1955, when Monte Meacham was killed in an automobile accident. The company kept its engagement at the Minnesota State Fair but officially disbanded in September of that year.

Children's World Theatre was originally headquartered at the Meacham's home at 4 Grove Street in New York City. The Meachams undertook a paternalistic type of management, wholeheartedly putting their energies into the organization, caring for actors, and using their home for rehearsals, costume building, and general management of company affairs. Even after their headquarters were moved to the Paramount Building, at 1501 Broadway, the Meacham home was a focal point for the company's activities. Later, professional management by Francis Schram of Briggs Management greatly enhanced Children's World Theatre's ability to reach audiences.

The founding members of the company had been well trained, had extensive theatrical backgrounds, and were responsive to the special needs of child audiences. Monte Meacham and Bette Butterworth had been trained at the Ohio State University, the University of Missouri, and the Academy of Dramatic Arts. Meacham had worked professionally in radio and television and on the stage. He served on the board of directors of the American Educational Theatre Association and on the governing board of the Children's Theatre Committee, held membership in the American National Theatre and Academy, and served as a consultant to the Junior League. Not only was he president of Children's World Theatre, but also its principal director. Bette Butterworth served Children's World Theatre as an actress, doing ingénue roles, as art director, as costumer, and, occasionally, as narrator, introducing shows. Both she and Meacham taught at the American Academy of Dramatic Arts, even after the company was formed, and several members of the acting staff were former students.

Sheldon Thompson, a graduate of the Philadelphia Museum School of Industrial Arts, designed sets for Children's World Theatre during its inaugural season. His wife, Julie, had been trained in dance and acting for children and had been a member of Clare Tree Majors' company. During her career she played more children's heroines than any other actress in the United States.

Sarah Newmeyer had been a publicist for the Museum of Modern Art before becoming vice president of Children's World Theatre. Jo Ann Sayers Bliss was responsible for fund-raising, publicity, and general guidance of Children's World Theatre operations.

While the Meachams and Thompsons were primarily responsible for artistic matters, Sayers Bliss and Newmeyer handled basic operational concerns. All, however, served in numerous capacities, wherever and however needed, to keep the operation functioning.

Incorporated in June 1947 as a nonprofit membership corporation, Children's World Theatre was organized as a permanent repertory children's theatre. "The theatre's sponsors began their operations with the firm conviction that Gotham, with an enrollment of 60,000 children in the elementary and junior high schools, was sadly in need of a children's theatre" (*New York Times*, October 17, 1948, Sec. II, p. 3). Their avowed purpose was to arouse children's imaginations through active entertainment, to increase understanding of national cultures and customs, to mold a future discriminating adult audience, and to provide good, professional entertainment. Adult actors were used in all roles, and children attending the theatre voted for plays they wanted to see on future bills. Adults were admitted to performances only when accompanied by children. Children's World Theatre provided an escort service for adults who wanted to attend but had no youngsters to bring with them.

When on tour the company was sponsored by parent-teacher organizations, junior leagues, civic theatres, the American Association of University Women, junior chambers of commerce, and similar associations. Educational materials were developed to assist the company and its sponsors. For example, Charlotte Chorpenning prepared a document on recognizing and controlling fear and restlessness in child audiences that Meacham and Butterworth had requested for use with the cast of *Jack and the Beanstalk*. Classroom study materials were developed for productions of *Ali Baba and the Forty Thieves* and *Aladdin*, both by Wadeesha Atieyh, and distributed to teachers in cities on the touring circuit.

The acting company was non-Equity, although professional performers were permitted by the actors' union to undertake roles because the group paid a salary close to union scale. The company fluctuated in size as additional casts were formed for new bookings or as actors left to undertake other opportunities. Productions were professionally reviewed, unlike most children's theatre performances of this period.

During the company's first year all shows on the November-to-April season were written by Charlotte Barrows Chorpenning, director of Children's Theatre at the Goodman Theatre in Chicago. Her plays were also an important part of subsequent seasons. In addition, Chorpenning directed *Jack and the Beanstalk* and her *Many Moons*, commuting from Chicago to New York to assist the new company during its premiere season. Chorpenning worked closely with Julie Thompson in this endeavor. Although Thompson cast the shows, Chorpenning had final approval of the selections. The concept of dual directorship (although Chorpenning is given credit as director in all programs and reviews) worked well. Chorpenning blocked a scene and Thompson directed it in her absence. On returning to New York City, Chorpenning polished the scene. Rehearsals were scheduled for evenings and weekends, thus enabling the actors to undertake or seek other jobs and giving the staff time to work on technical and financial aspects of production.

The Children's World Theatre pioneered in performances for handicapped populations when in December 1947 it arranged for one hundred hearing-impaired youngsters to be included in its audience for a production of *Many Moons*. "Under the auspices of the New York League for the Hard of Hearing, the performance was believed to be the first of its kind for such children, who ranged in age from 4 to 12 years" (*New York Times*, December 12, 1947, p. 36). These children used hearing aids or headphones on their chairs attached to microphones on stage, or they read lips. Actors accorded them no special treatment.

Admission charges to the Barbizon-Plaza productions ranged from 60 cents to $2.40, with the lower rates charged for Saturday morning performances. Before its opening production, the group announced that one hundred Founding Children would be chosen to purchase $100 certificates entitling them to a 20 percent reduction on tickets purchased during their lifetime for New York engagements. Founding Children also received a certificate, a badge, and membership with voting privileges and the opportunity to hold office in the Founder's Club.

Critical response to the Children's World Theatre was consistently favorable. The Children's Theatre Committee, as well as such noted critics as William Rose Benét, Jack Hawkins, and Brooks Atkinson, offered support. The company received enthusiastic responses both in New York and on tour. Reviews favorably cited broad, slapstick comedy, suspense, dance, magic, and energetic audience response.

Critics also remarked on the energy and enthusiasm of the adult actors, who were able to combine a broad style of playing with sincerity. The performers never condescended in performance, so the shows were enjoyable for both young and old. Adults in the audience found that the productions allowed them to recapture youthful memories, while child viewers were entranced by favorite stories coming to life on the stage. Seeing youngsters transformed by the action presented on the stage was, according to one critic, "a profound experience. The spell is a lasting one, too" (*New York Times*, October 25, 1948, p. 28). Strong direction, particularly by Monte Meacham, in combination with solid acting, became, according to the critical press, the trademark of the company.

The press likewise praised the company's technical achievements. Bette Butterworth's costumes received frequent mention for their beauty and authenticity. Set design and lighting in such shows as *King Midas and the Golden Touch*, *The Three Bears*, and *Rumpelstiltskin* drew critical compliments. Press notices generally attested to the company's commitment to excellence in unified productions.

Most of the scripts performed by Children's World Theatre were published by the Children's Theatre Press (later Anchorage Press), although at least three original scripts, including *Ali Baba and the Forty Thieves*, by Wadeesha Atieyh, and *Hansel and Gretel*, by Jack Alexander St. George, were written by members of the company. Most scripts were based on fairy tales and legends, though some, such as *The Indian Captive*, were based on true stories.

All productions were staged with an awareness of children's tastes. Virtue triumphed and evil was foiled, character comedy replaced foolishness, and harsh villainy was tempered by comedic devices to lessen the potential for frightening villainy was tempered by comedic devices to lessen the potential for frightening young viewers. According to founder Sarah Newmeyer, children enjoyed plays "in which the struggle between good and evil is fiercely fought out. The children want the hero to have a tough time, a real struggle to overcome the villain. Accordingly, the villain is most successful when he is a formidable villain. The kids want him to be so bad that he deserves punishment. They want to win a victory over him—the victory is theirs just as much as the hero's—and they want him thumped for the evil he has done. The crime must deserve the punishment, though, for otherwise the children's sense of justice is outraged" (*New York Times Magazine*, December 5, 1948, p. 26). Concern for the child manifested itself in such activities as allowing a child backstage to meet the heroine so as to be assured of her safety, or in having an Arabian actress perform an Arabian muezzin call and a wedding song during the intermission of *Aladdin*.

The strength of the company was its conscientious devotion to good theatre for young people. No expense was spared in mounting productions. Children derived the benefits of the company's work even if company members were, at times, called on to make personal sacrifices. Less successful were efforts at fundraising and sponsorship.

Several members of the company went on to make significant contributions in the areas of theatre, film, and television. Conrad Bain, Jason Robards, Jr., Tom Poston, and Lilia Skala achieved prominence. Canadian actor Henry Beckman appeared in television's *Peyton Place* and received awards in his native country. Founder Julie Thompson has been associated with the Children's Centre for Creative Arts at Adelphi University and has held national office in the Children's Theatre Association of America. Former actor Joseph Scully has worked as a producer, casting director, and talent executive, while William Robinson went on to become chairman of the department of speech and drama at Mesa College.

Children's World Theatre recognized and met the need for quality theatre for young people. Its professional attitude, its artistic commitment, and the energy of the company contributed significantly to the growth of the children's theatre movement while bringing countless hours of enjoyment to America's youngest theatregoers.

PERSONNEL

Management: Monte Meacham, president (1947–55); Sarah Newmeyer, vice president; Jo Ann Sayers Bliss; Bette Butterworth; Julie Thompson; Sheldon Thompson.

Costumer: Bette Butterworth.

Scenic Designers: Jesse Beers, Jr. (1948, 1949), Herman Husky, Doris Isaacson, Herald Perry (1948), Joseph Scully, Jr., Sheldon Thompson (1947).

Stage Directors: Charlotte Chorpenning (1947–48), Jack Edwards (1948), Monte Meacham (1947–55), Julie Thompson (1947–48), Sheldon Thompson (1948).

Actors and Actresses: *Wadeesha Atieyh* (1949), Charles Avery, Kenneth Bache, *Conrad Bain* (1947), Virginia Barrie, Jack Becker, Henry Beckman, Lynn Blanshard, Don Bouche, *Bette Butterworth* (1947–55), Robert Buzzel, Jane Compton, Joan Cullman, Kenneth Dobbs, Elhajayi, Heather Forgle, Miranne Forrest, *Nancy Graves* (1947–49), Toby Gould, Paula Houston, *Michael Howard* (1948–50), Robin Humphrey, Page Johnson, Bernard Kates, James Kazen, Herbert Lane, Stephen Lee, Paul Levitt, Mary Lowe, Ray Malon, Mary Lora Meacham, Kent More, Louise More, Ruth Morrison, Melvin Nadell, Franklin Nell, Burt Nodella, Jean Owens, *Robert Pastene* (1948), Murray Perlman, Mary Perrine, Sally Pomeranz (1947), *Tom Poston* (1947–48), Dorothy Powe, Jim Powell, Rosemary Prinz, Carl Redkoff, *Jason Robards, Jr.* (1948), *William Robinson* (1948–51), Susanne Rooney, Al Sargent, *Joseph Scully, Jr.* (1948–50), *Betty Serton* (1947–50), *Lilia Skala* (1949), La Vonne Slaybaugh, Stan Slorance, Billy Stockton, Suleman, Helen Thomas, *Julie Thompson* (1947–48), *Sheldon Thompson* (1947–48), Wendy Thompson, Eleanor Tulman, Wilson White.

REPERTORY

1947–48: *Jack and the Beanstalk, Many Moons, Little Red Riding Hood, Rumpelstiltskin.*

1948–49: *King Midas and the Golden Touch, Jack and the Beanstalk, The Indian Captive, Aladdin and the Wonderful Lamp.*

1949–50*: *Aladdin and the Wonderful Lamp, The Pied Piper of Hamelin.*

1950: *The Three Bears.*

1951: *Robin Hood, Ali Baba and the Forty Thieves, Dick Wittington and His Cat, Captain Kidd's Return, The Tinder Box* (played only at the Music Hall in Philadelphia), *Hansel and Gretel.*

1952: *Hiawatha, The Peace Maker, Rapunzel.*

1953: *Abe Lincoln—The River Years, The Red Shoes, Montezuma, The Aztec Prince, Tom Sawyer.*

1954: *Young Chris Columbus, Sinbad the Sailor, The Wizard's Ransom.*

BIBLIOGRAPHY

Published Sources:

Children's Theatre Review, 1951–55.

McCaslin, Nellie. *Historical Guide to Children's Theatre in America*. Westport, Conn.: Greenwood Press, 1987.

————. *Theatre for Children in the United States: A History*. Norman: University of Oklahoma Press, 1971.

Unpublished Source:

Rubin, Janet. "The Literary and Theatrical Contributions of Charlotte B. Chorpenning to Children's Theatre." Doctoral dissertation, The Ohio State University, 1978.

Archival Resource:

New York, New York. New York Public Library. Library and Museum of the Performing Arts. M. D. Howell Collection.

Janet E. Rubin

CIRCUIT PLAYHOUSE. See PLAYHOUSE ON THE SQUARE/CIRCUIT PLAYHOUSE.

---

* Beginning with the 1949–50 season, shows are listed in the approximate order in which they entered the repertory.

CIRCLE REPERTORY COMPANY was founded in 1969 in New York City by four young, unknown theatre artists: Marshall W. Mason, director; Lanford Wilson, playwright; Tanya Berezin, actress; and Robert Thirkield, director-actor. Their goal was to develop an ensemble of artists—actors, directors, playwrights, and designers—who would collectively create living theatre.

Calling themselves Circle Theatre Company, the group began in a loft on Broadway at Eighty-third Street in New York City. The first production, David Starkweather's *A Practical Ritual to Exorcise Frustration After Five Days of Rain*, opened on April 10, 1970. Robert Thirkield and the author directed and Lanford Wilson designed the scenery. A cast including Spalding Gray presented the play on two weekends. Tickets cost $20. Later the same year Marshall Mason staged two productions of Anton Chekhov's *The Three Sisters*, one traditional, the other an experiment using rock music, and presented them in repertory.

Mason, artistic director of the Circle, had directed his first play, Tennessee Williams' *Cat on a Hot Tin Roof*, while an undergraduate at Northwestern University, where he was a protégé of Alvina Krause. When he came to New York in 1961, his dream was to meet Tennessee Williams and direct his newest play. Actually, Mason's first job in New York was as an assistant stage manager for the Phoenix Theatre*. In 1962 he began to direct plays at the now legendary Cafe Cino. Lanford Wilson, who was also working at Cafe Cino, asked Mason to read his first full-length play, *Balm in Gilead*. In 1965 Mason directed it at LaMama, another new and experimental play venue, where the play sold out its two-week run. As he continued to direct Wilson's plays, Mason and the young playwright from Missouri formed their own company, The American Theatre Project, with Robert Thirkield and Tanya Berezin. They produced two of Wilson's plays, *Home Free* and *The Madness of Lady Bright*, in London, where they received good reviews.

After they returned to New York, Dr. Harry H. Lerner, founder of a humanist organization, the Council for International Recreation and Lifelong Education, Inc. (CIRCLE), invited the four to form a repertory theatre. Lerner found a loft space at 2307 Broadway, and the group took the name Circle Theatre Company. Three years later, in 1972, the group split from the parent organization and became Circle Repertory, Inc.

During its five seasons at 2307 Broadway the Circle presented classics such as August Strindberg's *The Ghost Sonata* and Henrik Ibsen's *When We Dead Awaken* as well as new American plays, including Berilla Kerr's *The Elephant in the House* and a number of Lanford Wilson's one-act plays.

The company produced only one or two classics each season while devoting itself mainly to new American dramas that dealt realistically with human situations and values. In fact, the Circle has become best known for its plays of "lyrical realism," particularly Wilson's *The Hot l Baltimore*, which won the 1973 Drama Critics' Award for Best American Play, and his *Talley's Folly*, 1979, which won the Pulitzer Prize.

In its early years the Circle's season ran from September to June, with performances Thursday through Sunday evenings. On the other nights the company often presented workshop productions of new American plays.

The company worked together daily, rehearsing, reading new plays, and taking classes, while also performing nightly in major productions or workshops. Unlike most off-off-Broadway theaters, the Circle paid its actors, although a bare minimum of $12.33 per performance.

The theatre was sixty-four feet by thirty feet, with neither wing space nor backstage. Both the stage and audience seating were often changed from one production to the next. It was impossible to anchor anything to the plaster walls, so sets had to be freestanding. Maximum seating capacity was just one hundred.

The highlight of the 1972–73 season was the production of *The Hot l Baltimore*, which transferred to the Circle in the Square Theatre in Greenwich Village and ran for more than 600 performances. The next season was also a success, with two critically acclaimed plays: Mark Medoff's *When You Comin' Back, Red Ryder?*, directed by Kenneth Frankel and featuring Kevin Conway; and Edward Moore's *The Sea Horse*, directed by Marshall Mason. Both plays moved to off-Broadway theatres for successful runs.

In 1974 the company moved to its current home in Greenwich Village at 99 Seventh Avenue South, the former Sheridan Square Playhouse, and became officially known as the Circle Repertory Company. The 1974–75 season opened with the New York premiere of Tennessee Williams' *Battle of Angels*, which won an Obie Award for director Marshall Mason. That season the group also presented the world premiere of Wilson's *The Mound Builders*.

For the next several years Circle Rep offered a season of six plays. In 1977 its production of Albert Innaurato's *Gemini* transferred to Broadway for a very long run. As part of its 1979–80 season, Circle Rep offered two classic plays in repertory, Shakespeare's *Hamlet* and Friedrich von Schiller's *Mary Stuart*. To prepare, actors worked with voice and movement specialists; nevertheless, some critics thought the company was not up to the vocal demands of the classic works. The next year the company also included a repertory of two classics, Shakespeare's *Twelfth Night* and *The Beaver Coat* by Gerhart Hauptmann.

Although Circle Repertory uses a core of directors, designers, and actors, it also hires other personnel to work on productions. Thus, for example, in 1982 Gordon Davidson staged a production of Michael Cristofer's *Black Angel* and Farley Granger starred in Lanford Wilson's *Talley & Son* in 1985.

In its 160-seat playhouse, Circle Repertory presents an annual subscription season that includes new plays, revivals, and classics, and a Projects in Progress Series. The company also operates the Circle LAB, a program in which new plays can be developed free from commercial and critical pressure. The LAB consists of play readings, playwrights' and directors' units, and actors' training workshops. In 1982 and 1983 Circle Rep, in conjunction with the Dramatists Guild, presented the Young Playwrights Festival.

Circle Repertory operated as an off-off-Broadway theatre with an Actors' Equity Association showcase contract until the 1976–77 season. At that time it began to operate under an Equity off-Broadway contract, which meant ticket prices could be increased from the usual $3.50 and actors' salaries would be raised. According to Mason, this new status also gave the Circle increased professional recognition and improved its chances for more foundation grants.

Although Circle Repertory has not become rich, it has fared better than many other theatre companies. After its first season the group received grants from the New York State Council on the Arts and the Peg Santvoord Foundation. However, during the first five seasons, most funds came from private contributions and ticket sales. For example, the budget for 1973–74 was $108,000, with only $20,850 coming from foundations. In 1977 the Ford Foundation awarded Circle Rep a grant of $250,000, to be spread over three years. For the 1978–79 season the group met its budget of $520,000, with $355,000 coming from grants and contributions. During the 1974–75 season Circle Repertory had 312 subscribers; by 1982 the subscription list had grown to 6,000. In 1985 Circle Repertory became one of eight American theatre companies selected by the National Endowment for the Arts to participate in its five-year Ongoing Ensembles Project. With the $260,000 received for 1985, the Circle established a resident ensemble of twenty-five actors working for twenty-five weeks at a weekly salary of $500.

For the 1985–86 season the group opened at its regular theatre with two premieres in repertory, Lanford Wilson's *Talley & Son* and Paul Osborn's *Tomorrow's Monday*. Requiring more backstage space to maintain repertory productions and seeking a larger seating capacity, Circle Rep also presented three plays in repertory at the 262-seat Triplex Theatre at Borough of Manhattan Community College: Albert Camus' *Caligula*, Anne Chislett's *Quiet in the Land*, and a revival of Wilson's *The Mound Builders*.

Over the years Circle Repertory Company has received much critical acclaim for its fine ensemble of actors, directors, playwrights and designers. The company has been the recipient of more than ninety major awards, including two Tony Awards, thirty-five Obie Awards, and twelve Drama Desk Awards. Lanford Wilson was awarded the Pulitzer Prize for *Talley's Folly*. Among the thirty-five Obie Awards, Marshall W. Mason received six for staging plays, including *Battle of Angels, The Mound Builders*, and *Serenading Louie*, all by Wilson. The many actors who were awarded Obies include Tanya Berezin in *The Mound Builders*, Kevin McCarthy in *Harry Outside*, and Helen Stenborg and Farley Granger in *Talley & Son*.

As for its significance, Circle Repertory has provided an environment in which actors, directors, playwrights, and designers could develop their talent. For Lanford Wilson, one of our finest American playwrights, Circle Rep has been a place to develop and present his many plays, including *The 5th of July* and *Talley's Folly*, part of his series of dramas about the Talley family. Also, the company has regularly produced the works of John Bishop, Milan Stitt, and

David Mamet. Among its talented actors are longtime members such as William Hurt and Judd Hirsch, who have gone on to television and film stardom and have continued to work in new plays at Circle Repertory.

The company has presented more than seventy-five world premieres, including landmark productions of *Talley's Folly;* two other plays by Wilson, *Angels Fall* and *A Tale Told;* and *The Sea Horse*. Circle Rep has also produced New York premieres of Sam Shepard's *Suicide in B-Flat* and *Fool for Love*, David Storey's *The Farm*, and Tennessee Williams' *Battle of Angels*.

PERSONNEL

Management: Marshall W. Mason, artistic director (1969–86); B. Rodney Marriott, associate artistic director (1982–86); Marshall Oglesby, general manager (1972–74); Jerry Arrow, executive director (1973–78); Lindsay Gambini, managing director (1978–79); Porter Van Zandt, executive director (1979–81); Richard Frankel, managing director (1981–84); Suzanne M. Sato, managing director (1984–86).

Set Designers: John Lee Beatty (1974–86), David Jenkins (1979), David Potts (1974–85), Ronald Radice (1971–73).

Lighting Designers: Arden Fingerhut (1976, 1977, 1980), Dennis Parichy (1974–86), Mal Sturchio (1982, 1985).

Costume Designers: Dina Costa (1971–73), Laura Crow (1974–85), Jennifer von Mayrhauser (1974–86).

Sound Designers: George Hansen (1975–78), Chuck London (1974–86), Stewart Werner (1981–86).

Stage Directors: John Bishop, Neil Flanagan, Kenneth Frankel, Daniel Irvine, John Malkovich (1984), David Mamet (1979–81), B. Rodney Marriott, Marshall W. Mason, Eve Merriam (1983), Marshall Oglesby, Elinor Renfield, Terry Schreiber (1977, 1978), Sam Shepard (1983), Joan Micklin Silver (1983), Robert Thirkield.

Actors and Actresses: Tom Aldredge (1982–83), *Michael Ayr* (1976–82), Henrietta Bagley, Margaret Barker, *Tanya Berezin* (1969–86), Gary Berner, Jacqueline Brookes, Paul Butler, William M. Carr, Roger Chapman, Mollie Collison, Kevin Conway (1973–74), Katherine Cortez, *Lindsay Crouse* (1979–81), Jeff Daniels, Jack Davidson, Jake Dengel, Brad Dourif, *Concheta Ferrell* (1969–78), Neil Flanagan, Mary Ellen Flynn, *Stephanie Gordon* (1971–86), Mari Gorman, Bruce Gray, Spalding Gray, George Grizzard (1986), Charles T. Harper, *Trish Hawkins* (1973–86), *Michael Higgins* (1979–81, 1983–84), *Judd Hirsch* (1973, 1976, 1979, 1983–84), Jonathan Hogan, Barnard Hughes (1982), Laura Hughes, *William Hurt* (1977–82), Kiya Ann Joyce, Nancy Killmer, Ken Kliban, Swoozie Kurtz (1986), Zane Lasky, Bobo Lewis, Robert Lu Pone, Kevin McCarthy (1975), Bruce McCarty, James McDaniel, *Sharon Madden* (1971–78, 1981), Ken Marshall, Paul Martell, Debra Mooney, Edward J. Moore, Jay Patterson, Burke Pearson, Lisa Pelikan, Scott Phelps, James Pickens, Jr., Joyce Reehling, Christopher Reeve (1977), Sharon Schlarth, Edward Seamon, Ron Seka, Timothy Shelton, Ben Siegler, Nancy Snyder, Mark J. Soper, June Stein, Helen Stenborg, Danton Stone, Beatrice Straight (1979–80), Elizabeth Sturges, Brian Tarantina, Antony Tenuta, Robert Thirkield, Richard Thomas, Douglass Watson, Fritz Weaver (1981, 1982), James Ray Weeks, Patricia Wettig, Amy Wright.

REPERTORY

1969–70: *A Practical Ritual to Exorcise Frustration After Five Days of Rain, The Three Sisters.*

1970–71: *Sextet (Yes), The Ghost Sonata, Princess Ivona.* Workshops: *Time Shadows, The Future Is in the Eggs,* adaptation workshop of *Death of a Salesman,* adaptation workshop of *Paderewski and the Garbage Thieves, Waiting for Godot.*

1971–72: *The Three Sisters, The Ghost Sonata, The Elephant in the House, Time Shadows, The Family Continues, Ikke, Ikke, Nye, Nye, Nye, The Great Nebula in Orion.* Workshops: *Howie's, Denim and Rose, The Empire Builders, Danny 405, Ludlow Fair.*

1972–73: *A Road Where Wolves Run, The Hot l Baltimore, When We Dead Awaken, The Tragedy of Thomas Andros.* Workshops: *Canvas, Icarus Nine, Peace at Hand, Great Jones Street, Offending the Audience, Mrs. Tidings Mason-Dixon Medicine Man, Smith Here!, Snow Angel, When You Comin' Back, Red Ryder?*

1973–74: *When You Comin' Back, Red Ryder?, Prodigal, The Amazing Activity of Charley Contrare and the Ninety-Eighth Street Gang, The Sea Horse, him, The Persians.* Workshops: *Straights of Massina, Hothouse, One Person, When Everything Becomes the City's Music, Not Enough Rope, The Summer Solstice, Busy Dyin'.*

1974–75: *Battle of Angels, The Mound Builders, Down by the River Where the Waterlilies Are Disfigured Every Day, Harry Outside, Not to Worry.* Workshops: *Innocent Thoughts, Harmless Intentions, Fire in the Mindhouse, Saint Freud, Scandalous Memories, Afternoon Tea, Spring Awakening.*

1975–76: *The Elephant in the House, Dancing for the Kaiser, Knock Knock, Who Killed Richard Cory?, Serenading Louie, Mrs. Murray's Farm.* Projects in Progress Series: *When I Dyed My Hair in Venice, Solo for Two, The Magic Formula, Terminal, Night Thoughts, The Confirmation, Fog and Mismanagement, Home Free!, Winners, Dark Room, Prague Spring.*

1976–77: *The Farm, A Tribute to Lili Lamont, My Life, Gemini, Exiles, Unsung Cole.* Projects in Progress Series: *Dead Sure, The Passing of Corky Brewster, For Love or Money, Suicide in B Flat, Allegro, To the Land, Fine Print, Mrs. Tidings Mason-Dixon Medicine Man, Celebration Off River Street, What the Babe Said, The Brixton Recovery.*

1977–78: *Feedlot, Ulysses in Traction, Lulu, Brontosaurus, Cabin 12, The 5th of July.* Projects in Progress Series: None.

1978–79: *Glorious Morning, In the Recovery Lounge, The Runner Stumbles, Winter Signs, Talley's Folly, Buried Child, Gertrude Stein Gertrude Stein Gertrude Stein.* Projects in Progress Series: *In Three Easy Lessons, Winter Signs, Perched on a Gabardine Cloud, American Options.*

1979–80: *Reunion, Hamlet, Mary Stuart, Innocent Thoughts, Harmless Intentions, Back in the Race, The Woolgatherer.* Projects in Progress Series: *Back in the Race, Mass Appeal, Some Sweet Time, Threads, Child of the Clay Country, In Vienna.* Festival of One-Acts: *The Coal Diamond, American Welcome, Breakfast Play, High Old Dance in the Afternoon, Am I Blue, On the Side of the Road, Diary of a Shadow Walker, Academy of Desire, Seduction Duet.*

1980–81: *The Diviners, Twelfth Night, The Beaver Coat, Childe Byron, In Connecticut, A Tale Told.* Projects in Progress Series: *The Diviners, Diary of a Shadow Walker, The Snow Orchid, The Great Grandson of Jedediah Kohler, Charlie McCarthy's Monocle.*

1981–82: *Threads, Thymus Vulgaris, Confluence, Am I Blue, Snow Orchid, Richard II, The Great Grandson of Jedediah Kohler.* Projects in Progress Series: *Bing and Walker,* *'night, Mother, What I Did Last Summer, Cat and Mouse, How Women Break Bad News, Presque Isle, Spookhouse.*

1982–83: *Angels Fall, Black Angel, What I Did Last Summer, Domestic Issues, Fool for Love* (Magic Theater of San Francisco production), *The Sea Gull.* Projects in Progress Series: *Rock County, The Paper Boy, Out of Order, In Place, Levitation, I Won't Be Here Forever, The Cherry Orchard,* Part II, *Faded Glory.*

1983–84: *Full Hookup, Levitation, The Harvesting, Balm in Gilead* (coproduced with the Steppenwolf Theater Company of Chicago), *Danny and the Deep Blue Sea* (coproduced with Circle in the Square). Projects in Progress Series: *The Harvesting, Dysan, Listen to the Lions, Save the World, Danny and the Deep Blue Sea, Hubbard, Ohio, The Early Girl, A Little Going Away Party.*

1984–85: *Love's Labour's Lost, Bing and Walker, Dysan, As Is, Angelo's Wedding.* Projects in Progress Series: *As Is, Rameau La Besque, The Musical Comedy Murders of 1940, An Evening of Short Plays* by Joe Pintauro, *To Culebra.*

1985–86: *Tomorrow's Monday, Talley & Son, The Beach House, Caligula, The Mound Builders, Quiet in the Land.* Projects in Progress Series: *Playing with Love, A Biography, Before I Got My Eye Put Out, Wandering Jew.*

BIBLIOGRAPHY

Published Source:
Moynihan, D. S. "Marshall Mason: The Inner River of Experience." *The Drama Review* 25 (Fall 1981): 29–38.

Archival Resource:
New York, New York. New York Public Library. Library and Museum of the Performing Arts. Clippings, press releases, brochures; photos and scrapbooks for Marshall Mason and Lanford Wilson.

Doris Hart

CIRCLE THEATRE COMPANY. See CIRCLE REPERTORY THEATRE.

CITY STAGE COMPANY. See CSC REPERTORY.

CLASSIC STAGE COMPANY. See CSC REPERTORY.

[THE] CLEVELAND PLAY HOUSE was initially organized in the first decade of this century by a small group of Ohioans convinced that most of the theatre being produced in Europe at the time was more important and vital than its American counterpart. By 1915, one year after the formation of the important Cleveland Foundation, Raymond O'Neil, drama and music critic for the *Cleveland Leader*, and his group organized to form an art theatre. O'Neil, who had seen the work of both Max Reinhardt, the internationally renowned German regisseur, and the influential Moscow Art Theatre, was elected director, while Charles Brooks was elected president. The Cleveland Play House was part of a renaissance, for in this same year the Cleveland Museum of Art was built and the Cleveland Symphony organized. In May 1916 the group presented Maurice Maeterlinck's *The Death of Tintagiles*, adapted especially for puppets. One month later the group adopted the motto "Art in Democracy" and the title "The Play House" (for years it would be called the "Cleveland Play House," a title made official in 1980). In 1917 a renovated barn, the home of Raymond and Ida O'Neil, became the scene of the production of two one-act plays, W. B. Yeats' *The Hour Glass* and Anton Chekhov's *The Bear*. Later that year two productions were mounted in the third-floor ballroom of a home at Euclid and East Twenty-fourth Street.

Under the leadership of Walter Flory, president of the board, the group sought more suitable production facilities. They finally purchased a small Lutheran church building at the corner of Cedar and East Seventy-third Street and converted it into a theatre with an initial seating capacity of 160 (a balcony added in 1923 increased the seating to about 225). The Cedar Avenue Play House was to be the home of the Cleveland Play House from December 1917 to April 1927. The first production there was the pantomime "The Garden of Semiramis." One year later the group incorporated under the laws of Ohio and established the board of trustees and its method for selecting the director. Financial support at this time came from membership dues, the box office, and donations.

Between 1917 and 1921, when a change in the directorship occurred, the Play House presented fourteen additional productions. In 1920 the group was deeply in debt and presented only six of twelve announced productions. In 1921, at which time the Play House was on the verge of collapse and discussions abounded about the group not fulfilling its promises to the audience and the community, O'Neil retired, noting that art theatre in America inevitably evolves from amateur to professional. In 1921 four theatres opened in downtown Cleveland (most of them on then fashionable Euclid Avenue): the State (movies, orchestras) on February 5, the Ohio (a 1,200-seat legitimate theatre) on February 12, the Hanna (a legitimate theatre replacing the old Euclid Avenue Opera House) on March 28, and the Allen (initially playing silent movies) on April 1. The Euclid Avenue Association was formed to promote "Playhouse Square," to which was added the Palace Theatre on November 6, 1922.

Frederic McConnell was chosen by the board, headed now by Leonard Smith, to begin in 1921 as director of the Cleveland Play House. McConnell, who had received a law degree from the University of Nebraska, became interested in theatre while continuing his academic studies at Carnegie Tech in Pittsburgh. Given a free hand by the board in selecting his staff, McConnell hired two persons who would eventually have a significant impact on the success of the theatre: K. Elmo Lowe, a recent graduate of Carnegie Tech, became associate director, and Max Eisenstat, also from Carnegie Tech, began as a technician and stage manager but became an important force in management. The board wanted to change the image of the Play House from that of an "amateur theatre club" with narrow community appeal to a professional theatre. To do this the group had to strengthen its economic position.

Under McConnell's direction, and with the able assistance of Lowe and Eisenstat, the Play House presented, between 1921 and 1958 (the year of Mc-

Connell's retirement), some 600 productions, including 40 American premieres and about 150 significant revivals. The first production under McConnell's aegis was that of Oscar Wilde's *The Importance of Being Earnest*. Each season during the period from 1921 to 1928 averaged about eight productions; this average increased to about twelve in the 1950s. With a permanent organization, the group developed a solid audience base. Playing only a few evenings a month at the beginning of this period, the group gradually lengthened its runs to a full week. The audience grew from 4,000 annually in 1921 to about 40,000 annually in 1928.

In 1924 the group paid off its mortgage on the Cedar Avenue Play House. The quest for an additional theatre began almost immediately. Mr. and Mrs. Francis Drury donated a plot of land valued at $50,000, and the newly established Cleveland Play House Foundation coordinated a fund drive. The new building, on East Eighty-sixth Street, was designed by Small, Reeb, and Draz (Francis Draz being the principal architect), with the advice of Frederic McConnell. It was built and fitted out for about $275,000. The building included two theatres, the larger Drury, seating 530, and the smaller Brooks, seating 160. Money for the building came from a $100,000 loan and gifts of $175,000. In 1929 the group initiated its summer productions at Chautauqua, New York, a program that flourished until 1981.

By the late 1930s the Play House was under firm direction. McConnell developed the budget, hired personnel, and scheduled plays and seasons. The acting company was, at this time, the core of the organization. This period also saw the establishment of an important wing of the Play House, the Women's Committee. Another important facet of the theatre, a program by and for children called "The Curtain Pullers" (later "Youtheatre"), was initiated by Esther Mullin. Famous alums of this program include Paul Newman, Joel Grey, and Joan Deiner.

The first increase in ticket prices since 1921 occurred in 1941, when the Federal Revenue Act forced a 10 percent surcharge. Ticket prices went to $1.10. Serious financial problems returned in the early 1940s, and members of the board personally contributed money to allay the situation. The board also launched a campaign in 1942 to raise $30,000. The popular Shakespeare Festival, established in 1933, was cancelled in 1943 (it would be reinstituted in 1962).

By 1945 audience support had increased to about 130,000, and the Play House played to about 87 percent of capacity. In this same year the concept of an additional theatre, first proposed in 1937 and again in 1940, was revived. This project led, with the assistance of a grant from the Rockefeller Foundation, to the opening in 1949 of the Euclid–77th Street Theatre. The 560-seat theatre was outfitted at a cost of $220,000 in a twenty-seven-year-old church purchased for $52,000. The theatre featured a deep and wide apron stage, a prototype of "open" or "thrust" stages to be built from the 1950s on. The new facility increased the financial strain on the organization and another fund drive was undertaken.

In 1950 K. Elmo Lowe became producing director, a move that allowed for Frederic McConnell's gradual withdrawal from the activities of the Play House. In the same year the Men's Committee was established, a group that would, in 1960, form the Play House Club, a profitable supper club built in an occasionally used rehearsal hall in the 77th Street Theatre. In this period of renewal under Lowe many new actors and technicians began working at the theatre. Principal directors were Lowe and Kirk Willis, a longtime Play House performer. In 1953 addition of an acoustically responsive false ceiling provided better lighting positions and improved the appearance of the Euclid–77th Street Theatre. With the death of Max Eisenstat in 1956, only McConnell, Willis, Lowe, and Dorothy Paxton (Lowe) remained of the leadership that emerged in the 1920s.

But in the mid-1950s overall theatre attendance declined and the Play House faced financial difficulties. The small Brooks Theatre was used infrequently, runs at the Euclid-77th Street Theatre were shortened, generally to an average of four and one-half weeks, and the professional production staff was reduced. In 1957, however, the Ford Foundation awarded the Play House its first-ever grant to a theatre. The grant of $130,000 paid the salaries of fifteen actors chosen to train at the Play House for two years, beginning in 1958, and to tour smaller cities in the Midwest with productions of the classics. The Play House assumed all other costs of the touring venture. For four years the Ford actors toured productions of plays by Henrik Ibsen, Christopher Marlowe, and Oscar Wilde, among others. The Ford Foundation grant and the tours it supported was a principal catalyst for the resident theatre movement in the United States, although the grant did not solve the economic problems of the Play House. The presence of the Ford actors altered the status of the Play House. Until 1958 it had been the only nonunion professional company in the United States. Since 1958 the Play House has operated under a contract with the Actors' Equity Association, the professional actors' union. The opening of the Play House Club in 1960, coupled with the favorable publicity generated by the national tour of the Ford actors and Lowe's use of star performers in plays with strong box-office appeal, turned the financial tide in the early 1960s.

With Lowe's retirement in 1969, the board faced for only the third time in the history of the Play House the task of selecting a director. William Greene, who worked with Lowe as executive director in 1969–70, prepared to succeed Lowe but met an untimely death. Rex Partington, the company's business manager, headed the organization through an artistically disastrous half-season in 1970–71. By this time the Great Lakes Shakespeare Festival, a summer theatre begun in 1962 in nearby Lakewood, was a firmly established and well-managed professional operation. In downtown Cleveland the curtain was coming down on the theatres in Playhouse Square, which had been Cleveland's own "Times Square" since the 1930s. Only the Hanna Theatre remained as a venue for major touring productions.

In January 1971 Richard Oberlin, who had been an actor with the Play House since 1954, was appointed managing director, and in the fall of 1971 he was named director. A student at the College of Wooster (Ohio) and Indiana University, Oberlin had served as the Play House's company manager for its National Touring Company from 1961–63 and was resident director of the Play House's Summer Theatre at the world-renowned Chautauqua Institute in Chautauqua, New York, from 1968 to 1972. The Summer Theatre had been established in 1929 and staffed since then by Cleveland Play House personnel, who produced an eight-week series of plays revived from the previous Cleveland season and provided a six-week, college-accredited theatre training school.

In the period from 1958 to 1971 the Cleveland Play House amassed a record of some 350 productions, including 15 American premieres, 1 world premiere, 4 musicals, an annual Shakespearean production, and many summer productions at Chautauqua, New York.

During the years of Oberlin's management, the Play House instituted the "Play House Comes to the School," which consisted of in-school sessions and student matinees. Expansion of student audiences, the utilization of Play House alumni, emphasis on the ensemble, and internal and financial stability were Oberlin's main achievements. Under Oberlin's direction the Play House began to receive grants from the National Endowment for the Arts, the Ohio Arts Council, and such local organizations as the Cleveland Foundation, the Jennings Foundation, and the Beaumont Foundation. Association with various theatre organizations and area colleges and universities also increased. By 1975 the theatre's audiences totaled about 150,000—a far cry from the few hundred that supported the group in the 1920s. From 1971 to 1981 the Play House mounted 127 productions (10 to 13 annually), including 13 American premieres and 4 world premieres.

To secure a building site adjacent to the Euclid-Eighty-sixth Street location of the Drury and Brooks Theatres for shops, storage, rehearsal space, and consolidated offices, and to build a new 650-seat theatre adjoining the forty-three-year-old Brooks and Drury were the aims of another substantial fund-raising campaign launched in 1979. The new $12.5 million Bolton Theatre complex, designed by Clevelander Philip Johnson, including a vast new Production Center for shops, opened in October 1983. In 1985, with annual attendance soaring past 200,000 and a budget pushing near $2.3 million, Richard Oberlin resigned as director. He was succeeded by William Rhys, his associate director and former (since 1969) Play House actor and director.

PERSONNEL and REPERTORY

Chloe Warner Oldenburg's *Leaps of Faith: History of the Cleveland Play House, 1915–85* (Pepper Pike, Ohio: Chloe Oldenburg, 1985) contains an exhaustive listing of the names of support and artistic staff from 1915 to 1985, as well as a year-by-year listing of plays produced.

BIBLIOGRAPHY

Published Sources:
Flory, Julia M. *The Cleveland Play House: How It Began*. Cleveland: Press of Western Reserve University, 1965.

Oldenburg, Chloe Warner. *Leaps of Faith: History of the Cleveland Play House, 1915–85*. Pepper Pike, Ohio: Chloe Oldenburg, 1985.

Unpublished Sources:

Allman, William A. "An Investigation of a Successful Civic Theatre as Exemplified by the Cleveland Play House." Master's thesis, Ohio University, 1951.

Clark, William B., Jr. "A History of the Cleveland Play House, 1936–1958." Master's thesis, Tulane University, 1968.

Herbst, Dorothy. "A History of the Play House from Its Origins to September, 1936." Master's thesis, Northwestern University, 1937.

Archival Resource:

Cleveland, Ohio. Cleveland Play House. Scrapbooks and files.

Wallace Sterling

[JEAN] COCTEAU REPERTORY COMPANY was organized in New York, New York, in June 1971 by Eve Adamson. She leased a storefront at 43 Bond Street, brought in rows of seats from a demolished movie theatre, and opened on June 17, 1971, with a double bill of Cocteau's *Orphee* and Michel de Ghelderode's *Christopher Columbus*. The next year the theatre was incorporated as the nonprofit Association for Development of Dramatic Arts, Inc., with a board of advisers, later the board of trustees.

Off-off-Broadway was flourishing by this time, with LaMama, the WPA Theatre, Truck and Warehouse Theatre, and Old Reliable Theatre in the immediate neighborhood. LaMama and Truck and Warehouse remain, as do later companies such as Dramatis Personnae, Colonades Theatre Lab, Wonderhorse Theatre, New York Theatre ensemble, the nearby Public Theatre, Open Space Theatre, First Amendment Company, and Improvisation Company. However, the Jean Cocteau Repertory quickly established itself as the company specializing in reviving classics and rarely produced foreign plays. When the Cocteau moved into the landmark Bouwerie Lane Theatre in the fall of 1973, it became one of the few true repertory companies in the nation with a resident company performing a season of plays in rotation.

Eve Adamson began directing at the Circle Theatre in Los Angeles, where she had grown up and done some acting before studying in New York. She operated a children's theatre in Los Angeles for two years after her theatre studies in New York and then she turned to writing. Still later she returned to New York, where she became involved with the Mainstream Theatre, a group producing new plays she considered flawed. Realizing that she wanted to concentrate on the more enduring plays of world theatre overlooked by conventional or experimental companies, she began the Cocteau as a showcase theatre with the intention of developing it into an ensemble. She was a founding member of the Off-off-Broadway Alliance, now The Alliance of Resident Theatres, New York.

At first the Cocteau presented plays on weekends, with one performance on Friday and two on Saturday. Sunday performances during the first few months were dramatic readings. In 1986 the company operated Thursday through Sunday and presented, as well, a series of Wednesday matinees for high school students. A subscription campaign begun in 1972–73 resulted in the sale of just nineteen season tickets. The company had 1,200 subscribers in 1984–85. Rotating repertory is too complicated and costly to sell through paid media advertising, so the Cocteau mainly relies on direct mail, free listings in city newspapers and magazines, and the Theatre Development Fund voucher system. Tickets cost about $3 in the early 1970s, reflecting then normal off-off-Broadway scale, but prices have slowly increased to $15 in 1986–87. A season subscription nets the customer a substantial discount. Beginning in 1983–84, the last play of the season has been free to new subscribers. The group accumulates a deficit that is carried over from season to season. The occasional profitable season reduces the deficit, as did grants from the National Endowment for the Arts in the early 1980s. In 1983–84 Adamson instituted an austerity budget and increased efforts to find corporate funding, especially to pay printing costs. Funding now comes from foundations, corporations, and individuals, as well as from the New York State Council on the Arts and the New York City Department of Cultural Affairs. Additionally, a city work program provides a person for janitorial duty and odd jobs.

Adamson began with an apprentice ensemble of about eight volunteers who also doubled as stage crew and helped with administration. The Cocteau company now includes the artistic director, Adamson; managing director, Robert H. Hupp; a technical director; seven actors, and—on a fee basis—set and costume designers for a six-play season, as well as jobbed-in directors for three of the plays produced each season. In 1974–75 Adamson asked members of the acting company to commit themselves for an entire season for a stipend primarily derived from school matinees. In 1982 she began paying a weekly salary, based on seniority. First-year members were paid only for school matinees and special performances. Although several actors have stayed with the company for several seasons, none are considered principal players because the rotating repertory allows everyone to participate in a variety of major and minor roles. Salaries remain nominal, so company members hold other jobs during the day. Rehearsals are held two evenings a week and Saturday afternoon, with some rehearsals added as needed. Plays are rehearsed for five to six weeks and each play runs from ten to forty-two performances. Occasionally a play is held over to the next season.

Each year the Cocteau presents more than 150 performances of plays chosen from well-known masterworks of the past (Shakespearean, Jacobean, and Georgian dramas), classics of the modern era (Samuel Beckett, G. B. Shaw, Jean-Paul Sartre), and forgotten plays by well-known playwrights (Oscar Wilde's *Vera* and August Strindberg's *Swanwhite*). Several productions have been world or American premieres of English translations. Henrik Ibsen's *Love's Comedy*, Sophocles' *Philoctetes*, and Aeschylus' *Oresteia* have graced the group's repertory, as have other world premieres of adaptations of Edna St. Vincent Millay's *No Fit Place for a Child to Play* and Jules Verne's *The Horrors of Doctor Moreau*. Productions of Alma Law's translations from the Russian of Edvard

Radzinsky's *Theatre in the Time of Nero and Seneca* and *Lunin: Theatre of Death* are further testimony of the group's extraordinary ambition. A revival of Tennessee Williams' *In the Bar of a Tokyo Hotel* was brought to Williams' attention when he read some of his material at the Bouwerie Lane Theatre for a German television documentary. He asked Adamson to revive the play once more, and she complied. Williams then gave the Cocteau permission to stage the world premieres of *Kirche, Kutchen und Kinder* in 1979 and *Something Cloudy, Something Clear* in 1981.

The Jean Cocteau Repertory is not reviewed on a regular basis, but revivals of Shakespeare and of lesser-known plays are noticed by the *New York Times*, the *Village Voice*, and other papers. The appeal of the company rests on the artistic challenges posed by its repertory, an appeal especially strong in the student population in the neighborhood. Because the company includes inexperienced players, the acting is often uneven, but increasingly the Cocteau has become one of New York's most distinguished off-off-Broadway troupes. Productions receiving particular praise were those accorded Ben Jonson's *Volpone*, Shakespeare's *Pericles*, Cyril Tourneur's *The Revenger's Tragedy*, and the Radzinsky plays.

PERSONNEL

Management: Eve Adamson, proprietor and artistic director (1971–86); Craig Smith, general manager (1974–86); Coral Potter, part-time administrator (1974–78); Steve Randolph, part-time administrator (1978–79); Carson Wiley, managing director (1979–80); Andrew Cohn, managing director (1980–82); Ben Carney, managing director (1982–83); John T. Bower, managing director (1983–84), also business manager (1982–83); Robert Hupp, managing director (1984–86); Andrea Tienan, administrative assistant (1983–84), box-office manager (1984–85), and business manager (1985–86).

Technical Directors: John Arndt (1984–85), Tom Keever (1977–80), Gregory Laird (1982–84), Edward R. F. Matthews (1980–81), James S. Payne (1971–77).

Directors: Eve Adamson, Gerald Chapman (*Epicoene*), Susan Flakes (*Swanwhite*), Giles Hogya (*The Beaux' Stratagem, The Importance of Being Earnest*, and *The Miser*), Daniel Irvine (*Six Characters in Search of an Author*), Christopher Martin (*New Way to Pay Old Debts*), Douglas McKeown (*The Witch of Edmonton, The Count of Monte Cristo, The Oresteia, Cymbeline*), Robert Moss (*The School for Scandal*), Anthony Naylor (*Under Milk Wood*), Martin L. Reymert (*Love's Comedy, The Cid, Ruy Blas*), Tony Robertson (*Pericles*, winner of an Obie Award, and *The Revenger's Tragedy*), Barbara Schofield (*The Maids*), Karen Sunde (*Exit the King, Philoctetes*),

Actors and Actresses: Leslie Appleby, *John Arndt* (1980–85), Margot Avery, Karla Barker, *Harris Berlinsky* (1977–86), Joe Bolduc, *John T. Bower* (1978–81), *Patrick Boyinton* (1981–85), George Brunner, Jonathan Cantor, Patricia Carey, Dominique Cieri, Michael F. Clarke, *Craig Cook* (1981–86), Craig Cormier, William Dante, *Phyllis Deitschel* (1978–83), Margaret Dulaney, J. D. Eiche, Barry Einstein, *John Emmert* (1982–85), John Fallon, Michelle Farr, Michael Fesenmeier, *Carmen Finestra* (1972–75), Meg Fisher, Kathleen Forbes, David Fuller, Gene Galusha, Jack Gooden, Joan Grant, Mary Gratch, Olivia Vergil Harper, Debora Houston, *Jere Jacob* (1971–75), Christopher Jarrett, *Judy Jones* (1979–83), Linda Jones, John Kadula, Scott Kanoff, *Tom Keever* (1976–80),

Boris Kinberg, Jim Klawin, Gretchen Krich, Stephanie Lett, Arthur Lundquist, *Andrew MacCracken* (1977–81), Douglas McKeown, *Miles Mason* (1982–86), Joseph Menino, R. Mack Miller, John Mitchell, Ceamus O'Brien, *James S. Payne* (1971–78), Elizabeth Pearson, Steve Pomerantz, Amy K. Posner, *Coral S. Potter* (1973–86), Steve Randolph, Donna Rowe, *John Schmerling* (1980–82, 1985–86), Barbara Schofield, Steven Silva, Deborah Singer, Barbara Sloane, Christina Sluberski, *Craig Smith* (1973–86), Roy Steinberg, Constance Stellas, Elise Stone, Sam Todd, Jim Toolen, Thomas Tresser, Lynn Treveal, Bob Tzudiker, Stuart Craig Wood, Mitchell Yaven.

REPERTORY

1971–72: *Orphee* with *Christopher Columbus, He Who Gets Slapped, The Eagle with Two Heads, No Fit Place for a Child to Play, Salome, The Winter's Tale.* Readings were given on Sunday evenings.

1972–73: *Orphee* with *The Human Voice, The Tragedy of Tragedies, or The Life and Death of Tom Thumb the Great, Coriolanus, Medea.*

1973–74: *Medea, Waiting for Godot, The Man Who Married a Dumb Wife, Astonishments* (act without words,-Part II, *Sweeney Agonistes*, and a magic act), *Ghosts, Cain, Suddenly Last Summer.*

1974–75: *A Midsummer Night's Dream, Waiting for Godot, Ghosts, The Doctor in Spite of Himself, Romeo and Juliet, The Firebugs, Winterset, In the Bar of a Tokyo Hotel.*

1975–76: *Twelfth Night, Brecht on Brecht, Desire Under the Elms, The Importance of Being Earnest, Endgame, The Count of Monte Cristo, Vera, or The Nihilists, Winterset, The Lesson.*

1976–77: *The Lesson, Macbeth, Rhinoceros, Androcles and the Lion, The Caretaker, The Cenci, She Stoops to Conquer, Salome, The Brass Butterfly.*

1977–78: *The Caretaker, The Cocktail Party, A New Way to Pay Old Debts, Love's Comedy, Hamlet, No Exit, Volpone, 'Tis Pity She's a Whore.*

1978–79: *Volpone, Hamlet, A Mad World, My Masters, Exit the King, The Cid, The Scarecrow, As You Like It, In the Bar of a Tokyo Hotel, The Changeling.*

1979–80: *Exit the King, Kirche, Kutchen und Kinder, Hamlet, He Who Gets Slapped, Ruy Blas, The Tempest, In the Bar of a Tokyo Hotel, The Roman Actor.*

1980–81: *The Witch of Edmonton, The Dybbuk, Pericles, Life Is a Dream, The Alchemist.*

1981–82: *Something Cloudy, Something Clear, Two Noble Kinsmen, The Revenger's Tragedy, The Golem, The Count of Monte Cristo.*

1982–83: *The Condemned of Altona, Swanwhite, Saint Joan, The School for Scandal, Don Carlos, Philoctetes.*

1983–84: *Judas, The Beaux' Stratagem, King John, Epicoene, The Oresteia, Antiquities.*

1984–85: *Theatre in the Time of Nero and Seneca, Cymbeline, Goat Song, The Importance of Being Earnest, L'Aiglon, The Maids.*

1985–86: *Lunin: Theatre of Death, Six Characters in Search of an Author, King Lear, The Miser, Rosencrantz and Guildenstern Are Dead, Under Milk Wood.*

BIBLIOGRAPHY

Published Sources:
New York Times, 1971–86.
Village Voice 1971–86.

Archival Resource:
New York, New York. New York Public Library. Library and Museum of the Performing
    Arts. Clipping and programs.

                                                                        Kevin J. Brady

CONTEMPORARY THEATRE, INC., See A CONTEMPORARY THEA-
TRE, INC.

CSC REPERTORY, also known as the Classic Stage Company and the City
Stage Company, was founded in New York, New York, in 1967 by Christopher
Martin, Harris Laskawy, and Kathryn Wyman.

The company presented its first season at Rutgers Presbyterian Church, 236
West Seventy-third Street, New York, under the name Classic Stage Company.
In November 1968 the company appeared briefly at a church in Brooklyn and
then moved in December to 273 Bleeker Street, with the new name CSC Repertory. In October 1969 CSC moved again, to 89 West Third Street. Finally, in
the summer of 1973, the company found a home at the Abbey Theatre, 136 East
Thirteenth Street, where it has remained. CSC moved from off-off-Broadway
to fully professional off-Broadway status in 1975–76, and since 1983 it has
called itself City Stage Company as well as CSC Repertory.

Martin, artistic director and major actor for CSC during most of its history,
came from a New York theatre family: his parents, Ian Martin and Inge Adams,
appeared on radio (with Orson Welles) and on the Broadway stage. While
continuing a career as a rock singer, the younger Martin attended New York
University, where he began working with Laskawy and Wyman. In 1967, after
a two-month visit by Martin to London's Royal Shakespeare Company and
National Theatre, the three formed the Classic Stage Company to give New
York a theatre nobody else was supplying.

CSC has defined and supplied that missing theatre in at least three ways: by
maintaining a true repertory company (at times the only one in the city) with as
many as six productions in rotation; by mounting full-scale productions, often
uncut, of rarely performed major dramatic classics; and by offering New York,
United States, and even English-language premieres of important recent European
plays. CSC's province has been those large, spare, textually oriented plays of
European origin.

Soon after its founding the company began gaining critical recognition. In
1970 *Cue* magazine theatre critic Marilyn Stasio recognized CSC as a stable
organization of dedicated classicists presenting well-mounted productions to a
loyal following. In 1970–71 Laskawy received an Obie Award for his title
performance in Anton Chekhov's *Uncle Vanya*, and in 1973–74 CSC as a whole
received an Obie for its achievements.

In 1977 Dennis Turner became executive director of CSC, bringing the company its first truly professional business management and assuring a strong
financial base for six subsequent years of artistic and box-office successes, in-

cluding Martin's productions of Shakespeare's *Richard II-Henry IV* trilogy, W. B. Yeats' Cuchulain plays, the Oedipus cycle, the complete *Peer Gynt* by Henrik Ibsen, Shakespeare's *King Lear*, and Goethe's *Faust* plays. In 1980 *New York Post* critic Clive Barnes touted CSC as the most significant of our classic repertory theatres, and he nominated Martin for leadership of a national theatre.

During these years Martin and Karen Sunde—the company's dramaturg, leading actress, and sometime playwright—also worked to establish strong CSC ties with several major European theatre companies. As part of that effort, CSC brought French playwright, director, and actor Roger Planchon to New York in early 1981 to assist with the production of his controversial work *Gilles de Rais*.

The company's high point, so far, has been the American premiere, in 1982, of the complete *Faust* plays. In recognition of this production and others the company received an Outer Critics Circle Special Award that year. Such acclaim helped make the 1982–83 season CSC's most financially successful to date, with a reported budget of $410,000, 31,000 in attendance, and 2,500 subscribers.

However, the next season, 1983–84, was only a limited success artistically and a failure financially; the season ended prematurely on January 29, 1984, amid serious managerial and directorial conflicts. All employee contracts were terminated, and the theatre building was rented out for February and March. In May the company reopened briefly with a low-budget mounting of August Strindberg's *Dance of Death*, its only offering for almost a year.

The 1984–85 season did not begin until January 1985, with an unacclaimed production of the Orestes plays of Aeschylus and Sophocles. By the end of that season Martin had resigned as artistic director; he was succeeded by Craig D. Kinzer, who had served the company as associate director. Since then CSC has struggled to regain its former financial condition and to continue its tradition of producing what one current company member calls "those oh-my-god-you-can't-do-that plays."

PERSONNEL

Management: William Snow, general manager (1967–68); William Glass, managing director (1973–75); Leonard Edelstein, managing director (1977); Dennis Turner, executive director (1977–81); Alberto Tore, general manager (1979–80); Stephen J. Holland, managing director (1981–82); Dan J. Martin, managing director (1982–83); Christopher Martin, Craig D. Kinzer, and Will Maitland Weiss, codirectors (1984–85); Will Maitland Weiss, managing director (1985–86); Carol Ostrow, managing director (1986).

Directors: Christopher Martin, artistic director (1967–84); Christopher Martin, Craig D. Kinzer, and Will Maitland Weiss, codirectors (1984–85); Craig D. Kinzer, artistic director (1985–86); Christopher Barns; Robert Bielecki; Julianne Boyd; Rene Buch; John Camera; Frank Dwyer; Robert Hall; Eric Krebs; Harris Laskawy; Paul Lazarus; Laurence Maslon; Laurence Sacharow; John Shannon; Karen Sunde; Marlene Swartz; Stuart Vaughan; David Villaire.

Dramaturgs: James W. Flannery, Laurence Maslon, Karen Sunde.

Designers: Lorraine Bege, Terry A. Bennett, Joe Bigelow, Blanche Blakeny, Rick Butler, David Chapman, Clay Coyle, Clarke Dunham, Robert Weber Federico, Tom

Gould, Philip Graneto, Joel Grynheim, Robert Hall, Pamela Howard, Kalina Ivanov, Barbara Kopit, Rachel Kurland, Harry Lines, Christopher Martin, Laurence Maslon, Donna Meyer, Miriam Nieves, Kay Pathanky, Lowell Patton, Marianne Powell-Parker, Seth Price, Whitney Quesenberry, Stephen Strawbridge, Evelyn Thompson, Kristina Watson, George D. Xenos, Catherine Zuber.

Actors and Actresses: David Aston-Reese, Mike Atkin, Mark Ballora, Nevada Rae Barr, Timothy Barrett, Cal Bedford, Paul Behar, Barbara Blackledge, Sam Blackwell, Jonathan Bolt, *Lance Brilliantine* (1967–71), Ted Britton, Alan Brooks, Susan Bruce, Masha Buell, Brenda Lynn Bynum, John Camera, Lisa Carling, Sally Chamberlin, Kathryn Chilson, Edward Cicciarelli, Irene Marcia Cooper, Geoffrey Cramer, Sheridan Crist, Ken Davis, Francois de Giroday, Ralph Dematthews, Deborah Dennison, Shelly Desai, Michael L. R. Devine, *Tom Donaldson* (1974–77), *Paul E. Doniger* (1967–74), Ray Dooley, Frank Dwyer, Patrick Egan, Paul Eickelberg, John Fitzgibbon, Carol Fleming, Patricia Fletcher, Thomas Francis, Pat Freni, David Friedlander, Dierdre Frouge, Peter Galman, Barbara Gambel, Jake Gardiner, Robert Gatto, Janet Geist, Gary Genard, Edward S. Gero, Laurence Gleason, Gina Gold, *Ginger Grace* (1981–85), Bruce Gray, Sheila Grenham, Arthur Hanket, Jeffrey Hayenga, Christina Heath, F. Richard Holland, Marcia Hyde, Jerri Iaia, Richard Johnson, *Stephen Joyce* (1978–79), *Phillip Kerr* (1979–80), Richard Kite, Ronald Klein, Kathryn Klvana, Michael Kolba, Esther Koslow, Julie Krasnow, Daniel Landon, Keith Langsdale, Linda Lashbrook, *Harris Laskawy* (1967–74), Dennis La Valle, Darrie Lawrence, Brian Lawson, Vivienne Lenk, Thomas Lenz, James Lieb, Nancy Linehan, Dennis Lipscomb, Katherine Marie Loague, Helmut Lohner, Peter Lopez, Larry Lott, Christy Lowery, Howard Lucas, Sandra McAllister, Kevin McClarnon, Lawrence McGlade, Michael McGuinness, John Mackay, Christiane McKenna, Mary McLain, Craig Marin, *Christopher Martin* (1968–85), Harriet Mason, Miles Mason, Roger Mason, Paul Meacham, Douglas Moore, Richard Mover, Brian Muehl, Barry Mulholland, Bill Nickerson, *Mary Eileen O'Donnell* (1978–84), Patricia O'Donnell, Owen O'Farrell, John Ryker O'Hara, Charles H. Patterson, Guy Paul, Tonia Payne, Ronald Perlman, Erika Petersen, Paul J. Pfadenhauer, Frank Pita, Blake Morgan Pitchford, Jack Powell, Jessica Powell, Robert Quinn, Essene R, Jennifer Reed, Diane Rieck, Jose Rodriguez, Brian Rose, Helene Rose, Michael Rothhaar, Catherine Rust, Susan Sadler, Van Santvoord, Claude-Albert Saucier, Harlan Schneider, Carol Schultz, Kurt Semel, David Sennett, Lisa Shea, Leslie Shreve, *Noble Shropshire* (1976–85), Gary Sloan, David Snizek, *Tom Spackman* (1981–85), *Tom Spiller* (1980–85), Diana Stagner, Ginny Stahlman, *Robert Stattel* (1978–82, 1984–85), Susan Stern, Shelley Stolaroff, *Karen Sunde* (1971–85), Rivka Szatmary, Eric Tavaris, Robert Todd, Alberto Tore, Andrew Traines, Martin Treat, Earl Trussell, Peter Tulipan, Patrick Tull, Debora Valle, Peter Van Norden, Susan Varon, Linda Varvel, John C. Vennema, William Verdeber, Amy Warner, Ara Watson, Pam Welch, Randall Wheatley, Jerry Whiddon, Christie Max Williams, Walter Williamson, Wayne Wofford, *Kathryn Wyman* (1967–74), Donn Youngstrom.

REPERTORY

1967–68: *Hamlet, Man and Superman, The Cavern, Tartuffe.*

1968–69: *Poor Bitos, Uncle Vanya, The Cavern, Tartuffe.*

1969–70: *The Revenger's Tragedy, Poor Bitos, Uncle Vanya, Man and Superman, Goat Island, Moby Dick.*

1970–71: *Hamlet, Rosencrantz and Guildenstern Are Dead, Moby Dick, Twelfth Night, Man and Superman, Pericles, Uncle Vanya.*

1971–72: *Marat/Sade, Julius Caesar, The Inspector General, Titus Andronicus.*

1972–73: *The Homecoming, Rosencrantz and Guildenstern Are Dead, The Tempest, Macbeth, The Devils, Rashomon, Loot, Measure for Measure, The Pool Hall of the Heart, Anna-Luse, Fire-Eater's Enemy.*

1973–74: *Moby Dick, Twelfth Night, The Misanthrope, Miss Julie, The Homecoming, Rosencrantz and Guildenstern Are Dead, The Revenger's Tragedy, Hedda Gabler, The Dwarfs* and *The Dumbwaiter, Under Milk Wood.*

1974–75: *Hedda Gabler, The Tempest, The Maids, Edward II, The Lady's Not for Burning, The Servant, Antigone, Woyzeck, The Dwarfs.*

1975–76: *Measure for Measure, Hedda Gabler, A Country Scandal, Antigone, The Hound of the Baskervilles.*

1976–77: *Heartbreak House, The Homecoming, Bingo, Tartuffe, The Balcony.*

1977–78: *A Midsummer Night's Dream, Rosmersholm, Serjeant Musgrave's Dance, The Maids, The Running of the Deer, The Madwoman of Chaillot.*

1978–79: *Richard II, Henry IV*, Parts I and II, *Wild Oats, The Marquis of Keith.*

1979–80: *Cuchulain the Warrior King, The Cavern, Doctor Faustus, Don Juan, The Merchant of Venice.*

1980–81: *Oedipus Rex, Oedipus at Colonus, Antigone, Gilles de Rais, Woyzeck* and *Leonce and Lena.*

1981–82: *Peer Gynt*, Parts I and II, *The Cherry Orchard, King Lear, Ghost Sonata.*

1982–83: *Faust*, Parts I and II, *Ghost Sonata, Wild Oats, Balloon, Danton's Death.*

1983–84: *Big and Little/Scenes, Faust*, Parts I and II, *Hamlet, Dance of Death.*

1984–85: *Agamemnon, Electra/Orestes, Georges Dandin, The Underpants, Frankenstein.*

1985–86: *Brand, Frankenstein, A Country Doctor, Divine Orlando.*

BIBLIOGRAPHY

Published Sources:
Best Plays, 1967–68 through *1985–86.* New York: Dodd, Mead, & Co., 1969–87.
Theatre Profiles. Vols. 1–7. New York: Theatre Communications Group, 1973–86.
Theatre World, 1967–68 through *1985–86.* New York: Crown Publishers, 1969–87.

Archival Resource:
New York, New York. Classic Stage Company. Scrapbooks.

Ken Davis

D

DALLAS THEATRE CENTER was founded in 1955 as civic leaders in Dallas, Texas, realized a need for a theatre in which groups of all ages could work and learn. Bea Handel, formerly a resident of Cleveland and there actively involved with the Cleveland Play House*, wanted a civic-operated, nonprofit community theatre, with a permanent professional staff and paid apprentices, where amateurs of all ages could participate. John Rosenfield, drama critic of *Dallas Morning News*, helped her to arrange a seminal meeting in August 1954. Dallas merchandising executive and art patron Robert Stecker later saw the need for a place where college-trained performers and technicians could acquire the experience necessary to prepare them for professional careers. After visits to theatre professionals and educators in the East, Stecker led a campaign, culminating February 21, 1955, to charter the Dallas Theatre Center (DTC) as a nonprofit educational theatre. The founders asked Paul Baker, director of the Baylor University Theatre in Waco, Texas, to become managing director. Baker, already a nationally and internationally known theatre artist and educator, shared Robert Stecker's belief that university-trained theatre artists needed additional nurturance and development. Furthermore, Baker's educational philosophy, founded on a belief in the creative potential—that "little bit of God" —in every person, appealed to businessmen in the Texas Bible Belt. Baker accepted and dedicated himself to the development of a repertory company, an organization he believed to be especially beneficial in developing versatile artists.

The founders opted to acquire land and build a theatre. Sylvan T. Baer donated a wooded tract of land on Turtle Creek Boulevard, and Frank Lloyd Wright, America's foremost architect, consented to design the building. Funds raised locally included a major bequest in memory of the late Kalita Humphreys, an actress after whom the building was named. Despite some difficulties in reconciling Wright's concept of "organic simplicity" with Baker's minimal needs for access to the stage from adjacent scenery shops, the founders built and equipped an open or thrust stage and an auditorium seating 416 for slightly less than $1 million. Faculty of the drama department at Baylor University in Waco, one hundred miles from Dallas, staffed the facility.

Baker then moved Baylor University's graduate program in drama to the DTC. Auditions held in Dallas, Los Angeles, New York, and London in 1959 recruited the first graduate class and company at DTC. Locally solicited gifts and grants provided for fellowships for the graduate student company, while tuition from students in the graduate program, in the Teen-Children's theatre program, and in the adult education program funded the startup. Heroic efforts on the part of Baker and his colleagues resulted in the unofficial opening of the center, for classes only, in September 1959. DTC's long struggle for artistic achievement, public acceptance, and critical esteem began December 27, 1959, with a production of an adaptation by Baker, Baylor playwriting teacher Eugene McKinney, and students at Baylor of Thomas Wolfe's sprawling novel *Of Time and the River*.

As the inaugural season progressed, Dallas critics, apparently wanting professional performers, not students in training, chided the company for its youthfulness, suggesting that many roles required maturer performers. Critics and patrons alike complained of the use of theatrical gimmickry to cover the inadequacy of the script and its direction. Overworked students quit in exhaustion. Some professionally experienced company members, convinced that their talent as actors exempted them from technical and front-of-house duties, chafed at Baker's insistence that each person perform a variety of duties. Nevertheless, 156 performances of nine productions played to 40,224 admissions. Box-office receipts were $143,770, about two-thirds of the cost of operations, or enough to permit the company to complete its first year without a deficit.

Baker recruited a new company for 1960–61, relying mainly on people he had known before coming to DTC, performers and technicians who understood and accepted DTC's limitations and challenges in order to be part of a developing theatre. The reconstituted company renewed its dedication to developing the training and production program for teens and children and, with a public acknowledgment of the influence of Dallasite Margo Jones, added a new program: the "Dark Night" staged readings of new plays. A production of Shakespeare's *The Taming of the Shrew* was popular, but attendance at all functions fell 8,000 short of the first year's mark. The glamorous new theatre was filled to only 35 percent of capacity. Baker had predicted it would taken ten years to develop a professional resident company out of local talent, but he had not anticipated the hostile press, unresponsive audiences, recalcitrant personnel, and inadequate rehearsal and technical space he was to encounter in the first two years.

In an effort to resuscitate the company, Baker used guest artists in six of the eight productions of 1961–62. Rick Besoyan's *Little Mary Sunshine*, the most popular show of the first three years, starred Miriam Gulager, wife of television actor Clu Gulager, a Baylor graduate. Guest director Pedro Mortheiru, an outstanding Latin-American theatre artist, directed Sergio Vodanovic's *Let the Dogs*

Bark, the first Chilean play to be staged in the United States. Burl Ives starred in *Joshua Beene and God*, written by Dallas playwright Hal Lewis, managing editor of *Dallas Times Herald*, while famed mime artist Angna Enters directed *The Snow Queen*, by Emily Jefferson and Beatrice Gaspar, the first Teen-Children's Theatre "Christmas Spectacular." Edmond Ryan starred in Howard Fast's *The Crossing*, a play about George Washington on the eve of the battle for Trenton. Norman Corwin, a Hollywood radio director and writer, directed Charles Ferguson's *Naked to Mine Enemies*, while Australian Robin Lovejoy directed Claire Booth Luce's *The Women*. In response to the guest artists, attendance and box-office income doubled. *Joshua Beene and God* and *The Snow Queen* were sold out and other productions played to an average 72 percent of capacity. The season established DTC as a playwright's theatre; four of the major productions were premieres. A tour of Philip C. Lewis' *Mirror Under the Eagle* was successful and enrollment in the graduate and other educational programs increased. In 1962 Paul Baker was awarded the Rodgers and Hammerstein Award for accomplishments in theatre in the Southwest.

The 1962–63 season saw the addition of the "Academy," a two-year certificate program for high school graduates and university undergraduates. Shakespeare's *Julius Caesar* was the most popular of twelve major productions; critics were more responsive but remained confused about the identity of the theatre. DTC claimed to be professional but was affiliated with no professional theatre unions.

In 1963 Baker and his entire staff resigned at Baylor over censorship of a production of Eugene O'Neill's *A Long Day's Journey into Night*. Trinity University in San Antonio engaged them and assumed support of the graduate program in theatre at DTC. The highlight of the year was an opportunity to present *Journey to Jefferson*, Robert Flynn's adaptation of William Faulkner's *As I Lay Dying*, at the Theatre of Nations in Paris and in other European cities. Grants and donations from leading Dallas citizens financed an unexpectedly successful European tour. In competition with such world-famous companies as the Moscow Art Theatre, the Abbey Theatre of Dublin, and the Shakespeare Festival Company of England, the DTC was awarded the Special Jury Prize for the best production of the festival. Baker, who regarded the European tour as DTC's greatest achievement, has written: "This play represented the best we could do. . . . We felt we were authorities in some ways on the Faulkner country and characters. . . . It was a play that we knew and understood" (*Dallas Theatre Center, 1959–79: Twenty Dynamic Years* [Dallas, Tex.: Dallas Theatre Center, 1979], p. 6). Meanwhile productions in the newly opened Down Center Stage, a proscenium theatre seating seventy-four in the basement of the Kalita Humphreys Theatre, largely supplanted the Dark Night readings. The 1963–64 season consisted of 418 performances for a then record attendance of 94,993. By this time company regulars Mary Sue Fridge (later Jones) and Ronald Wilcox had worked together for eight years and were mature performers. Numerous beneficent funds started by Dallas citizens for DTC suggested the growing status of the company.

Michael O'Sullivan, whose Tartuffe had astonished New York critics and audiences in 1964–65, came to Dallas in 1965 to play Prospero in an extravagant production of Shakespeare's *The Tempest*, which featured as well splendid costumes designed by Scandinavian artist Bjorn Wiinblad. In this sprawling, exhausting season, 408 performances of twenty-two productions played to 94,594 persons. Despite growing audiences and increasing critical esteem, costs increased faster than income, and the theatre experienced its first deficit.

In 1966–67 Trinity University built the Ruth Taylor Theatre in San Antonio and began engaging DTC actors and productions. In Dallas, audiences continued to grow as eighteen productions drew 112,227. West German Harry Buckwitz directed Bertolt Brecht's *The Caucasian Chalk Circle* and Jean-Pierre Granval of the Théâtre Français directed Georges Feydeau's *A Flea in Her Ear*, translated *A Bug in Her Ear* by company member Barnett Shaw. The work of these international visitors drew critical raves but a cool audience response. The hit of the season was the Preston Jones–directed copy of the Broadway production of Neil Simon's *Barefoot in the Park*.

By 1967 the graduate program had conferred fifty-one master's degrees; eleven of these persons remained at the theatre as part of the permanent repertory company, then numbering twenty-seven. *Village Voice* drama critic Julius Novick visited DTC in 1967 and observed: "Nowhere in this country, perhaps, are a professional theatre and a professional training program more closely integrated than at the Dallas Theatre Center. Of the twenty-seven actors, directors, designers, technicians, and administrators who form the permanent company, fourteen hold academic positions on the twenty-member faculty, and most of the remaining faculty members also work in various capacities with the company, as do students. . . . And though the Center does not operate under an Equity contract, it has a genuinely permanent professional company, with a core of members who have worked together for years" (*Beyond Broadway* [New York: Hill and Wang, 1969], p. 258). Novick went on to observe, however: "The Center is an anomalous institution, trying to perform two separate functions simultaneously; *R. U. Hungry*, in spite of some fine acting by some mature actors, made better sense as a drama-school exercise than as a professional production, but the Center does not make any such distinctions among its offerings." He concluded that the program of DTC was "ambitiously eclectic" (*Beyond Broadway*, p. 260).

By the season of 1967–68 DTC was fully committed to the Baker plan of operation. Operating on a slender budget of just over $349,000, Baker employed visiting directors Norman Ayrton, principal of the London Academy of Music and Dramatic Arts; Kosta Spaic, artistic director of the Dubrovnik (Yugoslavia) Festival; and renowned American actor-director Burgess Meredith in a bustling season of 432 performances of twenty plays, including several world premieres. Outreach programs continued to expand with a grant from the U.S. Department of Health, Education, and Welfare to take theatre to public schools in Dallas and funding from the Junior League of Dallas for creative dramatics classes in low-income housing projects in West Dallas. Baker received the Margo Jones Award for stimulating the production of new plays.

In 1968–69 an addition to the theatre provided two rehearsal studios and additional office space. Earned income accounted for 85 percent of the budget of the company, operating then, as were few in the growing regional theatre movement, without federal grants and without national foundation aid. However, operating expenses were rapidly increasing, while local resources were stable or declining. The success of the DTC company had been based on the relentless efforts of a hardworking company as Baker added more performances of more productions each year. Total audience increased and income mounted, but audience attendance, as a percentage of capacity, rose from 61 percent in 1959 to only 67 percent in 1969. The company added the Magic Turtle Series of Children's Theatre productions in 1969–70, thereby pushing the total of performances in the season to more than 500. However, three dinner theatres in the Dallas area offered competition with popular dramas and musicals, and area community and college theatre programs were growing. A revival of the previous season's *Macbeth* at the spacious Bronco Bowl Playhouse in suburban Dallas drew school audiences in large numbers, but the entire series of plays in the Kalita Humphreys Theatre played to only 51 percent of capacity. Overall attendance fell by 25,000 and the theatre experienced a significant budget deficit. Despite increased fund-raising efforts, increased attendance, and some budget slashing, DTC had a deficit in 1970–71 of $130,000. Local fund-raising was only modestly successful at best. Nevertheless, Baker established, with the aid of grants from the Moody Foundation of Galveston, the National Endowment for the Arts, and other organizations and individuals, the Janus Players, the first minority theatre in Texas.

In 1971–72 several new initiatives in publicity and public relations attracted a wider audience. DTC sold 7,500 season tickets, overall attendance picked up, and income increased. Additional fund-raising efforts and deep budget cuts permitted the DTC to realize a profit in 1971–72 and to retire a debt it had carried from deficits in previous years.

In 1973 the DTC board of directors deeded the theatre complex to the city of Dallas, which commenced to maintain the facility, and the board increased its participation in setting artistic and management policies. Baker's approach to solving DTC's financial and artistic problems by multiplying programs and productions alienated some board members, one of whom, Paul Corley, complained to the press that the DTC was an educational institution, not the professional theatre company Dallas wanted. Corley called for greater use of outside talent and suggested that the graduate program at DTC should be terminated. Baker's efforts to hush this popular Dallas businessman alienated portions of Dallas' corporate world and undermined the potential for financial support from that sector. In summarizing his investigation of DTC's first thirteen years of operation, John Carl Marder III, a graduate of Baker's program, noted a shroud of controversy and criticism. Supporters close to the organization had faulted it for its range of activities. Students complained of being underpaid and overworked;

critics disapproved of the kinds of plays produced and of the quality of productions; and Dallas audiences had silently ignored the Center's productions or expressed concern over the choice, staging, and casting of plays ("A History of the Development and Growth of the Dallas Theater Center." Doctoral dissertation, University of Kansas, 1972, p. 210). In 1974, at the board's behest, Baker, age sixty-three, agreed to retire on August 1, 1981.

An event called "The New Play Market" initiated in 1974 and repeated in 1976 and 1979 brought directors, writers, critics, and agents from throughout the United States and Great Britain to see six to ten full-length, fully produced new plays in less than a week. The first "Market" featured *Jack Ruby, All-American Boy*, by John Logan and Paul Baker; a rock musical version of *A Midsummer Night's Dream*, by Randolph Tallman and Steven Mackenroth; and two parts of Preston Jones's "Bradleyville Trilogy," *The Last Meeting of the Knights of the White Magnolia* and *Luann Hampton Laverty Oberlander*. Jon Jory witnessed the 1974 event and adapted it with great success at the Actors Theatre of Louisville*. More significantly, the DTC company was reborn to a new sense of independence and self-respect. Some spoke out for change in the Baker approach, especially more money, fewer hours, and affiliation with Actors' Equity, the union of professional actors. The new plays attracted more patrons, and in 1973–74 DTC sold 10,488 subscriptions and played to 80 percent of capacity. Succeeding Play Markets continued to break down the isolation of the company by focusing national and international attention on it. However, detractors claimed that in-breeding, long a bane of DTC, was in no way mitigated, for most of the plays featured in the Markets were written by DTC company members. Nevertheless, the outpouring of new plays was impressive: from 1973 to 1978 forty-two of ninety-one DTC productions were world premieres.

In 1976–77 the DTC budget surged past the $1 million mark; subscriptions stood at just above 10,000 and the theatres were filled to about 80 percent of capacity. In 1979 Baker added a 100-seat balcony to the Kalita Humphreys theatre, and in 1980 general manager Bruce Swerdfager negotiated an actor-teacher contract with Actors' Equity Association whereby the company became partially unionized. As might be expected, expenses zoomed upward past the $3 million mark in 1982–83. On the other hand, attendance increased to a total of 175,000, and subscriptions reached an all-time DTC high of 14,000. However, unionization did not quell persistent complaints about the quality of acting by student performers. Baker responded in 1980–81 with renewed dedication to improving the quality of productions through the use of distinguished guest directors, bringing in Anton Rodgers, Joan Vail Thorne, and Derek Goldby. This strategy left undisturbed the root of the problem of quality, which stemmed from Baker's persistence in attempting too many productions and outreach programs with too little financial backing. The company either had to attempt fewer different projects and exploit the acting strengths of its longtime members in more compact seasons of productions requiring smaller casts, or it had to solicit major foundation and government support to increase the size of the core professional company. Baker was an educator, however, and dedicated to heavy use of student performers in training. He was also dedicated to the despecialization of theatre training and practice, a dedication that thrust him far outside the mainstream of American professional theatre. Unionization and institutionalization along conventional resident theatre lines was anathema to Baker, who continued to resist the reformation of a company about which he was proudly possessive.

In 1980 the DTC board urged Baker to hire a dynamic and visionary general manager in the person of Bruce Swerdfager. Baker had a long history of regularly hiring and then dismissing general and business managers. Swerdfager lasted for seven months. At the beginning of the 1981–82 season the board intervened more deeply in company management in hiring Albert Milano, former managing director of the Dallas Symphony and an effective fund-raiser. Baker (still working months past his scheduled retirement date of August 1) briefly accepted Milano and then turned against him, thereby tilting the board of directors into a full-scale effort to force Baker's resignation and to affiliate the Center with nearby Southern Methodist University. Baker fought back, attempting to rally the company to strike if the board had its way. In May 1982 the board and Baker reached a compromise that held the company together. Mary Sue (Fridge) Jones, longtime assistant and associate director of the company, was named interim artistic director for 1982–83. Baker resigned on May 13, 1982, ending twenty-three years of leadership as managing director of the DTC.

In her year as interim managing director, Jones had little support from the board and little cooperation from Milano, and got little consideration in the search for a new artistic director.

The search committee located Adrian Hall, fifty-six-year-old artistic director and founder of the Trinity Square Repertory Company* in Providence, Rhode Island. The Texas-born Hall pledged to build in Dallas a nationally prestigious and internationally renowned resident company (despite the stipulation that he spend only half of each year in Dallas, as he planned to continue his work in Providence). Hall looked briefly at Baker's longtime associates and offered work to only a few, choosing to import talent from Providence until he could hire or develop better local performers, a decision that alienated local performers.

Hall insisted on a second, more "environmental" playing space, and Milano and the DTC board persuaded the city of Dallas to make room for a theatre in its new arts district. The Arts District Theatre, a flexible playing space in a prefabricated metal building, was hastily built and equipped according to plans drawn up by Eugene Lee, Hall's designer at Trinity Square. The location has not, however, proved attractive to Dallas theatre patrons, while low-flying aircraft and thunderstorms have on occasion briefly halted productions.

Hall and Milano fought over Milano's efforts to control costs and over Milano's involvement in the production of competing touring shows in the Majestic Theatre Broadway Series. Milano resigned in 1984, to be succeeded by Peter Donnelly as executive managing director. Hall changed the names of the theatres to the Frank Lloyd Wright Theatre and "In the Basement"; he terminated the graduate program in theatre and moved the Teen-Children's Theatre program out of the Center. Attendance and subscription sales dropped sharply. Observers concede that Hall has improved the artistic quality of DTC presentations, but the reception accorded him and his imported performers has been an apparent source of frustration for Hall.

Despite the turmoil and tension clouding its history, the DTC has been a force in the development of theatre in the Southwest. As a more or less university-based professional theatre, it has not achieved the fame and distinction of such organizations as the Yale Repertory Theatre*, the McCarter Theatre Company*, or the American Repertory Theatre*. Its distinction lies in its long survival as an anomaly in the resident theatre movement in America. Its dedication to graduate theatre education, to community outreach, and to the development of new plays and new playwrights, as well as its longtime resistance to the lure of unionization and institutionalization dependent on large federal and foundation subsidy, make it a truly distinctive element of the American theatre scene.

PERSONNEL

Managing Directors: Paul Baker (1959–82), Adrian Hall (1983–86), Mary Sue Fridge Jones (1982–83).

Executive Managing Director: Peter Donnelly (1984–86).

Assistant/Associate Director: Mary Sue Fridge Jones (1967–82).

Administrative Director: Gary Moore (1971–74).

Business Manager: Glenn Allen Smith (1974–75).

General Managers: Albert Milano (1981–84), Bruce Swerdfager (1980–81).

Directors: Larry Arrick (1983–84), Norman Ayrton (1967–68), Bob Baca (1965–66, 1967–68), *Paul Baker* (1959–71, 1972–76, 1977–79), Word Baker (1983–84), Joe Bousard (1973–74), Harry Buckwitz (1966–67, 1969–70), Ruth Byers, (1962–63, 1964–66), Fernando Colina (1968–69), Norman Corwin (1962), Hanna Cusick (1980–81), Linda Daugherty (1974–75), *Judith Kelly Davis* (1971–72, 1973–74, 1975–76, 1977–78, 1979–81), Don Davlin (1964–65), *Michael Dendy* (1966–69, 1971–74), Kaki Dowling (1964–65, 1969–70), Angna Enters (1961–62), Victor Fichtner (1965–66), *John Figlmiller* (1966–67, 1969–70, 1973–74), *Robyn Baker Flatt* (1964–66, 1976–77, 1979–81), Claudette Gardner (1969–70), Peter Gerety (1983–84), Derek Goldby (1980–81), Jean-Pierre Granval (1966–67), Cecile Guidote (1966–67), *Adrian Hall* (1983–86), Warren Hammack (1961–62, 1965–66), James Nelson Harrell (1967–68), C. P. Hendrie (1979–80), John Henson (1970–71, 1976–77, 1979–80), Edward Herrmann (1969–70), Mary Lou Hoyle (1980–81), Tom Hughes (1963–64), Richard Jenkins (1983–84), *Mary Sue Fridge Jones* (1968–70, 1972–73, 1979–80), *Preston Jones* (1963–64, 1965–66, 1967–70, 1971–72), Howard A. Karlsberg (1966–67), Jan Kessler (1962–63), Jeffrey Kinghorn (1980–81), *Ken Latimer* (1961–62, 1963–73, 1974–78), Barbara le Brun (1965–66), Irene Lewis, (1968–69), Eleanor Lindsay (1980–81), *John Logan* (1967–68, 1976–77, 1978–81), Rebecca Logan (1968–69), Robin Lovejoy (1962–63, 1964–66), Peter Lynch (1980–81), Theodore Mann (1969–70), Anna Paul Marsh–Neame (1967–69), David Martin (1962–63), Mark Medoff (1980–81), Burgess Meredith (1967–68), *Ryland Merkey* (1962–68, 1970–71, 1972–73, 1976–80), Albert Millaire (1977–78), Reginald Montgomery (1971–

72), Randall Moore (1962–63, 1964–65), Pedro Mortheiru (1961–62), Louise Mosley (1966–68), Paul Munger (1980–81), Sally Netzel (1969–71, 1972–73), Carveth Osterhaus (1964–65), David Pursley (1962–63, 1966–68, 1972–73), Mary Bozeman Raines (1963–64), Bryant J. Reynolds (1971–72, 1976–77, 1979–80), *Ivan Rider* (1961–64, 1966–67), Rosalie Robinson (1969–70), Anton Rodgers (1980–81), Anna Paul Rogers (1965–68), Frank Schaefer (1965–66, 1968–69), Michael Scudday (1980–81), John Shepherd (1969–70), Buddy Smith (1965–66), Glenn Allen Smith (1968–69), Kosta Spaic (1967–68), Randolph Tallman (1969–70, 1973–75, 1978–79), Campbell Thomas (1968–72), Joan Vail Thorne (1980–81), Lynn Trammell (1965–66), Evangelos Voutsinas (1969–70), Leonard T. Wagner (1966–67), George Webby (1966–68), David Wheeler (1983–84), Duk Hyung Yoo (1965–66).

Designers: (Nearly all DTC designers have credits in two or three areas of theatrical design, so no distinction as to design speciality is made here.) Deborah Allen (1979–80), Fil Alvarado (1969–70), Archie Andres (1968–69), *Yoichi Aoki* (1967–81), Sally Askins (1979–81), Bob Baca (1965–68), Pat Baca (1966–67), Word Baker (1983–84), Sally Dorothy Bailey (1980–81), *Virgil Beavers* (1964–81), Kathleen Benke (1965–68), Michael Bennett (1965–66), *Linda Blase* (1972–79), Ruthanne Boyles (1966–67), Ella-Mae Brainard (1964–68), Jere Broussard (1968–69), Paul Buboltz (1976–77), Anne Butler (1966–69), Gregory K. Caffy (1969–70), Gene Clampitt (1968–70), Charlotte Cole (1964–68), Marta Cole (1965–66), Fernando Colina (1968–69), Daryl Conner (1974–75), Irene Corey (1974–75, 1979–80), Ruthanne Cozine (1965–66), Robin Crews (1976–77), Judith Davis (1969–70), *Cheryl Denson* (1973–81), Deanna Devereaux (1975–76), Don Devlin (1968–69), Robert Dickson (1969–70, 1973–74), Denise Drennen (1976–77), John Duffy (1980–81), *Robert Duffy* (1975–76, 1978–81), Deanna Dunagan (1969–70), James Eddy (1979–80), David Edwards (1982–83), Zarin Engineer (1965–66), Bill Enix (1966–67), Leonard Feldman (1964–65), John Fish (1968–69), Richard Flatt (1964–65), *Robyn Baker Flatt* (1964–76), David Gibson (1964–66), George T. Green (1974–75), Russell Guinn (1971–72), Warren Hammack (1964–65), L. Scott Hammar (1980–81), Raynard Harper (1980–81), Tim Haynes (1979–81), *John Henson* (1969–81), Edward Herrmann (1966–67), Zak Herring (1980–81), *Allen Hibbard* (1969–84), John Holloway (1979–80), Mary Lou Hoyle (1980–81), Doug Jackson (1980–81), Charles Jarrell (1968–69), Pamela Jensen (1976–77), M. G. Johnston (1979–80), *Mary Sue Fridge Jones* (1965–79), Celia Karston (1974–75), Marshall Kaufman (1971–72), *Donna Kress* (1983–86), Michael Krueger (1976–77, 1979–80), Reta LaForce (1967–68), *Kathleen Latimer* (1967–79), Ken Latimer (1969–70), Sallie Laurie (1973–74, 1977–78), Renne LeCuyer (1980–81), *Eugene Lee* (1983–86), Lynn Lester (1969–71), *Nancy Levinson* (1964–70, 1973–75), Patricia Lobit (1972–73), Robin Lovejoy (1964–66), Peter Lynch (1979–81), Stella McCord (1980–81), Steven Mackenroth (1968–70), James Maronek (1983–84), Marian-Smith Martin (1971–72), Joan Meister (1969–70), Ryland Merkey (1964–67), Carol Miles (1980–81), Rayanne Miller (1977–78), Reginald Montgomery (1969–70), Gary Moore, (1965–66), *Randy Moore* (1966–67, 1968–81), Roger Morgan (1983–84), Louise Mosley (1969–70), Sam Nance (1971–76), Tina Navarro (1967–68), Lorenzo Nelson (1966–67), *Sally Netzel* (1965–67, 1969–78), Thomas Nichols (1966–67), Sharon O'Kelley (1964–65), Carveth Osterhaus (1964–65), Randolph Pearson (1975–76), George Pettit (1977–78), Sandra Pope (1964–65), Jean Progar (1969–70), David Pursley (1964–69, 1972–73), Mona Pursley (1965–66), Janice Rabinovitz (1966–67), Judith Rhodes (1973–74), A. J. Rogers (1967–71), Roberta Rude (1968–70), Martin L. Sachs (1980–81), Barbara Sanderson (1980–81), Anna Paul Schaefer (1964–66), Frank Schaefer (1965–66, 1968–

69), Gregory Schwab (1980–81), Michael Scudday (1979–81), Lavonia Shaw (1965–66), Robert Shook (1983–84), Cinda Siler (1964–66), Susan Sleeper (1978–79), Richard Slocum (1964–67), Cliff Smith (1979–80), Paul John Smith (1968–69), Nantawan Soonthorndhai (1969–70), Harold Carle Sparks (1969–70), Johanna Stalker (1968–72), Ann Stephens (1982–83), Jeff Storer (1980–81), Bonnie Stroup (1972–73), Margaret Tallman (1972–73), Carleton Tanner (1960–70), Gina Taulene (1975–76), Campbell Thomas 1969–70), Don Thomas (1979–80), Matt Tracy (1966–67), Leonard T. Wagner (1964–65), Steve Wallace (1976–77), Lydia Lee Weeks (1969–70), Larry Wheeler (1969–70), Bjorn Wiinblad (1965–66), Nancy Wilkins (1980–81), Rodger Wilson (1977–78), *Peter Wolf* (1973–79), Michael Wray (1969–71), Margaret Yount (1969–71), Duk Hyung Yoo (1965–67).

Guest Artists: Dale Barnhart (1971–72), Tom Bloom (1983–84), Candy Buckley (1982–83), Rocco Bufano (1971–72), Jeanne Cairns (1982–83), Carole Cook (1971–72), Christopher Councill (1982–83), Timothy Crowe (1983–84), Roger DeKoven (1981–82), Richard Dow (1981–82), Stephanie Dunnan (1984–85), Don Eitner (1971–72), Dolores Ferraro (1975–76), Anne Gerety (1984–85), Derek Goldby (1981–82), Jack Gwillim (1982–83), Warren Hammack (1981–82), Eric Hause (1981–82), David Healy (1975–76), Patrick Hines (1983–84), Gloria Hocking (1982–83), James Hurdle (1982–83), Burl Ives (1961–62), C. Bernard Jackson (1971–72), Richard Jenkins (1983–84), David C. Jones (1983–85), Stratis Karras (1970–71), Richard Kavanaugh (1983–85), Richard Kneeland (1983–85), Jerome Lawrence (1972–73), Walter Leaning (1981–82), Nancy Levinson (1972–73), Becca Lish (1983–84), Jo Livingston (1981–82), Robin Lovejoy (1975–76), Rallou Manou (1971–72), Molly McGreevy (1971–72), Theodore Mann (1970–71), Mark Medoff (1977–78), Barbara Meek (1983–84), Albert Millaire (1977–78), Moody Gary (1982–83), Norma Moore (1982–83), Takis Muzenidis (1971–72), Deirdre O'Connell (1983–84), Barbara Orson (1984–85), Cliff Osmond (1981–82), Michael O'Sullivan (1965–66), Jenny Pichanick (1982–83), David Pursley (1981–82), Ford Rainey (1984–85), John Reich (1972–73), Anton Rodgers (1981–82), Marcee Smith (1982–83), Steven Snyder (1983–84), Cliff Stephens (1982–83), Cynthia Strickland (1983–84), William Swetland (1984–85), Carol Teitel (1972–73), Lee Theodore (1971–72), Joan Vail Thorne (1981–82), Tom Troupe (1971–72), Daniel Von Bargen (1983–85), Norbert Weisser (1984–85), Lou Williford (1982–83), Paul Winfield (1982–83).

Musical Directors: Raymond Allen (1968–70), Russ Hoffman (1980–81).

Actors and Actresses: John Addington (1984–85), Cointon Anderson (1983–84), Yoichi Aoki (1976–80, 1981–82), Sally Askins (1981–83), Bob Baca (1965–68), Pat Baca (1966–67), Sally Dorothy Bailey (1980–81), Rita Barnes (1963–65), Susan Bayer (1983–84), Virgil Beavers (1978–82), Kathleen Benke (1965–66), Michael Bennett (1965–66), Garry Beveridge (1980–81), Annette Bishop (1980–81), Dale Blair (1966–67, 1968–69), *Linda Blase* (1974–80), Bill Bolender (1983–85), Randy Bonifay (1979–83), *Ella-Mae Brainard* (1962–70), Royal Brantley (1980–81), Victor Bravo (1982–83), John Brook (1980–81), Lisa Brown (1980–81), Candy Buckley (1983–85), Sharon Bunn (1983–84), Bob Burrus (1965–66), Alex Burton (1968–69), Peggy Ann Byers (1983–84), Ballard H. Byron (1980–81), Jeanne Cairns (1983–84), Henry Carter (1965–66), Bob Chapman (1983–84), Mary Cheatham (1963–64), Michael Cherkinian (1984–85), Sa'Mi Chester (1984–85), Margery Clive (1984–85), Richard Cohen (1968–69), Charlote Cole (1965–66, 1967–68), Chris Coleman (1984–85), Carole Cook (1962–63), Jon Stephen Crane (1966–67), John Cullum (1959–60), Hanna Cusick (1981–82), Melvin O. Dacus (1983–85), John S. Davies (1980–81, 1984–85), *Judith Davis* (1965–67, 1969–83), Don Davlin (1968–

70), *Michael Dendy* (1965–74), Felicia Denney (1980–81), *Cheryl Denson* (1976–82), Keith Dixon (1976–78), Kaki Dowling (1963–64, 1966–71), *Robert Duffy* (1979–83), Deanna Dunagan (1968–69), David Edwards (1980–81), Nancy Lewis Edwards (1980–81), R. Bruce Elliot (1983–84), Susan Engbrecht (1980–81), Zarin Engineer (1965–66), Sue Erdman (1963–64), Clyde Evans (1966–67), Scott Everhart (1984–85), Dwain Fall (1984–85), Hugh Feagin (1983–84), Victor Fichtner (1965–67), James Fields (1984–85), *John Figlmiller* (1964–84), Ann Fischer (1980–81), Niki Flacks (1983–84), *Robyn Baker Flatt* (1965–83), Robert Frost (1963–64, 1965–67), *Claudette Gardner* (1965–66, 1967–70), Andrew Christopher Gaupp (1981–83), Linda Gehringer (1983–85), Bo Gerard (1984–85), Peter Gerety (1983–84), Linda Giese (1965–67), Anna Gonyaw (1963–68), *Martha Robinson Goodman* (1976–82), Robert Graham (1983–85), *Tim Green* (1968–69, 1978–82), Art Greenhaw (1966–67), Cecile Guidote (1965–66), Miriam Gulager (1961–62, 1966–67), Paul Haggard (1983–84), Ann Hamilton (1983–85), *Warren Hammack* (1962–66), Marianne Hammock (1984–85), John Hancock (1968–69), Lou Hancock (1984–85), Dee Hannigan (1983–84), *James Nelson Harrell* (1962–70), Tim Haynes (1982–83), Susan A. Haynie (1975–76), Russell Henderson (1980–83), *C. P. Hendrie* (1968–69, 1977–81), Dee Hennigan (1984–85), Sean Hennigan (1984–85), *John Henson* (1972–84), Zak Herring (1980–83), *Edward Herrmann* (1965–67, 1969–70), Robert Hess (1980–81), *Allen Hibbard* (1974–82), Kenneth Hill (1980–83), Stanley Hill (1968–69), Susan McDaniel Hill (1980–83), Barry Hope (1965–66), Kaki Hopkins (1981–82), Ken D. Hornbeck (1983–84), Don Howell (1963–64), *Mary Lou Hoyle* (1979–83), Ken Hudson (1980–83), Penelope Hull (1962–63), Don Humphreys (1965–66), Pamela Hurst (1980–82), Lewis Hutcheson (1968–69), Rex Ingram (1965–66), Marian Jeffrey (1984–85), Richard Jenkins (1965–67), John Jenson (1977–78), Linda Johnson (1968–69), *Mary Sue Fridge Jones* (1959–83), *Preston Jones* (1962–79), Mary Sue Joris (1962–63), Stephen Kane (1983–84), Aro Kasper (1963–64), Tom Key (1983–85), Deborah A. Kinghorn (1981–83), Jeffrey Kinghorn (1980–83), Jon Krause (1983–84), Daniel Allen Kremer (1984–85), Reta LaForce (1968–69), *Betty June Lary* (1965–70), *Kathleen Latimer* (1969–79), *Ken Latimer* (1965–79), Sallie Laurie (1976–79), Gary LaVigne (1964–65), Barbara le Brun (1962–63, 1965–66), Linda LeNoir (1980–81), Jeri Leer (1984–85), *Gene Leggett* (1965–72), *Fritz Lennon* (1964–65, 1967–69, 1975–76), Irene Lewis (1969–70), Eleanor Lindsay (1980–83), Jo Livingston (1983–85), *John Logan* (1968–83), *Rebecca Logan* (1968–69, 1974–79), *Ronni Lopez* (1979–83), Robin Lovejoy (1962–63), Lee Lowrimore (1980–81), Elizabeth Lumpkin (1965–66), *Peter Lynch* (1979–83), Johnny McBee (1966–67), Andrea McCall (1984–85), Mary McClure (1980–81), Shelley McClure (1980–81), Stella McCord (1980–83), William McGuire (1962–63), *Steven Mackenroth* (1968–69, 1971–79), Mallory McMillan (1968–69), Jim McQueen (1984–85), Linda Mann (1968–69), Marilyn Markley (1966–67), Lisa Marsh (1980–81), David Martin (1961–63), Linda Martinsen (1964–66), John Marvin (1980–81), Kim Marvin (1981–82), Tom Matts (1983–84), Joan Meister (1974–75), *Ryland Merkey* (1963–82), Penny Metropulos (1965–67), Carol Miles (1980–83), Pat Miller (1965–66), Fred Mills (1968–69), Reginald Montgomery (1972–73), Lynne Moon (1980–83), *Gary Moore* (1965–66, 1972–75), *Norma Moore* (1974–85), *Randy Moore* (1959–85), Sandra Moore (1965–67), John Morrison (1984–85), *Louise Mosley* (later *Louise Mosley Smith*) (1962–82), Nancy Munger (1981–83), Paul Munger (1981–83), Alexis Munro (1965–66), Sam Nance (1975–76), *Sally Netzel* (1966–79), Thomas Nichols (1965–66), Patti O'Donnell (1975–78), Marshall Oglesby (1968–69), Michael O'Hara (1984–85), Arthur Olaisen (1982–83), Carveth Osterhaus (1963–65), Sam Patterson (1980–81), Patricia Pearcy (1968–69), Christopher

Pennywitt (1980–81), Jenny Pichanick (1984–85), Joel Plotkin (1965–66), Sandra Pope (1964–65), Spencer Prokop (1980–81), *David Pursley* (1959–73), *Mona Stiles Pursley* (1959–78), Janice Rabinovitz (1966–67), Mary Bozeman Raines (1961–63), John Rainone (1983–84), Mary Rausch (1964–65), Martin Rayner (1983–85), Patricia Ready (1964–65), Philip Reeves (1980–81), Tim Reischauer (1980–81), *Bryant J. Reynolds* (1972–82), Kurt Rhoads (1984–85), Stephanie Rich (1968–69), *Drexel H. Riley* (1962–63, 1965–67, 1968–69), Camilla Ritchey (1968–69), Jane Roberts (1984–85), Allen Robertson (1965–66), Anna Paul Rogers (1965–66), Arthur Jensen Rogers (1968–69), *Synthia Rogers* (1966–83), *Mary Rohde* (1976–82), Chelcie Ross (1973–75), Keith Rothschild (1968–69), *Roberta Rude* (1965–69), Jane Runnells (1968–69), Robert Runnells (1968–69), Julian Rush (1962–63), Edmond Ryan (1961–62), Dwight Sandell (1984–85), Anna Paul Schaefer (1965–66), *Frank Schaefer* (1963–65, 1968–71), Greg Schulte (1980–81), Bobbie Beth Scoggins (1980–81), Michael Scudday (1980–82), Dan Shackelford (1983–84), Barnett Shaw (1964–66, 1968–70), John Shepherd (1966–67, 1968–69), Cinda Siler (1963–66), Ashley Simmons (1965–66), Richard Slocum (1967–68), Buddy Smith (1966–68), *Glenn Allen Smith* (1975–82), Paul John Smith (1968–69), Robert A. Smith (1978–79), Sally Smith-Peterson (1980–81), Marie Hanes Smithers (1980–81), Octavio Solis (1980–81), George Speer (1980–81), Ann Stephens (1981–83), *John R. Stevens* (1975–80), David Stump (1983–85), Harold Suggs (1984–85), Gary Taggart (1984–85), Kenneth Tallman (1980–81), Margaret Tallman (1972–75), *Randolph Tallman* (1965–82), *Campbell Thomas* (1966–72), *Jacque Thomas* (1966–81), Sigrid Thor (1965–66), Matt Tracy (1975–77), *Lynn Trammell* (1963–83), Jerry Turner (1965–66), Cheryl Tyre (1968–69), Paula Unrau (1980–81), Terry Vandivort (1984–85), Dennis Vincent (1980–83), Leonard T. Wagner (1967–70), Lydia Lee Weeks (1968–69), James Werner (1983–85), Herman Wheatley (1968–69), Lee Wheatley (1978–82), Trudy Wheeler (1980–81), Gary Whitehead (1980–81), *Patti O'Donnell Wilcox* (1963–68), *Ronald Wilcox* (1959–71, 1978–82), Nance Williamson (1984–85), Lou Williford (1983–85), Dustye Winniford (1983–84), Gene Wolande (1982–83), Jenna Worthen (1984–85), Mike Wray (1968–69), John Wright (1980–81), Rudy Young (1983–84), Duk Hyung Yoo (1963–64).

REPERTORY

Kalita Humphreys Theatre (1959–86) and Arts District Theatre (1984–86) (@, world premiere; #, American premier):

1959–60: *Of Time and the River*, @*The Cross-Eyed Bear*, *Hamlet*, *The Importance of Being Earnest*, *Our Town*, *Under Milk Wood*, *A Solid House*, *The Bald Soprano*, *Hay Fever*.

1960–61: *Hay Fever*, *The Matchmaker*, @*A Waltz in the Afternoon*, *The Importance of Being Earnest*, *The Visit*, *A Phoenix Too Frequent*, *The Chairs*, @*Shadow of an Eagle*, *The Taming of the Shrew*, *Hamlet*, *The Mousetrap*, *The Unicorn*, *The Gorgon and the Manticore*, *Romanoff and Juliet*.

1961–62: *Little Mary Sunshine*, #*Let the Dogs Bark*, @*Joshua Beene and God*, @*The Snow Queen*, *The Madwoman of Chaillot*, @*The Crossing*, *The Mousetrap*, @*Naked to Mine Enemies*, *The Women*, *The Rivals*, *Krapp's Last Tape*, *The Man with a Flower in His Mouth*, *Village Wooing*, *Mirror Under the Eagle*.

1962–63: *Sister*, *Julius Caesar*, *The Women*, *The Wizard of Oz*, *As I Lay Dying*, *The Maids*, *The Sandbox*, *The Chairs*, *Auntie Mame*, *The Three Sisters*, *Blood Wedding*, *Under the Yum-Yum Tree*.

1963–64: *The Firebugs, Can-Can, Julius Caesar, @Hip-Hop-a-Hare, Medea, A Different Drummer, @The Tragedy of Thomas Andros, The Comedy of Errors, The Three Sisters, Journey to Jefferson* (formerly *As I Lay Dying*), *Night Must Fall, Come Blow Your Horn.*

1964–65: *Of Thee I Sing, Harvey, Julius Caesar, The Comedy of Errors, Peter Pan, A Different Drummer, Long Day's Journey into Night, What Price Glory? @Wheels a-Rollin', The Rivals, @The Days Between, Mary, Mary, The Marriage-Go-Round.*

1965–66: *The Tempest, The Rivals, Peter Pan, Oh Dad, Poor Dad, Mama's Hung You in the Closet and I'm Feelin' So Sad, Julius Caesar, The Physicists, You Can't Take It with You, @Creep Past the Mountain Lion, Rashomon, @The Golden Warriors, Who's Got the Pot?, Little Mary Sunshine, The Absence of a Cello.*

1966–67: *#A Bug in Her Ear, Blithe Spirit, @Alice in Wonderland, Journey to Jefferson* (formerly *As I Lay Dying*), *You Never Can Tell, The Tempest, Julius Caesar, Luv, The Caucasian Chalk Circle, Barefoot in the Park, Ben Bagley's "The Decline and Fall of the Entire World as Seen Through the Eyes of Cole Porter."*

1967–68: *Twelfth Night, The Odd Couple, A Delicate Balance, Pinocchio, A Streetcar Named Desire, #Vasco, @The Latent Heterosexual, Charley's Aunt, Spoon River Anthology, The Girl of the Golden West, Under the Yum-Yum Tree.*

1968–69: *Macbeth, Hippolytus, Iphigenia in Aulis, H.M.S. Pinafore, Journey to Jefferson* (formerly *As I Lay Dying*), *The Taming of the Shrew, Rags to Riches, Star-Spangled Girl, #A Gown for His Mistress, You Can't Take It with You, Cactus Flower.*

1969–70: *The Homecoming, @Project III: Is Law in Order @A Christmas Carol, She Stoops to Conquer, The Persecution and Assassination of Jean-Paul Marat as Performed by the Inmates of the Asylum of Charenton Under the Direction of the Marquis de Sade, Black Comedy, Greenski & the Hummingbird, On the Harmfulness of Tobacco, @The Top Loading Lover, Little Murders, The Boys from Syracuse.*

1970–71: *@Farce'n Flick, Fantoccini, @Hamlet ESP, Peter Pan, The Sea Gull, Harvey, The Night Thoreau Spent in Jail, The Apple Tree, Private Lives.*

1971–72: *The Night Thoreau Spent in Jail, The Lion in Winter, The School for Scandal, @Snow White and the Famous Fables, J.B., Lysistrata, Our Town, The House of Blue Leaves, #Wind in the Branches of the Sassafras.*

1972–73: *The Effect of Gamma Rays on Man-in-the-Moon Marigolds, The Happy Hunter, Life with Father, Summer and Smoke, @Jabberwock, How the Other Half Loves, Mary Stuart, Night Watch.*

1973–74: *John Brown's Body, Hadrian VII, @A Midsummer Night's Dream* (music and lyrics by Randolph Tallman and Steven Mackenroth), *The Crucible, Jacques Brel Is Alive and Well and Living in Paris, @Jack Ruby, All-American Boy, Arsenic and Old Lace, Tobacco Road.*

1974–75: *Jack Ruby, All-American Boy, @Chemin de Fer, The Last Meeting of the Knights of the White Magnolia, @The Oldest Living Graduate, Luann Hampton Laverty Oberlander, Inherit the Wind, Misalliance, Journey to Jefferson* (formerly *As I Lay Dying*), *The Amorous Flea, Promenade, All!.*

1975–76: *Count Dracula, Saturday, Sunday, Monday, @Manny, @A Place on the Magdalena Flats, Much Ado About Nothing, @Stillsong, Sherlock Holmes and the Curse of the Four, @Sam.*

1976–77: *Sherlock Holmes and the Curse of the Four, Once in a Lifetime, Scapino!, The Three Sisters, Something's Afoot, @Santa Fe Sunshine, Equus, Absurd Person Singular.*

1977–78: *Equus, The Imaginary Invalid, Vanities, The Night of the Iguana, Three Men on a Horse, @Firekeeper, The Royal Family.*

1978–79: *A Midsummer Night's Dream, A Texas Trilogy* (including *Luann Hampton Laverty Oberlander, The Last Meeting of the Knights of the White Magnolia, The Oldest Living Graduate), The Devil's General, As You Like It.*

1979–80: *To Kill a Mockingbird, Remember, A Man for All Seasons, A Christmas Carol, Ladybug, Ladybug, Fly Away Home, Sly Fox, @The Illusion.*

1980–81: *Da, Cyrano de Bergerac, On Golden Pond, The French Have a Word for It, The Incredible Murder of Cardinal Tosca, Children of a Lesser God.*

1981–82: *Deathtrap, War and Peace, Tintypes, Of Mice and Men, Tartuffe, Black Coffee, The Gin Game.*

1982–83: *The Three Musketeers, A Murder Is Announced, A Lesson from Aloes, The Threepenny Opera, The Dresser, Talley's Folly.*

1983–84: *Billy Bishop Goes to War, Galileo, The Wild Duck, Fool for Love, Seven Keys to Baldpate, Lady Audley's Secret, Cloud 9, Tom Jones.*

1984–85: *Misalliance, Amadeus, A Christmas Carol, Passion Play, Good, The Three Sisters, You Can't Take It with You.*

1985–86: *The Skin of Our Teeth, A Christmas Carol, The Marriage of Bette and Boo, The Glass Menagerie, The Tavern, @The Ups and Downs of Theophilus Maitland, @A Folk Tale, @Kith and Kin.*

Down Center Stage:

1964–65: *Oh Dad, Poor Dad, Mama's Hung You in the Closet and I'm Feelin' So Sad, The Typist, The Tiger, The Great God Brown, Rain, Talk to Me Like the Rain and Let Me Listen, Something Unspoken, This Property Is Condemned, @Epitaph, @Never Mind Tomorrow, @Telephones, Riverwind.*

1965–66: *@A Mime Show, La Ronde, The Birthday Party, @Sense and Nonsense, The House of Bernarda Alba, The Amorous Flea, @The Dance, @My Brother's Keeper, @One Dead Indian, The Subject Was Roses.*

1966–67: *Tiny Alice, The Amorous Flea, The World of Carl Sandburg, A Taste of Honey, @Fantoccini, @R. U. Hungry, Look Back in Anger.*

1967–68: *A Delicate Balance, Spoon River Anthology, The Private Ear, The Public Eye, The Knack, Chamber Music, The Day It Rained Forever, @The Finger Tomb, Crime on Goat Island.*

1968–69: *The Killing of Sister George, War, Muzeeka, A Taste of Honey, Summertree, @Black Reflections in a White Eye, @The Process Is the Product, Entertaining Mr. Sloane.*

1969–70: *The Promise, Halfway up the Tree, @The Field, Dear Liar, Lovers, #The Nightwatchmen, A Day in the Death of Joe Egg.*

1970–71: *The Late Christopher Bean, Waiting for Godot, Anna Christie, Dear Liar, #The Attendant, The Diary of a Madman.*

1971–72: *The Price, Exit the King, Dear Love, @I'm Read, You're Black, @Feathers, @Saloon.*

1972–73: *The Anniversary, The Marriage Proposal, Endgame, To Be Young, Gifted, and Black, Old Times, Moon on a Rainbow Shawl, @If You See Any Ladies, @The Novitiates, @Quincunx.*

1973–74: *@Getting to Know the Natives, @The Last Meeting of the Knights of the White Magnolia, @Dear Luger, @Luann Hampton Laverty Oberlander, @Curious in L. A., @Fuse, Enchanted Night, Charlie.*

1974–75: *My Drinking Cousin*, *@Why Don't They Ever Talk About the First Mrs. Phipps?*, *@Puppy Don't Live Here Anymore*, *@Sourwood Honey*, *La Turista*.

1975–76: *@A Marvelous War*, *@Standoff at Beaver and Pine*, *@Cazada and the Boys*, *@Faces of U.S.*, *Mirror Under the Eagle*.

1976–77: *@Ladyhouse Blues*, *Kennedy's Children*, *@Get Happy! @War Zone*, *@Hermit's Homage*.

1977–78: *@Door Play*, *@Cigarette Man*, *@The Night Visit*, *@Lady Bug, Lady Bug, Fly Away Home*, *@Inside the White Room*, *@Interweave*.

1978–79: *Blood Money*, *To Kill a Mockingbird*, *@Attic Aphrodite*, *@A Disposable Woman*, *@Remember*, *@Years in the Making*.

1980–81: *@Land of Fire*, *@Goya, Grandma Duck Is Dead*, *@Stagg and Stella*, *@The Chronicle of Queen Jane*.

1981–82: *@Under Distant Skies*, *@Pigeons on the Walk*, *@The Wisteria Bush*, *@Beowulf—Nocturnal Solstice*, *The Miracle Worker*, *Macbeth*, *A Christmas Carol*.

1982–83: *Embarcadero Fugue*, *@Topeka Scuffle*, *@The Pride of the Brittons*, *@Angel and Dragon*, *A Christmas Carol*.

Magic Turtle:

1969–70: *@Rumpelstiltskin*, *@Pecos Bill*, *Thumbelina*.

1970–71: *@Cinderella*, *@Beauty and the Beast*, *The Pied Piper of Hamelin*.

1971–72: *Sleeping Beauty*, *@Jack and the Beanstalk*, *@Little Red Riding Hood*, *@The Three Bears*, *The Adventures of Tom Sawyer*, *@Goose on the Loose*, *@Alice in Wonderland*.

1972–73: *Heidi*, *Winnie the Pooh*, *The Red Shoes*, *@The Adventures of Raggedy Ann and Raggedy Andy*, *@Tell Me a Story*.

1973–74: *Pinocchio*, *The Christmas Nightingale*, *Aesop's Fables*, *@Aladdin and His Wonderful Lamp*.

1974–75: *@Chi-Chin-Pui-Pui*, *@Grimm's Fairy Tales*, *Hans Brinker and the Silver Skates*, *@King Midas and the Golden Touch*.

1975–76: *@Lady Liberty*, *Celebration '76*, *Pocahontas*, *The Adventures of Br'er Rabbit*, *@Road to Yonder: The Boyhood Adventures of Abe Lincoln*.

1976–77: *Marco Polo*, *@Cinderella*, *@Hansel and Gretel*, *The Tale of the Mouse*, *Sleeping Beauty*.

1977–78: *@Equepoise*, *@Snow White*, *The Tiger in Traction*, *The Adventures of Tom Sawyer*.

1978–79: *Jack and the Beanstalk*, *Heidi*, *The New Adventures of Raggedy Ann and Raggedy Andy*, *The Squires and the Golden Kings*.

1980–81: *Beauty and the Beast*, *Winnie the Pooh*, *@The Wanderer's Stone*, *The Stonecutter* and *Peter and the Wolf*.

1981–82: *Oz—Land of Magic*, *Puss N. Boots*, *The Legend of Sleepy Hollow*, *Hansel and Gretel*, *Merlin and Arthur*.

1982–83: *The Lion, the Witch and the Wardrobe*, *@Jane Eyre*, *Step on a Crack*, *Oz—Land of Magic*.

The Janus Players:

1969–70: *The Blacks*, *Happy Ending*, *@Big Mamma, Big Man*.

1970–71: *Antigone*, *Day of Absence*.

1971–72: *Dracula*, *@Shades of Black and Brown*, *Ceremonies in Dark Old Men*, *@Frankenstein's Monster*, *La Conquista de Mexico*.

1972–73: *Day of Absence, The Marriage Proposal, @The People Speak.*
1973–74: *Enchanted Night, Charlie.*

BIBLIOGRAPHY

Published Sources:
American Theatre, 1984–86.
Theatre Communications, 1974–84.
Best Plays, 1961–62 through *1985–86*. New York: Dodd, Mead, & Co., 1963–87.
Dallas Theatre Center, 1959–1979: Twenty Dynamic Years. Dallas, Tex.: Dallas Theatre
    Center, 1979.
Donald, Mark. "Drama in Real Life." *D Magazine*, January 1985, pp. 79–90.
Northouse, Donna. "The Dallas Theatre Center." *Dictionary of Literary Biography*. Vol.
    7. Detroit: Gale Research Press, 1984.
Novick, Julius. *Beyond Broadway*. New York: Hill and Wang, 1969.
Theatre Profiles. Vols. 1–7. New York: Theatre Communications Group, 1973–85.

Unpublished Source:
Marder, John Carl III. "A History of the Development and Growth of the Dallas Theatre
    Center." Doctoral dissertation, University of Kansas, 1972.

Weldon B. Durham

[THE] DENVER CENTER THEATRE COMPANY is a satellite organization
of the Denver Center for the Performing Arts (DCPA), Denver, Colorado. It is
a professional regional theatre committed to maintaining an ensemble acting
company and producing American drama, world classics, and new plays examining the Colorado region. In 1987 more than 200 actors and actresses, resident
designers, directors, playwrights, technicians, and administrators made up the
organization, mainly funded by the Bonfils Foundation and season subscribers.
Currently the Denver Center Theatre Company is one of many divisions of the
DCPA, which includes the Recording and Research Center and Denver Center
Productions. All are united under a single board of trustees, chaired throughout
the history of the Denver Center Theatre Company by Donald R. Seawell, owner
and editor of the *Denver Post*.

DCPA's board of trustees began developing a plan for a regional theatre
company in Denver in the mid–1970s. In 1979 Seawell hired Edward Payson
Call as the company's artistic director and gave him absolute freedom to select,
manage, and develop the company. Edward Payson Call began his professional
career in 1963 as a stage manager and has since directed at the Guthrie Theatre
Company* in Minneapolis, Minnesota, and the San Diego (California) Repertory
Theatre*. At the same time, DCPA began to plan and build a theatre to house
the company.

Call first auditioned actors and actresses in Denver, Los Angeles, and New
York. Although Call hired three locals out of the seventy who auditioned in
Denver, he received complaints from the Denver community for not hiring more
Denver people. Call responded that the best regional theatres in the country must
employ people from the coasts, for Call believed the best performers migrate to
theatre centers in Los Angeles or New York.

While Call formed the company, the Bonfils Foundation built the Helen Bonfils Theatre Complex. Financed entirely by the Bonfils, the three-theatre complex cost $13 million. In 1979 the company used two theatres for productions and the third as a rehearsal space. The largest, a thrust theatre called the Stage, is the company's main venue. Originally designed to seat 642, it has since been redesigned to accommodate 543. The second largest area is called the Space. In 1979 the Space was a flexible, experimental space with bench-type seating on mobile risers. In 1981, DCPA replaced the benches with cushioned seats and fixed the space in an arena configuration. Unfortunately the new seats were constructed so that programs slipped off audience members' laps. In 1982 the seats were repitched and armrests added, but patrons continued to complain until the company replaced the seats in 1985. At that time the company remodeled the Space so that the 450-seat arena had features based on Shakespeare's Globe Theatre. The third area was called the Lab. Initially it served as a rehearsal space, but during the 1981–82 season the company began giving free staged readings of original scripts there. In 1984 the Lab was converted into a permanent, 156-seat theatre, renamed the Source, and dedicated to presenting fully mounted productions of new American plays.

The Denver Center Theatre Company opened December 31, 1979, with Bertolt Brecht's *The Caucasian Chalk Circle* performed in the Stage. Seawell opposed Call's choice of the inaugural production, but allowed Call a free hand to direct all aspects of the company. At the end of the first season Call admitted he should have opened with a different, more festive production.

The company followed with two more plays joining *The Caucasian Chalk Circle* in rotating repertory: Orson Welles' *Moby Dick—Rehearsed*, which played in the Space, and Molière's *The Learned Ladies*. A resident company of actors, directors, designers, and technicians was responsible for all productions. Tyne Daly, one of the leading actresses in the company's first season, commented that she came to Denver from the Mark Taper Forum in Los Angeles, where there was no resident company, seeking to develop artistic range and depth through true repertory casting and performance. However, after experimenting with a rotating repertory, Call changed to straight runs in February 1980. After the first, each season ran from November to May.

The company's major goal was to become an important part of the cultural life of Denver. The community wanted the company to expand its goal to be, at least in part, a unique expression of the culture of Colorado. During the 1981–82 season the company developed the Colorado Project Lab Series, an effort to define the character of the state by examining images rather than by recreating historical incidents. Four new plays, beginning November 11, 1981, with *A Ballad of Colorado*, by Frank X. Hogan, ran for nine or more free staged readings in the Lab. *Quilters*, by Molly Newman and Barbara Damashek, a musical drama based on oral histories of Colorado pioneer women, opened February 15, 1982, in the Lab as part of the Colorado Project. In 1982–83 the company staged a full production of *Quilters* in the Space, and in May 1985 a Broadway production of the musical was nominated for a Tony Award.

Call resigned as the company's artistic director in February 1983, and in October, Donovan Marley, founder and artistic director of the Pacific Conservatory of the Performing Arts at Santa Maria, California, became the new artistic director. By early 1984 Marley had assumed full control of the company. He told the Denver community that he aimed to lead artists to find significant ways to connect the community to its past. He also expressed an interest in choosing playscripts and developing new plays to define and celebrate what it means to live in the Rocky Mountain region and to prepare for the next century. Yet, according to the *Denver Post*, none of the plays chosen for 1984–85 lived up to this promise.

In May 1984 Marley reaffirmed the company's objective of nurturing a permanent group of resident performers. A few weeks later Marley dismissed twenty-five actors and actresses after the last performance of the season by slipping form letters under their doors at five o'clock in the morning. Of the 1983–84 company, Marley asked only four persons to return. Six more were given tentative assignments for 1984–85. Marley replaced those he had dismissed with people he had worked with in California.

Negative reaction in the community to Marley's "Saturday Night Massacre" forced Marley to seek and gain community approval before initiating drastic changes. For the 1984–85 season Marley returned the company to rotating repertory. He divided the eight-month season into four blocks; at the beginning of each block three shows opened within a week, one in each theatre (the Stage, Space, and Source). Each production ran for three to five months. Blocks overlapped, so that through most of the season six productions rotated in repertory. For the 1985–86 season Marley abandoned rotating repertory, and each production ran for six weeks.

When the Source became booked with fully mounted productions, it became necessary in May 1985 to move staged readings of original scripts to a hotel conference room at Denver's Executive Tower Inn. To help develop new dramas and to satisfy community mandate that the company support regional drama, Marley created the PrimaFacie (Latin for "at first sight") program in 1985. PrimaFacie presents staged readings of about ten dramas annually. From the plays presented, four are chosen for a full production in the Source in the next season.

Marley has also established the National Theatre Conservatory, a three-year actor training program leading to the degree of Master of Fine Arts. Third-year Conservatory students are members of the company.

PERSONNEL

Management: Donald R. Seawell, board chairman (1979–86).
Artistic Directors: Edward Payson Call (1979–83), Donovan Marley (1983–86).
Managing Director: Gully Stanford (1979–83).

Executive Director: Sarah Lawless (1983–86).

Directors: Bill Allard (1983–84), Larry Arrick (1981–82), John Broome (1983–84), *Edward Payson Call* (1979–83), Wallace Chappell (1983–84), Mark Cuddy (1980–82), *Barbara Damashek* (1981–84), Carolyn Eves (1983–84, 1984–85), Allen Fletcher (1984–85), Richard Owen Geer (1982–83), Peter Hackett (1983–86), Mark Harelick (1984–85), Edward Hastings (1982–83), Dan Hiester (1983–84), Sari Ketter (1985–86), Jerome Kilty (1980–81), Michael Lessac (1981–82), Gene Lesser (1979–80), Roberta Leviton (1983–84, 1985–86), Donald McKayle (1985–86), *Donovan Marley* (1982–86), James Moll (1984–86), Randal Myler (1984–86), Richard Russell Ramos (1981–82), *Walter Schoen* (1980–84), Bruce K. Sevy (1983–84, 1985–86), George Touliatos (1981–82), Stuart Vaughan (1980–81), Kenneth Welsh (1980–81), J. Steven White (1986), Laird Williamson (1980–81, 1984–86), William Woodman (1979–80), Garland Wright (1984–86), Jerry Zaks (1983–84).

Scenic Designers: Ursula Belden (1981–83), Susan Benson (1983–84), *Robert Blackman* (1979–86), Tom Buderwitz (1983–84), Kent Conrad (1983–84), Bill Curley (1985–86), *Peter A. Davis* (1979–83), Lowell Detweiler (1981–83), John Dexter (1984–86), Pavel M. Dobrusky (1984–86), Mark Donnelly (1983–84), Kent Dorsey (1983–84), Robert Ellsworth (1979–81), Eric Fielding (1984–85), Robert Franklin (1984–85), Ralph Funicello (1979–81), Christina Haatainen (1981–83), Van Hansen (1983–84), Richard L. Hay (1984–86), Christopher M. Idoine (1983–84), Judy Lowey (1985–86), Catherine Poppe (1984–86), Dan Reeverts (1985–86), Kevin Rupnik (1985–86), Bob Schmidt (1979–81), Clay Snider (1983–84), *Michael Stauffer* (1981–83, 1983–84), Douglas Stein (1984–86), Guido Tondino (1984–85), Warren Travis (1984–85), Thomas A. Walsh (1981–83), Laird Williamson (1985–86), Andrew V. Yelusich (1984–86).

Lighting Designers: Tom Buderwitz (1983–84), Dawn Chiang (1981–83), Kent Conrad (1983–84), Marty Contente (1984–85), Pamela Cooper (1979–81), Donald Darnutzer (1979–81), Pavel M. Dobrusky (1984–85), *Kent Dorsey* (1981–84), Dirk Epperson (1979–81), Eric Fielding (1984–85), Van Hansen (1983–84), Wendy Heffner (1985–86), *Allen Lee Hughes* (1981–84), Danny Ionazzi (1979–84), Robert Jared (1979–83), Charles MacLeod (1986), Peter Maradudin (1985–86), Scott Pinkney (1984–85), James Sale (1983–85), Duane Schuler (1979–83), Rodney J. Smith (1984–85), Clay Snider (1983–84), Greg Sullivan (1981–83), Michael W. Vennerstrom (1985–86).

Costume Designers: Nanzi Adzima (1979–81), Deborah Bays (1979–81), Susan Benson (1983–84), *Robert Blackman* (1979–86), Tom Buderwitz (1983–84), Elizabeth Covey (1983–84), *Lowell Detweiler* (1979–83), Pavel M. Dobrusky (1984–86), Deb Dryden (1983–84), Sam Fleming (1979–81), Robert Fletcher (1981–83), *Christina Haatainen* (1981–84), Ann Hould-Ward (1984–86), Janet S. Morris (1985–86), Kitty Murphy (1985–86), Merrily Ann Murray (1979–81), Elizabeth P. Palmer (1981–83), Judy Pederson (1983–84), John David Ridge (1981–83), Clay Snider (1983–84), Warren Travis (1984–85), Deborah Trout (1983–85), Hilary Waters (1983–84), Anne Thaxter Watson (1984–85), Kristina Watson (1979–81), Patricia Whitelock (1985–86), Andrew W. Yelusich (1984–86).

Actors and Actresses: Gregory Abels (1981–82), *Gregg Almquist* (1979–83), Stephen Anderson (1984–86), Stephen M. Ayers (1982–83), Dixie Baker (1982–83), Michael Lee Balch (1979–80), Kevin Bartlett (1982–84), Letitia Bartlett (1979–80), Benny Bell (1985–86), Annette Bening (1985–86), Mary Benson (1980–81), Marjorie Berman (1982–83), Donnie L. Betts (1979–80, 1985–86), *Duane Black* (1981–84), Mick Bolger (1982–83), Henri Bolzon (1984–86), Charlotte Booker (1982–83), Libby Boone (1984–85), Debra

Brickhaus (1981–82), Pamela Brook (1984–85), Maryedith Burrell (1984–85), Michael Butler (1982–83), Kathryn Cain (1981–82), Mark Capri (1982–83), Jeff Carey (1984–85), Tony Carpenter (1980–81), Jeannie Carson (1981–82), Jack Casperson (1985–86), Kay Casperson (1979–80, 1982–83), Emily Chatfield (1982–83), John A. Coe (1979–80), Gregory Cole (1980–81), Frank Collison (1983–84), David Connell (1982–83), *Maury Cooper* (1979–82), Wayne Cote (1983–84), Shelley Crandall (1981–83), Tandy Cronyn (1979–81), Tony Cummings (1979–80), Sheila Dabnew (1979–80), Tyne Daly (1979–80), Ted D'Arms (1979–80), Margo Davis (1979–80), Pater Davison (1982–83), Peggy Denious (1979–80), *Ted Denious* (1979–83), Craig Diffenderfer (1984–86), Jeff Dinmore (1981–84), James Doescher (1980–81), Kay Doubleday (1984–86), Lewis H. Dunlap (1981–82), Kevin Durkin (1979–80), George Ede (1983–84), Derek Edward-Evans (1981–82), Andrea Edwards (1980–81), Karen Erickson (1979–80, 1981–82), Lin Esser (1981–82, 1983–84), Mary Esterling (1982–83), Donna Falcon (1979–80), H. Mikel Feilen (1979–80), *Ken Fenwick* (1981–84), James Finnegan (1983–84), Karen Foster (1984–85), Patricia Fraser (1984–85), Mark Fuller (1981–82), John Galm (1979–80), Julian Gamble (1980–85), Richard K. Gardner (1985–86), Chris Gauthier (1979–80), Frank Georgianna (1985–86), Reno Goodale (1982–83), Kathryn Gray (1981–82), Stanford Green (1979–80), Lynnie Greene (1979–80), Ann Guilbert (1984–86), Carol Halstead (1984–86), Mark Harelik (1984–86), Wiley Harker (1985–86), Paul Hebron (1980–81), Barta Heiner (1985–86), Jon Held (1982–83), Gregg Henry (1980–81), Edward Hickok (1979–80), Leslie Hicks (1981–82), Bill Higham (1982–83), Malcolm Hillgartner (1983–84), Ingrid Hillhouse (1982–83), Jetta Hines (1981–82), Mary Gail Horan (1981–82), Bob Horen (1983–84), Jamie Horton (1983–86), Richard Hoyt-Miller (1981–82), Robert Jacobs (1984–86), Paul James (1983–84), Todd Jamieson (1980–81), Leticia Jaramillo (1984–85), Byron Jennings (1984–86), Frank Jermance (1979–80), Stephen Jimenez (1979–80), David Johnson (1979–80), Audre Johnston (1982–83), Maureen Kane (1981–82), Lisa Karen Kaufman (1984–85), Grace Keagy (1979–80), Robert Keagy (1979–80), Glenna Kelly (1982–83), Christopher Kendall (1981–82), *Jason Kenny* (1981–84), Steve Eugene Klotz (1979–80), Ravina Knueger (1983–84), David Kristin (1981–82), Tim LaBoria (1981–83), Sandra Ellis Lafferty (1985–86), Dorothy Lancaster (1982–83), Karen Landry (1979–80), Raymond Lang (1980–82), James Lawless (1979–81), *Darrie Lawrence* (1979–81, 1982–84), Ruth Margaret Lawyer (1979–80), Damien Leake (1979–80), *Judy Leavell* (1979–81, 1982–83), Alice Lenicheck (1979–80), Zoaunne LeRoy (1983–84), Philip LeStrange (1983–84), Kate Levy (1984–86), James K. Lewis (1984–85), Delroy Lindo (1979–80), Yolanda Lloyd (1983–84), Tara Loewenstern (1981–82), Rod Loomis (1980–81), Mary Lopez (1979–80), Allan Lurie (1979–80), William Lyman (1979–80), Michael McClure (1982–83), Mark McCoin (1982–84), Allen McCowan (1985–86), Bill McCutcheon (1981–82), Joseph McDonald (1981–82, 1983–84), Pirie MacDonald (1982–83), Biff McGuire (1981–82), Lisa McMillan (1983–84), Michael Maes (1982–84), Gus Malmgren (1983–84), Michael Mancuso (1981–82, 1983–84), Kathy Mar (1983–84), Lory Marie (1984–86), Stephen Markle (1979–80), Michael X. Martin 1984–86), Loraine M. F. Masterson (1979–81), Gary Mazzu (1981–82), Penelope Miller (1984–85), *Gary Montgomery* (1981–85), Randall Montgomery (1981–82), Cecelia Montoya (1979–80), Patricia Moren (1983–84), Gregory Mortensen (1983–84), Lisa Mounteer (1981–82), Margery Murray (1981–84), William Myers (1982–83), *John H. Napierala* (1979–82), *James Newcomb* (1979–83, 1985–86), William Newman (1982–83), Catherine O'Connell (1980–81), *Caitlin O'Connell* (1981–84, 1985–86), *Pamela O'Connor* (1979–82), Carolyn Odell (1982–83), Thomas S. Oleniacz (1979–80), Daniel

Onzo (1979–80), Luis Oropeza (1984–86), Art Andre Palmer (1985–86), Dougald Park (1984–86), Michael Parker (1981–82), Nigel Parr (1980–81), David J. Partington (1983–84), Rachael Patterson (1985–86), Will Patton (1979–80), Pippa Pearthree (1979–80), Paul Perri (1979–80), Lisa Jane Persky (1979–80), Ian Phares (1979–80), Larry Pine (1981–82), Lori Preisendorf (1984–85), Rebecca Prince (1984–85), Bruce C. Purcell (1981–82), Schyleen Qualls (1979–80), Tyson Douglas Rand (1981–82), Guy Raymond (1984–86), James Read (1979–81), Jeffrey Reese (1981–82), Mike Regan (1984–85), Ron Richardson (1979–80), Peter J. Rivard (1983–84), Linda O. Robinson (1980–81, 1983–84), *Robynn Rodriquez* (1983–86), Brenda Brock Rogers (1981–83), Renee Rose (1985–86), Raymond Ross (1982–83), Richard Ross (1979–80), Susan Ross (1979–80), Mercedes Ruehl (1980–82), Robert Rutland (1979–80), David Sage (1981–82), Diane Salinger (1982–83), Walter Schoen (1982–83), Tom Schuch (1982–83), Kym Schwartz (1979–81), David Seals (1979–80), Brockman Seawell (1979–81), Ruth Seeber (1982–84), Keith Ashley Sellon (1981–83), Earl Sennett (1980–81), Bruce K. Sevy (1982–83), Jeremy Shamos (1981–82), Tucker Shaw (1980–81), Jame Shepard (1982–84), Dutch Shindler (1979–80), Archie Smith (1983–86), Connor Smith (1980–81), Dick Smith (1979–80), Ken Sonkin (1984–85), Stan C. Soto (1981–82), Georgia Southcotte (1982–83), Tom Spackman (1980–81), Teig Stanley (1981–82), Michael Brennan Starr (1982–83), *Miles Stasica* (1980–81, 1982–84), Susan-Joan Stefan (1980–82), *Theodore Stevens* (1980–82, 1983–84), Mary Stribling (1982–83), Harold J. Surratt (1984–85), Glenn Tapley (1983–84), Kezia Tenenbaum (1982–83), *Hal Terrance* (1982–84), Adrienne Thompson (1984–86), Howard Thompson (1984–85), Bret Torbeck (1980–82), John Townsend (1984–85), David Trim (1981–82), Arnold E. Turner (1982–83), James Tyrone-Wallace II (1983–84), Angel Vigil (1979–80), Edward Vogels (1980–81), *Bill Walters* (1980–85), *W. Francis Walters* (1981–85), *Jerry Webb* (1979–83), Jack Welch (1982–83), Amelia White (1980–81), Darline White (1983–84), Melody Sue White (1983–84), Jonathan Wilhoft (1981–82), Gene Wilkins (1981–82), Fredye Jo Williams (1985–86), Penelope Windust (1979–80), Michael Winters (1984–86), G. Wood (1984–85), Robin Wood (1979–80), Dave Wright (1981–82), Michael Don Wymore (1979–80), D. Paul Yeuell (1984–85), Vince Zaffiro (1981–82), James H. (Buddy) Zimmer (1985–86), Peter Zimmerman (1984–85).

REPERTORY

1979–80: *The Caucasian Chalk Circle, Moby Dick—Rehearsed, The Learned Ladies, Passing Game, A Midsummer Night's Dream.*

1980–81: *Henry IV*, Part I, *Under Milk Wood, Misalliance, Loot, Medea, Wings, How to Succeed in Business Without Really Trying.*

1981–82: *Androcles and the Lion, Tartuffe, An Enemy of the People, The World of Sam Shepard: Patti's Poem to Sam* and *Suicide in B Flat, Antigone* (Jean Anouilh), *Much Ado About Nothing, Yanks 3, Detroit 0, Top of the Seventh, What the Babe Said.*

1982–83: *Quilters, The Tempest, The Hostage, Arms and the Man, Of Mice and Men, The Three Sisters, The Taming of the Shrew.*

1983–84: *Spokesong, Cyrano de Bergerac, The Front Page, The Night of the Iguana, Romeo and Juliet, The Importance of Being Earnest, Trumpets and Drums, Crossfire, Darwin's Sleepless Nights, Door Play, On the Verge, or, The Geography of Yearning.*

1984–85: *They Knew What They Wanted, Ringers, Hamlet, The Time of Your Life, Lahr and Mercedes, Design for Living, Pericles, The Immigrant, Painting Churches, Accidental Death of an Anarchist, The Female Entertainer, Don Juan, Quilters.*

1985–86: *The Petrified Forest, Christmas Miracles, The Emperor Jones, The Cherry Orchard, Pygmalion, Purlie, The Immigrant: A Hamilton County Album, Circe and Bravo, A Woman Without a Name, When the Sun Slides, Pleasuring Ground, Hope of the Future.*

BIBLIOGRAPHY

Published Sources:
Denver Post, 1979–86.
Best Plays, 1979–80 through *1985–86*. New York: Dodd, Mead, & Co., 1981–87.
Theatre Profiles. Vols 5–7. New York: Theatre Communications Group, 1982–86.
Theatre World, 1979–80 through *1985–86*. New York: Crown Publishers, 1981–87.

Debra L. Bruch

E

[THE] EMPTY SPACE ASSOCIATION was founded in Seattle, Washington, during the summer of 1970 by artistic director M. Burke Walker, along with James Royce, Julian Schembri, and Charles Younger. The theatre took its name from a statement in *The Empty Space*, by British director Peter Brook: ''I can take any empty space and call it a bare stage. A man walks across this empty space whilst someone else is watching, and this is all that is needed for an act of theatre to be engaged'' (New York: Atheneum, 1968, p. 9).

During the spring before founding the theatre, M. Burke Walker received his Master's degree from the University of Washington School of Drama. He had been drawn to Seattle because of its proximity to the Seattle Repertory Theatre* and the teaching of School of Drama executive director and professor Gregory A. Falls, founder of Seattle's A Contemporary Theatre*.

The Empty Space opened with a production of Harold Pinter's *The Dumb Waiter*, directed by Walker. The theatre was originally located in Stage I, a small, low-rent studio in the Pike Place Market in downtown Seattle. Eighteen productions were mounted in the sixty- to seventy-seat facility over two seasons before the theatre was forced to move. The diversity of productions presented during these first two years reflected the theatre's dedication to the professional presentation of contemporary plays and classics, as well as its strong commitment to the development of new playwrights and new plays.

After its initial two seasons in the downtown location, the theatre spent most of its third season performing in community centers, churches, and public parks. A remounted production of Robert Montgomery's *Subject to Fits* at A Contemporary Theatre brought the theatre critical recognition and a small grant of $7,500 from PONCHO (the Patrons of Northwest Civic, Cultural and Charitable Organizations), allowing the group to move to a renovated loft at 919 East Pike Street in Seattle's Capital Hill district. The new facility opened in 1973 with a sold-out production of the Manhattan Project's *Alice in Wonderland*. Subsequently the ninety-nine-seat house consistently averaged seasonal attendance in excess of 100 percent.

In its early seasons the Empty Space presented the initial Seattle productions of such playwrights as Sam Shepard, Lanford Wilson, Peter Handke, and Edward Bond. In addition to a number of world premieres by lesser-known playwrights, the theatre also presented English-language, West Coast, and Northwest premieres as well as original adaptations. These productions established the theatre's reputation as one of the leaders in the development and presentation of new plays and the encouragement of new playwrights.

In 1974 the theatre began operating as a resident theatre collective, employing six actors on small but regular stipends (no more than $60 per week). During this period the theatre added weekend midnight productions to supplement its regular fare. The number of resident actors grew to sixteen in 1976 when financial constraints and the limitation of artistic options forced abandonment of the resident company approach. During this period, for example, budgets grew from $23,000 in 1973 to $150,000 in 1976. After the dissolution of the acting ensemble the company rededicated itself to the production of new plays. In 1976 the entire mainstage season of ten plays consisted of premieres by writers, including David Mamet, Simon Gray, and Snoo Wilson, whose work had never been seen in Seattle.

The commitment of the Empty Space to the development of new playwrights and plays was formalized with the institution of the New Playwrights Forum in 1978 and the Northwest Playwrights Conference in 1981. The theatre also developed a One-Act Play Commission Project in 1982. The Empty Space has sponsored several residencies for playwrights such as Mabou Mines founder Lee Breuer and British playwright Snoo Wilson. Recognition of the Empty Space's commitment to new play development was highlighted by its selection as one of only five theatres in the country included in the New American Play Project, sponsored by CBS, Inc., and administered by the Foundation for the Dramatists Guild. Among the theatre's other awards have been grants from the Ford Foundation's New American Plays Program and a $100,000 National Endowment for the Arts Challenge Grant. Artistic director M. Burke Walker has also been individually honored. In 1978 he was selected as one of only four American directors to tour West German theatres as guests of the Federal Republic of Germany's cultural exchange program. He has also served on the board of directors of the Theatre Communications Group.

The Empty Space moved again in September 1984 to a new facility constructed especially for it in Merrill Place (the former Pacific Marine Schwabacher Building), a major renovation project in Seattle's Pioneer Square district. The construction costs for the latest move totaled nearly $1.5 million. The flexible auditorium currently seats 225 but can be expanded to accommodate 300. The group's fifteenth season opened with a remounted production of *The Day They Came from Way Out There*, a musical play by John Engerman, Rex McDowell,

Phil Shallat, and Bob Wright originally commissioned by the Empty Space as a touring park show. The rest of the season featured new works by American writers. The theatre's success in new play development was evidenced in 1984 by the New York productions of six plays produced at the Empty Space. *Woza Albert!*, by Percy Mawa, Mbongeni Ngema, and Barney Simon, whose American premiere was presented in association with A Contemporary Theatre, played to both public and critical praise. Two plays developed through the new play program, *The Longest Walk*, by Janet Thomas, and *A Country for Old Men*, by Anthony Doyle, also received New York productions. In addition, Harry Kondoleon's *The Vampires* and Roger Downey's translations of Franz Xaver Kroetz' *Mensch Meier* and *Through the Leaves* were produced in 1984.

Throughout its history the Empty Space has been a seminal source of new talent and a conduit for the development of new plays and playwrights. The theatre occupies an important position in Seattle cultural life and has become increasingly prominent in national artistic circles.

PERSONNEL

Directors: Shawn Austin-Olsen, John Aylward, Kurt Beattie, Jack Bender, Lee Breuer, Jody Briggs, Patrick Campbell, Clayton Corzatte, Ted D'Arms, Megan Dean, Randi Douglas, Roger Downey, Richard Edwards, Robert Egan, Anne-Denise Ford, Craig R. Gardner, Rita Giomi, Mark Harrison, Linda Hartzell, Jerry Jones, John Kauffman, John Kazanjian, Lori Larsen, Kathy Lichter, Robert Loper, Roberta McGuire, Emily Mann, Glenn Mazen, James W. Monitor, Robert Moss, William Partlan, Rod Pilloud, Susie Richardson-Glass, Carlo Scandiuzzi, Julian Schembri, Diane Schenker, Kathryn Shaw, Ruben Sierra, Barney Simon, Morgan Sloane, Jeff Steitzer, Anthony Taccone, Tom Towler, M. Burke Walker, Richard Watson, Robert Wright, Jace van der Veen.

Designers: Steve Bennett, William Bloodgood, James Ten Brooke, W. James Brown, Paul Bryan, David Butler, Tina Charney, Celeste Cleveland, Sheryl Collins, Marian Cottrell, Laura Crow, Michael Davidson, Julianne Dechaine, Ron Erickson, William Forrester, Deborah Gilbert, Karen Gjelsteen, Donna Grout, Carol Hanford, Mark Harrison, Cynthia Hawkins, Scott Hawthorne, Michael Holten, Julie James, Michael Johnson, Dennis Kambury, Rick Kennedy-Paulsen, Susan Min, Gary Mintz, Michael Murphy, Martin Pavloff, Mac Perkins, Carol Rathe, Sally Richardson, James Royce, Phillip Schermer, Frank Simons, James Verdery, Scott Weldin, Penny Wilson.

Actors and Actresses: Stephanie Adamek, Roderick Aird, Ramon Alvarez, Denis Arndt, Eric Augusztiny, Betsey Austin-Olsen, John Avinger, John Aylward, Laurence Ballard, Edward Baran, Don Bartholemew, Kurt Beattie, Michael Beaudreau, Jahnna Beecham, Gayle Bellows, Denby Bennett, Elliott Bennett, Cris Berns, David Bever, Gloria Biegler, Robin Biffle, Harvy Blanks, John Boylan, J. V. Bradley, Alan Brandon, Jane Bray, Bob Brombley, James Brousseau, Tamara Brown, Lemuel Buster, Joe Butcher, Jo Byars, James Cada, Vicki Carver, Pearl Castle, George Catalano, Paul Chadina, Kandis Chappell, Gordon Chase, David Paul Clark, Walter Cleveland, Karen Day Cody, David Colacci, Rosanne Conroy, Ann Convery, Frank Corrado, Lee Corrigan, Christopher Corzatte, Clayton Corzatte, Dana Cox, James Crabtree, Scott Creighton, Tony Cross, Amy Crumpacker, Daniel Daily, Robert Davidson, Megan Dean, Deidre Demetre, Cameron Dokey, Daniel Dorse, Inga Douglas, Randi Douglas, Toni Douglas, Roger Downey,

Anthony Doyle, Mark Drusch, Reuben Dumas, Michael Durovchic, Jack Dutt, Carole Etue, James Etue, Mary Ewald, Chuck Fader, Richard Farrell, Katherine Ferrand, Kevin Field, Paul Fleming, Nick Flynn, Joseph Franklin, Craig Gardner, John Gilbert, Sally Gladden, Tina Marie Goff, Peter Guss, Nathan Haas, Kathy Harris, Linda Hartzell, Daryl Hasten, Maureen Hawkins, Marcee Hayden, Christine Healy, Gail Hebert, Deborah Hedwall, Nels Hennum, Chad Henry, Mike Herger, Malcolm Hillgartner, Lisbeth Hinton, Pat Hodges, Dennis Hoerter, Virginia Hoffman, Scott Honeywell, Ron Hoover, Nancy Houfek, Brenda Hubbard, Wayne Hudgins, Molly Hughes, Suzy Hunt, Gwen Jackson, Sara O. Jackson, Charles Janasz, Charles Jenkins, Mark Jenkins, David Jepsen, Ted Jessen, Douglas Johnson, Jerry Mac Johnson, Raymond Johnson, Griff Kadnier, John Kauffman, Cecilie Keenan, Laura Kenny, Peggy Kessler, Maureen Kilmurray, Jean Marie Kinney, Jill Klein, Joanne Klein, Sally Kneist, Tobias Knight, Dianne Kohnke, Paula Kramer, Richard Kraus, Roza Kuring, Ken Kurtenback, Rene Laigo, Nancy Lane, Martin LaPlatney, Lori Larsen, Gary Larson, Nathan Larson, Michael Laskin, Adrian La-Tourelle, Jo Leffingwell, Roberta Levitow, Michael Longfield, S. W. Longfield, Robert Loper, Susan Ludlow, Kevin Hugh Lynch, Ann McCaffray, Glen McCord, Rex Mc-Dowell, Ruth McCree, Kyle MacLachlan, Ed Maran, Patti Mariano, Ruth Markoe, Douglas Marney, Brian J. Martin, Gilbert Martin, Jim Martin, John Martinuzzi, Don Matt, Glenn Mazen, Katherine Mesney, Mike Meyer, Ivars Mikelson, Melanie Milkie, Connie Miller, James Minahan, Hau Minn, Margit Moe, David Mong, Marnie Mosiman, Margaret Mostyn, Aloysius Mullally, Allen Nause, Marjorie Nelson, Courtney Nesbitt, Joan Norton, John Norwalk, Anne O'Connell, Peggy O'Connell, William O'Leary, Chris Olson, Linda Olson, William Ontiveros, Jr., Rise Paul, John Pendleton, Laurie Pilloud, Rod Pilloud, Demetra Pittman, Denise Pollack, Linda Pommerening, Sam Pond, Ben Prager, Jeffrey Prather, Barry Press, John Procaccino, Doug Pulse, Rex Rabold, Stephen Randoy, James Ranson, Pamela Reed, James Rice, John Rice, Clayton Richardson, Richard Riehle, Winston Rocha, Richard Rossi, John Rouse, Rex Rudeau, Elizabeth Rukavina, Gretchen Rumbaugh, Paul Russell, Janie Ryan, Ed Sampson, Carl Sander, Michael Santo, Alvin Saunders, Carlo Scandiuzzi, Michael Schauermann, Diane Schenker, Phil Shallat, Tressa Sharbaugh, Joanne Sharp, Coby Sheldt, Mark Sheppard, Larry Sherman, Jean Sherrard, Stephanie Shine, Bill Shoppert, Ruben Sierra, David Silverman, Curt Simmons, Cheri Sorenson, Tom Spiller, Andrea Stein, Jeff Steitzer, Peter Sullivan, Faye B. Summers, Jack Sydow, Jayne Taini, Fayra Teeters, Brian Thompson, Kevin Tighe, Deborah Tipton, Steve Tomkins, Steve Treacy, Craig Turner, Lyn Tyrell, Terres Unsoeld, Deems Urquhart, Peter van Slyke, Kelly Walters, Valery Wasilievsky, A. C. Weary, Rebecca Wells, Francia White, Rhonda White, Hannah Wiley, Amy Beth Williams, Randy Williams, Stuart Williams, Cal Winn, William Winship, Binky Wood, Jeffrey Woolf, Kathleen Worley, R. Hamilton Wright, Sue Yerxa.

REPERTORY

In the summary of plays presented, all titles are mainstage productions unless otherwise indicated.

1970–71: *The Dumb Waiter, Chamber Theatre, Cowboys #2* and *Icarus's Mother, The Tempest, This is the Rill Speaking, American Play, Melodrama Play, Self Accusation* and *My Foot, My Tutor, Three Hours After Marriage, The Wax Monkey.*

1971–72: *The White House Murder Case, This Is the Rill Speaking, Self Accusation, The Unseen Hand, Fando & Lis, The Lord of Misrule* (tour), *Happy Days, The Caretaker, Billy the Kid, Tom Thumb, Subject to Fits.*

1972–73: *Subject to Fits* (at A Contemporary Theatre), *Plum Pudding* (tour), *Oedipus* (tour), *Cole* (tour), *The Venetian Twins* (park show), *The Indian Wants the Bronx* (at Seattle Mayor's Festival).

1973–74: *Alice, Kaspar, Measure for Measure, The Glass Menagerie, Mandragola, The Tooth of Crime, A Midsummer Night's Dream, Ten Nights in a Barroom* (park show), *Tom Thumb* (park show).

1974–75: *Gertrude, The Alchemist, The Doctor in Spite of Himself* (with the Seattle Symphony Orchestra), *The Ride Across Lake Constance, Woyzeck, The Friend of Gotham* (park show), *Cheeze Whiz, or Putting on the Ritz, Ronnie B'wana, Jungle Guide, The Unseen Hand.*

1975–76: *Ronnie B'wana, Jungle Guide, Vampire, Gertrude, Dandy Dick, Bullshot Crummond, The Sea, Pilk's Madhouse, Yanks 3, Detroit O, Top of the Seventh, Fans, Gammer Gurton's Needle* (park show), *Molly Bloom.*

1976–77: *American Buffalo, Knuckle, School for Clowns, Heat, Butley, Klondike!* (tour), *Sexual Perversity in Chicago, Squirrels, Jesse and the Bandit Queen, Born to Maximize, The Amazing Faz* (park show and tour).

1977–78: *Ashes, The Misanthrope, Magic at Midnight, Gossip, The Landscape of the Body, Angel City, Oregon Gothic, The Pulse of New York* (park show). New Playwrights Forum staged readings: *Oregon Gothic, Guest of Honor, Free Parking, Dealing with Vincent van Gogh, A Case of Company.*

1978–79: *Illuminatus*, Parts I, II, and III, *A Prayer for My Daughter, Bonjour, là, Bonjour, Zastrozzi, Hooters, Psychosis Unclassified, Skungpoomery, The Voice of the Mountain* (park show). New Playwrights Forum staged readings: *Appalachian Ebenezer, Inalienable Rights and Wrongs, Tom and Sally and Tom, Heads and Tails, Father Dreams, The Cat's Meow.* New Playwrights Forum workshop productions: *Heads and Tails, Dear Child.*

1979–80: *The 5th of July, Heads and Tails, Comedians, Room Service, Dusa, Fish, Stas, and Vi, The Woods, An Evening of Improvisation with "None of the Above," Private Wars, Deadwood Dick, or The Curse of the Headless Horseman* (park show). New Playwrights Forum staged readings: *The Healer, Abstract—Memories of Weimar, The Sensitives, A Semblance of Order, Resurrection of Two Fools and a Blanket, Ophelia Kline.* In addition, The Empty Space sponsored the Seattle premiere performances of The Ridiculous Theatre Company production of *Camille.*

1980–81: *Agnes of God, The Workroom, Paranormal Review, Twelfth Night, Midnight Snack, Still Life, Back to Back, We Won't Pay!, We Won't Pay!* Northwest Playwrights Conference staged readings: *Brendan Behan, Ten Minutes for Twenty-Five Cents, Stand Still.* New Playwrights Forum staged reading: *The Killing Floor.*

1981–82: *The Day They Came from Way Out There* (park show), *Bent, Talley's Folly, Fefu and Her Friends, Mensch Meier, The Clown Show, Red Beads* (performance workshop), *A Well-Ordered Room.* Northwest Playwrights Conference staged readings: *Scenes of Departure and Arrival, A Country for Old Men, California.* New Playwrights Forum staged reading: *Life Science.*

1982–83: *Sister Mary Ignatius Explains It All for You* and *The Actor's Nightmare, Tartuffe, Woza Albert!* (coproduced with and presented at A Contemporary Theatre), *Through the Leaves, The Return of Pinocchio, Filthy Rich.* One-Act Play Commission Project workshop productions: *Delusion of Reference, Companion Piece, Dance in Winter, The Longest Walk.* Northwest Playwrights Conference staged readings: *Hear No, See No, Speak No, Uncle Happy, Help Wanted.*

1983–84: *Oktoberfest, The Fabulous Sateens Spill the Beans, The Vampires, Broadway, Kitchen, Church, and Kids, K2*. One-Act Play Commission Project workshop productions: *Postea Urgente, Something to Report, Precious Knees*. Northwest Playwrights Conference staged readings: *A Week in the Promised Land, Queen of Hearts, MOEXXV, Safety Rest, Blue Monday in a Sad Cafe, Sonata for Armadillos*.

1985–86: *Boesman and Lena, Sex Tips for Modern Girls, Queen of Hearts, American Buffalo, On the Verge, The Day They Came from Way Out There*.

1986–87: *The Rocky Horror Show, Have You Anything to Declare?, Don Juan, Aunt Dan and Lemon, Gloria Duplex*.

BIBLIOGRAPHY

Published Sources:
Seattle Post-Intelligencer, 1970–86.
Seattle Times 1970–86.
The Weekly, 1975–86.
Brook, Peter. *The Empty Space*. New York: Atheneum, 1968.
Glore, John. "The Empty Space and the Seattle Rep: or, Dionysus Meets the Bourgeois Gentleman." *Yale Theater* 10 (Summer 1979): 64–74.

Archival Resources:
Seattle, Washington. Empty Space Association. Programs, ephemera.
Seattle, Washington. Seattle Public Library. Programs, scrapbooks.
Seattle, Washington. University of Washington. School of Drama. Programs, scrapbooks.

Gene Burk

F

FEDERAL THEATRE PROJECT, DRAMATIC UNIT, SEATTLE was one of six Federal Theatre Units in Washington State under the supervision of Guy Williams, state director, George T. Hood, state supervisor, and Glenn Hughes, regional advisor. Harry Pfeil served as producer-director of the three vaudeville units—the Dixie Minstrels, the Hill Billies, and a Musical Comedy company—groups that played hundreds of performances. Both the Federal Theatre Project, Negro Theatre Unit, Seattle* and the Federal Theatre Players performed productions for adult and child audiences. Many of the better actors in the Federal Theatre Players also performed in the Variety Unit, which specialized in male quartets and song and dance numbers composed by Edward Chambreau.

The Federal Theatre Players did not officially organize until its production of James Warwick's melodrama, *Blind Alley*, when former members of the Tacoma Federal Theatre joined the company (*University District Herald*, March 5, 1937, p. 7). At that time the press considered the cast in its infancy except for Clarence Talbot, formerly of Seattle's Repertory Playhouse, the group's only seasoned performer (*The Argus*, March 13, 1937, p. 5). At the beginning of the Project the agency divided workers into skilled and unskilled and salaried them accordingly. Actors were paid from $66 to $77 per month. Directors were paid $72 each month. Salaries were later raised for chorus and minor actors to $72 and for directors to $96. The highest actor salary was $125.

In its early history the Federal Theatre Players was plagued by the lack of a permanent facility, by acting skills more suited to variety and vaudeville, by a repertory that appealed primarily to the upper classes, and by a crippling sensitivity to negative press coverage.

Early productions were staged in a variety of theatre or park facilities. *The Curtain Goes Up*, a variety show performed by the Variety Unit at the Repertory Playhouse, Fortieth and University Way Northeast, was the first production by white players involved in the Federal Theatre Project. The show was later revised and played at the Montlake Fieldhouse, 1618 East Calhoun. *Mother Goose on the Loose*, a musical fantasy composed of a series of vaudeville skits, rhymes, and verse, was performed more than twenty-five times between November 9, 1936, and April 1937, when it toured various Seattle parks. *Ali Baba*, a children's production sponsored by the Seattle Parks Department, was performed in the Collins Fieldhouse, 116 Avenue South and Washington Street, while *Blind Alley* and Julian Thompson's *The Warrior's Husband* were staged at the Moore, Second and Virginia, which also housed ballet groups. *Swing, Mikado, Swing*, an adaptation of the operetta by W. S. Gilbert and Arthur Sullivan, was performed at the Green Lake Center, 7201 East Green Lake Way North, under the sponsorship of the Seattle Parks Department. Arthur Arent's "living newspaper," *Power*, was performed at the Metropolitan Theatre, 411 University, which also housed road shows and opera. The Players moved into the Federal Theatre at Ranier and Atlantic, a converted movie theatre with a small auditorium, for their October 1937 production of *Help Yourself*. They remained at that location until December 1938, when they moved back to the Metropolitan Theatre to produce a revision of *See How They Run*, by George Savage, Jr. Thereafter children's productions played at the Federal and adult productions, at the Metropolitan.

Early press coverage consisted of press releases appearing regularly in *The Argus* and in the *Seattle Post-Intelligencer* but few productions were thoroughly reviewed. Criticism by J. Willis Sayre of the *Seattle Post-Intelligencer* consisted of comments on leading actors and stock characters attached to the end of the published press release. Reviews in *The Argus* consistently disparaged the quality of the music provided by the Federal Music Project orchestra performing before the show or at intermissions. *The Argus* reviewer went so far as to claim that the Project orchestra made music that was an insult to the ears (October 16, 1937, p. 5). At the opening of the second season *The Argus* observed that acting had improved because the vaudeville performers who filled the Project's relief roles had finally mastered some of the fundamentals of acting. *The Argus* noted, however, that an entertainment product meeting community standards seemed only a remote possibility.

Though sometimes beset with delays in scheduled openings and with late curtains, most of the productions ran from Monday through Saturday, with occasional matinees on Wednesday and Saturday. Children's Theatre performances were on Saturdays at 2:00 P.M., with additional productions at 11:00 A.M. for more popular shows. Admission was 25 cents and 40 cents and the season ran from September to July. The repertory consisted, for the most part, of plays recently seen on the Broadway stage and assumed, therefore, to be "popular." The Players attempted no classic drama. Gradually the Players gained in acting skill and began to perform with more regularity. By May 1937 the Players were sufficiently well established to present a "Carnival of Plays" from May 5 to May 29, during which they revived productions of *Blind Alley* and *The Warrior's Husband*. The plays alternated with *Stevedore*, by Paul Peters and George Sklar, and *In Abraham's Bosom*, Paul Green's Pulitzer Prize–winning folk-tragedy of Negro life in the Deep South, performed by the Negro Unit.

In an attempt to encourage growth in the Players, Florence B. James was selected to direct *Power*, the first opportunity for Seattle to see one of the celebrated and controversial political documentaries called "living newspapers." James, founder of Seattle's Repertory Playhouse, directed frequently for the Negro Unit. She made use of platform sets, movie and still projectors, and music by German-American composer Kurt Weill. James' organizational skills aided in promoting the production. Because the play dealt with the advantages of public ownership of electrical energy generating plants, James persuaded Seattle City Light to send advertising to its customers on forms similar to the monthly billing forms. The utility also provided generators and sodium lights used as displays in front of the Metropolitan Theatre. John F. Dore, mayor of Seattle, proclaimed June 21 through 24, the dates of the production, to be Power Week. This publicity coup went for naught, however, when J. Howard Miller, assistant national director of the Federal Theatre Project, declared that no new theatre project plays could be produced until the beginning of the fiscal year, July 1, 1937. Representatives from Federal Theatre Project headquarters in Washington, D.C., also criticized James for inappropriately using Project funds to buy new photographic equipment. She explained that slides sent from New York jammed in the projector, so she hired a local photographer to shoot and mount new slides. The Washington office had also objected to James' plans to integrate the cast of *Power*. Matters were further complicated by the reaction of the local press. The play, which employed seventy-five white actors, was the most ambitious production to date. It sold out and made $4,000, with standing room only on three of its five nights. *Post-Intelligencer* critic Sayre, while acknowledging the large and friendly audience, objected that *Power* had no plot; he also called the play propaganda for public ownership and a field day for government ownership (*Seattle Post-Intelligencer*, July 7, 1937, p. 4).

The reaction of the press caused a series of resignations and a reshuffling of personnel. Guy Williams, state director, resigned and went to Oregon to assist with the Project there. Florence B. James directed *Help Yourself*, the opening production for the next season, and then resigned from the Players. George T. Hood, the former state supervisor, served first as state director in October 1937 but by November he was demoted to acting director. Hallie Flanagan, piqued by Hood's inability to attract a large middle- and lower-class audience, imported Edwin O'Connor, a director from Los Angeles (*Arena*, pp. 307–8). O'Connor became supervisor of productions in November 1937, acting director of the Seattle Project in September 1938, and state director in February 1939. He remained in that position until the project closed. Esther Porter was brought in from Washington, D.C., to develop the children's theatre. Under Porter's tutelage additional plays were added to the children's theatre repertoire, the most popular being *Mother Goose Goes to Town*. It opened December 23, 1937, and was periodically revived until April 29, 1939. The Variety Unit continued to be active with its children's theatre productions.

Although *Pursuit of Happiness*, Lawrence Langner and Armina Marshall's American Revolution comedy, was held over an additional week, the quality and quantity of the Players' work suffered from the administrative shuffling. Eventually Hood concentrated on touring vaudeville and variety performances, while O'Connor gained control of the administration and began to woo the middle- and lower-class audience. It wasn't until *One Third of a Nation*, the closing show of the 1937–38 season, that the Players began to recover from the administrative changes. The production of Arthur Arent's living newspaper about the housing crisis in the United States combined stage documentary technique with vaudeville, the Players' strength. It had an unprecedented six-week run and was popular with both audiences and the press.

The combination of new management and a large audience restored the Players' confidence: they opened the next season with the premiere of George Savage, Jr.'s *See How They Run*, which had recently won the Dramatist Guild playwriting contest. The play was later to premiere in San Francisco, Los Angeles, and New York. The *Seattle Daily Times* called it one of the most important of the new season's events in theatre (September 20, 1938, p. 13), while the *Seattle Post-Intelligencer* considered it a "forceful labor play" (September 20, 1938, p. 22). Stuart Whitehouse of the *Seattle Star* called the cast excellent and the action well timed; he also praised the sets and the stage crew in heralding the unusually smooth finish given this production (September 20, 1938, p. 4).

Problems were slowly being overcome. The Players were attempting a less traditional repertoire and had established a permanent location. Reviews began to include commentary not only on the leading actors, but also on minor actors, on the ensemble quality of the company, and on the improved costumes and sets.

The final season of the Players was its best. *See How They Run* was revived in December. *Spirochete*, another Arent living newspaper, opened February 13, 1939, and played both matinee and evening performances for child and adult audiences. The production was sponsored by the Washington Medical Association, the State Board of Health, the County Medical Association, the City and County Health Department, and the Federated Women's Clubs (*Arena*, p. 309).

The popularity of both *Spirochete* and Eugene O'Neill's *Ah, Wilderness!*, which ran from March 29 to April 1, 1930, whetted the Players' appetite and they began making more ambitious plans. Edwin O'Connor planned a showboat tour through some of the smaller towns along Puget Sound. Rehearsals were under way for the Players' own living newspaper, *Timber*, by Burke Ormsby, while *The Flotilla of Faith*, which employed more than forty-two Project actors, played to a Vancouver audience of 8,000. A summer Drama Cycle scheduled to run from July 7 through August 5 was being planned when an act of Congress abolished the Project on June 30, 1939. The Seattle press made no mention of the demise of the Project.

PERSONNEL

Management: Guy Williams, state director (1936–37); George T. Hood, state supervisor (1936–37), state director (1937), acting state director (1937–38), tour director of Vaudeville and Variety Units (1938–39); Edwin O'Connor, supervisor of productions (1937–39), acting state director (1938), state director (1939); Glenn Hughes, regional advisor (1936–39); Esther Porter, assistant to state director (1937–39); Earle Cook, administrative assistant (1936–39); Harry Pfeil, producer-director of vaudeville (1936–39), production manager (1938–39); Ernest Amburg, agent cashier (1938–39); Fran Power, agent cashier (1936–38); Burke Ormsby, director of publicity (1936–39); Ralph Victor, treasurer (1936–38); George Bellman, press agent (1937–38); Fernetta Murphy, collection manager (1937); William Gowan, supervisor of production and assistant manager (1937); Fred Scudder, theatre manager (1937–38).

Set Designers: Virginia Miller (1937), Blanche Morgan (1937–39), Hovey Rich (1937).

Costumers: Blanche Morgan (1937–39), Virginia Opsvig (1937).

Scenic Artists: Leroy Carlisle (1937), Hovey Rich (1937–39).

Technical Directors: Lillian Deskin (1938), Flora Fulton (1937), Burton W. James (1937), Marion McGinnis (1939), Esther Porter (1938), Clarence H. Talbot (1937).

Master Carpenter: Walter Steffen (1937–39).

Master Electrician: James O'Malley (1937–39).

Sound Effects: Joe Staton (1938).

Property Master: Thomas Leach (1937–39).

Projectionist: Robert Cameron.

Stage Managers: Jane I. Chandler (1937), Flora Fulton (1939), Paul Travers (1937–38).

Musical Directors: Howard Biggs (1939), George McElroy (1937), George E. Metcalfe (1937–38).

Stage Directors: David Carroll (1938), Richard Glyer (1938), Florence Bean James (1937), Jan Norman (1939), Edwin O'Connor (1937–38), Burke Ormsby (1938), Harry A. Pfeil (1937–39), Irene Phillips (1938–39), Esther Porter (1938), Clarence Talbot (1937).

Actors and Actresses: Jean Allen (1938), Mark Allen (1938), *Sarah Allen* (1938), Becky Almoslino (1939), Sarah Almoslino (1937), David Alstrand (1938–39), Walter Andreson (1938), William Anthony (1937), Robert Arkell (1938), *Robert Banks* (1937–39), Fred Barron (1938–39), *Barbara Bettinger* (1937–39), Howard Biggs (1938), Elizabeth Bilkov (1938), Norris Blasdell (1939), Philip Bolton (1939), Doris Booker (1938–39, integrated productions), *Florence Bradbury* (1936–39), Theodore Brown (1938–39), Charles Browning (1938), Charles Cadle (1938), *Fred Carmela* (1937–38), *David Carroll* (1937–38), Ed Chambreau (1937), Jane Chandler (1938, integrated production), Betty Chapman (1937), Cherry Colclasure (1937), Herbert Coleman (1938), La Verne Coleman (1938, integrated production), Frank Collins (1938–39, integrated productions), Mary Corotola (1937–39), Walter Creddell (1937), *Truth Darling* (1937), Eileen Detchon (1937), Samuel Dew (1938), *Thomas Dew* (1936–39), Adrienne Downing (1937), Jack Dunbar (1939), Jim Fatore (1938), Helen Flannery (1939), Leo Fletcher (1938), Rex Foxley (1937), *Flora Fulton* (1937–39), Harper Gaston (1938, integrated production), Perry Gilliam (1938, integrated production), Richard Glyer (1938–39), *James Graham* (1936–39), Robert Graham (1938), Alvin Gregg (1938), Sirless Grove (1937–38, integrated productions), Mary Guilmat (1937), Wlyma Hamblin (1937), Beverly Harper (1937–38), Sandy Harper (1937–38), William Harper (1938–39), George Height (1938, integrated production), *Willis Higley* (1937–38), Ruth Hoffman (1937–38), Oswald Howick (1938), Effie Hoyt (1938), *Eleanor Hoyt* (1937–38), John Iacollucci (1939), King James (1939), Frank Jenkins, Jr. (1938, integrated production), Florence Johnson (1937), *John Johnson* (1936–39), Joe Kennedy (1939), Fred Kenzwick (1937–38), Earl Kinyon (1938), John La Fleur (1937), Henry Larnard (1938), Anna LaVaska (1939), Muriel Lazarius (1937), Tom Leach (1937), Rheba Lee (1939), *Toby Leitch* (1936–39), Adrienne Lillico (1937), Luther Losey (1937), Gertrude Lundberg (1937), Marion McGinnis (1937–38), Betty McKay (1937), *Charles Malott* (1937–39), Don Mastro (1937), Harold Moe (1939), Charlene Monroe (1938, integrated production), Herman Moore (1938, integrated production), Blanche Morgan (1937), Milton Moss (1938), *Myrtle Mary Moss* (1938–39), Lester Moyer (1937), Ewerth Mulligan (1938–39), Oliver Mulligan (1938), Penelope Murphy (1937), *Edwin G. O'Connor* (1938), Patrick O'Day (1937), Sarah Oliver (1937–39, integrated productions), *Edward O'Neill* (1937–39), *Burke Ormsby* (1938–39), Edward Page (1939), *Mildred Page* (1936–39), *Harold Petterson* (1938–39), Harry Phillips (1938), Alice Powell (1938–39, integrated productions), Allan Powers (1939), Ray Rathburn (1938), Barbara Roberts (1938), Becky Roberts (1937), Martha Roberts (1938, integrated production), Frances Robinson (1938), Lillian Rockwell (1938), Ed Russell (1937–39), John Russell (1938), Tex Russell (1938), Helen Saddoris (1937), Robert St. Clair (1938), Fred Scudder (1938), Thelma Seaman (1937), Harold Seeley (1938), Edward Shelverton (1938–39), Martha Shevlyn (1938), Roberta Shevlyn (1937–38), Donald Sloan (1938), Joseph Smith (1938), Leonard Spector (1938), Joe Staton (1938), Walter Steffen (1937), Becky Sweet (1938), Sara Sweet (1937), *Clarence H. Talbot* (1937), Evan Thompson (1938), *George Thomson* (1937), Edith May Thurston (1938), Wilson Todd (1937), *Paul Travers* (1937–39), Louie Traverso (1938), Thomas Trice (1938), Arthur Von Volkli (1938), Herman Wagner (1938), George Ward (1938), Herbert Ward (1938–39), Bruce Weir (1938), David Weir (1938), Edward White (1938), Douglas Wight (1938–39), Kathleen Wilson (1937), Oliver Wilson (1939), Evelyn Winston (1938–39, integrated productions), Gordon Wood (1937).

REPERTORY

1936–37: *The Curtain Goes Up, Mother Goose on the Loose, Ali Baba, Blind Alley, Sleeping Beauty, Katinka Comes to Town, The Warrior's Husband, Swing, Mikado, Swing, Power, We Dine at the Colonel's.*

1937–38: *Help Yourself, Clown Prince, Pursuit of Happiness, The Emperor's New Clothes*. The Sun and I*, Mother Goose Goes to Town, Swing on Down, Counsellor-at-Law, Radio Review, Flight* (integrated), *Tomorrow's a Holiday, Alice in Wonderland, One Third of a Nation.*

1938–39: *See How They Run, Christmas Carols* (Mummers performance), *Poor Little Consumer*, Mississippi Rainbow* (integrated), *Wives of the Caliph*, Pop Goes the Reason*, Clown Prince, Spirochete, Ah, Wilderness!.*

BIBLIOGRAPHY

Published Sources:
The Argus, 1936–39.
Seattle Daily Times, 1936–39.

---

* Productions listed as ''forthcoming'' in Project publicity, but for which no programs or press releases exist.

Seattle Post-Intelligencer, 1936–39.
Seattle Star, 1936–39.
University District Herald, 1936–39.
Flanagan, Hallie. *Arena*. New York: Duell, Sloan & Pearce, 1940.
Mathews, Jane De Hart. *The Federal Theatre, 1935–1939, Plays, Relief, and Politics*. Princeton, N.J.: Princeton University Press, 1967.

   Archival Resources:
Seattle, Washington. Seattle Public Library. J. Willis Sayre-Carkeek Collection contains programs of *Ah, Wilderness!*, *Blind Alley*, *Clown Prince*, *Counsellor-at-Law*, *The Curtain Goes Up*, *Flight*, *Help Yourself*, *Mississippi Rainbow*, *One Third of a Nation*, *Power*, *The Pursuit of Happiness*, *Radio Review*, *See How They Run*, *Spirochete*, *Tomorrow's a Holiday*, and *The Warrior's Husband*.
Seattle, Washington. University of Washington Libraries. Special Collection. Florence Bean James Papers.

Liz Fugate

FEDERAL THEATRE PROJECT, NEGRO THEATRE UNIT, NEW YORK CITY, also known as the Harlem Theatre Project of the Federal Theatre, was organized on October 23, 1935, when the New York Urban League submitted a project proposal for a Negro unit of government-sponsored theatre in Harlem. Negro actress Rose McClendon and white director-theatre entrepreneur John Houseman were chosen as codirectors of the project and assigned both administrative and artistic duties. McClendon, however, was never really involved in the Project, for shortly before the company took over the newly refurbished Lafayette Theatre on Seventh Avenue in Harlem, she succumbed to the ravages of cancer. On February 4, 1936, the Negro Theatre became the first of New York City's Federal Theatre units to raise its curtain. It opened with black actor-author Frank Wilson's *Walk Together Chillun*, a social drama with music.

   As a project for unemployed actors and other theatre professionals, Federal Theatre remains as the only truly national theatre the United States has ever had. The Negro Theatre was one of five large units originally formed in New York City. The others were the Living Newspaper, the Popular Price Theatre, the Experimental Theatre, and the Tryout Theatre. Each unit had its own director and staff of actors, playwrights, technicians, designers, costumers, clerical personnel, and housekeepers. The Negro Theatre was a stock company that initially employed 750 men and women in all capacities—some of them professionals, many not.

   Houseman, who had won respect among black theatre professionals for his production of the Virgil Thomson opera *Four Saints in Three Acts*, libretto by Gertrude Stein, accepted the position of joint head of the Project with McClendon because of an irresistible attraction to achieving the impossible. It should not be overlooked that late in his career Houseman turned to acting in motion pictures and on television and in the late 1970s won an Oscar for his supporting role in *The Paper Chase*. With more than 700 workers on the payroll, the most difficult task facing him was how to keep all of them working. Thus he chose to organize two production companies within the Harlem unit—the Contemporary Wing and the Classical Wing. The former was for plays written, directed, and performed by and for blacks, set in black locales, and preferably dealing with contemporary black subjects, while the latter would mount classic works that actors would interpret without concession or reference to color. Houseman remained in the position until August 1936, when he left to manage a new unit of Federal Theatre, the Classical Theatre, with Orson Welles. He was replaced, on his own recommendation, by the black triumvirate of Carlton Moss, Gus Smith, and Harry Edward. Moss was college educated and had some theatre background as a radio script writer and with the Civil Works Administration, the forerunner of the Project's parent, the Works Projects Administration (WPA). Smith was a professional actor, director, and writer, while Edward's forte was administration. They remained in their capacity as managing producers until the Project's close in June 1939.

Gainfully employing out-of-work theatre artists in their chosen profession was always the primary goal of the Federal Theatre Project. With large government subsidies, earning a profit was never a goal or a necessity. Even after huge federal budget cuts between 1937 and 1939, profits were still irrelevant. Tickets cost from 25 cents to 50 cents, and those showing welfare cards were admitted free of charge on Monday evenings. Ticket revenues were used for scenery, lighting, and costumes. After the budget cuts began, Federal Theatre Project administrators tried to maintain as many personnel as possible, but by the time the Project closed in 1939, fewer than 400 personnel remained on the payroll.

Through its four seasons, critics greeted productions of the Negro Unit with both critical superlatives and journalistic roasts, but never was a cast accused of being unenthusiastic, even when productions were cited as "uneven." As the Negro Theatre matured, it won a greater acceptance from the white press and, concomitantly, more laudatory notices in the drama pages. Certain critics, however, chose to temper their reviews with their own political and racial biases, never missing an opportunity to take a swipe at the New Deal or to make condescending remarks about the "dusky" players from uptown. Most critics agreed on the dexterity with which crowd scenes were handled. Other theatrical elements of set design, costumes, music, and dance frequently received favorable notices from the press. These, in fact, seemed to be the company's strong points. One of the main criticisms of many of the black critics, such as Edward Lawson of *Opportunity*, was that audiences at the Lafayette remained more white than black.

In four seasons the Negro Unit presented thirteen full-length productions and one series of four one-act plays. The first two years were the most prolific, with productions of the Welles–Houseman "Voodoo" *Macbeth*, social dramas and folk plays such as Gus Smith and Peter Morrell's *Turpentine*, Rudolph Fisher's mystery-comedy *Conjur Man Dies*, four Eugene O'Neill one-act plays, and the popular children's comedy *Horse Play*, by Dorothy Hailparn. The last two seasons saw only two productions: William Du Bois' historical melodrama *Haiti* and George Bernard Shaw's *Androcles and the Lion*, the unit's final production. In addition to performances at the Lafayette, traveling units, called Caravan productions, carried most of the plays to schools, parks, and community centers in all parts of the city. The "Voodoo" *Macbeth* had a Broadway run of some two months before going on tour to the Midwest and Texas, and the production of *Haiti* went on tour to Boston, where it was well received.

The Negro Project was the largest unit of Federal Theatre in New York, and it was completely self-sufficient. Of the 750 workers on the payroll, about 500 were officially classified as actors, singers, or dancers. One-third of these had no professional experience, while half of those with experience had only occasionally danced in a chorus, sung in a group, or worked as film extras. Theatre professionals in the group numbered about 150, including vaudevillians, cabaret entertainers, veteran stock actors, Broadway stars, and actors from the little theatre movement. Once installed as Project director, Houseman's most immediate task was to hire a creative and administrative staff to help him run the unit. Because of a special dispensation granted to the Arts Projects by the WPA, Houseman was permitted to hire up to 10 percent of his creative and executive personnel from outside the certified relief rolls at relief wages. This enabled him to hire actors, directors, and technicians from the professional theatre as well as experienced administrative personnel.

For the Project's production of *Macbeth*, Houseman hired Orson Welles as director, Nat Carson as designer, and Abe Feder as lighting designer. For their stars Welles and Houseman chose Jack Carter—the original Crown in George and Ira Gershwin's *Porgy and Bess*—to play Macbeth, Edna Thomas to play his lady, and Canada Lee, who in 1940 won acclaim on Broadway in the Welles–Houseman production of Richard Wright's *Native Son*, to appear as Banquo. A final count on the *Macbeth* company numbered 1,500. Almost every production boasted one or more actors who had achieved fame in the theatre or would later achieve it. These included Gus Smith, Dooley Wilson, Lionel Monagas, Maurice Ellis, Eric Burroughs, Thomas Moseley, Susie Sutton, and Frank Wilson. Dooley Wilson sang the Oscar-winning song, "As Time Goes By" in the 1941 film *Casablanca* and later starred on Broadway in the Lynn Root, John Latouche, Vernon Duke musical fantasy, *Cabin in the Sky*, for which Perry Watkins designed the set. Having polished his craft in the Federal Theatre Project, Watkins became the first black man to design a Broadway set.

Other artists employed by the Project for a single production included Eubie Blake, Cecil Mack, and Milton Reddie, who penned the popular musical *Swing It*, which played to appreciative audiences all over the city. Distinguished black actor Rex Ingram, who played "de Lawd" in Marc Connelly's *Green Pastures*, won rave notices for his interpretation of Henri Christophe in *Haiti*. P. Jay Sidney and Daniel Haynes won acclaim in *Androcles and the Lion* for their roles as the Captain and Ferrovious, respectively. White actress Elena Karam was also well received for her part in *Haiti*.

PERSONNEL

Management: John Houseman, producer and manager (1935–36); Harry Edward, administrator (1936–39); Carlton Moss and J. A. "Gus" Smith, producers (1936–39).

Scenic Technicians: James Cochrame (1938–39), Manuel Essman, Barry Farnol (1936), Abe Feder (1936), Maxine and Alexander Jones (1937), Walter Walden (1937), Perry Watkins, Byron Webb, Oscar Weidhaas (1937), Victor Zanoff (1937).

Musical Directors: George Courveur (1938–39), Leonard de Paur (1936–39), Joe Jordan (1936), Jean Stor (1936), Wen Talbert and Fred Ames (1936).

Stage Directors: William Challee (1937), Maurice Clark (1938), Hedley Gordon Graham (1937), Momodu Johnson (1936), Venzella Jones (1937), Cecil Mack and Jack Mason (1937), Samuel Rosen (1938–39), J. A "Gus" Smith (1936–37), Orson Welles (1936), Frank Wilson (1936), George Zorn (1936).

Actors and Actresses: Abdul, *James Adams* (1936), *John Alele* (1936), Ora Alexander, Frauline Alford, Alfred Allegro, Thomas Anderson, Jesse Austin, Leo Bailey, *Add Bates* (1938–39), Amy Bates, Norman Barksdale, Beryle Banfield, Mary Barnes, *Service Bell* (1936–37), George Booker, Alonzo Bosan, James Boxwell, Willis E. Bradley, Marion Brantley, Walter Brogsdale, Clarence Brown, Gabriel Brown, Helen Brown, William Brown, Ollie Burgoyne, Charles Burnham, Anita Bush, Lawrence Chenault, *Alvin Childress* (1937–38), Rita Christiani, Ernest J. Clark, William Clayton, *Norman Coker* (1936), George Colan, Charles Collins, Emma Collins, Julian Costello, Carl Crawford, Walter Crumbley, William Cumberbatch, Mary Davenport, Frank David, Clifton Davis, Viola Dean, Gerald De La Fontaine, Wilbur Derouge, Alma Dickson, Sherman Dirkson, Cornelius Donnelly, Abner Dorsey, Miriam Dugger, Walter Duke, Sidney Easton, Irving Ellis, *Maurice Ellis* (1936–39), Genora English (1937), David Enton, Frances Everett (1937), Edward Fleischer, Hugo Forde, John Fortune, Oliver Foster, Hilda French, *Edward Frye* (1937), Frederick Gibson, Virginia Girvin, Herbert Glynn, *Doe Doe Green* (1937), James Green, William Greene, Lisle Grenidge, Edna Guy, Joseph Hall, Lena Halsey, Ruby Harris, John Hayden, Estelle Hemsley, Emile Hirsch, Roy Holland, Algretta Holmes, Bertram Holmes, Mozelle Holmes, Hallie Howard, Theodore Howard, Frank Jackson, *Thurman Jackson* (1936–37), Herbert Jelley, Leroy Jenkins, Henry Jines, J. B. Johnson, J. Lewis Johnson, John D. Johnson, Paul Johnson, *Dorothy Jones* (1937), John Pope Jones, Lulu King, Zola King, Milton Lacey, Byron Lane, Larri Lauria, Catherine Lawrence, *Canada Lee* (1936–38), Edward H. Loeffler, Lawrence Lomax, *Joe Loomis* (1937), James McClean (1936), Albert McCoy, Richard McCracken, Muriel McCrory, Pat McCullough, Shirley Macey, Wanda Macey, James S. McLaughlin, Thelma MacQueens, Alberta Martin, Jacqueline Martin, William Melville, Ernest Mickens, Emanuel Middleton, Bertram Miller, *Lionel Monagas* (1936–37), Jay Mondaaye, James Mordecai, Alphonse Moore, Ruth Moore, Sybil Moore, *Thomas Moseley* (1936–39), DeWaymond Niles, George Nixon, Edmond Norris, *Hilda Offley* (1936–39), J. Francis O'Reilly, Lester Palmer, Cora Parks, Dorothy Paul, Ike Paul, Fanny Peele, Alberta Perkins, Laura Phauls, Tillmon Pittman, Edwin S. Platt, Rose Poindexter, Louis Polan, Hudson Prince, Kenneth Renwick, Lilly Robinson, Walter Robinson, Wardell Saunders, Archie Savage, Eleanor Scher, Frances Scott, William Sharon, *Louis Sharp* (1936–39), Ollie Simmons, Joseph Slocum, Carole Smith, Francis Smith, *J. A. "Gus" Smith* (1936–37), Louis Smith, Susie Sutton, Harris Talbert, Benny Tattnall, Charles Taylor, *Edna Thomas* (1936–39), George Thomas, Philandre Thomas, Sonny Thompson, Mable Thorne, Cherokee Thornton, Be-Be Townsend, Barclay Trigg, Dorothy Turner, Lavina Turner, Vergil Van Cleve, Robert Veritch, Percy Verwayne, Rosebud Washington, Al Watts, Charles Wayne, Richard Webb, Fritz Weller, Arnold Wiley, Christola Williams (1936), James Williams, Josephine Williams, Olena Williams, Wilhelmina Williams,

Arthur Wilson (1937–39), Elsie Winslow, James Wright, Clarence Yates, Al Young, Blanche Young, Marie Young.

REPERTORY

1936: *Walk Together Chillun, Conjur Man Dies, Macbeth, Turpentine, Noah, Bassa Moona.*

1937: *Sweet Land, The Case of Philip Lawrence, Swing It, Horse Play* (children's theatre). The Glencairn Cycle: *Moon of the Caribbees, In the Zone, Bound East for Cardiff, The Long Voyage Home; The Nativity Play.*

1938–39: *Haiti, Androcles and the Lion.*

BIBLIOGRAPHY

Published Sources:

Brooklyn Eagle, 1936–39.
New York Amsterdam News, 1936–39.
New York Daily Mirror, 1936–39.
New York Daily News, 1936–39.
New York Daily Worker, 1936–39.
New York Herald Tribune, 1936–39.
New York Journal American, 1936–39.
New York Post, 1936–39.
New York Sun, 1936–39.
New York Times, 1936–39.
New York World Telegram, 1936–39.

Archival Resources:

Fairfax, Virginia. George Mason University. Research Center for the Federal Theatre Project. Working scripts of *Androcles and the Lion, Haiti, Horse Play, Macbeth*, and the four O'Neill one-act plays.

New York, New York. New York Public Library. Library and Museum of the Performing Arts. Hallie Flanagan Collection. Scrapbooks, clippings, personal correspondence.

Washington, D.C. National Archives. Record Group 69, Federal Theatre Project.

Robert A. Adubato

FEDERAL THEATRE PROJECT, NEGRO THEATRE UNIT, SEATTLE, also known as the Negro Repertory Company, was organized and initially managed by Florence and Burton James in Seattle, Washington, in 1936. The Seattle Federal Theatre Project's Negro Unit was part of the Federal Theatre Project, itself a unit of the Works Progress Administration (WPA). The Negro Repertory Company initially rehearsed its plays and produced them at the 340-seat Seattle Repertory Playhouse, operated by Florence and Burton James, in January of 1936. Andre Obey's biblical fable, *Noah*, the company's first production, opened on April 28, 1936. The Negro Repertory Company used three other theatres in Seattle during its four-season history: the Moore Theatre, seating 1,425; the Metropolitan Theatre, seating 1,439; and the Federal Theatre Project Building, seating 496. The Federal Theatre Project theatre at 1321 Rainier Avenue, a former movie theatre, was too small and very remote.

The Federal Theatre Project founded fourteen Negro theatre units; the Seattle company was one of the three most successful, doing fifteen shows during its short existence. The unit provided work for black actors and technicians, work that had never been available to them before, and a quality, unique theatrical experience for Seattle audiences. When the Negro Repertory Company was created, Seattle had three resident theatrical organizations. The Cornish School and the Drama Division of the University of Washington were primarily involved in training people. The Seattle Repertory Theatre, run by Florence and Burton James, was a community theatre that maintained its production season under the Jameses even after they became involved with the Negro Repertory Company. The Negro Repertory Company even staged some of its plays as part of the Seattle Repertory Playhouse Summer Festival. It was also involved with four other Federal Theatre projects in Washington for white performers, a children's unit, a vaudeville unit, and a Tacoma-based unit that produced staged readings of locally written plays. The Negro Repertory Company helped with the production of Arthur Arent's living newspaper, *Power*, by working backstage and by selling tickets. When white actors were required for the Negro Repertory Company plays, they were borrowed from other local Federal Theatre projects.

Florence and Burton James were married in 1916 and created a performance group in New York, the Lennox Hill Players, which included the young James Cagney. They moved to Seattle in 1923 to work in the drama department of Cornish School. From there they went on to found the Seattle Repertory Playhouse. The Jameses were inspired to try a black Federal Theatre Project group because of the success of their Seattle Repertory Playhouse production of Paul Green's *In Abraham's Bosom*, a tragic folk play of Negro life in the Deep South. After becoming frustrated with red tape and politics, the Jameses left the Negro Repertory Company in 1937, and Hallie Flanagan, head of the Federal Theatre Project, sent Esther Porter, a former Vassar student and Federal Theatre Project administrator, to be the director of the Seattle project. She managed the Negro Repertory Company until she left the Federal Theatre Project in July of 1938 to become acting director of the Vassar College Experimental Theatre. Richard Glyer then became the director of the Negro Repertory Company. Glyer had acted professionally in New York and Los Angeles, but when acting jobs became scarce, he ended up in a WPA work gang. He became an actor in the Los Angeles Federal Theatre Project and was reassigned from there to the Seattle project.

The Federal Theatre Project aimed to provide jobs for unemployed theatrical workers, and the goal of the Negro theatre projects was to reflect the lives and concerns of black Americans. Before this time few blacks were employed in theatre, and when they were, most frequently they were assigned stereotyped and degrading roles. Flanagan wanted to provide additional training and experience for the blacks already in the entertainment industry and make them more employable in the future. When the Negro Repertory Company was founded in Seattle in 1936, it employed seventy-three actors, singers, and technicians.

The Federal Theatre Project was designed to take theatre people off the relief rolls; however, 40 percent of the original Negro unit in Seattle were not on relief or eligible for it. People became members of the company primarily because of their participation in the Seattle Repertory Company's production of *In Abraham's Bosom* and received jobs with a salary of from $55 to $94 a month. Florence James, in her unpublished manuscript "Fists upon a Star: The Making of a Theatre," told how the company was critically received. "Reviewers expressed amazement at the talent displayed by people taken from the scrap-heap of unemployment to the relief rolls of the W.P.A. The reviewer in the *Seattle Star* commented, 'This all-Negro cast put on a performance so rich, so full of promise, it was tragic in its implications. Tragic because these people who have so much to contribute have so long been wasted' (Cited in Evamarie Johnson, "A Production History of the Seattle Federal Theatre Project Negro Repertory Company: 1935–1939." Doctoral dissertation, University of Washington, 1981, p. 29). Comments published about the company's productions were generally favorable, but because the project took place in the 1930s in America, when black was usually regarded as inferior, newspapers did not provide in-depth reviews of the company's performances. Notices in the papers stated playing dates and casts, and sometimes described the play being presented.

Noah was the first play done by the Negro Repertory Company because it was "one of the few plays deemed suitable by white administrators for black casts" (Johnson, p. 29). The play, based on the biblical story, presented a traditional view of blacks and was well accepted by its audience. However, the company's second play, *Stevedore*, by Paul Peters and George Sklar, was inflammatory propaganda urging workers to unionize. The group's sincere, powerful production was so successful that the Negro Repertory Company revived it during the summer of 1936. *Swing, Gates, Swing*, a musical primarily written by company members Theodore Browne and Guy Williams with some help from other company members, closed the 1935–36 season.

The head of the WPA in Washington State closed, after one night, Aristophanes' sex comedy *Lysistrata*, the company's 1936–37 season opener, because the action of the play had been moved to Ethiopia. The WPA official believed the production was detrimental to the government's interests because of the delicacy of U.S. relations with Italy, then at war with Ethiopia. The Negro Repertory Company took part in a special project of the Federal Theatre Project: the simultaneous opening of Sinclair Lewis' *It Can't Happen Here* in twenty-two theatres in seventeen cities on October 27, 1936. After the presentation of Lewis' play about a fascist takeover, Theodore Browne adapted the legend of John Henry in an extremely powerful musical play, *Natural Man*. Critics felt the play suffered because audiences didn't know the playwright, but the next play on the 1936–37 schedule, *In Abraham's Bosom*, so successful for the Jameses, was better received because it was better known and because critics and audiences considered it a good "black" show to do.

In 1937–38 the company did the first all-black production of George Bernard Shaw's *Androcles and the Lion*. Critics were divided in response to the show, some feeling it was too sophisticated for black performers, while others were delighted the group was doing a strong, well-known play. The company, too, delighted in the challenges posed by Shaw's play. The Negro Repertory Company set *Is Zat So?* in Harlem. The popular 1925 farce by James Gleason and Richard Taylor became a big hit for the group. The next show of 1937–38, *Black Empire*, by Christine Ames and Clarke Painter, distorted the history of the Haitian Revolution, but it was a dynamic play and audiences thought it one of the group's best. *Br'er Rabbit and the Tar Baby*, by Ruth Mitchell and Alfred Allen, exemplified the attitude of America toward blacks in the thirties. Racial stereotyping and demeaning language that would never be accepted in America today were characteristic of this children's theatre production. As the first production of 1938–39, the company compiled *An Evening with Dunbar*, a theatricalization of the life and works of black poet Paul Lawrence Dunbar (1872–1906). It was a solid success; however, the white press, while unanimous in its praise of the musical aspects of the production, gave little credit to Dunbar's poetry or to the company's acting and staging. The inexperienced direction of Herman Moore seriously undermined the success of the company's next production, John C. Brownell's *Mississippi Rainbow*, a comedy. However, audiences loved the gay, sprightly style of the production of the children's play *The Dragon's Wishbone*, by Joan and Michael Slane, which the performers embellished with improvisations. The company's last production was a flawed production of an unworkable adaptation of Shakespeare's *The Taming of the Shrew* set in New Orleans.

The Negro Repertory Company gave its members an opportunity to try many different jobs in the theatre. In one show an actor would be a star; in the next he'd have a bit part. Some actors also stage-managed, directed, and wrote. The principal actors of the company were Theodore Browne, Sarah Oliver, and Joe Stanton, but little is known about them or any other members of the company after the demise of the Federal Theatre Project. Director Richard Glyer returned to Los Angeles and the University of Southern California and was later a member of the Actor's Workshop* in San Francisco. Howard Biggs went to New York, worked with Noble Sissle's band, and arranged nightclub acts. Joe Stanton went to work for Boeing Aircraft in Seattle.

The Federal Theatre Project was abruptly discontinued on June 30, 1939, after apparently unsubstantiated charges were made that its ranks were filled with Communists. The Negro Repertory Company had some success and abundant potential, but the untimely demise of the Federal Theatre Project destroyed its chances of becoming an independent regional company.

PERSONNEL

Management: Hallie Flanagan, national director of the Federal Theatre Project (1935–39); Richard Glyer, Negro Repertory Company director (1938–39); George Hood, Washington State Federal Theatre Project administrator (1935–38); Glenn Hughes, nominal director of Federal Theatre Project region 5 (1935–38); Burton James, Negro Repertory Company comanager (1935–37); Florence James, Negro Repertory Company comanager (1935–37); Ole Ness, regional Federal Theatre Project director (1939); Edwin O'Connor, Washington State director for the Federal Theatre Project (1938–39); Esther Porter, nonrelief director with the Seattle Federal Theatre Project (1937–38); Joe Stanton, company manager; Guy Williams, Washington State Federal Theatre Project director (1935–1938).

Stage Directors: Richard Glyer, Florence James, Herman Moore, Edwin O'Connor, Esther Porter, Joe Stanton.

Music Director: Howard Biggs.

Playwrights: Howard Biggs (*An Evening with Dunbar*), Theodore Browne (*Swing, Gates Swing, Lysistrata, Natural Man*), Richard Glyer (*The Taming of the Shrew*), Herman Moore (*The Taming of the Shrew*), Joe Stanton (*The Taming of the Shrew*), and Guy Williams (*Swing, Gates, Swing*).

Choreographers: Syvilla Fort, Mary Myrtle Moss.

Choral Directors: Julia White Gayton, Edward White.

Technical Effects Director: Burton James.

Orchestra Director: George Metcalf.

Costume and Scenic Designers: Virginia Miller, Blanche Morgan, Virginia Opsvig.

Scenic Artist: Hovey Rich.

Band Director: John Sparger.

Actors and Actresses: Sarah Allen, Barbara Bettinger, Howard Biggs, George Blackwell, Doris Booker, *Theodore Brown* (1936–37), Charles Browning, Jane Chandler, Harper Gaston, Perry Gilliam, Sirless Graves, Robert Hamlin, *Toby Leitch* (1936–38), Charles Monroe, Herman Moore, Mary Myrtle Moss, *Sarah Oliver* (1936–39), Esther Porter, Lucille Price, John Rustad, Robert St. Clair, Roberta Shevlyn, Joe Albert Smith, *Joe Stanton* (1936–39), Thomas Trice, *Alberta Walker* (1936–37), Evelyn Winston, Ed White.

REPERTORY

1936: *Noah, Stevedore, Swing, Gates, Swing.*

1936–37: *Lysistrata, It Can't Happen Here, Natural Man, In Abraham's Bosom.*

1937–38: *Androcles and the Lion, Is Zat So?, Black Empire, Br'er Rabbit and the Tar Baby.*

1938–39: *An Evening with Dunbar, Mississippi Rainbow, The Dragon's Wishbone, The Taming of the Shrew, Timber* (in rehearsal when the project was terminated).

BIBLIOGRAPHY

Unpublished Source:

Johnson, Evamarie Alexandria. "A Production History of the Seattle Federal Theatre Project Negro Repertory Company: 1935–39." Doctoral dissertation, University of Washington, 1981.

Emily Thiroux

FEDERAL THEATRE PROJECT, YIDDISH THEATRE UNITS, were located in New York City, Boston, Chicago, and Los Angeles. The origins of Yiddish federal theatre may be traced to 1934, when, about a year before the project got under way, a group associated with Yiddish theatre in New York City persuaded the New York City Civil Works Service to start a theatre unit for unemployed Yiddish theatre artists. Those who approached the city were Dan Tobin, a talent agent; Maurice Kurtz, formerly an actor with Arbeiter Theater Farband (ARTEF); Mordechai Yachson, a Yiddish actor; Boris Thomashefsky, known as the founder of Yiddish theatre in America; and Thomashefsky's son Harry, a director. Under the artistic direction of the two Thomashefskys, the Yiddish Drama Group was formed. With fifty actors, it opened its first production, *The Yiddish King Lear*, on December 4, 1934, in a hall at the Educational Alliance, 197 East Broadway. An English version was opened by the same actors on June 25, 1935. The Yiddish Drama Group became part of the Federal Theatre Project at the time of the project's birth in November 1935, with successive plays being staged at the Biltmore Theatre, the Maxine Elliot Theatre, and Daly's Theatre. The two Thomashefskys stayed on for a time but eventually were replaced by Yehuda Bleich, Wolf Barzell, Martin Wolfson, and Jacob Mestel.

Two other Yiddish companies were added to the list of New York City Yiddish federal theatre groups: *Geleibt un Gelacht* (We Live and Laugh), a satirical, intimate cabaret group directed by Zvee Scooler, Bleich, and Barzell, which opened on May 8, 1936, at the Public Theatre, and the Anglo-Yiddish Group, established for the purpose of staging Yiddish drama in translation or plays on Jewish themes. The latter group opened on March 10, 1936, at the Ansche Chesed Temple in Manhattan with *The Idle Inn*, a folk comedy by Peretz Hirschbein. The Anglo-Yiddish performed at a variety of community centers and synagogues as well as at Daly's. The Boston Yiddish Drama Group, under the artistic direction of Morris Schorr, opened on November 18, 1935, at the Repertory Playhouse with Samuel Becherman's *Golden Wedding*. On September 8, 1937, the Chicago Yiddish Drama Group opened under the artistic leadership of Adolph Gartner with *Monesh*, an adaptation by Jonah Spivak of a poem by I. L. Peretz, at the Great Northern Theatre. The Los Angeles Yiddish Drama Group, under the artistic direction of Adolph Freeman, opened on April 25, 1936, at the Figueroa Playhouse with the comedy *For Business Reasons*, by Charles Gottesfeld.

All of this activity marked the first time Yiddish theatre had been underwritten by the federal government. Moreover, as a result of its many English translations, it brought Yiddish theatre to new audiences on a wider scale than ever before. The Yiddish drama groups were not the only examples of ethnic theatre under Washington's banner; there were others, too, including units of Negro, Spanish, French, and German theatre. The Yiddishists, however, seem to have set a significant precedent in 1934 by setting up an ethnic theatre unit.

In most cases artistic directors of Yiddish federal theatre were selected from the ranks of professional Yiddish theatre, but in others the directors came from non-Yiddish theatre backgrounds. Some of these people were well established in their fields, while others had lesser artistic standing—including some with amateur standing. The directors of greatest standing were Zvee Scooler, Wolf

Barzell, Yehuda Bleich, and Jacob Mestel. As for Scooler, Bleich, and Barzell, this trio had already established a reputation as directors of a group known alternately as Die Boyes (The Boys), Zalts un Feffer (Salt and Pepper), and Die Tsulakhnekes (In Spite of Everything). A forerunner of We Live and Laugh, one of the last performances of The Boys was on September 21, 1935, in the Civic Repertory Theatre. Bleich and Barzell were also commissioned to direct the Yiddish version of Sinclair Lewis' *It Can't Happen Here*, which opened at the Biltmore Theatre on October 27, 1936, simultaneously with twenty other productions of the play across the country. Jacob Mestel, who directed the Yiddish version of Clifford Odets' *Awake and Sing!*, had helped to establish the ARTEF Yiddish workers' theatre company. Martin Wolfson, who directed *The Tailor Becomes a Storekeeper* for the New York Yiddish Drama Group, had no earlier Yiddish theatre experience, but had appeared in numerous New York plays, including Eugene O'Neill's *Marco Millions* for the Theatre Guild in 1930. A personal friend of Hallie Flanagan, head of the Federal Theatre Project, Wolfson had once lectured to her acting class at Vassar. The directors of the Anglo-Yiddish Group brought with them theatre backgrounds of a lesser degree. Julian Rochelle, who directed *The Idle Inn*, came to the project with a limited knowledge of theatre and perhaps some college experience. Harold Bolton, the director of the Anglo-Yiddish Group's production of Friedrich Wolf's *Professor Mamlock*, had appeared in minor roles before the federal theatre, including *Midnight*, a melodrama by Claire and Paul Sifton produced by the Theatre Guild in 1930. Morris Schorr of the Boston group had written a number of Yiddish plays of minor importance and appeared in Boston Yiddish theatre. Adolph Gartner of the Chicago group had appeared in German light operas in New York and later organized his own Yiddish theatre company at the Pavillion Theatre in Chicago. Adolph Freeman of the Los Angeles group had acted for many years in Yiddish theatre in Argentina and also appeared in Boris Thomashefsky's National Theatre in New York City.

There were many talented and highly experienced actors and other artistic personnel in Yiddish federal theatres whose presence provided a welcome balance to the essentially amateur standing of a high percentage of others, as was so typical of federal theatre in general. Among those with notable backgrounds were Maurice Strassberg and Emil Hirsch of the Anglo-Yiddish group, who had spent many years together as actors in Maurice Schwartz's New York Yiddish Art Theatre. Jacob Bergreen, Isaac Gladstone, and Ben Bassenko had all been seen in earlier versions of We Live and Laugh. Maurice Rauch, We Live and Laugh's musical director, and Lillian Shapero, its choreographer, were well-known figures in New York's Yiddish theatre world who had worked in ARTEF. Los Angeles Yiddish group actress Paula Walter was probably the artist of greatest standing there, having appeared with the famed Vilna Yiddish Troupe.

Each Yiddish unit operated as an independent company with its own actors and actresses. Design of sets and costumes, however, was left to central bureaus. This mode of organization, complicated by endless bureaucratic regulations, especially in the project's early months, made it difficult to requisition even the smallest stage properties. Publicity and theatre bookings, too, were handled by central offices detached from the performing units.

Although most actors on the project were on relief rolls, directors could hire nonrelief personnel to play certain parts or fill other needs. This was the case, for example, when Helen Blay, a respected actress with experience in Hirschbein plays, was taken on as a nonreliefer to play Meta in *The Idle Inn*. It was also true of Rauch and Shapero.

Yiddish actors, like their counterparts in other federal units, often struggled to find performance space, a factor inhibiting the business success of federal theatre. In Chicago, for example, there were three units on the project—English, Yiddish, and vaudeville—but only two available stages. The result was obvious: units had to wait for a free theatre. Because of the lack of performance space, they spent inordinately long periods in rehearsals or in green rooms. For the Yiddish actors, who by tradition were used to quick successions of plays, this was a particular problem. In New York City the difficulty of finding theatres was exacerbated by an agreement between commercial producers and the project in general that held the federal theatre to no more than two concurrent productions in stages located between Forty-second and Fifty-second Streets. According to George Kondolf, head of the New York City federal theatre, "as suitably appointed theatres outside of this area are extremely limited, we are continually running into the problem of having a show ready for production and then finding no theatre available to house it. The more successful are our plays, the fewer we are in a position to stage, since the 'hits' tie up the theatres we do have for months on end" (George Kondolf, "Federal Theatre—1939." Records of the Federal Theatre Project, Record Group No. 69, National Archives, Washington, D.C.). In the Yiddish groups some of this slack was taken up by group bookings by synagogues and Jewish educational associations in exchange for a percentage of the receipts.

Contemporary plays like *It Can't Happen Here, Professor Mamlock*, and *Awake and Sing!* seem to have brought the Yiddish units greater attention than offerings from the traditional, older Yiddish repertory. The Anglo-Jewish Play Department, which was the Yiddish counterpart of the National Service Bureau, tried to promote a fresh approach to Yiddish repertoire, circulating play lists of many contemporary plays and translating plays into Yiddish. This example was followed in a most pronounced manner by We Live and Laugh, which, as Maurice Rauch noted, tried to stage "better, more modern, more tasteful and literary Theatre than the going commodity" of melodramas in the commercial Yiddish theatre (Maurice Rauch, letter to the author, November 11, 1971). The first American theatre to experiment with the Chauve-Souris Russian cabaret style of intimate theatre, We Live and Laugh hoped to create what Scooler called, in the vernacular of the social-minded thirties, "wide-awake" theatre (Zvee Scooler, Radio Talk, n.d., gift to the author). Its repertoire included *America, America*, by Alfred Kreymborg, as well as dramatizations from many Yiddish writers and poets, including Moshe Nadir, I. L. Peretz, and Sholom Secunda. Other approaches to staging and interpretation were attempted here and there and thought to be innovative by the Yiddish unit directors. The Yiddish translation of *Awake and Sing!*, shared in productions by Yiddish groups in New York, Chicago, and Los Angeles, was thought to be somehow "closer" to the true flavor of Odets. This was interesting because Odets, in his later work, made a conscious effort to break away from what he perceived to be his identification as a Yiddish playwright writing in English. In Chicago, Nathan Vizonsky, Adolph Gartner's choreographer, saw *The Tailor Becomes a Storekeeper* as a choreographic unit with movement similar to that of kabuki. In Los Angeles, Adolph Freeman used wagon stages for *It Can't Happen Here* in an attempt, only minimally successful, to speed up the pace of the play.

Critics tended to give mixed reactions to the work of the Yiddish units. The work of the cabaret group We Live and Laugh, the Anglo-Yiddish Group's *Professor Mamlock*, the New York Yiddish Drama's *It Can't Happen Here*, and the Chicago Yiddish Drama Group's *Awake and Sing!* were singled out as particularly outstanding.

With federal money cut off in 1939, Yiddish federal theatre came to a halt with the rest of the project activities. As early as June 1937, congressional cuts in the appropriations for the project had forced units to let some personnel go in the interests of greater efficiency. The demise of the project meant the end of an experiment in federal sponsorship of one of America's oldest foreign-language theatres.

PERSONNEL

Stage Directors: Wolf Barzell, Yehuda Bleich, Adolph Freeman (1936–39), Adolph Gartner (1936–39), Jacob Mestel (1936–37), Morris Schorr (1935–38), Zvee Scooler (1936–37), Boris Thomashefsky, Harry Thomashefsky (1934–35), Martin Wolfson (1937–38).

Scene Designers: New York Yiddish Drama Group: Philip Gelb (1936), Paul Ouzounoff (1937). We Live and Laugh: Andrei Houdiakoff (1936–37). Anglo-Yiddish Group: Philip Gelb (1936–37). Chicago Yiddish Drama Group: Les Marzolf (1938–39), Clive Ricka-baugh (1936–38). Los Angeles Yiddish Drama Group: Frederick Stover (1936–39).

Musical Directors: New York Yiddish Drama Group: Maurice Rauch (1937–38). We Live and Laugh: Maurice Rauch (1936–37). Chicago Yiddish Drama Group: David Sheinfeld (1938). Los Angeles Yiddish Drama Group: George Dilworth (1936–39).

Choreographers: We Live and Laugh: Lillian Shapero (1936–37). New York Yiddish Drama Group: Lillian Shapero (1937–38). Chicago Yiddish Drama Group: Nathan Vi-zonsky (1936–39).

We Live and Laugh Actors and Actresses: Florence Abrams, Boris Auerbach, Ben Bassenko, Rose Becker, Harry Bender, Jacob Bergreen, Edward Bernard, Felix Bimko, Morris Bleiman, Henry Blum, Louis Brandt, Sam Bunin, Morris Chodak, Jacob Cohen, Rose Dickstein, Rubin Doctor, Zelda Durbin, Luba Eisenberg, Sol Eisikoff, Morris Feder, John Franzblau, Morris Ganz, Irvin Geist, Harry Gershonn, Betty Gladstone, Isaac Glad-stone, Benjamin Goichberg, Sol Goichberg, Max Gold, Aaron Goldblum, Carl Goldman,

Jacob Goldman, Ruth Gordon, Minna Guralnick, Max Hirsch, Samuel Horowitz, Benjamin Jacobs, Uri Kagan, Fishel Kanapoff, Morris Kirsch, Malka Kornstein, Berta Leltchuk, Dave Levine, Isidor Lillian, Sam Lowenwirth, Max Malinofsky, Israel Mandell, Julius Margolis, Isidore Meltzer, Sonia Mishel, Aaron Nager, Joseph Oberlander, Morris Paskin, Frances Pearlstein, Anna Raphael, Sylvia Schildwach, Chaim Schnayer, Lena Schoenfeld, Marcus Schwartz, Stella Schwartz, Joseph Shrogin, Elia Siegalow, Morrie Siegel, Jacob Silbert, Lyda Slava, Oscar Solomon, Morris Tayman, Lisa Varon, Charles Werlinsky, Mordechai Yachson.

New York Anglo-Yiddish Actors and Actresses: Joseph Anthony, Vivian Anthony, Archie Aronowitz, Maurice Barrett, Abe Barsukov, Albert Berman, Helen Blay, Herbert Breakstone, Mollie Buschbaum, Joseph Ceccacci, Barney Cohen, Robert Cohen, John Crawford, Benjamin Dansker, Dorothy Gammon, Virginia Gillies, Eleanor Gilmore, Joan Gilmore, Morris Gosfeld, Emil Hirsch, Jac Hoffman, Gretchen Karnot, Isidore Katz, Julius Kleinman, Maurice Lazarus, David Lipton, Nat Loesburg, William Mercur, David Meyrowitz, Lewis Parker, Benjamin Pestreich, Sadie Rosen, George Schlichting, Barney Silver, Sam Silverbush, *Maurice Strassberg* (1936–37), Jack Tammy, Morris Traum.

Chicago Yiddish Drama Group Actors and Actresses: Alexander Adams, Alex Amasia, Regina August, Leon E. Beach, John W. Bean, Constance Belmont, Jose Borcia, Barney Brown, Brenda Brown, Nell Calvin, Marian Cashman, Maurice Cazden, Charles Conklin, Carl Dahl, Sydney Ehrenberg, Charles Ernst, Isaac Fishelewitz, Josephine Flynn, Grant Foreman, Phyllis Franklin, Genevieve Gartner, Carl Goldman, Norman Hilgard, William Hiliard, Sam Kaplan, Dorothy Karl, Sandra Karyl, Jack Kroopkin, Stuart Langley, L. Louis, Gertrude Lyall, Ruby McMechan, Louis Marcus, Roy Moshel, Saul Nagoshiner, Francine Oliver, Silas Phelps, James Rice, Velma Replogle, David Schoenholtz, Stella Schulman, William Seabury, Edna Sexton, Elizabeth Sexton, Dorothy Silverman, Ruth Smyth, Albert Storch, Jennia Sweet, Harry Terman, Felicia Terry, Nathan Vizonsky, Opal Walker, Syde Walker, Wilder Walters, *David Yanover* (1936–39).

Los Angeles Yiddish Drama Group Actors and Actresses: Albert Aaron, Abraham Atlas, Philip Augenblick, Sam Bendel, Riva Brodsky, Laura Brookheart, Ralph Fitzsimmons, *Adolph Freeman* (1936–39), Bessie Gordon, Mark Grossman, Josephine Heath, Laura Howard, Wallace Kadel, Alexander Kopp, Beatrice Le Beaux, Bertha McKee, Jack Magee, Robert Perkoff, Dorothy Roche, Bernice Sachs, De Weese Seewir, Marion Sheldon, Richard Stirling, William Vine, Paula Walter, Nathan Weinstein, Dallas Welford, Fay Wishnevsky.

REPERTORY

New York Yiddish Drama Group: 1934–35: *The Yiddish King Lear*. 1935: *Uptown and Downtown*. 1936: *The Eternal Wanderer, It Can't Happen Here*. 1938: *The Tailor Becomes a Storekeeper, Awake and Sing!*.

We Live and Laugh: 1936–37.

New York Anglo-Yiddish Group: 1936: *The Idle Inn*. 1937: *Professor Mamlock*.

Chicago Yiddish Drama Group: 1937: *Monesh*. 1938: *The Tailor Becomes a Storekeeper*. 1938–39: *Awake and Sing!*.

Los Angeles Yiddish Drama Group: 1936: *When Will He Die?, A String of Pearls, Uriel Acosta, God of Vengeance, It Can't Happen Here, For Business Reasons*. 1936–37: *A Hidden Corner, Redemption*. 1937: *Relatives, The Treasure*. 1938: *Yankel Boyla, Professor Mamlock*. 1939: *Day Is Darkness, Awake and Sing!*.

Boston Yiddish Drama Group: 1935: *Too Late, Tragic Joke, The Client, Father in Disgrace, Golden Wedding, Greenfields, Hand of Destiny, The Idiot, The Stranger*. 1936: *The Blacksmith's Daughter, Blind Love, The Doctor, Each with His Own Belief, For Business Reasons, God, Man and Devil, God of Vengeance, The Idle Inn, Landsleit, The Lost Soul, The Prisoner, His Awakening*. 1936–37: *A Hidden Corner*. 1937: *Her Confessions, 200,000, The Two Kuni-Lemls*. 1938: *The Show-Off*.

BIBLIOGRAPHY

Published Source:
Flanagan, Hallie. *Arena*. New York: Duell, 1940.

Unpublished Sources:
Medovoy, George. "The Federal Theatre Project Yiddish Troupes (1935–1939)." Doctoral dissertation, University of California at Davis, 1975.
Rauch, Maurice. Letter to the author. November 11, 1971.
Scooler, Zvee. Radio talk. No date.

Archival Resources:
Fairfax, Virginia. George Mason University. Research Center for the Federal Theatre Project.
Washington, D.C. National Archives. Record Group 69, Federal Theatre Project.

George Medovoy

[THE] FREE SOUTHERN THEATRE (FST), New Orleans, originally known as the Tougaloo College Drama Workshop, was founded by John O'Neal, Doris Derby, Bill Hutchinson, and Gilbert Moses in October 1963 in Tougaloo, Mississippi. O'Neal and Derby were both field secretaries for the Student Non-Violent Coordinating Committee (SNCC) teaching English at Tougaloo College to nonliterate adults as part of SNCC's adult literacy project. Moses, an Oberlin College student, was in Jackson, Mississippi, writing for the *Mississippi Free Press*, owned by Oberlin College. Hutchinson was an English instructor and director of drama at Tougaloo College. Their first production, *Inherit the Wind*, by Jerome Lawrence and Robert E. Lee, opened in the fall of 1963. Moses directed, O'Neal was the business manager, Hutchinson served as technical director, and Derby, an artist, designed the set.

The FST was an outgrowth of the civil rights movement and always more an element of that movement than a theatre group. At the time few theatres were concerned with the arts as a force for social change. In New York only three theatres were politically oriented: Peter Schumann's Bread and Puppet Theatre; Amiri Baraka's short-lived Black Arts Repertory Theatre, founded in 1965 for Harlem youth; and the Living Theatre*. Outside of New York there were two nationally known groups: the San Francisco Mime Troupe*, and El Teatro Campesiño, founded in 1965 by Luis Valdez to politicize migrant farmworkers in California. Both the Black Arts Repertory Theatre and El Teatro Campesiño were oriented to specific racial groups and also attempted to instill a sense of racial esteem. As the decade progressed, other theatres were founded in other urban areas that mirrored the activities of these issue-oriented theatres.

The solidifying force in FST and the only person who stayed with FST from its inception to its demise was John O'Neal. The Mound City, Illinois, native was educated at Southern Illinois University in Carbondale (B.A. in English and Philosophy). After graduation, O'Neal joined SNCC and was sent to southwest Georgia. While at Tougaloo College, O'Neal attempted to reconcile his professional ambitions with his social concerns. He realized that achieving his goal of improved social justice for blacks would take a lifetime. He also realized that the best approach to his goal was through the arts.

FST's purpose was to stimulate critical and reflective thought about the civil rights movement. Most of the grass-roots activists associated with the civil rights movement were not from the middle class, although the leadership of the movement was. The motto of FST, "A theatre for those who have no theatre," illustrated its desire to make theatre available and pertinent to the lives of poor blacks in the rural and urban South. FST also sought to create theatrical forms allied with the experiences of its audiences. The organization was established as a permanent stock company whose primary outlet was a touring ensemble. After moving to New Orleans in January 1965, FST also operated a community workshop program. During the 1970s FST also had a regional television show, *Nation Time*, and a weekly radio show, *Plain Talk*.

The word free in the company's title meant that no admission was charged. Therefore, financial support came from foundations and private donors. FST's first contributed in 1963 was a check for $5 from poet Langston Hughes. With SNCC coordinating, O'Neal, the primary fund-raiser, traveled the breadth of the United States seeking contributions. In September 1964 FST incorporated; not-for-profit status came in December 1965. FST received its first grant from the Rockefeller Foundation in 1966 in the amount of $16,000. In subsequent years the Rockefeller Foundation, New York Foundation, National Endowment for the Arts, Ford Foundation, United Church of Christ, Episcopal Church, and the Rockefeller Family Fund supported the group. FST reached its peak funding year in 1969 when it received $227,754 in grants and private contributions.

FST's reputation is based on its courageous efforts to play in Southern communities violently opposed to its presenting theatre in the black communities. In some instances guards had to be posted during performances to protect both the audience and the players from violence. The most reliable criticism comes not from the newspaper critics, as the intent of FST was not to seek critical acclaim from established critics, but from the audiences who saw the productions. One viewer in New Orleans wrote: "[FST] has honored New Orleans by deciding to locate here. It has produced professional caliber plays presented to many persons who otherwise would never see a play" (Shirley Harrison, letter to the editor, *New Orleans Times-Picayune*, November 13, 1974, p. 4). Denying the role of mere propagandists, O'Neal stated that "our audiences were more grateful than critical. . . . We want to change that too" (cited in Elizabeth Switherland, "Theatre of the Meaningful," *Nation*, October 1964, p. 5).

In sixteen years FST, consisting of a paid staff and unpaid volunteers, including professional actors, produced forty-four plays as well as several poetry readings and dance concerts. Some of the productions were anthologies of black poetry works developed by the company. FST had a playwriting component that wrote scripts as part of a cultural program called Sunday Jambalaya. In addition, FST sponsored a workshop program, Blkartsouth, and published *Nkombo*, a literary journal.

Many people contributed time and expertise. Actress Denise Nicholas, who later married Gilbert Moses, joined FST in 1964 and toured in its first production, *In White America*, in the summer of 1964. In the winter of 1964 O'Neal asked Tulane University drama teacher Richard Schechner to join the managerial staff—which he did the next June. He convinced FST to move its headquarters to New Orleans. FST located first in the Seventh Ward, a middle-class black neighborhood, later in the Desire housing area, and finally, in 1966, in a storefront at 1240 Dryades, in the center of New Orleans. Schechner stayed with the group until Tulane reorganized its drama department. Schechner late served as chairman of the board of directors of FST. Tom Dent and his wife, Bobbie Jones, joined FST early in 1965. Dent served as chairman of the board and as playwriting director, while Jones was the administrative head of the New York office and worked as a fund-raiser. Actors, for the most part, were students from Tougaloo College, Dillard University, or Southern University, or from communities in which FST performed. However, during FST's early years, professional performers did work with FST, but not as principals or stars.

FST became inactive in September 1978 and ceased operations in 1980. Having prepared a one-man show, "Don't Start Me Talkin' or I'll Tell Everything I Know: Sayings from the Life and Writings of Junebug Jabbo Jones," O'Neal started touring independently of FST in 1980. A conference titled "The Role of Art in the Process of Social Change: A Valediction Without Mourning for the Free Southern Theatre, 1963–1980," featuring theatre workshops and a performance festival of groups inspired by FST, was held in New Orleans November 20–24, 1985. On the last day the FST was officially buried in a ritual based on the New Orleans "Second Line" Jazz Funeral.

PERSONNEL

Management: Tom Dent, producer and director of playwriting (1965–70); Gilbert Moses, producer, director, and actor (1963–69); John O'Neal, producer, director, actor (1963–80); Richard Schechner, producer and actor (1964–66); Frank Crump, tour manager (1965); Isaac Coleman, tour manager (1969); Richard Aronson, business manager (1966); Jesse Morrell, community relations director (1971–73).

Scene Technicians: McNeal Cayette (1971–73), Carmel Collins (1967), Raymond DuVernay (1967), Marie Evans (1971), Lester Galt (1964), Alvin James (1969), Gwendolyn Johnson (1971), Lewis Johnson (1971), Eric Lewis (1966), David McLaughlin (1965), Hammett Murphy (1965), Peter O'Grady (1965), Fred O'Neill (1969), Jose Sevilla (1969), Joe Stevens (1971–73), Stanley Taylor (1964).

Costume Staff: Lu Barre (1971), Willa Radin (1965), Sarallen (1969).

Musical Director: Jackie Washington (1964).

Stage Directors: Earl Billings (1973–74), Robert Cordier (1965), Robert Costley (1965–73), James Cromwell (1964), Scott Cunningham (1965), Severn Darden (1964), Lee Roy Giles (1969), Curtis King (1979–80), Alexander Peace (1969).

Stage Managers: Mathilde Shepard (1965), Sylvia Williams (1969), William Zukof (1965).

Staff: Sarah Allen (1973), Jeanne Breaker (1969), Ann Darden (1964), Carol Gaudin (1969), Rose Hicks (1969), Marge Jennings (1966), Mary Lovelace (1965), Roberta Jones (1969), Charlene Mays (1973–77), Wilma Moses (1969), LaVerne Neblett (1969), Marilyn O'Neal (1975–80), Ed Pearl (1965), Benjamin Rick (1966), Lionel Robinson (1969), Sara Rudner (1966), Lynn Sanzabacher (1965), Helen Brown Schechner (1965), Patricia Singler (1969), Cynthia Washington (1964).

Instructors: Betty Greenhoe (1965), Kate Pearl (1965), Paul Sills (1964).

Actors and Actresses: Gary Bolling (1967), Grace Brooks (1964), Tony Burton (1971), John Cannon (1964–65), Barbara Clarke (1969), Amos Coffee (1969), Bessie Dill (1965), Jaci Early (1967), T-C Ellis (1969), Richard Fells (1969), Leopoldo Flemming (1969), Joan Foreman (1965), Edna Gelhorn (1965), LeJuan Gilmore (1971), Yolanda Goff (1971), Betty Greenhoe (1965), Marie Hansell (1971), Penny Hartzell (1964), Emalyn Hawkins (1965), Sam Hill (1966–69), Marisa Joffrey (1965), Joan Johnson (1964), Roger Johnson (1964), Charles Lee (1969), Collin Lee (1965), Murray Levy (1964–66), Victor Lewis (1965), Detton Lieuteau (1966), Mary Lovelace (1965), Faye McNair (1971), Cynthia McPherson (1967), Denise Nicholas (1964–66), Roscoe Orman (1964–66), Joseph Perry (1965–66), Judith Richardson (1969), Francesca Roberts (1971), Melanie Roberts (1971), Peter de Rome (1964), Seret Scott (1969), Cynthia Small (1964), Ben Spillman (1971), Sally Summers (1965), Susan Tabor (1964), Billie Tyler (1969), Trish Van Devere (1965), Alana Villavasa (1971), Eric Weinberger (1964), James Williams (1969).

Auxillary Programs: Eluard Burt (1967), Tony Burton (1975), Chakula Cha Jua (McNeal Cayette) (1973–74, 1977), Norbert Davidson (1964, 1975–76), Val Ferdinand, Susan Ferrer (1965), Joanne Forman (1965), Quo Vadis Gex, David Henderson (poet in residence) (1967), Don Hubbard, Eartha Ison (1973–74), Octave Lilly (1973–74), Bayo Oduneye (1971–75), Dwight Ott (1969), Iona Reese (1969), Bill Rouselle (1972–76), Raymond Washington, Alvin Williams (1975).

FST's fund-raising activities and the many volunteers who served on its board, lending their names and credibility to the organization, were crucial to its success.

Sponsors and members of the board of directors of FST: Arthur Ashe, Wilfred Aubert, Robert Aulston, James Baldwin, Harry Belafonte, Theodore Bikel, Julian Bond, St. Clair Bourne, Grace Brooks, Ed Bullins, Juggy Butler, Oretha Castle, Mr. and Mrs. Randolph Compton, Maxine Copelin, Robert W. Corrigan, James Cromwell, Severn Darden, Leon Davis, Ossie Davis, Ruby Dee, Dave Dennis, Thomas C. Dent, Leonard Dreyfus, Rhoda Dreyfus, Norman Eisner, Carol Feinman, Mr. and Mrs. Thomas Fichandler, Garry Gaffman, Floyd Gaffney, Issac Garrison, Morton Gottlieb, Alan Greenberg, Joel Grey, Fannie Lou Hamer, Joe Hanlan, Penelope Hartzell, Margaret Helbach, Nat Hentoff, Mr. and Mrs. Dustin Hoffman, Langston Hughes, Jules Irving, Ernest Jones, Brenda Joyce, Tom Kefalas, Mr. and Mrs. John Killins, Mr. and Mrs. Arthur B. Krim, Jack Lemmon, Murray Levy, Joseph Liebman, Ernie McClintock, Alden McDonald, Alan Mandell,

Theodore Marchand, E. Howard Molisani, Gilbert Moses, Denise Nicholas, John O'Neal, Patrick O'Neal, Warren Parker, Gregory Peck, Robert Perkins, Brock Peters, Benjamin Pick, Robert Polk, Josephine Premice, Langston Reed, Issac Reynolds, Peter de Rome, Philip Rose, William Rucker, Robert Ryan, Rep. William F. Ryan, Richard Schechner, Madeleine Sherwood, Mrs. Timothy Slater, Hope R. Stevens, David Stone-Martin, Stanley Swerdow, Barbara Ann Teer, Milton Upton, Jack Valenti, Roxy Wright, Andrew Young, Wallace Young, Robert Zarem.

REPERTORY

1963–64: *Inherit the Wind.*

1964–65: *In White America, Purlie Victorious, Waiting for Godot.*

1965–66: *The Beauty and the Beast, The Rifles of Senora Carrar, In White America.*

1966–67: *An Evening of African and Afro-American Poetry, Roots, I Speak of Africa, Does Man Help Man?, An Evening of Robert Hayden's Poetry and Prose.*

1967–68: *Happy Ending, Uncle Tom's Second Line Funeral, The Lesson.*

1968–69: *Black Mind Jockeys, Lion in Winter, Mama, The Pill, The Picket.*

1969–70: *Feathers and Stuff, Ritual Murder, To Kill or Die, Slave Ship, Roots, Riot Duty, Proper and Fine, The Entourage of Fannie Lou Hamer, East of Jordan, Snapshot.*

1971–72: *The Warning . . . "A Theme for Linda," The Picket, To Kill a Devil, Minstrel Quintet, Rosalee Pritchett, Edifying Further Elaboration on the Mentality of a Chore, Black Love Song, Daddy Gander Raps.*

1972–73: *A Raisin in the Sun, Hurricane Season, A Black Experience, We Are the Suns.*

1973–74: *Where Is the Blood of Your Fathers?, When the Opportunity Scratches, Itch It, Black Cycles, Small Winds Before the Revolution.*

1974–75: *The Collected Works of Langston Hughes.*

1975–76: *Don't You Want to Be Free?.*

1976–77: *Our Lan', Hurricane Season, A Black Experience.*

1977–78: *Ritual Murder, An Evening of Black Dance, Tell Pharoah.*

1978–79: *Candle in the Wind.*

BIBLIOGRAPHY

Published Sources:

Dent, Thomas C., Richard Schechner, and Gilbert Moses, eds. *The Free Southern Theatre by the Free Southern Theatre.* New York: Bobbs-Merrill Co., 1969.

Fabre, G. "Free Southern Theatre, 1963–79." *Black American Literary Forum* 17 (Summer 1983):55–59.

Harrison, Shirley. Letter to the editor. *New Orleans Times-Picayune*, November 13, 1974, p. 4.

Sutherland, Elizabeth. "Theatre of the Meaningful." *Nation*, October 1964, p. 5.

Unpublished Sources:

O'Neal, John. Telephone interview. October 31, 1986.

Tripp, Ellen L. "Free Southern Theater: There Is Always a Message." Doctoral dissertation, University of North Carolina at Greensboro, 1986.

Archival Resource:
New Orleans, Louisiana. Amistad Research Center. Free Southern Theatre Records,
    1963–78 (microfilm). Register of documents may be ordered from the Center,
    400 Esplanade Avenue.

Barbara J. Molette

[THE] FRONT STREET THEATRE, Memphis, Tennessee, was founded as a summer stock operation called Theatre "12" by George Touliatos and Barbara Cason in 1954. Its first production, Christopher Fry's *The Lady's Not for Burning*, was performed in the basement (the former swimming pool area) of the old King Cotton Hotel, located on Front Street. As did similar operations in Houston (the Alley Theatre*) and San Francisco (the Actor's Workshop*), Theatre "12" began as an amateur organization with meager finances and in facilities not originally designed or intended for theatrical productions. This opening venture for Touliatos proved to be successful both critically and financially. The group incorporated as a not-for-profit organization in May 1955 (with Touliatos as president) and lasted for two years. During this period it presented fifteen additional productions. Theatre "12" dissolved in October 1956 with a bank balance of about $126, which the group donated to the Memphis Ballet Society. During the period of the group's existence, Touliatos was completing two master's degrees at the University of Iowa.

The Front Street Theatre of Memphis was chartered in May 1957, and the first season included seven plays produced by a company of ten, including Touliatos and his wife, the former Barbara Cason. The group presented two seasons of summer stock in the arena theatre, seating about 237, in the King Cotton Hotel. Approximately 20,000 patrons viewed these productions, which included the group's first musical. The stage musical would prove to be important to the financial health of the Front Street Theatre, one of few resident theatres producing them.

Four years as a quasi-professional theatre began with what the theatre called Season III (1959–60), a twenty-week term in which the group played to audiences that included 1,800 subscribers. Professional actors were paid $70 a week, musicals continued to dot the schedule, and the group produced *Othello*, its first play by Shakespeare. A revamped board of directors tried to stimulate better community relations. In the middle of Season IV the group moved to the old Idlewild Theatre at 1819 Madison Avenue (to be the group's home until 1968), with a seating capacity of about 375. The move greatly affected the financial condition of the company, though it always struggled. At this time Front Street Theatre became a charter member of Theatre Communications Group, and Touliatos announced expansion to a fifty-week season, despite a growing deficit and declining subscriptions. In Season V Front Street was still a non-Equity professional company, but 1,200 subscribers supported a season of eight productions, and the company played to about 51 percent of capacity. The group ended 1961 with a deficit of about $9,000.

At the same time the Front Street Theatre was trying to establish itself in its new location, the older and well-established Memphis Little Theatre continued to attract a large subscriber audience. The Front Street did initiate an apprentice program in 1961, as well as a small drama school, a ladies' auxiliary called the Dress Circle, and a children's theatre. The year's financial problems were alleviated in part by donations from the board of directors, a fund-raising drive, and by box-office receipts from several long-run musicals. Season VI saw subscriptions decrease to about 1,350. Musicals and light comedies began to dominate the theatre schedule.

The Front Street Theatre achieved full resident professional status in 1963 with an agreement between the theatre and Actors' Equity Association. Subscriptions increased to 2,500, and the theatre began an extensive children's theatre program under the direction of Barry Fuller, initiated the private Balcony Club (scene of numerous revues), and hired Bryan Clark as a full-time business manager. Despite the growth in memberships, the deficit at the end of the season rose substantially. Touliatos also faced difficulty in luring qualified professional actors to Memphis. Season VIII included a most successful subscription campaign, aided in part by the advice of Richard Kirschner and Danny Newman. Subscribers totaled about 4,400. Season IX reflected another substantial increase in audience support (5,800 subscribers paid $140,000 for their season tickets). Three revivals boosted income while keeping expenses low, and the Memphis Arts Council provided funding. However, staff dissension plagued the theatre this year, and Bryan Clark resigned.

Between 1963 and 1966, thirty productions, including twelve musicals, were presented to about 183,000 patrons. At the same time the theatre's indebtedness rose to about $40,000. In May 1966 the Rockefeller Foundation granted the theatre $18,000 for a summer youth program (directed by Peter Thompson); another grant supported an audience survey.

Season X (1966–67) was conducted under two general managers, first William Taylor and later Harvey Landa, as well as several guest directors. Audience development problems caused by schedule changes, a problem in previous seasons as well, continued to haunt management. Not long after the production of *Macbeth* the theatre's mounting deficit demanded a remedy. A last-ditch fund drive raised about $35,000, but before the money was collected, George Touliatos took a two-year leave of absence, leaving the theatre and its $200,000 deficit in the hands of Harvey Landa, the general manager.

In the fall of 1968 the group took up residence in a 500-seat theatre on the campus of Memphis State University; its director of theatre, Keith Kennedy, became the artistic director of the company and Landa stayed on as general manager. Although university affiliation was predicated on a break-even budget, and no university funds could be used to reduce the eleven-year-old deficit, an ambitious season of seven productions, including two musicals and a Shakespearean comedy, was announced. With only about 1,600 season tickets sold, the season ended after three productions, and the Front Street Theatre vanished from the scene. Only the memories of hundreds of performances and the spectre of a sizable deficit (to be paid by board members and friends of the theatre) remained of this short-lived theatre, which, according to J. W. Zeigler, was an organization "walking a high-tension wire" (*Regional Theatre: The Revolutionary Stage* [New York: DeCapo Press, 1977], p. 49).

PERSONNEL

Producers: Barbara Cason, George Touliatos.

Business Managers: Bryan Clark, Harvey Landa, William Taylor.

Directors: Robert Baker, Alan Bates, James Dyas, Louis Griss, Keith Kennedy, Jack Poggi, Curt Reis, *George Touliatos*, Carl Weber, William Woodman.

Designers: Evelyn Norton Anderson, Jim Boatman, Fran Brassard, Ralph Carter, Barbara Cason, Buck Clark, Tom Evans, Don Fibiger, Henry Fritzius, Francis Gassner, Edward Graczyk, Ron Jerit, Grady Larkins, Lynn lePelley, Andrew Loshbough, Jean Loshbough, Johnnie Lovelady, Mary Russell Ragsdale, Burt Rissman, Johnny Skinner, Ralph Swanson, James Tilton, George Touliatos, Kurt Wilhelm.

Actors and Actresses: Donna Alexander, Philip Arnoult, Gene Arturo, Nancy Baker, *Allen Bates*, Joe Bowman, Richard Briglea, Duane Campbell, *Tom Carson, Barbara Cason*, Linda Childress, Nancy Cole, Stephen Cole, Richard Coletti, Al Corbin, Pasha Davis, Harvey Dice, Ronnie Claire Edwards, Patricia Elliot, Bill Elwood, Jay Erlicher, Terrence Evans, Pam Fife, Jonathan Frid, *Barry Fuller*, Rita Gam, Karen Grassle, Jack Hallihan, Allen Hamilton, Jerry Hardin, George Hearn, Roland Hewgill, Raymond Hill, Polly Holliday, Liz Ingleson, Dana Ivey, Dennis Jones, Norman Jones, Robert Karnes, Sheila Larken, Dempster Leech, Robert Levine, *Macon (Sonny) McCalman*, Earl McCarroll, Nye McGeow, Cassandra Morgan, Nancy Nesbitt, Mike Norell, Ivan Paulsen, Robert Paulus, *Mary Russell Ragsdale*, Nancy Redfearn, Ben Reed, Gil Rogers, Leon Russom, Richard Sanders, William Shust, Wade Sides, Charles Stillwell, Ken Swafford, James Talkan, Marguerite Tarrant, Ron Thompson, *George Touliatos*, James Valentine, James Weiss, Patricia Weiting, Maggie West, Eleanor Williams, Ken Zimmerman.

REPERTORY

Season I (1957): *The Tender Trap, Mrs. McThing, Private Lives, A Streetcar Named Desire, Three for Tonight* (one-acts).

Season II (1958): *My Sister Eileen, The Boy Friend, Kiss Me Kate, Charley's Aunt, Arms and the Man, Will Success Spoil Rock Hunter?*

Season III (1959–60): *Cat on a Hot Tin Roof, Guys and Dolls, Othello, Call Me Madam, The Mousetrap, Fallen Angels, Don Juan in Hell, The Boy Friend.*

Season IV (1960–61): *The Solid Gold Cadillac, Carousel, Henry IV*, Part I, *The Man Who Came to Dinner, The Caine Mutiny Court Martial, Mister Roberts, Babes in Arms, Bus Stop, Brigadoon* (first production at the Madison Street location), *Waiting for Godot.*

Season V (1961–62): *Hay Fever, The Crucible, New Moon, Arsenic and Old Lace, The Tender Trap, The King and I, Wonderful Town, The Marriage-Go-Round, Auntie Mame, You Can't Take It with You, The Importance of Being Earnest, Ladies' Night in a Turkish Bath, Little Mary Sunshine.*

Season VI (1962–63): *Oklahoma, The Student Prince, Where's Charley, The Fourposter, Two for the Seesaw, I Am a Camera, Gypsy, Peter Pan, Come Blow Your Horn,*

The Fantasticks, The Caretaker, Period of Adjustment, Bye Bye Birdie, Gigi, South Pacific.

Season VII (1963–64): *Annie Get Your Gun, Three Men on a Horse, The Front Page, The Threepenny Opera, Kismet, My Three Angels, Misalliance, Irma La Douce, The Taming of the Shrew, Little Hut, Sound of Music, The Country Wife, Damn Yankees.*

Season VIII (1964–65): *My Fair Lady, The Seven Year Itch, Ah Wilderness!, Oh Dad, Poor Dad, Mama's Hung You in the Closet and I'm Feelin' So Sad, Roberta, The Music Man, Major Barbara, A Midsummer Night's Dream.*

Season IX (1965–66): *The King and I, The Glass Menagerie, The Cocktail Party, The Tavern, The Ballad of the Sad Cafe, Guys and Dolls, Becket, Antony and Cleopatra.*

Season X (1966–67): *A Funny Thing Happened on the Way to the Forum, Little Foxes, You Never Can Tell, A Streetcar Named Desire, Macbeth, The Miser, Six Characters in Search of an Author, Gypsy.*

Season XI (1967–68): *Luv, Who's Afraid of Virginia Woolf?, The Knack, The Subject Was Roses, The Imaginary Invalid, Twelfth Night.*

1967–68: Not available.

1968–69 (at Memphis State University): *Showboat, The Time of Your Life, A Moon for the Misbegotten.*

BIBLIOGRAPHY

Published Source:

Zeigler, Joseph Wesley. *Regional Theatre: The Revolutionary Stage*. New York: DeCapo Press, 1977.

Unpublished Source:

Sterling, Wallace. "The Front Street Theatre of Memphis." Doctoral dissertation, Southern Illinois University, 1966.

Archival Resources:

Memphis, Tennessee. Memphis State University Library. Front Street Theatre Collection.
Memphis, Tennessee. Private collection of Henry Swanson, professor of theatre, Memphis State University. Materials relating to the company's move to the campus of Memphis State University.

Wallace Sterling

G

[THE] GROUP THEATRE pursued its stormy existence during the 1930s in New York City, and despite the fact that it lasted for only ten years, it had a prolonged effect on the American theatre.

Harold Clurman (1901–80), Lee Strasberg (1901–82), and Cheryl Crawford (1902–86) organized the Group Theatre in 1930. The founders, all employees of the Theatre Guild, desired a more meaningful approach to theatre than they felt existed at that time in America. Earlier, in 1928, Clurman and Strasberg had experimented with the Stanislavski system, rehearsing Waldo Frank's *New Year's Eve* and Padraic Colum's *Balloon*. Later, during the 1928–29 theatrical season, Clurman and Crawford produced the Theatre Guild's first studio project, *Red Rust*, by Vladimir Kirshon and A. Ouspensky, a drama of student life in Russia.

After a series of meetings at Steinway Hall in New York in the spring of 1931, the group's leaders chose a company of twenty-seven members, and on June 8, 1931, they officially inaugurated the Group Theatre's first summer training session at Brookfield Center, Connecticut. There Strasberg rehearsed Paul Green's *The House of Connelly* and taught the basics of the Stanislavski system at the same time. On September 28, 1931, *The House of Connelly* opened at the Martin Beck Theatre in New York to critical plaudits. It ran for ninety-one performances. The Theatre Guild donated the rights to Green's play and paid one-half the production costs to support the fledgling group.

Later in the 1931–32 season the Group Theatre produced Claire and Paul Sifton's *1931*—(opened December 10, 1931; twelve performances) with settings by Mordecai Gorelik. Maxwell Anderson's *Night over Taos*, with settings by Robert Edmond Jones, followed on March 9, 1932 (thirteen performances). The Theatre Guild terminated its association with the Group Theatre at the end of the 1931–32 season. Cheryl Crawford resigned from the Theatre Guild at the same time.

In the spring of 1932 the Group Theatre began a subscription campaign. A $2 fee entitled a member to a 20 percent discount at the box office, an invitation seat during the season, and the privilege of submitting criticism of the Group Theatre's productions. After a summer session at Dover Furnace, New York, the Group returned to Broadway on September 26, 1932, in John Howard Lawson's *Success Story* (121 performances). Also during the fall of 1932 the Group held "Sunday Night Forums" for its membership audience. On January 17, 1933, the Group opened *Big Night*, by Dawn Powell, but the play—which Cheryl Crawford directed—failed after seven performances. Later Sidney Howard withdrew his *Yellow Jack*, and the Group suspended production for the 1932–33 season.

In 1933, despite hard times, the Group Theatre continued its summer training sessions by "singing for its supper" at Green Mansions, a resort near Lake George, New York. There Lee Strasberg rehearsed *Men in White*, by Sidney Kingsley, which opened to critical and popular acclaim in New York on September 26, 1933. Running for 351 performances, *Men in White* became the Group's first Broadway hit.

Between 1934 and 1936 a short-lived communist cell operated within the Group Theatre, hoping to influence the political stance of the organization. Later, during the House Un-American Activities Committee hearings of the 1950s, Elia Kazan revealed the presence of this cell, and some of the Group's members suffered blacklisting as a result (Morgan Y. Himelstein, *Drama Was a Weapon* [New Brunswick, N.J.: Rutgers University Press, 1963], pp. 159–60).

On March 22, 1934, the Group Theatre opened John Howard Lawson's *Gentlewoman* (twelve performances), with Stella Adler (a founding member of the Group) in the title role. Lloyd Nolan played the radical poet with whom she falls in love and became the first non-Group actor to play a leading role in a Group Theatre production.

During the spring of 1932 Strasberg, Clurman, and Stella Adler briefly toured the Soviet Union to observe theatrical activity. They were, however, unable to see Stanislavski, who was living abroad for reasons of health. Strasberg returned to the United States, but Clurman and Adler traveled on to Paris where they met Stanislavski, who, surprised at some of Adler's misgivings about his system, offered to coach her in his techniques. She remained in Paris for five additional weeks. In 1934, during a summer session at Ellensville, New York, Adler informed the Group that Strasberg had incorrectly interpreted Stanislavski's theories, especially as regards the use of "affective memory" in facilitating emotions in a performer.

The Group began the 1934–35 season with a six-week residence in Boston. Revivals of *Success Story* and *Men in White* played for two weeks each. Out-of-town try-outs of Melvin Levy's *Gold Eagle Guy*, a play set in the Gold Rush period of San Francisco, filled the final two weeks. The new production opened in New York on November 28, 1934, and ran for sixty-five performances.

The Groups's fortunes were, however, on the upswing. On January 5, 1935, the Group performed a new one-act play, *Waiting for Lefty*, by member Clifford Odets, at a benefit for the *New Theatre Magazine*. The play attracted widespread attention, and the Group continued to perform it on subsequent Sunday evenings. Clurman immediately began rehearsing Odets' longer play, *Awake and Sing!*. Opening on February 19, 1935, *Awake and Sing!* ran for 209 performances, establishing Odets as a promising new playwright and Clurman as a successful director. On March 26, 1935, the Group opened *Waiting for Lefty* on a double bill with another Odets' one-act, *Till the Day I Die*.

In the spring of 1935, Clurman and Cheryl Crawford once again visited the Soviet Union to see theatrical productions. The Group Theatre did not hold a summer session in 1935.

The Group Theatre resumed its Broadway career on November 30, 1935, with Nellise Child's *Weep for the Virgins*. Cheryl Crawford's second directorial effort fared no better than her first (*Big Night*); the play closed after nine performances. Luckily the Group's new playwright, Odets, provided another play, *Paradise Lost*, which opened on December 9, 1935, and ran a respectable seventy-three performances.

The Group seldom collaborated with other producers, but it did join with Milton Shubert to produce Erwin Piscator and Lena Goldschmidt's adaptation of Theodore Dreiser's *An American Tragedy*. Retitled *The Case of Clyde Griffiths*, the play related Griffiths' crime to the class struggle through the use of a "speaker" not present in the original novel. It opened on March 13, 1936, and ran for only nineteen performances.

For the remainder of the 1935–36 season the Group toured to Baltimore, Chicago, Cleveland, and Newark with *Awake and Sing!*. Also in the spring of 1936, Harold Clurman became the sole managing director of the Group Theatre. The Group Theatre spent the summer of 1936 at the Pinebrook Club Camp in Nichols, Connecticut.

Meanwhile the Group had commissioned Paul Green and Kurt Weill to write a musical play fashioned after Erwin Piscator's pioneering drama of epic realism, *The Good Soldier Schweik* (1928). On November 19, 1936, Green and Weill's play, *Johnny Johnson*, opened on Broadway. Despite critical acclaim, the play ran only a disappointing sixty-eight performances.

In the spring of 1936 internal dissension splintered the Group. The actors produced a critique analyzing every misstep or error along the organization's way, and they included a damning analysis of each director. As a result of the actors' stance, Strasberg, Clurman, and Crawford resigned their positions. The members elected a committee made up of Crawford, Strasberg, Clurman, Luther Adler, Roman Bohnen, and Elia Kazan to run the Group Theatre until further decisions could be made. However, in the spring of 1937, Clurman and three other members of the committee went to Hollywood for six months. During their absence Strasberg and Crawford withdrew altogether from the Group Theatre.

From 1937 Harold Clurman was the leader of the Group Theatre, and the organization strayed somewhat from its original objectives. Clurman struck gold on his first effort as sole director of the Group Theatre. Clifford Odets' *Golden Boy* opened November 4, 1937, and ran for 250 performances. Although many Group members were in the production, it featured a non-Group "star," Hollywood's Frances Farmer. In fact, many of the Group's subsequent productions featured non-Group stars.

The Group's financial success in *Golden Boy* led it to resurrect some of its original plans, and to that end, Bobby Lewis established a drama school for the Group Theatre. However, the Group had no permanent home. It simply occupied the theatre its current production was playing in. Consequently, when *Golden Boy* closed, Lewis' school had to be closed.

The Group's next production on Broadway arrived on February 19, 1938. Robert Ardrey's *Casey Jones* featured non-Group actors Charles Bickford, Van Heflin, and Peggy Conklin. Unfortunately the production survived only twenty-five performances. Later in 1938 the Group took *Golden Boy* to London, where it played successfully. They passed up their usual summer retreat in 1938.

In the fall of 1938 the Group scored a modest success with another Odets play, *Rocket to the Moon*, and on January 5, 1939, they opened Irwin Shaw's *The Gentle People*, starring one of the Group's charter members, Franchot Tone, by then a motion picture star. Shaw's polemic calling for a militant response to European fascism ran 141 performances and utilized non-Group actors Sam Jaffe and Silvia Sidney. On March 7, 1939, Clurman and company revived Odets' *Awake and Sing!* and ran it, with most of the original cast, in repertory with *Rocket to the Moon*. By late in the 1938–39 season the Group had fifteen actors under contracts that guaranteed them a minimum of thirty weeks of work yearly. Building on its financially successful year, the Group undertook two experimental productions. Irwin Shaw's *Quiet City* played only two Sunday nights, April 16 and April 23, 1939, but William Saroyan's *My Heart's in the Highlands*, produced under the sponsorship of the Theatre Guild, with Robert Lewis in his Broadway directing debut, ran forty-four performances. The production helped to establish Saroyan as a major new American playwright, though critical response was sharply divided. Clurman refused Saroyan's next play, but, under Theatre Guild production, *The Time of Your Life* won the Pulitzer Prize and the Drama Critics Circle Award as the best play of 1939–40.

In 1939 the Group Theatre returned to its practice of summering outside New York City, this time at Winwood, a Christian Science school in Lake Grove, on Long Island. They returned to Broadway on November 14, 1939, in Robert Ardrey's *Thunder Rock*, Elia Kazan directing. Ardrey's fantasy about the spiritual renewal of a disillusioned writer attempted to warn America of the heavy cost of political neutrality, but it ran for only twenty-three performances. Produced in wartime England, but not by the Group Theatre, the play was a great hit.

Also in 1939 a committee of Group Theatre actors drew up a constitution to provide for democratic and stable governance of the organization. The actors called for the election of a board of governors from the ranks of the Group Theatre; this body, in turn, would elect its executive officers. The constitution also established permanent committees to handle membership requests and deal with grievances. Although the actors ratified the constitution, Clurman ignored it. In May 1940 the Group's members again held a series of meetings to discuss the future of the organization. They elected a planning committee that proposed a five-production season for 1940–41. The shows would run for six weeks each, rather than just as long as the traffic would bear. The resultant thirty-week season would be guaranteed by advance sales to theatre parties and by benefits. The plan was not put into operation. The Group Theatre produced only one play in 1940–41, Irwin Shaw's *Retreat to Pleasure*, with Harold Clurman directing. This light comedy, the Group's final production, ran for only twenty-three performances.

The Group Theatre, according to Harold Clurman, who has told its story in *The Fervent Years*, wanted to develop and maintain a company that would keep its actors fresh with a variety of roles. It wanted to pay its actors according to their needs whether or not they appeared in the Group's current production, and it would have no stars. The Group also wanted to present timely, new American plays and to develop new playwrights to express the social and artistic intentions of the members. Adler, Strasberg, and Clurman, among others, were also dedicated to introducing the Stanislavski system of acting and Moscow Art Theatre principles of production to the American theatre. The Group labored to develop a common vocabulary, method, and style for rehearsing plays, and they wanted to rehearse each play unhurriedly until all parties reached a common understanding of the psychosocial truth of the drama under rehearsal. As the forerunner of the Actors' Studio, the center for the teaching of "Method" acting until Lee Strasberg's death in 1982, the Group Theatre exerted a powerful influence on the American theatre. They devoted summers to study and rehearsal away from New York, and they committed themselves to dignifying and professionalizing the art of acting. They achieved these goals, for the most part, but their goal of establishing a permanent theatre went unrealized. They failed to provide a durable financial base for their operations. Subscription campaigns modeled after those so successfully launched by the Theatre Guild developed no regular constituency. They also tried and failed to establish an endowment whose income would finance productions of commercially risky plays.

PERSONNEL

1931 Original Company
Directors: Harold Clurman, Cheryl Crawford, Lee Strasberg.

Actors and Actresses: Stella Adler, Margaret Barker, Phoebe Brand, J. Edward Bromberg, Morris Carnovsky, William Challee, Walter Coy, Virginia Farmer, Sylvia Fenningston, Friendly Ford, Gerritt Kraber, Lewis Leverett, Robert Lewis, Gertrude Maynard, Sanford Meisner, Paula Miller, Mary Morris, Ruth Nelson, Clifford Odets, Dorothy Patten, Herbert Ratner, Philip Robinson, Arthur Smith, Eunice Stoddard, Franchot Tone, Alixe Walker, and Clement Wilenchick.

Additional Members and Participants: Luther Adler, Kermit Bloomgarden, Roman Bohnen, Lee J. Cobb, Leif Ericson, Frances Farmer, John Garfield, Michael Gordon, Elia Kazan, Alexander Kirkland, Will Lee, Philip Loeb, Karl Malden, Martin Ritt, Howard da Silva.

Group Associates: Maxwell Anderson, Barrett Clark, Aaron Copland, Waldo Frank, Mordecai Gorelik, Theresa Helburn, Robert Edmond Jones, Dorothy Norman, Ralph Steiner, Alfred Stieglitz, Paul Strand, Gerald Sykes. (See *Educational Theatre Journal* 28 [December 1976]: 449–50.)

REPERTORY

1931–32: *The House of Connelly, 1931—, Night over Taos.*

1932–33: *Success Story, Big Night.*

1933–34: *Men in White, Gentlewoman.*

1934–35: *Gold Eagle Guy, Awake and Sing!, Waiting for Lefty, Till the Day I Die.*

1935–36: *Weep for the Virgins, Paradise Lost, The Case of Clyde Griffiths.*

1936–37: *Johnny Johnson.*

1937–38: *Golden Boy, Casey Jones.*

1938–39: *Rocket to the Moon, The Gentle People, Awake and Sing!* (revival), *My Heart's in the Highlands.*

1939–40: *Thunder Rock, Night Music.*

1940–41: *Retreat to Pleasure.*

BIBLIOGRAPHY

Published Sources:

Adler, Stella. "The Actor in the Group Theatre." In *Actors on Acting*, 3rd ed., edited by Toby Cole and Helen Krich Chinoy. New York: Crown Publishers, 1957.

Clurman, Harold. *The Fervent Years.* New York: Alfred A. Knopf, 1945.

Gassner, John. "The Group Theatre in Its Tenth Year: A Critical Estimate." *Theatre Arts* 24 (October 1940): 729–35.

Himelstein, Morgan Y. *Drama Was a Weapon.* New Brunswick, N.J.: Rutgers University Press, 1963.

"Reunion: A Self-portrait of the Group Theatre." Guest Editor, Helen Krich Chinoy. *Educational Theatre Journal* 28 (December 1976): 445–552.

Sievers, W. David. "Autopsy on 'The Group.' " *Quarterly Journal of Speech* 35 (December 1949): 470–76.

Unpublished Sources:

Sievers, W. David. "The Group Theatre of New York City, 1931–1941." Master's thesis, Stanford University, 1944.

Wolfe, Donald Howard. "The Significance of the Group Theatre." Doctoral dissertation, Cornell University, 1969.

Donald H. Wolfe

[THE] GROUP THEATRE COMPANY was founded in Seattle, Washington, in 1978 when an ensemble of eleven members from five ethnic backgrounds produced a three-week run of Miguel Pinero's *Short Eyes*. Maggie Hawthorn of the *Seattle Post-Intelligencer* wrote that "*Short Eyes* is probably the most gripping piece of theatre seen in town this year. . . . In addition to the individual performances, the ensemble works with a chemistry that would make bread rise'' (October 28, 1978, A15). The production played to sold-out houses.

In 1979 the Ethnic Cultural Center at the University of Washington invited the Group Theatre Company to become the resident company at the 197-seat, thrust-style Ethnic Culture Theatre. Although the theatre offered no fly space, little backstage area, and no scenery or costume shops, it provided a permanent home for the company.

Founding members of the Group Theatre Company were Robert Boneyard Beavers, L. A. (Leif) Bentsen, Scott Caldwell, Charles Canada, Tee Dennard, Richard Karl Greene, William Hall, Jr., Gil Rodriquez, Rubén Sierra, Will York, all actors, and Gilbert Wong, a scene designer. New members were elected by a two-thirds vote.

The Group Theatre Company dedicated itself to vibrant, socially relevant theatre, produced through artistic collaboration and focused on exploring the commonalities and universals of a multicultural world. From its inception The Group set out to provide training and experience for minority actors and to teach a white, middle-class audience to expect minority artists to contribute in all areas of theatre. From these roots it has evolved into a full-time professional theatre company.

Their second show, Bruce Jay Friedman's *Steambath*, in which God is represented as a Puerto Rican steambath proprietor, opened April 19, 1979, to excellent reviews. Some members were unhappy about the way profits were split, so the Group decided to write contracts for actors in future shows. Rubén Sierra became artistic director, Scott Caldwell secretary, Gil Rodriquez facilitator, and William Hall treasurer as the company formalized its structure. The Ethnic Culture Theatre budgeted $12,000 for three productions for 1979–80 and explored such options as a summer season and midnight shows. When the season opened July 19, 1979, with *Cops*, by Terry Curtis Fox, reviewers praised the work of the company but criticized the script. Closing night of *Cops* was a memorial for Gil Rodriquez, who had drowned on a company outing celebrating the close of the 1978–79 season.

The character of the company changed as actors left Seattle or developed other interests. Richard Karl Greene went to New York to act; Tee Dennard became inactive. The early seasons did not go well as The Group had difficulty finding scripts suitable for its multiethnic nature, but ''An Evening of One Acts,'' by Israel Horowitz, seen in April 1980, reclaimed for The Group some of its earlier promise.

The 1980–81 season consisted of five plays, each running for four weeks, Wednesday through Sunday. Subscriptions, sold for the first time, cost $20; students and senior citizens paid $12. The Group also began to use female directors and to search for scripts projecting less male chauvinism. Other efforts to liberate the theatre from stifling conventions met resistance as some reviewers were unable to accept a white actor and a black actor playing brothers in Arthur Miller's *The Price*. However, The Group's color-blind casting has been better received of late. Neither *The Price* nor Tom Cole's *Medal of Honor Rag* appealed to the critics; the remainder of the season was successful, however. The company incorporated in 1981 as a not-for-profit organization.

In 1981–82 a small grant from the Seattle Arts Commission supported the Seattle premiere of Marsha Norman's *Getting Out*, and, anticipating a successful production, the company scheduled additional performances before the show opened. Although the production opened to a small audience, it became a turning point for the company, when critics responded more favorably to it than to a production of the same play two months later by the much better known A Contemporary Theatre (ACT)*. Reviewers began to raise their expectations, and audiences enlarged. Beginning with *Getting Out*, The Group began auditioning and casting outside its membership. As Empty Space Association* and ACT became more conservative in their play selection, their younger audience members began to frequent The Group. When The Group negotiated a Letter of Agreement with Actors' Equity Association in December 1981, they became the only professional multiethnic theatre company in the Pacific Northwest. Because audiences flock to family Christmas productions, The Group developed an original variety musical called *Voices of Christmas*, in which the cast told stories of their favorite Christmases and sang carols from around the world. The production proved so profitable that it became an annual event. Season revenue in 1981–82 exceeded projections by $10,000, and the company ended the year in the black.

Discounting The Group's production of Percy Mackaye's *The Scarecrow* (1908), a type of Frankenstein story, 1982–83 was its most successful season. The 133-performance season ran for ten months and included, for the first time, reserved seating. Ticket prices were increased, though The Group played to only 41 percent of capacity. The season closed with a small deficit.

The Seattle Human Rights Commission began enforcing the city's affirmative action policy in 1982, and theatre companies not in compliance with the policy were threatened with having their Seattle Arts Commission funding withheld. Only The Group and Bathhouse were found to be in compliance. The Seattle Repertory Company and ACT claimed they couldn't afford to hire minority talent, although both theatres claimed to have used minority actors when the playwright's intent was served by such casting.

Much of the financial success of this period was due to the efforts of Elizabeth Brock, general manager from 1982–84. Her staff concentrated on increasing season subscriptions and unearned income. A $7,500 National Endowment for the Arts grant allowed playwright Derek Walcott to develop his play, *The Last Carnival*, while in residence with The Group. Local cosponsors of the world premiere of Walcott's work included PONCHO (Patrons of Northwest Civic, Cultural, and Charitable Organizations) and the King County Arts Commission. A Washington State Arts Commission grant allowed the company the luxury of increased support staff. The Northwest premiere of *Desert Fire*, by Roger Holzberg and Martin Casella, included a benefit for Greenpeace and a series of antiwar films during the run in September and October 1983. Despite its honorable intentions, the production was a critical flop and a financial liability. The remainder of 1982–83, however, was critically and financially successful. In 1983–84 Tom Topor's *Nuts* outsold any show in the company's six-year history and reduced The Group's debt to the University of Washington from $28,000 to $15,000. By the final week the show was playing to 97 percent of capacity. The West Coast premiere of Jane Martin's (pseudonym) *Talking With* played to 75 percent capacity. It was extended one week and then revived. Attendance rose to 13,800 and house capacity averaged 53 percent. Earned income rose 145 percent but unearned income dropped. Budget cuts forced the University of Washington to withdraw its support of The Group, and expenses increased almost $70,000 over the previous season. Although The Group launched an aggressive marketing program, and *Nuts* and *Talking With* were both financially and critically successful, 1983–84 ended with a $14,389 deficit.

The 1984–85 season opened to mixed reviews of the West Coast premiere of Kent Broadhurst's *Lemons*. In an attempt to reduce its debt The Group moved the *Voices of Christmas IV* to the larger Broadway Performance Hall. The hits of the season included Athol Fugard's *Sizwe Bansi Is Dead* and Emilio Carballido's *Orinoco!*, which was extended two weeks. The company's first annual American Minority Playwrights' Festival drew more than 250 scripts. Two finalists worked with Rubén Sierra, playwright in residence. Their scripts received workshop productions, and six scripts were given cold readings. A similar pattern prevailed in the second festival, held in 1986.

The Group has grown in size and sophistication. The budget for 1985–86 neared a half million dollars, and earned income was near 50 percent of total income. The Group has developed an enviable record of attracting both local and national grants, and its ability to attract corporate grants has grown. The company's audience is middle class, young, liberal, and strongly supportive of the company's message.

PERSONNEL

Artistic Director: Rubén Sierra (1979–86).
Associate Artistic Director: Tim Bond (1986).
General Manager: Elizabeth Brock (1982–84).
Managing Director: Scott Caldwell (1984–86).
Directors: Shaun Austin-Olsen (1980–81), Tim Bond (1983, 1985–86), Scott Caldwell (1980), Ron Antonio Castro (1985), Shawn Cleland (1982), Robert Egan (1979), Anne-Denise Ford (1986), Rita Giomi (1983–85), Joye Hardiman (1981), Linda Hartzell (1982, 1984), Jorge A. Huerta (1985), John Kauffman (1986), John Kazanjian (1982, 1985), Cecilie D. Keenan (1986), Jon Kretzu (1982), Robert Golden Leigh (1986), Don Matt (1985), David S. Moore (1980, 1982), Paul O'Connell (1985–86), Tawnya Pettiford-Wates (1985–86), Kay D. Ray (1986), Richard Riehle (1985), Eve Roberts (1981), Howard Chaim Rosemarin (1979), *Rubén Sierra* (1978–85), Steve Sneed (1986), Chris Sumption (1984).

Choreographers: Michelle Blackmon (1981), Nancy Cranbourne (1986), Edna Daigre (1984), Jesse Jaramillo (1985), Phillip Lewis (1985), David Moore (1981), Christopher Nardine (1984), Carmen Paris (1982), Kat Allen Pioro (1984), Craig Turner (1979–81, 1983).

Composers: Karen Cody (1979), Richard Karl Greene (1979), Chad Henry (1984), Teresa Metzger (1985), Lawrence Perkins (1985), Jim Ragland (1985), Joseph Seserko (1985–86).

Consultants: Tim Ford (1984), Dr. Jim Lurie (1984), Won-ldy Paye, (1986), Deborah A. Schwartz (1983).

Resident Designer: Gilbert Wong (1983–86).

Scene Designers: Robert Dahlstrom (1979), Karen Gjelsteen (1986), Alex W. Hutton (1979, 1982–85), David S. Moore (1981), Matthew Rawdon (1984), Shelley Henze Schermer (1981), Anna Scholbohm (1986), *Gilbert Wong* (1978–86).

Costume Designers: Marie Boucher (1978), Sheryl Collins (1983), Ron Erickson (1983), Marilyn Erly (1985), Becky Fuller (1980), Josie Gardner (1986), Gay Howard (1984–85), Frances Kenny (1986), Jan Locke (1979–80), Leslie McGovern (1986), Martha E. Mattus (1983), Nina Moser (1982, 1984), Michael Murphy (1984), Kathryn O'Connell (1981), Rose Ann Pederson (1980–81, 1984–85), Elaine Ramires (1979), Linda Sands (1979), *Mary Ellen Walter* (1982–85), Ann Thaxter Watson (1985).

Lighting Designers: Peter W. Allen (1985), Marie Bridgette Barrett (1979), Frank Butler (1984), *Rex Carleton* (1982–86), Michael Eichner (1979, 1981), Donna Grout (1980–81), Kurt Layton-Smith (1984), Darren McCroom (1986), Robin Macgregor (1985), Geoffrey Sedgwick (1984), Carmine Simone (1983–84), James Verdery (1979, 1981–82), Evelyn C. White (1978), Gilbert Wong (1980), Collier Woods (1986).

Sound Designers: Thomas Ager (1986), Steve Bennett (1979), Bill Carswell (1984–85), Amy Gonzalez (1981), Dennis Kambury (1982–83), Paul Prappas (1984), Jim Ragland (1985), *Joseph Seserko* (1983–86), Rubén Sierra (1979), Carmine Simone (1983), William Strock (1981).

Actresses/Actors/Singers: Jane Adams (1984), Roderick Aird (1982), David Arteaga (1984), Stan Asis (1985), Lyn Balesteri (1982), Douglas Q. Barett (1985), Robert Boneyard Beavers (1978), Barbara Becker-Frandeen (1981–82), *L. A. Bentsen* (Leif Bentsen) (1978–81), John Billingsley (1982), Jeff Bingham (1979), *Michelle Blackmon* (1981, 1984, 1986), Keith Bleyer (1985), Suzanne Bouchard (1985), John Boylan (1983), Geoffrey Bradley (1983), J. V. Bradley (1983), *Phyllis Brisson* (1983–85), James Brousseau (1982), *Roi-Martin Brown* (1979, 1981–82), Diane Caldwell (1984), *Scott Caldwell* (1978–83), Martha I. Campfield (1984), *(Frederick) Charles Canada* (1978–83, 1985–86), Rose E. Cano (1983, 1985), *Colleen Carpenter-Rodriguez* (1979–83), Betsey Cassell (1986), Jill Chan (1981), Karen Cody (1979), Ted Collins (1985), Rachel Coloff (1984), J. Lee Cook (1983), Lee Corrigan (1984), Karen Crewe (1984), Charlene Curtis (1985), Keith Dalhgren (1980), Ken Davidson (1984), J. David Dean (1982), Christine Deaver (1984), Tee Dennard (1978), Roger Downey (1979), *Sheryl Drummond Jenkins* (1981, 1983, 1986), *Reuben Renauldo Dumas* (1982–83, 1985–86), Dark Dumay (1985), Jerrilyn Eaglestaff (1985), James Etue (1983), Paul Fleming (1981–82), Adhania Frost (1981), Christina Gallegos (1985), Floyd Giannone-VanBuskirk (1983), John Gilbert (1986), Leontine Gilyard (1983), Heidi Godt (1984), Eddie Gove (1985), Tamu Gray (1981–82, 1984–86), *Richard Karl Greene* (1978–80, 1985), Nancy Griffiths (1986), Nathan Haas (1984), *William Hall, Jr.* (1978–81, 1983–84), John Harnagel (1979), Shirley Harned

(1985), Amy Harris (1986), Kit Harris (1982–84), Gregg Hashimoto (1983), Gail Hebert (1986), Brian Higham (1984–85), Patty Holley (1981), Scott Honeywell (1984), Kimberlee House (1984), Kathy Hsieh (1986), Michele Hurtado (1983, 1986), Sara O. Jackson (1984, 1986), Noya Jacobson (1984), Jesse Jaramillo (1986), Ron Ben Jarrett (1985), Jerry-Mac Johnson (1979, 1984–85), Joanne Kilgour (1983), Jean Marie Kinney (1981, 1984), Frieda Kirk (1985), Bea Kiyohara (1979, 1986), David S. Klein (1985), Jill Klein (1980), *David (Hunter) Koch* (1981–84), Roza Kuring (1981, 1984), Maggie Laird (1981), Robert I. Lee (1982), Jo Leffingwell (1985), Diana Lim (1986), James Liu (1984), Kim Loop (1986), Luis A. Lopez (1978), Lisa Loud (1985), Nikki Louis (1985–86), Kevin Hugh Lynch (1985), Helene McCardle (1983), Mary Machala (1982), Lachlan Macleay (1981–82), *Jimi Ray Malary* (1981–83, 1985), Anita Marti (1986), Michelina Wanda Martin (1985), Bruce Matley (1986), Kathryn Mesney (1983–84, 1986), Christian Mills (1982), Kathryn Minturn (1984), David Mong (1982, 1984), James W. Monitor (1984–86), David S. Moore (1980), Najja Morris (1984), William Morrow (1979), *Jacqueline D. Moscou* (1983–86), Jayne Muirhead (1985), Marjorie Nelson (1985), Keith Nicholai (1984), Nancy Nolan (1984), David Norfleet (1983), Steven W. Nourse (1985), Elizabeth Oakes (1986), Emily O'Connell (1985–86), Karen Oleson (1983), Shirley M. Oliver (1986), Marilyn Olson (1983, 1985), Bill Ontiveros (1982, 1984–85), Theresa Ontiveros (1985), Mark Padgett (1985), Kathleen Park (1984), Won-ldy Paye (1985), Tawnya Pettiford-Wates (1985–86), Kat Allen Pioro (1984), Demetra Pittman (1981, 1983, 1985), Sam Pond (1979), Amy Potozkin (1982), Ben Prager (1984), B. Marshall Press (1982), John Pribyl (1982–83), Josephine Ramirez (1986), Rick Ray (1981, 1983, 1985), William Ray (1985), Nora Rebusit (1985), Gary Reed (1986), Wesley Rice (1983), Christina Rich (1981–82), Jamie Richards (1979), Andrew Rivas (1984), *Dorothy Roberts* (1984–86), *Winston José Rocha* (1983–86), *Gil Rodriquez* (1978–79), Carmen Roman (1982, 1984), Cynthia Rose (1983), William Rowe (1986), Gretchen Rumbaugh (1982–83), Jane Ryan (1979), Edward Sampson (1981), Alvin Lee Sanders (1984–85), Michael V. Schauermann (1984), Coby Scheldt (1982, 1985), Jacalyn Schneider (1984), Mara Scott-Wood (1983–84), David Scully (1986), Nancy Seward (1985), Jean Sherrard (1982), Ed Shockley (1986), *Rubén Sierra* (1978–83, 1985–86), Tracy Sisley (1981), Jan Sizer (1984), Brad Smith (1979), Christine Smith (1982), Gary Baxter Smith (1985), Cheri Sorenson (1984), Sue Spencer (1979), Ralph Steadman (1984), Mark J. Sticklin (1984), Randall Stuart (1984), Sheila Stumvoll (1979), Laura J. Stusser (1983), Faye B. Summers (1983), Jayne Taini (1983), Kelly Tallariti (1984), Gary Taylor (1983), Mary Thielen (1985), Earl Thomas (1985), Donald M. Trujillo (1984), Daniel Turner (1983), Antonio Z. Valdez (1980), Leslie Vogel (1979), Mary Colleen Vreeland (1984), Paul Walsh (1981, 1983), Susan Wands (1982), Diane Weyrick (1984–85), Lloyd Williams (1985), Sara Wilson (1984–85), Christopher Wong (1984), Lily Woo (1981), Roald Wulff (1986), Will York (1978–79).

REPERTORY

1978: *Short Eyes.*

1979: *Steambath, Cops, Four Hubcaps and a Spare, The Lower Depths.*

1980: *Fanny Kemble, Rats, Line* and *The Indian Wants the Bronx, The Price, Medal of Honor Rag.*

1981: *The Blood Knot, Getting Out, The Primary English Class, Pantomime, Home, Voices of Christmas I.*

1982: *Scarecrow, A Lesson from Aloes, Division Street, How I Got That Story, Creeps, Voices of Christmas II.*

1983: *Nourish the Beast, Ladies in Waiting, The Last Carnival, Desert Fire, Strange Snow, Voices of Christmas III.*

1984: *Nuts, Talking With, Articus and the Angel, Reagan's Women, Lemons, Voices of Christmas IV.*

1985: *Sizwe Bansi Is Dead, Split Second, Orinoco!, I Am Celso, Self Portrait.* First Annual American Minority Playwrights' Festival Workshop Productions: *Stalking Horse* and *Going to Seed, Jacques Brel Is Alive and Well and Living in Paris, Staring Back, Voices of Christmas V.*

1986: *Nappy Edges, The Fifth Sun, A . . . My Name Is Alice.* Second Annual American Minority Playwright's Festival Workshop Productions: *Endings* and *Tea.*

BIBLIOGRAPHY

Published Sources:
Seattle Post Intelligencer, 1978–87.
Seattle Times, 1978–87.
Weekly, 1980–87.
Downey, Roger. "The Stages of Success." *Pacific Northwest*, September 1984, pp. 40–46.

Unpublished Sources:
The Group board minutes, 1980–86.
The Group press releases, October 1978–May 1987.
The Group programs, October 1978–June 1986.

Liz Fugate

THE GUTHRIE THEATRE COMPANY, originally known as the Minnesota Theatre Company, has often been referred to as the flagship of American regional theatre. The company and the theatre that houses it were developed primarily through the efforts of Sir Tyrone Guthrie (1900–71). His beliefs about theatre are incorporated in everything from the goals of the company and the building that houses it to its reputation for producing a classic repertory. Located in downtown Minneapolis, the theatre, with its three-quarter thrust stage, adjoins the distinguished Walker Art Museum cultural complex. The company opened its first season on May 6, 1963, with a production of *Hamlet*, with Guthrie directing George Grizzard in the title role. Since then the Minnesota Theatre Company has continued to present Midwestern audiences with successful professional theatre in seasons of up to ten productions in repertory.

Tyrone Guthrie began his theatre career as an actor at the Oxford Repertory Theatre in England, and the centrality of the actor in the theatrical event was a conviction he held all his life. Born and educated in Ireland, Guthrie quickly gained the respect of the English theatre community for his skills in both classic and commercial theatre. He was influential in the development of the Old Vic, the Scottish National Theatre, and the Stratford, Ontario, Shakespeare Festival, and in 1961 he was knighted by Queen Elizabeth for his contributions to the British and Canadian stage. It was his creative force that led the Minnesota Theatre Company to success in the early years. For its first three years he was the group's artistic director, and he remained active as a visiting director until his death, after which the theatre and the company itself was renamed in his memory.

Preparations for the Minnesota Theatre Company demanded four years of concentrated effort. In March 1959 Tyrone Guthrie invited his friends Oliver Rea, a knowledgeable theatre businessman, and Peter Zeisler, a highly skilled theatre technician, to a breakfast meeting to discuss a new theatre company. They talked about a theatre more permanent and more serious in aim than existing commercial theatres of Broadway or London's West End. Having agreed on the need for such an institution and on its initial principles, they met again the next July at Guthrie's home in Ireland, where they developed their goals and strategies.

Guthrie's book, *A New Theatre*, describes in explicit detail the entire process of creation, from his dissatisfaction with contemporary commercial theatre to the choice of location and the design specifications of the stage and auditorium. He also discusses the goals of the company and how "good plays" are selected for its repertory. A "good" play, decided Guthrie, Rea, and Zeisler, had stood the test of time, had displayed "serious merit," and could be labeled a classic. Initially each season would consist of three classics with contrast in origin, style, and content, and one American play of potential classic status, since, according to Guthrie, no American plays were yet old enough to have passed the test of time.

With these artistic goals in mind, they set out to locate a city in which to build their theatre. They met with Brooks Atkinson to discuss their plans, and he subsequently wrote an article in which he mentioned that interested groups were invited to respond. Seven cities expressed interest: San Francisco, Milwaukee, Boston, Minneapolis, Chicago, Cleveland, and Detroit. Guthrie admits that they had a hunch that Minneapolis was the place, but only after careful consideration under the influence of *Minneapolis Star and Tribune* vice president John Cowles, Jr., did they make their official decision.

Sensing the need for such a company in Minneapolis, Cowles organized the Steering Committee, a group of people from the business community committed to public service. The Steering Committee persuaded the Walker Foundation to donate land for the theatre and to make an initial contribution of $400,000. They promised to raise $900,000 to complete the theatre and were able to finance the final $2 million project with generous donations from large corporations and committed individual supporters. Because Minneapolis offered this kind of community support, because Minneapolis had already established itself as a cultural center with its symphony orchestra and opera company, and because Minneapolis could offer them a space built specifically for them, Guthrie, Rea, and Zeisler decided to go with their hunch and locate there.

Another part of the attraction of Minneapolis rested on Guthrie's belief that the gap between professional and academic theatre was too big. The chair of the University of Minnesota drama department, Frank Whiting, fully supported the venture, providing aid wherever possible. Relations between the university and the company have remained friendly, and someone from the department always sits on the governing board. In addition, the McKnight and Bush foundations have made it possible for advanced graduate students to work with the company.

Having decided on Minneapolis, they hired Ralph Rapson, professor of architecture at the university, to design their building. While Guthrie wanted a thrust stage similar to that at the Shakespeare festival in Stratford, Ontario, Rapson recommended a multiform stage. This, however, Guthrie would not approve, believing that such a building would limit, rather than expand, staging possibilities. Actor-director Douglas Campbell and designer Tanya Moiseiwitsch joined the team at this point. Having worked with Guthrie at Stratford, Ontario, both agreed that the Minnesota stage needed the intimacy offered by the thrust stage at Stratford, plus greater flexibility.

Using the thrust stage at Stratford as their model, they designed an auditorium that seats 1,441 spectators on an alpine slope with a 200-degree arc. None of the audience sits further than fifty-two feet from the stage. The stage is an asymmetrical seven-sided platform with steps leading up to it from an alley. Two vomitories open onto the alley, each approximately one-third of the way around the stage. Guthrie believed that this arrangement of stage and audience emphasized human interaction and favored movement over stasis. The proximity of the audience and its location on three sides of the stage would force designers to create sets more evocative than realistic. This, too, underscored Guthrie's conviction that acting is the center of the theatrical event.

In 1962 Guthrie began looking for actors of stature and plays of stature in which to feature them. Dedicated to the idea of ensemble production, he wanted to emulate the British model of repertory in order to avoid the star system. The first ensemble included Hume Cronyn, Jessica Tandy, George Grizzard, Rita Gam, and Zoe Caldwell, who took on the roles in *Hamlet*, Molière's *The Miser*, Anton Chekhov's *The Three Sisters*, and Arthur Miller's *Death of a Salesman*. The company studied voice, fencing, and movement while engaging as well in traditional rehearsals. Guthrie also instituted a daily ritual in which the acting company spent twenty minutes reciting Psalm 118, an exercise in preparation for the dedication ceremony, but also intended as vocal practice and as an aid in the development of ensemble spirit.

Opening night, May 7, 1963, featured the new company in its new building in a production of *Hamlet*. Twenty-two thousand season tickets had been sold through the efforts of the Stagehands volunteer organization, and a full house was on hand for what had become a media event. *Hamlet* was perhaps the wrong choice and Guthrie's four-hour production was not well received. However, Campbell's production of *The Miser*, opening on May 8, assured audiences that they had spent their money well. Two weeks later the opening of *The Three Sisters* and *Death of a Salesman* confirmed early reports: the Minnesota Theatre Company (as it was then called) was a success.

During the next two seasons, to continued applause, Guthrie repeated his formula: Shakespeare, a modern classic, a classic comedy, and a major American play. In 1964–65 he produced *Henry V*, G. B. Shaw's *Saint Joan*, Ben Jonson's *Volpone*, and Tennessee Williams' *The Glass Menagerie;* in 1965–66, *Richard III*, William Congreve's *The Way of the World*, Chekhov's *The Cherry Orchard*, and Bertolt Brecht's *The Caucasian Chalk Circle*. Feeling he had completed his task, Guthrie stepped down in 1966, leaving Douglas Campbell as artistic director. Without Guthrie's charismatic force, the company floundered and was without a strong artistic director until Michael Langham took the helm.

When Langham arrived in 1971, attendance had dropped to 61 percent of capacity, and the Ford Foundation had stopped covering the company's deficits. Although the period between the artistic direction of Guthrie and Langham had been rocky, several members of the artistic staff continued to return each year. Designer Tanya Moiseiwitsch remained with the company until 1970, and actors Paul Ballantyne, Len Cariou, Ellen Geer, Ed Flanders, and Ken Ruta were core company members. Langham had worked at Stratford, Ontario, and shared many of Guthrie's basic assumptions, so Langham was able to provide the direction the company needed. In 1972 Langham brought in Donald Schoenbaum as managing director, a position he still held in 1986.

Opening the 1972–73 season with Sophocles' *Oedipus the King* in a new translation by Anthony Burgess, Langham established a reputation for great success with the classics. He extended the company to eight productions per season in 1977–78, and he expanded other programs as well. Through negotiations with the McKnight Foundation, he instituted a fellowship for actors and apprenticeships for technicians studying theatre at the University of Minnesota. He initiated a community outreach program featuring signed performances for the hearing impaired and classes in acting, directing, mime, movement, prop construction, and costuming for the general public. He formed two tour groups, and established traveling exhibits and an artist-in-residence program for schools. In addition, he made a production of Charles Dickens' *A Christmas Carol* a regular part of each winter holiday season.

Langham was proud of the Guthrie's reputation as a classic theatre and of its second stage, The Other Place, which featured contemporary American and avant-garde plays. Audiences and finances had stabilized, but Langham saw that relations with the University of Minnesota were becoming strained. To repair the damage he used a 1976 Mellon Foundation grant to move The Other Place closer to the university and to begin the Guthrie 2, a theatre intended to tie the activities of the company and of the university closer together. Guthrie 2 did just that until 1978, when the building housing it was demolished during urban renewal.

In 1977, after six years as artistic director, Michael Langham resigned. The board of directors convinced Alvin Epstein to leave his position as assistant artistic director at the Yale Repertory Theatre* and take the job. Because Epstein was more interested in contemporary works than in classics and recognized a need to rejuvenate the company, his first season featured an unprecedented emphasis on contemporary plays. The 1977–78 season included Isaac Bashevis Singer's *Teibele and Her Demon*, Bella and Sam Spewack's *Boy Meets Girl*, and Michel Tremblay's *Bonjour, là, Bonjour*, along with more challenging classics such as Henrik Ibsen's *The Pretenders*, Nicolai Gogol's *Marriage*, and John Gay's *Beggar's Opera*. Revivals of *Hamlet* and *A Christmas Carol* fleshed out a season that was not well received. Epstein was artistic director for just one season.

The advent of the 1980s found the board of directors searching for a new hand to guide the company and a new outlook for the future. They hired internationally known teacher and director Liviu Ciulei as artistic director and the young, successful Garland Wright to share responsibilities as assistant artistic director. In addition, the University of Minnesota's Arthur Ballet was appointed dramaturg and the third member of the new artistic team. Together they developed a new policy for the 1980s that held that the mission of the Guthrie Theatre was to entertain Upper Midwest audiences with artistic productions of an eclectic repertory. They vowed to remain close to the classics, the Guthrie having established its reputation there, but Ciulei believed that each historical epoch has its own way of reading and seeing the classics, so that productions of them should extract from the classics ideas and meanings that belong to the current time.

The Guthrie Theatre Company has continued to grow and has been constantly in the national limelight because of Ciulei's daring and successful productions. In 1982 the company received a Tony Award for outstanding contribution to American regional theatre. Ciulei also instituted, in 1982, a program of telemarketing for audience development and has found that 26 percent of the people who answer their phones agree to purchase tickets. As a result, the theatre has continued to flourish and the financial troubles of the early eighties, which caused the company to disband its ensemble, have been eliminated. The company returned to the ensemble system in the 1985–86 season. However, Ciulei and the board of directors began to disagree over artistic matters, and these disagreements led to Ciulei's resignation in 1986. After a brief national search, Garland Wright was hired as artistic director.

In addition to the high quality of its productions, the company has distinguished itself throughout the world as an innovator of technical procedures. Because of the nature of the stage and the repertory system, sets must be minimal and mobile. To solve this problem, Guthrie technicians pioneered an air pressure system that lifts sets one-half inch off the stage floor and allows a heavy unit to be eased offstage by two or three stagehands. The McKnight Foundation and Bush Foundation fellowships have become internships solely for technical theatre, and students come from as far away as Europe and Asia to study in Minneapolis.

As the company enters its third decade, Minneapolis continues its initial generous corporate and individual support of the theatre. The women's volunteer organization, The Stagehands, has opened a gift shop and taken on ushering duties. The company has maintained a close relationship with the community through its outreach programs and through such projects as *Flashbacks*, based on stories from the elderly and performed by members of that segment of the population.

The Guthrie Theatre Company has established itself as a major force in American theatre. Since 1963 more than 7 million persons have seen its performances in Minneapolis, while another million have seen touring performances. Guthrie's vision has been realized and the future seems as bright as the past.

PERSONNEL

Artistic Directors: Douglas Campbell (1965–67), Liviu Ciulei (1980–86), Alvin Epstein (1978–80), Sir Tyrone Guthrie (1963–65), Michael Langham (1971–78).

Managing Directors: Oliver Rea (1963–66), Donald Schoenbaum (1969–86), Peter Zeisler (1963–69).

Designers: William Armstrong (1982–83), John Arnone (1981), Frances Aronson (1983), Jared Aswegan (1979–82), Leonard Auerbach (1967–68), Joyce Aysta (1970), James Bakkom (1970, 1972, 1974), Jack Barkla (1974–83), Jeff Bartlett (1976, 1978), William Barton (1969), John Lee Beatty (1981), Michael C. Beery (1981), Burton Bell (1968–69), Richard Borgen (1968, 1972, 1974), Miruna Boruzescru (1983), Radu Boruzescru (1983), *Lewis Brown* (1964–67, 1973, 1975, 1977, 1980), Zack Brown (1978), Ronald M. Bundt (1977, 1979), Robert Bye (1971, 1976–77), Geraldine Cain (1968, 1970, 1973), Lawrence Casey (1982), Ching Ho Chen (1974), Dawn Chiang (1983), Liviu Ciulei (1981, 1983), John Conklin (1976), Gregory M. Cummins (1977), Paul Daniels (1970), Dahl Delu (1966–67, 1969), Lowell Detweiler (1974), Dennis Dorn (1970), Kate Edmunds (1978), Ben Edwards (1968), *Jack Edwards* (1971–83), Karl Eigsti (1968–69, 1981), Robert T. Ellingsworth (1975, 1978), John F. Ferguson (1977), William Daniel File (1976), Robert Fletcher (1980), Richard Foreman (1981), Bruce Cana Fox (1974), Ralph Funicello (1976–77), Annette Garceau (1968), Hal George (1972), Eric Goldscheider (1976), Jane Greenwood (1968, 1980), Diana Grillé (1970), David Lloyd Gropman (1978), James Guenther (1979–81), Ron Hall (1970–71), Richard L. Hay (1968), *Desmond Heeley* (1971–76, 1978, 1980), Gilbert Hemsley (1973–74, 1979), Bill Henry (1974), Gregory Hill (1973), Richard Hoover (1976), Ann Hould-Ward (1982), John Jensen (1968–75), Virgil Johnson (1980), Bob Jorissen (1976, 1983), James Leonard Joy (1983), Marjorie Kellogg (1978), Sam Kirkpatrick (1973–74, 1976, 1980), Mary Rhopa laCiera (1980), Kerry Lafferty (1971), Gene Lakin (1983), Ming Cho Lee (1979, 1983), Valery Leventhal (1978), Arnold Levine (1970), Adrianne Lobel (1982), Santo Loquasto (1981–82), Tomás MacAnna (1973), John McLain (1980), Neil McLeod (1979), William Marshall (1976–77), Gorden Micunis (1970), Craig Miller (1979–83), Michael Miller (1983), Roberto Mitchell (1968), *Tanya Moiseiwitsch* (1963–66, 1968–69, 1973), Beni Montresor (1982), Robert Morgan (1976), Karlis Ozols (1981), Maurice Palinski (1976–77), Dennis Parichy (1981), Carolyn Parker (1967–69), Nancy Potts (1975), Frank Rahn (1976), Dunya Ramicova (1978, 1979), Richard Riddell (1981, 1983), Mary Rirard (1968), Carrie Fishbein Robbins (1969, 1978, 1983), Patrick Robertson (1977), Barry Robison (1976–77), Jean Rosenthal (1968), Paul Scharfenberger (1978, 1980–83), Robert Seales (1969–70, 1974), Douglas Schmidt (1969), Duane Schuler (1973–81), Patrick Shaughnessy (1982), Marjorie Slaiman (1981), Dan Snyder (1967), Eoin Sprott (1970, 1973), John Stark (1969–70), Michael Stauffer (1970), Douglas Stein

(1983), Tony Straiges (1978–79), Annena Stubbs (1977), Richard William Tidwell (1973–74), Hal Tine (1969), Jennifer Tipton (1981–82), Carl Toms (1972), Fred Voelpel (1968), Jennifer von Mayrhauser (1978–79, 1981), Ann Wallace (1983), Gil Wechsler (1971–72), Kurt Wilhelm (1981, 1983), Peter Wingate (1971), Michael Yeargan (1982), Paul Zalon (1983), Patricia Zipprodt (1973, 1981).

Stage Directors: Rae Allen (1979), Joseph Anthony (1969), Michael Bawtree (1974), Robert Benedetti (1974–75), Michael Blakemore (1977), Dan Bly (1969–70), Edward Payson Call (1965–66, 1968–69, 1983), *Douglas Campbell* (1963–68), Ken Campbell (1976), Len Cariou (1968, 1972, 1974), David Chambers (1974, 1982), Eric Christmas (1973), Liviu Ciulei (1981–83), Milt Commons (1970), Christopher Covert (1978), Jon Cranney (1977, 1979–81), Ron Daniels (1979), Cara Duff-MacCormick (1978–79), Anatoly Efros (1978–79), Alvin Epstein (1978–79), Michael Feingold (1978), David Feldshuh (1969–73, 1976, 1982), Richard Foreman (1981), Kenneth Frankel (1980), Edward Gilbert (1970, 1979–80), Gary Gisselman (1982), William Green (1968), Thomas Gruenwald (1975), *Sir Tyrone Guthrie* (1963–65, 1967–69), Adrian Hall (1976), Edward Hastings (1980–81), Nick Havinga (1977), Israel Hicks (1970), John Hirsch (1970, 1972), Loyce Houlton (1976), Stephen Kanee (1975–80), George Keathley (1980), Charles Keating (1970), Nicholas Kepros (1976), Mark Lamos (1976–77), Robert Lanchester (1968), Chris Langham (1976), *Michael Langham* (1970–77, 1980), Eugene Lion (1973, 1975–76), Tomás MacAnna (1973), Dugald MacArthur (1969), Robert David MacDonald (1970), Jack McLaughlin (1978), Emily Mann (1976–79), Christopher Markle (1981–83), Marshall Mason (1981), Philip Minor (1969–70), Tony Mockrus (1980), Tom Moore (1975), Peter Nichols (1976), Karlis Ozuls (1976), Michael Pierce (1968), Henry Pillsbury (1977), Lucian Pintilie (1983–84), Stephen Porter (1967–68), Richard Russell Ramos (1979), J. Ranelli (1977), Lee Richardson (1968), Steven Robman (1978–79), Scott Rubsam (1978), Ken Ruta (1975–77), Peter Mark Schifter (1978), Alan Schneider (1964, 1981), Andrei Serban (1982), Mel Shapiro (1967–69), Omar Shapli (1968), Bruce Siddons (1978–79), Gail Smogard (1978), Harold Stone (1982), Jim Wallace (1976), Kenneth Welsh (1975), David Wheeler (1971), Stephen Willems (1979–80), *Garland Wright* (1980–83).

Actors and Actresses: F. Murray Abraham (1978), Jim Ahrens (1980), Rod Aird (1973), James Alexander (1967–69), Lynn Alexander (1982), Richard Allan (1973), Lee Allen (1973), Penelope Allen (1971), Seth Allen (1982), Gregg Almquist (1968), Don Amendolia (1977), Maureen Anderman (1974), Alfred A. Anderson (1980), C. B. Anderson (1981), Deborah Anderson (1973), Dwight Anderson (1979), Erik Anderson (1973, 1977), Ian Anderson (1983), Richard Anderson (1964–65), Sarah Anderson (1981), Barbara Andres (1983), Jerome Anello (1969), Fred Applegate (1980–83), Richard Ashford (1968), Claudia Ashley (1969), Jared Aswegan (1973–74), Walter Atamaniuk (1982), Molly Atwood (1968), Jeni Austin (1976–79), Matthew Austin (1982), Richard Ayd (1979), Peter Aylward (1977–78), Arminae Azarian (1983), Dennis Babcock (1974, 1976), Edward Bach (1964), Helen Backlin (1963), Linda Backman (1980), Chuck Bailey (1981), Hillary Bailey (1981), Julian Bailey (1983), Jim Baker (1975–76), Mark Baker (1983), Scott Baker (1982), *Paul Ballantyne* (1963–77), Gerry Bamman (1979, 1982), Charles Bari (1983), Greg Barnell (1976–78), Evelyn Baron (1971), John Barone (1983), Joyce Barott (1981), Diana Barrington (1971), Don Barshay (1968), Gary Basaraba (1982), Emery Battis (1968–70), Matthew Beach (1982–83), Stephan Beach (1981), Andrea Bebel (1982), Leigh Beery (1973), Bernard Behrens (1971, 1973–74), *Fran Bennett* (1967–77), Robert Benson (1970), Walter Bera (1969), Karen Berg (1981), Paul

Berget (1973), Barbara Berlovitz (1976), Mark Berman (1966), Ed Bernard, Jacqueline
Bertrand (1979), Roger Beyer (1964), Ross Bickell (1969–71), Robert Binari (1981),
Theodore Bikel (1983), Wanda Bimson (1980), Edward Binns (1967), Raye Birk (1967),
Drew Birns (1974), Maria Bjornson (1981), Gerry Black (1970), Merrilly Blagen (1973),
Vernon Blake (1969), Sharon Faye Blaly (1982), James Blendick (1971–74), Peter Bloe-
doorn (1966), Mark Bloom (1976), Dan Bly (1970), Kathleen Bock (1980–81), Christian
Bode (1980), Steve Boe (1978–79), Earl Boen (1965–67), Peter Boesen, Jr. (1983), Tom
Bolstad (1973), Leta Bonynge (1976), Marshall Borden (1981), Paula Bormes (1979),
Alexandria Borrie (1981), Tom Bothof (1980), Ronald Boulden (1964–67), Ben Bowman
(1983), Gary Bowman (1968), Alan Brasington (1980), Matthew T. Brassil (1981), Mario
Bravo (1978–79), Michael Brennan (1973), Dori Brenner (1973), Robert Breuler (1977),
Roy Brocksmith (1980–81), Raina Brody (1983), Tanya Brody (1983), Doug Broe (1973),
Erik Brogger (1976), Ivan Brogger (1971–73), Bill Bromaghim (1982), Joel Brooks
(1977), Blair Brown (1973–74), Graham Brown (1963–65), Hosmer Andrew Brown IV
(1981–82), Richard Burton Brown (1975–76), Cara Mia Bruncati (1981), Trent Brunier
(1972–73), Gunar Bruvelis (1969), Gordon Bryars (1963), Oksana Bryn (1983), *Barbara
Bryne* (1970–80), Mark Buchanan (1969), Donald Buka (1978–79), Kathryn Ann Bulger
(1981–82), Bryce Bulles (1970), Yusef Bulos (1980), Donny Burks (1979–80), Catherine
Burns (1981–82), Helen Burns (1977), Robert Burns (1983), Thomas A. Burrington
(1981), James A. Bush (1981), Michael Butler (1981), William J. Butler (1982), Steven
Byrnes (1978–79), Adolph Caesar (1967), James Cahill (1973), Zoe Caldwell (1963,
1965), Kristina Callahan (1964–65), Jo Smith Cameron (1983), David Campbell (1971,
1981), Douglas Campbell (1964, 1967–68), J. Kenneth Campbell (1973), David Canary
(1978–79), John Cappelletti (1965), Christopher Cara (1980–81), *Helen Carey* (1966–
80), *Len Cariou* (1966–74), Cynthia Carle (1977–78), Johann Carlo (1981), Curtis Carlson
(1964), Linda Carlson (1972), Pamela Carlson (1970), Daniel Carroll (1978), Timothy
Casey (1969–70), Ann Casson (1968), Veronica Castang (1978), Jody Catlin (1981),
Rou Cato (1976), George Cattle (1981), Joe Anthony Cauise (1983), David Cecsarini
(1978–79), David E. Chadderdon (1983), Jeff Chandler (1973–75), Cindy Chapman
(1973), Douglas Cheek (1969), Cecilia Chejne (1979), Ann Cherne (1978–79), Bruce
Cherne (1978–79), Becky Cheston (1969), Yolanda Childress (1982), Timothy Christie
(1964–66), Eric Christmas (1975), Charles Cioffi (1963–65), Caitlin Clarke (1982), David
Clarke (1973), Patrick Clear (1977–78), Suzanna Clemin (1983), *Oliver Cliff* (1973–81),
Adrienne Cochran (1981), Lynn Cohen (1979–80, 1983), Polly Cohen (1982), Gilbert
Cole (1980), Olivia Cole (1966), Lucy Colfax (1970), Paul Collins (1980), Joel Colodner
(1981), Robert Colston (1976–77), John Command (1980), Jim Conklin (1980), Carey
Connell (1972), *Patricia Connolly* (1969–77), Neil Conrad (1978–79), Frances Conroy
(1981), William Converse-Roberts (1980), Maury Cooper (1975), Katherine Cortez
(1981), Clayton Corzatte (1963), Peggy Cosgrave (1971), Nicholas Coster (1963), Richard Cottrell (1968–69), Steve Coulter (1983), Richard Council (1975), Nathan Courtreau
(1981), Richard Cox (1981), *Jon Cranney* (1967–79), James Craven (1969, 1980–81),
Saylor Creswell (1971), Paddy Croft (1980), John Cromwell (1963–66), Harry Cronin
(1964), Hume Cronyn (1963, 1965, 1981), J. Stephen Crosby (1974), Dan Crowley
(1980–81), Dan Crowzie (1979), Ann Crumb (1979), Barbara Cullen (1980), Joseph
Culliton (1970), John Cunningham (1981), Richard Curnock (1973), Russell Curry (1977–
78), Robert Curtis-Brown (1983), Valery Daemke (1974–75), Paul Dallin (1972), Becka
Dalton (1978–80), Stephen D'Ambrose (1980–81, 1983), Michael Damon (1978–79),

Anita Dangler (1973), Paula Danser (1980), Richard M. Davidson (1980), Jeffrey Davies (1977–78), Dawn Davis (1979–80), Janette Davis (1980), Lance Davis (1970–77), Mark Davis (1983), Susan Davis (1969), Paula Dawn (1973), Libby Dean (1973), Justin Deas (1979), Susan Defoe (1976–79), Neil P. DeGroot (1981), Jossie de Guzman (1982) Kay de Lancey (1978–79), Michele Delattre (1980), Joseph Della Sorte (1973), Jake Dengel (1978–79), William Denis (1983), Frank Dent (1975–76), Steven Dietz (1980), Leigh Dillard (1981), Harold Dixon (1973), Lura Doebler (1969), Scott Doebler (1969), Madeline E. Doherty (1983), King Donovan (1975), Robert Dorfman (1981–82), Paula Dornisch (1972), Frank Dosse (1980), Mary Dosse (1980), Joel Dossi (1979), Judith Doty (1963), Sean Dowse (1976), Paul Drake (1980), Cara Duff-McCormick (1975, 1978–79), Mary Dykhouse (1964), James Eckhouse (1981), George Edwards (1972), Laurie Edwards-Wilson (1977), Michael Egan (1983), Doug Eha (1980), Abby Ehelick (1969), Jeffrey Eisenberg (1972), Patricia Elliot (1966–68), Scott Elliot (1983), Robert Ellis (1969), Katherine Emery (1963–64), Carol Emshoff (1963), Robert Engels (1974–75), Maury Engels (1977–78), Priscilla Entersz (1980), Alvin Epstein (1978), Sharon Ernster (1977), Laura Esterman (1978), Allan Estes (1970), Chris Evans (1976), Dillon Evans (1982), George Everett (1979–80), Phillip Fabel (1980), Ron Faber (1978–79), Steven Fagerberg (1981), Danielle Fagre (1981), Don R. Fallbeck (1977–80), Michelle Farr (1983), David Feldshuh (1968–73), Tovah Feldshuh (1971–73), David Fenley (1982), Larry Fergusson (1968), *Katherine Ferrand* (1968–74), Peter Filkins (1980–81), Donald Fischer (1983), Mary Beth Fischer (1983), John Fistos (1982), Lauren Fitzgerald (1980), Niki Flacks (1963), Pauline Flanagen (1973, 1983), Ed Flanders (1964–66), David Flaten (1967), Gus Fleming (1969), Henry Fleming (1980), Joe Foley (1979–80), Lois Foraker (1980–81), Bridget Foreman (1981), Johan Foreman (1978–79), Donald Forsberg (1963), Stacy Forster (1981–83), Gloria Foster (1982), Michelle Foster (1976), Tom Fox (1980), Linda Frailich (1972–73), Richard Frank (1982), Kenneth Frankel (1965), Patricia Fraser (1977–79), Michael Frederick (1969–70), Erik Fredericksen (1972–73), Mark Frost (1969), Warren Frost (1970–71), Ray Fry (1980), Kate Fuglei (1980, 1982–83), Randy Fuhrman (1983), Jonathon Fuller (1980–81), Lisa Fusaro (1977), Doug Gabrielli (1979), Boyd Gaines (1981), Frederick Gaines (1967), Michael Gallagher (1982–83), Michael Galloway (1979–80), Ann Galvin (1972), Rita Gam (1962), Robin Gamwell (1967–69), Jim Gardner (1973), Geoff Garland (1973), Katherine Garnett (1968–69), Larry Gates (1973–74), *Ellen Geer* (1963–66), Linda Gehringer (1979), Adam Geisness (1979), Marie Geist (1966), Gene Gentili (1972), Avril Gentles (1980), Elena Giannetti (1981–83), June Gibbons (1982–83), Allison Giglio (1970), Joseph Gillespie (1969), Jonathon Gillman (1968), David Gilmore (1980), J. Gilpin (1979–80), Manon Gimlet (1982), Francois de la Giraday (1981), Maxwell Glanville (1970), *Ron Glass* (1968–71), Doug Glore (1981), *Peter Michael Goetz* (1969–79), Steven Goldman (1971), John Going (1963), Russell Gold (1976–77), Sheila Goldes (1964), Maggi Good (1968), Michael Goodwin (1973–80), Ellin Gorky (1970–73), William Graham (1969), Kelsey Grammer (1980), Barbara Granning (1975–76), Gail Grate (1982), Giovanni Gray (1969), Dale Green (1983), Kenneth Green (1969), Kim Green (1982), William Greene (1967), Melody Greer (1967), Richard Grey (1976), Thomas Griffith (1983), John Grill (1973), Thomas Grimm (1969), Brian Grivna (1974, 1978–79), William Grivna (1969), George Grizzard (1963–64), Steve Gronwall (1980), Michael Gross (1976–77), Anita Grumish (1976), Karen Grumke (1972), Richard Gruslin (1979), Michael Guido (1980–81), Anne Gunderson (1983), Carol Gustafson (1968), Roxanne Patton Haine (1981), April Halcin (1981), Fiona Hale (1979–80), Donna Haley (1973), Brian Hall (1981), George Hall (1982–83),

William Halliday (1972), *Allen Hamilton* (1968–83), Douglas Hamilton (1973), Oren Hamson (1979), James Handy (1983), Carol Hanpeter (1981), Mary Hara (1977), Wiley Harker (1976), James Harper (1982), Helen Harrelson (1965–69), Peter Harren (1979), Delphi Harrinton (1982), James Harris (1977–79), *Rosemary Hartup* (1976–79), Michael Harvey (1964), Robert Haskin (1964), Curtis Hastings (1982), Nancy Hatch (1976), Naomi Hatfield (1979), Rana Haugen (1982), June Havoc (1973), Rob Haywood (1980), Virginia Heathman (1973), Paul Hecht (1971), *Thomas Hegg* (1969–78), Mark Heinzen (1979), Michael Hendricks (1975–76), Sara Hennessey (1981), Lance Henricksen (1971), Maxine Herman (1969), Scott Herner (1970–71), John Noah Herzler (1980–81), Eric Hetzler (1978–79), Munson Hicks (1982–83), Allen Hidalgo (1983), Dennis Jay Higgins (1973), Richard Hilger (1979–81), Terry Hill (1974), Mary Hitch (1971–72), Dennis Holland (1983), Prudence Wright Holmes (1974), Ann Homan (1974), Barbara Homes (1972), Richard Hoover (1971), Selma Hopkins (1963), James Horswill (1965, 1980–81), Eric House (1980), Bette Howard (1970), Jordan Howard (1964), Richard Howard (1981–82), Jo Howarth (1983), Kathleen Howell (1965), Joseph Hughes (1972–73), Steve Huke (1979–80), Hugh Hurd (1966), James Hurdle (1977), Barbara Hyslop (1977–78), Anthony Inneo (1973), Laura Innes (1983), Jerry Ion (1973), Greg Irwin (1977–78), Susan Isenberg (1978–79), Robert Jackson (1966), Paulette James (1968), Jeffrey Jamison (1977–78), Robert Jason (1980), Thomas Jasorka (1972), Josh Javits (1973), Joy Javits (1973), Mary Joel (1982), Bill Johnson (1980), Charles Johnson (1983), J. Warren Johnson (1972), Jody Johnson (1978–80), Tammy Johnson (1978–79), Teresa Johnson (1969), Cheryl Tafathale Jones (1976–77), James Earl Jones (1983), Jane Jones (1983), Jeffrey Jones (1967), Neal Jones (1973), Pam Jones (1969), Thornton Jones (1964), Henry J. Jordan (1974–75), Nancy L. Joseph (1972–73), Deborah Kafitz (1976), Ricky Kahn (1973), Stephen Kanee (1976), Terry Karn (1971), David Karr (1968), Greg Kassmar (1972), Art Kassul (1973), Carole Kastigar (1972), Grace Keagy (1967), Charles Keating (1968–69), Stephen Keep (1969–70), Eleni Kelakos (1983), Richard Kelsin (1969), Linda Kelsey (1969–70), Roberta Kendrick (1973), Dennis Kennedy (1976–77), *Nicholas Kepros* (1973–76), Philip Kerr (1966–67), Val Kilmer (1981), Randall Duk Kim (1978–79), Adam King (1980), Gary Kingsolver (1980), Katie Kladt (1978–79), Laurie Kladt (1978–79), Christopher Klein (1973), Joseph Klemowski (1966–68), Jacqueline Knapp (1982), T. R. Knight (1978–80), Kurt Koegel (1981), *Frederick Koivumaki* (1969–73), Victor Koivumaki (1964), Lara Kokernot (1980–81), Doug Korblick (1982), Kevin Korotev (1981), Sonja Kostich (1980–81), Linda Kozlowski (1982), Roger Kozol (1977–78), Stephen Kramer (1965), Warren Krech (1970), Ronald Kubler (1964), Rick Kurnow (1970), David Kwiat (1977–78), Matthew Kwiat (1977–78), Michael LaFleur (1983), *Mark Lambs* (1973–77), Robert Lancaster (1967), Timothy Landfield (1980–81), Karen Landry (1975–80), Colin Lane (1982), Meredith Lane (1976–77), Stephen Lang (1978–79), Frank Langella (1972), Randy Larsen (1980), Adrine Larson (1976), James Lashly (1980), Michael Laskin (1976–78), Paul Lasko (1981), *James Lawless* (1965–83), Charles Lawrence (1969), Kenneth Lazebnik (1983), Steve Lebens (1983), Joel Lee (1983), Mark Lee (1970), Patrick Leehan (1983), Russell Leib (1980), Gregory Leifeld (1981), Betty Leighton (1971–73), Arlene Lencioni (1980), Katherine Lenel (1972), Zara Lenfesty (1978–79), Michael Lenzen (1976–77), Cecil Lester (1981–82), Michael Levin (1976–77), William Levis (1970), Cindy Lew (1979), *John Lewin* (1963–82), Carol-Jean Lewis (1979–80), Pat Lewis (1973), Nancy Lillis (1979), Marie Lillo (1973), Delroy Lindo (1983), James Lineberger (1963–65), David Little (1969), Glen Lloyd (1968), Lee Lobenhofer (1983), Beverly Lockhart (1968), Kim Lockhart

(1973), Travis Lockhart (1967), Linda Lockman (1980), Tara Loewenstein (1978–79), John Long (1974), Alice Love (1970), Thomas Lubiano (1981), Peter Lucas (1982), Clark Luis (1969), Clyde Lund (1976), Jim Lund (1973), Chris Lundegaarde (1974), Patti LuPone (1981), Jesse Lykken (1974), Janet McCall (1973), Kim McCallum (1965), Sandy McCallum (1964–66), Macon McCalman (1974–75), Christopher McCann (1983), Laurie McCannell (1969), Laura McCarthy (1983), Steve McCloskey (1982), Kevin Robert McCormick (1982–83), Noel McCoy (1970), James McCreary (1967), Leroy McDonald (1970), Edwin J. McDonough (1980), Heather MacDonough (1978–79), Yvonne McElroy (1964–66), Bob McFadden (1973), Terry McGarity (1981), Randall McGee (1966), Tim McGee (1982), Shawn McGill (1973), Bob McGillivray (1980), Michael McGonagle (1969), Katherine McGrath (1980), Bill McGuire (1970), Joan Macintosh (1983), Bill McIntyre (1982), Jane MacIver (1980), Audrey Mack (1969), Bruce MacKay (1973), John MacKay (1964–65), James McKeel (1981), Richard McKenzie (1972), Janet MacLaughlin (1963), *Jack McLaughlin-Grey* (1977–80), *Jason McLean* (1973–80), R. Bruce McLean (1981), Jim McNee (1976–77), Norah McNellis (1981), Sean McNellis (1971, 1976), Peter MacNichol (1978–79), Peter McRobbie (1981–82), Richard McWilliams (1980), W. H. Macy (1978–79), Donald Madden (1981), Larkin Malloy (1979), Charles Maloney (1979), Joseph Maner (1971), Emily Mann (1978–79), Tia Mann (1976), Harold Manpin (1971), Tad Marburg (1976), Steven Marcus (1978–79), J. R. Marks (1973), Kaldin Marschel (1978–79), Dee Martin (1973), Donald Martin (1980), Greg Martin (1982), J. Patrick Martin (1976–81), Sandra Martin (1967), Gary Martinez (1974–75), Nancy Marvy (1972, 1978–79), Kristen Mathisen (1981), Marcy Mattox (1975), Abby Mauk (1982), *Roberta Maxwell* (1968–72), Daniel May (1983), Deborah May (1980–81), Jeanne Mayer (1982), John Mayer (1981–83), Mike Mazurki (1983), Fred Melamed (1981), David Melmer (1983), Frank Melodia (1980–81), Edna Reiss Merin (1974), Charles Merkle (1978–79), Robert John Metcalf (1972), Ed Meyer (1982), Karyn Meyer (1969), Lilian Mikiver (1972–73), David Milana (1981), Betsy Miller (1981), Fred Miller (1971), Robert Milli (1965), Laura Mirsky (1978–79), Marion Miska (1963), George Mitchell (1967), Tony Mockus (1976–83), David Monasch (1972), Isabelle Monk (1981–82), Patricia Monson (1983), Howard Moody (1963), Bill Moor (1982), Michael Moore (1976–77), Kathy Morath (1982), *Michael Moriarty* (1966–69), Jeannie Morick (1980), Barbara Morin (1976), Joan Morris (1978–79), Greg Morrisson (1973), Chuck Morrow (1983), Nancy Moyer (1981), Todd Murken (1980), Anne Murray (1982), Jane Murray (1976–77), Jason Murray (1976–78), Michelle Murray (1978), P. J. Murray (1978–79), Scott Murray (1977–78), Tena Murray (1977–78), George Muschamp (1969), Jean-Paul Mustone (1972), Robert Nadir (1980–81), William Nagel (1973), Lisa Naylor (1983), Timothy Near (1979), W. Alan Nebelthau (1981), Ross Neil (1973), Christopher Nelms (1978–79), Michael Nelms (1978–79), Chet Nelson II (1969), Connie Nelson (1983), Ruth Nelson (1963–69), Stan Nelson (1983), Tamara Nerby (1982), Virginia Ness (1979), John Newcome (1973–74, 1980–81), Audrey Newman (1968–69), Frederick Newman (1982), William Newman (1981), Paul Nickabonski (1973), Kristine Nielsen (1980–82), Amy Nissen (1978–79), Tim Nissen (1973), James Noah (1977–78), Michael Nolan (1973), Julie Ann Numbers (1980–81), Sheldon Nunn (1970), Pamela Nybery (1983), Thomas Nyman (1963), Gordon Oas-Heim (1978–79), Irene O'Brien (1976), Dennis O'Connell (1976), Peggy O'Connell (1981, 1983), Dana Offerman (1979–80), Lynn O'Heron (1981), Laurel Ollstein (1983), Allen Olsen (1973), Richard Ooms (1981–83), Sean O'Phelan (1978–79), Alexander Orfaly (1973), Kaarina Ornelas (1977), Marnie Osterberg (1980), John Ostrander (1979–80), Charlie Otte (1982),

Laurence Overmire (1981), Jenny Pageant (1981), Holly Palance (1977), Reid Papke (1971), Michael Paquin (1969), Michael Parish (1970), Peter Passi (1981), *Robert Pastene* (1963–82), Guy Paul (1976–77), Erika Paulson (1983), Virginia Payne (1975–76), J. Robert Pearce (1967), Jan Pearce (1966), Deborah Pedersen (1968), Tom Pedi (1979–80), Christopher Pennock (1976), Richard Perdue (1976), Mary Perez (1969), Kathleen Perkins (1976–77), Terry Perkins (1983), Fern Persons (1977–78), Brian Petchey (1970–71), Franklin Peters (1963–64), Lauri Peters (1968), Barry Peterson (1964), Deidre Peterson (1983), Jenny Peterson (1981), Susan Peterson (1980–81), Suzanne Petri (1981), Margaret Phillips (1969), Richard Phillips (1964), Stephen Phillips (1976), John Pielmeier (1976–77), David Pierce (1983), Michael Pierce (1966–67), Warren Pineus (1982), Fred Pinkard (1967–73), Scott Pionk (1969–70), Anne Pitoniak (1979), Christopher Plummer (1973), Brian Poffenberger (1980), Kenneth Pogue (1970–72), William Pogue (1963–64), Joy Pommerenke (1978–79), Wendy Pool (1970), Julie Populas (1981), Emand Poshek (1963), Mike Powell (1979), Leon Pownall (1971–72), Francisco Prado (1980–81), Ed Preble (1963), Alek Primrose (1968), Angie Prokop (1982), Ric Purdue (1980), Gerald Quimby (1971–73), John Rainer (1983), Clifford Rakerd (1980–81), *Richard Ramos* (1967–77), John Ramsey (1968–69), Darrell Ranum (1964), Garry Rayppy (1982), Eileen Reagan (1981), Nancy Reardon (1968), Adam Redfield (1981), Joseph Regalbuto (1978–79), Barton E. Reghr (1979), Floyd Reichman (1981), Barbara Reid (1977–78), Paul Reighard (1981), Dwyer Reilly (1976–77), Jon Reininga (1980), Sylvia Rhyne (1978–79), William Rhys (1971), Christopher Rich (1979), Lisa Richards (1969), Michael Richards (1976), James Richardson (1973), Lee Richardson (1963–69), Thomas L. Richern (1983), Nancy Ringham (1978–79), Ken Risch (1979–80), Kent Rizley (1976), Chad Roberts (1982), Linda Roberts (1982), Richard Rockwell (1983), George Roesler (1978–79), Jill Rogosheske (1973–74), Ronald Rogosheske (1963–64), Patricia Roos (1973), *Wilberto Rosario* (1973–76), Christine Rose (1982), Jill Rose (1973), Irene Roseen (1967–68), Ed Rosenberg (1972), Wendy Rosenberg (1983), Carol Rosenfeld (1981), Clive Rosengren (1981), Eliot Ross (1980–81), Judith Ross (1973), Alfred Rossi (1963), Gastone Rossilli (1972), Amy Rostron (1981), Theodore Rouse (1964), Mari Rovang (1972), Martin Ruben (1980–81), Amy Rudick (1976), David Rudick (1976), Marc Rush (1970), Stephen Rush (1978–79), *Ken Ruta* (1963–82), Steven Ryan (1971), Steven Rydberg (1971), Louella St. Ville (1982), Richard Sale (1982), Tina Saltin (1966), David Saltzman (1969), Ronald Oscar Sarum (1983), Nick Savian (1967, 1980), Mary Savidge (1971), August Schellenberg (1974), Martha Schlame (1978–79), E. Richard Schlattman (1975–76), Dale Walter Schmid (1983), Jana Schneider (1982), Carlotta Schoch (1977–79), Peggy Schoditsch (1980–81), David Schomaker (1980), William Schoppert (1974–75), 1977), Thomas Schreier (1973), Warren Schueneman (1981), Allen Schulte (1964), Brad Schultz (1981), Ron Schultz (1980–81), Robert Scogin (1980), Frank S. Scott (1974–78), Maurice Scroggins (1969–70), John Seitz (1981), Dominique Serrand (1976), Michael Sevareid (1968), Danny Sewell (1982), James Sewell (1976–77), Ryan Sexton (1980–81), Michele Seyler (1980), Maura Shaffer (1977–79), Harold Shallman (1974), Barbara Sharma (1983), Stockton Shaw (1979), Michele Shay (1970–72), Paul Shenar (1980), Terese Sherman (1983), Willis Sherman (1964), Armin Shimerman (1980, 1983), Sylvia Short (1983), Margaret Silk (1978–79), William Simington (1979–81), Marianne Simons (1981), Cleo Simonett (1974), Corey Simpson (1982–83), Scott Simpson (1978–79), T. J. Skinner (1976), Robert Skloot (1967), Thomas Slater (1965), Pat Slingsby (1963), Fern Sloan (1969–70), Robert Sloane (1966), Mim Sloberg (1980–81), William B. Smale (1981), Ben Smith (1978–79), Bo Smith (1980–81), Brian Smith (1980), Connor

Smith (1980), Craig Smith (1972), Doug Smith (1978–79), Fruud Smith (1981–82), J. Walter Smith (1967), Kim Smith (1978–79), Lois Smith (1983), Trevor Smith (1978–79), Bruce Somerville (1976), Melodie Sommers (1981), Gale Sondergaard (1967–68), Ingrid Helga Sonnichsen (1974), Ted Sothern (1981), Dale Souless (1981), Robert Spanelsel (1964), Adrian Sparks (1980), Denny Spence (1975–76), Debra Spencer (1980–81), John Spencer (1979–80), Neil Spencer (1980), Cherie Sprosty (1982), Brian Sprunek (1971), Katherine Squire (1967), Alvah Stanley (1964–65), Charles Stanley (1963–64), Michael Stayton (1981), Doug Steele (1980), Bronia Stefan (1971), Jody L. Steinke (1982–83), Ted Stelten (1968), Roy K. Stevens (1978–79), Jerry Stiller (1983), David Straka (1974), Henry Stram (1981–82), Mary Straten (1973), John E. Straub (1981), Dean Stricklin (1965–66), Ernest Stricklin (1964), Fred Stuthman (1979), Patrick Sullivan (1973), Lynda Sultze (1973–74), John Swanholm (1978–79), Kraig Swartz (1977, 1980–81), Tony Swartz (1968–69), Lyle Swedeen (1974), James Sweeney (1977–78), Donovan Sylvester (1973–74), Sandor Szabo (1970–72), Theodore Szymanski (1964), Robin Tagliente (1979–80), *Jessica Tandy* (1963, 1965, 1981), Jennifer Taylor (1979–80), Toni Taylor (1982), Tim Teachout (1969), Annie Thatcher (1978–79), Roy Thinnes (1983), Deborah Thoemke (1981), Lance Thoemke (1981), Madlynn Thoemke (1981), Peter Thoemke (1979–81), Robin Thomas (1971), Sheridan Thomas (1973–76), Paul Thompson (1969, 1973), Tom Thompson (1980–81), Victoria Thompson (1976), Scott E. Thun (1983), Sharon Tibesar (1980), Tara Tidgewell (1981), Todd Tidgewell (1981), Carl Tilli (1983), Barbara Tirrell (1983), Shirin Devrim Trainer (1979–80), Jan Triska (1979–81), Eugene Troobnick (1982–83), Christopher Troter (1982), Christine Tschida (1983), James Tucker (1972), Herb Tulien (1980), Louis Turenne (1973), Scott Turi (1979), Glynn Turman (1967), William Tynan (1973), Henrietta Valor (1983), Joan van Ark (1963), Kristin van de Plasch (1967), Raedell van de Plasch (1967), Granville Van Dusen (1967–69), Christy van House (1983), William Vanderber (1981), Harley Venton (1976–77), Carol Vincent (1977–78), Michael Vita (1973), George Vogel (1973), Hans von Mende (1963), Ralph Vucci (1983), James Walker (1981), Mary Walker (1981), Paul Walker (1983), James Wallace (1966–67, 1973), Donald Wallen (1964), Jack Walsh (1982), Joseph Walsh (1969), Keliher Walsh (1981), Maura Walsh (1969), Chris Ward (1980), Jaime Warhol (1981), Dennis Warning (1983), Jennifer Warren (1964), David Warrilow (1981–83), Danny Weathers (1983), Elizabeth Weger (1982), Maurice Weinblatt (1968), Hy Weingarden (1967–68), Christine Weller (1978–79), Cynthia Wells (1969–73), Kenneth Welsh (1973–74), Dona Werner (1982), Paul Wesman (1973), Donald West (1965–66), Tony Whitbeck (1972), Cynthia White (1980), Ann Whiteside (1965), Margaret Whitton (1980), Nancy Wickwine (1965–66), Dianne Wiest (1972), Fawn Wilderson (1981), Claudia Wilkens (1982–83), *Arnold Wilkerson* (1970–78), Jeffrey Wilkins (1983), Stephen Willems (1983), Hy Wingate (1970), James Winker (1980–81), Toni J. Wisti (1981), Thomas Witry (1982), Binky Wood (1981), Alan Woodward (1981), Claude Woolman (1963–64), Joyce Worsley (1983), Charles Michael Wright (1983), Mary Wright (1974), Max Wright (1971), Sally Ann Wright (1981), Todd Wronski (1983), Moira Wyle (1967–68), Ray Xifo (1981), Stephen Yoakam (1983), Edward Zang (1972), Nick Zanides (1966), Vito Zingarelli (1977).

REPERTORY

1963–64: Mainstage: *Hamlet, The Miser, The Three Sisters, Death of a Salesman.*
1964–65: Mainstage: *Henry V, Saint Joan, The Glass Menagerie, Volpone.*

1965–66: Mainstage: *Richard III, The Way of the World, The Cherry Orchard, The Caucasian Chalk Circle, The Miser* (revival).

1966–67: Mainstage: *The Skin of Our Teeth, The Dance of Death, As You Like It, The Doctor's Dilemma, S.S. Glencairn.*

1967–68: Mainstage: *Shoemaker's Holiday, Thieves' Carnival, Harpers Ferry, The House of Atreus, The Visit.*

1968–69: Mainstage: *Twelfth Night, Serjeant Musgrave's Dance, The Master Builder, The Resistible Rise of Arturo Ui, Merton of the Movies, The House of Atreus* (revival). Crawford Livingston Theatre: *She Stoops to Conquer, Tango, Enrico IV.* The Other Place: *Little Murders, Red Cross, The Indian Wants the Bronx, Quirk, Blood of an Englishman, The Flying Doctor* and *Jealous Husband, Charlie, Hallowe'en, Brecht on Brecht, Man with the Flower.* Tour: *The House of Atreus, The Resistible Rise of Arturo Ui.*

1969–70: Mainstage: *Julius Caesar, The Beauty Part, The Homecoming, Mourning Becomes Electra, Uncle Vanya.* Crawford Livingston Theatre: *The Alchemist, Ardele.* The Other Place: *The Measures Taken, The Dutchman, A Slight Ache, Krapp's Last Tape, The Hostage, The Ghost Dancer.*

1970–71: Mainstage: *The Venetian Twins, Ceremonies in Dark Old Men, The Tempest, A Man's a Man, A Play.* The Other Place: *Silence and Landscape, Don Perlimpin's Love for Belissa in His Garden, Kumaliza, The Madness of Lady Bright, Stars and Stripes Forever, The Labyrinth, Winners, Baal, Encore, Good for Thought* and *A Mild Case of Death, Madam Popov* and *Wet Dream by God.*

1971–72: Mainstage: *Cyrano de Bergerac, The Taming of the Shrew, A Touch of the Poet, Misalliance, The Diary of a Scoundrel, Fables Here and Then.* Tour: *Fables Here and Then* (mainstage).

1972–73: Mainstage: *A Midsummer Night's Dream, Of Mice and Men, The Relapse, An Italian Straw Hat, Oedipus the King, A Christmas Carol, Cyrano.* Tour: *Of Mice and Men.*

1973–74: Mainstage: *Becket, Oedipus the King, The Government Inspector, Juno and the Paycock, I, Said the Fly, Waiting for Godot, The Merchant of Venice, The Miracle Man.* Tour: *The Portable Pioneer and Prairie Show.*

1974–75: Mainstage: *King Lear, Love's Labour's Lost, The Crucible, Tartuffe, The School for Scandal.* Tour: *Everyman.*

1975–76: Mainstage: *Arsenic and Old Lace, The Caretaker, A Streetcar Named Desire, Loot, Mother Courage and Her Children, Under Milk Wood, Private Lives, A Christmas Carol, Measure for Measure.*

1976–77: Mainstage: *The Matchmaker, Doctor Faustus, Cat on a Hot Tin Roof, Rosencrantz and Guildenstern Are Dead, An Enemy of the People, The Winter's Tale, A Christmas Carol* (revival), *The National Health.* Guthrie 2: *The Collected Works of Billy the Kid, The Future Pit, Annulla Allen—Autobiography of a Survivor, Triple Feature— Cold—Glutt—Waterman, Ilk's Madhouse, Up the Seminole, Hello and Goodbye, Open Shut* (playwright in residence). Tour: *A Party for Two.*

1977–78: Mainstage: *She Stoops to Conquer, A Moon for the Misbegotten, La Ronde, Catsplay, The White Devil, Design for Living, A Christmas Carol* (revival), *Pantagleize.* Guthrie 2: *Ashes, Samuel Beckett . . . Mouth on Fire: Not I, Play, and Krapp's Last Tape, The Conversion of Aaron Weiss, Dear Liar, Reunion.* Tour: *A Moon for the Misbegotten Clowns, Lovers and Kings.*

1978–79: Mainstage: *The Pretenders, Teibele and Her Demon, Boy Meets Girl, Bonjour, là, Bonjour, Hamlet* (revival), *Marriage, A Christmas Carol* (revival), *The Beggar's*

Opera. Guthrie 2: *Flashbacks: A Christmas Past, Christmas Present, My Cup Runneth Over, Surprise, Surprise, Vienna Notes, Action, On Mount Chimborazo, Angel Honey, Baby, Darling, Dear, A Kurt Weill Cabaret, Little Eyolf, Emigres*. Tour: *Marriage, Under the Greenwood Tree, Americana*.

1979–80: Mainstage: *The Rivals, Right of Way, The Glass Menagerie* (revival), *Monsieur De Molière, Endgame, Romeo and Juliet, A Christmas Carol* (revival), *You Can't Take It with You*. Tour: *The Glass Menagerie, Americana* (revival). Guthrie Players on Tour: *I Remember, Even as the Sun*.

1980–81: Mainstage: *Wild Oats, Camille, The Tavern, Desire Under the Elms, Mary Stuart, A Christmas Carol, Arms and the Man, Macbeth*. Tour: *The Tavern, A Midsummer Night's Dream*. Guthrie Players on Tour: *Soldiering*.

1981–82: Mainstage: *The Tempest, Don Juan, Our Town, Foxfire, Eve of Retirement, Eli: A Mystery Play, A Christmas Carol, Candide, As You Like It*. Tour: *The Rainmaker*. Guthrie Players on Tour: *A Mark Twain Offering*.

1982–83: Mainstage: *Summer Vacation Madness, Requiem for a Nun, The Marriage of Figaro, Room Service, Heartbreak House, A Christmas Carol, Entertaining Mr. Sloane, Peer Gynt*. Tour: *Talley's Folly*.

1983–84: Mainstage: *The Threepenny Opera, Guys and Dolls, The Entertainer, The Sea Gull, A Christmas Carol, The Importance of Being Earnest, Hedda Gabler*. National Tour: *The Importance of Being Earnest*.

1984–85: Mainstage: *A Soldier's Play, Hang on to Me, The Three Sisters, Tartuffe, 'night, Mother, Twelfth Night, A Christmas Carol, Anything Goes*. Tour: *Foxfire*.

1985–86: *Great Expectations, Cyrano de Bergerac, A Midsummer Night's Dream, Candida, Execution of Justice, A Christmas Carol* (revival), *On the Razzle, The Rainmaker*. Tour: *Foxfire, Great Expectations*.

BIBLIOGRAPHY

Published Sources:

Forsythe, James. *Tyrone Guthrie: The Authorized Biography*. England: Hamish and Hamilton, 1978; New York: McGraw-Hill, 1964.

Guthrie, Tyrone. *A New Theatre*. New York: McGraw-Hill, 1964.

———. "Theatre in Minneapolis." In *Actor and Architect*, edited by Stephen Joseph. Manchester, U.K.: Manchester University Press, 1964.

Mould, William A. "The Guthrie Theatre." *Dictionary of Literary Biography*. Vol. 7. Detroit: Gale Research Press, 1981.

Rossi, Alfred. *Minneapolis Rehearsals: Tyrone Guthrie Directs Hamlet*. Berkeley: University of California Press, 1970.

Archival Source:

Minneapolis, Minnesota. Guthrie Theatre.

Juli A. Thompson

H

[THE] HARTMAN THEATRE COMPANY (HTC) was established in 1974 in Stamford, Connecticut, by Margot Hartman Tenney and her husband, Del Tenney. Margot Tenney's father, Stamford realtor Jesse Hartman, bequeathed resources to establish a service foundation to fund development projects for Stamford and the southwestern Connecticut area. The Tenneys, who had for several years promoted the idea of a resident theatre in Stamford, just fifty miles from Broadway, persuaded the foundation directors to support such a project. The Jesse and Dorothy Hartman Foundation provided major funding in the company's early years, including a $150,000 start-up grant. For 1975–76, its inaugural season, the company projected a $900,000 budget to support a full-time staff of forty administrators and artists. No resident company of actors was envisioned nor has one been maintained, although a number of actors appeared regularly in HTC productions, especially in the period from 1975 to 1980.

Del and Margot Tenney met at the Arena Stage* in Washington, D.C., where they were members of the 1956–57 acting company. These Stamford residents had acted on and off Broadway, in regional theatres, and on national tours. Del Tenney, an experienced stage and film director, directed several HTC productions from 1975 to 1980, and Margot Tenney acted regularly.

A grant of $400,000 from the Hartman Foundation funded conversion of the Palace Theatre at 61 Atlantic Street, originally a vaudeville house, to a flexible facility seating from 500 to 1,500 in thrust and proscenium arrangements. The Tenneys hoped the HTC would serve as a cultural and educational resource for the area and become a major component of a Performing Arts Center in a redeveloped downtown Stamford. To this end they established a theatre conservatory under the direction of Larry Arrick. Twenty-three students enrolled the first year and participated in productions of The Company Store in the 110-seat Landmark Square Theatre, just across the street from the Palace. Besides its short-lived actor training program, HTC has offered experimental productions, new play readings, internships, a children's theatre, educational programs in the local schools, and a teacher-training program.

The Tenneys dedicated HTC to the production of new plays and the revitalization of classics, so the first season included the world premiere of Milan Stitt's *The Runner Stumbles* and a seldom-staged musical adaptation by Larry Arrick and Barbara Damashek of Henry Fielding's *Tom Jones*. Patrons purchased 5,000 subscriptions to the seven-show season. Each show ran for three weeks. State officials greeted HTC's first production, Nicolai Gogol's *The Government Inspector*, with congratulatory telegrams, and local and national critics responded with enthusiastic reviews. One critic, however, felt the lavish production reflected "Broadway" values inappropriate to regional theatre and difficult to justify financially. The remainder of the season attracted several champions who praised the choice of material and the high quality of acting.

The organization flourished for but a year. Three poorly received new plays in the second season undermined subscriber confidence, and patronage slumped in 1977–78. The formula of new plays and revitalized classics seemed a commercial failure, so the Tenneys scrapped their model, trimmed their administrative staff, closed the second stage space dedicated to experimental projects, and, to win back their customers, turned to middle-of-the-road crowd-pleasers such as *The Diary of Anne Frank*, by Frances Goodrich and Albert Hackett. *The Diary of Anne Frank*, William Gibson's *The Miracle Worker*, and Agatha Christie thrillers, *The Mousetrap* and *The Unexpected Guest*, were the biggest hits of the Tenney years. The classics did not attract Stamford audiences: a revival of Georges Feydeau's *Monsieur Ribadier's System*, leading off in 1979–80, was the worst-attended production in the theatre's history, despite the group's move to the more attractive Stamford Theater at 307 Atlantic Street. In the five seasons the Tenneys managed the HTC, box-office receipts rose from 31 percent to 57 percent of the theatre's income, but the Hartman Foundation kept up its support. Nevertheless, HTC experienced an annual deficit ranging from $100,000 to $200,000 in its first five seasons. Efforts at fund-raising and subscription sales failed to close the gap between expenses and earned income, partly because the public saw the organization as well provided for by the Hartman Foundation. According to *New York Times* writer Haskel Frankel "no theatre in the state of Connecticut has suffered more from rumors of wealth it doesn't have than the Hartman" (June 18, 1978, XXIII, p. 12). In May 1980 the Tenneys resigned, citing apparently irresolvable financial difficulties brought on by their failure to win the support of a community they had come to see as uncaring.

The HTC board of directors hired fifty-year-old actor-director Edwin Sherin as artistic director. Sherin, at the pinnacle of a distinguished career that included a long association with Arena Stage, sought to revitalize the organization by bringing in star performers and by producing new plays by established playwrights. He also sought a venue for physically complex productions like that he had given Howard Sackler's *The Great White Hope* in Washington and in New York City. However, he faced an accumulated deficit of $900,000 and an organization without strong support in the community. Vehicles starring Henry Fonda, Richard Kiley, and Jane Alexander drew well, but Stamford did not respond so well to other stars. New plays by Neil Simon and Ira Levin were only modestly successful draws, while productions of Beddow Hatch's *Stem of a Briar* and Elia Kazan's *Chain* were critical and artistic failures, the latter provoking auditors to talk back to the performers and to noisily walk out during the show. However, Nell Dunn's *Steaming*, a British import featuring nudity and profanity, played to 88 percent of capacity, the best figure for 1982–83. The notoriety of the HTC production paved the way for a successful Broadway presentation of the play the next year. Herman Wouk's *The Caine Mutiny Court Martial*, revived in 1982–83, moved on to New York, making this season the best of the Sherin years. Sherin and his staff managed to trim the company's debt to around $230,000 in three years, but Sherin's efforts to build a subscription audience failed. His vision of stars, new plays by prominent playwrights, and physically complex productions required a subscription base of at least 16,000, and the best he could do was 9,295 in his second year. Sherin did establish a beneficial relationship between HTC and Boston University whereby the company built scenery in BU shops, provided instruction in the university's theatre program, and presented its plays for a two-week run at the university theatre before the regular four-week run in Stamford. Sherin also joined the BU faculty as director of the School of Theatre Arts. Under his leadership, HTC became the central element in a $10 million Stamford Center for the Arts, but on tendering his resignation in November 1984, Sherin admitted to his failure to identify an audience for the theatre company. He was able, however, to hold the accumulated deficit to just $200,000 in his last year as artistic director.

The board then hired Margaret Booker, founder of Seattle's Intiman Theatre Company*, to succeed Sherin. Booker took over on October 1, 1985, at which time she found the theatre in debt and subject to poor community relations. She set out to build stronger ties to the people of Connecticut by scheduling plays with an ''international'' flavor, that is, plays written, directed, and designed by non-Americans but executed by the HTC's technical staff and jobbed-in actors. During her two years as artistic director, the subscription base eroded frighteningly. The company had to move back to the Palace Theatre in 1986–87 and to cut its performance schedule to accommodate the Palace's busy schedule. In June 1987 the board of directors voted to cancel the 1987–88 season that Booker proposed, and the twelve-year effort to implant a resident theatre company in Stamford ended in defeat.

PERSONNEL

Producing Directors: Del Tenney (1975–80), Margot Tenney (1975–1980).
Producing Artistic Director: Edwin Sherin (1980–85).
Artistic Director: Margaret Booker (1985–87).
Managing Director: Roger Meeker (1975–80).
Executive Director: Harris Goldman (1980–85).

Directors: Charles Abbott, Alan Arkin, Monroe Arnold, Larry Arrick, Louis Beachner, John Beary, Melvin Bernhardt, Jerry Blunt, Margaret Booker, Mark Bramble, David Chambers, John Dillon, Gene Frankel, Gerald Freedman, Tony Giordano, John Going, James Hammerstein, Edward Hastings, William E. Hunt, Nagle Jackson, Glenn Jordan, Elia Kazan, Tom Kerr, Jerome Kilty, Darwin Knight, Ron Lagomarsino, Michael Lessac, Joe Patton, Pat Patton, Austin Pendleton, Leonard Peters, Peter Pope, Elinor Renfield, Byron Ringland, Louis W. Scheeder, Terry Schreiber, Mel Shapiro, Edwin Sherin, Arthur Sherman, Robert W. Smith, Roger Smith, Del Tenney, George C. White.

Lighting Designers: Francis Aronson, Sid Bennett, Richard Butler, Pat Collins, Jeff Davis, Arden Fingerhut, David Gauthier, John Gisondi, Allen Lee Hughes, John McLain, Marcia Madiera, Roger Meeker, Craig Miller, Roger Morgan, Denis Parichy, Andy Phillips, Marilyn Rennagel, James Sale, Jeffrey Schissler, Cheryl Thacker, James Tilton, Ruth A. Wells, Bill Williams, Andrea Wilson, Richard Winkler.

Scene Designers: Don Beaman, John Lee Beatty, Zack Brown, Victor Capeece, David Crank, Lowell Detweiller, Kate Edmunds, Kate Edwards, John Falabella, David N. Feight, J. D. Ferrara, Robert Fletcher, Peter Harvey, Richard M. Isackes, James Joy, Marjorie Bradley Kellogg, Hugh Landwehr, Hugh Lester, Santo Loquasto, David Loveless, Michael Miller, David Potts, Steven Rubin, Douglas W. Schmidt, Oliver Smith, John Wright Stevens, Tony Straiges, Robert U. Taylor, James Tilton, Guido Tondino, Robert VerBerkmoes, Robin Wagner, Nancy Winters, Akira Yoshimura.

Costume Designers: Annette Beck, Zack Brown, Clifford Capone, David Charles, Marie Anne Chimert, Elizabeth Covey, Judy Dearing, Kathleen Egan, Marianna Elliott, John Falabella, J. D Ferrara, Linda Fisher, Robert Fletcher, Cecilia Friederichs, Lana Fritz, Sarah Nash Gates, Dona Granata, Jane Greenwood, James Berton Harris, Rosemary Ingham, Rachel Kurland, David Loveless, Judianna Makovsky, Jennifer von Mayrhauser, Allen E. Munch, David Murin, Carol Oditz, Walter Pickette, Nancy Potts, Gerda Proctor, Ann Roth, Steven Rubin, June Stearns, John Carver Sullivan, Marianne Verheyen, Ann Wallace, Kurt Wilhelm, Freddy Wittop.

Actors and Actresses: David Ackroyd (1975–76), Robert Adamo (1985–86), Nat Adderly (1981–82), Tom Aldredge (1982–83, 1985–86), Jane Alexander (1981–82), Dion Anderson (1983–84), Leta Anderson (1981–82), Allan Arbus (1979–80), Adam Arkin (1975–76), Mathew Arkin (1975–76), Robert Armistead (1975–76), Deborah Arnold (1975–76), Mary Ellen Ashley (1982–83), Walter Atamaniuk (1984–85), Richard Backus (1984–85), Tom Bade (1980–81), Sally Bagot (1980–81), Blanche Baker (1983–84), *Robert Balaban* (1975–77), Judith Barcroft (1980–81), Geraldine Baron (1983–84), Lislie Barrett (1980–81), Elsa Bastone (1975–76), Charles Bateman (1978–79), Kathy Bates (1980–81), Danny Miller Beard (1981–82), John Bedford-Lloyd (1985–86), Glynis Bell (1979–80), Mark Bell (1977–78), Fran Bennett (1981–82), Mark Benninghofen (1984–85), Charles Berendt (1977–78), Stephen Berenson (1975–77), Nancy Berg (1983–84), Joseph Bergmann (1980–81), Aida Berlyn (1978–79), Deborah Blair (1979–80), Tom Blair (1979–80), Nesbitt Blaisdell (1980–81), Karl Blankenberg (1977–78), *John Blazo, Jr.* (1977–78, 1980–81), George Bliss (1975–76), Scotty Bloch (1985–86), Roberts Blossom (1980–81), Richard Bly (1983–84), Robert Boardman (1984–85), William Bogert (1975–76), Frank Borgman (1979–80), Sara Botsford (1979–80), Dennis Boutsikeris (1983–84), *Linda Bove* (1975–77), Clent Bowers (1982–83), *James Brick* (1975–77), Fran Brill (1982–83), Roy Brocksmith (1975–76), *Ivar Brogger* (1977–78, 1980–82), Pamela Brook (1984–85), Garrett M. Brown (1982–83), Shirley Bryan (1979–80), Joyce Bulifant (1984–85), Donna Bullock (1983–84), Yusef Bulos (1984–85), James C. Burge

(1979–80), Susan Burns (1983–84), Kate Burton (1985–86), Ralph Byers (1976–77), David Canary (1977–79), John C. Capodice (1979–80), Chet Carlin (1980–81), Allan Carlsen (1979–80), Lyle Carney (1976–77), David-James Carroll (1977–78), John Carroll (1979–80), Tiina Cartmell (1976–77), Marilyn Caskey (1980–81), Jacqueline Cassel (1980–81), Sally Chamberlin (1977–78), Sharon Chatten (1983–84), *Dominic Chianese* (1976–77, 1978–79), *Eric Christiansen* (1975–77), Ludi Claire (1978–79), Jane Clarke (1975–76), Richard Clarke (1984–85), Lynne Clifton (1982–83), Mel Cobb (1980–81), Richard Cochrane (1979–80), Peter Coffield (1977–78), Lynn Cohen (1980–81), Priscilla Cohen (1977–78), Patrick Collins (1975–76), Paul Collins (1976–77), David Combs (1984–85), *Katina Commings* (1975–76, 1979–80), Dino Condos (1983–84), Gordon Connell (1982–83), John P. Connolly (1980–81), Roderick Cook (1979–80), Dennis Cooney (1975–76), Carole Cortese (1975–76), Jacqueline Coslow (1978–80), Stephanie Cotsirilos (1977–78), Richard Council (1981–82), Barbara Covington (1983–84), Paul Craggs (1977–78), Saylor Creswell (1978–79), Paddy Croft (1984–85), David Cromwell (1979–80), Joan Croydon (1979–80), David Cryer (1984–85), John Cullum (1981–82), Steven Culp (1982–83), Leigh Curran (1980–81), Kelly Curtis (1985–86), Sheila Dabney (1984–85), Stephen Daley (1978–79), Barbara Damashek (1976–77), Barbara Dana (1975–76), Tony Darnay (1981–82), Keith David (1981–82), Diana Davila (1976–77), Harry Davis (1983–84), Jean DeBaer (1983–84), Gerrit de Beer (1979–80), Dana Delaney (1979–80, 1984–85), Jeffrey DeMunn (1980–81), Mark Diekmann (1979–80), J. Robert Dietz (1975–76), Denny Dillon (1985–86), James Doerr (1983–84), Lenny von Dohlen (1984–85), Nancy Donahue (1975–76), Robert Donley (1975–76), Mary Donnet (1981–82), Richard Dow (1984–85), Jay Doyle (1985–86), Timothy Doyle (1979–80), Joel Dramer (1976–77), Polly Draper (1982–83), *Leonard Drum* (1980–81, 1985–86), George Dvorsky (1982–83), George Dzundza (1976–77), George Ede (1981–82), Michael Edward-Stevens (1981–82), Jill Eikenberry (1975–76), Mercedes Ellington (1977–78), Patricia Englund (1978–79), Leann Enos (1975–76), Pierre Epstein (1979–80), Richard Esterbrook (1985–86), Ron Faber (1976–77), Sandy Faison (1979–80), Kathy Falk (1975–76), Rosalyn R. Farinella (1975–77), Michele Farr (1985–86), *Patrick Farrelly* (1977–78, 1979–80), Clarence Felder (1979–80), Douglas Fisher (1978–79), Frances Fisher (1983–84), Karen Fisher (1977–78), Pauline Flanagan (1982–83), *Mary Fogarty* (1981–82, 1984–85), Henry Fonda (1980–81), Monique Fowler (1984–85), Florence Fox (1975–76), Richard Frank (1980–81), Bernard Frawley (1975–76), Hand Frazier (1978–79), *Joan Friedman* (1975–77), Jonathan Fuller (1985–86), Anna Galiena (1983–84), Michael Galloway (1979–80), Kurt Garfield (1975–76), David Garrison (1982–83), *Deloris Gaskins* (1976–79), Peter Gatto (1975–76), Daniel Gerroll (1984–85), Joanne Gibson (1977–78), J. Gilpin (1978–79), Bruce Gooch (1985–86), Maurice Good (1981–82), Betty Gordon (1975–76), Haskell Gordon (1975–76), Breon Gormon (1984–85), Michael Granger (1975–76), Ernest Graves (1978–79), John Gray (1979–80), Marty Greene (1979–80), Edward Greenhalgh (1981–82), Sean Griffin (1981–82), *Tammy Grimes* (1981–82, 1984–85), Harry Groener (1980–81), Emily Hacker (1977–78), Jim Hale (1979–80), Ed Hall (1975–76), George Hamlin (1985–86), *Daniel P. Hannafin* (1977–78, 1979–80), Brian Hargrove (1981–82), Jeanne Harker (1975–76), Cecilia Hart (1980–81), Victoria Hawken (1975–76), Mel Haynes (1979–80), Rex D. Hays (1985–86), Deryck Hazel (1981–82), Curtis Hazell (1981–82), Paul Hecht (1985–86), Robert Heller (1983–84), Edward Herrmann (1981–82), John Hertzler (1979–80), Walker Hicklin (1980–81), Leslie Hicks (1985–86), Michael Higgins (1981–82), Malcolm Hilgartner (1985–86), Alfred Hinckley (1975–77), Patricia Hodges (1985–86), Jane Hoffman (1984–85), Leo Holder

(1976–77), Bob Horen (1977–78), John Horn (1975–76), Geoffrey Horne (1982–83), Celia Howard (1979–80), Denise Yvette Howell (1981–82), Richard Hoxie (1985–86), Laurence Hugo (1978–79), Dianne Hull (1983–84), Michael J. Hume (1979–80), Marcia Hyde (1980–81), *Earle Hyman* (1975–77), George S. Irving (1975–76), Judith Ivey (1982–83), Max Jacobs (1984–85), Robert Jason (1984–85), Mary Jay (1984–85), J. J. Jefferson (1977–78), Carol Mayo Jenkins (1978–79), Ebony Joann (1981–82), Vera Johnson (1985–86), Christine Jones (1983–84), Jerry-Allan Jones (1981–82), Jessi K. Jones (1981–82), Shami Jones (1975–76), Henry J. Jordan (1985–86), *Stephen Joyce* (1975–76, 1978–79), Linda Kamplay (1980–81), Caroline Kava (1976–77), Richard Kavanaugh (1975–77), Warren Kelley (1978–79), Mike Kellin (1976–77), Kathleen Kelly (1978–79), Laurie Kennedy (1977–78), Henson Keys (1976–77), Pamela Rose Kilburn (1980–81), Richard Kiley (1980–81), *Jerome Kilty* (1981–82, 1985–86), Shirley Knight (1982–83), Gilles Kohler (1985–86), Greg Kolb (1975–76), Roger Kozol (1980–81), Joel Kramer (1976–77), Tom Kremer (1977–78), Annette Kurek (1980–81), Swoosie Kurtz (1977–78), Berit Lagerwall (1980–81), Timothy Landfield (1985–86), Sofia Landon (1984–85), Ruth Landowne (1975–76), Nick La Padula (1983–84), Harris Laskawy (1983–84), Carmen de Lavellade (1976–77), Morcedai Lawner (1984–85), Michael Learned (1982–84), Jeanne Lehman (1977–78), Miriam Lehmann-Haupt (1979–80), Cathleen Leslie (1983–84), Robert Lesser (1975–76), Alde Lewis, Jr. (1981–82), Arden Lewis (1985–86), Edwina Lewis (1981–82), Gwendolyn Lewis (1979–80), Jenifer Lewis (1981–82), Matthew Lewis (1984–85), Ted Lewis (1976–77), Lawrence C. Lott (1979–80), Stafano LoVerso (1979–80), Carl Low (1977–79), Karen Ludwig (1977–78), Salem Ludwig (1983–84), Keith Luger (1977–78), Arthur E. Lund (1980–81), Denise Lute (1983–84), Susan Lynch (1980–81), Michael McCarty (1984–85), Wendell McCombas (1985–86), R. Bruce MacDonald (1980–81), William Forrest MacDonald (1981–82), Judith McGilligan (1979–80), Katherine McGrath (1981–82), Gannon McHale (1981–82), Richard McKenzie (1979–80), *John McMartin* (1979–80, 1983–84), Sam McMurray (1985–86), David MacNeill (1975–76), George Maguire (1980–81), Terrence Markovich (1979–80), Esther Marrow (1981–82), *Gary F. Martin* (1975–77), George Martin (1975–76), Robert Dale Martin (1975–76, 1983–84), Sandy Martin (1975–76), John Martinuzzi (1985–86), Jan Mason (1975–76), T. Richard Mason (1975–76), Tom Mason (1977–78), Ben Masters (1978–79), Michelle Maulucci (1980–81), Samuel Maupin (1981–82), *James Maxwell* (1980–81, 1985–86), Marilyn May (1975–76), James J. Mellon (1977–78), Stephen Mendillo (1982–83), Sally Mercer (1978–79), Richard Merrell (1981–82), Dina Merrill (1979–80), John Messenger (1982–83), *Jan Miner* (1980–82, 1984–85), Dan Mirro (1979–80), Donna Mitchell (1979–80), Sally Moffet (1983–84), Debra Monk (1980–81), Jonathan Moore (1980–81), L. Craig Moore (1981–82), Don Moran (1978–79), Gabor Morea (1980–81), *George Morforgen* (1976–78, 1979–80), Michael Moriarty (1982–83), Nat Morris (1981–82), Libby Moyer (1975–76), Kate Mulgrew (1977–78), Jane Murray (1985–86), James Naughton (1975–76), Julian Neil (1979–80), Corinne Neuchateau (1982–83), Katherine Neuman (1985–86), Stephen Newman (1984–85), William Newman (1979–80), Nancy Nichols (1978–79), Eulalie Noble (1983–84), James Noble (1975–76), Joyce Nolen (1977–78), Zack Norman (1979–80), Carrie Nye (1979–80), Carmel O'Brien (1975–76), Patricia O'Connell (1977–78), Deborah Offner (1976–77), Jill O'Hara (1978–79), Alexandra O'Karma (1984–85), John Oleson (1975–76), Fredi Olster (1981–82), Brian O'Mallon (1980–81), Ron O'Neal (1977–78), *Madelyn O'Neil* (1975–76, 1977–78), Eren Ozker (1975–76), Peter Pagan (1980–81), Giulia Pagano (1977–78), Joe Palmieri (1985–86), Estelle Parsons (1976–77), Bernie Passeltiner (1984–85), Moultrie Patten (1979–80), Casey Patterson (1977–78), Trina Patterson (1977–78), Bill Patton (1976–77), Pamela Payton-Wright (1981–82), Susan Pellegrino (1985–86), *Austin Pendleton* (1975–77), Edward Penn (1979–80), Seymour Penzer (1979–80), Lisa Jane Persky (1982–83), Lenka Peterson (1976–77), Richard Peterson (1980–81), Rico Peterson (1975–76), Florence Phillips (1975–76), Morrie Piersol (1975–76), David Pilot (1976–77), Charles Pistone (1975–77), Don Plumley (1984–85), Trip Plymale (1984–85), Vic Polizos (1979–80), Lewis Popelowsky (1977–78), William Preston (1984–85), Martin Priest (1983–84), Steve Pudenz (1979–80), Lori Putnam (1978–79), J. J. Quinn (1983–84), Rebecca Rabinowitz (1976–77), Michael Radigan (1977–78), *Joseph Ragno* (1979–80, (1983–84), Teri Ralston (1975–76), Ron Randell (1978–79), Gordana Rashovich (1980–81), Ricki G. Ravitts (1979–80), Stacy Ray (1985–86), John Rebinstein (1983–84), Morgan Redmond (1975–76), Robin Reif (1976–77), Jeffrey Reynolds (1982–83), Peter Reznikoff (1979–80), Ed Rice (1975–77), Lee Richardson (1980–82), Jeanne Riskin (1981–82), Sam Robards (1985–86), R. D. Robb (1982–83), Rex Robbins (1983–85), Judith Roberts (1985–86), Russell J. Roberts (1981–82), Alex Rocco (1975–76), Peter Rogan (1975–76), Cheryl Rogers (1984–85), David Romero (1983–84), Woody Romoff (1982–84), Mary Lou Rosato (1980–81), Tina Rose Rosselli (1976–77), Polly Rowles (1982–83), John Rubinstein (1982–83), Ken Ruta (1981–82), Jack Ryland (1979–80), Bill Sadler (1981–82), David Sage (1979–80), Gregory Salata (1976–77), Jay O. Sanders (1982–83), William Sandwick (1977–78), Bill Santoro (1979–80), Stanley Sayer (1979–80), Alan Scarfe (1981–82), Judith Scarpone (1979–80), Sasha von Scherler (1975–76), Laurel Schmidt (1976–77), David Schramm (1980–81), Shellie Sclan (1975–76), Anne Scurria (1975–76), Sanford Seeger (1980–81), Mark Segal (1975–76), David Selby (1981–82), Ed Setrakian (1983–84), James Seymour (1984–85), Nadya Sheehan (1975–76), Sloane Shelton (1975–76), Armin Shimerman (1981–82), Barbara Sieck (1975–76), Jack Sims (1983–84), Albert Sinkys (1979–80), Tucker Smallwood (1981–82), Des Smiley (1981–82), Cameron Smith (1978–79), Joy Smith (1975–76), Susan Smyth (1976–77), David Snell (1977–78), Barry Snider (1985–86), Norman Snow (1980–81), Barbara Sohmers (1984–85), Phil Soltanoff (1976–77), Josef Sommer (1975–76), *Theodore Sorel* (1976–77, 1979–80), Paul Sparer (1981–82), Frederic Sperberg (1977–78), Jonathan Sprague (1977–78), Katherine Squire (1983–84), Mike Starr (1979–80), Kim Staunton (1984–85), Charlie Stavola (1980–81), Doug Stender (1984–85), Susan Stevens (1975–76), Sam Stoneburner (1985–86), John Straub (1978–79), Dan Strickler (1982–83), Susan Strickler (1975–76), Bill Striglos (1979–80), Ian Sullivan (1979–80), Kim Sullivan (1984–85), Jane Summerhays (1985–86), John D. Swain (1979–80), Sally Ann Swarm (1977–78), William Swetland (1979–80), David Tabor (1975–76), Kristoffer Tabori (1983–84), Tom Tammi (1980–81), Lee Taylor (1981–82), Mark Taylor (1975–76), Carol Teitel (1976–77), Stephen Temperley (1977–80), *Margot Tenney* (1975–80), John Terranove (1979–80), Maggie Thatcher (1979–80), Diane Thompson (1979–80), Molly Thompson (1975–76), Linda Thorson (1982–83), Thomas Toner (1984–85), Ian Trigger (1984–85), Courtney Tucker (1975–76), Michael Tucker (1975–76), Louis Turenne (1975–76), Anne Twomey (1983–84, 1985–86), Lark Lee Tyrrell (1975–76), Eric Uhler (1980–81), Terres Unsoeld (1985–86), David Usdan (1979–80), Deborah Van Valkenbugh (1979–80), John C. Vennema (1985–86), John Vichiola (1976–77), Irving Harri Vincent (1975–76), George W. Vollano (1975–76), Jack Waltzer (1983–84), Jack Warden (1982–83), John Wardwell (1977–78), Tim Warren (1975–76), Ed Waterstreet, Jr. (1975–77), Douglass Watson (1977–78), Fritz Weaver (1984–85), Michelle Weeks

(1981–82), Peter Weller (1982–83), Ronald Wendschuh (1985–86), Debora Weston (1985–86), Jack Wetherall (1980–81), Margaret Whitton (1982–83), Ralph Williams (1980–81), K. C. Wilson (1980–81), Ruis Woertendyke (1979–80), Mary Catherine Wright (1985–86), Christopher Wynkoop (1979–80), Ray Zifo (1980–81).

REPERTORY

1975–76: *The Government Inspector, The Hostage, The Runner Stumbles, Tom Jones, Joan of Lorraine, An Evening with Tennessee Williams, Catch-22*.

1976–77: *The Reason We Eat, Arsenic and Old Lace, Tartuffe, As to the Meaning of Words, Death of a Salesman, He Who Gets Slapped*.

1977–78: *The Mousetrap, The Miracle Worker, The Middle Ages, Othello, The Animal Kingdom, Jerome Kern at the Hartman, The Servant of Two Masters, Yerma, Ribbons, The Maids, La Ronde, The Three Sisters, Mrile, Jumping Mouse*.

1978–79: *Two for the Seesaw, The Diary of Anne Frank, Absurd Person Singular, The Auction Tomorrow, The Little Foxes, The Fantasticks*.

1979–80: *Monsieur Ribadier's System, A View from the Bridge, Custer, Private Lives, Unexpected Guest, Uncle Vanya*.

1980–81: *Showdown at the Adobe Motel, Molière in Spite of Himself, Merton of the Movies, Semmelweiss*.

1981–82: *Hedda Gabler, Catholics, The Millionairess, Night Must Fall, The Magistrate, Mahalia*.

1982–83: *A Streetcar Named Desire, Steaming, A Christmas Carol, The Caine Mutiny Court Martial, Actors and Actresses, The Three Musketeers*.

1983–84: *Rocket to the Moon, The Chain, Bedrock, Cantorial, Stem of a Briar, The Me Nobody Knows*.

1984–85: *The Torch-Bearers, Over My Dead Body, Beloved Friend, Black Comedy* and *The Public Eye, The Team, Greater Tuna*.

1985–86: *The Imaginary Invalid, The Philadelphia Story, Fallen Angels, The Three Sisters, Careless Love*.

BIBLIOGRAPHY

Published Sources:
New York Times, 1975–87.
Best Plays 1975–76 through *1985–86*. New York: Dodd, Mead, & Co., 1977–87.
Theatre Profiles. Vols. 3–7. New York: Theatre Communications Group, 1977–85.
Theatre World, 1975–76 through *1985–86*. New York: Crown Publishers, 1977–87.

Archival Resource:
Stamford, Connecticut. Stamford Center for the Arts. Hartman Theatre Company archives
    includes programs, press releases, and clippings.

Janet Brown and Weldon B. Durhum

[THE] HIPPODROME THEATRE COMPANY, Gainesville, Florida, was organized in 1972 by novice professional actors Gregory Hausch, Mary Hausch, Kerry McKenney, Orin Wechsberg, Bruce Cornwell, and Marilyn Wall. By its official founding date of April 18, 1973, this group had converted a hardware-convenience store at 3401 Southeast Hawthorne Road into a flexible, open theatre space and named it the Hippodrome Theatre. During the summer of 1973 two productions for children, *A Land of Point* and *Hope for the Flowers*, toured shopping malls and recreation centers in Gainesville, and the company performed its first mainstage production, an original mime show titled *Did You Hear Something?*.

The Hippodrome Theatre was one of several regional theatres begun in the early 1970s by enterprising young artists who sought to bring to their home regions the excitement of alternative theatre techniques generated during the 1960s by New York groups such as Joseph Chaikin's Open Theatre*, Ellen Stewart's La Mama Experimental Theatre Club, Julian Beck and Judith Malina's Living Theatre*, and Richard Schechner's Performance Group. Repeating the birth pangs of earlier alternative regional theatres (Jo Ann Schmidman and Megan Terry's Omaha Magic Theatre, Ohio's feminist Earth Onion, the San Francisco Mime Troupe*, for example), the Hippodrome staff initially worked second jobs and taught children's theatre workshops to support the theatre. And the seven productions on the theatre's first season bill played to partial houses in a theatre that seated only seventy-five patrons. Unlike other alternative regional companies that remained uniquely experimental (Omaha's Magic Theatre, for example), the Hippodrome Theatre slowly emerged as a mainstream American regional company (in the mode of the Milwaukee Repertory Theatre* and Seattle Repertory Theatre*) producing classic, contemporary, and original plays.

The founders were all students of theatre at the University of Florida before their professional venture; they were also good friends who believed in the concept of ensemble, not only in acting, but also in management and every other phase of the theatrical enterprise. They initially ran the theatre democratically, putting every question to a vote, even a question as seemingly insignificant as whether to purchase a can of paint! The company's first production opened to an audience of eight (although the season's later productions eventually played to full houses of seventy-five), and the first season's expenses were about $15,000.

By its second season the Hippodrome had caught on with Gainesville theatre audiences. The company's environmental staging, audience involvement, and high-energy performing excited the community and provided a kind of theatre not available anywhere else locally. Sold-out houses that season dictated consideration of a larger facility. In 1974 the theatre incorporated as a nonprofit institution. In June 1975 the company moved into an empty warehouse space at 1540 Northwest Fifty-third Avenue, and by September of that year opened a facility with a flexible seating and staging that made it possible to vary capacity from 280 to 375. Tickets were priced at $4 to $6. The theatre's rapid growth and innovative programming began to attract out-of-state attention, and the National Endowment for the Arts (NEA) sent a representative to observe the theatre's work in February 1976. At that time the Hippodrome's artistic directorate took a new shape: Mary Hausch, Greg Hausch, Kerry McKenney, and Bruce Cornwell maintained their status as codirectors; Orin Wechsberg's association with the theatre ended; Marshall New became artistic codirector and publicity director; and Marilyn Wall emerged as the company's costumer. During the 1976–77 season the theatre's first subscription audience numbered 230, the nine-show season averaged 3,500 patrons per show, and the first NEA grant of $2,000 supported an annual budget of more than $100,000.

By its fifth season (1977–78) new subscription marketing techniques and public enthusiasm for the Hippodrome expanded the theatre's subscription membership to 1,800, and the company played to 85 percent of capacity. By July 1979 the theatre budget exceeded $200,000. That same year the city of Gainesville purchased the Old Post Office with the purpose of leasing it to the Hippodrome Theatre. On January 16, 1981, the company's production of Bernard Pomerance's *The Elephant Man* inaugurated the new 287-seat thrust theatre in the Corinthian-columned building at 25 Southeast Second Place. The theatre was officially recognized as Florida's State Touring Theatre. That year Carlos Asse became permanent scene designer, and Margaret Bachus took charge of the company's new Theatre in Education school touring program (which reached 20,000 students and teachers a year by 1986). The company added to its season a series of American and European art films, which played in the facility's Second Stage film theatre.

Since opening the new facility the Hippodrome staff has expanded to include about thirty full-time and five or six part-time employees. The theatre operates on an annual budget of more than $500,000, and season subscriptions average about 3,500. Currently the theatre presents a seven-play, year-round subscription season of straight-run repertory. Mainstage performances are scheduled Tuesday through Sundays. Tickets range from $7.75 for weekday evenings and weekend matinees to $12.75 for Friday and Saturday evening performances. Student tickets are priced at $5.

During its fourteen years of operation the Hippodrome's repertoire has tended to strike a balance between the experimental, the classic, the conventionally structured drama, and original works. Early productions performed in the converted hardware-convenience store included Jean-Claude van Italie's *The Serpent*, Jean Giraudoux's *The Madwoman of Chaillot*, and a lively adaptation of Aristophanes' *Lysistrata*. All three productions were performed in an environmental style (in the mode of the Open Theatre), so that the entire space became an environment for each production. The performances were highly energetic, the settings highly visual. This period also witnessed productions of Shakespeare's *Macbeth* and of contemporary plays that ranged in style from light comedy (Neil Simon's *The Odd Couple*) to significant drama (Peter Weiss' *Marat/Sade*). In their second facility, a warehouse space with greater flexibility in staging, the company produced experimental works such as the Living Theatre's *Frankenstein*, but began moving away from totally environmental pieces. Between 1975 and 1980 the company inaugurated its yearly production of Charles Dickens' *A Christmas Carol* and performed several classics (Shakespeare's *The Tempest* and *Two Gentlemen of Verona*) and significant contemporary successes (David Rabe's *In the Boom Boom Room*, David Mamet's *Duck Variations*, Jack Heifner's *Vanities*, Athol Fugard's *The Island*). The company also acquired the

Southeastern premiere rights to several Broadway productions (Peter Shaffer's *Equus*, Rabe's *Streamers*, Simon Gray's *Otherwise Engaged*, Larry Gelbart's *Sly Fox*, Lanford Wilson's *Talley's Folly*) and it produced world premieres of *Next Stop, Greenwich Village* (adapted by Marshall New from Paul Mazursky's film), Voltaire's *Candide*, Eric Bentley's *Lord Alfred's Lover*, and Tennessee Williams' *Tiger Tail*. For the latter two productions, Bentley and Williams served as visiting playwrights. Since moving into its current facility the company has continued to produce experimental works (Lee Breuer's *The Saint and the Football Player*), world premieres or American premieres of new plays (Adrian Mitchell's *Man Friday*, Mario Vargas Llosa's *Tango of Lies*), and classic and contemporary plays of merit (Shakespeare's *Comedy of Errors* and *Romeo and Juliet*, Tom Stoppard's *The Real Thing*, Harold Pinter's *Betrayal*, A. R. Gurney's *The Dining Room*, Peter Shaffer's *Amadeus*, Sam Shepard's *True West*).

Local critics have complained on occasion that some Hippodrome productions have emphasized production technique and ignored dramatic value. The company's production of the Living Theatre's *Frankenstein*, for example, was not well received by audiences or critics; and more recently, Lee Breuer's *The Saint and the Football Player* left most of its audiences and critics unexcited, even irritated. On occasion, too, the critics disliked an American premiere offered by the theatre's new play development program. Vargas Llosa's *Tango of Lies*, for example, elicited negative reactions from those who found unendurable its shifts between reality and fantasy and its intellectual subject matter. On the whole, however, local audiences and critics have been quick to approve an entertaining and significant production. And the theatre has achieved recognition throughout the Southeast for its high artistic standards and its aggressive efforts to bring contemporary theatre to the Southeast. Carlos Asse's settings and Marilyn Wall Asse's costumes are repeatedly cited by critics for detail and imagination in design and execution. And a local corps of actors has emerged to rival the resident companies of such excellent regional theatres as Florida's Asolo State Theatre*.

The Hippodrome's production wing is administered by two producing directors, Gregory Hausch and Mary Hausch. (Former artistic codirectors Bruce Cornwell, Marshall New, and Kerry McKenney are no longer associated with the theatre.) The Theatre for Young Audiences staff includes a producing director and tour director. And the theatre's Young Actors Ensemble Acting Workshops is staffed by a director-teacher and several interns. In addition, the theatre has employed several visiting directors and visiting playwrights, guest actors, music composers (most notably Eddie Gwaltney, who composed original music for Adrian Mitchell's *Man Friday* and David Mamet's *Revenge of the Space Pandas*), and a number of performance, design, and technical interns from the University of Florida theatre department's professional training program.

The Hippodrome draws its acting corps from among actors in the company who also serve in other capacities (stage managers, box-office manager, producing director, etc.) and from among Equity and non-Equity actors in the

Gainesville community. On occasion the theatre hires professional actors from New York or from other regional theatre companies; for example, for the production of D. L. Coburn's *The Gin Game* (1982) George Hall, a New York professional ("Uncle Freddie" in the New York production of Martin Sherman's *Bent*), and Marian Primont, who has performed at the New York Shakespeare Festival and the Cincinnati Playhouse, were engaged to play the roles originated by Hume Cronyn and Jessica Tandy. The most significant of the area Equity actors to perform at the Hippodrome are Jennifer Pritchett, Michael and Margaret Beistle, Michael Doyle, Malcolm Gets, Daniel Jesse, Dana Moser, Kurt Orwick, Chad Reed, and Michael Stevens. Those actors who also serve in other capacities with the theatre are Marilyn Wall Asse, Rena Carney, Mike Crider, Gregory Hausch, Mary Hausch, Kevin Rainsberger, Mariah Reed, and Rusty Salling.

The Hippodrome Theatre is a success story, one that is rare in a town the size of Gainesville (100,000 population). Thanks to the efforts of a small group of energetic actors, the theatre has grown from an environmental theatre housed in a convenience store to a major state theatre with more than a $500,000 annual budget and with numerous community, state, and regional outreach programs.

PERSONNEL

Management: Gregory Hausch, cofounder and producing director (1973–86); Mary Hausch, cofounder and producing director (1973–86); Bruce Cornwell, cofounder, artistic director, and grants specialist (1973–81); Kerry McKenney, cofounder, artistic director, and literary manager (1973–85); Marshall New, artistic director and publicity director (1975–84); Marilyn Wall Asse, cofounder and costume designer (1973–86); Orin Wechsberg, cofounder and artistic director (1973–75); Dan Schay, executive director (1980–82); Christina Tannen, administrative director (1979–84); Louis Tyrrell, director of Theatre in Education program (1980–81); Margaret Bachus, producing director of Theatre for Young Audiences (1980–86); Rena Carney, director-teacher, Young Actors Ensemble Acting Workshops (1983–86).

Resident Scene and Lighting Designer: Carlos Asse (1979–86).

Music Composer: Eddie Gwaltney (1981–86).

Costume Designer: Marilyn Wall Asse (1973–86).

Lighting Designers: Todd Bedell (1985), Brackley Frayer (1980–82), Robert Robins (1985–86), Sheldon Warshaw (1982).

Stage Directors: Bruce Cornwell (1973–81), Gregory Hausch (1973–86), Mary Hausch (1973–86), Kerry McKenney (1973–85), Marshall New (1975–84), Orin Wechsberg (1973–75).

Guest Directors: Sidney Homan (1985–86), John Staniunas (1985), Kent Stephens (1981).

Stage Managers: Peter Davis (1985), Julie Finfrock (1985–86), Victoria Pennington (1985–86), Kevin Rainsberger (1983–86), Rusty Salling (1973–86), Tony Waters (1980), Becky Barnett (1982–84).

Box-Office Manager: Rusty Salling (1973–86).

Actors and Actresses: *Kate Alexander* (1985), *Marilyn Wall Asse* (1973–86), Margaret Bachus, *Sondra Barrett* (1981), *Margaret Beistle* (1977–86), *Michael Beistle* (1977–86), *Richard Bowden* (1981), *Melanie Bridges* (1985–86), *Mark Capri* (1985), Margaret

Carey, *Rena Carney* (1973–86), *Bruce Cornwell* (1973–81), *Mike Crider* (1985–86), *Yvonne Dell* (1974–80), *Michael Doyle* (1976–86), *Malcolm Gets* (1979–85), Carolyn Griffin, *George Hall* (1982), *Lance Harmeling* (1984–86), Bernadette Harper, *Gregory Hausch* (1973–86), *Mary Hausch* (1973–86), Janet Hayes, Letitia Jaramillo, *Daniel Jesse* (1973–86), *Michael Johnson* (1985–86), Gregory Jones, Pradeep Kumar, Greta Lambert, *Debby Laumand* (1984–85), Rick Lotzkar, *Kerry McKenney* (1973–85), Jerry Mason, Maureen Matthews, *Dana Moser* (1974–79), *Marshall New* (1975–84), *Charles Noel* (1986), *Kurt Orwick* (1973–86), Theresa O'Shea, *Alex Pinkston* (1985), Lynn Pride, *Marian Primont* (1982), *Jennifer Pritchett* (1973–86), *Kevin Rainsberger* (1975–86), Galatea Ramphal, *Jim Randolph* (1984–86), *Chad Reed* (1974–86), *Mariah Reed* (1983–86), *Rusty Salling* (1973–86), *Daniel Sapecky* (1983–86), *Nell Page Sexton* (1979–83), Roz Simmons, John Staniunas, Linda Stephens, *Michael Stevens* (1979–86), Laura Shyte, Bert Taylor, *Louis Tyrrell* (1981), Andrew Watts, Phyllis Williams.

REPERTORY

*Theatre for Young Audiences (Education) Tour productions.

1973–74: *The Land of Point, Rapunzel* and *Snow White, Hope for the Flowers, Did You Hear Something?, The Odd Couple, Exit the King, Maid to Marry, Rats, The Caretaker, Sing to Me Through Open Windows, Steambath, The Owl and the Pussycat, The Madwoman of Chaillot, The Serpent.*

1974–75: *The Secret Affairs of Mildred Wild, Cop-Out, A Day for Surprises, The White House Murder Case, How the Grinch Stole Christmas, Marat/Sade, The Red Eye of Love, Papp, Macbeth, Lysistrata.*

1975–76: *Scuba Duba, Line, Ravenswood, A Midsummer Night's Dream, Catch–22, Frankenstein* (from The Living Theatre), *The Ruling Class, Calm Down, Mother, This Property Is Condemned, Tango Palace, Tom Jones.*

1976–77: *The Real Inspector Hound, Two Gentlemen of Verona, Feiffer's People, In the Boom Boom Room, The Duck Variations, Rubbers, Vanities, The Substitute Bunny, Butley.*

1977–78: *Soap, Equus, The Tempest, Steambath, Streamers, Otherwise Engaged, Gemini.*

1978–79: *The Last Meeting of the Knights of the White Magnolia, The Passion of Dracula, Cabrona, A Christmas Carol, The Island, Statements Made After an Arrest Under the Immorality Act, The Love Garden, Lord Alfred's Lover, The Norman Conquests, They Shoot Horses, Don't They?*

1979–80: *Same Time Next Year, Sleuth, Sly Fox, Belle of Amherst*, Tiger Tail, A Christmas Carol, Next Stop, Greenwich Village, Waking Up*, Game Play*, Clarence Darrow*, Talley's Folly, Loose Ends, Candide.*

1980–81: *Bedroom Farce, Deathtrap, As You Like It, Ernie Pyle: This Is My War*, Tree Tide*, A Christmas Carol, The Elephant Man, Betrayal, For Colored Girls Who Have Considered Suicide/When the Rainbow Is Enuf, Sign Posts*, Revenge of the Space Pandas.*

1981–82: *I Ought to Be in Pictures, Mornings at Seven, Whose Life Is It Anyway?, Pantomime, A Christmas Carol, Vaudeville Jazz*, Man Friday, Deathtrap, Terra Nova, The Gin Game, Robber Bridegroom.*

1982–83: Florida Festival of New Plays (six new works), *Beyond Therapy, The Dining Room, Stages*, A Christmas Carol, The Saint and the Football Player, Key Exchange, Portraits*, We Won't Pay! We Won't Pay!, Children of a Lesser God.*

1983–84: *Mass Appeal, I'm Getting My Act Together and Taking It on the Road, Amadeus, A Christmas Carol, The Servant of Two Masters, Cloud 9, Crimes of the Heart, True West, The Energy Carnival, The Water Log, Stages, Tree Tide.*

1984–85: *The Middle Ages, Isn't It Romantic, The Dresser, Turning Over, The Comedy of Errors, Rhinoceros, Sweet Tango of Lies, Sign Posts, The Energy Carnival*, The Water Log*.*

1985–86: *They're Playing Our Song, Ain't Misbehavin', The Real Thing, A Christmas Carol, Season's Greetings, Romeo and Juliet, Little Shop of Horrors, The Energy Carnival*, The Water Log*, Vaudeville Jazz*, Captain Jim's Fire Safety Review Revue*, A Period of Adjustment.*

BIBLIOGRAPHY

Published Source:
Gainesville Sun, 1973–86.

Unpublished Source:
Hausch, Gregory, and Kerry McKenney. Interview with author. Gainesville, Florida, December 27, 1982.

Archival Resource:
Gainesville, Florida. Hippodrome Theatre. Playbills, 1973–86; news clippings and reviews file, 1973–86; publicity brochure, 1980; commemorative program for the inauguration of the Hippodrome Theatre's new facility, January 16, 1981 (contains "History of the Hippodrome Theatre").

Alex Pinkston

HONOLULU THEATRE FOR YOUTH (HTY), one of the premiere theatre companies dedicated to the youth of America, has endeavored since 1955 to bring professional theatre to the schoolchildren of Hawaii. The company celebrates its own community and the world, and offers theatre in the schools in the Hawaiian islands, across the mainland of the United States, in Micronesia, and in American Samoa.

Nancy Corbett, then director of dramatic activities for the City of Honolulu Parks and Recreation Department, founded the company in 1955 with the help of Kathryn Kayser. Kayser, head of child drama at the University of Denver, traveled to Hawaii at Corbett's request to direct the company's first production, *Jack and the Beanstalk.* As the Honolulu Theatre for Youth's first artistic director, Kayser returned the next three summers to help launch the fledgling company.

Kayser's fifth season with Corbett and company in 1959 remains historic both for Hawaii and the Honolulu Theatre for Youth. During that year the company incorporated under the laws of the territory of Hawaii with the sponsorship of the City of Honolulu Parks and Recreation Department, Honolulu Community Theatre, University of Hawaii department of drama and theatre, and the Honolulu

---

* Theatre for Young Audiences (Education) Tour productions.

Junior League. Shortly thereafter Hawaii became the fiftieth state of the United States of America.

Nancy Corbett, Honolulu Theatre for Youth's executive director until 1966, remains as a life trustee and continues as an active participant in the growth of Hawaii's only fully professional theatre company. Having brought Kayser in from Denver, her foresight also led her to involve Frances Ellison in the new company. Ellison not only designed and constructed costumes throughout the group's first decade, but also advised directors and wrote many of the company's scripts. Ellison, like many of the company's original members, continues as a life trustee.

After Kayser's resignation in 1960, Jack Vaughn became artistic director. During his two years with the company he initiated a touring program that has grown to include tours throughout the world. The first tour took Vaughn's production of *The Emperor's New Clothes* to Maui. In addition to establishing the outreach program, Vaughn encouraged the company's concern for the ethnic diversity of the islands by incorporating non-Western theatre. With Ellison, he wrote and produced plays for the company, including two dragon plays, one Japanese and one Chinese.

The same year Vaughn joined the HTY, Jane Campbell, perhaps one of the most important company members in HTY history, had her first contact with the theatre. At the time a reporter with the Honolulu *Star Bulletin*, Campbell had been assigned to review the new company's production of *The Flying Prince*. She soon joined the company as Nancy Corbett's assistant and was named executive director and public relations director on Corbett's retirement.

Alfred Wheeler joined HTY as artistic director in 1962. Wheeler had written, acted, and served as guest director with the company when they appointed him artistic director. That year the company won the Winifred Ward Award for Best New Children's Theatre from the Children's Theatre Association.

In 1965 Thomas C. Kartak, who had also been actor, designer, technical director, and guest director with the company, succeeded Wheeler as artistic director. Kartak introduced a new dimension to the company's seasons in adapting four of Shakespeare's plays for HTY productions. Artistic directors Doug Kaya and Gary Anderson, who followed Kartak in the 1968 and 1969 seasons, also adapted Shakespeare for child audiences. Since then HTY has continued to include Shakespeare in their seasons, believing such exposure provides an early appreciation for classic drama.

During Kartak's second season the company received the first of many grants from the Hawaii State Legislature. Previously the company could afford to take productions only as far as Maui. These grants provided partial support to further extend quality cultural educational services to other island schoolchildren.

From 1970 to 1973 George M. Muschamp served as artistic director. His specialty was American classics, and he brought to Hawaii's schoolchildren productions of Washington Irving's *The Legend of Sleepy Hollow*, and *Wind in the Willows*.

Lorraine Dove, who had worked with HTY from the beginning as a member of the Children's Theatre Committee of Honolulu Community Theatre, joined HTY as production coordinator in 1968. She became managing director in 1972. During her five-year tenure she planned HTY's first mainland tour and affiliated the group with the national organization for nonprofit professional theatre in America, the Theatre Communications Group.

In the twenty years between 1955 and 1975 HTY diligently expanded its programs. In 1975 the company received a grant from the National Endowment for the Arts to fund a touring program of what the company calls Suitcase Productions. These small-cast productions tour Oahu and other Hawaiian islands in an effort to reach a new, older audience in the high schools. After each performance the actors and the audience discuss the issues raised by the productions. Recently the company toured Athol Fugard's *The Island*, a production that led to enthusiastic discussion of world politics.

The company received its first National Endowment for the Arts Award in 1976 under the auspices of artistic director Wallace K. Chappell. Chappell focused the company's attention on creating an ensemble of actors that reflected the ethnic diversity of Hawaii. With this aim in mind, and with the help of a federal grant, Chappell assembled the HTY's first full-time acting ensemble in 1977. Since that time the company has maintained an ethnically diverse professional acting ensemble.

One result of Chappell's dedication to the ethnic roots of Hawaii's population was a series of four plays developed from the legends of Hawaii and the Pacific Islands. The first, *Maui the Trickster*, was so successful in Hawaii that Chappell's next venture, *Tales of the Pacific*, toured to the mainland in 1977. During the tour the company performed at the American Theatre Association (ATA) Convention in Chicago, at Lincoln Center in New York City, and at the John F. Kennedy Center for the Performing Arts in Washington, D.C.

The same year *Tales of the Pacific* toured the mainland, HTY promoted Jane Campbell to the role of managing director. She had spent seven years specializing in publicity and government relations and heading the drive for a permanent home for the theatre. Campbell's dedication and hard work has been, and remains, the major force driving the continued success of this company.

The company's twenty-fifth anniversary year brought a new artistic director, Kathleen Collins, who came to Hawaii after three years as resident director and education director of Seattle, Washington's children's theatre, the PONCHO Theatre. In her first year Collins revived an old program designed to offer theatre training to the community. The new Theatre Arts Education Program, under the direction of Karen Yamamoto, provided creative expression sessions for teachers, students, recreation leaders, library groups, the handicapped, women in prisons, and gifted children. Since renewing the program HTY has expanded it to include students in secondary schools.

During her years with HTY Collins engendered in the company a tremendous sense of personal dedication far beyond their professional commitment. In 1982 this ensemble spirit brought the company the Jennie Heiden Award, given by the ATA for special achievement in the field of professional theatre for young audiences. The next year HTY's attendance passed 2 million.

When Collins returned to the mainland in 1983, HTY hired John Kauffman, a Seattle actor and director. In 1984 HTY performed at the World Festival of Theatre for Young Audiences at the New Orleans World Fair. This prestigious appearance and growing awareness of HTY as a leading children's theatre in America led the National Endowment for the Arts to award the company one of its Special Artistic Project Grants. This grant enabled the company to tour Micronesia with its production of Michael Cowell's *Song of the Navigator*.

As a result of the success of the tour of Micronesia, HTY was invited to represent America at the ninth World Congress of the French International Children's Theatre Association, held in Australia. The company has also participated in two invitational tours to American Samoa.

In an average year 95 percent of Hawaiian children attend HTY plays. The success of the HTY rests on the company's recognition of the human need for the theatre experience, the educational value of dialogue about theatre, and the imperative that theatre for young people be relevant to citizens of the Pacific basin.

PERSONNEL

Management: Gary D. Anderson, artistic director (1969–70); Jane Campbell, publicist, public relations director, executive director, managing director (1960–87); Wallace K. Chappell, artistic director (1975–78); Kathleen Collins, artistic director (1979–83); Nancy Corbett, founder, executive director (1955–66); Lorraine Dove, managing director (1972–77); Thomas C. Kartak, artistic director (1965–68); John Kauffman, artistic director (1983–87); Doug Kaya, artistic director (1968–69); Kathryn Kayser, artistic director (1955–60); George M. Muschamp, artistic director (1970–73); Jack Vaughn, artistic director (1960–62); Alfred Wheeler, artistic director (1962–64).

Designers: Eddie Barrows, Robert Campbell, Shell Dalzell, Frances Ellison, William Forrester, Colin Fraser, Roy Green, Michael Holten, Thomas C. Kartak, Ann Kimura, Mary Lewis, Grace Ligi [Yasuhara], Richard Mason, Bert Moon, Lloyd S. Riford, Don Slepian, Peter Treat, Charles Walsh, Virginia West, Don Yanik.

Guest Stage Directors: Bain Boehlke, Tim Bond, Jay Broad, Peter Charlot, Clayton Corzatte, Sneih Dass, Jo Diotalevi, Dave Donnelly, Denise Ford, Alan Grier, George Herman, Carole Huggins, Carl Hyman, Dando Kleuver, Tim Larson, Amiel Leonardia, Phyllis Look, Kermit Love, Ron Nakahara, Jim Nakamoto, Dale Ream, David Visser.

Choreographers: Akiko Masuda, Josephine Taylor.

Commissioned Playwrights: Max Bush, Wallace K. Chappell, Kathleen Collins, Michael Cowell, Nick diMartino, Frances Ellison, Jeffrey Fleece, Kermit Love, Ron Nakahara, Tremaine Tamayose, Janet Thomas.

Acting Company Members: Stephanie Akina, Jo Diotalevi, Dennis Duber, David Furumoto, Frank Kane, Phyllis Look, Ron Nakahara, Russell Omuri, Beryl Peralta-Murphy, James Pestana, Kevin Reese, Alan P. Ronquillo, Norris Shimabuku, Polly Sommerfeld, Tremaine Tamayose, Karima Tatum, Alison Uyeda, Cristine Wallis, Charles Walsh, Karen Yamamoto-Hackler.

REPERTORY

1955–56: *Jack and the Beanstalk*.

1956–57: *Cinderella, Aladdin*.

1957–58: *A Christmas Nightingale*.

1958–59: *Little Red Riding Hood, The Flying Prince*.

1959–60: *Rumpelstiltskin, Sleeping Beauty, Indian Captive, Marco Polo, The Flying Prince, Kalau and the Magic Numbers*.

1960–61: *Beauty and the Beast, Arthur and the Magic Sword, The Secret Scouts, Mask of the Gold Dragon, Queen with the Frozen Heart*.

1961–62: *Alice in Wonderland, The Phantom Officer, The Emperor's New Clothes, Young Abe Lincoln, Dragon of the Moon*.

1962–63: *Aladdin, Kalau and the Magic Numbers, Cinderella, Rip Van Winkle, Manjiro's Journey*. Tour: *Jack and the Beanstalk*.

1963–64: *Oliver Twist, The Magic Hat, Androcles and the Lion, Ke Alii Umi*. Tour: *The Mystery of Alhambra*.

1964–65: *Arthur and the Magic Sword, A Midsummer Night's Dream, Mask of the Gold Dragon, Beauty and the Beast, Young Jefferson, Escape at LaHaina Roads*.

1965–66: *Treasure Island, The Secret of Han Ho, The Christmas Nightingale, The Tempest, Manjiro's Journey*. Tour: *The Pied Piper of Hamelin*.

1966–67: *Harlequin, Young Abe Lincoln, The Emperor's New Clothes, As You Like It, Kalau and the Magic Numbers*. Tour: *Dragon of the Moon*.

1967–68: *The Miracle of San Fernando Mission, Ali Baba, Jack and the Beanstalk, Comedy of Errors, The Mystery of Alhambra*. Tour: *Young Mozart*.

1968–69: *The Magic Horn, The Dancing Monkey, The Magic Hat, William Tell*. Tour: *The Secret Scouts, The Taming of the Shrew*.

1969–70: *Cinderella, A Midsummer Night's Dream, Reynard the Fox, The Ice Wolf*. Tour: *The Prince Who Wouldn't Grow, Antigone*.

1970–71: *The Ballad of Robin Hood, Rapunzel and the Witch, Rip Van Winkle, The Pied Piper of Hamelin*. Tour: *William Shakespeare, Hiawatha*.

1971–72: *Androcles and the Lion, Rumpelstiltskin, The Legend of Sleepy Hollow, Beauty and the Beast, The Land of the Dragon*. Tour: *The Miracle Worker*.

1972–73: *Mo'o: A Modern Legend, Hansel and Gretel, The Wind in the Willows, The Royal Pardon*. Tour: *Manjiro's Journey, The Lark*.

1973–74: *The Honorable Urashima Taro, The Mysterious Piper, Arthur and the Magic Sword, Antelope Boy, Young Ben*. Tour: *Story Theatre*.

1974–75: *Maui the Trickster, Comedy of Errors, The Christmas Nightingale, The Doctor in Spite of Himself*. Tour: *Vasalisa, Alice in Wonderland*.

1975–76: *The Hobbit, A Christmas Carol, Tanuki, Hamlet, Cotton Blossom Floating Palace Theatre*. Tour: *Maui the Trickster, The Mirrorman*.

1976–77: *Marco Polo, The Tragical History of Doctor Faustus, The Lion, the Witch, and the Wardrobe, The Magic Circle*. Tour: *Tales of the Pacific*.

1977–78: *Scapino!, The Legend of Sleepy Hollow, Sleeping Beauty, Storytellers*. Tour: *Momotaro and Other Japanese Folktales*.

1978–79: *The Phantom Tollbooth, Horseopera, The Time Machine, Jack and the Beanstalk*. Tour: *Folktales of the Phillipines*.

1979–80: *The Nine Dragons, Halloween Tree, Transformations, Step on a Crack, Hansel and Gretel, Three Authors—One Drama*. Tour: *Snow White*.

1980–81: *Mark Twain in the Sandwich Islands, The Miracle Worker, Ozma of Oz, The Overcoat, Ama and the White Crane, The Dancing Frog of Iole Farm.*

1981–82: *A Midsummer Night's Dream, Dracula, Islands Further Farther and Beyond, The Hidden Place, Na Keiki Haku Mele O Ka Aina, In a Very Special House.*

1982–83: *Ali Baba and the Forty Thieves, The Masque of Beauty and the Beast, Chicken Skin, The Diary of Anne Frank, Clowns.*

1983–84: *Frankenstein, Newcomer, Pinocchio, Mime to the Max, Sparks, The Original Absurd Musical Revue for Children.*

1984–85: *Mime to the Max II, Flash Gordon Conquers the Planet of Evil, To Kill a Mockingbird, East of the Sun and West of the Moon, Sparks, Island Slices, The Best Christmas Pageant Ever, Raven the Hungry, The Code Breaker, The Belle of Amherst.*

1985–86: *Rashomon, Cinderella, Song of the Navigator, F.O.B., Charlotte's Web, The Story of Buck Buck Buh Deek.*

BIBLIOGRAPHY

Unpublished Source:

Muschamp, George M., Jr. "The Honolulu Theatre for Youth, 1955–1973." Doctoral dissertation, University of Minnesota, 1974.

Juli A. Thompson

HULL-HOUSE THEATRE, Chicago, began in 1963 as an attempt by a newly decentralized Hull-House social settlement to revitalize its dormant theatre program. Between 1963 and 1969 director Robert Sickinger, building on the huge success of his own directorial work at the settlement, developed a vast, multi-faceted amateur theatre program. At its peak the Hull-House program included four separate theatres, a chamber theatre, a playwright's workshop, a children's theatre, a touring company, an arts camp, and the arts publication *Intermission Magazine.* Each Hull-House theatre was situated in a community center. The program's cornerstone was the 110-seat Hallie Callner Memorial Theatre, usually referred to as the "Jane Addams Theatre" because it was in the Jane Addams Center (3212 North Broadway). Hull-House also built theatres in the Henry Booth House (located in the Harold Ickes Housing, 3238 South Dearborn) and in the Parkway Center (500 East Sixty-seventh Street). In 1967 the Leo Lerner Theatre opened in the Uptown Center (1257 West Wilson). The program's first major production was Frank Gilroy's *Who'll Save the Plowboy,* Sickinger directing, at the Jane Addams Theatre on November 15, 1963.

Though amateur, the Hull-House Theatre had enormous influence in shaping Chicago's professional theatre renaissance of the 1970s and 1980s. Its actors, directors, and designers included those who later made noteworthy professional careers, in Chicago and beyond. Among them are David Mamet and *Grease* coauthor Jim Jacobs; actors Robert Benedetti, Mike Nussbaum, Marilu Henner, Felton Perry, and Nate Davis; director Mike Miller; designer James Maronek; and musicians Ricky (Rocco) Jans and Jay Jans. The Hull-House Chamber Theatre, designed to perform privately in homes of the well-to-do, built a large, active, and wealthy audience for contemporary experimental theatre in Chicago.

Finally Sickinger introduced Chicago audiences to plays by Samuel Beckett, Harold Pinter, Edward Albee, and Athol Fugard, all done in a highly theatrical style that encouraged the emotional and physical acting later known as the trademark of Chicago theatre.

Robert Sickinger first turned to theatre while still teaching junior high school English in Philadelphia. He started the Abbey Theatre in 1952, the Philadelphia Civic Theatre in 1955, and then opened the Cricket Playhouse. Sickinger studied directing with Jose Quintero and Alan Schneider and won praise for his casting of the film *David and Lisa*. He then started the Theatre Workshop at Philadelphia's Lighthouse settlement, where he met its executive director, Paul Jans. When Jans was named to head Hull-House in 1962, he invited Sickinger to help him rebuild the Chicago settlement's theatre.

Both Sickinger and Jans argued that the Hull-House Theatre's work was consistent with the social service goals of the settlement itself. It is true that both the Henry Booth and Parkway theatres, situated in predominantly poor and black neighborhoods, did perform works relevant to local community concerns. However, the settlement theatre centered more on Sickinger's artistry than on social service. Neither the Jane Addams Theatre's avant-garde play selection nor the Uptown Theatre's focus on musicals had any direct bearing on local community concerns; they instead showcased Sickinger's work to audiences drawn from Chicago's more affluent areas. This discrepancy created resentment within Hull-House and in the communities the settlement served, and this antagonism proved damaging to the theatre program.

All Hull-House participants except Sickinger worked without fee. Nevertheless, the program required substantial funding. In 1964 tickets to Jane Addams Theatre productions sold for $3 during the week and $3.40 on Friday and Saturday; performances were given six days a week for five to six weeks. Hull-House began to offer a five-play subscription series in 1964. By 1967 its 4,500 subscribers represented 80 percent of the theatre's capacity. That same year the entire program's operating budget was $150,000, of which $100,000 came from ticket sales. With only occasional outside grants, most of the balance was paid by the settlement.

Lacking much home-grown serious theatre, Chicago critics expressed enthusiasm when the Hull-House Theatre program was first proposed. However, none anticipated the quality of play selection and production achieved by Sickinger. Nearly all of Sickinger's own productions were Chicago premieres. Not only did his productions of Jack Gelber's *The Connection*, Albee's *Tiny Alice*, Imamu Amiri Baraka's *Dutchman*, and Pinter's *The Birthday Party* win high critical acclaim, but they also packed the theatre, and this seemed to justify the theatre program's rapid expansion. Even Hull-House's Children's Theatre, for which playwright John Stasey created the popular *Captain Marbles* plays, proved fresh and inventive. Recognition came both locally and nationally: Mayor Daley proclaimed October 15, 1965, the start of "Hull-House Theatre Week in Chicago"; and in March 1965 producer David Susskind's *Esso Repertory Theatre* television show nationally broadcast Hull-House's production of Pinter's *The Dumb Waiter*, which won critical approval as well.

However, poor economics and social change caused the program to unravel. High costs forced the touring company to close in 1967. Then rioting after Martin Luther King's assassination forced both the Henry Booth and Parkway theatres to close in 1968. That same year the theatre reported annual losses of $25,000. When fiscal problems threatened the settlement's own survival in late 1968, Hull-House cut funding to all its arts programs. Jans resigned as executive director in April 1969; without Jans' support the theatre could not last at the social settlement. Sickinger left in July 1969, amid controversy. The settlement then refused to guarantee facilities for his replacement, Robert Benedetti, who in turn resigned. In September 1969 Hull-House officially withdrew from sponsoring theatre.

PERSONNEL

Management: Paul Jans, executive director; Robert Sickinger, artistic director; Beatrice Fredman, Chamber Theatre director; Selma Sickinger, Children's Theatre director; Marvin Foster, Touring Theatre director; Byron Tobin (1963), Antonio Desantis (1963–64), Fraser Kent (1964–69), Playwright Workshop directors; Gene Cole, *Intermission Magazine* editor.

Stage Directors: Robert Benedetti, Robert Sickinger, Selma Sickinger for the Jane Addams and Uptown theatres; Dick Gaffield, Elaine Goldman, Mike Miller, Gerald Wallace for the Parkway; George Starr, Gerald Wallace for the Henry Booth (also called "Underground"); Quinton Raines for the short-lived Sheridan theatre.

Actors and Actresses: Of the hundreds who performed, the most active or prominent were Cara Benedetti, *Robert Benedetti*, Christine Bergstrom, *Lake Bobbitt*, Tom Bradley, James Callahan, *Wilfred Cleary*, *Robert Curry*, Roberta Custer, Nate Davis, *Stuart Eckhaus*, Suzanne Faberson, Henry Fenwick, *Beatrice Fredman*, Marla Friedman, Arthur Geffen, Pauline Hague, Marilu Henner, *Jim Jacobs*, *Robert Kidder*, Catita Lord, *Richard Lucas*, David Mamet (understudy), Don Marston, Connie Mathieu, Richard Meyers, Mike Miller, Sally Mitchell, Candy Nichols, Kenneth Northcott, *Mike Nussbaum*, Terence Parker, *Felton Perry*, *Frank Reckett*, *Harvey Rubin*, Diane Rudall, *Tito Shaw*, Nancy Sherburne, Dorothy Mittleman Sigel, Kathryn Steindler, Ruth Stockard, *Bill Terry*, *Pat Terry*, Lorry Young, Jim Zerwin.

REPERTORY

Jane Addams Theatre (unless otherwise noted, all directed by Sickinger):

1963–64: *Who'll Save the Plowboy, Happy Days, The Connection, The Days and Nights of Beebee Fenstermaker, The Typist* and *The Tiger, The Death of Bessie Smith* and *The American Dream.*

1964–65: *The Threepenny Opera, Play* and *Endgame* (Benedetti, dir.), *The Brig, The Lover* and *The Collection, Home Free, Dutchman* and *Picnic on a Battlefield* (Selma Sickinger directed the last).

1965–66: *A Slight Ache* and *The Dumb Waiter, Tiny Alice, Victims of Duty, The Man with the Flower in His Mouth, Kids' Games, Caligula, The Child Buyer.*

1966–67: *The Birthday Party, Until the Monkey Comes, The Devils, The Typist* and *The Tiger* (revival).

1967–68: *Fortune and Men's Eyes, Electra.*

1968–69: *The Indian Wants the Bronx, It's Called the Sugar Plum, Johnny No Trump, Entertaining Mr. Sloane* (Selma Sickinger, dir.)

Uptown Theatre (all directed by Robert Sickinger):

1967–68: *Take Me Along, The Boy Friend.*

1968–69: *Flora, the Red Menace, The Desert Song.*

Parkway Center:

1965–66: *Sarah and the Sax, The Dirty Old Man, Tiger, Tiger Burning Bright, Call Me by My Rightful Name, Sponono, Miss Julie* and *The Slave, The Amen Corner.*

1966–67: *Don't Darken My Door, Blues for Mr. Charlie, Requiem for Brother X* and *Whisper in My Good Ear, My Sweet Charlie, Laundromat.*

1967–68: *Slow Dance on the Killing Ground, Viet Rock.*

Henry Booth/Underground Theatre:

1963–64: *Clandestine on the Morning Line, Seven Times Monday, Slaughter of the Innocents.*

1965: *Roots.*

1967 (now directed entirely by Gerald Wallace): *Kiss of the Rose, Libertyville, News of Marion Hill, If I Had a Hammer, Up the Hill to My House, The Sudden and Accidental Re-education of Horace Johnson.*

BIBLIOGRAPHY

Unpublished Sources:

Benson, Carol Angela. "Social Settlement Theatre: Hull House and Karamu House." Master's thesis, University of Wisconsin, 1965.

Flynn, Ruth Stockard. "A Historical Study of Dramatic Activities for Children at Hull-House Theatre, Chicago, Illinois, from 1889 to 1967." Master's thesis, University of Denver, 1967.

Hecht, Stuart J. "Hull-House Theatre: An Analytical and Evaluative History." Doctoral dissertation, Northwestern University, 1983.

Archival Resource:

Chicago, Illinois. Library of the University of Illinois, Chicago. Jane Adams Memorial Collection and Manuscript Collection.

Stuart J. Hecht

I

INDIAN MAGIQUE. See SAN DIEGO REPERTORY THEATRE.

INDIANA REPERTORY THEATRE (IRT), located in Indianapolis, Indiana, was founded in 1970 by Benjamin Mordecai and Gregory Poggi, doctoral students in theatre at Indiana University, and by Edward Stern, a recent graduate of IU's doctoral program in theatre. The group presented its first production, *Charley's Aunt*, by Brandon Thomas, on October 18, 1972, in the Atheneum Theatre at 411 East Michigan Street. The IRT was then and still is Indiana's only professional resident company. It produces a varied season of six to ten classics, established contemporary works, and original plays in Indianapolis, and it has served the state of Indiana with touring productions and workshops.

After eight productive years under the leadership of Stern and Mordecai, the limited space in the 396-seat Atheneum proved insufficient, and the IRT moved to a new home in the renovated Indiana Theatre, located at Washington Street and Capitol Avenue. New artistic director Tom Haas inaugurated the new theatre October 24, 1980, with a production of Adrian Mitchell's *Hoagy, Bix, and Wolfgang Beethoven Bunkhaus*, an original musical based on the life of Hoosier songwriter Hoagy Carmichael. The Indiana Theatre was built in 1927 as a 3,300-seat multipurpose entertainment center. It operated as a first-run movie palace and concert hall until 1976. The Spanish Baroque building, designed by Preston Rubush and Edgar O. Hunter, housed not only the theatre, but also a bowling alley and billiards room, restaurants, a soda fountain, and the glamorous Indiana Roof Ballroom. When the Indianapolis city government and the Downtown Merchants Association remodeled the building in 1980, three theatres were included in the $5.2 million project. The Mainstage boasts a 600-seat auditorium and a thrust-proscenium stage, where IRT continued to produce a wide range of plays, including classics such as *Hamlet* and Richard Brinsley Sheridan's *She Stoops to Conquer*, American favorites such as Eugene O'Neill's *Ah, Wilderness!*

and the Moss Hart–George S. Kaufman comedy, *You Can't Take It with You*, as well as contemporary works such as J. B. Ferzacca's *The Failure to Zigzag* and Ted Tally's *Coming Attractions*. The Upperstage, a proscenium theatre seating 245, is noted for smaller experimental productions of works such as Robert Montgomery's *Oedipus at the Holy Place*, a new adaptation of Sophocles' *Oedipus at Colonus*; *Live Tonight: Emma Goldman*, Michael Dixon's historical biography of the Russian-born American anarchist; and the American premiere of an Australian drama, Denis Whitburn's *The Siege of Frank Sinatra*. The Upperstage also serves as the home of Indiana's professional modern dance company, Dance Kaleidoscope. IRT's third theatre, the Cabaret, is a theatrical nightclub where original musical productions and revues paying tribute to American musical theatre are performed. Nightclub performers also work in this intimate 140-seat room, which operates fifty-two weeks a year. Only two other regional theatres operate a similar theatre.

Since the arrival of Haas, founder and director of Playmaker's Repertory Theatre at the University of North Carolina in Chapel Hill, IRT has attracted national press attention.

In 1972 IRT sold 5,000 season tickets. Today it has approximately 13,000 subscribers and reaches more than 200,000 persons annually. Similarly, IRT's operating budget has grown from $250,000 in its first season to $2,517,000 in 1986. In the mid-1980s IRT presented more than 700 performances of approximately twenty-two productions each season. The IRT in the Indiana Theatre, one of the largest not-for-profit regional theatres under one roof in the United States, is a member of the League of Resident Theatres, the Theatre Communications Group, the American Arts Alliance, and the Indiana Theatre Association.

PERSONNEL

Producing Directors: Len Alexander (1981–83), Jessica L. Andrews (1983–86), Benjamin Mordecai (1972–81).

Artistic Directors: Tom Haas (1980–86), Edward Stern (1972–80).

Directors: John Abajian (1975–76, 1979–81), Ben Cameron (1981–84, 1985–86), Gavin Cameron-Webb (1985–86), Marnie Carmichael (1983–84), Gerardine Clark (1976–77), Edward Cornell (1981–82), Jack L. Davis (1975–76), Frederick Farrar (1984–85), John Going (1973–75, 1976–77, 1978–81), Lynne Gould-Guerra (1979–81), Thomas Gruenewald (1977–81), William Guild (1976–78), Tom Haas (1975–76, 1979–86), Israel Hicks (1981–82), Bernard Kates (1975–76), Charles Kerr (1976–78), Woodie King, Jr. (1978–79), Pierre LeFeure (1972–73), Benjamin Mordecai (1972–75), Paul Moser (1975–76, 1984–85), Leland Moss (1976–77), Jim O'Connor (1983–84), John S. Patterson (1976–77), Leonard Peters (1979–81), William Peters (1981–82), Martin Platt (1983–84), David Rotenberg (1979–81, 1982–83, 1984–85), Amy Saltz (1984–85), Harold Scott (1979–81), Eric Steiner (1979–81), Edward J. Stern (1972–80), Daniel Sullivan (1978–79), Ted Weiant (1981–82), Scott Wentworth (1982–83), Garland Wright (1974–75).

Set Designers: John Arnone (1979–81), Bob Barnett (1979–83), Christopher Barreca (1985–86), Ursula Belden (1976–81), Keith Brumley (1975–76), James Burbeck (1984–

85), Virginia Dancy (1979–81), John Doepp (1976–79), Kate Edmunds (1980–83, 1984–85), Richard Ferguson-Wagstaffe (1973–75), Alison Ford (1985–86), Christopher Hacker (1976–77), Eric Head (1976–79), James Leonard Joy (1978–80), Marjorie Kellogg (1977–78), Heidi Landesman (1980–81), Ming Cho Lee (1981–82), Joe Dale Lunday (1972–73), Tom Lynch (1981–83), Richard F. Mays (1984–85), Russell Metheny (1980–86), Van Phillips (1976–78), David Potts (1977–80), Raymond C. Recht (1976–77), Steven Rubin (1980–84), William E. Schroder (1973–75, 1978–79), Karen Schulz (1980–85), Douglas Stein (1981–83), Thomas Taylor Targownik (1976–77), Leslie Taylor (1983–84), Elmon Webb (1979–81), Michael H. Yeargan (1982–83, 1984–85).

Costume Designers: Carol H. Beule (1976–77), Gail Brassard (1983–86), Leon I. Brauner (1980–84), Jeanne Button (1983–84), Lawrence Casey (1983–84), Michael Cesario (1978–79), Nan Cibula (1979–81), Elizabeth Covey (1977–80), Susan Denison (1976–77), Skip Gindhart (1979–81), Jess Goldstein (1978–79), James Berton Harris (1979–81), Susan Hilferty (1980–85), Sigrid Insull (1979–81), Shelley Joyce (1979–81), Martha Kelly (1981–83), Rachel Kurland (1979–81), Gene K. Lakin (1981–83), Arnold S. Levine (1977–78), Joe Dale Lunday (1972–73), Judianna Makovsky, (1981–83), Sherry Lynn Mordecai (1974–76), Sandra Mourey (1973–74), Carol Oditz (1979–81), Bobbi Owen (1985–86), Nancy Pope (1983–86), Steven Rubin (1980–83), Florence L. Rutherford (1975–77), Rita Ryack (1979–81), Tom Schmunk (1974–75), William Schroder (1978–79), Connie Singer (1985–86), Joan Thiel (1974–75), Dana Harnish Tinsley (1979–81), Susan Tsu (1976–78), Bill Walker (1981–83, 1984–85), Michel Yeuell (1981–83), Kenneth Yount (1978–80).

Lighting Designers: William Armstrong (1980–83), Frances Aronson (1981–83), Bridget Beier (1976–77), Judy Boese (1974–76), Rachel Budin (1980–86), Robert Owen Bye (1972–73), Carl Cindric (1972–73), Allen Cornell (1975–76), Geoffrey T. Cunningham (1977–80), Susan Dandridge (1976–77), Jeff Davis (1977–80), John Doepp (1977–78), Mary Jo Dondlinger (1984–85), Stuart Duke (1981–86), Richard Ferguson-Wagstaffe (1974–75), Arden Fingerhut (1977–78), Benjamin Ford (1972–73), Paul Gallo (1977–80), Charles Gotwald (1976–77), Joel Grynheim (1976–77, 1979–80), Robert Jared (1981–83), Timothy K. Joyce (1975–77), Michael Lincoln (1984–85), Steven D. Machlin (1979–81), Greg Marriner (1977–78), Ralph John Merkle (1976–77), Craig Miller (1981–84), Spencer Mosse (1979–81), Carl Roetter (1975–76), Robert Shook (1983–84), Johnny Walker (1973–74), Michael Orris Watson (1976–77), Lee Watson (1977–78).

Actors and Actresses: IRT maintained a resident acting company from 1972 to 1975. Since then directors have cast productions one at a time, but they use many performers with such consistency as to create a fluid casting company with an ensemble base. Performers appearing in at least two seasons include the following: John Abajian (1974–76, 1979–80), David Adamson (1981–82, 1983–84), Linda Atkinson (1975–77, 1978–79), Judith Marie Bergan (1972–74), Barbara Berge (1977–78, 1979–80), John Bergstrom (1977–78, 1979–80), Nancy Coleman (1974–76), Gloria Dorson (1983–85), Jennifer Dunegan (1982–84), *Rick Farrar* (1983–87), *Craig Fuller* (1981–87), *Bernadette Galanti* (1981–87), Allison Giglio (1977–80), *Mark Goetzinger* (1983–87), Max Gulack (1972–74), Michael Hendricks (1976–77, 1978–79), *Bella Jarrett* (1981–87), Howard Jenson (1984–86), Donald Christopher Johnson (1978–80), Henry Jordan (1981–83), *Bernard Kates* (1974–85), Dennis Kennedy (1972–74), Elaine Kilden (1973–75), Dorothy Lancaster (1982–85), *Priscilla Lindsay* (1974–86), Michael Lipton (1984–87), Barry McGuire (1982–85), Robert Machray (1974–76), *Lowry Miller* (1982–86), Terry Moore (1982–85), *Karen Nelson* (1981–87), *Gun-Marie Nilsson* (1974–78), Jon Oak (1973–75), Howard Pinhasik (1983–84, 1985–87), Stephen Preusse (1980–83), *Frank Raiter* (1981–87), Rae Randall (1981–83), Gerald Richards (1978–80), Robin Pearson Rose (1974–76), Donn Ruddy (1981–84), Steven Ryan (1973–76), Robert Scogin (1973–76), Linda Selman (1975–77), Raymond Singer (1972–75), Jill Tanner (1972–74), James Tasse (1981–83), Peter Thoemke (1977–80), Jeffery V. Thompson (1974–76), *Scott Wentworth* (1980–84), David Williams (1984–87), Mark Winkworth (1973–75), Sara Woods (1976–78, 1979–80).

REPERTORY

1972–73: *Charley's Aunt, Fables Here and Then, Scapin, House of Blue Leaves, The Glass Menagerie, Count Dracula.* Tour: *Shakespeare Alive, The World of Carl Sandburg, Fables Here and Then.*

1973–74: *Our Town, What the Butler Saw, Of Mice and Men, Jacques Brel Is Alive and Well and Living in Paris, The Servant of Two Masters, Sherlock Holmes.* Tour: *The Diaries of Adam and Eve, Lovers, Comedy Kaleidoscope, The Servant of Two Masters.*

1974–75: *Harvey, The Little Foxes, One Flew over the Cuckoo's Nest, The Taming of the Shrew, The Rainmaker, A Bird in the Hand.* Tour: *Musical Mirage Express '75, The Doctor in Spite of Himself.*

1975–76: *That Championship Season, Arms and the Man, Long Day's Journey into Night, The Envoi Messages, The Real Inspector Hound* and *Black Comedy, The Tavern.* Second Stage: *The Caretaker, The Old Jew, On the Harmfulness of Tobacco, The Man with the Flower in His Mouth, The Sea Horse.* Tour: *Musical Mirage Express '76, Women and Those Other People.*

1976–77: *The Last Meeting of the Knights of the White Magnolia, When You Comin' Back, Red Ryder?, The Threepenny Opera, The Tempest, Private Lives, Sleuth.* Second Stage: *Who's Afraid of Virginia Woolf?, The Brixton Recovery, Miss Julie.*

1977–78: *The Philadelphia Story, The Birthday Party, The Country Girl, Vanities, The Sea Gull, How the Other Half Loves.* Off Night Series: *Stepping Back, A Christmas Carol, An Evening with Dorothy Parker.* Tour: *To Kill a Mockingbird.*

1978–79: *13 Rue De L'Amour, Sizwe Bansi Is Dead, A Delicate Balance, The Importance of Being Earnest, Ten Little Indians, The Goodbye People.* Off Night Series: *Dear Liar, The Zoo Story.* Tour: *Scapin.*

1979–80: *Cold Storage, Descendants, Absurd Person Singular, Toys in the Attic, Twelfth Night, Born Yesterday.* Tour: *Musical Mirage Express '80.*

1980–81: Mainstage: *Hoagy, Bix, and Wolfgang Beethoven Bunkhaus, A Christmas Carol, Rocket to the Moon, Treats, The Failure to Zigzag, Ah, Wilderness!.* Upperstage: *Oedipus at the Holy Place, Live Tonight: Emma Goldman, Coming of Age.* Cabaret: *Murder in the Cabaret.* Tour: *Musical Mirage Express '81.*

1981–82: Mainstage: *Hamlet, A Lesson from Aloes, Coming Attractions, She Stoops to Conquer, Rain, Operetta, My Dear Watson, A Christmas Carol.* Upperstage: *The Siege of Frank Sinatra, Billy Bishop Goes to War, Home.* Cabaret: *Cole Porter, Native Son, Biodegradable: A Musical Soap Opera, Hilly Lili, and Lulu, Christmas Cheers, 2 × 4, The Music of Kander and Ebb, Maxine Andrews, The Radio Show, Murder in the Cabaret, Blue Suede Decade, Commercial Interruptions, The Manhattan Rhythm Kings.*

1982–83: Mainstage: *A Midsummer Night's Dream, Billy Bishop Goes to War, Tartuffe, You Can't Take It with You, Desire Under the Elms, Pal Joey, A Christmas Carol.* Cabaret: *Starting Here, Starting Now, Only When I Laugh, Key Changes and other Disasters, Come Rain or Come Shine: The Music of Harold Arlen, Christmas Presences,*

Stage Stricken, Murder in the Casbah, Herb and Potato, Murder Strikes Twice: Murder in the Cabaret and *Murder in the Casbah, Hey, Big Spender!: The Music of Cy Coleman, Kilroy Was Here, The Manhattan Rhythm Kings.*

1983–84: Mainstage: *Henry IV*, Parts I and II, *A Christmas Carol, Heartbreak House, Joan and Charles with Angels, Whodunnit.* Upperstage: *Mass Appeal, Pump Boys and Dinettes, The Island.* Cabaret: *The Manhattan Rhythm Kings, Love Songs, T-Bears, Maxine Andrews, In Jobs We Trust, Murder in the Kremlin, Herb and Potato, The Whole Earth Cabaret, Mimi Moyer, I Get a Kick Out of Cole.*

1984–85: Mainstage: *The Man Who Came to Dinner, A Christmas Carol, Painting Churches, The Three Sisters, The Diary of Anne Frank, The School for Wives.* Upperstage: *Fool for Love, Tintypes, 'night, Mother.* Cabaret: *The Manhattan Rhythm Kings, An Evening with Bernadette Galanti, Charles Busch Alone, The Steinettes, On the Air, Murder in the Capitol, Stage Stricken, Ho Ho Ho the Christmas Show, Another Evening with Bernadette Galanti, The Red Clay Ramblers, I Got Gershwin, Real to Reel, Modern Times, Annette Saves the World.*

1985–86: Mainstage: *The Front Page, Peter Pan, Dracula, The Boys in Autumn: Huck 'n' Tom Grow'd Up, Dial "M" for Murder, Romeo and Juliet.* Upperstage: *Virginia, Sister Mary Ignatius Explains It All for You* and *The Actor's Nightmare, Mourning Becomes Electra, Torch Song Trilogy.* Cabaret: *The Jerome Kern Songbook, Greater Tuna, Season's Greetings, Magic Child: An Evening with Teresa Burrell, Some Enchanted Evenings: The Songs of Rodgers and Hammerstein, Bullshot Crummond, A Little Sondheim Music, Together Again.*

BIBLIOGRAPHY

Published Sources:
Theatre Profiles. Vols. 4–7. New York: Theatre Communications Group, 1979–86.
Theatre World, 1975–76, 1976–77, and *1985–86.* New York: Crown Publishers, 1977, 1978, and 1987.

Unpublished Source:
Playbill Collection (microfiche) of the Theatre Communications Group, for programs 1972–75.

Archival Resource:
Indianapolis, Indiana. Indiana Repertory Theatre. IRT *Onstage,* papers, and clippings.

                                                           Alan C. English

[THE] INTIMAN THEATRE COMPANY, Seattle, Washington, was founded in December 1972 by Margaret Booker. A graduate of Stanford University, Booker spent two years as a Fulbright lecturer in Sweden, where she also produced radio dramas. After studying directing in Stanford's doctoral program, she was invited to study at the National Theatre in Stockholm under Ingmar Bergman and Alf Sjoberg. On returning to the United States she founded the Intiman, which means "intimate" in Swedish, taking the name from a theatre in Stockholm founded near the turn of the century by August Strindberg. The Intiman's first home was the Creative Arts League, a small theatre at 620 Market Street in Kirkland, Washington (a suburb of Seattle). The opening production of Henrik Ibsen's *Rosmersholm,* directed by Booker, played to a full house of sixty-five on its first night and was a critical success. Continued success marked Intiman's first season, which accumulated a total audience of 600 over four productions, on a total budget of $2,000. The critical and public response encouraged Margaret "Megs" Booker and confirmed her instincts: Seattle was ready and eager for a theatre that emphasized the "modern classics" of Ibsen, Strindberg, Anton Chekhov, G. B. Shaw, et al., performed in an intimate setting with contemporary production values. Also, from the start Booker emphasized the potential of an ensemble company consisting primarily of local talent, making use only occasionally of guest Equity artists.

For its second season the Intiman moved to the Cornish Institute in Seattle, a centrally located arts academy that adjusted its own theatre schedule to allow for Intiman's three productions. After searching for a more permanent home for her theatre, Booker moved Intiman for its third season to the Second Stage theatre on 801 Pike Street in downtown Seattle, where a larger house and inner-city location provided greater audience potential. Three productions and a holiday touring revue played to a total season's audience of 11,000, and the annual budget grew to $49,000. The 1975 season also saw Intiman become fully professional, negotiating agreements with Actors' Equity Association and the League of Resident Theatres.

In 1976 Booker added a third theatre program to the growing Mainstage season and popular Holiday Sampler tour. New Plays Onstage was created to provide a forum for new works as staged readings, directed and performed by members of the ensemble with minimal sets, props, and costumes. Often these were premieres, and the authors were always invited to attend rehearsals, performances, and postreading discussions with the actors and audience. By this time Intiman was also receiving acknowledgment and financial support from the King County Arts Commission, the Seattle Arts Commission, and the Washington State Cultural Enrichment Program, especially for its tours to promote theatre appreciation and cultural diversity for smaller communities. Recognition of Intiman's contribution to Seattle and to Washington State led in 1980 to its being awarded institutional status by the King County and Washington State arts commissions, as well as a Challenge Grant from the National Endowment for the Arts.

In the meantime Booker's search for innovative material took her to Germany in 1979 at the invitation of the German government to research plays for future seasons. This led to a staged reading of *Big and Little*, by Botho Strauss, in 1980, among others. She was also invited by the Swedish government in 1980 to tour Scandinavian theatres, and returned there in 1981 to contract directors, designers, and playwrights in preparation for the 1982 season and "Scandinavia Today." This international exposition of Nordic culture was then hosted in 1982 by five American cities, including Seattle, which has a large population of Scandinavian descent. The Intiman spearheaded the activities of "Scandinavia Today" in Seattle with a variety of theatre productions selected to promote Scandinavian culture. The Mainstage season included two lavish productions:

Ibsen's *The Wild Duck*, directed by Booker with costumes by Finnish guest designer Veronica Leo, and Strindberg's *A Dream Play*, directed by Peter Oskarson and designed by Peter Holm, both of Sweden. Their success was paralleled by a New Plays Onstage season made up entirely of new works by Scandinavian playwrights, one each from Iceland, Norway, Sweden, Denmark, and Finland. All of the playwrights were able to attend the readings and participate in the postproduction exchanges. A one-day symposium featuring guest speakers Bibi Andersson and Max Von Sydow drew a full house, and the Intiman was visited by Vigdis Finnbogadottir, president of Iceland and former director of that country's national theatre.

On the heels of such a major success for the Intiman, Booker traveled again to Germany, where she contracted various artists for the 1983 season. The German theatre program was sponsored by the Federal Republic of Germany to celebrate the 300th anniversary of German immigration to the United States, and included a Mainstage production of Bertolt Brecht's *In the Jungle of Cities*, along with works by contemporary German-language playwrights for New Plays Onstage. The Brecht play, directed by Christof Nel with scene design by Andreas Braito, aroused a storm of critical controversy over its acting style and production values. Lacking the widespread local support (and perhaps interest) that had attended "Scandinavia Today," the German program was less successful as a whole. Nevertheless, the Intiman in 1983 appeared firmly established as a major contributor to the Seattle cultural community, and Booker began a capital campaign for a new theatre.

In 1983 Booker continued to travel, as a guest director to Dubrovnik, Yugoslavia, and also to Caracas, Venezuela, where she was the guest of the Center for Inter-American Relations and the *Ateneo de Caracas*. In Venezuela she laid the groundwork for Intiman's 1984 International Theatre Festival, as these projects were now being called. The 1984 season thus included a Mainstage production from Venezuela, *Myth Weavers*, by Arturo Uslar-Pietri, staged by guest director Gustavo Tambascio with designs by Martin Lopez. The New Plays Onstage brought three American premieres from Mexico, Chile, and Argentina. Interestingly, the funding for the 1984 season's experiment was from a combination of local, state, and U.S. sources. In 1984 Booker again traveled to Yugoslavia for a two-week tour of theatres, in preparation for the next international theatre project.

However, the capital campaign for the new theatre space had fallen on difficult times by early 1984; and the Second Stage lease agreement expired at the end of the season. The projected new theatre space, on Third Avenue and Union Street in downtown Seattle, was considerably larger than the Second Stage, providing the increased number of house seats needed for future financial solvency. At approximately 28,000 square feet, the renovated new space would accommodate 450 to 500 seats with a thrust Greek-style stage area conducive to Intiman's staging demands. However, pending acquisition of appropriate funds for the new theatre, the Intiman's 1985 season had to be staged in an interim facility. The Mainstage productions were fewer in number, while the New Plays Onstage and International Theatre Festival had to be postponed. The continuation of support Intiman received from local, state, and even international sources seemed assured; and with the Seattle community solidly behind the Intiman, Booker had no cause to doubt that the Intiman would be successful in its campaign.

In 1985 a surprised Seattle learned that Margaret Booker had accepted the position of artistic director at the Hartman Theatre Company* in Stamford, Connecticut, and would leave Seattle at the end of the 1985 season. After a short national search, in December 1985 Elizabeth Huddle was named as the new artistic director of the Intiman. Huddle's credentials include long stints with the Actor's Workshop* of San Francisco, the Repertory Theatre of Lincoln Center*, and the American Conservatory Theatre* in San Francisco, where she functioned both as actor and as director, various television appearances (notably the series *Boone* and a recurring role on *Hill Street Blues*), and directing at the Oregon Shakespeare Festival.

Huddle immediately devoted her energies to finding a new home for the displaced Intiman and to recouping financial strength—the 1984 season had been particularly disastrous. Although the 1986 season was still staged in interim spaces, primarily the Broadway Theatre at Seattle Central Community College, arrangements were made for Intiman to occupy the Seattle Center Playhouse— a space left vacant by the Seattle Repertory Theatre when it moved into its new home, the Bagley Wright Theatre. Some renovation was necessary, but both the theatre and the location represented a step up for the Intiman, and came close to fulfilling Booker's earlier dream. Altered from a proscenium to a modified thrust stage, the house seats 405 in an intimate arrangement; and the Playhouse building accommodates all facets of the theatre's operations—scene shop, storage space, rehearsal rooms, and business offices—under one roof, a first for the Intiman.

Under Huddle's direction and drawing on the talents of new business manager Peter Davis, the Intiman has begun to thrive once again, adding new subscribers, maintaining full seasons, and reducing its debt. For the time being, some of the peripheral programs initiated by Booker have been shelved; but new programs, such as an acting internship agreement with the Cornish College of the Arts (Seattle), further indicate future continued growth and prosperity for the Intiman.

PERSONNEL

Management: Margaret Booker, founder and artistic director (1972–84); Elizabeth Huddle, artistic director (1985–86); John Booker, business manager (1972–76); Simon Siegl, general manager (1977–84); Peter Davis, managing director (1986).

Stage Directors: Margaret Booker (1972–84), Robert Brink (1983), Anthony Cornish (1978–79, 1984), Clayton Corzatte (1977), Richard Allen Edwards (1987), Robert J. Farley (1980), William Glover (1980), Elizabeth Huddle (1981), Nagle Jackson (1982– 83), George Kovach (1981), Sharon Ott (1982), Pat Patton (1976–77, 1981), Richard

Riehle (1982), Stephen Rosenfield (1976, 1978–79), Bruce Sevy (1982), Warner Shook (1987).

Designers: Peter W. Allen (1985–86); Carol H. Beule, costume (1982); Robert Blackman, set, costume (1980); William Bloodgood, set (1980–83); Martyn Bookwalter, set (1980); Dennis Bradford, set (1983); Nanrose Buchman, costume (1977–78); James Buss, hair (1979); Liz Covey (1985); Laura Crow, costume (1979–80, 1986); Robert A. Dahlstrom, principal designer, set, lighting, costume (1972–79, 1981, 1983); Ted D'Arms, visuals (1976); Michael Davidson, lighting (1981, 1985); Pete Davis, set (1978); Rondi Davis, costume (1979); Richard Devin, lighting (1977–80); Deborah Dryden, costume (1984); Ron Erickson, set, costume (1976–78, 1981, 1984); Donna Eskew, costume (1975–76); Sarah Nash Gates, costume (1985–86); Karen Gjelsteen, set (1975–80); Cynthia J. Hawkins, lighting (1976–77); Michael Holten, sound (1983–84); Jerry S. Hooker, set (1986); Robert Jackson, lighting (1975); Charles Kading, set (1976); John Kavelin, set (1980–81); Frances Kenney, costume (1986); Ellen M. Kozak, costume (1977); Alan Madsen, costume (1975); Michael Miller, set (1977, 1979, 1981–85); Michael Olich, costume (1979–80, 1984, 1986); Rick Paulsen, lighting (1986); Adam Pell, sound (1986); Robert Peterson, lighting (1981–84); Stephanie Poire, costume (1976); David Potts, set (1984–85); Lewis Rampino, costume (1979); Sally Richardson, costume (1974–75); James D. Sale, lighting (1979–85); Robert Scales, lighting (1981–82); Joseph Seserko, sound (1983); Greg Sullivan, lighting (1983–84); John Sullivan, costume (1982–83, 1985); D. Edmund Thomas, lighting (1975); Susan Tsu, costume (1980–81, 1983); James Verdery, lighting (1977–78, 1984); Kurt Wilhelm, costume (1982–83); Judy Wolcott, lighting (1975); Collier Woods, lighting (1986); Gilbert Wong, set (1985); Andrew Yelusich, costume (1980–81, 1983, 1986).

Literary Advisors: Roger Downey (1982), Alison Harris (1980), Karl Kramer (1983), Murray Morgan (1976).

Music Directors/Composers: James Kuhn (1984), Hub Miller (1981), Folke Rabe (1974), Gary Yershon (1984).

Choreographers: Leslie Bennet (1980), Lee Carrillo (1984), Valerie Dunne (1982), Charlotte Lewenhaupt (1982), Teodoro Morca (1984), Don Schwennesen (1983), Kent Stowell (1980), Jennifer Thienes (1974).

Production/Stage Management: Peter W. Allen (1984), K. Kevyne Baar (1984), Dennis Gill Booth (1982), J. V. Bradley (1974), Rita Calabro (1982), Kent Conrad (1985–86), Sandy Cruse (1975–77), Bruce Elsperger (1985–86), Diana Gervais (1982), Barbara Lutz (1983), Jane E. Maurer (1984), Michael Olich (1983), Dan Sedgwick (1978–1980), James Verdery (1980–83), Craig Weindling (1981).

Technical Directors: Dennis Gill Booth (1976–81), Robert Jackson (1975), Mark Putman (1984).

Scenic Technicians: John Booker (1974), Malcolm Brown (1978), Vicki Fowler (1980), Dan Goodwin (1975), Sue Grisvard (1976), Carolyn Keim (1982), Richard Klyce (1981–82), Carolyn MacLean (1982–83), Matt Moeller (1977), Martin Pavloff (1980–82), Jayna Orchard (1978), Peter S. Pentz (1978–82), Robert Reynolds (1982–84), Connie Rinchiuso (1981), Jeff Robbins (1976), Barry Rodgers (1980), John Savage (1979), Margaret Vincent (1976–77), Prue Warren (1979).

Production Assistants: Linda Briggs (1981), Betsy Hay (1981), Jerrie Kennedy (1981), Joe Koplowitz (1980), Stephen Oles (1979), Randy Paris (1979), Brian Rapalee (1980), Laurie Stusser (1980), John Teegarden (1979), Monika Willen (1982).

Administrative, House, and Publicity: Lin Bauer (1984), Chris Bennion (1974–84), Ruth Brinton (1975–79), Betsy Calloway (1977), Patricia Charlson (1974), Richard Crockett (1982), Lila Gault (1981–82), Lester Gruner (1983), Chad Henry (1976), Mary Lyn Hikel (1983), Barry Lynn Krich (1985), Cameron Mason (1982–83), Jan Matheson (1980–84), Marsha Morrison (1978–79), Gretchen Nordleaf (1984), Colette Ogle (1984), Philip Sanders (1975–76), Neil Savage (1984), Jerry Schwiebert (1979), Mark Sheppard (1980, 1983), Tobe Snow (1980–81), Jan Steadman (1987), Cindy Streltzov (1986), John L. Tamborelle (1983–84), Tracey Trudeau (1982–83), Christine Wheeler (1974), Beatrice Wallace (1983–84).

Actors and Actresses: Rex Allen (1980), Linda Alper (1982), Mark Anders (1987), Mike Anderson (1978), Dennis Arndt (1979), Marla Ashland (1978), John Aylward (1986–87), Barbara Bain (1984), *Laurence Ballard* (1979–83), Kurt Beattie (1986–87), Jahnna Beecham (1982), Barbara Bercu (1977), James Billingham (1982), Jeff Bingham (1977), Michelle Blackmon (1984), Suzanne Bouchard (1986–87), *J. V. Bradley* (1978–79, 1983), Marc Bridgham (1978), Suzie Cameron (1981), Rose E. Cano (1984), Mimi Carr (1983), Terry Caza (1983), Jeremy Clement (1982), *Megan Cole* (1976–84, 1987), *Clayton Corzatte* (1976–78, 1986–87), Amy Crumpacker (1982–84), *Ted D'Arms* (1974–80), Jeff David (1980), Regina David (1982), Jack Davidson (1984), Barbara Dirickson (1987), Cameron Dokey (1982), Paul Donahoe (1984), Toni Douglass (1982–84), Anthony Doyle (1978), Nick Erickson (1986–87), Mary Ewald (1982–84), R. A. Farrell (1980), Jay Fernandez (1977), Laura Ferri (1986), Lois Foraker (1986), Sharee Galpert (1986), Livia Genise-Andersen (1982), *John Gilbert* (1975–84), Tina Marie Goff (1981), Bruce Gooch (1984), James W. Gorgal (1975), Tammy Gray (1987), Nathan Haus (1976), Maureen Hawkins (1975), Gardner Hayes (1975), *Christine Healy* (1978–79, 1981), Mark Herrier (1978), Ken Hicks (1986), Malcolm Hillgartner (1980–82), *Margaret Hilton* (1977–83), *Patricia Hodges* (1974–75, 1981), Ruby Holbrook (1982), Scott Honeywell (1980), Will Huddleston (1981, 1983), Suzy Hunt (1979, 1983–84), Mark Jenkins (1982–83, 1987), Byron Jennings (1987), John Kauffman (1976), Brett Keogh (1984), Michael Kevin (1976), *Jean Marie Kinney* (1975–77, 1984), Laurie Lapinsky (1978), Martin LaPlatney (1977), Lori Larsen (1976), Carmen de Lavallade (1984), Jo Leffingwell (1980, 1986–87), *Zoaunne LeRoy* (1979–82, 1984), Roberta Levitow (1981), Jamie Lopez (1981), Susan Ludlow-Corzatte (1977, 1987), Scott Lykes (1979), Ann McCaffray (1974), Lachlan Macleay (1980), Gale McNeeley (1983), Sean Markland (1982), Susan Carr Marney (1975–76), Brian Martin (1982–83), Robert Martin (1975), Dale Matheson (1981), Mark Matheson (1981), Daniel Mayes (1984), Mark Mayo (1983), *Glenn Mazen* (1977–83, 1986–87), Margit Moe (1976, 1980), David Mong (1983–84), William Moreing (1978), Michael Morgan-Dunne (1982–84), Marguerite Morrissey (1979), *Marnie Mosiman* (1977, 1979–80), Barry Mulholland (1978), *Mark D. Murphey* (1976–77, 1979), Allen Nause (1980–81), Majorie Nelson (1979, 1983), Joan Norton (1976), Catherine O'Connell (1979, 1981), Peggy O'Connell (1978), Julia Odegard (1981), Shaun Austin Olsen (1980), Si Osborne (1979), Liann Pattison (1983), Demetra Pittman (1984), John Procaccino (1986), Rex Rabold (1982), Rick Ray (1979–80), Daniel Renner (1986), Rikki Ricard (1987), *Richard Riehle* (1976–78, 1982–84), *Eve Roberts* (1977, 1980–81), Judith Roberts (1983), Shirley Robertson (1979), Rick Rueben (1977), *Michael Santo* (1979–82, 1986–87), Ruben Sierra (1983–84), *Peter Silbert* (1977, 1980, 1982–84), Leah Sluis (1978, 1981), Jean Smart (1976, 1978–79), Ian Stuart (1981, 1983), Rebecca Stucki (1984), Gaynor Sturchi (1986), Jill Tanner (1983), William terKuile (1981–82), *Brian Thompson* (1978–80, 1984, 1986), Henry Tsu (1983), Brian Tyrrell (1983), Terres Unsoeld (1980), George Von Dassow (1982), Peter Von Dassow (1982), Paul Walsh (1982), Patrick Watkins (1983), Bill Watson (1983), A. C. Weary (1976), Amy Beth Williams (1980–81), Edward Williams (1986), Cal Winn (1983), R. Hamilton Wright (1983).

REPERTORY

1972–73: *Rosmersholm, The Creditors, The Underpants, Brecht on Brecht*.

1974: *Miss Julie, Tango, Candida*.

1975: *Uncle Vanya, The Philanderer, Hedda Gabler*. Tour: *Holiday Sampler*.

1976: *Arms and the Man, Electra, Anatol, Bus Stop, The Northwest Show*. New Plays Onstage: *Baudelaire*. Tour: *Holiday Sampler*.

1977: *Toys in the Attic, The Importance of Being Earnest, Ghosts, Playboy of the Western World, A Moon for the Misbegotten*. New Plays Onstage: *Wild Butterfly*. Tour: *Holiday Sampler, Villains, Victims, Heroes and Heroines*.

1978: *Henry IV, The Way of the World, The Three Sisters, The Country Girl, The Dance of Death*. New Plays Onstage: *Domino Courts, Canadian Gothic and American Modern*. Tour: *Holiday Sampler, Welcome to Our Theatre*.

1979: *The Loves of Cass McGuire, Tartuffe, Medea, Heartbreak House, Design for Living*. New Plays Onstage: *Two-Part Inventions, Mr. Krebs and Rosalie, Southern Cross, GBS, Bo*. Tour: *Holiday Sampler, Face Off: Man and Woman*.

1980: *Othello, The Lady's Not for Burning, Leonce and Lena, Mirandolina, The Cherry Orchard*. New Plays Onstage: *White Pelicans, Devour the Snow, Bloodletting, Twenty Minutes with an Angel, Big and Little, Mosaics*. Tour: *Holiday Sampler*.

1981: *Pygmalion, The Rose Tattoo, School for Wives, A Touch of the Poet, Damien*. New Plays Onstage: *In August We Play the Pyrenees, Pen Pals, Coming of Age*. Tour: *Holiday Sampler, Damien*.

1982: *Hay Fever, A Delicate Balance, She Stoops to Conquer, Shadow of a Gunman, The Wild Duck, A Dream Play*. New Plays Onstage: *A Brief Respite, Ballerina, Rain Snakes, And the Birds Are Singing Again, The Love Story of the Century*. Tour: *Holiday Sampler*.

1983: *Misalliance, Dear Liar, Crucifer of Blood, In the Jungle of Cities, The Ribadier System, The Sea Gull*. New Plays Onstage: *Iron Heart, The Correction, The Mission, The Medea Fragments, The Eve of Retirement*.

1984: *Long Day's Journey into Night, The Country Wife, Blood Wedding, Myth Weavers, The Dance and the Railroad*. New Plays Onstage: *Orinoco!, In the Country, Burning Patience*.

1985: *You Never Can Tell, Hedda Gabler, Duet for One*.

1986: *The Doctor in Spite of Himself, The Second Mrs. Tanqueray, The Play's the Thing, Mrs. Warren's Profession, Vikings*.

1987: *Man and Superman, The Little Foxes, The Sea Horse, A Doll's House, Private Lives*.

BIBLIOGRAPHY

Published Sources:
Seattle Post-Intelligencer, 1972–87.
Seattle Times, 1972–87.
The Weekly, 1985–87.

Jeanie K. Forte

J

[MARGO] JONES THEATRE. See MARGO JONES THEATRE.

L

[JOHN] LENTHIER TROUPE. See ACTORS' REPERTORY COMPANY.

[THE] LIVING THEATRE was founded in 1947 in New York City as Living Theatre Productions, Inc., by Judith Malina and Julian Beck (1925–85). Its first performance was held August 15, 1951, at the Becks' apartment at 789 West End Avenue. In late 1951 the Becks leased the Cherry Lane Theatre, where on December 2, 1951, they presented Gertrude Stein's *Doctor Faustus Lights the Lights*. They remained at the Cherry Lane producing avant-garde poetic drama until August 1952, when the landlord evicted the company because the rent wasn't paid.

From 1954 until late 1955 the Living Theatre continued to produce poetic drama in a loft at One Hundredth Street and Broadway. Fire marshals closed this theatre, insisting that only eighteen persons use a space in which the Becks were seating sixty-five. In 1957 the company found a spacious new theatre, the upper three floors of a former Hecht's department store at Sixth Avenue and Fourteenth Street, which they renovated under the guidance of architect Paul Williams. The Fourteenth Street theatre, capacity 162, also called the Living Theatre Playhouse, opened January 13, 1959, with William Carlos Williams' *Many Loves*. With the 1959 production of Jack Gelber's *The Connection* and the 1963 production of Kenneth Brown's *The Brig*, the Living Theatre achieved critical acclaim. European tours of *The Connection* in 1961 and 1962 brought the company international fame. In October 1963 the Fourteenth Street theatre was closed by the Internal Revenue Service in an effort to collect back taxes owed by the Becks. The closing of the Fourteenth Street theatre marked the end of the New York period of the company's work, but during this period, between 1951 and 1963, the Living Theatre had premiered twenty-nine plays.

In September 1964 the Becks and *The Brig* cast, a group of about twenty-five actors, went to London to perform *The Brig;* the company remained in Europe touring until September 1968. During this period the membership of the Living Theatre underwent many changes; some of the original members left the group, and some European actors joined. At one point, during its European phase, the Living Theatre had forty members. Also during this period the Living Theatre became overtly political and began to evolve into an anarchist commune as well as to create collectively pieces based on anarchist themes. In Europe the company created the pieces for which they are most famous: *Mysteries* (1964), *Frankenstein* (1965), *Antigone* (1967), and *Paradise Now* (1968).

In September 1968 the Living Theatre returned to the United States for a tour of American colleges and universities. They remained in America presenting the repertoire evolved in Europe until the end of March 1969, when they returned to Europe.

In January 1970 the Living Theatre divided into four cells to pursue diverse goals. The members issued the Living Theatre Action Declaration that stated their determination to find new theatrical forms and to perform in the streets for the underprivileged rather than in theatres for an elite.

In the spring of 1970 a group of Brazilian artists invited the surviving core of the Living Theatre—those who had remained with the Becks—to Brazil. The Living Theatre went to Brazil and worked with the people evolving pieces reflecting the people's concerns, pieces that became part of a projected cycle called *The Legacy of Cain*, 150 plays showing man's enslavement to man. The troupe's work in Brazil was cut short by their arrest on drug charges. After two months in Brazilian prisons the Living Theatre returned to the United States in August 1971, where they established themselves in Brooklyn.

From 1971 until late 1974 the Living Theatre Collective continued work on *The Legacy of Cain* cycle, gearing new sections of it to American industrial workers. In December 1974 the Living Theatre Collective moved to Pittsburgh, where, with the aid of a Mellon Foundation grant, they performed *The Destruction of the Money Tower* (1975) and *Six Public Acts* (1975).

In the fall of 1975 the collective returned to Europe, performing at several festivals. With Rome as its headquarters, since 1975, the Living Theatre has performed throughout Italy and other European countries. They have continued to do street theatre as well as to perform once again in theatres. The collective has introduced several new pieces into its repertory, including *Prometheus* (1978); *Masse Mensch* (1980), an adaptation of Ernst Toller's expressionist drama; *The Yellow Methuselah* (1982), Hanon Reznikov's collation of G. B. Shaw's *Back to Methuselah* and Wassily Kandinsky's *The Yellowsound;* and Julian Beck's *The Archeology of Sleep*, an effort to evaluate the dynamics of the sleeping being. In 1983 an offer of support from the French Ministry of Culture prompted a move to Paris, but the company was unable to find a suitable theatre. The group then returned to New York City, ending its fifteen-year self-imposed exile with a repertory of four pieces in January 1984. Critical and popular response prompted an early end to the Joyce Theatre stand, and many company members, citizens of European countries, left the United States to return home. Beck accepted work in motion pictures *(The Cotton Club)*, on television *(Miami Vice)*, and off-off-Broadway (in *The Beckett Trilogy* at La Mama E.T.C.), while Malina published her 1947–57 diaries and completed a video documentary on the Living Theatre, *Signals Through the Flames*.

During the late forties and the fifties the Living Theatre was a pioneer and leader of the avant-garde movement in the arts. Reacting against the commercialism of Broadway, the Living Theatre stood for experimentalism, the expansion of consciousness, poetic realism, and a commitment to effect greater audience involvement during performance. Beginning with its period of exile, 1964–68, the Living Theatre became a counterculture leader and a leader of the experimental theatre movement of the sixties. The Living Theatre influenced and was influenced by groups such as the Open Theatre*, the Bread and Puppet Theatre, and many others, both in America and in Europe. Of these, the Living Theatre is the oldest, the most influential, and the only one to survive for more than thirty years.

The Living Theatre's extreme longevity can be attributed largely to the dedication of the highly literate Becks, who, since the forties, have committed themselves and the Living Theatre to the alleviation of suffering and continual artistic experimentation. Judith Malina, an actress from her youth, and a gifted director, served an apprenticeship from 1945 to 1947 at Erwin Piscator's Dramatic Workshop in New York City. Julian Beck, a painter in his youth, and a gifted scene designer, poet, actor, and director, handled most administrative tasks of the Living Theatre until it became a collective. Both Becks have been pacifist-anarchists since the forties and have participated in many political protests against nuclear testing and war. Since the sixties their art and politics have been inseparable, and they have played a major role in the Living Theatre's evolution into a troupe dedicated to a peaceful, worldwide, anarchist revolution.

The Living Theatre has constantly struggled to raise funds and still remain faithful to its political and artistic ideals. The company was initially organized as a corporation in 1947, the Living Theatre Productions, Inc. During its loft period the Living Theatre depended entirely on the contributions of audience members and friends. During its Fourteenth Street phase the Living Theatre was reorganized as a corporation with a limited number of members. When the Fourteenth Street theatre was closed by the IRS, the Living Theatre Corporation was fined $12,500. In its European exile the group survived through box-office receipts, filmwork, odd jobs, and the support of friends. From 1965 actors were no longer paid salaries but shared equally in all receipts as the group strove to become an anarchist community. On its return to the United States in the seventies, the Living Theatre Collective raised money through lectures and workshops, as well as from a grant from the Mellon Foundation to produce theatre in Pittsburgh.

Critical controversy has raged about the Living Theatre. The company's early work was lauded by some reviewers for its bold experimentalism and panned by others as pretentious. *The Connection* (1959) and *The Brig* (1963) were praised by monthly reviewers for originality and boldness. The work created by the troupe at its peak in the sixties created much critical controversy both abroad and in the United States because of its political content as well as its use of audience confrontation tactics, its use of nudity, and an intensely kinetic style deemphasizing words.

In the more than thirty years of its existence the Living Theatre has evolved through several phases. From 1951 to 1963 the company experimented chiefly with avant-garde poetic drama, ranging from Paul Goodman's *Faustina* (1952) to Jean Cocteau's *Orpheus* (1954) to William Carlos Williams' *Many Loves* (1959). In 1960 the Living Theatre experimented with John Cage's theories of indeterminacy in its joint presentation of Jackson MacLow's *The Marrying Maiden* and Ezra Pound's *The Women of Trachis* (from Sophocles) as The Theatre of Chance. In Pirandello's *Tonight We Improvise* (1959) and Jack Gelber's *The Connection* (1959) the company experimented with the spectator-performer relationship. With both *The Connection* and *The Brig* (1963) the Living Theatre moved toward the presentation of contemporary social problems, deemphasis on script, experimentation with nonverbal techniques, and the elimination of a traditional performer-spectator relationship.

With *Mysteries, Frankenstein, Antigone*, and *Paradise Now* the art and politics of the Living Theatre became inseparable, audience confrontation reaching its peak in *Paradise Now*. The troupe's style in these works became highly Artaudian and visceral. In the seventies the Living Theatre experimented, in *The Legacy of Cain*, with audience participation in creating and performing pieces, as they experimented with street theatre, guerrilla theatre, and environmental theatre. Emphasis in the repertory shifted from confrontational politics to experimentation with spectator perception, with the goal of producing spiritual change that might lead to political change.

Although the Living Theatre began with the Becks in a dominant role, and with Julian Beck handling administration, since the mid-sixties the group has eschewed traditional forms of organization and striven for the anarchist ideal of voluntarism and egalitarian sharing. Thus those in the troupe with various skills have handled business and technical aspects for the troupe voluntarily, but there has been no formal role taking.

There are no stars in the troupe, owing to its anarchist orientation, but certain members have been with the troupe longer than others and some are more widely known than others. The Becks, of course, have been with the group since its inception. Members who have been Living Theatre members for a long time include Steven Ben Israel, who joined in 1963, and remained a member through much of the seventies; William Shari, who joined in 1959 and remained a member through much of the sixties' work; as well as Jim Anderson, Rufus Collins, Gene Gordon, Jim Tiroff, and Henry Howard, all of whom joined between 1959 and 1963 and were with the troupe through most of the sixties. Henry Proach joined the Living Theatre in 1952 and remained a member through 1963. Warren Finnerty, who won an Obie for his performance of Leach in *The Connection*, did not remain with the troupe past the early sixties. Joseph Chaikin, who later founded the Open Theatre, performed with the Living Theatre in the late fifties. Poet Jackson MacLow appeared in some fifties' productions.

PERSONNEL

European Exile: At the time of its creation of its most noted piece, *Paradise Now*, in 1968 in Europe, the Living Theatre consisted of the following members who contributed to its collective creation: Jim Anderson, Pamela Badyk, Cal Barber, Julian Beck, Rod Beere, Carol Berger, Odile Bingisser, Mel Clay, Rufus Collins, Pierre Devis, Echnaton, Carl Einhorn, Gene Gordon, Roy Harris, Jenny Hecht, Frank Hoogeboom, Henry Howard, Nona Howard, Steven Ben Israel, Birgit Knabe, Mary Krapf, Sandy Linden, Judith Malina, Gianfranco Mantegna, Michele Mareck, Gunter Pannewitz, Dorothy Shari, William Shari, Luke Theodore, Steve Thompson, Jim Tiroff, Diana Van Tosh, Petra Vogt, Karen Weiss, Peter Weiss, Souzka Zeller.

Spring 1975, the Living Theatre Collective consisted of Carlos Altamare, Pamela Badyk, Julian Beck, Isha Manna Beck, Anita Goldman, Carol Harris, Leroy House, Baruch Ben Israel, Steven Ben Israel, Mary Krapf, Judith Malina, Robert Massengale, Jeffrey Perlman, Howard Reznick, Stephen Schulberg, Eduardo da Silva, Chris Torch, Stephanette Vendeville, Tom Walker.

REPERTORY

At the Becks' Apartment, 789 West End Avenue:

1951: *Childish Jokes, Ladies Voices, He Who Says Yes and He Who Says No, The Dialogue of the Mannequin and the Young Man.*

At the Cherry Lane Theatre:

1951–52: *Doctor Faustus Lights the Lights, Beyond the Mountains,* An Evening of Bohemian Theatre (*Desire Trapped by the Tail, Ladies' Voices, Sweeney Agonistes), Faustina, Ubu the King, The Heroes.*

At the Loft, Broadway and One Hundredth Street:

1954–55: *The Age of Anxiety, The Spook Sonata, Orpheus, The Idiot King, Tonight We Improvise, Phedre, The Young Disciple.*

At the Fourteenth Street Theatre:

1959–60: *Many Loves, The Cave at Machpelah, The Connection, Tonight We Improvise.* The Theatre of Chance (*The Marrying Maiden, The Women of Trachis).*

1960–61: *In the Jungle of Cities.*

1961–62: *The Apple.* European Tour: *The Connection, Many Loves, In the Jungle of Cities.*

1962–63: *Man Is Man, The Brig.* European Tour: *The Connection, In the Jungle of Cities, The Apple.*

European Exile 1964–68:

1964–65: *The Brig, Mysteries and Smaller Pieces.*

1965–66: *Mysteries, The Brig, Frankenstein, The Maids.*

1966–67: *The Maids, Mysteries, The Brig, Frankenstein.*

1967–68: *Mysteries, Frankenstein, The Maids, Antigone, Paradise Now.*

American Tour 1968–69: *Antigone, Frankenstein, Paradise Now, Mysteries.*

Since 1970: *The Legacy of Cain* (1970), *Christmas Cake for the Hot Hole and the Cold Hole* (1970), *Rites and Visions of Transformation* (1970), *Six Dreams About Mother*

(1971), *Seven Meditations of Political Sado-Masochism* (1973), *Strike Support Oratorium* (1973), *Turning the Earth* (1975), *Six Public Acts* (1975), *The Destruction of the Money Tower* (1975), *Turning the Violence* (1976), *The End of the World* (1976), *Where Does the Violence Come From?* (1976), *Why Are We Afraid of Sexual Freedom?* (1976), *The New World* (1976), *Where Have We Come From? Why Are We Here? Where Are We Going?* (1976), *Monday, Tuesday, Wednesday, Is There Something Wrong with the Way We Work?* (1976), *Breaking Our Silence* (1976), *Unemployment, Work, Power and Exploitation* (1976), *Brothers, Don't Shoot!* (1977), *The Body of Giuseppe Pinelli* (1977), *Free Theatre* (1977), *Workers Working, Lovers Loving, Workers Not Working, Lovers Not Loving* (1977), *Can I Kill You?* (1977), *Fear and Flying* (1978), *The Box Play* (1978), *Prometheus* (1978), *Masse Mensch* (presented as *The One and the Many*) (1980), *The Yellow Methuselah* (1982), *The Archeology of Sleep* (1983).

BIBLIOGRAPHY

Published Sources:

Auslander, Philip. "Staying Alive: The Living Theatre in the Eighties." *American Theatre* 1 (July/August 1984): 10–14.
Beck, Julian. *The Life of the Theatre: The Relation of the Artist to the Struggle of the People*. San Francisco: City Lights, 1972.
———, Judith Malina, Franco Quadri, eds. *Il lavoro de Living Theatre (Materiali 1952–1962)*. Milan: Ubulibri, 1982.
Gelber, Jack. "Julian Beck, Businessman." *The Drama Review* 30 (Summer 1986): 6–29.
Malina, Judith. *The Diaries of Judith Malina, 1947–57*. New York: Grove Press, 1984.
———. *The Enormous Despair*. New York: Random House, 1972.
Neff, Renfreu. *The Living Theatre: U.S.A.* Indianapolis: Bobbs-Merrill, 1970.
Rostagno, Alto. *We, The Living Theatre*. New York: Ballantine Books, 1970.
Sainer, Arthur. "The Several Stages of the Embattled Living Theater." *Theater* 16 (Spring 1985): 52–57.

Videorecording:

Malina, Judith. "Signals Through the Flames." New York: Mystic Fire Video, 1985.

Archival Resources:

Davis, California. University of California. University Library. Living Theatre scripts, clippings, journals, notebooks, photos, tapes, and ephemera.
New York, New York. New York Public Library. Billy Rose Theatre Collection. The Living Theatre Collection includes production notes, press material, and correspondence.
———. Private Collection of Judith Malina. The Living Theatre Archive.

Ulrica Bell-Perkins

[THE] LONG WHARF THEATRE (LWT) was founded in New Haven, Connecticut, in the fall of 1964 by Jon Jory and Harlan Kleiman. After producing a successful season of summer stock in a small town near New Haven, the two former students of the Yale University School of Drama set out to establish a professional repertory company in New Haven (population 152,000). Initial reception of their public relations and fund-raising campaign was so positive that they incorporated on February 1, 1965, and called in the gifts that citizens and businesses of New Haven had pledged.

They located an ideal building for their theatre in the Long Wharf Terminal Market, an industrial area with ample parking space and easy access from the Connecticut Turnpike. Kleiman and Jory then established a fund-raising group called Hands (Helpers and Supporters). The women of Hands maintained the drive for financial support while Kleiman and Jory turned to the task of fitting a theatre into the building they had acquired. A subscription drive began in May 1965 in anticipation of an eight-week summer season. The first performance in the 441-seat Long Wharf Theatre was on July 6, 1965. The inaugural four-show season played to more than 99 percent of capacity, although receipts fell slightly short of expenses.

An eight-play winter season, ranging across the canon of Western dramatic literature from Noel Coward to Euripides, played to nearly 85,000 admissions, or better than 85 percent of capacity. Jory and Kleiman also established the Long Wharf Children's Theatre with fellow Yale Drama School student Arvin Brown at its head. A high school touring company visited thirty-six schools, and 17,000 high school students saw performances at the Long Wharf Theatre, their viewing guided by study aids given to schools in Connecticut. A grant from a New Haven foundation supported a program for culturally deprived high school students and for poverty-impacted elementary school students in New Haven. A program for senior citizens featured Sunday matinee performances of the company's productions. The brisk organization and burgeoning development of the Long Wharf Theatre made managing director Kleiman (Yale University, M.A. in industrial administration) a celebrity in theatre management circles.

Julius Novick has observed that the productions of the first season demonstrated that artistic director Jory and resident designer David Hager had not yet learned to use Long Wharf Theatre's large thrust stage. A production of Brendan Behan's *The Hostage* benefited most from Jory's explosive directorial style and from the broad acting style of the resident company (*Beyond Broadway: The Quest for Permanent Theatres* [New York: Hill and Wang, 1968], p. 167).

The summer season of 1966 featured four premieres, as LWT veered sharply away from their policy of producing well-known plays. These plays, including *The Happy Haven*, by one of England's leading dramatists, John Arden, were poorly received in New Haven, and the summer festival lost money playing to less than 60 percent of capacity. In a perhaps related development, subscriptions for the second season fell sharply and attendance ran at about 65 percent of capacity. Competition from the newly established Yale Repertory Theatre* also undermined the LWT. New Haven seemed too small to support two professional theatre companies. Bankruptcy loomed as the deficit grew, averted only by an heroic fund-raising campaign. Tensions developed between Kleiman and Jory, which led to Jory's resignation at the end of the second season. Arvin Brown was selected to succeed Jory, who directed free-lance for three years before becoming artistic director of the Actors Theatre of Louisville*. Kleiman's resignation followed shortly thereafter, as he left New Haven to begin a career as an off-Broadway producer.

Brown and LWT's new general manager, Douglas Buck, based the 1967–68 season on a tight budget by featuring small-cast shows, such as Tennessee Williams' *The Glass Menagerie* and Edward Albee's *Tiny Alice*. Brown also engaged famous Irish actress Siobhan McKenna to direct J. M. Synge's *The Playboy of the Western World*. Brown and his associates in management at the LWT have struggled and succeeded not only in keeping the theatre open, but also in establishing a unique identity and a worldwide reputation for the company.

Brown, recognizing that the proximity of the audience to the stage (as near as five feet) necessitated an intimate, realistic acting style, fashioned the production program and the acting company to capitalize on this feature of the theatre. As a result, LWT acquired and has maintained the identity of an "actor's theatre," a performance group dedicated to the exploration of personality in plays stressing psychological interaction. Brown made the revival of a classic a regular feature of each season, starting in 1967–68 with Molière's *A Doctor in Spite of Himself* and the "Don Juan in Hell" passage from Act III of G. B. Shaw's *Man and Superman*. However, seasonal balance, a common concern of artistic directors of regional repertory companies, has not concerned Brown. Several theatre companies near New Haven—Yale Rep, the Hartman Theatre Company* in Stamford, Connecticut, the Hartford Stage Company in Hartford, Connecticut, the Goodspeed Opera House in East Haddam, Connecticut, and the McCarter Theatre Company* in Princeton, New Jersey (to say nothing of Broadway theatre just sixty miles to the southwest)—provide patrons with ample opportunity to balance their diet of drama. The competition also permits LWT to concentrate on kinds of plays best suited to its performers, directors, and designers, and the space in which they present their work. Accordingly, the company has specialized in importing British plays such as *Epitaph for George Dillon*, by Anthony Creighton and John Osborne, seen in 1968–69; *A Day in the Death of Joe Egg*, by Peter Nichols, seen in 1969–70 and again in 1981–82; David Storey's *The Contractor*, seen in 1971–72; and Storey's *The Changing Room*, seen the next season.

In significant measure, the current reputation of the LWT rests not only on its American premieres of new British comedies and dramas, but also on the fact that several of these productions, as well as productions of new American plays, have been transferred from the LWT to Broadway: *The Changing Room*; Athol Fugard's *Sizwe Bansi Is Dead; The Island*, by Xhosa tribesmen John Kani and Winston Ntshona, and Afrikaaner director Athol Fugard; Robert Anderson's *Solitaire/Double Solitaire;* Peter Nichols' *The National Health, A Day in the Death of Joe Egg, Whistle in the Dark*, and *A Place Without Doors;* Stewart Parker's *Spokesong;* Eugene O'Neill's *Ah, Wilderness!* (1975 revival); David Mamet's *American Buffalo;* David Rabe's *Streamers;* Simon Gray's *Quartermaine's Terms* and *The Common Pursuit;* and Arthur Miller's *A View from the Bridge*. Two such transfers, Michael Cristofer's *The Shadow Box* and D. L.

Coburn's *The Gin Game*, seen in New Haven in 1976–77, won Pulitzer Prizes in drama after their presentation on Broadway. LWT has also acquired an international reputation through four productions transferred to the London stage and through a tour of *The Gin Game* to the Soviet Union. Despite the centrality of plays developed for Broadway in the LWT's image, Brown disclaims the idea that the potential for transfer is a priority in script selection or casting.

Brown maintained the Young People's Theatre he had headed before becoming artistic director until 1977, and he instituted a series of "Dark Night Readings," minimal stagings of new plays offered free to subscribers. In the seasons of 1969–70 and 1970–71 LWT committed itself to the reexamination of Maxim Gorky as a dramatist, with productions of Gorky's *Country People* and *Yegor Bulichov*. A 1974 production of D. H. Lawrence's *The Widowing of Mrs. Holroyd* created new interest in this novelist's playwriting. A revival of Edith Wharton's *The House of Mirth*, not seen professionally in the United States since 1906, further established LWT's interest in and capacity to present plays from the frontiers of dramatic literature.

In 1974 the theatre was expanded to provide 484 seats and additional lobby and office space; at that time LWT presentations were playing to 93 percent of capacity and the annual operating budget exceeded $1 million. Further expansion was necessary in 1977, when LWT built a permanent rehearsal hall and a flexible theatre space—Stage II, seating 199—for the development of new plays. Stage II offers two productions annually, each running for six weeks.

From 1965 to 1975 the theatre maintained a repertory company hired at the beginning of each season, but in another effort to turn a potential liability into an advantage, Brown acknowledged the depth and breadth of the talent available in New York City and began casting productions one at a time. Since 1975 casts have been selected from what Brown calls a "floating rep," a corps of about twenty-five performers who work at the LWT periodically but are free to accept more lucrative work in the commercial theatre or in motion pictures and television. Indeed, the company's corporate acting style accommodates the talents of performers who work regularly in motion pictures and television, and the popular appeal of LWT's productions has benefited from the regular use of performers, such as Richard Dreyfuss, who also work in mass entertainment media.

Sustaining a capacity to dip into the Broadway talent pool and to exploit the city's media facilities while retaining independence of Broadway's commercial pressures has been a persistent challenge to Brown and his executive director since 1970, M. Edgar Rosenblum. Resistance to external expansion—bigger facilities, longer runs, longer seasons—has been a hallmark of LWT leadership. Perhaps remaining small in the shadow of the Big Apple has been a key to the long-term and consistent financial and critical success of the LWT.

While most of its contemporaries must have support from federal and state sources and from foundations and corporations, the LWT has thrived on earned income, which consistently accounts for a very high percentage of its operating budget. The success of the organization seems attributable in part to a workable division of responsibilities among Brown, Rosenblum, associate artistic director Kenneth Frankel, and John Tillinger, resident director and literary manager. The achievements of LWT have been acknowledged by the Outer Circle Critics in 1975, by the Tony Award selection committee in 1978, and by the Jujamycn Theatres in 1986.

PERSONNEL

Artistic Directors: Arvin Brown (1967–86), Jon Jory (1965–67).

Executive Directors: Harlan P. Kleiman (1965–67), M. Edgar Rosenblum (1970–86).

Associate Artistic Directors: Maurice Breslow (1968–70), Arvin Brown (1966–67), Kenneth Frankel (1980–86).

Directors of Children's Theatre: Arvin Brown (1965–67), Peter Hajduk (1970–71), Isaac Schambalen (1970–71).

General Manager: Douglas L. Buck (1966–68).

Managing Director: Thayer Baldwin, Jr. (1968–69).

Directors: Patrick Adiarte (1977–78), Craig Anderson (1973–74), Harold Baldridge (1969–70), Peter Bennett (1978–79), Malcolm Black (1971–72), Jeff Bleckner (1967–68, 1970–71), Maurice Breslow (1969–70), *Arvin Brown* (1965–86), Edward Payson Call (1977–78), Morris Carnovsky (1971–72), Gilbert Cates (1970–71), Joseph Cazelet (1967–68), Wallace Chappell (1973–74), Meredith Dallas (1968–69), Virginia Dancy (1972–73), Ron Daniels (1974–75), Gordon Davidson (1976–77, 1982–84), Barry Davis (1969–70, 1971–72, 1974–75, 1980–81), John Dillon (1981–82), Allen Fletcher (1978–79), William Francisco (1973–74, 1978–79), *Kenneth Frankel* (1975–76, 1977–79, 1980–86), Martin Fried (1976–77), Athol Fugard (1974–75), Robin Gammell (1974–75), *Edward Gilbert* (1970–72, 1977–80, 1984–85), Bill Glassco (1979–80), Peter Hajduk (1969–70), Mark Healy (1969–70), Donald Howarth (1980–81), Waris Hussein (1975–76), Brooks Jones (1973–75), *Jon Jory* (1965–69), Peter Levin (1975–76), Michael Lindsay-Hogg (1976–77), John Lithgow (1973–74), Bill Ludel (1980–82), Joseph Maher (1983–84), Davey Marlin-Jones (1977–78), Vivian Matalon (1984–85), Nancy Meckler (1981–82), Arthur Miller (1982–84), Mike Nichols (1975–77, 1979–80), Rene Norman (1984–85), John Pasquin (1979–80, 1982–84), Kent Paul (1972–73), Austin Pendleton (1972–74, 1979–80), Nikos Psacharopoulos (1985–86), Jose Quintero (1984–85), Charles Nelson Reilly (1983–84), Steven Robman (1976–77, 1983–84), Michael Rudman (1972–73), Douglas Seale (1966), George Spalding (1969–70), Max Stafford-Clark (1972–73), Daniel Sullivan (1983–84), Eric Thompson (1976–77), *John Tillinger* (1980–84), Tommy Tune (1979–80), James Way (1967–68), Phil Young (1985–86), Michael Youngfellow (1967–69), Harris Yulin (1981–84).

Set Designers: Loy Arcenas (1984–85), Will Steven Armstrong (1967–69), Arthur Barrow (1967–68), John Lee Beatty (1984–85), D. Martyn Bookwalter (1985–86), Edward Burbridge (1976–77), Betsy Clinton (1967–68), *John Conklin* (1967–75, 1976–80, 1982–84, 1985–86), Robert Dahlstrom (1983–84), *Virginia Dancy* (1967–75), Robert Darling (1969–70), *Karl Eigsti* (1979–81, 1982–84), Eldon Elder (1979–80), Joe Erdey (1977–78), Kenneth Foy (1975–76), Philip Gilliam (1973–74), James Gohl (1967–68), Peter Gould (1973–74), David Gropman (1980–81), *David Hager* (1966–67), Douglas Heap (1974–75), George Hedges (1973–74), J. Allen Highfill (1980–81), Donald Howarth

(1980–81), Peter Hunt (1967–68), Andrew Jackness (1985–86), Vanessa James (1968–70), *David Jenkins* (1971–80, 1981–86), *John Jensen* (1977–84), *Marjorie Bradley Kellogg* (1971–73, 1974–79, 1980–85), Richard Klein (1967–68), *Hugh Landwehr* (1980–86), Ming Cho Lee (1976–77), Santo Loquasto (1967–68, 1969–70), Kert Lundell (1970–72), Laura Maurer (1981–82), David Mitchell (1976–77), Mark Louis Negin (1977–78), Thom Peterson (1969–70), *Steven Rubin* (1972–84, 1985–86), Tom Schwinn (1984–85), John Sherman (1969–70), David Taylor (1969–70), Hal Tine (1970–71), Therald Todd (1967–68), Ronald Wallace (1968–69), Tony Walton (1975–76, 1979–80), *Elmon Webb* (1967–75), Peter Wingate (1970–71), *Michael Yeargan* (1982–86).

Costume Designers: Will Steven Armstrong (1968–69), *Whitney Blausen* (1970–74, 1979–80), Elizabeth Clinton (1969–70), *John Conklin* (1974–75, 1977–78, 1979–80), *Linda Fisher* (1972–73, 1975–76, 1977–80, 1981–82, 1984–86), Jess Goldstein (1985–86), Dona Granata (1979–80), Jane Greenwood (1983–85), Marci Heiser (1969–70), Walker Hicklin (1984–85), J. Allen Highfill (1980–81), *Rosemary Ingham* (1966–68), Gary Jones (1982–84), *Rachel Kurland* (1979–82), Natasha Landau (1983–84), William Ivey Long (1983–84), Santo Loquasto (1970–71), Margaret Mahoney (1967–69), Jennifer von Mayrhauser (1984–86), Ruth Morley (1973–74), David Murin (1983–85), Carol Oditz (1978–79, 1981–82), Dunya Ramicova (1985–86), Lewis Rampino (1970–71), Michele S. Reisch (1976–77), Sally Richardson (1983–84), Carrie F. Robbins (1976–77), *Ann Roth* (1981–84), Mary Strief (1976–77, 1978–79), Michael Stuart (1979–80), *Alec Sutherland* (1967–70), *Jania Szatanski* (1973–76), Noel Taylor (1983–84), *Bill Walker* (1971–79, 1980–86), Peter Wingate (1970–71), Robert Wojewodski (1982–84).

Lighting Designers: Daniel Clayman (1980–81), *Pat Collins* (1982–86), Geoffrey T. Cunningham (1981–82), Joe Erdey (1977–78), *Jamie Gallagher* (1973–84), Paul Gallo (1982–84), John Hastings (1984–85), Debra J. Kletterm (1984–85), *Judy Rasmuson* (1970–73, 1974–76, 1978–86), Jennifer Tipton (1979–80), *Ronald Wallace* (1968–86).

Musical Directors: Tom Fay (1982–84, 1985–86), Murry Sidlin (1984–85).

Choreographer: Dan Siretta (1982–83).

Composer: Stanley Silverman (1982–83).

Actors and Actresses: Lucinda Adams (1984–85), Madeleine de Jean Adams (1970–72), Andra Akers (1978–79), Tom Aldredge (1984–85), Mary Alice (1974–75, 1982–84), Cosmo Allegretti (1983–84), Beth Allen (1985–86), Karen Allen (1985–86), Raymond Allen (1966–67), Robert Byron Allen (1982–84), Eunice Anderson (1978–79), Carol Androsky (1977–78), Victor Argo (1977–78), Bob Ari (1977–78), Mark Arnott (1984–85), Walter Atamaniuk (1981–82), William Atherton (1975–76), Eileen Atkins (1979–80), *Tom Atkins* (1967–69, 1970–73, 1982–83), Jayne Atkinson (1985–86), Richard Backus (1977–78, 1985–86), Kevin Bacon (1979–80), Maggie Baird (1983–84), Henry Bal (1968–69), Lisa Banes (1980–81), Margaret Barker (1980–81, 1984–85), Barbara Barrie (1985–86), *William Barry* (1980–84), D'Jamin Bartlett (1982–84), Phyllis Bash (1985–86), John Basinger (1981–82), Tom Batten (1983–84), *Emery Battis* (1971–82), *Louis Beachner* (1971–74, 1975–76, 1979–80, 1983–84), John Beal (1971–72), Alice Beardsley (1981–82), Graham Beckel (1977–78), Richard Bekins (1985–86), Paul Benedict (1982–84), Tom Berenger (1976–77), Tanya Berezin (1981–82), Alan Bergreen (1982–84), David Berman (1979–80), Clayton Berry (1982–84), Robert Beseda (1980–81), James Bigwood (1977–78), Benjamin Billingsley (1984–85), Ronald Bishop (1970–71), Robert Blackburn (1980–81), Ian Blackman (1979–80), Pamela Blafer (1968–69), Pamela Blair (1979–80), Paul Blake (1969–70), Larry Blauvelt (1967–68), Mark Blum (1980–81, 1982–84), Rudy Bond (1976–77), Curtis Borg (1980–82), Katherine Borowitz (1983–84), Alexandra Borrie (1980–81), John Bowman (1985–86), Nancy Boykin (1980–

81), *John Braden* (1968–69, 1971–75, 1978–79, 1983–84), Michael Bradshaw (1967–68), Thomas Brand (1984–86), Michael Brandon (1982–84), Alice Brereton (1977–78), Maurice Breslow (1968–69), Rand Bridges (1981–82), *Fran Brill* (1975–76, 1982–84, 1985–86), David Brizzolara (1985–86), Elaine Bromka (1977–78), Jacob Brooke (1976–77), Preston Brooks (1979–80), Peter Brouwer (1970–72), Arvin Brown (1969–70), Blair Brown (1975–76, 1977–78), Roscoe Lee Browne (1976–77), *Shirley Bryan* (1970–75, 1976–77, 1980–82), Larry Bryggman (1968–69), Stephen Burleigh (1984–85), Karen Burlingame (1985–86), Leo Burmester (1984–85), Robert Burns (1981–82), Jasper Burr (1981–82), Clyde Burton (1972–73), Timothy Busfield (1980–81), David A. Butler (1973–74, 1978–79), Michael Butler (1984–85), Ralph Byers (1981–82), David Byrd (1966–67, 1974–75), James Cahill (1976–77), William Cain (1984–85), Thomas Calabro (1982–84), Devern Cameron (1968–69), Joanne Camp (1982–84), William Carden (1979–80), Mary Carney (1983–84), Beeson Carroll (1977–78, 1984–85), Helena Carroll (1977–78), John Carroll (1979–80), Myra Carter (1977–78, 1984–85), Robert Caserta (1981–82), Dana Cashman (1982–84), Philip Casnoff (1982–84), Leslie Cass (1966–67), *Veronica Castang* (1973–74, 1978–80), Alan Castner (1972–73), *John Cazale* (1969–72), Sara Chaiken (1984–85), *Stockard Channing* (1981–84), John Charles-O'Leary (1983–84), Nora Chester (1977–78), Dominic Chianese (1981–82, 1983–84), Sarah Chodoff (1979–80), Octavio Ciano (1977–78), Leo Ciceri (1967–68), *Charles Cioffi* (1967–68, 1970–71, 1972–74, 1977–78, 1982–84), Josh Clark (1979–80), Caitlin Clarke (1983–84), *David Clennon* (1970–71, 1973–74, 1977–78), Glenn Close (1976–77), Carolyn Coates (1974–75, 1976–77), Frederick Coffin (1974–75, 1977–78), Megan Cole (1978–79), Olivia Cole (1970–71, 1973–74), Nancy Coleman (1973–74), Paul Collins (1974–75), Joel Colodner (1975–76), Robert Colston (1984–85), David Combs (1980–81), Katina Commings (1972–73), Matt Conley (1971–72), Jane Connell (1971–72), Frances Conroy (1981–82), Jarlath Conroy (1975–76), *Frank Converse* (1973–76, 1977–78), William Converse-Roberts (1984–85), John R. Conway (1983–84), Kevin Conway (1967–68), Fred Cook (1973–74), Roderick Cook (1976–77), Roy Cooper (1976–77), Gretchen Corbett (1973–74, 1981–82), Ted Cornell (1970–71), *Peggy Cosgrave* (1982–84, 1985–86), Staats Cotsworth (1971–72), Jack Coulter (1985–86), Richard Council (1979–80, 1983–84), Michael Countryman (1984–85), Margaret Cowles (1966), Tom Crawley (1969–70), Lou Criscuolo (1982–84), Paddy Croft (1980–81, 1983–84), Carey Cromelin (1985–86), David Cromwell (1985–86), John Cromwell (1969–71), *Jane Cronin* (1981–84), Hume Cronyn (1976–77), John Cunningham (1983–84), Leigh Curran (1977–78), William Cwikowski (1970–71), John D'Amico (1981–82), Cathryn Damon (1974–75, 1981–82), Jim Dale (1978–79), Susan Danielle (1982–84), Randy Danson (1984–85), Severn Darden (1981–82), Jennifer Darling (1966–67), Jack Davidson (1979–80, 1983–84), Lance Davis (1975–76, 1977–78), Bruce Davison (1981–82), Robertson Dean (1985–86), Dalton Dearborn (1966–67), Peter DeMaio (1972–73), Ray DeMatteis (1967–68, 1969–70), Jeffrey DeMunn (1981–82), Jake Dengel (1972–73, 1981–82), Brian Dennehy (1981–82), David DeRose (1974–75), Jon DeVries (1981–82, 1983–84), Colleen Dewhurst (1975–76, 1984–85), Dawn Didawick (1979–80), Ernie Dingo (1984–85), Tom Donaldson (1979–80), Peter Donat (1971–72), Nancy Donohue (1974–75), John Doolittle (1979–80, 1981–82), Richard Dow (1978–79), Richard Dreyfuss (1981–82, 1983–84), Ralph Drischell (1972–73), Alice Drummond (1976–77), Cara Duff-MacCormick (1981–82, 1983–84), Thyli Dumakude (1985–86), *Mildred Dunnock* (1968–71, 1972–73, 1975–76), le Clanche du Rand (1977–78), Richard Dysart (1970–71), Edward Earle (1981–82), Emery Ebert (1975–76), *Joyce Ebert* (1968–86), Jo-Ann Ebony (1985–86), January

Eckert (1973–74), Barbara eda-Young (1977–78), *George Ede* (1971–74), Michael Egan (1982–84), *Jill Eikenberry* (1979–80, 1982–84), Harrison Eldredge (1982–84), Kevin Ellicott (1974–75), Patricia Elliott (1976–77), Richard Eno (1967–68), Dan Entriken (1984–85), Alvin Epstein (1970–71), Pierre Epstein (1981–82), Jim Erickson (1971–72), Christine Estabrook (1981–82), Eleanor Evans (1966–67), Peter Evans (1975–76), Patricia Falkenhain (1985–86), Richard Fancy (1968–69), Kimberly Farr (1983–84), Michele Farr (1985–86), Jan Farrand (1966–67), Marjorie Lynne Feiner (1970–71), Alan Feinstein (1981–82), *Clarence Felder* (1975–76, 1977–78, 1981–82), Will Fenno (1970–72), Denise Ferguson (1966–68), James Ferrier (1975–76), Joyce Fidor (1979–80), Joe Fields (1975–76), Wendy Ann Finnegan (1982–84), J. J. Fiorello (1984–85), Jerry Fischer (1973–74), *Geraldine Fitzgerald* (1972–77, 1978–79), Louisa Flaningam (1982–84), Jane Fleiss (1985–86), Bill Flynn (1980–81), Steven Flynn (1983–84), *Mary Fogarty* (1973–78, 1979–80, 1981–82, 1983–84), Julie Follansbee (1977–78), Elizabeth Foster (1970–71), Monique Fowler (1980–81), Colin Fox (1983–84), Catherine Frankfurt (1982–83), Ron Frazier (1984–85), Erik Fredricksen (1977–78), Valerie French (1976–77), Leonard Frey (1983–84), *Peter Friedman* (1979–80, 1984–86), Vaughn Fritts (1984–85), Paula Fritz (1982–83), Anthony Fusco (1983–84), Boyd Gaines (1984–85), Megan Gallagher (1984–85), *Peter Gallagher* (1980–81, 1982–83, 1985–86), Jane Galloway (1979–80, 1984–85), Rosemarie Gambardella (1984–85), Robin Gammell (1973–75), Don Gantry (1974–76), Victor Garber (1974–76), David Gardiner (1968–69), Minnie Gaster (1971–72), Robert Gaus (1966–67), Kevin Geer (1982–83), Edmond Genest (1982–83), Avril Gentles (1976–77), Charles Gerald (1968–69), Daniel Gerroll (1983–84), Vicky Geyer (1973–74), Meg Gianotti (1982–83), Stefan Gierasch (1971–72, 1984–85), Steven Gillborn (1980–81), Paul Gleason (1982–83), *John Glover* (1970–71, 1972–73, 1981–82), Mal Goering (1981–82), Peter Michael Goetz (1980–82), Sharon Goldman (1978–79), Merwin Goldsmith (1983–84), Tony Goldwyn (1985–86), Rob Gomes (1982–83), Lisa Goodman (1982–83), Eve Bennet Gordon (1981–82), Haskell Gordon (1974–75), Gordon Gould (1971–72), Michael Govan (1977–78, 1979–80), Mark Graham (1978–79), Peter Graham (1985–86), Kelsey Grammer (1982–83), David Marshall Grant (1981–83), Grayce L. Grant (1969–70), Sarine Grant (1971–72), Ernest Graves (1977–78), Kenneth Gray (1977–78), James Greene (1975–76, 1984–85), Marvin Greene (1983–84), Rose Gregorio (1976–77), Joe Grifasi (1978–79), *Sean Griffin* (1972–76), Harry Groenier (1977–79), David Gropman (1980–81), Edward Grover (1973–74), Robin Groves (1980–81), Jon David Gruett (1984–85), Jonathan Hadary (1982–83), Karen Hageman (1982–83), Kenneth Haigh (1980–81), Donna Haley (1977–78), Pater Haller (1982–83), Dorothea Hammond (1981–82), *Bara-Cristin Hansen* (1975–76, 1980–81, 1983–84), *William Hansen* (1968–70, 1971–72), James Harker (1973–74), Jennie Harker (1977–78), James Harper (1979–80), Jessica Harper (1985–86), Robert Harper (1977–78, 1981–82), Baxter Harris (1981–82), Julie Harris (1983–84), David Hartman (1981–82), Christopher Hastings (1970–72), James Hayden (1981–82), William Hayes (1967–68), Anthony Heald (1982–83), John Heard (1975–76), *George Hearn* (1972–73, 1975–76, 1977–80), Robert Hearn (1984–85), Deborah Hedwall (1980–81), Bette Henritze (1976–77), Edward Herrmann (1978–80), Freda Herseth (1984–85), Roland Hewgill (1967–68, 1979–80), Gerald Hiken (1981–82), Margaret Hilton (1981–82), Rose Marie Himes (1980–81), Joseph Hindy (1967–68), Skip Hinnant (1977–78), Dale Hodges (1976–77), Jack Hoffmann (1973–74), Howard Hoig (1973–74), Ruby Holbrook (1972–73, 1975–76), Owen Hollander (1977–78), Tommy Hollis (1985–86), Frank Hooper (1970–71), John Horton

(1976–78), Ray Horvath (1981–82), David Houde (1982–83), Michael Houlihan (1975–76), Robin Howard (1978–79), Janet Hubert (1985–86), Marcie Hubert (1966–67), Walter Hudson (1985–86), David Huffman (1974–75), Tresa Hughes (1973–74), *Thomas Hulce* (1978–79, 1980–81, 1985–86), Michael Hume (1984–85), *James Hummert* (1972–76), *Linda Hunt* (1971–73, 1974–75, 1976–78), Neil Hunt (1976–78), Marsha Hunter (1984–85), Kristen Hurst-Hyde (1984–85), Mary Beth Hurt (1980–81), Laurie Hutchinson (1966–67), Peter Hydock (1983–84), Peter Iacangelo (1977–78), Andrea Iovine (1981–83), Paul Henry Itkin (1970–71), Dana Ivey (1982–83), Lisa Jablow (1984–85), Anne Jackson (1976–77), Clifton James (1976–77, 1980–81), Francesca James (1977–78), Stephen James (1984–85), Richard Jamieson (1977–78), Jim Jansen (1979–80), James Javore (1984–85), William Jay (1971–72), Annalee Jefferies (1984–85), John Jellison (1981–82), *Ken Jenkins* (1967–69), Richard Jenkins (1982–83), Lucinda Jenney (1984–85), John Jensen (1977–78), Timothy Jerome (1976–77), Jennifer Jestin (1973–74), J. S. Johnson (1966–67), Peter C. Johnson (1977–78), Jeffrey Jones (1984–85), Todd Jones (1973–74), Richard Jordan (1982–83), Betsy Joslyn (1982–83), Robert Joy (1978–79), Robert Judd (1979–80), Jane Kaczmarek (1985–86), Diane Kagan (1983–84), Gus Kaikonen (1979–80), Toni Kalem (1976–77), Nancy Elizabeth Kammer (1983–84), John Kani (1974–75, 1980–81), Ben Kapen (1975–77), Steve Karp (1973–74), Richard Kavanaugh (1978–79), *Stacey Keach* (1966–67, 1971–72), Steven Keats (1976–77), Harvey Keitel (1968–69), Nancy Kelly (1974–75), Linda Kelsey (1973–74), *Laurie Kennedy* (1967–72, 1977–78), Sean Kernan (1966–67), Kathleen Keske (1984–85), Daniel F. Keyes (1983–84), Ruth Kidder (1980–81), Richard Kiley (1985–86), Kim Kimbrough (1979–80), Charmion King (1979–80), Gary Kirsch (1982–83), Adelaide Klein (1969–70), Jacqueline Knapp (1978–79), Kurt Knudson (1978–80), Robert Koon (1981–83), Frank Kopye (1982–83), Jon Korkes (1983–84), Bruce Kramer (1984–85), William Krinsey (1966–67), Nancy Kulp (1983–84), Wally Kurth (1982–83), *Swoosie Kurtz* (1973–74, 1975–76, 1979–80), Richard Kuss (1971–72, 1978–79), Steven Kyprianides (1968–69), Caroline Lagerfelt (1982–83), Christine Lahti (1982–83, 1984–85), Sofia Landon (1982–83, 1985–86), Nathan Lane (1984–85), Robert Lansing (1977–78, 1983–84), Deborah Lapidus (1983–84), Lori Larsen (1983–84), Richard Larson (1969–70), Harris Laskawy (1979–80), Dick Latessa (1973–74), Frank Latimore (1978–79), Sue Lawless (1971–72), Emily Lay (1969–70), *David H. Leary* (1972–74), Robin Leary (1983–84), *Suzanne Lederer* (1972–76, 1977–78), Doug Lee (1974–75), *Will Lee* (1970–72), Adam LeFevre (1980–81), Johanna Leister (1978–79), *Joseph Leon* (1971–72, 1981–82, 1983–84), Thomas Leopold (1972–73), Calvin Levels (1982–83), Michael Levin (1966–67), Anna Levine (1977–78), Nicholas Levitin (1968–69), Carol-Jean Lewis (1977–78, 1984–85), Tommy Lewis (1984–85), Anna Lindig (1966–67), *John Lithgow* (1972–73, 1977–78, 1983–84), Christopher Lloyd (1975–76), Tony LoBianco (1981–82), John Long (1973–74), Robert P. Lonicki (1981–82), Christopher Loomis (1977–78), J. Frank Lucas (1976–77), Laurence Luckinbill (1976–77), Alvin K.U. Lu (1978–79), David Lurie (1981–82), Marlena Lustik (1977–78), Dorothy Lyman (1975–76), Annie McBreevey (1977–78), Paul McCrane (1983–84), J. Perry McDonald (1968–69), Ann McDonough (1985–86), Edwin J. McDonough (1977–78), Everett McGill (1976–77), Katherine McGrath (1977–78), Daniel McGuire (1980–81), *Linda McGuire* (1972–73, 1975–76, 1985–86), *Michael McGuire* (1966–68), *Stephen McHattie* (1974–76), Bernie McInerney (1981–82), Will McIntyre (1982–83), Siobhan McKenna (1967–68), Barbara MacKenzie (1973–74), Peter MacKenzie (1985–86), Albert Macklin (1982–83), Mark McLaughlin (1970–80), *John McMartin* (1976–77, 1978–79, 1980–82), Kenneth McMillan (1975–76), Sam McMurray (1983–84), Dermot McNamara (1967–68), Robert

Macnaughton (1984–85), Peter MacNicol (1982–83), W. H. Macy (1985–86), Valerie
Mahaffey (1981–82), *Joseph Maher* (1972–74, 1976–78), Kenneth R. Main (1983–84),
Vickie Mallory (1969–70), Graceanne Malloy (1981–82), Nancy Marchand (1984–85),
Jeanette Marcucci (1981–82), Lois Markle (1979–80), Jack Marks (1976–77), E. G.
Marshall (1973–74), Tom Martin (1975–76), Greg Martyn (1983–84), Cynthia Mason
(1977–78), Richard D. Masur (1972–73), *Carmen Mathews* (1973–75, 1976–77), *Richard
Mathews* (1976–78, 1979–81, 1984–85), *Roberta Maxwell* (1971–74, 1982–83), Beverly
May (1977–78), Elaine May (1970–80), Ruth Maynard (1968–69), Michael Medeiros
(1981–82), Heidi Mefford (1970–71), *Stephen Mendillo* (1973–76, 1978–80, 1981–82),
Eda Reiss Merin (1965–66), Joanna Merlin (1979–80), Mark Metcalf (1983–84), Nancy
Mette (1985–86), Kate Michelle (1966–67), *Lynn Milgrim* (1973–75), Michael J. Miller
(1977–78), Raleigh Miller (1968–69), Mary Jane Milli (1966–67), Robert Milli (1966–
67), Dana Mills (1977–78, 1980–81), *Jan Miner* (1975–76, 1977–78, 1979–80, 1984–
85), Evan H. Miranda (1982–83), Garry Mitchell (1967–68), *Robert Moberly* (1966–
67), Zakes Mokae (1970–71), David Monzione (1982–83), Charlotte Moore (1976–77,
1984–85), Carol Morell (1970–71), *Rita Moreno* (1973–74, 1976–77), George Morfogen
(1973–74), Mark Moses (1982–83), Tim Moses (1973–74), John Moskoff (1983–84),
Michael Mullins (1974–75), Robert Murch (1972–73, 1976–77), James Murphy (1968–
69), Brian Murray (1970–71, 1975–76), Peg Murray (1980–81), Tony Musante (1977–
78), Joseph F. Muzicar (1972–73), Tania Myren (1979–80), Tom Nardini (1980–81),
James Naughton (1971–72, 1982–83, 1985–86), Jeffrey Nelson (1970–71), *Ruth Nelson*
(1969–72), John Neville-Andrews (1976–77), Roger Newman (1978–79, 1980–81), Stephen Newman (1977–78), William Newman (1977–78, 1979–80), Mike Nichols (1979–
80), Walker Niehenke (1979–80), Kristine E. Nielson (1983–84), *James Noble* (1975–
78), Sally Noble (1966–67), Charles W. Noel (1982–83), Winston Ntshona (1974–75,
1980–81), Tom Offt (1982–83), Brad O'Hare (1984–85), Alexandra O'Karma (1985–
86), Michael O'Keefe (1975–76, 1980–81), Aideen O'Kelly (1980–81), Rochelle Oliver
(1980–81), Fredi Olster (1980–81), Eric O'Nanian (1974–75), Dick O'Neill (1981–82),
Ed O'Neill (1981–82), Milo O'Shea (1975–76), Susan O'Sullivan (1981–82), Jess Osuna
(1985–86), Albert Ottenheimer (1966–67), Timmy Ousey (1973–74), Meg Wynn Owen
(1980–81), Al Pacino (1980–81), Leland Palmer (1979–80), Antonino Pandolfo (1973–
74), David Parker (1972–73), Douglas Parker (1980–81), Ellen Parker (1984–85), Norman Parker (1985–86), Elizabeth Parrish (1975–76), Robert Pastene (1981–82), Mandy
Patinkin (1976–77), Mayme Paul (1982–83), Nancy Paul (1985–86), *Pamela Payton-
Wright* (1973–74, 1977–79, 1984–85), *Patricia Pearcy* (1970–72), Stephen Pearlman
(1981–82), Pippa Pearthree (1983–84), Carmen Pelton (1984–85), Austin Pendleton
(1971–72), Hannibal Penney, Jr. (1974–75), Susan Peretz (1978–79), Rick Pessagno
(1982–83), Ntombi Peters (1982–83), Sarah Peterson (1978–79, 1982–83), Silamour
Philander (1980–81), Peter Piccolo (1980–81), *Christina Pickles* (1972–74, 1976–77,
1981–82), David Pierce (1982–83), Wendell Pierce (1985–86), Richard Pizzini (1981–
82), Alice Playten (1980–81), Don Plumley (1967–68), Joel Polis (1979–80), Philip
Polito (1977–78), Graham Pollock (1973–74), Roy Poole (1982–83), Peggy Pope (1969–
70), Pamela Potillo (1982–83), C. H. Pounder (1977–78), Kobie Powell (1985–86),
Tyrone Power (1982–83), Bruce Probst (1979–80), John Procaccino (1983–84), Michael
Procaccino (1970–71), David Proval (1983–84, 1985–86), Paul Pryor (1984–85), Kathleen Quinlan (1983–84), Andy Rage (1982–83), Ramon Ramos (1981–82), Richard
Ramos (1981–82), Remak Ramsay (1982–83), John Ramsey (1966–67), Jerome Raphel
(1968–69), Marge Redmond (1985–86), Alexander Reed (1984–85), Gavin Reed (1978–

79, 1983–84), Kate Reid (1978–79), Joseph Remmes (1971–72), Judith Resnick (1970–71), Walter Rhodes (1965–67), Bill Rhys (1972–73), Christopher Rich (1979–80), Penelope Richards (1982–83), George C. Rieger (1981–82), Andrea Riskin (1981–82), Barrie Rivchun (1967–68), Jimmy Rivers (1985–86), *Rex Robbins* (1972–76, 1978–79, 1980–82, 1985–86), Tarah Roberts (1982–83), John Roddick (1974–75), Connie Roderick (1984–85), Peter Rogan (1983–84), Michele Roger (1982–83), Jeff Rohde (1980–81), Grant Roll (1970–71), Jay Romig (1971–72), Maury Rosenberg (1982–83), Paul Rosson (1975–76), John Rothman (1980–81), *Paul Rudd* (1971–75), Douglas Ruggiero (1966–67), Tait Rupert (1982–83), Jack Rushen (1981–82), Ellin Ruskin (1975–76, 1977–78), Jeanne Ruskin (1976–77), Leon Russom (1971–72, 1975–76), Steven Ryan (1977–78), David Sabin (1971–72), William Sadler (1978–79), Jose Santana (1980–81), Saundra Santiago (1981–82), *Chris Sarandon* (1968–70), Claude Saucier (1979–80), Justine Saunders (1984–85), John Sayward (1984–85), *Martha Schlamme* (1969–72), Rebecca Schull (1985–86), Jack Schultz (1972–73), Bobby Scott (1979–80), Gayton Scott (1985–86), Pippa Scott (1982–83), John Seitz (1981–82), Roger Omar Serbagi (1967–68), Carolyn Seymour (1980–81), James Seymour (1978–79, 1980–81), Barbara Shannon (1983–84), Michael Shannon (1972–73, 1977–78), *Susan Sharkey* (1974–78, 1979–80), William Sharp (1984–85), Sloane Shelton (1981–82), Paul Shenar (1978–79), John Shepard (1981–82), *Terrence Sherman* (1970–72, 1973–75), Larry Shue (1981–82), Richard B. Shull (1967–68), Ronald Siebert (1972–73, 1975–76), Maureen Silliman (1984–85), Tammy Silva (1982–83), James Silverstein (1973–74), Louis Simmon (1966–67), Charles Simon (1983–84), David Singer (1982–83), Michaelan Sisti (1976–77), Margo Skinner (1984–85), Benjamin Slack (1969–70), Gary Sloan (1980–81), Michael V. Smartt (1985–86), Dugg Smith (1980–81), Jeffrey Smith (1985–86), Laralu Smith (1980–81), Lois Smith (1978–79, 1980–81), Bill Smitrovich (1983–84), Timothy Smyth (1981–82), Donna Snow (1980–81), Monica Snowden (1979–80), Barbara Sohmers (1980–81), Phyllis Somerville (1977–78), *Josef Sommer* (1974–75, 1976–79, 1984–85), Ingrid Sonnichsen (1967–68), Mark Soper (1977–78), Adrian Sparks (1977–78), Frank Speiser (1971–72), John Spencer (1981–82), George Sperdakos (1979–80), *David Spielberg* (1966–67, 1977–78, 1979–80), Brent Spinner (1982–83), Dorothy Stanley (1982–83), *Joel Stedman* (1978–80, 1985–86), *Douglas Stender* (1972–73, 1975–76, 1977–79), Caryl Stern (1971–72), Vincent Stewart (1976–77), Colin Stinton (1983–84), Suzanne Stone (1978–79), Henry Stram (1979–81), David Strathairn (1981–82), James Sutorius (1978–79), Iralene Swain (1985–86), Eric Swanson (1985–86), Dolph Sweet (1975–76), *William Swetland* (1965–66, 1969–70, 1972–79, 1981–86), Anne Swift (1985–86), Donald Symington (1980–81), Eron Tabor (1977–78), Kristoffer Tabori (1976–77), Tony Taddei (1982–84), Jane Tamarkin (1980–81), Nicholas Tamarkin (1985–86), Jessica Tandy (1976–77), Eric Tavares (1968–69), *George Taylor* (1971–72, 1973–75, 1977–78), *Carol Teitel* (1970–72), Mary Testas (1976–77), Phyllis Thaxter (1982–83), *Henry Thomas* (1970–71, 1972–73, 1982–83), Owen Thompson (1982–83), Tazewell Thompson (1973–74), *John Tillinger* (1971–73, 1974–75, 1977–78, 1979–82), John Tillotson (1980–81), James Tolkan (1981–82), Ellen Tovatt (1968–69), Patricia Triana (1977–78), Steven Trinwith (1967–68), Eugene Troobnick (1978–79), *Maria Tucci* (1973–74, 1977–78, 1982–84), Mike Tucker (1966–67), Eric Tull (1980–81), Tamara Tunie (1985–86), Charles Turner (1971–72), Richard Bernard Turner (1976–77), Michael Tylo (1979–80), Paul F. Ugalde (1980–82), James Valentine (1968–69), Stephen Van Benschoten (1971–72), Ted van Griethuysen (1984–85), Nicolette Vannais (1981–82), *Cindy Veasey* (1970–72), *Richard Venture* (1969–71, 1973–75, 1983–84), Helen Verbit (1971–72), Virginia

Vestoff (1977–78), Steve Vilano (1981–82), Fiddle Viracola (1975–76), Christie Virtue (1973–74), James Vitale (1981–82), Jack Waddell (1985–86), Ralph Waite (1968–69), Thomas Waites (1980–81), Christopher Walken (1972–73), *Lee Wallace* (1966–67, 1971–72), Eli Wallach (1976–77), Richard Walley (1984–85), J. T. Walsh (1979–80, 1981–82), Tenney Walsh (1981–82), Scott Walters (1980–81), Janet Ward (1978–79), Laura Waterbury (1977–78), Peter Webster (1980–81), *Jean Weigel* (1968–70), Bruce Weitz (1966–67), Peter Weller (1984–85), Kenneth Welsh (1979–80), Donald West (1966–67), Jack Wetherall (1980–81), Laura White (1985–86), Christine Whitmore (1974–75), Kenneth Wickes (1969–70), *Dianne Wiest* (1968–70), Kate Wilkinson (1966–67, 1978–79), *Ellis "Skeeter" Williams* (1980–81, 1983–84, 1985–86), Treat Williams (1985–86), Carol Williard (1977–78), Rudolph Willrich (1974–75), Mary Louise Wilson (1973–74), Beatrice Winde (1974–75), Mark Windworth (1972–73), Kitty Winn (1971–72, 1976–77), Alex Wipf (1985–86), Brad Witsger (1982–83), Kelly Wolf (1983–84), Nancy Wolfe (1982–83), Angela Wood (1973–74), Grace Woodard (1976–77), Nicholas Woodeson (1977–79), Richard Woods (1981–82, 1983–84), Joanne Woodward (1985–86), Max Wright (1977–78, 1981–82), Michael Wright (1985–86), *Teresa Wright* (1971–72, 1974–75), Earl Wunderlee (1968–69), Thomas Young (1985–86), Michael Youngfellow (1966–67), Harris Yulin (1979–80, 1981–82), *Edward Zang* (1970–71, 1973–74), Nicki Lynn Zanni (1984–85), Anthony Zerbe (1979–80), Stephanie Zimbalist (1982–83), Randolyn Zinn (1974–75).

REPERTORY

1965–66: *The Crucible, The Hostage, Little Mary Sunshine, The Private Ear* and *The Public Eye, The Plough and the Stars, Volpone, The Pirates of Penzance, The Trojan Women, Hay Fever, The Rivals, Long Day's Journey into Night.*

1966–67: *The Loon Hunt* and *I'm Nobody, Thumby, The Happy Haven, Oh What a Lovely War, The Three Sisters, The Man Who Came to Dinner, Misalliance, Mother Courage and Her Children, The Tavern, The Night of the Iguana.*

1967–68: *The Glass Menagerie, The Rehearsal, The Playboy of the Western World, Room Service, A Whistle in the Dark, The Doctor in Spite of Himself* and *The Bald Soprano, Tiny Alice,* "Don Juan in Hell" from Act III of *Man and Superman.*

1968–69: *The Lion in Winter, The Play's the Thing, Epitaph for George Dillon, American Hurrah, The Indian Wants the Bronx* and *It's Called the Sugar Plum, Under Milk Wood, Ghosts.*

1969–70: *Tartuffe, Tango, The Pirate, Country People, Black Comedy* and *The White Liars, A Day in the Death of Joe Egg, Spoon River Anthology, A Thousand Clowns.*

1970–71: *The Skin of Our Teeth, A Place Without Doors* and *Yegor Bulichov, She Stoops to Conquer, Solitaire/Double Solitaire, The Blood Knot, Heartbreak House, The Price.*

1971–72: *You Can't Take It with You, The Contractor, A Streetcar Named Desire, Hamlet, The Way of the World, Troika: An Evening of Russian Comedy, The Iceman Cometh, Patrick's Day.*

1972–73: *The Lady's Not for Burning, The Changing Room, What Price Glory?, Trelawny of the "Wells," Juno and the Paycock, Forget-Me-Not, Dance to Death,* Part I, *Miss Julie.*

1973–74: *The Master Builder, The Widowing of Mrs. Holroyd, Mornings at Seven, A Pagan Place, The Sea Gull, The National Health, The Resistible Rise of Arturo Ui.*

1974–75: *The Soldier's Tale, The Knight of the Burning Pestle, Ah, Wilderness!, Pygmalion, You're Too Tall, but Come Back in Two Weeks, Afore Night Come, Richard III, Sizwe Bansi Is Dead, The Island.*

1975–76: *Artichoke, The Show-Off, What Every Woman Knows, Streamers, On the Outside, On the Inside, The House of Mirth, Daarlin' Juno.*

1976–77: *Alphabetical Order, The Autumn Garden, Home, The Shadow Box, Saint Joan, Absent Friends, The Rose Tattoo, The Gin Game.*

1977–78: *Hobson's Choice, The Lunch Girls, The Recruiting Officer, Spokesong, S.S. Glencairn: The Sea Plays, The Philadelphia Story, Two Brothers, Macbeth.*

1978–79: *Journey's End, I Sent a Letter To My Love, Summerfolk, Biography, Rosmersholm, Hillbilly Women, Privates on Parade.*

1979–80: *Watch on the Rhine, Jetters, Double Feature, The Beach House, The Caretaker, Mary Barnes, Who's Afraid of Virginia Woolf?, Cyrano de Bergerac.*

1980–81: *American Buffalo, Solomon's Child, Waiting for Godot, The Admirable Crichton, Close Ties, Romeo and Juliet, Bodies, A Life, The Lion in Winter, Private Lives.*

1981–82: *This Story of Yours, A Day in the Death of Joe Egg, A View from the Bridge, The Workroom, Lakeboat, The Doctor's Dilemma, The Carmone Brothers' Italian Food Products Corp's Annual Pasta Pageant, Ethan Frome, The Front Page, Molly.*

1982–83: *Open Admissions, Two by A. M., Holiday, Quartermaine's Terms, Another Country, The Lady and the Clarinet, The Guardsman, Free and Clear, Pal Joey, The Cherry Orchard.*

1983–84: *The Hostage, Not Quite Jerusalem, Accent on Youth, Requiem for a Heavyweight, Shivaree, The Homesteaders, The Bathers, Under the Ilex.*

1984–85: *Tobacco Road, Rainsnakes, Oliver, Oliver, The Common Pursuit, Blue Window, Cat on a Hot Tin Roof, Albert Herring, Bullie's House.*

1985–86: *Paris Bound, Pride and Prejudice, Crystal Clear, The Normal Heart, The Glass Menagerie, Fugue, Lost in the Stars.*

BIBLIOGRAPHY

Published Sources:

New York Times, 1965–86.

Barrett, Daniel. "Long Wharf Theatre." *Theatre Companies of the the World*, vol. 2, edited by Colby H. Kullman and William C. Young. Westport, Conn. Greenwood Press, 1986.

Novick, Julius. *Beyond Broadway: The Quest for Permanent Theatres*. New York: Hill and Wang, 1968.

Theatre Profiles, Vols. 1–7. New York: Theatre Communications Group, 1973–85.

Theatre World 1966–67 through *1985–86*. New York: Crown Publishers, 1967–87.

Weldon B. Durham

LORETTO-HILTON REPERTORY THEATRE. See REPERTORY THEATRE OF ST. LOUIS.

M

MABOU MINES had its origin in 1964 when Lee Breuer, Ruth Maleczech, and JoAnne Akalaitis, members of the Actor's Workshop* in San Francisco, began to experiment together and in collaboration with dancers, musicians, and visual artists on the development of new theatrical forms. In Europe, after the demise of the Actor's Workshop in 1966, these three were joined by composer Philip Glass and actor David Warrilow. The theatre collective, later called Mabou Mines, after the town in Nova Scotia near where the group rehearsed in the summer, was formed in New York City in 1969 to produce Breuer's *The Red Horse Animation*. The group's performance at the Paula Cooper Gallery prompted Ellen Stewart to invite the company to become a resident of her LaMama Experimental Theatre Club, the center of theatre experimentation in New York in the 1960s.

While a resident of LaMama, Mabou Mines received a three-year Ford Foundation grant, which provided a studio and a weekly salary of $50 for each member. At first the company found the theatre world unresponsive to its novelty, but the art world more receptive. Mabou Mines performed in galleries and museums in collaborations with visual artists. *The Arc-Welding Piece* (1972) included the work of sculptor Jene High Stein, while *Send/Receive/Send* (1974) relied on the contributions of visual artist Keith Sonnier. The Ford grant terminated in 1973, and Mabou Mines left LaMama. Then they received their first grant from the N.F.A. Artservices, and in 1974 the company moved from museums to theatres. *The Red Horse Animation* (the stability of the company allows it to keep pieces in repertory for years) and *The B. Beaver Animation* were performed together at the Theater of the New City, the Performing Garage, and the Byrd Hoffman School. Mabou Mines aligned with A Bunch of Experimental Theatres of New York, Inc., in the early 1970s. The Bunch (as it preferred to be known) included The Ridiculous Theatre Company, The Ontological-Hysteric Theatre, Richard Schechner's Performance Group, The Monk/The

House, and Mabou Mines. Quite diverse in their styles, the Bunch was united by "thinking of their work not as underground but as popular" (*New York Times*, July 30, 1974, p. 23). By the early 1980s the avant-garde had focused on a genre known as "performance art," merging theatre with music and dance, cinema and video, painting and sculpture. Since its formation Mabou Mines has remained in the forefront of this movement.

The work of Mabou Mines synthesizes motivational acting in the tradition of Konstantin Stanislavski with techniques borrowed from Jerzy Grotowski's more presentational approach to acting. Choral monologues rooted in the dramaturgy of Bertolt Brecht are joined with narrative dance adapted from Kabuki and Kathakali. Concern with acting styles, with postmodern music, and with abstract visual imagery coexists with a commitment to language as the basic ingredient of theatre. Mabou Mines is broadly eclectic in its efforts to extend the possibilities of theatre into the visual arts.

In 1975 *Mabou Mines Presents Samuel Beckett* opened at the Theatre for the New City in New York City, eliciting the group's first major response from the press and establishing it as a foremost interpreter of Beckett's work. Joseph Papp, producer of the New York Shakespeare Festival, saw the work and asked Mabou Mines to perform at the Public Theater. For the next decade the group performed at least once piece each year at the Public Theater.

In 1976 David Warrilow won a *Village Voice* "Obie" for his performance in *The Lost Ones*, JoAnne Akalaitis won for her direction of *Cascando*, and Philip Glass for his musical compositions for Mabou Mines. Breuer's *The Shaggy Dog Animation*, created in collaboration with puppetmaker-performer Linda Hartinian, artist Gordon Matta-Clark, and painter-sculptor L. B. Dallas, opened in January 1978. The work won a *Village Voice* "Obie," the Villager Theatre Award, and the *Soho News* Award for Best Ensemble. Since its founding, Mabou Mines has received fifteen "Obies" and numerous other awards, including the Brandeis University Creative Arts Awards' Citation in Theatre Arts in 1984. With the exception of an initial review by Clive Barnes in 1970, critical reception of the group's work has been generously receptive. In total, Mabou Mines has received forty-one awards, including an Obie for "Sustained Achievement."

Mabou Mines has remained a collective, a democracy. As of 1985, the company consisted of nine members: JoAnne Akalaitis, Lee Breuer, L. B. Dallas, Ellen McElduff, Ruth Maleczech, Greg Mehrton, Frederick Neumann, Terry O'Reilly, and William Raymond. Most members perform and involve themselves in technical theatre and publicity as well. When asked what it means to be a member, Greg Mehrton (the youngest member of Mabou Mines) replied: "You have to go to all the meetings, approve all the budgets, you're involved in everything. Yesterday I wrote three letters trying to raise money for my play, painted the bathroom at P.S. 122 [Mabou Mines' rehearsal studio] and interviewed people for the fund raising job" (quoted in Don Shewey, "The Many Voices of Mabou Mines." *American Theatre* 1 [June 1984]: 42).

Of the current members, Lee Breuer has directed thirteen of Mabou Mines' twenty-eight works. JoAnne Akalaitis has directed five; Ruth Maleczech, four; Greg Mehrton, one; and Frederick Neumann, one. Neumann also directed *Company* with Honora Ferguson, and Bill Raymond directed *Cold Harbor* with its author, Dale Worsley. Mabou Mines' one concession to standard theatre roles is that L. B. Dallas has emerged as a full-time technical advisor.

The company also collaborates quite frequently with artists outside the company: Michael Kuhling, John Fistos, Charles Cowing, Stephanie Rudolph, and Julie Archer. The company continues to expand its associations with new actors and new artists in other media.

PERSONNEL

JoAnne Akalaitis (1969–86), Lee Breuer (1969–86), L. B. Dallas (1979–86), Philip Glass (1969–86), Ruth Maleczech (1969–86), Ellen McElduff (1983–86), Greg Mehrton (1981–86), B.-St. John Schofield (1981–84), Frederick Neumann (1971–86), Terry O'Reilly (1972–86), William Raymond (1975–86), David Warrilow (1969–78).

REPERTORY

1969: *The Red Horse Animation.*
1972: *Music for Voices, The Arc-Welding Piece.*
1973: *Send/Receive/Send.*
1974: *Play, Come and Go, The Lost Ones.*
1975: *Cascando, The B. Beaver Animation.*
1976: *The Saint and the Football Player.*
1977: *Dressed Like an Egg.*
1979: *The Shaggy Dog Animation.*
1980: *Dead End Kids, A Prelude to Death in Venice, Vanishing Pictures.*
1981: *Wrong Guys.*
1982: *Keeper* and *The Joey Schmerda Story* (radio series), *The Tempest, Cold Harbor.*
1983: *Company, Hajj.*
1984: *Through the Leaves, Pretty Boy, Imagination Dead/Imagine.*
1985: *Flow My Tears, the Policeman Said.*
1985–86: *Starcock, Help Wanted.*

BIBLIOGRAPHY

Published Sources:
New York Times, 1970, 1974–87.
Soho News, April 29, May 5, 1981.
Shewey, Don. "The Many Voices of Mabou Mines." *American Theatre* 1 (June 1984): 5–11, 42.
Theatre Profiles. Vols. 3, 5–8. New York: Theatre Communications Group, 1977, 1982, 1984, 1986, 1988.

Unpublished Source:

"History and Artistic Mission." Mabou Mines Theatre Company. Updated regularly for
    press use.

Susan M. Thornton

[THE] MCCARTER THEATRE COMPANY'S founding resulted from
Princeton University's ownership of a theatre that had become an expensive
liability. Built in 1928 at a cost of $900,000, the 1,079-seat proscenium theatre
was named for Thomas N. McCarter, a wealthy alumnus whose estate provided
most of the funding for the playhouse's construction. This theatre served as the
home of Princeton's Triangle Club, an undergraduate dramatic society that has
produced an original satirical musical annually since 1888, and had contributed
$150,000 toward the building of the theatre. It also served as a road and try-out
house through the thirties and forties. After World War II outside bookings
decreased, and by the late fifties the theatre no longer generated sufficient income
to provide for its maintenance. A faculty committee, chaired by Alan S. Downer,
proposed a radical solution to the problem: the establishment of America's first
resident professional theatre on a university campus. Because Princeton had no
theatre arts department at the time, the new venture was not to be tied to the
university's instructional mission. The stated goal was to provide each undergraduate generation with exposure to a wide range of the world's great dramatic
repertory in high-quality productions. The university administration enthusiastically accepted the proposal, and in 1960 Milton Lyon, the Triangle Club's
professional director, became the first executive producer of the McCarter Theatre
Company.

Lyon solved the problem of instantly establishing a quality resident company
by contracting the APA* (Association of Producing Artists) to present a season
of plays in the McCarter. Because the theatre had to be available to the Triangle
Club for its annual musical, a fall season of plays was presented in October and
November and a spring season, from February through April. The university
provided the new venture with $115,000 and established ticket prices ranging
from $1.75 to $2.50. Opening in October of 1960, the APA company staged
simply mounted productions that emphasized good performances of significant
texts. The exuberantly youthful company captured the fancy of Princeton's undergraduates, and the plays attracted large audiences. But the enterprise lost
money, as expected. Nevertheless, the university's finance committee approved
funding for a second season. However, Lyon could not negotiate a new contract
with APA, and Ellis Raab took the company off to Ann Arbor to establish a
resident professional theatre on the University of Michigan's campus. Arthur
Lithgow, who had been founding director of both the Antioch Shakespeare
Festival and the Akron Shakespeare Festival, assembled a company for the
McCarter's second season. In addition to the evening series of plays, the company
provided low-cost matinees for high school students and furnished teachers with
scripts and teaching aids for each production. Within two years this innovative

policy was to attract more than 25,000 secondary students to the theatre. The resident company's split season format—necessitated by the Triangle Club's claims on the space through the winter holidays—resulted in four plays from the modern repertory in the fall, and three to five pieces from the classic and Elizabethan repertory in the spring.

Milton Lyon left as executive producer of the theatre at the end of the 1962–63 season, and Lithgow was named executive director of the resident company, a position he held until 1971.

Under Lithgow's leadership the company performed an annual season of simply produced, significant plays presented by a company hired for the entire season. Interestingly, the McCarter was not a founding member of the League of Resident Theatres in 1966, nor did the company receive any of the National Endowment for the Arts grants awarded to sixteen regional repertory companies in that year. Granting agencies may have assumed that Princeton University would continue to underwrite the resident company, but the school was becoming increasingly unwilling to do so. Lithgow continued to produce significant plays from a wide range of periods and genres, but only two new works appeared on the McCarter's stage during his regime. Without the often sizable grants that the National Endowment for the Arts and large private foundations were dispensing during the late sixties, Lithgow was forced to hire young, inexperienced performers at modest salaries who, after a season or two, moved on. The list of company alumni from his tenure who have gone on to highly visible and prosperous careers testifies to Lithgow's abilities as a nurturer of young professional actors.

With the death of Alan Downer in January of 1970, Lithgow lost his strongest and most influential supporter on the Princeton faculty. He took a leave of absence at the end of the 1970–71 season, never to return. Daniel Seltzer, a faculty member from Yale with extensive professional theatre experience, filled the vacancy in the English department created by Downer's death, and was named executive producer of the McCarter Theatre Company. Operations were suspended in 1971–72 while new strategies for the theatre's future were developed.

The resident company, bolstered by a Rockefeller Foundation grant of $200,000 over a four-year period, reopened on October 26, 1972, under the administrative direction of Seltzer and the artistic direction of Louis Criss. Rather than assemble a company for the entire season, Criss hired actors for each production. Few performers appeared in more than one play. The repertory differed from that of Lithgow's tenure. Of the five plays produced, only two were from the established canon. A world premiere, an American premiere, and the production of a relatively recent play by Joe Orton filled out Criss' initial season. The new regime differed from the previous twelve years in other important respects. Seltzer became executive producer of both the Resident Theatre and the McCarter Foundation, an administrative structure established to replace Princeton University as the theatre's financial guarantor. Nevertheless, the university continued to contribute approximately $115,000 to the resident company's annual operating budget, which had become, by 1973–74, $335,000. Grants from the Rockefeller Foundation, the Mellon Charitable Trust, the National Endowment for the Arts, and other sources provided $104,000, requiring the generation of approximately $105,000 from season subscriptions and general ticket sales. The New York press, which had paid only sporadic attention to the resident company during Lithgow's tenure, began to review productions regularly. Flattering critical notices, combined with increased season subscriptions, attest to a significant rise in the overall quality of the theatre's offerings. The spare physical productions that had supported Lithgow's youthful companies were replaced by lavishly mounted pieces performed by seasoned veterans. The company, however, continued to share the theatre with the Triangle Club, a film series, dance concerts, musical events, and occasional touring dramatic productions.

On July 1, 1974, Michael Kahn succeeded Louis Criss as artistic director of the company. The thirty-four-year-old Kahn, who planned to run the McCarter while retaining his position as artistic director of the American Shakespeare Theatre at Stratford, Connecticut, brought with him an enviable reputation as an exciting young director. With the announcement of Kahn's appointment, season subscriptions increased to more than 4,000. Kahn personally directed four of the five plays in his inaugural season, which included works by Eugene O'Neill, John Ford, Tennessee Williams, James Joyce, and William Shakespeare. Ticket prices remained modest and ranged from $2.50 to $6.75. Kahn's policies followed those of Criss: provocative modern pieces and occasional world or American premieres as well as plays from the classic repertory were played by actors hired more frequently for each production than for the entire season.

The grants that had contributed $150,000 to the theatre's precariously balanced operating budget were due to expire at the end of the 1975–76 season, and a financial crisis was imminent. General ticket sales and 8,000 season subscribers generated 65 percent of an operating budget, which had increased from $350,000 to $1.1 million in four years. Although a high inflation rate contributed to the meteoric rise in expenses, the McCarter Resident Theatre had become very expensive. In the midst of the pending financial crisis, Daniel Seltzer resigned as executive director in December of 1975, claiming he had fulfilled his intention of making the theatre one of the premiere resident companies in the country. By the end of the season half the money needed to bridge a projected $210,000 budget gap for the next campaign had been raised from a variety of sources, and a full season, featuring the world premiere of Sam Shepard's *Angel City*, was announced. A record high 9,600 season subscribers and grants totaling $82,000 from the National Endowment for the Arts and the New Jersey Council on the Arts enabled the theatre to open the 1976–77 with a projected budget shortfall of only $68,000. The crisis abated in April 1977 with the announcement of an $85,548 Ford Foundation Challenge Grant spread over four years and designed to enable the company to establish a cash reserve fund. To encourage financial responsibility, the Ford grant stipulated that annual installments would be awarded only if the company's budget balanced at the end of the prior fiscal year. Under Kahn's talented artistic direction, the quality of the company's productions continued to be consistently outstanding, and season subscriptions skyrocketed to 12,000. But Kahn's responsibility for both artistic and fiscal decisions took its toll, and in February 1979 he announced his resignation, claiming that management and fund-raising chores had left little time for artistic leadership. Several proposals for the future of the company, including a merger with the Philadelphia Drama Guild*, were made. Nevertheless, the McCarter opened 1979–80 as an independent entity under the artistic direction of Nagle Jackson.

The forty-two-year-old Jackson had earned his initial reputation as a resident director at San Francisco's American Conservatory Theatre*, and had served as artistic director of the Milwaukee Repertory Theatre* for six seasons before assuming leadership of the McCarter Theatre. In many ways his policies marked a return to those of Lithgow a decade earlier. He was interested in establishing a resident company and avoiding the expense of hiring performers on a production-to-production basis. Realizing that one could not forge a strong acting ensemble immediately, he hired sixteen actors as members of the resident company and an additional twenty-two performers for specific plays. His initial season of five plays included the premiere of James McClure's *1959 Pink Thunderbird; The Visions of Simone Machard*, a seldom-produced play by Bertolt Brecht and Lion Feuchtwanger; *The Miser;* Tom Stoppard's *Jumpers;* and Tad Mosel's *All the Way Home*. Achieving both critical acclaim and strong audience support during his initial season, Jackson managed to avoid the pitfall of having to split his energies between artistic and business management by hiring Alison Harris, former administrative assistant to Arvin Brown at the Long Wharf Theatre*, as the McCarter's managing director.

To date, Jackson's tenure has been characterized by the return to a resident company and a good mix of plays from the established repertory and some new pieces. A second season of staged readings and minimally produced new plays has been added to the theatre's offering. A capital funding campaign generated $3.8 million needed to renovate the interior of the aging theatre in 1986. With an annual operating budget of $2.5 million, a newly renovated home, and a strong resident acting ensemble, the McCarter Theatre Company continues to be a vital force among America's resident theatre troupes.

PERSONNEL

Executive Director: Arthur Lithgow (1961–71).
Artistic Directors: Louis Criss (1972–74), Nagle Jackson (1979–86).
Executive Producers: Milton Lyon (1961–63), Daniel Seltzer (1973–76).
Producing Director: Michael Kahn (1974–79).
General Manager/Managing Directors: Alison Harris (1979–86), Mrs. Herbert McAneny (1962–64), Edward Martensen (1974–79), Nancy Shannon (1964–71).
Associate Artistic Director: Robert Lanchester (1981–86).

Directors: Firth Banbury (1978–79), *Robert Blackburn* (1964–71), Barry Boys (1979–81), Tom Brennan (1963–70), Brendan Burke (1968–70), Ken Costigan (1966–68), *Louis Criss* (1971–73), Don Driver (1962–63), Edward Earle (1963–64), Sheldon Epps (1978–79), Alan Fletcher (1960–61), William Francisco (1963–64), *Kenneth Frankel* (1975–80), Hal George (1963–64), Gerald Guttierez (1978–79), Pat Hingle (1977–78), David Hooks (1962–63), *Nagle Jackson* (1977–86), Jon Jory (1967–68), *Michael Kahn* (1974–79), George Keathley (1962–63), *Robert Lanchester* (1981–86), Gene Lesser (1976–77), *Arthur Lithgow* (1961–71), John Lithgow (1968–70), Milton Lyon (1961–62), James McClure (1982–83), Donald Moffat (1963–64), Gordon Phillips (1966–69), Stephen Porter (1962–63, 1976–77), Eliss Rabb (1960–61, 1975–76), Mario Siletti (1964–65), Paul Widener (1982–83), Carl Weber (1972–74), *William Woodman* (1977–83), Garland Wright (1974–75).

Technical Directors/Production Supervisors: Clyde Blakely (1966–69), Gilbert Hemsley (1960–64), Mark Krause (1977–78), Michael Kurtz (1975–77), Leon Leake (1972–74), Rafe Schanblum (1978–82), John C. Schenck (1969–71), Robert E. Stanton (1962–63), Daniel York (1982–86).

Scene Designers: Howard Bay (1977–78), John Lee Beatty (1978–79), Clyde Blakely (1965–68), John Conklin (1972–73), Robert Edmonds (1968–69), Phillip Gilliam (1972–73), Hugh Hardy (1962–64), David Jenkins (1972–73), Marjorie Kellogg (1975–78), William D. Roberts (1960–64), Hunter Nesbitt Spense (1969–70), Robert U. Taylor (1972–75).

Costume Designers: Charles Blackburn (1967–70), Lawrence Casey (1974–76), Elizabeth Corey (1974–76), Linda Fisher (1972–74), Jane Greenwood (1974–79), Robin Hirsch (1979–81), David James (1974–75), Marny Wilmers (1967–68), Susan Rheauend (1982–86).

Lighting Designers: Clyde Blakely (1966–69), F. Mitchell Dana (1969–71), V. C. Fuqua (1962–63), Gilbert Hemsley (1960–65), John McClain (1972–80), Richard More (1982–86), John Schenck (1967–69), Marshall Williams (1966–67).

Actors and Actresses: Gregory Abels (1964–66), D'arcy Achziger (1973–75), Ann Adams (1981–83), Rudy Adams (1968–69), Marc Alaimo (1966–67), Philip Andreis (1960–61), Ray Aranha (1969–70), Edward D'Arms (1960–61), Tucker Ashworth (1960–61), Susan Babel (1966–68), Thomas Barbour (1963–64), Christine Barcuski (1975–77, 1982–83), Raymond Barry (1962–63), *Emery Battis* (1964–67), Lloyd Battista (1962–63), Mary Bell (1968–69), Ed Bernard (1968–69), Ramon Bieri (1961–62), Francis P. Bilancio (1979–80), Wanda Binson (1972–73), Suzanne Bishop (1964–65), *Robert Blackburn* (1963–65, 1968–71), Peter Blaxill (1972–73), Andrew Bloch (1972–73), Scotty Block (1970–71), Powers Booth (1975–77), *Barry Boys* (1979–81), Richard Brackus (1974–75), John Braden (1969–70), Tom Brennan (1970–71, 1972–73), Robert Bridges (1964–65), Peter Bailey Britton (1966–67), Jacqueline Brooks (1960–61), Sallie Brophy (1979–80), Brita Brown (1963–64), Mark A. Brown (1983–85), Yusef Bulos (1967–68), Raymond Burgin (1962–63), Brendan Burke (1968–71), Ann Gee Byrd (1965–68), David Byrd (1961–62, 1965–68), *Leila Cannon* (1968–71), Rudy Carigni (1967–68), *Barbara Caruso* (1962–63, 1964–65), Peggy Cass (1977–78), *Robin Chadwick* (1982–84), Pamela Christian (1977–78), Haig Chobanian (1962–64), Grady Clarkson (1967–69), Carolyn Coates (1977–78), Al Corbin (1961–62, 1972–73), Clayton Corbin (1966–67), Ken Costigan (1966–68), Peggy Cowles (1981–82), Diana Crane (1977–78), *Louis Criss* (1972–73), Chase Crosley (1960–61), *Ken Curtis* (1960–61), *Jon Cypher* (1961–62), Linda Dahl (1964–65), Angela D'Ambrosia (1963–64), Tamara Daniel (1966–67), Clifford

David (1972–73), Jeff David (1964–66), Thayer David (1960–61), Gideon Davis (1979–80), *Dom DeLuise* (1962–63), Jerome Dempsey (1972–73), Jack Dengel (1966–68), Richard Dix (1976–77), Beth Dixon (1968–71), MacIntyre Dixon (1964–65, 1972–73), *Jack Dodson* (1960–62), *Jay Doyle* (1979–85), Mary Doyle (1967–68), Ralph Drishell (1960–61), Alice Drummond (1973–74, 1977–78), Cara Duff-MacCormick (1972–73), David Duhaine (1972–73), *Richard Dysart* (1961–62), Edward Earle (1963–64), Richard Eaton (1960–61), Joyce Ebert (1960–61), *Ronnie Claire Edwards* (1962–63, 1964–65), Elizabeth Eisenman (1963–64), Alice Elliot (1970–71), George Ervin (1964–65), Gwyllum Evans (1961–63), Gordon Fearing (1966–67), *Clarence Felder* (1963–66, 1972–74), Michael Fender (1961–62), Michael Flanagan (1964–65), Thomas Ford (1962–63), *Herbert Foster* (1979–83), Judith Ann Frank (1961–62), Diane Franklin (1977–78), Karen Fraser (1964–65), Betty Fussell (1961–62), Gray Gage (1972–73), James Gallery (1972–73), Donald Gantry (1970–71), Mimi Garth (1967–68), Louis Gatterio (1966–67), Anne Gee (1961–62), John Genke (1966–67), *Leslie Geraci* (1979–83), *Richard Gere* (1975–76), Franklin Getchell (1972–73), Dennis Gilliland (1963–64), Charlotte Glenn (1965–66), James Goldsmith (1960–61), Richard Graham (1960–61), Gordon Gray (1973–74), Nancy Grey (1961–62), John Grimaldi (1967–68), Gene Gross (1972–73), Janet Groves (1960–61), Max Gulack (1968–69), Judy Guyll (1962–63), Chris Hagen (1977–78), Daniel Hamilton (1966–68), Georgine Hall (1961–62, 1977–78), Rosemary Harris (1960–61), Donald Hatch (1962–63), Pamela Hawthorne (1967–68), Mark David Healy (1961–62), George Hearn (1966–68), John Heffernan (1961–62), Betty Hellman (1960–61), Dale Helward (1962–73), *Charles Herrick* (1960–63), Keith Herrington (1962–63), Will Hicks (1966–69), Margeret Hilton (1981–82), I. M. Hobson (1972–74), Anne Hoffman (1969–70), Anne Jouise Hoffmaner (1972–73), Ruby Holbrook (1963–66), Laurence Holofcener (1976–78), David Hooks (1960–61, 1962–63), Michael Houlihan (1974–76), Duncan Hoxworth (1965–66), Harriet Hull (1980–81), Richard Jamieson (1970–71), Buddy Jarvis (1962–63), Timothy Jerome (1967–68), Eve Johnson (1966–67, 1968–69), Charlotte Jones (1974–75), Lauren Jones (1966–67), Susan Jordan (1981–82), Gretchen Kanne (1961–62), Susan Kaslow (1967–69), *Nicholas Kepros* (1964–65, 1972–73, 1977–78), Aldine King (1968–69), Norman Kingoff (1967–68), Martha Knight (1965–66), Terese Kreuzer (1964–65), James LaFerla (1969–70), *Gerald Lancaster* (1981–84), *Robert Lanchester* (1978–86), Jeanette Landes (1972–73), Judith Lane (1967–68), *Frank Langella* (1972–73), Penny Larsen (1965–67), William Larsen (1960–61, 1975–76), Paul Larson (1974–76), Joseph Leon (1972–73), Mark Leonard (1972–73), Peter Levin (1960–61), Arthur Lewis (1962–63), Derry Light (1982–85), *Karl Light* (1962–63, 1972–73, 1977–78, 1980–83), Arthur Lithgow (1961–62, 1964–65), *John Lithgow* (1969–70), Sarah Jane Lithgow (1964–65), David Little (1964–65), Dennis Longwell (1961–62), Julian Lopez-Morillos (1972–73), *Laurence Luckinbill* (1962–63), Jane McCarthur (1961–62), Sarah MacDonald (1964–65), Katherine McGrath (1980–81), W. G. McMillan (1970–71), Michael MacRae (1966–67), Gloria Maddox (1972–73), Mimi Maltby (1961–62), John Mansfield (1979–81), Tennyson Mare (1970–71), Nan Martin (1972–73), Nicholas Martin (1960–61), Madison Mason (1963–64), Richard Mathews (1968–70), Stephen Mendille (1979–80), Joanna Merlin (1960–61), Mark Metcalf (1972–73), Stuart Michaels (1961–62), Charles Miller (1962–63), Michael Miller (1963–64), Alan Mixon (1961–62), *Donald Moffat* (1960–61), Fred Morsell (1970–71), Anne Murray (1965–66, 1968–69), Tom Musante (1960–61, 1965–66), William Myers (1962–63, 1972–73), Rebecca Nibby (1981–82), Catherine Nisbit (1960–61), Eulalie Noble (1960–61), James

Noble (1977–78), E. E. Norris (1973–75), Francesca Norsa (1972–73), Frederic O'Brady (1965–66), K. Lyse O'Dell (1967–68), George Oliva (1977–78), Martin Oliver (1968–69), Tom Oliver (1969–70), Benton Palmer (1962–63), Joan Pape (1977–78), Portia Partersen (1978–79), Judy Parton (1972–73), Ricky Paul (1977–78), Seymour Penzner (1970–71), Elizabeth Pergerson (1967–68), Phillip Pero (1966–68), Gerald Peters (1963–64), Laurie Peters (1972–73), Sarah Peterson (1974–76), *Christine Pickles* (1961–63), Richard Pilcher (1969–71), *Gordon Phillips* (1966–67, 1968–70), Michael Plunkett (1979–80), *Ellis Rabb* (1960–61), Stacy Ray (1982–85), (1981–85), Jess Richards (1972–73), Marcia Rigsby (1980–81), Hugh Reilly (1974–75), *Richard Risso* (1980–85), Leslie Rivers (1968–69), Rex Robbins (1960–61), Eve Roberts (1960–61), Gary Roberts (1980–81), Joanna Ross (1960–61), Alice Ruby (1963–65), Tom Sawyer (1961–62), John Scanlan (1972–73), *Roy Scheider* (1961–62), Bob Schmidbauer (1970–71), *Dwight Schultz* (1972–74), Michael Schultz (1966–67), Don Seay (1961–62), *Daniel Seltzer* (1972–75), *Anne Shelden* (1961–62, 1972–73, 1978–80, 1982–83), Joseph Sicari (1963–64), Charles Siebert (1966–67), Mario Siletti (1963–66), Tom Slater (1961–62), Donegan Smith (1968–70), *Bruce Somerville* (1978–83), Theodore Sorel (1974–76), Paul Sparer (1960–61), Dionis Spitzer (1967–68), Ronald Steelman (1967–68), Douglas Stender (1964–65), Frances Sternhagen (1960–61), Anthony Stimac (1966–67), Stephen Stout (1979–80), Robert Summers (1964–65), Dolph Sweet (1972–73), Julie Tanner (1979–80), *Barbara Tarbuck* (1975–77), Tom Tarpey (1968–69), Helen Marie Taylor (1960–61), Carol Teitel (1961–62), Ray Thompson (1961–62), Tazewell Thompson (1970–71), *Greg Thornton* (1980–85), James Tripp (1964–66, 1967–68), *Maria Tucci* (1974–77), Dorothy Victor (1960–61), Holly Villaire (1968–70), Kathryn Walker (1968–70), Donald Warfield (1972–73), Joan Weisberg (1970–71), Roger Wellington (1974–75), Alice White (1969–70), Dorothy Whitney (1962–63), *Jo Beth Williams* (1975–78), Angela Wood (1966–67), George Wood (1978–81), Henry Yaeger (1964–65), David Young (1960–61), William Young (1960–61), Cole Younger (1963–64), Edward Zang (1972–73).

REPERTORY

1960–61: *Man and Superman, Anatol, The Lady's Not for Burning, The Sea Gull, Box and Cox, The Cat and the Moon, Scapin, The Importance of Being Earnest, A Midsummer Night's Dream, Twelfth Night, Hamlet, King Lear, As You Like It.*

1961–62: *Our Town, Pullman Car Hiawatha, The Happy Journey to Camden and Trenton, The Long Christmas Dinner, Androcles and the Lion, Saint Joan, Macbeth, The Merchant of Venice, The Duchess of Malfi, The Knight of the Burning Pestle, The Alchemist.*

1962–63: *The Fantasticks, Antigone, A Phoenix Too Frequent, The Comedy of Errors, Caligula, Desire Under the Elms, Galileo, Fuente Ovejuna, Julius Caesar, Le Bourgeois Gentilhomme.*

1963–64: *Hedda Gabler, Long Day's Journey into Night, She Stoops to Conquer, The Playboy of the Western World, Othello, Romeo and Juliet, Much Ado About Nothing, The Taming of the Shrew, Richard III.*

1964–65: *Three Men on a Horse, The Great God Brown, Death of a Salesman, A Streetcar Named Desire, The Marriage Proposal, The School for Wives, The Rivals, As You Desire Me, Macbeth.*

1965–66: *Mother Courage, Major Barbara, An Enemy of the People, Coriolanus, Lady Windermere's Fan, A Midsummer Night's Dream, Box and Cox, Candida, Arrah-Na-Pogue.*

1966–67: *Agamemnon, A View from the Bridge, Once in a Lifetime, Hamlet, Waiting for Godot, The Braggart Warrior, The Tempest, The Emperor Jones, The Servant of Two Masters.*

1967–68: *The Devil's Disciple, Twelfth Night, Enrico IV, The Words upon the Window Pane, It Should Happen to a Dog, Second Shepherd's Pageant, The Crucible, The Beggar's Opera, Dr. Faustus, The Marriage of Figaro.*

1968–69: *The Village: A Party* (world premiere), *The Glass Menagerie, As You Like It, Charley's Aunt, The Three Sisters, Oedipus the King, Krapp's Last Tape, The Scarecrow, The Plough and the Stars.*

1969–70: *The Birthday Party, Of Mice and Men, The Firebugs, The Way of the World, Pygmalion, Much Ado About Nothing, Ah, Wilderness!, Troilus and Cressida.*

1970–71: *All My Sons, A Raisin in the Sun, The Show-Off, Little Murders, The Importance of Being Earnest, The Homecoming, Macbeth, Caesar at the Rubicon* (world premiere).

1971–72: The Resident Theatre Company suspended operations during this season.

1972–73: William Alfred's *Agamemnon* (world premiere), *Tooth of Crime* (American premiere), *The Tempest, Loot, Rosmersholm.*

1973–74: *The Sea Gull, The Entertainer, Twelfth Night, You Never Can Tell, The Daughter-in-Law* (American premiere).

1974–75: *Beyond the Horizon, 'Tis Pity She's a Whore, Mother Courage, Kingdom of Earth, Romeo and Juliet.*

1975–76: *A Grave Undertaking* (world premiere), *The Royal Family, Section Nine* (American premiere), *The Heiress, Awake and Sing!, The Winter's Tale.*

1976–77: *A Streetcar Named Desire, Major Barbara, The Physicists, Design for Living, Night of the Tribades* (American premiere), *Angel City* (world premiere).

1977–78: *Infancy, Childhood, The Torch-Bearers, Much Ado About Nothing, The Confirmation* (world premiere), *The Utter Glory of Morrissey Hall* (world premiere).

1978–79: *A Month in the Country, The Aspern Papers, No Time for Comedy, Put Them All Together* (world premiere), *Blues in the Night, Heartbreak House.*

1979–80: *The Visions of Simone Machard, All the Way Home, Jumpers, The Miser, Hay Fever, 1959 Pink Thunderbird* (world premiere).

1980–81: *Taming of the Shrew, A Christmas Carol, Custer, The Play's the Thing, Putting on the Dog, Gertrude Stein Gertrude Stein Gertrude Stein.*

1981–82: *Just between Ourselves* (American premiere), *The Night of the Iguana, A Christmas Carol, Keystone, The Overland Rooms, Iphigenia at Aulis, Arms and the Man.*

1982–83: *Blithe Spirit, Hamlet, A Christmas Carol, The Day They Shot John Lennon* (world premiere), *The Three Sisters, A Delicate Balance.*

1983–84: *Play Memory, Saint Joan, Ah, Wilderness!, The Dining Room, At This Evening's Performance* (world premiere).

1984–85: *The School for Wives, The Dawns Are Quiet Here* (American premiere), *Faustus in Hell* (world premiere), *Under Milk Wood, A Raisin in the Sun.*

1985–86: *As You Like It, The Boys Next Door.*

BIBLIOGRAPHY

Published Sources:
New York Times, 1960–86.
Theatre World 1966–67 through *1983–84.* New York: Crown Publishers, 1968–85.

Unpublished Source:
Princeton, New Jersey. Princeton University Library. McIlhenny Theatre Collection.
    Programs, annual reports. The author gratefully acknowledges the research as-
    sistance of Philip Van Vleck.

David L. Rinear

[MAYDE] MACK MUMMERS. See MUMMERS THEATRE.

MARGO JONES THEATRE, Dallas, Texas, was renamed in each of its twelve
years of existence after the year of operation. On New Year's Eve 1948 the
theatre changed its name to Theatre '49, initiating an annual sign-changing
ceremony. Under the leadership of Margo Jones, a native Texan, and a committee
of seven prominent Dallasites, the theatre was officially chartered, a theatre
building was located, and a financial campaign was conducted between February
1945 and May 1947. Jones leased a small stucco and glass-brick building, located
at Grand and First avenues in Fair Park, which had been constructed in 1936
by the Magnolia Petroleum Company as a miniature theatre for the projection
of motion pictures and the display of exhibits. The interior was remodeled for
arena staging with a seating capacity of 198. Theatre '47 opened June 3, 1947,
with the premiere of William Inge's *Farther Off from Heaven* (later renamed
The Dark at the Top of the Stairs). In 1959, its last season, the theatre merged
with the Maple Street Theatre, a proscenium house with 414 seats.

No other regional theatre of the past fifty years had more influence on the
movement toward decentralized professional theatre than did the Margo Jones
Theatre in Dallas. It was the first professional nonprofit repertory theatre in the
United States to use arena staging (until its final disastrous season) as its sole
method of production. Although arena staging in the United States dates from
1925, when Gilmore Brown and Ralph Freud created The Playbox, an adjunct
to the Pasadena Playhouse, it began to become popular after Glenn Hughes
founded the Penthouse Theatre in 1940 at the University of Washington. No
professional theatre group, however, had successfully used arena staging until
Jones' effort. Furthermore, Margo Jones' operation was unique in presenting
primarily new scripts and classics in a city 1,500 miles from New York City.
Although this was not the first professional theatre in Dallas, it was the first
successful resident professional theatre. Theatre in Dallas dates from 1873, when
Tom Field, an early impresario of the Southwest, built a small opera house on
the second floor of a flimsy frame building. By the early 1900s Dallas had seen
Edwin Booth, Maurice Barrymore, Fanny Davenport, Tommaso Salvini, Clara
Morris, Johnston Forbes-Robertson, and Sarah Bernhardt, among others. Thereafter, before World War II, living theatre needs in Dallas were satisfied by
occasional road shows at the Melba or Majestic theatres or at the State Fair
Music Hall. In the 1920s the Dallas Little Theatre was formed. By the 1930s it
was internationally renowned, but by 1940 it had all but ceased operation. Civic
leaders wanted a new theatrical venture but realized that war conditions and the

absence of theatre activity in Dallas made a new project almost impossible. Dallas needed a special type of leadership to revive interest in theatre.

The moving force behind the creation of this new venture, Margo Jones, frequently referred to as a "Texas Tornado," was the ideal choice for this mission. Jones was obsessed with the theatre and "prone to sudden, vast enthusiasm that in a pinch became messianic conviction." (Murray Schumach, "A Texas Tornado Hits Broadway," *New York Times Magazine*, October 17, 1948, p. 19). She was called "The Margaret Webster of this American generation" (Fitzroy Davis, "A Texan Shows Enthusiasm for Round Theaters," *Chicago Sunday Tribune*, June 24, 1951), an idealist who was effective in raising money. In 1931 she received her Bachelor of Arts in drama and in 1932 her Master of Arts in psychology from Texas Woman's University. She received additional training at the Southwestern School of the Theatre in Dallas and at the Pasadena Playhouse. After touring the world extensively as a companion and secretary to a wealthy woman, she became assistant director of the Houston Little Theatre (of the Federal Theatre Project). In 1936 she attended the Moscow Art Theatre Festival, and for six years, until 1942, she directed the Houston Community Players, establishing there her interest in new scripts. From October 1942 to June 1944 she was an instructor in drama at the University of Texas in Austin. After a brief period as a director at the Pasadena Playhouse, she began her Dallas venture. John Rosenfield, the late drama critic for the *Dallas Morning News*, noted in his column on New Year's Eve of 1947 that she had the kind of persistence that could "conquer worlds or steel plants," and could accomplish about anything. Murray Schumach observed: "Her energy and enthusiasm for the theatre rise up and overwhelm one. There are no single impressions, but masses of them." It is little wonder that the annals of the Margo Jones Theatre are inseparable from the story of its founder.

From the beginning Margo Jones believed a non-profit professional theatre outside New York could sustain itself financially with little or no subsidy. The unusual financial solvency of the operation was due to Jones' ability to gain economic support from Dallasites, to interest Dallas playgoers in the production of new scripts, and to make artistic use of the relatively inexpensive production medium of the arena stage. While using arena staging, the organization was able to subsist solely on ticket sales, until the administration of Aaron Frankel in 1958–59. Unlike Jones and her assistant and immediate successor, Ramsey Burch, Frankel was unable to keep the business and artistic operations separate. A move to a converted motion picture theatre on Maple Street in 1959 had as one of its aims the separation of artistic and business responsibilities, but the move came too late to save the organization. Additional production costs in the proscenium theatre proved to be more than could be supported with ticket sales alone, and the theatre suspended operations. From the beginning, however, the theatre was able to obtain community support when needed. This was first illustrated in 1945, when Dallasites contributed $40,000 to the young project. At various times during the history of the theatre, especially after Jones' untimely death, board members gave money to meet small deficits or to pay for needed building expenses.

During the first four seasons critics praised the theatre for its imaginative productions, singling out the contribution of costumes and properties. For a number of years thereafter both the costumes and the properties were commonplace. From 1953 until the fateful move to the Maple Street Theatre, more attention was given to the settings, although the imaginative level of the first few seasons was never equaled.

Margo Jones intended her theatre to operate as a repertory company and attributed her success to the practice of allowing each play a limited run, regardless of popular acceptance. During its twelve years the theatre presented 2,882 performances of 124 full-length productions plus a number of shorter pieces. Only two plays had extended runs: Owen Crump's *Southern Exposure* in 1950 and Jerome Lawrence and Robert E. Lee's *Inherit the Wind* in 1955. At first Jones revived each of the season's plays after the initial run of each new production. She then devoted the last few weeks of the season to a repertory festival of the season's most popular plays. After the first year productions were rarely revived except in the season-ending repertory festival. After Jones' death the revivals and the repertory festival at the season's end were virtually eliminated. Margo Jones' major aim was to create a playwright's theatre, dedicated to the production of new plays and their classic models. The theatre produced eighty-six new scripts. Although not even Jones' most ardent admirer attributed perfect taste or infallible judgment to her play selection, only a small handful of her choices were complete failures. The least popular new plays at the box office were Vivian Johannes' *Skaal* (1949), Sari Scott's *An Old Beat-up Woman* (1949), Shirland Quinn's *Here's to Us!* (1948), Edward Caulfield's *The Blind Spot* (1952), William McCleery's *A Play for Mary* (1950), Anna Marie Barlow and S. Brooke White's *Cold Christmas* (1955), Gene Radan's *The World Is Yours* (1955), and Carl Oglesby's *Season of the Beast* (1958). Among the most popular at the box office were Loren Disney and George Sessions Perry's *My Granny Van* (1950), Owen Crump's *Southern Exposure* (1950), Frank Duane and Richard Shannon's *Walls Rise Up* (1951), A. B. Shiffrin's *The Willow Tree* (1951), Irving Phillip's *One Foot in Heaven* (1951), Rosemary Casey's *Late Love* (1953), Lawrence and Lee's *Inherit the Wind* (1955), Dorothy Parker and Ross Evans' *The Coast of Illyria* (1949), John Vari's *Farewell, Farewell, Eugene* (1955), Richard Reich's *The Tin Cup* (1957), and Paul Vincent Carroll's *The Devil Comes from Dublin* (1957). Eleven of the plays premiering at the Margo Jones Theatre were later produced on Broadway: William Inge's *The Dark at the Top of the Stairs*, Tennessee Williams' *Summer and Smoke*, Joseph Hayes' *Leaf and Bough*, Crump's *Southern Exposure*, *The Willow Tree* (under the title *Twilight Park*), *Late Love*, *Inherit the Wind*, *Farewell, Farewell, Eugene*, Eleanor and Leo Bayer's *Third Best Sport*, and Katherine Morrill's *And So, Farewell* (renamed *A Distant Bell*). The operation showcased young playwrights and introduced some of the country's most successful playwrights, such as

Tennessee Williams, William Inge, Ronald Alexander, Joseph Hayes, Sigmund Miller, Jerome Lawrence, and Robert E. Lee, and several European plays by such significant authors as Sean O'Casey, Bridget Boland, Paul Vincent Carroll, James Bridie, and Maura Laverty. The production of classics (both those plays more than fifty years old and later those termed "modern classics" by the management) was also a stated aim. Ten plays by Shakespeare; eight by G. B. Shaw; three by Molière; two each by Henrik Ibsen, Oscar Wilde, and Anton Chekhov; one each by Oliver Goldsmith, August Strindberg, Richard Brinsley Sheridan, Ben Jonson, and Royall Tyler were produced.

The Margo Jones Theatre was established as a civic, non-profit organization, with a board composed of local leaders who gave Jones a free hand and unquestioning support. During her management the board never interfered with the theatre's operation. After her death in 1955 the board began to take on more power and to attempt to control her successors. The result was the lack of clearcut policies. Declining emphasis on new scripts minimized the organization's uniqueness.

During the first decade of its operation, however, the theatre offered unusual opportunities for young theatre artists. It provided stability for the actor and technician alike. Jones did not believe in the star system or in visiting directors, although toward the end of its history both became the norm. During most seasons the staff included a production manager, a technical director, a business manager, a production designer, a lighting director (a position that lasted for only a few seasons), a costume designer, and a series of associate directors beginning in 1951. Both actors and technicians who trained at the Margo Jones Theatre discovered the experience was a boon to a professional career; however, few actors stayed for more than one or two seasons before moving on to more lucrative positions. The list of actors who later gained substantial professional reputations, or at least continued to work in professional theatre with some degree of success, is a lengthy one. Of the 300-plus actors who worked there, the following could be singled out as typical: Jack Warden, Tod Andrews, Mary Finney, John Hudson, Peggy McKay, Peter Donat, Rex Everhart, Ray MacDonnell, Clu Gulager, Charles Braswell, Larry Hagman, Rosemary Harris, George Mitchell, and Louise Latham. A complete staff change did not occur until the organization moved out of its original home in 1959.

The final production of the Margo Jones Theatre, *Othello*, opened December 8, 1959, at the Maple Street Theatre. Poor management and disinterest in the operation, which had been increasing since Margo Jones' death, coupled with the increased cost of a proscenium house, the selection of large cast plays, and the large payroll, which included guest stars and directors, spelled the theatre's doom. Another complication was the opening of Paul Baker's Dallas Theatre Center, which was taking a great deal of interest away from the Margo Jones Theatre. Consequently the board chose to terminate the operation before it was bankrupt.

PERSONNEL

Management: Margo Jones, managing director (1947–55); Ramsey Burch, managing director (1955–58): Alton Wilkes, managing director (1959); Manning Gurian, business manager (1947–49, 1950–51); J. B. Tad Adoue III, business manager (1949–50); Roy A. Somlyo, business manager (1951–58); Jean Elliott, business manager (1958–59); Robert C. Cairns, business manager (1959).

Production Designers: Tony Deeds, Vlada Dimac, Jed Mace.

Costume Designers: Andy Anderson, Kenn Barr, Dale Clement, Frederic Keck, Dhu Wray.

Lighting Designers: Richard Bernstein, Marshall Yokelson.

Technical Directors: Joseph Londin, H. R. Poindexter, James Pringle.

Stage Directors: Ronald Alexander (1954), Ramsey Burch (1951–58), Bill Butler (1959), John Denney (1956), Michael Ellis (1959), Aaron Frankel (1958–59), W. Broderick Hackett (1959), Spencer James (1950–51), Margo Jones (1947–55), James McAllen (1955–56), Jonathan Seymour (1950), Hall Shalton (1956–57), Milton Stiefel (1959).

Actors and Actresses: Bill Adair, Fred Aimsworth, James Alexander, Dean Lyman Almquist, Jill Alquist, Salvatore Amato, *Ruth Amos* (1956–57), Frank Amy, *Clinton Anderson* (1947–49), Judy Andrews, *Tod Andrews* (1947–48), *Edith Atwater* (1959), Raymond Bailey, *Katherine Balfour* (1947), Richard Banks, James Barbosa, Patricia Barclay, *Henry Barnard* (1958–59), Jonny Barta, Bruce Barton, Sherry Barton, Debbie Bennett, *Harry Bergman* (1954–57), *Evelyn Bettis* (1952–53, 1954–55), Robert Beyers, Bill Blankenship, Bill Blitch, Jack Boisseau, Barbara Borin, Kay Borman, Joyce Ann Boyd, John Bradford, Robert Brantley, *Charles Braswell* (1947–54, 1957–58), Bill Bray, Joan Breymer, Charles Brinkley, *Wilson Brooks* (1947, 1949), Howard P. Brown, Sam Brunstein, Will Bryant, *Martha Bumpus* (1952–57), Ramsey Burch, Barbara Burnett, Bill Butler, Ed Cantrell, Edythe Chan, Loia Cheaney, Darla Joyce Chick, Edgerley Clark, Marianne Clore, Mabel Cochran, Chevi Colton, Juleen Compton, Mady Correll, Bob Cotton, Ken Creighton, Pat Crowder, *Joan Croydon* (1953–54), *Edward Cullen* (1954–56), Winifred Cushing, *Henry Daniell* (1957), Martin David, *Alisa Dawson* (1956–57), Marga Ann Deighton, *Albert Dekker* (1959), *Joan Delehaunty* (1956, 1957–58), Frank DeLuca, *John Denney* (1949–51, 1954), George Devenney, Mavis Dion, Pat Dixon, Carolyn Dodge, *Mary Dolan* (1955), Michael Dolan, *Peter Donat* (1951–52), Robert Dracup, Dennis Drew, Ramon Eaves, *Ronnie Claire Edwards* (1956–58), Duane Ellason, *Ruthe Elliot* (1958–59), Cass Ellis, LeRoy Ellis, *Rex Everhart* (1952–53), Dick Ewell, Carroll Farr, *James Field* (1953–55), *Mary Finney* (1947–50), Taylor Flaniken, Sadie French, Carolyn Friday, Jeanne Gal, Eddie Gale, Michael Garth, Bennye Gatteys, Vaughan Glaser, Marianne Glenn, Julia Goldman, *Carol Goodner* (1947), Harry Goodwin, Nilmore Graham, *Grayce Grant* (1950–51), *Clu Gulager* (1956), Miriam Gulager, Gloria Gunshor, Larry Hagman, Bob Hall, Bruce Hall, James Hall, Jerry Hall, Charles Hamilton, Les Handy, James Harder, *Rebecca Hargis* (1947–48), Rosemary Harris, Mary Hartig, Bob Hartson, Bill Hayter, Marianne Heald, David Healy, S. K. Hershewe, Fred Hight, Arthur Hill, Boyd Hill, *Robert Van Hooten* (1955–56), Dorthy Hoskins, Fred Hoskins, Paula Houston, Joan Hovis, Norman Howard, Bob Howell, Donald Howell, *John Hudson* (1948–49), Al Hughes, David Hurst, Patricia Hyde, Katherine Hynes, Spencer James, James Jeffus, Jimmy Jeter, Mardi Bryant Jones, Gregg Juarez, Jewell Kelly, Bob Kendrick, Richard Kennedy, Mimi Key, *Maggie Kezer* (1955–56), Geoffrey Kilburn, George King, *Muriel Kirkland* (1954), Budd Kneisel, Patricia Kogin, David

Kurzon, *Jay Lanin* (1958–59), *Louise Latham* (1947–48, 1954–56), Pat Lawson, Marian Leeds, Randy Lewis, Richard Lilleskov, Dorothy Lincoln, *Betty Green Little* (1947, 1948–51), Lily Lodge, *Richard Longman* (1958–59), Daniel Love, Phyllis Love, *J. Frank Lucas* (1955–57), *Claire Luce* (1958), Geoffrey Lumb, James MacBerry, Richard McCook, Margaret McDonald, *Ray MacDonell* (1955–56), *Gene MacDonaugh* (1959), James McGee, LeRoy McGuire, *Peggy McKay* (1949–50), *John McQuade* (1958), Benedict MacQuarrie, Helen Maddox, John Maddox, Paul Manning, Mae Marmay, Nancy Marshall, Gay Martin, Karolyn Martin, Bill Mayhew, Dorothy Messick, Thomas Van Meter, Walter Miller, Gilbert Milton, *George Mitchell* (1947–48), Mabel Morris, Marion Morris, Bob Mullen, *John Munson* (1951–53), Joe Nash, Arthur Nations, *Louis Noble* (1953–54), Tom Noel, Rolla Nuckles, Hermes Nye, John O'Leary, Charles Olsen, Margaret O'Neill, Roddy Packer, Pat Papert, William Parker, Paul Peters, *Kathleen Phelan* (1954–55), Lillian Prather, *Charles Proctor* (1949–51), Marilyn Putnam, Louis Veda Quince, Elena Rafael, *Marion Randolph* (1955), James Ray, Glenn Reid, Ann Richardson, Romola Robb, Mary Dell Roberts, Virginia Robinson, Robert Rogers, Rod Rogers, Carol Jean Rosaire, Nathan V. Roth, Victor Roth, Anne Rovello, Jerry Rufus, Tom Ruisinger, Stanley Runkel, George Russell, Tommie Russell, Peter Sander, Paul Saye, Lil Schepps, Robert Scott, Lorraine Serabian, Jonathan Seymour, Nick Shavian, Bea Shaw, Jane Shaw, Richard Shepard, *Robert (Lester) Short* (1958–59), Jerice Shults, Raymond Van Sickle, Phil Slater, Harriet Slaughter, *Norman Smith* (1958–59), William Smithart, Arlen Dean Snyder, Carol Southard, Dee Sparks, *Guy Spaull* (1953–54), Eleanor Speers, *Katherine Squire* (1947–48), Margaret Starr, Ann Stephens, Claire Stewart, Darrell Stewart, Joe Sullivan, Pat Sully, Charles Taliaferro, Jerry Talley, Janet Taylor, Walter Taylor, Frank Tennant, Lynn Thatcher, Virginia Thompson, Bill Thornton, Pat Treston, *Richard Venture* (1950–51), Clyde Waddell, Dolores Walker, Joe Walker, Frances Waller, *Jack Warden* (1947–49), Earl F. Warren, Jean Washburn, Myrtolene Watson, Bobby Weaver, Harold Webster, Charlie West, Mrs. Claud C. Westerfield, Billie White, Bernedette Whitehead, *Erwin Whitner* (1948–53, 1954–57), Susan Wichman, Bill Willis, Jean Wilson, Oscar Wilson, Jr., *Norma Winters* (1951–53), Ethel Woodruff, Lee Woodward, Tommy Woodward, Tommy Wright, Ben Yafee, Marshall Yokelson, Pat Young, Quinda Young, Virginia Young.

Playwrights of Premiered Works: S. I. Abelow, Ronald Alexander, David Baker, Anna Marie Barlow, Eleanor and Leo Bayer, Muriel Roy Bolton, Kenneth Cameron, Robert Canedella, Alejandro Cansona, William Case, Rosemary Casey, Edward Caulfield, Joel Climenhaga, Martyn Coleman, Vivian Connell, Owen Crump, Jean Dalrymple, Reginald Denham, Albert Dickason, Loren Disney, Frank Duane, Ross Evans, Kate Farness, Norbert Faulkner, Sheridan Gibney, Samuel R. Golding, Harry Granick, Stephen Gray, Manning Gurian, John Briard Harding, Sheldon Harnick, Joseph Hayes, Edward Hunt, William Inge, Frederick Jackson, Vivian Johannes, Greer Johnson, Patricia Jourdry, Frederick Kohner, Jerome Lawrence, Robert E. Lee, Elinor Lenz, Don Liljenquist, William McCleery, Barton MacLane, Albert Mannheimer, Vera Marshall [Mathews], Robin Maugham, Edwin Justus Mayer, Sigmund Miller, Katherine Morrill, Alden Nash, Carl Oglesby, Dorothy Parker, George Sessions Perry, Irving Phillips, Tom Purefoy, Shirland Quinn, Gene Radano, Samson Raphaelson, Eugene Raskin, Richard Reich, Milton Robertson, Charles Robinson, John S. Rodell, Neal Roper, Bernard C. Schoenfield, Sari Scott, Richard Shannon, A. B. Shiffrin, Conrad Sutton-Smith, James Thurber, John Vari, William Walden, Ira Wallach, Violet Welles, Robert Penn Warren, S. Brooke White, Tennessee Williams.

REPERTORY

1947: *Farther Off from Heaven, How Now, Hecate, Hedda Gabler, Summer and Smoke, Third Cousin.*

1974–48: *The Master Builder*, Three Short Plays: *The Last of My Solid Gold Watches, This Property Is Condemned,* and *Portrait of a Madonna, Throng O'Scarlet, The Taming of the Shrew, Lemple's Old Man, The Importance of Being Earnest, Leaf and Bough, Black John.*

1948–49: *The Learned Ladies, Here's to Us!, Twelfth Night, Skaal, Sting in the Tail, The Sea Gull, She Stoops to Conquer, The Coast of Illyria.*

1949–50: *Heartbreak House, An Old Beat-up Woman, Romeo and Juliet, My Granny Van, Cock-a-Doodle Dandy, Ghosts, The Golden Porcupine, Southern Exposure.*

1950–51: *Lady Windermere's Fan, A Play for Mary, The Merchant of Venice, An Innocent in Time, The Willow Tree, One Bright Day, Candida, Walls Rise Up.*

1951–52: *The Sainted Sisters, One Foot in Heaven, A Midsummer Night's Dream, A Gift of Cathy, The Blind Spot, The Father, I Am Laughing, So in Love* (musical).

1952–53: *Goodbye, Your Majesty, Hamlet, The Rising Heifer, The Last Island, Uncle Marston, Late Love, The Day's Mischief, The Rivals.*

1953–54: *The Footpath Way, The Guilty, Happy We'll Be, Oracle Junction, The Heel, A Rainbow at Home, Horatio* (musical), *The Purification, The Apollo of Bellac, The Merry Wives of Windsor.* Summer season: *The Inevitable Circle, The Brothers, A Dash of Bitters, Sea-Change, Volpone.*

1954–55: *Marry-Go-Round, As You Like It, The Hemlock Cup, Inherit the Wind, The Feathered Fauna, The Summer of Fancy Dress, Misalliance, Ghost of a Chance, La Belle Lulu* (musical). Summer season: *Pygmalion, Whisper to Me, The Girl from Boston, Cold Christmas, Farewell, Farewell, Eugene.*

1955–56: *Somebody, The World Is Yours, The Dark Lady of the Sonnets* and *The Man of Destiny, Love in a Tutu, Tolka Row, The School for Wives, Mr. Gillie, The Sand Castle, The Spring Affair, Third Best Sport.* Summer season: *The Marriage Wheel, Love Goes to School, The Prisoner.*

1956–57: *Stalin Allee, Macbeth, The Small Servant, Woman Is My Idea, The Tin Cup, The Circle, Second Wind, The Most Fashionable Crime, Uncle Vanya, The Glass Menagerie.*

1957–58: *The Devil Comes from Dublin, Roadside, Androcles and the Lion, Heat of Noontide, And So, Farewell, The Doctor in Spite of Himself, Season of the Beast, The Hooper Law, A Waiter Not Named Julius.*

1958–59: *Penelope's Web, Willie Stark: His Rise and Fall, Legends and Fables: Down in the Valley* and *Fables in Our Time, The Millionairess, The Heiress, The Contrast, A Moon for the Misbegotten, The Mousetrap, Triangle, The Tridget of Greva, Overruled, The Browning Version.*

1959–60: *Physician for Fools, Leave It to Me* (musical), *A Few Days in Greece, Othello.*

BIBLIOGRAPHY

Published Sources:

Jones, Margo. *Theatre in the Round.* New York: Rinehart, 1951.

Magnus, Dorothy B. "Matriarchs of the Regional Theatre." In *Women in American Theatre,* edited by Helen Krich Chinoy and Linda Walsh Jenkins. New York: Crown Publishers, 1981.

Wilmeth, Don B. "The Margo Jones Theatre." *Southern Speech Journal* 31 (Spring 1967): 188–95.

———. "The Margo Jones Theatre." In *Theatrical Touring and Founding in North America*, edited by L. W. Conolly. Westport, Conn.: Greenwood Press, 1982.

Unpublished Sources:

Larsen, June Bennett. "Margo Jones: A Life in the Theatre." Doctoral dissertation, City University of New York, 1982.

Rudisell, Amanda. "The Contributions of Eva Le Gallienne, Margaret Webster, Margo Jones, and Joan Littlewood to the Establishment of Repertory Theatre in the United States and Great Britain." Doctoral dissertation, Northwestern University, 1972.

Wilmeth, Don B. "A History of the Margo Jones Theatre." Doctoral dissertation, University of Illinois, 1965.

Archival Resource:

Dallas, Texas. Dallas Public Library. Photographs, letters, newspaper clippings, reviews, scripts, promotional brochures, programs, financial records.

Don B. Wilmeth

MERCURY THEATRE ACTING COMPANY, New York City, was organized in 1937 by actor-producer-director Orson Welles and business and production manager John Houseman. Welles and Houseman acquired a lease on the proscenium-equipped Comedy Theatre (on West Forty-first Street), renamed it the Mercury Theatre, and opened it on November 11, 1937, with a production of Welles' adaptation of William Shakespeare's *Julius Caesar*.

The Mercury Theatre operated in New York City during the late 1930s, near the end of America's Great Depression. This period witnessed the continued presence in New York of art theatres such as the Theatre Guild and the development of politically oriented companies such as the Group Theatre*. The event that ultimately led to the creation of the Mercury Theatre, however, was the establishment of the Federal Theatre Project (governed by the Works Project Administration), a New Deal relief project that, under the leadership of Hallie Flanagan, sought to provide jobs for unemployed American theatre professionals. By 1936 the Federal Theatre Project was promoting and funding regional theatre companies throughout the United States, although the most productive and newsworthy units centered in New York City. The New York project originally established five major units: the Popular Price Theatre, which presented new plays in traditional formats; the Experimental Theatre, which produced new plays in novel styles; the Living Newspaper; the short-lived Manager's Tryout Theatre; and the Negro Theatre, under the direction of John Houseman and Rose McClendon. At the Negro Theatre, Houseman teamed with Orson Welles to produce an innovative production of Shakespeare's *Macbeth*, which was cast with the unit's black actors, set in the country of Haiti, and conceived to emphasize the power of voodoo over the play's characters. This hugely successful production resulted in Hallie Flanagan's decision to establish a new theatre project in New York City for the production of classic plays (Project #891), with Welles as actor-producer-director and Houseman as business and production manager. During the season of 1936–37 Welles and Houseman produced three plays at the Maxine Elliott Theater: *Horse Eats Hat*, an adaptation of Eugene Labiche's French farce, *The Italian Straw Hat;* Christopher Marlowe's *Doctor Faustus;* and Marc Blitzstein's *The Cradle Will Rock*, an opera that championed the aims of radical labor. The last of these productions was a significant event in the annals of American theatre history. *Cradle* appealed to the American Popular Front (the working masses and their sympathizers); accordingly, it "rocked" the Washington bureaucracy, and its scheduled opening was postponed by a Federal Theatre memorandum prohibiting openings of new works for several weeks because of budgetary concerns. Welles and Houseman bucked the edict and performed a special preview for an invited audience on June 14, 1937; the next day federal officers padlocked the Maxine Elliott Theater. Welles and Houseman responded by moving the play to the Venice Theatre, where they played the production without scenery and with most of the actors singing and acting from the auditorium seating. This rebellious act brought them considerable publicity and stimulated their decision to sever ties with the Federal Theatre Project and establish their own production company, the Mercury Theatre, in the fall of 1937.

During its two seasons as a New York producing organization the Mercury Theatre presented classic fare in innovative formats, and most of the innovations were the creative imaginings of producer Orson Welles. From its inception the Mercury established the practice of placing the legend "Production by Orson Welles" beneath the title of the play. This credit was originated by Welles' partner, John Houseman, who still maintains (despite his love-hate experience with Welles) that the legend meant exactly what it said: "they were Welles' shows." Both the initial concepts of a production and their eventual realization were largely Welles' doing. In this respect Welles was comparable to German director Max Reinhardt. But his approach also reflected the theories of Gordon Craig, who dreamed of a total artist for the theatre. Welles oversaw every aspect of production. He sought to control his designers and, indeed, was often unwilling to acknowledge designers' contributions. Moreover, he got along beautifully with actors who simply placed themselves in his hands, but very badly with others who demanded their share in the creative process.

Considered a boy genius by most of his mentors and colleagues, Welles received his early schooling and had his first theatrical experiences at the Todd School for Boys in Woodstock, Illinois. There, during the mid-1920s, he directed and acted in *Julius Caesar, Doctor Faustus*, and *Winter of Discontent*, a condensation of several of Shakespeare's histories. He made his first professional appearance at the age of sixteen in Dublin, Ireland, at the Gate Theatre, performing the Duke of Württemberg in *Jew Süss* to public and critical praise. Welles' subsequent work at the Gate Theatre, and particularly his associations with its producing directors-actors Hilton Edwards and Micheál MacLiammóir, opened his eyes to the new European stagecraft and reinforced his belief in innovative production. He played Mercutio, Eugene Marchbanks, and Octavius

Barrett on tour with Katharine Cornell in 1933–34, and over the next few years organized the Woodstock Theatre Festival in Illinois. Accordingly, when John Houseman saw Welles perform Tybalt in a 1936 New York revival of *Romeo and Juliet* and chose the actor to portray the role of MacGafferty in Archibald MacLeish's *Panic*, Welles was only twenty-one years of age. Subsequent to his Mercury venture in New York, Welles explored Hollywood filmmaking, completing the critically acclaimed *Citizen Kane* in 1941. His long career on the stage and in films, television, and radio has been thoroughly documented in various critical works and biographies (see the bibliography).

Before 1934 the intelligent, acutely cultivated, Rumanian-born John Houseman had worked in grain and commodity exports. He turned to the arts as a profession relatively late when, in 1934, Virgil Thomson invited him to direct and manage the opera *Four Saints in Three Acts*. On the strength of that venture and several other directorial successes in New York, Hallie Flanagan made Houseman managing producer of Federal Theatre Project's Negro Theatre. Houseman's function with the Negro Theatre, with Project #891, and the Mercury Theatre was primarily that of production and business manager. Most, if not all, of the artistic decisions were made by Welles. Since his association with Welles at the Mercury, Houseman has been active as artistic director of the American Shakespeare Festival in Hartford, Connecticut, and director of the drama division of Juilliard School of the Performing Arts; he has also produced, directed, or performed in film, television, and radio, and written significant volumes on his career in the theatre (*Run-Through* and *Front and Center*).

Conceived as a theatre primarily for the classics, like Project #891, the Mercury was nevertheless intended by Houseman and Welles to draw the same Popular Front audience that attended productions of the Federal Theatre and the Group Theatre. On August 29, 1937, courtesy of Welles' admirer Brooks Atkinson, the Mercury Theatre's *declaration of principles* appeared on the front page of the *New York Times*. Beginning with *Julius Caesar* that November, the producers asserted, the Mercury would mount each season four or five classic plays relevant to contemporary affairs. And, although politics was important, aesthetics would come first. The Mercury would never choose a particular drama just because it could be made to express ''proper'' political views. To recapture the heterogeneous audience that had flocked to Project #891, the Mercury would continue a low-price policy: the top ticket price would be $2. Finally the producers decided to perform the season's offerings in repertory, rather than extend the run of any ''hit'' production.

From a practical point of view, Welles and Houseman should have abandoned the Mercury's announced status as a repertory company. What they seemed to have forgotten was that, unlike Project #891, the Mercury was an independent enterprise, a business, without the cushion of government backing. The paradox of the Mercury was that it would consistently play to jam-packed houses and consistently lose money. From the beginning the Mercury enterprise operated on a shoestring. Houseman and Welles launched their new theatre in the fall of

1937 with capital of only $10,500. Although their first season was a popular, artistic, and critical success, their second season was a disappointment and failed to bring in sufficient box-office revenue to extend to a third season.

The Mercury's two-season repertory reflected Welles' commitment to classic production and continued the innovative approaches to staging he revealed with Project #891. The repertory also appealed to the Popular Front audiences that had flocked to Project #891. At the outset, Welles and Houseman intended to perform Ben Jonson's *The Silent Woman*, John Webster's *The Duchess of Malfi*, and Shakespeare's *Julius Caesar*. In addition, they announced their intention of producing George Bernard Shaw's *Heartbreak House* and a William Gillette farce, *Too Much Johnson*. Nothing came of their plans to produce *The Duchess of Malfi* and *The Silent Woman*, and *Too Much Johnson* (in which Welles utilized film footage within a stage production) did not survive try-out performances in a summer theatre at Stony Creek, Connecticut.

The productions that provide for the Mercury Theatre a place in American theatre history were *Julius Caesar* (1937), Thomas Dekker's *The Shoemaker's Holiday* (1938), Shaw's *Heartbreak House* (1938), and Georg Büchner's *Danton's Death* (1938). Additionally, Welles included Project #891's highly significant *The Cradle Will Rock* in the Mercury's first-season offerings; the show played only Sunday performances until Welles moved *Julius Caesar* and *The Shoemaker's Holiday* into other theatres and provided *Cradle* a continuous run at the Mercury. Finally the Mercury produced radio broadcasts of popular favorites and classics under the title "First Person Singular," which later became "Mercury Theatre of the Air." This program immortalized itself on Halloween Eve in 1938 with an adaptation of H. G. Wells' *The War of the Worlds*, which convinced thousands of listeners that the Martian invasion was an actuality.

The Mercury's first three offerings were enormously successful even though the theatre's low-priced ticket policy failed to provide financial profits. These three productions also demonstrated Welles' success in producing and directing in a range of production styles. Each production, too, demonstrated that, for Welles, a play's content served as little more than a vehicle for its expressive form. His adaptation of Shakespeare's *Julius Caesar* (which shortened the play, made considerable interpolations, and included lines from other Shakespeare plays) slanted the work to depict the atrocities of the modern fascist state. With his designers-collaborators Samuel Leve and Jean Rosenthal he set blocks and platforms on an open, blood-red stage (much the equivalent of Shakespeare's thrust stage) and illuminated this stark environment with beams of light shooting up through the floor, obvious reminders of the Nazi rallies at Nuremberg. The actors donned modern military uniforms and drab street clothes, and Welles dressed for Brutus in a dark overcoat. The lighting, which emphasized eerie shadows and half-shaded persons, and Marc Blitzstein's militaristic musical scoring created haunting environments for the play's events. Most critics applauded Welles' stunning visual and special effects and called the production an exciting evening in the theatre. And while no Welles production ever met with a unanimously positive reception from critics, *Julius Caesar* was the single most important Mercury production during the company's two-season tenure in New York. Critics responded favorably to the acting company and particularly to Welles' restrained performance. Brooks Atkinson accurately predicted that enthusiasm for acting and boldness in production would be the hallmarks of the Mercury. Finally, this production demonstrated the "master director" approach taken by Welles. As "producer," he took much credit for the show's design concepts, and he played the role of puppeteer to his puppet-like actors. He also apparently maintained an appalling lack of organization during rehearsals. Despite the brilliance of Welles' conceptions, the physical mountings of the Mercury productions were chaotic: a sense of improvisation was bound up in all his work.

Welles cut *The Shoemaker's Holiday* even more extensively than he did the text of *Julius Caesar*, reducing the playing time to well under two hours. A comparison of his script to Dekker's original also reveals that Welles practically rewrote the piece, reduced its sentimentality, and emphasized its bawdy humor. Brooks Atkinson called the production "an uproarious comic strip of Elizabethan fooling," and Welles' intentions were precisely that. He infused its characters with the sharp caricature of cartoon figures and emphasized the sexual double meanings in the dialogue. With respect to setting, Welles substituted natural textures for realistic details. The show played in repertory with *Julius Caesar;* accordingly, for *The Shoemaker's Holiday*, Caesar's blood-red stage was covered with burlap, and the resulting empty space was filled with an abstract rendering of an Elizabethan village. In opposition to the setting, costumes were realistic period recreations. After the successful opening of *Shoemaker*, the Mercury dispatched a road tour of *Julius Caesar* and moved *Cradle* to the Windsor Theater for a daily run. Soon thereafter the business for *Shoemaker* and *Caesar* was sufficiently brisk to move them to a larger theatre (the National, later the Billy Rose), so *Cradle* shifted back to the Mercury for a regular run. By January 1938 the Mercury had been operating for three months on Broadway and was running three hits. This pattern of several successful productions running simultaneously at different New York houses is reminiscent of the Theatre Guild's golden era of production during the late 1920s.

With *Heartbreak House* (1938) Welles proved his ability to maintain the integrity of a text (Shaw did not allow any tampering with his play) and demonstrated his fine taste in conventional production and in the acting of the eccentric Captain Shotover. But the Mercury production of *Danton's Death*, which underwent several script revisions to make its subject matter compatible with the views of the American Communist party (a strong supporter of the Mercury), was injured by script compromises and the resulting tension in rehearsal. The production received dull notices and closed early.

Welles and business manager Houseman employed a production manager, several stage managers, a musical director, a small orchestra, a costumer, several setting and lighting designers, twenty to twenty-five actors, and five to ten actresses. Some of the performers were engaged for a season, while others were engaged for a specific production. The acting company never actually attained the status of a repertory company. Indeed, Welles conceived of the Mercury as a director's theatre and did not originally hire his actors to fill the range of a repertory company. As he has admitted, "I had a company pretending to be an Abbey or a Moscow Art, and I knew perfectly well it was a group of people cast for *Julius Caesar*." Later he began to desire a true repertory company, but by that time the Mercury was experiencing insurmountable financial problems. While none of the Mercury actors were major stars when they were first engaged, several went on to distinguished careers. Welles, Joseph Cotton, Vincent Price, Geraldine Fitzgerald, Will Geer, and Howard da Silva attained renown as stars of stage, film, and television after their Mercury years. Cotton appeared in Welles' *Citizen Kane* and *Magnificent Ambersons*, was Katherine Hepburn's choice for Dexter Haven in the original New York production of Philip Barry's *The Philadelphia Story*, and has appeared in significant films such as *The Third Man* and *Portrait of Jenny*. Vincent Price's fame as an actor of horror films was preceded by his significant work in such films as *Song of Bernadette* and *Keys of the Kingdom*. Geraldine Fitzgerald has performed in both classic and contemporary plays in New York and in various regional theatre companies; her film work includes roles in *Wuthering Heights, Watch on the Rhine*, and *The Pawnbroker*. Other notable performers with the Mercury were husband and wife Martin Gabel and Arlene Francis (best remembered as panelists on television's *What's My Line*), Ruth Ford, and Brenda Forbes. Those who remained with the Mercury for both New York seasons and continued to act for Welles in his subsequent stage and film productions were Joseph Cotton, Martin Gabel, Erskine Sanford, and George Coulouris (an English actor by birth who has appeared in major roles at the Old Vic and Edinburgh Festival, has performed in various American regional theatres, and has acted fifty film roles).

With the failure of *Danton's Death* in 1938, the Mercury Theatre as it had been constituted came to an end. Houseman and Welles were forced to seek financial backing from the Theatre Guild for Welles' adaptation and condensation of several Shakespeare histories (*Five Kings*, 1939), but because of an overly long running time, insufficient rehearsals, and unmanageable scenery, the Guild opted to withdraw financial support, and the show never reached New York. In 1941 Welles and Houseman teamed for the last time to produce Paul Green's *Native Son*, which utilized white actors who were formerly Mercury players and black actors from the Federal Theatre's Negro unit, but this offering was not actually a Mercury Theatre production. For several years thereafter the name "Mercury Theatre" continued to be associated with Welles' productions, but the original New York experiment came to an end in 1939 with the failure of *Five Kings*.

PERSONNEL

Management: Orson Welles, producing director (1937–39); John Houseman, business manager (1937–39); Jean Rosenthal, production manager (1937–39).

Scenic Designers: John Koenig (1937–38), Samuel Leve (1937–39), James Morcom (1938–39), Ed Schruers (1937–38), Stephen Jan Tichacek (1938).

Lighting Designers: Abe Feder (1937–38), Samuel Leve (1937–39), Jean Rosenthal (1938–39).

Musical Director: Lehman Engel (1937–39).

Stage Director: Orson Welles (1937–39).

Actors and Actresses (this list does not include the names of company members from *Too Much Johnson* and *Five Kings*, the two projects that failed to achieve a New York production. Because the Mercury operated for only two seasons, years of residency for leading actors have not been indicated): Kent Adams, John Addair, Guido Alexander, William Alland, Evelyn Allen, Arthur Anderson, Ellen Andrews, Leopold Badia, Richard Baer, Charles Baker, Fay Baker, Edith Barrett, Edgar Barrier, John Berry, Howard Bird, Muriel Brassler, Grover Burgess, Francis Carpenter, Rosemary Carver, Mady Christians, Blanche Collins, *Joseph Cotton*, Peggy Coudray, Helen Coule, *George Coulouris, Howard da Silva*, George Duthie, Robert Earle, Ross Elliott, George Fairchild, Morgan Farley, Robert Farnsworth, *Geraldine Fitzgerald, Brenda Forbes, Ruth Ford*, Dulce Fox, *Arlene Francis*, Alice Frost, Edward Fuller, *Martin Gabel*, Betty Garrett, *Will Geer*, MacGregor Gibbs, Warren Goddard, Sparke Hastings, Josephine Heathman, Louis Hefter, Edward Hemmer, William Herz, Arthur Hoffe, *Joseph Holland*, Robert Hopkins, William Howell, John Hoysradt, Phyllis Joyce, *Whitford Kane*, Guy Kingsley, Wallace Lawder, Norman Lloyd, Clifford Mack, Frank Marvel, Jack Mealy, William Mowry, James O'Rear, Edgerton Paul, Tileston Perry, Stanley Poss, Geoffrey Powers, *Vincent Price*, Elliott Reid, Stephen Roberts, Frederick Ross, Marion Grant Rudley, *Erskine Sanford*, Stefan Schnabel, Hiram Sherman, Sanford Siegel, Howard Smith, George Smithfield, *Vladamir Sokoloff*, Anna Stafford, Olive Stanton, Frederick Thompson, Victor Thorley, Frederic Tozere, Evelyn Wahle, Marian Warring-Manley, *Orson Welles*, Norman Wess, Frank Westbrook, Bert Weston, Huntley Weston, John A. Willard, Hansford Wilson, Richard Wilson, Eustace Wyatt.

REPERTORY

1937–38: *Julius Caesar, The Cradle Will Rock, The Shoemaker's Holiday, Heartbreak House*.

1938–39: *Too Much Johnson* (did not play in New York), *Danton's Death, Five Kings* (did not play in New York).

BIBLIOGRAPHY

Published Sources:

France, Richard. *The Theatre of Orson Welles*. London: Associated University Presses, 1977.

Goldstein, Malcolm. *The Political Stage*. New York: Oxford University Press, 1974.

Leaming, Barbara. *Orson Welles*. New York: Viking Press, 1985.

Notable Names in the American Theatre. Clifton, N.J.: James T. White & Co., 1976.

Alex Pinkston

[FRED] MILLER THEATRE COMPANY. See MILWAUKEE REPERTORY THEATRE.

MILWAUKEE REPERTORY THEATRE. The Fred Miller Theatre Company (forerunner of the Milwaukee Repertory Theatre) was organized in the summer and fall of 1954 by Mary Widrig John, a Milwaukee native who had been very active in that city's community theatre and moderately active in New York's professional theatre. With her associates Dori Hersch and Van Conway and her attorney, Milton Padway, John established Drama, Incorporated, a nonprofit stock corporation, to serve as the parent organization for the theatre. Drama, Inc., founded the Frederick C. Miller Memorial Theatre in a converted movie house at 2842 North Oakland shortly after the untimely death of Fred Miller, president of the Miller Brewery and chairman of the new theatre's fund-raising campaign. Drama, Inc., renovated the movie house to effect a 346-seat arena theatre, and opened it on January 25, 1955, with a production of Samuel Taylor's *Sabrina Fair*, starring Jeffrey Lynn.

The first of the nonprofit, professional resident theatres in America were Theatre 47, established by Margo Jones in Dallas, 1947 (see Margo Jones Theatre*); the Alley Theatre*, begun by Nina Vance in Houston, 1947; and the Arena Stage*, established by Zelda Fichandler in Washington, D.C., 1950. Each of these early ventures was begun by an industrious and talented woman; each was housed in an arena-style theatre; and each became an Equity company after several years of nonunion operation. This model approach was repeated by companies in several other cities: the Mummers Theatre* in Oklahoma City, Herbert Blau and Jules Irving's Actor's Workshop* in San Francisco, and the Front Street Theatre* in Memphis. Such ventures also inspired a number of amateur companies to transform themselves into professional theatres; for example, the Cleveland Play House* moved from community theatre to professional theatre status in 1958. But the Fred Miller Theatre was one of only a few theatres to begin as a professional stock company and later reorganize as a nonprofit repertory theatre.

For the first seven years of its existence the Fred Miller Theatre booked individually cast productions with guest stars from Broadway or Hollywood. A show's selection depended not on the caliber of the play, its appropriateness for Milwaukee, or its relation to the rest of the season's offerings but on whether it was an appealing vehicle for a star. Until 1961 the Fred Miller presented light dramatic fare usually presented by star-attraction, summer-stock houses. The theatre jobbed-in additional actors (some from the Milwaukee area), several directors, and the necessary design and technical staff to accomplish the productions, so it was considerably more than a roadhouse, but somewhat less than a regional repertory company.

The Fred Miller's first season (1954–55), was twenty weeks long and consisted of ten plays, each running for two weeks. That season was so successful (it played to 91 percent of capacity and had a paid attendance of 50,507) that each of the ten shows the next season was presented for three weeks. During its second season the Fred Miller also began a rather modest professional drama school that accommodated approximately twelve full-time and twenty-five part-time students. For four seasons Mary John ran the Fred Miller, and on occasion she also directed productions. She was the major stockholder in Drama, Inc., and so maintained decisive power in all matters. The third and fourth years of the theatre's existence witnessed a growing dissension among the staff and the board of directors regarding John's authority. The crucial question to be answered was whether the theatre belonged to John or to the public. In July 1958, after the attorney general of the state of Wisconsin had entered the scene as counsel on behalf of the board of Drama, Inc., the courts directed that Drama, Inc., change its status from a stock corporation to a nonstock, non-profit organization operated by a board of directors elected from the public. After this legal decision John resigned and the management of the theatre was vested in a thirty-member board of directors. For the next three years the theatre continued to operate as a stock-star company, under the managements of Edward Mangum (1958–59) and Ray Boyle (1959–61). At the end of its first seven years the Fred Miller had presented 75 percent of all professional drama in Milwaukee. Seventy-one major productions, mostly popular commercial plays with well-known guest stars, had been presented to 450,927 paying patrons.

During Ray Boyle's management the board began to feel the Fred Miller should present more serious theatre, classics and recent plays drawing critical acclaim for their message and dramatic potency. In 1961 the board opted to drop the star system and employ a resident ensemble. During the 1961–62 season actor-director Ellis Rabb's APA* (Association of Producing Artists) repertory company was engaged for a fall drama festival. The company included Rosemary Harris, Will Geer, and Richard Dysart; John A. McQuiggan was production manager. Later, a repertory company formed by William Ball and Alan Fletcher presented a spring season. Although proclaimed an artistic success by the critics, this season was financially devastating. Average attendance was only 46 percent of capacity. Without the appeal of a star, many people would not come to the theatre.

Over the next six years the board worked on audience development and searched for a strong artistic director. The board of directors engaged John McQuiggan as managing director in 1961, and he remained with the company during its developmental phase. The theatre's lowest period occurred during Paul Shyre's tenure as artistic director (1962–63), when attendance averaged only 44 percent of capacity. In July 1964 the organization became the Milwaukee Repertory Theatre (MRT) in conformity with the trend away from the use of persons' names in theatre titles, and also to incorporate the name of the city in the theatre's name. In the fall of 1964 Charles Ray McCallum, former president of Drama, Inc., was named general manager in charge of administration. John McQuiggan continued as producer. This administration, an artistic corps headed by actor-director Philip Minor, and a new emphasis on subscription sales succeeded in increasing attendance from the low 44 percent of capacity of 1962–63 to 76 percent of capacity in 1965–66. This period also witnessed the formation of a finance committee and the recognition on the part of the board and the public that the theatre would have to be regularly subsidized.

The subsequent history of the MRT may be divided into three periods, each headed by a dynamic artistic director who continued the traditions of ensemble acting, audience growth, and a mixed classic and contemporary repertoire. Each of these directors also introduced new programs that have become stock components of the MRT. Tunc Yalman (artistic director, 1966–71) was born in Istanbul, Turkey, and educated at the Yale School of Drama. He worked as actor, writer, designer, teacher, and director in Turkey and France before coming to the United States. His open-air production of Shakespeare's *Coriolanus* in the courtyard of a fifteenth-century fortress in Istanbul attracted international attention in 1964. He directed at Istanbul's Municipal Theatre and Dormen Theatre; in New York he directed the Broadway production of *The Trial of Lee Harvey Oswald* by Amram Ducovny and Leon Friedman. As the Rep's artistic director, Yalman inaugurated the new play series "Theatre for Tomorrow" and conducted the Rep's first statewide tour with a production of Samuel Beckett's *Waiting for Godot* in 1968. His tenure also witnessed the company's move, in 1969, to the Todd Wehr Theatre in Milwaukee's Performing Arts Center, the expansion of subscribers from 9,500 to 16,000 in a single season (1969–70), and an increased emphasis on performing and developing new works.

Nagle Jackson (artistic director, 1971–77) studied drama in Paris on a Fulbright Fellowship and was a member of the Circle-in-the-Square Director's Workshop in New York City. A featured performer with the Julius Monk revues from 1963 to 1966, he spent eight summers with the Oregon Shakespeare Festival, appearing in twenty-two productions and directing such works as Ben Jonson's *Volpone* and Shakespeare's *Richard II*. During his first season at the MRT he directed his original adaptation of the *The English Mystery Plays*. Before his tenure at the MRT, Jackson was a resident director at the American Conservatory Theatre* in San Francisco; he also directed at other regional theatres: the Hartford Stage Company in Connecticut, the Old Globe in San Diego, and the Seattle Repertory Theatre* among others. At the MRT Jackson concentrated on strong ensemble acting and introduced the second-stage Court Street Theatre in 1974. His tenure also witnessed the hiring of Sara O'Connor as managing director (1974) and the use of the historic Pabst Theatre for the MRT's annual production of Charles Dickens' *A Christmas Carol*.

John Dillon (artistic director, 1977–86) has directed at more than a dozen of the nation's top resident theatres. He acquired graduate degrees in theatre from Northwestern and Columbia universities and began his professional career as a member of Joseph Chaikin's award-winning Open Theatre*. He is especially fond of his work with new plays, having staged premieres of works by David Mamet and Israel Horowitz, and, at the MRT, works by resident playwrights Amlin Gray, Tom Cole, and Larry Shue, among others. His major artistic policy at the MRT was to include playwrights as integral, continuing members of the company. Also interested in international theatre exchange, Dillon has toured an MRT production to Japan (Tennessee Williams' *The Glass Menagerie*, 1983) and has collaborated with the Royal Exchange Theatre Company, Manchester, England (1982). His tenure witnessed the formation of The Lab, a theatre research and development wing; the establishment of a resident acting ensemble of twelve members (1985); the selection of playwright Amlin Gray and director Sharon Ott as artistic associates; and the development of training, the organization of workshops, and the exchange of observerships with other theatres, as well as numerous experimental projects.

The increased attendance and expressions of public support that preceded Tunc Yalman's appointment in 1966 encouraged the board to extend the run of each production to four weeks with additional weeks for those shows having a special appeal for students. Student tickets ran $1.75, and the range of regular ticket prices was $2.50 to $3.90. The subscription drive that accompanied the company's move to the Todd Wehr Theatre (1969) increased subscription sales to nearly 16,000. An unprecedented 87 percent of all seats for performances were sold out before the season began, and, with additional single ticket purchases, the theatre played to 96.4 percent of capacity that season. Single tickets remained a reasonable $2.50 to $4.50; student tickets were $2. For the 1970–71 season the MRT decided to increase its capacity by reducing the number of plays to six and increasing the run of each play to six weeks. The previous season's experiment with alternating repertory was dropped, and the MRT returned to a straight-run policy. The usual performance week, which ran from Wednesday through Sunday in 1966, expanded to include a Tuesday evening performance in 1969. Matinees were held Wednesday at 2:00 and Saturday at 5:15; Tuesday, Wednesday, and Sunday evening performances were at 7:30; Saturday's late performance occurred at 9:15; and all other evening performances were at 8:30. This schedule remained fairly consistent through the 1985–86 season. Although the price of the least expensive tickets has not risen appreciably since 1969 (from $2.50 to $4.75), the price of the better seats has tripled ($4.50 in 1969 to $14.25 in 1986). Subscription sales have not boomed since 1969–70, although they have increased a substantial 3,500, averaging between 19,000 and 20,000 between 1975 and 1986.

The MRT's excellence as a producing organization has garnered positive critical response, not only locally, but also nationally and internationally. In the February 1965 *Saturday Review* Henry Hewes applauded the MRT's high artistic standards, substantial dramatic fare, initiative in performing new works and adaptations of classics, and originality in production. In particular, he asserted that the MRT's production of Anton Chekhov's *Uncle Vanya* attested to "the continuing vitality and excellence of this company." Reviewers almost always praised the Fred Miller's star-system productions (1954–61); indeed, many of the early reviews were chatty, "isn't our company wonderful" articles. These productions were, for the most part, packaged touring shows with only a few local actors; accordingly, the novelty of having stars appear in Milwaukee affected the city's social elite. During the theatre's years of struggle to acquire an identity as a repertory company, and to gain focus and leadership, reviewers generally praised an artistic effort, even if audiences stayed away. By the 1964–65 season, for example, local critics had acquired such an appreciation of MRT's artistic efforts that they praised productions of classics and panned productions of a popular comedy and a light musical. Throughout the period during which the theatre attained artistic maturity (1966–86), the MRT received consistently favorable reviews, not only for its fine acting companies and consistently high production standards, but also for the originality of its productions and its emphasis on new plays. And from 1983 to 1986 the MRT has achieved a degree of international fame.

Since 1961 MRT's repertoire has been a mixture of historical classics (both European and American), twentieth-century (or "modern") classics, serious contemporary works, and premieres of new works and adaptations/translations of classic plays. Included among the historical classics have been works by Sophocles, Shakespeare (almost the entire canon), Molière, Richard Brinsley Sheridan, William Congreve, Carlo Goldoni, Chekhov, Henrik Ibsen, and Arthur Schnitzler. Modern "classics" have included works by Luigi Pirandello (*Six Characters in Search of an Author*), Eugene O'Neill (*Long Day's Journey into Night*), Tennessee Williams (*A Streetcar Named Desire, The Glass Menagerie*), Arthur Miller (*Death of a Salesman*), Bertolt Brecht (*Mother Courage*), Noel Coward (*Design for Living*), Lillian Hellman (*The Little Foxes*), and Peter Weiss (*Marat/Sade*). Serious contemporary works have included David Mamet's *American Buffalo*, Athol Fugard's *Master Harold . . . and the boys*, Sam Shepard's *Buried Child*, Peter Nichols' *A Day in the Death of Joe Egg*, David Rabe's *Sticks and Bones*, and Edward Albee's *A Delicate Balance*. Among the new works featured at the MRT have been resident playwright Amlin Gray's *Kingdom Come* and Larry Shue's *The Foreigner*. The 1985–86 resident acting ensemble of twelve was assisted by associate guest actors and a number of acting interns. Most of the MRT's resident actors and actresses arrived in Milwaukee with excellent professional credentials.

Of the company actors who performed during the MRT's star-system days, Karl and Evelyn King Redcoff were perhaps the most notable. Leading actors whose residencies coincided with Tunc Yalman's tenure as artistic director (1966–71) were Michael Fairman, Charles and Mary Jane Kimbrough, and Diana Kirkwood. Penelope Reed's and William McKereghan's tenures as the company's leading performers (1967–77) overlapped the tenures of Yalman and Nagle Jackson. Jim Baker, Judith Light, John Mansfield, Durward McDonald, and G. Wood were the company's major performers during Jackson's directorship in the 1970s. Peggy Cowles, Montgomery Davis, and Ruth Schudson played leading roles for both Jackson and current artistic director John Dillon. And leading players since 1977 have included James and Rose Herron Pickering (who also performed under Jackson's directorship), Peter Callender, Ellen Lauren, William Leach, Daniel Mooney, Larry Shue, Peter Silbert, and Henry Strozier. Film and television stars James Broderick, Richard Dysart, Rosemary Harris,

Rosemary Prinz, and Franklyn Seales are MRT alumni. The late Will Geer, known for his role as Grandpa Walton on television's *The Waltons*, appeared with Ellis Rabb's APA company in 1961–62. Oscar nominee Thomas Hulce (Mozart in the film *Amadeus*) played Romeo in the MRT's production of *Romeo and Juliet* during the 1978–79 season. And Sada Thompson, known for her role as the mother in television's *Family* series, played Amanda Wingfield in the MRT's production of *The Glass Menagerie* (1965–66).

Today the MRT stands among the vanguard of American regional theatre companies. Its influence and impact are not just local, but regional, national, and even international. The theatre's 1984–85 six-play subscription season extended from September to May and played to more than 95 percent of capacity in the Todd Wehr Theatre (124,290 admissions); the Court Street Theatre operates from six to twelve weeks each spring (3,675 admissions in 1984–85); and the annual four-week run of *A Christmas Carol* at the Pabst Theatre serves approximately 41,000 persons. The 1984–85 operating budget totaled $2.3 million. Each season the MRT employs about 160 persons, plus occasional temporary help. Over the years the MRT's innovative programs, services, and artistic endeavors have earned the generous support of leading funding sources across the nation. The National Endowment for the Arts has consistently supported the theatre's production activities over the past two decades, awarding the group $215,000 in 1985–86. Other supporters have included the Wisconsin Arts Board and Wisconsin Humanities Committee, and the Andrew W. Mellon, Shubert, and Rockefeller foundations.

The MRT and the company opened its 1987–88 season in new quarters on the east bank of the Milwaukee River, adjacent to the Wells Street Bridge. The new facility, a renovation of the old Wisconsin Electric Wells Street Power Plant, includes a 720-seat thrust theatre, a 200-seat second stage, a 100-seat cabaret space, lobbies, three rehearsal halls, full scene, costume, paint, and properties shops, lounges and meeting areas, office space, and dressing rooms.

PERSONNEL

Management: Ray Boyle, managing director (1959–61); John Dillon, artistic director (1977–86); Amlin Gray, artistic associate (1985–86); Nagle Jackson, artistic director (1971–77); Mary John, founder and managing director, Fred Miller Theatre (1954–58); Edward Mangum, managing director (1958–59); Charles Ray McCallum, general manager and managing director (1964–74); John A. McQuiggan, managing director (1961–63) and producer (1963–66); Sara O'Connor, managing director (1974–86); Sharon Ott, artistic associate (1985–86); Peggy Haessler Rose, business manager (1964–85); Paul Shyre, artistic director (1962–63); Tunc Yalman, artistic director (1966–71).

Stage Directors: Kenneth Albers (1984–86), Rod Alexander (1971–73), Word Baker (1962–63), William Ball (1961–62), Dale Bellaire (1970–71), Robert Benedetti (1966–68), Ray Birk (1971–73), Thomas Bissinger (1966–67), Gregory Boyd (1984–86), Ray Boyle (1959–61), Tom Brennan (1965–66), Rocco Bufano (1963–64), Louis Criss (1966–67), *John Dillon* (1977–86), Gordon Duffy (1963–64), Susan Einhorn (1978–79), Nick Faust (1981–85), Alan Fletcher (1961–62), Tullio Garzone (1964–65), William Glover

(1976–77), Rob Goodman (1982–84), Wayne Grice (1968–69), Tom Gruenewald (1966–67, 1973–74), Adrian Hall (1963–66), Dilys Hamlett (1985–86), Jay Harnick (1964–65), Israel Hicks (1984–85), Patrick Hines (1963–64), Ronald Hufham (1969–71), *Nagle Jackson* (1971–77), Mary John (1954–55), Robert Kalfin (1966–67), Hy Kalus (1966–68), Stephen Katz (1983–84), Charles Kimbrough (1971–73), Robert Lanchester (1976–77), *Eugene Lesser* (1966–70), Peter Link (1978–79), John Lion (1973–74), Bill Ludel (1978–80, 1983–84), Hale McKeen (1954–55), John McQuiggan (1965–66), Timothy Mayer (1970–71), Philip Minor (1963–66), Daniel Mooney (1979–80), Craig Noel (1961–62), Kevin O'Connor (1970–71), John Olan-Scrymgeour (1969–70), Charles Olsen (1962–63), *Sharon Ott* (1979–86), John Pasquin (1970–71), Kent Paul (1976–77), Anthony Perkins (1968–70), Stephen Porter (1963–66), Ellis Rabb (1961–62), Byron Ringland (1963–65), Richard Risso (1972–74), Sanford Robbins (1978–80), Edwin Sherin (1962–63), Geoffrey Sherman (1978–79), Paul Shyre (1962–63), Mary Tigar (1970–71), Boris Tumarin (1968–70), John Ulmer (1968–69), M. Burke Walker (1985–86), Paul Weidner (1970–71), Richard White (1985–86), Garland Wright (1979–80), *Tunc Yalman* (1966–71).

Resident Playwrights: *Tom Cole* (1978–83), Kermit Frazier (1985–86), *Amlin Gray* (1978–86), John Leicht (1985–86), Peter Link (1978–79), Felipe Santander (1985–86), *Larry Shue* (1981–85), William Stancil (1982–83), Daniel Stein (1976–77).

Music Composers: Richard Cumming (1962–66), Michael Hammond (1964–68), James Reichert (1970–71), Allan Smallwood (1979–80), William Stancil (1982–83), John Tanner (1985–86), Mark Van Hecke (1978–85), G. Wood (1972–77).

Scene Designers: John Lee Beatty (1978–79), Jay Depenbrock (1969–70), Charles Dox, Jr. (1965–66), Kate Edmunds (1984–85), John Ezell (1984–85), Ralph Funicello (1983–84), Peter Gared (1985–86), Robert Paine Grose (1960–61), Richard Hoover (1983–84), Christopher Idoine (1970–78, 1981–82), David Jenkins (1982–83), Hugh Landwehr (1982–83), *Laura Maurer* (1979–86), Cynthia Merritt (1966–67), Michael Merritt (1985–86), Bill Michelewicz (1984–85), Kenneth Mueller (1967–69), Robert Soule (1964–65), *Tim Thomas* (1982–86), Anna Von Kanel (1966–67), *William James Wall* (1966–71).

Lighting Designers: Rachel Budin (1982–84), Dawn Chiang (1984–86), Derek Duarte (1985–86), Victor En Yu Tan (1984–85), Arden Fingerhut (1978–80), John Gisondi (1983–84), R. H. Graham (1976–77), Vern Huntsinger (1962–63), *Christopher Idoine* (1972–78), Robert Jared (1985–86), Dan Kotlowitz (1983–86), *William Mintzer* (1966–72), Spencer Mosse (1980–86), Dennis Parichy (1983–84), Rick Paulsen (1985–86).

Costume Designers/Costumers: James Edmund Brady (1971–74), Robert Colbath (1968–69), Charlotte Cole (1969–70), Elizabeth Covey (1981–83), Sam Fleming (1983–86), Donna A. Gresham (1970–71), Ellen M. Kozak (1974–77), John Lehmeyer (1964–66), *Colleen Muscha* (1979–84), Michael Olich (1984–85), Joan Pavelin (1967–68), Sally Richardson (1985–86), Patricia Risser (1983–84), Linda Rogers (1970–71), Hillary Sherred (1971–72), Susan Tsu (1978–79), Evelyn Wachs (1964–67), Janet Warren (1968–70), Kurt Wilhelm (1982–85).

Production Stage Managers: James Doolan (1967–68), John Economos (1966–67), Robert Goodman (1979–86), Richard Nesbitt (1964–66), Frederic H. Orner (1976–77), Rod Pilloud (1978–79), Norman Rothstein (1962–63), Merry Tigar (1967–74).

Actors and Actresses (selected list includes significant company members through 1985 and all the names of the 1985–86 company): *Marc Alaimo* (1967–70), *Catherine Albers* (1984–85), *Kenneth Albers* (1984–86), Raymond Allen, Raul Aranas, *Jim Baker* (1971–

77), Lawrence Ballard, Candace Barrett, *Dana Barton* (1979–80), *Dale J. Bellaire* (1970–71), *Raye Birk* (1971–73), Tom Blair, Ritch Brinkley, *James Broderick* (1962–63), *Jacqueline Brooks* (1961–62), *Emma Angeline Butler* (1976–77), *James Cahill* (1963–64, 1968–69), *Peter Callender* (1983–86), *Linda Carlson* (1970–71), Rhoada B. Carrol, *Jeff Chandler* (1967–68), *Colin Chase* (1962–63), *Nancy Coleman* (1962–63), *Roy Cooper* (1978–79), *Albert Corbin* (1982–83), *Clayton Corbin* (1967–68), *Clayton Corzatte* (1961–62), *Peggy Cowles* (1975–80), *Catherine Lynn Davis* (1985–86), *Montgomery Davis* (1972–77, 1981–84), Ellen Dolan, *Jay Doyle* (1961–64), *Mary Doyle* (1963–66), *Richard Dysart* (1961–64), *Michael Ebert* (1961–62), *Earle Edgerton* (1978–79), Joseph Endes, *Michael Fairman* (1966–70), Albert Farrar, Joanna Featherstone, *Kay Feinberg* (1962–63), *Lori Ferguson* (1984–85), *Pauline Flanagan* (1962–63), *Harry Frazier* (1962–65), *Ronald Frazier* (1977–79), *Jane Gabbert-Wilson* (1981–82), Eduardo Gallardo, James Gallery, *Robin Gammell* (1964–65), *Julie Garfield* (1979–80), *Will Geer* (1961–62), *Stefan Gierasch* (1964–66), Robert Ground, *Davis Hall* (1972–73, 1983–84), Ric Hamilton, *Mark Hammer* (1964–65), *Rosemary Harris* (1961–62), Eric Hill, *Nicholas Hormann* (1983–84), *Thomas Hulce* (1978–79), Robert Jackson (1968–69), Jim Jansen, *Page Johnson* (1961–62), *Janet Kapral* (1966–67), Stuart Kendall, *Sharon Kent* (1962–63), Miki Kim, *Charles Kimbrough* (1966–73), *Mary Jane Kimbrough* (1966–73), *Diana Kirkwood* (1967–70), *Marge Kotlisky* (1979–80), William Lafe, *Ellen Lauren* (1980–85), *William Leach* (1979–82), Damien Leake, *Judith Light* (1970–74), *Anne Lilley* (1964–65), Matthew Loney, *Anne Lynn* (1962–64), *Durward McDonald* (1973–77), *William McHale* (1960–61), *William McKereghan* (1968–77), *Peter MacLean* (1964–65), *Valerie Mahaffey* (1978–79), *John Mansfield* (1974–77), Nicholas Martin, Mary Mathay, *Anne Meacham* (1962–63), Johanna Melamed, *Mark Metcalf* (1970–71), *Philip Minor* (1963–66), *Robert Moberly* (1964–65), *Daniel Mooney* (1967–86), *Judy Mueller* (1968–69), *Josephine Nichols* (1971–73), Charles Noel, *Patricia O'Connell* (1963–65), Maggie Oleson, *Fredi Olster* (1971–73), Virginia Payne, *James Pickering* (1973–86), *Rose Herron Pickering* (1973–86), *Christine Pickles* (1961–62), Michael Pierce, Demetra Pittman, F. J. Pratt, Marian Primont, *Rosemary Prinz* (1982–83), Victor Raider-Wexler, Matthew Redding, *Evelyn King Redcoff* (1959–62), *Karl Redcoff* (1959–62), *Penelope Reed* (1967–77), *Gail Rice* (1964–65), *Steven Ryan* (1976–77), Peter Rybolt, *Ruth Schudson* (1973–77, 1985–86), *Franklin Seales* (1976–77), *James Secrest* (1976–77), *Anne Shropshire* (1970–71, 1973–74), *Larry Shue* (1977–83), *Charles E. Siegel* (1970–71), *Peter Silbert* (1982–86), *Erika Slezak* (1966–69), *Ahvi Spindell* (1983–84), *Robert Stattel* (1963–64), *Ronald Steelman* (1968–70), *Jack Stehlin* (1983–84), *Henry Strozier* (1977–82), Jack Swanson, *Jeffrey Tambor* (1971–74), Michael Tezla, Kristine Thatcher, *Sada Thompson* (1965–66), *Martha Tippin* (1971–73), Edmund Torrance, Michael Tucker, Ron Van Lieu, *Ralph Williams* (1964–65), *Eleanor Wilson* (1966–70), *G. Wood* (1972–77), *Charles Michael Wright* (1984–85), *Tunc Yalman* (1966–71), *Lois Zetter* (1964–65).

REPERTORY

For seasons 1954–61 (under the star system), names of guest stars are listed in parentheses after the title of the play in which they appeared.

1954–55: *Sabrina Fair* (Jeffrey Lynn), *Cyprienne* (Uta Hagen and Herbert Berghof), *Kind Lady* (Fay Bainter), *Affairs of State* (Shepperd Strudwick), *Shadow and Substance* (Julie Haydon), *Late Love* (Signe Hasso), *The White Sheep of the Family* (Edward Everett Horton), *The Philadelphia Story* (Geraldine Brooks), *Angel Street* (Sylvia Sidney), *Oh, Men! Oh, Women!* (Jeffrey Lynn).

1955–56: *King of Hearts* (Buff Cobb), *The Corn Is Green* (Eva Le Gallienne), *Nina* (Edward Everett Horton), *The Damask Cheek* (Nancy Coleman), *The Fifth Season* (Tod Andrews), *The Little Foxes* (Ruth Chatterton), *Bernardine* (Vickie Cummings), *Summer and Smoke* (Geraldine Page), *Night Must Fall* (Florence Reed), *Three Men on a Horse* (Frank McHugh).

1956–57: *Detective Story* (Chester Morris), *Jenny Kissed Me* (Leo G. Carroll), *Ghosts* (Eva Le Gallienne), *Harvey* (Edward Everett Horton), *Clutterbuck* (Arthur Treacher), *The Glass Menagerie* (Fay Bainter), *Arms and the Man* (Jeffrey Lynn), *A Roomful of Roses* (Louise Allbritton), *The Member of the Wedding* (Ethel Waters), *Bell, Book and Candle* (K. T. Stevens and Hugh Marlowe).

1957–58: *The Reluctant Debutante* (Edward Everett Horton), *A View from the Bridge* (Luther Adler), *Light Up the Sky* (Diana Barrymore), *Picnic* (John Ireland), *The Happy Time* (Jules Munshin), *Will Success Spoil Rock Hunter?* (Ann Corio), *O Mistress Mine* (Sylvia Sidney).

1958–59: *Visit to a Small Planet* (Eddie Mayehoff), *The Chase* (John Beal), *The Country Girl* (Nancy Coleman), *My Three Angels* (John Carradine), *Last Days of a Young Man* (Vicki Cummings), *The Rainmaker* (Meg Mundy), *The Hasty Heart* (John Kerr), *Dial "M" for Murder* (Judith Evelyn), *The Seven Year Itch* (Gene Raymond), *Pal Joey* (Ken Hamilton and Susan Willis).

1959–60: *Bells Are Ringing* (June Ericson and Tony Travis), *Once More, with Feeling* (Vicki Cummings), *Dark of the Moon* (Rita Moreno), *Our Town* (Tom Tully), *The Tender Trap* (Robert Q. Lewis), *Damn Yankees* (Betty Koerber), *Kind Sir* (Sylvia Sidney), *Born Yesterday* (Monique Van Vooren), *Hamlet* (Ray Boyle), *Who Was That Lady I Saw You With?* (Betty White), *Brigadoon*.

1960–61: *Two for the Seesaw* (Pat Carroll), *Death of a Salesman* (Walter Abel), *Bus Stop* (John Kerr), *Song of Norway*, *Othello* (Lee Henry), *The Marriage-Go-Round* (Gloria Grahame), *The Pajama Game* (Karen Morrow), *Rain* (Monique Van Vooren), *Send Me No Flowers* (Robert Q. Lewis), *Adam, the Creator* (David Hooks), *The Boy Friend* (Helen Strine and John Baylis), *Fallen Angels* (Ann B. Davis), *Under the Yum-Yum Tree* (Peggy Ann Garner).

1961–62: *A Midsummer Night's Dream, The Sea Gull, The Tavern, The School for Scandal, Fashion, The Matchmaker, Six Characters in Search of an Author, The Taming of the Shrew, The Crucible, Charley's Aunt.*

1962–63: *Beyond the Horizon, U.S.A., The Fantasticks, The Comedy of Errors, As You Desire Me, Major Barbara, The Elder Statesman, The Show-Off.*

1963–64: *The Madwoman of Chaillot, Twelfth Night, A Thurber Carnival, Tartuffe, The Hostage, Right You Are (If You Think You Are), Long Day's Journey into Night, The Fantasticks.*

1964–65: *The Playboy of the Western World, Oh, Dad, Poor Dad . . . ,Once upon a Mattress, Uncle Vanya, The Tempest, Under Milk Wood, Pantagleize, Anatol.*

1965–66: *Saint Joan, The Diary of a Scoundrel, The Time of Your Life, Mother Courage, The Servant of Two Masters, Henry IV,* Part I, *The Glass Menagerie.*

1966–67: *Electra, The Physicists, Design for Living, The Merchant of Venice, The Miser, Puntila and His Hired Man, Hedda Gabler.*

1967–68: *Othello, A Streetcar Named Desire, Amphitryon 38, Mary Stuart, Waiting for Godot, The Big Knife, The Importance of Being Earnest.*

1968–69: *The Skin of Our Teeth, Dulcy, The Imaginary Invalid, The Three Sisters, Marat/Sade, Dangerous Corner.*

1969–70: *A Midsummer Night's Dream, The Burgomaster, The Kitchen, Misalliance, The Prince of Peasantmania, She Stoops to Conquer, The Lesson* and *The Chairs.*

1970–71: *Medea, You Can't Take It with You, As You Like It, Spoon River Anthology, The Liar, A Doll's House.*

1971–72: *Cat Among the Pigeons, The English Mystery Plays, The White House Murder Case, Measure for Measure, A Delicate Balance, The Journey of the Fifth Horse.*

1972–73: *Two Gentlemen of Verona, Scenes from American Life, The Play's the Thing, The Cherry Orchard, Sticks and Bones, All Together Now. . . .*

1973–74: *Prisoner of the Crown, Knock, Our Town, The Tragical Historie of Dr. Faustus, La Turista, The Little Foxes.*

1974–75: *Down by the Gravois (Under the Anheuser-Busch), The Rehearsal, Androcles and the Lion, Richard II, Big Fish, Little Fish, A Day in the Death of Joe Egg.*

1975–76: *King Lear, Democracy, The School for Wives, The Visions of Simone Machard, Never a Snug Harbor, My Sister, My Sister.*

1976–77: *Death of a Salesman, The Trial of the Moke, Private Lives, Volpone, Vanities, The Dog Ran Away.*

1977–78: *Richard III, Long Day's Journey into Night, Ah, Wilderness!, Friends, High Time, Namesake.*

1978–79: *Romeo and Juliet, The Freeway, Island, Fighting Bob, Merton of the Movies, The Taming of the Shrew.*

1979–80: *The Recruiting Officer, The Dance of Death, On the Road to Babylon, Dead Souls, The Workroom, Of Mice and Men.*

1980–81: *Cyrano de Bergerac, Mother Courage, Children of a Lesser God, Julius Caesar, A Streetcar Named Desire, The Nerd.*

1981–82: *Fridays, Have You Anything to Declare?, Boesman and Lena, Kingdom Come, Born Yesterday, Secret Injury, Secret Revenge.*

1982–83: *Miss Lulu Bett, Buried Child, The Glass Menagerie, The Foreigner, Uncle Vanya, The Government Man.*

1983–84: *Much Ado About Nothing, American Buffalo, The Splintered Wood, The Forest, The Rules of the Game, Translations.*

1984–85: *The Revenger's Tragedy, Wenceslas Square, Master Harold . . . and the boys, The Devil's Disciple, Top Girls, A Woman Without Means.*

1985–86: *Henry IV*, Part I, *Two Brothers, The Art of Dining, The Crucible, A Flea in Her Ear, Joe's Remains.*

BIBLIOGRAPHY

Published Sources:

Berkowitz, Gerald M. *New Broadways*. Totowa, N.J.: Rowman & Littlefield, 1982.

Novick, Julius. *Beyond Broadway*. New York: Hill and Wang, 1968.

Ziegler, Joseph W. *Regional Theatre: The Revolutionary Stage*. Minneapolis: University of Minnesota Press, 11973.

Unpublished Sources:

Henry, Joyce E. "The Milwaukee Repertory Theatre and the Company It Keeps; A Chronicle: 1954–1971," Doctoral dissertation, University of Wisconsin-Milwaukee, 1972.

Milwaukee Repertory Theatre. "About the Milwaukee Repertory Theatre." Annual Report of the Milwaukee Repertory Theatre, 1985.

Milwaukee Repertory Theatre. *Playbills*, 1964–86.
Milwaukee Repertory Theatre. *Prologue Magazine*, 1975–86.

Archival Resource:
Milwaukee, Wisconsin. Milwaukee Central Library. Milwaukee Repertory Theatre Col-
    lection. News releases, clippings, reviews, and the "Milwaukee Repertory Theatre
    Chronology," updated each year by the Milwaukee Repertory Theatre staff.

Alex Pinkston

MINNESOTA THEATRE COMPANY. See GUTHRIE THEATRE COM-
PANY.

MISSOURI REPERTORY THEATRE grew out of the Summer Repertory
Theatre inaugurated by the University of Missouri-Kansas City (UMKC) in the
summer of 1964. Under the artistic direction of Patricia McIlrath, and with a
budget of $8,000, UMKC produced *The Corn Is Green*, by Emlyn Williams, and
Private Lives, by Noel Coward, in the University Playhouse on the UMKC campus. McIlrath, chair of the university's speech and drama department, proposed
to establish professional standards in theatrical production and to provide a nucleus
for a permanent, year-round company to be developed in the future.

The success of the first season prompted expansion in 1965 to four plays, one
of which was directed by guest professional director Rod Alexander. Guest
directors such as Alexander, John Houseman, Alan Schneider, Vincent Dowling,
John O'Shaughnessy, and Adrian Hall contributed significantly to the group's
measured progress toward full professionalization over the next few years.

The installation of much needed air conditioning in the University Playhouse
in 1967 cleared the way for the employment of some Equity professional performers. McIlrath believed the professional performers would enhance the impact
of training and experience imparted to students performing in the Summer Repertory Theatre and would facilitate the transition of students from amateur to
professional status. In 1968 McIlrath changed the name of the organization to
Missouri Repertory Theatre (MRT), expanded to a twelve-week season, and
introduced, with the aid of generous gifts and a grant from the Missouri Arts
Council, the Missouri Vanguard Theatre, a touring satellite of MRT under the
direction of James Assad. Over the next few years MRT seasons continued to
expand and to include increasing numbers of well-known guest directors from
the United States and abroad. In 1969, for instance, Alexis Minotis, former
general director of the Greek National Theatre, directed August Strindberg's *The
Father*, while Tone Brulin of the National Theatre of Belgium directed John
Osborne's *Look Back in Anger*. The Vanguard tour began February 28 and lasted
for seven weeks; the summer season of twelve weeks commenced July 4.

In 1977, with a new fine arts center under construction on the UMKC campus,
the University Playhouse was declared structurally unsound and had to be abandoned at the close of the summer season. A frantic search for alternate space
ended when MRT leased Danciger Auditorium at the Kansas City Jewish Com-

munity Center, where it made the transition to a two-season calendar that included both a twelve-week summer season and a month-long winter season in February 1978.

MRT's current home, the 595-to 733-seat, flexible-stage Helen F. Spencer Theatre, opened July 5, 1979, with a gala production of *Hamlet*, directed by Ellis Rabb. The same year McIlrath established MRT, Inc., a not-for-profit corporation, independent of UMKC. Each of MRT's two seasons was fourteen weeks long, a calendar that prevailed until 1986. MRT introduced its short-lived Showcase Theatre in 1980. Showcase Theatre afforded company apprentices and interns more opportunity to perform and permitted MRT to stage new plays in development. MRT added a production of Charles Dickens' *A Christmas Carol* in 1981. It became an annual event. MRT also produced David Edgar's adaptation of Dickens' *The Life and Adventures of Nicholas Nickleby*, with the help of Leon Rubin, one of the three original directors of the Royal Shakespeare Company production. McIlrath experimented further by presenting two productions in straight runs rather than in the repertory format used since the group's inception.

McIlrath retired in 1985 and George Keathley replaced her as artistic director of the repertory company while Jacques Burdick succeeded her as chair of the UMKC theatre department. As both chair of the UMKC department of theatre and artistic director of MRT, McIlrath had been a pioneer in the integration of professional theatre into an academic theatre program (see also American Repertory Theatre*, Dallas Theatre Center*, McCarter Theatre Company*, and Yale Repertory Theatre*). In her twenty-two years McIlrath managed the growth of an organization that has become nationally prominent, especially for the prestige of guest directors she has employed. MRT under McIlrath also established and maintained a strong base of community and university support.

George Keathley had trained with Maria Ouspenskaya, Erwin Piscator, and Lee Strasberg. In 1950 he founded his own theatre in Miami, Florida, which he headed for six years. Subsequently he directed in New York, where his revivals of *The Glass Menagerie* by Tennessee Williams and the Ruth and Augustus Goetz adaptation of Andre Gide's *The Immoralist* had lengthy runs. He then served as artistic director of the Philadelphia Playhouse in the Park and of Chicago's Ivanhoe Theatre, where he won a Joseph Jefferson Award for his directing. Keathley also won an Emmy in 1984 for directing the daytime drama *One Life to Live*. Keathley was immediately faced with sharp cutbacks in university support, forcing MRT to reduce the size of the 1985–86 resident and touring seasons. The 1986–87 season, the first chosen under Keathley's direction, marked a major change in MRT production policy, for Keathley instituted a seven-play season of straight, limited runs. The abandonment of repertory, a cost-cutting measure, met with audience approval, for subscription sales were up about 16 percent over 1985–86. Additionally, the season opener, Neil Simon's *Brighton Beach Memoirs*, has been the biggest seller in MRT history. Keathley believes straight runs will be more attractive to quality actors who may have

avoided MRT because of the lengthier commitment required by repertory cal-
endaring, but he admits the change may result in fewer acting opportunities for
UMKC theatre students. In 1986 MRT began a ''Second Stage'' program devoted
to developing new plays and playwrights. More than 400 new scripts were
reviewed and seven were selected for rehearsed readings. Second Stage, under
the direction of Beverly Shatto, asks audiences to participate in discussions after
readings and to fill out response forms. Scripts may be revived in more fully
staged readings, and then they may be selected for full production in the regular
season. In addition to the change in production format and the plan to include
more new plays in the regular season, Keathley also wants to employ stars to
improve the commercial attractiveness and the artistic quality of MRT productions.

MRT auditions under McIlrath's artistic direction were held in Kansas City
and in New York. Keathley has vowed to continue to use local talent whenever
possible. MRT tours, which covered ten states and went as far afield as Fort
Meyers, Florida, in 1985–86, will continue, as will MRT's extensive in-school
programs.

PERSONNEL

Artistic Directors: George Keathley (1985–86), Patricia McIlrath (1964–85).

Executive Director: James D. Costin (1964–86).

Directors: Rod Alexander (1965–66, 1970), Ray Aranha (1975), *James Assad* (1958,
1975–78, 1980–82, 1984), Norman Ayrton (1980), Peter Bennett (1986), Tone Brulin
(1969), Gavin Cameron-Webb (1977), Richard Carrothers (1969), *Francis Cullinan*
(1975–83, 1985–86), *Vincent Dowling* (1972–75, 1979, 1983), Robert Elliott (1970),
William Glover (1972), Thomas Gruenewald (1973–76), Gerald Gutierrez (1979), Adrian
Hall (1974), Joseph Hamer (1969), George Hamlin (1979, 1981), Pamela Hawthorn
(1984–85), Norris Houghton (1982), John Houseman (1971), Robin Humphrey (1970–
72, 1975), George Keathley (1979, 1983, 1986), Jerome Kilty (1985), Fritz Andre Kracht
(1967), Michael Langham (1978), *Patricia McIlrath* (1964–68, 1970, 1972–75, 1980–
81, 1983–84), Albert Marre (1979), Cedric Messina (1981, 1983), Alexis Minotis (1968–
69), J. Sterling Morton (1969), Kevin O'Morrison (1976), *John O'Shaughnessy* (1969–
74, 1976), Albert Pertalion (1982–85), Ellis Rabb (1979–80), John Reich (1976–78,
1981, 1984), Cyril Ritchard (1977), Leon Rubin (1983–85), Ying Ruocheng (1984),
Alan Schneider (1973), Harold Scott (1977), Robert Smith (1977), Robert Speaight
(1972), Alvah Stanley (1967–68), Andrew T. Tsubaki (1978), Boris Tumarin (1978),
Erik Vos (1980, 1982, 1985), *J. Morton Walker* (1964–68, 1973), William Woodman
(1970), Tunc Yalman (1975).

Designers: William D. Anderson (1983–85), *Joseph Appelt* (1973–86), Les Appelt
(1978–79), Jack Ballance (1984–86), Howard Bay (1983–84), *Max Beatty* (1964–67,
1969–71, 1974, 1976–77), Michele Bechtold (1979–82), Barry Bengston (1978–79),
James Blackwood (1967–70, 1976), Nigel Boyd (1983–84), S. O. Butler (1973), Herbert
L. Camburn (1984–85), Suellen Childs (1968–69), Franco Colavecchia (1980–81), Barbara J. Costa (1971), *Judith Dolan* (1972–75, 1977–80, 1982–83), Douglas E. Ederle
(1981–82), *John Ezell* (1972, 1974–86), *Harry Feiner* (1981–85), Steven B. Feldman
(1984–85), Richard Ferguson-Wagstaffe (1973–74), Daniel Thomas Field (1978–79),
Arden Fingerhut (1980–81), Karen Gerson (1984–85), Max Gile (1965), James F. Gohl

(1979–80, 1983–84), Wray Steven Graham (1982–84), Niels Hamel (1985–86), Kathleen Harrington (1965), Richard Hay (1980–81), Richard Hieronymous (1968–71), Frederic James (1968–69, 1975–77), Robert Jared (1982–83), Howard Jones (1981–82), *James Leonard Joy* (1976–81), Judy A. Juracek (1976), J. Henry Kester (1985–86), Robert LaVoie (1984–85), Ruth Ludwick (1980–83), Thomas MacAnna (1972), Jackie Manassee (1985–86), Victoria Marshall (1982–84), Barbara E. Medlicott (1975–77), Jack Montgomery (1970–71, 1978–79), Robert Moody (1984–85), Richard Moore (1983–84), Keri Muir (1981–83), Eden Lee Murray (1978–79), Michael J. O'Kane (1975), Curt Ostermann (1975–77), David Potts (1982–83), *Carolyn Leslie Ross* (1978–84), Philippe de Rozier (1976), Douglas A. Russell (1973–74, 1980–81), Robert R. Scales (1984–85), *Vincent J. Scasselatti* (1964–86), Tom Schenk (1982–83), Max Schlackman (1974), Michael Schweppe (1978–79), James Shehan (1977), Kenneth Slattery (1967), Baker S. Smith (1976, 1978–85), Paige Southard (1975), James Hart Stearns (1975), John Carver Sullivan (1981–84), Jon Terry (1984–85), Delbert L. Unruh (1978–79), Mariann Verheyen (1981–82), J. Morton Walker (1965, 1968, 1970–71, 1974–75), Donnell Walsh (1973), Janet Warren (1972), Anne Thaxter Watson (1975), Lee Watson (1970), Charles Weeks (1971–72), Susan A. White (1981–82), James Zeiger (1966).

Actors and Actresses: Mary Adams-Smith (1983–84), Rod Alexander (1965), Richard K. Allison (1976), Andy Alsup (1983–85), Joicie Appell (1968, 1974), Ray Aranha (1970), Jack Aranson (1982–83), *James Assad* (1964–65, 1967, 1969, 1975, 1983–84), *Walter Atamaniuk* (1974–80), Irwin Atkins (1968), Peter Aylward (1978–80, 1981–82), Irene Ballenger (1966), Daniel Barnett (1979–80), David Baron (1982–83), Roger Michael Baron (1985–86), Peter Bartlett (1968), Geoffrey Beauchamp (1979–80, 1982–83, 1984–85), Stephen Benson (1976), Harriet Biggus (1967), *Jim Birdsall* (1979–85), Charlotte Booker (1973–80), Ed Bordo (1967, 1969), Susan Borneman (1975–76), Barry Boys (1977), John Brandon (1972), Rand Bridger (1983–84), Joseph Brockett (1966), *Richard C. Brown* (1965–67, 1975–76, 1978–80, 1984–85), Caren Browning (1984–85), *John Q. Bruce, Jr.* (1966, 1969–76, 1982–83), Vicki Bruce (1966), Floyd Bunce (1964), Carolgene Burd (1976, 1982–83, 1984–85), Gerard A. Burke (1980–81), Robert Burke (1979–80), Al Burns (1976), James Burr (1970), Jackie Burroughs (1977), George Word Byers, Jr. (1974), Peter Byger (1983–84), Sharon Calloway (1966), Richard Calvin (1968), Richard Carrothers (1965), Paul Carson (1969–70), Dalton Cathey (1976), David Chadderdon (1976), Daryl Champine (1984–85), Leah Chandler (1966), Kay Christ (1981–82), Philip Christopher (1970), Al Christy (1971, 1974, 1975), Jim Clancy (1984–85), Stella Clancy (1984–85), Laurence P. Clement (1984–85), Lynn Cohen (1964, 1966, 1975, 1976), Toby Cohen (1966), Liza Cole (1975, 1976, 1979–80), Robert Cole (1964), Jerome Collamore (1980–81, 1983–84), Rosanne E. Coppage (1983–85), *John Cothran, Jr.* (1977–80, 1982–83, 1985–86), David Doxwell (1979–81), Ellen Crawford (1976–79), J. B. Crump (1964), Christopher Cull (1984–86), Brian Cutler (1984–85), Sidney Cutright (1971), James Robert Daniels (1973, 1977–79, 1981–82), Joan Darrow (1964–65), Jo Ella Deffenbaugh (1966–67, 1969–71), Cecelia DeLaurier (1972), David Des Jardins (1969), Richard Dix (1984–85), Vincent Dowling (1974), *Cynthia Dozier* (1979–83), James Duley (1966), Ron Durbin (1976), Richard Durham (1967), *Robert Elliott* (1966–79, 1982–83), *Art Ellison* (1965–74, 1976, 1978–80), Gene L. Eugene (1971), Valarie Fagan (1985–86), Jonathan Farwell (1984–85), Charles Fee (1985–86), Vivian Ferrara (1971), James Fields (1983–84), Bramwell Fletcher (1975), Jane Fopeano (1984–85), Craig French (1964–65), Marla Frumkin (1975, 1977), Nina Furst (1978–79), Michelle Garrison (1974), Mike Genovese (1977–78), Buckner Gibbs (1977), Steven Gilborn

(1972), Max Gile (1966), C. B. Gilford (1964), Christopher Glendon (1969), Sally
Gordon (1970), Ken Graham (1974, 1976), Rebecca Graham-Cronin (1984–85), Marty
Greene (1976), *Susan Rae Greve* (1983–86), Kathryn Grody (1972), *Richard Gustin*
(1980–83, 1985–86), Jeffrey Guyton (1984–85), *Richard Halverson* (1967–69, 1971,
1981–82, 1983–85), Craig Handel (1981–82), Michael Haney (1979–80), Larry Hansen
(1985–86), Carl Harms (1983–84), Olivia Virgil Harper (1985–86), Jeffrey Hayenza
(1982–83), Lambry Hedge (1984–85), Tracy Lynne Hill (1984–85), Kevin Hofeditz
(1984–85), Frederic Homan (1970), Walter Hook (1979–80), Karen Hopper (1965), Paul
Hough (1976), *Barbara Houston* (1980–85), John Houston, Jr. (1977), Mark Houston
(1985–86), Earnest L. Hudson (1976), Evelyn Huffman (1964), *Robin Humphrey* (1965–
67, 1969–70, 1972–73, 1977–81, 1982–84), Margaret Humphreys (1982–83, 1984–85),
Glenn Hunt (1966), *Jeannine Hutchings* (formerly *Jeannine Weeks*) (1974–76, 1981–
84), John Ingle (1966), Patricia Ingraham (1965, 1967), Lynna Jackson (1983–84),
Rosemary John (1981–82), Gary Neal Johnson (1982–85), Ronald M. Johnson (1976),
Sandee Johnson (1985–86), George Kahn (1981–82, 1984–85), *Robert Lewis Karlin*
(1979–84, 1985–86), Dewey Keener (1979–80), Stephen Keener (1978–80), Chuck Kee-
ton (1965), Hubert Kelly, Jr. (1984–85), William Kiehl (1983–84), Rob Knepper (1982–
83), Jim Korinke (1976), William Kuhlke (1983–84), *Michael LaGue* (1973–76, 1979–
80, 1983–85), Sherry Lambert (1979–80), Dottie Lane (1966), Philip Larson (1970),
Ken Latimer (1982–83), James La Vaggi (1979–80), *Charles Leader* (1982–86), Robin
League (1967–68), Stephen Lee (1979–80), *Harriet Levitt* (1965–67, 1969–75, 1977),
J. Stanley Levitt (1965, 1971), Robert M. Lewis (1964), Priscilla Lindsay (1973), Richard
Lippman (1964), Gary Logan (1983–85), David Lyman (1966), Marilyn Lynch (1977–
78), Joyce McBroom (1979–80), Melinda McCrary (1983–85), Jerry McGonigle (1983–
84), Molly McGrevy (1970), Linda McGuire (1964), Katie Madden (1966, 1974), Lou
Malandra (1976), Graeme Malcolm (1984–85), Martin Marinaro (1971, 1982–83), Doris
Martin (1980–81), Wilbert L. Mathews (1973), Paul Meacham (1984–85), Kirk Mee
(1966–67), Michael Mertz (1972–73), Sally Mertz (1972–73), Randy Messersmith (1984–
85), William Metzo (1980–81, 1985–86), Steve Meyer (1977), Christine Michael (1978–
79), Damon Millican (1983–85), James F. Mitchell (1983–84), Merle Moores (1978–
80), Ryan Morgan (1980–81, 1982–83), Eden Lee Murray (1977–78), Michael Murray
(1965), Lina Murrish (1964, 1966), Meg Myles (1975), Sarah Nall (1982–83, 1984–85),
Duncan Naylor (1980–81), Alan Nichols (1978–79), Josephine Nichols (1985–86), Nancy
Nichols (1980–81), Rolla Nuckles (1966, 1977), Tony Nugent (1964), Michael O'Hare
(1982–83), Oliver O'Herlihy (1975), Etain O'Malley (1983–84), Holmes Osborne (1971–
72, 1978–79), Tom Otteson (1966), Edith Owen (1977–78, 1980–83), Meg Wynn Owen
(1979–80), Angie Pallett (1966), Herbert Mark Parker (1981–85), Steven Passer (1984–
85), Marisa Pavan (1983–84), Hannibal Penney, Jr. (1973), Frances Peter (1974, 1977,
1981), Carol Pfander (1966–67, 1969, 1974), Richard Pilcher (1966), Madelyn Porter
(1977), Dan Putman (1979–80), *Juliet Randall* (1977–84, 1985–86), Mary-Linda Rapelye
(1974, 1978), Je. Raphael (1981–83), Ray-Roy (1964), Nancy Reardon (1978–80), Cynthia M. Rendlen (1982–84), Howard Renensland (1974), Loren Reyher (1985–86), Walter
Rhodes (1975), Jacqueline Riggs (1982–83), Patricia Ripley (1968), *Mark Robbins* (1979–
85), Judy Roberts (1964–65), Leslie Robinson (1975), Libby Roman (1982–84), Joanna
Roos (1967), *Becca Ross* (later Elizabeth Robbins) (1981–83, 1984–85), Cherie Ross
(1983–84), Steven Ryan (1972–75), Peter Sanders (1983–85), Laura San Giocomo (1984–
85), John Scanlon (1982–83, 1984–85), David Schramm (1981–82), Carl Schurr (1977),
David Schuster (1981–82, 1984–85), *Robert Scogin* (1970–74), Steve Searcy (1975),

Susan K. Selvey (1982–83, 1984–85), Roger Seward (1966), Beverly Shatto (1981–83), Curtis Shaw (1985–86), Cherie Shuck (1968), William Simington (1982–85), Peg Small (1981–84), Tom Small (1981–84), Donegan Smith (1969), Kenneth Smith (1983–85), Robert L. Smith (1973, 1981–82), Felicia Soper (1974), Kathryn C. Sparer (1979–81), Sylvia Spencer (1968), *Alvah Stanley* (1967–71), Jack Stehlin (1983–84), Edward Stevlingson (1970), Dorothy Stinette (1969), Carolyn Stockwell (1965), Henry Strozier (1975), John Sullivan (1965), James M. Symons (1983–84), Todd Taylor (1979–80), Gloria P. Terrell (1975–76), Eberle Thomas (1975), Heidi Thomas (1984–85), Donna Thomason (1976), *Don Tomei* (1980–85), Norman Trigg (1965), William Turner (1977), Michael Tylo (1977), Peter Umbras (1982–85), Holly Villaire (1968–69), Ray Virta (1984–85), Valerie Von Volz (1971, 1973), J. Morton Walker (1965, 1967, 1970, 1972), *Ronetta Wallman* (1970–76, 1978–84), Frederick Walters (1983–84), Susan Waren (1983–85), Von H. Washington (1975–77), Ronald Wendschuh (1978–80, 1982–84), Alice White (1976–77, 1981–82), Eva Wielgat (1984–86), Curt Williams (1968), Frederic Winslow-Oram (1982–83, 1984–85), Donald Woods (1980–81), Claude Woolman (1973, 1982–83), Laura Ann Worthen (1983–84), John Yadrick (1965–66), Alan Zampese (1978), James Zvanut (1982–83).

REPERTORY

1964: *The Corn Is Green, Private Lives.*

1965: *Twelfth Night, Tartuffe, Candida, The Lady's Not for Burning.*

1966: *Marat/Sade, She Stoops to Conquer, Crime on Goat Island, Camille.*

1967: *The Physicists, You Can't Take It with You, The Importance of Being Earnest, Richard III.*

1968: *Oedipus Rex, The Miser, Aegina, Philadelphia, Here I Come!.* Vanguard Touring Productions: *The Glass Menagerie, The White House.*

1969: *The Father, Our Town, A Flea in Her Ear, Look Back in Anger, The Taming of the Shrew.* Vanguard Touring Productions: *J.B., Blithe Spirit.*

1970: *The Skin of Our Teeth, Harvey, Indians, Exit the King, The Tempest, Arms and the Man.* Vanguard Touring Productions: *Arms and the Man, Spoon River Anthology, The Marriage Proposal.*

1971: *Measure for Measure, The Subject Was Roses, The Waltz of the Toreadors, The Night Thoreau Spent in Jail, The School for Wives, An Enemy of the People.* Vanguard Touring Productions: *The Subject Was Roses, See How They Run.*

1972: *Murder in the Cathedral, Cat Among the Pigeons, Barefoot in the Park, Long Day's Journey into Night, The House of Blue Leaves, Borstal Boy.* Vanguard Touring Productions: *Tartuffe, Angel Street, The Strolling Players, The Director, Dandelion Wine.*

1973: *Straight Up, Pygmalion, One Flew over the Cuckoo's Nest, Othello, Hedda Gabler, Jabberwock, Henry V.* Vanguard Touring Productions: *Charley's Aunt, The Fourposter.*

1974: *The Rivals, Peg o' My Heart, That Championship Season, A Midsummer Night's Dream, The Effect of Gamma Rays on Man-in-the-Moon Marigolds, Peer Gynt.* Vanguard Touring Productions: *Pygmalion, Hedda Gabler, Androcles and the Lion.*

1975: *Born Yesterday, The Cherry Orchard, Much Ado About Nothing, The Last Meeting of the Knights of the White Magnolia, A Streetcar Named Desire, In the Well of the House;* Vanguard Bonus: *Dear Liar, I Am Black.* Vanguard Touring Productions: *Peg o' My Heart, Dear Liar.*

1976: *The Rainmaker, The Morgan Yard, The Drunkard, Don Juan of Flatbush, The Great White Hope, The Heiress, Who's Afraid of Virginia Woolf?, Once in a Lifetime.* Vanguard Touring Productions: *The Rainmaker, The Morgan Yard.*

1977: *The Glass Menagerie, The Orphans, The Misanthrope, Old Times, Mary Stuart, The Hostage, The Morning Star, Purlie Victorious.* Vanguard Touring Productions: *The Orphans, The Glass Menagerie.*

1978: *The Imaginary Invalid, All My Sons.* Vanguard Touring Productions: *The Imaginary Invalid, All My Sons.*

1978–79: *Julius Caesar, Light Up the Sky, The Shadow Box, The Sea Gull, Rashomon, The Happy Hunter, Bus Stop, The Little Foxes.* Vanguard Touring Productions: *Bus Stop, The Little Foxes.*

1979–80: *Hamlet, Rosencrantz and Guildenstern Are Dead, The New York Idea, The Chalk Garden, Oh, Coward!, The Visit, Twelfth Night, Look Homeward, Angel.* Vanguard Touring Productions: *Hamlet, Twelfth Night.*

1980–81: *Medea, What Every Woman Knows, The Learned Ladies, Catsplay, Clearview Heights, The Fall of Troy, Choices, Lady Audley's Secret, The Night of the Iguana, Wings, A Perfect Gentleman.* Touring: *What Every Woman Knows, The Learned Ladies.*

1981–82: *The Three Sisters, Talley's Folly, Picnic, The Good Person of Szechwan, The Dinner Party, The Cruise, The Dove Gifts, A Dream of Vermillion Splendor, A Christmas Carol, The Royal Family, Loose Ends, Crown of Thorn, Macbeth.* Touring: *Talley's Folly, Picnic.*

1982–83: *Antony and Cleopatra, Hay Fever, The Magnificent Yankee, Terra Nova, And Miss Reardon Drinks a Little, The Enchanted, Gardens Wither, A Christmas Carol, The Innocents, Translations, The Life and Adventures of Nicholas Nickleby.* Touring: *Hay Fever, Terra Nova.*

1983–84: *Sea Marks, The Importance of Being Earnest, The Dresser, The Speckled Band: An Adventure of Sherlock Holmes, The Showman, Soldaderas, A Christmas Carol, Life with Father, Retro, Trio, The Taming of the Shrew.* Touring: *The Importance of Being Earnest.*

1984–85: *Strider, True West, Come Back, Little Sheba, Fifteen Strings of Cash, A Cabaret Evening, Duse and D'Annunzio, Miss Julie, A Christmas Carol, Romeo and Juliet, Crimes of the Heart, Masters of the Sea, Peter Pan.* Touring: *Come Back, Little Sheba.*

1985–86: *Agamemnon, Foxfire, Side by Side by Sondheim, The Good Doctor, A Candle for Jimmy Dean, Gods and Unbelievers, Miss Millay Was Right, A Christmas Carol, Fallen Angels, Master Harold . . . and the boys, Othello.* Touring: *Side by Side by Sondheim, Foxfire.*

1986–87: *Brighton Beach Memoirs, Equus, Fool for Love, A Christmas Carol, A Class "C" Trial in Yokohama, And Miss Reardon Drinks a Little, The Glass Menagerie.*

BIBLIOGRAPHY

Published Sources:
Kansas City Star, 1964–86.
Kansas City Magazine, November 1986.
Backstage Banner, MRT Subscriber Newsletter.

Unpublished Source:
Kansas City, Missouri. University of Missouri-Kansas City Archives. MRT Programs, 1964–86; Raymond R. Gould, "Missouri Repertory Theatre: A History of Productions."

Timothy D. Connors

MOPPETT PLAYERS. See CHILDREN'S THEATRE COMPANY.

MUMMERS THEATRE, Oklahoma City, Oklahoma, began operation in 1949 when a group of amateurs known as the Mayde Mack Mummers produced 1890s-style melodramas in a tent theatre. During its twenty-three-year history the Mummers achieved professional status and national recognition. Although the Mummers began as a community theatre under the direction of elected officers, Mack Scism, a member of the group, soon assumed the role of managing director, a position he retained until the demise of the Mummers in 1972.

The Mummers staged melodramas in a tent for two summer seasons. Then, for four seasons the group performed in a room in the Municipal Auditorium building. During the first winter season the bill of plays changed to more standard theatrical fare. The search for a more permanent home brought the Mummers to a warehouse they remodeled as a theatre in the round and occupied for sixteen years. In 1970 the Mummers moved into a new theatre built with funds supplied by the Ford Foundation and local fund-raising campaigns. The organization ceased operation in 1972 after two years in the new building.

Mack Scism, who assumed the direction of the Mummers in its early days, was a native of Oklahoma, educated in the public schools of Oklahoma City and at the University of Oklahoma, where he majored in engineering. Scism acquired an informal education in theatre through experience, reading, and travel. At the time he joined the Mummers, Scism headed the department of speech at Capitol Hill High School in Oklahoma City.

In later years the Mummers employed personnel who were trained in university theatres as well as in the commercial theatres of New York, Chicago, and Los Angeles. These salaried employees served as designers, technicians, costumers, directors, and publicity directors.

The first members of the Mummers theatre espoused a threefold purpose. They wanted to establish a theatre in Oklahoma City that would be a civic asset, they wanted a vehicle for self-expression, and, ultimately, they wanted theatre training for youth of the area. While in its formative stages the Mummers, and especially Mack Scism, sought and received advice from several sources, especially from Margo Jones, who had started a professional theatre in Dallas (see Margo Jones Theatre). As early as 1951 the purposes of the organization began to shift when Scism began to agitate for professional status; in 1964 the Mummers became a resident professional theatre.

During the early years critical evaluations of the performances were limited to reviews by local reporters. In 1970, on the occasion of the premiere production in the new theatre, a writer for the Associated Press noted that Oklahoma's resident professional theatre set a standard any of the nation's leading regional companies should be pleased to maintain.

During its twenty-three-year history the Mummers Theatre had little competition in Oklahoma City. The Jewel Box community theatre operated as an adjunct to a local church, providing an outlet for amateur actors after the Mummers became professionals. The Lyric Theatre, a summer music theatre, operated while the Mummers was closed for the season.

Initially, elected officers governed the Mummers, and all the production work was handled by volunteers. By 1958 the Mummers employed a staff of five, including the director, a technical director, a teacher of children's theatre, a box-office manager, and an office assistant. Production chores were done by volunteers until 1962, when the Mummers employed a production staff that included a technical director, a stage manager, a costume designer, and two production assistants. After 1962 the affairs of the organization were directed by a board of trustees and an administrative staff, an arrangement that characterized the operation of the Mummers until its demise in 1972.

Although the members of the fledgling community theatre started with a debt in the hundreds of dollars in 1949, they could not know their venture would collapse with a debt of hundreds of thousands of dollars. After starting with nothing in 1949, the Mummers Tent Theatre finished the first summer in the black, so it proceeded to plan a winter season. The early years were difficult, but by 1962, when the members voted to change from amateur to professional status, the expenses of production and operation were budgeted at $57,800 and income from all sources was $58,000. Between 1948 and 1955 the organization saved $23,000 in cash reserves. In 1962 the Mummers received a grant of $1,250,000 to build a new theatre in Oklahoma City, but Scism's dream was not realized until 1970. By then, operational deficits extending back to 1964, when Scism first hired actors, had reduced the cash reserves to such an extent that the Mummers folded after only two brief seasons in its new home.

The Mummers produced 150 plays between the summer of 1949 and February 1972. During the first five years the selection of plays included several previously unproduced scripts. Broadway comedies, such as Joseph Kesselring's *Arsenic and Old Lace* and Garson Kanin's *Born Yesterday*, were staples on the annual play lists. Plays that Scism called "classics" were also prominent in the seasonal lists, including works by Noel Coward, George Bernard Shaw, Shakespeare, and Luigi Pirandello. Plays by contemporary American playwrights William Inge, Arthur Miller, and Tennessee Williams also appeared frequently in the Mummers roster of plays. In twenty-three years the Mummers offered a variety of well-mounted productions to the theatregoer in Oklahoma City. Attendance records were established by productions of such well-known plays as *Hamlet*, *Macbeth*, Robert Bolt's *A Man for All Seasons*, Mary Chase's *Harvey*, and

Williams' *Cat on a Hot Tin Roof*. Plays that drew low-capacity houses included some of the original scripts mounted in the early years as well as better-known works such as Paul Osborn's *Mornings at Seven, My Three Angels*, by Sam and Bella Spewack, and Harry Kurnitz's *Reclining Figure*.

From 1949 until 1964 the actors and actresses performing in plays at the Mummers, primarily under the direction of Mack Scism, came from metropolitan Oklahoma City. For the most part they were teachers, lawyers, businessmen, secretaries, housewives, schoolchildren, and local television and radio personalities. Although most of the performers played only a few roles, a few appeared frequently enough to attract a local following, for example, Jerry Allred (thirty-three roles), Mary Weeks Ingle (twenty-one roles), Clyde Martin (thirty-five roles), Stanley Zenor (forty-three roles).

From 1964 to 1972 Scism employed a company of actors composed of local residents, people from other resident professional theatres, and an occasional star, such as Edward Mulhare (Sir Thomas More in *A Man for All Seasons*) or Dody Goodman (Dolly Levi in Thornton Wilder's *The Matchmaker*). In 1964, when Scism first employed actors at the Mummers, he drew his company primarily from the pool of local talent. Of the nine actors and actresses who constituted the first company, six were local and three were hired from auditions in New York and Chicago. Scism reversed this pattern by 1972, when he had seventeen in his company, only two of whom were local. Scism was never able to attract nationally known performers in any numbers to his theatre in the heartland. The Mummers Theatre closed February 12, 1972, during the repertory run of Neil Simon's *The Odd Couple* and Wilder's *The Matchmaker*.

PERSONNEL

Management: Presidents: Bonnie Allred (1956), Jim Booher (1959), Ruth Dropkin (1957–58), Jack Durland (1963–69), Glen Finefrock (1960–61), Mack Jones (1949–54), E. C. Ted Smith (1962), Hortense Taylor (1955–56), Sidney Upsher (1970–71). Treasurers: Bryan Arnn (1970–71), Lamar Cory (1953), Ruth Dropkin (1959–60), Frank J. Hightower (1963–69), Doris Johnson (1949–50), Paul Oakes (1954–55), John Orr (1957–58), Paul Perkins (1951–52), Leo Shultz (1961).

Business Managers: Louise Johnson (1970), John Orr (1959–66), Dianne Schonwald (1971), Mack Scism (1952).

Stage Directors: Anne Ault (1961), David Christmas (1972), Joanne Combs (1966), Saylor Creswell (1971), William Duell (1950), Joan Finefrock (1960), Jack Going (1972), Nagle Jackson (1971), Jack Jones (a/k/a Andrew Way [1962–69]), Charles Kephart (1963), Gene Lasko (1967), Jean McFaddin (1968–70), John Mosely (1949), Dollett Norris (1967), Ron Pitts (1962), Joseph B. Sax (1966–67), Lee Schirk (1951–53), Mack Scism (1949–51, 1953–72), Judge Springer (1964), Larry Suffill (1949), Porter Van Zandt (1970), John Wylie (1969–72).

Designers (Costumes, Lights, Sets, and Sound): Olga Alfreff (1967), Dean Andrew (1958), George Ashton (1960), Ben Benson (1955, 1962, 1963, 1965, 1969), Ed Bohling (1953), Joe Carder (1963), Bill Dallas (1950–52, 1956–68), Don Davis (1951), Bill

Dawson (1952), Madeline Dougherty (1949), Diann Fay (1970–71), Jack Haggard, Jr. (1952), Katherine Hammett (1968), Rick Hardin (1970–72), Nikki Harmon (1971), Glenda Highland (1967), Jean McFadden (1967–69), Stephen A. Milam (1971), Gene Nowell (1949, 1952), John Pittman, Jr. (1956–57, 1966–67), Glenard Quiette (1952), William Schroder (1959, 1970–72), Mack Scism (1959), Pamela Scofield (1971), Lorene Seago (1951), Robert Steinberg (1968–71), Gary Stevens (1968), Charles Stockton (1971–72), Warren Stroud (1952), Clara Tokken (1959–60, 1962), Gene Tomlins (1959), Jeri Walker (1967–68), La Verne Walker (1952), Helene Wilkinson (1967–69), John Wylie (1970–71).

Actors and Actresses (The Mummers Theatre operated as a community theatre using local talent from 1949 until the spring of 1964): Professional Company: Raymond Allen (1968–69), *Anne Ault* (1967–71), Tony Aylward (1971), Joanna Bayless (1969), Charles Berendt (1970), Susan Brown (1964–66), Saylor Creswell (1970), Jack Davidson (1967), Stephen DePue (1969), Maurice Eaves (1964–65), George Ede (1971), Carolyn Ellis (1964), Laura Esterman (1967), Gwyllum Evans (1971), Sean Griffin (1968), Jack Hammett (1967), Charles Hyden (1966), *Jack Jones* (a/k/a Andrew Way [1964–68]), *Tom Kroutil* (1964–69), Bob Lashbrook (1966), Dennis Longwell (1968), Robert Machray (1970), Mary Michaels (1970), Vincent Duke Milana (1971), John Milligan (1968–69), Garry Moore (1969), Pamela Muench (1969), Ken Parker (1964–66), Garry Phillips (1971), Carl Reggiardo (1969), Joseph B. Sax (1965–66), Grant Sheehan (1968), Christopher Shelton (1970), Benjamin Slack (1970), Fern Sloan (1968), *Louise Speed* (1964–70), Judge Springer (1964–66), Bille Dee Stone (1964), Peter Stuard (1971), Angela Wood (1970), Claude Woolman (1970), *John Wylie* (1967–71). Guest Actresses and Actors: Joan Bassie (1971), Jack Carruthers (1972), Ethel Barrymore Colt (1971), Clarence Felder (1971), Maxwell Glanville (1967), Dody Goodman (1971), Earl Hindman (1971), Gertrude Jeanette (1967), Tamara Long (1972), Edward Mulhare (1970), Michael Parish (1971), Virginia Payne (1969), Kathleen Phelan (1967), Jane Marla Robbins (1971), Rudolph Willrich (1971).

REPERTORY

Summer 1949; *The Drunkard, East Lynne, Ten Nights in a Barroom, Fashion, Dirty Work at the Crossroads.*

1949–50: *Louder Please, Summer and Smoke.*

Summer 1950: *The Drunkard, Maria Marten, The Streets of New York, Lost in Egypt, Uncle Tom's Cabin, Sweeney Todd, Nick of the Woods, Ticket-of-Leave Man.*

1950–51: *Light up the Sky, Rope's End, Blithe Spirit, Joan of Lorraine, You Touched Me, Two Blind Mice.*

1951–52: *The Women, Arsenic and Old Lace, Ah, Wilderness!, Private Lives, The Silver Cord, Roadside.*

1952–53: *Heaven Can Wait, Child's Play* (original script), *Heartbreak House, Starfish* (original script), *Hay Fever, Sainted Sisters* (original script).

1953–54: *No Room for Peter Pan* (original script), *Philadelphia Story, The Pursuit of Happiness, Bell, Book, and Candle, The World Within* (original script), *Claudia.*

1954–55: *Voice of the Turtle, Dark of the Moon, Illusion* (original script), *She Stoops to Conquer, Anna Christie, My Three Angels.*

1955–56: *An Italian Straw Hat, King of Hearts, The Rainmaker, Pelleas and Melisande, Misalliance, The Time of the Cuckoo.*

1956–57: *The Solid Gold Cadillac, Man of Destiny, Mornings at Seven, Macbeth, Cradle Song, The Happy Time, Getting Married.*

1957–58: *The Madwoman of Chaillot, Julius Caesar, The Glass Menagerie, Janus, Inherit the Wind, Bus Stop.*

1958–59: *The Boy Friend, The Hasty Heart, The Fourposter, The Merchant of Venice, The Country Girl, The Corn Is Green, The Moon Is Blue.*

1959–60: *Middle of the Night, Reclining Figure, Othello, Visit to a Small Planet, A Streetcar Named Desire, Born Yesterday.*

1960–61: *The Boy Friend, The Lady's Not for Burning, Kind Sir, Death of a Salesman, The Women, As You Like It, Picnic.*

1961–62: *Detective Story, The Marriage-Go-Round, The Matchmaker, Hamlet, The American Dream, Krapp's Last Tape, The Crucible, The Seven Year Itch.*

1962–63: *The Fantasticks, Invitation to a March, Gallows Humor, Summer and Smoke, The Importance of Being Earnest, The Caine Mutiny Court Martial, The Mousetrap, The Man Who Came to Dinner.*

1963–64: *Dark of the Moon, Antigone, Life with Father, Cat on a Hot Tin Roof, The Chalk Garden, Twelve Angry Men, The Miracle Worker, The Best Man.*

1964–65: *Only in America, Who'll Save the Plowboy?, Harvey, Long Day's Journey into Night, Bus Stop, The Diary of Anne Frank, Night of the Iguana, The Remarkable Mr. Pennypacker.*

1965–66: *The Disenchanted, The Little Foxes, Arsenic and Old Lace, Volpone, The Devil's Disciple, Hay Fever, The Glass Menagerie, Look Homeward, Angel.*

1966–67: *The Fantasticks, Rashomon, The Tavern, Mademoiselle Colombe, Ah, Wilderness!, Two for the Seesaw, Major Barbara, You Can't Take It with You.*

1967–68: *The Member of the Wedding, In White America, Night of the Dunce, Life with Mother, The Three Sisters, Arms and the Man, Right You Are (If You Think You Are), A Brecht Syntopicon* (original script), *Strange Bedfellows.*

1968–69: *State of the Union, Misalliance, Our Town, The Sea Gull, Big Fish, Little Fish, Hedda Gabler, A Thousand Clowns.*

1969–70: *Blithe Spirit, Charley's Aunt, Spoon River Anthology, The Pursuit of Happiness, The World of Sholom Aleichem, Black Comedy, The Lady's Not for Burning, The Marriage-Go-Round.*

1970–71: *A Man for All Seasons, Dear Liar, The Rivalry, The Misanthrope, The World of Carl Sandburg, A Phoenix Too Frequent, Bedtime Story, Arsenic and Old Lace, Star-Spangled Girl, See How They Run.*

1971–72: *The Taming of the Shrew, The Man Who Came to Dinner, Dames at Sea, The Odd Couple, The Matchmaker.*

BIBLIOGRAPHY

Published Sources:

Advertiser (Oklahoma City, Oklahoma), 1953, 1963, 1964, 1966.

Daily Oklahoman (Oklahoma City, Oklahoma), 1949–72.

Journal (Oklahoma City, Oklahoma), 1965.

Monitor (Moore, Oklahoma), 1966–67.

New York Times, 1963.

Times (Oklahoma City, Oklahoma), 1972.

Women's Wear Daily (New York), 1967.

Blake, Peter. "The Mummers Theatre." *Architectural Forum*, March 1971, pp. 30–36.

Daily Oklahoman (Oklahoma City, Oklahoma), 1949–72.

Johansen, John. "Mummers Theatre: A Fragment, Not a Building." *Architectural Forum*, May 1968, pp. 64–69.

MacKay, Patricia J. "Oklahoma City's New Mummers Theatre." *Theatre Crafts*, May-June 1971, pp. 6–13.

"New Plays Staged at Two Theatres." *Theatre Arts*, February 1953, p. 86.

Novick, Julius. *Beyond Broadway*. New York: Hill and Wang, 1968.

Schechner, Richard. "Ford, Rockefeller and Theatre." *Tulane Drama Review* 10 (Fall 1965): 23–49.

Schmidt, Sandra. "The Regional Theatre: Some Statistics." *Tulane Drama Review* 10 (Fall 1965): 50–61.

Welsh, Willard. "Mummers Theatre, Oklahoma City." *Players Magazine*, June-July 1969, pp. 190–94, 218–19.

Unpublished Source:

Alexander, Darrel Eugene. "A History of the Mummers' Theatre, Oklahoma City, Oklahoma, 1949–1972." Doctoral dissertation, Louisiana State University, 1974.

Archival Resources:

Oklahoma City, Oklahoma. Oklahoma Christian College. Speech Department. Darrel E. Alexander. Taped interviews with Mack Scism and other Mummers Theatre personnel. Manuscript history of Mummers Theatre by Mack Scism.

Oklahoma City, Oklahoma. Oklahoma Theatre Center. Minutes of meetings 1950–62 (incomplete), financial records, attendance records, correspondence, photographs, playbills, and miscellaneous materials.

Oklahoma City, Oklahoma. Personal collection of Florene Garner. Scrapbook.

Oklahoma City, Oklahoma. Personal collection of Gweneth Geller. Scrapbook.

Darrel E. Alexander

N

NEGRO ENSEMBLE COMPANY, New York City, also known as the NEC, was founded in 1967 by Douglas Turner Ward, actor-director-playwright; Robert Hooks, actor-producer; and Gerald S. Krone, producer-manager. They leased The St. Marks Playhouse (built in 1958 at 133 Second Avenue), which contained a 145-seat theatre with an open playing area and space to accommodate rehearsals, workshops, offices, and set storage. The company's initial production, on January 2, 1968, was the premiere of Peter Weiss' *Song of the Lusitanian Bogey*, a play vehemently attacking colonialism in Africa.

Founded during the fervent 1960s during which increased numbers of blacks in the diaspora began to explore their African ancestry and assert their identities as individuals and as part of a major cultural group, the NEC, the New Lafayette Theatre (1966–73), and the New Federal Theatre of the Henry Street Settlement (founded 1970) expanded the employment opportunities of black artists of the theatre. The NEC, however, remains the only fully professional black theatre company in the United States. The company's longevity is remarkable, but its accomplishments are even more notable in the development of black and American drama and theatre. The group developed several black playwrights and a large body of plays concerned with contemporary and historical Afro-American, Afro-Caribbean, and African life. More than 5,000 actors, directors, designers, technicians, theatre managers, and other business personnel have received training and/or the opportunity to apply and develop skills at the NEC. Finally, the development of black audiences nationally and internationally through the company's tours of selected plays is a significant accomplishment.

In November 1965 Robert Hooks produced two one-act plays written by Douglas Turner Ward, *Happy Ending* and *Day of Absence*. Gerald S. Krone and Dorothy Olim managed the plays that were presented at St. Marks Playhouse in the East Village. Ward had acted in several significant productions in New York, while Hooks had created the role of Clay in Imamu Amiri Baraka's (at the time LeRoi Jones') *Dutchman* and had organized the Group Theatre Work-shop, which offered tuition-free acting instruction. Krone-Olim Associates had produced several productions off- and off-off-Broadway.

Ward's satiric plays ran for more than 500 performances, and during the run Ward was invited by the *New York Times* to write an article on the status of the black artist in the American theatre. Ward's "American Theatre: For Whites Only?" (August 14, 1966) enumerated reasons a professional theatre company connected to a training program is required to develop black audiences, play-wrights, actors, designers, stage managers, and other theatre personnel. Ward recognized the need for a permanent theatre committed to producing plays whose primary audience would be black, basing his vision on the practicalities that he, Hooks, and Krone had experienced producing *Happy Ending* and *Day of Absence*.

Ward's article was the key to a Ford Foundation grant of $434,000, which provided the financial base on which the NEC was established as a professional theatre and workshop on April 1, 1967. Douglas Turner Ward was the artistic director of the new group, Robert Hooks the executive director, and Gerald S. Krone the administrative director.

The NEC was to utilize professional theatre artists for productions and in its training programs. The four major thrusts of the company were to maintain a resident acting company of fifteen; to provide instruction and training for the resident company; to train an apprentice company, using students of Hook's Group Theatre Workshop as the nucleus; and to support the experimental work of a playwrights' and directors' unit.

The instruction and training of the resident company began in the fall of 1967. For three months the members took classes six days a week. Paul Mann conducted the acting classes, Louis Johnson the dance and movement, Kristin Linklater the voice, and John Blair the classes in karate. The intensive training created a common vocabulary and frame of reference for the resident company. The ap-prentice classes, conducted by Lloyd Richards and Ron Mack, were in acting, voice, dance, and technical aspects of the theatre. Apprenticeships in theatre administration; press relations; set, costume, and lighting design; box-office and house management; wardrobe; and stage management were offered. Lonne Elder III coordinated the playwrights' and directors' unit.

During its first four years the NEC employed a resident acting company, members of which were given alphabetical billing and identical salaries. The company gave eight performances per week (Tuesdays through Fridays and Sundays at 8:30, and Saturdays at 7:00 and 10:30; matinees on Sundays at 3:00). Four major plays were presented in runs of four to six weeks each in a twenty-six-week season. Only once since its beginning years has the company been able to sustain a resident company. During the 1978–79 season thirteen actors were employed for five months. Since that time the company auditions and employs actors for each play. The minimum LORT (League of Resident Theatres) Equity salary for each category of artist and alphabetical listing is still maintained. Over

the years the Saturday matinee has replaced the second Saturday evening performance.

The Ford Foundation granted NEC $1.2 million during its first three years.
Financial management was difficult in the early 1970s, but worsened during the
mid-1970s when the Ford Foundation reduced its support of the company and
the nation's economy began to decline. The company had to subsist on its box-
office receipts and on contributions that the Ford Foundation only matched. To
extend its resources, the company reduced its staff, selected plays with small
casts, and reduced the cost of scenic designs. During the 1977–78 season rehearsals were compressed. Each of the four plays offered had only a two-week
run, and Ward and the company's office staff declined their salaries for three
months. The company increased its income when, in September 1980, it moved
to Theatre Four (built in 1962 at 424 West Fifty-fifth Street) and more than
doubled its seating capacity (from 145 to 299 seats). The move to the current
theatre also drew NEC closer to Broadway and Lincoln Center and made the
group more accessible to more theatregoers.

The company's top ticket price before its move to Theatre Four was less than
$8. After the move, ticket prices ranged from $7.95 to $12. Higher production
costs have necessitated subsequent increases, but the NEC's policy is to maintain
the lowest feasible ticket prices. The company is determined not to become a
totally "sold-out" subscription theatre, so that tickets are available to those who
can afford to purchase tickets only a short time before or on the day of a
performance.

Even though the company does realize profits from its national tours, free
training of theatre artists and personnel was impossible to support from a budget
of solely earned income. Although only the Playwrights' Workshop is operative
now, the company does plan to restore other workshops when it is financially
able to do so. Apprenticeships in theatre management and production have
continued since the founding of the company. The NEC considers grants from
the New York State Council on the Arts, the National Endowment for the Arts,
and other foundations essential; nevertheless, the company is striving toward
financial independence. A primary goal of establishing permanence appears to
have been accomplished, for the company has survived for nineteen years,
through several financial crises.

The most unfortunate effect of insufficient funding was the termination of the
company's tuition-free training programs. In 1972, 125 students were enrolled
in the company's various training programs, including the productive "works
in progress" component of the Playwrights' Workshop. The Playwrights' Workshop was the last to be terminated, indicating the emphasis the company places
on the development of black American plays. Several of the NEC's critically
successful plays originated in its Playwrights' Workshop. Samm-Art Williams,
author of *Home*, attributes much of his development as a playwright to NEC
workshops. Charles Fuller, author of *Zooman and the Sign* and *A Soldier's Story*,

also values the NEC and Douglas Turner Ward's role as artistic director in his development as a playwright.

Fortunately the Playwrights' Workshop was restored and is, today, the sole workshop of the company. It is coordinated by Leslie Lee, author of *The First Breeze of Summer* and *Colored People's Time*. Participants read their works in weekly seminars, after which fellow playwrights and Lee analyze and evaluate them and offer suggestions for improvement. At the end of the season NEC subscribers are invited to closed readings of the works. Selected plays may then receive staged readings or workshop productions; exceptional ones may undergo additional work and be mounted as a main production of the company.

In addition to the plays of its developing playwrights, the company's literary manager and its play readers screen from seventy-five to one hundred scripts per year. Currently the chief literary manager is Gus Edwards. Lonne Elder III and Steve Carter have also held the post. The literary manager relays the recommendations of the readers to managing director Leon Denmark. Denmark may make additional recommendations to Douglas Turner Ward, but Ward sees all the scripts and decides ultimately which plays will be produced and which actors will perform the roles. The plays produced by the company indicate its commitment to produce works illuminating all aspects of black life. Although the NEC reserves the right to produce plays by anyone, primarily it has produced plays by black Americans.

The satiric *Day of Absence* (1969–70), a one-act play by Ward; the ritualistic *Ododo* (1970–71), by Joseph A. Walker and Dorothy A. Dinroe; the folkloric *Dream on Monkey Mountain* (1970–71), by Derek Walcott; the realistic *The River Niger* (1972–73), by Walker; the romantic *Home* (1979–80), by Samm-Art Williams; and the mixed genres of *Zooman and the Sign* (1980–81) and *A Soldier's Play* (1981–82), by Charles Fuller, exemplify the diversity of the forms, styles of production, theme, characterization, and structure in the body of plays produced by the company. Although the company has produced a wide variety of types and styles of plays, Ward believes that realistic works have been the most influential. He feels that the critical and popular acceptance of NEC productions has influenced Broadway to return to realism as its dominant mode, after it had embraced avant-garde European influences in the 1960s. A consensus of critics' opinions is that the NEC's productions are usually superior to the plays themselves; but considering the awards its plays have won and the fact that the NEC produces primarily new works, its accomplishments are extraordinary.

More plays about contemporary black life in America have come from the NEC than from any other source. Quantity has not precluded quality, for excellence in the company's work has been nationally and internationally recognized, as this listing of the group's awards will attest:

1967–68: Vernon Rice Drama Desk Award; Obie Award (Special Citation for Excellence) to the NEC.

1968–69: Tony Award (Special Achievement in the Theatre) to the NEC; Premio Roma Award—Artistic Excellence and Production of *Song of the Lusitanian Bogey*, by Peter Weiss; Vernon Rice Drama Desk Award for *Ceremonies in Dark Old Men*, by Lonne Elder III.

1969–70: Brandeis University Creative Award to the NEC.

1970–71: Obie Award (Outstanding New Play), *Dream on Monkey Mountain*, by Derek Walcott; Guggenheim Fellowship to Lonne Elder III.

1971–72: Dramatists' Guild Award; Vernon Rice Drama Desk Award for *Sty of the Blind Pig*, by Phillip Hayes Dean.

1972–73: Vernon Rice Drama Desk Award, Obie Award (Outstanding New Play), and Dramatists' Guild Award for *The River Niger*, by Joseph A. Walker (off-Broadway production).

1973–74: 1973 Tony Award (Best Play) for *The River Niger* (Broadway production); Obie Award (Outstanding New Play) for *The Great MacDaddy*, by Paul Carter Harrison; Guggenheim Fellowship to Joseph A. Walker.

1974–75: Obie Award (Outstanding New Play) and Margo Jones Award for *The First Breeze of Summer*, by Leslie Lee (off-Broadway production).

1975–76: New York State Arts Council Award to the NEC; Tony Award Nomination (Best Play) and Clarence Derwent Award for *The First Breeze of Summer* (Broadway production).

1976–77: Obie Award (Outstanding New Play) and Audelco Black Audience Award for *Eden*, by Steve Carter; Bronze Medallion of New York City to the NEC.

1977–78: Eudora Welty Television Award to Charles Fuller, author of *The Brownsville Raid*.

1978–79: Obie Awards (Outstanding New Play and Outstanding Ensemble Performance) for *Nevis Mountain Dew*, by Steve Carter, and for the cast of *Nevis Mountain Dew*.

1979–80: Outer Circle Critics John Gassner Playwriting Medallion; Drama Desk Award Nominations and Tony Award Nominations for Best Play for *Home*, by Samm-Art Williams, and for Best Actor, Charles Brown. Schubert Organization's James N. Vaughn Award for Excellence in the American Theatre to the NEC; Obie Award (Outstanding Play) for *LaGrima del Diablo*, by Dan Owens; 1980 Creative Artist Public Service Grant/Award to Ali Wadud, author of *Companions of the Fire*.

1980–81: Obie Awards (Outstanding New Play), *Zooman and the Sign*, by Charles Fuller, (Outstanding Performance) for Giancarlo Esposito as Zooman, and (Sustained Achievement in the Theatre) for NEC; Delta Sigma Theta Sorority Osceola Award for Artistic Achievement for NEC; Guggenheim Fellowship for Samm-Art Williams.

1981–82: New England Theatre Conference Special Award to the NEC; Pulitzer Prize to Charles Fuller for *A Soldier's Play*.

1982–83: Theatre Club Award for *A Soldier's Play;* American Theatre Wing Award to the NEC; NAACP Image Award to the NEC; Citations of Excellence from the cities of Atlanta, Chicago, Detroit, Hartford, Los Angeles, New York, Philadelphia, St. Louis, and Washington, D.C.

1984–85: Colonial Theatre Award, Boston, for *A Soldier's Play;* American Theatre Wing Award of $1,000 to the NEC; New York Urban League's Frederick Douglass Award for Distinguished Leadership Toward Equal Opportunity to the NEC; Academy Award Nominations for *A Soldier's Story*—Best Picture, Best Supporting Actor (Adolph Caesar), and Best Screenplay (Charles Fuller); Obie Award (Sustained Excellence) to Frances Foster; Doctoral Theatre Students of City University of New York, Third Annual Edwin Booth Award (Contributions to the New York Theatre) to the NEC and Douglas Turner Ward; Drama League Award to Karen Jones-Meadows for *Henrietta;* Boston Theatre Critics' Circle Awards to Douglas Turner Ward for Outstanding Presentation of *A Soldier's Play* at the Colonial Theatre and to Allen Hughes for Outstanding Lighting of *A Soldier's Play;* American Theatre Wing Award Grant to Consistently Nurture and Develop Talent for the Theatre to NEC.

1985–86: Rockefeller Foundation Fellowship to Paul Carter Harrison.

In addition to its national tours and recognition in the United States, the NEC, on invitation, has toured internationally and has participated in world dramatic festivals. The company was also invited to present plays as part of the official cultural program presented in conjunction with the Olympic Games of 1972 and 1984.

After just five years of existence the company had developed a large body of plays and numerous black artists in every aspect of the theatre. In ten years the company had produced about fifty plays and had screened more than 5,000 scripts.

The growth of the company's black audience is the most reliable test of the relevance and significance of the company's plays to blacks. For the first productions 80 percent of the NEC's audiences were white; however, by the end of the first season its audiences were 60 percent black. In five years 80 percent of the NEC's audiences were black, 20 percent white. Generally this ratio has remained in subsequent years. The rate of growth of the NEC's black audience is even greater than it appears, for the company's seating capacity has more than doubled since its founding.

The effect of the NEC on black theatre and American theatre has been gargantuan. Before the NEC there were few roles for blacks, other than those of a servile, one-dimensional nature. Frances Foster, a member of the original resident company who still performs regularly with the NEC, refers to the majority of the roles available to black actresses in pre-NEC days as "dinner-is-served roles" (Interview, July 18, 1982). Not only has there been much critical acclaim for the company and its members, but the majority of blacks who work in theatre, film, and television have studied and/or worked at the NEC. Ward recognizes the economic appeal to work in film and television, and he finds it gratifying that many return to work at the NEC.

Theatre artists and historians recognize that the long-term achievements of the NEC—the great body of premieres, body of plays, the company's excellence in production, and its accomplished alumni of more than 5,000 persons—are attributable in significant measure to the inspiration of the founders of the NEC, but especially the dedication of artistic director Douglas Turner Ward.

Ward was born on May 5, 1930, in Burnside, Louisiana. He came to New York aspiring to become a journalist and evolved into a playwright. To facilitate his writing for the stage, he became an actor and was known professionally until 1972 as Douglas Turner as an actor, and as Douglas Turner Ward as a playwright and director. Since 1972 he has been known in all his artistic endeavors by his full name.

Before he was known as the author of the highly acclaimed *Happy Ending* and *Day of Absence*, Ward had been involved in several productions significant in the history of black and American theatre: he was Joe Mott in *The Iceman Cometh* at the Circle in the Square (New York City, 1956); the Moving Man in the Broadway production of Lorraine Hansberry's *A Raisin in the Sun*, which opened in 1959; and an understudy to Sidney Poitier in the role of Walter Lee Younger. He played Walter Lee with Claudia McNeil (as Mama) in the national tour of the play. It was during the Broadway production and national tour of *A Raisin in the Sun* that Ward and Robert Hooks became acquainted. Ward replaced Roscoe Lee Browne in Jean Genet's *The Blacks*. After James Earl Jones, he played Zachariah Pieterson in *The Blood Knot* in 1963. Since the NEC's founding, Ward has been not only president of the board of directors and an acclaimed actor in several of the company's productions, but also a brilliant director and, indisputably, the guiding force of the NEC.

Robert Hooks was born on April 18, 1937, and reared in Washington, D.C. He attended Temple University before coming to New York in 1959, where, as Bobbie Dean Hooks, he was a replacement in the role of George Murchison in *A Raisin in the Sun*. He then performed in the national tour of the play. Hooks replaced Lincoln Kilpatrick as Deodatus Village in *The Blacks* (New York City, 1961) and he was the Boy in *A Taste of Honey* during the tour of the play to Washington, D.C., in 1962. He appeared as Dewey Chipley in *Tiger, Tiger Burning Bright* (New York City, 1962), as Dennis Thornton in *Ballad for Bimshire* (New York City, 1962), and as the Stage Assistant in *The Milk Train Doesn't Stop Here Anymore* (New York City, 1964).

As Robert Hooks, he created the role of Clay in *Dutchman* (New York City, 1964), and he played the title role in *Henry V* (New York City, 1965). Hooks performed several roles at the NEC and served as its executive director before founding the D.C. Black Repertory Company (1973–77) in Washington, D.C. Since then he has acted numerous roles in film and television, has directed, and has formed a film production company with Lonne Elder III. Hooks serves as a lifetime member of the NEC's board of directors.

Gerald S. Krone, born February 25, 1933, in Memphis, Tennessee, spent some formative years in Los Angeles, where he developed an interest in theatre, but he was primarily reared near Memphis. Krone attended Washington University in St. Louis, Missouri, where he received a B.A. in English and sociology. During his first trip abroad he lived in England, studied Shakespearean drama, and was an observer of the Royal Shakespeare Company in London. Krone also received an M.A. degree from Washington University, where he then taught. With Dorothy Olim, his former wife, he formed Krone-Olim Associates, a production and management company. He and Olim managed Ward's plays *Happy Ending* and *Day of Absence*. Krone served as administrative director from the NEC's inception and intermittently to 1981; he is also a life member of the board of directors. Krone is director of creative services for Geller Media Management, Incorporated.

Developing more female black playwrights, launching a classics series, and purchasing its own theatre are three projects that the company has recently undertaken.

PERSONNEL

Artistic Director: Douglas Turner Ward (1967–86).

Active Executive Director: Robert Hooks (1967–73).

Administrative Director: Gerald S. Krone (1967–81).

Managing Directors: Leon Denmark (1981–86), Fred Garrett (1967–76).

Literary Managers: Steve Carter, Gus Edwards, Lonne Elder III.

Directors: *Edmund Cambridge*, Walter Dallas, *Clinton Turner Davis, Hal DeWindt*, Glenda Dickerson, Bill Dukes, Richard Gant, *Paul Carter Harrison, Israel Hicks, Dean Irby*, Regge Life, *Gilbert Moses, Shaunielle Perry, Lloyd Richards, Michael Schultz, Horacena J. Taylor, Douglas Turner Ward*.

Designers: *Martin Aronstein*, Ernest Baxter, Ken Billington, *Bertha Brock*, LaDonna Brown, Jeanne Button, Steve Carter, Felix E. Cochren, *Judy Dearing*, Michael DeVine, *Jules Fisher*, Paul Gallo, Joe Gandy, Samuel Gonzalez, William H. Grant III, Bernard Hall, Gary Harris, Allen Lee Hughes, Neil Peter Jampolis, *Bernard Johnson*, Larry Johnson, *Dik Krider, Whitney LeBlanc, Regge Life*, Tommie Louie, Rodney J. Lucas, Arthur McGee, Tharon Musser, Dennis Ogburn, Pamela Peniston, Kathy Perkins, Alvin Perry, *Shirley Prendergast*, Judy Rasmuson, Raymond G. Recht, William Ritman, *Sandra L. Ross*, Betty Sample, Clyde Santana, Eric Stephenson, Wynn Thomas, Jennifer Tipton, Charles Vincent, Mary Mease Warren, Edna Watson, Lisa Watson, Sylvester Weaver, Jr., Gary James Wheeler, Marshall Williams.

Playwrights: Michael J. Abbensetts, Janus Adams, Ade Adembla, *Ray Aranha*, Ben Bates, Calvin Beckett, Lennox Brown, *Ed Bullins, Steve Carter, Alice Childress*, Buriel Clay II, Gail Davis, *Philip Hayes Dean*, Alexis DeVeaux, *Gus Edwards, Lonne Elder III*, E. Ernest, *Don Evans*, Laura Fowler, *J. E. Franklin, Charles Fuller, J. E. Gaines*, Clay Goss, Jackie Greene, Gertrude Greenidge, Bonnie Greer, *Bill Gunn*, Bill Harris, *Paul Carter Harrison, Errol Hill*, Weldon Irvine, Julie Jensen, Herman Johnson, Reginald Vel Johnson, Ramona King, Roy R. Kuljian, Gyavira Lasana, Jim Lee, *Leslie Lee*, Karmyn Lott, Winston Lovett, Theresa McGriff, *Judi Ann Mason*, Mustapha Matura, *Barbara Molette, Carlton Molette*, Katherine Peppers, *Trevor Rhone, Ted Shine, Wole Soyinka, Ali Wadud, Derek Walcott, Joseph A. Walker, Douglas Turner Ward, Peter Weiss, Richard Wesley*, Grady Whitfield, *Samm-Art Williams, Richard Wright*.

Musicians: *Margaret Harris, Pat Patrick, Coleridge-Taylor Perkinson.*

Choreographers: Mary Barnett, Talley Beatty, *George Faison, Louis Johnson, Diane McIntyre*, John Parks, *Eleo Pomare, Rod Rodgers*, Shawneequa Baker Scott, Andy Torres.

Photographer: *Burt Andrews.*

Actors and Actresses (partial listing; # denotes original members of the acting company): David Ackroyd, Alvin Alexis, *Mary Alice, Ray Aranha, Ethel Ayler*, Paul Benjamin, Earl Billings, George Bowe, *Charles Brown, Graham Brown, Roscoe Lee Browne, #Norman Bush*, Betty K. Bynam, *Adolph Caesar, L. Scott Caldwell, Godfrey Cambridge, #Rosalind Carter, Steve Carter*, Brian Evaret Chandler, Robert Christian, Bill Cobbs, Chuck Cooper, Clayton Corbin, David Davies, Peter DeMaio, Carla Deon, John Dewey-Carter, *#David Downing, Ja'net DuBois*, O. L. Duke, Ventura Edgerson, *#Judyann (Jonsson) Elder*, Terrance (Terry) Ellis, Ben E. Epps, *Giancarlo Esposito*, Gwyllum Evans, *Antonio Fargas*, Laurence Fishburne, Kathleen Forbes, *#Frances Foster, Al Freeman, Jr., #Arthur French*, Peter Friedman, *Minnie Gentry*, Jesse D. Goins, Danny Goldring, Carl Gordon, Robert Gordon, Robert Gossett, *Elain Graham*, Reuben Green, David Alan Grier, *#Moses Gunn*, Jeffrey St. L. Anderson Gunter, Olivia Virgil Harper, Berkeley Harris, *Julius Harris, Jackée Harry*, Lorey Hayes, *Sherman Hemsley*, Kene Holliday, *Robert Hooks*, Samuel Jackson, Robert Jason, *#William Jay*, Brent Jennings, Lauren Jones, Steven Jones, Herb Kerr, Janet League, Eugene Lee, Gil Lewis, *Cleavon Little*, Dan Lutzky, Timothy Lynch, James McDaniel, Sam McMurray, Juanita Mahone, Carol L. Maillard, Dana Manns, Jeffrey Mathews, *Hazel J. Medina, Stephanie Mills, Barbara Montgomery*, Leon Morenzie, *Debbie Morgan, Garrett Morris, #Denise Nicholas, Ron O'Neal*, Roscoe Orman, Bill Overton, Chuck Patterson, James Pickens, Jr., *Phylicia Rashad, Rayno, Larry Riley*, Naomi Riseman, Maree Rogers, *Roxie Roker, Richard Roundtree*, Shirley Rushing, Fran Salisbury, *Sarallen, Seret Scott*, Frances Sharp, *Michele Shay*, Jean Smart, Cotter Smith, Kim Staunton, *#Clarice Taylor, Glynn Turman, Sullivan H. Walker, Douglas Turner Ward, Denzel Washington*, Charles Weldon, Curt Williams, *Samm-Art Williams*, Anita Wilson, *Teddy Wilson, #Hattie Winston*, Terry Woodberry, *#Allie Woods*, Stephen Zettler.

REPERTORY

1967–68: *Song of the Lusitanian Bogey*, by Peter Weiss; *Summer of the Seventeenth Doll*, by Ray Lawler; *Kongi's Harvest*, by Wole Soyinka; *Daddy Goodness*, by Richard Wright. Monday Playwrights' Series: *One Last Look*, by Steve Carter; *Ladies in Waiting*, by Peter deAnda; *Two in a Trap*, by Ted Shine; *Black Is . . . We Are* (workshop project).

1968–69: *God Is a (Guess What?)*, by Ray McIver; *Ceremonies in Dark Old Men*, by Lonne Elder III; *String*, by Alice Childress; *Contribution*, by Ted Shine; *Malcochon*, by Derek Walcott. Workshop Festival: *The Mau Mau Room*, by J. E. Franklin; *Maggie*, by Lee Hunkins; *The Last Dragon* (workshop project); *Black Circles Around Angela*, by Hazel Bryant; *Man Better Man*, by Errol Hill.

1969–70: *The Harangues*, by Joseph A. Walker; *Brotherhood*, by Douglas Turner Ward; *Day of Absence*, by Douglas Turner Ward; *Akokowe* (coordinated by Afolabi Ajayi).

1970–71: *Ododo*, by Joseph A. Walker; *Perry's Mission*, by Clarence Young III; *Rosalie Pritchett*, by Carlton and Barbara Molette; *The Dream on Monkey Mountain*, by Derek Walcott; *Ride a Black Horse*, by John Scott. Repertory Workshop: *The Terraced*

Apartment, by Steve Carter; *Us vs. Nobody*, by Hal de Windt; *His First Step*, by Oyamo; *The Corner*, by Ed Bullins; *Dreams*, by Bill Duke.

1971–72: *The Sty of the Blind Pig*, by Phillip Hayes Dean; *A Ballet Behind the Bridge*, by Lennox Brown; *Frederick Douglass . . . Through His Own Words*, by Arthur Burghardt; Special Attractions Festival; Music and Dance Festival.

1972–73: *The River Niger*, by Joseph A. Walker. Repertory Workshop: *Laundry*, by Gertrude Greenidge; *Wild Flower*, by Robbie McCauley; *Indiana Avenue*, by Debbie Wood; *Galavantin' Husband*, by Milburn Davis; *The Death of Little Marcus*, by Herman Johnson; *Funnytime*, by Seret Scott; *Johnnas*, by Bill Gunn; *Playstreet*, by Ted Harris; *Crocodiles*, by Femi Euba; *The Riddle of the Palm Leaf*, by Femi Euba; *The Yellow Pillow*, by John Perkins; *Buy a Little Tenderness*, by Buriel Clay II.

1973–74: *The Great MacDaddy*, by Paul Carter Harrison. Season-Within-a-Season: *Black Sunlight*, by Al Davis; *Nowhere to Run, Nowhere to Hide*, by Herman Johnson; *Terraces*, by Steve Carter; *Heaven and Hell's Agreement*, by J. E. Gaines; *In the Deepest Part of Sleep*, by Charles Fuller.

1974–75: *The First Breeze of Summer*, by Leslie Lee. Season-Within-a-Season: *Liberty Call*, by Buriel Clay II; *Sugar Mouth Sam Don't Dance No More*, by Don Evans; *Orrin*, by Don Evans; *The Moonlight Arms*, by Rudy Wallace; *The Dark Tower*, by Rudy Wallace; *Welcome to Black River*, by Samm-Art Williams; *Waiting for Mongo*, by Silas Jones.

1975–76: *Eden*, by Steve Carter. Season-Within-a-Season: *The Trap Play*, by Reginald Vel Johnson; *A Love Play*, by Samm-Art Williams; *A Fictional Account of the Lives of Richard and Sarah Allen*, by Sylvia-Elaine Foard; *Kingdom*, by Ali Wadud; *Sunshine, Moonbeam*, by Alberta Hill; *Livin' Fat*, by Judi Ann Mason.

1976–77: *The Brownsville Raid*, by Charles Fuller; *The Great MacDaddy*, by Paul Carter Harrison; *The Square Root of Soul*, by Adolph Caesar. Playwrights' Unit Presentation: *1280 on Your Dial*, by William A. Walker.

1977–78: *The Offering*, by Gus Edwards; *Black Body Blues*, by Gus Edwards; *Twilight Dinner*, by Lennox Brown. Playwrights' Series: *Pathetique*, by Samm-Art Williams; *Sherry and Wine*, by Jimi Rand; *As Time Goes By*, by Mustapha Matura; *Bread*, by Mustapha Matura; *Mr. E.*, by Michael Abbensetts; *Last Brownstone in Brooklyn*, by Grady Whitfield; *Haliki*, by Mae Jackson; *A Long Way Home*, by Reginald Vel Johnson.

1978–79: Readings and Staged Readings: *The Pathetique*, by Samm-Art Williams; *The Ceremony*, by Ali Wadud; *Daughters of the Mock*, by Judi Ann Mason; *Nevis Mountain Dew*, by Steve Carter; *Faith and the Good Thing*, by Robert Glenn; *The Afrindi Aspect*, by Silas Jones; *Old Phantoms*, by Gus Edwards; *Brother Righteous*, by W. B. Burdine; *Masada*, by Edgar White; *Redeemer*, by Douglas Turner Ward; *Big City Blues*, by Roy R. Kuljian; *A Season to Unravel*, by Alexis DeVeaux; *The Imprisonment of Obatala*, by Obotunde Ijimere; *Everyman*, by Obotunde Ijimere; *Ozidi*, by J. P. Clarke; *The Raft*, by J. P. Clarke; *Willie*, by Leslie Lee; *Trade-Offs*, by Lonnie Carter; *Upon This Rock*, by Derek Walcott; *Woyengi*, by Obotunde Ijimere. Four Play Festival: *Nevis Mountain Dew*, by Steve Carter; *The Daughters of the Mock*, by Judi Ann Mason; *Plays from Africa: Everyman/Imprisonment of Obatala*, by Obotunde Ijimere; *A Season to Unravel*, by Alexis DeVeaux. Developmental Stages—Monday Evening Readings: *The Rain Stole Otis Moon*, by Calvin Beckett; *Steal Away*, by Ramona King; *The Will*, by Weldon Irvine; *Mainstream*, by Gyavira Lasana; *Pictures*, by Bonnie Greer; *Miss Lydia*, by Don Evans; *Old Phantoms*, by Gus Edwards.

1979–80: Readings and Staged Readings: *What Can You Call This . . . ?*, by Suhuba Tillar; *Renaissance*, by Elmo Terry Morgan; *Jeff and Jenny*, by Brenda Collie; *The Noirhommes*, by Dan Owens; *Home*, by Samm-Art Williams; *Mainstream*, by Gyavira Lasana; *LaGrima del Diablo*, by Dan Owens; *Signs of Preparation*, by Gyavira Lasana; *The Michigan*, by Dan Owens; *The Drink That Follows*, by Suhuba L. Pertillar; *Echoes and Memories*, by Gus Edwards; *It All Comes Out in the Wash*, by Michael Darrell; *The Truth About the Truth*, by Harold Stuart. Four Play Productions: *The Michigan*, by Dan Owens; *Home*, by Samm-Art Williams; *La Grima del Diablo*, by Dan Owens; *Companions of the Fire*, by Ali Wadud; *Big City Blues*, by Roy Kuljian. Developmental Stages: *Daniel and Simara*, by Ramona King; *The Comic*, by Winston Lovett; *1919*, by Bonnie Greer; *Chasing Dreams Is the Message*, by Grady Whitfield; *Fixed Income*, by Jim Lee; *Hot Sauce*, by Karmyn Lott; *Able to Leap from Tall Buildings in a Single Bound*, by Theresa C. McGriff.

1980–81: *The Sixteenth Round*, by Samm-Art Williams; *Zooman and the Sign*, by Charles Fuller; *Weep Not for Me*, by Gus Edwards. Developmental Stages Readings and Staged Readings: *Hush Sweet Baby*, by Karmyn Lott; *St. Steven: A Passion Play*, by Janus Adams; *Della*, by Ben Bates; *Strings*, by Ramona King; *The Favorite*, by Gyavira Lasana; *A Cup Full of Empty*, by Laura L. Fowler; *The Hunchback of Harlem*, by Winston Lovett; *Giant*, by Ade Ademola; *What Goes Around*, by Bill Harris; *Capricorn's Livery*, by E. Ernest; *Extentions*, by Jackie Greene; *Night of the Wizard Fantasy*, by Clyde Santana and Gail Davis; *In an Upstate Motel*, by Larry Neal.

1981–82: "A Salute to Black Classics in Music/Dance"; *A Soldier's Play*, by Charles Fuller; *Colored People's Time (C.P.T.)*, by Leslie Lee; *Abercrombie Apocalypse*, by Paul Carter Harrison.

1982–83: *A Soldier's Play*, by Charles Fuller; *Sons and Fathers of Sons*, by Ray Aranha; *About Heaven and Earth*, three one-acts including: *The Redeemer*, by Douglas Turner Ward; *Tigus*, by Ali Wadud; and *Night Line*, by Julie Jensen; *Manhattan Made Me*, by Gus Edwards.

1983–84: *Puppet Play*, by Pearl Cleage; *American Dreams*, by Velina Houston; *Colored People's Time (C.P.T)*, by Leslie Lee. Developmental Stages Readings: *Jonah Howard and His Wonder Dog*, by Judi Ann Mason; *Henrietta*, by Karen Jones-Meadows; *Creedmore*, by Ray Aranha; *My Girlish Days*, by Karen L.B. Evans; *Moody's Mood Cafe*, by Gus Edwards; *Longtime Since Yesterday*, by P. J. Gibson; *Eyes of the American*, by Samm-Art Williams; *D-E-L*, by Dan Owens.

1984–85: *District Line*, by Joseph L. Walker; *Henrietta*, by Karen Jones-Meadows; *Two Can Play*, by Trevor Rhone; *Ceremonies in Dark Old Men*, by Lonne Elder III.

1985–86: *Eyes of the American*, by Samm-Art Williams; *House of Shadows*, by Steve Carter; *Jonah and the Wonder Dog*, by Judi Ann Mason; *Louie and Ophelia*, by Gus Edwards.

BIBLIOGRAPHY

Published Sources:
Amsterdam News (New York, New York), 1967–86.
Daily News (New York, New York), 1967–86.
Long Island Press, 1967–77.
New York Times, 1967–86.
Post (New York, New York), 1967–86.

Village Voice, 1967–86.

The Negro Ensemble Company. Documentary film directed by Richard Kilberg. RKB
    Productions. September 14, 1987.

Unpublished Sources:

Andrews, Bert (company photographer). Personal interview. April 23, 1985.

Aubrey, Diane (director of development). Personal interview. April 30, 1985.

Card, Mary (company manager). Personal interview. May 2, 1985.

Crane, Cathy Lee (assistant controller/bookkeeper). Personal interview. May 2, 1985.

Davis, Clinton (director). Personal interview. May 20, 1985.

Denmark, Leon (managing director). Personal interview. April 22, 1985.

Foster, Frances (actress in original resident company). Personal interview. July 18, 1982.

French, Arthur (actor in original resident company). Personal interview. July 28, 1987.

Hayes-Dean, Phillip (playwright). Personal interview. July 25, 1987.

Howard, Portia (marketing director). Personal interview. April 24, 1985.

Hughley, Stephanie S. (general manager). Personal interview. April 30, 1985.

Krone, Gerald S. (cofounder). Personal interview. April 10, 1985.

Lee, Leslie (playwright/coordinator of Playwrights' Workshop). Personal interview. April
    29, 1985.

Misani (audience development). Personal interview. May 7, 1985.

Richardson, LaTanya (assistant to artistic director). Personal interview. April 29, 1985.

Walden, Larry (company manager). Personal interview. June 3, 1985.

Ward, Douglas Turner (cofounder/artistic director). Personal interview. May 4, 1984 and
    May 30, 1985.

Washington, Jennifer (assistant office manager/secretary). Personal interview. May 8,
    1985.

Visser, David (tour representative). Personal interview. May 2, 1985.

Archival Resources:

New York, New York. New York Public Library. Library and Museum of the Performing
    Arts. Clippings, programs (incomplete).

New York, New York. Schomburg Center for Black Research. Clippings, programs
    (incomplete), raw footage of scores of interviews filmed in making of documentary
    film, *The Negro Ensemble Company*.

The author acknowledges Douglas Turner Ward, Leon Denmark, and Deborah McGee,
    who graciously consented to allow her to examine the NEC's collection of pro-
    grams and national and international news articles.

                                                                    C. Joyce D. White

[THE] NEW AMERICAN THEATRE (NAT) was founded by actor-director-
manager J. R. Sullivan in Rockford, Illinois, in 1972. With little local theatrical
interest and Chicago only an hour's drive away, a resident theatre in Rockford,
a working-class city with a population of less than 150,000, seemed a dubious
enterprise. Karen and Bill Howard and Stephen Powers, a high school friend of
Sullivan's, were planning to open a coffeehouse called Charlotte's Web on the
first floor of an abandoned synagogue at 728 First Avenue in downtown Rockford.
Sullivan, a recent graduate of the theatre program at nearby Beloit College, saw
his chance, and, with the support of his friends, began renovating the second
floor of the building in the summer of 1972. The first production of the NAT,

Room Service, a comedy by John Murry and Allen Boretz, opened October 20, 1972, and generated strong public response. In each of the next two seasons the NAT produced ten plays and gave thirteen performances of each.

Though the NAT achieved popular and artistic success in its first two seasons, it was not, because of the small capacity of the theatre, a solvent operation: box-office receipts could not support the cost of the productions. The Howards financed most of the first two seasons, but they found it difficult to support the theatre with profits from the coffeehouse, and two businesses under one roof was a heavy responsibility.

For its third season the NAT moved to the larger Rockford Women's Club Theatre, opening there with a production of the Stephen Sondheim musical *Company*. The new, larger theatre caused new problems. In its first two seasons the NAT had developed an intimacy with its audience, a quality lost in the vast Rockford Theatre. In an effort to solve some of its financial problems, the NAT acquired not-for-profit tax status, but the burden of operating the Rockford Theatre forced them further into debt. The Rockford Park Service gave NAT a helpful enabling grant in 1975, but the group was still awash in debt. A frustrated Sullivan rested for a summer and then returned to Rockford to resume the struggle. The group renovated and adapted an old hotel at 118 South Main Street in Rockford's downtown shopping area where it opened its fourth season with its second production of Edgar Lee Masters' *Spoon River Anthology*. In this new space the financial fortunes of the group were righted.

The NAT tends to produce safe and relatively well-known works such as the Tom Jones and Harvey Schmidt musical, *The Fantasticks*, Shakespeare's *Two Gentlemen of Verona*, and Tennessee Williams' *The Glass Menagerie*. A few lesser-known classics such as John O'Keeffe's *Wild Oats* (1791) or more controversial plays such as Athol Fugard's *Master Harold . . . and the boys* and Stephen Metcalfe's *Strange Snow*, as well as new plays by "regional" writers such as Terrence Ortwein and Amlin Gray, are artistic and commercial experiments.

Shakespeare's *As You Like It*, opening in the middle of its fourteenth season, was the group's first production in the "New" New American Theatre, located on the site of the old hotel at 118 North Main Street. Designed by Larson and Barby Architects for the NAT, it houses all offices, rehearsal and support spaces, and two theatres: a proscenium stage before a 300-seat auditorium and a 125-seat auditorium wrapped around an arena stage. The smaller theatre also functions as a 200-seat cabaret named "Charlotte's Web" in acknowledgment of the coffeehouse origins of the group.

The NAT runs a seven-to ten-production season, September through June, playing to more than 40,000 admissions each year. Subscriptions numbered 3,650 in 1984–85. NAT sponsors a summer festival theatre at Beloit College, Beloit, Wisconsin. It also uses special programs to bolster local support and participation: touring productions, children's theatre, the Young American Theatre for children and teens, the Black Theatre Ensemble, and theatre workshops.

The NAT employs a large staff with a producing director, marketing director, production manager and assistant, box-office manager and assistant, production stage manager, various resident and guest directors, designers, actors, and, beginning with the 1986–87 season, two or three interns. A governing board of twenty patrons helps Sullivan set priorities and plan and sell the work of the group. In 1983 NAT negotiated a small professional theatre contract with Actors' Equity Association; in 1986 the company engaged six to eight Equity professional performers.

PERSONNEL

Management: J. R. Sullivan, producing director; Judith Barnard, marketing and development director; Robert Morgan, business manager.

Directors: Ted Bacino (1973), Carl Balson (1973), Allan Carlsen (1983, 1985–86), Kirk Denmark (1973), G. Michael Johnson (1979), B. J. Jones (1977, 1979, 1983), Ginny MacDonald (1981), Rod MacDonald (1973), Tim Olds (1984), Ricki Ravitts (1977–78), J. R. Sullivan (1972–86), James E. Sullivan (1972, 1975–76), Matt Swan (1981).

Designers: Jon R. Accardo (1976–86), Alan Bluestone (1973, 1977), Joy Butler (1973), Marie Hilgeman (1976–77), Marcia Hinds (1974–76), Theodor R. Hoerl (1972–73), Dan Kasten (1983–84), Kenneth Kloth (1975–76), Sue Ann Kreitlow (1974), Rod Maynard (1972–73), Lynn Means (1972), John Mitchell (1975–76), Bill Monroe (1973), Karen Nelson (1975–76), Michael S. Philippi (1982–86), David Radunsky (1985–86), Ellen Regan (1973–74), Matthew Rosmus (1972–73), Jim Russel (1972), Debora Threedy (1972–73), Stephen Ware (1976), James Wolk (1976–86).

Actors and Actresses (making long-term or otherwise significant contributions): Peter Aylward (1984–85), Carl Balson (1974–80), Dale Benson (1980), Allan Carlsen (1982–85), Brooks Gardner (1978), Richard Henzel (1980, 1984), Celia Howard (1982), B. J. Jones (1977–79), Roone (Ann) O'Donnell (1978), F. William Parker (1980), Michael Pierce (1977–82), Margaret Raether (1972–84), Richard Raether (1972–84), Ricki G. Ravitts (1973–85), Ellen Regan (1972–74), Ann Risley (1979), Matt Swan (1972–82), Hugh Thompson (1972–82), Suzanne-Theus Thompson (1979–85), William Windom (1980), Amy Wright (1972–74).

REPERTORY

1972–73: *Room Service, Adaptation, Next, Spoon River Anthology, Ben Hecht—Child of the Century, The Subject Was Roses, The American Dream, The Zoo Story, The Front Page, The Effect of Gamma Rays on Man-in-the-Moon Marigolds, Star-Spangled Girl, Death of a Salesman.*

1973–74: *Man of La Mancha, Who's Afraid of Virginia Woolf?, Boy Meets Girl, Wait Until Dark, House of Blue Leaves, . . . And Miss Reardon Drinks a Little, The Skin of Our Teeth, U.S.A., The Gingerbread Lady, A Streetcar Named Desire.*

1974–75: *Company, A Thousand Clowns, Arms and the Man, Sticks and Bones, Ah, Wilderness!, Hughie, A Flea in Her Ear, The Time of Your Life, The Tender Trap.*

1975–76: *Spoon River Anthology, The Fantasticks, The Miracle Worker, You Can't Take it with You, That Championship Season, The Sunshine Boys, The Liar.*

1976–77: *The Subject Was Roses, Candide, The Little Foxes, Three Men on a Horse, Sleuth, The Real Inspector Hound, A Day in the Death of Joe Egg, Scapino!.*

1977–78: *Winesburg, Ohio, Anyone Can Whistle, Hay Fever, The Hostage, Equus, The Good Doctor, The Brute, The Marriage Proposal, Firehouse Rites, Born Yesterday, The Belle of Amherst, Vanities, Picnic.*

1978–79: *Of Mice and Men, Two Gentlemen of Verona, Absurd Person Singular, The School for Wives, The Shadow Box, Dunelawn, The Duck Variations, Lovers, The Last Meeting of the Knights of the White Magnolia, Sizwe Bansi Is Dead, Same Time, Next Year.*

1979–80: *The Glass Menagerie, The Great White Hope, Side by Side by Sondheim, Sly Fox, The Belle of Amherst, The Norman Conquests, The Water Engine, The Time of Your Life, Ben Hecht—Child of the Century.*

1980–81: *Clarence Darrow, Mistress of the Inn, Rosencrantz and Guildenstern Are Dead, A Midwinter Night's Dream, Da, My Sister, My Sister, Deathtrap, Getting Out, The Philadelphia Story.*

1981–82: *On Golden Pond, Wild Oats, Lester and the Winter Visitors, Room Service, A Man for All Seasons, Whose Life Is It Anyway?, Talley's Folly.*

1982–83: *Mornings at Seven, Bedroom Farce, The Gift of the Magi, Ludlow Ladd, The Miser, Clara's Play, Home, The 5th of July, A Life.*

1983–84: *Mass Appeal, Have You Anything to Declare?, The Gift of the Magi, Ludlow Ladd, Charlotte Sweet, Amadeus, New Spoon River, Careless Love, Blithe Spirit.*

1984–85: *The Taming of the Shrew, Foxfire, Huckleberry Finn, Translations, Master Harold . . . and the boys, Black Coffee, Crimes of the Heart, Boys in Autumn.*

1985–86: *Sly Fox, Painting Churches, Great Expectations, As You Like It, Broadway Comedy, And a Nightingale Sang, Strange Snow.*

BIBLIOGRAPHY

Published Source:
The Story. New American Theatre Commemorative Publication. Rockford, Illinois: New American Theatre, 1982.

Archival Resource:
Rockford, Illinois. New American Theatre. Programs, production books, directors' notes.

William T. Clow

[THE] NEW MEXICO REPERTORY THEATRE (NMRT) of Santa Fe and Albuquerque, New Mexico, was founded in February 1984 by Andrew Shea, Clayton Karkosh, and Steven Schwartz-Hartley. The company opened in August 1984 in Santa Fe with a production of Mark Medoff's *Children of a Lesser God.*

The NMRT is the first full-time permanent professional theatre in New Mexico, and the vitality of several amateur theatres in the area, most notably the Albuquerque Little Theatre, the Vortex Theatre, and La Compañia de Teatro de Albuquerque, promised a strong public welcome for the new theatre. Dividing its performances equally between the Johnson Street Theatre in Santa Fe and the KiMo Theatre in Albuquerque, the NMRT plays two weeks in each city. Additionally, selected productions are taken on tour to smaller cities and towns in the state.

Andrew Shea, trained in stage direction at the California Institute of the Arts, became the artistic director of the theatre and has directed several productions.

Clayton Karkosh, professor of technical theatre at the University of New Mexico, has provided technical supervision, while Steven Schwartz-Hartley has acted in many productions. All three founders sit on the board of directors of the nonprofit corporation that arranges funding for the company. Additionally, John P. Beauchamp, who also sits on the board of directors, serves as managing director.

Although NMRT faced serious financial problems at the end of the first season, attendance steadily increased, growing by 10 percent in the second season over the first season. The NMRT has found a dedicated following in its season ticket holders. Contributors providing additional support represent a broad spectrum of the residents and businesses in the Santa Fe–Albuquerque area.

Critics have praised NMRT productions, commenting on the strength of acting, the apparently effortless ensemble work, and the imagination behind the play selection. "Impressive," "engaging," and "joy of theatre" are terms that appear in reviews of repertory productions.

In its first two seasons the NMRT mounted twelve productions. The majority of these were contemporary, some controversial (*Cloud 9, Master Harold . . . and the boys*). More traditional works, whether by William Shakespeare or Tennessee Williams, have not been ignored, however.

The company is organized around a core of directors, designers, actors and actresses, and a dramaturg. Additional cast members, guest stars, and guest directors or designers appear at times. Also, when necessary, musical directors and choreographers are hired. Chief among the company's actors and actresses are Kip Allen, Adan Sanchez, Laura Ann Worthen, Anthony Forkush, and Steven Schwartz-Hartley. Company members have appeared at theatres such as the Missouri Repertory Theatre*, the South Coast Repertory*, the Los Angeles Theatre Centre, and the Melrose Theatre before coming to the NMRT.

Despite a rocky financial start, the NMRT has weathered two well-received seasons, and anticipates further growth.

PERSONNEL

Management: John P. Beauchamp, managing director (1984–86); Andrew Shea, artistic director (1984–86).

Production Managers: Bob Davis (1984–85), Howard Wellman (1985–86).

Dramaturg: David Richard Jones (1985–86).

Stage Directors: Paul Baker (1984–85), Philip Chapman (1984–85), Jim Holmes (1985–86), Mark Medoff (1985–86), Roxanne Rogers (1985–86), Andrew Shea (1984–86).

Musical Director: Michele Larsson (1985–86).

Technical Directors: Bob Davis (1984–85), Howard Wellman (1985–86).

Choreographer: Michele Larsson (1985–86).

Production Designers: Jim Billings (1985–86), Bob Davis (1984–85), Brian Jeffries (1985–86), Mary Sue Jones (1984–85), John Malolepsy (1984–86), Cheryl Lee Odom (1984–86), Thomas C. Umfrid (1985–86).

Lighting Designers: Richard Bernstein (1984–85), Dante Cardone (1985–86), Rush Dudley (1985–86), John Malolepsy (1985–86), M. Jason Sturm (1985–86).

Costume Designers: Joan Catanzariti (1985–86), Genera Gutierrez (1984–85), Mary Sue Jones (1984–85), David Kay Mickelson (1984–86), Gwendolyn Nagle (1984–86), Cheryl Dee Odom (1984–85).

Sound Designers: John Malolepsy (1984–86), Mark Putnam (1985–86), William H. Scott (1984–85), Stewart Warner (1984–85).

Actors and Actresses: *Kip Allen* (1984–86), Robert Althouse, David Andrews, Ken Bader, Gregory Bell, Jason Bernard, *Salley Bissell* (1984–86), Deborah Blanche, Michael Blum, Harry Booker, Amelia Bornstein, Don Boughton, *Susan Bruyn* (1984–85), Kevin Carrigan, Laurie Daniels, Daniel Paul Davis, Radha Delamarter, *Anthony Forkush* (1984–86), Steve Foster, William Frankfather, Lois Geary, Grant Gottschall, David Haney, Susan Hartley, David Harum, Richard Herkert, Dominic Hoffman, Larry Holgerson, *Jim Holmes* (1984–86), Logan Houston, Patrick Husted, Patti Johns, Curt Karibalis, Jackie Kinner, Dennis Lebby, *C. Michael Leopard* (1985–86), Robert Lesser, Margaret Lewis, Susie Lunt, Kim McCallum, Christopher McCarty, John Mahan, David Mallon, Marcos Martinez, Patricia Martinez, Molly Mathiesen, *Roger Michelson* (1984–85), Richard Molinare, Jack Murdock, Sabra Parks, Elena Parres, Bill Pearlman, David Pinchette, Ralitsa Popcheva, Phillip Reeves, Melody Ryane, *Adan Sanchez* (1984–86), *Steven Schwartz-Hartley* (1984–86), Kirk Sutton, Norma Taylor, Angie Torres, William Verderber, Michael Vodde, Harry Waters, Jr., John Wojda, *Laura Ann Worthen* (1984–85), Ray Zuppa.

REPERTORY

1984–85: *Children of a Lesser God, The Last Meeting of the Knights of the White Magnolia, A Streetcar Named Desire, Cloud 9, A Midsummer Night's Dream, Talley's Folly.*

1985–86: *Master Harold . . . and the boys, Twelfth Night, Happy End, Orphans, The Rainmaker, The Heart Outright* (world premiere).

BIBLIOGRAPHY

Published Sources:
Albuquerque *Journal*, 1984–86.
Albuquerque *Tribune*, 1984–86.
Santa Fe *New Mexican*, 1984–86.

Krystan V. Douglas

O

OPEN THEATRE, New York City. The group that was soon to become the Open Theatre first met in February 1963. Seventeen actors and four writers, many of whom had worked with acting teacher Nola Chilton before her emigration to Israel, met to explore nonnaturalistic acting techniques. The next fall the members reorganized as the Open Theatre, a name intended to reflect their commitment to experimentation. Friends sometimes observed the early workshops, which were held in borrowed space at the Living Theatre* and later in a loft on West Twenty-fourth Street, but the first public performance was in December 1963 at the Sheridan Square Playhouse. During the ten years of its existence the company rehearsed and performed in a variety of New York locations (a major location was a loft on Fourteenth Street), and toured the United States and Europe as well.

Although the Open Theatre was loosely organized and anyone could conduct a project, Joseph Chaikin quickly became its most visible leader. By the company's close in 1973 he was its sole director. Chaikin had been an actor with the Living Theatre since 1959, and had unsuccessfully attempted to create an acting workshop within that company. When the Living Theatre left in 1964 for self-exile in Europe, Chaikin stayed behind to continue the Open Theatre work. By 1970 the director felt the group had become unmanageable. It was reorganized, and some of the members who left formed a new company called the Medicine Show.

The Open Theatre was part of a vigorous theatrical avant-garde that began in New York City in 1958 with three important events: the English publication of Antonin Artaud's *The Theatre and Its Double*, the opening of Joe Cino's Cafe Cino, and the presentation of New York's first Happening (by Allan Kaprow) at the Judson Gallery (later to become the Judson Poets' Theatre). A year later the Living Theatre, which had performed poetic and nonnaturalistic drama since 1946, opened a new theatre, and in 1961 Ellen Stewart opened the Cafe LaMama.

These theatres, however, focused on staging experimental scripts. The Open Theatre was more than a production company; it was also an experimental laboratory, and members often considered the workshop explorations to be as valuable as performances. Moreover, the Open Theatre was the first well-known American group fully to explore collaborative creation of theatre pieces. From the beginning the workshops included actors, directors, playwrights, and critics working together improvisationally to find common images that could also become meaningful for an audience. Although the theatre was also to produce plays and playlets by its own members as well as by nonmembers, its most innovative work resulted in five full-length collaborative plays: *Viet Rock, The Serpent, Terminal, Mutation Show*, and *Nightwalk. (America Hurrah* was not strictly an Open Theatre production, although parts of it were influenced by workshop sessions.)

The earliest Open Theatre performances were combinations of group exercises, structured improvisations (often with scenarios by Jean-Claude van Itallie), open improvisations, and scripted playlets. By the third season production commitments had expanded at the expense of workshop explorations, and most performances were of short plays. At the end of the season, however, the first major collaborative work was produced: *Viet Rock*, developed from a workshop directed by Megan Terry. Partially because of pressures resulting from commercial productions of this play, the group decided that obligatory performances threatened exploratory work. Performance commitments were reduced while workshop activity increased, resulting eventually in the final four collaborative works. Between 1968 and 1970 the ensemble also performed Alfred Jarry's *Ubu Cocu* and Samuel Beckett's *Endgame*. Although they continued occasionally to present collections of improvisations, scripted playlets, and songs, these performances were secondary to those of the longer works.

The collaborative pieces had a nonlinear structure, with scenes loosely related to a core idea or mood. Actors transformed readily from one character to another, and sections often alternated between satirical "character" sketches and more lyrical, rhythmic evocations. The actors were not interested in naturalistic behavior, but in presenting gestural or aural "emblems" of character or situation. The group defined as an early objective "to concentrate on a theatre of ritual, myth, illusion, and mystery (as opposed to a theatre of behavioral or psychological motivation)" (Program, December 1963, Open Theatre Papers, Kent State University Library, Kent, Ohio). From the earliest exercises to the final collaborative pieces, certain interrelated concerns permeated the ensemble's work: role-playing and the interchangeability of roles, presence-absence, inside-outside, community-isolation, creativity-mechanization, process-stagnation, waking-sleeping, life-death.

Reviewers generally praised the Open Theatre's work, especially the four final plays. Walter Kerr labeled the group "the finest company of its kind," and further stated: "Of all the work now being done in this vein, the Open Theatre's seems to be plainly the best.... If you are at all interested in the theatre's latest attempt to remake itself, this is the company to watch" (Walter Kerr, "The Finest Company of Its Kind," *New York Times*, May 14, 1970, Sec. 2, p. 3; and "What If Cain Did Not Know How to Kill Abel?" *New York Times*, February 9, 1969, Sec. 2, p. 1). The group's positive critical reception probably resulted from its ability to combine inner exploration with outer form; through the precision of its images the ensemble respected the audience's experience as much as its own, and thus avoided the criticism of self-indulgence that many other experimental groups received. (An important goal of the company, in fact, was to explore the subtleties of various audience-actor relationships, and Chaikin designed exercises to achieve this end.) The company won several awards, and Chaikin was selected in 1977 to receive the first Obie Award for lifetime achievement in the theatre.

The entire group or a committee made all financial and organizational decisions. One major commitment was to avoid commercial pressure. Chaikin especially wanted people in the ensemble who were not grooming themselves for a successful career, since he felt that goal forced the actor into a restrictive mold. He also felt that the group itself could only suffer by allowing its productions to depend on money, since it would be forced to please a paying audience (or grant-givers). In the early days actors received no salaries, but paid $3 to $5 a week for loft rental and other expenses. Finally, workshop member Jacques Levy secured substantial grants, and the money paid for babysitter fees, insurance policies, or workshop instructors (including Polish director Jerzy Grotowski), or it was given to other groups who had difficulty securing funds. When the company did receive a salary or divided box-office income, everyone in the group received an equal amount, with some adjustment for a member's number of dependents. Performances were often free, or admission was by donation, unless the group was on tour and/or being produced by someone else. The company also gave several benefit performances for political causes and performed for free in prisons, hospitals, and schools.

Because the Open Theatre's methods were communal and because the company was loosely organized until 1970, designating certain actors and actresses as stars of the ensemble is difficult. Certainly some members had greater longevity than others: Joyce Aaron, James Barbosa, Ron Faber, Barbara Vann, and Lee Worley were with the theatre from its first season until its restructuring in 1970. Ray Barry, Tina Shepard, and Paul Zimet were involved from work on *The Serpent* until the theatre's close, and so acted in the four final collaborative works. Shami Chaikin was the only company member to perform in all five of the major collaborative pieces. Moreover, various directors worked with performances, and still other company members conducted important workshops that fed directly or indirectly into the public shows. Chaikin, Peter Feldman, Jacques Levy, Roberta Sklar, and Sydney Shubert Walter were among the most active of the directors, while Chaikin, Feldman, Levy, Megan Terry, and Lee Worley were some of the key workshop leaders. A number of playwrights were active in the ensemble, while others had only tenuous connections with the exploratory work. Among the most active were Jean-Claude van Itallie, Megan Terry, and Michael Smith.

The only company member continuously involved with the Open Theatre from the first meeting to the last performance was Joseph Chaikin. Members of the company seemed to respond most to Chaikin's leadership, and those projects most flourished that received at least tacit approval from him. Burdened by the company's increasing success, which brought an inflated budget and a temptation to stick with forms it already knew, Chaikin felt the group should disband. In November 1972, the company reached a consensus about the matter, and the final performance was of *Nightwalk* at the University of California, Santa Barbara, on December 1, 1973.

Many Open Theatre members went on to act and direct—on, off, and off-off Broadway or in films—and to participate in or found other experimental companies such as the Medicine Show, the Bridge Collective, the Quena Company, the Women's Experimental Theatre, the Working Theatre, the Talking Band, and the Winter Project. Through the work of the Open Theatre and its satellites, and through the writings and interviews by its members (Chaikin's book, *The Presence of the Actor*, was one of the major American treatises on acting during the 1970s), the company was an important force in developing nonnaturalistic theatre in America.

PERSONNEL

Management: Michael Bartuccio, Patricia Berman, Kenneth Glickfeld, Stephen Rich, Richard Snyder, John Stoltenberg.

Scenic Technicians: Michael Bartuccio, Gwen Fabricant (1966–73), Arden Fingerhut, Esther Gilman, Bil Mikulewicz.

Musical Directors: Susan Ain, Ellen Maddow, Richard Peaslee, Marianne de Pury, Stanley Walden.

Stage Directors: Tom Bissinger, Joseph Chaikin (1963–73), Peter Feldman (1964–70), Jacques Levy, Roberta Sklar (1965–72), Megan Terry, Jean-Claude van Itallie, Sydney Shubert Walter, Ira Zuckerman.

Playwrights: Patricia Cooper, Marc Kaminsky, W. E. R. La Farge, Nancy Fales Martin, Sam Shephard, Michael Smith, John Stoltenberg, Megan Terry, Sharon Thie, Jean-Claude van Itallie, Susan Yankowitz.

Dramaturg: Mira Rafalowicz.

Actors and Actresses (dates are appearances for public performances): Joyce Aaron (1964–70), Seth Allen (1966), James Barbosa (1964–70), Ray Barry (1967–73), Valerie Belden (1964–65), Jenn Ben-Yakov (1967–68), Isabelle Blau (1963–65), Paul Boesing (1963–65), Michael Bradford (1964–65), Kay Carney (1966), Joseph Chaikin (1969–70), Shami Chaikin (1965–73), Mimi Cozzins (1963), Brenda Dixon (1967–70), Pat Donegan (1963–65), Ron Faber (1964–70), Fred Forrest (1966), Sharon Gans (1964–68), Cynthia Harris (1964–68), Philip Harris (1967–68), Robert Hart (1966), Jayne Haynes (1967–70), Leonard Hicks (1964–66), John Kramer (1966), Ralph Lee (1967–70, 1972–73), Roy London (1965–66), Dorothy Lyman (1967–68), John McCurry (1966), Ellen Maddow (1973), Peter Maloney (1967–70), Muriel Miguel (1966–70), Murray Paskin (1964–65), Suzanne Pred (1966), Gerome (Jerry) Ragni (1963–66), Barbara Ralley

(1966), Howard Roy (1966), Mark Samuels (1969–70), Ellen Schindler (1967–70), JoAnn Schmidman (1969–73), Ed Setrakian (1966), Tina Shepard (1967–73), David Spielberg (1963–65), Jack Tetarsky (1966), Alice Tweedey (1966), Lois Unger (1963–65), Barbara Vann (1963–70), Sydney Shubert Walter (1963–65), Lee Worley (1963–70), Paul Zimet (1967–73).

REPERTORY

1963–64: "Ritual Hello" (a group warmup). Structured improvisations: "Variations on a Clifford Odets' Theme," "An Airplane, Its Passengers and Its Portent," "The Perfect People," "A Man Sometimes Turns into the Machine He Is Using," "Commercials," "A Dream, in Which the Actors Realize the Dreamer's Illusion," "Liebestod Mountain," "Contest," "Picnic in Spring." Open improvisations: "Story," "Party and Dream." Plays: *Eat at Joe's, The Murdered Woman, The Clown Play*.

1964–65: "Ritual Hello" (a group warmup). Singing transformations. Open transformations. Dream improvisations. Unnoticed actions. Styles transformation: "Free-for-All." Structured improvisations: "Contest," "An Airplane," "From an Odets' Kitchen," "Rip van Winkle," "The Trial of Agreement," "The Exorcism," "Panel Show." Plays: *The First Fool, The Hunter and the Bird, I'm Really Here, Almost Like Being, Pavane: A Fugue for Eight Actors, Calm Down, Mother, Keep Tightly Closed in a Cool Dry Place, The Successful Life of 3, The Clown Play, Sweeney Agonistes, Ars Longa Vita Brevis*.

1965–66: Structured improvisations: "Life Styles," and revisions of previously performed works. Plays: *Dream* (later retitled *Where Is de Queen?*), *Soon Jack November, The Magic Realists, The Next Thing, The Trial of Judith and Julian Beck, Comings and Goings, The Clown Play, Viet Rock*.

1966–67: *Viet Rock* (the off-Broadway production), *America Hurrah* (the off-Broadway performances of *Viet Rock* and *America Hurrah* were not officially by the Open Theatre, although both depended heavily on earlier Open Theatre work); "Angry Artists Against the War in Vietnam" performances (mainly structured improvisations around the form of a party from which various nonparty sequences emerged, including the plays, *Thoughts on the Instant of Greeting a Friend in the Street, Building the Soldiers, State of the Union, The Clown Play*).

1967–68: "Informal Evenings" (varying collections of musical numbers: "Zapping the Cong," "Wild Mountain Thyme"; improvisations: "The Opening Argument," "State of the Union," "Sunday Morning," "Locked Action"; plays: *Foursome, The Clown Play*; poetry: "Wichita Vortex Sutra"); *Masks* (varying collections of musical numbers: "Zapping the Cong," "Wild Mountain Thyme"; improvisations: "State of the Union," "Sunday Morning," "Locked Action," "Contest"; plays: *Foursome, The Clown Play, Keep Tightly Closed in a Cool Dry Place, Interview, The Red Burning Light, Witness*); *The Serpent*.

1968–69: *The Serpent, Masks, Ubu Cocu*.

1969–70: *The Serpent, Endgame, Ubu Cocu, Terminal*.

1970–71: *Terminal, Mutations* (work in progress).

1971–72: *The Mutation Show, Terminal*.

1972–73: *Terminal, The Mutation Show, Nightwalk*.

BIBLIOGRAPHY

Published Source:

Gildzen, Alex. "The Open Theatre." In *Three Works by the Open Theatre*. New York: Drama Book Specialists/Publishers, 1974, pp. 188–191. A published bibliography of works by and about the Open Theatre and its members.

Archival Resource:

Kent, Ohio. Kent State University Library. Joseph Chaikin Papers, Open Theatre Papers, Jean-Claude van Itallie Papers. The Kent State collections include notes, letters, minutes of group meetings, programs, clippings of reviews and articles, videotapes and films, early drafts of van Itallie's plays and of Chaikin's *The Presence of the Actor*, unpublished interviews and theses, and some costumes and properties.

Erlene Laney Hendrix

P

[THE] **PAPER BAG PLAYERS,** New York City, was founded in 1958 when modern dancer Judith Martin asked a number of artists from various mediums to improvise with her to create theatre pieces for children.

The founders of the company were all professional artists with a common background in modern dance. Judith Martin, after studying dance with Martha Graham and theatre at the Neighborhood Playhouse and the New Theatre School, had danced with Merce Cunningham and founded her own dance troupe. Artist and children's book author Remy Charlip had developed simultaneous careers in theatre, notably with the Living Theatre*, and in modern dance, notably with the Merce Cunningham Company. Painter Shirley Kaplan had begun to direct and design for theatre while studying at La Grand Chaumiere in Paris. Broadway actress Sudie Bond had danced in Martin's company and acted with Charlip in an early Living Theatre production at the Cherry Lane Theatre. Pianist and composer Daniel Jahn had specialized in improvising and composing music for modern dancers. Those five founding members were joined by a young actress, Joyce Aaron, who had also studied dance at the Martha Graham school and acting at the Neighborhood Playhouse.

In the fall of 1959 this group of artists hired Frances Schram of Briggs Management as their booking agent and, at her insistence, chose a name, the Paper Bag Players. Beginning in September, they held previews of their work in their Manhattan studio. The company debuted officially on December 28, 1959, at the Living Theatre, 520 Sixth Avenue, New York, where they played a series of holiday matinees titled *Cut-ups*.

Out of the tradition-breaking background and the early collaborations of the founding members, a new kind of children's theatre emerged, one that had little in common with other children's theatre of the times. The Paper Bag Players offered a fresh and innovative approach in a field dominated by traditional fairy-tale productions. They replaced familiar stories and fairy tales with original

contemporary skits, songs, and dances based on a child's own everyday experiences, sense of humor, and ideas of the world. In place of traditionally elaborate
costumes and settings, the company pioneered in performing in basic "uniforms"
in front of a simple, curtained background. The company trademark came from
their transformation of simple materials—commonplace objects, paper, and card-
board—into brilliant, visually exciting, innovative theatre.

The Paper Bag Players worked outside the established tradition of both adult
and children's theatre. They were most closely allied with other improvisational
theatre groups that emerged during the late 1950s and early 1960s, such as the
Bread and Puppet Theatre (1961), the San Francisco Mime Troupe* (1959), and
Second City (1959). Those groups all worked independently and developed their
own unique style, yet all were part of the experimental trends toward improvisation, toward a variety of loosely structured formats, toward political and social
significance, and toward an emphasis on the actor-audience relationship.

In the beginning, company members supported themselves with outside jobs
while devoting themselves to the group, rehearsing and creating new materials
daily in their studio and performing on weekends. The early company was
organized along egalitarian lines. Company members performed all functions—
collaborating on new material, building props and costumes, providing transportation, and performing. Other than booking agent Schram, all management
functions were also performed by the company. The musician, Daniel Jahn, was
designated as the bookkeeper. Early accounting was simple—the proceeds from
any given production were divided equally among company members with an
extra portion set aside to cover all costs.

For their first three seasons in New York (1959–62), the Paper Bag Players
presented Christmas and Easter shows at the Living Theatre, where they performed matinees amid the sets for such productions as *The Connection* and *The
Brig*. In addition, the company established an early tradition of local and regional
touring through sponsorship by colleges, schools, and community groups.

In 1962 the Paper Bag Players were incorporated as a nonprofit organization.
That fall they attempted their first full New York season, which was to be held
in the newly renovated Pocket Theatre. The theatre was never completed, however, and their first New York season was held in three theatres consecutively:
the Living Theatre, the Masque Theatre, and the East End Theatre. For that
season the company maintained Frances Schram as their agent for out-of-town
bookings but hired Judith Liss to book large groups for their New York season.
Gradually Liss assumed all management responsibilities for the company, serving
unassisted as company administrator for ten years. From 1972 on she hired aides
such as a secretary and an assistant manager. Judith Liss provided a stability in
management that undoubtedly helped the group survive for over two decades.

The performance company was sustained from 1965 on by the leadership of
Judith Martin, who served as artistic director, designer, author, and actress. The
original company had attempted to work as a true ensemble with all members
being equal. From the beginning, however, two members emerged as leaders—

Judith Martin and Remy Charlip. Martin's guiding hand was the stabilizing factor in the group, however, and after Charlip's resignation in 1965, Martin provided continuity for the group. In order to ensure that the older, more experienced members stayed with the company, salaries and working conditions were superior to other off-Broadway and children's theatres. Eventually regular thirty-six week guaranteed contracts were offered to the principals.

From 1965 to 1969 the principals included artistic director-actress Judith Martin, actress Betty Osgood, actor Irving Burton, and musician Donald Ashwander. Burton and Osgood, both exceptional comedians trained as modern dancers, had joined the company in its second season (1960–61). Osgood had performed for several years as a featured dancer with the Charles Weidman Company, while Burton had trained with a number of famous dancers, including Martha Graham, and had taught at the New Dance Group Studio. Ashwander, who joined the company in 1966, had studied classical music at the Manhattan School of Music, but his interest in ragtime, sacred harp, jazz, and other forms of American folk and popular music also influenced his work. He brought an upbeat contemporary sound to the company with his original electronic harpsichord music.

When Betty Osgood resigned in 1969, the other principals remained with the company. Each season a young actor and actress were hired to fill out the performing company. With a few exceptions, those young professionals stayed in the company for only one or two seasons. The Paper Bag Players remained a non-Equity company throughout most of its history, hiring Equity actors on a guest artist contract.

For many years no technical staff was hired. Martin designed and executed the costumes, sets, and properties with assistance from the company. From about 1967, however, Martin hired usually one young man who served simultaneously as stage manager, light technician, builder of props and costumes, driver, and stagehand. A series of "stage managers" followed, with part-time scenic technicians and lighting consultants hired as needed.

The Paper Bag Players early evolved a season that consisted of one or two public runs in New York, a series of free school shows in disadvantaged neighborhoods, and touring outside the city. Though the company remained small by choice, the scope of its activities widened considerably as public and private support for its work increased. The 1962–63 budget was just over $10,000. By 1966–67 it had risen to more than $60,000 and by the mid-1970s it had stabilized at an annual average of $250,000. From 1965 to 1970, with state and local government support, the company expanded its program of free shows in the schools to an average of sixty performances annually. The group also became nationally and internationally recognized through media coverage and expanded touring. A highlight was its critically acclaimed appearance at the Royal Court Theatre in London, December 1967 to January 1968.

From 1970 to 1975 the work of the company continued to expand. Its average season consisted of more than 160 performances of three productions, including one new or substantially revised show. Its activities expanded to include regular classes and workshops, some television work, and numerous educational publications. As its primary funding source shifted to the federal government, it concurrently put more emphasis on national touring.

During the latter half of the 1970s and the early 1980s expansion of activities halted as inflation eroded the financial base of the company. Its program of free school shows was drastically curbed. Sponsorship, booking, and grants all became more difficult to obtain. While financial reserves were depleted and the company had to struggle to make ends meet, it continued to perform on a fairly regular basis, maintaining consistently high standards and supporting its principals on thirty-six-week contracts.

While Judith Martin devoted her genius to sustaining and developing the Paper Bag Players, the other original company members pursued interesting careers. As an author and artist, Remy Charlip published more than twenty-four children's books. As a choreographer, he designed more than eighty new dances, danced with many leading companies, and formed his own dance troupe. In theatre, Charlip directed, acted, and designed for a number of well-known off-Broadway theatres, including the Judson Poet's Theatre, the American Place Theatre, LaMama, and the National Theatre of the Deaf. Artist Shirley Kaplan had an active career in theatre as a designer, writer, director, and teacher. She collaborated with Ben Bagley on his Cole Porter cabaret theatre productions and founded the Painter's Theatre, an ensemble theatre company. Sudie Bond, after performing in the original casts of Edward Albee's *The Sandbox* (1959), *The American Dream* (1960), and *Box/Mao* (1968), went on to a long career in conventional theatre, performing on Broadway, in touring companies and dinner theatres, and in a situation comedy series on television. Joyce Aaron pursued a career in avant-garde, off-Broadway theatre: she was in the original cast of Jean-Claude van Itallie's *America Hurrah* as well as a number of Sam Shepard plays; she won an Obie for her acting in *Acrobatics* (1975), a play she coauthored; and she worked with Joseph Chaikin in the original Open Theatre* and later in the Winter Project.

The Paper Bag Players never had a permanent theatre of its own, but several New York theatres and institutions gave it steady performance space: the Living Theatre, 1959–63; the Henry Street Settlement House Playhouse, 1963–68; Hunter College Playhouse, 1968–75; the Ninety-second Street YW-YMCA, 1975–78; and Lincoln Center, 1968–80, intermittently. Occasionally the company rented theatres for short runs in New York, such as the Marymount Manhattan Theatre and Town Hall.

In more than twenty-two seasons of production the Paper Bag Players mounted twelve original productions, averaging about one every two years. All twelve productions were in the company's original style of comedy, in which a series of simple stories, songs, dances, and cartoon-like sketches are joined together in a revue format. Its one attempt to create a full-length narrative theatre piece, *Guffawhaw*, led to the group's least successful show. It was quickly reduced to twenty minutes with additional sketches added to create a full-length revue. Most of the shows remained in repertory, and remounted productions were often changed considerably with pieces added, deleted, and rearranged. Consequently the total creative output of the company was considerably more than twelve shows. All material was original, often based on the ideas of Judith Martin and developed and polished for performance by the company in improvisational and working sessions. The diverse elements in the productions were unified by the extensive use of movement and music, by the ingenious use of paper props and costumes, and by the fast-paced, highly theatrical style of acting.

For more than two decades the Paper Bag Players maintained a reputation for professionalism and innovation in children's theatre. An early review called them "probably the best, certainly the most original children's theatre group in this country" (*Newsweek*, December 28, 1964). The group was regularly reviewed throughout its career, critics consistently noting its imagination and ingenuity, the appeal and insight of its contemporary content, the intelligence and respect accorded its audiences, the freshness and clarity with which the performers appealed equally to preschoolers and adults, and the infectious joy of its humor. Over the years some critics noted that the Paper Bag Players seemed unwilling to go beyond its established style; that there was a certain amount of repetition in its work. But most reviewers found the group to be far above the standard in children's theatre and many considered it an outstanding example of contemporary American theatre.

PERSONNEL

Founders: Sudie Bond, Remy Charlip, Daniel Jahn, Shirley Kaplan, Judith Martin.

Artistic Directors: Judith Martin and Remy Charlip (1959–65), Judith Martin (1965–81).

Management: Judith Liss, manager and administrator (1962–81).

Musical Directors: Donald Ashwander (1966–81), Daniel Jahn (1959–65).

Technical Staff: Jack Andrews, John Armstrong, David Bradford, William Dunas, Danny Fennell, Jack Fiala, Paul Fitzmaurice, Lee Guilliant, Peter Jablonski (stage manager) (1974–79), David Kellman, Mac Kerr, John W. Lloyd, Adam Perl, Jim Ray, Daniel Rosenfels, Debra Schechner, James Shearwood, Peter Sibley, Gene Smith.

Management Staff: Susan Baerwald, coordinator (1976–78); Charlotte Bandler, secretary (1978–81); Michele Brustein, assistant manager (1972–73); Judy Felsenfeld, assistant manager (1980–81); Edith Harnik, executive secretary to associate administrator (1973–81); Jan Liss, audience development (1979); Nancy Lloyd, assistant administrator (1975–77); Elinor Rogosin, coordinator (1977).

Actors and Actresses: *Joyce Aaron* (1958–61), Christopher Allport, Aileen Armstrong, *Donald Ashwander* (1966–81), David Bates, *Sudie Bond* (1958–60), Pat Brodhead, Marcia Burr, *Irving Burton* (1961–81), *Remy Charlip* (1959–65), Adrienne Doucette, Samir Elias, Sara Farwell, Leslie Flanders, Bruce Fuller, *Pilar Garcia* (1962–72, 1980), Betsy Henn, Buck Hobbs, *Daniel Jahn* (1959–65), *Shirley Kaplan* (1958–61, 1964–65), James Lally, Charles Leipart, J. C. McCord, Janet Mackenzie, Marne Mahaffey, *Judith Martin* (1958–81), Gary Maxwell, Jan Maxwell, Joseph Medalis, *Jeanne Michols* (1972–77, 1980), *Court Miller* (1973–75, 1979–80), *Douglas Norwick* (1974–77), *Betty Osgood*

(1960–69), Douglas Richardson, Virgil Roberson, Sharon Watroba, Micki Wesson, Carolyn Yeager, Cy Young.

REPERTORY

1959–60: †*Cut-ups*.

1960–61: †*Scraps, Cut-ups*.

1961–62: †*Group Soup, Scraps*.

1962–63: *Group Soup, Scraps*.

1963–64: *Scraps, Group Soup,* †*The Paper Bag Players Ride Again* (later called *Fortunately*).

1964–65: *Group Soup,* †*Fortunately, Scraps*.

1965–66: †*My Horse Is Waiting, Group Soup, Fortunately*.

1966–67: †*Guffawhaw, Scraps, Group Soup, Fortunately*.

1967–68: *Guffawhaw, Scraps, Fortunately, My Horse Is Waiting,* "Summer 1968 in the Streets."

1968–69: *Scraps,* †*Baked Alaska* (later called *Dandelion*), †*Hot Feet*.

1969–70: †*Dandelion, Group Soup, Hot Feet*.

1970–71: *Dandelion, Hot Feet*.

1971–72: *Hot Feet, Dandelion, Group Soup*.

1972–73: *Dandelion, Group Soup,* †*To the Rescue* (later called *I Won't Take a Bath*).

1973–74: *Dandelion, Hot Feet,* †*I Won't Take a Bath*.

1974–75: *I Won't Take a Bath,* †*Everybody, Everybody, Hot Feet*.

1975–76: *Everybody, Everybody, Dandelion*.

1976–77: *Everybody, Everybody,* †*Grandpa*.

1977–78: *I Won't Take a Bath, Everybody, Everybody, Hot Feet*.

1978–79: "A Christmas Review," *Dandelion, Everybody, Everybody*.

1979–80: †*Mama's Got A Job, Dandelion, Everybody, Everybody*.

1980–81: *Hot Feet, Everybody, Everybody*.

†indicates the twelve original shows as each entered the repertory.

BIBLIOGRAPHY

Published Sources:

Christian Science Monitor, 1958–81.

Daily News (New York), 1958–81.

Dance Magazine, 1958–81.

Herald Tribune (New York), 1958–81.

New York Times, 1958–81.

Post (New York), 1958–81.

Village Voice (New York), 1958–61.

Women's Wear Daily (New York), 1958–81.

Unpublished Sources:

Osgood, Betty. "The Paper Bag Players: A New Concept in Theatre for Young Audiences." Unpublished manuscript, New York University, 1968.

Parchem, Georga Larsen. "The Development of a Unique American Children's Theatre, The Paper Bag Players of New York: 1958–81." Doctoral dissertation, The Ohio State University, 1982.

Archival Resources:

New York, New York. New York Public Library. Library and Museum of the Performing
     Arts. Scrapbooks, programs, films, videos.
New York, New York. The Paper Bag Players, 50 Riverside Drive (office) and 185 East
     Broadway (studio). Scrapbooks, correspondence, financial records, programs,
     posters, educational materials, press releases, slides, films, video and audio tapes,
     scripts.

Georga Larsen Parchem

PHILADELPHIA DRAMA GUILD (known regionally simply as the Drama
Guild), founded in 1956 by local dentist Sidney S. Bloom, acquired a reputation
as one of the Delaware Valley's most prestigious and accomplished amateur
community theatres. However, the 1970 bankruptcy and dispersal of Philadelphia's only professional resident theatre company at the Theatre of the Living
Arts* sparked the Drama Guild's interest in upgrading to professional status.
Bloom's business relationship with a key member of the Hass Foundation, the
organization then restoring the Walnut Street Theatre, and his personal friendship
with the well-connected New York actor John Randolph helped convert this
interest into reality. It was at the historic, 1,054-seat Walnut Street Theatre,
located at 825 Walnut Street in downtown Philadelphia, that the Drama Guild
opened its first professional season on December 1, 1971, with a production of
Molière's *The Imaginary Invalid*.

The professional Drama Guild remained under the producership of Bloom,
who accepted no salary. Not surprisingly, he initially repeated many of his
amateur group's policies. As in the past, the organization's primary home was
a rented office and rehearsal space at 220 South Sixteenth Street. The theatre
itself was secured for performances only. (Previously the Drama Guild had rented
performances space at a local YM-YWHA and YMCA, and, later, secured larger
blocks of theatre performance time from the amateur Plays and Players, who
owned the Playhouse on Delancey Street.)

The Drama Guild's initial repertory also mirrored that of the amateur years
in concentrating on classics of western European theatre. A few Broadway hits,
such as Garson Kanin's *Born Yesterday* and Lillian Hellman's *The Little Foxes*,
provided a slightly more "popular" tone. Nonetheless, the group's demeanor
was overtly educational. The amateur Drama Guild had a close association with
Philadelphia's conservative board of education, and the professional group maintained that tie.

The practice prevailed of casting each show separately, from a pool of local,
semiprofessional actors. Several performers made a direct transition from amateur
to professional status, notably local radio personality Doug Wing and actor
Dennis Cunningham, who became a nationally televised movie critic. The policy
of presenting four shows per year, each running for three weeks, also persisted.

Convinced that local audiences demanded celebrities as proof of professionalism, the Drama Guild used Randolph's influence to secure for its leading roles
many of Broadway's most renowned performers. E. G. Marshall, Anne Jackson,

Eli Wallach, Geraldine Fitzgerald, Geraldine Page, Maureen Stapleton, Rip Torn, Tom Ewell, Bernadette Peters, and Martin Balsam were but a few of the stars who were paid weekly salaries of $1,000 for their time with the Guild. A guest director policy likewise lured to Philadelphia such New York directing "stars" as Stephen Porter, Brian Murray, Jeff Bleckner, and George C. Scott. Ironically, although the Drama Guild promoted itself as a local institution, the only truly professional resident artists were on the scenic and technical staffs. Clarke Dunham was resident scenic and lighting designer, and Joseph F. Bella the resident costumer.

Although the Drama Guild maintained a board of directors, the bulk of both artistic and managerial decision-making rested with Bloom during the first three seasons, 1971–74, even after he formally hired artistic director William Ross in 1972. Attendance grew, but local critics complained that the albeit solid productions were bland and predictable. Indeed, only the black drama *Ceremonies in Dark Old Men*, by Lonne Elder III, and a controversial interracial production of Shakespeare's *The Taming of the Shrew* drew the sort of enthusiasm for things experimental that local critics, from their experience with the Theatre of the Living Arts, had come to expect. Critics more strenuously faulted the Guild's failure to develop an ensemble with a distinctive personality and especially to distinguish its productions from those of the New York touring shows that played the Walnut while the Guild rehearsed. Furthermore, critics were exasperated by the Guild's kowtowing to stars' whims, notably their exercising of "out clauses" that, according to one critic, "were invoked often enough to make the Guild look the foolish . . . autograph hound" (*Philadelphia Inquirer*, July 28, 1974).

The 1974 appointment of Douglas Seale as artistic director was evidently aimed at the resolution of these aesthetic difficulties. Simultaneously, the board hired a managing director, James B. Freydberg, who set out to alleviate the deficits that mounted despite a hefty subscription audience (approximately 17,000) and significant funding from federal, state, and city sources. Former artistic director of the famed Birmingham Repertory Company as well as an associate director of the Old Vic, the British-born Seale also brought sterling American credentials as the former artistic director of Baltimore's Center Stage* and Chicago's Goodman Theatre. His reputation clearly awed both Bloom and the board, who gave him full rein. Seale swiftly wiped away past legacies, greatly reducing star appearances and creating a tightly knit ensemble of resident actors selected from both the New York and the Canadian stage. The repertory swerved sharply toward British staples, especially Shaw and high comedy. Seale tempered this pattern with Irish pieces, especially those of Hugh Leonard, and new Afro-American dramas. The Guild increased its offerings from four to five plays per season and established a secondary series of smaller, limited-run offerings, called "Second Stage." These were put on by resident company regulars in Theatre 5, an intimate, eighty-five-seat performing area in the Walnut Street Theatre building.

The Drama Guild's board seemed highly pleased with Seale's performance and perfunctorily renewed his contract in 1976. However, a power struggle emerged between Bloom and managing director Freydberg over budget priorities, fund-raising, deposit-handling, and play selection. At first, Freydberg was fired. But when Seale backed Freydberg he was reinstated, and Bloom resigned. These developments at first seemed provident, for the 1976–77 season proved to be one of the Guild's most popular: it played to 89.1 percent of capacity, up from the roughly 85 percent capacities of previous years. Not unexpectedly, the board renewed Seale and Freydberg in 1978.

Ironically, flagging subscription sales, mounting deficits, and inflation undermined the directors' hitherto sure authority. In 1979 Freydberg relinquished his post and, later that year, the board decided that Philadelphians wanted a more immediate theatrical experience and advised Seale to inject newer American plays into his essentially traditional repertories. However, his first attempt to do so, a production of Val Coleman's drama of the civil rights movement, *The Last Few Days of Willie Callendar*, drew sharp criticism. Local critics decried its aesthetic qualities while the Philadelphia School District, a longtime Guild supporter, complained about the play's profanity. Seale's 1980 contract was not renewed.

Clearly aiming for a break with tradition, the board hired Irene Lewis, a young, relatively inexperienced (she had been associate director of the Hartford Stage Company), and uncharacteristically, female graduate of the Yale School of Drama. In fact, the Drama Guild would be Lewis' first try at resident theatre directorship. Further severing ties with the past, the organization simultaneously moved from the Walnut to the 944-seat, thrust-staged Zellerbach Theatre on the campus of the University of Pennsylvania in West Philadelphia and dismantled the resident company policy. Once again actors and directors were jobbed-in for each production.

Critics chastised Lewis for the 1980–81 season of more popular but pedestrian plays by Lillian Hellman, Brian Friel, Peter Nichols, and Ben Hecht. However, the board seemed to approve the more down-to-earth aura of the season. Her decision to leave in the middle of her two-year contract was publicized as "strictly personal," although she had found the administrative duties of an artistic director ill-befitting her particular talents as a stage director. Because it was too late in the season to conduct a search for a new artistic director, artistic directorship temporarily fell to managing director Gregory Poggi, who had replaced Freydberg in 1979.

Termed the "businessman's businessman," Poggi paradoxically suited the Drama Guild board's specifications perfectly. A founder of the Indiana Repertory Theatre* in Indianapolis and the former general manager of Canada's Manitoba Theatre Center, Poggi brought to the Guild a keen awareness of more recent resident theatre trends and of marketing research techniques. In the hope that Poggi could translate his skills and experience into policy more effectively under one leader than, as in the past, under two, Poggi was elevated to the title of producing director in 1982. Poggi stressed local responsivity, attempting as never before to tap younger audiences, especially the young professionals populating Philadelphia's gentrified downtown. He concentrated on newer, American plays, especially those recently seen off-Broadway or in regional repertory theatres and new to Philadelphia, such as Albert Innaurato's *Gemini*, A. R. Gurney, Jr.'s *The Dining Room*, and Larry Sarson, Levi Lee, and Rebecca Wackler's *Tent Meeting*. New plays, too, appeared frequently on main season rosters. To further encourage new dramatic talent, Poggi instituted a Playwright's Project whereby selected new playscripts received professional staged readings which were open to public critique. In effect, Poggi sought to give Philadelphia theatregoers a more active voice in the selection and development of new plays.

By choosing plays that appealed to various Philadelphia ethnic sensibilities, Poggi strove to create new audiences and to more intimately involve old ones. Jewish plays prevailed, followed closely by plays about Italian and Catholic experiences and, somewhat more recently, about black urban experiences. Poggi's Drama Guild catered as well to Philadelphians' pleasure in seeing New York theatrical stars on the hometown stage. He engaged both younger talents, such as Glenn Close and Mary Beth Hurt, and more seasoned celebrities, such as Nancy Marchand, Esther Rolle, and Howard da Silva. However, Poggi balanced his stars with equally strong support for Philadelphia performers by initiating local auditions for other than minor roles. Actors continued to be hired only for individual shows, however. Continuity was maintained, instead, through a corps of directors such as Steven Schachter, Charles Karchmer, William Woodman, and actor-director Jerry Zaks, as well as a group of affiliated designers. Poggi himself did not direct.

Despite competition from a professional theatre troupe at the Walnut Street Theatre, the Guild (which moved its office to 112 South Sixteenth Street in 1984) has prospered under Poggi. Reviews of Guild productions continue to run the gamut from excellent to mixed, with the productions of new scripts viewed most skeptically. However, because of Poggi's successful campaign to generate corporate support of the local professional arts, the Philadelphia Drama Guild now operates in the black. In 1975–76 the Guild's earned income accounted for 75 percent of the budget. Such heavy demand on box-office support was unworkable. Deficits mounted and expansion was impeded. But as early as 1982–83, under Poggi's management, it raised more than one-third of a $1,360,000 budget outside the box office. This allowed the Guild to expand its audience base by means of subsidized admission for students, seniors, and the needy; to implement a transportation program; and to interpret performances for the deaf. Consequently, with subscription sales roughly equal in number to those of the best seasons of the 1970s, the company of the mid-1980s could boast of attendance at 93 percent of capacity and justifiably could extend its runs by five performances each. By proving its assessment of itself as a "strong theatre for everyone," the Philadelphia Drama Guild has continued its artistic health and productivity.

PERSONNEL

Management: Sidney S. Bloom, producer (1971–76); John Randolph, artistic consultant (1971–74); William Ross, artistic director (1972–74); Douglas Seale, artistic director (1974–80); James Freydberg, managing director (1974–79); David Hale, interim managing director (1979); Irene Lewis, artistic director (1980–81); Gregory Poggi, managing director (1979–81) and producing director (1982–87).

Stage Directors: Malcolm Black, Jeff Bleckner, Thomas Bullard, Edmund Cambridge, Douglas Campbell, Andre Ernotte, Tony Giordano, John Going, Michael Kahn, Robert Kalfin, Charles I. Karchmer, Irene Lewis, Richard Maltby, Jr., Vivian Matalon, Michael Montel, Brian Murray, Michael Murray, Shauneille Perry, Daniel M. Petrie, Stephen Porter, Kurt Reis, William Ross, Steven Schachter, George C. Scott, Douglas Seale, Tony Van Bridge, Paxton Whitehead, William Woodman, Jerry Zaks.

Scenic Artists (resident or frequent): William Armstrong (lights, 1982–86), David Ballou (sets, 1974–75), F. Mitchell Dana (lights, 1981–86), Jeff Davis (lights, 1983–86), Clarke Dunham (sets and lights, 1971–74), John Kasarda (sets, 1975–80), Spencer Mosse (lights, 1975–80), Lee Watson (lights, 1974–75), Ann Wrightson (lights, 1981–84).

Costumers (resident or frequent): Joseph F. Bella (1971–74), David Charles (1975–76), Frankie Fehr (1982–86), Linda Fisher (1980–82), Jess Goldstein (1980–86), Dona Granata (1976–79), Jane Greenwood (1974–76), David Murin (1976–83).

Actors and Actresses (resident or frequent): Edward Atienza, Ronald Bishop, Domini Blythe, William Buell, Leah Chandler, *Carolyn Coates* (1976–77), Ann Crumb, Lois de Banzie, Virginia Downing, Donald Ewer, Gillie Fenwick, Moya Fenwick, Boyd Gaines, Robert Gerringer, *John Glover* (1974–77), Susan Greenhill, *Tana Hicken* (1980–81), *Munson Hicks* (1980–82), Linda Hunt, Gerry Iaia, Philip Kerr, David Leary, Russell Leib, *Betty Leighton* (1974–80), John Leighton, William Le Massina, Thomas Markus, Jonathan Moore, Robert Pastene, Lu Ann Post, William Preston, *John Randolph* (1971–74), *David Rounds* (1977–79), Douglas Seale, Sherry Steiner, Lee Toombs, *Louise Troy* 1974–80), Eric Uhler, *James Valentine* (1974–80), *Tony Van Bridge* (1976–80), Valerie von Volz, Paxton Whitehead, Douglas Wing, Jerry Zaks.

Selected Guest Performers: Edward Albert, Martin Balsam, Rosalind Cash, Leonardo Cimino, Glenn Close, Imogene Coca, Howard da Silva, Ruby Dee, David Dukes, Patricia Elliott, Tom Ewell, Geraldine Fitzgerald, Ed Flanders, Leonard Frey, Tammy Grimes, Ken Howard, Mary Beth Hurt, Anne Jackson, Richard Kiley, Swoosie Kurtz, Margaret Ladd, Vera Lockwood, Nancy Marchand, E. G. Marshall, Roberta Maxwell, Judy Mills, Charlotte Moore, Jenny O'Hara, Ron O'Neal, Jerry Orbach, Geraldine Page, Betsy Palmer, Bernadette Peters, Kate Reid, Chita Rivera, Esther Rolle, Maureen Stapleton, Kristoffer Tabori, Rip Torn, Eli Wallach, Ray Walston, Douglas Turner Ward, Fritz Weaver, Jobeth Williams, Teresa Wright.

REPERTORY

1971–72: *The Imaginary Invalid, Born Yesterday, The Rivals, Volpone.*

1972–73: *Tartuffe, Waltz of the Toreadors, Ceremonies in Dark Old Men, Juno and the Paycock.*

1973–74: *The Rose Tattoo, The Taming of the Shrew, Death of a Salesman, The Little Foxes.*

1974–75: *Misalliance, Ardele, Long Day's Journey into Night, The Importance of Being Earnest.*

1975–76: *The Royal Family, The Glass Menagerie, The Birthday Party, Hedda Gabler, The Miser.*

1976–77: *Heartbreak House, Enter a Free Man, Five Finger Exercise, Blithe Spirit, Hamlet.*

1977–78: *The Show-Off, Travesties, Saint Joan, Hobson's Choice, Uncle Vanya.*

1978–79: *The Au Pair Man, Arms and the Man, Private Lives, Blood Knot, The Night of the Iguana.*

1979–80: *The Last Few Days of Willie Callendar, You Can Never Tell, Summer, Twelfth Night, Thark.*

1980–81: *Watch on the Rhine, Joe Egg, Philadelphia, Here I Come!, The Front Page, Old World.*

1981–82: *Of Mice and Men, Gemini, Dear Daddy, Servant of Two Masters, The Contest.*

1982–83: *The Keeper, The Diary of Anne Frank, Talley's Folly, Daughters, All My Sons.*

1983–84: *Teibele and Her Demon, The Member of the Wedding, The Dining Room, Black Comedy, The Father.*

1984–85: *Oliver Oliver, The Power and the Glory, Love Gifts, The Price, Arsenic and Old Lace.*

1985–86: *Tent Meeting, A Raisin in the Sun, Absurd Person Singular, A Delicate Balance, Hot l Baltimore.*

1986–87: *The Shayna Maidel, The Amen Corner, The Foreigner, The Crucible, The Middle Ages.*

BIBLIOGRAPHY

Published Sources:
Philadelphia Evening Bulletin, 1971–87.
Philadelphia Inquirer, 1971–87.

Archival Resource:
Philadelphia, Pennsylvania. Free Library of Philadelphia. Philadelphia Theatre Collection. Programs, theatre files, actor files, and Philadelphia Drama Guild file.

Mari Kathleen Fielder

PHOENIX THEATRE. In August 1953 T. Edward Hambleton phoned Norris Houghton, offering to put up $50,000 to establish a theatre in New York City if Houghton could raise an equal amount. A total of $125,000 was raised, with Roger Stevens bringing in $25,000. Funds came from a variety of people, including Jo Mielzener, Richard Rodgers, Elia Kazan, Mildred Dunnock, Howard Lindsay, and Russel Crouse.

Houghton would take charge of artistic matters and Hambleton would be responsible for business management, although no major step could be taken without joint approval. Both men were highly experienced in theatre. Hambleton had studied at the Yale School of Drama in the 1930s and received his first professional training as manager of a summer theatre in Rhode Island. Later he turned to producing plays in New York, including the Broadway production of Bertolt Brecht's *Galileo*, starring Charles Laughton.

Norris Houghton, after graduating from Princeton in 1931, joined the University Players at Falmouth, Massachusetts, where he was a stage manager and designer. After designing seven productions on Broadway, he turned to directing, staging a notable production of *Macbeth* with Michael Redgrave and Flora Robson. Houghton was also a lecturer on drama at Princeton and at Columbia University and had written books on theatre practice in the USA and in the Soviet Union.

Their purpose was to present quality plays that would not be produced on Broadway, which preferred money-making hits. At the new theatre, stars would have a chance to perform in classics and in new plays without the pressures of Broadway. With a low budget, a top weekly salary of $100, even for stars, and a theatre with a large seating capacity, Hambleton and Houghton planned to present fine plays at reasonable prices. Because they believed a repertory company would be too expensive, Hambleton and Houghton decided to hire actors for productions presented in straight runs of about four weeks each.

They selected the 1,200-seat Stuyvesant Theatre, formerly the Yiddish Art Theatre, on Second Avenue and Twelfth Street. After renovations, the Phoenix Theatre opened on December 1, 1953, with Sidney Howard's comedy, *Madam, Will You Walk*, starring Hume Cronyn and Jessica Tandy. This was followed by a highly acclaimed *Coriolanus*, directed by John Houseman and featuring Robert Ryan and Mildred Natwick. In the cast were three unknowns: Jack Klugman, Gene Saks, and Jerry Stiller. They were the first of many gifted young actors the Phoenix would help make visible during its thirty-year history, future stars such as Joel Grey, Tammy Grimes, Carol Burnett, and Meryl Streep.

The third production, *The Golden Apple*, a musical by John Fatouche and Jerome Moross, ran for six weeks, transferred to Broadway, and won the Drama Critics' Circle Award. The final production that first season, Anton Chekhov's *The Sea Gull*, was chosen because movie star Montgomery Clift, who had just received rave notices in *From Here to Eternity*, wanted to appear in a Chekhov play. With Houghton directing, the cast included Judith Evelyn, Maureen Stapleton, and George Voskovec. Even though reviewers criticized the different acting styles, theatregoers flocked to see the play.

Despite an auspicious first year, the Phoenix retrieved only $85,000 of its $125,000 investment. By the end of the second season the theatre was further in debt, and rarely thereafter did it ever make a profit. During the second season the Phoenix inaugurated its Side Shows on Monday nights when the theatre was usually dark. Events included staged readings, dramas, ballets, and puppet shows. Geraldine Fitzgerald, with others, read Eugene O'Neill's *Anna Christie*. A Side Shows highlight the next year was a presentation of the Virgil Thomson–Gertrude Stein opera, *The Mother of Us All*.

During its first five years the Phoenix focused on European classics featuring renowned performers: August Strindberg's *Miss Julie* with Viveca Lindfors, Friedrich von Schiller's *Mary Stuart* starring Eva Le Gallienne as Elizabeth and Irene Worth as Mary, G. B. Shaw's *The Doctor's Dilemma* featuring Geraldine

Fitzgerald and Roddy McDowell, and Ivan Turgenev's *A Month in the Country* with Uta Hagen and Alexander Scourby. Outstanding directors included Sidney Lumet and Tyrone Guthrie.

With deficits continuing to mount, despite many rave reviews among the unfavorable ones, Houghton and Hambleton sought advice from Tyrone Guthrie and came to the decision that a permanent acting company was necessary for further development of the Phoenix. As a first step, the theatre became a nonprofit organization, thereby hoping to attract large tax-deductible donations.

For the 1958–59 season Houghton and Hambleton hired a permanent director, Stuart Vaughan. Vaughan selected the members of the repertory company, which included Fritz Weaver, Patricia Falkenheim, Robert Gerringer, and, the next year, Donald Madden. Nevertheless, the season was a financial disaster, and the Phoenix, unable to complete its subscription series, was forced to make refunds and suspend operations.

Later that season, however, Houghton and Hambleton produced *Once upon a Mattress*, a musical by Jay Thompson, Mary Rodgers, and Marshall Barer. George Abbott directed, and when Carol Burnett belted out ''I'm Shy,'' the show became an overnight sensation. It was transferred to Broadway, where it was a money-maker.

The Phoenix launched a major subscription drive in 1959–60, and the Ford Foundation granted funds to support the repertory company. The company received a setback, though, when Norris Houghton resigned to accept a position at Vassar College. The repertory company continued under the artistic direction of Stuart Vaughan through the 1960–61 season.

With deficits over $100,000 despite Ford Foundation funding, Hambleton decided the Phoenix could not afford to maintain a permanent company in a large theatre. In 1961 the Phoenix moved to a 299-seat theatre on East Seventy-fourth Street. Here Hambleton produced new plays, with a different director and cast for each production.

During the first season in its new home the Phoenix had a hit in Arthur Kopit's fantasy, *Oh Dad, Poor Dad, Mamma's Hung You in the Closet and I'm Feelin' So Sad*. The comedy filled the house for more than a year and was both a financial and a theatrical success. Because *Oh Dad* continued its run during the 1962–63 season, Hambleton rented the Phyllis Anderson Theatre, just south of the old playhouse, and presented two classics, Robert E. Sherwood's *Abe Lincoln in Illinois* and Shakespeare's *The Taming of the Shrew*. Although critically well received, the productions lost money.

When the next season at the Seventy-fourth Street playhouse started off unsuccessfully, the Phoenix formed an alliance with Ellis Rabb's Association of Producing Artists (APA),* a company of talented actors, including Nancy Marchand, Paul Sparer, and Rosemary Harris. In March 1964 the combined group presented a five-play repertory: Luigi Pirandello's *Right You Are (If You Think You Are)*, George M. Cohan's *The Tavern*, Molière's *Scapin* and *The Impromptu at Versailles*, and Maxim Gorky's *The Lower Depths*.

Despite growing audience support, the 299-seat theatre could not sustain a repertory company of thirty members. A successful revival of *You Can't Take It with You*, by George S. Kaufman and Moss Hart, at the Lyceum provided funds for the company's move to the Broadway Theatre. In three seasons, from 1965 to 1969, despite fine notices and several hits, especially a revival of George Kelly's *The Show-Off*, with Helen Hayes, deficits mounted to more than $2 million. At the end of the 1969 season, on the heels of a poorly received production of *Hamlet*, starring Ellis Rabb, Hambleton and Rabb dissolved their alliance. In addition to their financial problems, the Phoenix and the APA had disagreed over production methods and objectives and had made a number of costly errors.

The next season, the Phoenix received an infusion of funds from a highly successful limited engagement of the comedy *Harvey*, by Mary Chase, starring Helen Hayes and James Stewart. During the next few years the Phoenix, with Hambleton still managing director, presented plays in different spaces: *Harvey* played at the ANTA Theatre, *The Criminals* (1970) at Sheridan Square Theatre, *The Persians* (1970) at St. George's Church on Stuyvesant Square, Daniel Berrigan's *The Trial of the Catonsville Nine* (1971) at the Good Shepherd–Faith Church near Lincoln Center, and *Murderous Angels* (1971) at the Playhouse Theatre.

For the next three seasons (1972–75) the Phoenix returned to Broadway, calling itself the New Phoenix Repertory Company. Under the aegis of three artistic directors, Harold Prince, Stephen Porter, and Michael Montel, a permanent company, consisting of such fine actors as David Dukes, Glenn Close, and Mary Beth Hurt, was maintained. The group presented brief runs of revivals, including Eugene O'Neill's *The Great God Brown*, John Dryden's *Love for Love*, and Carson McCullers' *The Member of the Wedding*.

Still faced with debts, the Phoenix underwent another change. Daniel Freudenberger became the producing director, and for the 1975–76 season a new company of actors was formed, which included Meryl Streep, Roy Poole, and John Lithgow. At the Playhouse Theatre, with a different director for each production, the revivals included Sidney Howard's *They Knew What They Wanted* and William Gillette's *Secret Service*.

The next season the Phoenix moved to permanent quarters at Marymount Manhattan College. Here the Phoenix decided to concentrate on new plays, and it helped develop the careers of Wendy Wasserstein (*Uncommon Women and Others, Isn't It Romantic*) and Johanna M. Glass (*Canadian Gothic, American Modern*). Nonetheless, the theatre had financially and aesthetically disastrous seasons.

In 1982, hoping for a new start, the Phoenix moved to St. Peter's Church on East Fifty-third Street. Its first production, *Two Fish in the Sky*, closed quickly after receiving poor reviews. Finally, on December 8, 1982, after thirty seasons, out of funds and out of energy, the Phoenix closed. One critic noted that for the past several seasons the Phoenix had generated little popular or critical enthusiasm

(*Variety*, December 15, 1982). Another critic, Clive Barnes, pointed out that the Phoenix lacked consistency over the years (*New York Post*, December 18, 1982).

The Phoenix never developed a unique style or an identifiable personality. Aside from this, it presented many remarkable productions with outstanding directors, actors, and designers and helped develop the careers of talented new actors and playwrights.

PERSONNEL

Management: T. Edward Hambleton, managing director (1953–82); artistic directors: Daniel Freudenberger (1975–80), Norris Houghton (1953–59), Michael Montel (1972–75), Stephen Porter (1972–75), Harold Prince (1972–75), Ellis Rabb (APA) (1964–69), Steven Robman (1980–82), Stuart Vaughan (1959–61); Marilyn S. Miller, executive director (1975–78).

Set Designers: *Will Steven Armstrong* (1958–60), Boris Aronson, *Edward Burbridge* (1973–74), Jean Eckart, William Eckart, Ben Edwards, Judith Haugan, David Hays, *Klaus Holm* (1955–56), Norris Houghton, David Jenkins, John Kasarda, *Marjorie Kellogg* (1980–82), Hugh Landwehr, Ming Cho Lee, Donald Oenslager, Karen Schulz, *James Tilton* (1964–70, 1975–79), *Peter Wexler* (1963, 1971), *Peter Wingate* (1960–61).

Lighting Designers: *Ken Billington* (1973–75), Ronald Bundt, Arden Fingerhut, Jules Fisher, *Gilbert Hemsley* (1964–67, 1971), Klaus Holm (1954–58, 1964), *Joan Larkey* (1960–61), Spencer Mosse, *Tharon Musser* (1957–60, 1971–72), Dennis Parichy, Jean Rosenthal, *James Tilton* (1965, 1967–70, 1975–79), Jennifer Tipton.

Costume Designers: Will Steven Armstrong (1958–60), Alvin Colt (1953–58, 1963), *Linda Fisher* (1979–82), Jane Greenwood, *Jennifer Von Mayrhauser*, (1977–78, 1980–82), *Nancy Potts* (1964–70, 1971, 1974), Denise Romano, Frances Ellen Rosenthal, *Julie Weiss* (1977–79), Peter Wingate (1960–61), Albert Wolsky, Patricia Zipprodt (1962–64).

Stage Directors: George Abbott, Word Baker, Eric Bentley, Herbert Berghof, Arvin Brown, Peter Coe, Hume Cronyn, Howard da Silva, Gordon Davidson, Gerald Freedman, *Daniel Freudenberger* (1973, 1975–80), Tony Giordano, Ulu Grosbard, Tyrone Guthrie, Oscar Homolka, John Houseman, Jack Landau, Eva Le Gallienne, John Lithgow, Sidney Lumet, *Michael Montel* (1972–74), Jack O'Brien, *Stephen Porter* (1964, 1966–68, 1970, 1972–76), *Harold Prince* (1972–74), *Ellis Rabb* (1964–69), Michael Redgrave, Tony Richardson, Jerome Robbins, *Steven Robman* (1978–82), Gene Saks, Burt Shevelove, George Tabori, *Stuart Vaughan* (1958–63), Jerry Zaks.

Actors and Actresses: Luther Adler, Alvin Ailey, Tom Aldredge, Jean-Pierre Aumont, Conrad Bain, Kaye Ballard, Christine Baranzki, Brian Bedford, Jacob Ben-Ami, *Eric Berry* (1958–60), Leon Bibb, Joseph Bird, Robert Blackburn, Barry Bostwick, J. D. Cannon, Len Cariou, Vinnette Carroll, Jack Cassidy, Leonardo Cimino, *Glenn Close* (1974–75, 1977–80), Patricia Connolly, Clayton Corzatte, Franklin Cover, Michael Cristofer, Alma Cuervo, Robert Culp, Keene Curtis, Irene Dailey, James Daly, Meredith Dallas, Howard da Silva, Dom DeLuise, Alice Drummond, *David Dukes* (1971–72, 1974–75), Mildred Dunnock, Joyce Ebert, Barbara eda-Young, George Ede, Maurice Edwards, Jill Eikenberry, Christine Estabrook, Laura Esterman, Rex Everhart, Peter Falk, *Patricia Falkenheim* (1959–61), Jan Farrand, Eliot Feld, Ed Flanders, Will Geer, *Robert Gerringer* (1958–59), Alice Ghostly, Jack Gilford, Jack Gilpin, Lillian Gish, Lou Gossett,

Gordon Gould, Farley Granger, James Greene, Rose Gregorio, Ted van Griethuysen, Joe Grifasi, Bob Gunton, Barbara Harris, *Rosemary Harris* (1965–66), June Havoc, John Heard, *John Heffernan* (1959–61), Bette Henritze, Eileen Herlie, Michael Higgins, *Patrick Hines* (1957, 1959, 1960, 1977–78), Hal Holbrook, Oscar Homolka, David Hooks, Marcie Hubert, *Mary Beth Hurt* (1974–76), Earle Hyman, Sam Jaffe, Gerry Jedd, James Earl Jones, Raul Julia, Kurt Kasznar, Nicholas Kepros, John Kerr, Richard Kiley, Swoosie Kurtz, William Larsen, *John Lithgow* (1976, 1981–82), Cleavon Little, Tony Lo Bianco, Jane McArthur, David McCallum, Kevin McCarthy, Ann McDonough, Siobhan McKenna, *John McMartin* (1964, 1973–75), *Donald Madden* (1959–61, 1976–77), *Nancy Marchand* (1964), *Nan Martin* (1959–60, 1963), Anne Meara, James Mitchell, Donald Moffat, Michael Moriarty, Zero Mostel, Mary-Joan Negro, *Lois Nettleton* (1976), Estelle Parsons, Pamela Payton-Wright, Austin Pendleton, George Pentecost, Christine Pickles, Joan Plowright, Roy Poole, Albert Quinton, *Ellis Rabb* (1964–69), Charlotte Rae, John Ragin, Juliet Randall, Don Redlich, Jared Reed, Pamela Reed, Ray Reinhardt, Lee Richardson, Eve Roberts, Joanna Roos, Janice Rule, Wallace Shawn, Ed Sherin, *Paul Sparer* (1964), Frances Sternhagen, Larry Storch, Beatrice Straight, Meryl Streep, Elliott Sullivan, Sandor Szabo, Sada Thompson, Joan Van Ark, Jo Van Fleet, June Walker, Nancy Walker, Sydney Walker, Eli Wallach, Jack Warden, Frederic Warriner, Sam Waterson, *Fritz Weaver* (1955, 1958–60), Sigourney Weaver, Dianne Wiest, Richard Woods, Harris Yulin, Jerry Zaks, Louis Zorach.

REPERTORY

1953–54: *Madam, Will You Walk, Coriolanus, The Golden Apple, The Sea Gull*.

1954–55: *Sing Me No Lullaby, Sandhog, The Doctor's Dilemma, The Master Builder, Phoenix '55*. Side Shows: *Angna Enters, The White Devil, Moby Dick*.

1955–56: *The Carefree Tree, Six Characters in Search of an Author, Miss Julie, The Stronger, A Month in the Country, The Littlest Revue*. Side Shows: *Anna Christie, Venice Preserv'd, Queen After Death, The Mother of Us All, The Terrible Swift Sword, The Adding Machine*.

1956–57: *Saint Joan, Diary of a Scoundrel, The Good Woman of Setzuan, The Duchess of Malfi, Livin' the Life*.

1957–58: *Mary Stuart, The Makropoulos Secret, The Chairs, The Lesson, The Infernal Machine, Two Gentleman of Verona*. Side Shows: *Tobias and the Angel, A Sleep of Prisoners, Everyman Today, The World of Cilly Wang, The Transposed Heads*.

1958–59: *The Family Reunion, The Power and the Glory, The Beaux' Stratagem, Once upon a Mattress*.

1959–60: *The Great God Brown, Lysistrata, Pictures in the Hallway, Peer Gynt, Henry IV*, Parts I and II.

1960–61: *She Stoops to Conquer, The Plough and the Stars, The Octoroon, or Life in Louisiana, Hamlet*.

1961–62: *Androcles and the Lion, The Policemen, The Dark Lady of the Sonnets, Who'll Save the Plowboy?, Oh Dad, Poor Dad, Mamma's Hung You in the Closet and I'm Feelin' So Sad*. Side Show: *But It's Nothing*.

1962–63: *Abe Lincoln in Illinois, The Taming of the Shrew, The Dragon*. Side Show: *Persephone*.

1963–64: *Morning Sun, Next Time I'll Sing to You, Too Much Johnson, The Brontes*. With APA: *Right You Are (If You Think You Are), The Tavern, Scapin, Impromptu at Versailles, The Lower Depths*.

1964–65: *Doctor Faustus*. With APA: *Man and Superman, War and Peace, Judith*.

1965–66: With APA: *You Can't Take It with You*.

1966–67: With APA: *The School for Scandal, Right You Are (If You Think You Are), We Comrades Three, The Wild Duck, War and Peace, You Can't Take It with You*.

1967–68: With APA: *Pantagleize, The Show-Off, Exit the King, The Cherry Orchard*.

1968–69: With APA: *Pantagleize, The Show-Off, The Cocktail Party, The Misanthrope, Cock-a-Doodle Dandy, Hamlet*.

1969–70: *Harvey, The Criminals, The Persians*.

1970–71: *The Trial of the Catonsville Nine, The School for Wives*.

1971–72: *Murderous Angels*.

1972–73: *The Great God Brown, Don Juan*. Side Shows: *Games/After Liverpool, Strike Heaven*.

1973–74: *The Visit, Chemin de Fer, Holiday*. Side Shows: *Miracle Play, The Removalists, In the Voodoo Parlor of Marie Leveau, Gris-Gris, The Commedia World of Lafcadio Beau, Pretzels*.

1974–75: *Love for Love, The Rules of the Game, The Member of the Wedding*. Side Shows: *Knuckle, Dandelion Wine, Meeting Place, Macrune's Guevara, Flux*.

1975–76: *27 Wagons Full of Cotton, A Memory of Two Mondays, They Knew What They Wanted, Secret Service, Boy Meets Girl*.

1976–77: *Ladyhouse Blues, Canadian Gothic, American Modern, Marco Polo, A Sorrow Beyond Dreams, G. R. Point, Scribes*.

1977–78: *Hot Grog, Uncommon Women and Others, The Elusive Angel, One Crack Out, City Sugar*.

1978–79: *Getting Out, Later, Says I, Says He, Big and Little, Chinchilla*.

1979–80: *The Winter Dancers, Shout Across the River, The Trouble with Europe, Save Grand Central, Second Avenue Rag*.

1980–81: *Bonjour, là, Bonjour, Beyond Therapy, The Captivity of Pixie Shedman, Meetings, Isn't It Romantic*.

1981–82: *Maggie and Pierre, After the Prize, Kaufman at Large, Weekends Like Other People*.

1982: *Two Fish in the Sky*.

BIBLIOGRAPHY

Published Sources:

Feingold, Michael. "The Phoenix Theater 1953–1982." *The Village Voice*, December 21, 1982, p. 117.

Little, Stuart W. *Off-Broadway: The Prophetic Theatre*. New York: Coward, McCann & Geoghegan, 1972, pp. 137–60.

"Stages: Phoenix Grounded," *Theatre Communications*, February 1983, p. 6.

Vaughan, Stewart. *A Possible Theatre*. New York: McGraw-Hill Book Co., ch. 7, pp. 88–136.

Archival Resource:

New York, New York. New York Public Library. Library and Museum of the Performing Arts. Photos, posters, and programs, as well as scrapbooks containing news clippings, reviews, press releases, brochures, and letters.

Doris Hart

PLAYHOUSE ON THE SQUARE/CIRCUIT PLAYHOUSE. Circuit Playhouse, so named because it originally performed at different locations throughout Memphis, Tennessee, was formed in 1963 as a summer acting troop by Jackie

Nichols, a local actor-director who had had experience with Memphis' Front Street Theatre*. In 1968 the Playhouse moved to a permanent location on Walker Street, near Memphis State University, and filed as a nonprofit corporation, Circuit, Inc. In 1970 the company moved again to 1947 Poplar Avenue. In addition to its main-stage activities, the group opened a workshop theatre and Theatre II for children. The company further expanded by opening Playhouse on the Square in 1975 in Overton Square, thereby becoming the only nonprofit professional theatre in a 150-mile radius. In 1976 Circuit, Inc., produced Lanford Wilson's *Hot l Baltimore* at the King Cotton Hotel; subsequently eight environmental productions were produced.

Circuit, Inc., established Show of Hands, a Theatre of the Deaf troupe, in 1978, and in 1983 Marc Martinez, head of the troupe, was awarded the Governor's Award for outstanding contributions to the arts in Tennessee. Show of Hands was established to heighten awareness of the problems of the hearing impaired, as well as to provide entertainment and teach better communication skills to the hearing impaired, the handicapped, nonnative speakers, and young children. The company performs throughout Tennessee and the South.

In 1979 Circuit Playhouse won a state competition for community theatres with an original play by John Fergus Ryan, *Baby Dave*. Ryan's play won the Tennessee Theatre Association competition the next year and the regional award in the Southeastern Theatre Competition in 1981. Executive producer Jackie Nichols won the Tennessee Theatre Association's Distinguished Service Award for his contributions to theatre in the state in 1981 as well.

In 1981 the company purchased the Evergreen Theatre as a permanent home for the Circuit Playhouse and as a technical facility for both the Circuit Playhouse and the Playhouse on the Square. In 1982 the company established its Student Matinee Program and its first-run foreign film series. The Playhouse on the Square moved, in 1985, to the Memphian Theatre at 51 South Cooper, spending $150,000 on renovations and expanding its seating from 88 to 240, and replacing the twenty-two-foot-wide stage with one forty-three feet wide. Because of this increased capacity, the Playhouse on the Square was able, in 1986, to expand its Theatre for Youth program to include workshops for students in all areas of theatre and to establish a workshop for teachers. The matinee program was able to accommodate 27,000 students. A new "theatre conservatory" opened in the summer of 1987.

Both playhouses emphasize new theatrical works and those previously unproduced in Memphis. Playhouse on the Square attempts to aid developing actors, directors, designers, and technicians to make a living in the profession while improving their craft, and the Circuit Playhouse attempts to provide an opportunity for community participation in all aspects of the theatre while serving as a second stage for intern programs. Both playhouses present a September-to-July season of seven shows, and each produces a summer show as well. The Circuit Playhouse also stages annually an original work chosen through a playwrights' competition.

Broadly based and carefully expanding and diversifying to serve the needs of the area, both playhouses receive solid support from the Memphis area.

PERSONNEL

Staff: Jackie Nichols, executive director and producer; Michael J. Vails, managing director; Mindy C. Moore, director of marketing; Angela Powers Ward, director of subscriptions and promotions; Archie Grinalds, director of publicity; Jay M. Kinney, Youth Theatre director; Ken Zimmerman, artistic director; Karin Barile Hill, director, Theatre of the Deaf; Elizabeth Howard, business manager.

Production Staff: Lois Mytas, stage manager; Renee E. Weiss, costumer; Peter Bowman, technical director; Steve Forsyth, master electrician.

Actors and Actresses: Beverly Baxter, Brent Blair, Leila Boyd, Leonard Bracken, Jerry Bradley, Jeff Braun, *Linda Brinkerhoff* (1983–85), *Bates Brooks* (1979–86), Maureen Burns, *Mark Chambers* (1981–85), Pepi Chitwood, Shannon Cochran, Angie Cockroft, Catherine Coscarelly, Stefan Cotner, Irene Crist, Michael Darling, John Dunavent, Cathryn Ann Fleuchaus, *Stephan Foster* (1977–80), Ray Fuller, John Gibson, Thomas Hammond, Matha Hester, Anne Marie Hehir, Trula Housier, Robert Hutchens, *Michael Jeter* (1975–76), Dale Johnson, Mark Johnson, Ridge Johnson, A. Victer Jones, Jane Jones, Stephen Kean, Nita Koon, Elly Koslo, Tom Lawson, Maggie McMillian, Ken Miller, *Allen Mullikin* (1980–86), Harry Murphy, Maggie Murphy, George Naylor, Donna Nerwith, Michael O'Brien, Jim Palmer, Tom Parkhill, David Lancaster Phillips, Blaine Pickett, David Poirer, Angela Powers, Robert Reynolds, *Larry Riley* (1975–76), Richard Roberts, Reginald Robinson, James Vivrant, Ron Wachholtz, *Alvin Walker* (1981–82), Jane Wallace, *Steve Wilkerson* (1983–85), Gene Wilkins.

REPERTORY

1965: *Fashion*.

1966: *The Glass Menagerie, The Importance of Being Earnest, The Wizard of Oz*.

1967: *Babes in Arms*.

1968: *The Roar of the Greasepaint, the Smell of the Crowd*.

1969–70: *The Fantasticks, The Owl and the Pussycat, We Bombed in New Haven, Encounters, Bus Stop, The Giant's Dance, Your Own Thing, Bell, Book and Candle*.

1970–71: *Of Mice and Men, Loot, The Boys in the Band, Marat/Sade, The Rainmaker, Slow Dance on the Killing Ground, Celebration, Steambath*.

1971–72: *Charlie Brown, A Streetcar Named Desire, Rosencrantz and Guildenstern Are Dead, The Three Sisters, Feiffer's People, The Miracle Worker, Who's Afraid of Virginia Woolf?, You Can't Take It with You*.

1972–73: *One Flew over the Cuckoo's Nest, The Lion in Winter, The Price, I Never Sang for My Father, The Serpent, The Threepenny Opera, Member of the Wedding, Dylan*.

1973–74: *Waiting for Godot, Old Times, Fortune and Men's Eyes, Alice in Wonderland, The Real Inspector Hound, The Only Game in Town*.

1974–75: *Tiny Alice, Private Lives, Godspell, Look Back in Anger, The Taming of the Shrew, When You Comin' Back, Red Ryder?, The Creation of the World and Other Business, Butley, Biederman and the Firebugs, The Imaginary Invalid, Little Murders, No Place to be Somebody*.

1975–76: *After the Fall, Sweet Bird of Youth, Sleuth, The Ruling Class, The Sea Horse, America Hurrah!, The Hostage, All My Sons, Doctor Holocaust, Godspell, A Shot in the Dark, Tobacco Road, The Fantasticks, Bus Stop, Once upon a Mattress, Jacques Brel, Evening of Soul.*

1976–77: *El Grande de Coca Cola, Find Your Way Home, The Tavern, Clarence Darrow, Two for the Seesaw, A Moon for the Misbegotten, Seascape, A Streetcar Named Desire, Happy Birthday, Wanda June, Two Gentlemen of Verona, Hay Fever, Thurber Carnival, The Misanthrope, The Threepenny Opera, Candide, Fallen Angels, Of Mice and Men, The School for Wives.*

1977–78: *Suddenly Last Summer, The Runner Stumbles, Streamers, Enter a Free Man, Room Service, Counterfeit Rose, And Miss Reardon Drinks a Little, Scuba Duba, One Flew over the Cuckoo's Nest, Angel Street, Man of La Mancha, Twelfth Night, Summer and Smoke, Waltz of the Toreadors, Marat/Sade, Southern Comfort, The King Is a Fink, Evening of Soul.*

1978–79: *Don't Bother Me, I Can't Cope, The Children's Hour, Women Behind Bars, The Hobbit, Dracula, Come Back, Little Sheba, Lenny, The Marriage of Mr. Mississippi, Jesse and the Bandit Queen, Diamond Studs, Much Ado About Nothing, Light Up the Sky, Another Part of the Forest, Oliver, The Oldest Living Graduate, Dames at Sea, El Grande de Coca Cola, Harry Bryce, Evening of Soul.*

1979–80: *The 5th of July, Indulgences in a Louisville Harem, In the Restroom at Rosenbloom's, American Buffalo, Art of Murder, Oedipus, On Borrowed Time, Ernest in Love, Jesus Christ, Superstar, Romeo and Juliet, Present Laughter, The Hot l Baltimore, Jumpers, Death of a Salesman, Company, For Colored Girls Who Have Considered Suicide, Joseph, Baby Dave.*

1980–81: *Luann Hampton Laverty Oberlander, Dirty Linen, Into Thy Narrow Bed, The Club, Othello, Runaways, Getting Out, Holy Ghosts, The Play's the Thing, Pippin, Sherlock Holmes, Sly Fox, A Funny Thing Happened on the Way to the Forum, Cyrano, Cat on a Hot Tin Roof, Grease, Ernest in Love, The Club.*

1981–82: *Loose Ends, The Gin Game, Bent, Alice in Wonderland, The Emperor Jones, The Women, California Suite, The Wiz, Born Yesterday, Tribute, God Bless You, Mr. Rosewater, Arsenic and Old Lace, Frankenstein, Comedy of Errors, The Little Foxes, Fiddler on the Roof, The Fantasticks, Jacques Brel.*

1982–83: *Arts and Leisure, Talley's Folly, Cinderella, Home, Betrayal, Wings, Uncommon Women, Treasure Island, Chicago, To Kill a Mockingbird, Cabaret, The Lion in Winter, The Elephant Man, Mister Roberts, 1776, The Wiz.*

1983–84: *The Dresser, Peter Pan, Terra Nova, Something's Afoot, Angel's Fall, The Wind in the Willows, The March of the Falsettos, Arpeggio Major, The Pirates of Penzance, The Miracle Worker, 1940's Radio Hour, Black Coffee, Julius Caesar, Ain't Misbehavin', Children of a Lesser God, Getting My Act Together.*

1984–85: *Mass Appeal, Peter Pan, Nuts, How I Got That Story, To Gillian on Her 37th Birthday, Agnes of God, Amen Corner, The Rose Tattoo, The Mikado, Hedda Gabler, Two X Two, Coup/Clucks, Diary of Anne Frank, Hollywood/Ukraine, The Dining Room.*

1985–86: *Baby with the Bathwater, Peter Pan, K2, Extremities, Cloud 9, The Curse of the Starving Class, Key Exchange, Evita, Of Mice and Men, Gypsy, A Spider's Web, A Midsummer Night's Dream, Purlie.*

BIBLIOGRAPHY

Information drawn from archival resources in author's possession.

Rodney Simard

R

REPERTORY THEATRE AT LORETTO-HILTON CENTER. See REP-
ERTORY THEATRE OF ST. LOUIS.

REPERTORY THEATRE IN THE SQUARE. See TRINITY SQUARE REP-
ERTORY COMPANY.

[THE] REPERTORY THEATRE OF LINCOLN CENTER grew out of a
network of cultural and philanthropic organizations in New York City. In 1956,
after years of planning, New York's civic, business, and cultural leaders created
Lincoln Center for the Performing Arts, Inc., a nonprofit institution. The founders
of Lincoln Center hoped it would become a model of organizational planning
and managerial efficiency as well as "a symbol of American cultural maturity,
affirming for people everywhere our faith in the life of the spirit . . . and helping
fulfill some of the needs of an anxious age" (John D. Rockefeller III, quoted
in "Center Viewed as Arts Capital," *New York Times*, December 14, 1956,
p. 62). They acquired a fourteen-acre site bounded by West Sixty-second and
Sixty-fifth streets and Columbus and Amsterdam avenues, and, in 1959, began
construction of Philharmonic Hall. When the building was completed in 1962,
it became the new home of the New York Philharmonic Orchestra. Subsequently
the Center became the home of the New York City Ballet, the Library and
Museum of the Performing Arts (a branch of the New York Public Library), the
Metropolitan Opera, and the Julliard School of Music, in addition to the Repertory
Theatre of Lincoln Center (RTLC).

A substantial monetary gift from May Company department store heiress
Vivian Beaumont Allen was instrumental in launching the repertory theatre
portion of the center project and in maintaining the repertory company in its
years of operation (1963–73). On May 16, 1958, the Lincoln Center board appointed Broadway producer Robert Whitehead as a consultant on repertory theatre.

The Lincoln Center board also empaneled a Repertory Theatre board that included Walter Kerr, drama critic of the *New York Herald Tribune;* Sanford Meisner, director of The Neighborhood Playhouse; Eva Le Gallienne, actress, founder of the Civic Repertory Theatre and cofounder of the American Repertory Theatre*; Cheryl Crawford, producer, cofounder of the American Repertory Theatre, of the Actors Studio, Inc., and of the Group Theatre*; Elia Kazan, director, cofounder of the Actors Studio, Inc.; Jo Mielziner, scene designer; producers Roger L. Stevens and Robert W. Dowling; and Vivian Beaumont Allen.

Whitehead believed a well-planned and financed theatre company at Lincoln Center should facilitate the continuing maturation of already accomplished native talent, so preference for new works by American authors was a feature of early announcements about the aims of the organization. A tour of European theatre centers in 1959 confirmed Whitehead's belief in the value of the resident company, but he believed Lincoln Center should produce plays in serial fashion rather than in rotating repertory. Whitehead also naively suggested the company would be financially self-sustaining after an initial first-year subsidy of $750,000.

Elia Kazan became a coconsultant to the Lincoln Center board in October 1959. Together, Kazan and Whitehead refined a strategy for developing a company, though Kazan gradually replaced Whitehead as Lincoln Center's theatre spokesman. Kazan persuaded Whitehead of the value of a two-play repertory, with each playing half a week. They agreed that classics of the American drama and new plays by leading American writers should be featured. The pair envisioned a company with no stars, but with, nevertheless, leading Broadway performers, who would rehearse for periods much longer than the prevailing standard on Broadway. The company would be pitched to an audience that did not frequent Broadway, so there would be no direct competition with commercial theatre. Critics, intellectuals, and theatre professionals responded skeptically to these announcements.

The Lincoln Center board selected Eero Saarinen to design the theatre in Lincoln Center and named Jo Mielziner as theatrical consultant. While Saarinen, a renowned architect, had few theatre designs to his credit, Mielziner was Broadway's most famous scenic designer. Saarinen faced the problem of designing a building at once distinctive yet in harmony with the appearance of the other five, each being designed by a different renowned architect. Both Sarrinen and Mielziner opposed a multiform stage as being costlier to build and operate, but the building committee of the Lincoln Center board overruled them. Mielziner also encountered grave difficulties in blending the axial vision of the proscenium stage with the radial vision of the thrust stage. Repertory functioning also necessitated a vast and costly backstage where sets not immediately in use could be stored.

After approval of the final plans for the physical plant, Kazan and Whitehead began in May 1962 to select members of a company. Robert Lewis, cofounder of the Actors Studio, headed the actor training program; dancer-choreographer Anna Sokolow became movement instructor; and Arthur Lessac became voice instructor. Whitehead and Kazan planned a company including fifteen experienced performers and fifteen younger performers to be selected from the training program. Auditions for the training program began in May 1962; by September Kazan and Lewis had selected thirty-five trainees from more than 1,500 applicants. Both looked for young performers with training in and a gift for contemporary realism, but also with aptitude and skill for work in classic and other modern styles.

Performers in the school Lewis formed complained that the close scrutiny to which they were continually submitted made it more like one long audition than like a school, and that techniques of stylization were poorly taught. Lewis left the organization after eight months. As rehearsals began October 24, 1963, training ceased, though the young performers were still not adept at classic styles. Performers selected from the training program included Faye Dunaway, Barbara Loden, Austin Pendleton, and Barry Primus.

The first play Kazan and company produced was a new work by Arthur Miller, *After the Fall*, and most of the established actors joining the company in October 1963 signed not for seasonal contracts, but for roles in *After the Fall*. These included Jason Robards, Jr., Hal Holbrook, Salome Jens, Zohra Lampert, Paul Mann, Ralph Meeker, David Wayne, and Joseph Wiseman.

Construction delays at the site of the Lincoln Center theatre forced Kazan and Whitehead to seek an alternate theatre in which to present optioned plays by Miller and S. N. Behrman. An option to construct a temporary steel building in which the stage of the projected Vivian Beaumont Theatre could be approximated emerged as the most attractive, but the Lincoln Center board would not allow such a structure on the Lincoln Square site. New York University offered a site on Washington Square, but the Repertory Theatre board opposed this solution. Whitehead and Kazan, recognizing the widening rift between company needs as they perceived them and the interests of the two boards to whom the RTLC was responsible, proceeded with an independent fund-raising campaign. The American National Theatre and Academy sponsored the campaign, and real estate tycoon and financier Robert W. Dowling chaired it. Ground was broken at the Washington Square site on July 10, 1963. Kazan and Whitehead hired Robert Downing and Frederic de Wilde as production stage managers and then sent them on a tour of repertory theatres at Stratford, Connecticut, Stratford, Ontario, and Minneapolis. They also retained director and critic Harold Clurman as a consultant and to direct a play in the company's second season.

A subscription campaign for a three-show season (*After the Fall*, Behrman's *But for Whom Charlie*, and Eugene O'Neill's *Marco Millions*) resulted in the early sale of 71 percent of the total available capacity of the new theatre. Ticket prices were scaled about a third lower than those prevailing on Broadway.

The ANTA-Washington Square Theatre was a simple but unimpressive building with inadequate public facilities, poor soundproofing, a cramped auditorium, and awkward access to the stage for performers. The thrust stage, edged with permanent steps, worked beautifully for *After the Fall*, but posed problems for subsequent productions. It seemed to be a stage for epic confrontations, not for intimate realism and muted conflict. Nevertheless, critics and the public at large generally approved the temporary theatre.

Miller's play was a hit, but dissatisfaction with the repertory situation and with exclusive contracts awarded some actors swept the company. Some critics complained that Behrman's play was outmoded and banal, while others suggested it should have been produced in a Broadway proscenium theatre. O'Neill's bitter satirizing of the philistine businessman proved as tedious in revival as it had seemed when first produced in 1928. The new plays by Miller and Behrman were attacked by commercial producers and by critics alike as commercial properties inappropriate in the repertory of a resident company. The O'Neill and Behrman works were withdrawn after brief runs, but *After the Fall* held up for a long run.

As the first season ended, the organization seemed uncertain of its purpose, and play selection for the second season, labeled "World Theatre Repertory," differed so markedly from the first that concerns about the integrity of the company's artistic point of view were confirmed. Kazan and Whitehead met with disdain from the artistic and intellectual establishment and jealousy from the entertainment world. The venom in some of the commentary suggested to Walter Kerr that Whitehead and Kazan seemed to have been singled out as bloodsacrifices for the accumulated sins of the American theatre (*Thirty Plays Hath November*, pp. 167–68).

Total cost of the first year's operation was $1,750,000. Operating at capacity, the theatre could earn only about 90 percent of such expenses, and in its first season the RTLC experienced a deficit of $600,000. Moreover, subscriptions for the second season dropped to about 55 percent of capacity, suggesting that the deficit would be even larger in the year to come. The Vivian Beaumont Allen Foundation contributed $300,000 toward balancing the budget, leaving the remainder to be raised by the Repertory Theatre board. Tension developed between George Woods, chairman of the Repertory Theatre board, and Robert Whitehead over the size of the budget and the necessity of a deficit. Increasingly the board expressed dissatisfaction over Whitehead's apparent inability to establish a budget and then perform within its limits.

As plans for the second season progressed, so did construction on the Vivian Beaumont Theatre, which was projected for completion in the spring of 1965. Kazan and Whitehead wanted to defer its opening until the fall; the Lincoln Center board and the Repertory Theatre board wanted it opened sooner, with a visiting troupe or production, if necessary. Robert L. Hoguet, Jr., executive vice president of the First National City Bank of New York, succeeded George Woods as president of the Repertory Theatre board, with no apparent easing of tensions between the Repertory Theatre board and its theatre managers.

Response to the October opening of *The Changeling* (1622), by Thomas Middleton and William Rowley, featuring performers from the original training program, was uniformly critical. It was withdrawn after thirty-two performances.

The Clurman-directed *Incident at Vichy*, using the senior company in Arthur Miller's contemporary realistic drama, was better received. Then William Schuman, president of the Lincoln Center board, offered the position of head of the Repertory Theatre to Herman Krawitz, assistant manager of the Metropolitan Opera. An uproar ensued. Krawitz declined amid a public furor raised by all those persons and boards at Lincoln Center that believed they should have been party to a decision to replace Whitehead and "transfer" Krawitz. Whitehead publicly resigned but named himself as the object of a "wrongful discharge" (*New York Times*, December 8, 1964, p. 55). Maureen Stapleton, signed to play the leading role in Jean Giraudoux' *The Madwoman of Chaillot*, withdrew in protest, while Kazan, too, resigned. The company, now performing *The Changeling* and *Incident at Vichy* in repertory and rehearsing *Tartuffe* for a January opening, was leaderless. Charges that Kazan and Whitehead had squandered a great opportunity to build a fine company capable of presenting the classics of drama were mitigated somewhat by the success of the William Ball–directed *Tartuffe*, featuring the regular company in support of Joyce Ebert, Michael O'Sullivan, and Sada Thompson. *Madwoman* was canceled. The second season ended May 29, 1965.

The Repertory Theatre board began a search for a new manager and artistic director. Favorable reviews of the recently published *The Impossible Theatre: A Manifesto*, by Herbert Blau, producing director of the Actor's Workshop* of San Francisco, as well as favorable reviews in the national press of recent productions of the group, focused attention on Blau and his associate, Jules Irving. Visits to San Francisco to see rehearsals and productions of the Actor's Workshop confirmed Hoguet's interest in Blau and Irving. Despite some reservations that Blau and Irving could not, because of the intensity of public scrutiny in New York, do in Manhattan what they had done in California, Hoguet offered Blau and Irving the job. After a period of agonizing consideration, Blau and Irving accepted Hoguet's offer, and on January 25, 1965, Hoguet announced their appointment as directors of the Repertory Theatre. Blau and Irving signed three-year contracts commencing March 1, 1965. Reaction in New York ranged from unalloyed approval to open hostility.

Blau and Irving were hardly the sun-tanned amateurs their detractors depicted them to be. Both were native New Yorkers and alumni of New York University. Irving had made his Broadway acting debut at age thirteen and had appeared both on and off Broadway and in summer stock. Both had attended Stanford University after World War II, both had taught at San Francisco State College, and both had married New York actresses. The Actor's Workshop, established in 1952, had garnered an international reputation for excellence in the production of a wide range of drama, but the group seemed especially adept in productions of then avant-garde drama of Harold Pinter, Bertolt Brecht, and Samuel Beckett. At first glance, Blau appeared to be the idealistic intellectual and Irving the practical man of the theatre, but no such easy division of functions actually existed. Both were adept managers and both were gifted with fine minds and driven by high ideals.

Blau and Irving agreed to release from their long-term contracts those of the Lincoln Center company who wanted to be released, and to work with those who wanted to continue. Several performers opted out, including David Wayne and Hal Holbrook.

Blau, often maligned for his devotion to alienating and negativistic drama, had revised his approach in the course of writing *The Impossible Theatre*. His new approach stressed activism and affirmation, and plays were chosen for the third season of the RTLC for their capacity to represent social action and probe the issues of individual responsibility. Georg Büchner's *Danton's Death* posed reservations about a revolution that degenerates into a reign of terror. William Wycherly's *The Country Wife* satirized a corrupt culture in which lying and hypocrisy are pervasive but funny, nevertheless. Jean-Paul Sartre's *The Condemned of Altona* was a modern parable probing the problem of the legitimate uses of violence and the morally ambiguous consequences of political action. Brecht's *The Caucasian Chalk Circle* was another parable that explored the impact of social change on the most fundamental cultural assumptions. These were indeed the kinds of plays critics of the RTLC thought it should have been producing, but observers were chagrined to learn that each production would be presented for a six-week run rather than in repertory.

Season ticket sales increased, though not to first-season levels. One of the big attractions was the new Vivian Beaumont Theatre, built entirely with private funds and costing $10,326,000. The capacity of the main theatre was 1,140; of the Forum, a second theatre in the Beaumont building, 299. The Eero Saarinen design was singled out as the best in the Lincoln Center complex, but the main auditorium and stage was criticized for its poor sight lines and for the awkward compromise effected between the thrust stage and the proscenium stage. Blau and Irving soon found that the acoustics were not good and that the stage machinery and the machinery for altering the auditorium configuration were flawed. Designers found that the width and height of the stage forced them to reduce the volume of the stage space to bring it into scale for the actors performing on the stage; directors found that only the most heroic actor could command an audience's attention in this space. Gordon Rogoff called it "the all-purpose theatre that absolutely defines lack of purpose" (*New York Times*, December 19, 1965, Section 2, p. 1). Furthermore, the theatre's George Izenour–designed lighting system was, in the view of John Gleason, resident lighting designer for six years, "ill-conceived, ill-designed, and ill-built . . . [and] out of date by the time [it] was installed" (private interview, quoted in Saraleigh Carney, "The Repertory Theatre of Lincoln Center: Aesthetics and Economics, 1960–1973," doctoral dissertation, City University of New York, 1976, p. 271). For all its design flaws, it was the cost of maintenance that would be crucial, for the building committee of the Repertory Theatre board had never adequately assessed the cost of operating and maintaining a repertory company in a multipurpose facility.

Meanwhile, Blau and Irving set up a training program for their new company, a program consisting in part of mime classes with Carlo Mazzone and voice classes with Henry Jacobi. Fusion of the Actor's Workshop contingent of performers with those remaining from the Whitehead-Kazan regime was effected through work on small practice scenes and then, later, on crowd and battle scenes under the direction of Irving (working on a section of Brecht's *A Man's a Man*) and Blau (working on a portion of Shakespeare's *Troilus and Cressida*). This experimental and instructional work also allowed Blau and Irving to explore the uses of the new stage.

The company of forty-nine for the first production (*Danton's Death*) included eleven from the Whitehead-Kazan company, fifteen from the Actor's Workshop, and fourteen new players from New York. No stars were engaged, and the salary scale was considerably lower than during the first two seasons. Moreover, principal roles in the first production were distributed so as to allay charges that "alien" performers were being forced on New York audiences: three principals were from the old company, four from San Francisco, and nine from the corps of new actors from New York. Frederic de Wilde, production stage manager, and Howard Fischer, stage manager, were held over from the old company, while Jo Mielziner was invited to design the scenery and lights for the Beaumont's inaugural production.

Rehearsals for *Danton's Death* went well, according to Blau, but critics reported disquietude in the company. Controversy sprang up over a portion of Blau's program note for the first preview of *Danton's Death*, in which Blau drew a parallel between revolutionary terrorists and then-President Lyndon Johnson. Objections of several patrons forced the withdrawal of the note, and the withdrawal of the note offended those who had agreed with Blau's assessment of Johnson.

The Vivian Beaumont Theatre was dedicated on October 14, 1964; a gala benefit of *Danton's Death* was held on October 20, raising $100,000 toward the anticipated deficit; and on October 21 the play officially opened. The response was almost uniformly negative, and virtually no aspect of the enterprise escaped denunciation. *The Country Wife*, directed by Robert Symonds, followed. The production, which had been such a success in San Francisco a year earlier, was swallowed up by the new theatre. The small reservoir of critical tolerance in New York was drained dry by these two productions. *The Condemned of Altona* was another failure, but the Irving-directed *The Caucasian Chalk Circle* was well received, and this modest success allowed the new directors to catch their breath after such a devastating premiere season. Former supporters of Blau and Irving questioned the artistic competency of the directors and of their company, and the deficit for the season was $722,000, nearly double what had been anticipated. An additional grant from the Vivian Beaumont Foundation and other contributions erased the deficit. The only bright note in the chorus of gloomy failure was that nearly 40 percent of the subscribers renewed.

Blau and Irving started several auxiliary projects in their first season: a secondary school touring company, cosponsored by the Lincoln Center Fund and the New York Department of Education; an arrangement with Pratt Institute to use student graphic artwork for the theatre's promotional posters; and a thirty-minute weekly radio program broadcast in New York City.

Blau, deeply dissatisfied with developments at Lincoln Center and battered and berated in the press, resigned on January 12, 1966. Irving elected to stay on as director of the Repertory Theatre. He had enjoyed greater success as an artist and as an administrator, his style suited his superiors on the Repertory Theatre board, critics had been less censorious, and he liked his job. The world premiere of Leo Lehman's *The East Wind* was not a critical success, but *Galileo*, with Anthony Quayle in the title role, was well received and its run extended. Irving thought his success with *Galileo* and the later success of G. B. Shaw's *Saint Joan* indicated that the company had at last conquered the problems of the vast Vivian Beaumont Theatre stage.

In his first season as solo director, Irving did not himself direct a play; he used rather a series of distinguished guest directors such as John Hirsch and Carl Weber. The plays selected were theatrical and grand. Actors from outside the company were used more liberally, and fewer actors were engaged on seasonal contracts. He also hired resident scenic and lighting designers David Hays and John Gleason. An all-star production of Lillian Hellman's *The Little Foxes*, with Mike Nichols directing Anne Bancroft, Margaret Leighton, E. G. Marshall, and George C. Scott, was a sold-out hit, owing largely to the mystique of Nichols' infallibility hovering over the production and protecting it from critical disdain. As had virtually all prior expediencies, scheduling of a guest production with stars provoked harsh criticism from those who saw it as a betrayal of the aims of the RTLC. The remainder of the productions of 1967–68 fared well in the press and at the box office.

In 1967 Irving finally opened the Forum Theatre with a grant from the Rockefeller Foundation to underwrite the expenses of a production of two one-acts by May Simon, *Happiness* and *Walking to Waldheim*. The production was well received, but the Forum was dark until March 1968, when Ron Cowen's *Summertree* was premiered. Critics lauded the play and actor David Birney in the lead role. The production's run was extended for two months, Birney won two prestigious acting awards, and the theatre was cited by the Outer Critic's Circle for its outstanding contribution to the American theatre.

Play selection under Irving tended largely toward the classics and depended partly on the availability of directors willing to work at the theatre and capable of doing good work without creating controversy. John Lahr described Irving's regime as one of "participatory autocracy," in which staff consensus nearly always accorded with what Irving wanted to do.

The 1968–69 season ended with two critically acclaimed productions: Heinar Kipphardt's *In the Matter of J. Robert Oppenheimer*, with Gordon Davidson directing, and Molière's *The Miser*, with Carl Weber directing. In 1969–70 the physical productions overshadowed the plays, even in the Forum, where Irving directed Vaclev Havel's *The Increased Difficulty of Concentration.* The world premiere of Sam Shepard's *Operation Sidewinder* alienated subscribers and the Repertory Theatre board. Finally, Hopi Indians protested Shepard's use of a sacred snake ritual, and the critics responded negatively. The company was once again beset by controversy.

The 1970–71 season featured an especially experienced company of actors, some of whom had worked at the theatre previously and with John Hirsch, who was scheduled to direct two mainstage productions. The RTLC also benefited from an influx of performers formerly associated with the recently defunct APA* (Association of Producing Artists). The average salary was about $215 per week; the top was $500 per week. Few performers signed for the whole season, however, for motives of professional survival and advancement steered them away from long-term commitments to a company. It is likely that a nuclear acting company was never realized at Lincoln Center, even though a few actors stayed with the organization for several years. The company ideal was realized most fully in the technical and production areas, where Douglas Schmidt and John Gleason gathered and headed a stable staff. Irving felt the critical reception accorded J. M. Synge's *The Playboy of the Western World,* John Hirsch directing, marked a developmental moment for his acting company.

The company continued to struggle with inadequate funding for productions and for staffing, while expending one-quarter of its budget to operate and maintain the Beaumont building. Irving's cost just "to open the doors" was about $560,000 per year, or about 300 percent more than the cost of operation of a comparably sized Broadway theatre. Corporate, foundation, and government support was available, but in nothing like the amounts the theatre needed. Contributions steadily decreased throughout the Irving regime, while Irving struggled to make ends meet by cutting costs and attracting helpful but annually shrinking amounts of government and foundation support. Failure of the Repertory Theatre board and the Lincoln Center board to aggressively pursue a subsidy for the theatre imperiled the future of the organization.

Budgets had a direct effect on play selection, for the ideal play became a well-known classic (no royalty for the playwright and reduced risks at the box office) utilizing a single set and a small cast. Average Broadway production costs for straight drama in 1970 were about $175,000; the Repertory Theatre cost was about $121,000, despite requirements of period productions for larger casts and more costumes. In fact, average production costs per season never exceeded $128,000. Irving also shortened the season from thirty-four weeks to thirty-two in 1970–71, while sustaining attendance at 82 percent of capacity, a decline from the best year for the RTLC, when audiences filled the Vivian Beaumont Theatre to an average 92 percent of capacity.

The 1971–72 season was another season of mixed artistic success and nerve-racking political struggle. Irving and the RTLC board became embroiled in protracted negotiations to transfer responsibility for the Beaumont to City Center, to remodel the building to provide for greater usability, and then to rent the building to constituents such as the Repertory Theatre. Irving and his board posed many objections to the plan but met with heavy resistance to any alteration to the City Center proposal. Ultimately the Lincoln Center board accepted the City Center proposal, citing the economic infeasibility of the Beaumont building, even though the board recognized that the City Center proposal might mean the death of the Repertory Theatre. Irving was about to acquire a new landlord and a new, potentially beneficial rental agreement. He was also about to lose the Forum Theatre in the City Center remodeling plans. In the midst of these negotiations he was awarded a three-year extension of his contract as director of the RTLC.

On September 16, 1971, the Lincoln Center board sold the Vivian Beaumont Theatre to the City Center for $1. However, the city council of New York had to approve the plan, and persons outside the RTLC administration mounted a campaign to fight the proposal before the finance committee of the city council. The battle ended in December when Irving withdrew his support of the City Center plan. City Center forthwith withdrew its plan to purchase and renovate the Beaumont. The defeat of the City Center plan by friends of the Repertory Theatre further strained relations between the Repertory Theatre and the Lincoln Center board.

The 1971–72 season went on despite these political battles. The RTLC inaugurated a new "Explorations" series of works in progress and continued a full calendar of productions on the mainstage and in the Forum. Controversy welled up over Peter Handke's challenging *The Ride Across Lake Constance* and over Gilbert Moses' staging of Ed Bullins' *The Duplex*. Nevertheless, Irving brought the season in $20,000 under the agreed-on deficit, but the board fell $164,000 short of raising funds to retire the deficit. Irving had found in Ellis Rabb, formerly artistic director of the APA, a director who could work with Irving's pool of actors and former APA actors and do so without stirring up trouble. A new light control system and a new sound system vastly improved the theatre's technical capacity. The sound system was especially important because it allowed actors to be heard without speaking with extraordinary effort, thereby radically altering the conditions governing stylization in the theatre.

Then the failure of a key grant request wrecked the company's budget for the 1972–73 season. Irving resigned as artistic director on October 26, 1972, when it became necessary to cancel three productions in the Forum season. The Repertory Theatre board continued to seek funds to complete the season planned for the mainstage and for the Forum while reevaluating the philosophy of a theatre at Lincoln Center and seeking a successor to Irving. The season was a box-office success, ironically enough, and the theatre closed its doors on July 29, 1973, with a $200,000 surplus, even after wiping out all its former deficits and debts. Joseph Papp, president and producer of the New York Shakespeare Festival, was asked to succeed Irving as artistic director, and he consented. The Lincoln Center board replaced the Repertory Theatre board with the New York Shakespeare Festival board, upped the allowable annual deficit from $750,000 to $1.5 million, and assumed the maintenance costs of the theatre building. The Vivian Beaumont Theatre thus became a production facility for the New York Shakespeare Festival.

PERSONNEL

Managing Directors: Herbert Blau (1965–66), Jules Irving (1965–72), Elia Kazan (1963–65), Robert Whitehead (1963–65).

Associate Director: Robert Symonds (1969–72).

Managing Director: Alan Mandell (1965–66).

General Managers: Stanley Gilkey (1964–66), Alan Mandell (1969–73), Oscar Oleson (1963).

Directors: William Ball (1965), John Berry (1971–72), Herbert Blau (1965–66), Harold Clurman (1964), Gordon Davidson (1969), Gene Frankel (1968), Gerald Freedman (1968), Jack Gelber (1971), Peter Gill (1970), *John Hirsch* (1966–71), *Jules Irving* (1966, 1969, 1971), Glen Jordan (1970), Milton Katselas (1970), *Elia Kazan* (1963–65), Gilbert Moses (1972), Anthony Quayle (1968), Jose Quintero (1964), *Ellis Rabb* (1972–73), Alan Schneider (1972), Michael A. Schultz (1970), Mel Shapiro (1969), George Sherman (1968), Paul Shyre (1971), Anna Sokolow (1972), *Robert Symonds* (1966–68, 1970), Stephen Varble (1971), Tim Ward (1969), Carl Weber (1968–69, 1972).

Designers: Theoni Aldredge (1968), Michael Annals (1967, 1970), Boris Aronson (1964), Martin Aronstein (1966–67), Sara Brook (1972), Jeanne Button (1971), Deidre Cartier (1966), Dahl Delu (1972), Marsha Louis Eck (1970), Ben Edwards (1964), Karl Eigsti (1968), *John Gleason* (1965–73), James F. Gohl (1966–67), Jane Greenwood (1964–65, 1971), Charles Gross (1966), Holly Haas (1968, 1969), James Berton Harris (1971), *David Hays* (1964–66, 1968–69), Bernard Johnson (1972), Anna Hill Johnstone (1964), Willa Kam (1970), Ming Cho Lee (1968), Ralph Lee (1967), Kert Lundell (1972), Malcolm McCormick (1971), *Jo Mielziner* (1963–65, 1972), David I. Mitchell (1969), Beni Montresor (1964), Tom Munn (1968), Richard Nelson (1966), Nancy Potts (1973), *Carrie Robbins* (1969–73), Jean Rosenthal (1964, 1966), Constance Ross (1969), Ann Roth (1972, 1973), *Douglas W. Schmidt* (1969–73), *James Hart Stearns* (1965–70), Patricia Quinn Stuart (1968), James Tilton (1973), Fred Voelpel (1968), Robin Wagner (1966, 1967), Peter Wexler (1969–70).

Stage Managers: Craig Anderson (1971–72), Frank Bayer (1966, 1968–69, 1971), Stanley Beck (1965), Paul Bengston (1970, 1971), Robert Benson (1971), Christopher Bernau (1965), Janis Checkanow (1971), Jeff David (1965), *Frederic de Wilde* (1964–66), *Robert Downing* (1963–66), Barnett Epstein (1968–70), John Felton (1968), Howard Fischer (1963–65), Jon Froscher (1968), Kenneth Haas (1966–67), Frank Hamilton (1964–65), Jay Harnick (1965), Martin Herzer (1968–70), *Patrick Horrigan* (1968–72), Michael Judson (1970), Christopher Kelly (1968–69), *James Kershaw* (1965–68), Richard Levy (1966), Robert Lowe (1972), Macon McCalmon (1971), Don McGovern (1964–65, 1967), Russell McGrath (1966), Michael Mauer (1968), Brian Meister (1971–72), Jean-Daniel Noland (1969–71), *Barbara-Mae Phillips* (1968–73), Judith Propper (1966), Ronald Schaeffer (1968–69), Fred Seagraves (1968), Bruce W. Stark (1963–64), David Sullivan (1966–67), Brent Sutton (1968), Robert Walter (1972), Jack Waltzer (1965), Jane Ward (1969–70), *Timothy Ward* (1966–70).

Technical Director: Jose Sevilla (1965–67).

Composers: William Bolcom (1968–69), John Duffy (1971, 1973), Lukas Foss (1971), James Hodges (1968), The Holy Modal Rounders (1970), Cathy MacDonald (1972), John Herbert McDowell (1967), Gilbert Moses (1972), Richard Peaslee (1962), Herbert Pelhofer (1970), John Morris (1968), George Rockberg (1966), Bernardo Segall (1970), *Stanley Silverman* (1966–68, 1970–72), Morton Subotnick (1966).

Actors and Actresses: Charles Abruzzo (1966–67), Daniel Ades (1964–65), Frank Adu (1971–72), Mary Alice (1971–72), Penelope Allen (1972–73), Seth Allen (1972–73), Jane Altman (1968–69), Dimitra Arliss (1970–71), William Atherton (1971–72), Tom Atkins (1967–68), *Ruth Attaway* (1963–68), Joseph Attles (1968–69, 1971–72), Rene Auberjonois (1968–69, 1971–72), Jean-Pierre Aumont (1969–70), *Luis Avalos* (1969–72), Phylicia Ayers-Allen (1971–72), Antonio Azito (1971–72), Conrad Bain (1970–71), Lenny Baker (1968–70), Anne Bancroft (1968–69), Jose Barrera (1969–70), George Bartenieff (1969–70), Gary Barton (1967–68), Lloyd Battista (1968–69), *Frank Bayer* (1965–67, 1969–70), John Beal (1969–70), *Stanley Beck* (1963–66), John Beecher (1969–70), Cynthia Belgrave (1971–72), *Ralph Bell* (1968–70, 1971–72), Paul Benjamin (1969–70), Esther Benson (1970–71), Robert Benson (1967–68, 1970–71), Margo Ann Berdeshevsky (1966–67), Charles Berendt (1971–72), Herbert Berghof (1968–70), Alan Bergmann (1965–66), Christopher Bernau (1967–68), *David Birney* (1968–69, 1970–71), Gerry Black (1968–69), C. Thomas Blackwell (1964–65), James Blendick (1970–71), Verna Bloom (1971–72), Roberts Blossom (1969–70), Samual Blue, Jr. (1968–69), Joseph Boley (1970–71), Leta Bonynge (1968–70), Gregory Borst (1969–70), *Philip Bosco* (1966–73), Richard Bowler (1970–71), John Braden (1967–68), Roger Braun (1969–70), Tommy Breslin (1969–70), Tony van Bridge (1967–69), James Broderick (1969–71), Jacqueline Brookes (1969–70), Roscoe Lee Browne (1965–66), Brian Brownlee (1972–73), Richard Buck (1967–68), Victor Buono (1969–70), Robert Burgos (1971–72), Charles Burks (1967–68), Howard Burnham (1970–71), Catherine Burns (1969–70), Alan Cabal (1966–67), Adolph Caesar (1971–72), James Cahill (1968–71), Roberta Callahan (1966–68), Northern Calloway (1967–68), Nick Cantrell (1969–70), John Carpenter (1965–66), Helena Carroll (1970–71), Barbara Cason (1970–71), Albert Cavens (1967–68), Dorothy Chace (1967–68), Virgilia Chew (1966–67, 1968–69), Robert Christian (1971–72), Edward Cicciarelli (1965–66), Leonardo Cimino (1965–66), Charles Cioffi (1968–69, 1970–71), Oliver Clark (1965–66), Richard Clarke (1967–68), Michael Clarke-Laure (1972–73), Crickett Coan (1971–72), Carolyn Coates (1965–66, 1969–70), Lee J. Cobb (1968–69), Peter Coffield (1972–73), Olivia Cole (1972–73), Jacque Lynn Colton (1969–70), Whitfield Connor (1968–69), Barbara Conrad (1966–67), Kevin Conway (1972–73), Barbara Cook (1972–73), *James Cook* (1967–69, 1970–71), Dennis Cooney (1967–68), Maury Cooper (1970–71), Al Corbin (1967–68), Blaine Cordner (1970–71), *Mariclare Costello* (1963–66), Thomas Costello (1967–68), George Coulouris (1965–66), Richard Council (1972–73), Matthew Cowles (1969–70), Paddy Croft (1972–73), Hume Cronyn (1972–73), Tandy Cronyn (1970–71), Edward Crowley (1968–69), Calvin Culver (1972–73), Bill Cunningham (1969–70), Scott Cunningham (1963–65), Keene Curtis (1971–72), Bob Daley (1969–70), Leora Dana (1969–70), Edgar Daniels (1967–68), Blythe Danner (1967–69, 1971–72), Ted D'Arms (1967–68), Lili Darvas (1968–69), Clifford David (1969–70), Jeff David (1965–66), Diana Davila (1971–72), Cherry Davis (1969–70), Bruce Davison (1967–68), Roger DeKoven (1967–68), Lee Delmer (1963–64), Jerome Dempsey (1968–69, 1971–72), Robert DeNiro (1971–72), Frank DeSal (1963–64), John Devlin (1965–66, 1968–69), Colleen Dewhurst (1970–71), Eileen Dolphin (1967–68), Norma Donaldson (1971–72), John Dorrin (1967–68), Nina

Dova (1966–67), Mel Dowd (1967–68), Kathleen Doyle (1971–72), *Ralph Drischell* (1966–67, 1969–70), James Dukas (1964–66), Faye Dunaway (1963–65), Pamela Dunlap (1966–67), Michael Dunn (1968–69), Mildred Dunnock (1969–70), Stan Dworkin (1968–69), Frank Dwyer (1972–73), Paul Dwyer (1965–66), Joyce Ebert (1964–65), *Barbara eda-Young* (1969–70, 1971–73), Michael Egan (1968–69), Elain Eldridge (1965–66), Alix Elias (1969–70), Patricia Elliott (1968–69), *Stephen Elliott* (1968–72), Rene Enriquez (1963–64), Michael Enserro (1969–70), Barnett Epstein (1968–69), Mark Epstein (1964–65), Pierre Epstein (1964–65), Carl Esser (1966–67), Laura Esterman (1969–70), James Farentino (1972–73), Margaret Fargnoli (1971–72), Brendan Fay (1968–69), Patricia Fay (1963–65), John Felton (1967–68), Betty Field (1970–71), Crystal Field (1963–65), Pamela Fife (1967–68), Gail Fisher (1965–66), Richard Fitz (1968–69), Pauline Flanagan (1970–73), Gus Fleming (1969–70), Jack Fletcher (1969–70), Henderson Forsythe (1972–73), Frances Foster (1970–71), Gloria Foster (1966–67), Herbert Foster (1970–71), Robert Foxworth (1971–72), Dorothy Frank (1969–70), Carl Mikal Franklin (1971–72), Eduard Franz (1968–69), Ronald Frazier (1970–71), Leonard Frey (1969–72), Phillip H. Frey (1963–64), Lou Frizzell (1963–64), Jon Froscher (1967–68), *Ray Fry* (1970–73), Tom Fuccello (1967–68), Lorenzo Fuller (1969–70), Les "Bubba" Gaines (1969–70), Alexander Gam (1964–65), Sharon Gans (1971–72), John Garces (1963–65), Jay Garner (1969–70), Larry Gates (1964–65), Patricia Gaul (1971–72), Jennifer Gaus (1966–67), Murrell Gehman (1972–73), Lou Gilbert (1970–71), Lee Goodman (1966–67), Michael Gorrin (1966–67), Harold Gould (1969–70), Michael Granger (1965–67), Leslie Graves (1968–69), Howard Green (1967–68), *James Greene* (1963–66), Richard Greene (1971–72), Edith Gresham (1965–66), Ted van Griethuysen (1966–67), Donald M. Griffith (1972–73), Suzanne Grossmann (1967–68), Moses Gunn (1971–72), Jack Gwillim (1971–72), William Haddock (1965–66), Mervyn Haines (1968–69), Ronald Hale (1969–70), Albert Hall (1971–72), Ben Hammer (1969–70, 1971–72), Elain Handel (1969–70), John Harkins (1970–71), Robert Harley (1970–71), Rosemary Harris (1972–73), Jack Harrold (1970–71), Johnny Hartman (1971–72), Robert Harwood (1966–67), Judith Hastings (1966–67), *Robert Haswell* (1965–68), Douglas Hayle (1968–69), Paul Hecht (1971–72), John Heffernan (1967–68), Nora Heflin (1971–72), *Martha Henry* (1970–72), Martin Herzer (1968–70), Joseph Hindy (1966–67), Linda Hodes (1963–64), James Hodges (1968–69), Jane Hoffman (1969–70), *Hal Holbrook* (1963–65), Lloyd Hollar (1967–68), Gail Honig (1967–68), Patrick Horrigan (1968–70), Russell Horton (1966–67), Kathryn Howell (1971–72), Margaret Howell (1971–72), Marcie Hubert (1965–66), *Elizabeth Huddle* (1965–67, 1970–71), Tresa Hughes (1969–70), Kate Hurney (1966–67), William Hutt (1967–68), Earle Hyman (1967–68), Amy Irving (1965–66), George S. Irving (1966–67), Anne Ives (1970–71), Scott Jacoby (1969–70), Jude Jade (1971–72), *Graham Jarvis* (1963–65), Joan Jeffri (1968–69), *Salome Jens* (1963–65, 1971–72), James Earl Jones (1965–66), Stephen Joyce (1966–68), Diane Kagan (1967–68), Richard Kahn (1963–64), Jane Karel (1967–68), Caroline Kava (1972–73), Virginia Kaye (1963–65), Stacy Keach (1968–69), Robert Keesler (1969–70), Christopher Kelly (1967–68), Nicholas Kepros (1967–68), Richard Khan (1964–65), Lincoln Kilpatrick (1965–66), Marketa Kimbrell (1965–67), Clinton Kimbrough (1963–65), Sally Kirkland (1971–72), Kirk Kirksey (1971–72), Diana Kirkwood (1970–71), Richard Kline (1971–72), Martin Kove (1971–72), Marcia Jean Kurtz (1968–69), Tom Lacy (1972–73), Joseph Lambrie (1972–73), Zohra Lampert (1963–65), Leonora Landau (1963–64), Frank Langella (1966–67, 1968–69), Noemi Lapzeson (1963–64), Robert LaTourneaux (1972–73),

John Phillip Law (1963–65), Lee Lawson (1970–73), Janet League (1967–68), David H. Leary (1972–73), Bobby Lee (1969–70), Will Lee (1964–65, 1972–73), Robert Legionaire (1970–71), Brad Leigh (1964–65), Stephen Lemberg (1967–68), Rosetta LeNoire (1968–69, 1972–73), Michael Levin (1969–71), *Robert Levine* (1968–72), Amy Levitt (1972–73), Richard Levy (1965–67), Marcia Lewis (1969–70), Ira Lewis (1964–65), Leo Leyden (1972–73), Marilyn Lightstone (1968–69), Cec Linder (1968–70), Margaret Linn (1969–70), Ryan Listman (1967–68), Cleavon Little (1971–72), David Little (1970–71), Tony Lo Bianco (1964–65), Elvira Lockwood (1967–68), Vera Lockwood (1966–67), Barbara Loden (1963–65), Judith Lowry (1965–66), Laurence Luckinbill (1964–65), Clark Luis (1969–70), Macon McCalman (1970–71), John McCurry (1963–64), Everett McGill (1972–73), Don McGovern (1963–65, 1966–67), Jack MacGowran (1972–73), Biff McGuire (1969–70), Maeve McGuire (1967–69), Michael McGuire (1970–71), Stephen McHattie (1970–72), Don McHenry (1968–69), *Aline MacMahon* (1966–69, 1970–72), Dermot McNamara (1970–71), Patrick McVey (1969–70), Joseph Maher (1971–72), Alan Mandell (1972–73), Anthony Manionis (1966–67), *Beatrice Manley* (1965–67), *Paul Mann* (1963–66), Winifred Mann (1967–68), Ruth Manning (1966–67), *Nancy Marchand* (1966–68, 1971–73), Bryan Marks (1966–68), Joseph Mascolo (1969–71), Richard Mason (1969–70), Michael Maurer (1967–68), Kenneth H. Maxwell (1970–71), Roberta Maxwell (1972–73), Jim May (1971–72), Lorry May (1972–72), Jerry Mayer (1967–68), *Glenn Mazen* (1965–67), Carlo Mazzone-Clementi (1965–66), Ralph Meeker (1963–65), Donnie Melvin (1966–68), John Merensky (1969–70), Eda Reiss Merin (1968–69, 1970–71), Theresa Merritt (1971–72), Marilyn Meyers (1971–72), Michael Meyers (1970–71), Kim Michaels (1967–68), Muriel Miguel (1969–70), Judith Mihalyi (1968–69), Harold Miller (1971–72), Michael Miller (1969–71), Ronnie Misa (1965–66), Louis Mofsie (1969–70), Robert Molock (1968–69), *Earl Montgomery* (1965–68), Bill Moor (1968–69), Deidre Moore (1964–65), Santos Morales (1969–70), Garrett Morris (1969–70), Fred Morsell (1972–73), William Myers (1968–69), Lois Nettleton (1972–73), Claudette Nevins (1965–66), Ellen Newman (1972–73), John Newton (1971–73), Jean-Daniel Noland (1969–71), Peter Norman (1969–70), Peter Nyberg (1966–67, 1970–71), Toby Obayashi (1970–71), Carole Ocewieja (1972–73), Kevin O'Connor (1971–72), Art Ostrin (1969–70), Michael O'Sullivan (1964–65, 1966–67), Timmy Ousey (1970–71), Al Pacino (1969–70), Joseph Palmieri (1967–68), Stuart Pankin (1971–72), Joan Pape (1971–72), William Pardue (1966–67), Jackie Paris (1968–69), Michael Parish (1966–67), Tom Parrish (1971–72), Estelle Parsons (1966–67, 1971–72), James Patterson (1969–70), Pamela Payton-Wright (1971–72), Michon Peacock (1969–70), Charles Pegues (1969–70), George Pentecost (1971–73), Jose Perez (1969–70), Brock Peters (1965–66), Stephen Peters (1964–65), *Robert Phalen* (1965–73), Barbara-Mae Phillips (1967–68), Wendell Phillips (1964–65, 1971–72), Larry Pine (1967–68), Don Plumley (1969–71), *Priscilla Pointer* (1965–73), Sasha Pressman (1963–64), Alek Primrose (1964–65), Barry Primus (1963–65), Joan Pringle (1969–70), Judith Propper (1965–67), Robert Puleo (1966–67), Anthony Quayle (1966–67), J. K. Quinn (1971–72), Herbert Ratner (1964–65), James Ray (1969–70), Jim Ray-James (1963–64), Antonia Rey (1969–70, 1972–73), Ruby Lynn Reyner (1971–72), Roberto Reys (1969–70), Roger Ricci (1970–72), Doris Rich (1965–66, 1971–72), Robert Riggs (1969–70), Jason Robards, Jr. (1963–65), Arthur Roberts (1966–67), Les Roberts (1971–72), Andy Robinson (1969–70, 1971–72), Larry Robinson (1968–69), Roger Robinson (1968–69), Sandy Rochelle (1967–68), *Patricia Roe* (1963–65, 1968–69), Peter Rogan (1971–73), Casper Roos (1972–73), Jane Rose (1972–73), *Tom Rosqui* (1965–67, 1972–73), Gastone Rossilli (1972–73), Ronald

Roston (1971–72), Myra Rubin (1970–71), Paul Rudd (1968–69, 1970–71), Emily Ruhberg (1966–67), Leon Russom (1967–68), John P. Ryan (1966–67), Jack Ryland (1967–68), Sterling St. Jacques (1972–73), Diana Sands (1967–68), John Sarno (1964–65), Lanna Saunders (1964–65), Tom Sawyer (1968–69), Sam Schacht (1969–70), Ronald Schaeffer (1968–69), Roy R. Scheider (1964–65, 1968–69), Stefan Schnabel (1968–69, 1972–73), *Joseph Schorer* (1968–70), *Harold Scott* (1963–65), Sandra Seacat (1972–73), Fred Seagraves (1967–68), Arthur Sellers (1969–70), *Diane Shalet* (1963–66), *Susan Sharkey* (1970–73), Paul Shenar (1964–65), Sasha von Sherler (1967–68), Charles Siebert (1966–67), Raymond Singer (1969–70), Henry Smith (1971–72), Arnold Soboloff (1968–70), Marilyn Sokol (1968–69), Rudy Solari (1972–73), Josef Sommer (1972–73), Paul Sparer (1969–70), Barbara Spiegel (1969–70), Robert Stattell (1969–66, 1968–69), Frances Sternhagen (1970–71, 1972–73), *David J. Stewart* (1963–66), Fred Stewart (1966–67), Jean-Pierre Stewart (1968–69), Ray Stewart (1968–69, 1971–72), Alexandra Stoddart (1971–72), *Michael Strong* (1963–65), Sheppard Strudwick (1966–67, 1969–70), *Dan Sullivan* (1969–73), *David Sullivan* (1965–66, 1967–68), Megan Sullivan (1972–73), Brent Sutton (1967–68), Barry Symonds (1970–71), Rebecca Symonds (1970–71), *Robert Symonds* (1965–73), Victoria Symonds (1965–66), Sylvia Syms (1969–70), Sandor Szabo (1969–70), Kristoffer Tabori (1968–69), Jessica Tandy (1969–70, 1972–73), Barbara Tarbuck (1969–71), Florence Tarlow (1970–71), Clarice Taylor (1971–72), George Taylor (1972–73), Marie Thomas (1971–72), Vickie Thomas (1969–70), Arthur C. Thompson (1966–67), Sada Thompson (1964–65, 1968–69), Barbara Thurston (1967–68), James Tolkan (1971–72), Beryl Towbin (1969–70), Harry Townes (1968–69), Gene Troobnick (1969–70), Maria Tucci (1966–67), Boris Tumarin (1965–66), Louis Turenne (1972–73), Charles Turner (1971–72), Barbette Tweed (1968–69), Susan Tyrrell (1968–69), Sam Umani (1969–70), Marc L. Vahanian (1969–70), George Van Den Hout (1966–67, 1970–71), John Vari (1964–65), Edmond Varrato (1967–68), David Vilner (1967–68), George Voskovec (1966–67), Andreas Voutsinas (1964–65), Murvyn Vye (1965–66), Warren Wade (1966–67), *Shirley Jac Wagner* (1965–68), Christopher Walken (1970–71, 1972–73), *Sydney Walker* (1970–73), William Walsh (1967–68), *Jack Waltzer* (1963–66), Craig Ward (1965–66), Susan Watson (1969–70), David Wayne (1963–65), Alyce E. Webb (1972–73), James Ray Weeks (1972–73), Peter Weil (1971–72), Robert Weil (1969–70), Peter Weller (1972–73), Frank T. Wells (1970–71), Jennifer West (1967–68), *Ronald Weyand* (1965–68), Jerry Whelan (1971–72), James Whittle (1972–73), Kate Wilkinson (1965–66), Rico Williams (1970–71), Elizabeth Wilson (1970–71), Mary Louise Wilson (1968–69), Helene Winston (1969–70), Edward Winter (1965–66), Joseph Wiseman (1963–65, 1968–69, 1972–73), Lawrence Wolf (1971–72), Angela Wood (1965–66), Eugene R. Wood (1970–71), Mark Woods (1971–72), Richard Woods (1968–69), Claude Woolman (1964–65), William Wright (1972–73), Erica Yohn (1965–67), Edward Zang (1967–68), Louis Zorich (1965–66).

REPERTORY

At ANTA Washington Square Theatre:
1963–64: *After the Fall, Marco Millions, But for Whom Charlie.*
1964–65: *The Changeling, Incident at Vichy, Tartuffe.*
At the Vivian Beaumont Theatre:
1965–66: *Danton's Death, The Country Wife, The Condemned of Altona, The Caucasian Chalk Circle.*
1966–67: *The Alchemist, Yerma, The East Wind, Galileo.*

1967–68: *The Little Foxes* (guest production), *Saint Joan, Tiger at the Gates, Cyrano de Bergerac*.

1968–69: *King Lear, A Cry of Players, In the Matter of J. Robert Oppenheimer, The Miser*.

1969–70: *In the Matter of J. Robert Oppenheimer, The Time of Your Life, Operation Sidewinder, Camino Real, Beggar on Horseback*.

1970–71: *The Good Woman of Setzuan, The Playboy of the Western World, An Enemy of the People, Antigone*.

1971–72: *Mary Stuart, Narrow Road to the Deep North, Twelfth Night, The Crucible*.

1972–73: *Enemies, The Plough and the Stars, The Merchant of Venice, A Streetcar Named Desire*.

At the Forum Theatre:

1967–68: *Happiness* and *Walking to Waldheim, Summertree*.

1968–69: *An Evening for Merlin Finch, The Inner Journey, The Year Boston Won the Pennant*.

1969–70: *Bananas, The Disintegration of James Cherry, The Increased Difficulty of Concentration, Landscape* and *Silence*.

1970–71: *The Birthday Party, Landscape* and *Silence, Play Strindberg*.

1971–72: *Play Strindberg, Kool Aid* (consisting of *Grail Green* and *Three Street Koans*), *People Are Living There, Delicate Champion, The Ride Across Lake Constance*, Anna Sokolow's Players Project, *The Duplex, Suggs*.

1972–73: The Samuel Beckett Festival (consisting of *Happy Days, Act Without Words I, Krapp's Last Tape*, and *Not I* [world premiere]).

BIBLIOGRAPHY

Published Sources:

American Theatre Planning Board, Inc. *Theatre Check List*. Middletown, Conn.: Wesleyan University Press, 1969, pp. 14–17. Plans, diagrams, sections, photographs of the Vivian Beaumont Theatre building.

Hyams, Barry, ed. *Theatre: The Annual of the Repertory Theatre of Lincoln Center*. Vol. 1. New York: Playbill, 1964.

———. *Theatre: The Annual of the Repertory Theatre of Lincoln Center*. Vol. 2. New York: Hill and Wang, 1965.

Kaminsky, Laura J., ed. *Nonprofit Repertory Theatre in North America, 1958–75: A Bibliography and Indexes to the Playbill Collection of the Theatre Communications Group*. Westport, Conn.: Greenwood Press, 1977.

Martin, Ralph G. *Lincoln Center for the Performing Arts*. Englewood Cliffs, N.J.: Prentice-Hall, 1971.

Theatre World 1963–64 through *1972–73*. Philadelphia: Chilton Books, 1964; New York: Crown Publishers, 1965–73.

Zeigler, Joseph Wesley. *Regional Theatre: The Revolutionary Stage*. Minneapolis: University of Minnesota Press, 1973.

Unpublished Sources:

Carney, Saraleigh. ''The Repertory Theatre of Lincoln Center: Aesthetics and Economics, 1960–73.'' Doctoral dissertation, City University of New York, 1976. This item, from which most of the information in the narrative is taken, includes an exhaustive listing of archival resources.

Playbill Collection of the Theatre Communications Group (microfiche), includes programs
from 1964 through 1973.

Weldon B. Durham

REPERTORY THEATRE OF ST. LOUIS, formerly known as the Repertory
Theatre at Loretto-Hilton Center (1966–73) and the Loretto-Hilton Repertory
Theatre (1973–81), was established in May 1966 on the campus of Webster
University in Webster Groves (a suburb of St. Louis, Missouri). Before its
partnership in the repertory company, this small liberal arts school operated by
the Sisters of Loretto became involved in professional theatre through the efforts
of faculty members Marita Woodruff and Wayne Loui. Creating a company from
a handful of New York professionals and her own students, Woodruff initiated
Theatre Impact, a summer stock operation, in 1962. The success of this venture
and its continued progress inspired interest in building a campus facility capable
of housing both a professional company and a conservatory for Webster theatre
majors. The theatre building was primarily financed through a $1.5 million
donation by Conrad Hilton, hotel magnate and former student of the Sisters of
Loretto—thus the designation Loretto-Hilton. Under the guidance of artistic
director Michael Flanagan, the premiere season commenced on July 1, 1966,
with a bill of eight plays in rotating repertory.

The development of this theatre company follows a predictable trend in American theatrical expansion during the 1960s. A strong economy, combined with
a construction boom and available foundation subsidies, created a receptive
atmosphere for the arts. Large urban areas erected theatres, museums, and concert
halls with increasing frequency, and the Loretto-Hilton Center opened at the
peak of this activity. Its most renowned predecessor was the Guthrie Theatre
Company* in Minneapolis, which had opened three years earlier, although cities
of comparable size constructed or renovated more than 170 theatres and art
centers to accommodate resident companies between 1962 and 1969.

The St. Louis operation stands apart in one respect. Since its inception it has
maintained a partnership with the Webster theatre conservatory. The conservatory
students gain valuable experience working with the professionals and, in some
cases, they build impressive professional résumés by the time they receive their
diplomas. The repertory theatre utilizes college facilities and personnel, while
the availability of large numbers of undergraduates makes possible some of the
more ambitious productions. A 1982 adaptation of *A Tale of Two Cities* utilized
a cast of eighty-five. Such an undertaking would severely strain the budget of
most theatre companies, but by casting conservatory students the repertory company can sustain projects of this magnitude.

With a stated purpose to be a truly regional theatre by serving the St. Louis
community (an area of more than 2.5 million persons with varied, if conservative,
tastes), the company expanded its interests in the 1970s to include the Imaginary
Theatre Company (a touring children's troupe) and a studio season that presented
avant-garde plays. The 1970s also saw the evolution of the St. Louis Opera

Theatre at the Loretto-Hilton Center, a company that accelerated into international acclaim within a few years. Though the opera company is a separate entity, it shares space with the repertory theatre and the conservatory.

In its first four seasons Webster University financed the repertory theatre. During this early period the company accumulated a deficit that placed an unmanageable burden on the university. In March 1970 the school suspended the company while seeking a solution. The theatre reopened in October 1971 as an operation fiscally independent of Webster University and has remained so.

The 1972 arrival of David Frank, managing director, began a period of fiscal stability that has continued. Frank, a young and personable Englishman, arrived by way of the Center Stage* in Baltimore. When he began his tenure the subscription list numbered barely 3,000 patrons. At the end of his third year this number had dramatically increased to 14,500. By the end of his eighth and final season there were more than 16,000 subscribers. The sound fiscal practices David Frank initiated stabilized the organization and ticket sales provided more than 60 percent of its revenue, an exemplary achievement for a not-for-profit regional theatre. The annual budget currently stands at more than $2 million.

Few seasons pass without the presentation of at least one American classic. In a flurry of patriotism during the bicentennial of the American Revolution, eight out of eleven plays presented in the period from 1975 to 1977 were American. The American playwright has always commanded attention in this theatre. The 1967–68 season included Tennessee Williams' *A Streetcar Named Desire* and William Saroyan's *The Time of Your Life*. Other years have witnessed American classics such as *You Can't Take It with You*, by George S. Kaufman and Moss Hart, *The Crucible*, by Arthur Miller, and *The Iceman Cometh*, by Eugene O'Neill. *Luann Hampton Laverty Oberlander*, by Preston Jones, *The Runner Stumbles*, by Milan Stitt, and *The Curse of the Starving Class*, by Sam Shepard, are from the American new wave.

A typical season also includes one or two foreign classics, with Shakespearean plays receiving the most productions, including three separate stagings of *Twelfth Night* and two each of *Othello* and *A Midsummer Night's Dream*. The plays of Molière have been staged periodically (*The School for Wives, The Miser, The Imaginary Invalid*, and *Tartuffe*), as have the plays of George Bernard Shaw (*Misalliance, Arms and the Man, Major Barbara, Caesar and Cleopatra*, and *The Devil's Disciple*). Plays by more recent European writers such as Bertolt Brecht, Peter Weiss, and Tom Stoppard have been presented only occasionally.

At the top of the organizational structure of the repertory company is its artistic or managing director, who, although accountable to a board of directors, is in charge of all production personnel. The theatre's history falls into three distinct eras of management. First, the Flanagan-Perner period, which covered the initial four years of operation and the year after its reopening. Michael Flanagan served as artistic director for three years, followed by Walter Perner for two years. As he weathered the financial crisis, Perner was listed as managing director. Clearly the emphasis shifted from artistic direction to budget management while the company faced its mounting deficit.

Perner's successor proved highly successful. David Frank came to the company as a managing director with a view toward building subscriptions and improving finances. He did both. Seldom involving himself directly in production, Frank engaged a consultant to administer the company's artistic direction. During most of Frank's career in St. Louis he employed Davey Marlin-Jones in this capacity.

Wallace Chappell succeeded David Frank in 1980 but stayed for only three seasons. Hired as the artistic director, Chappell made several alterations: he disbanded the resident company, changed the theatre's name, and staged three world premieres in his initial season. In addition, Chappell redefined his position by taking a more active interest in production and by personally staging three plays in his first year. With the exception of *Under the Ilex* (a star vehicle for Leonard Fry and Julie Harris), his several productions of premiere plays made little impact. Chappell was replaced by David Chambers, who stayed only one season. Steven Woolf was contracted to begin the 1986–87 season as artistic director.

The Repertory Theatre of St. Louis has employed many guest actors over the years, some familiar to Broadway and film audiences. Well-known artists include Imogene Coca, Georgia Engel, Leonard Fry, Julie Harris, Philip Kerr, Donna McKechnie, Cara Duff-MacCormick, Brett Somers, and Paul Winfield. Until 1980, however, the theatre employed a resident contract company of actors, many of whom returned year after year and became favorites of St. Louis audiences. J. Robert Dietz, Marian Mercer, Robert Murch, Arthur A. Rosenberg, and James Scott all contributed to the company's early years. In the 1970s the company expanded and several actors made St. Louis their home. Notable performers from this era include Lewis Arlt, Brendan Burke, Alan Clarey, Robert Darnell, Joneal Joplin, Wil Love, Robert Spencer, Susan Maloy Wall, Addie Walsh, and Margaret Winn.

PERSONNEL

Artistic Directors: David Chambers (1985–86), Wallace Chappell (1980–83), Michael Flanagan (1966–69), Steven Woolf (1983–86).

Managing Directors: James Bernardi (1966–67), David Frank (1972–80), Walter Perner, Jr. (1969–72), Michael P. Pitek III (1980–1981), Steven Woolf (1981).

Associate Directors: James Bernardi (1967–69), Jan Eliasberg (1981–83), Michael P. Pitek III (1978–79).

Administrative Directors: John Economos (1971–72), M. Rose Jonas (1972–73), Robert Olin (1969–70), Walter Perner, Jr. (1968–69), Charles Seymour, Jr. (1976–77), George Spaulding (1973–75), Thomas K. Warner (1978–79).

Stage Directors: Craig Anderson, Larry Arrick, James Bernardi, Gregory Boyd, David Chambers, *Wallace Chappell* (1980–83), Louis Criss, Robert Darnell, Bob DeFrank, *J. Robert Dietz* (1966–70), John Dillon, Jan Eliasberg, Peter Farago, *Michael Flanagan* (1966–69), *David Frank* (1972–80), Norman Gevanthor, John Going, Susan Gregg,

Charles Haid, Bert Houle, Pamela Hunt, Nagle Jackson, *Davey Marlin-Jones* (1972–80), Neal Kenyon, Phillip Kerr, Tony Kushner, Sheldon Larry, Gene Lesser, Rene Lewis, Larry Lillo, Robert H. Livingston, Wayne Loui, Milton Lyon, Charles Martan, Phillip Minor, Charles Werner Moore, *Timothy Near* (1981–85), Jack O'Brien, Jim O'Connor, John Olan-Scrymgeour, Leonard Peters, Jackson Phippin, Michael P. Pitek III, Charles Nelson Reilly, Byron Ringland, Frederick Rolf, Dennis Rosa, Sarah Sanders, Dwight Schultz, Carl Schurr, Hal Scott, Geoffrey Sherman, Edward Stern, Fontaine Syer, Ian Trigger, Clyde Ventura, W. Burke Walker, R. Stuart White, Sophie Wilbaux, William Woodman, *Marita Woodruff* (1966–85), Steven Woolf, Milton R. Zoth.

Music Directors: *Byron Grant* (1981–85), Manny Mendelsohn, Terrance Sherman, David Stein, John R. Tickner, Tony Zito.

Choreographers: Sarah Barker, Gail Cronauer, Marcia Milgrom Dodge, Peter Hamilton, David Holdgrive, Pamela Hunt, Darwin Knight, Swen Swenson.

Scenic Designers: Jim Bakkom, Gary Barten, John Conant, Karen R. Connolly, Lewis Crickard, Peggy DePuy, Clark Dunham, John Ezell, Michael Ganio, Tim Jozwick, *John Kavelin* (1974–85), Raymond Jens Klausen, Heidi Landesman, *Grady Larkins* (1967–79), Sandi Marks, Atkin Pace, Arthur Ridley, *John Roslevich* (1978–85), Carolyn Ross, Bill Schmiel, Oliver Smith, Paul Staheli, John Wright Stevens, Richard Tolkkuhn, James Walker, Paul Wonsek.

Costume Designers: James Edmund Brady, Jeanne Button, Marie Anne Chiment, Bonnie J. Cutter, Elizabeth Eisloeffel, Steven Epstein, Michael Ganio, Carr Garnett, Laura Hanson, Bruce Harrow, Sigrid Insull, Dorothy L. Marshall, Lawrence Miller, Katherine Reich, John David Ridge, Arthur Ridley, Vance Sorrells, Mary Strieff, *John Carver Sullivan* (1975–85), Allison Todd, Vita, Bill Walker.

Lighting Designers: Max DeVolder, Clark Dunham, Glenn Dunn, Gilbert V. Hemsley, Jr., David Hitzert, Stephen Ross, *Peter Sargent* (1966–85), Jennifer Tipton.

Playwrights, Composers, Lyricists: Larry Arrick, Norman L. Berman, Adrien Burgess, Wallace Chappell, Arthur Custer, Barbara Damashek, Dennis DeBrito, Jan Eliasberg, Victor Gialanella, A. E. Hotchner, Ron Mark, Davey Marlin-Jones, Mel Marvin, James Moberly, Max Morath, James Nicholson, Geoffrey Sherman, Clyde Talmadge, Addie Walsh, Ron Whyte.

Actors and Actresses: George Addis, *James Anthony* (1974–76), Bob Ari, *Lewis Arlt* (1972–75), Humbert Allen Astrada, Laurinda Barrett, B. Constance Barry, Raymond Barry, Lloyd Battista, *Beth Bauer* (1980–83), Robert Bays, Kurt Beattie, Maxwell Beaver, Peter Beiger, Paul Blake, Charlotte Booker, Eric Brooks, Bruce Brown, Robert Browning, Yusef Bulos, *Brendan Burke* (1971–85), *Madelaine Cain* (1966–68), Diane Carr, Rocky Carroll, James Carruthers, Thelma Carter, Barbara Caruso, Susan Cash, Martin J. Cassidy, Gian Cavallini, Marie Chambers, *Grace Chapman* (1968–70), Marilyn Chris, *Alan Clarey* (1976–85), Imogene Coca, Peter Coffeen, Lynn Cohen, *John Cothran, Jr.* (1976–85), Stephan A. Cowan, Ellen Crawford, Valery Daemke, Jonathon Daly, Mary D'Arcy, *Robert Darnell* (1972–79, 1985), Bob DeFrank, Roni Dengel, *Patrick Desmond* (1973–77), Anthony J. DeStefanis, John Devlin, Doris Diener, Grace DiGig, *J. Robert Dietz* (1967–74), James Donohue, King Donovan, Jane Dreyer, *Cara Duff-MacCormick* (1976–1978), Peter Duncan, Paddy Edwards, *Patricia Egglinger* (1966–69), Gwyllam Evans, Lillian Evans, Mary Ellen Falk, Elizabeth Farley, Patrick Farrelly, David Faulkner, Christopher Fields, Michael Flanagan, Pauline Flanagan, Mary Fogarty, *Skip Foster* (1980–83), *Elizabeth Franz* (1968–70), Leonard Frey, Donald Gantry, Tony Geary, *Mike Genovese* (1969–81), Michelle Giannini, Ronnie Gilbert, *Jonathan Gillard* (1978–81),

George Gito, Al Grab, Ronny Graham, Michael Granger, *Byron Grant* (1981–85), Linnie Green, William Grivna, Edward Grover, Les Gruner, *Sarah-Jane Gwillim* (1981–83), *Joan Hanson* (1967–69, 1972), Kathleen Harper, Julie Harris (1982), *Mickey Hartnet* (1973–74, 1978, 1979–80), Lee Patton Hasegawa, *Stephen McKinley Henderson* (1977–81, 1984), Eric Hill, Tony Hoty, *Bert Houle* (1973–75), J. C. Hoyt, David Huffman, Edith Taylor Hunter, *Keith Jochim* (1977–80), *Peter Johl* (1983–85), Glenn Johnson, *Duane Jones* (1971–73, 1976–77), *John Christopher Jones* (1981–83), *Joneal Joplin* (1972–85), *Thomas Kampman* (1966–69), Caroline Kava, Stephen Keep, *Phillip Kerr* (1980–83), Patricia Kilgarriff, Jeffrey King, Myron Kozman, *Susan Leigh* (1981–83), *Lynn Ann Leveridge* (1978, 1980, 1981, 1984), Bernard Levine, Pamela Lewis, *Chris Limber* (1980–84), Kristan Linklater, Lawrence Linville, Wayne Loui, *Wil Love* (1973–79), Michael Makman, Patrick Manion, *Lilene Mansell* (1971–73), Susanne Marley, J. Patrick Martin, Pamela Mathews, Joan Mathieson, Tanny McDonald, Ann McDonough, Richard McGougan, Donna McKechnie, Dermot McNamara, *Marian Mercer* (1966–68, 1969–70), Carla Meyer, Page Miller, Jan Miner, Robert Moberly, Zakes Mokae, Martin Molson, Pamela R. Moore, Max Morath, *Robert Murch* (1966–69), Timothy Near, Timothy Neller, Christopher Nickel, Bill Nunnery, Patricia O'Connell, Beverly Ostraka, Jackie Parker, *Bernie Passeltiner* (1966–69), *James Paul* (1966–67, 1981–85), Don Perkins, Anthony Ponzini, Dennis Predovic, Lawrence Pressman, Gerald J. Quimby, John Ramsey, Gavin Reed, *Jack Reidelberger* (1979, 1980–81), Seth Richards, Jessica Richman, Mark Robbins, *Judith Roberts* (1981–83, 1984), Scott Robertson, *Arthur A. Rosenberg* (1968–74, 1975–76), David Sabin, *Wayne Salomon* (1981–85), Sarah Sanders, *James Scott* (1967–73), April Shawhan, *Nelson Sheehy* (1974–76), *Gerald Simon* (1966–68), Eric Singerman, *Vance Sorrells* (1973–75), *Robert Spencer* (1974–80), Gray Stephens, *Stephanie Stoyanoff* (1966–68), *Henry Strozier* (1974–77), Swen Swenson, Renee Tadlock, Jill Tanner, Trinity Thompson, John Tickner, Ian Trigger, *George Vafiadis* (1969–72), Paul Vincent, George Vogel, Stephen Walker, *Susan Maloy Wall* (1977–81, 1982), *Addie Walsh* (1978–80), Frank Warninsky, Paulette Waters, Carlene Watkins, Richard Wharton, Christine Wiedeman, Arnold Wilkerson, *Bari K. Willerford* (1978–80), Judith Willis, Paul Winfield, *Margaret Winn* (1973–77), William Wolack, G. Wood, John Libson Wood, Brian Worley, Steven Worth.

REPERTORY

1966–67: *The Private Ear, The Public Eye, Waiting for Godot, The School for Wives, The Cage, A Midsummer Night's Dream, Oh What a Lovely War, Twelfth Night.*

1967–68: *The Hostage, Rashomon, A Streetcar Named Desire, The Caucasian Chalk Circle, The Time of Your Life, The Miser, The Merchant of Venice, Six Characters in Search of an Author, Misalliance.*

1968–69: *Ring Round the Moon, The World of Sholom Aleichem, Long Day's Journey into Night, The Miser, Major Barbara, The Lower Depths, Albee Before Guare (The Zoo Story, The Loveliest Afternoon of the Year, Muzeeka), Much Ado About Nothing.*

1969–70: *Ides of March, You Can't Take It with You, Once upon a Mattress, Othello, Arms and the Man.*

1970–71: Season suspended.

1971–72: *Sherlock Homes, Marat/Sade, After the Rain, Room Service, Horatio.*

1972–73: *Of Mice and Men, Twelfth Night, One Flew over the Cuckoo's Nest, The Mousetrap, A Flea in Her Ear.*

1973–74: *Detective Story, The Imaginary Invalid, The Hot l Baltimore, Henry V, Irma La Douce.*

1974–75: *Indians, Caesar and Cleopatra, The Crucible, Trevor* and *The Real Inspector Hound, Have I Stayed too Long at the Fair?.*

1975–76: *A Midsummer Night's Dream, Desire Under the Elms, Tom Jones, A Memory of Two Mondays* and *Brandy Station, Once in a Lifetime.*

1976–77: *Billy Budd, The Eccentricities of a Nightingale, The Beaux' Stratagem, The House of Blue Leaves, The Front Page.*

1977–78: *Macbeth, Luann Hampton Laverty Oberlander, The Devil's Disciple, The Runner Stumbles, Canterbury Tales, Ashes.*

1978–79: *The Iceman Cometh, A Penny for a Song, Father's Day, The Three Sisters, Frankenstein, Curse of the Starving Class, Old Times, By Grand Central Station I Sat Down and Wept.*

1979–80: *Crimes of the Heart, A Christmas Carol, Put Them All Together, A View from the Bridge, A Servant of Two Masters, Masquerade, Sizwe Bansi Is Dead, Father Dreams.*

1980–81: *Othello, A Midsummer Night's Dream, Eve, Sweet Prince, A Christmas Carol, Happy Ending, Richard III, Talley's Folly, The Island, American Soap, A Life in the Theatre.*

1981–82: *The Threepenny Opera, Buried Child, A Christmas Carol, One for the Road, Romeo and Juliet, Charley's Aunt, Brecht on Brecht, A Lesson from Aloes.*

1982–83: *Tartuffe, A Tale of Two Cities, A Christmas Tapestry, Present Laughter, Hedda Gabler, Under the Ilex, Sore Throats.*

1983–84: *The Glass Menagerie, The Dining Room, Tintypes, Sleuth, Medea, The Importance of Being Earnest, True West, The Unseen Hand* and *Killer's Head, Tongues* and *Savage Love.*

1984–85: *A Raisin in the Sun, Master Harold . . . and the boys, The 1940's Radio Hour, Dial "M" for Murder, The Price, The Comedy of Errors, Waiting for Godot, Still Life, Annulla, an Autobiography.*

1985–86: *Twelfth Night, Understatements, The Little Shop of Horrors, The Mighty Gents, Golden Boy, A Streetcar Named Desire, The Marriage of Bette and Boo, Tom and Viv, Miss Julie Bodiford.*

BIBLIOGRAPHY

Published Sources:

St. Louis Post-Dispatch, 1966–86.

Archer, Stephen M. "The Loretto-Hilton Center at St. Louis." *Players* 15.4 (1970): 155–61, 199.

———. "The Loretto-Hilton Repertory Theatre." *Educational Theatre Journal* 22.3 (1970): 319–20.

"Webster College and the Loretto-Hilton Repertory." *Theatre Crafts* 9.1 (1975): 12–17, 43–50.

Woodward, Jenine. "Report on The Rep." *St. Louis Commerce*, September 1982, pp. 128–30.

Archival Resource:

St. Louis, Missouri. Repertory Theatre of St. Louis. Playbills and subscription brochures.

John M. Heidger

S

SAN DIEGO REPERTORY THEATRE. Sam Woodhouse, a recent graduate of the California Institute of the Arts (MFA in directing), joined Indian Magique, a troubador group of actors, in 1973. They produced original works, improvised dramas, and miniconcerts, in parks, schools, recreation centers, and cafes, "passing the hat" for their livelihood. Douglas Jacobs, who had received his MFA in the same class with Woodhouse, joined the company in 1975 when the group began to call itself the San Diego Repertory Theatre (SDRT). Woodhouse became the producing director and Jacobs the artistic director. The company toured to schools and colleges doing such plays as Bertolt Brecht's adaptation of John Ford's *Duchess of Malfi*, Jean Genet's *The Maids*, and *Gold!*, a play created by the company.

In 1976 they offered fifty performances in repertory at San Diego City College. Included were George M. Cohan's *Seven Keys to Baldpate, The Maids*, a company adaptation of Molière's *That Scoundrel Scapin!*, and Jacobs' own adaptation of Charles Dickens' *A Christmas Carol*.

Permanent quarters for the troupe were established in 1977 when they leased St. Cecilia's Chapel, a former mortuary near downtown San Diego. With volunteer help and donated funds they remodeled the building as a 200-seat proscenium theatre. They called it the San Diego Repertory Theatre. "Repertory" is a misnomer, for the group has never offered two to three plays per month on an alternating schedule. The plays offered during their first year of operation were an eclectic mixture ranging from Oscar Wilde's *The Importance of Being Earnest* and Tennessee Williams' *The Glass Menagerie* to company-created plays called *The California Medicine Show* and *How I Lost My Sock at the Malt Shop but Found True Love at the Hop*.

The 1978 season consisted of fifteen productions, three of which were world premieres. Four were West Coast premieres, and five were San Diego premieres. During the next ten years the company matured and developed its propensity for new, experimental, and sometimes controversial work. And although its offerings lean toward contemporary plays that examine the challenges and joys of living in the late twentieth century, it is also committed to revitalizing the classics. The excellence of the execution of its mission has garnered SDRT numerous grants from the California Arts Council and the National Endowment for the Arts.

In May of 1987 the company moved into two new theatre spaces: The Lyceum Stage, which has a 540-seat auditorium and a modified thrust stage, and the Lyceum Space, a 220-seat flexible space. Both are located in Horton Plaza, a new $90 million shopping complex in downtown San Diego. The Lyceum theatres are so named after the original 400-seat theatre that was one of the antiquated structures destroyed in the redevelopment project. The company also maintains its former theatre, now renamed the Sixth Avenue Playhouse.

SDRT has participated in the revitalization of downtown San Diego and aided in the cultural renaissance of the city. It views one of its functions as that of an "artistic swapmeet." It has rented the Lyceum spaces to such groups as the San Diego Jazz Festival, the San Diego Chamber Orchestra, the Spanish Ballet, the Pacific Chamber Opera, the Southeast Community Theatre, Boxing Day Productions, Pipeline Theatre, and Sledgehammer. Even the theatre lobby serves as an art gallery showing the works of local artists.

The SDRT is one of the first year-round professional theatres in San Diego. Over the first eight years actors' salaries have grown from the initial $100 per show to up to $1,000 for rehearsals and a run of approximately twenty-four performances. In 1984 SDRT signed a Letter of Agreement with Actors' Equity Association.

Another unique facet of SDRT is its actor training program, through which it hires outside teachers to give its professional actors training. The training incorporates voice, movement, music, and dance workshops for four to six hours per week, depending on the rehearsal schedule. Actors in rehearsal or in performance are paid to attend, and others in the company may attend free.

The quality of SDRT's productions on recent record is such that from 1985 to 1986 its attendance doubled to more than 100,000. In 1986 SDRT received thirteen San Diego Theatre Critic's Circle Nominations, and twenty-one Drama Logue Awards for Outstanding Achievement in acting, directing, and design.

PERSONNEL

Board of Trustee Presidents: Jane Applegate, Roger Graham, Jennifer Hamkins, John Messner.

Producing Director: Sam Woodhouse.
Artistic Director: Douglas Jacobs.

Directors: Michael Addison, Ron Arden, Frank Condon, Tony Curiel, Sabin Epstein, George Ferencz, Floyd Gaffney, Joseph Hanreddy, David Hay, Douglas Jacobs, James C. Manley, Peter Robinson, Tavis Ross, Walter Schoen, Will Simpson, Frolic Taylor, Andrew J. Traister, Meg Wilbur, Sam Woodhouse.

Production Managers: John Forbes, Parris Zirkenback.

Managing Directors: Roberta Liscz, John McCann, James Priebe.

Teachers: Ron Arden, Judith Greer Essex, Bonnie Johnston, Vikram Singh, Linda Vickerman, Meg Wilbur.

Associate Directors: Scott Feldsher, Will Roberson.

Composers/Musical Directors: Richard Jennings, Burnham Joiner, Polly Pen, Max Roach, Jonathan Sacks, Linda Vickerman, Victor Zupanc.

Technical Directors: Reid Bartlett, Willa Mann Day, Michael Faw, Rob Murphy, Parris Zirkenback.

Designers: D. Martyn Bookwalter, Don Childs, Willa Mann Day, Mark Donnelly, Kent Dorsey, Dan Dryden, Fred Duer, Robert Earl, Uta Fink, John Forbes, Mary Gibson, Robert Green, Claire Henkel, Dianne Holly, Tom Kamm, Gordon Lusk, Charles P. McCall, Lynn McLeod, Peter Maradudin, Ingrid Melton, Rob Murphy, Ray Naylor, Patrick Nollet, Margaret Perry, Steve Peterson, Eric Sinkonnen, Nancy Jo Smith, Sally Rosen Thomas, Christopher Villa, Ladislav Vyckodil.

Actors and Actresses: William Anton, Ian Arrow, Bernard Baldan, Ric Barr, Olenn Beatty, Jim Brown, Darla Cash, Diana Castle, Kathie Danger, Bill Dunnan, Frederick Edmund, Patricia Elmore, Richard Farrell, Kabe Frank, Whoopi Goldberg, Haskell Gordon, Lauren Hamilton, Amy Herzberg, W. Dennis Hunt, Tom Hutchinson, Douglas Jacobs, Peter Jacobs, Michael Kilpatrick, Francine Lembi, Michael Lewis, Marcy MacDonald, Don McManus, James Manley, Gloria Mann, Jeanne Mori, Barbara Murray, Thom Murray, Ollie Nash, Steve Papaleo, David Ann Reeves, J. Michael Ross, Tavis Ross, Peter Samuel, Marie Selland, Spike Sorrentino, James A. Strait, Wayne Tibbitts, Biff Whiff, Barbara Wilson, Sam Woodhouse.

REPERTORY

1976: *Seven Keys to Baldpate, That Scoundrel Scapin!, The Knack, The Maids, Come and Go, A Christmas Carol.*

1977: *City: Population 5, The California Medicine Show, Arsenic and Old Lace, The Importance of Being Earnest, The Glass Menagerie, How I Lost My Sock at the Malt Shop but Found True Love at the Hop, The Happy Haven, A Christmas Carol.*

1978: *Trevor!, Mimosa Pudica, The Dark of the Moon and the Full, The Unseen Hand, Voices, Truffles* (adaptation of *Servant of Two Masters), The Stingaree* (company-developed), *American Buffalo, Sun Spots* (company-developed), *The Bean Bag Stories, The Matchmaker, Hold Me, Tragedy of Tragedies or the Life and Death of Tom Thumb the Great, Waiting for Godot, A Christmas Carol.*

1979: *Private Lives, Gold!, Curse of the Starving Class, Ladyhouse Blues, Bleacher Bums, Tartuffe, The Club, A Christmas Carol.*

1980: *Hay Fever, Getting Out, Of Mice and Men, Wings, What the Butler Saw, Androcles and the Lion, The Lady Cries Murder, Bonjour, là, Bonjour, A Christmas Carol.*

1981: *Working, The Petrified Forest, The School for Wives, Mother Courage, Talley's Folly, Funeral March for a One Man Band, The Elephant Man, A Christmas Carol.*

1982: *Tintypes, True West, Death of a Salesman, Home, Division Street, Titus Andronicus, The Club, A Christmas Carol.*

1983: *Crossing Niagara, The Death of a Miner, Children of a Lesser God, Mrs. Warren's Profession, A Funny Thing Happened on the Way to the Forum, In the Matter of J. Robert Oppenheimer, A Christmas Carol.*

1984: *K2, Beyond Therapy, The Tooth of Crime, Crimes of the Heart, America I Like to Think of You Naked* (company-developed), *Ah, Wilderness!, Long Day's Journey into Night, A Christmas Carol.*

1985: *The Time of Your Life, Extremities, Cloud 9, Woody, Baby with the Bathwater, Rap Master Ronnie, A Christmas Carol.*

1986: *To Gillian On Her 37th Birthday, Quilters, Holy Ghosts, Top Girls, The Little Shop of Horrors, Fool for Love, The Strange Case of Dr. Jekyll and Mr. Hyde, Master Harold . . . and the boys, A Christmas Carol.*

BIBLIOGRAPHY

Unpublished Sources:
Jacobs, Douglas. Personal interviews. December 1986–March 1987.
Woodhouse, Sam. Personal interviews. December 1986–March 1987.

Archival Resource:
San Diego, California. San Diego Repertory Theatre playbills, 1977–86.

Joseph J. Bellinghiere

SAN FRANCISCO MIME TROUPE. Many theatre companies formed during the 1960s and 1970s consciously reflected the social tensions of the period. Some of these companies drew on the model of the workers' theatre of the Depression years of the 1930s; the later plays and theoretical writings of Bertolt Brecht have added immeasurably to this tradition by demonstrating an aesthetic involving social analysis. By critical consent, the San Francisco Mime Troupe is the most important of the new groups reviving the workers' theatre concept.

The Mime Troupe gave its first performance in San Francisco in 1959, making it one of the oldest of the contemporary theatres dedicated to bringing about collective social action. Founder R. G. Davis, formerly a member of the Actor's Workshop*, but disenchanted with the aesthetic and political conservatism of that group, initially projected no political intentions or any desire to perform for a nontraditional audience, but these objectives were soon evident. The Troupe gradually became known for controversial sociopolitical messages skillfully conveyed through presentational performance techniques derived from the *commedia dell'arte*, circus, carnival sideshows, minstrel shows, music hall, buskers, vaudeville, brass bands, comic strips, and nineteenth-century melodrama.

At first, Davis explored a theatrical form in clear contrast to the psychological realism of the established theatre. His company mimed in the common man tradition of Charlie Chaplin and Buster Keaton, using body movement alone to convey action, character, and attitude. Soon, however, they added words to their performances, and their model became the *commedia dell'arte*.

In 1962 the Mime Troupe broadened its audience by giving free performances on a portable stage in the parks of San Francisco. Whereas its indoor audiences had been predominantly young, middle-class intellectuals, the audience in the parks varied, depending on the neighborhood. In the North Beach area, for instance, they attracted beatniks and hippies, as well as working people of Italian and Chinese extraction. The group's core audience of young intellectuals fol-

lowed them wherever they played, however. The transition to open air performances was difficult because there was no local tradition of theatre in the parks
and because the plays the Mime Troupe performed were provocative in their
language and politics. The resulting struggle with authorities brought the company the support of the New Left. In 1965 Davis was arrested when the group
performed without a permit, denied them because of the "vulgar" material in
the script. The denial was ruled an unconstitutional attempt at censorship.

From 1962 until 1970 the repertoire of the group consisted of adaptations of
scripts by Molière, Carlo Goldoni, Niccolo Machiavelli, Angelo Beolco, Giordano Bruno, and Lope de Rueda, performed in the manner of *commedia dell' arte*
with traditional masked characters and exaggerated movement and voice. The
commedia style served to hold an audience's attention in competition with the
usual outdoor distractions. It also included sufficient flexibility to incorporate
news events of the day and to permit impromptu responses to unplanned events
during performances. These adaptations of seventeenth- and eighteenth-century
plays, while keeping the traditional characters and costuming, were infused with
political radicalism.

The 1967 adaptation of Goldoni's *L'Amant Militaire* may be taken as representative. The plot is mostly from Goldoni: the Spanish army is fighting in Italy,
a clear parallel with the presence of the U.S. army in Vietnam, and Pantalone,
the major, connives with the old Spanish general to profit from the war. Pantalone
plots to marry his daughter to the old general, who "pursues peace" with every
weapon at his disposal, but she is secretly in love with a young lieutenant. The
wily Arlecchino disguises himself as a woman in order to avoid military service.
Finally, in a confusion of cross purposes, the soubrette, dressed as the pope,
appears and stops the war. The *commedia* stereotypes—authoritarian, well-to-
do old man, old warrior, young lovers, scheming soubrette, and tricky servant—
had undergone some changes, but were still traditional *commedia* figures in half-
masks and period costumes. Further, the names were unchanged and the plots,
although somewhat adapted, were more rooted in an Italian past than in an
American present.

In 1969 the group began experimenting with other styles. They spent months
working on a production of Bertolt Brecht's last, unfinished play, *The Congress
of the Whitewashers*, a play with a Marxist message written in the style of a
Chinese opera. Work on the play emphasized ideological divisions in the company, and led to a series of meetings to resolve differences about the focus and
organization of the company. The Marxists believed they should focus on playing
for the working class. Davis, however, was convinced they should aim their
work at the revolutionary, young, middle-class intellectuals. Some were determined the Mime Troupe should be a collective in which all decisions were made
by the group. Davis was equally determined to continue as the company's sole
director and make all important decisions himself. The conflicts ended when
Davis and the most militant of the Marxists left the company.

Those who remained felt leaderless. Partly for this reason and partly on principle they formed a theatre collective. The structure of the organization came to reflect the ideals presented in their plays, as the members of the new, politically active troupe abandoned their identity as artist intellectuals with a proprietary attitude about their individual contributions and became "art workers" with a common objective of bringing about social change.

Since 1970 each of the Mime Troupe's productions has focused on a political problem selected by the group. Most often the plays have been written by Joan Holden, sometimes in collaboration with other company members. Playbills have rarely carried the name of any individual, since company members have preferred to take collective credit for their productions. Despite scripting by individuals, the plays express the consensus of the group as developed through study and discussion of the political issues by all members.

The first production after reorganization as a collective was also the first of their productions to break with the *commedia* style. *Commedia* characters were clear and broadly comic, but they were foreign. The troupe searched for an American model, and they found it in nineteenth-century melodrama. In 1970 Holden wrote *The Independent Female, or, A Man Has His Pride!* in this style. American stereotypes—the capitalist, the naive young man, and the strong woman—were used as had been stereotypes from the *commedia*. This women's liberation play set in the nineteenth century featured a heroine, a working woman, who is asked by her fiancé to leave her job when they are married. She rebels and leads a women's strike for equal pay and free nurseries. When her chauvinist fiancé fails to understand her needs, she renounces him forever and vows to work for women's rights.

The first version of the play followed the melodrama form very closely, but feminists suggested changes. The heroine was a manipulative, almost villainous woman, out to destroy all men. The play had a mock happy ending in which the heroine gives up her fight and is reconciled to her betrothed. In the course of discussions with feminists, it became clear that parody of the melodrama form could undermine the seriousness of the political statement and the whole be taken as a spoof of the women's liberation movement. The Mime Troupe decided to further alter the parody to be sure the feminist message was clear.

In the next major play, *The Dragon Lady's Revenge* (1971), this problem was averted. The piece borrowed elements from the nineteenth-century melodrama, from *commedia*, from the spy movie, and even from comic strips. In part, this diffuse form may have come about because the scenario of the play was developed collectively by five members through discussion, after which each wrote assigned scenes. *The Dragon Lady's Revenge* was set in the present (1971) in the capital of a mythical country in Southeast Asia. A young American lieutenant, the son of the U.S. ambassador, attempts to find the man who murdered his friend with an overdose of heroin. He becomes a pawn in the power struggle between those running the drug traffic: the Dragon Lady, General Rong Q (who is head of the country), and the CIA. In the end all are exposed by Blossom, a member of the

National Liberation Front who works as a B-girl in the den of iniquity run by the Dragon Lady. When Mr. Big, the man behind the drug traffic, is revealed to be the American ambassador, his son changes sides and joins Blossom. The lieutenant and Blossom are the young lovers from *commedia*. The U.S. ambassador is a blend of Pantalone and the capitalist boss of *The Independent Female*. General Rong Q is a cross between the Capitano of *commedia* and the intriguing villain of foreign espionage movies. An agent of the ambassador who makes each appearance in a different disguise is like one of the *commedia zanni*. The Dragon Lady is the evil woman of Josef von Sternberg films and of the comic strip "Terry and the Pirates." Although masks were not used in *The Independent Female* or *The Dragon Lady's Revenge*, the acting style was broad enough to accommodate a man in the role of the mother and a woman as General Rong Q. Both pieces used devices such as overheard conversations, disguises, mock heroic speeches, slapstick comedy, surprise revelations, and endings that provided models for action by the spectators.

Although Mime Troupe members thought of themselves as art workers, their plays came more from the intellectual Left than from the working class. The Mime Troupe found that working people are difficult to reach, that they watch television and attend sports events but think theatre is for an educated elite. Nevertheless, the Mime Troupe continued to look for ways to serve a working-class audience.

The attempt to serve workers forced the Troupe to resolve a related issue concerning the composition of the company. As they performed in 1971 for striking longshoremen, they and their critics noticed that they were white, whereas most of the longshoremen were black. In fact, the working people in San Francisco were largely nonwhite. The Mime Troupe had to become multiracial. Their "affirmative action" program got under way in 1974, and by 1980 the membership of the company included seven whites, five Latinos, and three blacks.

The mixed company put on a succession of productions dealing with issues of concern to working-class, multiethnic audiences. They played for a black church in Illinois, a Mexican farmworkers' picnic in Texas, a Filipino organization in Oakland, California, throughout the California prison system, and for anybody in San Francisco. The black hero of *The Great Air Robbery* (1974) strikes out against capitalist society and racial discrimination; *Frijoles or Beans* (1975) condemns the United States' economic manipulation of Third World countries; and in 1976, to commemorate the American bicentennial year, the Troupe created its longest and most complex play, *False Promises/Nos Enganeron* (Spanish: "We've been had"), on the subjects of racism and the materialistic, expansionist policies the United States maintained toward Puerto Rico, the Philippines, and Cuba at the turn of the century. The central characters are miners, and the Troupe drew on the American western movie and on Bertolt Brecht in stylizing the material. As with Brecht, the aim was serious analysis, but the method incorporated skillful acting, dancing, and singing to forge entertaining connections between historical events and the present-day interests of workers.

In form and style as well as in content, *False Promises* represented a synthesis of several years' work. Discussions that ultimately led to its composition began in 1973 when the group considered the possibility of making a play on the history of the U.S. labor movement. But having insufficient time for such a large project, they produced Brecht's *The Mother* instead. When discussions resumed in the summer of 1975 they set out to make a "people's history" for the American bicentennial. In January 1976, after an intervening tour, they began their research by reading histories of the United States and inviting speakers from the labor movement—mainly from union "radical caucuses"—to give political education seminars.

The company divided up into smaller groups that met separately in order to develop possible scenario ideas. These scenarios were then presented to the entire company for discussion. Inevitably, there were frictions as members became advocates for competing scenarios. After weeks of discussion the scenario that had been put forward by Joan Holden prevailed, and she was assigned to write the script. However, the play came from a collective concept developed and tested through months of reading, discussion, and rehearsals in which members of the company continued to raise and resolve questions.

False Promises is stylistically the most complex of the Mime Troupe's plays. Holden used the Shakespearean form of a main plot, presenting heroic figures speaking in blank verse and a subplot of low characters speaking in prose. However, in *False Promises* the "heroic" figures are treated comically, and the "low" characters are taken seriously. The group had learned in its production of Brecht's *The Mother* that the style of "epic" realism could work outdoors, so they could abandon the older styles that they now found too limiting. As a result, the working-class characters in the new play, although based on comic types, were made realistically complex, but not simplistically good.

The energetic, heightened realism of *False Promises* became the style of all subsequent plays of the Troupe, most of which focus on working-class issues. Holden's *Hotel Universe* (1977), for example, explores the issue of urban renewal. The events of the play loosely parallel actual events surrounding the destruction of San Francisco's International Hotel. The multiracial residents of this hotel, instead of being intimidated by the capitalists who threaten to demolish their home, unite the working community in opposition. Although they eventually lose their battle, as did the tenants of the International Hotel, they see their fight as a model. *Electro-Bucks* (1978), by Holden and Peter Solomon, is set in an electronics factory in "Silicon Valley" (the Santa Clara valley just south of San Francisco) that, as is typical of the industry, employs mostly minority women at low wages. When business exigencies result in mass layoffs, the workers revolt and take charge of the factory. While the characters in these plays are dimensional and realistic, the productions included band music, songs, and comic pantomime, additions that heightened the scale of the event, while introducing

Brechtian manipulation of aesthetic distance and an exuberance extending the literal boundaries of realism. This amalgamated idiom has been the common mode of expression of the Troupe in recent years, but the style of the company continues to evolve.

In 1984 the Mime Troupe celebrated its twenty-five years of theatre of social change with two major productions. Both *Steeltown*, a musical about the current crisis in the labor movement, and *1985*, an updating of Charles Dickens' *A Christmas Carol*, deal with compromise and co-option in Left-wing politics.

Members of the Mime Troupe have worked full time at theatre for many years, but their economic conditions are difficult. Passing the hat in the parks does not pay salaries and other expenses. During the autumn and spring they usually tour the United States and Europe; in 1980 they became the first American theatre to tour Cuba since the 1959 revolution, and in 1986 the collective traveled to Nicaragua. Although their work is well received—their awards include a 1987 Tony—they barely survive financially.

The Troupe has played several winters at the Victoria Theatre, formerly a burlesque house, in San Francisco's Mission District, where it has been encouraged by a broad-based audience. Despite more than twenty years of poverty, the San Francisco Mime Troupe has continued its commitment to audiences of the culturally disenfranchised. The Mime Troupe strives to help those who do not benefit from the American class system to recognize their self-interest and to see that change is possible. Although such audiences are probably the least lucrative, they are essential to the company's objective of bringing about social change. The Troupe also announced in 1984 that the National Endowment for the Arts had granted it an Ongoing Ensemble Award for use in 1986. Since its founding the Mime Troupe had declined, on principle, to apply for federal subsidy.

The San Francisco Mime Troupe remains firm in its belief that theatre can restore a sense of community to people who have been deprived of it. The Troupe is dedicated to change, not to art. It continues its search for better ways of making the theatre, in content and style, a living, radical force.

PERSONNEL

Management: R. G. Davis (1959–70). Since the reorganization of the Troupe as a "theatre collective" in 1970, the administrative and artistic leadership has been shared by the company.

Stage Directors: 1959–70: Sandra Archer, Joe Bellan, Peter Berg, Peter Cohon, R. G. Davis, Arthur Holden, Nina Serrano Landau, Tom Purvis, Judy Rosenberg-Goldhaft, Juris Svendsen. 1970–87: Sandra Archer, Dan Chumley, Brian Freeman, Steve Friedman, Arthur Holden, Joan Holden, Sharon Lockwood, Denny Stevens, Joel Weisman.

Scenic Designers/Technicians: 1959–70: John Barrow, Richard Beggs, John Connell, William Geis III, Wally Hedrick, Jerome Marcel, Fred Reichman, Karl Rosenberg, Barbara Scales, Megan Snider, Coni Spiegel, William Wiley. 1970–87: David Brune, Dan Chumley, Valentine Hooven, Renaldo Iturrino, Trina Johnson, Larry Montgomery, Larry Pisoni, Alain Schons, Patricia Silver, Peggy Snider, Peter Snider.

Costume Designers/Craftspersons: 1959–70: Judy Collins, Judy Davis, Nancy Dikler, Francesca Greene, Ann Horton, Larry Keck, David Maclay, Sara Morris, Bruce Newell, Judy Rosenberg-Goldhaft, Susan Roth, Marina Sender, Megan Snider, Coni Spiegel, Kathryn Stuntz, Caralie Tarble, William Wiley, Anne Willock, Joan Wright. 1970–87: Wilma Bonet, Sharon Lockwood, Nora Long, Jennifer Telford.

Composers/Musicians: 1959–70: Jeanne Brechan, John Flores, David Jenkins, Leonard Kline, Saul Landau, Phil Lesh, Charles McDermott, Pauline Oliveros, Gayle Pearl, Steven Reich, William Spenser, Juris Svendsen. 1970–87: Glenn Appell, Bruce Barthol, Randall Craig, Barry Glick, Phil Marsh, Javier Pacheco, Eduardo Robledo, Andrea Snow, Theodore Sobel, Jack Wickert.

Actors and Actresses: 1959–70: Michael Alaimo, *Sandra Archer* (1964–70), Steve Bailey, *Joe Bellan* (1962–70), *Peter Berg* (1965–67), Lorne Berkun, Eric Berne, Anne Bernstein, Lee Bouterse, Jean Brechan, Ruth Breuer, John Broderick, Manny Brookman, Lynn Brown, Mia Carlisle, Dan Chumley, *Peter Cohon* (1966–67), John Condrin, Don Crawford, *Susan Darby* (1959–63), *R. G. Davis* (1959–70), Charlie Degelman, Billie Dixon, *Robert Doyle* (1959–62), Serge Echeverria, Nick Eldridge, Ellen Ernest, Sam Erwin, William Freese, Steve Friedman, Paula Gilbert, Dawn Grey, Emmett Grogan, Roger Guy-Bray, Merle Harding, Willie B. Hart, Jr., Fred Hayden, Jim Haynie, Kay Hayward, Darryl Henriques, Victoria Hochberg, *Arthur Holden* (1960–70), Robert Hurwitt, Bollette Jacobson, Melody James, J. Jeffrey Jones, *Jerry Jump* (1961–66), Buck Lacey, Robert LaMorticello, Bob Lanchester, Jane Lapiner, Michael Lawrence, Norma Leistiko, Larry Lewis, Bill Lindyn, Marc Ling, Sharon Lockwood, *Joe Lomuto, Jr.* (1963–70), Dave Love, Tom Luce, Daniel McDermott, Jason Marc-Alexander, Julio Martinez, George Matthews, Barbara Melandry, Norma Middlebrook, Jamie Miller, Jeanne Milligan, Kent Minault, Boris Morris, Yvette Nachmias, Keith Nason, Terry O'Keefe, Richard Olsen, Mary Overlie, Gayle Pearl, Ron Poindexter, *Tom Purvis* (1963–64), Judy Quick, Gary Rappy, Chuck Ray, William Raymond, Ronald Reese, Georges Rey, Chuck Richardson, Val Riseley, *John Robb* (1964–67), Earl Robertson, *Judy Rosenberg-Goldhaft* (1962–67), Erica Rosqui, John Schonenberg, Shirley Shaw, Ruth Sicular, Marvin Silber, Robert Slattery, Marlene Slivers, Kai Spiegel ("Malachi Spicer"), Caraline Straley, Marilyn Sydney, Marc Truman, Fred Unger, Luis Valdez, Jael Weisman, Donald Weygandt, Jo Ann Wheatley, Norma Whittaker, Ann Willock, Ken Wydro. 1970–87: *Marie Acosta-Colon* (1975–87), Glenn Appell, Juaquin Aranda, Sandra Archer, Bruce Barthol, Joe Bellan, Lorne Berkun, Paul Binder, *Wilma Bonet* (1981–84), Mary Burnley, Michael Christiansen, *Dan Chumley* (1970–87), John Condrin, Randall Craig, Jack Dowding, Chris Fitzsimmons, Lonnie Ford, Brian Freeman, Steve Friedman, Deborah Gilyard, Merle Gladstone, Al Guzman, Jay Hamburger, *Jason Harris* (1970–72), *Arthur Holden* (1970–87), Joan Holden, *Melody James* (1970–82), Gus Johnson, Crain Knudsen, *Ed Levey* (1971–87), Barry Levitan, *Sharon Lockwood* (1970–87), *Joan Mankin* (1970–73), Tripp Mikich, Ingrid Monson, Jesse Moore, Michael Nolan, *Esteban Oropeza* (1973–87), Ilka Payan, Larry Pisoni, Muziki Roberson, Ed Robledo, Felipe Rodriquez, David Rokeach, Shabaka, Patricia Silver, *Audrey Smith* (1981–87), Peggy Snider, *Andrea Snow* (1970–82), Theodore Sobel, David Topham, Jeff Unger, Jeff Veale, Phil Walker, Joel Weisman, Bennett Yahya.

REPERTORY

1959: *Mime and Words.*
1960: *11th Hour Mime Show.*

1961: *Act Without Words, Purgatory* and *Krapp's Last Tape, Event I.*

1962: *The Dowry.*

1963: *Plastic Haircut* (film), *Event II, The Root, Ruzzante's Maneuvers, Ubu King.*

1964: *Mime (s) and Movie, Event III, Chorizos.*

1965: *Tartuffe, The Exception and the Rule, Candelaio, Chronicles of Hell.*

1966: *What's That, a Head?, Jack Off!, Mirage and Centerman* (film), *Olive Pits, Search and Seizure, The Miser, Out Put You.*

1967: *The Minstrel Show, or, Civil Rights in a Cracker Barrel, The Condemned, The Vaudeville Show, L'Amant Militaire.*

1968: *Ruzzante, or, the Veteran, Gutter Puppets (Metermaid, Little Black Panther, Meat), The Farce of Patelin.*

1969: *The Third Estate, The Congress of the Whitewashers.*

1970: *The Independent Female, or, A Man Has His Pride!, Eco Man, Telephone, or, Ripping Off Ma Bell, La Siete.*

1971: *Dragon Lady's Revenge, Clown Show (Highway Robbery* and *Soledad).*

1972: *Highrises, Frozen Wages, American Dreamer.*

1973: *San Fran Scandals of 1973, The Mother.*

1974: *The Great Air Robbery.*

1975: *Frijoles, or, Beans to You, Power Play.*

1976: *False Promises/Nos Enganeron.*

1977: *Hotel Universe.*

1978: *Electro-Bucks.*

1979: *Squash, TV Dinner, We Can't Pay, We Won't Pay.*

1980: *Factperson.*

1981: *Americans, or, Last Tango in Huahuatenango, Ghosts, Factwino Meets the Moral Majority.*

1982: *Factwino vs. Armageddonman.*

1983: *Secrets in the Sand.*

1984: *Steeltown, 1985.*

1985: *Factwino: The Opera, Crossing Borders (A Domestic Farce).*

1986: *Spain/'36, Hotel Universe, The Mozamgola Caper.*

1987: *The Mozamgola Caper, Dragon Lady's Revenge.*

BIBLIOGRAPHY

Published Sources:

Production calendars, photographs, and brief production accounts may be found in *California Theatre Annual* and *Theatre Directory of the San Francisco Bay Area.*

Barthol, Bruce. "In the Face of Fear and Struggle, Art." *American Theatre* 4.3 (1987): 26, 28.

Davis, R. G. *The San Francisco Mime Troupe: The First Ten Years.* Palo Alto, Calif.: Ramparts, 1975.

Holden, Joan. "Comedy and Revolution." *Arts in Society* 2 (1969): 175–82.

Kleb, William. "The San Francisco Mime Troupe: A Quarter of a Century Later; An Interview with Joan Holden." *Theater* 16 (Spring 1985): 58–61.

San Francisco Mime Troupe. *By Popular Demand.* San Francisco, Calif.: San Francisco Mime Troupe, 1980.

Shank, Theodore. *American Alternative Theatres.* New York: Grove Press, 1982.

Theatre Profiles, Vols. 1–8. New York: Theatre Communications Group, 1973–88.
Troupers, directed by Glenn Silber and Claudia Vianello. Icarus Films, 1986. 84 min.

Archival Resource:
Madison, Wisconsin. Wisconsin State Historical Society. Business records, correspondence, programs, photographs, production ephemera.

Lawrence Jasper

SEATTLE REPERTORY THEATRE (SRT) was organized in the summer of 1963 by Stuart Vaughan and a group of prominent Seattle, Washington, citizens who wanted to establish a resident acting company to perform in the 800-seat playhouse built for the 1962 World's Fair. The company incorporated as a nonprofit organization and opened on November 13, 1963, with a production of *King Lear*.

Vaughan, who had previously directed for the Phoenix Theatre* in New York City and for Joseph Papp's Shakespeare in the Park, was excited by the idea of a permanent theatre outside the commercial pressures of New York, and he initially established a thirty-week season (November to June) with six productions alternating in repertory. He had studied a number of European companies, including the Berliner Ensemble, as models for the Seattle experiment, and he was determined to employ his actors on a yearly basis. By paying them over the "dark" summer months he hoped to foster a sense of continuity and to create a feeling of genuine community. The Rep was also part of a general return to resident companies in America after World War II and opened only weeks before a similar and more highly publicized venture at Lincoln Center in New York (See Repertory Theatre of Lincoln Center).

The first company was composed of fifteen professional actors drawn largely from the New York area and four resident journeymen from Seattle. The journeyman contract Vaughan negotiated with Actors' Equity in Seattle pioneered a concept copied by many other resident companies. It allowed a theatre to hire talented amateurs from local communities in proportion to its Equity membership. Members of the original company included Conrad Bain, Stephen Joyce, Thomas Hill, and Andre Gregory, who served briefly as associate director.

From the outset, however, financial problems created tensions between Vaughan and the board of directors. Although the SRT sold approximately 9,000 subscriptions for the initial season, this was far short of its goal, and Century 21 Center, the parent group, withdrew its support at the end of the first year. Vaughan accused the SRT board of interfering in the artistic decisions of the company, and they, distrusting his fiscal sense, complained that he was unwilling to make concessions—such as adjusting the play rotation—in order to save funds. Midway through the third year of his contract Vaughan was fired and, after a highly publicized national search, replaced by Alan Fletcher.

Fletcher, who had degrees from Stanford University and teaching experience at Purdue University and Carnegie Institute of Technology, was a skillful director with a solid reputation at regional theatres like the Association of Producing

Artists (APA)* and San Francisco's American Conservatory Theatre* (ACT). He signed a two-year contract in February 1966 and announced that the SRT would be more contemporary in its play selection. He proposed a split season in which three plays alternated in repertory from November to February before the final three were introduced. And he expanded the size of the resident company so they could do a larger variety of plays.

Despite successful productions of Arthur Miller's *The Crucible*, Brendan Behan's *The Hostage*, and Molière's *Tartuffe*, financial difficulties continued to plague SRT. After Fletcher's first season the deficit exceeded $150,000, and in July 1967 there were more administrative changes. Donald Foster was appointed executive director and Peter Donnelly, who had joined the theatre from the Ford Foundation, became general manager. At the outset of the fifth season, in the fall of 1967, season subscribers numbered approximately 11,500, a slight falling off from the nearly 13,000 at the height of Vaughan's tenure.

Fletcher continued to introduce imaginative changes, however, and his productions were generally highly regarded. The resident company eventually grew to thirty, and he inaugurated a second season called Off Center, which performed avant-garde works such as Jean Genet's *The Blacks*, Jules Feiffer's *Little Murders*, Samuel Beckett's *Krapp's Last Tape*, John Osborne's *Look Back in Anger*, and Eugene O'Neill's *Mourning Becomes Electra*. In addition, SRT's production of Edward Albee's *Who's Afraid of Virginia Woolf?* was invited to the Bergen (Norway) International Theatre Festival in May 1969, thereby becoming the first American resident company to perform at the *Festspillene*.

At the start of SRT's seventh season (1969–70) Fletcher abandoned the repertory concept that had been the hallmark of the company since its inception and went to straight runs of six plays. But the change of fare did not attract a significantly larger audience, and with a deficit of $265,000 looming at year's end, the board again moved for a change. In a very close secret ballot Fletcher was retired after his fourth season and replaced by W. Duncan Ross, who was then head of the Professional Actor Training Program at the nearby University of Washington Drama School. The title of artistic director was dropped and Ross was appointed managing director.

Ross was English-trained and opposed to the repertory system, which he felt dissipated artistic and managerial energies. He began to reshape SRT around a small core of actors (six to eight) and to fill remaining roles in open casting. He also hired guest stars to gain a higher visibility for SRT and to increase audience attendance. Maureen O'Sullivan came for Noel Coward's *Hay Fever* in Ross' first season, while Douglas Watson appeared in Arthur Kopit's *Indians* and Myrna Loy was seen in a special production of Jerome Kilty's *Dear Love*. But the most significant event of the 1970–71 season was Richard Chamberlain's American Shakespeare debut in *Richard II*, which played for fifty-five sold-out performances in the spring and received nationwide press coverage.

Over the next several years Ross, Donnelly, and the SRT board pursued their starring system with sometimes uneven artistic results but with increasingly beneficial box-office support. Rita Gam was featured in Tennessee Williams' *Camino Real;* Christopher Walken in *Hamlet;* and Hume Cronyn and Jessica Tandy re-created their Broadway roles in David V. Robison's *Promenade, All!* Ross directed in each season, but he also brought in guest artists to support his vision of a revitalized company. George Abbott staged *Life with Father*, by Howard Lindsay and Russel Crouse, Eva Le Gallienne directed Henrik Ibsen's *A Doll's House*, and Robert Patrick supervised his own *Kennedy's Children*.

Seattle audiences responded to Ross' starring seasons, and ticket sales climbed. By his fourth year as managing director subscriptions totaled just under 20,000, a figure that would expand to 22,000 by the end of the 1975–76 season. Moreover, walk-up ticket business increased, as did the number of sold-out performances. Peter Donnelly, now functioning as producing director, estimated that the SRT had played to 240,000 persons at the conclusion of its thirteenth season.

In 1974 they leased a second building in downtown Seattle, redesigned the interior, and christened it the 2nd Stage. Ross hired a former colleague at the University of Washington, Arne Zaslove, to supervise the operation that produced five plays per season over the next three years, including Tom Stoppard's *The Real Inspector Hound*, Joe Orton's *Entertaining Mr. Sloan*, and Edward Bond's *Bingo*.

Ross and Donnelly also increased the SRT's activities in area touring, summer park shows, and special benefits for season ticket holders. And they campaigned vigorously for a new physical plant to replace the Paul Hayden Kirk structure inherited from the World's Fair. In 1977 Seattle passed a bond issue with $4.8 million earmarked for a new theatre. But after nine seasons Ross' efforts to develop audiences seemed to have reached a plateau. He had radically changed the nature of SRT as it had been conceived by Vaughan and then modified by Fletcher, and he had worked hard at improving community relations. But his stamina suffered, and on March 15, 1979, he resigned to accept an appointment at the University of Southern California.

After Ross' resignation the board of trustees appointed Daniel Sullivan as resident director and then hired John Hirsch as consulting artistic director. Sullivan, who had previously directed at ACT and Lincoln Center, was a veteran of several regional theatre productions and had also taught at the California Institute of the Arts. He had guest-directed at the SRT during Ross' tenure, and his work was widely known and respected. But he was perceived as a caretaker by many who believed policy would be determined by Hirsch, who commuted to Seattle from Toronto, Stratford, and New York.

Hirsch and Sullivan continued the performance calendar Ross had standard-ized—six plays from October through May—but they used fewer stars and employed more local actors. And they introduced a vigorous new plays workshop to stimulate scripts from national and international writers. Their seasons were typical of many regional theatres: a musical, a new play, and several standards that appealed to the subscription ticket buyer. Midway through their second year, however, Hirsch accepted the prestigious directorship of the Stratford (Canada) Shakespeare Festival and Sullivan was appointed artistic director of the SRT.

On October 26, 1983, the $8 million Bagley Wright Theatre opened as the new home for the SRT. Named after the first board president, the Bagley Wright is a proscenium house, built in reaction to the open stages that had proliferated after World War II, seating 856. The premiere production, Michael Weller's *The Ballad of Soapy Smith*, signaled a commitment to new plays that characterized Sullivan's leadership. Over the next three years his skillful blending of classic and original works boosted the SRT's audience and its artistic reputation. When Herb Gardner's *I'm Not Rappoport* won the Tony Award in 1986—after long development in Seattle—it was public recognition of Sullivan's support of original scripts and of such writers as Weller, William Mastrosimone, and Ted Gross.

Seattle audiences responded enthusiastically to Sullivan's leadership, and the theatre's subscription list grew to 25,000. But in 1985 Peter Donnelly, who had been the theatre's financial steward through many hard times and had led the campaign for the new building, left Seattle for new challenges at the Dallas Theatre Center. He was replaced by Benjamin Moore, formerly of ACT in San Francisco, who joined Sullivan in moving the SRT into other ventures: producing contemporary plays in the theatre's second space; developing tours for both child and adult audiences; and refining the new plays program. As the SRT looked forward to its twenty-fifth anniversary, however, Sullivan's highest priority was the rebuilding of a resident company, a goal that—ironically—had preoccupied Stuart Vaughan in the very first year of the theatre's existence.

PERSONNEL

Management: Peter Donnelly, Robert Egan, Alan Fletcher, Donald Foster, John Hirsch, Douglas Hughes, Benjamin Moore, W. Duncan Ross, Daniel Sullivan, William Taylor, Stuart Vaughan.

Designers: John Lee Beatty, Robert Blackman, Pat Collins, Laura Crow, Robert Dahlstrom, Robert Darling, Pete Davis, Richard Devin, Eldon Elder, Thomas Fichter, Ralph Funicello, Karen Gjelsteen, Allan Granstrom, Michael Holton, Allen Lee Hughes, James Ingalls, Neil Peter Jampolis, James Joy, Alan Kimmel, Steven Klein, Hugh Landwehr, Eugene Lee, John McLain, Robert Morgan, Spencer Mosse, Dennis Parichy, Robert Peterson, Lewis Rampino, Sally Richardson, W. Scott Robinson, Loren Sherman, Jennifer Tipton, Tony Walton, Kurt Wilhelm, Peter Wingate, Ed Wittstein, Robert Wojewodski, Paul Zalon.

Performers: Roderick Aird, Jane Alexander, Dennis Arndt, Mark Arnott, John Aylward, Conrad Bain, Kurt Beattie, J. V. Bradley, Jane Bray, James Brousseau, Kim Burroughs, Christina Burz, Scott Caldwell, Jeanne Carson, Veronica Castang, Malachy Cleary, Karen Kay Cody, Gordon Coffey, Megan Cole, Patricia Conolly, Christopher Cooper, Frank Corrado, Lee Corrigan, Clayton Corzatte, Ted D'Arms, Daniel Davis, George Deloy, William Dennis, Corky Dexter, Judith Doty, Kay Doubleday, David Downing, Stuart Duckworth, Starletta DuPois, Woody Eney, Mary Ewald, Richard Farrell, Katherine Ferrand, Pauline Flanagan, Bernard Frawley, Maureen Frawley, Patricia

Gage, Richard Gere, Anne Gerety, Cheryl Giannini, John Gilbert, Tina Marie Goff, Harold Gould, Sean Griffin, Harry Groener, Ed Hall, William Hall, Jr., Helen Harrelson, Yvette Hawkins, Thomas Hill, Pat Hinds, Ellen Holly, Paul Hostetler, Laura Hughes, Suzy Hunt, Laura Innes, William Jay, Mark Jenkins, Stephen Joyce, Valerie Karasek, William Keeler, David Hunter Koch, Lori Larsen, Damien Leake, John Lee, John Leonard, BoBo Lewis, Delroy Lindo, Cleavon Little, Robert Loper, Susan Ludlow, Pirie MacDonald, Scott MacDonald, Bianca Tampico McGinnis, Biff McGuire, Gale McNeeley, Deborah May, Glenn Mazen, Betty Miller, Robert Moberly, Donald Moffat, Stillman Moss, Kate Mulgrew, William Myers, Marjorie Nelson, William Ontiveros, Barney O'Sullivan, Marianne Owen, Holly Palance, Tony Pasqualini, Liann Pattison, Rod Pilloud, Nina Polan, John Procaccino, Rick Ray, Paul Redford, Richard Riehle, Eve Roberts, Mary Lou Rosato, Michael Santo, Raynor Scheine, Cambell Scott, Jean Sherrard, Kate Skinner, Michael J. Smith, Tony Soper, Jackie Sorel, Ted Sorel, Kevin Spacey, David Spielberg, David Strathairn, Daniel Sullivan, Joseph Summers, Joseph Tanner, Kevin Tighe, Elizabeth Van Dyke, George Vogel, Bill Watson, June White, Mel Winkler, Kathleen Worley, R. Hamilton Wright, William Wright.

REPERTORY

1963–64: *King Lear, The Firebugs, The Lady's Not for Burning, Death of a Salesman, Shadow of Heroes.* Bonus Programs (free to subscribers): *The Battle of the Sexes from Shakespeare to Shaw, A Sleep of Prisoners, The Lily and the Rose.*

1964–65: *Twelfth Night, Man and Superman, Ah, Wilderness!, The Cherry Orchard, Hamlet.* Special Events: *Bedtime Story, Twelfth Night* and *Ah, Wilderness!* (tour of Northwest cities). Bonus Programs: *Don Juan in Hell, Who Was Joan?, One Times One (An Illusion of a Play).* Summer Tour, "Theatre-in-the-Park": *The Taming of the Shrew.*

1965–66: *Julius Caesar, The Importance of Being Earnest, Long Day's Journey into Night, Heartbreak House, Galileo.* Special Event: *The Tinder Box.* Bonus Programs (free to subscribers): *Under Milk Wood, Northwest Poets.* Summer Tour, "Theatre-in-the-Park": *She Stoops to Conquer.*

1966–67: *The Crucible, The Hostage, Blithe Spirit, Tartuffe, The Visit, The Night of the Iguana.* Bonus Program (free to subscribers): *Moby Dick Rehearsed, Three by Chekhov, One Times One (An Illusion of a Play).* Summer Tour, "Theatre-in-the-Park": *The Merry Wives of Windsor.*

1967–68: *Henry IV*, Part I, *The Rehearsal, You Can't Take It with You, The Rivals, The Father, The Threepenny Opera.* Off Center Theatre—First Season: *The Death of Bessie Smith* and *The American Dream* (one-acts), *U.S.A.* (a musical revue), *Little Murders, Christopher, Infancy and Childhood, Krapp's Last Tape, Brecht on Brecht.* Summer Tour, "Theatre-in-the-Park": *The Imaginary Invalid.*

1968–69: *Our Town, Juno and the Paycock, A Midsummer Night's Dream, Serjeant Musgrave's Dance, Lysistrata, A View from the Bridge.* Off Center Theatre, Second Season: *Mourning Becomes Electra, Three Cheers for What's-Its-Name* (one-acts—premiere), *Look Back in Anger, Big Nose Mary Is Dead, And the Quickies* (eleven one-acts), *The Blacks.* Bergen International Festival: *Who's Afraid of Virginia Woolf?, Short Sacred Rite of Search and Destruction/A Little Set-To* (premiere). Summer Tour, "Theatre-in-the-Park": *The Servant of Two Masters.*

1969–70: *Volpone, The Three Sisters, Once in a Lifetime, In the Matter of J. Robert Oppenheimer, The Little Foxes, The Country Wife.* Off Center Theatre, Third Season: *Joe Egg, Summertree, Initiation.* Summer Tour, "Theatre-in-the-Park": *Misalliance.*

1970–71: *Indians, A Flea in Her Ear, The Miser, Hay Fever, The Price, Happy Ending* and *Days of Absence*. Special Presentations: *Dear Love, Emlyn Williams in Charles Dickens, Richard II*. Summer Tour, "Rep 'n Rap": *A Village Wooing*.

1971–72: *Ring 'Round the Moon, The House of Blue Leaves, Hotel Paradiso, Getting Married, And Miss Reardon Drinks a Little, Adaptation* and *Next*. Special Presentation: *I Am a Woman*. Special Event: *Adaptation* and *Next* (tour of Washington state). Summer Tour, "Rep'n Rap": *Thurbermania*.

1972–73: *Macbeth, Camino Real, Charley's Aunt, Child's Play, All Over, The Tavern*. Special Presentation: *Promenade, All!*. Special Event: *The Tavern* (tour of Washington state). Summer Tour, "Rep'n Rap": *Love, Life and Other Laughing Matters*.

1974–75: *Hamlet, A Grave Undertaking, Life with Father, Waltz of the Toreadors, A Doll's House, The Matchmaker*. Special Event: *The Matchmaker* (tour of Washington state). Summer Tour, "Rep'n Rap": *Crazyquilt* (collection of American humor). The 2nd Stage, first season: *After Magritte* and *The Real Inspector Hound, The Architect and the Emperor of Assyria, A Look at the Fifties*. 2nd Stage "Extra": *Halloween* and *Lunchtime*.

1975–76: *Cyrano de Bergerac, Jumpers, Seven Keys to Baldpate, The Last Meeting of the Knights of the White Magnolia, The Madwoman of Chaillot, Private Lives*. Special Presentation: *The Many Faces of Love*. Special Event: *Seven Keys to Baldpate* (tour of five Western states). The 2nd Stage, second season: *Benito Cereno, Entertaining Mr. Sloane, Made for TV* (an ensemble work created by the 2nd Stage Company), *Kennedy's Children, The Collected Works of Billy the Kid*.

1976–77: *Music Is* (world premiere of a new musical based on *Twelfth Night)*, *Anna Christie, The Mousetrap, Cat on a Hot Tin Roof, The Show-Off, Equus*. Special Event: *The Show-Off* (tour of five Western states). Special Tours: *The Rhythm Show* (thirteen-day Alaskan tour sponsored by National Endowment for the Arts). The 2nd Stage, third season: *Bingo, Once upon a Time, Suzanna Andler* (premiere), *Boesman and Lena, Vanities*. Summer Tour, "Rep'n Rap": *Just Between Us* (one-woman show with Peggy Cowles). Special Presentation: *By-Line, Ernie Pyle* (one-man show with William Windom).

1977–78: *The Royal Family, The Dream Watcher, The National Health, Uncle Vanya, Much Ado About Nothing, 13 Rue de L'Amour*. Special Event: *Much Ado About Nothing* (tour of Washington and Idaho). The 2nd Stage, play in progress: *Eminent Domain*. Summer Tour, "Rep 'n Rap": *Discovering Tutankhamun*.

1978–79: *A Penny for a Song, The Master Builder, Side by Side by Sondheim, The Glass Menagerie, Catsplay, Fallen Angels*. Special Events: *The Glass Menagerie* (tour of Washington and Idaho), *The Energy Show—MOB* (Mobile Outreach Bunch, created and performed by SRT actors for tour of Washington and Idaho junior high schools).

1979–80: *Saint Joan, A History of the American Film, An Enemy of the People, The Taming of the Shrew, Spokesong, Pal Joey*. Special Events: *The Taming of the Shrew* (tour of Washington and Idaho), *Top of the Charts—MOB* (Mobil Outreach Bunch, specially created show toured to schools). Sundays at Three: *The Lion and the Portuguese* (later developed into full-length play), *Transformations, Brush Up Your Shakespeare, We're Here Because We're Here, Pleasure and Repentance, Was Ever Woman in This Humor Wooed?, Mr. Joyce Is Leaving Paris, Always Take Mother's Advice, Pride and Prejudice, The King Baggy Pants Revue, With a Song in My Heart*. Plays in progress: *The American Clock, The Lion and the Portuguese, Dud Shuffle*.

1980–81: *Strider: The Story of a Horse, The Grand Hunt, Ah, Wilderness!, Born Yesterday, The Dance of Death, Up from Paradise.*

1981–82: *Another Part of the Forest, Two Gentlemen of Verona, Awake and Sing!, Bedroom Farce, Savages, Major Barbara.* New Plays in Process Project: *The Duel, The Grass Widow, An Ounce of Prevention, What I Did Last Summer.* Sundays at Three: *Lillian Hellman: A Memoir of Art, Love and Politics, The Yoked Fool: Shakespeare on Love, The 30's: Odets and the Theatre of the Left, None of the Above, Everything You Always Wanted to Know About Indian Education, Shaw on Women and War.* Mobile Outreach Bunch (MOB) tour: *Newcomer.* Special Events: *An Evening with Barbara Cook.*

1982–83: *Romeo and Juliet, The Front Page, Death of a Salesman, Taking Steps, Translations, The Vinegar Tree.* New Plays in Process Project: *Crossfire, The Ballad of Soapy Smith, My Uncle Sam, Shivaree.* Sundays at Three: *Shakespeare's Contemporary: Christopher Marlowe, The Other Voice, The Freedom and Power of the Press: The Critical Decades 1950–1980, Arthur Miller and the American Myth: The Critical Controversy, Love and Marriage in the 80's, The Poetry and Song of Irish Liberation, Utopian Visions of the American Community.* Mobile Outreach Bunch (MOB) tour: *Everything Nice.* Special Events: *Barbara Cook Onstage.*

1983–84: *The Ballad of Soapy Smith, The Adventures of Huckleberry Finn, Make and Break, The Misanthrope, Master Harold . . . and the boys, As You Like It.* New Plays in Process Project: *Coming of Age in Soho, Splittin' Hairs, Between East and West, Abingdon Square.* Sundays at Three: *Gold Rush: Easy Money in America, An Hour with Mark Twain, None of the Above.* Improvisational Theatre Company: *Molière: The Art of Social Critique, Fugard and the South African Struggle, Shakespeare and the Poetry of Love.* Mobile Outreach Bunch (MOB) tour: *Aesop's Fantastic Fables.* Special Events: *Appearing Nitely* (Lily Tomlin's award-winning Broadway one-woman show). Inaugural Production in the PONCHO (Patrons of Northwest Civic, Cultural, and Charitable Organizations) Forum: *Shivaree* (world premiere).

1984–85: *Our Town, Passion Play, I'm Not Rappaport, The Mandrake* and *The Wedding, 'night, Mother, Guys and Dolls.* The Other Season: *Discovered, The Nice and the Nasty, Cat's Paw, Bearclaw* (formerly *My Father in the Tate*). The Dollar Theatre: *Big and Little, Greetings from Elsewhere, Standing Up Walking Out, Longshots* (comedian Rod Long in an original one-man show), *Alan Lande* (an evening of performance art). Mobile Outreach Bunch (MOB) Tour: *Oldies.* Special Events: *The Texas Chainsaw Manicurist* (a musical cabaret), *The Search for Signs of Intelligent Life in the Universe* (Lily Tomlin's one-woman show).

1985–86 (Mainstage): *The Merry Wives of Windsor, All My Sons, The Real Thing, The Forest, Fences, Girl Crazy.* PONCHO Forum: *Endgame, Cat's Paw.* Mobile Outreach Bunch (MOB) Tour: *Homegirl.* The Dollar Theatre: *Thanatophobia: Fear of Death* (with magician Kirk Charles), *Krapp's Last Tape, Theatresports, Ruth* (Alazais Azema Theatre Company). The "Other Season": *The Understanding, A Peep into the Twentieth Century, Remote Conflict.*

BIBLIOGRAPHY

Published Sources:
Seattle Post-Intelligencer, 1964–86.
Seattle Times, 1964–86.
Vaughan, Stuart. *A Possible Theatre*. New York: McGraw-Hill, 1969.

Archival Resource:

Seattle, Washington. University of Washington Library. Papers, promptbooks, and records.

Barry B. Witham

SHOCK TROUPE. See WORKERS' LABORATORY THEATRE.

SOUTH COAST REPERTORY has grown in twenty years from a tiny, struggling touring company to a multimillion-dollar professional resident theatre in Costa Mesa, California, an Orange County suburb about thirty-five miles from downtown Los Angeles, on the southeastern edge of the metropolitan area. Founders David Emmes, producing artistic director, and Martin Benson, artistic director, have guided the group through several stages of fiscal and artistic growth.

Emmes and Benson met at San Francisco State College, where they enrolled as theatre students in 1960, studying under Jules Irving, who, with Herbert Blau, dominated the theatre arts department while running the Actor's Workshop*. Emmes finished his M.A. in 1962 and accepted a teaching position at Long Beach City College; Benson finished his B.A. in the same year and moved to Los Angeles to seek work as an actor. In the spring of 1963 the Off-Broadway Theatre in Long Beach, a small, semiprofessional company, invited Emmes to direct a production. He chose a play to showcase Benson and other actors he had known in San Francisco. Arthur Schnitzler's *La Ronde* opened on August 15, 1963, and ran for four weeks. The production's success inspired the participants to organize a group called the Theatre Workshop, composed of former students from both San Francisco State College and Long Beach City College. In a promotional brochure published in August 1964, Emmes declared that the company would choose plays for their artistic integrity, relevance to contemporary life, and capacity to stimulate the audience. They returned to the Off-Broadway Theatre in the summer of 1964, this time renting the space and acting as their own producers, to test the potential audience and their own mettle with three plays in repertory: Brendan Behan's *The Hostage*, Ben Jonson's *The Alchemist*, and George Bernard Shaw's *Major Barbara*. The latter was only the third directing assignment of Benson's young career; earlier that year he had directed John Osborne's *Look Back in Anger* at the Off-Broadway and Sean O'Casey's *Shadow of a Gunman* at Long Beach City College. As the leaders of the group planned to develop the company from a summer troupe to a full-year operation, they confronted the question of location. The rich cultural climate of Los Angeles made it a likely home for one more small, independent theatre company, but Emmes urged that they remain in Orange County, a less urban but potentially affluent area known principally, at that time, as the home of Disneyland. The suburbs offered more opportunity and less competition than Los Angeles, and economists predicted local growth that would provide the money and the middle-class audience that resident theatres seemed to need. At Jules Irving's suggestion, the group changed its name to South Coast Repertory (SCR).

SCR's first production was Molière's *Tartuffe*. It opened on November 12, 1964, at the Ebell Club, a sixty-seat meeting house for a women's civic group in Newport Beach. The production ran for two weekends and then toured to Orange Coast College in Costa Mesa and to the Laguna Beach Playhouse.

The company's first permanent home was the "Second Step," converted from a secondhand marine hardware store located on the beachfront in the cannery district of Newport Beach. In January 1965 the nearly bankrupt company raised money to reconstruct the building by selling 119 season subscriptions at $7 each. John Arthur Davis (also a graduate of San Francisco State College and an SCR artistic director until 1969) designed a theatre seating seventy-five in seven rows. The farthest seat was only twenty-four feet from a small stage measuring twenty-three and a half feet wide, sixteen feet deep, and eleven feet high. The Second Step opened with a production of Samuel Beckett's *Waiting for Godot* on March 12, 1965. The company struggled, paying production expenses out of each week's box-office receipts, and some of the performers lived in rooms above the theatre. Although SCR paid none of its personnel at this point, the company called itself professional because of its aesthetic objectives and potential capabilities.

In 1967 SCR opened the "Third Step," a theatre in a converted variety store at 1827 Newport Boulevard in Costa Mesa. Davis' new design included a stage forty feet wide and thirty-two feet deep, and a seating area with a flexible capacity of 175 to 200.

By 1970 not only had the company survived, but it had received significant acclaim in the form of awards from the Los Angeles Critics' Circle. Furthermore, Orange County's growth made it possible for Emmes and Benson to expand the company. They hired a secretary and a part-time managing director, and in 1972 they organized the first board of trustees, relinquishing autonomy in order to create a supportive link between the company and the community. They joined the Theatre Communications Group and made plans for developing a substantial subscription audience. The National Endowment for the Arts granted them $2,500 to fund an outreach program to bring the theatre closer to the people of Orange County.

The early 1970s became a period of rapid growth and development. The company began to pay actors, directors, and designers at the rate of approximately $50 per week. In 1972 the company established two training programs: the Summer Conservatory offered an intensive, eight-week session to aspiring professional actors, and the Young Conservatory trained talented children and complemented the Educational Touring Program that had been initiated in 1969 to bring theatre directly to the schools. The company numbered sixty in 1973, and in 1974 mounted its first production sanctioned by the Actors' Equity Association—Tom Stoppard's *The Real Inspector Hound*. During the same year SCR hired its first Equity guest artist, Herb Voland, to play the Coach in Jason Miller's *That Championship Season*.

In 1976 Emmes and Benson decided that the physical limitations of the Third Step were preventing the company from achieving further artistic progress. Financier Henry T. Segerstrom, wanting to encourage a cultural organization to complement the growth of business in Costa Mesa, donated more than an acre of land for a new theatre complex. SCR launched the largest cultural fund-raising campaign in Orange County's history, and in twenty-eight months they collected $3.5 million. In October 1978 SCR opened the Main Stage of the "Fourth Step" complex with William Saroyan's *The Time of Your Life*. The Main Stage, a proscenium theatre with a nineteen-line counterweight system, offers a wide, shallow auditorium holding 507 seats in thirteen rows. In 1979 the Second Stage went into operation with David Mamet's *A Life in the Theatre*. The Second Stage is a smaller space, containing a thrust stage surrounded on three sides by 161 seats in five rows.

SCR's financial base has grown each year, reflecting the increasing support of its affluent audience. The total box-office receipts grew from just over $8,000 in 1964–65 to nearly $34,000 in 1967–68 (their first season at the Third Step), to more than $66,000 in 1971–72. From the mid-1970s the annual budget grew from $267,000 in 1974 to $1 million in 1978 and $3.4 million in 1984. Subscriptions grew from 10,000 in 1977 to 17,000 in 1978, and reached 21,500 for the twentieth anniversary season of 1984–85. From 1980 to 1985 between 65 and 83 percent of subscribers renewed subscriptions.

Emmes and Benson run the theatre cooperatively. Their ability to agree on plays, directors, and designers and the serene longevity of their partnership have impressed the volatile southern California theatre community. Emmes has assumed more administrative responsibility, leaving him time to direct only two productions each year to Benson's three. Emmes also supervises four staff members who manage the day-to-day operations: a director of development, a business director, a production manager, and a marketing director.

The company is now operating on two Equity contracts: LORT-B for the Main Stage and LORT-D for the Second Stage. In effect, most roles are played by Equity actors, with some small parts taken by non-Equity performers. A core company of nine performers (including six of the original founding members) is guaranteed twenty-six weeks of work each season. Emmes and Benson foster continuity and company identity by casting people who have worked with them before, so the "extended" company includes every actor who has ever acted with SCR.

The company offers one or two classics annually but concentrates on contemporary material, including five to eight premieres in each season. Over the twenty-two seasons from 1964 through 1986 the company has produced 211 plays. Twenty-five percent have been local or national premieres and nearly 15 percent have been world premieres. They have presented the southern California premieres of Harold Pinter's *The Birthday Party*, Sam Shepard's *True West*, and

Tom Stoppard's *Jumpers*, and the West Coast premieres of Bertolt Brecht's *Baal*, Arthur Kopit's *Indians*, Slawomir Mrozek's *Tango*, David Rabe's *The Basic Training of Pavlo Hummel* and *Sticks and Bones*, and Jean-Claude van Itallie's *America Hurrah*. SCR has produced only twenty-two plays from the era before Henrik Ibsen's *A Doll's House* (1879), mostly those of Shakespeare (ten plays) and Molière (seven productions of five plays), who, with Pinter (seven productions of six plays), have been the most frequently produced playwrights in SCR's repertory.

SCR must look almost exclusively to the Los Angeles press for its influential critical reception, but the critics tend to give SCR less regard and interest than smaller companies in their own city. Although Gordon Davidson's Center Theatre Group/Mark Taper Forum was founded only three years after SCR, the Los Angeles company reached national stature much earlier and its southern neighbor has lived in its shadow. The journalists have never faulted SCR's administration, its continuity, or its endurance, but they have been slow to praise the artistic results, thereby leaving the impression of a company that runs very well yet fails to inspire. Lawrence Christon has praised the actors for not using their performances to audition for potential Hollywood casting agents, has asserted that "production design is always uniquely expressive," and has noted the group's "discipline, taste [and] intelligence." Yet he has gone on to say that "despite the thoroughness and discipline of SCR productions one may still cite the lack of mature actors . . . who are complete and work well within the classical idiom" (*Los Angeles Times*, March 7, 1976, "Calendar" section, p. 46). Sylvie Drake has referred to "the successful mixture of artistic perspicacity and administrative efficiency that has characterized the operation of Orange County's only resident professional theater" (*Los Angeles Times*, April 15, 1976, section IV, p. 15), but when she reviewed *The Time of Your Life* she complained about the lack of excitement and concluded by saying, "Given the tenaciousness of this outfit, it can be counted on to keep trying" (*Los Angeles Times*, November 13, 1978, section IV, p. 12). Dan Sullivan has adopted a similar point of view, referring to SCR's production of Peter Shaffer's *Amadeus* as "a very capable account" (*Los Angeles Times*, September 16, 1983, section IV, p. 1), but he changed his tone when he saw Martin Benson's interpretation of John Millington Synge's *The Playboy of the Western World*. He announced that "South Coast Repertory has come of age," and followed with an unreservedly laudatory review (*Los Angeles Times*, November 1, 1983, section VI, p. 1). That production won eight nominations in the competition for the Los Angeles Drama Critics' Circle Awards, and it inspired Drake to write that "South Coast is a theater that has come up through the ranks over the last 15 years. . . . Artistic maturity was slower to follow, but in the last two seasons, South Coast Repertory has increasingly hit its stride" (*Los Angeles Times*, February 23, 1984, section VI, p. 1). *Playboy* subsequently won in every category for which it was nominated, and its success represented the artistic growth that SCR had achieved since moving into the Fourth Step and developing into a major resident theatre. During the three seasons from 1983 to 1986 the company won fifteen Los Angeles Drama Critics' Circle awards and more than seventy Dramalogue awards, surpassing all other theatres in southern California.

Emmes would like SCR to be known as an innovative company, willing to take risks while developing new plays through readings and workshops. The company prefers text-based, "literary" drama that permits production in a presentational or theatrical style. There is a separate endowment (at $1.4 million as of 1986) intended expressly for the development of new scripts, and playwrights in residence received $4,000 to $12,000 per script. During the 1985–86 season, the company initiated the Collaboration Laboratory (Colab), a program designed to offer playwrights a means to test their work as they go. Two of Colab's activities included the Hispanic Playwrights Project, a week-long summer workshop for three plays chosen from more than eighty entries by Hispanic-American writers, and NewSCRipts, a series of play readings presented to a subscription audience. One of the first plays featured in NewSCRipts was Keith Reddin's *Highest Standard of Living*, which went on to open SCR's 1986–87 season on the Main Stage. In late 1986 Colab moved into the new Artists Center, an 11,000-square-foot addition to the main building that offers rehearsal space and work space for writers.

Under the consistent leadership of Emmes and Benson, SCR has grown into a multifaceted organization of artistic prominence and civic significance. The company takes theatre to the schools and invites schoolchildren to the theatre, providing a salutary community service to the families of SCR's suburban surroundings. The conservatories offer training programs to children and adults throughout the year. SCR stands out as the only professional ensemble company in southern California, and the theatre keeps expanding its work in the development of new playwrights and new plays.

PERSONNEL

Artistic Management: David Emmes, producing artistic director; Martin Benson, artistic director; Cliff Faulkner, resident scenic designer; Tom Ruzika, resident lighting director; Jerry Patch, Dramaturg.

Directors: John Allison (1981–82, 1983–85), *Martin Benson* (1964–86), Robert Bonaventura (1970–71, 1973–75), John Arthur Davis (1965–68), Warren Deacon (1966–67, 1970–72), James De Priest (1967–70, 1971–75), *David Emmes* (1964–70, 1971–86), *John-David Keller* (1974–86), Hal Landon, Jr. (1969–70, 1972–75), Mathias Reit (1966–68, 1972–73), Reginald Rook (1973–76), Lee Shallat (1975–76, 1979–86), Daniel Sullivan (1973–74, 1975–78), Ron Thronson (1967–71).

Designers: George Barcos (1969–72), Martin Benson (1967–68, 1969–71), Greg Bolton (1971–74), David Clements (1964–67), Barbara Cox (1979–80, 1981–86), John Arthur Davis (1964–65, 1966–67, 1968–69), *Michael Devine* (1964–66, 1967–68, 1977–86), Mark Donnelly (1979–86), Kent Dorsey (1982–85), David Emmes (1966–71), Cliff Faulkner (1978–86), Ralph Funicello (1981–84, 1985–86), Cameron Harvey (1979–86), Paulie Jenkins (1981–86), Merrily Ann Murray (1980–83), Sergio O'Cadiz (1966–68), Dwight Richard Odle (1978–86), Sandra Parker (1968–71), Trina Portillo (1965–67,

1970–71), Reginald Rook (1970–73), Robinson Royce (1970–73), Donna Ruzika (1980–86), *Tom Ruzika* (1975–86), Stephen Shaffer (1983–86), Maggi Stamm (1968–69, 1973–75), Charles Tomlinson (1975–78, 1981–82, 1985–86), *Susan Tuohy* (1972–86), Shigeru Yaji (1983–86).

Actors and Actresses: Nathan Adler (1981–82, 1983–86), Wayne Alexander (1980–85), George Archambeault (1978–81), Elaine Bankston (1967–71), George Barcos (1968–70, 1971–73), James Baxes (1967–71), George Bell (1971–77), Martin Benson (1964–69, 1971–72), *Ron Boussom* (1965–69, 1970–73, 1976–86), William Brady (1969–75, 1976–77), Wynne Broms (1974–79), Pat Brown (1966–72), Pat Brumbaugh (1972–74, 1975–76), Ron Chipres (1975–78), David Clements (1964–67), Megan Cole (1980–81, 1983–84, 1985–86), Jeffrey Combs (1982–85), Gary Cotter (1968–73), Sharon Crabtree (1973–74, 1975–77), John Arthur Davis (1964–70), Warren Deacon (1965–67, 1972–73), *Steve De Naut* (1971–85), Diane De Priest (1973–74, 1975–79, 1981–82), *James De Priest* (1967–68, 1970–74, 1975–80), Michael Douglass (1967–71), Toni Douglass (1967–72), Diane Doyle (1982–85), *Richard Doyle* (1964–66, 1970–75, 1976–86), Pamela Dunlap (1983–86), *John Ellington* (1971–77, 1978–86), Ellen Elliott (1972–75), David Emmes (1964–66, 1968–69, 1970–72), Marilyn Fox (1983–86), Patricia Fraser (1980–81, 1982–83, 1985–86), Squire Fridell (1968–75), Jake Gardiner (1973–78), Wayne Grace (1978–81, 1982–86), Paul Gracey (1972–76), Noreen Hennessy (1979–84), Karen Hensel (1980–81, 1984–86), Patti Johns (1980–85), Kathryn Johnson (1978–79, 1981–82, 1984–85), *Leslie Jones* (1964–68, 1971–79), *John-David Keller* (1974–75, 1976–86), David Kettles (1965–68), Scotty King (1975–79), *Art Koustik* (1964–68, 1969–72, 1974–86), Pam Krumb (1973–77), *Hal Landon, Jr.* (1966–86), Charles Lanyer (1976–78, 1979–81), Barbara Leva (1970–72, 1973–77), Francesca L'Hoir (1964–66, 1968–69), *Dennis Long* (1975–86), Kristen Lowman (1982–86), *Martha McFarland* (1964–71, 1974–86), Robert Machray (1981–82, 1983–84, 1985–86), Morgan Mackay (1975–78), James McKie (1966–68, 1970–71, 1973–74), Rosemary Mallett (1974–77, 1978–79), Sandra Marino (1967–74), *Ron Michaelson* (1974–86), Billy Miller (1967–71), Marnie Mosiman (1980–82, 1983–84), Heath Park (1967–77), Cherie Patch (1972–73, 1976–79), Steve Patterson (1970–75, 1978–81, 1985–86), Alan Paul (1971–74), Reginald Rook (1970–75, 1976–78), Irene Roseen (1978–81, 1983–84), Tom Rosqui (1982–86), Paul Rudd (1981–84), Richard Ryan (1975–78), Lee Shallat (1976–82), Howard Shangraw (1975–86), *Ann Siena-Schwartz* (1972–82, 1983–84), Gabrielle Sinclair (1983–86), Caroline Smith (1977–79, 1980–81), Mimi Smith (1972–75), *Don Took* (a.k.a. Don Tuche) (1964–86), George Woods (1981–82, 1984–86), Cameron Young (1969–73).

REPERTORY

1964–65: *Tartuffe, Waiting for Godot, Volpone, The Trial of Gabriel Kapuniak, The Glass Menagerie, The Hostage, Ring 'Round the Moon.*

1965–66: *Othello, The Birthday Party, Candida, Baal, Chocolates, Juno and the Paycock, Mandragola.*

1966–67: *Let's Get a Divorce, The Caretaker, The Playboy of the Western World, Act Without Words, Last Day of the Year, A Moon for the Misbegotten, Serjeant Musgrave's Dance, Red Magic, The Miser, The Typist* and *The Tiger.*

1967–68: *Big Soft Nellie, Entertaining Mr. Sloane, Arms and the Man, Hail Scrawdyke, Pictures from the Walls of Pompeii, The Time of Your Life, The Knack, A Taste of Honey, Macbeth, A Streetcar Named Desire, Adventures in a Paper Bag, America Hurrah.*

1968–69: *The Homecoming, The Three Cuckolds, The Incredible Reign of Good King Ubu, Death of a Salesman, La Turista, Room Service, The Threepenny Opera, We Bombed in New Haven.*

1969–70: *A Funny Thing Happened on the Way to the Forum, An Evening of Arrabal, Spoon River Anthology, A Day in the Death of Joe Egg, The Glass Menagerie, One Flew over the Cuckoo's Nest, Saved, Rosencrantz and Guildenstern Are Dead.*

1970–71: *The Boys in the Band, Indians, The Birthday Party, Mother Earth, Snowman in the Empty Closet, The Imaginary Invalid, Next, The Indian Wants the Bronx, Luv, The Ginger Man, Charley's Aunt.*

1971–72: *Feiffer's People, Tommy, Our Town, Mother Earth, The White House Murder Case, The Innocents, Oli's Ice Cream Suit, Uncle Vanya, Actor's Mime Theatre, Pueblo, Happy Birthday, Wanda June.*

1972–73: *The Torch-Bearers, Tango, Moonchildren, Play Strindberg, The Basic Training of Pavlo Hummel, The Tempest, In the Midst of Life, The Clowns, Catch-22.*

1973–74: *The Tavern, The Would-Be Gentleman, Sticks and Bones, The Taming of the Shrew, The Philanthropist, The House of Blue Leaves, Godspell.*

1974–75: *The Real Inspector Hound* and *After Magritte, That Championship Season, The Hot l Baltimore, Tartuffe, Subject to Fits, The Cave Dwellers, Godspell.*

1975–76: *Jumpers, Scenes from American Life, The Wager, The National Health, A Midsummer Night's Dream, Rubbers* and *Yanks 3, Detroit 0, Top of the Seventh, In Fashion.*

1976–77: *The Ruling Class, Saturday, Sunday, Monday, Old Times, Two Gentlemen of Verona, The Daring Dardolases (Or Love Finds Cosmo C. Cosmo), Equus, Jacques Brel Is Alive and Well and Living in Paris, Vanities, James Joyce's Women.*

1977–78: *Private Lives, The Last Meeting of the Knights of the White Magnolia, A Doll's House, Volpone, Comedians, A Macbeth, Otherwise Engaged.*

1978–79: *The Time of Your Life, The Contractor, The Sorrows of Frederick, The Learned Ladies, Brecht on Brecht, Peg o' My Heart, Spokesong.*

1979–80: *Wild Oats, A Life in the Theatre, Wings, Forever Yours, Marie-Lou, Side by Side by Sondheim, Points in Time, Right of Way, No Man's Land, Much Ado About Nothing, Time Was, Ladyhouse Blues.*

1980–81: *Hotel Paradiso, American Buffalo, The Glass Menagerie, A Christmas Carol, Bosoms and Neglect, The Elephant Man, Screwball, The Merchant of Venice, Ashes, Childe Byron, Chevaliere, Anything Goes!.*

1981–82: *Ah, Wilderness!, True West, Loose Ends, A Christmas Carol, The Play's the Thing, Bodies, Henry IV,* Part I, *The Blood Knot, Da, Coming Attractions, Tintypes, The Man Who Could See Through Time.*

1982–83: *All in Favour Said No!, The Diviners, Brothers, A Christmas Carol, Boy Meets Girl, She Also Dances, Betrayal, Closely Related, The Imaginary Invalid, Goodbye Freddy, Major Barbara, April Snow.*

1983–84: *Amadeus, Men's Singles, The Playboy of the Western World, Christmas on Mars, A Christmas Carol, Becoming Memories, Life and Limb, Good, Sally and Marsha, The Sea Gull, Bing and Walker, Angels Fall.*

1984–85: *Saint Joan, Top Girls, The Gigli Concert, Shades, A Christmas Carol, The Show-Off, Reckless, The Importance of Being Earnest, Salt-Water Moon, The Debutante Ball, Rum and Coke, Master Harold . . . and the boys.*

1985–86: *Galileo, Blue Window, Before I Got My Eye Put Out, Painting Churches, A Christmas Carol, The Foreigner, Driving Around the House, As You Like It, Unsuitable for Adults, Buried Child, Virginia, Jitters, Tomfoolery.*

BIBLIOGRAPHY

Published Source:
Los Angeles Times, 1972–86.

Unpublished Sources:
Emmes, David Michael, Personal interview. July 24, 1986.
————. "South Coast Repertory, 1963–1972: A Case Study." Doctoral dissertation,
    University of Southern California, 1973.
Weiner, Sydell. "South Coast Repertory Theatre: Growth and Development 1973–1985."
    Doctoral dissertation, New York University, 1986.

Archival Resource:
Costa Mesa, California. South Coast Repertory. Programs, annual reports, special report
    for the company's twentieth anniversary.

Jeffrey D. Mason

STATE THEATRE OF VIRGINIA. See BARTER THEATRE.

STEPPENWOLF THEATRE COMPANY, Chicago, Illinois, was founded in 1974 by actors Terry Kinney, Jeff Perry, and Gary Sinise. In their first year they presented four plays in eight months, beginning with Paul Zindel's *And Miss Reardon Drinks a Little*. However, in 1976 the company reorganized, expanded, and began to operate on a regular basis. In 1976 they opened an eighty-eight-seat theatre, located in the basement of the Immaculate Conception School in the Chicago suburb of Highland Park, with Eugene Ionesco's *The Lesson*.

A nonprofit theatre, Steppenwolf played a key part in Chicago's booming "off-Loop" theatre movement of the 1970s and 1980s. Dedicated to developing group skills, Steppenwolf built its reputation as a permanent acting ensemble. Directors were usually drawn from the company, thereby reinforcing the group's style. When Steppenwolf opened its 1982 production of Sam Shepard's *True West* in New York City, the company earned national acclaim; the production won Obie Awards for best actor (John Malkovich) and best director (Gary Sinise). Later Steppenwolf productions also found success in New York. In 1985 Steppenwolf received a Tony Award as best American regional theatre. Though retaining their ties to the group, many Steppenwolf members have won national recognition. These include John Malkovich, Joan Allen, John Mahoney, Laurie Metcalf, Kevin Anderson, and Glenne Headly.

Steppenwolf's three founding members all studied theatre at Illinois State University and later recruited other alumni in building the ensemble, including Malkovich, Metcalf, Randy Arney, Francis Guinan, Moira Harris, Tom Irwin, Rondi Reed, and Alan Wilder. Using the Group Theatre* and the Moscow Art Theatre as models, Steppenwolf sought to work collectively in the creation of innovative theatre. Play selection favored established contemporary works, especially those that featured a range of well-drawn characters. The result was a performer's theatre committed to realizing the play's intent.

In 1976 the three original members of Steppenwolf added six new members to the group. One of them, H. E. Baccus, was named artistic director. Kevin Rigdon was also added that year as resident designer. The actors supported themselves doing odd jobs, giving all their free time to rehearsing and doing all technical and administrative work. Averaging five productions a year, Steppenwolf slowly built an audience. In addition to the productions themselves, its audiences enjoyed the experience of recognizing the work of individual ensemble members from play to play.

Five more members were added in 1979. That season culminated in a very successful production of Ralph Pape's *Say Goodnight, Gracie*, which brought the company added attention because it also featured the skills of guest director Austin Pendleton. Seeking a larger audience and a better facility, the company moved in 1980 from its suburban location to the 134-seat Jane Addams Theatre (formerly home of the Hull-House Theatre*), located in Chicago at 3212 North Broadway. Though their reputation and following grew, by 1982 the annual income of Steppenwolf actors averaged only $3,000.

However, 1982 proved a pivotal year for Steppenwolf. The Company again moved, this time to the 211-seat former home of the recently closed St. Nicholas Theatre, located at 2851 North Halsted. It also first drew national attention in October when its production of *True West* moved to New York. National recognition improved working conditions. By 1985 Steppenwolf actors averaged $10,000 a year in salary. Furthermore, Steppenwolf now included nineteen actors and a full-time staff of fifteen. Its annual operating budget had grown to almost $1 million with an annual attendance of 55,000, including 5,300 subscribers.

Steppenwolf has achieved marked critical success, both locally and nationally. By 1986 the company had won twenty-six Joseph Jefferson Awards for excellence in Chicago theatre. Five Steppenwolf productions went on to New York (*True West*, C. P. Taylor's *And a Nightingale Sang . . .*, Lanford Wilson's *Balm in Gilead*, Lyle Kessler's *Orphans*, and Harold Pinter's *The Caretaker*), where their honors have included four Theatre World Awards, four Obie Awards, and two Drama Desk Awards. Finally, in the summer of 1985, Steppenwolf presented Lynn Siefert's *Coyote Ugly* and David Rabe's *Streamers* at the AT&T Performing Arts Festival held at the Kennedy Center in Washington.

The Steppenwolf performance style stressed strong individual character work combined with ensemble interaction. It epitomized the Chicago acting style, which emphasized the expression of concentrated emotion more than the spoken word. The company's play selection reflects this by favoring dramas that portray danger, like *True West, Orphans*, and *Balm in Gilead*. However, it has proved equally capable of achieving the softer lyricism of *And a Nightingale Sang . . .* and the sad irony of Athol Fugard's *A Lesson from Aloes*.

National success has altered the group's makeup and orientation. Individual actors have moved on to work in film and television and on the New York stage. Though they have kept their Steppenwolf affiliation, Malkovich, Mahoney, and

Allen work only occasionally at the Chicago theatre. The company has tried to balance this by adding new members. Still, though the company remains intact on paper, it no longer regularly features the tight interplay of an ensemble accustomed to working together over a period of years. Perhaps because of this the company announced in July 1984 that it would become more of a director's theatre concerned with the presentation of new scripts.

PERSONNEL

Management: Timothy Evans, executive manager (1977–79); Robert Maxey, general manager (1979–82); Russell Smith, business manager (1979–82); John Economos, executive manager (1982–83); Stephan Eich, executive manager (1983–86).

Artistic Directors: H. E. Baccus (1976–79), Terry Kinney (1985–86), Jeff Perry (1982–86), Gary Sinise (1980–82, 1985–86). Others include Dan Ursini, playwright in residence (1978–79); Kevin Rigdon, resident designer (1976–86); Kathryn Richey, assistant to the artistic director (1986); Aubrey Payne, dramaturg (1985–86).

Actors and Actresses: In addition to the ensemble, occasionally other actors performed at Steppenwolf, such as Danny Glover in *A Lesson from Aloes*, Dennis Farina in *Streamers*, and William L. Petersen in *Fool for Love*. However, the ensemble was composed of the following performers: Joan Allen (1977–86), Kevin Anderson (1984–86), Randall Arney (1984–86), H. E. Baccus (1976), Gary Cole (1985–86), Nancy Evans (1976), Frank Galati (1986), Francis Guinan (1979–86), Moira Harris (1976–86), Glenne Headly (1979–86), Tom Irwin (1979–86), Terry Kinney (1974–86), John Mahoney (1979–86), John Malkovich (1976–86), Laurie Metcalf (1976–86), Jeff Perry (1974–86), Rondi Reed (1979–86), Molly Regan (1985–86), Gary Sinise (1974–86), Rick Snyder (1983–86), Alan Wilder (1976–86).

REPERTORY

1974: *And Miss Reardon Drinks a Little, Grease, Rosencrantz and Guildenstern Are Dead, The Glass Menagerie.* (There wasn't a 1975 season.)

1976: *The Lesson, The Indian Wants the Bronx, Birdbath, The Lover, Look, We've Come Through, The Dumbwaiter, The Loveliest Afternoon of the Year.*

1977: *The Seahorse, Birdbath* and *The Indian Wants the Bronx, Our Late Night, Mack, Anything Goes, Over the Rainbow, Rosencrantz and Guildenstern Are Dead.*

1978: *Sandbar Flatland, Home Free* and *Krapp's Last Tape, The Caretaker, The 5th of July, Philadelphia, Here I Come!.*

1979: *Exit the King, The Caretaker, The Glass Menagerie, Waiting for Lefty, Say Goodnight, Gracie.*

1980: *Bonjour, là, Bonjour, Death of a Salesman, Quiet Jeannie Green, Balm in Gilead, Absent Friends.*

1981: *Savages, No Man's Land, Arms and the Man, Of Mice and Men, Waiting for the Parade.*

1982: *Loose Ends, True West, The House, A Prayer for My Daughter, And a Nightingale Sang . . . .*

1983: *Cloud 9, A Moon for the Misbegotten, The Miss Firecracker Contest, The Hothouse, Our Town.*

1984: *Tracers, Fool for Love, Stage Struck, The Three Sisters.*

1985: *Orphans, Coyote Ugly, Miss Julie, The Caretaker, You Can't Take It with You.*

1986: *A Lesson from Aloes, Lydie Breeze, Frank's Wild Years.*

Stuart J. Hecht

T

THEATRE COLLECTIVE. See WORKERS' LABORATORY THEATRE.

THEATRE '47—'59, DALLAS, TEXAS. See MARGO JONES THEATRE.

THEATRE OF ACTION. See WORKERS' LABORATORY THEATRE.

THEATRE OF THE LIVING ARTS. Paradoxically, two suburban housewives with only amateur theatrical experience brought Philadelphia, in 1963 the nation's fourth largest city, into the post–World War II professional repertory theatre movement. Former Cheltenham Playhouse and Hedgerow Theatre producers Jean Goldman and Celia Silverman believed their city's theatrical reliance on flagging Broadway try-outs was a serious detriment to its indigenous culture. To remedy this situation they organized in 1963 the Philadelphia Council for the Performing Arts (PCPA), a nonprofit educational corporation that would act as the sponsor for their projected professional resident theatre. As the PCPA's ranks grew to nearly 700 individual members, private citizens all, a disused movie theatre located along the southern periphery of Philadelphia's eastern downtown at 334 South Street was rented to house the proposed resident troupe. Mayor James H. J. Tate and 350 civic leaders gave their blessings on March 19, 1964, officially launching Philadelphia's Theatre of the Living Arts (TLA).

PCPA raised funds and hired architect Frank Weise to accomplish a $20,000 renovation of the theatre. Theatre professionals, mostly from New York, were secured to select plays and to recruit professional actors, again primarily from New York. Nonetheless, Philadelphia volunteers supplied the free labor needed to open the theatre and maintain it. While the Philadelphia Chapter of the Brandeis University's National Women's Committee executed a subscription drive, with prices for the as-yet-unspecified five-play season set at $6 to $22.50, PCPA members and their families carried out much of the theatre renovation work themselves. This amateur undertaking delayed the renovation process (which was further compromised by union protests), and the theatre's opening was postponed several times. Finally, the new Theatre of the Living Arts and its resident troupe, the Southwark Company, premiered at a black-tie affair on January 6, 1965. Not until January 12, 1965, however, were critics invited to view on the TLA's new open-thrust stage the troupe's demanding first production, Bertolt Brecht's philosophical examination of science's responsibility to humanity, *Galileo*.

Theatre of the Living Arts derived its name from its proposed goal: to bring to Philadelphia live performing arts in all categories, new art distinguished from the old—especially from empty museum pieces—by a "living" relevance to modern life. Although live theatre was to have priority, music and dance programs were presented on Monday and Tuesday evenings while the Southwark Company rested. If the theatre's title captured the spirit of the new, the company's title captured the spirit of history pervading Philadelphia. Southwark was the colonial designation of that area just south of Penn's green country town. Outside city parameters, it escaped theatre censorship and consequently hosted many of America's first professional theatre companies. Indeed, it was on this very same South Street—above Fourth Street, less than a block from the TLA—that the country's first permanent theatre, the New Theatre in Southwark (also called the Southwark Theatre), was built in 1766. And it was in this theatre that America's first indigenous professional play, Thomas Godfrey's *Prince of Parthia*, premiered in 1767. The Southwark Company, it was intimated, would carry on this time-honored professional tradition of contributing to American culture and creating new "firsts." Perhaps unconsciously the name also suggested that this Southwark Company, like those of old, would remain just far enough beyond society's fringe to be its conscience.

Artistic director Andre Gregory molded the TLA into a theatre of intellectual query and spiritual quest. The young Gregory had impeccable credentials: he had been a member of the directors' unit of the Actors' Studio and he was a cofounder and former director for the Seattle Repertory Theatre*. But it was the Paris-born, Harvard-educated Gregory's commitment to an expansive internationalism in the arts that shaped his TLA directorship. Gregory had studied dramatic theory, especially that of Antonin Artaud and Brecht, and had observed firsthand the workings of such varied modern companies as the Gate Theatre, Dublin, the Berliner Ensemble, and the San Francisco Actor's Workshop*. Gregory synthesized new performance theory and avant-garde performance practice in a personal vision. His theatre aimed at communal inspiration and political change, accomplished through sometimes jarring, always rousing sensuality.

Gregory's staging rather than his repertory choices built an early avant-garde reputation for TLA. Although the troupe's productions frequently espoused antiwar themes, and Gregory often commented publicly on the nuclear threat, most of TLA's initial plays strayed little from the European and American "masterpieces" that conventionally constituted the repertory of regional and amateur art theatres. Guests directed many critically well-received productions. Gregory's own productions, however, prompted the most critical enthusiasm, and his style and tone established the troupe's orientation. Even unsuccessful productions were lauded for their freshness, originality, and unreserved international flavor. Critics would eventually term Gregory's direction "a Coney Island of the senses," but even in the first season Gregory's rich carnival scene in *Galileo* and his humorous interpretation of Samuel Beckett's dark *Endgame* characters as vaudeville comics convinced commentators everywhere that TLA was extraordinary. Indeed, *Endgame* convinced the Rockefeller Foundation's representatives to provide funding for an associate director and a resident set designer for the company's second season.

Gregory's Marxist leanings prompted a strong preference for an ensemble that resembled an egalitarian artists' collective. Initially, Southwark Company actors forsook the usual program biographies for simple alphabetical listings. Although this practice was dropped, strong ensemble performance highlighted Gregory's tenure, a feat especially remarkable because financial constraints dictated a permanent Equity ensemble of less than ten. An ascetic and naturalistic acting style emerged, and several of Gregory's core performers, notably Ron Leibman, Anthony Zerbe, and David Hurst, went on to distinguished careers on Broadway and in Hollywood.

Gregory, recognizing always the importance of widespread exposure, tempted critics to come to TLA from as far away as London, Seattle, and Washington, D.C. He also promoted visits by well-known playwrights, such as Jack Gelber, Maria Irene Fornes, and Robert Lowell. The troupe also hosted the Royal Shakespeare Company. Gregory further enhanced TLA's status by securing such celebrities as Ben Gazzara, Rod Steiger, Stella Adler, and Arthur Miller to promote the troupe on Philadelphia radio and television. But Gregory tempered this cosmopolitanism with programs of strictly local appeal, such as a radio show on the local WUHY-FM, a Southwark Theatre School (added in 1965) offering Philadelphians acting, speech, and movement courses taught by TLA actors, and a study guide and workshop project for area high school and college teachers.

TLA radiated success in its early seasons, boasting a growing subscription list that numbered more than 8,000, one of the five largest subscription lists among the more than forty regional theatres then operating in the United States. TLA ran five productions for three weeks each in 1964–65 and then escalated each run to five weeks in 1965–66. In 1966–67 the number of productions rose to six and a sixth week of performance was slated for each.

Nevertheless, TLA's achievements began to be tarnished by internal difficulties. The PCPA's board was altered by a series of replacements. Meanwhile the managing director in 1964–65, A. Gino Giglio, was replaced by public relations director David Lunney. Lunney, too, soon came under fire, accused by the board of exercising too little fiscal responsibility. In truth, TLA had raised only $200,000 of $250,000 needed in its first season and had allowed this deficit to rise in each subsequent season. By 1966–67 operating expenses grew to

$360,000, severely complicating the deficit situation. Audience numbers remained high and several shows each season played to capacity, but the small, 431-seat (sometimes 486-seat) theatre simply could not prosper on box-office receipts alone. Although governmental and philanthropic grants assisted greatly, the fervent local corporate and communal support needed to sustain TLA was not forthcoming. The board believed this to be the fault of the managing director and, to a lesser degree, the artistic director. In late June 1966 Fred Goldman, by then vice president of the PCPA board, formally charged both Lunney and Gregory with mismanagement.

Board president Thomas Fleming initially backed Gregory, but questions regarding the direction in which Gregory led the company remained unanswered. The PCPA board focused concern on Gregory's plan to tour successful productions to colleges, thereby stripping the company of many of its most accomplished actors and weakening the ensemble. Gregory had toured his own *Endgame* to Yale University in the fall of 1966 while, at TLA, William Carlos Williams' *A Dream of Love* floundered badly. However, when the TLA's first new play, the controversial *Beclch*, by off-off-Broadway playwright Rochelle Owens, premiered as part of Gregory's novel 1966–67 all-American season, tensions particularly heightened. Called by the theatre's own public relations staff "brazen" and "erotic," *Beclch* attempted to expose Man's savage nature by enacting the wanton murders and ritualistic tortures of Beclch, a cruel Mother Earth figure who rules the jungle. As if near-nudity, erotic dancing, and sadomasochistic rituals were not enough to make staid Philadelphians disgruntled, an onstage cockfight and a goat sacrifice provoked sharp protests from local animal lovers. The play, furthermore, opened during Christmas week, making it, for many, an obvious effort to undercut traditional values.

Critics who found *Beclch* flawed and formless nevertheless upheld Gregory's artistic prerogative in producing the piece. Nonetheless, it was immediately after *Beclch's* run that Gregory effected what the press termed an emotional departure. Quite a few troupe actors, Leibman and Hurst among them, resigned as well. (Gregory, of course, went on to form the Manhattan Project, a theatre group affiliated with New York University, whose achievements included the famed 1970 *Alice in Wonderland* as well as revised stagings of several TLA productions, notably those of *Endgame* and Anton Chekhov's *Uncle Vanya*.)

The PCPA board envisioned an easy transition, fairly certain they could replace Gregory with George L. Sherman, formerly of Washington's Arena Stage*. During Sherman's stint as the TLA's associate artistic director in 1965–66, he had directed several well-received productions, especially that of Richard Brinsley Sheridan's *The Critic*, and had withdrawn from the troupe only because he and Gregory quarreled over artistic control. However, after several months of negotiations, during which Sherman selected the 1967–68 season, he withdrew, citing the board's failure to grant him the creative freedom he needed. New managing director John Bos was left, in June 1967, not only severely in debt, but also without any artistic leadership.

An undaunted Bos encouraged the board, by now fed up with what they viewed as artistic butterflies, to hire a resident rather than an artistic director. This resident director would be paid less because he would be "but another member of the ensemble" and not responsible for administrative decision-making. (This now would rest totally with managing director Bos.) When the bearded, twenty-nine-year-old Art Wolff arrived at TLA he had only to direct the plays selected by Sherman. A change to a rotating repertory policy in which two or three plays would alternate performances during most weeks was meant to give more variety and to deemphasize any one production. However, all of the first three productions, John Osborne's *The Entertainer*, Harold Pinter's *The Caretaker*, and Oscar Wilde's *The Importance of Being Earnest*, received rancorous reviews, despite a rash of last-minute actor firings and rehirings. TLA was left for most of the season with three weak shows in repertory.

In a belated attempt to appease critical disdain at its safe, dull lineup, TLA secured a play by ex-convict C. Lester Franklin to replace the scheduled *Twelfth Night*. *A Scaffold for Marionettes: A Myth*, which revolved around the 1963 caning death of a Negro waitress by a wealthy white man at a Baltimore society ball, took a startling, expressionistic look at American racial relations. But if this play fit the bill for relevance, it failed to meet critical requirements for form and style. Attendance continued to drop sharply, despite TLA's last-ditch effort to import actress-director Sarah Sanders from the National Theatre of France to direct Jean Anouilh's *The Rehearsal* (in which she had originally starred). The season closed three weeks early, on April 7, 1968.

Location remained a key problem for TLA. In the mid-1960s TLA's immediate neighborhood was only beginning gentrification. Later commentators would credit the theatre with aiding the redevelopment of southern Society Hill and especially South Street, which by the 1980s had become one of the most upscale and trendy shopping districts in the city. But when TLA opened, the street and its community remained predominantly working class with only the most adventuresome and resourceful bohemians willing to convert dusty retail stores into makeshift art galleries, restaurants, and boutiques. Indeed, when TLA opened, it was sandwiched between a junk-filled, grimy Richie's Electrical Shop and Max Brookstein's King of Dresses. (Philadelphia's mostly immigrant Jewish garment industry branched directly off this portion of South Street.) It was little wonder that commentators observed that Philadelphia's typical socialite theatre-goers, even those who resided only a few blocks to the north in Society Hill, termed South Street "that awful neighborhood."

TLA's location, thus, dictated a youthful, open-minded, and bohemian clientele. This tendency toward an audience of students and artistes was further enhanced by the troupe's consistently young leadership and by its daring, experimental, antiwar, anti-Establishment persona. But as TLA became more and more aligned in the public view with the aims and style of the hippie movement, its financial footing became increasingly precarious. Its failure to win the sponsorship of the mainstream social set led to its inability to secure adequate corporate sponsorship.

TLA, housed in a former movie house, also lacked adequate backstage and dressing facilities, which encouraged PCPA's contemplation of new quarters for its theatre group. Negotiations to secure the Walnut Street Theatre, located in the heart of Philadelphia's downtown at Ninth and Walnut streets, commenced in 1968 but came to no avail when corporate backing for TLA failed to materialize. The niggardly support granted TLA by wealthy Philadelphians was pointed up by the Federal Council on the Arts when, in 1967–68, it gave TLA a matching rather than an outright grant (for $15,000) to spur local contributions.

Meanwhile TLA continued to operate under severe cost-cutting measures. From early 1968 PCPA rented the theatre to touring dance and musical groups. Finally, touring dramatic bookings, notably those of the National Theatre of the Deaf, were incorporated into TLA's season. In 1968–69 six of eleven offerings were imports, and the five resident productions were crammed into a January–May calendar. Neither an artistic nor a resident director was employed, and a no-frills program replaced the glossy *Playbill*. Critics generally were kinder than in the previous season, but still took exception to the guest director policy that they thought responsible for an enfeebled ensemble.

To allay such criticism, a relatively new PCPA board again hired an artistic director in 1969–70. But they now chose to embellish rather than downplay TLA's hippie image. Their choice was Tom Bissinger, a young San Franciscan whose directorial experience included stints at the LaMama and American Place theatres in New York. Bissinger had been introduced to Philadelphia audiences during the previous season when his staging of Jean-Claude van Itallie's irreverent *America Hurrah* toured to the TLA. Later that season he guest-directed TLA's public premiere of Sam Shepard's avant-garde fantasy-comedy, *La Turista*. His first act as artistic director was to string up across South Street TLA's new motto, ''Go with the Beat,'' and he facilitated his stated goal of fusing theatre and rock music by hiring a resident rock group.

Under Bissinger's guidance even a production of George Farquhar's eighteenth-century comedy, *The Recruiting Officer*, was termed ''psychedelic.'' The emphasis shifted further toward new American plays of the off-off-Broadway type, which the troupe encouraged by supporting a public playwrights' workshop (it introduced the works of Albert Innaurato) and by opening a hundred-seat, environmental, nominal-admission performance area called The Space in TLA's scenery and costume building on Oriana Street. A new program format highlighted hippie-era priorities, with actors' horoscopes and personal views taking precedence over summaries of their theatrical backgrounds. When Danny DeVito, shortly to become a television star on *Taxi*, appeared as part of the troupe, his program biography read ''a Scorpio . . . a very hip sex nut . . . a most charming hound.'' Not surprisingly, rock musicals were to be a part of TLA's new bill, and the troupe jubilantly accepted a $22,000 National Endowment for the Arts grant to produce Rosalyn Drexler's *The Line of Least Existence*, about the adventures of a female hippie runaway. Bissinger's improvisational directing style garnered critical praise, as did the band of youthful new actors, among them Judd Hirsch, who also would come to national attention on the sitcom *Taxi*.

Again, however, glowing prospects darkened. The Space, which had opened with *Gargoyle Cartoons*, a collection of Michael McClure playlets, was closed by city building officials for code violations. New plays proved problematic for local critics, especially Ronald Ribman's *Harry, Noon and Night* and Drexler's musical. That the musical was mercilessly panned was particularly crucial, for these reviews not only negatively colored future grant chances, but also cost the troupe additional funding, for they had purchased its future production rights. Accommodation to patrons' whims, to the point of making dinner reservations for them, could not make up for the constant scheduling changes. Play runs shrank to a mere three weeks, and TLA increasingly relied on intern actors. TLA's mounting deficit and diminishing audiences forced it to close its 1969–70 season in February after only three resident productions. Despite yet another new PCPA president and a Hass Foundation grant of $75,000, TLA officially filed for bankruptcy on August 14, 1970, leaving Philadelphia as it had found it: devoid of any resident professional theatre.

PERSONNEL

Management: Philadelphia Council for the Performing Arts, producer (1964–70); Andre Gregory, artistic director (1964–67); A. Gino Giglio, managing director (1964–65); David Lunney, managing director (1965–67); Art Wolff, resident director (1967–68); John Bos, managing director (1967–68) and producing director (1968–70); Tom Bissinger, artistic director (1969–70).

Stage Directors: Jim Ambandos, Tom Bissinger, Mark Epstein, André Gregory, Jerome Guardino, Lawrence Kornfield, Gene Lasko, Charles Maryan, Gennaro Montanino, Charles Olsen, John O'Shaughnessy, Stephen Porter, Dennis Rosa, Ronald Roston, Sarah Sanders, George L. Sherman, Harold Stone, James D. Waring, Art Wolff.

Scenic Artists (sets and lights): Jack Bates, John Bos, John Conklin, Robert E. Darling, Don Earl, Marsha L. Eck, William Eggleston, Karl Eigsti, Holly Haas, Neil Peter Jampolis, D. Atwood Jenkins, Eugene Lee, Eric Martin, David Mitchell, Roger Morgan, Richard Nelson, Frank Quinlan, Wolfgang Roth, Nicholas Russiyan, Douglas W. Schmidt, Fred Voelpel, Robert Wagner, James D. Waring.

Costumers: Nancy Christoffersen, John Conklin, Robert E. Darling, Melly Eigsti, William French, Holly Haas, Eric Martin, Franne Newman, Leigh Rand, Domingo Rodriguez, Adam Sage, Pearl Somner, Caley Summers, Dorothy Summers, Fred Voelpel.

Actors and Actresses: Alfonso Akeela, Kevin Allen, Anatole, Michael Bacon, Ruth Baker, Susan Barrister, *George Bartenieff* (1965–67), Ed Bernard, Linda Berry, Ed Blair, Peter Blaxill, Lawrence Block, Celeste Bonnaire, *Tom Brannum* (1965–67), Peter Bailey Britton, Marc Brown, Mark Carvel, Kevin Coleman, Marilyn Coleman, David Congdon, Daryle Ann Corr, William Countryman, Ed Crowley, Gretel Cummings, Jo Ann Cunningham, Joan Darling, Jeanne De Baer, Bob DeFrank, *Jerome Dempsey* (1964–67), Danny DeVito, Dan Dietrich, Rachel Drexler, Flora Elkins, Heidi Endress, Ted Fertik, Crystal Field, Frank Freda, Morgan Freeman, *Jonathan Frid* (1965–66), Sharon Gans,

Sylvia Gassell, George Gaynes, William Gearhart, Robert Gentry, Alan Glass, James Glenn, Ken Goldman, Merwin Goldsmith, Adam Gopnick, Alison Gopnik, Hilary Gopnik, Morgan Gopnik, Richard Granat, Micki Grant, Dylan Green, Gene Gross, Philip Baker Hall, *Brendan Hanlon* (1967–69), Marcia Haufrecht, Bruce Heighley, Betsy Henn, *Judd Hirsch* (1969–70), Ken Horning, Judy Howshall, *David Hurst* (1964–67), Richard Huttinger, Zviah Igdalsky, Arnette Jens, Stacey Jones, Terry Jones, Andrew Kahn, *Marion Killinger* (1969–70), *Sally Kirkland* (1964–66, 1969–70), Virginia Kiser, Adelaide Klein, Edward Kovens, Simm Landres, Bob Latch, Ralph Lee, Andrew Lenton, *Ron Leibman* (1964–67), James John Little, Betty Liveright, Michael McGuire, Don McHenry, Marianne MacPhail, *Gloria Maddox* (1967–69), Valerie Mamches, Ruth Manning, Janice Mars, David Matson, Mary Lou Metzger, Brian Mitchell, Wendy Mitchell, Sylvia Montgomery, Philip Morgan, Jeremiah Morris, Patsy Perkins, *Miriam Phillips* (1964–67), Wendell K. Phillips, H. Latta Pinkerton, Joan Poor, Paul B. Price, *Michael Procaccino* (1968–69), Nicholas Pryor, Anne Ramsey, Logan Ramsey, Jerome Raphael, Michael Reed, Linda Richardson, Andrew Robinson, Paul Rodger-Reid, Kathleen Roland, Allen Rosenblum, *Ronald Roston* (1966–69), *David Rounds* (1969–70), Harvey Rovine, Sam Rulon, Frank Savino, Sam Schacht, Susan Sharkey, Audrey Shaw, Vivienne Shub, James Simmons, Pamela Simpson, Benjamin Slack, Peggy Slack, Larry Smith, *Lois Smith* (1964–67), Mitchell Smith, Lorraine Spritze, Dimitra Steris, Andrea Stonorov, Sonny Streater, Deborah Sussel, David Swenson, Susan Tait, Amy Taubin, David Tress, Nadyne Turney, James Valentine, Richard Voronkov, M. Emmet Walsh, Cheryl Lynn White, Ann Whiteside, Kate Wilkinson, Hilda Young, Janis Young, Harris Yulin, *Anthony Zerbe* (1965–66).

Guest Performers: Georgia Burke, Paddy Croft, Robert Fields, Gertrude Jeanette, Lee Kissman, Dermot McNamara, Estelle Parsons, Diana Sands.

REPERTORY

1964–65: *Galileo, Tiger at the Gates, The Misanthrope, Desire Under the Elms, Endgame.*

1965–66: *Uncle Vanya, The Critic* and *They, The Stronger* and *Miss Julie, The Last Analysis.*

1966–67: *A Dream of Love, Room Service, Beclch, The Time of Your Life, U.S.A., Phaedra.*

1967–68: *The Entertainer, The Caretaker, The Importance of Being Earnest, A Scaffold for Marionettes, The Rehearsal.*

1968–69: *Six Characters in Search of an Author, Little Murders, The Collection* and *Muzeeka, La Turista, The Hostage.*

1969–70: *The Recruiting Officer, Gargoyle Cartoons, Harry, Noon and Night, The Line of Least Existence.*

BIBLIOGRAPHY

Published Sources:
Philadelphia Evening Bulletin, 1964–70.
Philadelphia Inquirer, 1964–70.

Archival Resource:
Philadelphia, Pennsylvania. Free Library of Philadelphia. Philadelphia Theatre Collection.
    Programs, actor files, and Theatre of the Living Arts file.

                                                            Mari Kathleen Fielder

THEATRE "12." See FRONT STREET THEATRE.

THEATRE UNION. During the depths of the Depression the commercial theatre's failure to address social issues stimulated Charles R. Walker to create a
theatre that would. A young scholar and novelist, Walker and his wife, Adelaide,
spent eighteen months raising money and securing the off-Broadway Civic Repertory Theatre at 166 West Fourteenth Street to house the Theatre Union's first
production in November 1933.

A group of similarly minded young playwrights joined the Walkers on the
Theatre Union's executive board. George Sklar, Michael Blankfort, Albert
Maltz, and Paul Peters were joined in 1934 by Victor Wolfson, another play-
wright. Others, besides the Walkers, included Margaret Larkin, a writer; Liston
M. Oak, a journalist of leftist bent; Mary Fox, executive director of the League
for Industrial Democracy; Sylvia Fennigston, a former Group Theatre* actress;
Eleanor Fitzgerald, formerly of the Provincetown Players; Samuel Friedman;
Manuel Gomez; Martin Wolfson; and Charles Friedman. The executive board
also appointed an advisory board covering a considerable range of political
viewpoints: Sidney Howard, a successful Broadway playwright; Lynn Riggs,
author of *Green Grow the Lilacs*; Rose McClendon, the noted black actress;
actor Paul Muni; Joseph Freeman from the *New Masses*, a newspaper of the
workers' movement; and H.W.L. Dana, a proponent of Soviet drama.

The Theatre Union manifesto proposed that the group would produce plays
dealing boldly with social conflicts, the economic, emotional, and cultural problems confronting the majority of the people. The Union set prices deliberately
low, from 30 cents to $1.50, with more than half the seats priced under a dollar,
in hopes of attracting those who did not normally attend any theatre. Subscription
memberships and benefit theatre parties would, it was hoped, organize the audiences.

Almost from the start the Theatre Union excited controversy. The ultra-Left
Theatre Collective, incensed by socialists on the executive board and the salaries
paid to the Theatre Union employees, demanded an investigation before the
Theatre Union had staged its first production.

In their first season the Theatre Union produced two scripts for a total of 300
performances, drawing 300,000 audience members. The first, *Peace on Earth*,
by Sklar and Maltz (both former students of George Pierce Baker at Yale University), depicted an ordinary citizen's conversion to political activism to protest
arms sales to foreign powers. The second offering, *Stevedore*, by Sklar and
Peters, was to be the Theatre Union's only production concerned with the black
dilemma in the United States, a matter of no concern to the professional theatre

at the time. The Theatre Union also desegregated seating at a time when blacks were seated only in balconies of professional theatres. Any white organization that complained of this policy was refused tickets from the Theatre Union.

The second season opened with Friedrich Wolf's *Sailors of Cattaro*, a blunt statement of the superiority of totalitarianism over democracy. The script, which had received more than 1,000 performances in Moscow, presented a Marxist view of the failed uprising of 6,000 Austrian sailors just before World War I. The Union's second production of 1934–35 was Maltz's *Black Pit*, a depiction of West Virginian coal-mining in which a miner betrays his fellow workers and is ostracized by them. Both plays ran less than one hundred performances.

The Theatre Union initiated a one-act script contest in 1934, hoping to discover new talent. The first winner was *God's in His Heaven*, by Philip Stevenson, published by the Theatre Union. The company also began a dance unit and held regular acting classes, concentrating on the Stanislavski system. As well, they held an annual costume ball to supplement box-office income.

By January 1936 the executive board claimed attendance of 523,000 for their first five plays, but also an annual deficit of $15,000. Figures published by the Theatre Union suggested their productions cost an average of $6,000 each to stage, including design and construction of settings, crew and actors' rehearsal salaries, costumes and props, advertising, and general overhead during rehearsals. By contrast, settings alone might cost $6,000 in the commercial theatre at this time.

Average running costs were $3,000 a week, with the maximum weekly salary for staff or actors being $40. Since the average Theatre Union season was thirty-one weeks, average annual costs came to $128,500.

Of the total audience to this point of 523,000, 23,000 saw the Theatre Union productions free with tickets distributed each week through settlement houses and trade unions. A quarter of a million audience members bought their tickets at the box office; the others bought theirs through professional organizations, unions, and other groups who regularly purchased large blocks of tickets. Some 200 such groups regularly saw shows at the Theatre Union. Audiences averaged 990 in a house seating 1,100. Average weekly income was $3,650; a thirty-one-week season grossed $113,150, leaving a deficit of $15,350.

Six months after *Black Pit* closed, the Theatre Union opened its fifth production, *The Mother*, dramatized by Bertolt Brecht from Maxim Gorky's novel of the same name. The production failed miserably, the company failing to comprehend Brecht's intended *verfremdungseffekt*. Brecht himself visited rehearsals but condemned the entire effort, stating, "Dass ist scheisse."

When *Mother* closed after twenty-nine performances, the Theatre Union had nothing ready to replace it, so they took over the failing Broadway production of Albert Bein's *Let Freedom Ring*. The production ran a mere 79 performances, having run 108 uptown. The script dealt with the displacement of Carolina mountaineers forced to work in cotton mills.

On February 16, 1936, the Theatre Union offered a Sunday night special program, repeating it on March 3. *Picket Line* presented strikers' oratory as it might have been written by Shakespeare, Chekhov, and Noel Coward. A dance, *Strange American Funeral*, was premiered by Anna Sokolow and her company. "Letter to the President," a song written by Sklar and Peters, was sung by Juanita Hall and danced by Miriam Blecher. Finally, John Wexley's *Running Dogs*, concerning Mao-Tse Tung, was directed by Anthony Brown and acted by members of the Theatre Union Studio. Although planned as a regular offering, only one such bill was ever presented.

The Theatre Union closed the 1935–36 season with Victor Wolfson's *Bitter Stream*, the board having rejected Irwin Shaw's *Bury the Dead*. *Bitter Stream* depicted the daily living conditions under Mussolini, the first play seen in New York on the subject. Although the leftist press lauded the piece, the mainstream newspapers found little to praise, and the show closed after sixty-one performances.

As the 1936–37 season began, the Theatre Union found itself without a home, the owner of the Civic Rep having decided to tear down the building to make room for a parking lot. The company decided to move uptown and produce two plays, John Howard Lawson's *Marching Song* and Sklar's *Life and Death of an American*. Keeping their top ticket price at $1.50, they hoped to sign up 10,000 subscribers. They also hoped to form a permanent acting company and a mobile group to perform in union halls. Of all these plans, only one took place.

In February 1937 the Theatre Union opened *Marching Song*, their last production, a proletariat drama about out-of-work auto workers. Such leftist organs as the *New Theatre*, the *New Masses*, and the *Daily Worker* praised it highly; again, the commercial press found it tepid. After sixty-one performances the show closed, and with it ended the Theatre Union.

Adding to their difficulties was the Theatre Union practice of appointing a production committee from the executive board for each play. All decisions had to come from this committee, although the actual work was done by volunteers and office staff. The result was extremely difficult and complex administrative action. Eventually Lem Ward was designated as producer, cutting through much of the red tape, but the damage had been done. The Depression made it difficult to find financial backing; the Federal Theatre was in full operation with a 55-cent top ticket price, and the New Theatre League offered more radical drama at similar prices. In August 1937 the executive board announced the group's demise.

PERSONNEL

Producers: Charles R. Walker (1933–36), Lem Ward (1936–37).

Business Manager: Victor Wolfson.

Directors: Jacob Ben-Ami, Michael Blankfort, Anthony Brown, Charles Friedman, Irving Gordon, Worthington Miner, Robert Sinclair, Victor Wolfson.

Scenic Designers: Howard Bay, Tom Adrian Crecraft, Mordecai Gorelik, S. Syrjain, Cleon Throckmorton.

Composer: Hans Eisler.

Actors and Actresses (Italics indicates appearances in two or more Theatre Union productions): Frieda Allman, Richard Barrows, Paula Bauersmith, *Frances Bavier*, Alan Baxter, *Walter Beck*, Malcolm Lee Beggs, Abner Biberman, Tommi Bissell, Donald A. Black, G. I. Harry Boiden, *Isabel Bonner, John Boruff*, Halliam Bosworth, Aldrich Bowker, Dorothy Brackett, Alice Brooks, Gena Brown, Hubert Brown, John Brown, Arthur Bruce, Grover Burgess, Robert Calle, Jack Carter, Norma Chambers, Fanya Cherenko, *Lee J. Cobb*, Frank Conlan, Cario Conte, Curt Conway, Thomas Coffin Cooke, Edwin Cooper, Theodore Corday, Maria Coxe, *Howard Da Silva, Alvin Dexter*, Charles Dingle, Lew Eckels, Nonnie Edwards, William C. Elkins, Tom Ewell, Alfonso Fenderson, Elvin Field, *Elliott Fisher*, Gertrude Flynn, Bart Ford, Clyde Franklin, Frank Gabrielson, Ernest Gann, Will Geer, Toni Gilman, Irving Gordoe, *Millicent Green*, Edward Everett Hale, Robert Harris, Jack Hartley, Georgette Harvey, Robert Hayes, Helen Henry, Alfred Herrick, Fred Herwick, David Hoffman, John Huntington, *Rex Ingram*, Ethel Intrepidi, Dean Jenks, *Harold Johnerud*, Phil Jones, *Charles Jordan*, Rose Keane, Robert Keith, Victor Kilian, Manart Kippler (or Masart Kippen?), *Charles Kuhn*, Harry LeMay, Harry Levian, Carrington Lewis, *Lester Lonergan, Jr.*, Lester Lonergan III, *James MacDonald*, W. H. Malone, Lisa Markah, Sidney Mason, June Meier, Dodson Mitchell, Russell Morrison, Caroline Newcombe, Charles Niemeyer, Neill O'Malley, John O'Shaughnessy, *Sidney Packer*, Douglas Parkhurst, Mary Perry, Shirley Poirier, Robert Porterfield, Tom Powers, *Robert Reed*, Frederich Roland, Amelia Romana, *Tony Ross*, Herbert Rudley, Eddie Ryan, Jr., Bigelow Sayre, John Scruff, *Vincent Sherman*, Charles Smith, *Hester Sondergaard*, Leslie Stafford, *Paul Stein*, Royal C. Stout, Lucille Strudwick, Sheppard Strudwick, Susie Sutton, Jerry Sylvan, Maria Tartar, Joseph Taulane, George Oliver Taylor, Edna Thomas, *Charles Thompson*, Robert Thomsen, *George Tobias, Frank Tweddell*, Lili Eisenlohr Valenty, Albert Van Dekker, Walter Vonnegut, Herta Ware, Helen Waren, Al Watts, Leigh Whippen, *Jack Williams*, Robert B. Williams, *Martin Wolfson*, Marjorie Wood, *Stanley G. Wood*, Ray Yeats, P. A. Xanthe.

REPERTORY

1933: *Peace on Earth*.
1934: *Stevedore, Sailors of Cattaro*.
1935: *Black Pit, Let Freedom Ring*.
1936: *Mother, Bitter Stream*.
1937: *Marching Song*.

BIBLIOGRAPHY

Published Sources:
New York Times, 1935–37.
Goldstein, Malcolm. *The Political Stage: American Drama and Theatre of the Great Depression*. New York: Oxford University Press, 1974, ch. 3 and 8.
Himelstein, Morgan Y. *Drama Was a Weapon: The Left-Wing Theatre in New York, 1929–1941*. New Brunswick, N.J.: Rutgers University Press, 1963, ch. 4.

Archival Resource:
New York, New York. New York Public Library. Billy Rose Theatre Collection. Scrapbooks of newspaper clippings, 1933–35.

Stephen M. Archer

THEATRE WORKSHOP, LONG BEACH. See SOUTH COAST REPER-
TORY.

TRINITY SQUARE PLAYHOUSE. See TRINITY SQUARE REPERTORY
COMPANY.

TRINITY SQUARE REPERTORY COMPANY, Providence, Rhode Island,
was originally known as "The Repertory Theatre in the Square," and subsequently as "Trinity Square Playhouse." In the fall of 1963 a group of citizens,
including lawyers, doctors, businessmen, and members of several community
theatre groups, formed a nonprofit corporation called the Foundation for Repertory Theatre of Rhode Island. Dedicated to the formation of a professional
theatre with a professional director and to the production of new plays as well
as the classics, the board of trustees of the Foundation—with Milton Stanzler
as coordinating chairman of the executive committee—invited Adrian Hall to
direct several plays in the spring of 1964. Although Hall's other professional
commitments prevented his coming to Providence until April 1964, the Repertory
Theatre in the Square opened its first production, Brendan Behan's *The Hostage*,
on March 14, 1964. With Ira Zuckerman as the professional guest director from
New York and with local actors and actresses as members of the company, *The
Hostage* was staged in the social hall of the Trinity Union Methodist Church on
Trinity Square (at the corners of Broad and Bridgham streets in Providence).
The theatre's second production, Federico García Lorca's *The House of Bernarda
Alba*, also directed by Zuckerman, opened April 10, 1964.

   The final two productions of this first season, Tennessee Williams' *Orpheus
Descending* (opening May 8, 1964) and a double bill of Edward Albee's *The
Death of Bessie Smith* and *The American Dream* (opening June 5, 1964), were
directed by Adrian Hall. Because the Hall productions were especially well
received and gate receipts and favorable reviews indicated that the community
would support the new theatre, Hall and the members of the board of trustees
began to plan for the next season with a more professional organization.

   The modern regional theatre movement had begun with the Margo Jones
Theatre* in Dallas, Texas. During the 1950s and 1960s this movement continued
to flourish in the major urban centers nationwide. Although the Charles Playhouse
in Boston was the first regional theatre in New England, during the 1960s other
resident repertory companies established in the northeast included the Theatre
Company of Boston, the Hartford Stage Company, and the Long Wharf Theatre*
in New Haven, Connecticut. As part of this widespread theatre movement Adrian

Hall came to Providence, where he has continued to serve as the director of the Trinity Square Repertory Company throughout its twenty-two-year history.

After graduating from college, Hall, a native of Van, Texas, had studied at the Pasadena Playhouse and at the Actors' Studio in New York. During the 1950s he had worked with Margo Jones in Dallas. Having successfully directed several widely acclaimed off-Broadway productions, national touring productions, and professional productions for theatre companies in Arizona, Nebraska, North Carolina, and New Hampshire and for the Milwaukee Repertory Theatre*, Hall found in Rhode Island a place where he could develop his artistic talents without the pressures of New York commercialism and where the community was enthusiastic about establishing a professional theatre with a permanent ensemble.

In July 1964, at Hall's suggestion, the Foundation for Repertory Theatre of Rhode Island hired as the first managing director of the new Providence company Donald H. Schoenbaum (who had been producer of The Repertory Players of Omaha, where Hall had previously directed). The first full season of the newly named Trinity Square Playhouse with Adrian Hall as artistic director opened on October 14, 1964. Hall's production of *Dark of the Moon*, by Howard Richardson and William Berney, was staged in the annex of the Trinity Union Methodist Church in a space that had been newly renovated to include a 300-seat house, a thrust stage, dressing rooms, and new lighting equipment. With a professional director and business manager and with the addition of three members of the Actors' Equity Association (Richard Kneeland, William Cain, and J. Frank Lucas), by December of 1964 the company had established itself as a professional organization.

Under Schoenbaum's management, season subscriptions rose from 200 to 1,350. Performances were scheduled for Wednesday through Saturday evenings, and the average attendance in 1964–65 was 3,000 per production. In 1965–66 Schoenbaum was replaced by David Tausig Frank as executive director and Douglas Buck as general manager. Performances were scheduled for Thursday through Saturday (with two performances on Saturday), and season subscriptions increased to 1,800.

In 1966 Frank and Buck left the company, and John McQuiggan came to Providence from his successful five-year position as director and producer of the Milwaukee Repertory Theatre to become codirector with Adrian Hall of the newly renamed Trinity Square Repertory Company. Subscriptions for the season increased to 3,150 and the company tripled in size. The eight-play season was performed in two separate theatre spaces: four in the 300-seat Trinity Square Playhouse and four in the 1,000-seat auditorium of the Rhode Island School of Design on North Main Street in Providence.

This sudden expansion was the result of a $2 million, three-year grant from the National Endowment for the Arts and the U.S. Office of Education in support of the Educational Laboratory Theatre Project, which Trinity Square Repertory Company named "Project Discovery." In 1965–66 the company, supported by a grant from the Rockefeller Foundation and the U.S. Office of Education, had tested a pilot project, with 30,000 students from the high schools of Rhode Island attending twenty performances of the company's production of Shakespeare's *Twelfth Night* at the Albee Theatre (an old vaudeville house converted to a movie theatre) in downtown Providence. During the next three seasons (1966–69) the company played 440 performances to more than 350,000 high school students.

While the financial resources of the company were ensured by the Project Discovery grant and by the continuing outstanding artistic quality of the productions, the company continued to have difficulty maintaining a permanent managing director. Between 1964 and 1975 twelve individuals assumed the position of business manager. During this period the annual budgets increased from less than $7,000 to more than $865,000.

In 1971 the board of trustees purchased the Majestic Theatre, a former vaudeville house/movie theatre originally built in downtown Providence in 1917, launched a capital fund drive, and made plans to renovate the Majestic. By 1973 the company had moved into its new home, christened the Lederer Theatre Project (for its chief donor, the B. B. Lederer family). The new theatre complex, located at 201 Washington Street, contained two theatre spaces: the 280-seat Lederer Playhouse (downstairs) with a thrust stage, in an arrangement resembling the former Trinity Square Playhouse; and the Lederer Upstairs Theatre, a modular design with flexible seating that could accommodate an audience of 800. By 1975 the upstairs theatre was renovated to seat 485 and the downstairs theatre to seat 297; in 1982 new renovations resulted in a seating capacity upstairs of 544.

Between 1975 and 1979 the managing director of the company was G. David Black. With rising production costs and capital expenditures, growing deficits, and increasing tension between the trustees and the artistic and managerial staffs, Adrian Hall decided to create a new organizational structure. From 1964 to 1975 the company had been governed and supported by the trustees of the Foundation for Repertory Theatre of Rhode Island, Inc. Desiring more autonomy from the trustees of the Foundation, Hall in 1975 formed the Trinity Personna Company, which continued to produce theatre as Trinity Square Repertory Company, with its own operating budget. The responsibility of the Foundation was to be primarily fund-raising and the continued ownership, oversight, and maintenance of the Lederer Theatre complex, which it rented to the Trinity Square Repertory Company.

The open conflict between Hall and the trustees reached a climax in the spring and summer of 1976, with some members of the board of trustees insisting that Hall and his company leave the Lederer Theatre. After months of heated debate in public meetings and in the local press, the community came to the defense of Hall and the company with increased contributions, season subscriptions, and ticket sales. Although Hall survived this crisis, over the next three years the deficit continued to increase, so that by 1979 the company was threatened with bankruptcy by an accumulated operating deficit of $408,000. Under this financial pressure G. David Black resigned in the spring of 1979, and E. Timothy Langan (who had been general manager since 1976) took over as managing director. Under Langan's managerial leadership the company's deficit was eliminated within the next three years. Since 1982 the company has continued to operate without a deficit. Surpluses have been used for facility renovation and other special projects.

The Trinity Personna Company and the Foundation for Repertory Theatre of Rhode Island, Inc., continued to operate separately until 1981, when they united for a joint fund-raising campaign and began to explore the possibilities of a merger. The merger occurred in July 1984, with the formation of the Trinity Repertory Company board of trustees, a twenty-five-member board with Adrian Hall as president and Bruce G. Sundlun as chairman.

By 1985 Trinity Repertory Company had become a $2.5 million operation, with 72 percent of its income generated by earned revenues, 17 percent from government and national foundation grants (such as the National Endowment for the Arts, the National Endowment for the Humanities, the Rhode Island State Council on the Arts, the Rhode Island Committee for the Humanities, the Ford Foundation, the Andrew W. Mellon Foundation, and the Shubert Foundation), and 11 percent from private and public local community gifts. In twenty-one seasons, from 1964 to 1985, attendance has increased from 24,000 to 160,000 and season subscriptions from 1,350 to 19,300.

From the small 1964 organization consisting of the artistic director, a managing director, several professional actors, and a production staff made up primarily of volunteers, the company of 1985 had grown to include a management and support staff of twenty seven full-time employees, an artistic staff of sixty (including actors, directors, and designers), and a full-time production staff of fifteen. In addition to volunteer assistance, paid personnel are hired for specific large-cast productions or special projects.

As a self-proclaimed devotee of Brecht, Adrian Hall has become known for his use of epic, environmental, and experimental theatre techniques in his production of both classics and new plays. As author, adaptor, and collaborator, as well as director, Hall has been recognized by local and national critics for his unique contribution to the American theatre. Reviewers not only have praised the company for the theatrical excellence of its productions, but they have also noted the superiority of the ensemble and the adventurousness and inventiveness of production concepts and designs.

Since its inception the company has usually included in each season revivals of European and American classics, as well as modern and contemporary plays. The unique feature for which the company has achieved national and international renown, however, has been its production of new plays and of new adaptations and translations of older works. Of 180 works mounted during twenty-two seasons, the company has produced twenty-eight world premieres and four American premieres.

Some of the best received premieres have been Norman Holland's *Years of the Locust*, a play about Oscar Wilde, which, in 1968, became the first production by an American regional theatre to be included in the Edinburgh Festival; Robert Penn Warren's *Brother to Dragons*, first produced in 1968 and revived in 1973–74 and again in 1975–76; an Adrian Hall–Timothy Taylor adaptation of Herman Melville's *Billy Budd*, also included in the 1968–69 season; Robert Van Zandt's *Wilson in the Promised Land* (1969); an Adrian Hall–Richard Cumming original, *Feasting with Panthers* (1973); and a Hall–Cumming adaptation of Dickens' *A Christmas Carol* first produced in 1977 and performed annually since then.

The most controversial productions of both new works and revivals of Shakespeare directed by Hall have included *Son of Man and the Family*, a 1970 original play by Adrian Hall and Timothy Taylor based on the life of Charles Manson; Shakespeare's *Troilus and Cressida* (1971); James Schevill's *Cathedral of Ice*, a 1975 world premiere based on Hitler's rise to power; a Hall–Cumming adaptation of James Purdy's novel *Eustace Chisholm and the Works* (1976); Shakespeare's *King Lear* (1977) and *The Tempest* (1983); and the Hall adaptation of Jack Henry Abbott's *In The Belly of the Beast: Letters from Prison* (1983).

While Hall has directed the company in more than eighty productions (in addition to overseeing forty touring productions), he has invited guest artists and also established members of the company to direct certain productions each season. The most frequent guest directors have been Philip Minor and Larry Arrick (fourteen productions each), David Wheeler (five), and Word Baker (four). Members of the acting company who have also directed productions have included George Martin (twelve); Peter Gerety (seven); William Radka (six); Melanie Jones and Sharon Jenkins (three each); Richard Jenkins and Timothy Crowe (two each); and William Damkoehler, Richard Kneeland, William Cain, and Louis Beachner (one each).

Some of the most important individuals in the history of the company include Marion Simon, assistant to Adrian Hall since 1966 and also at various times chief administrator and director of development, of grants, and of public relations; Richard Cumming, composer-in-residence since 1966, who has also served as musical director, dramaturg, director of educational services, musician, and actor; E. Timothy Langan, managing director from the spring of 1979 to 1986; and resident designers Eugene Lee, Robert Soule, John Custer, William Lane, and Sandra Nathanson.

The only two performers who have continued as members of the acting company since its beginning are Barbara Orson (one of the founders of the company) and Richard Kneeland. The other performers who have been with the company for the longest period of time and continue to be part of the resident ensemble are Timothy Crowe, William Damkoehler, Peter Gerety, Tom Griffin, Ed Hall, Richard Jenkins, David C. Jones, Richard Kavanaugh, David Kennett, Howard London, George Martin, and Barbara Meek.

In addition to its regular season the company has toured extensively and has filmed four television productions. Its international tours have included the 1968

Edinburgh Festival and a 1981 tour of India and Syria with Sam Shepard's *Buried Child* and John Steinbeck's *Of Mice and Men*. The company has also taken productions to Boston (1966, 1974, 1977, and 1979), to New York City (1970 and 1982), to Cincinnati and Phoenix (1972), to Philadelphia (1973, 1974, 1978, 1979, and 1980), to Washington, D.C. (1980), and to Dallas (1983 and 1984), plus additional tours to schools and colleges throughout New England (1965–70 and 1972–74). The television films that have been shown nationally are *Feasting with Panthers* (1974), *Brother to Dragons* (1975), *Life Among the Lowly* (1976), and *The House of Mirth* (1981).

In the summer of 1978 the company began its first full summer season as "Trinity Summer Rep." Each summer since then it has produced revivals of musicals, mysteries, farces, and commercial plays from New York. In 1983 one of these summer musicals, *Billy Bishop Goes to War*, by John Gray and Eric Peterson, received the Boston Theatre Critics' Circle Award.

Throughout its history the company has actively engaged in numerous educational programs. During the summer of 1965 the company was in residence at the University of Rhode Island and was featured in the summer theatre festival. Between 1967 and 1973 special workshops for high school students and their teachers, plus internship programs with high schools and colleges throughout the region, became a vital part of the company's activities. Also between 1970 and 1985, supported by funds from the state and from local school districts, the company has continued its Project Discovery program, averaging forty-eight matinee performances for 17,000 students each season. Since its beginning the company has also been associated with special educational workshops in conjunction with local hospitals and the medical programs at Brown University.

During the summer of 1978 the Trinity Rep Conservatory was begun under the directorship of Larry Arrick, with David Eliet as his assistant. When Arrick left Providence in 1983 to join the Pittsburgh Public Playhouse, Eliet became the director of the two-year program. Conservatory students have the opportunity to audition for and perform in company productions, as well as to participate in other production activities; they can also receive graduate credit for their course of study from Rhode Island College, which has been affiliated with the conservatory since 1982.

In addition to the numerous special local and regional awards received by individual members of the company, Trinity Square Repertory Company has been the recipient of several national awards, including the first Margo Jones Award for production of new plays (1969–70), the Antoinette Perry ("Tony") Award for distinguished contribution to the American theatre (1981), and the first award for "the best public humanities program" in the nation (1982), a program initiated in 1978, titled "The Dramatic Work as a Historical Cultural Document," and funded by the Rhode Island Committee for the Humanities, an affiliate of the National Endowment for the Humanities. Beginning with the 1985–86 season the company received one of the first five-year ongoing ensemble grants ever awarded by the National Endowment for the Arts, so that the company can ensure the established members of the company ten-month contracts on a weekly salaried basis.

Since the 1983–84 season Adrian Hall, in addition to remaining as director and president of the Trinity Repertory Company in Providence, has also been named artistic director of the Dallas Theatre Center*.

PERSONNEL

Director: Adrian Hall (1966–86).

Assistant to the Director: Marion Simon (1966–86).

Managing Directors: G. David Black (1975–79), Newell Cook (1966–67), Barton H. Emmet (1968–70), David Tausig Frank (1965–66), David H. Harper (1967–68), E. Timothy Langan (1979–86), John A. McQuiggan (1966), Daniel B. Miller (1972–74), Hilmar Sallee (1967), Donald H. Schoenbaum (1964–65), Stanley D. Silver (1974–75), Marion Simon (1970), Lamont E. Smith (1970–72), Milton Stanzler (1967).

Set Designers: John Braden (1965–66), Stewart Brecher (1965–66), David Christian (1965–66), Patrick Firpo (1964–65), Marc S. Harrison (1964–65), Matthew Jacobs (1978–79), David Jenkins (1971–72), *Eugene Lee* (1967–86), Kert F. Lundell (1967–68), Abe Nathanson (1964–65), Morris Nathanson (1964–65), Lynn Pecktal (1966–67), David D. Rotondo (1985), Michael Scott (1965–66), *Robert D. Soule* (1968–86), Robert R. Troie (1964–65).

Lighting Designers: Tom Aubin (1964–65), Jody Briggs (1965–66), *John F. Custer* (1975–86), Richard Devin (1973–75), Gene Jalesky (1964–65), Barry Kearsley (1965–66), Kevin S. Keating (1976–78), *Eugene Lee* (1967–86), John McLain (1974–75), *Roger Morgan* (1966–74), Shirley Prendergast (1972–73), Mark Rippe (1975–78), Michael Tschudin (1965–66).

Costume Designers: John Braden (1965–66), Ellen Brecher (1965–66), Mary Aiello Bruce (1978–79), Vittorio Capecce (1978–79), A. Christiana Giannini (1971–73), *James Berton Harris* (1973–78), Rosemary Ingham (1965–66), *William Lane* (1979–86), Franne Newman Lee (1970–71, 1975–77), *John Lehmeyer* (1966–72), Ann Morrell (1977–79), *Betsey Potter* (1971–78), Annette Rossi (1978–79), Gere Schoenbaum (1964–65), Sunny B. Warner (1964–66, 1972–73).

Property Designers: Sandra Nathanson (1965–86), Cheryl Ottaviano (1977–83), Robert H. Schleinig (1983–86), Tom Waldon (1976–80), William Wieters (1983–84).

Stage Managers: Bernard Jay Adler (1976–77), Beverly Andreozzi (1974–78), Robert Applegarth (1967–71), Dennis Blackledge (1976–79), Ken Bryant (1983–84), David A. Butler (1973–74), Carroll L. Cartwright III (1982–83), Bree Cavazos (1970–72), Wendy Cox (1984–85), Robert Crawley (1981–82), Patrick Firpo (1964–65), Maureen F. Gibson (1976–79), Joseph Kavanaugh (1979–81), Franklin Keysar (1965–71, 1973–74, 1979–80), Donald King (1966–67), Carolyn Knox (1973–74), Rebecca Linn (1980–82), Howard London (1973–74), Dian Miller (1964–67), Mary O'Leary (1981–83), Florine Pulley (1967–68), William Radka (1970–80), Louis Scenti (1979–80), Edgar F. Staff (1964–65), Sandra Tilles (1964).

Technical Directors: David Christian (1965–66), Steve Crowley (1966–71), Shaun B. Curran (1974–75), Joseph W. Landry, Jr. (1971–72), George Marks (1971–74), Richard Rogers (1981–83), *David A. Rotondo* (1980–86), Douglas Smith (1975–76), Arthur Torg (1964), David Ward (1976–80).

Musical Directors: Daniel Birnbaum (1983–84), *Richard Cumming* (1966–86), William Damkoehler (1984–85), Robert M. Kaplan (1964–65), Theodore Saidenberg (1966–67), Stephen Snyder (1983–84).

Choreographers: Doris Holloway (1964–65), Sharon Jenkins (1974–75, 1977–86), Brian Jones (1975–76, 1984–85), Zoya Leporska (1966–67), Julie Strandberg (1973–74).

Guest Directors: Paul Benedict, Ann McBey Brebner, Rocco Bufano, Henry Butler, Wayne Carson, Jacques Cartier, Vincent Dowling, James Hammerstein, Patrick Hines, Brooks Jones, Jonas Jurasas, George Keathley, James Howard Laurence, Pirie Mac-Donald, Robert Mandel, Jack O'Brien, Ron Pember, Stephen Porter, Don Price, Dennis Rosa, Suzanne Shepherd, Stuart Vaughan, Henry Velez, Tunc Yalman.

Actors and Actresses: Jane Abrams, Nancy Acly, Barbara Aiello, Andra Akers, Victor Allen, *Clinton Anderson* (1966–69), Joyce Anderson, Leta Anderson, Rob Anderson, Robert Applegarth, Katherine Argo, Mary Armitage, David Baccari, Mildred Bailey, Kyle Baker, Beatrice Ballance, Myrna Barenbaum, Hadler Barnes, James O. Barnhill, Hoda Baron, Louis Beachner, Robert Becker, William R. Begley, Margo Bennett, Richard P. Bennett, Ruth Benson, Donald R. Benway, Lou Birtwell, *Bonnie Sacks Black* (1975–79, 1982–83), *Robert Black* (1969–79, 1982–83), Richard Blackburn, Gloria Bloom, Tom Bloom, *Barbara Blossom* (1979–86), Virginia Blue, Malcolm Bowes, Ken Bradford, Florence Bray, Ellen Brecher, Carol Brice, Frederick Brink, Steven D. Brown, Ed Budz, Dan Butler, *William Cain* (1964–72, 1975–76), Cait Calvo, Lori Cardille, James Carruthers, Joan Carter, Elwin Causey, *Bree Cavazos* (1966–72, 1977–78, 1980–81), Vince Ceglie, Michael Champagne, Jean Cheeseman, Ken Cheeseman, Nancy Chesney, David Christian, Michael Cobb, Paul Collins, *Robert J. Colonna* (1966–76, 1978–79), Edward Conaty, Margaret Cool, Brenda Jean Corwin, Walter Covell, *Timothy Crowe* (1970–86), Joseph Culliton, *Richard Cumming* (1981–86), *Timothy Daly* (1981–86), Barbara Damashek, *William Damkoehler* (1967–80, 1983–86), Lila Daniels, *Blythe Danner* (1966–67), George F. Darling, Judith Davidson, David Davies, Lane Davies, Sylvia Davis, Gary deLena, Paul DePasquale, Roslyn Dickens, Margot Dionne, Steve Dobey, Maurice Dolbier, Timothy John Donahue, Michael D'Orlando, David Doyle, Mary Doyle, Carol J. Drowne, Jeffrey Duarte, Dortha Duckworth, Patricia Echeverria, *James Eichelberger* (1967–74), Elizabeth Eis, David Eliet, Winifred Elze, June Emery, Bettie Endrizzi, Victor Eschbach, Robert Farber, Joanna Featherstone, Roland Fernandez, *Richard Ferrone* (1981–86), Bill Finlay, Monique Fowler, Joseph Fowlkes, Elizabeth Franz, *Ron Frazier* (1967–70), Violet Fritz, *James Gallery* (1966–71), Alexis Gantry, Donald Gantry, John Garrick, Anthony George, *Anne Gerety* (1977–78, 1982–86), *Peter Gerety* (1965–69, 1974–86), Stefan Gierasch, Harris Ginsberg, Ralph Glickman, Russell Gold, Roz Goldberg, Tom Goode, Michael Gorrin, Bradford Gottlin, Ann Gravel, *Tom Griffin* (1974–86), Paul Haggard, *Ed Hall* (1965–86), Dorcas Haller, William Haller, Robert Hargraves, Tony Harrington, Jr., Carol Harris, Ronald Harris, Ruth Healy, *Katherine Helmond* (1965–69), John Hickok, Skip Hinnant, Alexandra Holland, David Hooks, Jacques Hopkins, Lura Bane Howes, Terrie Hoxie, Richard Hoyt-Miller, Giboney Hykin, Martin Hykin, Judith Israel, Zina Jasper, Barbara Jean, *Richard Jenkins* (1970–86), Michael Jepson, *Keith Jochim* (1981–86), Vera Johnson, Peter Jolly, *David C. Jones* (1969–86), *Melanie Jones* (1974–84), Suzanne Juhasz, Dorothy Jungles, Robert M. Kaplan, Dorrie Kavanaugh, *Richard Kavanaugh* (1969–86), Drew Keil, Earl Kells, Richard Kennedy, *David Kennett* (1968–86), Franklin Keysar, Jegana Khan-Khozsky, *Jon Kimbell* (1970–72), Maury Klein, *Richard Kneeland* (1964–86), Stephen Knox, Bernie Kolb, James

Howard Laurence, Joel Leffert, *Marguerite H. Lenert* (1965–76), Geraldine Librandi, Vernon J. Lisbon, *Becca Lish* (1982–86), Terry Lomax, *Howard London* (1970–86), Dennis Longwell, Paul Lovett, Henry Lowder, Charles Lowe, *J. Frank Lucas* (1964–65), Jack McCullough, John McDonald, Tim McDonough, Brian McEleney, Bruce McGill, Cynthia McKay, David McKenna, David Mack, Anthony Mancini, Janice Mancini, *Mina Manente* (1970–81), Lois Markle, Despina Marsella, Vassa Marsella, Dana Martin, *George Martin* (1969–86), Hope G. Martin, Linda Martin, David Marsoli, Margaret Marx, Madison P. Mason, *Thomas Richard Mason* (1970–74), Kate Matthews, *Ruth Maynard* (1979–86), Marius F. Mazmanian, *Derek Meader* (1974–86), Ruth Meader, Marilyn Meardon, *Barbara Meek* (1968–86), Marian Mercer, Marge Merdinyan, William Meyers, Dian Miller, Gertrude Miller, Mary Miller, *Philip Minor* (1982–86), Kevin Mitchell, Julie Miterko, Robert Moberly, *Martin Molson* (1968–71), Elizabeth Moore, Richard Morse, Chris Murney, Bill Murphy, Leah Mushnick, John A. Mutter, Phyllis Myers, Tom Neely, Dawn Nelson, *Nancy Nichols* (1974–78, 1981–82), Deirdre O'Connell, Halcyon Oldham, John Oldham, Tom O'Leary, *Barbara Orson* (1964–86), Mairin D. O'Sullivan, Michael Paliotti, Anthony Palmer, Glenn Palmer, Joel Parks, Robin Patrick, Moultrie Patten, Robert Patterson, Susan Payne, *Pamela Payton-Wright* (1966–67, 1969–70, 1973–74), Richard Pearl, Julie Pember, Al Pereira, Nancy Pereira, Bond Perry, Lenka Peterson, Tom Pezzulo, James Pickering, Richard Pinter, Charles Pistone, *Ricardo Pitts-Wiley* (1974–79, 1983–86), Dan Plucinski, Edie Pool, *Ben Powers* (1972–75), *Ford Rainey* (1978–86), Norman Ranone, Bob Reed, Sean M. Reilly, Arthur H. Roberts, Dorothea Roberts, Andrew Robinson, Edward L. Rondeau, James Roos, Ina B. Rosenthal, Gene Rousseau, Ken Rubenfeld, Carlton Russell, Ellye Russell, Elizabeth Ann Sachs, William Sadler, Nina Salter, Linda Saposhkov, Gail Sauer, Marcia Savella, Schorling Schneider, Lola Schwartz, Charles Scovil, *Anne Scurria* (1979–86), James Seymour, Daniel Shane, *April Shawhan* (1979–82), Samuel Sherman, Judith Shroeder, *Margo Skinner* (1972–83), Neva Small, Edward Smith, Jr., Marran Smith, *Norman B. Smith* (1976–81), Stephen Snyder, Sylvia Ann Soares, *Donald Somers* (1966–73), Richard Steele, *David P. B. Stephens* (1982–86), Deborah Strang, *Cynthia Strickland* (1975–78, 1983–86), Bonnie Strickman, Brad Sullivan, Frank L. Sullivan, Michael Surgento, Jill Tanner, Timothy Taylor, Warren Teixeira, Deborah Templin, Editha Thomas, *Patricia Ann Thomas* (1981–86), Anne Thompson, Allen Thornton, Calvin Tillotson, Alan Tongret, Arthur Torg, Esther Torg, Michael Tschudin, Terrence Turner, *Robert Van Hooten* (1964–66, 1967–68), *Amy Van Nostrand* (1977–86), Ancelin Vogt, *Daniel Von Bargen* (1972–86), John Walsh, Howard Walters, Sunny B. Warner, Diane Warren, *Rose Weaver* (1973–84), Christopher Wells, *Cynthia Wells* (1970–72, 1974–75, 1977–78), Raymond Wells, Kimber Wheelock, Sheila Whitcomb, Robert Whitney, Margaret L. Wilbur, Joanna Williams, *Jobeth Williams* (1970–74), Rick Williamson, Alexander Wolfson, John Woodson, *Mary Wrubel* (1964–67), Greg Young.

Guest Artists: Gerardine Arthur, Barbara Baxley, Paul Benedict, James Broderick, Carol Bruce, Cynthia Carle, Nancy Cushman, Carmen de Lavallade, Sheryl Dold, Stephanie Dunnam, Jan Farrand, Michele Fraioli, Vincent Gardenia, Martyn Green, Robin Groves, Ann Hamilton, Patrick Hines, Richard Loder, Conrad MacLaren, Jean Marsh, Zakes Mokae, Daniel Nagrin, Georgia Neu, Margaret Phillips, Christina Pickles, Alyssa Roth, Hilmar Sallee, Marian Seldes, Kevin Sessums, Vivienne Shub, Elaine Stritch, Angela Thornton, Naomi Thornton, Mark Torres, Maria Tucci, Myra Turley, Joan White, Kate Young.

REPERTORY

Spring 1964: *The Hostage, The House of Bernarda Alba, Orpheus Descending, The Death of Bessie Smith* and *The American Dream.*

1964–65: *Dark of the Moon, The Rehearsal, The Caretaker, Uncle Vanya, Desire Under the Elms, Don Juan in Hell, All to Hell Laughing* (world premiere), *The Zoo Story* and *The American Dream.*

Summer 1964: *Don Juan in Hell, The Caretaker, The Glass Menagerie, The Zoo Story* and *The American Dream, Rhinoceros, The Time of Your Life, Happy Days* and *Dutchman.*

1965–66: *The Crucible, Tartuffe, The Balcony, Twelfth Night, Long Day's Journey into Night, The Eternal Husband* (world premiere), *The Playboy of the Western World.*

1966–67: *Saint Joan, A Streetcar Named Desire, The Grass Harp* (world premiere), *Ah, Wilderness!, A Midsummer Night's Dream, The Questions* and *Dutchman, The Birthday Party, The Three Sisters.*

1967–68: *The Threepenny Opera, Julius Caesar, The Importance of Being Earnest, Years of the Locust* (world premiere), *An Enemy of the People, Phaedra.*

1968–69: *Red Roses for Me, Brother to Dragons* (world premiere), *Macbeth, The Homecoming, Billy Budd* (world premiere), *Exiles.*

1969–70: *The Old Glory, House of Breath Black/White* (world premiere), *Wilson in the Promised Land* (world premiere), *The Skin of Our Teeth, Lovecraft's Follies* (world premiere).

1970–71: *You Can't Take It with You, Son of Man and the Family* (world premiere), *Little Murders, The Taming of the Shrew, Adaptation/Next, Love for Love, The Good and Bad Times of Cady Francis McCullum and Friends* (world premiere), *The Threepenny Opera, Harvey.*

1971–72: *Child's Play, Troilus and Cressida, Down by the River Where the Waterlilies Are Disfigured Every Day* (world premiere), *Child's Play, The School for Wives, The Price.*

1972–73: *Old Times, The School for Wives, Lady Audley's Secret, The Royal Hunt of the Sun, Feasting with Panthers* (world premiere).

1973–74: *Brother to Dragons, Ghost Dance* (world premiere), *Alfred the Great* (world premiere), *Aimee* (world premiere), *For the Use of the Hall* (world premiere), *The Tooth of Crime, A Man for All Seasons, Sherlock Holmes.*

1974–75: *Well Hung* (American premiere), *Jumpers, Peer Gynt* (world premiere of adaptation by Adrian Hall and Richard Cumming), *The Emperor Henry, Tom Jones* (world premiere of adaptation by Larry Arrick), *Seven Keys to Baldpate.*

1975–76: *Cathedral of Ice* (world premiere), *Another Part of the Forest, The Little Foxes, Two Gentlemen of Verona, Bastard Son* (world premiere), *Eustace Chisholm and the Works* (world premiere of adaptation by Adrian Hall and Richard Cumming).

1976–77: *Seven Keys to Baldpate, A Flea in Her Ear, Of Mice and Men, Knock Knock, The Boys from Syracuse, Rich and Famous, King Lear, Bad Habits, Of Mice and Men.*

1977–78: *Ethan Frome, The Show-Off, Rosmersholm, Boesman and Lena, A Christmas Carol, Vanities, Equus, American Buffalo, As You Like It, Seduced* (world premiere).

Summer 1978: *Vanities, The Shock of Recognition* and *The Real Inspector Hound, Whiskey.*

1978–79: *A Life in the Theatre, Uncle Tom's Cabin: A History* (world premiere), *Father's Day, A Christmas Carol, The Shadow Box, Awake and Sing!, Jack the Ripper* (American premiere), *Death of a Salesman, Who's Afraid of Virginia Woolf?.*

Summer 1979: *Side by Side by Sondheim, Same Time, Next Year, Dial "M" for Murder*.

1979–80: *Bosoms and Neglect, Born Yesterday, Sly Fox, A Christmas Carol, The Suicide* (American premiere), *Buried Child, The Night of the Iguana, Sea Marks, Waiting for Godot*.

Summer 1980: *El Grande de Coca Cola, An Almost Perfect Person, Deathtrap*.

1980–81: *Betrayal, Arsenic and Old Lace, A Christmas Carol, On Golden Pond, The Iceman Cometh, The Whales of August* (world premiere), *Inherit the Wind, How I Got That Story, Whose Life Is It Anyway?*.

Summer 1981: *The Elephant Man, Talley's Folly*.

1981–82: *Of Mice and Men, Buried Child, L'Atelier, The Gin Game, A Christmas Carol, A Lesson from Aloes, The Hothouse* (American premiere), *Dead Souls, True West, The 5th of July*.

Summer 1982: *Tintypes, Crucifer of Blood, 13 Rue De L'Amour*.

1982–83: *The Web* (world premiere), *The Dresser, A Christmas Carol, The Front Page, Translations, The Tempest, In the Belly of the Beast: Letters from Prison* (world premiere), *Pygmalion, Mass Appeal*.

Summer 1983: *Tintypes, Billy Bishop Goes to War*.

1983–1984: *Bus Stop, Galileo, The Wild Duck, A Christmas Carol, Fool for Love, Cloud 9, Amadeus, Crimes of the Heart, Jonestown Express* (world premiere).

Summer 1984: *Beyond Therapy, What the Butler Saw*.

1984–1985: *Terra Nova, Passion Play, Tartuffe, A Christmas Carol, Misalliance, And a Nightingale Sang..., The Country Wife, Master Harold...and the boys, Present Laughter*.

Summer 1985: *Baby, Not by Bed Alone*.

1985–1986: *The Marriage of Bette and Boo, Cat on a Hot Tim Roof, The Beauty Part, A Christmas Carol, The Crucible, Life and Limb, The Tavern, Pasta* (world premiere), *The Country Girl*.

Summer 1986: *Noises Off, A Funny Thing Happened on the Way to the Forum*.

1986–1987: *The Visit, The Real Thing, A Christmas Carol, Hurlyburly, Our Town, Glengarry Glen Ross, All the King's Men, Quartermaine's Terms, A Lie of the Mind, The Lady from Maxim's*.

BIBLIOGRAPHY

Published Sources:

[Providence] *Journal*, 1964–85.

Best Plays of 1964–65 through *1983–84*. New York: Dodd, Mead & Co., 1966–86.

Educational Laboratory Theatre Project: 1966–1970. St. Louis: CEMREL, Inc., 1970.

Theatre Profiles. Vols. 1–7. New York: Theatre Communications Group, 1973–86.

Theatre World. Vols. 23–40. New York: Crown Publishers, 1967–84.

Zeigler, Joseph W. *Regional Theatre: The Revolutionary Stage*. Minneapolis: University of Minnesota Press, 1973.

Archival Resource:

Providence, Rhode Island. Trinity Square Repertory Company. Programs, business records.

P. William Hutchinson

W

WISDOM BRIDGE THEATRE, Chicago, was founded by David Beaird and Rebecca Smiser in 1974. Beaird named the theatre after a contemporary painting he saw at the Art Institute of Chicago. Located at 1559 West Howard, the old building had housed a speakeasy, a Chinese restaurant, and an occult bookstore before Beaird transformed its second floor into a 150-seat theatre. It opened on June 7, 1974, with William Hanley's *Slow Dance on the Killing Ground.*

Beginning as part of the burgeoning "off-Loop" movement, Wisdom Bridge evolved into one of the city's premiere theatres during Chicago's theatre renaissance of the 1970s and 1980s. Its stage showcased the directorial talents of Robert Falls, Beaird's successor, and featured many actors who later gained national recognition, including John Malkovich, William L. Petersen, Laurie Metcalf, Glenne Headly, Aidan Quinn, Gary Cole, Alan Ruck, Gary Sinise, Megan Mullaly, and Steve Fletcher. Wisdom Bridge was also successful in bringing prominent performers such as Brian Dennehy, Dorothy Louden, John O'Neal, and Japan's Suzuki Company of Toga to appear in new works on its small stage.

In 1974 Beaird was a twenty-one-year-old from Shreveport, Louisiana, still enrolled at the Goodman School of Drama, with a few Chicago acting credits to his name. In his three seasons as Wisdom Bridge artistic director Beaird worked for high standards on a slim budget. After the first two Wisdom Bridge productions failed to draw audiences, Beaird opened *The Fantasticks*, the musical by Tom Jones and Harvey Schmidt, which ran for four months and brought both money and name recognition. Operating on a shoestring, Beaird worked constantly at fund-raising. In addition to his directing, Beaird wrote original works based on Edmond Rostand's *Cyrano de Bergerac*, on Sophocles' *Oedipus Rex*, on the life of Socrates (called *Dignity*), and on *The Wizard of Id* comic strip, by Brant Parker and Johnny Hart. However, the heavy work load taxed Beaird's already poor health and he resigned after the 1976–77 season.

Robert Falls replaced Beaird as artistic director of Wisdom Bridge. The selection of Falls was logical; Beaird had hired Falls to direct John Steinbeck's *Of Mice and Men* in 1977, for which Falls won Chicago's prestigious Joseph Jefferson (''Jeff'') Award Citation for best direction. He was a newcomer to Chicago theatre. After studying theatre at the University of Illinois, Falls quickly established himself in Chicago by directing Michael Weller's *Moonchildren* and Charles Dickens' *A Christmas Carol* at the since-defunct St. Nicholas Theatre. When Wisdom Bridge appointed Falls he was regarded as being one of the finest young directors in the city.

Wisdom Bridge became substantially more successful under Falls, both artistically and commercially. He shaped a theatre committed to presenting an eclectic mixture of serious, often provocative plays, staged with theatricality and verve. Despite this challenging approach, the theatre drew large audiences. Striving to make Wisdom Bridge artistically innovative, Falls' play selection increasingly favored the latest work of America's best young dramatists, along with thoughtful new stagings of classic dramas.

The theatre's financial picture also improved. The entire budget for *Of Mice and Men* was $50. In 1977 both Falls and stage manager Mary Badger's salary came from the government's CETA (Comprehensive Employment Training Act) program. The situation improved when Kevin O'Morrison's *Ladyhouse Blues*, the 1977–78 season's first show, became a hit. Audiences continued to pack the tiny theatre for all but the last show of that season. As a result, Wisdom Bridge became a not-for-profit Equity theatre the next season. In late 1979 Jeffrey Ortmann became executive director of Wisdom Bridge and began to build its foundation grant support. This, combined with strong ticket sales in 1979–80, enabled Wisdom Bridge to launch a $40,000 renovation: the stage was altered from a three-quarter thrust to a modified proscenium, and the seating capacity was increased to 196. By 1984 Wisdom Bridge averaged eight performances a week, with a top ticket price of $12. It boasted 6,000 subscribers, an annual attendance of 60,000, and total operating expenses of $1.2 million a year. In addition, between 1980 and 1984 Wisdom Bridge sponsored an actor training center, begun by Edward Kaye-Martin and later led by Dan LaMorte.

Ladyhouse Blues was the first of many Wisdom Bridge hits. In its first ten years alone the theatre won thirteen Jeff awards, sixteen citations (awarded when non-Equity), and seventy Jeff nominations. Its peak Jeff season was 1979–80 when it earned seventeen nominations and had six winners, including best production and best direction (by Falls) for Marsha Norman's *Getting Out*, best actor for Frank Galati in Tom Stoppard's *Travesties*, and best actress for Roz Alexander in Arthur Kopit's *Wings*. Meanwhile the theatre's reputation grew with each season. The 1978 musical *Bagtime*, by Alan Rosen and Louis Rosen, based on columnist Bob Greene's book, brought Wisdom Bridge fully into the Chicago theatre limelight. It again drew public acclaim in 1978 for presenting *Travesties* and the play it travesties, Oscar Wilde's *The Importance of Being Earnest*, in repertory with the same cast. Subsequent successes include *Yentl*, by Leah Napolin, Isaac Bashevis Singer, and Mel Marvin; Martin Sherman's *Bent;* Bertolt Brecht's *Mother Courage and Her Children; Kabuki Macbeth* and *Kabuki Medea* (both conceived and directed by Shozo Sato); John Olive's *Standing on My Knees;* Keith Reddin's *Life and Limb; In the Belly of the Beast: Letters from Prison* (which Falls adapted from a work by Jack Henry Abbott at the request of Adrian Hall, its first stage creator); and *Hamlet.* Michael Merritt won special praise for designing all aspects of Falls' productions of *Mother Courage and Her Children* and *Hamlet.*

Wisdom Bridge gained considerable recognition for its achievements. In 1982 the Wisdom Bridge production of John Olive's *Standing on My Knees* appeared at the Manhattan Theatre Club. The next year Wisdom Bridge was a recipient of a CBS–Dramatists Guild grant designed to discover new playwrights (the winner was Jon Klein for *Losing It)*. In May 1985 *In the Belly of the Beast* (still featuring William L. Petersen) was presented as part of Glasgow, Scotland's Mayfest and London's American Festival. That same summer it was again presented as part of the AT&T Performing Arts Festival at the Kennedy Center in Washington, D.C., along with *Kabuki Medea.* Falls himself served on the board of the Theatre Communications Group as well as on the Theatre Program Panel for the National Endowment for the Arts.

In January 1986 Robert Falls resigned to become artistic director of Chicago's Goodman Theatre. In November 1986 the Wisdom Bridge board of directors announced the appointment of Richard E. T. White, formerly resident director of the Berkeley Repertory Theatre* (Berkeley, California), as Wisdom Bridge artistic director.

PERSONNEL

Management: David Beaird, artistic director (1974–77); Robert Falls, artistic director (1977–86); Mary Pat Byrne, business manager (1975–76); Lisa Malkis, business manager (1976–78); Jeffrey Ortmann, executive director (1979–86); Susan Hope, associate artistic director (1981–84); Douglas Finlayson, assistant artistic director (1984–86); Stuart J. Hecht, dramaturg (1983–86); John Olive, playwright in residence (1984–85); Steven Robman, artistic associate (1985–86).

Stage Technicians: Mary Badger, Abby Farber, Larry Shaden, Karl Sullivan.

Stage Directors: David Beaird, Allen Belknap, Aubrey Berg, Anne Claus, David Colacci, Robert Falls, Doug Finlayson, Tracey Friedman, Gail Isaacson, Edward Kaye-Martin, Steve Kent, Michael Maggio, Jim O'Connor, Patrick O'Gara, Judd Parkin, Jerry Proffit, Steve Robman, Lou Salerni, Shozo Sato, Ned Schmidtke, Mel Shapiro, Jeff Steitzer, J. R. Sullivan.

Actors and Actresses: Ortez Alderson, *Roslyn Alexander*, Steven Anders, Ray Andrecheck, Sarajane Avidon, *Peter Aylward*, Chuck Bailey, James M. Barry, Joshua Bartz, Bernard Beck, Tom Benich, Jerome Bernstein, *Gisli Bjorgvinsson*, David Bodin, Darryl Boehmer, Peter G. Boekhoff, Charlotte Booker, Richard Brambert, Peter Brandon, Margo Buchanan, *Peter Burnell*, Dale Calandra, Janis Carr, Matthew Causey, David Chadderdon, Lorraine Clark, *Del Close*, Leona Coakley, *David Colacci, Gary Cole*, Dan Conway, John Copeland, John Cothran, Jr., Larry Coven, *Leland Crooke*, Jodean Culbert, C.

Thomas Cunliffe, Susan Dafoe, *David Darlow*, Dawn David, Nathan Davis, Deanna Deignan, Mike Dempsey, *Brian Dennehy*, James Deuter, Colleen Dodson, *Lisa A. Dodson*, Diane Dorsey, *Deanna Dunagan*, Kevin Dunn, Judith Easton, Howard Elfman, Norman Engstrom, Diane Fahnstrom, Krishna Fairchild, *Stewart Figa, Kit Flanagan*, Donald Flayton, Suzanna Fleck, *Steve Fletcher, Gregg Flood*, Neil Flynn, Peter Fogel, *Dean Fortunato*, Michael Fosberg, Norm Fox, Douglas Frank, Don Franklin, *Ray Frewen*, Danny Frohman, Jonathon Fuller, *Frank Galati*, Julie Geiser, Mike Genovese, J. Michael Gerrity, Ira Goldstein, John Green, Brian Greene, Marla Greenspan, Kevin Gudahl, Chuck Hall, *Tim Halligan*, Dennis Hamel, Jan Ellen Hand, Scott Harlan, Caitlin Hart, *Glenne Headly*, K. C. Helmeid, Stephen M. Henderson, Richard Henzel, Jack Hickey, John Hines, Ron Hirsen, Phillip Hoffman, *Isabella Hofmann*, Jill Holden, Mark J. Holstein, Eleah Horwitz, Donald Humbertson, Phil Hurlbut, Diane Hurley, Jeffrey Hutchinson, Roy Hytower, Paul Ilmer, *Laura Innes, Scott Jaeck*, Ina Jaffe, *B. J. Jones*, John M. Jones, Martin Jones, Lee Kanne, Chris Karchmar, Bob Keenan, Elizabeth Kelly, Leonard Kelly, Michael Kendricks, Mark Kenmore, Sheila Kennan, *Linda Kimbrough*, Barbara Kingsley, John Kunik, Robert Kurcz, *Felicity LaFortunate*, John Lanahan, *James Lancaster*, Ruth Landis, *Sonja Lanzener*, Martha Lavey, *James J. Lawless*, Rich Leff, Mindy Levin, *Ted Levine*, Herb Lichtenstein, Jami Lieder, Nancy Linari, *Dorothy Louden*, Elizabeth Lynde, Clayton McAllister, *Lawrence McCauley*, Gordon McClure, Durward McDonald, Linsay McGee, Barbara McGreevy, Christine McHugh, Christopher McIntyre, Kenned MacIver, Tom McKeon, *Megan McTavish, John Malkovich*, Barrie Mason, Marie Mathay, Don Mayo, Robert Meitzer, Kathleen Melvin, *Laurie Metcalf, Edgar Meyer*, Ernie Miller, *J. Pat Miller*, Donald Moffett, Leyla Modir, *Amy Morton*, John Mueller, *Tom Mula, Megan Mullaly*, James D. Murphy, *Robert Neches, Audrie J. Neenan*, John Nesci, *Alan Novak*, Roone O'Donnell, *John O'Neal, James O'Reilly*, Phyllis Parmer, David Pearson, Carmen Pecchio, Marty Peifer, *William L. Petersen, Byrne Piven, Joyce Piven*, Les Podewell, *Aidan Quinn*, Robin Rauch, Hollis Resnik, Maria Ricossa, Rob Riley, *Barbara E. Robertson*, Chelcie Ross, *Alan Ruck*, Janice St. John, Kathy Santen, Nancy Schieber, Patrick Schmitt, Gene Schuldt, Irene Schweyer, Pamela Shaffer, Elizabeth Shaw, Nancy Sigworth, *Gary Sinise*, Eileen Smith, Lionel Smith, Bryan Sorenson, Rick Sparks, Joan Spatafora, Walton Stanley, John Starrs, Barbara Steele, Stephen Stout, *David Studwell*, Pat Sturgis, *James Sudik*, Jeff Sumner, Kenji Suzuki, Nabuko Suzuki, Nancy Sybeg, Pamela Szarzak, Scott Tauber, Michael Tezla, *Mary Ann Thebus*, Charles Thomas, Jim True, Joe van Slyke, Greg Vinkler, Vince Viverito, Marcia Waller, G. J. Walsh, Susan Wells, *Natalie West*, David Westgoer, *Jack Wetherall*, Tod Wheeler, Thomas White, *Alan Wilder*, Darlene Williams, David Wirth, Mike Wise, *Bruce A. Young*, Will Zahrn, Paul Zegler, Peter Zopp.

REPERTORY

1974–75: *Slow Dance on the Killing Ground, Woyzeck, The Fantasticks, Oscar Wilde: In Person, De Bergerac.*

1975–76: *Dignity, The Merchant of Venice, The Wizard of Id, The Threepenny Opera.*

1976–77: *The Wager, Oedipus Rex, Twelfth Night, Of Mice and Men.*

1977–78: *Ladyhouse Blues, The Idiots Karamazov, The Crucible, Carmilla.*

1978–79: *The Runner Stumbles, Tartuffe, Comedians, Bagtime, Suburbs of Heaven, Breaking Out.*

1979–80: *Wings, Travesties, The Importance of Being Earnest, Getting Out, Treats.*

1980–81: *Yentl, Bent, One-Reel Romance, Mother Courage and Her Children, The Faith Healer.*

1981–82: *Kabuki Macbeth, Standing on My Knees, A Streetcar Named Desire, Sister Mary Ignatius Explains It All for You, Sizwe Bansi Is Dead* and *The Island,* the Suzuki company's *The Trojan Women.*

1982–83: *Princess Grace and the Fazarris, Awake and Sing!, We Won't Pay! We Won't Pay!, Losing It, Clarence Darrow.*

1983–84: *In the Belly of the Beast: Letters from Prison, Kabuki Medea, Billy Bishop Goes to War, Life and Limb* (performed with the Remains Theatre Company), *Careless Love.*

1984–85: *Terra Nova, Hamlet, Painting Churches, You Can't Judge a Book by Looking at Its Cover.*

1985–86: *Rat in the Skull, The Middle of Nowhere in the Middle of the Night, 'night, Mother, Kabuki Faust, Hamlet* (revival), *The Immigrant.*

BIBLIOGRAPHY

Archival material is in the author's possession.

Stuart J. Hecht

WOOSTER GROUP, New York, was founded by Elizabeth LeCompte and Spalding Gray as a parallel development to and a reaction against Richard Schechner's Performance Group. The first production of the Wooster Group, *Sakonnet Point,* opened on May 29, 1975, and ran for forty-eight performances. From the first, the Group realized it had a clear and separate identity, more in line with Richard Foreman than with Richard Schechner. LeCompte, Gray, and the five other members took on the corporate name, The Wooster Group, in June 1980. Along with Foreman's Ontological-Hysteric Theatre and a group of artists loosely associated with Richard Wilson, the Wooster Group was one of several theatre collectives in the 1970s to challenge the theatre of the 1960s by further developing the idea of seeing themselves as creative artists rather than as mere interpreters of dramatic roles. The Group, along with Mabou Mines* and Meredith Monk, remains the most active experimental company in New York.

Elizabeth LeCompte, born in 1944 and raised in New Jersey, studied painting at Skidmore College, where she received her bachelor's degree in fine arts. She was also interested in photography. Coming to New York in 1967, she joined the Performance Group in 1970. Her technique as a director is to develop strong, emotionally charged images through the juxtaposition of words, images, and movements suggested by the actors, and to combine them in a mixed-media collage. The working process begins by assembling a pool of "source" texts that can be pictorial, literary, choreographic, or structural. These are then explored, reworked, and rearranged with images from cultural history, images of public events, and with other ideas that emerge from the collective experiences of Group members. LeCompte also adds the influence of television to that of painting and of photography as she uses television techniques of cutting, editing, distancing, storytelling, the combination of live characters and animation in commercials, and quick pacing. This process began in the mid-1970s in improvisations based on material by Spalding Gray. LeCompte served as an "outside eye" who could observe and shape the emotional impact of moments. Before opening, the ensemble pieces are typically rehearsed over long periods, from six to eighteen months, and in the final stage a physical score is choreographed and the various elements are fused.

The 150-seat Performing Garage, bought by the Group's seven members in the late 1970s and run as a collective as part of the Grand Street Artists Co-op, provides flexible design possibilities for the innovative performances staged by the Group. At first, members of the Group received intermittent salaries. Performances were usually presented Thursday through Saturday or Sunday. Tickets cost $2.50 at first, but prices increased to $4 and then $8. The 1986 range was $5 to $15, and performances were often presented throughout the week. Funding for some seasons has been received from the New York and Massachusetts councils on the arts, from the city of New York, the Wallace Fund, and several other foundations and corporations. In September 1984 the National Endowment for the Arts, a longtime supporter, announced a $170,000 matching grant to the Group as part of a five-year Ongoing Ensembles Grant of $475,000. This allowed the Group to pay its personnel more regularly.

Over a period of time, performances outside New York brought the Group a wider audience, and subsequently the Group performed at the Mickery Theatre in Amsterdam in 1978, the Kaai Theatre Festival in Brussels, the Adelaide Festival in Australia, and the Kennedy Center in Washington, where LeCompte was an associate director of the American National Theatre during its existence. The Group's *Route 1 & 9 (The Last Act)* was an official production of the 1982 Holland-America Bicentennial. When not in residence, the Group sponsors a program at the Garage consisting of experimental theatre, dance, music, and performance art and called the Visiting Artists Season.

In addition to a New York Dance and Performance Award ("Bessie") presented to the Group as a whole, several Group members have received growing attention. LeCompte and Gray received a Creative Artists Public Service (CAPS) Multimedia Fellowship and a Rockefeller Foundation fellowship, and in 1980 LeCompte won an Obie Award for directing *Point Judith*. Spalding Gray, who began in 1979 to explore his personal history in a series of autobiographic monologues, won an Obie in 1985 for one of them, *Swimming to Cambodia*, and in 1986 he presented his one-man series at Lincoln Center, where *Sex and Death to the Age of 14* and *A Personal History of the American Theatre* stood out among other monologues. All Group members have appeared in other theatre and film activities: Willem Dafoe in the motion pictures *Platoon* and *To Live and Die in L.A.*, Peyton Smith with the Ontological-Hysteric Theatre, and Ron Vawter, who received an Obie in 1985 for sustained excellence in performing with the Group, are more familiar. Jim Clayburgh won an Obie in 1982 for sustained excellence in set design.

The Group's experimental work has met with diverse critical and public re-action. *Route 1 & 9 (The Last Act)* was embroiled in a controversy over its use of blackface, and the Group's use of scenes from conventional scripts as one of the bases for its reinterpretation and deconstruction process resulted in the Thornton Wilder Estate threatening action for the use of excerpts from *Our Town*. Premiering in 1981, *Route 1 & 9 (The Last Act)* was hailed variously as "intriguing," "disturbing," "dangerous," and "aggressive." Some critics praised as "inventive" the presentation of excerpts from Eugene O'Neill's *Long Day's Journey into Night* and Arthur Miller's *The Crucible*, but the presentation of an excerpt from T. S. Eliot's *The Cocktail Party* prompted Mel Gussow of the *New York Times* to wish the Group "would sweep the stage of avant-garde detritus—and present a play" (October 31, 1984, III, 28). Arthur Miller's threat of legal action against *LSD (Part One)* resulted in the Group withdrawing the play and revising it as *The Road to Immortality—Part Two (. . . Just the High Points . . .)*. Perhaps the most highly acclaimed Group piece was *Rumstick Road*, which Richard Eder described in the *New York Times* as "visually haunting" and suggestive of "both the intensity of childhood pain, and the odd, generating glow that it possesses in the memory" (December 19, 1978, III, 7). Some critics have found the Group's presentations self-serving and inartistic. Others support and applaud the Wooster Group for its imaginative and resourceful explorations of the possibility of a postmodern theatre.

PERSONNEL

The Group's collective members are the principal management of the organization: Jim Clayburgh, Willem Dafoe, Spalding Gray, Elizabeth LeCompte, Peyton Smith, Kate Valk, and Ron Vawter.

Management: Elizabeth LeCompte, artistic director (1975–86); general managers: Linda Chapman (1983–86), Jeff Jones (1980–83), Debbie Loctizer (1977–80), Ron Vawter (1973–77); office assistants: Pam Calvert (1984–85), Courtenay McPherson (1985–86), Lynn Rublee (1980–83); box office: Dennis Dermody (1980–86), Mary Ann Hestand (1985–86); Berenice Reynaud, director of development (1984–86); Cynthia Hedstrom, director of special projects (1986).

Technical Directors: Scott Breindel (1979–82), Paul Gordon (1985–86), Michael Nishball (1985–86), Bruce Porter (1976–79), Jeff Webster (1983–86).

Designer: Jim Clayburgh (1975–86).

Filmmaker: Ken Kobland (1975–86).

Playwright: Jim Strahs (1978–86).

Dramaturg: Norman Frisch (1983–86).

Guest Director: Richard Foreman (*Miss Universal Happiness*, 1985).

Actors and Actresses: Steve Buscemi, Jim Clayburgh (1975–86), Tena Cohen (1978–83), Willem Dafoe (1978–86), Ursula Easton (1978–83), Norman Frisch (1983–86), Spalding Gray (1975–86), Matthew Hansell (1978–86), Libby Howes (1975–81), Jim Johnson, Joan Jonas, Michael Kirby (1983–86), Anna Köhler (1983–86), Erik Moskowitz (1975–79), Bruce Porter, Nancy Reilly (1983–86), Michael Rivkin (1978–81), Elion Sacker, Irma St. Paule, Peyton Smith (1980–86), Michael Stumm (1983–86), Kate Valk (1978–86), Ron Vawter (1977–86), Jeff Webster (1983–86).

REPERTORY

In addition to the premieres listed below, the Wooster Group presents retrospectives (revivals) of plays each season.

1975: *Sakonnet Point.*

1977: *Rumstick Road.*

1978: *Nayatt School.*

1979: *Point Judith.*

1981: *Hula, Route 1 & 9 (The Last Act)*, later retitled *The Road to Immortality—Part One.*

1982: *For the Good Times.*

1983: *LSD (Part 1), North Atlantic.*

1984: *LSD (. . . Just the High Points . . .)*, later retitled *The Road to Immortality—Part Two (. . . Just the High Points . . .).*

1985: *Miss Universal Happiness.*

1986: *The Road to Immortality—Part Three: The Temptation of Saint Anthony.*

BIBLIOGRAPHY

Published Sources:

Christian Science Monitor, 1975–86.

New York Times, 1975–86.

Village Voice, 1975–86.

Aronson, Arnold. "The Wooster Group's *LSD (. . . Just the High Points . . .)*." *The Drama Review* 29 (Summer 1985): 65–77.

Bierman, James. "*Three Places in Rhode Island*." *The Drama Review* 23 (March 1979): 13–30.

Gray, Spalding. "About *Three Places in Rhode Island*." *The Drama Review* 23 (March 1979): 31–42.

LeCompte, Elizabeth. "Rhode Island Trilogy: An Introduction." *Performing Arts Journal* 8 (Fall 1978): 81–86.

Leverett, James. "The Wooster Group's 'Mean Theatre.' " *Theatre Communications* 5 (July–August 1982): 16–20.

Mehta, Xerxes. "Notes from the Avant-Garde." *Theatre Journal* 31 (March 1979): 5–24.

Rabkin, Gerald. "Is There a Text on This Stage?" *Performing Arts Journal* 26/27 (1985): 142–59.

Savran, David. *The Wooster Group, 1975–1985: Breaking the Rules*. Ann Arbor, Michigan: UMI Research Press, 1986.

David M. Price

WORKERS' LABORATORY THEATRE (WLT), New York City, gave birth to the Shock Troupe and the Theatre Collective, and later became The Theatre of Action. Organized in 1928 by individuals who had worked on Michael Gold's pageant, *Strike!*, in Paterson, New Jersey, two years earlier, it did not assume the collective style of organization nor the style of production for which it was noted until 1930–31. Alfred Saxe, who joined the group at that time, became its leader. After 1932 it was housed in a second floor loft at 42 East Twelfth

Street, which contained offices and a hall that seated 150 persons opposite a low platform stage.

The WLT was one of a number of groups that aimed to use theatre as a weapon in the class struggle by promoting class consciousness among working people. These groups were nationally organized in the League of Workers' Theatres (LOWT, 1932–35), which became the New Theatre League (NTL, 1935–40). Their preferred style of performance was called "agitprop" (agitation-propaganda), a form originating in Russia during its civil war and popularized by Communist trade unions in Germany after 1925. The first group in America to produce this type of theatre was the Proletbuehne (1928–35), directed by John E. Bonn, who had been active in the Berlin theatre between 1923 and 1928. During the thirties the Proletbuehne and the WLT shared artistic resources, and members of the Group Theatre* (1931–40) and the Theatre Union* (1933–37) were also active in WLT projects. WLT members participated in the work of the Federal Theatre Project* (FTP, 1935–39) and Labor Stage (1937–40).

The history of the WLT can be divided into two periods that reflect the strategy of the Communist Party International. Between 1928 and 1933 the International advocated a radical "turn to the Left" that emphasized the irreconcilable nature of class conflict. This was translated into a theatrical style that decisively rejected the values and techniques of bourgeois theatre. During this period the WLT gathered its forces, defined its style, and developed its audience. Its original repertory was made up of conventional one-act plays on social themes, but contact with the Proletbuehne in 1929 introduced its members to agitprop. By 1932 the WLT was organized into two sections. The Evening Section was composed of some fifty working people, who devoted several nights a week to rehearsal and performance. The heart of the organization was the Shock Troupe of between a dozen and eighteen members, who devoted themselves entirely to theatre, lived collectively, and were supported by contributions. The members of the Shock Troupe established policy, gave a majority of the performances, and conducted classes and rehearsals for the evening group. Performances were given on all sorts of occasions for working-class and Left-wing organizations. Normally a booking fee was charged, but free performances were given for rent parties and strike benefits.

During this period there were major changes and achievements in the group. At the end of 1932 the brothers Hiram and Jack Shapiro formed the Theatre Collective as a separate group. It had a membership of about seventy-five, including Mordecai Gorelik. The addition of Stephen and Greta Karnot to the WLT in 1933 stimulated both the theoretical and practical work of the Shock Troupe, and it developed its most successful agitprop piece, *Newsboy*, based on a poem by V. J. Jerome.

The second period of the WLT's history (1933–36) coincided with the International's switch to a popular-front strategy that deemphasized class conflict in favor of an alliance among all progressive segments of society in a war against fascism. This was translated into a rejection of the agitprop style in favor of socialist realism. The political rapprochement with the middle class coincided with rising artistic ambitions among some people in the workers' theatre movement. Between 1930 and 1935 members of various groups debated the permissibility of a relationship with bourgeois theatre. Those whose primary orientation was political argued that in order to participate effectively in the overthrow of capitalist society, it was necessary for workers' theatres to develop a revolutionary theatrical style in no way connected with conventional theatre. Others, with a primarily artistic orientation, argued that a knowledge of theatrical and dramatic techniques gained from the establishment theatre could be put to revolutionary use. As the International took a posture of collaboration with all antifascists, the latter arguments prevailed, and the productions of the Theatre Union, which were class conscious and revolutionary in content but bourgeois in production values, became the norm.

Every group was affected by this shift. The Proletbuehne ceased to exist during 1933–34, and Bonn associated himself with the Theatre Collective. At the end of 1934 the Shock Troupe renamed itself the Theatre of Action for the production of its first full-length play, *The Young Go First*, by Peter Martin, George Sendder, and Charles Friedman. During a stormy rehearsal period Elia Kazan emerged as the dominant director of the newly christened group. Because of his work with the Group Theatre, he was experienced in the craft of representational production, and the WLT actors, who had never before created or sustained realistic characters, turned to him for help. The play opened at the Park Theatre (formerly the Cosmopolitan) on Columbus Circle in May 1935. The last act was admittedly weak, but the group had exhausted its funds and could not afford further rehearsals. Consequently the play's critical and commercial failure plunged them into serious debt, which led to the end of the WLT. The Evening Section was dissolved, and members of the Shock Troupe retained the name Theatre of Action, reverting to mobile production of representational one-act plays.

Financial difficulties only stimulated an existing trend. The FTP was competing with the workers' theatre groups for both performers and audience. Because the FTP could offer a steady wage, members of workers' groups began to defect during 1935–36. By the spring of 1936 neither the Theatre of Action nor the Theatre Collective existed. The former had entered the New York FTP as the Experimental One-Act Play Group, while the latter had dissolved, most of its members finding FTP employment.

Members of the WLT were young (most between the ages of eighteen and twenty-eight), and came from diverse backgrounds. They were neither trained for theatre nor had they much experience in it. Alfred Saxe was a rabbi's son from Illinois who had done some acting at the University of Wisconsin's Experimental College. Will Lee had taught drama at a summer camp. The Shapiros were veterans of the same Chrystie Street Settlement House theatre group as Lee Strasberg. Harry Lessin had been to DePauw University, and had toured with Fritz Lieber's Shakespearean company. Mary Virginia Farmer had broken into dramatic stock in 1921, and had been in Broadway companies since 1925. The most highly trained members of the company did not join until 1933. Stephen Karnot, the group's theorist, had studied at Richard Boleslavsky's American Laboratory Theatre, and had spent eight months at the Meyerhold Theatre in Moscow. His wife, Greta, had been a dance student of both Doris Humphrey and Charles Weidman. Earl Robinson was a musician trained at the University of Washington. After 1933 new members were trained in the WLT's own classes, which included voice (Rhoda Rammelkamp), singing (Earl Robinson), dance (Greta Karnot), fencing (Harold Jacobson), and acting (Robert Lewis and Morris Carnovsky from the Group Theatre).

Because of its members' lack of training and experience, the theatre was collectively organized. The WLT was administered by an elected executive committee that appointed committees and heads of departments for playwriting, directing, and technical production. Usually the membership decided on a subject and its ideological treatment. One or two members then did the actual writing, and their product was submitted to the rest, who were free to suggest changes that would then be tested by improvisation, and either adopted or rejected by majority vote. Directing was also collective. In the WLT Saxe was the principal director, but he was always assigned a colleague for each piece. In the Theatre of Action the only directors were Saxe and Kazan. The former provided the ideological or thematic interpretation of the script, while the latter elicited the desired results from the performers.

A combination of ideology, inexperience, and poverty determined the WLT's performance style. Scenery was minimal, not only because there was little money, but also because it was not practical to transport it from one union or fraternal hall to another. What scenery they did use had to be small enough to fit through the doors of the subway train. Costumes were either uniforms or actual clothes of the actors, augmented by symbolic indication of social type, such as a top hat for a capitalist. The plays were short and featured choral recitation, songs, chants, expressionistic dialogue, and coordinated rhythmic movement.

The Shock Troupe led the most rigorous life. Rising at eight, the group devoted the first part of the morning to cleaning both its apartment and its theatre. By midmorning it was engaged in classes, both technical (acting, makeup) and theoretical (current politics, dialectical materialism). After lunch players rehearsed the material to be performed that night or during the rest of the week. Usually the Shock Troupe gave two performances an evening, but open nights were devoted to classes and rehearsals with members of the Evening Section.

Such intensive work was necessary to meet the demands of its booking schedule. The Shock Troupe had a repertory of eighty-three pieces in 1934, according to one source. Thirty-eight can be identified, and many were published in *Workers Theatre* and *New Theatre*. The earliest of these (1931–32) included *Unemployed, Scottsboro, Help the Miners, Fight Against Starvation*, and *I'll Tell You How to Vote*. In 1933 the Shock Troupe focused on the New York City mayoral election. The piece it played during the campaign was *Who's Got the Baloney?* After the votes were counted it was revised as *LaGuardia's Got the Baloney*, and featured Perry Bruskin's impersonation of the Little Flower.

The most successful piece was *Newsboy*, a twelve-minute montage of the evils of capitalism, but the group continued to be topical with *Free Thaelmann, Jews at the Crossroads*, and the minimusical *Hollywood Goes Red*, all in 1934. It varied its style with excursions into vaudeville (*Mr. Fixemup and Mr. Mixemup*), commedia (*Hot Pastrami*), and classics (Molière's *The Miser*). Its one conventional play, *The Young Go First*, was the topical, realistic story of a young city boy in a CCC (Civilian Conservation Corps) camp.

An agitprop play was always short and directed to a specific point. It dramatized the class consciousness and conflict in a current situation of concern to a specific group. Each character was identified by a typology of attitude, speech, gesture, and costume derived from its economic class. Once the nature of the conflict between classes was established, the piece could conclude in one of two ways: the audience was offered a specific solution to the problem, usually in the form of an exhortation to organize or join a union, or a direction to vote for a specific candidate or group of candidates. On the other hand, the audience could be wrought to an emotional pitch and told that the responsibility for finding a solution was theirs. Although *Newsboy* was the best known of these pieces, the overall framework, as well as the individual episodes of *Waiting for Lefty*, by Clifford Odets, accurately represents the agitational script, though in a sophisticated form.

The subsequent theatrical careers of members of the WLT and its associated groups were insignificant. Most of them vanished after the closing of the FTP. Only Mordecai Gorelik figured prominently on Broadway. A student of Robert Edmond Jones and Norman Bel Geddes, his most successful designs were for John Howard Lawson's *Loud Speaker* (1927), Sidney Kingsley's *Men in White* (1933), Clifford Odets' *Golden Boy* (1937), and Michael Gazzo's *A Hatful of Rain* (1955). From 1960 until the early 1980s he was on the faculty of Southern Illinois University, and he is the author of *New Theatres for Old* (1940). Three of the WLT's actors had subsequent careers that can be traced. Perry Bruskin studied at the Neighborhood Playhouse School of Theatre after leaving the FTP, and then worked as an actor and stage manager on Broadway and in summer stock. Curt Conway and Will Lee had successful Broadway and Hollywood careers as actors. Alfred Saxe continued to work in the political theatre after the demise of the WLT. Between 1940 and 1943 he founded and directed the Popular Theatre, which seems to have been a continuation of the San Francisco Theatre Union, and between 1948 and 1950 he led the Jefferson Theatre Workshop in New York. Of the many notable members of the Group Theatre who worked with the WLT, Elia Kazan was subsequently the most notable. Primarily as the result of his work with the plays of Tennessee Williams and Arthur Miller in the late forties and early fifties, he became the leading Broadway director of serious drama. He was a founder of the Actors' Studio (1947), and was the first artistic director of the Repertory Theatre of Lincoln Center*.

PERSONNEL

Because of the collective nature of the WLT's work, it is not possible to distinguish most people by function. Nearly all performed and also lent a hand at whatever else had to be done. Similarly, membership among groups was so fluid that it is often not possible to distinguish members of the Evening Section from those of the Shock Troupe, the Theatre Collective, or the Theatre of Action. Dates are also a problem. Where possible, the date of earliest participation is given.

Management: Lucy Kaye, secretary (1932); Peter Hyun, the Evening Section (1934); Charles Friedman, Shock Troupe/Theatre of Action (1934).

Musical Director: Earl Robinson (1933).

Choreographer: Greta Karnot (1933).

Stage Directors: Elia Kazan (1935), Alfred Saxe (1930).

Stage Designer: Mordecai Gorelik (1933).

Actors and Actresses: Philip Barber (1933), Rose Beigel (1931), *Ben Berenberg* (1933), Cecilia Bluestone (1933–34), *Perry Bruskin* (1932), Maurice Clark (1933–34), Curt Conway (1932), Louis DeSantes (1928), *Harry Elion* (1932), Mary Virginia Farmer (1933), Peter Frye (1933–34), Ann Gold (1932), Jean Harper (1932), Harold Jacobson (1933–34), Florence Kamlot (1932), Stephen Karnot (1933), David Kerman (1933–34), Lou Lantz (1933–34), Gil Laurence (1933–34), *Will Lee* (1930), Harry Lessin (1932), Edward Mann (1933–34), Peter Martin (1933–34), Harry Nance (1932), *Al Prentiss* (1930), *Rhoda Rammelkamp* (1932), Florence Rauh (1928), Nick Ray (1932), *Bernard Reins* (1930), Oscar Saul (1933–34), *Hiram Shapiro* (1930), *Jack Shapiro* (1930), Johnny Topa (1933–34), Arthur Vogel (1934–35).

REPERTORY

1928–30: *Marching Men, 100,000, S.S. Hellenback, Revolutionary Interlude, ROR, White Trash.*

1930–32: *Unemployed, It's Funny as Hell, Help the Miners, Fight Against Starvation, I'll Tell You How to Vote, The Fight Goes On, Three of a Kind, Step on It, Mr. Box, Mr. Fox, and Mr. Nox, The Big Stiff, Tempo! Tempo!, The Miners Are Striking, We Demand, Scottsboro, Charity, The Sell-Out.*

1933–36: *The Big Fight, The Side Show, Sweet Charity, Whose Got the Baloney?, LaGuardia's Got the Baloney, Newsboy, Life Is Just a Bowl of Neuroses, Intervention, The Miser, Jews at the Crossroads, Daughter, Free Thaelmann, Hot Pastrami, Hollywood Goes Red, Mr. Mixemup and Dr. Fixemup, The Young Go First, The Crime, The Little Green Bundle, Snickering Horses, The Great Catherine, Casey Jones, The Triangle.*

BIBLIOGRAPHY

Published Sources:
The Daily Worker, 1928–36.
New Masses, 1929–36.
New Theatre and Film, April/May 1937.
New Theatre Magazine, January 1934–November, 1936.
New Theatre News, November 1938–January 1939, November 1939.

TAC, July 1938–August 1940.

Theatre Workshop, October/December 1936–April/June 1938.

Workers' Theatre, April 1931–December 1933.

Goldstein, Malcolm. *The Political Stage: American Drama and Theatre of the Great Depression*. New York: Oxford University Press, 1974.

Himelstein, Morgan Y. *Drama Was a Weapon: The Left-Wing Theatre in New York, 1929–1941*. New Brunswick, N.J.: Rutgers University Press, 1974.

McDermott, Douglas. "Agitprop: Production Practice in the Workers' Theatre, 1932–42." *Theatre Survey* 7 (May 1966): 115–24.

Williams, Jay. *Stage Left*. New York: Scribner, 1974.

   Archival Resource:

New York, New York. New York Public Library. Library and Museum of the Performing Arts. Plays, photographs, and clipping files.

Douglas McDermott

Y

YALE REPERTORY THEATRE (YRT), New Haven, Connecticut, was founded in 1966 by Robert Brustein, then newly appointed dean of the Yale School of Drama, as part of his plan to transform the school from an academically structured graduate institution into a professional conservatory. A former actor, professor of dramatic literature at Columbia University, and drama critic for the *New Republic* since 1959, Brustein envisioned the YRT as a model for students in the conservatory, as a source of instructors, as a laboratory for adventurous productions and for testing student talent, and as a potential employer of conservatory graduates. Brustein's ideal of a professional theatre organically linked to a theatre conservatory informed the company's growth under his leadership from 1966 to 1979 and distinguished it from New Haven's other resident company, the Long Wharf Theatre*. Under the artistic direction of Lloyd Richards from 1979 to 1986, the YRT has continued to articulate its role as "master teacher" to the Yale School of Drama.

From 1966 to 1969 YRT used the University Theatre, a 700-seat proscenium house built in 1925–26 for Yale's department of drama. In 1969 the university donated the recently acquired Calvary Baptist Church, located at the corner of Chapel and York streets, a half block from the school. Though originally intended as a temporary home for YRT, the church was renovated in 1969, again in 1972, and once more in 1975, when, with 491 seats before an apron stage, it became YRT's permanent production center. YRT has continued to use the University Theatre for proscenium productions.

Before the establishment of a resident company, the Yale School of Drama employed two visiting companies. Philadelphia's Theatre of the Living Arts* presented Samuel Beckett's *Endgame*, directed by Andre Gregory, and the Open Theatre* of New York City presented Megan Terry's *Viet Rock*. The first work (opening December 6, 1966) produced wholly under the auspices of YRT was the antiwar "actors' opera," *Dynamite Tonite!*, by Arnold Weinstein and William Bolcom. Paul Sills directed William Redfield, George Gaynes, Linda Lavin, Eugene Troobnick, Alvin Epstein, and three drama school students. Two revitalized classics followed: Clifford Williams of the Royal Shakespeare Company directed Ben Jonson's *Volpone*, setting it in a Federico Fellini–like Venice; and British director Jonathan Miller set Robert Lowell's new adaptation of *Prometheus Bound* in a seventeenth-century prison.

The first season's range in play selection was matched by a variety of acting styles. Many in the cast of *Dynamite Tonite!* had been members of an improvisational troupe run by Sills at Chicago's Second City. Two expert comic stylists, David Hurst and Ron Leibman, formerly with the Theatre of the Living Arts, where they had portrayed Hamm and Clov in *Endgame*, played Volpone and Mosca at Yale. They also played Ocean and Hermes opposite the classically trained Kenneth Haigh and Irene Worth, Prometheus and Io in Lowell's *Prometheus Bound*.

In 1967 Brustein hired what he hoped would become a permanent company. Larry Arrick, formerly an associate of Sills at Second City, became resident artistic director, and Kathleen Widdoes, Richard Jordan, Michael Lombard, Paul Mann, Anthony Holland, Barry Morse, Jeanne Hepple, Estelle Parsons, John Karlen, Harris Yulin, Roger Hendricks, Tom Rosqui, and Stacy Keach joined Haigh and Leibman to form the acting company. The first full season produced by the Yale School of Drama Repertory Theatre (a name changed to Yale Repertory Theatre in 1968) included Kenneth Haigh's first directing effort, a reconceptualization of John Ford's *'Tis Pity She's a Whore;* Arrick's improvisation-based production of Joseph Heller's first play, *We Bombed in New Haven;* Luigi Pirandello's *Henry IV* (with a highly praised performance by Haigh in the title role); and Shakespeare's *Coriolanus*, with Stacy Keach in the title role. Though *New York Times* critic Clive Barnes called the Yale group one of the best repertory companies in the country (February 7, 1968, p. 40), by season's end everyone except Keach, Morse, Yulin, and Lombard had left and Arrick had stepped down. In his memoir of his Yale years Brustein claims that a lack of enough large roles, unfriendly tension between actors and some students, and limited access to the University Theatre undermined the group (*Making Scenes: A Personal History of the Turbulent Years at Yale, 1966–1979* [New York: Limelight Editions, 1984], pp. 53, 58).

Brustein became artistic director for the controversy-rocked 1968–69 season. YRT hosted the Living Theatre*, recently returned to the United States, and ten performers and spectators were arrested for indecent exposure after a performance of *Paradise Now*. A production of *God Bless*, Jules Feiffer's satire on Washington politics and radical revolutionaries, brought bomb threats to the theatre. Finally, Sam Shepard canceled a production of *Operation Sidewinder*, under pressure of mounting complaints that the play stereotyped blacks.

These events reflected not only the tense national mood of the time, but also tensions between theatre students and theatre professionals. Both parties resisted integration, though signs of successful cooperation were plentiful. Students designed sets, costumes, and lights, and played small roles from the beginning, and the 1968–69 company included four recent graduates. Resident director Jeff Bleckner, one of those graduates, directed the American premiere of Edward Bond's *Saved*, which featured former conservatory students David Clennon and Joan Pape. *Saved* appeared on a bill of one-act plays directed and acted by students. Moreover, Brustein canceled a production of Ronald Ribman's *The Inheritors* because it had too few roles for students. Critics praised the ensemble work of Paul Sills' *Story Theatre*, with its mixed cast of professionals, graduates, and advanced students narrating and acting out selections of Grimm's fairy tales. *Story Theatre* productions appeared regularly until 1974–75. Their success highlighted the growth of student-professional integration at YRT in these years, for each production blended the talents of professionals with those of students and recent graduates. Conversely, no students appeared in *God Bless*, and Andre Gregory's electrifying production of Euripides' *The Bacchae* was prepared in two rehearsal periods, one for principals, played by professionals, and one for the student chorus.

In 1969–70 students began to appear regularly in significant roles; in 1976 Brustein institutionalized the method by which students were chosen to act: first-year students played small roles and walk-ons; second-year students worked as understudies; and third-year (and selected second-year) students played substantial parts. Some third-year students became members of the acting company and played two or more roles in the season. After graduation these students often became professional members of the company. Almost 300 of the more than 400 actors who appeared at the YRT from 1966 to 1979 were students. Although the majority played small parts and walk-ons, the students were the backbone of YRT.

In addition to the names of Clennon, Pape, and David Ackroyd, a list of conservatory graduates and students who acted at the YRT under Brustein would include such now well-known television and film actors as Ken Howard, Henry Winkler, Jill Eikenberry, Michael Gross, Christine Estabrook, James Naughton, John Shea, Mark Linn-Baker, William Converse-Roberts, Sigourney Weaver, and Meryl Streep, as well as playwright Christopher Durang. Winkler's fame as television's "Fonzie" was hardly foreshadowed by the classic roles he played at the YRT. These included both Bobchinsky and Dobchinsky in the same production of Nikolai Gogol's *The Government Inspector (Revizor)*, Pedro in Molière's *Don Juan*, and Andres in Georg Buchner's *Woyzeck*. In contrast, Streep's great range as a film actress was anticipated by the range of her roles, as, among others, the senile Constance Garnett in *The Idiots Karamazov*, by Christopher Durang and Albert Innaurato; Bertha in August Strindberg's *The Father;* and Helena in *A Midsummer Night's Dream*.

The involvement of student actors in YRT productions was matched only by that of student designers. Only six non-students—Michael Annals, Ming Cho Lee, Krystyna Zachwatowicz, Ariel Ballif, Jeanne Button, and William Warfel—designed sets, costumes, and lights. Most of these were conservatory teachers and advisors to student designers such as Santo Loquasto, Jeffrey Higginbottom, Michael H. Yeargan, Tony Straiges, William Ivey Long, and Dunya Ramicova, all of whom have acquired significant national and international reputations. Yeargan, who has served as resident set designer since 1973, has uniquely conceptualized and artfully designed sets and costumes for almost forty productions of classic, modern, and new texts.

Although *Story Theatre* became the hallmark of Yale's student-professional ensemble work, the YRT under Brustein received even more critical attention for its innovative interpretations of classic and modern plays. Williams' *Volpone* and Miller's *Prometheus* began a tradition whose most emphatic continuator was Brustein himself. Between 1969 and 1979 he directed a highly praised Black Mass version of Molière's *Don Juan;* a less favorably received production of Cyril Tourneur's *The Revenger's Tragedy* that stressed the work's debt to the medieval morality play; a controversial *Macbeth* that portrayed the weird sisters as extraterrestrials exerting power over a prehistoric civilization; a production of Henrik Ibsen's *The Wild Duck* that presented the play through a gigantic camera lens; and a "dream-play" version of Chekhov's *The Sea Gull.*

One of YRT's leading actors, Alvin Epstein, became another of YRT's innovative directors. Epstein, who trained with Etienne Decroux in Paris and performed with the Habimah Theatre in Israel, was an accomplished mime and a well-established New York actor when he first appeared at Yale in *Dynamite Tonite!.* His career at Yale began in earnest in 1968–69, when he portrayed the 110-year-old statesman in *God Bless*, Dionysus in *The Bacchae*, and various roles in *Story Theatre* and the Weinstein–Bolcom opera, *Greatshot*. From 1969 to 1977, when he left Yale to become artistic director of the Guthrie Theatre Company*, Epstein continued to perform a wide range of roles, including Khlestakov in *The Government Inspector*, Maurice in August Strindberg's *There Are Crimes and Crimes*, Don Juan, Woyzeck, Prospero, the title role in Eugene Ionesco's *Macbett*, Shakespeare in Bond's *Bingo*, and Ivanov in Anton Chekhov's play of the same title.

Epstein's first directing assignment, in 1969–70, was Richard Brinsley Sheridan's *The Rivals*, presented, according to Brustein, in a fashion reminiscent of the Old Vic of the 1950s (*Making Scenes*, p. 97). From this conventional beginning, he went on to direct a variety of less orthodox productions. These included Albert Camus' *Caligula*, with a highly praised performance by Christopher Walken, and Michael Feingold's colloquial adaptation of Molière's *The Bourgeois Gentleman*. Epstein also served as acting artistic director (1972–73) and associate director (1973–77).

Yet Epstein's work as a director is significant primarily because of his involvement with two of the theatre's most successful projects in reinterpretation of modern and classic drama: its productions of the works of Bertolt Brecht and Kurt Weill and of William Shakespeare. In 1968 Epstein and Martha Schlamme opened the first season of the Yale Cabaret with "An Evening of Kurt Weill Songs," which later toured the country as "The Kurt Weill Cabaret." In 1970–

71 Epstein directed part of a YRT outgrowth from this cabaret: a *Story Theatre*–style version of Brecht and Weill's *The Seven Deadly Sins*, which appeared on the same bill with Michael Feingold's translation of *The Little Mahagonny*, also by Brecht and Weill. These productions were the first in a series of collaborations with the Yale School of Music: the American premiere, twenty-three years after its writing, of Elizabeth Hauptmann, Brecht, and Weill's *Happy End*, adapted by Michael Feingold (with Epstein in a leading role); Feingold's adaptation of *The Rise and Fall of the City of Mahagonny*, with Epstein directing YRT actors and the professional singers Gilbert Price and Grace Keagy; and a chamber version of *The Rise and Fall of the City of Mahagonny*, titled *Mahagonny*, adapted and directed by Keith Hack. These productions led music critic Alan Rich to observe: "Yale has become a cornerstone for a splendid new style of restoring life to the Brecht-Weill repertory" (*New York*, March 11, 1974, p. 82).

Elements of the "Yale" style included setting productions in a new locale and time period (Epstein set *Mahagonny* in Alaska during the Gold Rush) and using YRT actors rather than professional singers to stress energetic, evocative acting over precise singing. Efforts to find new life in an old play characterized Epstein's productions of Shakespeare as well. In addition to playing Prospero, Epstein combined the text of *The Tempest* with the score of Henry Purcell's operatic version of the play. This production was generally well received, as was *Troilus and Cressida*, which Epstein set in a deteriorating world, symbolized by a crumbling wall. Far less successful was Epstein's *Julius Caesar*, set in a chaotic, phantasmagoric world, evoked partly by a cacophonous chorus of natural sounds created by avant-garde composer Kirk Nurock. The YRT's greatest critical and popular success with Shakespeare came when Epstein integrated the score of Purcell's *The Fairy Queen*, performed by a full orchestra and chorus from the Yale School of Music, with *A Midsummer Night's Dream* and set the whole in an eerily beautiful nightscape designed by Tony Straiges.

Innovative directors have been a hallmark of the YRT. Englishman Ron Daniels expanded YRT's exploration of Brecht with productions of *Mr. Puntila and His Chauffeur Matti* and *Man Is Man*, staging the first as a carnival and the second as an epic, revolutionary spectacle. In both he created a totally anti-illusionistic environment, exposing entirely the YRT stage and its source of scenic effects. After Epstein left Yale, Rumanian Andrei Belgrader continued the theatre's exploration of Shakespeare with an experimental version of *As You Like It*. Another Rumanian, Andrei Serban, widely known for his performance group interpretations of modern and classic plays at LaMama and at Lincoln Center, succeeded Epstein as associate director in 1977–78. That season he directed an imagistic production of Strindberg's *The Ghost Sonata* and a highly successful evening of four of Molière Sganarelle farces. One of these pieces, *A Dumb Show*, was loosely adapted by Serban and composer Elizabeth Swados from Molière's *A Doctor in Spite of Himself*, and consisted of knockdown antics and an innovative text of grunts and Slavic-sounding neologisms. Loose adaptation was also the keynote of Burt Shevelove's work. In the style of *A Funny*

Thing Happened on the Way to the Forum, Shevelove, Larry Gelbart, and composer Stephen Sondheim created a musical version of Aristophanes' *The Frogs*, which Shevelove staged in and around the swimming pool of Yale's Payne-Whitney gymnasium.

Polish director Andrzej Wajda's work included an adaptation of Camus' dramatization of Fyodor Dostoyevsky's *The Possessed*, and a new play, Tadeuscz Rozewicz' *White Marriage*. Collaborating with his wife, designer Krystyna Zachwatowicz, Wajda reproduced the spare, metaphorical design—mud floor, luminous skies—of his earlier production of the play at Cracow's Stary Theatre. For *White Marriage*, an investigation into the development of two adolescent girls toward sexual awareness, Wajda and Zachwatowicz created a fantasy world of material objects transformed into erotic imagery. Jan Kott's observation that *The Possessed* was the best thing he had ever seen in the United States (cited in *Making Scenes*, p. 187) is representative of the praise YRT received for the theatrical power of these productions.

In addition to its efforts to revitalize the classics, YRT maintained a strong commitment to theatrical adaptation of narrative masterpieces and to new plays. *Story Theatre* was the model of several adventurous theatricalizations: Arnold Weinstein and Kenneth Cavender's adaptation of Ovid's *Metamorphoses*, Cavender's adaptation of Gustave Flaubert's *Saint Julian the Hospitaler*, Larry Arrick's adaptation of Isaac Bashevis Singer's *Gimpel the Fool*, and Alvin Epstein and Walt Jones' adaptation of Joseph Conrad's novel *Victory*. Notable new American works produced by the YRT included Eric Bentley's *Are You Now or Have You Ever Been?*, Sam Shepard's *Suicide in B-Flat* and *Buried Child*, Arthur Kopit's *Wings*, David Mamet's *Reunion* and *Dark Pony*, Christopher Durang and Albert Innaurato's *The Idiots Karamazov*, Durang's *The Vietnamization of New Jersey*, and Ted Tally's *Terra Nova*. The 1968 production of *Saved* was the first of a series of controversial plays by English playwright Edward Bond. The series lasted to the end of Brustein's tenure and included *Passion, Lear, Bingo*, and *The Bundle*. An annual grant of $100,000 from the CBS Foundation supported CBS Fellows who taught playwriting and wrote plays for potential production at Yale from 1973 to 1978. E. L. Doctorow, Jack Gelber, John Ford Noonan, Thomas Babe, Robert Penn Warren, William Hauptmann, Derek Walcott, Charles Ludlam, and Dwight Macdonald were CBS Fellows, among others. The CBS fellowships were representative of Brustein's efforts to maintain a nearly self-sufficient company of resident artists.

After the dissolution of the 1967–68 acting company the dream of a permanent acting ensemble remained unfulfilled, yet from 1968 to 1979 YRT signed almost half of its more than one hundred visiting actors for two or more roles in a season. At the heart of acting ensembles were, in addition to Alvin Epstein, five actors who made their careers throughout the 1970s mainly through acting at Yale: Jeremy Geidt, Eugene Troobnick, Carmen de Lavallade, Elizabeth Parrish, and Norma Brustein. Geidt, a former teacher at the Old Vic School, came to Yale with Brustein in 1966 as a teacher of acting and left with Brustein in 1979.

This former member of the English satirical group "The Establishment" played a variety of classic and modern roles, many of them comic. He was seen as Bob Acres in *The Rivals*, as Duncan and the Porter in *Macbeth*, as Stephano in *The Tempest*, as Pandarus in *Troilus and Cressida*, as Julius Caesar, as Old Ekdal in *The Wild Duck*, and as Sorin in *The Sea Gull*. Troobnick, one of the veterans of the Second City improvisational troupe, came to Yale for *Dynamite Tonite!* and returned regularly until 1978 to play roles comparable to Geidt's: the mayor in *The Government Inspector*, Sganarelle in both Brustein's *Don Juan* and Serban's evening of Molière farces, Agamemnon in *Troilus and Cressida*, and Hjalmar Ekdal in *The Wild Duck*.

De Lavallade was a distinguished dancer with Alvin Ailey, Martha Graham, and Robert Joffrey before she made a striking midcareer shift to acting with the YRT. From 1969 to 1977 she moved from small roles to Lady Macbeth, Maia in Ibsen's *When We Dead Awaken*, Ariel in *The Tempest*, Titania in *A Midsummer Night's Dream*, and Helen in *Troilus and Cressida*. She also danced as "the dancing Anna" in *The Seven Deadly Sins*. Both Elizabeth Parrish and Norma Brustein had wide experience in New York theatre before coming to Yale. From 1968 to 1975 Parrish's roles included Mrs. Malaprop in *The Rivals*, Lady Macbeth, and "the singing Anna" in *The Seven Deadly Sins*. From 1973 to 1979 Norma Brustein moved from supporting roles into the roles of Mrs. Sorby in *The Wild Duck* and Arkadina in *The Sea Gull*.

In 1969 the theatre was one of the first in the country to employ a literary manager (sometimes called a dramaturg), a person responsible for script preparation (including translation), researching and writing program notes, and consultation with directors and the artistic director on historical and aesthetic matters. The use of production dramaturgs gradually increased until 1975, when it became a season-long practice, drawing on students from Yale's doctor of fine arts program in dramatic literature and criticism.

Following the standard model of resident theatre organization in the United States, the YRT employed a managing director in charge of business operations. Until 1973, when this position was filled by a recent graduate of Yale's master of fine arts program in theatre administration (established by Brustein in 1966), Brustein himself bore much of the burden of fund-raising. Between 1967 and 1973 the YRT received sizable grants from the National Endowment for the Arts and from the Rockefeller Foundation as well as private gifts from donors such as Paul Newman, Joseph E. Levine, and David Merrick. Though box-office sales were strong and steadily increased, total funding levels were never high enough to make the theatre consistently solvent. The 1970–71 season ended with YRT $110,000 in the red, and in the spring of 1973 the company lost more than 1,000 subscribers. Brustein has observed that funding agencies, especially city and state arts commissions, commonly perceive the YRT as an educational institution, and therefore beyond their funding purview (*Making Scenes*, p. 135). Between 1973 and 1979 the theatre received support for special programs not only from the CBS Foundation, but also from the Mellon Foundation. However,

neither public nor foundation funding was YRT's financial mainstay during the
Brustein years. Moreover, until 1979, it never had more than 6,000 subscribers,
and about 50 percent of these were Yale students attending the theatre on deeply
discounted passes. By comparison, the Long Wharf Theatre had 14,000 subscribers in 1978. The YRT has depended on increasing audiences for its survival,
managing to end every season without debt. After a change to rotating repertory
in 1973, YRT's attendance totals grew annually.

In 1978 Yale's new president, A. Bartlett Giamatti, decided he would not
renew Brustein's contract in 1979. In the fall of 1978 Harvard University accepted
Brustein's proposal for the formation of a professional company and conservatory
at Harvard's Loeb Drama Center. Brustein's "new" organization, the American
Repertory Theatre (ART)*, opened its first season on March 21, 1980, with the
Alvin Epstein–directed *A Midsummer Night's Dream*. The initial ART season
included a revival of Brecht's *Happy End* and involved more than thirty YRT
actors, directors, designers, dramaturgs, technicians, playwrights, and administrators, who moved to Cambridge with Brustein.

Since 1978, the YRT has flourished not as a resident theatre company, but
as a single-play-producing organization under the leadership of Lloyd Richards,
Giamatti's appointee as dean of the drama school and artistic director of YRT.
In 1980–81 Richards suspended efforts to maintain a permanent acting company
and elected sequential production over rotating repertory, although he has maintained rotating repertory for an annual "Winterfest" of three or four new American plays. Between 1979 and 1986 Yale has seen American and/or world
premieres of South African Athol Fugard's *A Lesson from Aloes*, *Master Harold
. . . and the boys*, *The Road to Mecca*, and *The Blood Knot*, all directed by
Fugard. Richards has directed significant world premieres of August Wilson's
Ma Rainey's Black Bottom, *Fences*, and *Joe Turner's Come and Gone*. The
transfer to Broadway of Fugard's and Wilson's works has earned the YRT
Antoinette Perry ("Tony") Awards and other national critical accolades. YRT
has staged American premieres of Austrian Peter Handke's *They Are Dying Out*,
Italian Dario Fo's *About Face*, and Nigerian Wole Soyinka's *A Play of Giants*,
new work by American writers John Guare, Corinne Jacker, Richard Nelson,
and James Yoshimura, as well as by West Indian Derek Walcott, among others.
The repertory has continued to include productions of dramatic masterpieces of
the past.

A few directors have returned from the Brustein years: Andrei Belgrader, for
example, has directed Alfred Jarry's *Ubu Rex*, Joe Orton's *What the Butler Saw*,
and Gogol's *Marriage;* Alvin Epstein has directed Oscar Wilde's *The Importance
of Being Earnest* and Shaw's *Heartbreak House*. Returning from the Brustein
years to act have been, among others, Christopher Walken, Ron Faber, Harris
Yulin, Swoosie Kurtz, Addison Powell, Bob Balaban, and Thomas Hill, as well
as numerous Yale students and graduates. According to the policy established
by Brustein, drama school students continue to act with professionals in YRT

productions. Especially successful conservatory graduates under Richards, all of whom have acted at the YRT, are Kate Burton, Charles S. "Roc" Dutton, Sabrina LeBeauf, John Turturro, and Courtney Vance. Thus a strong relationship between the conservatory and a professional theatre persists at Yale.

PERSONNEL

Artistic Directors: Larry Arrick, resident artistic director (1968); Robert Brustein, artistic director (1968–79); Alvin Epstein, acting artistic director (1972–73), associate director (1973–77); Keith Hack, associate director (1978–79); Walt Jones, associate director (1977–78); Lloyd Richards, artistic director (1979–86); Andrei Serban, associate director (1977–78).

Managing Directors: Thomas R. Burrows, Jr. (1966–71), Sheldon Kleinman (1971–73), Edward A. Martenson (1979–82), Benjamin Mordecai (1982–86), Robert J. Orchard (1973–79).

Dramaturgs: Philip Blumberg, associate literary manager (1975–76); Michael Cadden, associate literary manager (1976–77, 1980–83); Barbara Davenport, associate literary manager (1979–83), associate dramaturg (1983–86); Michael Feingold, literary manager (1969–75); Gitta Honegger, resident dramaturg (1983–86); Stephen R. Lawson, associate literary manager (1978–79); Jonathan Marks, literary manager (1975–80); Joel Schechter, associate literary manager (1977–83), associate dramaturg (1983–86).

Production Supervisors: F. Mitchell Dana (1969–70), John Robert Hood (1970–80), Bronislaw J. Sammler (1980–86).

Technical Directors: A. D. Carson (1984–86), Robin Lacy (1966–67), Robert D. McClintock (1982–84), George Moredock (1970–73), Bronislaw J. Sammler (1973–80), William Taylor (1967–70), David Ward (1980–82).

Resident Set Designers: Santo Loquasto (1970–71); Steven Rubin (1971–73); Tony Straiges, associate resident designer (1974–1976); *Michael H. Yeargan* (1973–86).

Resident Costume Designer: *Dunya Ramicova* (1977–86).

Scene Design Advisor: *Ming Cho Lee* (1973–86).

Costume Design Advisors: Ariel Ballif (1970–72), Jeanne Button (1974–78), *Jane Greenwood* (1978–86).

Lighting Design Advisors: Tom Skelton (1977–81); Jennifer Tipton (1981–86); *William B. Warfel*, lighting advisor (1968–73), lighting director (1973–86).

Set Designers: Michael Annals (1966–67), Ming Cho Lee (1972–73), Krystyna Zachwatowicz (1974–75, 1976–77).

Set Designers—Yale School of Drama Students and Graduates: Timothy Averill (1984–85), Christopher H. Barreca (1982–83), John Beatty (1972–73), Ursula Belden (1975–76), Robert Blackman (1968–69), Scott Bradley (1985–86), Zack Brown (1973–74), Andrew Carter (1983–84), Lawrence Casey (1979–80), Jane Clark (1981–82), Christopher Phelps Clavens (1976–77), Elizabeth Doyle (1983–84), Randy Drake (1979–80), Gary C. Eckhardt (1969–70), Kate Edmunds (1977–78), Kenneth Emmanule (1969–70), Heidi Ettinger (1975–76), Joel Fontaine (1981–83), Alison Ford (1981–82), Bill Forrester (1968–69), Jess Goldstein (1977–78), Peter Gould (1969–70), David Lloyd Gropman (1975–77), Jeffrey Higginbottom (1969–70), Douglas Higgins (1966–67), Andrew Jackness (1977–79), John W. Jacobsen (1967–68), Stewart Wayne Johnson (1969–70), Philipp Jung (1982–83), Elina Katsioula (1985–86), Lawrence Station King (1969–70), Raymond M. Kluga (1980–81), Susan Condie Lamb (1984–85), Wing Lee (1982–83), Adrianne Lobel (1978–79), William Ivey Long (1973–74), Santo Loquasto (1968–69, 1970–71),

Tom Lynch (1978–80), Charles E. McCarry (1979–80, 1984–86), Charles Henry McClennahan (1983–84), Derek McLane (1983–84), Peter Maradudin (1983–84), Richard F. Mays (1983–84), G. W. Mercier (1982–83), Ricardo Morin (1981–83), Tina Navarro (1985–86), Atkin Pace (1974–75), David Peterson (1985–86), Pamela Peterson (1984–86), Rosario Provenza (1985–86), Ellis M. Pryce-Jones (1971–72), Raymond C. Recht (1971–72), Richard L. Rowsell (1972–73), Andrew Rubenoff (1981–82), Steven Rubin (1970–73), Kevin Rupnik (1980–81, 1984–85), Steve Saklad (1980–81), James D. Sandefur (1984–85), Tim Saternow (1985–86), Clare Scarpulla (1984–85), Karen Schultz (1980–81), Loren Sherman (1979–80), Paul Shortt (1966–68), Rusty Smith (1985–86), Douglas O. Stein (1981–82), Tony Straiges (1973–77, 1978–79, 1981–82), Robert R. Struble (1968–69), Robert U. Taylor (1967–68), Nancy Thun (1977–78), Gil Weschler (1966–67), Gary James Wheeler (1971–72), Robert M. Wierzel (1982–84), Michael H. Yeargan (1970–71, 1972–86), Leo Yoshimura (1970–71), Basha Zmyslowski (1984–85).

Costume Designers: Michael Annals (1966–67), Ariel Ballif (1970–71), *Jeanne Button* (1972–78), Krystyna Zachwatowicz (1974–75, 1976–77).

Costume Designers—Yale School of Drama Students and Graduates: Tove Ahlback (1973–74), Kathleen Armstrong (1976–77), Anette Beck (1975–76), Robert Blackman (1968–69), Scott Bradley (1984–86), Claudia Marlow Brown (1984–85), Zack Brown (1974–75), Vittorio Capecce (1974–75), Nan Cibula (1978–80), Jane Clark (1981–82), Candice Donnelly (1983–85), Arnall Downs (1984–86), Gary C. Eckhardt (1968–70), Kate Edmunds (1977–78), Kenneth Emmanule (1969–70), Linda Fisher (1967–68), Quina Fonseca (1981–82), Jess Goldstein (1975–76, 1977–78), Peter Gould (1969–70), Marjorie Graf (1978–79), Michelle Guillot (1971–72), Jeffrey Higginbottom (1969–70), Douglas Higgins (1967–68), Susan Hilferty (1978–80, 1985–86), Philipp Jung (1982–83), Martha Kelly (1980–81), Lawrence Station King (1969–70), Raymond M. Kluga (1980–81), Gene K. Lakin (1981–82), Susan Condie Lamb (1984–85), Wing Lee (1981–82), Adrianne Lobel (1978–79), William Ivey Long (1973–75), Santo Loquasto (1968–69, 1970–71), Jac McAnelly (1968–69), Charles E. McCarry (1985–86), Charles Henry McClennahan (1983–84), Sheila McLamb (1981–82), Derek McLane (1983–84), Judianna Makovsky (1978–80), Richard F. Mays (1982–84), G. W. Mercier (1982–83), Carl Michna Michell (1968–69), Ricardo Morin (1982–83), Tina Navarro (1985–86), Tony Negron (1973–74), Atkin Pace (1974–75), Suzanne Palmer (1975–76), Daphne Pascucci (1983–84), David Peterson (1984–85), Pamela Peterson (1985–86), Thom Peterson (1966–68), Enno Poersch (1972–73), Ellis M. Pryce-Jones (1971–72), Dunya Ramicova (1976–86), Tom Rasmussen (1967–68), Dean H. Reiter (1979–80), Richard L. Rowsell (1972–73), Steven Rubin (1969–73), Rita Ryack (1979–80), Steve Saklad (1980–81), James D. Sandefur (1983–84), Cara Z. Shubin (1966–67), Connie Singer (1982–83), Rusty Smith (1984–86), Douglas O. Stein (1980–81), Tony Straiges (1973–74, 1975–76), Alec Sutherland (1967–68), Kenneth Thompson (1969–70), Michael H. Yeargan (1971–72, 1973–76), Donna Zakowski (1982–83), Catherine Zuber (1981–84).

Lighting Designers: Jennifer Tipton (1981–86), *William B. Warfel* (1969–86), Krystyna Zachwatowicz (1974–75).

Lighting Designers—Yale School of Drama Students and Graduates: William Armstrong (1978–80), Ting Barrow (1966–67), Michael H. Baumgarten (1980–81), William J. Buck (1983–84), Paul Butler (1970–71), Rick Butler (1979–81), Ian Rodney Calderon (1971–72), Andrew Carter (1982–83), Suellen Childs (1968–69), Michael R. Chybowski (1985–86), William Conner (1977–78), Dennis G. Dalusio (1970–71), F. Mitchell Dana (1966–67), Richard Devin (1968–69), Phil Dixson (1966–67), Dennis L. Dorn (1971–

72), Nathan L. Drucker (1971–73), Dirk Epperson (1973–74), Lewis Folden (1975–77), James H. Gage (1976–78), Paul Gallo (1975–77), Mary Louise Geiger (1984–85), Michael Gianitti (1985–86), Barb Harris (1972–74), Robert Allen Heaton (1967–68), Donald Holder (1984–86), Timothy J. Hunter (1980–82), James F. Ingalls (1974–75), Laura Mae Jackson (1967–68), Robert Jared (1977–79), Stewart Wayne Johnson (1969–70), Al Kibbe (1971–72), Donald Bondy Lowy (1975–76), T. J. McHose (1968–69), Peter Maradudin (1982–84), Edwin C. Meyer (1967–68), Jeffrey Milet (1968–69), Danianne Mizzy (1984–86), George Moredock (1969–70), Spencer Mosse (1967–68), David Noling (1980–82), Steve Pollock (1975–76), Lloyd S. Riford III (1974–76), Tom Roscher (1983–84), Bronislaw J. Sammler (1973–74), Robert W. Scheeler (1970–71), Tom Schraeder (1977–78), Laurence F. Schwartz (1982–83), Loren Sherman (1979–80), Thomas Skelton (1976–80), David Alan Stach (1984–85), Stephen Strawbridge (1981–83), Jenie Swartz (1969–70), Edgar Swift (1970–72), D. Edmund Thomas (1972–74), John Tissot (1979–81), Rick Ulrich (1968–69), Carol M. Waaser (1969–70, 1973–74), Steven Waxler (1967–68), Gil Weschler (1966–67), Robert M. Wierzel (1982–84), Peter Edmond Winter (1969–70), Stephen R. Woody (1974–76).

Composers: Dwight Andrews (1980–81, 1985–86), William Bolcom (1966–67, 1968–69, 1975–77), Marion Brown (1970–71), Barbara Damashek (1969–71), Jack Feldman (1974–75), George Griggs (1982–83), Lenny Hat (1973–74), Walt Jones (1972–73, 1974–75), Vasil Kazandgiev (1980–81), Zigmund Konieczny (1974–75), Carol Lees (1975–76), Mark Levinson (1969–70), Rusty Magee (1980–81), Sarah S. Meneely (1971–72), Steven Michaels (1969–70), Robert Montgomery (1969–70), Carman Moore (1979–80), Grafton Mouen (1981–82), Kirk Nurock (1976–77), Bobby Paul (1973–74), Richard Peaslee (1968–71, 1977–78), Krzysztof Penderecki (1975–76), Herb Pilhofer (1977–78), Michael Posnick (1969–70), Paul Schierhorn (1974–76, 1977–80), Paul Severtson (1971–72), Craig Shapiro (1982–83), Stephen Sondheim (1973–74), Elizabeth Swados (1977–78), Preston A. Trombly (1972–73), Lawrence Wolf (1976–77), Yehudi Wyner (1972–73), Maury Yeston (1971–72, 1973–74).

CBS Playwriting Fellows: Robert Auletta (1974–76), Thomas Babe (1975–76), Eric Bentley (1976–77), Lonnie Carter (1974–75), Charles Dizenzo (1975–76), E. L. Doctorow (1973–74), Christopher Durang (1975–76), David Epstein (1973–74), Jack Gelber (1974–75), William Hauptmann (1976–77), Adrienne Kennedy (1973–74), Arthur Kopit (1976–77), Charles Ludlam (1977–78), Dwight Macdonald (1977–78), Terrence McNally (1973–74), David Mamet (1976–77), John Ford Noonan (1974–75), Ted Tally (1977–78), Derek Walcott (1977–78), Robert Penn Warren (1975–76).

Resident Directors: Jeff Bleckner (1968–69), Ali Taygun (1969–70).

Directors: Robert Alan Ackerman (1980–81), Larry Arrick (1967–68, 1969–71), *Andrei Belgrader* (1978–80, 1982–83, 1984–86), *Robert Brustein* (1969–72, 1975–76, 1977–79), Jacques Burdick (1971–72), Ron Daniels (1975–78), *Alvin Epstein* (1969–76, 1985–86), Kenneth Frankel (1976–77), *Athol Fugard* (1979–80, 1981–82, 1983–84, 1985–86), David Giles (1972–73), Richard Gilman (1969–70), Tony Giordano (1979–80, 1982–84), Goran Graffman (1983–84), Andre Gregory (1968–69), Tom Haas (1970–73), Keith Hack (1978–79), Kenneth Haigh (1967–68), Adrian Hall (1978–79), *David Hammond* (1981–85), Anthony Holland (1973–74), David Jones (1981–82), Jonas Jurasas (1980–81), Mladen Kiselov (1980–82), Lawrence Kornfeld (1975–76, 1982–83), Robert Lewis (1969–70), *John Madden* (1977–81, 1984–85), Jonathan Miller (1966–67), Andre Mtumi (1973–74), William Partlan (1984–85), *Lloyd Richards* (1979–86), Stanley Rosenberg (1968–69), Dennis Scott (1981–82, 1983–86), Andrei Serban (1977–78), Isaiah Sheffer

(1973–74), Arthur Sherman (1972–73), Burt Shevelove (1973–74), Paul Sills (1966–67, 1968–69), Wole Soyinka (1984–85), Harold Stone (1968–69), Frank Torok (1978–79), Andrzej Wajda (1974–75, 1976–77), Julian Webber (1984–85), Carl Weber (1967–68, 1979–80), Clifford Williams (1966–67), Moni Yakim (1973–74).

1709 Directors—Yale School of Drama Students and Graduates: Robert Alford II (1983–84), Christian Angerman (1982–83), Jeff Bleckner (1967–68, 1974–75), Mark Brokaw (1985–86), Robert Gainer (1978–79), Walt Jones (1975–78, 1980–83, 1984–85), Barnet Kellman (1980–81), William Ludel (1980–81, 1982–83), John McAndrew (1972–73), Jim Peskin (1981–82), William Peters (1972–73, 1974–75), Stephen Porter (1981–82), *Michael Posnick* (1968–69, 1970–75), Travis Preston (1977–78, 1985–86), Steven Robman (1979–80, 1985–86), David Schweizer (Yale College graduate; 1971–72, 1973–75), Roger Hendricks Simon (1971–72), James Simpson (1980–81, 1983–84), Ali Taygun (1968–70), Evan Yinoulis (1984–85), Dana B. Westberg (1980–81).

Actors and Actresses: *Mary Alice* (1983–85), *Seth Allen* (1980–82), *William Andrews* (1979–80, 1984–85), *William Atherton* (1985–86), Andy Backer, *Blanche Baker* (1976–78), *Bob Balaban* (1972–73), *Gerry Bamman* (1979–80, 1981–82), *Thomas Barbour* (1971–72), *George Bartenieff* (1968–69), *Robin Bartlett* (1980–81, 1983–84), *Barbara Baxley* (1981–82, 1983–84), Susan Blommaert, *Larry Blyden* (1973–74), Tom Brennan, *Norma Brustein* (1973–79), *Robert Brustein* (1973–77), Robert Burr, *L. Scott Caldwell* (1984–86), *Miles Chapin* (1972–73), Dominic Chianese, *Glenn Close* (1981–82), *Frances Conroy* (1979–80, 1984–85), Maury Cooper, *Roy Cooper* (1982–84), *Tandy Cronyn* (1982–83), *Lindsay Crouse* (1977–78), *Constance Cummings* (1977–78), *Elzbieta Czyzewska* (1974–75, 1976–77), *Clifford David* (1976–77), *Richard M. Davidson* (1979–80, 1983–84), *Donald Davis* (1972–73), *Jean De Baer* (1979–80, 1984–85), *Carmen de Lavallade* (1969–77), *Jerome Dempsey* (1973–75, 1980–81, 1984–85), *Jon De Vries* (1982–83, 1985–86), *Ralph Drischell* (1966–67, 1974–75), *Robert Drivas* (1970–71, 1976–77), Alice Drummond, *Mildred Dunnock* (1968–70), *Alvin Epstein* (1966–67, 1968–77), *Rex Everhart* (1982–83), *Ron Faber* (1976–77, 1979–80, 1983–84), *Clarence Felder* (1978–79, 1980–81, 1983–84), Niki Flacks, *Dann Florek* (1980–81, 1982–84), *Elizabeth Franz* (1978–79), *Al Freeman, Jr.* (1972–73), *Leonard Frey* (1972–73), *Athol Fugard* (1985–86), *George Gaynes* (1966–67, 1968–69), *Jeremy Geidt* (1968–79), *Anne Gerety* (1975–76, 1979–80), *Anita Gillette* (1983–84), *Danny Glover* (1981–82), *John Glover* (1978–79, 1980–81, 1982–83), *Mari Gorman* (1968–69), *James Greene* (1979–80, 1981–82), *Tammy Grimes* (1985–86), *George Grizzard* (1982–83), *Moses Gunn* (1978–79), *Kenneth Haigh* (1966–68, 1970–71), *Dan Hamilton* (1975–76), Berkeley Harris, *Hurd Hatfield* (1974–75), Roger Hendricks (1967–68), *Jeanne Hepple* (1967–68), *William Hickey* (1976–77), *Michael Higgins* (1977–78), *Arthur Hill* (1977–78), *Thomas Hill* (1975–77), *Anthony Holland* (1967–68, 1973–74), *Katherine Houghton* (1982–83), Earnest L. Hudson, *Kim Hunter* (1984–85), *David Hurst* (1966–67, 1971–72), *Zeljko Ivanek* (1981–82), *Leonard Jackson* (1979–80, 1983–84), *Richard Jenkins* (1980–81, 1982–83), *James Earl Jones* (1979–81, 1983–85), *Richard Jordan* (1967–68), *Stephen Joyce* (1971–74), *Robert Judd* (1983–84), *John Karlen* (1966–67), *Kurt Kasznar* (1973–74), *Andreas Katsulas* (1982–83), *Stacy Keach* (1967–68), *Grace Keagy* (1973–74), *Philip Kerr* (1975–76), *Jerome Kilty* (1969–70), *Polina Klimovitskaya* (1976–77), Tom Klunis, John Kuhner, *Swoosie Kurtz* (1972–73, 1980–81), *Linda Lavin* (1966–67, 1975–76), *Ron Leibman* (1966–68, 1976–77), *Hal Linden* (1984–85), *Delroy Lindo* (1983–84, 1985–86), Jack Litten, *Christopher Lloyd* (1974–75), *Michael Lombard* (1967–68), Paul Mann, *Frank Maraden* (1981–82, 1985–86), *Joan McIntosh* (1984–85), *Theresa*

Merritt (1983–84, 1985–86), *Allan Miller* (1972–73), *Leon Morenzie* (1981–82, 1984–85), Michael Morgan, *Barry Morse* (1967–68), *Zakes Mokae* (1980–82, 1985–86), *Michael Murphy* (1982–83), John Neville-Andrews, *Lynn Oliver* (1975–77), Marion Paone, *Ellen Parker* (1980–81), *Elizabeth Parrish* (1968–73, 1974–75), *Estelle Parsons* (1967–68, 1977–78), *Austin Pendleton* (1984–85), Wyman Pendleton, Don Plumley, *Addison Powell* (1978–79, 1982–83, 1984–85), *Gilbert Price* (1973–74), *Ford Rainey* (1978–79), *William Redfield* (1966–67), *Beah Richards* (1983–84), *Lee Richardson* (1970–71, 1977–78), *Tony Roberts* (1973–74), Reno Roop, *Tom Rosqui* (1966–67), David Sabin, *John Seitz* (1977–79, 1981–82), *Joe Seneca* (1983–84), *Karen Shallo* (1982–83, 1985–86), *Dick Shawn* (1971–72), Sloane Shelton, *David Spielberg* (1968–69), Richard Spore, *Shepperd Strudwick* (1977–78), *Rip Torn* (1974–75), *Eugene Troobnick* (1966–67, 1969–70, 1972–73, 1975–78), *Maria Tucci* (1979–80), Michael Vale, Mary Van Dyke, *Richard Venture* (1972–73), *Michael Wager* (1978–79), *Christopher Walken* (1971–72, 1977–78, 1979–80, 1981–82), J. T. Walsh, *Frederic Warriner* (1973–76), *Nancy Wickwire* (1967–68, 1971–72), *Kathleen Widdoes* (1967–68), *Dianne Wiest* (1980–81, 1982–83), *Irene Worth* (1966–67), *Max Wright* (1977–78), *Harris Yulin* (1967–68, 1979–80, 1981–82).

Actors and Actresses—Yale School of Drama Students and Graduates: *David Ackroyd* (1967–71), *Sarah Albertson* (1970–72), Jerome Anello, *Linda Atkinson* (1974–76), Dylan Baker, William Ballantyne, Bever-leigh Banfield, Zakiah Barksdale, Gary Basaraba, Spencer Beglarian, Diana Belshaw, *Richard Bey* (1975–77), Peter Blanc, Charlene Fredericka Bletson, Stephen R. Blye, Katherine Borowitz, *Julie Boyd* (1982–84), Allison Brennan, *James Brick* (1967–72), John J. Brown, Meredith E. Burns, Kimberleigh Burroughs, *Kate Burton* (1980–82), Michael Cadden, Jay Cady, Peter Cameron, Joseph Capone, Lisa Carling, Marilyn Carter, Reg E. Cathey, Edward Chell, *Caitlin Clarke* (1978–79), *Patricia D. Clarkson* (1984–85), Christian Clemenson, *David Clennon* (1966–69, 1978–79), Bill Cohen, *William Converse-Roberts* (1976–79), *Caris Corfman* (1977–80), Joseph Costa, *Stephanie Cotsirilos* (Yale School of Music graduate; 1970–72, 1973–75), Peter Covette, Peter C. Crawford, Peter Crombie, *Kitty Crooks* (1984–86), *Alma Cuervo* (1973–77), Marycharlotte Cummings, Robert Curtis-Brown, *Barbara Damashek* (1968–71), Andrew Davis, *Robert Dean* (1978–79), Katherine De Hetre, Bill De Luca, Thomas Derrah, *Dan Desmond* (1973–74), *John Dolittle* (1976–77, 1985–86), Franchelle Stewart Dorn, Tim Douglas, *Herb Downer* (1970–72, 1981–82, 1984–85), *Polly Draper* (1977–80), *Christopher Durang* (1973–75), Charles S. Dutton (1981–84, 1985–86), Jan Egleson, *Jill Eikenberry* (1968–70), Abba Elfman, Eric Elice, Jonathan Emerson, *Christine Estabrook* (1974–76), Allen Evans, Joyce Fideor, *Lydia Fisher* (1967–71), R. N. Foerster, Marc Flannagan, William Foeller, Robert Gainer, Bill Gearhart, *Steven J. Gefroh* (1983–85), Marcus Giamatti, Aloysius Gigl, Jeff Ginsberg, Eve Gordon, Anneke Gough, David Marshall Grant, *Keith Grant* (1979–80, 1981–82), Dennis Green, *David Alan Grier* (1978–82), *Joe Grifasi* (1972–73, 1974–75, 1976–78, 1980–81, 1982–83), *Michael Gross* (1972–73, 1977–79), Rick Grove, *Richard Grusin* (1976–79), Linda Gulder, *Ben Halley, Jr.* (1975–77, 1985–86), John Harnagel, Don Harvey, Alan Haufrect, Avram J. Hellerman, Steven Hendrickson, *Darryl Hill* (1973–74), Robert Hitt, Nicholas Hormann, Ken Howard, Tom Isbell, Kirk Jackson, David Jaffe, Bill Jarvis, Andrew Johnson, Anthony Johnson, Pamela Jones, *Jane Kaczmarek* (1979–82), Warren Keith, Bill Keller, Patrick Kerr, Michael C. Knight, Jon Krupp, William Kux, Joanna Kyd, Marty Lafferty, Michael Lassell, Stephen R. Lawson, Katharin Leavelle, Sabrina LeBeauf, Sue Lefebvre, *Charles Levin* (1973–77), Mitchell Lichtenstein, *Maxine Lieberman* (1968–72), Amandina Lihamba, *Mark Linn-Baker* (1976–79), J. J. Linsalata, John Lloyd,

Becky London, William Ludel, Everette Lunning, Jr., John McAndrew, *Frances McDormand* (1980–82), Theresa McElwee, Eric McFarland, William McGlinn, *Kate McGregor-Stewart* (1973–75, 1976–77), Lizbeth Mackay, *Warren Manzi* (1977–80, 1982–86), Shaine Marinson, Christopher J. Markle, Jonathan Marks, Ken L. Marks, Barry E. Marshall, Thomas O. Martin, Richard D. Masur, Nancy Mayans, Deborah Mayo, Fred Melamed, Stephen Mendillo, William Mesnik, James Metzner, David K. Miller, *Devora Millman* (1984–86), Stephen Mills, Sharon Mitchell, Isabell Monk, H. S. Murphy, Jeff Natter, *James Naughton* (1968–71), David Wayne Nelson, Rebecca Nelson, Robert Nersesian, Mordecai Newman, Kristine Nielsen, Patrizia Norcia, Elizabeth Norment, Stephen D. Nowicki, David Officer, Timothy O'Hagan, Damon Ortega, Carol Ostrow, *Marianne Owen* (1976–79, 1983–84), *Joan Pape* (1966–70, 1971–72, 1980–81), Hannibal Penney, Jr., William Peters, *Geoffrey Pierson* (1977–80), *Louis Plante* (1966–71), Joel Polis, Barry M. Press, David Prittie, Ellis M. Pryce-Jones, *Darcy Pulliam* (1978–79), Michael Quigley, Dean L. Radcliffe, Mark Rafael, Theodore Ravinett, *Ron Recasner* (1973–74), Ralph Redpath, Kathleen Reiter, *Laila Robbins* (1983–84), Steven Robman, Robin Pearson Rose, Alan Rosenberg, Marcell Rosenblatt, John Rothman, *Stephen Rowe* (1973–78, 1980–81), John Gould Rubin, *Cecilia Rubino* (1980–82), *Vytautus Ruginis* (1979–82), Kenneth Ryan, Gabrielle Schafer, *Paul Schierhorn* (1971–77), Peter Schifter, Carol Schlanger, Asante Scott, Kimberly Scott, James R. Shaffer, *Tony Shalhoub* (1977–80), *John Shea* (1972–73, 1977–78), Tony Sherer, Susan Sherry, Talia Shire, Charles Siegel, Douglas Simes, Roger Hendricks Simon, Yannis Simonides, *Melissa Smith* (1980–82), Robert Snow, Marilyn Sommer, *Barbara Somerville* (1982–83), Frank Speiser, Roy Steinberg, Rosemary Stewart, *Meryl Streep* (1973–75), Larry Strichman, Matt Sussman, Ted Tally, Richard Taus, Meral Taygun, David Thornton, Charles Turner, John Turturro, *Joseph Urla* (1982–85), *Stephen Van Benschoten* (1968–71), *Courtney B. Vance* (1983–85), Ruth Wallman, Donald Warfield, Sigourney Weaver, *Joan Welles* (1966–67, 1968–69, 1971–72), Scott Rickey Wheeler, Robert Whittembre, Stanley E. Wiklinski, David Wiles, Tyrone Wilson, *Henry Winkler* (1968–72), James Zitlow.

REPERTORY

1966–67: *Dynamite Tonite!, Volpone, Prometheus Bound.*

1967–68: *'Tis Pity She's a Whore, We Bombed in New Haven, Henry IV, The Three Sisters, Coriolanus.*

1968–69: *God Bless, The Great Chinese Revolution* and *They Told Me That You Came This Way* (two one-acts), *Saved, Story Theatre, Bacchae, Greatshot.*

1969–70: *The Rivals, Ovid's Metamorphoses, Transformations: The Rhesus Umbrella, Clutches,* and *Iz She Izzy or Iz He Ain'tszy or Iz They Both?* (three one-acts), *Crimes and Crimes, The Government Inspector, Don Juan.*

1970–71: *Story Theatre Repertory: Two Saints (Gimpel the Fool* and *Saint Julian the Hospitaler)* and *Olympian Games; The Revenger's Tragedy, Where Has Tommy Flowers Gone?, Macbeth, Woyzeck* and *Play, Two by Bertolt Brecht and Kurt Weill: The Little Mahagonny* and *The Seven Deadly Sins.*

1971–72: *When We Dead Awaken, The Big House, Caligula, Repertory Holiday: Two by Brecht and Weill (The Little Mahagonny* and *The Seven Deadly Sins), Passion* and *Stops* (two one-acts), and *Jacques Brel: Songs; Life Is a Dream, I Married You for the Fun of It, Happy End.*

1972–73: *The Bourgeois Gentleman, A Break in the Skin, Are You Now or Have You Ever Been?, In the Clap Shack, The Mirror, Baal, Macbett, Lear.*

1973–74: *The Tempest, Darkroom, Watergate Classics* (songs and sketches), *The Tubs, The Rise and Fall of the City of Mahagonny, Geography of a Horse Dreamer* and *An Evening with Dead Essex, Shleimel the First, The Frogs.*

1974–75: *The Possessed, The Idiots Karamazov, Story Theatre IV: Victory, Happy End, The Father, The Shaft of Love, A Midsummer Night's Dream.*

1975–76: *A Midsummer Night's Dream, Don Juan, Bingo: Scenes of Money and Death, Walk the Dog, Willie, General Gorgeous, Troilus and Cressida.*

1976–77: *Julius Caesar, Suicide in B-Flat, Ivanov, The Banquet Years* (texts by Alfred Jarry, Pierre Louys, Max Jacob, and Erik Satie), *The Vietnamization of New Jersey (An American Tragedy), The Durango Flash, Mr. Puntila and His Chauffeur Matti, White Marriage.*

1977–78: *The Ghost Sonata, Reunion* and *Dark Pony, Terra Nova, The 1940's Radio Hour, Sganarelle* (an evening of Molière farces: *The Flying Doctor, The Forced Marriage, Sganarelle, or The Imaginary Cuckold,* and *A Dumb Show,* loosely based on *The Doctor in Spite of Himself), Man Is Man, Wings, The Wild Duck.*

1978–79: *Tales from the Vienna Woods, Mistaken Identities: 'dentity Crisis* and *Guess Work, Mahagonny* (a chamber version of *The Rise and Fall of the City of Mahagonny), Jacques Brel . . .* (a tribute to the author of *Jacques Brel Is Alive and Well and Living in Paris), Buried Child, The Sea Gull, The Bundle, As You Like It.*

1979–80: *Bosoms and Neglect, They Are Dying Out, Measure for Measure, Curse of the Starving Class, Ubu Rex, A Lesson from Aloes, Timon of Athens.*

1980–81: *Boesman and Lena, The Suicide, Twelfth Night,* Winterfest I: *The Resurrection of Lady Lester, Rococo, Sally and Marsha,* and *Domestic Issues; The Magnificent Cuckold, Hedda Gabler, An Attempt at Flying.*

1981–82: *Uncle Vanya, Mrs. Warren's Profession, Rip Van Winkle or "The Works,"* Winterfest II: *Beef, No Chicken, Flash Floods, Going Over,* and *The Man Who Could See Through Time; Master Harold . . . and the boys, Johnny Bull, Love's Labour's Lost.*

1982–83: *A Doll's House, Hello and Goodbye, The Philanderer,* Winterfest III: *Astapovo, Coyote Ugly,* and *Playing in Local Bands; Much Ado About Nothing, About Face, A Touch of the Poet.*

1983–84: *Major Barbara, A Raisin in the Sun* (twenty-fifth anniversary production), *Richard II,* Winterfest IV: *The Sweet Life, Chopin in Space,* and *The Day of the Picnic; Night Is Mother to the Day, Ma Rainey's Black Bottom, The Road to Mecca.*

1984–85: *Tartuffe, Henry IV, Part I, A Play of Giants,* Winterfest V: *Between East and West, Faulkner's Bicycle, Rum and Coke,* and *Vampires in Kodachrome; What the Butler Saw, Talley's Folly, Fences.*

1985–86: *The Blood Knot* (twenty-fifth anniversary production), *Little Eyolf, Marriage,* Winterfest VI: *A Child's Tale, Crazy from the Heart, Stitchers and Starlight Talkers,* and *Union Boys; Othello, The Importance of Being Earnest, Joe Turner's Come and Gone.*

BIBLIOGRAPHY

Published Sources:
Hartford Courant, 1967–86.
The Nation, 1967–78.
New Haven Journal-Courier, 1967–86.

New Haven Register, 1967–86.
Newsweek, 1966–86.
New York, 1974, 1978.
New York Times, 1966–86.
Time, 1967–86.
Village Voice, 1967–86.
Yale Daily News, 1967–86.
Yale School of Drama/Yale Repertory Theatre. *Annual Report*, 1980–86.
Brustein, Robert. *Making Scenes: A Personal History of the Turbulent Years at Yale, 1966–1979*. New York: Limelight Editions, 1984.

Archival Resource:
New Haven, Connecticut. Yale University. The Yale Repertory Theatre. Press office. Production photographs. The Yale School of Drama Library. Scrapbooks containing reviews of YRT productions and other press material on the theatre and the School of Drama; a complete collection of programs; a collection of dramaturgs' logbooks, which document rehearsals; and a nearly complete collection of scripts, ranging from early drafts and cuttings to clean copies of final scripts, to stage managers' production books, to student stage managers' master of fine arts theses (production books *and* specially prepared acting editions based on them). The only scripts missing are *Story Theatre, The Seven Deadly Sins, When We Dead Awaken*, and *Passion*.

Dramaturgs' logbooks are available for *Volpone, Are You Now or Have You Ever Been?, The Father, A Midsummer Night's Dream* (1974–75 and 1975–76), *Don Juan* (1975–76), *Walk the Dog, Willie, Bingo, General Gorgeous, Julius Caesar, Suicide in B-Flat, Ivanov, The Durango Flash, Puntila, White Marriage, The Ghost Sonata, Reunion, Terra Nova, Man Is Man, Wings, The Wild Duck, Tales from the Vienna Woods, Mistaken Identities, Mahagonny* (the 1978–79 chamber version), *Buried Child, The Sea Gull*, and *The Bundle*.

Student stage managers' theses are available for *The Tempest, The Tubs, Shlemiel the First, General Gorgeous, Suicide in B-Flat, Ivanov, The Durango Flash, Terra Nova, Wings, Mahagonny* (chamber version), *Buried Child, Measure for Measure, Curse of the Starving Class, Boesman and Lena, The Suicide, The Magnificent Cuckold, Hedda Gabler, Rip Van Winkle, Hello and Goodbye, Playing in Local Bands, Much Ado About Nothing, About Face, Richard II, Ma Rainey's Black Bottom, A Play of Giants, Faulkner's Bicycle, Talley's Folly, Little Eyolf, A Child's Tale, Othello*, and *Joe Turner's Come and Gone*. There is a student director's master of fine arts thesis on *Crazy from the Heart*.

The musical scores for *The Little Mahagonny, The Rise and Fall of the City of Mahagonny, The Frogs, Dynamite Tonite!* (1966–67 and 1975–76), and *The Banquet Years* are also available.

Art Borreca

YIDDISH THEATRE UNITS, NEW YORK CITY, BOSTON, CHICAGO, LOS ANGELES. See FEDERAL THEATRE PROJECT, YIDDISH THEATRE UNITS.

APPENDIX I

CHRONOLOGY OF THEATRE COMPANIES

1915   Cleveland Play House
1928   Workers' Laboratory Theatre
1931   Group Theatre
1933   Barter Theatre
       Theatre Union
1935   Actors' Repertory Company
       Federal Theatre Project, Negro Theatre Unit, New York City
       Federal Theatre Project, Yiddish Theatre Units
1936   Federal Theatre Project, Dramatic Unit, Seattle
       Federal Theatre Project, Negro Theatre Unit, Seattle
1937   Mercury Theatre Acting Company
1938   American Actors Company
1939   Chekhov Theatre Players
1940   American Negro Theatre
1941   Actors' Laboratory, Inc.
1945   American Repertory Theatre, Inc.
1947   Alley Theatre
       Children's World Theatre
       Living Theatre
       Margo Jones Theatre
1949   Mummers Theatre
1950   Arena Stage
1952   Actor's Workshop

1953 Artists' Theatre
      Phoenix Theatre
1954 Front Street Theatre
      Milwaukee Repertory Theatre
1955 Dallas Theatre Center
      Honolulu Theatre for Youth
1956 Philadelphia Drama Guild
1958 Paper Bag Players
1959 San Francisco Mime Troupe
1960 APA (Association of Producing Artists)
      Asolo State Theatre
      McCarter Theatre Company
1961 Children's Theatre Company
1962 Center Stage
1963 Free Southern Theatre
      Guthrie Theatre Company
      Hull-House Theatre
      Open Theatre
      Playhouse on the Square/Circuit Playhouse
      Repertory Theatre of Lincoln Center
      Seattle Repertory Theatre
      Theatre of the Living Arts
      Trinity Square Repertory Company
1964 Actors Theatre of Louisville
      Long Wharf Theatre
      Missouri Repertory Theatre
      South Coast Repertory
1965 A Contemporary Theatre
      American Conservatory Theatre
1966 Boarshead: Michigan Public Theatre
      Repertory Theatre of St. Louis
      Yale Repertory Theatre
1967 Arizona Theatre Company
      CSC Repertory
      Negro Ensemble Company
1968 American Theatre Company
      Berkeley Repertory Theatre
1969 Circle Repertory Company

Mabou Mines
1970   Empty Space Association
        Indiana Repertory Theatre
1971   Baltimore Theatre Project
        Cocteau Repertory Company
1972   Intiman Theatre Company
        New American Theatre
1973   Hippodrome Theatre Company
        San Diego Repertory Theatre
1974   At the Foot of the Mountain
        Hartman Theatre Company
        Steppenwolf Theatre Company
        Wisdom Bridge Theatre
1975   Wooster Group
1976   Alaska Repertory Theatre
1977   Actors Theatre of St. Paul
        BAM (Brooklyn Academy of Music)
1978   The Group Theatre Company
1979   American Repertory Theatre
        Denver Center Theatre Company
1984   New Mexico Repertory Theatre

APPENDIX II

THEATRE COMPANIES
BY STATE

Alaska	Alaska Repertory Theatre
Arizona	Arizona Theatre Company
California	Actors' Laboratory, Inc.
	Actor's Workshop
	American Conservatory Theatre
	Berkeley Repertory Theatre
	Federal Theatre Project, Yiddish Theatre Unit, Los Angeles
	San Diego Repertory Theatre
	San Francisco Mime Troupe
	South Coast Repertory
Colorado	Denver Center Theatre Company
Connecticut	Chekhov Theatre Players
	Hartman Theatre Company
	Long Wharf Theatre
	Yale Repertory Theatre
District of Columbia	Arena Stage
Florida	Asolo State Theatre
	Hippodrome Theatre Company
Hawaii	Honolulu Theatre for Youth
Illinois	American Conservatory Theatre
	Federal Theatre Project, Yiddish Theatre Unit, Chicago
	Hull-House Theatre

	New American Theatre
	Steppenwolf Theatre Company
	Wisdom Bridge Theatre
Indiana	Indiana Repertory Theatre
Kentucky	Actors Theatre of Louisville
Maryland	Baltimore Theatre Project
	Center Stage
Massachusetts	American Repertory Theatre
	Federal Theatre Project, Yiddish Theatre Unit, Boston
Michigan	Boarshead: Michigan Public Theatre
Minnesota	Actors Theatre of St. Paul
	At the Foot of the Mountain
	Children's Theatre Company
	Guthrie Theatre Company
Mississippi	Free Southern Theatre
Missouri	Missouri Repertory Theatre
	Repertory Theatre of St. Louis
New Jersey	McCarter Theatre Company
New Mexico	New Mexico Repertory Theatre
New York	Actors' Repertory Company
	American Actors Company
	American Negro Theatre
	American Repertory Theatre, Inc.
	American Theatre Company
	APA (Association of Producing Artists)
	Artists' Theatre
	BAM (Brooklyn Academy of Music)
	Children's World Theatre
	Circle Repertory Theatre
	Cocteau Repertory Company
	CSC Repertory
	Federal Theatre Project, Negro Theatre Unit, New York City
	Federal Theatre Project, Yiddish Theatre Unit, New York City
	Group Theatre
	Living Theatre
	Mabou Mines

	Mercury Theatre Acting Company
	Negro Ensemble Company
	Open Theatre
	Paper Bag Players
	Phoenix Theatre
	Repertory Theatre of Lincoln Center
	Theatre Union
	Wooster Group
	Workers' Laboratory Theatre
Ohio	Cleveland Play House
Oklahoma	Mummers Theatre
Pennsylvania	American Conservatory Theatre
	Philadelphia Drama Guild
	Theatre of the Living Arts
Rhode Island	Trinity Square Repertory Company
Tennessee	Front Street Theatre
	Playhouse on the Square/Circuit Playhouse
Texas	Alley Theatre
	Dallas Theatre Center
	Margo Jones Theatre
Virginia	Barter Theatre
Washington	A Contemporary Theatre
	Empty Space Association
	Federal Theatre Project, Dramatic Unit, Seattle
	Federal Theatre Project, Negro Theatre Unit, Seattle
	The Group Theatre Company
	Intiman Theatre Company
	Seattle Repertory Theatre
Wisconsin	Milwaukee Repertory Theatre

Index of Personal Names and Play Titles

About the Contributors

ROBERT A. ADUBATO is associate professor of English, theatre, and speech at Essex County College in Newark, New Jersey, and coordinator of the English Department and of the theatre program. His book, play reviews, and articles have appeared in *Theatre Journal, Theatre News,* and *College English Notes.*

DARREL E. ALEXANDER is professor of speech and theatre at Oklahoma Christian College in Oklahoma City, Oklahoma, where he is a teacher, director, and costumer. He received his Ph.D. from Louisiana State University and his M.A. from the University of Denver.

STEPHEN M. ARCHER is professor of theatre at the University of Missouri-Columbia, where he teaches theatre history and playwriting. He has published *American Actors and Actresses: A Guide to Information Sources* (Gale, 1983), *How Theatre Happens* (Macmillan, 1983), as well as numerous articles and reviews. He is presently preparing a comprehensive biography of J. B. Booth, Sr.

JOSEPH J. BELLINGHIERE is graduate coordinator of the drama department at San Diego State University. He is the editor of *A Practical Introduction to the Theatre* (Harcourt Brace Jovanovich, forthcoming), and he has presented papers at conventions of the American Theatre in Higher Education, the Southeast Theatre Conference, the Children's Theatre Association of America, and the American Conference on Aging.

ULRICA BELL-PERKINS is professor of English at Cerro Coso Community College's Southern outreach at Edwards Air Force Base in California. She has a B.A. in English literature from Bryn Mawr College, a Master of Arts in Teaching from Harvard University, and a Ph.D. in Theatre History and Dramatic Literature from the University of California at Davis. She is an artist and writer, currently completing a biography of artist Charles La Monk.

FREDRIC BERG is an actor, director, and teacher who lives and works in New York City. He is currently completing his doctorate at the City University of New York.

ART BORRECA has served as a Production Dramaturg and Assistant Literary Manager at the Yale Repertory Theatre, and he has been a Teaching Fellow in the Theatre Studies Program in Yale College. He has also contributed articles to *Theater* and *Before His Eyes: Essays in Honor of Stanley Kauffmann* and taught literature and drama at Wesleyan University and Albertus Magnus College.

KEVIN J. BRADY teaches in the Department of English at the Marymount College of Virginia in Arlington, Virginia.

JANET BROWN is director of the Greater Hartford Academy of Performing Arts, a regional magnet school she originated in Hartford, Connecticut, in 1985. She is author of *Feminist Drama* (Scarecrow Press, 1979), soon to appear in a second edition, and of numerous articles and two produced plays. One of these, *Cora's Blues, Rising* was winner of the Market House Theatre One-Act Play Competition in 1988. She received her Ph.D. in Speech and Dramatic Art from the University of Missouri-Columbia.

DEBRA L. BRUCH is assistant professor of theatre at Michigan Technological University, Houghton, Michigan. She contributed to *American Theatre Companies, 1888–1930*. She received her Ph.D. in Theatre at the University of Missouri-Columbia in 1987.

TIM BUDKE is a graduate of the University of Minnesota-Twin Cities with an M.F.A. in Acting and a Ph.D. candidate in Theatre at the University of Missouri-Columbia.

GENE BURK received his Ph.D. from the School of Drama at the University of Washington, where he specialized in dramatic theory. He currently serves as dramaturg for Kumu Kahua Theatre in Honolulu, Hawaii.

BENJAMIN F. CARNEY is assistant professor of speech and theatre at Bernard M. Baruch College of the City University of New York and an associate of the Klausner International Literary Agency in New York. He is active as an independent producer, director, and writer in theatre and film.

WILLIAM T. CLOW is a scenic and lighting designer trained at Illinois State University. He has designed numerous productions including the University of Missouri-Columbia's award-winning *Eleven Zulu* and *Cyrano de Bergerac* at Illinois State University.

TIMOTHY D. CONNORS is associate professor of theatre at Northern Arizona University, Flagstaff, where he teaches directing, playwriting, and theatre history. An active actor and director, he has also presented several papers on contemporary Soviet and Polish theatre at national conventions, and he maintains a research interest in American vaudeville managers and management.

KEN DAVIS is associate professor of English at Indiana University-Purdue University at Indianapolis. He has worked as a director, stage manager, actor, and dramaturg in amateur and professional theatre and has earned the Faculty Service Award of the National University Continuing Education Association for his theatre courses and tours in the United States, Canada, and Great Britain. His books include *Rehearsing the Audience: Ways to Develop Student Perceptions of Theatre*, published in 1988.

KRYSTAN V. DOUGLAS is lecturer in English at the University of New Mexico, Albuquerque. She is author of several papers on film and American drama and editor of a forthcoming collection of essays on American drama, *Splintered Images: Dramatic Visions of the West*.

WELDON B. DURHAM is professor of theatre and associate dean for academic programs in the Graduate School of the University of Missouri-Columbia. He teaches American theatre history, dramatic literature, and dramatic theory and criticism. Dr. Durham is general editor of *American Theatre Companies, 1749–1887* (Greenwood Press, 1986) and *American Theatre Companies, 1888–1930* (Greenwood Press, 1987). His articles have appeared in *Theatre History Studies* (of which he is also associate editor), *Quarterly Journal of Speech*, and *Theatre Journal*.

ALAN C. ENGLISH is associate professor of theatre at Ball State University in Muncie, Indiana. He has published several articles on the dramas of Harold Pinter. Educated at the University of Arkansas (M.A.) and the University of Missouri-Columbia (Ph.D.), his teaching specialties are acting and directing.

ROBERT F. FALK is professor of theatre at Lycoming College, Pennsylvania, where he serves as the chair of the Department of Theatre. He is an active stage director and producer for the Arena Theatre and the Arena Summer Theatre at Lycoming College. He has served as a regional cochair for the American College Theatre Festival and as an adjudicator. He is also a member of the Association for Theatre in Higher Education.

MARI KATHLEEN FIELDER is an independent historian of the performing arts currently conducting research in ethnic studies. Her articles and reviews have appeared in *Theatre Journal, Theatre Studies, Theatre History Studies*, and *Eire-Ireland*. She hold an M.A. in Theatre from Ohio State University and a Ph.D. in Theatre Arts from the University of California, Los Angeles.

JEANIE FORTE is assistant professor of modern drama in the English Department of the University of Tennessee, Knoxville. She is author of *Women in Performance Art: Feminism and Postmodernism*, and she has contributed articles and reviews to *Theater, Theatre Journal, Women & Performance*, and *High Performance*. She is active in the Women's Theatre Program of the Association of Theatre in Higher Education and in the Modern Language Association.

LIZ FUGATE is Drama Librarian at the University of Washington, Seattle. She contributes articles to *Script*, the Northwest Playwright Guild's newsletter, and she advises Seattle-area freelance writers and publishers of theatre material. She has contributed book reviews to *Theatre Journal*.

DORIS HART is assistant professor of English at Manhattan Community College, New York. She received her Ph.D. in Educational Theatre from New York University and conducts research on the plays of Eugene O'Neill. She has written more than twenty-five plays and is a member of the Dramatists Guild.

STUART J. HECHT is assistant professor of theatre at Boston College. He received his Ph.D. in theatre from Northwestern University before spending several years as Resident Dramaturg for Chicago's Wisdom Bridge Theatre. He has contributed articles to *Theatre Journal and Chicago History*.

JOHN M. HEIDGER is associate professor and Director of Theatre at St. Louis Community College at Florissant Valley. He received his B.A. and M.A. in theatre at Southern Illinois University-Edwardsville, and his Ph.D. in theatre history from the University of Missouri-Columbia.

ERLENE LANEY HENDRIX is chair of the department of speech communication and theater arts at Old Dominion University in Norfolk, Virginia. She earned her doctorate in Speech and Dramatic Art at the University of Missouri-Columbia in 1977 for her research on the Open Theatre. Since then she has published reviews of Joseph Chaikin's post-Open Theatre work in *Theatre Journal*, and she has been invited to speak on the director at the Open Theatre Conference, Kent State University (1983) and at the Edwin Booth Award ceremony at the City University of New York (1987).

P. WILLIAM HUTCHINSON is professor of theatre at Rhode Island College, where he teaches acting, directing, dramatic and performance criticism, and the history of theatre. He has served the profession as a member of the board of directors of the New England Theatre conference and the national committee of the American College Theatre Festival. He received a national directing award for his production of *Mindbender*. His theatre reviews and articles have appeared in

Theatre Journal and in the *Black Theatre Newsletter*. In 1987 he was inducted into the College of Fellows of the New England Theatre Conference.

LAWRENCE JASPER is associate professor of theatre at California State University in Fullerton. He has made numerous contributions to panels and projects for ATA and ATHE and is active in the leadership of both the Southern California Educational Theatre Association and ACTF, Region VIII-S. He received his M.A. in theatre from the University of California and his Ph.D. from the University of Kansas.

NANCY KINDELAN is assistant professor of theatre and dance at Northeastern University, Boston, where she teaches acting and dramatic literature. She is also a freelance director. Her articles have appeared in *Comparative Drama* and in *Children's Theatre Review*.

NANCY R. McCLAVE is an attorney in Coral Gables, Florida, where she heads her own legal research bureau. She received her B.A. in English from Ohio State University, Columbus; her M.A. in English and her Ph.D. in theatre from Kent State University, Kent, Ohio; and her J.D. from the University of Miami Law School, Coral Gables, Florida.

DOUGLAS McDERMOTT is professor of drama at California State University, Stanislaus, where he teaches theatre history and directs. He has published articles on American theatre and drama in various journals. He has served both on the Executive Committee of the American Society for Theatre Research and on the editorial board of its journal, *Theatre Survey*.

JEFFREY D. MASON is associate professor of theatre at California State University, Bakersfield, where he teaches acting, directing, playwriting, American theatre and theatre history. He is the author of *Wisecracks: The Farces of George S. Kaufman* (UMI Research Press, 1988), and he has contributed articles and reviews to *Theatre Journal, Theatre Annual*, and *Themes in Drama*. He has either directed or acted in over sixty productions and is founder and artistic director of the Kern Art Theatre. He is currently preparing a study of myth and ideology in American melodrama.

GEORGE MEDOVOY received his doctorate in dramatic art from the University of California at Davis. His dissertation dealt with the Yiddish troupes of the Federal Theatre Project. His articles on theatre have appeared in *Federal One* and *The Los Angeles Times*. A journalist and international travel writer, his writings have appeared in *Newsday*, the *San Jose* (California) *Mercury News*, and the *Toronto Globe and Mail* and other newspapers.

BARBARA J. MOLETTE is director for the arts-in-education programs for the Mayor's Committee on Art and Culture for the city of Baltimore, Maryland.

She is coauthor of *Black Theatre: Premise and Presentation* (Wyndham Hall Press, 1986), and she has written plays performed by the Negro Ensemble Company, the Free Southern Theatre, and several college and university theatre groups. She is active in the National Conference on African-American Theatre, and she is a member of the Dramatists Guild.

GEORGA LARSEN PARCHEM received her doctorate from the College of Education at The Ohio State University for her research on the Paper Bag Players. She resides in Oak Park, Illinois.

ALEX PINKSTON is assistant professor of theatre at Davidson College, Davidson, North Carolina, where he serves as acting specialist and dramatic theorist. He has contributed articles to *Theatre Journal, Theatre Survey, Nineteenth Century Theatre Research*, and *Theatre History Studies*. He is a member of the American Society for Theatre Research and he performs periodically with regional theatre companies.

DAVID M. PRICE is adjunct associate professor of English at the Borough of Manhattan Community College of the City University of New York. A graduate of the University of Wisconsin and the City University of New York, Dr. Price writes about theatre and is involved with off-Broadway theatre companies. He is a member of the East Coast Theatre Conference.

DAVID RINEAR is professor of drama at Trinity University, San Antonio, Texas, where he teaches theatre history, dramatic theory, acting, and directing. He directs for the university theatre and continues to work as a freelance actor and director. Author of *The Temple of Momus: Mitchell's Olympic Theatre* (Scarecrow Press, 1987), his historical articles have appeared in several major theatre journals.

JANET E. RUBIN is professor of communication and theatre at Saginaw Valley State University, University Center, Michigan, where she serves as artistic director of the theatre program. She has been an exchange professor at Ballarat College of Advanced Education in Australia. She has also delivered numerous conference presentations, authored several articles, undertaken guest artist appointments, and is active in the American Alliance for Theatre and Education. She received her Ph.D. from The Ohio State University.

DELIA N. SALVI, Ph.D., is professor of directing and acting in the Department of Theatre, Film and Television at the University of California, Los Angeles, and she teaches in both the theatre and film divisions of that department. Master classes conducted throughout the United States, Canada, and Europe in "Directing the Actor for Film and Television," a course she originated at UCLA, have brought her an international reputation. A member of the Actors Studio, she continues to work as a professional actress.

RODNEY SIMARD is assistant professor of English at California State University, San Bernardino. Author of *Postmodern Drama: Contemporary Playwrights in America and Britain* (ATA-UPA, 1984), he has contributed articles and reviews to a number of journals and collections, including *Shakespeare-Jharbuch, Modern Drama, Theatre Journal*, and *Theatre Research International*.

WALLACE STERLING is associate professor of theatre arts at the University of Akron. He has presented papers and chaired panels on theatre history and dramatic literature at regional and national theatre conferences. He received his B.A. and M.A. from the University of Florida and his Ph.D. from Southern Illinois University. He has followed the fortunes of the Cleveland Play House for many years.

EMILY THIROUX is lecturer in English at California State University and instructor in English at Bakersfield College. She received her B.A. and M.A. from California State University, Bakersfield, and she serves on the board of directors for Bakersfield Community Theatre. She has been active in Kern Art Theatre, the Great American Melodrama, and the Kern Shakespeare Festival.

JAMES THOMAS is associate dean for academic affairs and associate professor in the School of Theatre at Florida State University. He is author of *The Art of the Actor-Manager* (UMI Research Press, 1984), and he has published articles and reviews in *Theatre Journal* and *Library Chronicle*. He is currently working on *Principles of Play Analysis*, a comprehensive textbook for drama and English students.

JULI A. THOMPSON is professor of dramatic theory at the University of Hawaii at Manoa. In addition to teaching and directing at the university, she serves as Executive Director of Kumu Kahua Theatre, a company that produces five new plays each season.

SUSAN M. THORNTON has studied theatre at the graduate level at the University of Missouri-Columbia and at New York University. She has also taught acting and play production at Hazelwood Central High School in St. Louis, Missouri.

C. JOYCE D. WHITE is a doctoral degree candidate in theatre history and criticism at the City University of New York, where she is researching the history of the Negro Ensemble Company. Educated at Florida A. & M. University and at Purdue University, White has taught in high schools in Florida, at Purdue University, at the City College of the City University of New York, and at Kingsborough Community College of the City University of New York, Brooklyn.

ANNE ST. CLAIR WILLIAMS is the owner of Staging Assistance and Design Services, Durham, North Carolina, providing set, lighting, costume design, scene painting, and general technical services to area theatres and schools. She holds an M.A. in Dramatic Art from the University of North Carolina and a Ph.D. in Speech and Theatre from the University of Illinois.

DON B. WILMETH is professor of theatre arts and English and chair (1979–1987) of the Theatre, Speech and Dance Department at Brown University, Providence, Rhode Island. A 1982 Guggenheim Fellow, he received the 1981 Barnard Hewitt Theatre History Award for his *George Frederick Cooke: Machiavel of the Stage*. He is also an editor for *The Cambridge Guide to World Theatre* and a contributor to *Documents of American Theatre*.

BARRY B. WITHAM is director of Ph.D. studies in the school drama department at the University of Washington, Seattle. He is coauthor of *Uncle Sam Presents* (University of Pennsylvania, 1982) and has published articles in *Modern Drama, Theatre Journal*, and *Theatre History Studies*. He has served on the Executive Committee of the American Society for Theatre Research, chaired the American Theatre Association Commission on Theatre Research, and is currently general editor of *Documents of American Theatre* to be published by Cambridge University Press.

DONALD H. WOLFE is professor of theatre arts at Wake Forest University in Winston-Salem, North Carolina, where he has served as chair of the Department of Speech Communication and Theatre Arts since 1974. He has served as an officer of the North Carolina Theatre Conference, the Southeastern Theatre Conference, and the Theatre Arts Panel of the North Carolina Arts Council.